G000019615

Collins

*gem*

# Collins
# English
# Thesaurus

Collins
*gem*

# Collins
# English
# Thesaurus

**HarperCollins Publishers**
Westerhill Road
Bishopbriggs
Glasgow
G64 2QT

**Fifth Edition 2006**

© WilliamCollins Sons & Co. Ltd.
Publishers 1987

© HarperCollins Publishers 1994,
1999, 2004, 2006

ISBN-10 0-00-720876-6
ISBN-13 978-0-00-720876-0

Collins® is a registered trademark of
HarperCollins Publishers Limited

www.collins.co.uk

A catalogue record for this book is
available from the British Library.

Computing support by
Thomas Callan and Mark Taylor

Typeset by Wordcraft, Glasgow

Printed and bound by Legoprint S.P.A.

**Acknowledgements**
We would like to thank those authors
and publishers who kindly gave
permission for copyright material to
be used in the Collins Word Web. We
would also like to thank Times
Newspapers Ltd for providing
valuable data.

All rights reserved. No part of this
publication may be reproduced,
stored in a retrieval system or
transmitted, in any form or by any
means, electronic, mechanical,
photocopying, recording or
otherwise, without the prior
permission of the publisher. This
book is sold subject to the
conditions that it shall not, by way
of trade or otherwise, be lent, re-
sold, hired out or otherwise
circulated without the publisher's
prior consent in any form of
binding or cover other than that in
which it is published and without
a similar condition including this
condition being imposed on the
subsequent purchaser.

Entered words that we have reason
to believe constitute trademarks
have been designated as such.
However, neither the presence nor
absence of such designation
should be regarded as affecting
the legal status of any trademark.

## Editorial Staff

*Editor*
**Lorna Gilmour**

*Publishing Manager*
Elaine Higgleton

*Series Editor*
Lorna Sinclair Knight

*Editorial Assistance*
Jennifer Baird    Kay Cullen

William Collins' dream of knowledge for all began with the publication of his first book in 1819. A self-educated mill worker, he not only enriched millions of lives, but also founded a flourishing publishing house. Today, staying true to this spirit, Collins books are packed with inspiration, innovation, and practical expertise. They place you at the centre of a world of possibility and give you exactly what you need to explore it.

Language is the key to this exploration, and at the heart of Collins Dictionaries is language as it is really used. New words, phrases, and meanings spring up every day, and all of them are captured and analysed by the Collins Word Web. Constantly updated, and with over 2.5 billion entries, this living language resource is unique to our dictionaries.

Words are tools for life. And a Collins Dictionary makes them work for you.

**Collins. Do more.**

# Contents

# Introduction

When this thesaurus was first published in 1992, it proved to be an immensely popular language resource. This new edition has been completely revised to give you even more ways of expressing yourself, with a clear and attractive layout which highlights its many extra features.

The headword list has been selected on the basis of frequency as verified by the *Collins Word Web*, which means that the entry words given are those most likely to be looked up by the user. The key synonym for each sense is shown first, which not only offers you the most helpful alternative but also lets you identify the sense in question at a glance. Other synonyms are arranged in order of their frequency of occurrence. In addition, all main entry words are printed in colour so that they are quick and easy to find.

The thesaurus offers extensive coverage of English as a world language, with words and phrases from all over the English-speaking world making this a truly international language resource.

As well as generous synonym lists, key antonyms are included for many entry words. But this new edition gives you much more than just synonyms and antonyms.

The *Related Words* feature enables you to find information such as adjectives and collective nouns connected with many main entry words.

Informative subject word lists provide a wealth of material connected with many entry words. In addition, the new *Word Power* supplement lists famous people such as actors, novelists, and politicians, all arranged by their occupations. It also lists geographical information such as countries, capitals, and currencies, arranged by subject. It is therefore a source of invaluable information for solving general-knowledge clues in crosswords and puzzles, and for boosting home study.

Helpful *Word Power* notes are also included at key entries. These give advice on good English and help you to avoid some of the more common language mistakes.

All these features mean that this new thesaurus is a treasury of useful and practical words and information, arranged in the most helpful way possible.

# Features of the Thesaurus

**Entry words**
in colour

**speed** NOUN 1= <u>rate</u>, pace
2= <u>swiftness</u>, rush, hurry, haste,
rapidity, quickness ≠ slowness
• VERB 1= <u>race</u>, rush, hurry, zoom,
career, tear, barrel (along)
(*informal, chiefly U.S. & Canad.*),
gallop ≠ crawl 2= <u>help</u>, advance,
aid, boost, assist, facilitate,
expedite ≠ hinder

**Synonyms** offer a
wide range of
alternatives

**Regional labels**

**Word Power notes**
give advice on
good English

### Word Power

**speed**– The past tense of
*speed up* is *speeded up* (not *sped
up*), for example *I speeded up to
overtake the lorry.* The past
participle is also *speeded up*, for
example *I had already speeded
up when I spotted the police car.*

**Related words**
expand your
vocabulary

**spider**► **spiders and other**
**arachnids**

*Related Words*

fear of: arachnophobia

**Cross**
**references**

#### Spiders and other arachnids

| | |
|---|---|
| black widow | red-back (spider) |
| chigger, chigoe, *or (U.S. &* | spider |
| *Canad.)* redbug | spider mite |
| chigoe, chigger, jigger, *or sand* | tarantula |
| flea | tick |
| harvestman *or (U.S. & Canad.)* | trap-door spider |
| daddy-longlegs | whip scorpion |
| katipo | wolf spider *or hunting spider* |
| mite | |

**Sense numbers**

**spin** VERB 1= <u>revolve</u>, turn, rotate,
reel, whirl, twirl, gyrate, pirouette
2= <u>reel</u>, swim, whirl
• NOUN 1(*informal*) = <u>drive</u>, ride,
joy ride (*informal*) 2= <u>revolution</u>,
roll, whirl, gyration
• PHRASES **spin something out**
= prolong, extend, lengthen,
draw out, drag out, delay, amplify

**Subject word lists**
add an extra
dimension to
your vocabulary

**Idioms and**
**phrases** add
colour to your
language

x

# Features of the Thesaurus

**International English** from all regions of the world where English is spoken

**Key synonyms** given first

**Part of speech labels**

**Fixed phrases**

**spirit** NOUN 1 = <u>soul</u>, life 2 = <u>life force</u>, vital spark, mauri (N.Z.) 3 = <u>ghost</u>, phantom, spectre, apparition, atua (N.Z.), kehua (N.Z.) 4 = <u>courage</u>, guts (informal), grit, backbone, spunk (informal), gameness 5 = <u>liveliness</u>, energy, vigour, life, force, fire, enthusiasm, animation 6 = <u>attitude</u>, character, temper, outlook, temperament, disposition 7 = <u>heart</u>, sense, nature, soul, core, substance, essence, quintessence 8 = <u>intention</u>, meaning, purpose, purport, gist 9 = <u>feeling</u>, atmosphere, character, tone, mood, tenor, ambience

• PLURAL NOUN = <u>mood</u>, feelings, morale, temper, disposition, state of mind, frame of mind

**spite** NOUN = <u>malice</u>, malevolence, ill will, hatred, animosity, venom, spleen, spitefulness ≠ kindness

• VERB = <u>annoy</u>, hurt, injure, harm, vex ≠ benefit

• PHRASES **in spite of** = <u>despite</u>, regardless of, notwithstanding,

**Labels** identify areas of usage

**Opposites** given for many key words

# Lists in the Thesaurus

# Lists in the Thesaurus

# A

**abandon** VERB 1 = <u>leave</u>, strand, ditch, forsake, run out on, desert, dump 2 = <u>stop</u>, give up, halt, pack in (*Brit. informal*), discontinue, leave off ≠ continue 3 = <u>give up</u>, yield, surrender, relinquish ≠ keep

● NOUN = <u>recklessness</u>, wildness ≠ restraint

**abandonment** = <u>desertion</u>, leaving, forsaking

**abbey** = <u>monastery</u>, convent, priory, nunnery, friary

**abduct** = <u>kidnap</u>, seize, carry off, snatch (*slang*)

**abide** VERB = <u>tolerate</u>, suffer, accept, bear, endure, put up with, take, stand

● PHRASES **abide by something** = <u>obey</u>, follow, agree to, carry out, observe, fulfil, act on, comply with

**abiding** = <u>enduring</u>, lasting, continuing, permanent, persistent, everlasting ≠ brief

**ability** 1 = <u>capability</u>, potential, competence, proficiency ≠ inability 2 = <u>skill</u>, talent, expertise, competence, aptitude, proficiency, cleverness

**able** = <u>capable</u>, qualified, efficient, accomplished, competent, skilful, proficient ≠ incapable

**abnormal** = <u>unusual</u>, different, odd, strange, extraordinary, remarkable, exceptional, peculiar ≠ normal

**abnormality** 1 = <u>strangeness</u>, peculiarity, irregularity, singularity 2 = <u>anomaly</u>, oddity, exception, peculiarity, deformity, irregularity

**abolish** = <u>do away with</u>, end, destroy, eliminate, cancel, get rid of, ditch (*slang*), throw out ≠ establish

**abolition** = <u>eradication</u>, ending, end, destruction, wiping out, elimination, cancellation, termination

**abort** 1 = <u>terminate</u> (*a pregnancy*), miscarry 2 = <u>stop</u>, end, finish, check, arrest, halt, cease, axe (*informal*)

**abortion** = <u>termination</u>, miscarriage, deliberate miscarriage

**abound** = <u>be plentiful</u>, thrive, flourish, be numerous, proliferate, be abundant, be thick on the ground

**about** PREPOSITION 1 = <u>regarding</u>, on, concerning, dealing with, referring to, relating to, as regards 2 = <u>near</u>, around, close to, nearby, beside, adjacent to, in the neighbourhood of

● ADVERB = <u>approximately</u>, around, almost, nearly, approaching, close to, roughly, just about

**above** 1 = <u>over</u>, upon, beyond, on top of, exceeding, higher than

≠ under 2 = <u>superior to</u>, over, ahead of, in charge of, higher than, superior to, more powerful than

**abroad** = <u>overseas</u>, out of the country, in foreign lands

**abrupt** 1 = <u>sudden</u>, unexpected, rapid, surprising, quick, rash, precipitate ≠ <u>slow</u> 2 = <u>curt</u>, brief, short, rude, impatient, terse, gruff, succinct ≠ polite

**absence** 1 = <u>time off</u>, leave, break, vacation, recess, truancy, absenteeism, nonattendance 2 = <u>lack</u>, deficiency, omission, scarcity, want, need, shortage, dearth

**absent** ADJECTIVE 1 = <u>away</u>, missing, gone, elsewhere, unavailable, nonexistent ≠ present 2 = <u>absent-minded</u>, blank, vague, distracted, vacant, preoccupied, oblivious, inattentive ≠ alert

● PHRASES **absent yourself** = <u>stay away</u>, withdraw, keep away, play truant

**absolute** 1 = <u>complete</u>, total, perfect, pure, sheer, utter, outright, thorough 2 = <u>supreme</u>, sovereign, unlimited, ultimate, full, unconditional, unrestricted, pre-eminent 3 = <u>autocratic</u>, supreme, all-powerful, imperious, domineering, tyrannical

**absolutely** = <u>completely</u>, totally, perfectly, fully, entirely, altogether, wholly, utterly

≠ somewhat

**absorb** 1 = <u>soak up</u>, suck up, receive, digest, imbibe 2 = <u>engross</u>, involve, engage, fascinate, rivet, captivate

**absorbed** = <u>engrossed</u>, lost, involved, gripped, fascinated, caught up, wrapped up, preoccupied

**absorbing** = <u>fascinating</u>, interesting, engaging, gripping, compelling, intriguing, enticing, riveting ≠ boring

**absorption** 1 = <u>soaking up</u>, consumption, digestion, sucking up 2 = <u>immersion</u>, involvement, concentration, fascination, preoccupation, intentness

**abstract** ADJECTIVE 1 = <u>theoretical</u>, general, academic, speculative, indefinite, hypothetical, notional, abstruse ≠ actual

● NOUN = <u>summary</u>, résumé, outline, digest, epitome, rundown, synopsis, précis ≠ expansion

● VERB = <u>extract</u>, draw, pull, remove, separate, withdraw, isolate, pull out ≠ add

**absurd** = <u>ridiculous</u>, crazy (*informal*), silly, foolish, ludicrous, unreasonable, irrational, senseless ≠ sensible

**abundance** = <u>plenty</u>, bounty, exuberance, profusion, plethora, affluence, fullness, fruitfulness ≠ shortage

**abundant** = plentiful, full, rich, liberal, generous, ample, exuberant, teeming ≠ scarce

**abuse** NOUN 1 = maltreatment, damage, injury, hurt, harm, exploitation, manhandling, ill-treatment 2 = insults, blame, slights, put-downs, censure, reproach, scolding, defamation 3 = misuse, misapplication

● VERB 1 = ill-treat, damage, hurt, injure, harm, molest, maltreat, knock about or around ≠ care for 2 = insult, offend, curse, put down, malign, scold, disparage, castigate ≠ praise

**abusive** 1 = violent, rough, cruel, savage, brutal, vicious, destructive, harmful ≠ kind 2 = insulting, offensive, rude, degrading, scathing, contemptuous, disparaging, scurrilous ≠ complimentary

**academic** ADJECTIVE 1 = scholastic, educational 2 = scholarly, learned, intellectual, literary, erudite, highbrow, studious 3 = theoretical, abstract, speculative, hypothetical, impractical, notional, conjectural

● NOUN = scholar, intellectual, don, master, professor, fellow, lecturer, tutor, acca (Austral. slang)

**accelerate** 1 = increase, grow, advance, extend, expand, raise, swell, enlarge ≠ fall 2 = expedite,

further, speed up, hasten ≠ delay 3 = speed up, advance, quicken, gather momentum ≠ slow down

**acceleration** = hastening, hurrying, stepping up (informal), speeding up, quickening

**accent** NOUN 1 = pronunciation, tone, articulation, inflection, brogue, intonation, diction, modulation

● VERB = emphasize, stress, highlight, underline, underscore, accentuate

**accept** 1 = receive, take, gain, pick up, secure, collect, get, obtain 2 = acknowledge, believe, allow, admit, approve, recognize, yield, concede

**acceptable** = satisfactory, fair, all right, suitable, sufficient, good enough, adequate, tolerable ≠ unsatisfactory

**acceptance** 1 = accepting, taking, receiving, obtaining, acquiring, reception, receipt 2 = acknowledgement, agreement, approval, recognition, admission, consent, adoption, assent

**accepted** = agreed, common, established, traditional, approved, acknowledged, recognized, customary ≠ unconventional

**access** 1 = admission, entry, passage 2 = entrance, road, approach, entry, path, gate, opening, passage

**accessible** = handy, near,

nearby, at hand, within reach, at your fingertips, reachable, achievable ≠ inaccessible

**accessory** 1 = <u>extra</u>, addition, supplement, attachment, adjunct, appendage 2 = <u>accomplice</u>, partner, ally, associate (*in crime*), assistant, helper, colleague, collaborator

**accident** 1 = <u>crash</u>, smash, wreck, collision 2 = <u>misfortune</u>, disaster, tragedy, setback, calamity, mishap, misadventure 3 = <u>chance</u>, fortune, luck, fate, hazard, coincidence, fluke, fortuity

**accidental** 1 = <u>unintentional</u>, unexpected, incidental, unforeseen, unplanned ≠ deliberate 2 = <u>chance</u>, random, casual, unplanned, fortuitous, inadvertent

**accidentally** = <u>unintentionally</u>, incidentally, by accident, by chance, inadvertently, unwittingly, randomly, haphazardly ≠ deliberately

**acclaim** VERB = <u>praise</u>, celebrate, honour, cheer, admire, hail, applaud, compliment
● NOUN = <u>praise</u>, honour, celebration, approval, tribute, applause, kudos, commendation ≠ criticism

**accommodate** 1 = <u>house</u>, put up, take in, lodge, shelter, entertain, cater for 2 = <u>help</u>,

support, aid, assist, cooperate with, abet, lend a hand to 3 = <u>adapt</u>, fit, settle, alter, adjust, modify, comply, reconcile

**accommodating** = <u>obliging</u>, willing, kind, friendly, helpful, polite, cooperative, agreeable ≠ unhelpful

**accommodation** = <u>housing</u>, homes, houses, board, quarters, digs (*Brit. informal*), shelter, lodging(s)

**accompaniment** 1 = <u>backing</u>, music, backing, support, obbligato 2 = <u>supplement</u>, extra, addition, companion, accessory, complement, decoration, adjunct

**accompany** 1 = <u>go with</u>, lead, partner, guide, attend, conduct, escort, shepherd 2 = <u>occur with</u>, belong to, come with, supplement, go together with, follow

**accompanying** = <u>additional</u>, extra, related, associated, attached, attendant, complementary, supplementary

**accomplish** = <u>realize</u>, produce, effect, finish, complete, manage, achieve, perform ≠ fail

**accomplished** = <u>skilled</u>, able, professional, expert, masterly, talented, gifted, polished ≠ unskilled

**accomplishment**
1 = <u>achievement</u>, feat, act, stroke, triumph, coup, exploit, deed 2 = <u>accomplishing</u>, finishing,

carrying out, conclusion, bringing about, execution, completion, fulfilment

**accord** NOUN 1 = <u>treaty</u>, contract, agreement, arrangement, settlement, pact, deal (*informal*) 2 = <u>sympathy</u>, agreement, harmony, unison, rapport, conformity ≠ conflict

● PHRASES **accord with something** = <u>agree with</u>, match, coincide with, fit with, correspond with, conform with, tally with, harmonize with

**accordingly** 1 = <u>consequently</u>, so, thus, therefore, hence, subsequently, in consequence, ergo 2 = <u>appropriately</u>, correspondingly, properly, suitably, fitly

**account** NOUN 1 = <u>description</u>, report, story, statement, version, tale, explanation, narrative 2 = <u>importance</u>, standing, concern, value, note, worth, weight, honour

● PLURAL NOUN (*Commerce*) = <u>ledgers</u>, books, charges, bills, statements, balances, tallies, invoices

● VERB = <u>consider</u>, rate, value, judge, estimate, think, count, reckon

**accountability** = <u>responsibility</u>, liability, culpability, answerability, chargeability

**accountable** = <u>answerable</u>, subject, responsible, obliged, liable, amenable, obligated, chargeable

**accountant** = <u>auditor</u>, book-keeper, bean counter (*informal*)

**accumulate** = <u>build up</u>, increase, be stored, collect, gather, pile up, amass, hoard ≠ disperse

**accumulation** 1 = <u>collection</u>, increase, stock, store, mass, build-up, pile, stack 2 = <u>growth</u>, collection, gathering, build-up

**accuracy** = <u>exactness</u>, precision, fidelity, authenticity, correctness, closeness, veracity, truthfulness ≠ inaccuracy

**accurate** 1 = <u>precise</u>, close, correct, careful, strict, exact, faithful, explicit ≠ inaccurate 2 = <u>correct</u>, true, exact, spot-on (*Brit. informal*)

**accurately** 1 = <u>precisely</u>, correctly, closely, truly, strictly, exactly, faithfully, to the letter 2 = <u>exactly</u>, closely, correctly, precisely, strictly, faithfully, explicitly, scrupulously

**accusation** = <u>charge</u>, complaint, allegation, indictment, recrimination, denunciation, incrimination

**accuse** 1 = <u>point at or the finger</u> at, blame for, denounce, hold responsible for, impute blame to ≠ exonerate 2 = <u>charge with</u>, indict for, impeach for, censure

**accustom** 1 = familiarize, train, discipline, adapt, instruct, school, acquaint, acclimatize

**accustomed** 1 = used, trained, familiar, given to, adapted, acquainted, in the habit of, familiarized ≠ unaccustomed 2 = usual, established, expected, common, standard, traditional, normal, regular ≠ unusual

**ace** NOUN 1 (*Cards, dice*) = one, single point 2 (*Informal*) = expert, star, champion, authority, professional, master, specialist, guru
• ADJECTIVE (*Informal*) = great, brilliant, fine, wonderful, excellent, outstanding, superb, fantastic (*informal*), bonzer (*Austral. slang*), exo (*Austral. slang*), sik (*Austral. slang*), ka pai (*N.Z.*)

**ache** VERB = hurt, suffer, burn, pain, smart, sting, pound, throb
• NOUN = pain, discomfort, suffering, hurt, throbbing, irritation, tenderness, pounding

**achieve** = accomplish, fulfil, complete, gain, perform, do, get, carry out

**achievement** = accomplishment, effort, feat, deed, stroke, triumph, coup, exploit

**acid** 1 = sour, tart, pungent, acerbic, acrid, vinegary ≠ sweet 2 = sharp, cutting, biting, bitter,

harsh, barbed, caustic, vitriolic ≠ kindly

**acknowledge** 1 = admit, own up, allow, accept, reveal, grant, declare, recognize ≠ deny 2 = greet, address, notice, recognize, salute, accost ≠ snub 3 = reply to, answer, notice, recognize, respond to, react to, retort to ≠ ignore

**acquaintance** 1 = associate, contact, ally, colleague, comrade ≠ intimate 2 = relationship, connection, fellowship, familiarity ≠ unfamiliarity

**acquire** = get, win, buy, receive, gain, earn, secure, collect ≠ lose

**acquisition** 1 = acquiring, gaining, procurement, attainment 2 = purchase, buy, investment, property, gain, prize, asset, possession

**acquit** VERB = clear, free, release, excuse, discharge, liberate, vindicate ≠ find guilty
• PHRASES **acquit yourself** = behave, bear yourself, conduct yourself, comport yourself

**act** VERB 1 = do something, perform, function 2 = perform, mimic
• NOUN 1 = deed, action, performance, achievement, undertaking, exploit, feat, accomplishment 2 = pretence, show, front, performance, display, attitude, pose, posture 3 = law,

bill, measure, resolution, decree, statute, ordinance, enactment **4** = _performance_, show, turn, production, routine, presentation, gig (_informal_), sketch

**acting** NOUN = _performance_, playing, performing, theatre, portrayal, impersonation, characterization, stagecraft
● ADJECTIVE = _temporary_, substitute, interim, provisional, surrogate, stopgap, pro tem

**action 1** = _deed_, act, performance, achievement, exploit, feat, accomplishment **2** = _measure_, act, manoeuvre **3** = _lawsuit_, case, trial, suit, proceeding, dispute, prosecution, litigation **4** = _energy_, activity, spirit, force, vitality, vigour, liveliness, vim **5** = _effect_, working, process, operation, activity, movement, functioning, motion **6** = _battle_, fight, conflict, clash, contest, encounter, combat, engagement

**activate** = _start_, move, initiate, rouse, mobilize, set in motion, galvanize ≠ stop

**active 1** = _busy_, involved, occupied, lively, energetic, bustling, on the move, strenuous ≠ sluggish **2** = _energetic_, quick, alert, dynamic, lively, vigorous, animated, forceful ≠ inactive **3** = _in operation_, working, acting, at work, in action, operative, in force, effectual

**activist** = _militant_, partisan

**activity 1** = _action_, labour, movement, energy, exercise, spirit, motion, bustle ≠ inaction **2** = _pursuit_, project, scheme, pleasure, interest, hobby, pastime

**actor** _or_ **actress** = _performer_, player, Thespian, luvvie (_informal_)
➤ **WORD POWER SUPPLEMENT actors**

### Word Power

**actor/actress** – The use of _actress_ is now very much on the decline, and women who work in the profession invariably prefer to be referred to as _actors_.

**actual** = _real_, substantial, concrete, definite, tangible

### Word Power

**actual** – The words _actual_ and _actually_ are often used when speaking, but should only be used in writing where they add something to the meaning of a sentence. For example, in the sentence _he actually rather enjoyed the film_, the word _actually_ is only needed if there was originally some doubt as to whether he would enjoy it.

**actually** = _really_, in fact, indeed, truly, literally, genuinely, in reality, in truth

**acute** 1 = <u>serious</u>, important, dangerous, critical, crucial, severe, grave, urgent 2 = <u>sharp</u>, shooting, powerful, violent, severe, intense, fierce, piercing 3 = <u>perceptive</u>, sharp, keen, smart, sensitive, clever, astute, insightful ≠ slow

**adamant** = <u>determined</u>, firm, fixed, stubborn, uncompromising, resolute, unbending, obdurate ≠ flexible

**adapt** 1 = <u>adjust</u>, change, alter, modify, accommodate, conform, acclimatize 2 = <u>convert</u>, change, transform, alter, modify, tailor, remodel

**adaptation** 1 = <u>acclimatization</u>, naturalization, familiarization 2 = <u>conversion</u>, change, variation, adjustment, transformation, modification, alteration

**add** 1 = <u>count up</u>, total, reckon, compute, add up, tot up ≠ take away 2 = <u>include</u>, attach, supplement, adjoin, augment, affix, append

**addict** 1 = <u>junkie</u> (*informal*), freak (*informal*), fiend (*informal*) 2 = <u>fan</u>, lover, nut (*slang*), follower, enthusiast, admirer, buff (*informal*), junkie (*informal*)

**addicted**

● PHRASES **addicted to** = <u>hooked on</u>, dependent on, accustomed to (*slang*), habituated to

**addiction** = <u>dependence</u>, habit, obsession, craving, enslavement with to = <u>love of</u>, passion for, attachment to

**addition** NOUN 1 = <u>extra</u>, supplement, increase, gain, bonus, extension, accessory, additive 2 = <u>inclusion</u>, adding, increasing, extension, attachment, insertion, incorporation, augmentation ≠ removal 3 = <u>counting up</u>, totalling, adding up, computation, totting up ≠ subtraction

● PHRASES **in addition to** = <u>as well as</u>, along with, on top of, besides, to boot, additionally, over and above, to say nothing of

**additional** = <u>extra</u>, new, other, added, further, fresh, spare, supplementary

**address** NOUN 1 = <u>location</u>, home, place, house, point, position, situation, site 2 = <u>speech</u>, talk, lecture, discourse, sermon, dissertation, homily, oration

● VERB = <u>speak to</u>, talk to, greet, hail, approach, converse with, korero (*N.Z.*)

**adept** ADJECTIVE = <u>skilful</u>, able, skilled, expert, practised, accomplished, versed, proficient ≠ unskilled

● NOUN = <u>expert</u>, master, genius, hotshot (*informal*), dab hand (*Brit. informal*)

**adequate** 1= passable, acceptable, average, fair, satisfactory, competent, mediocre, so-so (*informal*) ≠ inadequate ≠ sufficient, enough ≠ insufficient

**adhere to** = stick to, attach to, cling to, glue to, fix to, fasten to, hold fast to, paste to

**adjacent** ADJECTIVE = adjoining, neighbouring, nearby ≠ far away
● PREPOSITION with to= next to, touching, close to, neighbouring, beside, near to, adjoining, bordering on

**adjoin** = connect with *or* to, join, link with, touch on, border on

**adjoining** = connecting, touching, bordering, neighbouring, next door, adjacent, abutting

**adjourn** = postpone, delay, suspend, interrupt, put off, defer, discontinue ≠ continue

**adjust** 1= adapt, change, alter, accustom, conform 2= change, reform, alter, adapt, revise, modify, amend, make conform 3= modify, alter, adapt

**adjustable** = alterable, flexible, adaptable, malleable, movable, modifiable

**adjustment** 1= alteration, change, tuning, repair, conversion, modifying, adaptation, modification 2= acclimatization, orientation,

change, regulation, amendment, adaptation, revision, modification

**administer** 1= manage, run, control, direct, handle, conduct, command, govern 2= dispense, give, share, provide, apply, assign, allocate, allot 3= execute, give, provide, apply, impose, carry out, impose, implement

**administration**
1= management, government, running, control, handling, direction, conduct, application 2= directors, board, executive(s), employers 3= government, leadership, regime

**administrative** = managerial, executive, directing, regulatory, governmental, organizational, supervisory, directorial

**administrator** = manager, head, official, director, executive, boss (*informal*), governor, supervisor, baas (*S. African*)

**admirable** = praiseworthy, good, great, fine, wonderful, excellent, brilliant, outstanding, booshit (*Austral. slang*), exo (*Austral. slang*), sik (*Austral. slang*), ka pai (*N.Z.*) ≠ deplorable

**admiration** = regard, wonder, respect, praise, approval, recognition, esteem, appreciation

**admire** 1= respect, value, prize, honour, praise, appreciate, esteem, approve of ≠ despise 2= adore, like, love, take to, fancy

(*Brit. informal*), treasure, cherish, glorify 3 = <u>marvel at</u>, look at, appreciate, delight in, wonder at, be amazed by, take pleasure in, gape at

**admirer** 1 = <u>fan</u>, supporter, follower, enthusiast, partisan, disciple, devotee 2 = <u>suitor</u>, lover, boyfriend, sweetheart, beau, wooer

**admission** 1 = <u>admittance</u>, access, entry, introduction, entrance, acceptance, initiation, entrée 2 = <u>confession</u>, declaration, revelation, allowance, disclosure, acknowledgement, unburdening, divulgence

**admit** 1 = <u>confess</u>, confide, own up, come clean (*informal*) 2 = <u>allow</u>, agree, accept, reveal, grant, declare, acknowledge, recognize ≠ deny 3 = <u>let in</u>, allow, receive, accept, introduce, take in, initiate, give access to ≠ keep out

**adolescence** = <u>teens</u>, youth, minority, boyhood, girlhood

**adolescent** ADJECTIVE 1 = <u>young</u>, junior, teenage, juvenile, youthful, childish, immature, boyish 2 = <u>teenage</u>, young, teen (*informal*)
● NOUN = <u>teenager</u>, girl, boy, kid (*informal*), youth, lad, minor, young man

**adopt** 1 = <u>take on</u>, follow, choose, maintain, assume, take up, engage in, become involved

in 2 = <u>take in</u>, raise, nurse, mother, rear, foster, bring up, take care of ≠ abandon

**adoption** 1 = <u>fostering</u>, adopting, taking in 2 = <u>embracing</u>, choice, taking up, selection, assumption, endorsement, appropriation, espousal

**adore** = <u>love</u>, honour, admire, worship, esteem, cherish, revere, dote on ≠ hate

**adoring** = <u>admiring</u>, loving, devoted, fond, affectionate, doting ≠ hating

**adorn** = <u>decorate</u>, array, embellish, festoon

**adrift** ADJECTIVE 1 = <u>drifting</u>, afloat, unmoored, unanchored 2 = <u>aimless</u>, goalless, directionless, purposeless
● ADVERB = <u>wrong</u>, astray, off course, amiss, off target, wide of the mark

**adult** NOUN = <u>grown-up</u>, mature person, person of mature age, grown or grown-up person, man or woman
● ADJECTIVE 1 = <u>fully grown</u>, mature, grown-up, of age, ripe, fully fledged, fully developed, full grown 2 = <u>pornographic</u>, blue, dirty, obscene, filthy, indecent, lewd, salacious

**advance** VERB 1 = <u>progress</u>, proceed, come forward, make inroads, make headway ≠ retreat

2 = <u>accelerate</u>, speed, promote, hasten, bring forward
3 = <u>improve</u>, rise, develop, pick up, progress, upgrade, prosper, make strides 4 = <u>suggest</u>, offer, present, propose, advocate, submit, prescribe, put forward ≠ withhold 5 = <u>lend</u>, loan, supply on credit ≠ withhold payment
● NOUN 1 = <u>down payment</u>, credit, loan, fee, deposit, retainer, prepayment 2 = <u>attack</u>, charge, strike, assault, raid, invasion, offensive, onslaught
3 = <u>improvement</u>, development, gain, growth, breakthrough, step, headway, inroads
● ADJECTIVE = <u>prior</u>, early, beforehand
● PHRASES in advance = <u>beforehand</u>, earlier, ahead, previously
**advanced** = <u>sophisticated</u>, foremost, modern, revolutionary, up-to-date, higher, leading, recent ≠ backward
**advancement** = <u>promotion</u>, rise, gain, progress, improvement, betterment, preferment
**advantage** 1 = <u>benefit</u>, help, profit, favour ≠ disadvantage
2 = <u>lead</u>, sway, dominance, precedence 3 = <u>superiority</u>, good
**adventure** 1 = <u>venture</u>, experience, incident, enterprise, undertaking, exploit, occurrence, caper 2 = <u>excitement</u>, action,

passion, thrill, animation, commotion
**adventurous** = <u>daring</u>, enterprising, bold, reckless, intrepid, daredevil ≠ cautious
**adversary** = <u>opponent</u>, rival, enemy, competitor, foe, contestant, antagonist ≠ ally
**adverse** 1 = <u>harmful</u>, damaging, negative, destructive, detrimental, hurtful, injurious, inopportune ≠ beneficial
2 = <u>unfavourable</u>, hostile, unlucky 3 = <u>negative</u>, opposing, hostile, contrary, dissenting, unsympathetic, ill-disposed
**advert** (*Brit. informal*) = <u>advertisement</u>, notice, commercial, ad (*informal*), announcement, poster, plug (*informal*), blurb
**advertise** = <u>publicize</u>, promote, plug (*informal*), announce, inform, hype, notify, tout
**advertisement** = <u>advert</u> (*Brit. informal*), notice, commercial, ad (*informal*), announcement, poster, plug (*informal*), blurb
**advice** = <u>guidance</u>, help, opinion, direction, suggestion, instruction, counsel, counselling
**advise** 1 = <u>recommend</u>, suggest, urge, counsel, advocate, caution, prescribe, commend 2 = <u>notify</u>, tell, report, announce, warn, declare, inform, acquaint
**adviser** = <u>counsellor</u>, guide,

consultant, aide, guru, mentor, helper, confidant

**advisory** = advising, helping, recommending, counselling, consultative

**advocate** VERB = recommend, support, champion, encourage, propose, promote, advise, endorse ≠ oppose

● NOUN 1 = supporter, spokesman, champion, defender, campaigner, promoter, counsellor, proponent 2 (*Law*) = lawyer, attorney, solicitor, counsel, barrister

**affair** 1 = matter, business, happening, event, activity, incident, episode, topic 2 = relationship, romance, intrigue, fling, liaison, flirtation, amour, dalliance

**affect**[1] 1 = influence, concern, alter, change, manipulate, act on, bear upon, impinge upon 2 = emotionally move, touch, upset, overcome, stir, disturb, perturb

**affect**[2] 1 = put on, assume, adopt, pretend, imitate, simulate, contrive, aspire to

**affected** = pretended, artificial, contrived, put-on, mannered, unnatural, feigned, insincere ≠ genuine

**affection** = fondness, liking, feeling, love, care, warmth, attachment, goodwill, aroha (*N.Z.*)

**affectionate** = fond, loving,

kind, caring, friendly, attached, devoted, tender ≠ cool

**affiliate** = associate, unite, join, link, ally, combine, incorporate, amalgamate

**affinity** 1 = attraction, liking, leaning, sympathy, inclination, rapport, fondness, partiality, aroha (*N.Z.*) ≠ hostility 2 = similarity, relationship, connection, correspondence, analogy, resemblance, closeness, likeness ≠ difference

**affirm** 1 = declare, state, maintain, swear, assert, testify, pronounce, certify ≠ deny 2 = confirm, prove, endorse, ratify, verify, validate, bear out, substantiate ≠ refute

**affirmative** = agreeing, confirming, positive, approving, consenting, favourable, concurring, assenting ≠ negative

**afflict** = torment, trouble, pain, hurt, distress, plague, grieve, harass

**affluent** = wealthy, rich, prosperous, loaded (*slang*), well-off, opulent, well-heeled (*informal*), well-to-do ≠ poor

**afford** 1 = have the money for, manage, bear, pay for, spare, stand, stretch to 2 = bear, stand, sustain, allow yourself 3 = give, offer, provide, produce, supply, yield, render

**affordable** = inexpensive,

cheap, reasonable, moderate, modest, low-cost, economical ≠ expensive

**afraid** 1 = <u>scared</u>, frightened, nervous, terrified, shaken, startled, fearful, cowardly ≠ unafraid 2 = <u>reluctant</u>, frightened, scared, unwilling, hesitant, loath, disinclined, unenthusiastic 3 = <u>sorry</u>, apologetic, regretful, sad, distressed, unhappy ≠ pleased

**after** PREPOSITION = <u>at the end of</u>, following, subsequent to ≠ before

● ADVERB = <u>following</u>, later, next, succeeding, afterwards, subsequently, thereafter

*Related Words*

prefix: post-

**aftermath** = <u>effects</u>, results, wake, consequences, outcome, sequel, end result, upshot

**again** 1 = <u>once more</u>, another time, anew, afresh 2 = <u>also</u>, in addition, moreover, besides, furthermore

**against** 1 = <u>beside</u>, on, up against, in contact with, abutting 2 = <u>opposed to</u>, anti (*informal*), hostile to, in opposition to, averse to, opposite to 3 = <u>in opposition to</u>, resisting, versus, counter to, in the opposite direction of 4 = <u>in preparation for</u>, in case of, in anticipation of, in expectation of, in provision for

*Related Words*

prefixes: anti-, counter-

**age** NOUN 1 = <u>years</u>, days, generation, lifetime, length of existence 2 = <u>old age</u>, experience, maturity, seniority, majority, senility, decline (*of life*), advancing years ≠ youth 3 = <u>time</u>, day(s), period, generation, era, epoch

● VERB 1 = <u>grow old</u>, decline, weather, fade, deteriorate, wither 2 = <u>mature</u>, season, condition, soften, mellow, ripen

**aged** = <u>old</u>, getting on, grey, ancient, antique, elderly, antiquated ≠ young

**agency** 1 = <u>business</u>, company, office, firm, department, organization, enterprise, establishment 2 (*Old-fashioned*) = <u>medium</u>, means, activity, vehicle, instrument, mechanism

**agenda** = <u>programme</u>, list, plan, schedule, diary, calendar, timetable

**agent** 1 = <u>representative</u>, rep (*informal*), negotiator, envoy, surrogate, go-between 2 = <u>author</u>, worker, vehicle, instrument, operator, performer, catalyst, doer 3 = <u>force</u>, means, power, cause, instrument

**aggravate** 1 = <u>make worse</u>, exaggerate, intensify, worsen, exacerbate, magnify, inflame, increase ≠ improve 2 (*Informal*)

= <u>annoy</u>, bother, provoke, irritate, nettle, get on your nerves (*informal*) ≠ please

**aggregate** NOUN = <u>total</u>, body, whole, amount, collection, mass, sum, combination

● ADJECTIVE = <u>collective</u>, mixed, combined, collected, accumulated, composite, cumulative

● VERB = <u>combine</u>, mix, collect, assemble, heap, accumulate, pile, amass

**aggression** 1 = <u>hostility</u>, malice, antagonism, antipathy, ill will, belligerence, destructiveness, pugnacity 2 = <u>attack</u>, campaign, injury, assault, raid, invasion, offensive, onslaught

**aggressive** 1 = <u>hostile</u>, offensive, destructive, belligerent, unfriendly, contrary, antagonistic, pugnacious, aggers (*Austral. slang*), biffo (*Austral. slang*) ≠ friendly 2 = <u>forceful</u>, powerful, convincing, effective, enterprising, dynamic, bold, militant ≠ submissive

**agitate** 1 = <u>stir</u>, beat, shake, disturb, toss, rouse 2 = <u>upset</u>, worry, trouble, excite, distract, unnerve, disconcert, fluster ≠ calm

**agony** = <u>suffering</u>, pain, distress, misery, torture, discomfort, torment, hardship

**agree** 1 = <u>concur</u>, be as one,
sympathize, assent, see eye to eye, be of the same opinion ≠ disagree 2 = <u>correspond</u>, match, coincide, tally, conform 3 = <u>suit</u>, get on, befit

**agreement** 1 = <u>treaty</u>, contract, arrangement, alliance, deal (*informal*), understanding, settlement, bargain 2 = <u>concurrence</u>, harmony, compliance, union, agreeing, consent, unison, assent ≠ disagreement 3 = <u>correspondence</u>, similarity, consistency, correlation, conformity, compatibility, congruity ≠ difference

**agricultural** = <u>farming</u>, country, rural, rustic, agrarian

**agriculture** = <u>farming</u>, culture, cultivation, husbandry, tillage

**ahead** 1 = <u>in front</u>, in advance, towards the front, frontwards 2 = <u>at an advantage</u>, in advance, in the lead 3 = <u>in the lead</u>, winning, leading, at the head, to the fore, at an advantage 4 = <u>in front</u>, before, in advance, in the lead

**aid** NOUN = <u>help</u>, backing, support, benefit, favour, relief, promotion, assistance ≠ hindrance

● VERB 1 = <u>help</u>, support, serve, sustain, assist, avail, subsidize, be of service to ≠ hinder 2 = <u>promote</u>, help, further, forward, encourage, favour, facilitate, pave the way for

**aide** = <u>assistant</u>, supporter, attendant, helper, right-hand man, second

**ailing** 1 = <u>weak</u>, failing, poor, flawed, unstable, unsatisfactory, deficient 2 = <u>ill</u>, poorly, sick, weak, crook (*Austral. & N.Z. informal*), unwell, infirm, under the weather (*informal*), indisposed

**ailment** = <u>illness</u>, disease, complaint, disorder, sickness, affliction, malady, infirmity

**aim** VERB 1 = <u>try for</u>, seek, work for, plan for, strive, set your sights on 2 = <u>point</u>
• NOUN = <u>intention</u>, point, plan, goal, design, target, purpose, desire

**air** NOUN 1 = <u>wind</u>, breeze, draught, gust, zephyr 2 = <u>atmosphere</u>, sky, heavens, aerosphere 3 = <u>tune</u>, song, theme, melody, strain, lay, aria 4 = <u>manner</u>, appearance, look, aspect, atmosphere, mood, impression, aura
• PLURAL NOUN = <u>affectation</u>, arrogance, pretensions, pomposity, swank (*informal*), hauteur, haughtiness, superciliousness
• VERB 1 = <u>publicize</u>, reveal, exhibit, voice, express, display, circulate, make public 2 = <u>ventilate</u>, expose, freshen,

aerate

(Related Words)
*adjective:* aerial

**airborne** = <u>flying</u>, floating, in the air, hovering, gliding, in flight, on the wing

**airing** 1 = <u>ventilation</u>, drying, freshening, aeration 2 = <u>exposure</u>, display, expression, publicity, vent, utterance, dissemination

**airplane** (*U.S. & Canad.*) = <u>plane</u>, aircraft, jet, aeroplane, airliner

**aisle** = <u>passageway</u>, path, lane, passage, corridor, alley, gangway

**alarm** NOUN 1 = <u>fear</u>, panic, anxiety, fright, apprehension, nervousness, consternation, trepidation ≠ calmness 2 = <u>danger signal</u>, warning, bell, alert, siren, alarm bell, hooter, distress signal
• VERB = <u>frighten</u>, scare, panic, distress, startle, dismay, daunt, unnerve ≠ calm

**alarming** = <u>frightening</u>, shocking, scaring, disturbing, distressing, startling, horrifying, menacing

**alcoholic** NOUN = <u>drunkard</u>, drinker, drunk, toper, lush (*slang*), tippler, wino (*informal*), inebriate, alko *or* alco (*Austral. slang*)
• ADJECTIVE = <u>intoxicating</u>, hard, strong, stiff, brewed, fermented, distilled

**alert** ADJECTIVE 1 = <u>attentive</u>,

awake, vigilant, watchful, on the lookout, circumspect, observant, on guard ≠ careless 2 = <u>quick-witted</u>, bright, sharp
- **NOUN** = <u>warning</u>, signal, alarm, siren ≠ all clear
- **VERB** = <u>warn</u>, signal, inform, alarm, notify, tip off, forewarn ≠ lull

**alien** ADJECTIVE 1 = <u>foreign</u>, strange, imported, unknown, exotic, unfamiliar 2 = <u>strange</u>, new, foreign, novel, unknown, exotic, unfamiliar, untried ≠ similar
- **NOUN** = <u>foreigner</u>, incomer, immigrant, stranger, outsider, newcomer, asylum seeker ≠ citizen

**alienate** = <u>antagonize</u>, anger, annoy, offend, irritate, hassle (*informal*), estrange

**alienation** = <u>estrangement</u>, setting against, separation, turning away, disaffection, remoteness

**alight**[1] 1 = <u>get off</u>, descend, get down, disembark, dismount 2 = <u>land</u>, light, settle, come down, descend, perch, touch down, come to rest ≠ take off

**alight**[2] = <u>lit up</u>, bright, brilliant, shining, illuminated, fiery

**align** 1 = <u>ally</u>, side, join, associate, affiliate, cooperate, sympathize 2 = <u>line up</u>, order, range, regulate, straighten, even up

**alike** ADJECTIVE = <u>similar</u>, close, the same, parallel, resembling, identical, corresponding, akin ≠ different
- **ADVERB** = <u>similarly</u>, identically, equally, uniformly, correspondingly, analogously ≠ differently

**alive** 1 = <u>living</u>, breathing, animate, subsisting, existing, functioning, in the land of the living (*informal*) ≠ dead 2 = <u>in existence</u>, existing, functioning, active, operative, in force, on-going, prevalent ≠ inoperative 3 = <u>lively</u>, active, vital, alert, energetic, animated, agile, perky ≠ dull

**all** PRONOUN 1 = <u>the whole amount</u>, everything, the total, the aggregate, the totality, the sum total, the entirety, the entire amount 2 = <u>every</u>, each, every single, every one of, each and every
- **ADJECTIVE** = <u>complete</u>, greatest, full, total, perfect, entire, utter
- **ADVERB** = <u>completely</u>, totally, fully, entirely, absolutely, altogether, wholly, utterly

**allegation** = <u>claim</u>, charge, statement, declaration, accusation, assertion, affirmation

**allege** = <u>claim</u>, charge, challenge, state, maintain, declare, assert, uphold ≠ deny

**alleged** = <u>claimed</u>, supposed, declared, assumed, so-called, apparent, stated, described

**allegiance** = <u>loyalty</u>, devotion, fidelity, obedience, constancy, faithfulness ≠ disloyalty

**allergic** = <u>sensitive</u>, affected by, susceptible, hypersensitive

**allergy** = <u>sensitivity</u>, reaction, susceptibility, antipathy, hypersensitivity, sensitiveness

**alleviate** = <u>ease</u>, reduce, relieve, moderate, soothe, lessen, lighten, allay

**alley** = <u>passage</u>, walk, lane, pathway, alleyway, passageway, backstreet

**alliance** = <u>union</u>, league, association, agreement, marriage, connection, combination, coalition ≠ division

**allied** 1 = <u>united</u>, linked, related, combined, integrated, affiliated, cooperating, in league 2 = <u>connected</u>, linked, associated

**allocate** = <u>assign</u>, grant, distribute, designate, set aside, earmark, give out, consign

**allocation** 1 = <u>allowance</u>, share, portion, quota, lot, ration 2 = <u>assignment</u>, allowance, allotment

**allow** VERB 1 = <u>permit</u>, approve, enable, sanction, endure, license, tolerate, authorize ≠ prohibit 2 = <u>let</u>, permit, sanction, authorize, license, tolerate, consent to, assent to ≠ forbid 3 = <u>give</u>, provide, grant, spare, devote, assign, allocate, set aside 4 = <u>acknowledge</u>, accept, admit, grant, recognize, yield, concede, confess

● PHRASES **allow for something** = <u>take something into account</u>, consider, plan for, accommodate, provide for, make provision for, make allowances for, make concessions for

**allowance** 1 = <u>portion</u>, lot, share, amount, grant, quota, allocation, stint 2 = <u>pocket money</u>, grant, fee, payment, ration, handout, remittance 3 = <u>concession</u>, discount, reduction, repayment, deduction, rebate

**all right** 1 = <u>satisfactory</u>, O.K. or okay (informal), average, fair, sufficient, standard, acceptable, good enough ≠ unsatisfactory 2 = <u>well</u>, O.K. or okay (informal), whole, sound, fit, safe, healthy, unharmed ≠ ill

**ally** NOUN = <u>partner</u>, friend, colleague, associate, mate, comrade, helper, collaborator, cobber (Austral. & N.Z. old-fashioned informal), E hoa (N.Z.) ≠ opponent

● PHRASES **ally yourself with something** or **someone** = <u>unite with</u>, associate with, unify, collaborate with, join forces with, band together with

**almost** = <u>nearly</u>, about, close to, virtually, practically, roughly, just about, not quite

**alone** ADJECTIVE 1 = <u>solitary</u>, isolated, separate, apart, by

yourself, unaccompanied, on your tod (*slang*) ≠ **accompanied** 2 = **lonely**, abandoned, isolated, solitary, desolate, forsaken, forlorn, destitute
● ADVERB 1 = **solely**, only, individually, singly, exclusively, uniquely 2 = **by yourself**, independently, unaccompanied, without help, on your own, without assistance ≠ **with help**

**aloud** = **out loud**, clearly, plainly, distinctly, audibly, intelligibly

**already** = **before now**, before, previously, at present, by now, by then, even now, just now

**also** = **and**, too, further, in addition, as well, moreover, besides, furthermore

**alter** 1 = **modify**, change, reform, vary, transform, adjust, adapt, revise 2 = **change**, turn, vary, transform, adjust, adapt

**alternate** VERB 1 = **interchange**, change, fluctuate, take turns, oscillate, chop and change 2 = **intersperse**, interchange, exchange, swap, stagger, rotate
● ADJECTIVE = **alternating**, interchanging, every other, rotating, every second, sequential

**alternative** NOUN = **substitute**, choice, other (*of two*), option, preference, recourse
● ADJECTIVE = **different**, other, substitute, alternate

**alternatively** = **or**, instead,

otherwise, on the other hand, if not, then again, as an alternative, as another option

**although** = **though**, while, even if, even though, whilst, albeit, despite the fact that, notwithstanding

**altogether** 1 = **absolutely**, quite, completely, totally, perfectly, fully, thoroughly, wholly 2 = **completely**, fully, entirely, thoroughly, wholly, in every respect ≠ **partially** 3 = **on the whole**, generally, mostly, in general, collectively, all things considered, on average, for the most part 4 = **in total**, in all, all told, taken together, in sum, everything included

---

### Word Power

**altogether** – The single-word form *altogether* should not be used as an alternative to *all together* because the meanings are very distinct. *Altogether* is an adverb meaning 'absolutely' or, in a different sense, 'in total'. *All together*, however, means 'all at the same time' or 'all in the same place'. The distinction can be seen in the following example: *altogether there were six or seven families sharing the flat's facilities* means 'in total', while *there were six or seven families all together in one flat*, means 'all crowded in together'.

**always** 1 = <u>habitually</u>, regularly, every time, consistently, invariably, perpetually, without exception, customarily ≠ seldom 2 = <u>forever</u>, for keeps, eternally, for all time, evermore, till the cows come home (*informal*), till Doomsday 3 = <u>continually</u>, constantly, all the time, forever, repeatedly, persistently, perpetually, incessantly

**amass** = <u>collect</u>, gather, assemble, compile, accumulate, pile up, hoard

**amateur** = <u>nonprofessional</u>, outsider, layman, dilettante, layperson, non-specialist, dabbler

**amaze** = <u>astonish</u>, surprise, shock, stun, alarm, stagger, startle, bewilder

**amazement** = <u>astonishment</u>, surprise, wonder, shock, confusion, admiration, awe, bewilderment

**amazing** = <u>astonishing</u>, surprising, brilliant, stunning, overwhelming, staggering, sensational (*informal*), bewildering

**ambassador** = <u>representative</u>, minister, agent, deputy, diplomat, envoy, consul, attaché

**ambiguity** = <u>vagueness</u>, doubt, uncertainty, obscurity, equivocation, dubiousness

**ambiguous** = <u>unclear</u>, obscure, vague, dubious, enigmatic, indefinite, inconclusive, indeterminate ≠ clear

**ambition** 1 = <u>goal</u>, hope, dream, target, aim, wish, purpose, desire 2 = <u>enterprise</u>, longing, drive, spirit, desire, passion, enthusiasm, striving

**ambitious** 1 = <u>enterprising</u>, spirited, daring, eager, intent, enthusiastic, hopeful, striving ≠ unambitious

**ambush** VERB = <u>trap</u>, attack, surprise, deceive, dupe, ensnare, waylay, bushwhack (*U.S.*)
● NOUN = <u>trap</u>, snare, lure, waylaying

**amend** VERB = <u>change</u>, improve, reform, fix, correct, repair, edit, alter
● PLURAL NOUN (usually in *make amends*) = <u>compensation</u>, redress, reparation, restitution, atonement, recompense

**amendment** 1 = <u>addition</u>, change, adjustment, attachment, adaptation, revision, modification, alteration 2 = <u>change</u>, improvement, repair, edit, remedy, correction, revision, modification

**amenity** = <u>facility</u>, service, advantage, comfort, convenience

**amid** or **amidst** 1 = <u>during</u>, among, at a time of, in an atmosphere of 2 = <u>in the middle of</u>, among, surrounded by, amongst, in the midst of, in the thick of

**ammunition** = <u>munitions</u>, rounds, shot, shells, powder, explosives, armaments

**amnesty** = <u>general pardon</u>, mercy, pardoning, immunity, forgiveness, reprieve, remission (of penalty), clemency

**among** or **amongst** 1 = <u>in the midst of</u>, with, together with, in the middle of, amid, surrounded by, amidst, in the thick of 2 = <u>in the group of</u>, one of, part of, included in, in the company of, in the class of, in the number of 3 = <u>between</u>, to

**amount** NOUN = <u>quantity</u>, measure, size, supply, mass, volume, capacity, extent

● PHRASES **amount to something** 1 = <u>add up to</u>, mean, total, equal, constitute, comprise, be equivalent to 2 = <u>come to</u>, become, develop into, advance to, progress to, mature into

> ### Word Power
>
> **amount** – Although it is common to use a plural noun after *amount of*, for example in *the amount of people* and *the amount of goods*, this should be avoided. Preferred alternatives would be to use *quantity*, as in *the quantity of people*, or *number*, as in *the number of goods*.

**amphibian ▸ amphibians**

**ample** 1 = <u>plenty of</u>, generous, lavish, abundant, plentiful, expansive, copious, profuse ≠ insufficient 2 = <u>large</u>, full, extensive, generous, abundant, bountiful

**amply** = <u>fully</u>, completely, richly, generously, abundantly, profusely, copiously ≠ insufficiently

**amuse** 1 = <u>entertain</u>, please, delight, charm, cheer, tickle

### Amphibians

| | |
|---|---|
| axolotl | midwife toad |
| brown-striped frog (*Austral.*) | natterjack |
| bullfrog | newt or (*dialect or archaic*) eft |
| caecilian | olm |
| cane toad (*Austral.*) | Queensland cane toad |
| congo eel or snake | salamander |
| frog or (*Caribbean*) crapaud | siren |
| Goliath frog | toad or (*Caribbean*) crapaud |
| hairy frog | tree frog |
| hyla | |

≠ bore 2 = <u>occupy</u>, interest, involve, engage, entertain, absorb, engross

**amusement** 1 = <u>enjoyment</u>, entertainment, cheer, mirth, merriment ≠ boredom 2 = <u>diversion</u>, fun, pleasure, entertainment 3 = <u>pastime</u>, game, sport, joke, entertainment, hobby, recreation, diversion

**amusing** = <u>funny</u>, humorous, comical, droll, interesting, entertaining, comic, enjoyable ≠ boring

**anaesthetic** NOUN = <u>painkiller</u>, narcotic, sedative, opiate, anodyne, analgesic, soporific
● ADJECTIVE = <u>pain-killing</u>, dulling, numbing, sedative, deadening, anodyne, analgesic, soporific

**analogy** = <u>similarity</u>, relation, comparison, parallel, correspondence, resemblance, correlation, likeness

**analyse** 1 = <u>examine</u>, test, study, research, survey, investigate, evaluate, inspect 2 = <u>break down</u>, separate, divide, resolve, dissect, think through

**analysis** = <u>examination</u>, test, inquiry, investigation, interpretation, breakdown, scanning, evaluation

**analytical** or **analytic** = <u>rational</u>, organized, exact, precise, logical, systematic, inquiring, investigative

**anarchy** = <u>lawlessness</u>, revolution, riot, disorder, confusion, chaos, disorganization ≠ order

**anatomy** 1 = <u>structure</u>, build, make-up, frame, framework, composition 2 = <u>examination</u>, study, division, inquiry, investigation, analysis, dissection

**ancestor** = <u>forefather</u>, predecessor, precursor, forerunner, forebear, antecedent, tupuna or tipuna (*N.Z.*) ≠ descendant

**ancient** 1 = <u>classical</u>, old, former, past, bygone, primordial, primeval, olden 2 = <u>very old</u>, aged, antique, archaic, timeworn 3 = <u>old-fashioned</u>, dated, outdated, obsolete, out of date, unfashionable, outmoded, passé ≠ up-to-date

**and** 1 = <u>also</u>, including, along with, together with, in addition to, as well as 2 = <u>moreover</u>, plus, furthermore

---

### Word Power

**and** – The forms *try and do something* and *wait and do something* should only be used in informal or spoken English. In more formal writing, use *try to* and *wait to*, for example: *we must try to prevent this happening* (not *try and prevent*).

---

**anecdote** = <u>story</u>, tale, sketch,

short story, yarn, reminiscence, urban myth, urban legend

**angel** 1 = <u>divine messenger</u>, cherub, archangel, seraph 2 (*Informal*) = <u>dear</u>, beauty, saint, treasure, darling, jewel, gem, paragon

**anger** NOUN = <u>rage</u>, outrage, temper, fury, resentment, wrath, annoyance, ire ≠ calmness

● VERB = <u>enrage</u>, outrage, annoy, infuriate, incense, gall, madden, exasperate ≠ soothe

**angle** 1 = <u>gradient</u>, bank, slope, incline, inclination 2 = <u>intersection</u>, point, edge, corner, bend, elbow, crook, nook 3 = <u>point of view</u>, position, approach, direction, aspect, perspective, outlook, viewpoint

**angry** = <u>furious</u>, cross, mad (*informal*), outraged, annoyed, infuriated, incensed, enraged, tooshie (*Austral. slang*), off the air (*Austral. slang*) ≠ calm

> ### Word Power
> **angry** – Some people feel it is more correct to talk about being *angry with* someone than being *angry at* them. In British English, *angry with* is still more common than *angry at*, but *angry at* is used more commonly in American English.

**angst** = <u>anxiety</u>, worry, unease, apprehension ≠ peace of mind

**anguish** = <u>suffering</u>, pain, distress, grief, misery, agony, torment, sorrow

**animal** NOUN 1 = <u>creature</u>, beast, brute 2 = <u>brute</u>, devil, monster, savage, beast, bastard (*informal, offensive*), villain, barbarian

● ADJECTIVE = <u>physical</u>, gross, bodily, sensual, carnal, brutish, bestial

> **amphibians ▸ animals**
> **birds ▸ dinosaurs ▸ fish**
> **insects ▸ invertebrates**
> **mammals ▸ reptiles**

**animate** ADJECTIVE = <u>living</u>, live, moving, alive, breathing, alive and kicking

● VERB = <u>enliven</u>, excite, inspire, move, fire, stimulate, energize, kindle ≠ inhibit

**animated** = <u>lively</u>, spirited, excited, enthusiastic, passionate, energetic, ebullient, vivacious ≠ listless

**animation** = <u>liveliness</u>, energy, spirit, passion, enthusiasm, excitement, verve, zest

**announce** = <u>make known</u>, tell, report, reveal, declare, advertise, broadcast, disclose ≠ keep secret

**announcement** 1 = <u>statement</u>, communication, broadcast, declaration, advertisement, bulletin, communiqué, proclamation 2 = <u>declaration</u>, report, reporting, revelation, proclamation

# Animals

## Collective animals

| | | | |
|---|---|---|---|
| antelopes | herd | geese | gaggle *or* skein |
| apes | shrewdness | giraffes | herd |
| asses | pace *or* herd | gnats | swarm *or* cloud |
| badgers | cete | goats | herd *or* tribe |
| bears | sloth | goldfinches | charm |
| bees | swarm *or* grist | grouse | brood, covey, |
| birds | flock, | | *or* pack |
| | congregation, | gulls | colony |
| | flight, *or* volery | hares | down *or* husk |
| bitterns | sedge *or* siege | hawks | cast |
| boars | sounder | hens | brood |
| bucks | brace *or* lease | herons | sedge *or* siege |
| buffaloes | herd | herrings | shoal *or* glean |
| capercailzies | tok | hounds | pack, mute, *or* |
| cats | clowder | | cry |
| cattle | drove *or* herd | insects | swarm |
| choughs | chattering | kangaroos | troop |
| colts | rag | kittens | kindle |
| coots | covert | lapwings | desert |
| cranes | herd, sedge, *or* | larks | exaltation |
| | siege | leopards | leap |
| crows | murder | lions | pride *or* troop |
| cubs | litter | mallards | sord *or* sute |
| curlews | herd | mares | stud |
| curs | cowardice | martens | richesse |
| deer | herd | moles | labour |
| dolphins | school | monkeys | troop |
| doves | flight *or* dule | mules | barren |
| ducks | paddling *or* team | nightingales | watch |
| dunlins | flight | owls | parliament |
| elk | gang | oxen | yoke, drove, |
| fish | shoal, draught, | | team, *or* herd |
| | haul, run, *or* | partridges | covey |
| | catch | peacocks | muster |
| flies | swarm *or* grist | pheasants | nye *or* nide |
| foxes | skulk | pigeons | flock *or* flight |

## Animals (continued)

*Collective animals*

| | | | |
|---|---|---|---|
| pigs | litter | sparrows | host |
| plovers | stand *or* wing | starlings | murmuration |
| pochards | flight, rush, bunch, *or* knob | swallows | flight |
| | | swans | herd *or* bevy |
| ponies | herd | swifts | flock |
| porpoises | school *or* gam | swine | herd, sounder, *or* dryft |
| poultry | run | | |
| pups | litter | teal | bunch, knob, *or* spring |
| quails | bevy | | |
| rabbits | nest | whales | school, gam, *or* run |
| racehorses | field *or* string | | |
| ravens | unkindness | whelps | litter |
| roes | bevy | whiting | pod |
| rooks | building *or* clamour | wigeon | bunch, company, knob, *or* flight |
| ruffs | hill | wildfowl | plump, sord, *or* sute |
| seals | herd *or* pod | | |
| sheep | flock | wolves | pack, rout, *or* herd |
| sheldrakes | dopping | | |
| snipe | walk *or* wisp | woodcocks | fall |

**annoy** = irritate, trouble, anger, bother, disturb, plague, hassle (*informal*), madden ≠ soothe

**annoying** = irritating, disturbing, troublesome, maddening, exasperating ≠ delightful

**annual** 1 = once a year, yearly 2 = yearlong, yearly

**annually** 1 = once a year, yearly, every year, per year, by the year, every twelve months, per annum 2 = per year, yearly, every year, by the year, per annum

**anomaly** = irregularity, exception, abnormality, inconsistency, eccentricity, oddity, peculiarity, incongruity

**anonymous** 1 = unnamed, unknown, unidentified, nameless, unacknowledged, incognito ≠ identified 2 = unsigned, uncredited, unattributed ≠ signed

**answer** VERB = reply, explain, respond, resolve, react, return, retort ≠ ask

● NOUN 1 = reply, response,

reaction, explanation, comeback, retort, return, defence ≠ question
2 = solution, resolution, explanation 3 = remedy, solution

**ant ▸ ants, bees, and wasps**

**anthem** = song of praise, carol, chant, hymn, psalm, paean, chorale, canticle

**anthology** = collection, selection, treasury, compilation, compendium, miscellany

**anticipate** 1 = expect, predict, prepare for, hope for, envisage, foresee, bank on, foretell

2 = await, look forward to, count the hours until

**anticipation** = expectancy, expectation, foresight, premonition, prescience, forethought

**antics** = clowning, tricks, mischief, pranks, escapades, playfulness, horseplay, tomfoolery

**antique** NOUN = period piece, relic, bygone, heirloom, collector's item, museum piece

● ADJECTIVE = vintage, classic,

---

## Ants, bees, and wasps

| | |
|---|---|
| Amazon ant | kootchar (*Austral.*) |
| ant *or* (*archaic or dialect*) emmet | leafcutter ant |
| army ant *or* legionary ant | leafcutter bee |
| bee | mason bee |
| blue ant (*Austral.*) | mason wasp |
| bulldog ant, bull ant, *or* (*Austral.*) bull Joe | minga (*Austral.*) |
| | mining bee |
| bumblebee *or* humblebee | mud dauber |
| carpenter bee | native bee *or* sugarbag fly (*Austral.*) |
| cicada hunter (*Austral.*) | |
| cuckoo bee | Pharaoh ant |
| digger wasp | policeman fly (*Austral.*) |
| driver ant | ruby-tail wasp |
| flower wasp (*Austral.*) | sand wasp |
| gall wasp | Sirex wasp (*Austral.*) |
| honeypot ant *or* honey ant (*Austral.*) | slave ant |
| | spider-hunting wasp |
| honeybee *or* hive bee | termite *or* white ant |
| horntail *or* wood wasp | velvet ant |
| ichneumon fly *or* ichneumon wasp | wasp |
| | wood ant |
| killer bee | yellow jacket (*U.S. & Canad.*) |

antiquarian, olden

**anxiety** = <u>uneasiness</u>, concern, worry, doubt, tension, angst, apprehension, misgiving ≠ confidence

**anxious** 1 = <u>eager</u>, keen, intent, yearning, impatient, itching, desirous ≠ reluctant 2 = <u>uneasy</u>, concerned, worried, troubled, nervous, uncomfortable, tense, fearful ≠ confident

**apart** 1 = <u>to pieces</u>, to bits, asunder 2 = <u>away from each other</u>, distant from each other 3 = <u>aside</u>, away, alone, isolated, to one side, by yourself 4 *with from* = <u>except for</u>, excepting, other than, excluding, besides, not including, aside from, but

**apartment** 1 (*U.S.*) = <u>flat</u>, room, suite, penthouse, crib 2 = <u>rooms</u>, quarters, accommodation, living quarters

**apathy** = <u>lack of interest</u>, indifference, inertia, coolness, passivity, nonchalance, torpor, unconcern ≠ interest

**apiece** = <u>each</u>, individually, separately, for each, to each, respectively, from each ≠ all together

**apologize** = <u>say sorry</u>, express regret, ask forgiveness, make an apology, beg pardon

**apology** NOUN = <u>regret</u>, explanation, excuse, confession
● PHRASES **apology for**

**something** *or* **someone** = <u>mockery of</u>, excuse for, imitation of, caricature of, travesty of, poor substitute for

**appal** = <u>horrify</u>, shock, alarm, frighten, outrage, disgust, dishearten, revolt

**appalling** 1 = <u>horrifying</u>, shocking, alarming, awful, terrifying, horrible, dreadful, fearful ≠ reassuring 2 = <u>awful</u>, dreadful, horrendous

**apparatus** 1 = <u>organization</u>, system, network, structure, bureaucracy, hierarchy, setup (*informal*), chain of command 2 = <u>equipment</u>, tackle, gear, device, tools, mechanism, machinery, appliance

**apparent** 1 = <u>seeming</u>, outward, superficial, ostensible ≠ actual 2 = <u>obvious</u>, marked, visible, evident, distinct, manifest, noticeable, unmistakable ≠ unclear

**apparently** = <u>seemingly</u>, outwardly, ostensibly

**appeal** VERB = <u>plead</u>, ask, request, pray, beg, entreat ≠ refuse
● NOUN 1 = <u>plea</u>, call, application, request, prayer, petition, overture, entreaty ≠ refusal 2 = <u>attraction</u>, charm, fascination, beauty, allure ≠ repulsiveness
● PHRASES **appeal to someone** = <u>attract</u>, interest, draw, please,

charm, fascinate, tempt, lure

**appealing** = <u>attractive</u>, engaging, charming, desirable, alluring, winsome ≠ repellent

**appear** 1 = <u>look (like or as if)</u>, seem, occur, look to be, come across as, strike you as 2 = <u>come into view</u>, emerge, occur, surface, come out, turn up, be present, show up (*informal*) ≠ disappear

**appearance** 1 = <u>look</u>, form, figure, looks, manner, expression, demeanour, mien (*literary*) 2 = <u>arrival</u>, presence, introduction, emergence 3 = <u>impression</u>, air, front, image, illusion, guise, façade, pretence

**appease** 1 = <u>pacify</u>, satisfy, calm, soothe, quiet, placate, mollify, conciliate ≠ anger 2 = <u>ease</u>, calm, relieve, soothe, alleviate, allay

**appendix** = <u>supplement</u>, postscript, adjunct, appendage, addendum, addition

**appetite** 1 = <u>hunger</u> 2 = <u>desire</u>, liking, longing, demand, taste, passion, stomach, hunger ≠ distaste

**applaud** 1 = <u>clap</u>, encourage, praise, cheer, acclaim ≠ boo 2 = <u>praise</u>, celebrate, approve, acclaim, compliment, salute, commend, extol ≠ criticize

**applause** = <u>ovation</u>, praise, cheers, approval, clapping, accolade, big hand

**appliance** = <u>device</u>, machine, tool, instrument, implement, mechanism, apparatus, gadget

**applicable** = <u>appropriate</u>, fitting, useful, suitable, relevant, apt, pertinent ≠ inappropriate

**applicant** = <u>candidate</u>, claimant, inquirer

**application** 1 = <u>request</u>, claim, appeal, inquiry, petition, requisition 2 = <u>effort</u>, work, industry, trouble, struggle, pains, commitment, hard work

**apply** VERB 1 = <u>request</u>, appeal, put in, petition, inquire, claim, requisition 2 = <u>be relevant</u>, relate, refer, be fitting, be appropriate, fit, pertain, be applicable 3 = <u>use</u>, exercise, carry out, employ, implement, practise, exert, enact 4 = <u>put on</u>, work in, cover with, lay on, paint on, spread on, rub in, smear on

● PHRASES **apply yourself to something** = <u>work hard at</u>, concentrate on, try at, commit yourself to, buckle down to (*informal*), devote yourself to, be diligent in, dedicate yourself to

**appoint** 1 = <u>assign</u>, name, choose, commission, select, elect, delegate, nominate ≠ fire 2 = <u>decide</u>, set, choose, establish, fix, arrange, assign, designate ≠ cancel

**appointed** 1 = <u>decided</u>, set, chosen, established, fixed, arranged, assigned, designated

2= <u>assigned</u>, named, chosen, selected, elected, delegated, nominated 3= <u>equipped</u>, provided, supplied, furnished, fitted out

**appointment** 1= <u>selection</u>, naming, election, choice, nomination, assignment 2= <u>job</u>, office, position, post, situation, place, employment, assignment 3= <u>meeting</u>, interview, date, arrangement, engagement, fixture, rendezvous, assignation

**appraisal** = <u>assessment</u>, opinion, estimate, judgment, evaluation, estimation

**appreciate** 1= <u>enjoy</u>, like, value, respect, prize, admire, treasure, rate highly ≠ scorn 2= <u>be aware of</u>, understand, realize, recognize, perceive, take account of, be sensitive to, sympathize with ≠ be unaware of 3= <u>be grateful</u>, be obliged, be thankful, give thanks, be indebted, be in debt, be appreciative ≠ be ungrateful for 4= <u>increase</u>, rise, grow, gain, improve, enhance, soar ≠ fall

**appreciation** 1= <u>admiration</u>, enjoyment 2= <u>gratitude</u>, thanks, recognition, obligation, acknowledgment, indebtedness, thankfulness, gratefulness ≠ ingratitude 3= <u>awareness</u>, understanding, recognition, perception, sympathy,

consciousness, sensitivity, realization ≠ ignorance 4= <u>increase</u>, rise, gain, growth, improvement, escalation, enhancement ≠ fall

**apprehension** 1= <u>anxiety</u>, concern, fear, worry, alarm, suspicion, dread, trepidation ≠ confidence 2= <u>arrest</u>, catching, capture, taking, seizure ≠ release 3= <u>awareness</u>, understanding, perception, grasp, comprehension ≠ incomprehension

**apprentice** = <u>trainee</u>, student, pupil, novice, beginner, learner, probationer ≠ master

**approach** VERB 1= <u>move</u> <u>towards</u>, reach, near, come close, come near, draw near 2= <u>make a</u> <u>proposal to</u>, speak to, apply to, appeal to, proposition, solicit, sound out, make overtures to 3= <u>set about</u>, tackle, undertake, embark on, get down to, launch into, begin work on, commence on

● NOUN 1= <u>advance</u>, coming, nearing, appearance, arrival, drawing near 2= <u>access</u>, way, drive, road, passage, entrance, avenue, passageway 3*often plural* = <u>proposal</u>, offer, appeal, advance, application, invitation, proposition, overture 4= <u>way</u>, means, style, method, technique, manner

**appropriate** ADJECTIVE

= <u>suitable</u>, fitting, relevant, to the point, apt, pertinent, befitting, well-suited ≠ unsuitable

● VERB 1 = <u>seize</u>, claim, acquire, confiscate, usurp, impound, commandeer, take possession of ≠ relinquish 2 = <u>allocate</u>, allow, budget, devote, assign, designate, set aside, earmark ≠ withhold 3 = <u>steal</u>, take, nick (*slang, chiefly Brit.*), pocket, pinch (*informal*), lift (*informal*), embezzle, pilfer

**approval** 1 = <u>consent</u>, agreement, sanction, blessing, permission, recommendation, endorsement, assent 2 = <u>favour</u>, respect, praise, esteem, acclaim, appreciation, admiration, applause ≠ disapproval

**approve** VERB = <u>agree to</u>, allow, pass, recommend, permit, sanction, endorse, authorize ≠ veto

● PHRASES **approve of something** *or* **someone** = <u>favour</u>, like, respect, praise, admire, commend, have a good opinion of, regard highly

**apt** 1 = <u>appropriate</u>, fitting, suitable, relevant, to the point, pertinent ≠ inappropriate 2 = <u>inclined</u>, likely, ready, disposed, prone, liable, given, predisposed 3 = <u>gifted</u>, skilled, quick, talented, sharp, capable, smart, clever ≠ slow

**arbitrary** = <u>random</u>, chance,

subjective, inconsistent, erratic, personal, whimsical, capricious ≠ logical

**arbitration** = <u>decision</u>, settlement, judgment, determination, adjudication

**arc** = <u>curve</u>, bend, bow, arch, crescent, half-moon

**arcade** = <u>gallery</u>, cloister, portico, colonnade

**arch**[1] NOUN 1 = <u>archway</u>, curve, dome, span, vault 2 = <u>curve</u>, bend, bow, crook, arc, hunch, sweep, hump

● VERB = <u>curve</u>, bridge, bend, bow, span, arc

**arch**[2] = <u>playful</u>, sly, mischievous, saucy, pert, roguish, frolicsome, waggish

**archetypal** = <u>typical</u>, standard, model, original, classic, ideal, prototypic *or* prototypical

**architect** = <u>designer</u>, planner, draughtsman, master builder

**architecture** 1 = <u>design</u>, planning, building, construction 2 = <u>construction</u>, design, style 3 = <u>structure</u>, design, shape, make-up, construction, framework, layout, anatomy

**archive** NOUN = <u>record office</u>, museum, registry, repository

● PLURAL NOUN = <u>records</u>, papers, accounts, rolls, documents, files, deeds, chronicles

**arctic** (*Informal*) = <u>freezing</u>, cold, frozen, icy, chilly, glacial, frigid

**Arctic** = polar, far-northern, hyperborean

**ardent** 1= enthusiastic, keen, eager, avid, zealous ≠ indifferent 2= passionate, intense, impassioned, lusty, amorous, hot-blooded ≠ cold

**area** 1= region, quarter, district, zone, neighbourhood, locality 2= part, section, sector, portion 3= realm, part, department, field, province, sphere, domain

**arena** 1= ring, ground, field, theatre, bowl, pitch, stadium, enclosure 2= scene, world, area, stage, field, sector, territory, province

**argue** 1= quarrel, fight, row, clash, dispute, disagree, squabble, bicker 2= discuss, debate, dispute 3= claim, reason, challenge, insist, maintain, allege, assert, uphold

**argument** 1= reason, case, reasoning, ground(s), defence, logic, polemic, dialectic 2= debate, questioning, claim, discussion, dispute, controversy, plea, assertion 3= quarrel, fight, row, clash, dispute, controversy, disagreement, feud ≠ agreement

**arise** 1= happen, start, begin, follow, result, develop, emerge, occur 2(*Old-fashioned*) = get to your feet, get up, rise, stand up, spring up, leap up 3= get up, wake up, awaken, get out of bed

**aristocrat** = noble, lord, lady, peer, patrician, grandee, aristo (*informal*), peeress

**aristocratic** = upper-class, lordly, titled, elite, gentlemanly, noble, patrician, blue-blooded ≠ common

**arm**¹ = upper limb, limb, appendage

**arm**²VERB = equip, provide, supply, array, furnish, issue with, deck out, accoutre

● PLURAL NOUN = weapons, guns, firearms, weaponry, armaments, ordnance, munitions, instruments of war

**armed** = carrying weapons, protected, equipped, primed, fitted out

**armour** = protection, covering, shield, sheathing, armour plate, chain mail, protective covering

**armoured** = protected, mailed, reinforced, toughened, bulletproof, armour-plated, steel-plated, ironclad

**army** 1= soldiers, military, troops, armed force, legions, infantry, military force, land force 2= vast number, host, gang, mob, flock, array, legion, swarm

**aroma** = scent, smell, perfume, fragrance, bouquet, savour, odour, redolence

**around** PREPOSITION 1= surrounding, about, enclosing, encompassing, framing, encircling, on all sides of, on every side of **2** = <u>approximately</u>, about, nearly, close to, roughly, just about, in the region of, circa (*used with dates*)

● ADVERB **1** = <u>everywhere</u>, about, throughout, all over, here and there, on all sides, in all directions, to and fro **2** = <u>near</u>, close, nearby, at hand, close at hand

**arouse 1** = <u>stimulate</u>, encourage, inspire, prompt, spur, provoke, rouse, stir up ≠ quell **2** = <u>inflame</u>, move, excite, spur, provoke, stir up, agitate **3** = <u>awaken</u>, wake up, rouse, waken

**arrange 1** = <u>plan</u>, agree, prepare, determine, organize, construct, devise, contrive, jack up (*N.Z. informal*) **2** = <u>put in order</u>, group, order, sort, position, line up, organize, classify, jack up (*N.Z. informal*) ≠ disorganize **3** = <u>adapt</u>, score, orchestrate, harmonize, instrument

**arrangement 1** *often plural* = <u>plan</u>, planning, provision, preparation **2** = <u>agreement</u>, contract, settlement, appointment, compromise, deal (*informal*), pact, compact **3** = <u>display</u>, system, structure, organization, exhibition, presentation, classification, alignment **4** = <u>adaptation</u>, score,

version, interpretation, instrumentation, orchestration, harmonization

**array** NOUN **1** = <u>arrangement</u>, show, supply, display, collection, exhibition, line-up, mixture **2** (*Poetic*) = <u>clothing</u>, dress, clothes, garments, apparel, attire, finery, regalia

● VERB **1** = <u>arrange</u>, show, group, present, range, display, parade, exhibit **2** = <u>dress</u>, clothe, deck, decorate, adorn, festoon, attire

**arrest** VERB **1** = <u>capture</u>, catch, nick (*slang, chiefly Brit.*), seize, detain, apprehend, take prisoner ≠ release **2** = <u>stop</u>, end, limit, block, slow, delay, interrupt, suppress ≠ speed up **3** = <u>fascinate</u>, hold, occupy, engage, grip, absorb, entrance, intrigue

● NOUN **1** = <u>capture</u>, bust (*informal*), detention, seizure ≠ release **2** = <u>stoppage</u>, suppression, obstruction, blockage, hindrance ≠ acceleration

**arresting** = <u>striking</u>, surprising, engaging, stunning, impressive, outstanding, remarkable, noticeable ≠ unremarkable

**arrival 1** = <u>appearance</u>, coming, arriving, entrance, advent, materialization **2** = <u>coming</u>, happening, taking place, emergence, occurrence, materialization 3= <u>newcomer</u>, incomer, visitor, caller, entrant

**arrive** 1= <u>come</u>, appear, turn up, show up (*informal*), draw near ≠ depart 2= <u>occur</u>, happen, take place 3(*Informal*) = <u>succeed</u>, make it (*informal*), triumph, do well, thrive, flourish, be successful, make good

**arrogance** = <u>conceit</u>, pride, swagger, insolence, high-handedness, haughtiness, superciliousness, disdainfulness ≠ modesty

**arrogant** = <u>conceited</u>, proud, cocky, overbearing, haughty, scornful, egotistical, disdainful ≠ modest

**arrow** 1= <u>dart</u>, flight, bolt, shaft (*archaic*), quarrel 2= <u>pointer</u>, indicator, marker

**arsenal** = <u>armoury</u>, supply, store, stockpile, storehouse, ammunition dump, arms depot, ordnance depot

**art** 1= <u>artwork</u>, style of art, fine art, creativity 2= <u>skill</u>, craft, expertise, competence, mastery, ingenuity, virtuosity, cleverness

**article** 1= <u>feature</u>, story, paper, piece, item, creation, essay, composition 2= <u>thing</u>, piece, unit, item, object, device, tool, implement 3= <u>clause</u>, point, part, section, item, passage, portion, paragraph

**articulate** ADJECTIVE

= <u>expressive</u>, clear, coherent, fluent, eloquent, lucid ≠ incoherent

● VERB 1= <u>express</u>, say, state, word, declare, phrase, communicate, utter 2= <u>pronounce</u>, say, talk, speak, voice, utter, enunciate

**artificial** 1= <u>synthetic</u>, manufactured, plastic, man-made, non-natural 2= <u>insincere</u>, forced, affected, phoney *or* phony (*informal*), false, contrived, unnatural, feigned ≠ genuine 3= <u>fake</u>, mock, imitation, bogus, simulated, sham, counterfeit ≠ authentic

**artillery** = <u>big guns</u>, battery, cannon, ordnance, gunnery

**artist ▸ WORD POWER SUPPLEMENT artists**

**artistic** 1= <u>creative</u>, cultured, original, sophisticated, refined, aesthetic, discerning, eloquent ≠ untalented 2= <u>beautiful</u>, creative, elegant, stylish, aesthetic, tasteful ≠ unattractive

**as** CONJUNCTION = <u>when</u>, while, just as, at the time that

● PREPOSITION 1= <u>in the role of</u>, being, under the name of, in the character of 2= <u>in the way that</u>, like, in the manner that 3= <u>since</u>, because, seeing that, considering that, on account of the fact that

**ashamed** 1= <u>embarrassed</u>, sorry, guilty, distressed,

humiliated, self-conscious, red-faced, mortified ≠ proud
2 = <u>reluctant</u>, embarrassed

**ashore** = <u>on land</u>, on the beach, on the shore, aground, to the shore, on dry land, shorewards, landwards

**aside** ADVERB = <u>to one side</u>, separately, apart, beside, out of the way, on one side, to the side
● NOUN = <u>interpolation</u>, parenthesis

**ask** 1 = <u>inquire</u>, question, quiz, query, interrogate ≠ answer
2 = <u>request</u>, appeal to, plead with, demand, beg 3 = <u>invite</u>, bid, summon

**asleep** = <u>sleeping</u>, napping, dormant, dozing, slumbering, snoozing (*informal*), fast asleep, sound asleep

**aspect** 1 = <u>feature</u>, side, factor, angle, characteristic, facet
2 = <u>position</u>, view, situation, scene, prospect, point of view, outlook 3 = <u>appearance</u>, look, air, condition, quality, bearing, attitude, cast

**aspiration** = <u>aim</u>, plan, hope, goal, dream, wish, desire, objective

**aspire to** = <u>aim for</u>, desire, hope for, long for, seek out, wish for, dream about, set your heart on

**ass** 1 = <u>donkey</u>, moke (*slang*)
2 = <u>fool</u>, idiot, twit (*informal, chiefly Brit.*), oaf, jackass,

blockhead, halfwit, numbskull or numskull, dorba or dorb (*Austral. slang*), bogan (*Austral. slang*)

**assassin** = <u>murderer</u>, killer, slayer, liquidator, executioner, hit man (*slang*), hatchet man (*slang*)

**assassinate** = <u>murder</u>, kill, eliminate (*slang*), take out (*slang*), terminate, hit (*slang*), slay, liquidate

**assault** NOUN = <u>attack</u>, raid, invasion, charge, offensive, onslaught, foray ≠ defence
● VERB = <u>strike</u>, attack, beat, knock, bang, slap, smack, thump

**assemble** 1 = <u>gather</u>, meet, collect, rally, come together, muster, congregate ≠ scatter
2 = <u>bring together</u>, collect, gather, rally, come together, muster, amass, congregate
3 = <u>put together</u>, join, set up, build up, connect, construct, piece together, fabricate ≠ take apart

**assembly** 1 = <u>gathering</u>, group, meeting, council, conference, crowd, congress, collection, hui (*N.Z.*), runanga (*N.Z.*) 2 = <u>putting together</u>, setting up, construction, building up, connecting, piecing together

**assert** VERB 1 = <u>state</u>, argue, maintain, declare, swear, pronounce, affirm, profess ≠ deny
2 = <u>insist upon</u>, stress, defend, uphold, put forward, press, stand

up for ≠ retract

● **PHRASES assert yourself** = be forceful, put your foot down (*informal*), put yourself forward, make your presence felt, exert your influence

**assertion** 1 = <u>statement</u>, claim, declaration, pronouncement 2 = <u>insistence</u>, stressing, maintenance

**assertive** = <u>confident</u>, positive, aggressive, forceful, emphatic, insistent, feisty (*informal, chiefly U.S. & Canad.*), pushy (*informal*) ≠ meek

**assess** 1 = <u>judge</u>, estimate, analyse, evaluate, rate, value, check out, weigh up 2 = <u>evaluate</u>, rate, tax, value, estimate, fix, impose, levy

**assessment** 1 = <u>judgment</u>, analysis, evaluation, valuation, appraisal, rating, opinion, estimate 2 = <u>evaluation</u>, rating, charge, fee, toll, levy, valuation

**asset** NOUN = <u>benefit</u>, help, service, aid, advantage, strength, resource, attraction ≠ disadvantage

● **PLURAL NOUN** = <u>property</u>, goods, money, funds, effects, capital, riches, finance

**assign** 1 = <u>give</u>, set, grant, allocate, give out, consign, allot, apportion 2 = <u>select for</u>, post, commission, elect, appoint, delegate, nominate, name

3 = <u>attribute</u>, credit, put down, set down, ascribe, accredit

**assignment** = <u>task</u>, job, position, post, commission, exercise, responsibility, duty

**assist** 1 = <u>help</u>, support, aid, cooperate with, abet, lend a helping hand to 2 = <u>facilitate</u>, help, further, serve, aid, forward, promote, speed up ≠ hinder

**assistance** = <u>help</u>, backing, support, aid, cooperation, helping hand ≠ hindrance

**assistant** = <u>helper</u>, ally, colleague, supporter, aide, second, attendant, accomplice

**associate** VERB 1 = <u>connect</u>, link, ally, identify, join, combine, attach, fasten ≠ separate 2 = <u>socialize</u>, mix, accompany, mingle, consort, hobnob ≠ avoid

● **NOUN** = <u>partner</u>, friend, ally, colleague, mate (*informal*), companion, comrade, affiliate, cobber (*Austral. & N.Z. old-fashioned informal*), E hoa (*N.Z.*)

**association** 1 = <u>group</u>, club, society, league, band, set, pack, collection 2 = <u>connection</u>, union, joining, pairing, combination, mixture, blend, juxtaposition

**assorted** = <u>various</u>, different, mixed, varied, diverse, miscellaneous, sundry, motley ≠ similar

**assume** 1 = <u>presume</u>, think, believe, expect, suppose, imagine, fancy, take for granted ≠ know 2 = take on, accept, shoulder, take over, put on, enter upon 3 = simulate, affect, adopt, put on, imitate, mimic, feign, impersonate 4 = take over, take, appropriate, seize, commandeer ≠ give up

**assumed** = false, made-up, fake, bogus, counterfeit, fictitious, make-believe ≠ real

**assumption** 1 = presumption, belief, guess, hypothesis, inference, conjecture, surmise, supposition 2 = taking on, managing, handling, shouldering, putting on, taking up, takeover, acquisition 3 = seizure, taking, takeover, acquisition, appropriation, wresting, confiscation, commandeering

**assurance** 1 = promise, statement, guarantee, commitment, pledge, vow, declaration, assertion ≠ lie 2 = confidence, conviction, certainty, self-confidence, poise, faith, nerve, aplomb ≠ self-doubt

**assure** 1 = convince, encourage, persuade, satisfy, comfort, reassure, hearten, embolden 2 = make certain, ensure, confirm, guarantee, secure, make sure, complete, seal 3 = promise to, pledge to, vow to, guarantee to, swear to, confirm to, certify to, give your word to

**assured** 1 = confident, certain, positive, poised, fearless, self-confident, self-assured, dauntless ≠ self-conscious 2 = certain, sure, ensured, confirmed, settled, guaranteed, fixed, secure ≠ doubtful

**astonish** = amaze, surprise, stun, stagger, bewilder, astound, daze, confound

**astounding** = amazing, surprising, brilliant, impressive, astonishing, staggering, sensational (informal), bewildering

**astute** = intelligent, sharp, clever, subtle, shrewd, cunning, canny, perceptive ≠ stupid

**asylum** 1 (Old-fashioned) = mental hospital, hospital, institution, psychiatric hospital, madhouse (informal) 2 = refuge, haven, safety, protection, preserve, shelter, retreat, harbour

**athlete** = sportsperson, player, runner, competitor, sportsman, contestant, gymnast, sportswoman

**athletic** ADJECTIVE = fit, strong, powerful, healthy, active, trim, strapping, energetic ≠ feeble
● PLURAL NOUN = sports, games, races, exercises, contests, sporting events, gymnastics, track and field events

**atmosphere** 1 = air, sky, heavens, aerosphere 2 = feeling, character, environment, spirit, surroundings, tone, mood, climate

**atom** = <u>particle</u>, bit, spot, trace, molecule, dot, speck

**atrocity** 1 = <u>act of cruelty</u>, crime, horror, evil, outrage, abomination 2 = <u>cruelty</u>, horror, brutality, savagery, wickedness, barbarity, viciousness, fiendishness

**attach** 1 = <u>affix</u>, stick, secure, add, join, couple, link, tie ≠ detach 2 = <u>ascribe</u>, connect, attribute, assign, associate

**attached** ADJECTIVE = <u>spoken for</u>, married, partnered, engaged, accompanied

● PHRASES **attached to** = <u>fond of</u>, devoted to, affectionate towards, full of regard for

**attachment** 1 = <u>fondness</u>, liking, feeling, relationship, regard, attraction, affection, affinity, aroha (*N.Z.*) ≠ aversion 2 = <u>accessory</u>, fitting, extra, component, extension, supplement, fixture, accoutrement

**attack** VERB 1 = <u>assault</u>, strike (at), mug, ambush, tear into, set upon, lay into (*informal*) ≠ defend 2 = <u>invade</u>, occupy, raid, infringe, storm, encroach 3 = <u>criticize</u>, blame, abuse, condemn, knock (*informal*), put down, slate (*informal*), have a go (at) (*informal*)

● NOUN 1 = <u>assault</u>, charge, campaign, strike, raid, invasion, offensive, blitz ≠ defence 2 = <u>criticism</u>, censure, disapproval, abuse, bad press, vilification, denigration, disparagement 3 = <u>bout</u>, fit, stroke, seizure, spasm, convulsion, paroxysm

**attacker** = <u>assailant</u>, assaulter, raider, intruder, invader, aggressor, mugger

**attain** 1 = <u>obtain</u>, get, reach, complete, gain, achieve, acquire, fulfil 2 = <u>reach</u>, achieve, acquire, accomplish

**attempt** VERB = <u>try</u>, seek, aim, struggle, venture, undertake, strive, endeavour

● NOUN 1 = <u>try</u>, go (*informal*), shot (*informal*), effort, trial, bid, crack (*informal*), stab (*informal*) 2 = <u>attack</u>

**attend** VERB 1 = <u>be present</u>, go to, visit, frequent, haunt, appear at, turn up at, patronize ≠ be absent 2 = <u>pay attention</u>, listen, hear, mark, note, observe, heed, pay heed ≠ ignore

● PHRASES **attend to something** = <u>apply yourself to</u>, concentrate on, look after, take care of, see to, get to work on, devote yourself to, occupy yourself with

**attendance** 1 = <u>presence</u>, being there, attending,

appearance 2= <u>turnout</u>, audience, gate, congregation, house, crowd, throng, number present

**attendant** NOUN = <u>assistant</u>, guard, servant, companion, aide, escort, follower, helper
• ADJECTIVE = <u>accompanying</u>, related, associated, accessory, consequent, resultant, concomitant

**attention** 1= <u>thinking</u>, thought, mind, consideration, scrutiny, heed, deliberation, intentness 2= <u>care</u>, support, concern, treatment, looking after, succour, ministration 3= <u>awareness</u>, regard, notice, recognition, consideration, observation, consciousness ≠ inattention

**attic** = <u>loft</u>, garret, roof space

**attitude** 1= <u>opinion</u>, view, position, approach, mood, perspective, point of view, stance 2= <u>position</u>, bearing, pose, stance, carriage, posture

**attract** 1= <u>allure</u>, draw, persuade, charm, appeal to, win over, tempt, lure (informal) ≠ repel 2= <u>pull</u>, draw, magnetize

**attraction** 1= <u>appeal</u>, pull (informal), charm, lure, temptation, fascination, allure, magnetism 2= <u>pull</u>, magnetism

**attractive** 1= <u>seductive</u>, charming, tempting, pretty, fair, inviting, lovely, pleasant ≠ unattractive 2= <u>appealing</u>, pleasing, inviting, tempting, irresistible ≠ unappealing

**attribute** VERB = <u>ascribe</u>, credit, refer, trace, assign, charge, allocate, put down
• NOUN = <u>quality</u>, feature, property, character, element, aspect, characteristic, distinction

**audience** 1= <u>spectators</u>, company, crowd, gathering, gallery, assembly, viewers, listeners 2= <u>interview</u>, meeting, hearing, exchange, reception, consultation

**aura** = <u>air</u>, feeling, quality, atmosphere, tone, mood, ambience

**austerity** 1= <u>plainness</u>, simplicity, starkness 2= <u>asceticism</u>, self-discipline, sobriety, puritanism, self-denial

**authentic** 1= <u>real</u>, pure, genuine, valid, undisputed, lawful, bona fide, dinkum (Austral. & N.Z. informal), true-to-life ≠ fake 2= <u>accurate</u>, legitimate, authoritative

**authenticity** 1= <u>genuineness</u>, purity 2= <u>accuracy</u>, certainty, validity, legitimacy, faithfulness, truthfulness

**author** 1= <u>writer</u>, composer, novelist, hack, creator, scribbler, scribe, wordsmith 2= <u>creator</u>, father, producer, designer, founder, architect, inventor, originator

**authoritarian** ADJECTIVE = strict, severe, autocratic, dictatorial, dogmatic, tyrannical, doctrinaire ≠ lenient

● NOUN = disciplinarian, dictator, tyrant, despot, autocrat, absolutist

**authoritative**

1 = commanding, masterly, imposing, assertive, imperious, self-assured ≠ timid 2 = reliable, accurate, valid, authentic, definitive, dependable, trustworthy ≠ unreliable

**authority** 1 usually plural = powers that be, government, police, officials, the state, management, administration, the system 2 = prerogative, influence, power, control, weight, direction, command, licence, mana (N.Z.) 3 = expert, specialist, professional, master, guru, virtuoso, connoisseur, fundi (S. African) 4 = command, power, control, rule, management, direction, mastery

**authorize** 1 = empower, commission, enable, entitle, mandate, accredit, give authority to 2 = permit, allow, grant, approve, sanction, license, warrant, consent to ≠ forbid

**automatic** 1 = mechanical, automated, mechanized, push-button, self-propelling ≠ done by

hand 2 = involuntary, natural, unconscious, mechanical, spontaneous, reflex, instinctive, unwilled ≠ conscious

**autonomous** = self-ruling, free, independent, sovereign, self-sufficient, self-governing, self-determining

**autonomy** = independence, freedom, sovereignty, self-determination, self-government, self-rule, self-sufficiency, home rule, rangatiratanga (N.Z.) ≠ dependency

**availability** = accessibility, readiness, handiness, attainability

**available** = accessible, ready, to hand, handy, at hand, free, to be had, achievable ≠ in use

**avalanche** 1 = snow-slide, landslide, landslip 2 = large amount, barrage, torrent, deluge, inundation

**avant-garde** = progressive, pioneering, experimental, innovative, unconventional, ground-breaking ≠ conservative

**avenue** = street, way, course, drive, road, approach, route, path

**average** NOUN = standard, normal, usual, par, mode, mean, medium, norm

● ADJECTIVE = usual, standard, general, normal, regular, ordinary, typical, commonplace ≠ unusual 2 = mean, middle, medium, intermediate, median

≠ minimum

● **VERB** 1= <u>make on average</u>, be on average, even out to, do on average, balance out to

● **PHRASES on average** = <u>usually</u>, generally, normally, typically, for the most part, as a rule

**avert** 1= <u>ward off</u>, avoid, prevent, frustrate, fend off, preclude, stave off, forestall 2= <u>turn away</u>, turn aside

**avoid** 1= <u>prevent</u>, stop, frustrate, hamper, foil, inhibit, avert, thwart 2= <u>refrain from</u>, bypass, dodge, eschew, escape, duck (out of) (*informal*), fight shy of, shirk from 3= <u>keep away from</u>, dodge, shun, evade, steer clear of, bypass

**await** 1= <u>wait for</u>, expect, look for, look forward to, anticipate, stay for 2= <u>be in store for</u>, wait for, be ready for, lie in wait for, be in readiness for

**awake ADJECTIVE** = <u>not sleeping</u>, sleepless, wide-awake, aware, conscious, aroused, awakened, restless ≠ asleep

● **VERB** 1= <u>wake up</u>, come to, wake, stir, awaken, rouse 2= <u>alert</u>, stimulate, provoke, revive, arouse, stir up, kindle

**awaken** 1= <u>stimulate</u>, provoke, alert, stir up, kindle 2= <u>awake</u>, wake, revive, arouse, rouse

**award NOUN** = <u>prize</u>, gift, trophy, decoration, grant, bonsela (*S. African*), koha (*N.Z.*)

● **VERB** 1= <u>present with</u>, give, grant, hand out, confer, endow, bestow 2= <u>grant</u>, give, accord

**aware** = <u>informed</u>, enlightened, knowledgeable, learned, expert, versed, up to date, in the picture ≠ ignorant

**awareness**

● **PHRASES awareness of** = <u>knowledge of</u>, understanding of, recognition of, perception of, consciousness of, realization of, familiarity with

**away ADJECTIVE** = <u>absent</u>, out, gone, elsewhere, abroad, not here, not present, on vacation

● **ADVERB** 1= <u>off</u>, elsewhere, abroad, hence, from here 2= <u>aside</u>, out of the way, to one side = <u>at a distance</u>, far, apart, remote, isolated 4= <u>continuously</u>, repeatedly, relentlessly, incessantly, interminably, unremittingly, uninterruptedly

**awe NOUN** = <u>wonder</u>, fear, respect, reverence, horror, terror, dread, admiration ≠ contempt

● **VERB** = <u>impress</u>, amaze, stun, frighten, terrify, astonish, horrify, intimidate

**awesome** = <u>awe-inspiring</u>, amazing, stunning, impressive, astonishing, formidable, intimidating, breathtaking

**awful** 1= <u>disgusting</u>, offensive, gross, foul, dreadful, revolting, sickening, frightful, festy (*Austral. slang*), yucko (*Austral. slang*) **2** = **bad**, poor, terrible, appalling, foul, rubbish (*slang*), dreadful, horrendous ≠ **wonderful**, ka pai (*N.Z.*) **3** = **shocking**, dreadful **4** = **unwell**, poorly (*informal*), ill, terrible, sick, crook (*Austral. & N.Z. informal*), unhealthy, off-colour, under the weather (*informal*)

**awfully 1** (*Informal*) = **very**, extremely, terribly, exceptionally, greatly, immensely, exceedingly, dreadfully **2** = **badly**, woefully, dreadfully, disgracefully, wretchedly, unforgivably, reprehensibly

**awkward 1** = **embarrassing**, difficult, sensitive, delicate, uncomfortable, humiliating, disconcerting, inconvenient, barro (*Austral. slang*) ≠ **comfortable 2** = **inconvenient**, difficult, troublesome, cumbersome, unwieldy, unmanageable, clunky (*informal*) ≠ **convenient 3** = **clumsy**, lumbering, bumbling, unwieldy, ponderous, ungainly, gauche, gawky, unco (*Austral. slang*) ≠ **graceful**

**axe NOUN** = **hatchet**, chopper, tomahawk, cleaver, adze
● **VERB 1** (*Informal*) = **abandon**, end, eliminate, cancel, scrap, cut back, terminate, dispense with

**2** (*Informal*) = **dismiss**, fire (*informal*), sack (*informal*), remove, get rid of
● **PHRASES the axe** (*Informal*) = **the sack** (*informal*), dismissal, the boot (*slang*), termination, the chop (*slang*)

**axis** = **pivot**, shaft, axle, spindle, centre line

# B

**baas** (*S. African*) = **master**, bo (*informal*), chief, ruler, commander, head, overlord, overseer

**baby NOUN** = **child**, infant, babe, bairn (*Scot.*), newborn child, babe in arms, ankle-biter (*Austral. slang*), tacker (*Austral. slang*)
● **ADJECTIVE** = **small**, little, minute, tiny, mini, wee, miniature, petite

**back NOUN 1** = **spine**, backbone, vertebrae, spinal column, vertebral column **2** = **rear** ≠ **front 3** = **reverse**, rear, other side, wrong side, underside, flip side
● **ADJECTIVE 1** = **rear** ≠ **front 2** = **rearmost**, hind, hindmost **3** = **previous**, earlier, former, past, elapsed ≠ **future 4** = **tail**, end, rear, posterior
● **VERB 1** = **support**, help, aid, champion, defend, promote, assist, advocate ≠ **oppose 2** = **subsidize**, help, support, sponsor, assist

**backbone** 1= <u>spinal column</u>, spine, vertebrae, vertebral column 2= <u>strength of character</u>, character, resolution, nerve, daring, courage, determination, pluck

**backer** 1= <u>supporter</u>, second, angel (*informal*), patron, promoter, subscriber, helper, benefactor 2= <u>advocate</u>, supporter, patron, sponsor, promoter

**backfire** = <u>fail</u>, founder, flop (*informal*), rebound, boomerang, miscarry, misfire

**background** 1= <u>upbringing</u>, history, culture, environment, tradition, circumstances 2= <u>experience</u>, grounding, education 3= <u>circumstances</u>, history, conditions, situation, atmosphere, environment, framework, ambience

**backing** 1= <u>support</u>, encouragement, endorsement, moral support 2= <u>assistance</u>, support, help, aid, sponsorship, patronage

**backlash** = <u>reaction</u>, response, resistance, retaliation, repercussion, counterblast, counteraction

**backward** 1= <u>underdeveloped</u>, undeveloped 2= <u>slow</u>, behind, retarded, underdeveloped, subnormal, half-witted, slow-witted

**backwards** *or* **backward** = <u>towards the rear</u>, behind you, in reverse, rearwards

**bacteria** = <u>microorganisms</u>, viruses, bugs (*slang*), germs, microbes, pathogens, bacilli

> ### *Word Power*
>
> **bacteria**– *Bacteria* is a plural noun. It is therefore incorrect to talk about *a bacteria*, even though this is quite commonly heard, especially in the media. The correct singular is *a bacterium*.

**bad** 1= <u>harmful</u>, damaging, dangerous, destructive, unhealthy, detrimental, hurtful, ruinous ≠ beneficial 2= <u>poor</u> 3= <u>unfavourable</u>, distressing, unfortunate, grim, unpleasant, gloomy, adverse 4= <u>inferior</u>, poor, inadequate, faulty, unsatisfactory, defective, imperfect, substandard, bush-league (*Austral. & N.Z. informal*), half-pie (*N.Z. informal*), bodger or bodgie (*Austral. slang*) ≠ satisfactory 5= <u>incompetent</u>, poor, useless, incapable, unfit, inexpert 6= <u>grim</u>, severe, hard, tough 7= <u>wicked</u>, criminal, evil, corrupt, immoral, sinful, depraved ≠ virtuous 8= <u>naughty</u>, defiant, wayward, mischievous, wicked, unruly, impish, undisciplined ≠ well-behaved 9= <u>rotten</u>, off, rank, sour, rancid, mouldy, putrid, festy (*Austral. slang*)

**badge** 1 = <u>image</u>, brand, stamp, identification, crest, emblem, insignia 2 = <u>mark</u>, sign, token

**badger** = <u>pester</u>, harry, bother, bug (*informal*), bully, plague, hound, harass

**badly** 1 = <u>poorly</u>, incorrectly, carelessly, inadequately, imperfectly, ineptly ≠ well 2 = <u>severely</u>, greatly, deeply, seriously, desperately, intensely, exceedingly 3 = <u>unfavourably</u>, unsuccessfully

**baffle** = <u>puzzle</u>, confuse, stump, bewilder, confound, perplex, mystify, flummox ≠ explain

**bag** NOUN = <u>sack</u>, container, sac, receptacle
● VERB 1 = <u>get</u>, land, score (*slang*), capture, acquire, procure 2 = <u>catch</u>, kill, shoot, capture, acquire, trap

**baggage** = <u>luggage</u>, things, cases, bags, equipment, gear, suitcases, belongings

**baggy** = <u>loose</u>, slack, bulging, sagging, sloppy, floppy, roomy, ill-fitting ≠ tight

**bail** NOUN (*Law*) = <u>security</u>, bond, guarantee, pledge, warranty, surety
● PHRASES **bail out** = <u>escape</u>, withdraw, get away, retreat, make your getaway, break free *or* out
◆ **bail something** *or* **someone out** (*Informal*) = <u>save</u>, help, release, aid, deliver, recover, rescue, get out

**bait** NOUN = <u>lure</u>, attraction, incentive, carrot (*informal*), temptation, snare, inducement, decoy
● VERB = <u>tease</u>, annoy, irritate, bother, mock, wind up (*Brit. slang*), hound, torment

**baked** = <u>dry</u>, desert, seared, scorched, barren, sterile, arid, torrid

**bakkie** (*S. African*) = <u>truck</u>, pick-up, van, lorry, pick-up truck

**balance** VERB 1 = <u>stabilize</u>, level, steady ≠ overbalance 2 = <u>weigh</u>, consider, compare, estimate, contrast, assess, evaluate, set against 3 (*Accounting*) = <u>calculate</u>, total, determine, estimate, settle, count, square, reckon
● NOUN 1 = <u>equilibrium</u>, stability, steadiness, evenness ≠ instability 2 = <u>stability</u>, equanimity, steadiness 3 = <u>parity</u>, equity, fairness, impartiality, equality, correspondence, equivalence 4 = <u>remainder</u>, rest, difference, surplus, residue 5 = <u>composure</u>, stability, restraint, self-control, poise, self-discipline, equanimity, self-restraint

**balcony** 1 = <u>terrace</u>, veranda 2 = <u>upper circle</u>, gods, gallery

**bald** 1 = <u>hairless</u>, depilated, baldheaded 2 = <u>plain</u>, direct, frank, straightforward, blunt, rude, forthright, unadorned

**ball** = <u>sphere</u>, drop, globe, pellet, orb, globule, spheroid

**balloon** = <u>expand</u>, rise, increase, swell, blow up, inflate, bulge, billow

**ballot** = <u>vote</u>, election, voting, poll, polling, referendum, show of hands

**ban** VERB 1 = <u>prohibit</u>, bar, block, veto, forbid, boycott, outlaw, banish ≠ permit 2 = <u>bar</u>, prohibit, exclude, forbid, disqualify, preclude, debar, declare ineligible
• NOUN = <u>prohibition</u>, restriction, veto, boycott, embargo, injunction, taboo, rahui (*N.Z.*) ≠ permission

**band**[1] 1 = <u>ensemble</u>, group, orchestra, combo 2 = <u>gang</u>, company, group, party, team, body, crowd, pack

**band**[2] = <u>headband</u>, strip, ribbon

**bandage** NOUN = <u>dressing</u>, plaster, compress, gauze
• VERB = <u>dress</u>, cover, bind, swathe

**bandit** = <u>robber</u>, outlaw, raider, plunderer, mugger (*informal*), looter, highwayman, desperado

**bang** NOUN 1 = <u>explosion</u>, pop, clash, crack, blast, slam, discharge, thump 2 = <u>blow</u>, knock, stroke, punch, bump, sock (*slang*), smack, thump
• VERB 1 = <u>resound</u>, boom, explode, thunder, thump, clang

2 = <u>bump</u>, knock, elbow, jostle 3 often with *on* = <u>hit</u>, strike, knock, belt (*informal*), slam, thump, clatter
• ADVERB = <u>exactly</u>, straight, square, squarely, precisely, slap, smack, plumb (*informal*)

**banish** 1 = <u>exclude</u>, ban, dismiss, expel, throw out, eject, evict 2 = <u>expel</u>, exile, outlaw, deport ≠ admit 3 = <u>get rid of</u>, remove

**bank**[1] NOUN 1 = <u>financial institution</u>, repository, depository 2 = <u>store</u>, fund, stock, source, supply, reserve, pool, reservoir
• VERB = <u>deposit</u>, keep, save

**bank**[2] NOUN 1 = <u>side</u>, edge, margin, shore, brink 2 = <u>mound</u>, banking, rise, hill, mass, pile, heap, ridge, kopje or koppie (*S. African*) 3 = <u>mass</u>
• VERB = <u>tilt</u>, tip, pitch, heel, slope, incline, slant, cant

**bank**[3] = <u>row</u>, group, line, range, series, file, rank, sequence

**bankrupt** = <u>insolvent</u>, broke (*informal*), ruined, wiped out (*informal*), impoverished, in the red, destitute, gone bust (*informal*) ≠ solvent

**bankruptcy** = <u>insolvency</u>, failure, disaster, ruin, liquidation

**banner** = <u>flag</u>, standard, colours, placard, pennant, ensign, streamer

**banquet** = <u>feast</u>, spread (*informal*), dinner, meal, revel, repast, hakari (*N.Z.*)

**bar** NOUN 1 = <u>public house</u>, pub (*informal, chiefly Brit.*), counter, inn, saloon, tavern, canteen, watering hole (*facetious slang*) 2 = <u>rod</u>, staff, stick, stake, rail, pole, paling, shaft 3 = <u>obstacle</u>, block, barrier, hurdle, hitch, barricade, snag, deterrent ≠ aid
● VERB 1 = <u>lock</u>, block, secure, attach, bolt, blockade, barricade, fortify 2 = <u>block</u>, restrict, restrain, hamper, thwart, hinder, obstruct, impede 3 = <u>exclude</u>, ban, forbid, prohibit, keep out of, disallow, shut out of, blackball ≠ admit

**barbarian** 1 = <u>savage</u>, monster, beast, brute, yahoo, swine, sadist 2 = <u>lout</u>, yahoo, bigot, philistine, hoon (*Austral. & N.Z.*), cougan (*Austral. slang*), scozza (*Austral. slang*), bogan (*Austral. slang*), boor, vulgarian

**bare** 1 = <u>naked</u>, nude, stripped, uncovered, undressed, unclothed, unclad, without a stitch on (*informal*) ≠ dressed 2 = <u>simple</u>, spare, stark, austere, spartan, unadorned, unembellished, unornamented ≠ adorned 3 = <u>plain</u>, simple, basic, obvious, sheer, patent, evident, stark

**barely** = <u>only</u>, just, just, hardly, scarcely, at a push ≠ completely

**bargain** NOUN 1 = <u>good buy</u>, discount purchase, good deal, steal (*informal*), snip (*informal*),

giveaway, cheap purchase 2 = <u>agreement</u>, deal (*informal*), promise, contract, arrangement, settlement, pledge, pact
● VERB = <u>negotiate</u>, deal, contract, mediate, covenant, stipulate, transact, cut a deal

**barge** = <u>canal boat</u>, lighter, narrow boat, flatboat

**bark**[1] VERB = <u>yap</u>, bay, howl, snarl, growl, yelp, woof
● NOUN = <u>yap</u>, bay, howl, snarl, growl, yelp, woof

**bark**[2] = <u>covering</u>, casing, cover, skin, layer, crust, cortex (*Anatomy, botany*), rind

**barracks** = <u>camp</u>, quarters, garrison, encampment, billet

**barrage** 1 = <u>bombardment</u>, attack, bombing, assault, shelling, battery, volley, blitz 2 = <u>torrent</u>, mass, burst, stream, hail, spate, onslaught, deluge

**barren** 1 = <u>desolate</u>, empty, desert, waste ≠ fertile 2 (*Old-fashioned*) = <u>infertile</u>, sterile, childless, unproductive

**barricade** NOUN = <u>barrier</u>, wall, fence, blockade, obstruction, rampart, bulwark, palisade
● VERB = <u>bar</u>, block, defend, secure, lock, bolt, blockade, fortify

**barrier** = <u>barricade</u>, wall, bar, fence, boundary, obstacle, blockade, obstruction

**base**[1] NOUN 1 = <u>bottom</u>, floor, lowest part ≠ top 2 = <u>support</u>,

stand, foot, rest, bed, bottom, foundation, pedestal
**3 =** <u>foundation</u>, institution, organization, establishment
**4 =** <u>centre</u>, post, station, camp, settlement, headquarters, starting point **5 =** <u>home</u>, house, pad (*slang*), residence
**6 =** <u>essence</u>, source, basis, root, core

● **VERB 1 =** <u>ground</u>, found, build, establish, depend, construct, derive, hinge **2 =** <u>place</u>, set, post, station, establish, locate, install

**base² =** <u>dishonourable</u>, evil, disgraceful, shameful, immoral, wicked, sordid, despicable, scungy (*Austral. & N.Z.*)
≠ honourable

**bash NOUN** (*Informal*) **=** <u>attempt</u>, go (*informal*), try, shot (*informal*), bid, crack (*informal*), stab (*informal*)

● **VERB** (*Informal*) **=** <u>hit</u>, beat, strike, knock, smash, belt (*informal*), slap, sock (*slang*)

**basic ADJECTIVE 1 =** <u>fundamental</u>, main, essential, primary, vital, principal, cardinal, elementary
**2 =** <u>vital</u>, needed, important, key, necessary, essential, primary, crucial **3 =** <u>essential</u>, key, vital, fundamental ≠ secondary
**4 =** <u>main</u>, key, essential, primary
**5 =** <u>plain</u>, simple, classic, unfussy, unembellished

● **PLURAL NOUN =** <u>essentials</u>, principles, fundamentals, nuts and bolts (*informal*), nitty-gritty (*informal*), rudiments, brass tacks (*informal*)

**basically =** <u>essentially</u>, mainly, mostly, principally, fundamentally, primarily, at heart, inherently

**basis 1 =** <u>arrangement</u>, way, system, footing, agreement
**2 =** <u>foundation</u>, support, base, ground, footing, bottom, groundwork

**bask =** <u>lie</u>, relax, lounge, sprawl, loaf, lie about, swim in, sunbathe, outspan (*S. African*)

**bass =** <u>deep</u>, low, resonant, sonorous, low-pitched, deep-toned

**bat**

| *Bats* | |
|---|---|
| flying fox | noctule |
| fruit bat | pipistrelle |
| hammerhead | serotine |
| horseshoe bat | vampire bat |
| kalong | |

**batch =** <u>group</u>, set, lot, crowd, pack, collection, quantity, bunch

**bath NOUN =** <u>wash</u>, cleaning, shower, soak, cleansing, scrub, scrubbing, douche

● **VERB =** <u>clean</u>, wash, shower, soak, cleanse, scrub, bathe, rinse

**bathe 1 =** <u>swim</u> **2 =** <u>wash</u>, clean, bath, shower, soak, cleanse, scrub, rinse 3 = <u>cleanse</u>, clean, wash, soak, rinse 4 = <u>cover</u>, flood, steep, engulf, immerse, overrun, suffuse, wash over

**baton** = <u>stick</u>, club, staff, pole, rod, crook, cane, mace, mere (*N.Z.*), patu (*N.Z.*)

**batter** = <u>beat</u>, hit, strike, knock, bang, thrash, pound, buffet

**battery** = <u>artillery</u>, ordnance, gunnery, gun emplacement, cannonry

**battle** NOUN 1 = <u>fight</u>, attack, action, struggle, conflict, clash, encounter, combat, biffo (*Austral. slang*) ≠ peace 2 = <u>conflict</u>, campaign, struggle, dispute, contest, crusade 3 = <u>campaign</u>, drive, movement, push, struggle
● VERB 1 = <u>wrestle</u>, war, fight, argue, dispute, grapple, clamour, lock horns 2 = <u>struggle</u>, work, labour, strain, strive, toil, go all out (*informal*), give it your best shot (*informal*)
➤ **famous battles**

**battlefield** = <u>battleground</u>, front, field, combat zone, field of battle

**batty** = <u>crazy</u>, odd, mad, eccentric, peculiar, daft (*informal*), touched, potty (*Brit. informal*), off the air (*Austral. slang*), porangi (*N.Z.*)

**bay**[1] = <u>inlet</u>, sound, gulf, creek, cove, fjord, bight, natural harbour

**bay**[2] = <u>recess</u>, opening, corner, niche, compartment, nook, alcove

**bay**[3] VERB = <u>howl</u>, cry, roar (*used of hounds*), bark, wail, growl, bellow, clamour
● NOUN = <u>cry</u>, roar (*used of hounds*), bark, howl, wail, growl, bellow, clamour

**bazaar** 1 = <u>market</u>, exchange, fair, marketplace 2 = <u>fair</u>, fête, gala, bring-and-buy

**be** = <u>be alive</u>, live, exist, survive, breathe, be present, endure

**beach** = <u>shore</u>, coast, sands, seaside, water's edge, seashore

**beached** = <u>stranded</u>, grounded, abandoned, deserted, wrecked, ashore, marooned, aground

**beacon** = <u>signal</u>, sign, beam, flare, lighthouse, bonfire, watchtower

**bead** = <u>drop</u>, tear, bubble, pearl, dot, drip, blob, droplet

**beam** VERB 1 = <u>smile</u>, grin 2 = <u>transmit</u>, show, air, broadcast, cable, send out, relay, televise 3 = <u>radiate</u>, flash, shine, glow, glitter, glare, gleam
● NOUN 1 = <u>ray</u>, flash, stream, glow, streak, shaft, gleam, glint 2 = <u>rafter</u>, support, timber, spar, plank, girder, joist 3 = <u>smile</u>, grin

**bear** VERB 1 = <u>carry</u>, take, move, bring, transfer, conduct, transport, haul ≠ put down 2 = <u>support</u>, shoulder, sustain, endure, uphold, withstand ≠ give up 3 = <u>display</u>, have, show, hold, carry, possess

# Famous battles

| | | | |
|---|---|---|---|
| Aboukir Bay *or* | 1798 | Manassas | 1861; 1862 |
|   Abukir Bay | | Marathon | 490 B.C. |
| Actium | 31 B.C. | Marengo | 1800 |
| Agincourt | 1415 | Marston Moor | 1644 |
| Alamo | 1836 | Missionary Ridge | 1863 |
| Arnhem | 1944 | Naseby | 1645 |
| Austerlitz | 1805 | Navarino | 425 B.C. |
| Balaklava *or* Balaclava | 1854 | Omdurman | 1898 |
| Bannockburn | 1314 | Passchendaele | 1917 |
| Barnet | 1471 | Philippi | 42 B.C. |
| Bautzen | 1813 | Plains of Abraham | 1759 |
| Belleau Wood | 1918 | Plassey | 1757 |
| Blenheim | 1704 | Plataea | 479 B.C. |
| Borodino | 1812 | Poltava | 1709 |
| Bosworth Field | 1485 | Prestonpans | 1745 |
| Boyne | 1690 | Pydna | 168 B.C. |
| Cannae | 216 B.C. | Quatre Bras | 1815 |
| Crécy | 1346 | Ramillies | 1706 |
| Culloden | 1746 | Roncesvalles | 778 |
| Dien Bien Phu | 1954 | Sadowa *or* Sadová | 1866 |
| Edgehill | 1642 | Saint-Mihiel | 1918 |
| El Alamein | 1942 | Salamis | 480 B.C. |
| Falkirk | 1298; 1746 | Sedgemoor | 1685 |
| Flodden | 1513 | Sempach | 1386 |
| Gettysburg | 1863 | Shipka Pass | 1877–78 |
| Guadalcanal | 1942–3 | Somme | 1916; 1918 |
| Hastings | 1066 | Stamford Bridge | 1066 |
| Imphal | 1944 | Tannenberg | 1410; 1914 |
| Inkerman | 1854 | Tewkesbury | 1471 |
| Issus | 333 B.C. | Thermopylae | 480 B.C. |
| Jemappes | 1792 | Tobruk | 1941; 1942 |
| Jena | 1806 | Trafalgar | 1805 |
| Killiecrankie | 1689 | Trenton | 1776 |
| Kursk | 1943 | Verdun | 1916 |
| Ladysmith | 1899–1900 | Vitoria | 1813 |
| Leipzig | 1813 | Wagram | 1809 |
| Lepanto | 1571 | Waterloo | 1815 |
| Leyte Gulf | 1944 | Ypres | 1914;1915; |
| Little Bighorn | 1876 | | 1917;1918 |
| Lützen | 1632 | Zama | 202 B.C. |

4 = <u>suffer</u>, experience, go through, sustain, stomach, endure, brook, abide 5 = <u>bring yourself to</u>, allow, accept, permit, endure, tolerate 6 = <u>produce</u>, generate, yield, bring forth 7 = <u>give birth to</u>, produce, deliver, breed, bring forth, beget 8 = <u>exhibit</u>, hold, maintain 9 = <u>conduct</u>, carry, move, deport ● PHRASES **bear something out** = <u>support</u>, prove, confirm, justify, endorse, uphold, substantiate, corroborate

**bearer** 1 = <u>agent</u>, carrier, courier, herald, envoy, messenger, conveyor, emissary 2 = <u>carrier</u>, runner, servant, porter

**bearing** NOUN 1 *usually with on or upon* = <u>relevance</u>, relation, application, connection, import, reference, significance, pertinence ≠ irrelevance 2 = <u>manner</u>, attitude, conduct, aspect, behaviour, posture, demeanour, deportment
● PLURAL NOUN = <u>way</u>, course, position, situation, track, aim, direction, location

**beast** 1 = <u>animal</u>, creature, brute 2 = <u>brute</u>, monster, savage, barbarian, fiend, swine, ogre, sadist

**beastly** = <u>unpleasant</u>, mean, awful, nasty, rotten, horrid, disagreeable ≠ pleasant

**beat** VERB 1 = <u>batter</u>, hit, strike, knock, pound, smack, thrash, thump 2 = <u>pound</u>, strike, hammer, batter, thrash 3 = <u>throb</u>, thump, pound, quake, vibrate, pulsate, palpitate 4 = <u>hit</u>, strike, bang 5 = <u>flap</u>, thrash, flutter, wag 6 = <u>defeat</u>, outdo, trounce, overcome, crush, overwhelm, conquer, surpass
● NOUN 1 = <u>throb</u>, pounding, pulse, thumping, vibration, pulsating, palpitation, pulsation 2 = <u>route</u>, way, course, rounds, path, circuit
● PHRASES **beat someone up** (*Informal*) = <u>assault</u>, attack, batter, thrash, set about, set upon, lay into (*informal*), beat the living daylights out of (*informal*)

**beaten** 1 = <u>stirred</u>, mixed, whipped, blended, whisked, frothy, foamy 2 = <u>defeated</u>, overcome, overwhelmed, cowed, thwarted, vanquished

**beautiful** = <u>attractive</u>, pretty, lovely, charming, tempting, pleasant, handsome, fetching ≠ ugly

**beauty** 1 = <u>attractiveness</u>, charm, grace, glamour, elegance, loveliness, handsomeness, comeliness ≠ ugliness 2 = <u>good-looker</u>, lovely (*slang*), belle, stunner (*informal*)

**because** CONJUNCTION = <u>since</u>, as, in that
● PHRASES **because of** = <u>as a</u>

result of, on account of, by reason of, thanks to, owing to

> ### Word Power
>
> **because**– The phrase *on account of* can provide a useful alternative to *because of* in writing. It occurs relatively infrequently in spoken language, where it is sometimes followed by a clause, as in *on account of I don't do drugs*. However, this use is considered nonstandard.

**beckon** = gesture, sign, wave, indicate, signal, nod, motion, summon

**become** 1 = come to be, develop into, be transformed into, grow into, change into, alter to, mature into, ripen into 2 = suit, fit, enhance, flatter, embellish, set off

**becoming** 1 = flattering, pretty, attractive, enhancing, neat, graceful, tasteful, well-chosen ≠ unflattering 2 = appropriate, seemly, fitting, suitable, proper, worthy, in keeping, compatible ≠ inappropriate

**bed** 1 = bedstead, couch, berth, cot, bunk, divan 2 = plot, area, row, strip, patch, ground, land, garden 3 = bottom, ground, floor 4 = base, footing, basis, bottom, foundation, underpinning, groundwork, bedrock

**bee** ► ants, bees, and wasps

**beetle** ► beetles

**before** PREPOSITION 1 = earlier than, ahead of, prior to, in advance of ≠ after 2 = in front of, ahead of, in advance of 3 = in the presence of, in front of 4 = ahead of, in front of, in advance of
● ADVERB 1 = previously, earlier, sooner, in advance, formerly ≠ after 2 = in the past, earlier, once, previously, formerly, hitherto, beforehand

( Related Words )
*prefixes*: ante-, fore-, pre-

**beforehand** = in advance, before, earlier, already, sooner, ahead, previously, in anticipation

**beg** 1 = implore, plead with, beseech, request, petition, solicit, entreat 2 = scrounge, bum (*informal*), touch (someone) for (*slang*), cadge, sponge on (someone) for, freeload (*slang*), seek charity, solicit charity ≠ give

**beggar** = tramp, bum (*informal*), derelict, drifter, down-and-out, pauper, vagrant, bag lady (*chiefly U.S.*), derro (*Austral. slang*)

**begin** 1 = start, commence, proceed ≠ stop 2 = commence, start, initiate, embark on, set about, instigate, institute, make a beginning 3 = start talking, start, initiate, commence 4 = come into existence, start, appear, emerge, arise, originate, come into being

## Beetles

| | |
|---|---|
| ambrosia beetle | dung beetle *or* chafer |
| Asiatic beetle | firefly |
| bacon beetle | flea beetle |
| bark beetle | furniture beetle |
| bee beetle | glow-worm |
| black beetle *or* (*N.Z.*) kekerengu *or* Māori bug | gold beetle *or* goldbug |
| blister beetle | goldsmith beetle |
| bloody-nosed beetle | ground beetle |
| boll weevil | Japanese beetle |
| bombardier beetle | June bug, June beetle, May bug, *or* May beetle |
| burying beetle *or* sexton | ladybird *or* (*U.S. & Canad.*) ladybug |
| cabinet beetle | leaf beetle |
| cardinal beetle | leather beetle |
| carpet beetle *or* (*U.S.*) carpet bug | May beetle, cockchafer, *or* June bug |
| chafer | scarab |
| Christmas beetle *or* king beetle | scavenger beetle |
| click beetle, snapping beetle, *or* skipjack | snapping beetle |
| cockchafer, May beetle, *or* May bug | water beetle |
| Colorado beetle *or* potato beetle | weevil *or* snout beetle |
| deathwatch beetle | weevil, pea weevil, *or* bean weevil |
| diving beetle | |

5 = <u>emerge</u>, start, spring, stem, derive, originate ≠ end

**beginner** = <u>novice</u>, pupil, amateur, newcomer, starter, trainee, apprentice, learner ≠ expert

**beginning** 1 = <u>start</u>, opening, birth, origin, outset, onset, initiation, inauguration ≠ end
2 = <u>outset</u>, start, opening, birth, onset, commencement
3 = <u>origins</u>

**behave** 1 = <u>act</u> 2 *often reflexive* = <u>be well-behaved</u>, mind your manners, keep your nose clean, act correctly, conduct yourself properly ≠ misbehave

**behaviour** 1 = <u>conduct</u>, ways, actions, bearing, attitude, manner, manners, demeanour
2 = <u>action</u>, performance, operation, functioning

**behind** PREPOSITION 1 = <u>at the</u>

rear of, at the back of, at the heels of 2 = <u>after</u>, following 3 = <u>supporting</u>, for, backing, on the side of, in agreement with 4 = <u>causing</u>, responsible for, initiating, at the bottom of, instigating 5 = <u>later than</u>, after
● ADVERB 1 = <u>after</u>, next, following, afterwards, subsequently, in the wake (of) ≠ in advance of 2 = <u>behind schedule</u>, delayed, running late, behind time ≠ ahead 3 = <u>overdue</u>, in debt, in arrears, behindhand
● NOUN (Informal) = <u>bottom</u>, butt (U.S. & Canad. informal), buttocks, posterior

**being** 1 = <u>individual</u>, creature, human being, living thing 2 = <u>life</u>, reality ≠ nonexistence 2 = <u>soul</u>, spirit, substance, creature, essence, organism, entity

**beleaguered** 1 = <u>harassed</u>, troubled, plagued, hassled (informal), badgered, persecuted, pestered, vexed 2 = <u>besieged</u>, surrounded, blockaded, beset, encircled, assailed, hemmed in

**belief** 1 = <u>trust</u>, confidence, conviction ≠ disbelief 2 = <u>faith</u>, principles, doctrine, ideology, creed, dogma, tenet, credo 3 = <u>opinion</u>, feeling, idea, impression, assessment, notion, judgment, point of view

**believe** 1 = <u>think</u>, judge, suppose, estimate, imagine, assume, gather, reckon 2 = <u>accept</u>, trust, credit, depend on, rely on, have faith in, swear by, be certain of ≠ disbelieve

**believer** = <u>follower</u>, supporter, convert, disciple, devotee, apostle, adherent, zealot ≠ sceptic

**bellow** VERB = <u>shout</u>, cry (out), scream, roar, yell, howl, shriek, bawl
● NOUN = <u>shout</u>, cry, scream, roar, yell, howl, shriek, bawl

**belly** = <u>stomach</u>, insides (informal), gut, abdomen, tummy, paunch, potbelly, corporation (informal), puku (N.Z.)

**belong** = <u>go with</u>, fit into, be part of, relate to, be connected with, pertain to

**belonging** = <u>fellowship</u>, relationship, association, loyalty, acceptance, attachment, inclusion, affinity

**belongings** = <u>possessions</u>, goods, things, effects, property, stuff, gear, paraphernalia

**beloved** = <u>dear</u>, loved, valued, prized, admired, treasured, precious, darling

**below** PREPOSITION 1 = <u>under</u>, underneath, lower than 2 = <u>less than</u>, lower than 3 = <u>subordinate to</u>, subject to, inferior to, lesser than
● ADVERB 1 = <u>lower</u>, down, under, beneath, underneath

2= <u>beneath</u>, following, at the end, underneath, at the bottom, further on

**belt** 1= <u>waistband</u>, band, sash, girdle, girth, cummerbund 2= <u>conveyor belt</u>, band, loop, fan belt, drive belt 3(*Geography*) = <u>zone</u>, area, region, section, district, stretch, strip, layer

**bemused** = <u>puzzled</u>, confused, baffled, at sea, bewildered, muddled, perplexed, mystified

**bench**NOUN 1= <u>seat</u>, stall, pew 2= <u>worktable</u>, stand, table, counter, trestle table, workbench

• PHRASES **the bench** = <u>court</u>, judges, magistrates, tribunal, judiciary, courtroom

**benchmark** = <u>reference point</u>, gauge, yardstick, measure, level, standard, model, par

**bend**VERB 1= <u>twist</u>, turn, wind, lean, hook, bow, curve, arch

• NOUN = <u>curve</u>, turn, corner, twist, angle, bow, loop, arc

**beneath**PREPOSITION 1= <u>under</u>, below, underneath, lower than ≠ over 2= <u>inferior to</u>, below 3= <u>unworthy of</u>, unfitting for, unsuitable for, inappropriate for, unbefitting

• ADVERB = <u>underneath</u>, below, in a lower place

(*Related Words*)

*prefix:* sub-

**beneficial** = <u>favourable</u>, useful, valuable, helpful, profitable, benign, wholesome, advantageous ≠ harmful

**beneficiary** = <u>recipient</u>, receiver, payee 2= <u>heir</u>, inheritor

**benefit**NOUN 1= <u>good</u>, help, profit, favour ≠ harm 2= <u>advantage</u>, aid, favour, assistance

• VERB 1= <u>profit from</u>, make the most of, gain from, do well out of, reap benefits from, turn to your advantage 2= <u>help</u>, aid, profit, improve, enhance, assist, avail ≠ harm

**benign** 1= <u>benevolent</u>, kind, kindly, warm, friendly, obliging, sympathetic, compassionate ≠ unkind 2(*Medical*) = <u>harmless</u>, innocent, innocuous, curable, inoffensive, remediable ≠ malignant

**bent**ADJECTIVE 1= <u>misshapen</u>, twisted, angled, bowed, curved, arched, crooked, distorted ≠ straight 2= <u>stooped</u>, bowed, arched, hunched

• NOUN = <u>inclination</u>, ability, leaning, tendency, preference, penchant, propensity, aptitude

• PHRASES **bent on** = <u>intent on</u>, set on, fixed on, predisposed to, resolved on, insistent on

**bequeath** 1= <u>leave</u>, will, give, grant, hand down, endow, bestow, entrust 2= <u>give</u>, accord, grant, afford, yield, lend, pass on, confer

**berth** NOUN 1 = <u>bunk</u>, bed, hammock, billet 2 (*Nautical*) = <u>anchorage</u>, haven, port, harbour, dock, pier, wharf, quay

● VERB (*Nautical*) = <u>anchor</u>, land, dock, moor, tie up, drop anchor

**beside** PREPOSITION = <u>next to</u>, near, close to, neighbouring, alongside, adjacent to, at the side of, abreast of

● PHRASES **beside yourself** = <u>distraught</u>, desperate, distressed, frantic, frenzied, demented, unhinged, overwrought

---

### Word Power

**beside** – People occasionally confuse *beside* and *besides*. *Besides* is used for mentioning something that adds to what you have already said, for example: *I didn't feel like going and besides, I had nothing to wear*. *Beside* usually means *next to* or *at the side of something or someone*, for example: *he was standing beside me* (not *besides me*).

---

**besides** PREPOSITION = <u>apart from</u>, barring, excepting, other than, excluding, as well (as), in addition to, over and above

● ADVERB = <u>also</u>, too, further, otherwise, in addition, as well, moreover, furthermore

**besiege** 1 = <u>harass</u>, harry, plague, hound, hassle (*informal*),

badger, pester 2 = <u>surround</u>, enclose, blockade, encircle, hem in, shut in, lay siege to

**best** ADJECTIVE = <u>finest</u>, leading, supreme, principal, foremost, pre-eminent, unsurpassed, most accomplished

● NOUN = <u>finest</u>, top, prime, pick, flower, cream, elite, crème de la crème (*French*)

● ADVERB = <u>most highly</u>, most fully, most deeply

**bestow** = <u>present</u>, give, award, grant, commit, hand out, lavish, impart ≠ obtain

**bet** VERB = <u>gamble</u>, chance, stake, venture, hazard, speculate, wager, risk money

● NOUN = <u>gamble</u>, risk, stake, venture, speculation, flutter (*informal*), punt, wager

**betray** 1 = <u>be disloyal to</u>, dob in (*Austral. slang*), double-cross (*informal*), stab in the back, be unfaithful to, inform on or against 2 = <u>give away</u>, reveal, expose, disclose, uncover, divulge, unmask, let slip

**betrayal** = <u>disloyalty</u>, sell-out (*informal*), deception, treason, treachery, trickery, double-cross (*informal*), breach of trust ≠ loyalty

**better** ADVERB 1 = <u>to a greater degree</u>, more completely, more thoroughly 2 = <u>in a more excellent manner</u>, more effectively, more attractively, more advantageously, more competently, in a superior way ≠ worse

● ADJECTIVE **1**= well, stronger, recovering, cured, fully recovered, on the mend (*informal*) ≠ worse **2**= superior, finer, higher-quality, surpassing, preferable, more desirable ≠ inferior

**between**= amidst, among, mid, in the middle of, betwixt

*Related Words*

prefix- inter-

---

**Word Power**

**between**– After *distribute* and words with a similar meaning, *among* should be used rather than *between*: share out the sweets among the children (not *between the children*, unless there are only two children).

---

**beverage**= drink, liquid, liquor, refreshment

**beware 1**= be careful, look out, watch out, be wary, be cautious, take heed, guard against something **2**= avoid, mind

**bewilder**= confound, confuse, puzzle, baffle, perplex, mystify, flummox, bemuse

**bewildered**= confused, puzzled, baffled, at sea, muddled, perplexed, at a loss, mystified

**beyond 1**= on the other side of **2**= after, over, past, above **3**= past **4**= except for, but, save, apart from, other than, excluding, besides, aside from **5**= exceeding, surpassing, superior to, out of reach of **6**= outside, over, above

**bias**NOUN **1**= prejudice, leaning, tendency, inclination, favouritism, partiality ≠ impartiality

● VERB = influence, colour, weight, prejudice, distort, sway, warp, slant

**biased**= prejudiced, weighted, one-sided, partial, distorted, slanted

**bid**NOUN **1**= attempt, try, effort, go (*informal*), shot (*informal*), stab (*informal*), crack (*informal*) **2**= offer, price, amount, advance, proposal, sum, tender

● VERB **1**= make an offer, offer, propose, submit, tender, proffer **2**= wish, say, call, tell, greet **3**= tell, ask, order, require, direct, command, instruct

**bidding**= order, request, command, instruction, summons, beck and call

**big 1**= large, great, huge, massive, vast, enormous, substantial, extensive ≠ small **2**= important, significant, urgent, far-reaching ≠ unimportant **3**= powerful, important, prominent, dominant, influential, eminent **4**= grown-up, adult, grown, mature, elder, full-grown

≠ young **5** = <u>generous</u>, good, noble, gracious, benevolent, altruistic, unselfish, magnanimous

**bill¹** NOUN **1** = <u>charges</u>, rate, costs, score, account, statement, reckoning, expense **2** = <u>act of parliament</u>, measure, proposal, piece of legislation, projected law **3** = <u>list</u>, listing, programme, card, schedule, agenda, catalogue, inventory **4** = <u>advertisement</u>, notice, poster, leaflet, bulletin, circular, handout, placard
• VERB **1** = <u>charge</u>, debit, invoice, send a statement to, send an invoice to **2** = <u>advertise</u>, post, announce, promote, plug (*informal*), tout, publicize, give advance notice of

**bill²** = <u>beak</u>, nib, neb (*archaic, dialect*), mandible

**bind** VERB **1** = <u>oblige</u>, make, force, require, engage, compel, constrain, necessitate **2** = <u>tie</u>, join, stick, secure, wrap, knot, strap, lash ≠ untie
• NOUN (*Informal*) = <u>nuisance</u>, inconvenience, hassle (*informal*), drag (*informal*), spot (*informal*), difficulty, bore, dilemma, uphill (*S. African*)

**binding** = <u>compulsory</u>, necessary, mandatory, obligatory, irrevocable, unalterable, indissoluble ≠ optional

**binge** (*Informal*) = <u>bout</u>, spell,

fling, feast, stint, spree, orgy, bender (*informal*)

**biography** = <u>life story</u>, life, record, account, profile, memoir, CV, curriculum vitae

**bird** = <u>feathered friend</u>, fowl, songbird
*Related Words*
*adjective:* avian
*male:* cock
*female:* hen
*young:* chick, fledg(e)ling, nestling
*collective nouns:* flock, flight
*habitation:* nest
  ‣ birds ‣ birds of prey
  ‣ seabirds ‣ types of fowl

**bird of prey** ‣ **birds of prey**

**birth 1** = <u>childbirth</u>, delivery, nativity, parturition ≠ death **2** = <u>ancestry</u>, stock, blood, background, breeding, pedigree, lineage, parentage
*Related Words*
*adjective:* natal

**bit¹ 1** = <u>slice</u>, fragment, crumb, morsel **2** = <u>piece</u>, scrap **3** = <u>jot</u>, iota **4** = <u>part</u>

**bit²** = <u>curb</u>, check, brake, restraint, snaffle

**bite** VERB = <u>nip</u>, cut, tear, wound, snap, pierce, pinch, chew
• NOUN **1** = <u>snack</u>, food, piece, taste, refreshment, mouthful, morsel, titbit **2** = <u>wound</u>, sting, pinch, nip, prick

**biting 1** = <u>piercing</u>, cutting, sharp, frozen, harsh, penetrating,

## Birds

accentor
amokura (N.Z.)
apostle bird or happy family bird (Austral.)
avocet
axebird (Austral.)
banded dotterel (N.Z.)
banded rail (N.Z.)
bee-eater
bellbird or (N.Z.) koromako or makomako
bittern
blackbird
blackcap
black-fronted tern or tara (N.Z.)
black robin (N.Z.)
blue duck, mountain duck, whio or whistling duck (N.Z.)
boobook (Austral.)
brain-fever bird or (Austral.) pallid cuckoo
brambling
brolga, Australian crane, or (Austral.) native companion
brown creeper or pipipi (N.Z.)
brown duck (N.Z.)
brown kiwi (N.Z.)
budgerigar or (Austral.) zebra parrot
bunting
bush wren (N.Z.)
bustard or (Austral.) plain turkey, plains turkey, or wild turkey
button quail or (Austral.) bustard quail
Californian quail (N.Z.)
canary

capercaillie or capercailzie
chaffinch
chicken or (Austral. informal) chook
chiffchaff
chough
chukar
crane
crossbill
crow or (Scot.) corbie
cuckoo
curlew
dipper or water ouzel
diver
dove or (archaic or poetic) culver
dunlin or red-backed sandpiper
egret
fernbird (N.Z.)
fieldfare
finch
firecrest
flamingo
flycatcher
galah or (Austral.) galar or gillar
godwit
goldcrest
grebe
greenshank
grey-crowned babbler, happy family bird, Happy Jack, or parson bird (Austral.)
grey warbler or riroriro (N.Z.)
grouse
hen harrier or (U.S. & Canad.) marsh harrier
heron
hoopoe

## Birds (continued)

jabiru or (Austral.) policeman
 bird
jackdaw
jaeger (U.S. & Canad.)
jay
kaka (N.Z.)
kakapo (N.Z.)
kakariki (N.Z.)
karoro or blackbacked gull (N.Z.)
kea (N.Z.)
kingfisher or (N.Z.) kotare
kiwi or apteryx
knot
koel or (Austral.) black cuckoo or
 cooee bird
kokako or blue-wattled crow
 (N.Z.)
kookaburra, laughing jackass, or
 (Austral.) bushman's clock,
 settler's clock, goburra, or great
 brown kingfisher
kotuku or white heron (N.Z.)
lapwing or green plover
lark
linnet
lorikeet
lyrebird or (Austral.) piping shrike
 or piping crow-shrike
magpie lark or (Austral.)
 mudlark, Murray magpie, mulga,
 or peewit
Major Mitchell or Leadbeater's
 cockatoo
makomako (Austral.)
martin
metallic starling or shining
 starling (Austral.)

miromiro (N.Z.)
mistletoe bird (Austral.)
mohua or bush canary (N.Z.)
New Zealand pigeon or
 kereru (N.Z.)
nightingale
nightjar, (U.S. & Canad.)
 goatsucker, or (Austral.)
nighthawk
noisy miner or (Austral.) micky or
 soldier bird
nutcracker
nuthatch
ouzel or ousel
paradise duck or putangitangi
 (N.Z.)
pardalote (Austral.)
partridge
pheasant
pigeon
pipit or (N.Z.) pihoihoi
pipiwharauroa or bronze-winged
 cuckoo (N.Z.)
pitta (Austral.)
plover
ptarmigan
puffin
quail
rainbow lorikeet
raven
redpoll
redshank
redstart
redwing
ringneck parrot, Port Lincoln
 parrot, or buln-buln (Austral.)
robin or robin redbreast
roller

## Birds (continued)

| | |
|---|---|
| rook | thrush *or* (*poetic*) throstle |
| ruff | tit |
| saddlebill *or* jabiru | topknot pigeon (*Austral.*) |
| sanderling | tree creeper |
| sandpiper | tui *or* parson bird (*N.Z.*) |
| serin | twite |
| shrike *or* butcherbird | wagtail |
| silver-eye (*Austral.*) | warbler |
| siskin *or* (*formerly*) aberdevine | waxwing |
| skylark | weka, weka rail, Maori hen, *or* |
| snipe | wood hen (*N.Z.*) |
| sparrow | whinchat |
| spoonbill | white-eye *or* (*N.Z.*) blighty, |
| spotted crake *or* (*Austral.*) water | silvereye, tauhou *or* waxeye |
| crake | white-fronted tern *or* kahawai |
| starling | bird (*N.Z.*) |
| stint | whitethroat |
| stonechat | woodcock |
| stork | woodlark |
| sulphur-crested cockatoo *or* white | woodpecker |
| cockatoo | wren |
| superb blue wren (*Austral.*) | yellowhammer |
| superb lyrebird (*Austral.*) | yellowtail *or* yellowtail kingfisher |
| swallow | (*Austral.*) |
| swift | |

arctic, icy ≉ = <u>sarcastic</u>, cutting, stinging, scathing, acrimonious, incisive, virulent, caustic

**bitter** 1= <u>resentful</u>, angry, offended, sour, sore, acrimonious, sullen, miffed (*informal*) ≠ happy 2= <u>freezing</u>, biting, severe, intense, raw, fierce, chill, stinging ≠ mild 3= <u>sour</u>, sharp, acid, harsh, tart, astringent, acrid, unsweetened ≠ sweet

**bitterness** 1= <u>resentment</u>, hostility, indignation, animosity, acrimony, rancour, ill feeling, bad blood 2= <u>sourness</u>, acidity, sharpness, tartness, acerbity

**bizarre**= <u>strange</u>, unusual, extraordinary, fantastic, weird, peculiar, eccentric, ludicrous ≠ normal

**black** 1= <u>dark</u>, raven, ebony, sable, jet, dusky, pitch-black,

## Shades from black to white

| | | | |
|---|---|---|---|
| ash | gunmetal | pitch-black | slate |
| black | iron | platinum | steel grey |
| charcoal | ivory | putty | white |
| cream | jet | raven | |
| ebony | off-white | sable | |
| grey | pearl | silver | |

**swarthy** ≠ **light** 2 = gloomy, sad, depressing, grim, bleak, hopeless, dismal, ominous ≠ happy 3 = terrible, bad, devastating, tragic, fatal, catastrophic, ruinous, calamitous 4 = wicked, bad, evil, corrupt, vicious, immoral, depraved, villainous ≠ good 5 = angry, cross, furious, hostile, sour, menacing, moody, resentful ≠ happy

> **shades from black to white**

### Word Power

**black** – When referring to people with dark skin, the adjective *black* or *Black* is used. For people of the US whose origins lie in Africa, the preferred term is *African American*.

**blackmail** NOUN = threat, intimidation, ransom, extortion, hush money (slang)
• VERB = threaten, squeeze, compel, intimidate, coerce, dragoon, extort, hold to ransom

**blame** VERB 1 = hold responsible, accuse, denounce, indict, impeach, incriminate, impute ≠ absolve 2 = attribute to, credit to, assign to, put down to, impute to 3 (used in negative constructions) = criticize, condemn, censure, reproach, chide, find fault with ≠ praise
• NOUN = responsibility, liability, accountability, onus, culpability, answerability ≠ praise

**bland** 1 = dull, boring, plain, flat, dreary, run-of-the-mill, uninspiring, humdrum ≠ exciting 2 = tasteless, insipid, flavourless, thin

**blank** ADJECTIVE 1 = unmarked, white, clear, clean, empty, plain, bare, void ≠ marked 2 = expressionless, empty, vague, vacant, deadpan, impassive, poker-faced (informal) ≠ expressive
• NOUN 1 = empty space, space, gap 2 = void, vacuum, vacancy, emptiness, nothingness

**blanket** NOUN 1 = cover, rug, coverlet 2 = covering, sheet, coat, layer, carpet, cloak, mantle, thickness

● **VERB** = <u>coat</u>, cover, hide, mask, conceal, obscure, cloak

**blast** NOUN 1= <u>explosion</u>, crash, burst, discharge, eruption, detonation 2= <u>gust</u>, rush, storm, breeze, puff, gale, tempest, squall 3= <u>blare</u>, blow, scream, trumpet, wail, resound, clamour, toot

● **VERB** = <u>blow up</u>, bomb, destroy, burst, ruin, break up, explode, shatter

**blatant** = <u>obvious</u>, clear, plain, evident, glaring, manifest, noticeable, conspicuous ≠ subtle

**blaze** VERB 1= <u>burn</u>, glow, flare, be on fire, go up in flames, be ablaze, fire, flame 2= <u>shine</u>, flash, beam, glow, flare, glare, gleam, radiate

● **NOUN** 1= <u>inferno</u>, fire, flames, bonfire, combustion, conflagration 2= <u>flash</u>, glow, glitter, flare, glare, gleam, brilliance, radiance

**bleach** = <u>lighten</u>, wash out, blanch, whiten

**bleak** = <u>dismal</u>, dark, depressing, grim, discouraging, gloomy, hopeless, dreary ≠ cheerful 2= <u>exposed</u>, empty, bare, barren, desolate, windswept, weather-beaten, unsheltered ≠ sheltered 3= <u>stormy</u>, severe, rough, harsh, tempestuous, intemperate

**bleed** 1= <u>lose blood</u>, flow, gush, spurt, shed blood 2= <u>blend</u>, run, meet, unite, mix, combine, flow, fuse 3(*Informal*) = <u>extort</u>, milk, squeeze, drain, exhaust, fleece

**blend** VERB 1= <u>mix</u>, join, combine, compound, merge, unite, mingle, amalgamate 2= <u>go well</u>, match, fit, suit, go with, correspond, complement, coordinate 3= <u>combine</u>, mix, link, integrate, merge, unite, amalgamate

● **NOUN** = <u>mixture</u>, mix, combination, compound, brew, union, synthesis, alloy

**bless** 1= <u>sanctify</u>, dedicate, ordain, exalt, anoint, consecrate, hallow ≠ curse 2= <u>endow</u>, give to, provide for, grant for, favour, grace, bestow to ≠ afflict

**blessed** = <u>holy</u>, sacred, divine, adored, revered, hallowed, sanctified, beatified

**blessing** 1= <u>benefit</u>, help, service, favour, gift, windfall, kindness, good fortune ≠ disadvantage 2= <u>approval</u>, backing, support, agreement, favour, sanction, permission, leave ≠ disapproval 3= <u>benediction</u>, grace, dedication, thanksgiving, invocation, commendation, consecration, benison ≠ curse

**blight** NOUN 1= <u>curse</u>, suffering, evil, corruption, pollution, plague, hardship, woe ≠ blessing

2 = <u>disease</u>, pest, fungus, mildew, infestation, pestilence, canker
● VERB = <u>frustrate</u>, destroy, ruin, crush, mar, dash, wreck, spoil, crool or cruel (Austral. slang)

**blind** 1 = <u>sightless</u>, unsighted, unseeing, eyeless, visionless ≠ sighted 2 often with to = <u>unaware of</u>, unconscious of, ignorant of, indifferent to, insensitive to, oblivious of, unconcerned about, inconsiderate of ≠ aware 3 = <u>unquestioning</u>, prejudiced, wholesale, indiscriminate, uncritical, unreasoning, undiscriminating

**blindly** 1 = <u>thoughtlessly</u>, carelessly, recklessly, indiscriminately, senselessly, heedlessly 2 = <u>wildly</u>, aimlessly

**blink** VERB 1 = <u>flutter</u>, wink, bat 2 = <u>flash</u>, flicker, wink, shimmer, twinkle, glimmer
● PHRASES **on the blink** (Slang) = <u>not working (properly)</u>, faulty, defective, playing up, out of action, malfunctioning, out of order

**bliss** 1 = <u>joy</u>, ecstasy, euphoria, rapture, nirvana, felicity, gladness, blissfulness ≠ misery 2 = <u>beatitude</u>, blessedness

**blister** = <u>sore</u>, boil, swelling, cyst, pimple, carbuncle, pustule

**blitz** = <u>attack</u>, strike, assault, raid, offensive, onslaught, bombardment, bombing campaign

**bloc** = <u>group</u>, union, league, alliance, coalition, axis

**block** NOUN 1 = <u>piece</u>, bar, mass, brick, lump, chunk, hunk, ingot 2 = <u>obstruction</u>, bar, barrier, obstacle, impediment, hindrance
● VERB 1 = <u>obstruct</u>, close, stop, plug, choke, clog, stop up, bung up (informal) ≠ clear 2 = <u>obscure</u>, bar, obstruct 3 = <u>shut off</u>, stop, bar, hamper, obstruct

**blockade** = <u>stoppage</u>, block, barrier, restriction, obstacle, barricade, obstruction, impediment

**bloke** (Informal) = <u>man</u>, person, individual, character (informal), guy (informal), fellow, chap

**blonde** or **blond** 1 = <u>fair</u>, light, flaxen 2 = <u>fair-haired</u>, golden-haired, tow-headed

**blood** 1 = <u>lifeblood</u>, gore, vital fluid 2 = <u>family</u>, relations, birth, descent, extraction, ancestry, lineage, kinship

**bloodshed** = <u>killing</u>, murder, massacre, slaughter, slaying, carnage, butchery, blood-letting

**bloody** 1 = <u>cruel</u>, fierce, savage, brutal, vicious, ferocious, cut-throat, warlike 2 = <u>bloodstained</u>, raw, bleeding, blood-soaked, blood-spattered

**bloom** NOUN 1 = <u>flower</u>, bud, blossom 2 = <u>prime</u>, flower,

beauty, height, peak, flourishing, heyday, zenith 3= <u>glow</u>, freshness, lustre, radiance ≠ pallor
● VERB 1= <u>flower</u>, blossom, open, bud ≠ wither 2= <u>grow</u>, develop, wax 3= <u>succeed</u>, flourish, thrive, prosper, fare well ≠ fail

**blossom**NOUN 1= <u>flower</u>, bloom, bud, efflorescence, floret
● VERB 1= <u>bloom</u>, grow, develop, mature 2= <u>succeed</u>, progress, thrive, flourish, prosper 3= <u>flower</u>, bloom, bud

**blow¹**VERB 1= <u>move</u>, carry, drive, sweep, fling, buffet, waft 2= <u>be carried</u> 3= <u>exhale</u>, breathe, pant, puff 4= <u>play</u>, sound, pipe, trumpet, blare, toot
● PHRASES **blow something up** 1= <u>explode</u>, bomb, blast, detonate, blow sky-high 2= <u>inflate</u>, pump up, fill, expand, swell, enlarge, puff up, distend 3= <u>magnify</u>, increase, extend, expand, widen, broaden, amplify
◆ **blow up** 1= <u>explode</u>, burst, shatter, erupt, detonate 2(informal) = <u>lose your temper</u>, rage, erupt, see red (informal), become angry, hit the roof

(informal), fly off the handle (informal), go crook (Austral. & N.Z. slang), blow your top

**blow²** 1= <u>knock</u>, stroke, punch, bang, sock (slang), smack, thump, clout (informal) 2= <u>setback</u>, shock, disaster, reverse, disappointment, catastrophe, misfortune, bombshell

**bludge**(Austral. & N.Z. informal) = <u>slack</u>, skive (Brit. informal), idle, shirk

**blue**ADJECTIVE 1= <u>depressed</u>, low, sad, unhappy, melancholy, dejected, despondent, downcast ≠ happy 2= <u>smutty</u>, obscene, indecent, lewd, risqué, X-rated (informal) ≠ respectable
● PLURAL NOUN = <u>depression</u>, gloom, melancholy, unhappiness, low spirits, the dumps (informal), doldrums
➤ **shades of blue**

**blueprint** 1= <u>scheme</u>, plan, design, system, programme, proposal, strategy, pattern 2= <u>plan</u>, scheme, pattern, draft, outline, sketch

**bluff¹**NOUN = <u>deception</u>, fraud,

---

### Shades of blue

| | | | |
|---|---|---|---|
| aqua | cobalt blue | perse | steel blue |
| aquamarine | indigo | royal blue | teal |
| azure | navy blue | sapphire | turquoise |
| Cambridge blue | Oxford blue | saxe blue | ultramarine |
| clear blue | peacock blue | sky blue | |

sham, pretence, deceit, bravado, bluster, humbug

● VERB = <u>deceive</u>, trick, fool, pretend, cheat, con, fake, mislead

**bluff²** NOUN = <u>precipice</u>, bank, peak, cliff, ridge, crag, escarpment, promontory

● ADJECTIVE = <u>hearty</u>, open, blunt, outspoken, genial, ebullient, jovial, plain-spoken ≠ tactful

**blunder** NOUN = <u>mistake</u>, slip, fault, error, oversight, gaffe, slip-up (*informal*), indiscretion ≠ correctness

● VERB 1 = <u>make a mistake</u>, blow it (*slang*), err, slip up (*informal*), foul up, put your foot in it (*informal*) ≠ be correct 2 = <u>stumble</u>, fall, reel, stagger, lurch

**blunt** ADJECTIVE 1 = <u>frank</u>, forthright, straightforward, rude, outspoken, bluff, brusque, plain-spoken ≠ tactful 2 = <u>dull</u>, rounded, dulled, edgeless, unsharpened ≠ sharp

● VERB = <u>dull</u>, weaken, soften, numb, dampen, water down, deaden, take the edge off ≠ stimulate

**blur** NOUN = <u>haze</u>, confusion, fog, obscurity, indistinctness

● VERB 1 = <u>become indistinct</u>, become vague, become hazy, become fuzzy 2 = <u>obscure</u>, make indistinct, mask, obfuscate, make vague, make hazy

**blush** VERB = <u>turn red</u>, colour, glow, flush, redden, go red (as a beetroot), turn scarlet ≠ turn pale

● NOUN = <u>reddening</u>, colour, glow, flush, pink tinge, rosiness, ruddiness, rosy tint

**board** NOUN 1 = <u>plank</u>, panel, timber, slat, piece of timber 2 = <u>council</u>, directors, committee, congress, advisers, panel, assembly, trustees 3 = <u>meals</u>, provisions, victuals, daily meals

● VERB = <u>get on</u>, enter, mount, embark ≠ get off

**boast** VERB 1 = <u>brag</u>, crow, vaunt, talk big (*slang*), blow your own trumpet, show off, be proud of, congratulate yourself on, skite (*Austral. & N.Z. informal*) ≠ cover up 2 = <u>possess</u>, exhibit

● NOUN = <u>bragging</u> ≠ disclaimer

**bob** = <u>bounce</u>, duck, hop, oscillate

**bodily** = <u>physical</u>, material, actual, substantial, tangible, corporal, carnal, corporeal

**body** 1 = <u>physique</u>, build, form, figure, shape, frame, constitution 2 = <u>torso</u>, trunk 3 = <u>corpse</u>, dead body, remains, stiff (*slang*), carcass, cadaver 4 = <u>organization</u>, company, group, society, association, band, congress, institution 5 = <u>main part</u>, matter, material, mass, substance, bulk, essence 6 = <u>expanse</u>, mass, sweep

*Related Words*

adjectives: corporal, physical

**bog** = <u>marsh</u>, swamp, slough,

wetlands, fen, mire, quagmire, morass, pakihi (*N.Z.*)

**bogey**= bugbear, bête noire, horror, nightmare, bugaboo

**bogus**= <u>fake</u>, false, artificial, forged, imitation, sham, fraudulent, counterfeit ≠ genuine

**Bohemian**ADJECTIVE *often not cap.* = <u>unconventional</u>, alternative, artistic, unorthodox, arty (*informal*), offbeat, left bank, nonconformist ≠ conventional

● NOUN *often not cap.*
= <u>nonconformist</u>, rebel, radical, eccentric, maverick, hippy, dropout, individualist

**boil**¹= <u>simmer</u>, bubble, foam, seethe, fizz, froth, effervesce

**boil**²= pustule, gathering, swelling, blister, carbuncle

**bold** 1= <u>fearless</u>, enterprising, brave, daring, heroic, adventurous, courageous, audacious ≠ timid 2= <u>impudent</u>, forward, confident, rude, cheeky, brazen, shameless, insolent ≠ shy

**bolster**= <u>support</u>, help, boost, strengthen, reinforce, shore up, augment

**bolt**NOUN 1= <u>pin</u>, rod, peg, rivet 2= <u>bar</u>, catch, lock, latch, fastener, sliding bar

● VERB 1= <u>lock</u>, close, bar, secure, fasten, latch 2= <u>dash</u>, fly 3= <u>gobble</u>, stuff, wolf, cram, gorge, devour, gulp, guzzle

**bomb**NOUN = <u>explosive</u>, mine, shell, missile, device, rocket, grenade, torpedo

● VERB = <u>blow up</u>, attack, destroy, assault, shell, blitz, bombard, torpedo

**bombard** 1= <u>attack</u>, assault, besiege, beset, assail 2= <u>bomb</u>, shell, blitz, open fire, strafe, fire upon

**bombardment**= <u>bombing</u>, attack, assault, shelling, blitz, barrage, fusillade

**bond**NOUN 1= <u>tie</u>, union, coupling, link, association, relation, connection, alliance 2= <u>fastening</u>, tie, chain, cord, shackle, fetter, manacle 3= <u>agreement</u>, word, promise, contract, guarantee, pledge, obligation, covenant

● VERB 1= <u>form friendships</u>, connect 2= <u>fix</u>, hold, bind, connect, glue, stick, paste, fasten

**bonus** 1= <u>extra</u>, prize, gift, reward, premium, dividend 2= <u>advantage</u>, benefit, gain, extra, plus, asset, icing on the cake

**book**NOUN 1= <u>work</u>, title, volume, publication, tract, tome 2= <u>notebook</u>, album, journal, diary, pad, notepad, exercise book, jotter

● VERB = <u>reserve</u>, schedule, engage, organize, charter, arrange for, make reservations

●PHRASES **book in**= <u>register</u>,

enter

**booklet** = <u>brochure</u>, leaflet, hand-out, pamphlet, folder, mailshot, handbill

**boom** NOUN 1 = <u>expansion</u>, increase, development, growth, jump, boost, improvement, upsurge ≠ decline 2 = <u>bang</u>, crash, clash, blast, burst, explosion, roar, thunder

● VERB 1 = <u>increase</u>, flourish, grow, develop, expand, strengthen, swell, thrive ≠ fall 2 = <u>bang</u>, roll, crash, blast, explode, roar, thunder, rumble

**boon** 1 = <u>benefit</u>, blessing, godsend, gift 2 = <u>gift</u>, favour

**boost** VERB = <u>increase</u>, develop, raise, expand, add to, heighten, enlarge, amplify ≠ decrease

● NOUN 1 = <u>rise</u>, increase, jump, addition, improvement, expansion, upsurge, upturn ≠ fall 2 = <u>encouragement</u>, help

**boot** = <u>kick</u>, punt, put the boot in(to) (slang), drop-kick

**border** NOUN 1 = <u>frontier</u>, line, limit, bounds, boundary, perimeter, borderline 2 = <u>edge</u>, margin, verge, rim

● VERB = <u>edge</u>, bound, decorate, trim, fringe, rim, hem

**bore**[1] VERB = <u>drill</u>, mine, sink, tunnel, pierce, penetrate, burrow, puncture

**bore**[2] VERB = <u>tire</u>, fatigue, weary, wear out, jade, be tedious, pall

on, send to sleep ≠ excite

● NOUN = <u>nuisance</u>, pain (informal), yawn (informal), anorak (informal)

**bored** = <u>fed up</u>, tired, wearied, uninterested, sick and tired (informal), listless, brassed off (Brit. slang), hoha (N.Z.)

**boredom** = <u>tedium</u>, apathy, weariness, monotony, sameness, ennui, flatness, world-weariness ≠ excitement

**boring** = <u>uninteresting</u>, dull, tedious, tiresome, monotonous, flat, humdrum, mind-numbing

**borrow** 1 = <u>take on loan</u>, touch (someone) for (slang), scrounge (informal), cadge, use temporarily ≠ lend 2 = <u>steal</u>, take, copy, adopt, pinch (informal)

**boss** NOUN = <u>manager</u>, head, leader, director, chief, master, employer, supervisor, baas (S. African)

● PHRASES **boss someone around** (Informal) = <u>order around</u>, dominate, bully, oppress, push around (informal)

**bother** VERB 1 = <u>trouble</u>, concern, worry, alarm, disturb, disconcert, perturb 2 = <u>pester</u>, plague, harass, hassle (informal), inconvenience ≠ help

● NOUN = <u>trouble</u>, problem, worry, difficulty, fuss, irritation, hassle (informal), nuisance, uphill (S. African) ≠ help

**bottle shop** *(Austral. & N.Z.)* = <u>off-licence</u> *(Brit.)*, liquor store *(U.S. & Canad.)*, bottle store *(S. African)*, package store *(U.S. & Canad.)*, offie or offy *(Brit. informal)*

**bottle store** *(S. African)* = <u>off-licence</u> *(Brit.)*, liquor store *(U.S. & Canad.)*, bottle shop *(Austral. & N.Z.)*, package store *(U.S. & Canad.)*, offie or offy *(Brit. informal)*

**bottom** NOUN 1= <u>lowest part</u>, base, foot, bed, floor, foundation, depths ≠ top 2= <u>underside</u>, sole, underneath, lower side 3= <u>buttocks</u>, behind *(informal)*, rear, backside, rump, seat, posterior
● ADJECTIVE = <u>lowest</u>, last ≠ higher

**bounce** VERB 1= <u>rebound</u>, recoil, ricochet 2= <u>bound</u>, spring, jump, leap, skip, gambol
● NOUN 1= <u>springiness</u>, give, spring, resilience, elasticity, recoil 2 *(Informal)* = <u>life</u>, go *(informal)*, energy, zip *(informal)*, vigour, exuberance, dynamism, vivacity

**bound**[1] 1= <u>compelled</u>, obliged, forced, committed, pledged, constrained, beholden, duty-bound 2= <u>tied</u>, fixed, secured, attached, tied up, fastened, pinioned 3= <u>certain</u>, sure, fated, doomed, destined

**bound**[2] 1= <u>surround</u>, confine, enclose, encircle, hem in,
demarcate 2= <u>limit</u>, restrict, confine, restrain, circumscribe

**bound**[3] VERB = <u>leap</u>, bob, spring, jump, bounce, skip, vault
● NOUN = <u>leap</u>, bob, spring, jump, bounce, hurdle, skip, vault

**boundary** 1= <u>frontier</u>, edge, border, barrier, margin, brink 2= <u>edges</u>, limits, fringes, extremities 3= <u>dividing line</u>, borderline

**bounds** = <u>boundary</u>, limit, edge, border, confine, verge, rim, perimeter

**bouquet** 1= <u>bunch of flowers</u>, spray, garland, wreath, posy, buttonhole, corsage, nosegay 2= <u>aroma</u>, smell, scent, perfume, fragrance, savour, odour, redolence

**bourgeois** = <u>middle-class</u>, traditional, conventional, materialistic, hidebound

**bout** 1= <u>period</u>, term, fit, spell, turn, interval 2= <u>round</u>, series, session, cycle, sequence, stint 3= <u>fight</u>, match, competition, struggle, contest, set-to, encounter, engagement

**bow**[1] VERB = <u>bend</u>, bob, nod, stoop, droop, genuflect
● NOUN = <u>bending</u>, bob, nod, obeisance, kowtow, genuflection

**bow**[2] *(Nautical)* = <u>prow</u>, head, stem, fore, beak

**bowels** 1= <u>guts</u>, insides *(informal)*, intestines, innards

(*informal*), entrails, viscera, vitals
**2**= depths, hold, inside, deep, interior, core, belly

**bowl¹**= basin, plate, dish, vessel

**bowl²**= throw, hurl, launch, cast, pitch, toss, fling, chuck (*informal*)

**box¹NOUN** = container, case, chest, trunk, pack, package, carton, casket
● **VERB** = pack, package, wrap, encase, bundle up

**box²**= fight, spar, exchange blows

**boxer**= fighter, pugilist, prizefighter

**boy**= lad, kid (*informal*), youth, fellow, youngster, schoolboy, junior, stripling

**boycott**= embargo, reject, snub, black ≠ support

**boyfriend**= sweetheart, man, lover, beloved, admirer, suitor, beau, date

**brace**VERB **1**= steady, support, secure, stabilize **2**= support, strengthen, steady, reinforce, bolster, fortify, buttress
● **NOUN** = support, stay, prop, bolster, bracket, reinforcement, strut, truss

**bracing**= refreshing, fresh, stimulating, crisp, brisk, exhilarating, invigorating ≠ tiring

**brain**= intelligence, understanding, sense, intellect

**brake**NOUN = control, check, curb, restraint, constraint, rein

● **VERB** = slow, decelerate, reduce speed

**branch 1**= bough, shoot, arm, spray, limb, sprig, offshoot
**2**= office, department, unit, wing, chapter, bureau **3**= division, part, section, subdivision, subsection
**4**= discipline, section, subdivision

**brand**NOUN **1**= trademark
**2**= label, mark, sign, stamp, symbol, logo, trademark, marker
● **VERB 1**= stigmatize, mark, expose, denounce, disgrace, discredit, censure **2**= mark, burn, label, stamp, scar

**brash**= bold, rude, cocky, pushy (*informal*), brazen, impertinent, insolent, impudent ≠ timid

**brave**ADJECTIVE = courageous, daring, bold, heroic, adventurous, fearless, resolute, audacious ≠ timid
● **VERB** = confront, face, suffer, tackle, endure, defy, withstand, stand up to ≠ give in to

**bravery**= courage, nerve, daring, pluck, spirit, fortitude, heroism, mettle ≠ cowardice

**brawl**NOUN = fight, clash, fray, skirmish, scuffle, punch-up (*Brit. informal*), fracas, altercation, biffo (*Austral. slang*)
● **VERB** = fight, scrap (*informal*), wrestle, tussle, scuffle

**breach 1**= nonobservance, abuse, violation, infringement,

trespass, transgression, contravention, infraction
≠ **compliance** 2 = <u>opening</u>, crack, split, gap, rift, rupture, cleft, fissure

**bread** 1 = <u>food</u>, fare, kai (*N.Z. informal*), nourishment, sustenance 2 (*Slang*) = <u>money</u>, cash, dough (*slang*)

**breadth** 1 = <u>width</u>, spread, span, latitude, broadness, wideness 2 = <u>extent</u>, range, scale, scope, compass, expanse

**break** VERB 1 = <u>shatter</u>, separate, destroy, crack, snap, smash, crush, fragment ≠ **repair** 2 = <u>fracture</u>, crack, smash 3 = <u>burst</u>, tear, split 4 = <u>disobey</u>, breach, defy, violate, disregard, flout, infringe, contravene ≠ **obey** 5 = <u>stop</u>, cut, suspend, interrupt, cut short, discontinue 6 = <u>disturb</u>, interrupt 7 = <u>end</u>, stop, cut, drop, give up, abandon, suspend, interrupt 8 = <u>weaken</u>, undermine, tame, subdue, demoralize, dispirit 9 = <u>be revealed</u>, be published, be announced, be made public, be proclaimed, be let out 10 = <u>reveal</u>, tell, announce, declare, disclose, proclaim, make known 11 = <u>beat</u>, top, better, exceed, go beyond, excel, surpass, outstrip

● NOUN 1 = <u>fracture</u>, opening, tear, hole, split, crack, gap, fissure 2 = <u>interval</u>, pause, interlude,

intermission 3 = <u>holiday</u>, leave, vacation, time off, recess, awayday 4 (*Informal*) = <u>stroke of luck</u>, chance, opportunity, advantage, fortune, opening

● PHRASES **break off** = <u>stop talking</u>, pause ◆ **break out** = <u>begin</u>, start, happen, occur, arise, set in, commence, spring up
◆ **break something off** = <u>detach</u>, separate, divide, cut off, pull off, sever, part, remove
◆ **break something up** = <u>stop</u>, end, suspend, dismantle, terminate, disband, diffuse
◆ **break up** 1 = <u>finish</u>, be suspended, adjourn 2 = <u>split up</u>, separate, part, divorce

**breakdown** = <u>collapse</u>

**break-in** = <u>burglary</u>, robbery, breaking and entering

**breakthrough** = <u>development</u>, advance, progress, discovery, find, invention, step forward, leap forwards

**breast** = <u>bosom(s)</u>, front, chest, bust

**breath** = <u>inhalation</u>, breathing, pant, gasp, gulp, wheeze, exhalation, respiration

**breathe** 1 = <u>inhale and exhale</u>, pant, gasp, puff, gulp, wheeze, respire, draw in breath 2 = <u>whisper</u>, sigh, murmur

**breathless** 1 = <u>out of breath</u>, panting, gasping, gulping, wheezing, short-winded

2= <u>excited</u>, curious, eager, enthusiastic, impatient, on tenterhooks, in suspense

**breathtaking**= <u>amazing</u>, exciting, stunning (*informal*), impressive, thrilling, magnificent, astonishing, sensational

**breed** NOUN 1= <u>variety</u>, race, stock, type, species, strain, pedigree 2= <u>kind</u>, sort, type, variety, brand, stamp
● VERB 1= <u>rear</u>, tend, keep, raise, maintain, farm, look after, care for 2= <u>reproduce</u>, multiply, propagate, procreate, produce offspring, bear young, bring forth young 3= <u>produce</u>, cause, create, generate, bring about, arouse, give rise to, stir up

**breeding**= <u>refinement</u>, culture, taste, manners, polish, courtesy, sophistication, cultivation

**breeze** NOUN = <u>light wind</u>, air, draught, gust, waft, zephyr, breath of wind, current of air
● VERB = <u>sweep</u>, move briskly, pass, sail, hurry, glide, flit

**brew** VERB 1= <u>boil</u>, make, soak, steep, stew, infuse (*tea*) 2= <u>make</u>, ferment 3= <u>start</u>, develop, gather, foment 4= <u>develop</u>, form, gather, foment
● NOUN = <u>drink</u>, preparation, mixture, blend, liquor, beverage, infusion, concoction

**bribe** NOUN = <u>inducement</u>, pay-off (*informal*), sweetener (*slang*), kickback (*U.S.*), backhander (*slang*), enticement, allurement
● VERB = <u>buy off</u>, reward, pay off (*informal*), corrupt, suborn, grease the palm or hand of (*slang*)

**bribery**= <u>corruption</u>, inducement, buying off, payola (*informal*), palm-greasing (*slang*)

**bridge** NOUN = <u>arch</u>, span, viaduct, flyover, overpass
● VERB 1= <u>span</u>, cross 2= <u>reconcile</u>, resolve

**brief** ADJECTIVE = <u>short</u>, quick, fleeting, swift, short-lived, momentary, ephemeral, transitory ≠ long
● VERB = <u>inform</u>, prime, prepare, advise, fill in (*informal*), instruct, put in the picture (*informal*), keep (someone) posted
● NOUN = <u>summary</u>, résumé, outline, sketch, abstract, digest, epitome, rundown

**briefing** 1= <u>conference</u>, priming 2= <u>instructions</u>, information, priming, directions, preparation, guidance, rundown

**briefly** 1= <u>quickly</u>, shortly, hastily, momentarily, hurriedly 2= <u>in outline</u>, in brief, in a nutshell, concisely

**brigade** 1= <u>corps</u>, company, force, unit, division, troop, squad, team 2= <u>group</u>, band, squad, organization

**bright** 1= <u>vivid</u>, rich, brilliant,

glowing, colourful 2 = **shining**, glowing, dazzling, gleaming, shimmering, radiant, luminous, lustrous 3 = <u>intelligent</u>, smart, clever, aware, sharp, enlightened, astute, wide-awake ≠ stupid 4 = <u>clever</u>, smart, ingenious 5 = <u>sunny</u>, clear, fair, pleasant, lucid, cloudless, unclouded ≠ cloudy

**brighten** 1 = <u>light up</u>, shine, glow, gleam, lighten ≠ dim 2 = <u>enliven</u>, animate, make brighter, vitalize 3 = <u>become brighter</u>, light up, glow, gleam

**brilliance** or **brilliancy** 1 = <u>cleverness</u>, talent, wisdom, distinction, genius, excellence, greatness, inventiveness ≠ stupidity 2 = <u>brightness</u>, intensity, sparkle, dazzle, lustre, radiance, luminosity, vividness ≠ darkness 3 = <u>splendour</u>, glamour, grandeur, magnificence, éclat, illustriousness

**brilliant** 1 = <u>intelligent</u>, sharp, intellectual, clever, profound, penetrating, inventive, perspicacious ≠ stupid 2 = <u>expert</u>, masterly, talented, gifted, accomplished ≠ untalented 3 = <u>splendid</u>, famous, celebrated, outstanding, superb, magnificent, glorious, notable 4 = <u>bright</u>, shining, intense, sparkling, glittering, dazzling, vivid, radiant ≠ dark

**brim** NOUN = <u>rim</u>, edge, border, lip, margin, verge, brink
● VERB 1 = <u>be full</u>, spill, well over, run over 2 = <u>fill</u>, well over, fill up, overflow

**bring** VERB 1 = <u>fetch</u>, take, carry, bear, transfer, deliver, transport, convey 2 = <u>take</u>, guide, conduct, escort 3 = <u>cause</u>, produce, create, effect, occasion, result in, contribute to, inflict
● PHRASES **bring someone up** = <u>rear</u>, raise, support, train, develop, teach, breed, foster
◆ **bring something about** = <u>cause</u>, produce, create, effect, achieve, generate, accomplish, give rise to ◆ **bring something off** = <u>accomplish</u>, achieve, perform, succeed, execute, pull off, carry off ◆ **bring something up** = <u>mention</u>, raise, introduce, point out, refer to, allude to, broach

**brink** = <u>edge</u>, limit, border, lip, margin, boundary, skirt, frontier

**brisk** 1 = <u>quick</u>, lively, energetic, active, vigorous, bustling, sprightly, spry ≠ slow 2 = <u>short</u>, brief, blunt, abrupt, terse, gruff, brusque, monosyllabic

**briskly** = <u>quickly</u>, smartly, promptly, rapidly, readily, actively, efficiently, energetically

**bristle** NOUN = <u>hair</u>, spine, thorn, whisker, barb, stubble, prickle
● VERB 1 = <u>stand up</u>, rise, stand on

end **2=** be angry, rage, seethe, flare up, bridle, see red

**brittle=** fragile, delicate, crisp, crumbling, frail, crumbly, breakable, friable ≠ tough

**broad 1=** wide, large, ample, generous, expansive **2=** large, huge, vast, extensive, ample, spacious, expansive, roomy ≠ narrow **3=** full, general, comprehensive, complete, wide, sweeping, wide-ranging, thorough **4=** universal, general, common, wide, sweeping, worldwide, widespread, wide-ranging **5=** general, loose, vague, approximate, indefinite, ill-defined, inexact, unspecific

**broadcast**NOUN = transmission, show, programme, telecast
● VERB **1=** transmit, show, air, radio, cable, beam, send out, relay **2=** make public, report, announce, publish, spread, advertise, proclaim, circulate

**broaden=** expand, increase, develop, spread, extend, stretch, swell, supplement ≠ restrict

**brochure=** booklet, advertisement, leaflet, hand-out, circular, pamphlet, folder, mailshot

**broekies**(S. African informal) = underpants, pants, briefs, drawers, knickers, panties, boxer shorts, Y-fronts®, underdaks (Austral. slang)

**broke**(Informal) = penniless, short, ruined, bust (informal), bankrupt, impoverished, in the red, insolvent ≠ rich

**broken 1=** interrupted, incomplete, erratic, intermittent, fragmentary, spasmodic, discontinuous **2=** imperfect, halting, hesitating, stammering, disjointed **3=** smashed, burst, shattered, fragmented, fractured, severed, ruptured, separated **4=** defective, not working, imperfect, out of order, on the blink (slang), kaput (informal)

**broker=** dealer, agent, trader, supplier, merchant, negotiator, mediator, intermediary

**bronze=** reddish-brown, copper, tan, rust, chestnut, brownish
> shades of brown

**brood**NOUN **1=** offspring, issue, clutch, litter, progeny **2=** children, family, nearest and dearest, flesh and blood, ainga (N.Z.)
● VERB = think, obsess, muse, ponder, agonize, mull over, mope, ruminate

**brook=** stream, burn (Scot. & Northern English), rivulet, beck, watercourse, rill

**brother 1=** male sibling **2=** monk, cleric, friar, religious
(Related Words)
adjective: fraternal

## Shades of brown

| | | | |
|---|---|---|---|
| amber | café au lait | ginger | rust |
| auburn | camel | hazel | sable |
| bay | chestnut | henna | sepia |
| beige | chocolate | khaki | sienna |
| biscuit | cinnamon | liver | tan |
| bisque | cocoa | mahogany | taupe |
| bronze | coffee | mocha | tawny |
| buff | copper | nutbrown | terracotta |
| burnt sienna | dun | oxblood | tortoiseshell |
| burnt umber | fawn | russet | walnut |

**brotherly** = <u>fraternal</u>, friendly, neighbourly, sympathetic, affectionate, benevolent, kind, amicable

**brown** ADJECTIVE 1 = <u>brunette</u>, bay, coffee, chocolate, chestnut, hazel, dun, auburn 2 = <u>tanned</u>, bronze, tan, sunburnt
● VERB = fry, cook, grill, sear, sauté
➤ **shades of brown**

**browse** 1 = <u>skim</u>, scan, glance at, survey, look through, look round, dip into, leaf through 2 = <u>graze</u>, eat, feed, nibble

**bruise** NOUN = <u>discoloration</u>, mark, injury, blemish, contusion
● VERB 1 = <u>hurt</u>, injure, mark 2 = <u>damage</u>, mark, mar, discolour

**brush**[1] NOUN 1 = <u>broom</u>, sweeper, besom 2 = <u>conflict</u>, clash, confrontation, skirmish, tussle 3 = <u>encounter</u>, meeting, confrontation, rendezvous
● VERB 1 = <u>clean</u>, wash, polish, buff 2 = <u>touch</u>, sweep, kiss, stroke,

glance, flick, scrape, graze
● PHRASES **brush someone off** (Slang) = <u>ignore</u>, reject, dismiss, snub, disregard, scorn, disdain, spurn ◆ **brush something up** or **brush up on something** = <u>revise</u>, study, go over, cram, polish up, read up on, relearn, bone up on (informal)

**brush**[2] = <u>shrubs</u>, bushes, scrub, undergrowth, thicket, copse, brushwood

**brutal** 1 = <u>cruel</u>, savage, vicious, ruthless, callous, sadistic, heartless, inhuman ≠ kind 2 = <u>harsh</u>, tough, severe, rough, rude, indifferent, insensitive, callous ≠ sensitive

**brutality** = <u>cruelty</u>, atrocity, ferocity, savagery, ruthlessness, barbarism, inhumanity, viciousness

**bubble** NOUN = <u>air ball</u>, drop, bead, blister, blob, droplet, globule

● **VERB** 1= <u>boil</u>, seethe 2= <u>foam</u>, fizz, froth, percolate, effervesce 3= <u>gurgle</u>, splash, murmur, trickle, ripple, babble, burble, lap

**bubbly** 1= <u>lively</u>, happy, excited, animated, merry, bouncy, elated, sparky 2= <u>frothy</u>, sparkling, fizzy, effervescent, carbonated, foamy

**buckle** NOUN = <u>fastener</u>, catch, clip, clasp, hasp

● **VERB** 1= <u>fasten</u>, close, secure, hook, clasp 2= <u>distort</u>, bend, warp, crumple, contort 3= <u>collapse</u>, bend, twist, fold, give way, subside, cave in, crumple

**bud** NOUN = <u>shoot</u>, branch, sprout, sprig, offshoot

● **VERB** = <u>develop</u>, grow, shoot, sprout, burgeon, burst forth

**budding** = <u>developing</u>, beginning, growing, promising, potential, burgeoning, fledgling, embryonic

**budge** 1= <u>move</u>, stir 2= <u>dislodge</u>, move, push, transfer, shift, stir

**budget** NOUN = <u>allowance</u>, means, funds, income, finances, resources, allocation

● **VERB** = <u>plan</u>, estimate, allocate, cost, ration, apportion

**buff**[1] ADJECTIVE = <u>fawn</u>, tan, beige, yellowish, straw-coloured, sand-coloured, yellowish-brown

● **VERB** = <u>polish</u>, smooth, brush, shine, rub, wax, brighten, burnish

➤ **shades of brown** ➤ **shades of yellow**

**buff**[2] (*Informal*) = <u>expert</u>, fan, addict, enthusiast, admirer, devotee, connoisseur, aficionado, fundi (*S. African*)

**buffer** = <u>safeguard</u>, screen, shield, cushion, intermediary, bulwark

**buffet** 1= <u>smorgasbord</u> 2= <u>snack bar</u>, café, cafeteria, brasserie, refreshment counter

**bug** NOUN 1(*Informal*) = <u>illness</u>, disease, virus, infection, disorder, sickness, ailment, affliction 2= <u>fault</u>, error, defect, flaw, glitch, gremlin

● **VERB** 1= <u>tap</u>, eavesdrop, listen in on 2(*Informal*) = <u>annoy</u>, bother, disturb, irritate, hassle (*informal*), pester, vex, get on your nerves (*informal*)

**build** VERB 1= <u>construct</u>, make, raise, put up, assemble, erect, fabricate, form ≠ demolish

● **NOUN** = <u>physique</u>, form, body, figure, shape, structure, frame

**building** = <u>structure</u>, house, construction, dwelling, erection, edifice, domicile

**build-up** = <u>increase</u>, development, growth, expansion, accumulation, enlargement, escalation

**bulge** VERB 1= <u>swell out</u>, project, expand, stick out, protrude, puff out, distend 2= <u>stick out</u>, stand out, protrude

● NOUN 1 = <u>lump</u>, swelling, bump, projection ≠ hollow, hump, protuberance, protrusion ≠ hollow ≠ <u>increase</u>, rise, boost, surge, intensification

**bulk** 1 = <u>size</u>, volume, dimensions, magnitude, substance, immensity, largeness 2 = <u>weight</u>, size, mass, heaviness, poundage 3 = <u>majority</u>, mass, most, body, best part, lion's share, better part, preponderance

---

### Word Power

**bulk** – The use of a plural noun after *bulk*, as in sense 3, although common, is considered by some to be incorrect and should be avoided. This usage is most commonly encountered, according to the Bank of English, when referring to *funds* and *profits*: *the bulk of our profits stem from the sale of beer*. The synonyms *majority* and *most* would work better in this context.

---

**bullet** = <u>projectile</u>, ball, shot, missile, slug, pellet

**bulletin** = <u>report</u>, account, statement, message, communication, announcement, dispatch, communiqué

**bully** NOUN = <u>persecutor</u>, tough, oppressor, tormentor, bully boy, browbeater, coercer, ruffian

● VERB 1 = <u>persecute</u>, intimidate, torment, oppress, pick on, victimize, terrorize, push around (*slang*) 2 = <u>force</u>, coerce, browbeat, hector, domineer

**bump** VERB 1 = <u>knock</u>, hit, strike, crash, smash, slam, bang 2 = <u>jerk</u>, shake, bounce, rattle, jog, lurch, jolt

● NOUN 1 = <u>knock</u>, blow, impact, collision, thump 2 = <u>thud</u>, crash, knock, bang, smack, thump 3 = <u>lump</u>, swelling, bulge, hump, nodule, protuberance, contusion

**bumper** = <u>exceptional</u>, excellent, exo (*Austral. slang*), massive, jumbo (*informal*), abundant, whopping (*informal*), bountiful

**bunch** NOUN 1 = <u>group</u>, band, crowd, party, team, gathering, gang, flock 2 = <u>bouquet</u>, sheaf 3 = <u>cluster</u>, clump

●PHRASES **bunch together** *or* **up** = <u>group</u>, mass, collect, assemble, cluster, huddle

**bundle** NOUN = <u>bunch</u>, group, collection, mass, pile, stack, heap, batch

● VERB = <u>push</u>, thrust, shove, throw, rush, hurry, jostle, hustle

●PHRASES **bundle someone up** = <u>wrap up</u>, swathe

**bungle** = <u>mess up</u>, blow (*slang*), ruin, spoil, blunder, botch, make a mess of, muff, crool *or* cruel (*Austral. slang*) ≠ accomplish

**bungling** = <u>incompetent</u>, blundering, clumsy, inept, cack-handed (*informal*), maladroit, ham-fisted (*informal*), unco (*Austral. slang*)

**bunk** or **bunkum** (*Informal*) = nonsense, rubbish, garbage (*informal*), hot air (*informal*), twaddle, moonshine, baloney (*informal*), hogwash, bizzo (*Austral. slang*), bull's wool (*Austral. & N.Z. slang*), kak (*S. African taboo slang*)

**buoy** = float, guide, signal, marker, beacon

**buoyant** ADJECTIVE = cheerful, happy, upbeat (*informal*), carefree, jaunty, chirpy (*informal*), light-hearted ≠ gloomy
● ADJECTIVE = floating, light

**burden** NOUN 1= trouble, worry, weight, responsibility, strain, affliction, onus, millstone 2= load, weight, cargo, freight, consignment, encumbrance
● VERB = weigh down, worry, load, tax, bother, handicap, oppress, inconvenience

**bureau** 1= agency 2= office, department, section, branch, station, unit, division, subdivision 3= desk, writing desk

**bureaucracy** 1= government, officials, authorities, administration, the system, civil service, corridors of power 2= red tape, regulations, officialdom

**bureaucrat** = official, officer, administrator, civil servant, public servant, functionary, mandarin

**burglar** = housebreaker, thief, robber, pilferer, filcher, cat burglar, sneak thief

**burglary** = breaking and entering, housebreaking, break-in

**burial** = funeral, interment, obsequies, entombment, exequies

**burn** 1= be on fire, blaze, be ablaze, smoke, flame, glow, flare, go up in flames 2= set on fire, light, ignite, kindle, incinerate 3= scorch, toast, sear, char, singe 4= be passionate, be aroused, be inflamed 5= seethe, fume, be angry, simmer, smoulder

**burning** 1= intense, passionate, eager, ardent, fervent, impassioned, vehement ≠ mild 2= blazing, fiery, smouldering, glowing 3= flashing, blazing, flaming, gleaming, fiery 4= crucial, important, pressing, significant, essential, vital, critical, acute

**burrow** NOUN = hole, shelter, tunnel, den, lair, retreat
● VERB 1= dig, tunnel, excavate 2= delve, search, probe, ferret, rummage, forage, fossick (*Austral. & N.Z.*)

**burst** VERB 1= explode, blow up, break, split, crack, shatter, puncture, rupture 2= rush, run, break, break out, erupt, spout, gush forth 3= barge, charge,

rush, shove
● NOUN 1 = <u>rush</u>, surge, outbreak, outburst, spate, gush, torrent, spurt 2 = <u>explosion</u>, crack, blast, bang, discharge
● ADJECTIVE = <u>ruptured</u>, flat, punctured, split, rent

**bury** 1 = <u>inter</u>, lay to rest, entomb, consign to the grave, inhume ≠ dig up 2 = <u>hide</u>, cover, conceal, stash (*informal*), secrete, stow away ≠ uncover 3 = <u>sink</u>, embed, immerse, enfold 4 = <u>forget</u>

**bush** NOUN = <u>shrub</u>, plant, hedge, thicket, shrubbery
● PHRASES **the bush** = <u>the wilds</u>, brush, scrub, woodland, backwoods, scrubland

**business** 1 = <u>trade</u>, selling, industry, manufacturing, commerce, dealings 2 = <u>establishment</u>, company, firm, concern, organization, corporation, venture, enterprise 3 = <u>profession</u>, work, job, line, trade, career, function, employment 4 = <u>matter</u>, issue, subject, point, problem, responsibility, task, duty 5 = <u>concern</u>, affair

**businessman** = <u>executive</u>, director, manager, merchant, capitalist, administrator, entrepreneur, tycoon

**bust**[1] = <u>bosom</u>, breasts, chest, front

**bust**[2] (*Informal*) VERB 1 = <u>break</u>, smash, split, burst, shatter, fracture, rupture 2 = <u>arrest</u>, catch, raid
● PHRASES **go bust** = <u>go bankrupt</u>, fail, be ruined, become insolvent

**bustle** VERB = <u>hurry</u>, rush, fuss, hasten, scuttle, scurry, scamper ≠ idle
● NOUN = <u>activity</u>, to-do, stir, excitement, fuss, flurry, commotion, ado ≠ inactivity

**bustling** = <u>busy</u>, full, crowded, active, lively, buzzing, humming, swarming

**busy** ADJECTIVE 1 = <u>active</u>, industrious, rushed off your feet ≠ idle 2 = <u>occupied with</u>, working, engaged in, on duty, employed in, hard at work ≠ unoccupied 3 = <u>hectic</u>, full, exacting, energetic
●PHRASES **busy yourself** = <u>occupy yourself</u>, be engrossed, immerse yourself, involve yourself, absorb yourself, employ yourself, engage yourself

**but** CONJUNCTION = <u>however</u>, still, yet, nevertheless
● PREPOSITION = <u>except (for)</u>, save, bar, barring, excepting, excluding, with the exception of
● ADVERB = <u>only</u>, just, simply, merely

**butcher** NOUN = <u>murderer</u>, killer, slaughterer, slayer, destroyer,

### Butterflies and moths

| | | |
|---|---|---|
| argus | house moth | skipper |
| bag moth (*N.Z.*) | lackey moth | small white |
| brown-tail moth | large white or | snout |
| cabbage white | cabbage white | speckled wood |
| cactoblastis | leopard moth | swallowtail |
| cardinal | magpie moth | swift |
| carpet moth | marbled white | tapestry moth |
| clearwing *or* | monarch | tiger (moth) |
| clearwing moth | orange-tip | umber (moth) |
| death's-head moth | painted lady | wax moth |
| ermine moth *or* | peacock butterfly | honeycomb moth, *or* |
| ermine | peppered moth | bee moth |
| ghost moth | privet hawk | white |
| gipsy moth | processionary moth | white admiral |
| grayling | purple emperor | winter moth |
| hairstreak | puss moth | yellow underwing |
| herald moth | red admiral | |
| hawk moth, sphinx | red underwing | |
| moth, *or* | ringlet | |
| hummingbird moth | silver-Y | |

executioner, cut-throat,
exterminator

● VERB 1= <u>slaughter</u>, prepare,
carve, cut up, dress, cut, clean,
joint 2= <u>kill</u>, slaughter, massacre,
destroy, cut down, assassinate,
slay, liquidate

**butt¹** 1= <u>end</u>, handle, shaft, stock,
shank, hilt, haft 2= <u>stub</u>, tip,
leftover, fag end (*informal*)

**butt²**= <u>target</u>, victim, dupe,
laughing stock, Aunt Sally

**butt³**VERB = <u>knock</u>, push, bump,
thrust, ram, shove, poke, prod

●PHRASES **butt in** 1= <u>interfere</u>,
meddle, intrude, heckle, barge in

(*informal*), stick your nose in, put
your oar in 2= <u>interrupt</u>, cut in,
break in, chip in (*informal*)

**butt⁴**= <u>cask</u>, barrel

**butterfly**

(*Related Words*)

*young*: caterpillar, chrysalis *or*
chrysalid

*enthusiast*: lepidopterist

➤ **butterflies and moths**

**buy**VERB = <u>purchase</u>, get, pay for,
obtain, acquire, invest in, shop
for, procure ≠ sell

● NOUN = <u>purchase</u>, deal, bargain,
acquisition, steal (*informal*), snip
(*informal*), giveaway

**by** PREPOSITION 1 = <u>through</u>,
through the agency of 2 = <u>via</u>,
over, by way of 3 = <u>near</u>, past,
along, close to, closest to,
neighbouring, next to, beside
● ADVERB = <u>nearby</u>, close, handy,
at hand, within reach

**bypass** 1 = <u>get round</u>, avoid
2 = <u>go round</u>, circumvent, depart
from, deviate from, pass round,
detour round ≠ cross

# C

**cab** = <u>taxi</u>, minicab, taxicab,
hackney carriage

**cabin** 1 = <u>room</u>, berth, quarters,
compartment 2 = <u>hut</u>, shed,
cottage, lodge, shack, chalet,
shanty, whare (N.Z.)

**cabinet** 1 = <u>cupboard</u>, case,
locker, dresser, closet, press,
chiffonier 2 often cap. = <u>council</u>,
committee, administration,
ministry, assembly, board

**cad** (Old-fashioned, informal)
= <u>scoundrel</u> (slang), rat (informal),
bounder (Brit. old-fashioned
slang), rotter (slang, chiefly Brit.),
heel

**café** = <u>snack bar</u>, restaurant,
cafeteria, coffee shop, brasserie,
coffee bar, tearoom, lunchroom

**cage** = <u>enclosure</u>, pen, coop,
hutch, pound

**cake** = <u>block</u>, bar, slab, lump,

cube, loaf, mass

**calculated** = <u>deliberate</u>,
planned, considered, intended,
intentional, designed, aimed,
purposeful ≠ unplanned

**calculating** = <u>scheming</u>, sharp,
shrewd, cunning, sly, devious,
manipulative, crafty ≠ direct

**calculation** 1 = <u>computation</u>,
working out, reckoning, estimate,
forecast, judgment, result, answer
2 = <u>planning</u>, intention,
deliberation, foresight,
contrivance, forethought,
premeditation

**calibre** or (U.S.) **caliber**
1 = <u>worth</u>, quality, ability, talent,
capacity, merit, distinction,
stature 2 = <u>standard</u>, level,
quality, grade 3 = <u>diameter</u>, bore,
gauge, measure

**call** VERB 1 = <u>name</u>, entitle, dub,
designate, term, style, label,
describe as 2 = <u>cry</u>, shout, scream,
yell, whoop ≠ whisper 3 = <u>phone</u>,
telephone, ring (up) (informal,
chiefly Brit.) 4 = <u>hail</u>, summon
5 = <u>summon</u>, gather, rally,
assemble, muster, convene
≠ dismiss 6 = <u>waken</u>, arouse,
rouse
● NOUN 1 = <u>visit</u> 2 = <u>request</u>, order,
demand, appeal, notice,
command, invitation, plea
3 (usually used in a negative
construction) = <u>need</u>, cause,
reason, grounds, occasion,

excuse, justification
4= <u>attraction</u>, pull (*informal*), appeal, lure, allure, magnetism
5= <u>cry</u>, shout, scream, yell, whoop ≠ whisper
● **PHRASES call for someone** = <u>fetch</u>, pick up, collect ◆ **call for something** 1= <u>demand</u>, order, request, insist on, cry out for 2= <u>require</u>, need, involve, demand, occasion, entail, necessitate

**calling**= <u>profession</u>, trade, career, mission, vocation, life's work

**calm**ADJECTIVE 1= <u>cool</u>, relaxed, composed, sedate, collected, dispassionate, unemotional, self-possessed ≠ excited 2= <u>still</u>, quiet, smooth, mild, serene, tranquil, balmy, windless ≠ rough
● NOUN 1= <u>peacefulness</u>, peace, serenity 2= <u>stillness</u>, peace, quiet, hush, serenity, tranquillity, repose, peacefulness 3= <u>peace</u>, calmness ≠ disturbance
● VERB 1= <u>soothe</u>, quiet, relax, appease, still, allay, assuage, quieten ≠ excite 2= <u>placate</u>, hush, pacify, mollify ≠ aggravate

**camouflage**NOUN
1= <u>protective colouring</u>
2= <u>disguise</u>, cover, screen, blind, mask, cloak, masquerade, subterfuge
● VERB = <u>disguise</u>, cover, screen, hide, mask, conceal, obscure, veil

≠ reveal

**camp**[1]= <u>camp site</u>, tents, encampment, bivouac, camping ground

**camp**[2](*Informal*) = <u>affected</u>, mannered, artificial, posturing, ostentatious, effeminate

**campaign** 1= <u>drive</u>, appeal, movement, push (*informal*), offensive, crusade 2= <u>operation</u>, drive, attack, movement, push, offensive, expedition, crusade

**canal**= <u>waterway</u>, channel, passage, conduit, duct, watercourse

**cancel**VERB 1= <u>call off</u>, drop, forget about 2= <u>annul</u>, abolish, repeal, abort, do away with, revoke, eliminate
● **PHRASES cancel something out**= <u>counterbalance</u>, offset, make up for, compensate for, neutralize, nullify, balance out

**cancellation** 1= <u>abandonment</u> 2= <u>annulment</u>, abolition, repeal, elimination, revocation

**cancer** 1= <u>growth</u>, tumour, malignancy 2= <u>evil</u>, corruption, sickness, pestilence

**candidate**= <u>contender</u>, competitor, applicant, nominee, entrant, claimant, contestant, runner

**cannabis**= <u>marijuana</u>, pot (*slang*), dope (*slang*), grass (*slang*), hemp, dagga (*S. African*)

**cannon**= <u>gun</u>, big gun, field

gun, mortar

**canon** 1 = <u>rule</u>, standard, principle, regulation, formula, criterion, dictate, statute 2 = <u>list</u>, index, catalogue, roll

**canopy** = <u>awning</u>, covering, shade, sunshade

**cap** 1 (*Informal*) = <u>beat</u>, top, better, exceed, eclipse, surpass, transcend, outstrip 2 = <u>top</u>, crown 3 = <u>complete</u>, crown

**capability** = <u>ability</u>, means, power, potential, capacity, qualification(s), competence, proficiency ≠ inability

**capable** 1 = <u>able</u> ≠ incapable 2 = <u>accomplished</u>, qualified, talented, gifted, efficient, competent, proficient ≠ incompetent

**capacity** 1 = <u>ability</u>, facility, gift, genius, capability, aptitude, aptness, competence *or* competency 2 = <u>size</u>, room, range, space, volume, extent, dimensions, scope 3 = <u>function</u>, position, role, post, office

**cape** = <u>headland</u>, point, head, peninsula, promontory

**capital** NOUN = <u>money</u>, funds, investment(s), cash, finances, resources, assets, wealth

● ADJECTIVE (*Old-fashioned*) = <u>first-rate</u>, fine, excellent, superb

> **WORD POWER SUPPLEMENT**
**capital cities**

**capitalism** = <u>private enterprise</u>,

free enterprise, private ownership, laissez faire *or* laisser faire

**capsule** 1 = <u>pill</u>, tablet, lozenge 2 (*Botany*) = <u>pod</u>, case, shell, vessel, sheath, receptacle, seed case

**captain** 1 = <u>leader</u>, boss, master, skipper, head, chief 2 = <u>commander</u>, skipper

**captivate** = <u>charm</u>, attract, fascinate, entrance, enchant, enthral, beguile, allure ≠ repel

**captive** ADJECTIVE = <u>confined</u>, caged, imprisoned, locked up, enslaved, incarcerated, ensnared, subjugated

● NOUN = <u>prisoner</u>, hostage, convict, prisoner of war, detainee, internee

**captivity** = <u>confinement</u>, custody, detention, imprisonment, incarceration, internment

**capture** VERB = <u>catch</u>, arrest, take, bag, secure, seize, collar (*informal*), apprehend ≠ release

● NOUN = <u>arrest</u>, catching, trapping, imprisonment, seizure, apprehension, taking, taking captive

**car** 1 = <u>vehicle</u>, motor, wheels (*informal*), auto (*U.S.*), automobile, jalopy (*informal*), motorcar, machine 2 (*U.S. & Canad.*) = <u>(railway) carriage</u>, coach, cable car, dining car, sleeping car, buffet car, van

**cardinal**= principal, first, leading, chief, main, central, key, essential ≠ secondary

**care**VERB = be concerned, mind, bother, be interested, be bothered, give a damn, concern yourself

• NOUN 1= custody, keeping, control, charge, management, protection, supervision, guardianship 2= caution, attention, pains, consideration, heed, prudence, vigilance, forethought ≠ carelessness 3= worry, concern, pressure, trouble, responsibility, stress, anxiety, disquiet ≠ pleasure

• PHRASES **care for someone** 1= look after, mind, tend, attend, nurse, minister to, watch over 2= love, desire, be fond of, want, prize ♦ **care for something or someone**= like, enjoy, take to, relish, be fond of, be keen on, be partial to ♦ **take care of** 1= look after, mind, watch, protect, tend, nurse, care for, provide for 2= deal with, manage, cope with, see to, handle

**career**NOUN = occupation, calling, employment, pursuit, vocation, livelihood, life's work

• VERB = rush, race, speed, tear, dash, barrel (along) (*informal, chiefly U.S. & Canad.*), bolt, hurtle

**careful** 1= cautious, scrupulous, circumspect, chary, thoughtful, discreet ≠ careless 2= thorough, full, particular, precise, intensive, in-depth, meticulous, conscientious ≠ casual 3= prudent, sparing, economical, canny, provident, frugal, thrifty

**careless** 1= slapdash, irresponsible, sloppy (*informal*), cavalier, offhand, neglectful, slipshod, lackadaisical ≠ careful 2= negligent, hasty, thoughtless, unthinking, forgetful, absent-minded, remiss ≠ careful 3= nonchalant, casual, offhand, artless, unstudied ≠ careful

**caretaker**NOUN = warden, keeper, porter, superintendent, curator, custodian, watchman, janitor

**cargo**= load, goods, contents, shipment, freight, merchandise, baggage, consignment

**caricature**NOUN = parody, cartoon, distortion, satire, send-up (*Brit. informal*), travesty, takeoff (*informal*), lampoon

• VERB = parody, take off (*informal*), mock, distort, ridicule, mimic, send up (*Brit. informal*), lampoon

**carnage**= slaughter, murder, massacre, holocaust, havoc, bloodshed, shambles, mass murder

**carnival**= festival, fair, fête, celebration, gala, jubilee, jamboree, revelry

**carnivore ► carnivores**

**carol** = <u>song</u>, hymn, Christmas song

**carp** = <u>find fault</u>, complain,

criticize, reproach, quibble, cavil, pick holes ≠ praise

**carpenter** = <u>joiner</u>, cabinet-maker, woodworker

**carriage** 1 = <u>vehicle</u>, coach, trap,

## Carnivores

| | | |
|---|---|---|
| aardwolf | grizzly bear or grizzly | polar bear or (N. Canad.) nanook |
| arctic fox | hyena or hyaena | polecat |
| badger | ichneumon | prairie dog |
| bear | jackal | puma or cougar |
| binturong | jaguar | raccoon, racoon, or coon |
| black bear | jaguarondi, jaguarundi, or (Austral.) eyra | raccoon dog |
| bobcat | | ratel |
| brown bear | | red fox |
| caracal or desert lynx | kinkajou, honey bear, or potto | sable |
| cat | Kodiak bear | sea otter |
| catamount, catamountain, or cat-o'-mountain | laughing hyena or spotted hyena | serval |
| | | silver fox |
| cheetah or chetah | leopard or panther | skunk |
| cinnamon bear | linsang | sloth bear |
| civet | lion | snow leopard or ounce |
| coyote or prairie wolf | lynx | stoat |
| dhole | margay | strandwolf |
| dingo or (Austral.) native dog or warrigal | marten | sun bear |
| | meerkat | swift fox or kit fox |
| | mink | tayra |
| dog | mongoose | teledu |
| ermine | mountain lion | tiger |
| fennec | ocelot | tiger cat |
| ferret | otter | timber wolf |
| fox | otter shrew | weasel |
| genet or genette | palm civet | wolf |
| giant panda | panda | wolverine, glutton, or carcajou |
| grey fox (U.S.) | panther | |
| grey wolf or timber wolf | pine marten or sweet marten | |

gig, cab, wagon, hackney, conveyance **2** = <u>bearing</u>, posture, gait, deportment, air

**carry** VERB **1** = <u>convey</u>, take, move, bring, bear, transfer, conduct, transport **2** = <u>transport</u>, take, transfer **3** = <u>transmit</u>, transfer, spread, pass on **4** = <u>win</u>, gain, secure, capture, accomplish
● PHRASES **carry on**
**1** = <u>continue</u>, last, endure, persist, keep going, persevere
**2** (*Informal*) = <u>make a fuss</u>, misbehave, create (*slang*), raise Cain ◆ **carry something on** = <u>engage in</u>, conduct, carry out, undertake, embark on, enter into ◆ **carry something out** = <u>perform</u>, effect, achieve, realize, implement, fulfil, accomplish, execute

**carry-on** (*Informal, chiefly Brit.*) = <u>fuss</u>, disturbance, racket, commotion

**carton** = <u>box</u>, case, pack, package, container

**cartoon 1** = <u>drawing</u>, parody, satire, caricature, comic strip, takeoff (*informal*), lampoon, sketch **2** = <u>animation</u>, animated film, animated cartoon

**carve 1** = <u>sculpt</u>, cut, chip, whittle, chisel, hew, fashion **2** = <u>etch</u>, engrave

**cascade** NOUN = <u>waterfall</u>, falls, torrent, flood, shower, fountain, avalanche, deluge

● VERB = <u>flow</u>, fall, flood, pour, plunge, surge, spill, tumble

**case$^1$ 1** = <u>situation</u>, event, circumstance(s), state, position, condition, context, contingency **2** = <u>instance</u>, example, occasion, specimen, occurrence **3** (*Law*) = <u>lawsuit</u>, trial, suit, proceedings, dispute, action

**case$^2$ 1** = <u>cabinet</u>, box, chest, holder **2** = <u>container</u>, carton, canister, casket, receptacle **3** = <u>suitcase</u>, bag, grip, holdall, portmanteau, valise **4** = <u>crate</u>, box **5** = <u>covering</u>, casing, shell, jacket, envelope, capsule, sheath, wrapper

**cash** = <u>money</u>, funds, notes, currency, silver, brass (*Northern English dialect*), dough (*slang*), coinage

**cast** NOUN **1** = <u>actors</u>, company, players, characters, troupe, dramatis personae **2** = <u>type</u>, sort, kind, style, stamp
● VERB **1** = <u>choose</u>, name, pick, select, appoint, assign, allot **2** = <u>bestow</u>, give, level, direct **3** = <u>give out</u>, spread, deposit, shed, distribute, scatter, emit, radiate **4** = <u>throw</u>, launch, pitch, toss, thrust, hurl, fling, sling **5** = <u>mould</u>, set, found, form, model, shape

**caste** = <u>class</u>, order, rank, status, stratum, social order

**castle** = <u>fortress</u>, keep, palace,

tower, chateau, stronghold, citadel

**casual** 1= <u>careless</u>, relaxed, unconcerned, blasé, offhand, nonchalant, lackadaisical ≠ serious 2= <u>chance</u>, unexpected, random, accidental, incidental ≠ planned 3= <u>informal</u>, leisure, sporty, non-dressy ≠ formal

**casualty** 1= <u>fatality</u>, death, loss, wounded 2= <u>victim</u>, sufferer

**cat**= <u>feline</u>, pussy (*informal*), moggy (*slang*), puss (*informal*), ballarat (*Austral. informal*), tabby

*Related Words*
adjective: feline
male: tom
female: tabby
young: kitten

**catalogue**or (*U.S.*) **catalog**
NOUN = <u>list</u>, record, schedule, index, register, directory, inventory, gazetteer
● VERB = <u>list</u>, file, index, register, classify, inventory, tabulate, alphabetize

**catastrophe**= <u>disaster</u>, tragedy, calamity, cataclysm, trouble, adversity, fiasco

**catch** VERB 1= <u>capture</u>, arrest, trap, seize, snare, apprehend, ensnare, entrap ≠ free 2= <u>trap</u>, capture, snare, ensnare, entrap 3= <u>seize</u>, get, grab, snatch 4= <u>grab</u>, take, grip, seize, grasp, clutch, lay hold of ≠ release

5= <u>discover</u>, surprise, find out, expose, detect, catch in the act, take unawares 6= <u>contract</u>, get, develop, suffer from, incur, succumb to, go down with ≠ escape
● NOUN 1= <u>fastener</u>, clip, bolt, latch, clasp 2(*Informal*) = <u>drawback</u>, trick, trap, disadvantage, hitch, snag, stumbling block, fly in the ointment ≠ advantage
● PHRASES **catch on** 1(*Informal*) = <u>understand</u>, see, find out, see through, comprehend, twig (*Brit. informal*), get the picture 2= <u>become popular</u>, take off, become trendy, come into fashion

**catching**= <u>infectious</u>, contagious, transferable, communicable, transmittable ≠ non-infectious

**category**= <u>class</u>, grouping, heading, sort, department, type, division, section

**cater**
● PHRASES **cater for something** or **someone** 1= <u>provide for</u>, supply, purvey 2= <u>take into account</u>, consider, bear in mind, make allowance for, have regard for

**cattle**= <u>cows</u>, stock, beasts, livestock, bovines
*Related Words*
adjective: bovine

*collective nouns*: drove, herd

**cause** NOUN 1 = <u>origin</u>, source, spring, agent, maker, producer, root, beginning ≠ result 2 = <u>reason</u>, call, need, grounds, basis, incentive, motive, motivation 3 = <u>aim</u>, movement, principle, ideal, enterprise
● VERB = <u>produce</u>, create, lead to, result in, generate, induce, bring about, give rise to ≠ prevent

**caution** NOUN 1 = <u>care</u>, discretion, heed, prudence, vigilance, alertness, forethought, circumspection ≠ carelessness 2 = <u>reprimand</u>, warning, injunction, admonition
● VERB 1 = <u>warn</u>, urge, advise, alert, tip off, forewarn 2 = <u>reprimand</u>, warn, admonish, give an injunction to

**cautious** = <u>careful</u>, guarded, wary, tentative, prudent, judicious, circumspect, cagey (*informal*) ≠ careless

**cavalry** = <u>horsemen</u>, horse, mounted troops ≠ infantrymen

**cave** = <u>hollow</u>, cavern, grotto, den, cavity

**cavity** = <u>hollow</u>, hole, gap, pit, dent, crater

**cease** 1 = <u>stop</u>, end, finish, come to an end ≠ start 2 = <u>discontinue</u>, end, stop, finish, conclude, halt, terminate, break off ≠ begin

**celebrate** 1 = <u>rejoice</u>, party, enjoy yourself, carouse, live it up (*informal*), make merry, put the flags out, kill the fatted calf 2 = <u>commemorate</u>, honour, observe, toast, drink to, keep 3 = <u>perform</u>, observe, preside over, officiate at, solemnize

**celebrated** = <u>renowned</u>, popular, famous, distinguished, well-known, prominent, acclaimed, notable ≠ unknown

**celebration** 1 = <u>party</u>, festival, gala, jubilee, festivity, revelry, red-letter day, merrymaking 2 = <u>commemoration</u>, honouring, remembrance 3 = <u>performance</u>, observance, solemnization

**celebrity** 1 = <u>personality</u>, star, superstar, big name, dignitary, luminary, big shot (*informal*), V.I.P. ≠ nobody 2 = <u>fame</u>, reputation, distinction, prestige, prominence, stardom, renown, repute ≠ obscurity

**cell** 1 = <u>room</u>, chamber, lock-up, compartment, cavity, cubicle, dungeon, stall 2 = <u>unit</u>, group, section, core, nucleus, caucus, coterie

**cement** NOUN 1 = <u>mortar</u>, plaster, paste 2 = <u>sealant</u>, glue, gum, adhesive
● VERB = <u>stick</u>, join, bond, attach, seal, glue, plaster, weld

**cemetery** = <u>graveyard</u>,

churchyard, burial ground, necropolis, God's acre

**censor** = expurgate, cut, blue-pencil, bowdlerize

**censure** VERB = <u>criticize</u>, blame, condemn, denounce, rebuke, reprimand, reproach, scold ≠ applaud
● NOUN = <u>disapproval</u>, criticism, blame, condemnation, rebuke, reprimand, reproach, stick (*slang*) ≠ approval

**central** 1= <u>inner</u>, middle, mid, interior ≠ outer 2= <u>main</u>, chief, key, essential, primary, principal, fundamental, focal ≠ minor

**centre** NOUN = <u>middle</u>, heart, focus, core, nucleus, hub, pivot, kernel ≠ edge
● VERB = <u>focus</u>, concentrate, cluster, revolve, converge

**ceremonial** ADJECTIVE = <u>formal</u>, public, official, ritual, stately, solemn, liturgical, courtly ≠ informal
● NOUN = <u>ritual</u>, ceremony, rite, formality, solemnity

**ceremony** 1= <u>ritual</u>, service, rite, observance, commemoration, solemnities 2= <u>formality</u>, ceremonial, propriety, decorum

**certain** 1= <u>sure</u>, convinced, positive, confident, satisfied, assured ≠ unsure 2= <u>bound</u>, sure, fated, destined ≠ unlikely 3= <u>inevitable</u>, unavoidable,

inescapable 4= <u>known</u>, true, positive, conclusive, unequivocal, undeniable, irrefutable, unquestionable ≠ doubtful 5= <u>fixed</u>, decided, established, settled, definite ≠ indefinite

**certainly** = <u>definitely</u>, surely, truly, undoubtedly, without doubt, undeniably, indisputably, assuredly

**certainty** 1= <u>confidence</u>, trust, faith, conviction, assurance, sureness, positiveness ≠ doubt 2= <u>inevitability</u> ≠ uncertainty 3= <u>fact</u>, truth, reality, sure thing (*informal*), banker

**certificate** = <u>document</u>, licence, warrant, voucher, diploma, testimonial, authorization, credential(s)

**certify** = <u>confirm</u>, declare, guarantee, assure, testify, verify, validate, attest

**chain** NOUN 1= <u>tether</u>, coupling, link, bond, shackle, fetter, manacle 2= <u>series</u>, set, train, string, sequence, succession, progression
● VERB = <u>bind</u>, confine, restrain, handcuff, shackle, tether, fetter, manacle

**chairman** or **chairwoman** 1= <u>director</u>, president, chief, executive, chairperson 2= <u>master of ceremonies</u>, spokesman, chair, speaker, MC, chairperson

### Word Power

**chairman/chairwoman** –
The general trend of nonsexist
language is to find a term which
can apply to both sexes equally,
as in the use of *actor* to refer to
both men and women.
*Chairman* can seem
inappropriate when applied to a
woman, while *chairwoman*
specifies gender, and so, as the
entry above illustrates, the terms
*chair* and *chairperson* are often
preferred as alternatives.

**challenge** NOUN 1 = <u>dare</u>,
provocation, wero (*N.Z.*) 2 = <u>test</u>,
trial, opposition, confrontation,
ultimatum
● VERB 1 = <u>dispute</u>, question,
tackle, confront, defy, object to,
disagree with, take issue with
2 = <u>dare</u>, invite, defy, throw down
the gauntlet 3 = <u>test</u>
4 = <u>question</u>, interrogate

**chamber** 1 = <u>hall</u>, room
2 = <u>council</u>, assembly, legislature,
legislative body 3 = <u>room</u>,
bedroom, apartment, enclosure,
cubicle 4 = <u>compartment</u>

**champion** NOUN 1 = <u>winner</u>,
hero, victor, conqueror, title
holder 2 = <u>defender</u>, guardian,
patron, backer, protector,
upholder
● VERB = <u>support</u>, back, defend,
promote, advocate, fight for,

uphold, espouse

**chance** NOUN 1 = <u>probability</u>,
odds, possibility, prospect,
likelihood ≠ certainty
2 = <u>opportunity</u>, opening,
occasion, time 3 = <u>accident</u>,
fortune, luck, fate, destiny,
coincidence, providence ≠ design
4 = <u>risk</u>, speculation, gamble,
hazard
● VERB = <u>risk</u>, try, stake, venture,
gamble, hazard, wager

**change** NOUN 1 = <u>alteration</u>,
innovation, transformation,
modification, mutation,
metamorphosis, difference,
revolution 2 = <u>variety</u>, break
(*informal*), departure, variation,
novelty, diversion ≠ monotony
3 = <u>exchange</u>, trade, conversion,
swap, substitution, interchange
● VERB 1 = <u>alter</u>, reform, transform,
adjust, revise, modify, reorganize,
restyle ≠ keep 2 = <u>shift</u>, vary,
transform, alter, modify, mutate
≠ stay 3 = <u>exchange</u>, trade,
replace, substitute, swap,
interchange

**channel** NOUN 1 = <u>means</u>, way,
course, approach, medium, route,
path, avenue 2 = <u>strait</u>, sound,
route, passage, canal, waterway
3 = <u>duct</u>, artery, groove, gutter,
furrow, conduit
● VERB = <u>direct</u>, guide, conduct,
transmit, convey

**chant** NOUN = <u>song</u>, carol, chorus,

melody, psalm
● VERB = sing, chorus, recite, intone, carol

**chaos** = disorder, confusion, mayhem, anarchy, lawlessness, pandemonium, bedlam, tumult ≠ orderliness

**chaotic** = disordered, confused, uncontrolled, anarchic, tumultuous, lawless, riotous, topsy-turvy

**chap** (*Informal*) = fellow, man, person, individual, character, guy (*informal*), bloke (*Brit. informal*)

**chapter** 1 = section, part, stage, division, episode, topic, segment, instalment 2 = period, time, stage, phase

**character** 1 = personality, nature, attributes, temperament, complexion, disposition 2 = nature, kind, quality, calibre 3 = reputation, honour, integrity, good name, rectitude 4 = role, part, persona 5 = eccentric, card (*informal*), original, oddball (*informal*) 6 = symbol, mark, sign, letter, figure, device, rune, hieroglyph

**characteristic** NOUN = feature, mark, quality, property, attribute, faculty, trait, quirk
● ADJECTIVE = typical, special, individual, representative, distinguishing, distinctive, peculiar, singular ≠ rare

**characterize** = distinguish, mark, identify, brand, stamp, typify

**charge** VERB 1 = accuse, indict, impeach, incriminate, arraign ≠ acquit 2 = attack, assault, assail ≠ retreat 3 = rush, storm, stampede 4 = fill, load
● NOUN 1 = price, rate, cost, amount, payment, expense, toll, expenditure 2 = accusation, allegation, indictment, imputation ≠ acquittal 3 = care, trust, responsibility, custody, safekeeping 4 = duty, office, responsibility, remit 5 = ward, pupil, protégé, dependant 6 = attack, rush, assault, onset, onslaught, stampede, sortie ≠ retreat

**charisma** = charm, appeal, personality, attraction, lure, allure, magnetism, force of personality

**charismatic** = charming, appealing, attractive, influential, magnetic, enticing, alluring

**charitable** 1 = benevolent, liberal, generous, lavish, philanthropic, bountiful, beneficent ≠ mean 2 = kind, understanding, forgiving, sympathetic, favourable, tolerant, indulgent, lenient ≠ unkind

**charity** 1 = charitable organization, fund, movement, trust, endowment 2 = donations, help, relief, gift, contributions, assistance, hand-out,

philanthropy, koha (*N.Z.*)
≠ meanness 3 = <u>kindness</u>,
humanity, goodwill, compassion,
generosity, indulgence, altruism,
benevolence, aroha (*N.Z.*) ≠ ill will

**charm** NOUN 1 = <u>attraction</u>,
appeal, fascination, allure,
magnetism ≠ repulsiveness
2 = <u>talisman</u>, trinket, amulet,
fetish 3 = <u>spell</u>, magic,
enchantment, sorcery, makutu
(*N.Z.*)
● VERB 1 = <u>attract</u>, delight,
fascinate, entrance, win over,
enchant, captivate, beguile
≠ repel 2 = <u>persuade</u>, seduce,
coax, beguile, sweet-talk
(*informal*)

**charming** = <u>attractive</u>, pleasing,
appealing, fetching, delightful,
cute, seductive, captivating
≠ unpleasant

**chart** NOUN = <u>table</u>, diagram,
blueprint, graph, plan, map
● VERB 1 = <u>plot</u>, map out,
delineate, sketch, draft, tabulate
2 = <u>monitor</u>, follow, record, note,
document, register, trace, outline

**charter** NOUN 1 = <u>document</u>,
contract, permit, licence, deed,
prerogative 2 = <u>constitution</u>,
laws, rules, code
● VERB 1 = <u>hire</u>, commission,
employ, rent, lease 2 = <u>authorize</u>,
permit, sanction, entitle, license,
empower, give authority

**chase** VERB 1 = <u>pursue</u>, follow,

track, hunt, run after, course
2 = <u>drive away</u>, drive, expel,
hound, send away, send packing,
put to flight 3 = <u>rush</u>, run, race,
shoot, fly, speed, dash, bolt
● NOUN = <u>pursuit</u>, race, hunt,
hunting

**chat** VERB = <u>talk</u>, gossip, jaw
(*slang*), natter, blather, blether
(*Scot.*)
● NOUN = <u>talk</u>, tête-à-tête,
conversation, gossip, heart-to-
heart, natter, blather, blether
(*Scot.*), korero (*N.Z.*)

**chatter** VERB = <u>prattle</u>, chat,
rabbit on (*Brit. informal*), babble,
gab (*informal*), natter, blather,
schmooze (*slang*)
● NOUN = <u>prattle</u>, chat, gossip,
babble, gab (*informal*), natter,
blather, blether (*Scot.*)

**cheap** 1 = <u>inexpensive</u>, reduced,
keen, reasonable, bargain, low-
priced, low-cost, cut-price
≠ expensive 2 = <u>inferior</u>, poor,
worthless, second-rate, shoddy,
tawdry, tatty, trashy, bodger or
bodgie (*Austral. slang*) ≠ good
3 (*Informal*) = <u>despicable</u>, mean,
contemptible, scungy (*Austral. &
N.Z.*) ≠ decent

**cheat** VERB = <u>deceive</u>, trick, fool,
con (*informal*), mislead, rip off
(*slang*), fleece, defraud
● NOUN = <u>deceiver</u>, sharper, shark,
charlatan, trickster, con man
(*informal*), double-crosser

(*informal*), swindler, rorter (*Austral. slang*)

**check** VERB 1 often with *out* = <u>examine</u>, test, study, look at, research, investigate, monitor, vet ≠ overlook 2 = <u>stop</u>, limit, delay, halt, restrain, inhibit, hinder, obstruct ≠ further

● NOUN 1 = <u>examination</u>, test, research, investigation, inspection, scrutiny, once-over (*informal*) 2 = <u>control</u>, limitation, restraint, constraint, obstacle, curb, obstruction, stoppage

**cheek** (*Informal*) = <u>impudence</u>, nerve, disrespect, audacity, lip (*slang*), temerity, chutzpah (*U.S. & Canad. informal*), insolence

**cheeky** = <u>impudent</u>, rude, forward, insulting, saucy, audacious, pert, disrespectful ≠ respectful

**cheer** VERB 1 = <u>applaud</u>, hail, acclaim, clap ≠ boo 2 = <u>hearten</u>, encourage, comfort, uplift, brighten, cheer up, buoy up, gladden ≠ dishearten

● NOUN = <u>applause</u>, ovation, plaudits, acclamation

● PHRASES **cheer someone up** = <u>comfort</u>, encourage, hearten, enliven, gladden, gee up, jolly along (*informal*) ◆ **cheer up** = <u>take heart</u>, rally, perk up, buck up (*informal*)

**cheerful** 1 = <u>happy</u>, optimistic, enthusiastic, jolly, merry, upbeat (*informal*), buoyant, cheery ≠ sad 2 = <u>pleasant</u> ≠ gloomy

**chemical** = <u>compound</u>, drug, substance, synthetic substance, potion

**chemist** = <u>pharmacist</u>, apothecary (*obsolete*), dispenser

**cherish** 1 = <u>cling to</u>, prize, treasure, hold dear, cleave to ≠ despise 2 = <u>care for</u>, love, support, comfort, look after, shelter, nurture, hold dear ≠ neglect 3 = <u>harbour</u>, nurse, sustain, foster, entertain

**chest** 1 = <u>breast</u>, front 2 = <u>box</u>, case, trunk, crate, coffer, casket, strongbox

*(Related Words)*

*adjective*: pectoral

**chew** = <u>munch</u>, bite, grind, champ, crunch, gnaw, chomp, masticate

**chic** = <u>stylish</u>, smart, elegant, fashionable, trendy (*Brit. informal*) ≠ unfashionable

**chief** NOUN = <u>head</u>, leader, director, manager, boss (*informal*), captain, master, governor, baas (*S. African*), ariki (*N.Z.*) ≠ subordinate

● ADJECTIVE = <u>primary</u>, highest, leading, main, prime, key, premier, supreme ≠ minor

**chiefly** 1 = <u>especially</u>, essentially, principally, primarily, above all 2 = <u>mainly</u>, largely, usually, mostly, in general, on the whole, predominantly, in the main

**child** 1 = <u>youngster</u>, baby, kid (*informal*), infant, babe, juvenile, toddler, tot, littlie (*Austral. informal*), ankle-biter (*Austral. slang*), tacker (*Austral. slang*) 2 = offspring

*Related Words*

*adjective*: filial

*prefix*: paedo-

**childbirth** = <u>child-bearing</u>, labour, delivery, lying-in, confinement, parturition

**childhood** = <u>youth</u>, minority, infancy, schooldays, immaturity, boyhood *or* girlhood

**childish** 1 = <u>youthful</u>, young, boyish *or* girlish 2 = <u>immature</u>, juvenile, foolish, infantile, puerile ≠ mature

**chill** VERB 1 = <u>cool</u>, refrigerate, freeze 2 = <u>dishearten</u>, depress, discourage, dismay, dampen, deject

● NOUN 1 = <u>coldness</u>, bite, nip, sharpness, coolness, rawness, crispness, frigidity 2 = <u>shiver</u>, frisson

● ADJECTIVE = <u>chilly</u>, biting, sharp, freezing, raw, bleak, chilly, wintry

**chilly** 1 = <u>cool</u>, fresh, sharp, crisp, penetrating, brisk, draughty, nippy ≠ warm 2 = <u>unfriendly</u>, hostile, unsympathetic, frigid, unresponsive, unwelcoming ≠ friendly

**china**[1] = <u>pottery</u>, ceramics, ware, porcelain, crockery, tableware, service

**china**[2] (*Brit. & S. African informal*) = <u>friend</u>, pal, mate (*informal*), buddy (*informal*), companion, best friend, intimate, comrade, cobber (*Austral. & N.Z. old-fashioned informal*), E hoa (*N.Z.*)

**chip** NOUN 1 = <u>fragment</u>, shaving, wafer, sliver, shard 2 = <u>scratch</u>, nick, notch 3 = <u>counter</u>, disc, token

● VERB 1 = <u>nick</u>, damage, gash 2 = <u>chisel</u>, whittle

**choice** NOUN 1 = <u>range</u>, variety, selection, assortment 2 = <u>selection</u>, preference, pick 3 = <u>option</u>, say, alternative

● ADJECTIVE = <u>best</u>, prime, select, excellent, exclusive, elite, booshit (*Austral. slang*), exo (*Austral. slang*), sik (*Austral. slang*)

**choke** 1 = <u>suffocate</u>, stifle, smother, overpower, asphyxiate 2 = <u>strangle</u>, throttle, asphyxiate 3 = <u>block</u>, clog, obstruct, bung, constrict, congest, stop, bar

**choose** 1 = <u>pick</u>, prefer, select, elect, adopt, opt for, designate, settle upon ≠ reject 2 = <u>wish</u>, want

**chop** = <u>cut</u>, fell, hack, sever, cleave, hew, lop

**chore** = <u>task</u>, job, duty, burden, hassle (*informal*), errand

**chorus** NOUN 1 = <u>refrain</u>, response, strain, burden 2 = <u>choir</u>, singers, ensemble, vocalists, choristers

• **PHRASES in chorus**: = in unison, as one, all together, in concert, in harmony, in accord, with one voice

**christen** 1= baptize, name 2= name, call, term, style, title, dub, designate

**Christmas** = festive season, Noël, Xmas (*informal*), Yule (*archaic*), Yuletide (*archaic*)

**chronicle** VERB = record, tell, report, enter, relate, register, recount, set down

• NOUN = record, story, history, account, register, journal, diary, narrative

**chuck** (*Informal*) 1= throw, cast, pitch, toss, hurl, fling, sling, heave 2 *often with* away *or* out= throw out, dump (*informal*), scrap, get rid of, ditch (*slang*), dispose of, dispense with, jettison 3= give up *or* over, leave, abandon, cease, resign from, pack in 4 (*Austral. & N.Z. informal*) = vomit, throw up (*informal*), spew, heave (*slang*), puke (*slang*), barf (*U.S. slang*), chunder (*slang, chiefly Austral.*)

**chuckle** = laugh, giggle, snigger, chortle, titter

**chum** (*Informal*) = friend, mate (*informal*), pal (*informal*), companion, comrade, crony, cobber (*Austral. & N.Z. old-fashioned informal*), E hoa (*N.Z.*)

**chunk** = piece, block, mass, portion, lump, slab, hunk, nugget

**churn** 1= stir up, beat, disturb, swirl, agitate 2= swirl, toss

**cinema** 1= pictures, movies, picture-house, flicks (*slang*) 2= films, pictures, movies, big screen (*informal*), motion pictures, silver screen

**circle** NOUN 1= ring, disc, hoop, halo 2= group, company, set, club, society, clique, coterie

• VERB 1= go round, ring, surround, enclose, envelop, encircle, circumscribe, circumnavigate 2= wheel, spiral

**circuit** 1= course, tour, track, route, journey 2= racetrack, course, track, racecourse 3= lap, tour, revolution, orbit

**circular** ADJECTIVE 1= round, ring-shaped 2= circuitous, cyclical, orbital

• NOUN 1= advertisement, notice, ad (*informal*), announcement, advert (*Brit. informal*), press release

**circulate** 1= spread, issue, publish, broadcast, distribute, publicize, disseminate, promulgate 2= flow, revolve, rotate, radiate

**circulation** 1= distribution, currency, readership 2= bloodstream, blood flow 3= flow, circling, motion, rotation 4= spread, distribution, transmission, dissemination

**circumstance** 1 *usually plural* = situation, condition, contingency, state of affairs, lie of the land 2 *usually plural* = detail, event, particular, respect 3 *usually plural* = situation, state, means, position, station, status 4 = chance, the times, accident, fortune, luck, fate, destiny, providence

**cite** = quote, name, advance, mention, extract, specify, allude to, enumerate

**citizen** = inhabitant, resident, dweller, denizen, subject, townsman

*Related Words*
adjective: civil

**city** = town, metropolis, municipality, conurbation

*Related Words*
adjective: civic

**civic** = public, municipal, communal, local

**civil** 1 = civic, political, domestic, municipal ≠ state 2 = polite, obliging, courteous, considerate, affable, well-mannered ≠ rude

**civilization** 1 = society, people, community, nation, polity 2 = culture, development, education, progress, enlightenment, sophistication, advancement, cultivation

**civilize** = cultivate, educate, refine, tame, enlighten,

sophisticate

**civilized** 1 = cultured, educated, sophisticated, enlightened, humane ≠ primitive 2 = polite, mannerly, tolerant, gracious, courteous, well-behaved, well-mannered

**claim** VERB 1 = assert, insist, maintain, allege, uphold, profess 2 = demand, call for, ask for, insist on

● NOUN 1 = assertion, statement, allegation, declaration, pretension, affirmation, protestation 2 = demand, application, request, petition, call 3 = right, title, entitlement

**clamour** = noise, shouting, racket, outcry, din, uproar, commotion, hubbub

**clamp** NOUN = vice, press, grip, bracket, fastener

● VERB = fasten, fix, secure, brace, make fast

**clan** 1 = family, group, society, tribe, fraternity, brotherhood, ainga (N.Z.), ngai (N.Z.) 2 = group, set, circle, gang, faction, coterie, cabal

**clap** = applaud, cheer, acclaim ≠ boo

**clarify** = explain, interpret, illuminate, clear up, simplify, make plain, elucidate, throw or shed light on

**clarity** 1 = clearness, precision, simplicity, transparency, lucidity,

straightforwardness ≠ obscurity
2= transparency, clearness
≠ cloudiness

**clash** VERB 1= conflict, grapple, wrangle, lock horns, cross swords, war, feud, quarrel 2= disagree, conflict, vary, counter, differ, contradict, diverge, run counter to 3= not go, jar, not match 4= crash, bang, rattle, jar, clatter, jangle, clang, clank
● NOUN 1= conflict, fight, brush, confrontation, collision, showdown (informal) 2= disagreement, difference, argument, dispute, dissent, difference of opinion

**clasp** VERB = grasp, hold, press, grip, seize, squeeze, embrace, clutch
● NOUN 1= grasp, hold, grip, embrace, hug 2= fastening, catch, grip, hook, pin, clip, buckle, brooch

**class** NOUN 1= group, set, division, rank 2= type, set, sort, kind, category, genre
● VERB = classify, group, rate, rank, brand, label, grade, designate

**classic** ADJECTIVE 1= typical, standard, model, regular, usual, ideal, characteristic, definitive, dinki-di (Austral. informal)
2= masterly, best, finest, world-class, consummate, first-rate ≠ second-rate 3= lasting, enduring, abiding, immortal,

undying, ageless, deathless
● NOUN = standard, masterpiece, prototype, paradigm, exemplar, model

**classification**
= categorization, grading, taxonomy, sorting, analysis, arrangement

**classify** = categorize, sort, rank, arrange, grade, catalogue, pigeonhole, tabulate

**classy** (Informal) = high-class, exclusive, superior, elegant, stylish, posh (informal, chiefly Brit.), up-market, top-drawer

**clause** = section, condition, article, chapter, passage, part, paragraph

**claw** NOUN 1= nail, talon
2= pincer
● VERB = scratch, tear, dig, rip, scrape, maul, mangulate (Austral. slang), lacerate

**clean** ADJECTIVE 1= hygienic, fresh, sterile, pure, purified, antiseptic, sterilized, uncontaminated ≠ contaminated 2= spotless, fresh, immaculate, impeccable, flawless, unblemished, unsullied ≠ dirty 3= moral, good, pure, decent, innocent, respectable, upright, honourable ≠ immoral 4= complete, final, whole, total, perfect, entire, decisive, thorough
● VERB = cleanse, wash, scrub, rinse, launder, scour, purify,

disinfect ≠ dirty

**cleanse** = purify, clear, purge
1 = absolute, clear, purge, purify
2 = clean, wash, scrub, rinse, scour

**clear** ADJECTIVE
1 = comprehensible, explicit, understandable ≠ confused
2 = distinct ≠ indistinct
3 = obvious, plain, apparent, evident, distinct, pronounced, manifest, blatant ≠ ambiguous
4 = certain, sure, convinced, positive, satisfied, resolved, definite, decided ≠ confused
5 = transparent, see-through, translucent, crystalline, glassy, limpid, pellucid ≠ opaque
6 = unobstructed, open, free, empty, unhindered, unimpeded ≠ blocked
7 = bright, fine, fair, shining, sunny, luminous, cloudless, light ≠ cloudy
8 = untroubled, clean, pure, innocent, immaculate, unblemished, untarnished
● VERB 1 = unblock, free, loosen, extricate, open, disentangle
2 = remove, clean, wipe, cleanse, tidy (up), sweep away
3 = brighten, break up, lighten
4 = pass over, jump, leap, vault, miss
5 = absolve, acquit, vindicate, exonerate ≠ blame

**clear-cut** = straightforward, specific, plain, precise, black-and-white, explicit, definite, unequivocal

**clearly** 1 = obviously, undoubtedly, evidently, distinctly, markedly, overtly, undeniably, beyond doubt
2 = legibly, distinctly
3 = audibly, distinctly, intelligibly, comprehensibly

**clergy** = priesthood, ministry, clerics, clergymen, churchmen, the cloth, holy orders

**clever** 1 = intelligent, bright, talented, gifted, smart, knowledgeable, quick-witted ≠ stupid
2 = shrewd, bright, ingenious, resourceful, canny ≠ unimaginative
3 = skilful, talented, gifted ≠ inept

**cliché** = platitude, stereotype, commonplace, banality, truism, hackneyed phrase

**client** = customer, consumer, buyer, patron, shopper, patient

**cliff** = rock face, overhang, crag, precipice, escarpment, scar, bluff

**climate** = weather, temperature

**climax** = culmination, top, summit, height, highlight, peak, high point, zenith

**climb** VERB 1 = ascend, scale, mount, go up, clamber, shin up
2 = clamber, descend, scramble, dismount ≠ rise, go up, soar, ascend, fly up
● PHRASES **climb down** = back down, withdraw, yield, concede, retreat, surrender, give in, cave in (informal)

**clinch** 1 = secure, close, confirm,

conclude, seal, sew up (*informal*), set the seal on **2=** <u>settle</u>, decide, determine

**cling 1=** <u>clutch</u>, grip, embrace, grasp, hug, hold on to, clasp **2=** <u>stick to</u>, adhere to

**clinical=** <u>unemotional</u>, cold, scientific, objective, detached, analytic, impersonal, dispassionate

**clip¹VERB 1=** <u>trim</u>, cut, crop, prune, shorten, shear, snip, pare **2**(*Informal*) **=** <u>smack</u>, strike, knock, punch, thump, clout (*informal*), cuff, whack

● NOUN (*Informal*) **=** <u>smack</u>, strike, knock, punch, thump, clout (*informal*), cuff, whack

**clip²=** <u>attach</u>, fix, secure, connect, pin, staple, fasten, hold

**cloakNOUN 1=** <u>cape</u>, coat, wrap, mantle **2=** <u>covering</u>, layer, blanket, shroud

● VERB **1=** <u>cover</u>, coat, wrap, blanket, shroud, envelop **2=** <u>hide</u>, cover, screen, mask, disguise, conceal, obscure, veil

**clog=** <u>obstruct</u>, block, jam, hinder, impede, congest

**close¹VERB 1=** <u>shut</u>, lock, fasten, secure ≠ open **2=** <u>shut down</u>, finish, cease ≠ <u>wind up</u>, finish, shut down, terminate **4=** <u>block up</u>, bar, seal ≠ open **5=** <u>end</u>, finish, complete, conclude, wind up, terminate ≠ begin **6=** <u>clinch</u>, confirm, secure, conclude, seal,

sew up (*informal*), set the seal on **7=** <u>come together</u>, join, connect ≠ separate

● NOUN **=** <u>end</u>, ending, finish, conclusion, completion, finale, culmination, denouement

**close² 1=** <u>near</u>, neighbouring, nearby, handy, adjacent, adjoining, cheek by jowl ≠ far **2=** <u>intimate</u>, loving, familiar, thick (*informal*), attached, devoted, confidential, inseparable ≠ distant **3=** <u>noticeable</u>, marked, strong, distinct, pronounced **4=** <u>careful</u>, detailed, intense, minute, thorough, rigorous, painstaking **5=** <u>even</u>, level, neck and neck, fifty-fifty (*informal*), evenly matched **6=** <u>imminent</u>, near, impending, at hand, nigh ≠ far away **7=** <u>stifling</u>, oppressive, suffocating, stuffy, humid, sweltering, airless, muggy ≠ airy

**closed 1=** <u>shut</u>, locked, sealed, fastened ≠ open **2=** <u>shut down</u>, out of service ≠ open **3=** <u>exclusive</u>, select, restricted **4=** <u>finished</u>, over, ended, decided, settled, concluded, resolved, terminated

**cloth=** <u>fabric</u>, material, textiles

**clothe=** <u>dress</u>, array, robe, drape, swathe, attire, fit out, garb ≠ undress

**clothes=** <u>clothing</u>, wear, dress, gear (*informal*), outfit, costume, wardrobe, garments

**clothing=** <u>clothes</u>, wear, dress,

gear (*informal*), outfit, costume, wardrobe, garments

**cloud** NOUN = <u>mist</u>, haze, vapour, murk, gloom

● VERB 1 = <u>confuse</u>, distort, impair, muddle, disorient 2 = <u>darken</u>, dim, be overshadowed

**clout** (*Informal*) VERB = <u>hit</u>, strike, punch, slap, sock (*slang*), smack, thump, clobber (*slang*)

● NOUN 1 = <u>thump</u>, blow, punch, slap, sock (*slang*), wallop (*informal*) 2 = <u>influence</u>, power, authority, pull, weight, prestige, mana (*N.Z.*)

**clown** NOUN 1 = <u>comedian</u>, fool, comic, harlequin, joker, jester, prankster, buffoon 2 = <u>fool</u>, idiot, twit (*informal*, *chiefly Brit.*), imbecile (*informal*), ignoramus, dolt, blockhead, dorba or dorb (*Austral. slang*), bogan (*Austral. slang*)

● VERB usually with *around* = <u>play the fool</u>, mess about, jest, act the fool

**club** NOUN 1 = <u>association</u>, company, group, union, society, lodge, guild, fraternity 2 = <u>stick</u>, bat, bludgeon, truncheon, cosh (*Brit.*), cudgel

● VERB = <u>beat</u>, strike, hammer, batter, bash, bludgeon, pummel, cosh (*Brit.*)

**clue** = <u>indication</u>, lead, sign, evidence, suggestion, trace, hint, suspicion

**clump** NOUN = <u>cluster</u>, group, bunch, bundle

● VERB = <u>stomp</u>, thump, lumber, tramp, plod, thud

**clumsy** = <u>awkward</u>, lumbering, bumbling, ponderous, ungainly, gauche, gawky, uncoordinated, unco (*Austral. slang*) ≠ skilful

**cluster** NOUN = <u>gathering</u>, group, collection, bunch, knot, clump, assemblage

● VERB = <u>gather</u>, group, collect, bunch, assemble, flock, huddle

**clutch** VERB 1 = <u>hold</u>, grip, embrace, grasp, cling to, clasp 2 = <u>seize</u>, catch, grab, grasp, snatch

● PLURAL NOUN = <u>power</u>, hands, control, grip, possession, grasp, custody, sway

**clutter** NOUN = <u>untidiness</u>, mess, disorder, confusion, litter, muddle, disarray, jumble ≠ order

● VERB = <u>litter</u>, scatter, strew, mess up ≠ tidy

**coach** NOUN 1 = <u>instructor</u>, teacher, trainer, tutor, handler 2 = <u>bus</u>, charabanc

● VERB = <u>instruct</u>, train, prepare, exercise, drill, tutor

**coalition** = <u>alliance</u>, union, association, combination, merger, conjunction, bloc, confederation

**coarse** 1 = <u>rough</u>, crude, unfinished, homespun, impure, unrefined, unprocessed, unpolished ≠ smooth 2 = <u>vulgar</u>, rude, indecent, improper, earthy, smutty, ribald, indelicate

**coast** NOUN = <u>shore</u>, border, beach, seaside, coastline, seaboard
● VERB = <u>cruise</u>, sail, drift, taxi, glide, freewheel

**coat** NOUN 1= <u>fur</u>, hair, skin, hide, wool, fleece, pelt 2= <u>layer</u>, covering, coating, overlay
● VERB = <u>cover</u>, spread, plaster, smear

**coax** = <u>persuade</u>, cajole, talk into, wheedle, sweet-talk (*informal*), prevail upon, entice, allure ≠ bully

**cobber** (*Austral. & N.Z. old-fashioned informal*) = <u>friend</u>, pal, mate (*informal*), buddy (*informal*), china (*Brit. & S. African informal*), best friend, intimate, comrade, E hoa (*N.Z.*)

**cocktail** = <u>mixture</u>, combination, compound, blend, mix

**cocky** or **cockie** (*Austral. & N.Z. informal*) = <u>farmer</u>, smallholder, crofter (*Scot.*), grazier, agriculturalist, rancher

**code** 1= <u>principles</u>, rules, manners, custom, convention, ethics, maxim, etiquette, kawa (*N.Z.*), tikanga (*N.Z.*) 2= <u>cipher</u>, cryptograph

**coherent** 1= <u>consistent</u>, reasoned, organized, rational, logical, meaningful, systematic, orderly ≠ inconsistent

2= <u>articulate</u>, lucid, comprehensible, intelligible ≠ unintelligible

**coil** 1= <u>wind</u>, twist, curl, loop, spiral, twine 2= <u>curl</u>, wind, twist, snake, loop, twine, wreathe

**coin** NOUN = <u>money</u>, change, cash, silver, copper, specie
● VERB = <u>invent</u>, create, make up, forge, originate, fabricate

**coincide** 1= <u>occur simultaneously</u>, coexist, synchronize, be concurrent 2= <u>agree</u>, match, accord, square, correspond, tally, concur, harmonize ≠ disagree

**coincidence** = <u>chance</u>, accident, luck, fluke, stroke of luck, happy accident

**cold** ADJECTIVE 1= <u>chilly</u>, freezing, bleak, arctic, icy, frosty, wintry, frigid ≠ hot 2= <u>distant</u>, reserved, indifferent, aloof, frigid, undemonstrative, standoffish ≠ emotional 3= <u>unfriendly</u>, indifferent, frigid ≠ friendly
● NOUN = <u>coldness</u>, chill, frigidity, frostiness, iciness

**collaborate** 1= <u>work together</u>, team up, join forces, cooperate, play ball (*informal*), participate 2= <u>conspire</u>, cooperate, collude, fraternize

**collaboration** 1= <u>teamwork</u>, partnership, cooperation, association, alliance 2= <u>conspiring</u>, cooperation, collusion, fraternization

**collaborator** 1= <u>co-worker</u>, partner, colleague, associate, team-mate, confederate
2= <u>traitor</u>, turncoat, quisling, fraternizer

**collapse**VERB 1= <u>fall down</u>, fall, give way, subside, cave in, crumple, fall apart at the seams
2= <u>fail</u>, fold, founder, break down, fall through, come to nothing, go belly-up (*informal*)
● NOUN 1= <u>falling down</u>, ruin, falling apart, cave-in, disintegration, subsidence
2= <u>failure</u>, slump, breakdown, flop, downfall 3= <u>faint</u>, breakdown, blackout, prostration

**collar**(*Informal*) = <u>seize</u>, catch, arrest, grab, capture, nail (*informal*), nab (*informal*), apprehend

**colleague** = <u>fellow worker</u>, partner, ally, associate, assistant, team-mate, comrade, helper

**collect** 1= <u>gather</u>, save, assemble, heap, accumulate, amass, stockpile, hoard ≠ scatter
2= <u>assemble</u>, meet, rally, cluster, come together, convene, converge, congregate ≠ disperse

**collected** = <u>calm</u>, cool, composed, poised, serene, unperturbed, unruffled, self-possessed ≠ nervous

**collection** 1= <u>accumulation</u>, set, store, mass, pile, heap, stockpile, hoard 2= <u>compilation</u>, accumulation, anthology
3= <u>group</u>, company, crowd, assembly, cluster, assortment
4= <u>gathering</u> 5= <u>contribution</u>, donation, alms 6= <u>offering</u>, offertory

**collective** 1= <u>joint</u>, united, shared, combined, corporate, unified ≠ individual
2= <u>combined</u>, aggregate, composite, cumulative ≠ separate

**collide** 1= <u>crash</u>, clash, meet head-on, come into collision
2= <u>conflict</u>, clash, be incompatible, be at variance

**collision** 1= <u>crash</u>, impact, accident, smash, bump, pile-up (*informal*), prang (*informal*)
2= <u>conflict</u>, opposition, clash, encounter, disagreement, incompatibility

**colony** = <u>settlement</u>, territory, province, possession, dependency, outpost, dominion, satellite state

**colour**(*U.S.*) **color**NOUN 1= <u>hue</u>, tone, shade, tint, colourway 2= <u>paint</u>, stain, dye, tint, pigment, colorant
● VERB = <u>blush</u>, flush, redden
> shades from black to white> shades of blue
> shades of brown> shades of green> shades of

orange ➤ shades of purple
➤ shades of red ➤ shades of
yellow

**colourful** 1 = <u>bright</u>, brilliant,
psychedelic, variegated,
multicoloured ≠ drab
2 = <u>interesting</u>, rich, graphic,
lively, distinctive, vivid,
picturesque ≠ boring

**column** 1 = <u>pillar</u>, support, post,
shaft, upright, obelisk 2 = <u>line</u>,
row, file, rank, procession,
cavalcade

**coma** = <u>unconsciousness</u>, trance,
oblivion, stupor

**comb** 1 = <u>untangle</u>, arrange,
groom, dress 2 = <u>search</u>, hunt
through, rake, sift, scour,
rummage, ransack, forage, fossick
(*Austral. & N.Z.*)

**combat** NOUN = <u>fight</u>, war,
action, battle, conflict,
engagement, warfare, skirmish
≠ peace
● VERB = <u>fight</u>, oppose, resist, defy,
withstand, do battle with
≠ support

**combination** 1 = <u>mixture</u>, mix,
blend, composite, amalgamation,
coalescence 2 = <u>association</u>,
union, alliance, coalition,
federation, consortium,
syndicate, confederation

**combine** 1 = <u>amalgamate</u>, mix,
blend, integrate, merge
≠ separate 2 = <u>join together</u>, link,
connect, integrate, merge,

amalgamate 3 = <u>unite</u>, associate,
team up, get together,
collaborate, join forces, join
together, pool resources ≠ split
up

**come** VERB 1 = <u>approach</u>, near,
advance, move towards, draw
near 2 = <u>arrive</u>, turn up
(*informal*), show up (*informal*)
3 = <u>reach</u>, extend, come up to,
come as far as 4 = <u>happen</u>, fall,
occur, take place, come about,
come to pass 5 = <u>be available</u>, be
made, be offered, be produced,
be on offer
● PHRASES **come across
something** or **someone**
= <u>seem</u>, look, seem to be, appear
to be, give the impression of
being ◆ **come across
someone** = <u>meet</u>, encounter,
run into, bump into (*informal*)
◆ **come across something**
= <u>find</u>, discover, notice, unearth,
stumble upon, chance upon = <u>be
obtained</u>, be from, issue, emerge,
flow, arise, originate, emanate

**comeback** 1 (*Informal*)
= <u>return</u>, revival, rebound,
resurgence, rally, recovery,
triumph 2 = <u>response</u>, reply,
retort, retaliation, riposte,
rejoinder

**comedian** = <u>comic</u>, wit, clown,
funny man, humorist, wag, joker,
jester, dag (*N.Z. informal*)

**comedy** 1 = <u>light entertainment</u>

≠ tragedy, soapie (*Austral. slang*)
2= <u>humour</u>, fun, joking, farce, jesting, hilarity ≠ **seriousness**

**comfort**NOUN 1= <u>ease</u>, luxury, wellbeing, opulence
2= <u>consolation</u>, succour, help, support, relief, compensation ≠ annoyance
● VERB = <u>console</u>, reassure, soothe, hearten, commiserate with ≠ distress

**comfortable** 1= <u>pleasant</u>, homely, relaxing, cosy, agreeable, restful ≠ unpleasant 2= <u>at ease</u>, happy, at home, contented, relaxed, serene ≠ uncomfortable 3(*Informal*) = <u>well-off</u>, prosperous, affluent, well-to-do, comfortably-off, in clover (*informal*)

**comforting** = <u>consoling</u>, encouraging, cheering, reassuring, soothing, heart-warming ≠ upsetting

**comic**ADJECTIVE 1= <u>funny</u>, amusing, witty, humorous, farcical, comical, droll, jocular ≠ sad
● NOUN = <u>comedian</u>, funny man, humorist, wit, clown, wag, jester, dag (*N.Z. informal*), buffoon

**coming**ADJECTIVE
= <u>approaching</u>, near, forthcoming, imminent, in store, impending, at hand, nigh
● NOUN = <u>arrival</u>, approach, advent

**command**VERB 1= <u>order</u>, tell, charge, demand, require, direct, bid, compel ≠ beg 2= <u>have authority over</u>, lead, head, control, rule, manage, handle, dominate ≠ be subordinate to
● NOUN 1= <u>order</u>, demand, instruction, requirement, decree, directive, ultimatum, commandment 2= <u>domination</u>, control, rule, mastery, power, government 3= <u>management</u>, power, control, charge, authority, supervision

**commander**= <u>leader</u>, chief, officer, boss, head, captain, bass (*S. African*), ruler

**commanding**= <u>dominant</u>, controlling, dominating, superior, decisive, advantageous

**commemorate**= <u>celebrate</u>, remember, honour, recognize, salute, pay tribute to, immortalize ≠ ignore

**commence** 1= <u>embark on</u>, start, open, begin, initiate, originate, instigate, enter upon ≠ stop 2= <u>start</u>, open, begin, go ahead ≠ end

**commend** 1= <u>praise</u>, acclaim, applaud, compliment, extol, approve, speak highly of ≠ criticize 2= <u>recommend</u>, suggest, approve, advocate, endorse

**comment**VERB 1= <u>remark</u>, say, note, mention, point out, observe, utter 2 *usually with on* = <u>remark on</u>, explain, talk about, discuss, speak about, say something about, allude to, elucidate

● NOUN 1 = <u>remark</u>, statement, observation 2 = <u>note</u>, explanation, illustration, commentary, exposition, annotation, elucidation

**commentary** 1 = <u>narration</u>, report, review, explanation, description, voice-over 2 = <u>analysis</u>, notes, review, critique, treatise

**commentator** 1 = <u>reporter</u>, special correspondent, sportscaster 2 = <u>critic</u>, interpreter, annotator

**commercial** 1 = <u>mercantile</u>, trading 2 = <u>materialistic</u>, mercenary, profit-making

**commission** VERB = <u>appoint</u>, order, contract, select, engage, delegate, nominate, authorize

● NOUN 1 = <u>duty</u>, task, mission, mandate, errand 2 = <u>fee</u>, cut, percentage, royalties, rake-off (*slang*) 3 = <u>committee</u>, board, representatives, commissioners, delegation, deputation

**commit** 1 = <u>do</u>, perform, carry out, execute, enact, perpetrate 2 = <u>put in custody</u>, confine, imprison ≠ release

**commitment** 1 = <u>dedication</u>, loyalty, devotion ≠ indecisiveness

2 = <u>responsibility</u>, tie, duty, obligation, liability, engagement

**common** 1 = <u>usual</u>, standard, regular, ordinary, familiar, conventional, routine, frequent ≠ rare 2 = <u>popular</u>, general, accepted, standard, routine, widespread, universal, prevailing 3 = <u>shared</u>, collective 4 = <u>ordinary</u>, average, typical, dinki-di (*Austral. informal*) ≠ important 5 = <u>vulgar</u>, inferior, coarse, plebeian ≠ refined 6 = <u>collective</u>, public, community, social, communal ≠ personal

**commonplace** ADJECTIVE = <u>everyday</u>, common, ordinary, widespread, mundane, banal, run-of-the-mill, humdrum ≠ rare

● NOUN = <u>cliché</u>, platitude, banality, truism

**common sense** = <u>good sense</u>, sound judgment, level-headedness, prudence, gumption (*Brit. informal*), horse sense, native intelligence, wit

**communal** = <u>public</u>, shared, general, joint, collective ≠ private

**commune** = <u>community</u>, collective, cooperative, kibbutz

**communicate** = <u>contact</u>, talk, speak, make contact, get in contact 2 = <u>make known</u>, declare, disclose, pass on, proclaim, transmit, convey, impart ≠ keep secret **3**= <u>pass on</u>, transfer, spread, transmit

**communication 1**= <u>contact</u>, conversation, correspondence, link, relations **2**= <u>passing on</u>, circulation, transmission, disclosure, imparting, dissemination, conveyance **3**= <u>message</u>, news, report, word, information, statement, announcement, disclosure

**communism** *usually cap.* = <u>socialism</u>, Marxism, collectivism, Bolshevism, state socialism

**communist** *often cap.* = <u>socialist</u>, Red (*informal*), Marxist, Bolshevik, collectivist

**community**= <u>society</u>, people, public, residents, commonwealth, general public, populace, state

**commuter**= <u>daily traveller</u>, passenger, suburbanite

**compact¹** ADJECTIVE **1**= <u>closely packed</u>, solid, thick, dense, compressed, condensed, pressed together ≠ loose **2**= <u>concise</u>, brief, to the point, succinct, terse ≠ lengthy

● VERB = <u>pack closely</u>, stuff, cram, compress, condense, tamp ≠ loose

**compact²**= <u>agreement</u>, deal, understanding, contract, bond, arrangement, treaty, bargain

**companion 1**= <u>friend</u>, partner, ally, colleague, associate, mate (*informal*), comrade, accomplice, cobber (*Austral. & N.Z. old-fashioned informal*) **2**= <u>assistant</u>, aide, escort, attendant

**company 1**= <u>business</u>, firm, association, corporation, partnership, establishment, syndicate, house **2**= <u>group</u>, set, community, band, crowd, collection, gathering, assembly **3**= <u>troop</u>, unit, squad, team **4**= <u>companionship</u>, society, presence, fellowship **5**= <u>guests</u>, party, visitors, callers

**comparable 1**= <u>equal</u>, equivalent, on a par, tantamount, a match for, proportionate, commensurate, as good as ≠ unequal **2**= <u>similar</u>, related, alike, corresponding, akin, analogous, of a piece, cognate

**comparative**= <u>relative</u>, qualified, by comparison

**compare** VERB = <u>contrast</u>, balance, weigh, set against, juxtapose

● PHRASES **compare to something**= <u>liken to</u>, parallel, identify with, equate to, correlate to, mention in the same breath as ◆ **compare with something**= <u>be as good as</u>, match, approach, equal, compete with, be on a par with, be the equal of, hold a candle to

**comparison** 1 = <u>contrast</u>, distinction, differentiation, juxtaposition 2 = <u>similarity</u>, analogy, resemblance, correlation, likeness, comparability

**compartment** 1 = <u>section</u>, carriage, berth 2 = <u>bay</u>, booth, locker, niche, cubicle, alcove, pigeonhole, cubbyhole

**compass** = <u>range</u>, field, area, reach, scope, limit, extent, boundary

**compassion** = <u>sympathy</u>, understanding, pity, humanity, mercy, sorrow, kindness, tenderness, aroha (*N.Z.*) ≠ indifference

**compassionate** = <u>sympathetic</u>, understanding, pitying, humanitarian, charitable, humane, benevolent, merciful ≠ uncaring

**compatible** 1 = <u>consistent</u>, in keeping, congruous ≠ inappropriate 2 = <u>like-minded</u>, harmonious, in harmony ≠ incompatible

**compel** = <u>force</u>, make, railroad (*informal*), oblige, constrain, coerce, impel, dragoon

**compelling** 1 = <u>convincing</u>, telling, powerful, forceful, conclusive, weighty, cogent, irrefutable 2 = <u>pressing</u>, binding, urgent, overriding, imperative, unavoidable, coercive, peremptory 3 = <u>fascinating</u>, gripping, irresistible, enchanting, enthralling, hypnotic, spellbinding, mesmeric ≠ boring

**compensate** 1 = <u>recompense</u>, repay, refund, reimburse, remunerate, make good 2 = <u>make amends</u>, make up for, atone, make it up to someone, pay for, do penance, cancel out, make reparation 3 = <u>balance</u>, cancel (out), offset, make up for, redress, counteract, counterbalance

**compensation** 1 = <u>reparation</u>, damages, recompense, remuneration, restitution, reimbursement 2 = <u>recompense</u>, amends, reparation, restitution, atonement

**compete** 1 = <u>contend</u>, fight, vie, challenge, struggle, contest, strive 2 = <u>take part</u>, participate, be in the running, be a competitor, be a contestant, play

**competence** 1 = <u>ability</u>, skill, talent, capacity, expertise, proficiency, capability ≠ incompetence 2 = <u>fitness</u>, suitability, adequacy, appropriateness ≠ inadequacy

**competent** 1 = <u>able</u>, skilled, capable, proficient ≠ incompetent 2 = <u>fit</u>, qualified, suitable, adequate

≠ unqualified

**competition** 1= <u>rivalry</u>, opposition, struggle, strife 2= <u>opposition</u>, field, rivals, challengers 3= <u>contest</u>, event, championship, tournament, head-to-head

**competitive** 1= <u>cut-throat</u>, aggressive, fierce, ruthless, relentless, antagonistic, dog-eat-dog 2= <u>ambitious</u>, pushing, opposing, aggressive, vying, contentious, combative

**competitor** 1= <u>rival</u>, adversary, antagonist 2= <u>contestant</u>, participant, contender, challenger, entrant, player, opponent

**compilation**= <u>collection</u>, treasury, accumulation, anthology, assortment, assemblage

**compile**= <u>put together</u>, collect, gather, organize, accumulate, marshal, garner, amass

**complacency**= <u>smugness</u>, satisfaction, contentment, self-congratulation, self-satisfaction

**complacent**= <u>smug</u>, self-satisfied, pleased with yourself, contented, satisfied, serene, unconcerned ≠ insecure

**complain**= <u>find fault</u>, moan, grumble, whinge (*informal*), carp, groan, lament, whine

**complaint** 1= <u>protest</u>, objection, grievance, charge 2= <u>grumble</u>, criticism, moan, lament, grievance, grouse, gripe (*informal*) 3= <u>disorder</u>, problem, disease, upset, illness, sickness, ailment, affliction

**complement**VERB = <u>enhance</u>, complete, improve, boost, crown, add to, set off, heighten
● NOUN 1= <u>accompaniment</u>, companion, accessory, completion, finishing touch, rounding-off, adjunct, supplement 2= <u>total</u>, capacity, quota, aggregate, contingent, entirety

> ### Word Power
>
> **complement**– This is sometimes confused with *compliment* but the two words have very different meanings. As the synonyms show, the verb form of *complement* means 'to enhance' and 'to complete' something. In contrast, common synonyms of *compliment* as a verb are *praise*, *commend*, and *flatter*.

**complementary**= <u>matching</u>, companion, corresponding, compatible, reciprocal, interrelating, interdependent, harmonizing ≠ incompatible

**complete**ADJECTIVE 1= <u>total</u>,

perfect, absolute, utter, outright, thorough, consummate, out-and-out 2 = whole, full, entire ≠ partial 3 = entire, full, whole, intact, unbroken, faultless ≠ incomplete 4 = unabridged, full, entire 5 = finished, done, ended, achieved, concluded, fulfilled, accomplished ≠ unfinished 6 = perfect, finish off, round off, crown ≠ spoil
● VERB 1 = finish, conclude, end, close, settle, wrap up (*informal*), finalize ≠ start 2 = fill in, fill out

**completely** = totally, entirely, wholly, utterly, perfectly, fully, absolutely, altogether

**completion** = finishing, end, close, conclusion, fulfilment, culmination, fruition

**complex** ADJECTIVE
1 = compound, multiple, composite, manifold, heterogeneous, multifarious 2 = complicated, difficult, involved, elaborate, tangled, intricate, tortuous, convoluted ≠ simple
● NOUN 1 = structure, system, scheme, network, organization, aggregate, composite 2 (*Informal*) = obsession, preoccupation, phobia, fixation, fixed idea, idée fixe (*French*)

> ### Word Power
>
> **complex** – Although *complex* and *complicated* are close in meaning, care should be taken when using one as a synonym of the other. *Complex* should be used to say that something consists of several parts rather than that it is difficult to understand, analyse, or deal with, which is what *complicated* inherently means. In the following real example a clear distinction is made between the two words: *the British benefits system is phenomenally complex and is administered by a complicated range of agencies.*

**complexion** 1 = skin, colour, colouring, hue, skin tone, pigmentation 2 = nature, character, make-up 3 = perspective, look, light, appearance, aspect, angle, slant

**complexity** = complication, involvement, intricacy, entanglement

**complicate** = make difficult, confuse, muddle, entangle, involve ≠ simplify

**complicated** 1 = involved, difficult, puzzling, troublesome, problematic, perplexing ≠ simple 2 = complex, involved, elaborate, intricate, convoluted, labyrinthine ≠ understandable

**complication** 1= <u>problem</u>, difficulty, obstacle, drawback, snag, uphill (*S. African*)
2= <u>complexity</u>, web, confusion, intricacy, entanglement

**compliment** NOUN 1= <u>praise</u>, honour, tribute, bouquet, flattery, eulogy ≠ criticism
● PLURAL NOUN 1= <u>greetings</u>, regards, respects, good wishes, salutation ≠ insult
2= <u>congratulations</u>, praise, commendation
● VERB = <u>praise</u>, flatter, salute, congratulate, pay tribute to, commend, extol, wax lyrical about ≠ criticize

> ### Word Power
> **compliment**– *Compliment* is sometimes confused with complement.

**complimentary** 1= <u>flattering</u>, approving, appreciative, congratulatory, commendatory ≠ critical
2= <u>free</u>, donated, courtesy, honorary, on the house, gratuitous, gratis

**comply** = <u>obey</u>, follow, observe, submit to, conform to, adhere to, abide by, acquiesce with ≠ defy

**component** NOUN = <u>part</u>, piece, unit, item, element, ingredient, constituent
● ADJECTIVE = <u>constituent</u>, inherent, intrinsic

**compose** VERB 1= <u>put together</u>, make up, constitute, comprise, make, build, form, fashion ≠ destroy
2= <u>create</u>, write, produce, invent, devise, contrive
3= <u>arrange</u>, make up, construct, put together, order, organize
● PHRASES **compose yourself** = <u>calm</u>, control, collect, quiet, soothe, pull yourself together

**composed** = <u>calm</u>, cool, collected, relaxed, poised, at ease, serene, sedate ≠ agitated

**composition** 1= <u>design</u>, structure, make-up, organization, arrangement, formation, layout, configuration
2= <u>creation</u>, work, piece, production, opus, masterpiece
3= <u>essay</u>, exercise, treatise, literary work
4= <u>production</u>, creation, making, fashioning, formation, putting together, compilation, formulation

**compound** NOUN = <u>combination</u>, mixture, blend, composite, fusion, synthesis, alloy, medley ≠ element
● ADJECTIVE = <u>complex</u>, multiple, composite, intricate ≠ simple
● VERB 1= <u>intensify</u>, add to, complicate, worsen, heighten, exacerbate, aggravate, magnify ≠ lessen
2= <u>combine</u>, unite, mix, blend, synthesize, amalgamate, intermingle ≠ divide

**comprehend** = <u>understand</u>,

see, take in, perceive, grasp, conceive, make out, fathom ≠ misunderstand

**comprehension** = understanding, grasp, conception, realization, intelligence, perception, discernment ≠ incomprehension

**comprehensive** = broad, full, complete, blanket, thorough, inclusive, exhaustive, all-inclusive ≠ limited

**compress** 1 = squeeze, crush, squash, press 2 = condense, contract, concentrate, shorten, abbreviate

**comprise** 1 = be composed of, include, contain, consist of, take in, embrace, encompass 2 = make up, form, constitute, compose

---

### Word Power

**comprise** – The use of *of* after *comprise* should be avoided: *the library comprises* (not *comprises of*) *6,500,000 books and manuscripts. Consist*, however, should be followed by *of* when used in this way: *Her crew consisted of children from Devon and Cornwall.*

---

**compromise** NOUN = give-and-take, agreement, settlement, accommodation, concession, adjustment, trade-off ≠ disagreement

● VERB 1 = meet halfway, concede, make concessions, give and take, strike a balance, strike a happy medium, go fifty-fifty (*informal*) ≠ disagree 2 = undermine, expose, embarrass, weaken, prejudice, discredit, jeopardize, dishonour ≠ support

**compulsive** 1 = obsessive, confirmed, chronic, persistent, addictive, uncontrollable, incurable, inveterate 2 = fascinating, gripping, absorbing, compelling, captivating, enthralling, hypnotic, engrossing 3 = irresistible, overwhelming, compelling, urgent, neurotic, uncontrollable, driving

**compulsory** = obligatory, forced, required, binding, mandatory, imperative, requisite, de rigueur (*French*) ≠ voluntary

**compute** = calculate, total, count, reckon, figure out, add up, tally, enumerate

**comrade** = companion, friend, partner, ally, colleague, associate, fellow, co-worker, cobber (*Austral. & N.Z. old-fashioned informal*)

**con** (*Informal*) VERB = swindle, trick, cheat, rip off (*slang*), deceive, defraud, dupe, hoodwink

● NOUN = swindle, trick, fraud, deception, scam (*slang*), sting (*informal*)

**conceal** 1 = hide, bury, cover, screen, disguise, obscure, camouflage ≠ reveal 2= keep secret, hide, disguise, mask, suppress, veil ≠ show

**concede** 1= admit, allow, accept, acknowledge, own, grant, confess ≠ deny 2= give up, yield, hand over, surrender, relinquish, cede ≠ conquer

**conceive** 1= imagine, envisage, comprehend, visualize, think, believe, suppose, fancy 2= think up, create, design, devise, formulate, contrive 3= become pregnant, get pregnant, become impregnated

**concentrate** 1= focus your attention on, focus on, pay attention to, be engrossed in, put your mind to, keep your mind on, apply yourself to, give your mind to ≠ pay no attention to 2= focus, centre, converge, bring to bear 3= gather, collect, cluster, accumulate, congregate ≠ scatter

**concentrated** 1= condensed, rich, undiluted, reduced, evaporated, thickened, boiled down 2= intense, hard, deep, intensive, all-out (*informal*)

**concentration** 1= attention, application, absorption, single-mindedness, intentness ≠ inattention 2= focusing, centring, consolidation, convergence, bringing to bear, intensification, centralization 3= convergence, collection, mass, cluster, accumulation, aggregation ≠ scattering

**concept** = idea, view, image, theory, notion, conception, hypothesis, abstraction

**conception** 1= idea, plan, design, image, concept, notion 2= impregnation, insemination, fertilization, germination

**concern**NOUN 1= anxiety, fear, worry, distress, unease, apprehension, misgiving, disquiet 2= worry, care, anxiety 3= affair, issue, matter, consideration 4= care, interest, attentiveness 5= business, job, affair, responsibility, task 6= company, business, firm, organization, corporation, enterprise, establishment 7= importance, interest, bearing, relevance

● VERB 1= worry, trouble, bother, disturb, distress, disquiet, perturb, make anxious 2= be about, cover, deal with, go into, relate to, have to do with 3= be relevant to, involve, affect, regard, apply to, bear on, have something to do with, pertain to

**concerned** 1= worried, troubled, upset, bothered, disturbed, anxious, distressed, uneasy ≠ indifferent 2= involved, interested, active, mixed up, implicated, privy to

**concerning**= regarding, about, re, touching, respecting, relating to, on the subject of, with reference to

**concession** 1 = <u>compromise</u>, agreement, settlement, accommodation, adjustment, trade-off, give-and-take 2 = <u>privilege</u>, right, permit, licence, entitlement, indulgence, prerogative 3 = <u>reduction</u>, saving, grant, discount, allowance 4 = <u>surrender</u>, yielding, conceding, renunciation, relinquishment

**conclude** 1 = <u>decide</u>, judge, assume, gather, work out, infer, deduce, surmise 2 = <u>come to an end</u>, end, close, finish, wind up ≠ begin 3 = <u>bring to an end</u>, end, close, finish, complete, wind up, terminate, round off ≠ begin 4 = <u>accomplish</u>, effect, bring about, carry out, pull off

**conclusion** 1 = <u>decision</u>, opinion, conviction, verdict, judgment, deduction, inference 2 = <u>end</u>, ending, close, finish, completion, finale, termination, bitter end 3 = <u>outcome</u>, result, upshot, consequence, culmination, end result

**concrete** 1 = <u>specific</u>, precise, explicit, definite, clear-cut, unequivocal ≠ vague 2 = <u>real</u>, material, actual, substantial, sensible, tangible, factual ≠ abstract

**condemn** 1 = <u>denounce</u>, damn, criticize, disapprove, censure, reprove, upbraid, blame ≠ approve 2 = <u>sentence</u>, convict, damn, doom, pass sentence on ≠ acquit

**condemnation** = <u>denunciation</u>, blame, censure, disapproval, reproach, stricture, reproof

**condition** NOUN 1 = <u>state</u>, order, shape, nick (*Brit. informal*), trim 2 = <u>situation</u>, state, position, status, circumstances 3 = <u>requirement</u>, terms, rider, restriction, qualification, limitation, prerequisite, proviso 4 = <u>health</u>, shape, fitness, trim, form, kilter, state of health, fettle 5 = <u>ailment</u>, problem, complaint, weakness, malady, infirmity ● PLURAL NOUN = <u>circumstances</u>, situation, environment, surroundings, way of life, milieu ● VERB = <u>train</u>, teach, adapt, accustom

**conditional** = <u>dependent</u>, limited, qualified, subject to, contingent, provisional, with reservations ≠ unconditional

**condone** = <u>overlook</u>, excuse, forgive, pardon, turn a blind eye to, look the other way, make allowance for, let pass ≠ condemn

**conduct** VERB 1 = <u>carry out</u>, run, control, manage, direct, handle, organize, administer

2= accompany, lead, escort, guide, steer, convey, usher

• NOUN 1= management, running, control, handling, administration, direction, organization, guidance

2= behaviour, ways, bearing, attitude, manners, demeanour, deportment

• PHRASES conduct yourself = behave yourself, act, carry yourself, acquit yourself, deport yourself, comport yourself

confer 1= discuss, talk, consult, deliberate, discourse, converse 2= grant, give, present, accord, award, hand out, bestow

conference= meeting, congress, discussion, convention, forum, consultation, seminar, symposium, hui (N.Z.)

confess 1= admit, acknowledge, disclose, confide, own up, come clean (informal), divulge ≠ cover up 2= declare, allow, reveal, confirm, concede, assert, affirm, profess

confession= admission, revelation, disclosure, acknowledgment, exposure, unbosoming

confidant or confidante = close friend, familiar, intimate, crony, alter ego, bosom friend

confide= tell, admit, reveal, confess, whisper, disclose, impart, divulge

confidenceNOUN 1= trust, belief, faith, dependence, reliance, credence ≠ distrust 2= self-assurance, courage, assurance, aplomb, boldness, self-possession, nerve ≠ shyness 3= secret

• PHRASES in confidence= in secrecy, privately, confidentially, between you and me (and the gatepost), (just) between ourselves

confident 1= certain, sure, convinced, positive, secure, satisfied, counting on ≠ unsure 2= self-assured, positive, assured, bold, self-confident, self-reliant, sure of yourself ≠ insecure

confidential 1= secret, private, intimate, classified, privy, off the record, hush-hush (informal) 2= secretive, low, soft, hushed

confineVERB 1= imprison, enclose, shut up, intern, incarcerate, hem in, keep, cage 2= restrict, limit

• PLURAL NOUN = limits, bounds, boundaries, compass, precincts, circumference, edge

confirm 1= prove, support, establish, back up, verify, validate, bear out, substantiate 2= ratify, establish, sanction, endorse, authorize 3= strengthen, establish, fix, secure, reinforce, fortify

confirmation 1= proof,

evidence, testimony, verification, ratification, validation, corroboration, authentication ≠ repudiation 2 = affirmation, approval, acceptance, endorsement, ratification, assent, agreement ≠ disapproval

**confirmed** = long-established, seasoned, chronic, hardened, habitual, ingrained, inveterate, dyed-in-the-wool

**confiscate** = seize, appropriate, impound, commandeer, sequester ≠ give back

**conflict** NOUN 1 = dispute, difference, opposition, hostility, disagreement, friction, strife, fighting ≠ agreement
2 = struggle, battle, clash, strife
3 = battle, war, fight, clash, contest, encounter, combat, strife ≠ peace
● VERB = be incompatible, clash, differ, disagree, collide, be at variance ≠ agree

**conflicting** = incompatible, opposing, clashing, contrary, contradictory, inconsistent, paradoxical, discordant ≠ agreeing

**conform** 1 = fit in, follow, adjust, adapt, comply, obey, fall in with, toe the line 2 = fulfil, meet, match, suit, satisfy, agree with, obey, abide by

**confound** = bewilder, baffle, confuse, astound, perplex,

mystify, flummox, dumbfound

**confront** 1 = tackle, deal with, cope with, meet head-on
2 = trouble, face, perturb, bedevil
3 = challenge, face, oppose, tackle, encounter, defy, stand up to, accost ≠ evade

**confrontation** = conflict, fight, contest, set-to (*informal*), encounter, showdown (*informal*), head-to-head

**confuse** 1 = mix up with, take for, muddle with 2 = bewilder, puzzle, baffle, perplex, mystify, fluster, faze, flummox
3 = obscure, cloud, make more difficult

**confused** 1 = bewildered, puzzled, baffled, at sea, muddled, perplexed, taken aback, disorientated ≠ enlightened
2 = disorderly, disordered, chaotic, mixed up, jumbled, untidy, in disarray, topsy-turvy ≠ tidy

**confusing** = bewildering, puzzling, misleading, unclear, baffling, contradictory, perplexing ≠ clear

**confusion** 1 = bewilderment, doubt, uncertainty ≠ enlightenment 2 = disorder, chaos, turmoil, upheaval, muddle, shambles, commotion ≠ order

**congestion** = overcrowding, crowding, jam, clogging, bottleneck

**congratulate**= compliment, pat on the back, wish joy to

**congratulations** PLURAL NOUN = good wishes, greetings, compliments, best wishes, felicitations

● INTERJECTION = good wishes, greetings, compliments, best wishes, felicitations

**congregation**= parishioners, brethren, crowd, assembly, flock, fellowship, multitude, throng

**congress** 1= meeting, council, conference, assembly, convention, conclave, hui (N.Z.), runanga (N.Z.) 2= legislature, council, parliament, House of Representatives (N.Z.)

**conjure** VERB = produce, generate, bring about, give rise to, make, create, effect, produce as if by magic

● PHRASES **conjure something up**= bring to mind, recall, evoke, recreate, recollect, produce as if by magic

**connect** 1= link, join, couple, attach, fasten, affix, unite ≠ separate 2= associate, join, link, identify, lump together

**connected**= linked, united, joined, coupled, related, allied, associated, combined

**connection** 1= association, relationship, link, bond, relevance, tie-in 2= communication, alliance, attachment, liaison, affinity, union 3= link, coupling, junction, fastening, tie 4= contact, friend, ally, associate, acquaintance

**conquer** 1= seize, obtain, acquire, occupy, overrun, annex, win 2= defeat, overcome, overthrow, beat, master, crush, overpower, quell ≠ lose to 3= overcome, beat, defeat, master, overpower

**conquest** 1= takeover, coup, invasion, occupation, annexation, subjugation 2= defeat, victory, triumph, overthrow, rout, mastery

**conscience** 1= principles, scruples, moral sense, sense of right and wrong, still small voice 2= guilt, shame, regret, remorse, contrition, self-reproach

**conscious** 1 often with of = aware of, alert to, responsive to, sensible of ≠ unaware 2= deliberate, knowing, studied, calculated, self-conscious, intentional, wilful, premeditated ≠ unintentional 3= awake, wide-awake, sentient, alive ≠ asleep

**consciousness**= awareness, understanding, knowledge, recognition, sensibility, realization, apprehension

**consecutive**= successive, running, succeeding, in turn, uninterrupted, sequential, in sequence

**consensus**= agreement,

general agreement, unanimity, common consent, unity, harmony, assent, concord, kotahitanga (*N.Z.*)

> ### Word Power
>
> **consensus** – The original meaning of the word *consensus* is *a collective opinion*. Because the concept of 'opinion' is contained within this word, a few people argue that the phrase *a consensus of opinion* is incorrect and should be avoided. However, this common use of the word is unlikely to jar with the majority of speakers.

**consent** NOUN = <u>agreement</u>, sanction, approval, go-ahead (*informal*), permission, compliance, assent, acquiescence ≠ refusal

● VERB = <u>agree</u>, approve, permit, concur, assent, acquiesce ≠ refuse

**consequence** 1 = <u>result</u>, effect, outcome, repercussion, issue, sequel, end result, upshot 2 = <u>importance</u>, concern, moment, value, account, weight, import, significance

**consequently** = <u>as a result</u>, thus, therefore, hence, subsequently, accordingly, for that reason, thence

**conservation** 1 = <u>preservation</u>, saving, protection, maintenance, safeguarding, upkeep, guardianship, safekeeping 2 = <u>economy</u>, saving, thrift, husbandry

**conservative** ADJECTIVE = <u>traditional</u>, conventional, cautious, sober, reactionary, die-hard, hidebound ≠ radical

● NOUN = <u>traditionalist</u>, reactionary, die-hard, stick-in-the-mud (*informal*) ≠ radical

**Conservative** ADJECTIVE = <u>Tory</u>, Republican (*U.S.*), right-wing

● NOUN = <u>Tory</u>, Republican (*U.S.*), right-winger

**conserve** 1 = <u>save</u>, husband, take care of, hoard, store up, use sparingly ≠ waste 2 = <u>protect</u>, keep, save, preserve

**consider** 1 = <u>think</u>, see, believe, rate, judge, suppose, deem, view as 2 = <u>think about</u>, reflect on, weigh, contemplate, deliberate, ponder, meditate, ruminate 3 = <u>bear in mind</u>, remember, respect, think about, take into account, reckon with, take into consideration, make allowance for

**considerable** = <u>large</u>, goodly, great, marked, substantial, noticeable, plentiful, appreciable ≠ small

**considerably** = <u>greatly</u>, very much, significantly, remarkably, substantially, markedly, noticeably, appreciably

**consideration** 1 = <u>thought</u>,

review, analysis, examination, reflection, scrutiny, deliberation 2 = <u>thoughtfulness</u>, concern, respect, kindness, tact, considerateness 3 = <u>factor</u>, point, issue, concern, element, aspect 4 = <u>payment</u>, fee, reward, remuneration, recompense, tip

**considering** = <u>taking into account</u>, in the light of, bearing in mind, in view of, keeping in mind, taking into consideration

**consist** VERB

● PHRASES **consist in something** = <u>lie in</u>, involve, reside in, be expressed by, subsist in, be found *or* contained in

♦ **consist of something** = <u>be made up of</u>, include, contain, incorporate, amount to, comprise, be composed of

**consistency** 1 = <u>agreement</u>, regularity, uniformity, constancy, steadiness, steadfastness, evenness 2 = <u>texture</u>, density, thickness, firmness, viscosity, compactness

**consistent** 1 = <u>steady</u>, even, regular, stable, constant, persistent, dependable, unchanging ≠ erratic 2 = <u>compatible</u>, agreeing, in keeping, harmonious, in harmony, consonant, in accord, congruous ≠ incompatible 3 = <u>coherent</u>, logical, compatible, harmonious, consonant

≠ contradictory

**consolation** = <u>comfort</u>, help, support, relief, cheer, encouragement, solace, succour

**console** = <u>comfort</u>, cheer, soothe, support, encourage, calm, succour, express sympathy for ≠ distress

**consolidate** 1 = <u>strengthen</u>, secure, reinforce, fortify, stabilize 2 = <u>combine</u>, unite, join, merge, unify, amalgamate, federate

**conspicuous** = <u>obvious</u>, clear, patent, evident, noticeable, blatant, salient ≠ inconspicuous

**conspiracy** = <u>plot</u>, scheme, intrigue, collusion, machination

**conspire** 1 = <u>plot</u>, scheme, intrigue, manoeuvre, contrive, machinate, plan 2 = <u>work together</u>, combine, contribute, cooperate, concur, tend

**constant** 1 = <u>continuous</u>, sustained, perpetual, interminable, unrelenting, incessant, ceaseless, nonstop ≠ occasional 2 = <u>unchanging</u>, even, fixed, permanent, stable, steady, uniform, invariable ≠ changing 3 = <u>faithful</u>, true, devoted, loyal, stalwart, staunch, trustworthy, trusty ≠ undependable

**constantly** = <u>continuously</u>, always, all the time, invariably, continually, endlessly, perpetually, incessantly

≠ occasionally

**constituent** NOUN 1 = voter, elector, member of the electorate 2 = component, element, ingredient, part, unit, factor
• ADJECTIVE = component, basic, essential, integral, elemental

**constitute** 1 = represent, be, consist of, embody, exemplify, be equivalent to 2 = make up, form, compose, comprise

**constitution** 1 = state of health, build, body, frame, physique, physical condition 2 = structure, form, nature, make-up, composition, character, disposition

**constitutional** = legitimate, official, legal, chartered, statutory, vested

**constrain** 1 = restrict, confine, curb, restrain, constrict, straiten, check 2 = force, bind, compel, oblige, necessitate, coerce, impel, pressurize

**constraint** 1 = restriction, limitation, curb, rein, deterrent, hindrance, check 2 = force, pressure, necessity, restraint, compulsion, coercion

**construct** 1 = build, make, form, create, fashion, shape, manufacture, assemble ≠ demolish 2 = create, make, form, compose, put together

**construction** 1 = building, creation, composition 2 (Formal)

= interpretation, reading, explanation, rendering, inference

**constructive** = helpful, positive, useful, practical, valuable, productive ≠ unproductive

**consult** 1 = ask, refer to, turn to, take counsel, pick (someone's) brains, question 2 = confer, talk, compare notes 3 = refer to, check in, look in

**consultant** = specialist, adviser, counsellor, authority

**consultation** 1 = discussion, talk, council, conference, dialogue 2 = meeting, interview, session, appointment, examination, deliberation, hearing

**consume** 1 = eat, swallow, devour, put away, gobble (up), eat up 2 = use up, spend, waste, absorb, exhaust, squander, dissipate, expend 3 = destroy, devastate, demolish, ravage, annihilate, lay waste 4 often passive = obsess, dominate, absorb, preoccupy, eat up, monopolize, engross

**consumer** = buyer, customer, user, shopper, purchaser

**consumption** 1 = using up, use, loss, waste, expenditure, exhaustion, depletion, dissipation 2 (Old-fashioned) = tuberculosis, T.B.

**contact** NOUN 1 = communication, link,

association, connection, correspondence 2 = <u>touch</u>, contiguity 3 = <u>connection</u>, colleague, associate, liaison, acquaintance, confederate
- **VERB** = <u>get</u> *or* be in touch with, call, reach, approach, write to, speak to, communicate with

**contain** 1 = <u>hold</u>, incorporate, accommodate, enclose, have capacity for 2 = <u>include</u>, consist of, embrace, comprise, embody, comprehend 3 = <u>restrain</u>, control, hold in, curb, suppress, hold back, stifle, repress

**container** = <u>holder</u>, vessel, repository, receptacle

**contaminate** = <u>pollute</u>, infect, stain, corrupt, taint, defile, adulterate, befoul ≠ purify

**contamination** = <u>pollution</u>, infection, corruption, poisoning, taint, impurity, contagion, defilement

**contemplate** 1 = <u>consider</u>, plan, think of, intend, envisage, foresee 2 = <u>think about</u>, consider, ponder, reflect upon, ruminate (upon), muse over, deliberate over 3 = <u>look at</u>, examine, inspect, gaze at, eye up, view, study, regard

**contemporary** ADJECTIVE 1 = <u>modern</u>, recent, current, up-to-date, present-day, à la mode, newfangled, present ≠ old-fashioned 2 = <u>coexisting</u>, concurrent, contemporaneous
- **NOUN** = <u>peer</u>, fellow, equal

> ### Word Power
>
> **contemporary** – Since *contemporary* can mean either 'of the same period' or 'of the present period', it is best to avoid it where ambiguity might arise, as in *a production of Othello in contemporary dress*. A synonym such as *modern* or *present-day* would clarify if the first sense were being used, while a specific term, such as *Elizabethan*, would be appropriate for the second sense.

**contempt** = <u>scorn</u>, disdain, mockery, derision, disrespect, disregard ≠ respect

**contend** 1 = <u>argue</u>, hold, maintain, allege, assert, affirm 2 = <u>compete</u>, fight, struggle, clash, contest, strive, vie, jostle

**content**[1] NOUN 1 = <u>subject matter</u>, material, theme, substance, essence, gist 2 = <u>amount</u>, measure, size, load, volume, capacity
- **PLURAL NOUN** = <u>constituents</u>, elements, load, ingredients

**content**[2] ADJECTIVE = <u>satisfied</u>, happy, pleased, contented, comfortable, fulfilled, at ease, gratified
- **NOUN** = <u>satisfaction</u>, ease,

pleasure, comfort, peace of mind, gratification, contentment

● PHRASES **content yourself with something** = satisfy yourself with, be happy with, be satisfied with, be content with

**contented** = satisfied, happy, pleased, content, comfortable, glad, thankful, gratified ≠ discontented

**contentious** = argumentative, wrangling, bickering, quarrelsome, querulous, cavilling, disputatious, captious

**contest** NOUN 1 = competition, game, match, trial, tournament 2 = struggle, fight, battle, conflict, dispute, controversy, combat

● VERB 1 = compete in, take part in, fight in, go in for, contend for, vie in 2 = oppose, question, challenge, argue, debate, dispute, object to, call in or into question

**contestant** = competitor, candidate, participant, contender, entrant, player

**context** 1 = circumstances, conditions, situation, ambience 2 = frame of reference, background, framework, relation, connection

**contingency** = possibility, happening, chance, event, incident, accident, emergency, eventuality

**continual** 1 = constant, interminable, incessant, unremitting ≠ erratic 2 = frequent, regular, repeated, recurrent ≠ occasional

**continually** 1 = constantly, always, all the time, forever, incessantly, nonstop, interminably 2 = repeatedly, often, frequently, many times, over and over, persistently

**continuation** 1 = continuing, lasting, carrying on, keeping up, endurance, perpetuation, prolongation 2 = addition, extension, supplement, sequel, resumption, postscript

**continue** 1 = keep on, go on, maintain, sustain, carry on, persist in, persevere, stick at ≠ stop 2 = go on, progress, proceed, carry on, keep going 3 = resume, return to, take up again, proceed, carry on, recommence, pick up where you left off ≠ stop 4 = remain, last, stay, survive, carry on, live on, endure, persist ≠ quit

**continuing** = lasting, sustained, enduring, ongoing, in progress

**continuity** = cohesion, flow, connection, sequence, succession, progression

**continuous** = constant, extended, prolonged, unbroken, uninterrupted, unceasing ≠ occasional

**contract** NOUN = agreement, commitment, arrangement,

settlement, bargain, pact, covenant

● **VERB** 1 = <u>agree</u>, negotiate, pledge, bargain, undertake, come to terms, covenant, make a deal ≠ refuse 2 = <u>constrict</u>, confine, tighten, shorten, compress, condense, shrivel 3 = <u>tighten</u>, narrow, shorten ≠ stretch 4 = <u>lessen</u>, reduce, shrink, diminish, decrease, dwindle ≠ increase 5 = <u>catch</u>, get, develop, acquire, incur, be infected with, go down with, be afflicted with ≠ avoid

**contraction** 1 = <u>tightening</u>, narrowing, shortening, constricting, shrinkage 2 = <u>abbreviation</u>, reduction, shortening, compression

**contradict** 1 = <u>dispute</u>, deny, challenge, belie, fly in the face of, be at variance with 2 = <u>negate</u>, deny, rebut, controvert ≠ confirm

**contradiction** 1 = <u>conflict</u>, inconsistency, contravention, incongruity 2 = <u>negation</u>, opposite, denial

**contradictory** = <u>inconsistent</u>, conflicting, opposed, opposite, contrary, incompatible, paradoxical

**contrary** ADJECTIVE 1 = <u>opposite</u>, different, opposed, clashing, counter, reverse, adverse, contradictory ≠ in agreement 2 = <u>perverse</u>, difficult, awkward,

intractable, obstinate, stroppy (*Brit. slang*), cantankerous, disobliging ≠ cooperative

● NOUN = <u>opposite</u>, reverse, converse, antithesis

**contrast** NOUN = <u>difference</u>, opposition, comparison, distinction, foil, disparity, divergence, dissimilarity

● **VERB** 1 = <u>differentiate</u>, compare, oppose, distinguish, set in opposition 2 = <u>differ</u>, be contrary, be at variance, be dissimilar

**contribute** VERB = <u>give</u>, provide, supply, donate, subscribe, chip in (*informal*), bestow

● PHRASES **contribute to something** = <u>be partly responsible for</u>, lead to, be instrumental in, be conducive to, help

**contribution** = <u>gift</u>, offering, grant, donation, input, subscription, koha (*N.Z.*)

**contributor** = <u>donor</u>, supporter, patron, subscriber, giver

**contrive** 1 = <u>devise</u>, plan, fabricate, create, design, scheme, manufacture, plot 2 = <u>manage</u>, succeed, arrange, manoeuvre

**contrived** = <u>forced</u>, planned, laboured, strained, artificial, elaborate, unnatural, overdone ≠ natural

**control** NOUN 1 = <u>power</u>, authority, management, command, guidance, supervision, supremacy, charge 2 = <u>restraint</u>, check, regulation, brake, limitation, curb 3 = <u>self-discipline</u>, self-restraint, restraint, self-command 4 = <u>switch</u>, instrument, button, dial, lever, knob

● PLURAL NOUN = <u>instruments</u>, dash, dials, console, dashboard, control panel

● VERB 1 = <u>have power over</u>, manage, direct, handle, command, govern, administer, supervise 2 = <u>limit</u>, restrict, curb 3 = <u>restrain</u>, limit, check, contain, curb, hold back, subdue, repress

**controversial** = <u>disputed</u>, contentious, at issue, debatable, under discussion, open to question, disputable

**controversy** = <u>argument</u>, debate, row, dispute, quarrel, squabble, wrangling, altercation

**convene** 1 = <u>call</u>, gather, assemble, summon, bring together, convoke 2 = <u>meet</u>, gather, assemble, come together, congregate

**convenience** 1 = <u>benefit</u>, good, advantage 2 = <u>suitability</u>, fitness, appropriateness 3 = <u>usefulness</u>, utility ≠ uselessness 4 = <u>accessibility</u>, availability, nearness 5 = <u>appliance</u>, facility, comfort, amenity, labour-saving device, help

**convenient** 1 = <u>suitable</u>, fit, handy, satisfactory 2 = <u>useful</u>,

practical, handy, serviceable, labour-saving ≠ useless 3 = <u>nearby</u>, available, accessible, handy, at hand, within reach, close at hand, just round the corner ≠ inaccessible 4 = <u>appropriate</u>, timely, suitable, helpful

**convention** 1 = <u>custom</u>, practice, tradition, code, usage, protocol, etiquette, propriety, kawa (N.Z.), tikanga (N.Z.) 2 = <u>agreement</u>, contract, treaty, bargain, pact, protocol 3 = <u>assembly</u>, meeting, council, conference, congress, convocation, hui (N.Z.), runanga (N.Z.)

**conventional** 1 = <u>proper</u>, conservative, respectable, genteel, conformist 2 = <u>ordinary</u>, standard, normal, regular, usual 3 = <u>traditional</u>, accepted, orthodox, customary 4 = <u>unoriginal</u>, routine, stereotyped, banal, prosaic, run-of-the-mill, hackneyed ≠ unconventional

**converge** VERB = <u>come together</u>, meet, join, combine, gather, merge, coincide, intersect

● PHRASES **converge on something** = <u>close in on</u>, arrive at, move towards, home in on, come together at

**conversation** = <u>talk</u>, discussion, dialogue, tête-à-tête, conference, chat, gossip, discourse, korero (*N.Z.*)

**Related Words**
*adjective*: colloquial

**conversion** 1 = change, transformation, metamorphosis 2 = adaptation, reconstruction, modification, alteration, remodelling, reorganization

**convert VERB** 1 = change, turn, transform, alter, transpose 2 = adapt, modify, remodel, reorganize, customize, restyle 3 = reform, convince, proselytize
● NOUN = neophyte, disciple, proselyte

**convey** 1 = communicate, impart, reveal, relate, disclose, make known, tell 2 = carry, transport, move, bring, bear, conduct, fetch

**convict VERB** = find guilty, sentence, condemn, imprison, pronounce guilty
● NOUN = prisoner, criminal, lag (*slang*), felon, jailbird

**conviction** 1 = belief, view, opinion, principle, faith, persuasion, creed, tenet, kaupapa (*N.Z.*) 2 = certainty, confidence, assurance, firmness, certitude

**convince** 1 = assure, persuade, satisfy, reassure 2 = persuade, induce, coax, talk into, prevail upon, bring round to the idea of

> **Word Power**
>
> **convince** – The use of *convince* to talk about persuading someone to do something is considered by many British speakers to be wrong or unacceptable. It would be preferable to use an alternative such as *persuade* or *talk into*.

**convincing** = persuasive, credible, conclusive, telling, powerful, impressive, plausible, cogent ≠ unconvincing

**cool ADJECTIVE** 1 = cold, chilled, refreshing, chilly, nippy ≠ warm 2 = calm, collected, relaxed, composed, sedate, self-controlled, unruffled, unemotional ≠ agitated 3 = unfriendly, distant, indifferent, aloof, lukewarm, offhand, unenthusiastic, unwelcoming ≠ friendly 4 = unenthusiastic, indifferent, lukewarm, unwelcoming
● VERB 1 = lose heat, cool off ≠ warm (up) 2 = make cool, freeze, chill, refrigerate, cool off ≠ warm (up)
● NOUN = coldness, chill, coolness 2 (*Slang*) = calmness, control, temper, composure, self-control, poise, self-discipline, self-possession

**cooperate** = work together, collaborate, coordinate, join forces, conspire, pull together, pool resources, combine your efforts ≠ conflict

**cooperation** = teamwork, unity, collaboration, give-and-take, combined effort, esprit de corps, kotahitanga (*N.Z.*) ≠ opposition

**cooperative** 1 = shared, joint, combined, collective, collaborative 2 = helpful, obliging, accommodating, supportive, responsive, onside (*informal*)

**cope VERB** = manage, get by (*informal*), struggle through, survive, carry on, make the grade, hold your own

● **PHRASES cope with something** = deal with, handle, struggle with, grapple with, wrestle with, contend with, weather

**copy NOUN** = reproduction, duplicate, replica, imitation, forgery, counterfeit, likeness, facsimile ≠ original

● **VERB** 1 = reproduce, replicate, duplicate, transcribe, counterfeit ≠ create 2 = imitate, act like, emulate, behave like, follow, repeat, mirror, ape

**cord** = rope, line, string, twine

**cordon NOUN** = chain, line, ring, barrier, picket line

● **PHRASES cordon something off** = surround, isolate, close off, fence off, separate, enclose, picket, encircle

**core** 1 = centre 2 = heart, essence, nucleus, kernel, crux, gist, nub, pith

**corner NOUN** 1 = angle, joint, crook 2 = bend, curve 3 = space, hideaway, nook, hide-out

● **VERB** 1 = trap, catch, run to earth 2 (*usually with market as object*) = monopolize, take over, dominate, control, hog (*slang*), engross

**corporation** 1 = business, company, concern, firm, society, association, organization, enterprise 2 = town council, council, municipal authorities, civic authorities

**corps** = team, unit, regiment, detachment, company, band, division, troop

**corpse** = body, remains, carcass, cadaver, stiff (*slang*)

**correct ADJECTIVE** 1 = accurate, right, true, exact, precise, flawless, faultless, O.K. or okay (*informal*) ≠ inaccurate 2 = right, standard, appropriate, acceptable, proper, precise 3 = proper, seemly, standard, fitting, kosher (*informal*) ≠ inappropriate

● **VERB** 1 = rectify, remedy, redress, right, reform, cure, adjust, amend ≠ spoil 2 = rebuke, discipline, reprimand, chide, admonish, chastise, chasten, reprove ≠ praise

**correction** 1 = rectification, improvement, amendment, adjustment, modification, alteration, emendation 2 = punishment, discipline, reformation, admonition, chastisement, reproof, castigation

**correctly** = rightly, right, perfectly, properly, precisely, accurately

**correctness** 1 = truth, accuracy, precision, exactitude, exactness, faultlessness 2 = decorum, propriety, good manners, civility, good breeding

**correspond** 1 = be consistent, match, agree, accord, fit, square, tally, conform ≠ differ 2 = communicate, write, keep in touch, exchange letters

**correspondence** 1 = communication, writing, contact 2 = letters, post, mail 3 = relation, match, agreement, comparison, harmony, coincidence, similarity, correlation

**correspondent** 1 = reporter, journalist, contributor, hack 2 = letter writer, pen friend or pen pal

**corresponding** = equivalent, matching, similar, related, complementary, reciprocal, analogous

**corridor** = passage, alley, aisle, hallway, passageway

**corrupt** ADJECTIVE 1 = dishonest, bent (slang), crooked (informal), fraudulent, unscrupulous, venal, unprincipled ≠ honest 2 = depraved, vicious, degenerate, debased, profligate, dissolute 3 = distorted, doctored, altered, falsified

● VERB 1 = bribe, fix (informal), buy off, suborn, grease (someone's) palm (slang) 2 = deprave, pervert, subvert, debauch ≠ reform 3 = distort, doctor, tamper with

**corruption** 1 = dishonesty, fraud, bribery, extortion, venality, shady dealings (informal) 2 = depravity, vice, evil, perversion, decadence, wickedness, immorality 3 = distortion, doctoring, falsification

**cosmetic** = superficial, surface, nonessential

**cosmic** 1 = extraterrestrial, stellar 2 = universal, general, overarching

**cosmopolitan** = sophisticated, cultured, refined, cultivated, urbane, well-travelled, worldly-wise ≠ unsophisticated

**cost** NOUN 1 = price, worth, expense, charge, damage (informal), amount, payment, outlay 2 = loss, suffering, damage, injury, penalty, hurt, expense, harm

● **PLURAL NOUN** = <u>expenses</u>, spending, expenditure, overheads, outgoings, outlay, budget

● **VERB** 1 = <u>sell at</u>, come to, set (someone) back (*informal*), be priced at, command a price of 2 = <u>lose</u>, deprive of, cheat of

**costly** 1 = <u>expensive</u>, dear, stiff, steep (*informal*), highly-priced, exorbitant, extortionate ≠ inexpensive 2 = <u>damaging</u>, disastrous, harmful, catastrophic, loss-making, ruinous, deleterious

**costume** = <u>outfit</u>, dress, clothing, uniform, ensemble, livery, apparel, attire

**cosy** 1 = <u>comfortable</u>, homely, warm, intimate, snug, comfy (*informal*), sheltered 2 = <u>snug</u>, warm, comfortable, sheltered, comfy (*informal*), tucked up 3 = <u>intimate</u>, friendly, informal

**cottage** = <u>cabin</u>, lodge, hut, shack, chalet, whare (*N.Z.*)

**cough** **VERB** = <u>clear your throat</u>, bark, hack

● **NOUN** = <u>frog or tickle in your throat</u>, bark, hack

**council** 1 = <u>committee</u>, governing body, board 2 = <u>governing body</u>, parliament, congress, cabinet, panel, assembly, convention, conference, runanga (*N.Z.*)

**counsel** **NOUN** 1 = <u>advice</u>, information, warning, direction, suggestion, recommendation, guidance 2 = <u>legal adviser</u>, lawyer, attorney, solicitor, advocate, barrister

● **VERB** = <u>advise</u>, recommend, advocate, warn, urge, instruct, exhort

**count** **VERB** 1 *often with up* = <u>add (up)</u>, total, reckon (up), tot up, calculate, compute, tally, number 2 = <u>matter</u>, be important, carry weight, tell, rate, weigh, signify 3 = <u>consider</u>, judge, regard, deem, think of, rate, look upon 4 = <u>include</u>, number among, take into account or consideration

● **NOUN** = <u>calculation</u>, poll, reckoning, sum, tally, numbering, computation, enumeration

● **PHRASES** **count on** or **upon something** or **someone** = <u>depend on</u>, trust, rely on, bank on, take for granted, lean on, reckon on, take on trust

**counter** **VERB** 1 = <u>oppose</u>, meet, block, resist, parry, deflect, repel, rebuff 2 = <u>retaliate</u>, answer, reply, respond, retort, hit back, rejoin, strike back ≠ yield

● **ADVERB** = <u>opposite to</u>, against, versus, conversely, in defiance of, at variance with, contrariwise ≠ in accordance with

**counterpart** = <u>opposite number</u>, equal, twin, equivalent, match, fellow, mate

**countless** = innumerable, legion, infinite, myriad, untold, limitless, incalculable, immeasurable ≠ limited

**country** 1 = nation, state, land, commonwealth, kingdom, realm, people 2 = people, community, nation, society, citizens, inhabitants, populace, public 3 = countryside, provinces, sticks (*informal*), farmland, outback (*Austral. & N.Z.*), green belt, backwoods, bush (*N.Z. & S. African*) ≠ town 4 = territory, land, region, terrain

➤ **WORD POWER SUPPLEMENT countries**

**countryside** = country, rural areas, outback (*Austral. & N.Z.*), green belt, sticks (*informal*)

**county** = province, district, shire

➤ **WORD POWER SUPPLEMENT counties**

**coup** = masterstroke, feat, stunt, action, exploit, manoeuvre, deed, accomplishment

**couple** NOUN = pair, two, brace, duo, twosome

● PHRASES **couple something to something** = link to, connect to, pair with, unite with, join to, hitch to, yoke to

**coupon** = slip, ticket, certificate, token, voucher, card

**courage** = bravery, nerve, resolution, daring, pluck, heroism,

mettle, gallantry ≠ cowardice

**courageous** = brave, daring, bold, gritty, fearless, gallant, intrepid, valiant ≠ cowardly

**courier** 1 = messenger, runner, carrier, bearer, envoy 2 = guide, representative, escort, conductor

**course** NOUN 1 = route, way, line, road, track, direction, path, passage 2 = procedure, plan, policy, programme, method, conduct, behaviour, manner 3 = progression, order, unfolding, development, movement, progress, flow, sequence 4 = classes, programme, schedule, lectures, curriculum 5 = racecourse, circuit 6 = period, time, duration, term, passing

● VERB 1 = run, flow, stream, gush, race, speed, surge 2 = hunt, follow, chase, pursue

● PHRASES **of course** = naturally, certainly, obviously, definitely, undoubtedly, needless to say, without a doubt, indubitably

**court** NOUN 1 = law court, bar, bench, tribunal 2 = palace, hall, castle, manor 3 = royal household, train, suite, attendants, entourage, retinue, cortege

● VERB 1 = cultivate, seek, flatter, solicit, pander to, curry favour with, fawn upon 2 = invite, seek, attract, prompt, provoke, bring about, incite 3 = woo, go (out) with, date, take out, run after, walk out with, set your cap at

**courtesy** 1 = <u>politeness</u>, good manners, civility, gallantry, graciousness, affability, urbanity 2 = <u>favour</u>, kindness, indulgence

**courtyard** = <u>yard</u>, square, piazza, quadrangle, plaza, enclosure, cloister, quad (*informal*)

**cove** = <u>bay</u>, sound, inlet, anchorage

**covenant** = <u>promise</u>, contract, agreement, commitment, arrangement, pledge, pact

**cover** VERB 1 = <u>conceal</u>, hide, mask, disguise, obscure, veil, cloak, shroud ≠ <u>reveal</u> 2 = <u>clothe</u>, dress, wrap, envelop ≠ <u>uncover</u> 3 = <u>overlay</u>, blanket 4 = <u>coat</u>, cake, plaster, smear, envelop, spread, encase, daub 5 = <u>submerge</u>, flood, engulf, overrun, wash over 6 = <u>travel over</u>, cross, traverse, pass through or over 7 = <u>protect</u>, guard, defend, shield 8 = <u>consider</u>, deal with, investigate, describe, tell of 9 = <u>report on</u>, write about, commentate on, relate, tell of, narrate, write up 10 = <u>pay for</u>, fund, provide for, offset, be enough for

• NOUN 1 = <u>protection</u>, shelter, shield, defence, guard, camouflage, concealment 2 = <u>insurance</u>, protection, compensation, indemnity,

reimbursement 3 = <u>covering</u>, case, top, coating, envelope, lid, canopy, wrapper 4 = <u>bedclothes</u>, bedding, sheets, blankets, quilt, duvet, eiderdown 5 = <u>jacket</u>, case, wrapper 6 = <u>disguise</u>, front, screen, mask, veil, façade, pretext, smoke screen

**covering** NOUN = <u>cover</u>, coating, casing, wrapping, layer, blanket
• ADJECTIVE = <u>explanatory</u>, accompanying, introductory, descriptive

**covet** = <u>long for</u>, desire, envy, crave, aspire to, yearn for, lust after, set your heart on

**coward** = <u>wimp</u>, chicken (*slang*), scaredy-cat (*informal*), yellow-belly (*slang*)

**cowardly** = <u>faint-hearted</u>, scared, spineless, soft, yellow (*informal*), weak, chicken (*slang*), fearful, sookie (*N.Z.*) ≠ <u>brave</u>

**cowboy** = <u>cowhand</u>, drover, rancher, stockman, cattleman, herdsman, gaucho (*S. American*)

**crack** VERB 1 = <u>break</u>, split, burst, snap, fracture, splinter 2 = <u>snap</u>, ring, crash, burst, explode, pop, detonate 3 (*Informal*) = <u>hit</u>, clip (*informal*), slap, smack, clout (*informal*), cuff, whack 4 = <u>break</u>, cleave 5 = <u>solve</u>, work out, resolve, clear up, fathom, decipher, suss (out) (*slang*), get to the bottom of 6 = <u>break down</u>, collapse, yield, give in, give way, succumb, lose control, be overcome

● NOUN 1 = break, chink, gap, fracture, rift, cleft, crevice, fissure 2 = split, break, fracture 3 = snap, pop, crash, burst, explosion, clap, report 4 (*Informal*) = blow, slap, smack, clout (*informal*), cuff, whack, clip (*informal*) 5 (*Informal*) = joke, dig, gag (*informal*), quip, jibe, wisecrack, witticism, funny remark

● ADJECTIVE (*Slang*) = first-class, choice, excellent, ace, elite, superior, world-class, first-rate

**crackdown** = clampdown, crushing, repression, suppression

**cracked** = broken, damaged, split, chipped, flawed, faulty, defective, imperfect

**cradle** NOUN 1 = crib, cot, Moses basket, bassinet 2 = birthplace, beginning, source, spring, origin, fount, fountainhead, wellspring

● VERB = hold, support, rock, nurse, nestle

**craft** 1 = vessel, boat, ship, plane, aircraft, spacecraft 2 = occupation, work, business, trade, employment, pursuit, vocation, handicraft 3 = skill, art, ability, technique, know-how (*informal*), expertise, aptitude, artistry

**craftsman** = skilled worker, artisan, master, maker, wright, technician, smith

**cram** 1 = stuff, force, jam, shove, compress 2 = pack, fill, stuff 3 = squeeze, press, pack in 4 = study, revise, swot, bone up (*informal*), mug up (*slang*)

**cramp**[1] = spasm, pain, ache, contraction, pang, stitch, convulsion, twinge

**cramp**[2] = restrict, hamper, inhibit, hinder, handicap, constrain, obstruct, impede

**cramped** = restricted, confined, overcrowded, crowded, packed, uncomfortable, closed in, congested ≠ spacious

**crash** NOUN 1 = collision, accident, smash, wreck, prang (*informal*), bump, pile-up (*informal*) 2 = smash, clash, boom, bang, thunder, racket, din, clatter 3 = collapse, failure, depression, ruin, downfall

● VERB 1 = fall, plunge, topple, lurch, hurtle, overbalance, fall headlong 2 = plunge, hurtle 3 = collapse, fail, go under, be ruined, go bust (*informal*), fold up, go to the wall, go belly up (*informal*)

● PHRASES **crash into** = collide with, hit, bump into, drive into, plough into

**crate** = container, case, box, packing case, tea chest

**crater** = hollow, hole, depression, dip, cavity

**crave** 1 = long for, yearn for,

hanker after, want, desire, hope for, lust after 2 (*Informal*) = **beg**, ask for, seek, petition, pray for, plead for, solicit, implore

**craving** = <u>longing</u>, hope, desire, yen (*informal*), hunger, appetite, yearning, thirst

**crawl** VERB 1 = <u>creep</u>, slither, inch, wriggle, writhe, worm your way, advance slowly ≠ run
● PHRASES **crawl to someone** = <u>grovel</u>, creep, fawn, toady, humble yourself

**craze** = <u>fad</u>, fashion, trend, rage, enthusiasm, vogue, mania, infatuation

**crazed** = <u>mad</u>, crazy, raving, insane, lunatic, berko (*Austral. slang*), off the air (*Austral. slang*), porangi (*N.Z.*)

**crazy** 1 (*Informal*) = <u>ridiculous</u>, absurd, foolish, ludicrous, senseless, preposterous, idiotic, nonsensical, porangi (*N.Z.*) ≠ sensible 2 = <u>insane</u>, mad, unbalanced, deranged, nuts (*slang*), crazed, demented, off the air (*Austral. slang*), out of your mind, porangi (*N.Z.*) ≠ sane 3 = <u>fanatical</u>, wild (*informal*), mad, devoted, enthusiastic, passionate, infatuated ≠ uninterested

**cream** NOUN 1 = <u>lotion</u>, ointment, oil, essence, cosmetic, paste, emulsion, salve 2 = <u>best</u>, elite, prime, pick, flower, crème de la crème (*French*)

● NOUN or ADJECTIVE = <u>off-white</u>, ivory, yellowish-white
➤ **shades from black to white**

**creamy** 1 = <u>milky</u>, buttery 2 = <u>smooth</u>, soft, velvety, rich

**crease** NOUN 1 = <u>fold</u>, line, ridge, groove, corrugation 2 = <u>wrinkle</u>, line, crow's-foot
● VERB 1 = <u>crumple</u>, rumple, fold, double up, corrugate 2 = <u>wrinkle</u>, crumple, screw up

**create** 1 = <u>cause</u>, lead to, occasion, bring about 2 = <u>make</u>, produce, invent, compose, devise, originate, formulate, spawn ≠ destroy 3 = <u>appoint</u>, make, establish, set up, invest, install, constitute

**creation** 1 = <u>universe</u>, world, nature, cosmos 2 = <u>invention</u>, production, achievement, brainchild (*informal*), concoction, handiwork, pièce de résistance (*French*), magnum opus 3 = <u>making</u>, generation, formation, conception, genesis 4 = <u>setting up</u>, development, production, institution, foundation, establishment, formation, inception

**creative** = <u>imaginative</u>, gifted, artistic, inventive, original, inspired, clever, ingenious

**creativity** = <u>imagination</u>, inspiration, ingenuity, originality, inventiveness, cleverness

**creator** 1= <u>maker</u>, father, author, designer, architect, inventor, originator 2 *usually with cap.* = <u>God</u>, Maker

**creature** 1= <u>living thing</u>, being, animal, beast, brute 2= <u>person</u>, man, woman, individual, soul, human being, mortal

**credentials** 1= <u>qualifications</u>, ability, skill, fitness, attribute, capability, eligibility, aptitude 2= <u>certification</u>, document, reference(s), papers, licence, passport, testimonial, authorization

**credibility** = <u>believability</u>, reliability, plausibility, trustworthiness

**credible** 1= <u>believable</u>, possible, likely, reasonable, probable, plausible, conceivable, imaginable ≠ unbelievable 2= <u>reliable</u>, honest, dependable, trustworthy, sincere, trusty ≠ unreliable

**credit** NOUN 1= <u>praise</u>, honour, recognition, approval, tribute, acclaim, acknowledgment, kudos 2= <u>source of satisfaction</u> *or* pride, asset, honour, feather in your cap 3= <u>prestige</u>, reputation, standing, position, influence, regard, status, esteem 4= <u>belief</u>, trust, confidence, faith, reliance, credence

● VERB = <u>believe</u>, rely on, have faith in, trust, accept

● PHRASES **credit someone with something** = <u>attribute to</u>, assign to, ascribe to, impute to

**creed** = <u>belief</u>, principles, doctrine, dogma, credo, catechism, articles of faith

**creek** 1= <u>inlet</u>, bay, cove, bight, firth *or* frith (*Scot.*) 2 (*U.S., Canad., Austral., & N.Z.*) = <u>stream</u>, brook, tributary, bayou, rivulet, watercourse, runnel

**creep** VERB = <u>sneak</u>, steal, tiptoe, slink, skulk, approach unnoticed

● NOUN (*Slang*) = <u>bootlicker</u> (*informal*), sneak, sycophant, crawler (*slang*), toady

● PHRASES **give someone the creeps** (*Informal*) = <u>disgust</u>, frighten, scare, repel, repulse, make your hair stand on end, make you squirm

**crescent** = <u>meniscus</u>, sickle, new moon

**crest** 1= <u>top</u>, summit, peak, ridge, highest point, pinnacle, apex, crown 2= <u>tuft</u>, crown, comb, plume, mane 3= <u>emblem</u>, badge, symbol, insignia, bearings, device

**crew** 1= <u>(ship's) company</u>, hands, (ship's) complement 2= <u>team</u>, squad, gang, corps, posse 3 (*Informal*) = <u>crowd</u>, set, bunch (*informal*), band, pack, gang, mob, horde

**crime** 1= <u>offence</u>, violation, trespass, felony, misdemeanour, misdeed, transgression, unlawful act 2 = **lawbreaking**, corruption, illegality, vice, misconduct, wrongdoing

**criminal** NOUN = **lawbreaker**, convict, offender, crook (*informal*), villain, culprit, sinner, felon, rorter (*Austral. slang*), skelm (*S. African*)

● ADJECTIVE 1 = **unlawful**, illicit, lawless, wrong, illegal, corrupt, crooked (*informal*), immoral ≠ lawful 2 (*Informal*) = **disgraceful**, ridiculous, foolish, senseless, scandalous, preposterous, deplorable

**cripple** 1 = **disable**, paralyse, lame, maim, incapacitate, weaken, hamstring ≠ **damage**, destroy, ruin, spoil, impair, put paid to, put out of action ≠ help

**crippled** = **disabled**, handicapped, paralysed, lame, incapacitated

**crisis** 1 = **emergency**, plight, predicament, trouble, deep water, meltdown (*informal*), dire straits 2 = **critical point**, climax, height, crunch (*informal*), turning point, culmination, crux, moment of truth

**crisp** 1 = **firm**, crunchy, crispy, crumbly, fresh, brittle, unwilted ≠ soft 2 = **bracing**, fresh, refreshing, brisk, invigorating ≠ warm 3 = **clean**, smart, trim, neat, tidy, spruce, well-groomed, well-pressed

**criterion** = **standard**, test, rule, measure, principle, gauge, yardstick, touchstone

---

### Word Power

**criterion**–The word *criteria* is the plural of *criterion* and it is incorrect to use it as an alternative singular form; *these criteria are not valid* is correct, and so is *this criterion is not valid*, but not *this criteria is not valid*.

---

**critic** 1 = **judge**, authority, expert, analyst, commentator, pundit, reviewer, connoisseur 2 = **fault-finder**, attacker, detractor, knocker (*informal*)

**critical** 1 = **crucial**, decisive, pressing, serious, vital, urgent, all-important, pivotal ≠ unimportant 2 = **grave**, serious, acute, precarious ≠ safe 3 = **disparaging**, disapproving, scathing, derogatory, nit-picking (*informal*), censorious, fault-finding, captious ≠ complimentary 4 = **analytical**, penetrating, discriminating, discerning, perceptive, judicious ≠ undiscriminating

**criticism** 1 = **fault-finding**, censure, disapproval, disparagement, stick (*slang*), flak (*informal*), bad press, character assassination 2 = <u>analysis</u>, assessment, judgment, commentary, evaluation, appreciation, appraisal, critique

**criticize** = <u>find fault with</u>, censure, disapprove of, knock (*informal*), condemn, carp, put down, slate (*informal*) ≠ praise

**crook** NOUN (*Informal*) = <u>criminal</u>, rogue, cheat, thief, shark, villain, robber, racketeer, skelm (*S. African*)

● ADJECTIVE (*Austral. & N.Z. informal*) = <u>ill</u>, sick, poorly (*informal*), unhealthy, seedy (*informal*), unwell, queasy, out of sorts (*informal*)

● PHRASES **go (off) crook** (*Austral. & N.Z. informal*) = <u>lose your temper</u>, be furious, rage, go mad, lose it (*informal*), crack up (*informal*), see red (*informal*), blow your top

**crooked** 1 = <u>bent</u>, twisted, curved, irregular, warped, out of shape, misshapen ≠ straight 2 = <u>deformed</u>, distorted 3 = <u>zigzag</u>, winding, twisting 4 = <u>at an angle</u>, uneven, slanting, squint, awry, lopsided, askew, off-centre 5 (*informal*) = <u>dishonest</u>, criminal, illegal, corrupt, unlawful, shady (*informal*), fraudulent, bent (*slang*) ≠ honest

**crop** NOUN = <u>yield</u>, produce, gathering, fruits, harvest, vintage, reaping

● VERB 1 = <u>graze</u>, eat, browse, feed on, nibble 2 = <u>cut</u>, trim, clip, prune, shear, snip, pare, lop

● PHRASES **crop up** (*Informal*) = <u>happen</u>, appear, emerge, occur, arise, turn up, spring up

**cross** VERB 1 = <u>go across</u>, pass over, traverse, cut across, move across, travel across 2 = <u>span</u>, bridge, go across, extend over 3 = <u>intersect</u>, intertwine, crisscross 4 = <u>oppose</u>, interfere with, obstruct, block, resist, impede 5 = <u>interbreed</u>, mix, blend, cross-pollinate, crossbreed, hybridize, cross-fertilize, intercross

● NOUN 1 = <u>crucifix</u> 2 = <u>trouble</u>, worry, trial, load, burden, grief, woe, misfortune 3 = <u>mixture</u>, combination, blend, amalgam, amalgamation 4 = <u>crossroads</u>, crossing, junction, intersection

● ADJECTIVE = <u>angry</u>, annoyed, put out, grumpy, short, ill-tempered, irascible, tooshie (*Austral. slang*), in a bad mood, hoha (*N.Z.*) ≠ good-humoured

● PHRASES **cross something out** *or* **off** = <u>strike off</u> *or* <u>out</u>, eliminate, cancel, delete, blue-pencil, score off *or* out

**crouch** = <u>bend down</u>, kneel, squat, stoop, bow, duck, hunch

**crow** = <u>gloat</u>, triumph, boast, swagger, brag, exult, blow your own trumpet

**crowd** NOUN 1 = <u>multitude</u>, mass,

throng, army, host, pack, mob, swarm 2= group, set, lot, circle, gang, bunch (informal), clique 3= audience, spectators, house, gate, attendance
• VERB 1= flock, mass, collect, gather, stream, surge, swarm, throng 2= squeeze, pack, pile, bundle, cram 3= congest, pack, cram

**crowded** = packed, full, busy, cramped, swarming, teeming, congested, jam-packed

**crown** NOUN 1= coronet, tiara, diadem, circlet 2= laurel wreath, trophy, prize, honour, garland, laurels, wreath 3= high point, top, tip, summit, crest, pinnacle, apex
• VERB 1= install, honour, dignify, ordain, inaugurate 2= top, cap, be on top of, surmount 3= cap, finish, complete, perfect, round off, put the finishing touch to, be the climax or culmination of 4(Slang) = strike, belt (informal), bash, hit over the head, box, punch, cuff, biff (slang)
• PHRASES the Crown 1= monarch, ruler, sovereign, emperor or empress, king or queen 2= monarchy, sovereignty, royalty

**crucial** 1(Informal) = vital, important, pressing, essential, urgent, momentous, high-priority 2= critical, central, key,

psychological, decisive, pivotal

**crude** 1= rough, basic, makeshift 2= simple, rudimentary, basic, primitive, coarse, clumsy, rough-and-ready 3= vulgar, dirty, rude, obscene, coarse, indecent, tasteless, smutty ≠ tasteful 4= unrefined, natural, raw, unprocessed ≠ processed

**crudely** 1= roughly, basically 2= simply, roughly, basically, coarsely 3= vulgarly, rudely, coarsely, crassly, obscenely, lewdly, impolitely, tastelessly

**cruel** 1= brutal, ruthless, callous, sadistic, inhumane, vicious, monstrous, unkind ≠ kind 2= bitter, ruthless, traumatic, grievous, unrelenting, merciless, pitiless

**cruelly** 1= brutally, severely, mercilessly, in cold blood, callously, monstrously, sadistically, pitilessly 2= bitterly, deeply, severely, ruthlessly, mercilessly, grievously, pitilessly, traumatically

**cruelty** = brutality, ruthlessness, depravity, inhumanity, barbarity, callousness, spitefulness, mercilessness

**cruise** NOUN 1= sail, voyage, boat trip, sea trip
• VERB 1= sail, coast, voyage 2= travel along, coast, drift, keep a steady pace

**crumb** = bit, grain, fragment,

shred, morsel 2 = <u>morsel</u>, scrap, shred, snippet, soupçon (*French*)

**crumble** 1 = <u>disintegrate</u>, collapse, deteriorate, decay, fall apart, degenerate, tumble down, go to pieces 2 = <u>crush</u>, fragment, pulverize, pound, grind, powder, granulate 3 = <u>collapse</u>, deteriorate, decay, fall apart, degenerate, go to pieces, go to wrack and ruin

**crumple** 1 = <u>crush</u>, squash, screw up, scrumple 2 = <u>crease</u>, wrinkle, rumple, ruffle, pucker 3 = <u>collapse</u>, sink, go down, fall 4 = <u>break down</u>, fall, collapse, give way, cave in, go to pieces 5 = <u>screw up</u>

**crunch** VERB = <u>chomp</u>, champ, munch, chew noisily, grind
● NOUN (*Informal*) = <u>critical point</u>, test, crisis, emergency, crux, moment of truth

**crusade** NOUN 1 = <u>campaign</u>, drive, movement, cause, push 2 = <u>holy war</u>
● VERB = <u>campaign</u>, fight, push, struggle, lobby, agitate, work

**crush** VERB 1 = <u>squash</u>, break, squeeze, compress, press, pulverize 2 = <u>crease</u>, wrinkle, crumple 3 = <u>overcome</u>, overwhelm, put down, subdue, overpower, quash, quell, stamp out 4 = <u>demoralize</u>, depress, devastate, discourage, humble, put down (*slang*), humiliate, squash
● NOUN = <u>crowd</u>, mob, horde, throng, pack, mass, jam, huddle

**crust** = <u>layer</u>, covering, coating, skin, surface, shell

**crustacean ► crustaceans**

**cry** VERB 1 = <u>weep</u>, sob, shed tears, blubber, snivel ≠ laugh 2 = <u>shout</u>, scream, roar, yell, howl,

---

### Crustaceans

| | |
|---|---|
| barnacle | lobster |
| crab | oyster crab |
| crayfish, crawfish, (*U.S.*) or (*Austral. & N.Z. informal*) craw | prawn |
| | robber crab |
| freshwater shrimp | sand shrimp |
| hermit crab | scorpion |
| horseshoe crab *or* king crab | sea spider |
| king prawn | shrimp |
| koura (*N.Z.*) | soft-shell crab |
| krill | spider crab |
| land crab | spiny lobster, rock lobster, crawfish, *or* langouste |
| langoustine | |

call out, exclaim, shriek ≠ whisper
- **NOUN** 1 = weep, sob, bawl, blubber 2 = shout, call, scream, roar, yell, howl, shriek, bellow 3 = appeal, plea
- **PLURAL NOUN** = weeping, sobbing, blubbering, snivelling
- **PHRASES** cry off (*Informal*) = back out, withdraw, quit, excuse yourself

**cuddle VERB** 1 = hug, embrace, fondle, cosset 2 = pet, hug, bill and coo
- **PHRASES** cuddle up = snuggle

**cue** = signal, sign, hint, prompt, reminder, suggestion

**culminate** = end up, close, finish, conclude, wind up, climax, come to a head, come to a climax

**culprit** = offender, criminal, felon, guilty party, wrongdoer, miscreant, evildoer, transgressor

**cult** 1 = sect, faction, school, religion, clique, hauhau (*N.Z.*) 2 = craze, fashion, trend, fad 3 = obsession, worship, devotion, idolization

**cultivate** 1 = farm, work, plant, tend, till, plough 2 = develop, establish, foster 3 = court, seek out, run after, dance attendance upon 4 = improve, refine

**cultural** 1 = ethnic, national, native, folk, racial 2 = artistic, educational, aesthetic, enriching, enlightening, civilizing, edifying

**culture** 1 = the arts

2 = civilization, society, customs, way of life 3 = lifestyle, habit, way of life, mores 4 = refinement, education, enlightenment, sophistication, good taste, urbanity

**cultured** = refined, intellectual, educated, sophisticated, enlightened, well-informed, urbane, highbrow ≠ uneducated

**cunning ADJECTIVE** 1 = crafty, sly, devious, artful, sharp, wily, Machiavellian, shifty ≠ frank 2 = ingenious, imaginative, sly, devious, artful, Machiavellian 3 = skilful, clever ≠ clumsy
- **NOUN** 1 = craftiness, guile, trickery, deviousness, artfulness, slyness ≠ candour 2 = skill, subtlety, ingenuity, artifice, cleverness ≠ clumsiness

**cup** 1 = mug, goblet, chalice, teacup, beaker, bowl 2 = trophy

**cupboard** = cabinet, press

**curb VERB** = restrain, control, check, restrict, suppress, inhibit, hinder, retard
- **NOUN** = restraint, control, check, brake, limitation, rein, deterrent, bridle

**cure VERB** 1 = make better, correct, heal, relieve, remedy, mend, ease 2 = restore to health, restore, heal 3 = preserve, smoke, dry, salt, pickle
- **NOUN** = remedy, treatment, antidote, panacea, nostrum

**curiosity** 1 = inquisitiveness, interest, prying, snooping (*informal*), nosiness (*informal*) 2 = oddity, wonder, sight, phenomenon, spectacle, freak, novelty, rarity

**curious** ADJECTIVE 1 = inquisitive, interested, questioning, searching, inquiring, meddling, prying, nosy (*informal*) ≠ uninterested 2 = strange, unusual, bizarre, odd, novel, rare, extraordinary, unexpected
● ADJECTIVE ≠ ordinary

**curl** NOUN 1 = ringlet, lock 2 = twist, spiral, coil, kink, whorl 3 = crimp, wave, perm
● VERB 1 = twirl, turn, bend, twist, curve, loop, spiral, coil 2 = wind

**curly** = wavy, curled, curling, fuzzy, frizzy

**currency** 1 = money, coinage, legal tender, notes, coins 2 = acceptance, popularity, circulation, vogue, prevalence
➤ WORD POWER SUPPLEMENT
**currencies**

**current** NOUN 1 = flow, course, undertow, jet, stream, tide, progression, river 2 = draught, flow, breeze, puff 3 = mood, feeling, spirit, atmosphere, trend, tendency, undercurrent
● ADJECTIVE 1 = present, fashionable, up-to-date, contemporary, trendy (*Brit. informal*), topical, present-day, in fashion ≠ out-of-date

2 = prevalent, common, accepted, popular, widespread, customary, in circulation

**curse** VERB 1 = swear, cuss (*informal*), blaspheme, take the Lord's name in vain 2 = abuse, damn, scold, vilify
● NOUN 1 = oath, obscenity, blasphemy, expletive, profanity, imprecation, swearword 2 = malediction, jinx, anathema, hoodoo (*informal*), excommunication 3 = affliction, plague, scourge, trouble, torment, hardship, bane

**cursed** = under a curse, damned, doomed, jinxed, bedevilled, accursed, ill-fated

**curtail** = reduce, diminish, decrease, dock, cut back, shorten, lessen, cut short

**curtain** = hanging, drape (*chiefly U.S.*), portière

**curve** NOUN = bend, turn, loop, arc, curvature
● VERB = bend, turn, wind, twist, arch, snake, arc, coil

**curved** = bent, rounded, twisted, bowed, arched, serpentine, sinuous

**cushion** NOUN = pillow, pad, bolster, headrest, beanbag, hassock
● VERB 1 = protect 2 = soften, dampen, muffle, mitigate, deaden, suppress, stifle

**custody** 1 = care, charge,

protection, supervision, safekeeping, keeping **2** = <u>imprisonment</u>, detention, confinement, incarceration

**custom 1** = <u>tradition</u>, practice, convention, ritual, policy, rule, usage, kaupapa (*N.Z.*) **2** = <u>habit</u>, way, practice, procedure, routine, wont **3** = <u>customers</u>, business, trade, patronage

**customary 1** = <u>usual</u>, common, accepted, established, traditional, normal, ordinary, conventional ≠ unusual **2** = <u>accustomed</u>, regular, usual

**customer 1** = <u>client</u>, consumer, regular (*informal*), buyer, patron, shopper, purchaser

**customs** = <u>import charges</u>, tax, duty, toll, tariff

**cut VERB 1** = <u>slit</u>, score, slice, slash, pierce, penetrate **2** = <u>chop</u>, split, slice, dissect **3** = <u>carve</u>, slice **4** = <u>sever</u>, cut in two **5** = <u>shape</u>, carve, engrave, chisel, form, score, fashion, whittle **6** = <u>slash</u>, wound **7** = <u>clip</u>, mow, trim, prune, snip, pare, lop **8** = <u>trim</u>, shave, snip **9** = <u>reduce</u>, lower, slim (down), diminish, slash, decrease, cut back ≠ increase **10** = <u>abridge</u>, edit, shorten, curtail, condense, abbreviate ≠ extend **11** = <u>delete</u>, take out, expurgate **12** = <u>hurt</u>, wound, upset, sting, hurt someone's feelings **13** (*Informal*) = <u>ignore</u>, avoid, slight, blank

(*slang*), snub, spurn, cold-shoulder, turn your back on ≠ greet **14** = <u>cross</u>, bisect

● **NOUN 1** = <u>incision</u>, nick, stroke, slash, slit **2** = <u>gash</u>, nick, wound, slash, laceration **3** = <u>reduction</u>, fall, lowering, slash, decrease, cutback **4** (*Informal*) = <u>share</u>, piece, slice, percentage, portion **5** = <u>style</u>, look, fashion, shape

**cutback** = <u>reduction</u>, cut, retrenchment, economy, decrease, lessening

**cute** = <u>appealing</u>, sweet, attractive, engaging, charming, delightful, lovable, winsome

**cutting** = <u>hurtful</u>, wounding, bitter, malicious, scathing, acrimonious, barbed, sarcastic ≠ kind

**cycle** = <u>series of events</u>, circle, revolution, rotation

**cynic** = <u>sceptic</u>, doubter, pessimist, misanthrope, misanthropist, scoffer

**cynical 1** = <u>sceptical</u>, mocking, pessimistic, scoffing, contemptuous, scornful, distrustful, derisive ≠ trusting **2** = <u>unbelieving</u>, sceptical, disillusioned, pessimistic, disbelieving, mistrustful ≠ optimistic

**cynicism 1** = <u>scepticism</u>, pessimism, misanthropy **2** = <u>disbelief</u>, doubt, scepticism, mistrust

# D

**dab** VERB 1 = <u>pat</u>, touch, tap 2 = <u>apply</u>, daub, stipple
● NOUN 1 = <u>spot</u>, bit, drop, pat, smudge, speck 2 = <u>touch</u>, stroke, flick

**daft** (*Informal, chiefly Brit.*) 1 = <u>stupid</u>, crazy, silly, absurd, foolish, idiotic, witless, crackpot (*informal*), off the air (*Austral. slang*) 2 = <u>crazy</u>, mad, touched, nuts (*slang*), crackers (*Brit. slang*), insane, demented, deranged, off the air (*Austral. slang*), porangi (*N.Z.*)

**dag** NOUN (*N.Z. informal*) = <u>joker</u>, comic, wag, wit, comedian, clown, humorist, prankster
● PHRASES **rattle your dags** (*N.Z. informal*) = <u>hurry up</u>, get a move on, step on it (*informal*), get your skates on (*informal*), make haste

**dagga** (*S. African*) = <u>cannabis</u>, marijuana, pot (*slang*), dope (*slang*), hash (*slang*), grass (*slang*), weed (*slang*), hemp

**daily** ADVERB = <u>every day</u>, day by day, once a day
● ADJECTIVE = <u>everyday</u>, diurnal, quotidian

**dam** NOUN = <u>barrier</u>, wall, barrage, obstruction, embankment
● VERB = <u>block up</u>, restrict, hold back, barricade, obstruct

**damage** VERB = <u>spoil</u>, hurt, injure, harm, ruin, crush, devastate, wreck ≠ fix
● NOUN 1 = <u>destruction</u>, harm, loss, injury, suffering, hurt, ruin, devastation ≠ improvement 2 (*Informal*) = <u>cost</u>, price, charge, bill, amount, payment, expense, outlay
● PLURAL NOUN (*Law*) = <u>compensation</u>, fine, satisfaction, amends, reparation, restitution, reimbursement, atonement

**damaging** = <u>harmful</u>, detrimental, hurtful, ruinous, deleterious, injurious, disadvantageous ≠ helpful

**dame** = <u>lady</u>, baroness, dowager, grande dame (*French*), noblewoman, peeress

**damn** = <u>criticize</u>, condemn, blast, denounce, put down, censure ≠ praise

**damned** (*Slang*) = <u>infernal</u>, detestable, confounded, hateful, loathsome

**damp** ADJECTIVE = <u>moist</u>, wet, soggy, humid, dank, sopping, clammy, dewy ≠ dry
● NOUN = <u>moisture</u>, liquid, drizzle, dampness, wetness, dankness ≠ dryness
● VERB = <u>moisten</u>, wet, soak, dampen, moisturize
● PHRASES **damp something down** = <u>curb</u>, reduce, check,

diminish, inhibit, stifle, allay, pour cold water on

**dampen** 1 = <u>reduce</u>, check, moderate, dull, restrain, stifle, lessen 2 = <u>moisten</u>, wet, spray, make damp

**dance** VERB 1 = <u>prance</u>, trip, hop, skip, sway, whirl, caper, jig 2 = <u>caper</u>, trip, spring, jump, bound, skip, frolic, cavort
● NOUN = <u>ball</u>, social, hop (*informal*), disco, knees-up (*Brit. informal*), discotheque, B and S (*Austral. informal*)

**dancer** = <u>ballerina</u>, Terpsichorean

**danger** 1 = <u>jeopardy</u>, vulnerability 2 = <u>hazard</u>, risk, threat, menace, peril, pitfall

**dangerous** = <u>perilous</u>, risky, hazardous, vulnerable, insecure, unsafe, precarious, breakneck ≠ safe

**dangerously** = <u>perilously</u>, alarmingly, precariously, recklessly, riskily, hazardously, unsafely

**dangle** 1 = <u>hang</u>, swing, trail, sway, flap, hang down 2 = <u>wave</u> 3 = <u>offer</u>, flourish, brandish, flaunt

**dare** 1 = <u>risk doing</u>, venture, presume, make bold (*archaic*), hazard doing 2 = <u>challenge</u>, provoke, defy, taunt, goad, throw down the gauntlet

**daring** ADJECTIVE = <u>brave</u>, bold, adventurous, reckless, fearless, audacious, intrepid, daredevil ≠ timid
● NOUN = <u>bravery</u>, nerve (*informal*), courage, spirit, bottle (*Brit. slang*), pluck, audacity, boldness ≠ timidity

**dark** ADJECTIVE 1 = <u>dim</u>, murky, shady, shadowy, grey, dingy, unlit, poorly lit 2 = <u>black</u>, brunette, ebony, dark-skinned, sable, dusky, swarthy 3 = <u>evil</u>, foul, sinister, vile, wicked, infernal 4 = <u>secret</u>, hidden, mysterious, concealed 5 = <u>gloomy</u>, sad, grim, miserable, bleak, dismal, pessimistic, melancholy ≠ cheerful
● NOUN 1 = <u>darkness</u>, shadows, gloom, dusk, obscurity, murk, dimness, semi-darkness 2 = <u>night</u>, twilight, evening, evo (*Austral. slang*), dusk, night-time, nightfall

**darken** 1 = <u>cloud</u>, obscure, dim, overshadow, blacken ≠ brighten 2 = <u>make dark</u>, blacken

**darkness** = <u>dark</u>, shadows, shade, gloom, blackness, murk, duskiness

**darling** NOUN = <u>beloved</u>, love, dear, dearest, angel, treasure, precious, sweetheart
● ADJECTIVE = <u>beloved</u>, dear, treasured, precious, adored, cherished

**dart** = <u>dash</u>, run, race, shoot, fly, speed, spring, tear

**dash** VERB 1 = <u>rush</u>, run, race, shoot, fly, career, speed, tear ≠ dawdle 2 = <u>throw</u>, cast, pitch, slam, toss, hurl, fling, chuck (*informal*) 3 = <u>crash</u>, break, smash, shatter, splinter

● NOUN 1 = <u>rush</u>, run, race, sprint, dart, spurt, sortie 2 = <u>drop</u>, little, bit, shot (*informal*), touch, spot, trace, hint ≠ lot 3 (*Old-fashioned*) = <u>style</u>, spirit, flair, flourish, verve, panache, élan, brio

**dashing** 1 (*Old-fashioned*) = <u>stylish</u>, smart, elegant, flamboyant, sporty, jaunty, showy 2 = <u>bold</u>, spirited, gallant, swashbuckling, debonair ≠ dull

**data** = <u>information</u>, facts, figures, details, intelligence, statistics

**date** NOUN 1 = <u>time</u>, stage, period 2 = <u>appointment</u>, meeting, arrangement, commitment, engagement, rendezvous, tryst, assignation 3 = <u>partner</u>, escort, friend

● VERB 1 = <u>put a date on</u>, assign a date to, fix the period of 2 = <u>become dated</u>, become old-fashioned

● PHRASES **date from or date back to** (with a *time* or *date* as object) = <u>come from</u>, belong to, originate in, exist from, bear a date of

**dated** = <u>old-fashioned</u>, outdated, out of date, obsolete, unfashionable, outmoded, passé,

old hat ≠ modern

**daunting** = <u>intimidating</u>, alarming, frightening, discouraging, unnerving, disconcerting, demoralizing, off-putting (*Brit. informal*) ≠ reassuring

**dawn** NOUN 1 = <u>daybreak</u>, morning, sunrise, daylight, aurora (*poetic*), crack of dawn, sunup, cockcrow 2 (*Literary*) = <u>beginning</u>, start, birth, rise, origin, emergence, advent, genesis

● VERB 1 = <u>begin</u>, start, rise, develop, emerge, unfold, originate 2 = <u>grow light</u>, break, brighten, lighten

● PHRASES **dawn on or upon someone** = <u>hit</u>, strike, occur to, register (*informal*), become apparent, come to mind, come into your head

**day** 1 = <u>twenty-four hours</u> 2 = <u>daytime</u>, daylight 3 = <u>date</u> 4 = <u>time</u>, age, era, period, epoch

**daylight** = <u>sunlight</u>, sunshine, light of day

**daze** VERB = <u>stun</u>, shock, paralyse, numb, stupefy, benumb

● NOUN (usually used in the phrase *in a daze*) = <u>shock</u>, confusion, distraction, trance, bewilderment, stupor, trancelike state

**dazzle** VERB 1 = <u>impress</u>, amaze, overwhelm, astonish, overpower, bowl over (*informal*), take your breath away **2** = <u>blind</u>, confuse, daze, bedazzle

● NOUN = <u>splendour</u>, sparkle, glitter, brilliance, magnificence, razzmatazz (*slang*)

**dazzling** = <u>splendid</u>, brilliant, stunning, glorious, sparkling, glittering, sensational (*informal*), virtuoso ≠ ordinary

**dead** ADJECTIVE **1** = <u>deceased</u>, departed, late, perished, extinct, defunct, passed away ≠ alive **2** = <u>boring</u>, dull, dreary, flat, plain, humdrum, uninteresting **3** = <u>not working</u>, useless, inactive, inoperative ≠ working **4** = <u>numb</u>, frozen, paralysed, insensitive, inert, deadened, immobilized, unfeeling **5** (usually used of *centre*, *silence*, or *stop*) = <u>total</u>, complete, absolute, utter, outright, thorough, unqualified **6** (*Informal*) = <u>exhausted</u>, tired, worn out, spent, done in (*informal*), all in (*slang*), drained, knackered (*slang*)

● NOUN = <u>middle</u>, heart, depth, midst

● ADVERB (*Informal*) = <u>exactly</u>, completely, totally, directly, fully, entirely, absolutely, thoroughly

**deadline** = <u>time limit</u>, cutoff point, target date or time, limit

**deadlock 1** = <u>impasse</u>, stalemate, standstill, gridlock, standoff **2** = <u>tie</u>, draw, stalemate,

impasse, standstill, gridlock, standoff, dead heat

**deadly 1** = <u>lethal</u>, fatal, deathly, dangerous, devastating, mortal, murderous, malignant **2** (*Informal*) = <u>boring</u>, dull, tedious, flat, monotonous, uninteresting, mind-numbing, wearisome

**deaf 1** = <u>hard of hearing</u>, without hearing, stone deaf **2** = <u>oblivious</u>, indifferent, unmoved, unconcerned, unsympathetic, impervious, unhearing
> disabled

**deal** NOUN **1** (*Informal*) = <u>agreement</u>, understanding, contract, arrangement, bargain, transaction, pact **2** = <u>amount</u>, quantity, measure, degree, mass, volume, share, portion

● PHRASES **deal in something** = <u>sell</u>, trade in, stock, traffic in, buy and sell ◆ **deal something out** = <u>distribute</u>, give, share, assign, allocate, dispense, allot, mete out ◆ **deal with something** = <u>be concerned with</u>, involve, concern, touch, regard, apply to, bear on, pertain to ◆ **deal with something or someone** = <u>handle</u>, manage, treat, cope with, take care of, see to, attend to, get to grips with

**dealer** = <u>trader</u>, merchant, supplier, wholesaler, purveyor, tradesman

**dear** ADJECTIVE 1 = <u>beloved</u>, close, valued, favourite, prized, treasured, precious, intimate ≠ hated 2 (*Brit. informal*) = <u>expensive</u>, costly, high-priced, pricey (*informal*), at a premium, overpriced, exorbitant ≠ cheap
● NOUN = <u>darling</u>, love, dearest, angel, treasure, precious, beloved, loved one

**dearly** (*Formal*) 1 = <u>very much</u>, greatly, extremely, profoundly 2 = <u>at great cost</u>, at a high price

**death** 1 = <u>dying</u>, demise, end, passing, departure ≠ birth 2 = <u>destruction</u>, finish, ruin, undoing, extinction, downfall ≠ beginning

*(Related Words)*
*adjectives*: fatal, lethal, mortal

**deathly** = <u>deathlike</u>, white, pale, ghastly, wan, pallid, ashen

**debacle** *or* **débâcle** = <u>disaster</u>, catastrophe, fiasco

**debate** NOUN = <u>discussion</u>, talk, argument, dispute, analysis, conversation, controversy, dialogue
● VERB 1 = <u>discuss</u>, question, talk about, argue about, dispute, examine, deliberate 2 = <u>consider</u>, reflect, think about, weigh, contemplate, deliberate, ponder, ruminate

**debris** = <u>remains</u>, bits, waste, ruins, fragments, rubble, wreckage, detritus

**debt** NOUN = <u>debit</u>, commitment, obligation, liability
● PHRASES in debt = <u>owing</u>, liable, in the red (*informal*), in arrears

**debtor** = <u>borrower</u>, mortgagor

**debut** = <u>entrance</u>, beginning, launch, coming out, introduction, presentation, first appearance, initiation

**decay** VERB 1 = <u>rot</u>, spoil, crumble, deteriorate, perish, decompose, moulder, go bad 2 = <u>decline</u>, diminish, crumble, deteriorate, fall off, dwindle, lessen, wane ≠ grow
● NOUN 1 = <u>rot</u>, corruption, mould, blight, decomposition, gangrene, canker, caries 2 = <u>decline</u>, collapse, deterioration, failing, fading, degeneration ≠ growth

**deceased** = <u>dead</u>, late, departed, expired, defunct, lifeless

**deceive** = <u>take in</u>, trick, fool (*informal*), cheat, con (*informal*), mislead, dupe, swindle

**decency** 1 = <u>propriety</u>, correctness, decorum, respectability, etiquette 2 = <u>courtesy</u>, politeness, civility, graciousness, urbanity, courteousness

**decent** 1 = <u>satisfactory</u>, fair, all right, reasonable, sufficient, good enough, adequate, ample ≠ unsatisfactory 2 = <u>proper</u>, becoming, seemly, fitting, appropriate, suitable, respectable,

**befitting** ≠ **improper** 3 (*Informal*)
= **good**, kind, friendly,
neighbourly, generous, helpful,
obliging, accommodating
4 = **respectable**, pure, proper,
modest, chaste, decorous

**deception** 1 = **trickery**, fraud,
deceit, cunning, treachery, guile,
legerdemain ≠ **honesty** 2 = **trick**,
lie, bluff, hoax, decoy, ruse,
subterfuge

**decide** 1 = **make a decision**,
make up your mind, reach *or*
come to a decision, choose,
determine, conclude ≠ **hesitate**
2 = **resolve**, answer, determine,
conclude, clear up, ordain,
adjudicate, adjudge 3 = **settle**,
determine, resolve

**decidedly** = **definitely**, clearly,
positively, distinctly, downright,
unequivocally, unmistakably

**decision** 1 = **judgment**, finding,
ruling, sentence, resolution,
conclusion, verdict, decree
2 = **decisiveness**, purpose,
resolution, resolve,
determination, firmness,
forcefulness, strength of mind *or*
will

**decisive** 1 = **crucial**, significant,
critical, influential, momentous,
conclusive, fateful ≠ **uncertain**
2 = **resolute**, decided, firm,
determined, forceful, incisive,
trenchant, strong-minded
≠ **indecisive**

**deck** = **decorate**, dress, clothe,
array, adorn, embellish, festoon,
beautify

**declaration**
1 = **announcement**,
proclamation, decree, notice,
notification, edict,
pronouncement 2 = **affirmation**,
profession, assertion, revelation,
disclosure, acknowledgment,
protestation, avowal
3 = **statement**, testimony

**declare** 1 = **state**, claim,
announce, voice, express,
maintain, assert, proclaim
2 = **testify**, state, swear, assert,
affirm, bear witness, vouch
3 = **make known**, reveal, show,
broadcast, confess, communicate,
disclose

**decline** VERB 1 = **fall**, drop, lower,
sink, fade, shrink, diminish,
decrease ≠ **rise** 2 = **deteriorate**,
weaken, pine, decay, worsen,
languish, degenerate, droop
≠ **improve** 3 = **refuse**, reject, turn
down, avoid, spurn, abstain, say
'no' ≠ **accept**
● NOUN 1 = **depression**, recession,
slump, falling off, downturn,
dwindling, lessening ≠ **rise**
2 = **deterioration**, failing,
weakening, decay, worsening,
degeneration ≠ **improvement**

**décor** *or* **decor** = **decoration**,
colour scheme, ornamentation,
furnishing style

**decorate** 1 = <u>adorn</u>, trim, embroider, ornament, embellish, festoon, beautify, grace 2 = <u>do up</u>, paper, paint, wallpaper, renovate (*informal*), furbish 3 = <u>pin a medal on</u>, cite, confer an honour on *or* upon

**decoration** 1 = <u>adornment</u>, trimming, enhancement, elaboration, embellishment, ornamentation, beautification 2 = <u>ornament</u>, trimmings, garnish, frill, bauble 3 = <u>medal</u>, award, star, ribbon, badge

**decorative** = <u>ornamental</u>, fancy, pretty, attractive, for show, embellishing, showy, beautifying

**decrease** VERB 1 = <u>drop</u>, decline, lessen, lower, shrink, diminish, dwindle, subside 2 = <u>reduce</u>, cut, lower, moderate, weaken, diminish, cut down, shorten ≠ increase

● NOUN = <u>lessening</u>, decline, reduction, loss, falling off, dwindling, contraction, cutback ≠ growth

**decree** NOUN 1 = <u>law</u>, order, ruling, act, command, statute, proclamation, edict 2 = <u>judgment</u>, finding, ruling, decision, verdict, arbitration

● VERB = <u>order</u>, rule, command, demand, proclaim, prescribe, pronounce, ordain

**dedicate** 1 = <u>devote</u>, give, apply, commit, pledge, surrender, give over to 2 = <u>offer</u>, address, inscribe

**dedicated** = <u>committed</u>, devoted, enthusiastic, single-minded, zealous, purposeful, wholehearted ≠ indifferent

**dedication** 1 = <u>commitment</u>, loyalty, devotion, allegiance, adherence, single-mindedness, faithfulness, wholeheartedness ≠ indifference 2 = <u>inscription</u>, message, address

**deduct** = <u>subtract</u>, remove, take off, take away, reduce by, knock off (*informal*), decrease by ≠ add

**deduction** 1 = <u>conclusion</u>, finding, verdict, judgment, assumption, inference 2 = <u>reasoning</u>, thinking, thought, analysis, logic 3 = <u>discount</u>, reduction, cut, concession, decrease, rebate, diminution 4 = <u>subtraction</u>, reduction, concession

**deed** 1 = <u>action</u>, act, performance, achievement, exploit, feat 2 (*Law*) = <u>document</u>, title, contract

**deep** ADJECTIVE 1 = <u>big</u>, wide, broad, profound, yawning, bottomless, unfathomable ≠ shallow 2 = <u>intense</u>, great, serious (*informal*), acute, extreme, grave, profound, heartfelt ≠ superficial 3 = <u>sound</u>, profound, unbroken, undisturbed, untroubled 4 = <u>absorbed</u>, lost, gripped, preoccupied, immersed, engrossed, rapt 5 = <u>dark</u>, strong, rich, intense, vivid ≠ light 6 = <u>low</u>, booming, bass, resonant, sonorous, low-pitched ≠ high 7 = <u>secret</u>, hidden, mysterious, obscure, abstract, esoteric, mystifying, arcane 8 = <u>far</u>, a long way, a good way, miles, a great distance

• NOUN = <u>middle</u>, heart, midst, dead

• PHRASES **the deep** (*Poetic*) = <u>the ocean</u>, the sea, the waves, the main, the high seas, the briny (*informal*)

**deepen** 1 = <u>intensify</u>, increase, grow, strengthen, reinforce, escalate, magnify 2 = <u>dig out</u>, excavate, scoop out, hollow out

**deeply** = <u>thoroughly</u>, completely, seriously, sadly, severely, gravely, profoundly, intensely

**de facto** ADJECTIVE = <u>actual</u>, real, existing

• ADVERB = <u>in fact</u>, really, actually, in effect, in reality

**default** VERB = <u>fail to pay</u>, dodge, evade, neglect

• NOUN 1 (usually in phrase *by default* or *in default of*) = <u>failure</u>, neglect, deficiency, lapse, omission, dereliction 2 = <u>nonpayment</u>, evasion

**defeat** VERB 1 = <u>beat</u>, crush, overwhelm, conquer, master, rout, trounce, vanquish

≠ surrender 2 = <u>frustrate</u>, foil, thwart, ruin, baffle, confound, balk, get the better of

• NOUN 1 = <u>conquest</u>, beating, overthrow, rout ≠ victory 2 = <u>frustration</u>, failure, reverse, setback, thwarting

**defect** NOUN = <u>deficiency</u>, failing, fault, error, flaw, imperfection

• VERB = <u>desert</u>, rebel, quit, revolt, change sides

**defence** or (*U.S.*) **defense** NOUN 1 = <u>protection</u>, cover, security, guard, shelter, safeguard, immunity 2 = <u>armaments</u>, weapons 3 = <u>argument</u>, explanation, excuse, plea, justification, vindication, rationalization 4 = <u>plea</u> (*Law*), testimony, denial, alibi, rebuttal

• PLURAL NOUN = <u>shield</u>, barricade, fortification, buttress, rampart, bulwark, fortified pa (*N.Z.*)

**defend** 1 = <u>protect</u>, cover, guard, screen, preserve, look after, shelter, shield 2 = <u>support</u>, champion, justify, endorse, uphold, vindicate, stand up for, speak up for

**defendant** NOUN = <u>the accused</u>, respondent, prisoner at the bar

**defender** 1 = <u>supporter</u>, champion, advocate, sponsor, follower 2 = <u>protector</u>, guard, guardian, escort, bodyguard

**defensive** 1 = <u>protective</u>, watchful, on the defensive, on guard 2 = **oversensitive**, uptight (*informal*)

**defer** = **postpone**, delay, put off, suspend, shelve, hold over, procrastinate, put on ice (*informal*)

**defiance** = **resistance**, opposition, confrontation, contempt, disregard, disobedience, insolence, insubordination ≠ obedience

**defiant** = **resisting**, rebellious, daring, bold, provocative, audacious, antagonistic, insolent ≠ obedient

**deficiency** 1 = **lack**, want, deficit, absence, shortage, scarcity, dearth ≠ sufficiency 2 = **failing**, fault, weakness, defect, flaw, drawback, shortcoming, imperfection

**deficit** = **shortfall**, shortage, deficiency, loss, arrears

**define** 1 = **mark out**, outline, limit, bound, delineate, circumscribe, demarcate 2 = **describe**, interpret, characterize, explain, spell out, expound 3 = **establish**, specify, designate

**definite** 1 = **specific**, exact, precise, clear, particular, fixed, black-and-white, cut-and-dried (*informal*) ≠ vague 2 = **clear**, black-and-white, unequivocal, unambiguous, guaranteed, cut-and-dried (*informal*)

3 = **noticeable**, marked, clear, decided, striking, particular, distinct, conspicuous 4 = **certain**, decided, sure, settled, positive, confident, assured ≠ uncertain

**definitely** = **certainly**, clearly, surely, absolutely, positively, without doubt, unquestionably, undeniably

**definition** 1 = **description**, interpretation, explanation, clarification, exposition, elucidation, statement of meaning 2 = **sharpness**, focus, clarity, contrast, precision, distinctness

**definitive** 1 = **final**, convincing, absolute, clinching, decisive, definite, conclusive, irrefutable 2 = **authoritative**, greatest, ultimate, reliable, exhaustive, superlative

**deflect** = **turn aside**, bend

**defy** = **resist**, oppose, confront, brave, disregard, stand up to, spurn, flout

**degenerate** VERB = **decline**, slip, sink, decrease, deteriorate, worsen, decay, lapse
● ADJECTIVE = **depraved**, corrupt, low, perverted, immoral, decadent, debauched, dissolute

**degrade** = **demean**, disgrace, humiliate, shame, humble, discredit, debase, dishonour ≠ ennoble

**degree** = <u>amount</u>, stage, grade

**delay** VERB 1 = <u>put off</u>, suspend, postpone, shelve, defer, hold over 2 = <u>hold up</u>, detain, hold back, hinder, obstruct, impede, bog down, set back ≠ speed (up)
● NOUN = <u>hold-up</u>, wait, setback, interruption, stoppage, impediment, hindrance

**delegate** NOUN = <u>representative</u>, agent, deputy, ambassador, commissioner, envoy, proxy, legate
● VERB 1 = <u>entrust</u>, transfer, hand over, give, pass on, assign, consign, devolve 2 = <u>appoint</u>, commission, select, contract, engage, nominate, designate, mandate

**delegation** 1 = <u>deputation</u>, envoys, contingent, commission, embassy, legation 2 = <u>commissioning</u>, assignment, devolution, committal

**delete** = <u>remove</u>, cancel, erase, strike out, obliterate, efface, cross out, expunge

**deliberate** ADJECTIVE 1 = <u>intentional</u>, meant, planned, intended, conscious, calculated, wilful, purposeful ≠ accidental 2 = <u>careful</u>, measured, slow, cautious, thoughtful, circumspect, methodical, unhurried ≠ hurried
● VERB = <u>consider</u>, think, ponder, discuss, debate, reflect, consult, weigh

**deliberately** = <u>intentionally</u>, on purpose, consciously, knowingly, wilfully, by design, in cold blood, wittingly

**deliberation** 1 = <u>consideration</u>, thought, reflection, calculation, meditation, forethought, circumspection 2 = <u>discussion</u>, talk, conference, debate, analysis, conversation, dialogue, consultation

**delicacy** 1 = <u>fragility</u>, flimsiness 2 = <u>daintiness</u>, charm, grace, elegance, neatness, prettiness, slenderness, exquisiteness 3 = <u>difficulty</u> 4 = <u>sensitivity</u>, understanding, consideration, diplomacy, discretion, tact, thoughtfulness, sensitiveness 5 = <u>treat</u>, luxury, savoury, dainty, morsel, titbit 6 = <u>lightness</u>, accuracy, precision, elegance, sensibility, purity, subtlety, refinement

**delicate** 1 = <u>fine</u>, elegant, exquisite, graceful 2 = <u>subtle</u>, fine, delicious, faint, refined, understated, dainty ≠ bright 3 = <u>fragile</u>, weak, frail, brittle, tender, flimsy, dainty, breakable 4 = <u>skilled</u>, precise, deft 5 = <u>diplomatic</u>, sensitive, thoughtful, discreet, considerate, tactful ≠ insensitive

**delicious** = <u>delectable</u>, tasty, choice, savoury, dainty, mouthwatering, scrumptious (*informal*), appetizing, lekker (*S. African slang*), yummo (*Austral. slang*) ≠ unpleasant

**delight** NOUN = <u>pleasure</u>, joy, satisfaction, happiness, ecstasy, enjoyment, bliss, glee ≠ displeasure

● VERB = <u>please</u>, satisfy, thrill, charm, cheer, amuse, enchant, gratify ≠ displease

● PHRASES **delight in** or **take (a) delight in something** or **someone** = <u>like</u>, love, enjoy, appreciate, relish, savour, revel in, take pleasure in

**delightful** = <u>pleasant</u>, charming, thrilling, enjoyable, enchanting, agreeable, pleasurable, rapturous ≠ unpleasant

**deliver** 1 = <u>bring</u>, carry, bear, transport, distribute, convey, cart 2 *sometimes with up* = <u>hand over</u>, commit, give up, yield, surrender, turn over, relinquish, make over 3 = <u>give</u>, read, present, announce, declare, utter 4 = <u>strike</u>, give, deal, launch, direct, aim, administer, inflict 5 (*Dated*) = <u>release</u>, free, save, rescue, loose, liberate, ransom, emancipate

**delivery** 1 = <u>handing over</u>, transfer, distribution, transmission, dispatch, consignment, conveyance 2 = <u>consignment</u>, goods, shipment, batch 3 = <u>speech</u>,

utterance, articulation, intonation, elocution, enunciation 4 = <u>childbirth</u>, labour, confinement, parturition

**delusion** = <u>misconception</u>, mistaken idea, misapprehension, fancy, illusion, hallucination, fallacy, false impression

**demand** VERB 1 = <u>request</u>, ask (for), order, expect, claim, seek, insist on, exact 2 = <u>challenge</u>, ask, question, inquire 3 = <u>require</u>, want, need, involve, call for, entail, necessitate, cry out for ≠ provide

● NOUN 1 = <u>request</u>, order 2 = <u>need</u>, want, call, market, claim, requirement

**demanding** = <u>difficult</u>, trying, hard, taxing, wearing, challenging, tough, exacting ≠ easy

**demise** 1 = <u>failure</u>, end, fall, defeat, collapse, ruin, breakdown, overthrow 2 (*Euphemistic*) = <u>death</u>, end, dying, passing, departure, decease

**democracy** = <u>self-government</u>, republic, commonwealth

**Democrat** ADJECTIVE = <u>left-wing</u>, Labour

● NOUN = <u>left-winger</u>

**democratic** = <u>self-governing</u>, popular, representative, autonomous, populist, egalitarian

**demolish** 1 = <u>knock down</u>, level, destroy, dismantle, flatten, tear down, bulldoze, raze ≠ build

2 = <u>destroy</u>, wreck, overturn, overthrow, undo

**demolition** = <u>knocking down</u>, levelling, destruction, explosion, wrecking, tearing down, bulldozing, razing

**demon** 1 = <u>evil spirit</u>, devil, fiend, goblin, ghoul, malignant spirit, atua (*N.Z.*), wairua (*N.Z.*) 2 = <u>wizard</u>, master, ace (*informal*), fiend

**demonstrate** 1 = <u>prove</u>, show, indicate, make clear, manifest, testify to 2 = <u>show</u>, express, display, indicate, exhibit, manifest 3 = <u>march</u>, protest, rally, object, parade, picket, remonstrate, express disapproval, hikoi (*N.Z.*) 4 = <u>describe</u>, show, explain, teach, illustrate

**demonstration** 1 = <u>march</u>, protest, rally, sit-in, parade, picket, mass lobby, hikoi (*N.Z.*) 2 = <u>display</u>, show, performance, explanation, description, presentation, exposition 3 = <u>indication</u>, proof, testimony, confirmation, substantiation 4 = <u>exhibition</u>, display, expression, illustration

**den** 1 = <u>lair</u>, hole, shelter, cave, haunt, cavern, hide-out 2 (*Chiefly U.S.*) = <u>study</u>, retreat, sanctuary, hideaway, sanctum, cubbyhole

**denial** 1 = <u>negation</u>, contradiction, dissent, retraction, repudiation ≠ admission

2 = <u>refusal</u>, veto, rejection, prohibition, rebuff, repulse 3 = <u>renunciation</u>, giving up, rejection, abdication, repudiation, forswearing, disavowal, relinquishment

**denomination** 1 = <u>religious group</u>, belief, sect, persuasion, creed, school, hauhau (*N.Z.*) 2 = <u>unit</u>, value, size, grade

**denounce** 1 = <u>condemn</u>, attack, censure, revile, vilify, stigmatize 2 = <u>report</u>, dob in (*Austral. slang*)

**dense** 1 = <u>thick</u>, heavy, solid, compact, condensed, impenetrable, close-knit ≠ thin 2 = <u>heavy</u>, thick, opaque, impenetrable 3 = <u>stupid</u> (*Informal*), thick, dull, dumb (*informal*), dozy (*Brit. informal*), stolid, dopey (*informal*), moronic ≠ bright

**density** 1 = <u>tightness</u>, thickness, compactness, impenetrability, denseness 2 = <u>mass</u>, bulk, consistency, solidity

**dent** VERB = <u>make a dent in</u>, press in, gouge, hollow, push in ● NOUN = <u>hollow</u>, chip, indentation, depression, impression, pit, dip, crater, ding (*Austral. & N.Z. dated informal*)

**deny** 1 = <u>contradict</u>, disagree with, rebuff, negate, rebut, refute ≠ admit 2 = <u>renounce</u>, reject, retract, repudiate, disown, recant, disclaim 3 = <u>refuse</u>, forbid, reject,

149

depart → depot

rule out, turn down, prohibit, withhold, preclude ≠ permit

**depart** 1 = <u>leave</u>, go, withdraw, retire, disappear, quit, retreat, exit ≠ arrive 2 = <u>deviate</u>, vary, differ, stray, veer, swerve, diverge, digress

**department** = <u>section</u>, office, unit, station, division, branch, bureau, subdivision

**departure** 1 = <u>leaving</u>, going, retirement, withdrawal, exit, going away, removal, exodus ≠ arrival 2 = <u>retirement</u>, going, withdrawal, exit, going away, removal 3 = <u>shift</u>, change, difference, variation, innovation, novelty, deviation, divergence

**depend** 1 = <u>be determined by</u>, be based on, be subject to, hang on, rest on, revolve around, hinge on, be subordinate to 2 = <u>count on</u>, turn to, trust in, bank on, lean on, rely upon, reckon on

**dependent** or (U.S. sometimes)
**dependant** ADJECTIVE = <u>reliant</u>, vulnerable, helpless, powerless, weak, defenceless ≠ independent
● PHRASES **dependent on** or **upon** 1 = <u>reliant on</u>, relying on 2 = <u>determined by</u>, depending on, subject to, influenced by, conditional on, contingent on

**depict** 1 = <u>illustrate</u>, portray, picture, paint, outline, draw, sketch, delineate 2 = <u>describe</u>, present, represent, outline,

characterize

**deplete** = <u>use up</u>, reduce, drain, exhaust, consume, empty, lessen, impoverish ≠ increase

**deplore** = <u>disapprove of</u>, condemn, object to, denounce, censure, abhor, take a dim view of

**deploy** (used of troops or military resources) = <u>use</u>, station, position, arrange, set out, utilize

**deployment** (used of troops or military resources) = <u>use</u>, stationing, spread, organization, arrangement, positioning, utilization

**deport** = <u>expel</u>, exile, throw out, oust, banish, expatriate, extradite, evict

**depose** = <u>oust</u>, dismiss, displace, demote, dethrone, remove from office

**deposit** NOUN 1 = <u>down payment</u>, security, stake, pledge, instalment, retainer, part payment 2 = <u>accumulation</u>, mass, build-up, layer 3 = <u>sediment</u>, grounds, residue, lees, precipitate, silt, dregs
● VERB 1 = <u>put</u>, place, lay, place 2 = <u>store</u>, keep, put, bank, lodge, entrust, consign

**depot** 1 = <u>arsenal</u>, warehouse, storehouse, repository, depository 2 (Chiefly U.S. & Canad.) = <u>bus station</u>, station, garage, terminus

**depreciation** = <u>devaluation</u>, fall, drop, depression, slump, deflation

**depress** 1 = <u>sadden</u>, upset, distress, discourage, grieve, oppress, weigh down, make sad ≠ cheer 2 = <u>lower</u>, cut, reduce, diminish, decrease, lessen ≠ raise 3 = <u>devalue</u>, depreciate, diminish 4 = <u>press down</u>, push, squeeze, lower, flatten, compress, push down

**depressed** 1 = <u>sad</u>, blue, unhappy, discouraged, fed up, mournful, dejected, despondent 2 = <u>poverty-stricken</u>, poor, deprived, disadvantaged, run-down, impoverished, needy 3 = <u>lowered</u>, devalued, weakened, depreciated, cheapened 4 = <u>sunken</u>, hollow, recessed, indented, concave

**depressing** = <u>bleak</u>, sad, discouraging, gloomy, dismal, harrowing, saddening, dispiriting

**depression** 1 = <u>despair</u>, misery, sadness, dumps (*informal*), the blues, melancholy, unhappiness, despondency 2 = <u>recession</u>, slump, economic decline, stagnation, inactivity, hard *or* bad times 3 = <u>hollow</u>, pit, dip, bowl, valley, dent, cavity, indentation

**deprivation** 1 = <u>lack</u>, denial, withdrawal, removal, expropriation, dispossession 2 = <u>want</u>, need, hardship, suffering, distress, privation, destitution

**deprive** = <u>dispossess</u>, rob, strip, despoil, bereave

**deprived** = <u>poor</u>, disadvantaged, needy, in need, lacking, bereft, destitute, down at heel ≠ prosperous

**depth** 1 = <u>deepness</u>, drop, measure, extent 2 = <u>insight</u>, wisdom, penetration, profundity, discernment, sagacity, astuteness, profoundness ≠ superficiality 3 = <u>breadth</u>

**deputy** = <u>substitute</u>, representative, delegate, lieutenant, proxy, surrogate, second-in-command, legate

**derelict** ADJECTIVE = <u>abandoned</u>, deserted, ruined, neglected, discarded, forsaken, dilapidated
● NOUN = <u>tramp</u>, outcast, drifter, down-and-out, vagrant, bag lady, derro (*Austral. slang*)

**descend** VERB 1 = <u>fall</u>, drop, sink, go down, plunge, dive, tumble, plummet ≠ rise 2 = <u>get off</u> 3 = <u>go down</u>, come down, walk down, move down, climb down 4 = <u>slope</u>, dip, incline, slant
● PHRASES be descended from = <u>originate from</u>, derive from, spring from, proceed from, issue from

**descent** 1 = <u>fall</u>, drop, plunge, coming down, swoop 2 = <u>slope</u>, drop, dip, incline, slant, declivity

3 = **decline**, deterioration, degeneration 4 = **origin**, extraction, ancestry, lineage, family tree, parentage, genealogy, derivation

**describe** 1 = **relate**, tell, report, explain, express, recount, recite, narrate 2 = **portray**, depict 3 = **trace**, draw, outline, mark out, delineate

**description** 1 = **account**, report, explanation, representation, sketch, narrative, portrayal, depiction 2 = **calling**, naming, branding, labelling, dubbing, designation 3 = **kind**, sort, type, order, class, variety, brand, category

**desert**[1] = **wilderness**, waste, wilds, wasteland

**desert**[2] 1 = **abandon**, leave, quit (*informal*), forsake 2 = **leave**, abandon, strand, maroon, walk out on (*informal*), forsake, jilt, leave stranded ≠ take care of 3 = **abscond**

**deserted** 1 = **empty**, abandoned, desolate, neglected, vacant, derelict, unoccupied 2 = **abandoned**, neglected, forsaken

**deserve** = **merit**, warrant, be entitled to, have a right to, rate, earn, justify, be worthy of

**deserved** = **well-earned**, fitting, due, earned, justified, merited, proper, warranted

**deserving** = **worthy**, righteous, commendable, laudable, praiseworthy, meritorious, estimable ≠ undeserving

**design** VERB 1 = **plan**, draw, draft, trace, outline, devise, sketch, formulate 2 = **create**, plan, fashion, propose, invent, conceive, originate, fabricate 3 = **intend**, mean, plan, aim, purpose

● NOUN 1 = **pattern**, form, style, shape, organization, arrangement, construction 2 = **plan**, drawing, model, scheme, draft, outline, sketch, blueprint 3 = **intention**, end, aim, goal, target, purpose, object, objective

**designate** 1 = **name**, call, term, style, label, entitle, dub 2 = **choose**, reserve, select, label, flag, assign, allocate, set aside 3 = **appoint**, name, choose, commission, select, elect, delegate, nominate

**designer** 1 = **couturier** 2 = **producer**, architect, deviser, creator, planner, inventor, originator

**desirable** 1 = **advantageous**, useful, valuable, helpful, profitable, of service, convenient, worthwhile ≠ disadvantageous 2 = **popular** ≠ unpopular 3 = **attractive**, appealing, pretty, fair, inviting, lovely, charming, sexy (*informal*) ≠ unattractive

**desire** NOUN 1 = <u>wish</u>, want, longing, hope, urge, aspiration, craving, thirst 2 = <u>lust</u>, passion, libido, appetite, lasciviousness

• VERB = <u>want</u>, long for, crave, hope for, ache for, wish for, yearn for, thirst for

**despair** NOUN = <u>despondency</u>, depression, misery, gloom, desperation, anguish, hopelessness, dejection

• VERB = <u>lose hope</u>, give up, lose heart

**despatch ▸ dispatch**

**desperate** 1 = <u>grave</u>, pressing, serious, severe, extreme, urgent, drastic 2 = <u>last-ditch</u>, daring, furious, risky, frantic, audacious

**desperately** = <u>gravely</u>, badly, seriously, severely, dangerously, perilously

**desperation** 1 = <u>misery</u>, worry, trouble, despair, agony, anguish, unhappiness, hopelessness 2 = <u>recklessness</u>, madness, frenzy, impetuosity, rashness, foolhardiness

**despise** = <u>look down on</u>, loathe, scorn, detest, revile, abhor ≠ admire

**despite** = <u>in spite of</u>, in the face of, regardless of, even with, notwithstanding, in the teeth of, undeterred by

**destination** = <u>stop</u>, station, haven, resting-place, terminus,

journey's end

**destined** = <u>fated</u>, meant, intended, certain, bound, doomed, predestined

**destiny** 1 = <u>fate</u>, fortune, lot, portion, doom, nemesis 2 *usually cap.* = <u>fortune</u>, chance, karma, providence, kismet, predestination, divine will

**destroy** 1 = <u>ruin</u>, crush, devastate, wreck, shatter, wipe out, demolish, eradicate 2 = <u>slaughter</u>, kill

**destruction** 1 = <u>ruin</u>, havoc, wreckage, demolition, devastation, annihilation 2 = <u>slaughter</u>, extermination, eradication 3 = <u>slaughter</u>

**destructive** = <u>devastating</u>, fatal, deadly, lethal, harmful, damaging, catastrophic, ruinous

**detach** 1 = <u>separate</u>, remove, divide, cut off, sever, disconnect, tear off, disengage ≠ attach 2 = <u>free</u>, remove, separate, isolate, cut off, disengage

**detached** 1 = <u>objective</u>, neutral, impartial, reserved, impersonal, disinterested, unbiased, dispassionate ≠ subjective 2 = <u>separate</u>, disconnected, discrete, unconnected, undivided

**detachment** 1 = <u>indifference</u>, fairness, neutrality, objectivity, impartiality, coolness, remoteness, nonchalance 2 (*Military*) = <u>unit</u>, party, force, body, squad, patrol, task force

**detail** NOUN 1 = point, fact, feature, particular, respect, factor, element, aspect 2 = fine point, particular, nicety, triviality 3 (*Military*) = party, force, body, duty, squad, assignment, fatigue, detachment

● VERB = list, relate, catalogue, recount, rehearse, recite, enumerate, itemize

**detailed** = comprehensive, full, complete, minute, particular, thorough, exhaustive, all-embracing ≠ brief

**detain** 1 = hold, arrest, confine, restrain, imprison, intern, take prisoner, hold in custody 2 = delay, hold up, hamper, hinder, retard, impede, keep back, slow up *or* down

**detect** 1 = discover, find, uncover, track down, unmask 2 = notice, see, spot, note, identify, observe, recognize, perceive

**detective** = investigator, cop (*slang*), private eye, sleuth (*informal*), private investigator, gumshoe (*U.S. slang*)

**detention** = imprisonment, custody, quarantine, confinement, incarceration ≠ release

**deter** 1 = discourage, inhibit, put off, frighten, intimidate, dissuade, talk out of 2 = prevent, stop

**deteriorate** = decline, worsen, degenerate, slump, go downhill ≠ improve

**determination** = resolution, purpose, resolve, dedication, fortitude, persistence, tenacity, perseverance ≠ indecision

**determine** 1 = affect, decide, regulate, ordain 2 = settle, learn, establish, discover, find out, work out, detect, verify 3 = decide on, choose, elect, resolve 4 = decide, conclude, resolve, make up your mind

**determined** = resolute, firm, dogged, intent, persistent, persevering, single-minded, tenacious

**deterrent** = discouragement, obstacle, curb, restraint, impediment, check, hindrance, disincentive ≠ incentive

**devastate** = destroy, ruin, sack, wreck, demolish, level, ravage, raze

**devastation** = destruction, ruin, havoc, demolition, desolation

**develop** 1 = grow, advance, progress, mature, evolve, flourish, ripen 2 = establish, set up, promote, generate, undertake, initiate, embark on, cultivate 3 = form, establish, breed, generate, originate 4 = expand, extend, work out, elaborate, unfold, enlarge, broaden, amplify

**development** 1 = growth,

increase, advance, progress, spread, expansion, evolution, enlargement 2 = <u>establishment</u>, forming, generation, institution, invention, initiation, inauguration, instigation 3 = <u>event</u>, happening, result, incident, improvement, evolution, unfolding, occurrence

**deviant** ADJECTIVE = <u>perverted</u>, sick (*informal*), twisted, warped, kinky (*slang*) ≠ normal
• NOUN = <u>pervert</u>, freak, misfit

**device** 1 = <u>gadget</u>, machine, tool, instrument, implement, appliance, apparatus, contraption 2 = <u>ploy</u>, scheme, plan, trick, manoeuvre, gambit, stratagem, wile

**devil** NOUN 1 = <u>evil spirit</u>, demon, fiend, atua (*N.Z.*), wairua (*N.Z.*) 2 = <u>brute</u>, monster, beast, barbarian, fiend, terror, swine, ogre 3 = <u>person</u>, individual, soul, creature, thing, beggar 4 = <u>scamp</u>, rogue, rascal, scoundrel, scallywag (*informal*), nointer (*Austral. slang*)
• PHRASES **the Devil** = <u>Satan</u>, Lucifer, Prince of Darkness, Mephistopheles, Evil One, Beelzebub, Old Nick (*informal*)

**devise** = <u>work out</u>, design, construct, invent, conceive, formulate, contrive, dream up

**devoid** with of = <u>lacking in</u>, without, free from, wanting in,

bereft of, empty of, deficient in

**devote** = <u>dedicate</u>, give, commit, apply, reserve, pledge, surrender, assign

**devoted** = <u>dedicated</u>, committed, true, constant, loyal, faithful, ardent, staunch ≠ disloyal

**devotee** = <u>enthusiast</u>, fan, supporter, follower, admirer, buff (*informal*), fanatic, adherent

**devotion** NOUN 1 = <u>love</u>, passion, affection, attachment, fondness 2 = <u>dedication</u>, commitment, loyalty, allegiance, fidelity, adherence, constancy, faithfulness ≠ indifference 3 = <u>worship</u>, reverence, spirituality, holiness, piety, godliness, devoutness ≠ irreverence
• PLURAL NOUN = <u>prayers</u>, religious observance, church service, divine office

**devour** 1 = <u>eat</u>, consume, swallow, wolf, gulp, gobble, guzzle, polish off (*informal*) 2 = <u>enjoy</u>, take in, read compulsively *or* voraciously

**devout** = <u>religious</u>, godly, pious, pure, holy, orthodox, saintly, reverent ≠ irreverent

**diagnose** = <u>identify</u>, determine, recognize, distinguish, interpret, pronounce, pinpoint

**diagnosis** = <u>identification</u>, discovery, recognition, detection

**diagram** = <u>plan</u>, figure, drawing,

chart, representation, sketch, graph

**dialogue** 1 = <u>discussion</u>, conference, exchange, debate 2 = <u>conversation</u>, discussion, communication, discourse

**diary** 1 = <u>journal</u>, chronicle 2 = <u>engagement book</u>, Filofax®, appointment book

**dictate** VERB = <u>speak</u>, say, utter, read out

● NOUN 1 = <u>command</u>, order, decree, demand, direction, injunction, fiat, edict

2 = <u>principle</u>, law, rule, standard, code, criterion, maxim

● PHRASES **dictate to someone** = <u>order (about)</u>, direct, lay down the law, pronounce to

**dictator** = <u>absolute ruler</u>, tyrant, despot, oppressor, autocrat, absolutist, martinet

**dictatorship** = <u>absolute rule</u>, tyranny, totalitarianism, authoritarianism, despotism, autocracy, absolutism

**dictionary** = <u>wordbook</u>, vocabulary, glossary, lexicon

**die** VERB 1 = <u>pass away</u>, expire, perish, croak (slang), give up the ghost, snuff it (slang), peg out (informal), kick the bucket (slang), cark it (Austral. & N.Z. slang) ≠ live 2 = <u>stop</u>, fail, halt, break down, run down, stop working, peter out, fizzle out 3 = <u>dwindle</u>, decline, sink, fade,

diminish, decrease, decay, wither ≠ increase

● PHRASES **be dying for something** = <u>long for</u>, want, desire, crave, yearn for, hunger for, pine for, hanker after

**diet¹** NOUN 1 = <u>food</u>, provisions, fare, rations, kai (N.Z. informal), nourishment, sustenance, victuals 2 = <u>fast</u>, regime, abstinence, regimen

● VERB = <u>slim</u>, fast, lose weight, abstain, eat sparingly ≠ overindulge

**diet²** often cap. = <u>council</u>, meeting, parliament, congress, chamber, convention, legislature

**differ** 1 = <u>be dissimilar</u>, contradict, contrast with, vary, belie, depart from, diverge, negate ≠ accord 2 = <u>disagree</u>, clash, dispute, dissent ≠ agree

**difference** 1 = <u>dissimilarity</u>, contrast, variation, change, variety, diversity, alteration, discrepancy ≠ similarity 2 = <u>remainder</u>, rest, balance, remains, excess 3 = <u>disagreement</u>, conflict, argument, clash, dispute, quarrel, contretemps ≠ agreement

**different** 1 = <u>dissimilar</u>, opposed, contrasting, changed, unlike, altered, inconsistent, disparate 2 = <u>various</u>, varied, diverse, assorted, miscellaneous, sundry 3 = <u>unusual</u>, special, strange, extraordinary, distinctive, peculiar, uncommon, singular

> ### Word Power
>
> **different** – On the whole, *different from* is preferable to *different to* and *different than*, both of which are considered unacceptable by some people. *Different to* is often heard in British English, but is thought by some people to be incorrect; and *different than*, though acceptable in American English, is often regarded as unacceptable in British English. This makes *different from* the safest option: *this result is only slightly different from that obtained in the US* – or you can rephrase the sentence: *this result differs only slightly from that obtained in the US.*

**differentiate** 1 = distinguish, separate, discriminate, contrast, mark off, make a distinction, tell apart, set off or apart 2 = make different, separate, distinguish, characterize, single out, segregate, individualize, mark off 3 = become different, change, convert, transform, alter, adapt, modify

**difficult** 1 = hard, tough, taxing, demanding, challenging, exacting, formidable, uphill ≠ easy 2 = problematical,

involved, complex, complicated, obscure, baffling, intricate, knotty ≠ simple 3 = troublesome, demanding, perverse, fussy, fastidious, hard to please, refractory, unaccommodating ≠ cooperative

**difficulty** 1 = problem, trouble, obstacle, hurdle, dilemma, complication, snag, uphill (*S. African*) 2 = hardship, strain, awkwardness, strenuousness, arduousness, laboriousness

**dig** VERB 1 = hollow out, mine, quarry, excavate, scoop out 2 = delve, tunnel, burrow 3 = turn over 4 = search, hunt, root, delve, forage, dig down, fossick (*Austral. & N.Z.*) 5 = poke, drive, push, stick, punch, stab, thrust, shove
● NOUN 1 = cutting remark, crack (*slang*), insult, taunt, sneer, jeer, barb, wisecrack (*informal*)
2 = poke, thrust, nudge, prod, jab, punch

**digest** VERB 1 = ingest, absorb, incorporate, dissolve, assimilate 2 = take in, absorb, grasp, soak up
● NOUN 1 = summary, résumé, abstract, epitome, synopsis, précis, abridgment

**dignity** 1 = decorum, gravity, majesty, grandeur, respectability, nobility, solemnity, courtliness 2 = self-importance, pride, self-esteem, self-respect

**dilemma** = predicament,

problem, difficulty, spot (*informal*), mess, puzzle, plight, quandary

> ### Word Power
>
> **dilemma** – The use of *dilemma* to refer to a problem that seems incapable of solution is considered by some people to be incorrect. To avoid this misuse of the word, an appropriate alternative such as *predicament* could be used.

**dilute** 1 = <u>water down</u>, thin (out), weaken, adulterate, make thinner, cut (*informal*) ≠ condense 2 = <u>reduce</u>, weaken, diminish, temper, decrease, lessen, diffuse, mitigate ≠ intensify

**dim ADJECTIVE** 1 = <u>poorly lit</u>, dark, gloomy, murky, shady, shadowy, dusky, tenebrous 2 = <u>cloudy</u>, grey, gloomy, dismal, overcast, leaden ≠ bright 3 = <u>unclear</u>, obscured, faint, blurred, fuzzy, shadowy, hazy, bleary ≠ distinct 4 = <u>stupid</u> (*Informal*), thick, dull, dense, dumb (*informal*), daft (*informal*), dozy (*Brit. informal*), obtuse ≠ bright
● **VERB** 1 = <u>turn down</u>, fade, dull 2 = <u>grow or become faint</u>, fade, dull, grow or become dim 3 = <u>darken</u>, dull, cloud over

**dimension** 1 = <u>aspect</u>, side, feature, angle, facet 2 = <u>extent</u>, size

**diminish** 1 = <u>decrease</u>, decline, lessen, shrink, dwindle, wane, recede, subside ≠ grow 2 = <u>reduce</u>, cut, decrease, lessen, lower, curtail ≠ increase

**din** = <u>noise</u>, row, racket, crash, clamour, clatter, uproar, commotion ≠ silence

**dine** = <u>eat</u>, lunch, feast, sup

**dinkum** (*Austral. & N.Z. informal*) = <u>genuine</u>, honest, natural, frank, sincere, candid, upfront (*informal*), artless

**dinner** 1 = <u>meal</u>, main meal, spread (*informal*), repast 2 = <u>banquet</u>, feast, repast, hakari (*N.Z.*)

**dinosaur ► dinosaurs**

**dip VERB** 1 = <u>plunge</u>, immerse, bathe, duck, douse, dunk 2 = <u>drop (down)</u>, fall, lower, sink, descend, subside ≠ slope (down), descend, fall, decline, sink, incline, drop away
● **NOUN** 1 = <u>plunge</u>, ducking, soaking, drenching, immersion, douche 2 = <u>nod</u>, drop, lowering, slump, sag 3 = <u>hollow</u>, hole, depression, pit, basin, trough, concavity
● **PHRASES dip into something** = <u>sample</u>, skim, glance at, browse, peruse

**diplomacy** 1 = <u>statesmanship</u>, statecraft, international negotiation 2 = <u>tact</u>, skill,

## Dinosaurs

| | | |
|---|---|---|
| allosaur(us) | elasmosaur(us) | protoceratops |
| ankylosaur(us) | hadrosaur(us) | stegodon or |
| apatosaur(us) | ichthyosaur(us) | stegodont |
| atlantosaur(us) | iguanodon or | stegosaur(us) |
| brachiosaur(us) | iguanodont | theropod |
| brontosaur(us) | megalosaur(us) | titanosaur(us) |
| ceratosaur(us) | mosasaur(us) | trachodon |
| compsognathus | oviraptor | triceratops |
| dimetrodon | plesiosaur(us) | tyrannosaur(us) |
| diplodocus | pteranodon | velociraptor |
| dolichosaur(us) | pterodactyl or | |
| dromiosaur(us) | pterosaur | |

sensitivity, craft, discretion, subtlety, delicacy, finesse ≠ tactlessness

**diplomat** = <u>official</u>, ambassador, envoy, statesman, consul, attaché, emissary, chargé d'affaires

**diplomatic** 1 = <u>consular</u>, official, foreign-office, ambassadorial, foreign-politic 2 = <u>tactful</u>, politic, sensitive, subtle, delicate, polite, discreet, prudent ≠ tactless

**dire** = <u>desperate</u>, pressing, critical, terrible, crucial, extreme, awful, urgent

**direct** ADJECTIVE = <u>quickest</u>, shortest

● ADVERB 1 = <u>straight</u>, through ≠ circuitous 2 = <u>first-hand</u>, personal, immediate ≠ indirect 3 = <u>clear</u>, specific, plain, absolute, definite, explicit, downright, point-blank ≠ ambiguous 4 = <u>straightforward</u>, open,

straight, frank, blunt, honest, candid, forthright ≠ indirect 5 = <u>verbatim</u>, exact, word-for-word, strict, accurate, faithful, letter-for-letter 6 = <u>non-stop</u>, straight

● VERB 1 = <u>aim</u>, point, level, train, focus 2 = <u>guide</u>, show, lead, point the way, point in the direction of 3 = <u>control</u>, run, manage, lead, guide, handle, conduct, oversee 4 = <u>order</u>, command, instruct, charge, demand, require, bid 5 = <u>address</u>, send, mail, route, label

**direction** NOUN 1 = <u>way</u>, course, line, road, track, bearing, route, path 2 = <u>management</u>, control, charge, administration, leadership, command, guidance, supervision

● PLURAL NOUN = <u>instructions</u>, rules, information, plan, briefing, regulations, recommendations, guidelines

**directive** = <u>order</u>, ruling, regulation, command, instruction, decree, mandate, injunction

**directly** 1 = <u>straight</u>, unswervingly, without deviation, by the shortest route, in a beeline 2 = <u>immediately</u>, promptly, right away, straightaway 3 (*Old-fashioned*) = <u>at once</u>, as soon as possible, straightaway, forthwith 4 = <u>honestly</u>, openly, frankly, plainly, point-blank, unequivocally, truthfully, unreservedly

**director** = <u>controller</u>, head, leader, manager, chief, executive, governor, administrator, baas (*S. African*)

**dirt** 1 = <u>filth</u>, muck, grime, dust, mud, impurity, kak (*S. African taboo slang*) 2 = <u>soil</u>, ground, earth, clay, turf, loam

**dirty** ADJECTIVE 1 = <u>filthy</u>, soiled, grubby, foul, muddy, polluted, messy, grimy, festy (*Austral. slang*) ≠ clean 2 = <u>dishonest</u>, illegal, unfair, cheating, crooked, fraudulent, treacherous, unscrupulous ≠ honest 3 = <u>obscene</u>, indecent, blue, offensive, filthy, pornographic, sleazy, lewd ≠ decent

● VERB = <u>soil</u>, foul, stain, spoil, muddy, pollute, blacken, defile

≠ clean

**disability** = <u>handicap</u>, affliction, disorder, defect, impairment, infirmity

**disable** = <u>handicap</u>, cripple, damage, paralyse, impair, incapacitate, immobilize, enfeeble

**disabled** = <u>differently abled</u>, physically challenged, handicapped, weakened, crippled, paralysed, lame, incapacitated ≠ able-bodied

---

### Word Power

**disabled** – Referring to people with disabilities as *the disabled* can cause offence and should be avoided. Instead, refer to them as people *with disabilities* or *who are physically challenged*, or, possibly, *disabled people* or *differently abled people*. In general, the terms used for disabilities or medical conditions should be avoided as collective nouns for people who have them – so, for example, instead of *the blind*, it is preferable to refer to *sightless people*, *vision-impaired people*, or *partially-sighted people*, depending on the degree of their condition.

---

**disadvantage** 1 = <u>drawback</u>, trouble, handicap, nuisance, snag, inconvenience, downside

≠ **advantage** 2 = <u>harm</u>, loss, damage, injury, hurt, prejudice, detriment, disservice ≠ benefit

**disagree** 1 = <u>differ (in opinion)</u>, argue, clash, dispute, dissent, quarrel, take issue with, cross swords ≠ agree 2 = <u>make ill</u>, upset, sicken, trouble, hurt, bother, distress, discomfort

**disagreement** 1 = <u>argument</u>, row, conflict, clash, dispute, dissent, quarrel, squabble ≠ agreement

**disappear** 1 = <u>vanish</u>, recede, evanesce ≠ appear 2 = <u>pass</u>, fade away 3 = <u>cease</u>, dissolve, evaporate, perish, die out, pass away, melt away, leave no trace

**disappearance** 1 = <u>vanishing</u>, going, passing, melting, eclipse, evaporation, evanescence 2 = <u>flight</u>, departure 3 = <u>loss</u>, losing, mislaying

**disappoint** = <u>let down</u>, dismay, fail, disillusion, dishearten, disenchant, dissatisfy, disgruntle

**disappointment** 1 = <u>regret</u>, discontent, dissatisfaction, disillusionment, chagrin, disenchantment, dejection, despondency 2 = <u>letdown</u>, blow, setback, misfortune, calamity, choker (*informal*) 3 = <u>frustration</u>

**disapproval** = <u>displeasure</u>, criticism, objection, condemnation, dissatisfaction, censure, reproach, denunciation

**disapprove** = <u>condemn</u>, object to, dislike, deplore, frown on, take exception to, take a dim view of, find unacceptable ≠ approve

**disarm** 1 = <u>demilitarize</u>, disband, demobilize, deactivate 2 = <u>win over</u>, persuade

**disarmament** = <u>arms reduction</u>, demobilization, arms limitation, demilitarization, de-escalation

**disarming** = <u>charming</u>, winning, irresistible, persuasive, likable *or* likeable

**disarray** 1 = <u>confusion</u>, disorder, indiscipline, disunity, disorganization, unruliness ≠ order 2 = <u>untidiness</u>, mess, chaos, muddle, clutter, shambles, jumble, hotchpotch ≠ tidiness

**disaster** 1 = <u>catastrophe</u>, trouble, tragedy, ruin, misfortune, adversity, calamity, cataclysm 2 = <u>failure</u>, mess, flop (*informal*), catastrophe, debacle, cock-up (*Brit. slang*), washout (*informal*)

**disastrous** 1 = <u>terrible</u>, devastating, tragic, fatal, catastrophic, ruinous, calamitous, cataclysmic 2 = <u>unsuccessful</u>

**disbelief** = <u>scepticism</u>, doubt, distrust, mistrust, incredulity, unbelief, dubiety ≠ belief

**discard** = <u>get rid of</u>, drop, throw away *or* out, reject, abandon, dump (*informal*), dispose of, dispense with ≠ keep

**discharge** VERB 1 = <u>release</u>, free, clear, liberate, pardon, allow to go, set free 2 = <u>dismiss</u>, sack (*informal*), fire (*informal*), remove, expel, discard, oust, cashier 3 = <u>carry out</u>, perform, fulfil, accomplish, do, effect, realize, observe 4 = <u>pay</u>, meet, clear, settle, square (up), honour, satisfy, relieve 5 = <u>pour forth</u>, release, leak, emit, dispense, ooze, exude, give off 6 = <u>fire</u>, shoot, set off, explode, let off, detonate, let loose (*informal*)
● NOUN 1 = <u>release</u>, liberation, clearance, pardon, acquittal 2 = <u>dismissal</u>, notice, removal, the boot (*slang*), expulsion, the push (*slang*), marching orders (*informal*), ejection 3 = <u>emission</u>, ooze, secretion, excretion, pus, seepage, suppuration 4 = <u>firing</u>, report, shot, blast, explosion, volley, salvo

**disciple** 1 = <u>apostle</u> 2 = <u>follower</u>, student, supporter, pupil, devotee, apostle, adherent ≠ teacher

**discipline** NOUN 1 = <u>control</u>, authority, regulation, supervision, orderliness, strictness 2 = <u>punishment</u>, penalty, correction, chastening, chastisement, castigation 3 = <u>self-control</u>, control, restraint, self-discipline, willpower, self-restraint, orderliness 4 = <u>training</u>, practice, exercise, method, regulation, drill, regimen 5 = <u>field of study</u>, area, subject, theme, topic, course, curriculum, speciality
● VERB 1 = <u>punish</u>, correct, reprimand, castigate, chastise, chasten, penalize, bring to book 2 = <u>train</u>, educate

**disclose** 1 = <u>make known</u>, reveal, publish, relate, broadcast, confess, communicate, divulge ≠ keep secret 2 = <u>show</u>, reveal, expose, unveil, uncover, lay bare, bring to light ≠ hide

**disclosure** 1 = <u>revelation</u>, announcement, publication, leak, admission, declaration, confession, acknowledgment 2 = <u>uncovering</u>, publication, revelation, divulgence

**discomfort** 1 = <u>pain</u>, hurt, ache, throbbing, irritation, tenderness, pang, malaise ≠ comfort 2 = <u>uneasiness</u>, worry, anxiety, doubt, distress, misgiving, qualms, trepidation ≠ reassurance 3 = <u>inconvenience</u>, trouble, difficulty, bother, hardship, irritation, nuisance, uphill (*S. African*)

**discontent** = <u>dissatisfaction</u>, unhappiness, displeasure, regret, envy, restlessness, uneasiness

**discontented** = <u>dissatisfied</u>, unhappy, fed up, disgruntled, disaffected, vexed, displeased

≠ satisfied

**discount** NOUN = <u>deduction</u>, cut, reduction, concession, rebate

● VERB 1 = <u>mark down</u>, reduce, lower 2 = <u>disregard</u>, reject, ignore, overlook, discard, set aside, dispel, pass over

**discourage** 1 = <u>dishearten</u>, depress, intimidate, overawe, demoralize, put a damper on, dispirit, deject ≠ hearten 2 = <u>put off</u>, deter, prevent, dissuade, talk out of ≠ encourage

**discourse** 1 = <u>conversation</u>, talk, discussion, speech, communication, chat, dialogue 2 = <u>speech</u>, essay, lecture, sermon, treatise, dissertation, homily, oration, whaikorero (N.Z.)

**discover** 1 = <u>find out</u>, learn, notice, realize, recognize, perceive, detect, uncover 2 = <u>find</u>, come across, uncover, unearth, turn up, dig up, come upon

**discovery** 1 = <u>finding out</u>, news, revelation, disclosure, realization 2 = <u>invention</u>, launch, institution, pioneering, innovation, inauguration 3 = <u>breakthrough</u>, find, development, advance, leap, invention, step forward, quantum leap 4 = <u>finding</u>, revelation, uncovering, disclosure, detection

**discredit** VERB 1 = <u>disgrace</u>, shame, smear, humiliate, taint, disparage, vilify, slander ≠ honour 2 = <u>dispute</u>, question, challenge,

deny, reject, discount, distrust, mistrust

● NOUN = <u>disgrace</u>, scandal, shame, disrepute, stigma, ignominy, dishonour, ill-repute ≠ honour

**discreet** = <u>tactful</u>, diplomatic, guarded, careful, cautious, wary, prudent, considerate ≠ tactless

**discrepancy** = <u>disagreement</u>, difference, variation, conflict, contradiction, inconsistency, disparity, divergence

**discretion** 1 = <u>tact</u>, consideration, caution, diplomacy, prudence, wariness, carefulness, judiciousness ≠ tactlessness 2 = <u>choice</u>, will, pleasure, preference, inclination, volition

**discriminate** VERB = <u>differentiate</u>, distinguish, separate, tell the difference, draw a distinction

● PHRASES **discriminate against someone** = <u>treat differently</u>, single out, victimize, treat as inferior, show bias against, show prejudice against

**discriminating** = <u>discerning</u>, particular, refined, cultivated, selective, tasteful, fastidious ≠ undiscriminating

**discrimination** 1 = <u>prejudice</u>, bias, injustice, intolerance, bigotry, favouritism, unfairness 2 = <u>discernment</u>, taste, judgment, perception, subtlety, refinement

**discuss** = <u>talk about</u>, consider, debate, examine, argue about, deliberate about, converse about, confer about

**discussion** 1 = <u>talk</u>, debate, argument, conference, conversation, dialogue, consultation, discourse, korero (N.Z.) 2 = <u>examination</u>, investigation, analysis, scrutiny, dissection

**disdain** NOUN = <u>contempt</u>, scorn, arrogance, derision, haughtiness, superciliousness
● VERB = <u>scorn</u>, reject, slight, disregard, spurn, deride, look down on, sneer at

**disease** = <u>illness</u>, condition, complaint, infection, disorder, sickness, ailment, affliction

**diseased** = <u>unhealthy</u>, sick, infected, rotten, ailing, sickly, unwell, crook (Austral. & N.Z. informal), unsound

**disgrace** NOUN 1 = <u>shame</u>, degradation, disrepute, ignominy, dishonour, infamy, opprobrium, odium ≠ honour 2 = <u>scandal</u>, stain, stigma, blot, blemish
● VERB = <u>shame</u>, humiliate, discredit, degrade, taint, sully, dishonour, bring shame upon ≠ honour

**disgraceful** = <u>shameful</u>, shocking, scandalous, unworthy, ignominious, disreputable,

# discuss → disintegrate

contemptible, dishonourable

**disgruntled** = <u>discontented</u>, dissatisfied, annoyed, irritated, put out, grumpy, vexed, displeased, hoha (N.Z.)

**disguise** NOUN = <u>costume</u>, mask, camouflage
● VERB = <u>hide</u>, cover, conceal, screen, mask, suppress, withhold, veil

**disguised** = <u>in disguise</u>, masked, camouflaged, undercover, incognito 2 = <u>false</u>, artificial, forged, fake, mock, imitation, sham, counterfeit

**disgust** NOUN 1 = <u>loathing</u>, revulsion, hatred, dislike, nausea, distaste, aversion, repulsion ≠ liking 2 = <u>outrage</u>, shock, anger, hurt, fury, resentment, wrath, indignation
● VERB = <u>sicken</u>, offend, revolt, put off, repel, nauseate ≠ delight

**disgusting** 1 = <u>sickening</u>, foul, revolting, gross, repellent, nauseating, repugnant, loathsome, festy (Austral. slang), yucko (Austral. slang) 2 = <u>appalling</u>, shocking, awful, offensive, dreadful, horrifying

**dish** 1 = <u>bowl</u>, plate, platter, salver 2 = <u>food</u>, fare, recipe

**dishonest** = <u>deceitful</u>, corrupt, crooked (informal), lying, bent (slang), false, cheating, treacherous ≠ honest

**disintegrate** = <u>break up</u>,

crumble, fall apart, separate, shatter, splinter, break apart, go to pieces

**dislike** VERB = hate, object to, loathe, despise, disapprove of, detest, recoil from, take a dim view of ≠ like
● NOUN = hatred, hostility, disapproval, distaste, animosity, aversion, displeasure, antipathy ≠ liking

**dismal** 1 = bad, awful, dreadful, rotten (informal), terrible, poor, dire, abysmal 2 = sad, gloomy, dark, depressing, discouraging, bleak, dreary, sombre ≠ happy 3 = gloomy, depressing, dull, dreary ≠ cheerful

**dismantle** = take apart, strip, demolish, disassemble, take to pieces or bits

**dismay** NOUN 1 = alarm, fear, horror, anxiety, dread, apprehension, nervousness, consternation 2 = disappointment, frustration, dissatisfaction, disillusionment, chagrin, disenchantment, discouragement
● VERB 1 = alarm, frighten, scare, panic, distress, terrify, appal, startle 2 = disappoint, upset, discourage, daunt, disillusion, let down, dishearten, dispirit

**dismiss** 1 = reject, disregard 2 = banish, dispel, discard, set aside, cast out, lay aside, put out

of your mind 3 = sack, fire (informal), remove (informal), axe (informal), discharge, lay off, cashier, give notice to 4 = let go, free, release, discharge, dissolve, liberate, disperse, send away

**dismissal** = the sack, removal, notice, the boot (slang), expulsion (informal), the push (slang), marching orders (informal)

**disobey** 1 = defy, ignore, rebel, disregard, refuse to obey 2 = infringe, defy, refuse to obey, flout, violate, contravene, overstep, transgress

**disorder** 1 = illness, disease, complaint, condition, sickness, ailment, affliction, malady 2 = untidiness, mess, confusion, chaos, muddle, clutter, shambles, disarray 3 = disturbance, riot, turmoil, unrest, uproar, commotion, unruliness, biffo (Austral. slang)

**disorderly** 1 = untidy, confused, chaotic, messy, jumbled, shambolic (informal), disorganized, higgledy-piggledy (informal) ≠ tidy 2 = unruly, disruptive, rowdy, turbulent, tumultuous, lawless, riotous, ungovernable

**dispatch** or **despatch** VERB 1 = send, consign 2 = kill, murder, destroy, execute, slaughter, assassinate, slay, liquidate 3 = carry out, perform, fulfil, effect, finish, achieve, settle, dismiss

● **NOUN** = <u>message</u>, news, report, story, account, communication, bulletin, communiqué

**dispel** = <u>drive away</u>, dismiss, eliminate, expel, disperse, banish, chase away

**dispense VERB** 1 = <u>distribute</u>, assign, allocate, allot, dole out, share out, apportion, deal out 2 = <u>prepare</u>, measure, supply, mix 3 = <u>administer</u>, operate, carry out, implement, enforce, execute, apply, discharge

● **PHRASES dispense with something** or **someone** 1 = do away with, give up, cancel, abolish, brush aside, forgo 2 = <u>do without</u>, get rid of, dispose of, relinquish

**disperse** 1 = <u>scatter</u>, spread, distribute, strew, diffuse, disseminate, throw about 2 = <u>break up</u>, separate, scatter, dissolve, disband ≠ gather 3 = <u>dissolve</u>, break up

**displace** 1 = <u>replace</u>, succeed, supersede, oust, usurp, supplant, take the place of 2 = <u>move</u>, shift, disturb, budge, misplace

**display VERB** 1 = <u>show</u>, present, exhibit, put on view ≠ conceal 2 = <u>expose</u>, show, reveal, exhibit, uncover 3 = <u>demonstrate</u>, show, reveal, register, expose, disclose, manifest 4 = <u>show off</u>, parade, exhibit, sport (*informal*), flash (*informal*), flourish, brandish, flaunt

● **NOUN** 1 = <u>proof</u>, exhibition, demonstration, evidence, expression, illustration, revelation, testimony 2 = <u>exhibition</u>, show, demonstration, presentation, array 3 = <u>ostentation</u>, show, flourish, fanfare, pomp 4 = <u>show</u>, exhibition, parade, spectacle, pageant

**disposable** 1 = <u>throwaway</u>, nonreturnable 2 = <u>available</u>, expendable, consumable

**disposal NOUN** = <u>throwing away</u>, dumping (*informal*), scrapping, removal, discarding, jettisoning, ejection, riddance

● **PHRASES at your disposal** = <u>available</u>, ready, to hand, accessible, handy, at hand, on tap, expendable

**dispose VERB** = <u>arrange</u>, put, place, group, order, distribute, array

● **PHRASES dispose of someone** = <u>kill</u>, murder, destroy, execute, slaughter, assassinate, slay, liquidate ◆ **dispose of something** 1 = <u>get rid of</u>, destroy, dump (*informal*), scrap, discard, unload, jettison, throw out or away 2 = <u>deal with</u>, manage, treat, handle, settle, cope with, take care of, see to

**disposition** 1 = <u>character</u>, nature, spirit, make-up, constitution, temper, temperament 2 = <u>tendency</u>, inclination, propensity, habit, leaning, bent, bias, proclivity 3 = <u>arrangement</u>, grouping, ordering, organization, distribution, placement

**dispute** NOUN 1 = <u>disagreement</u>, conflict, argument, dissent, altercation 2 = <u>argument</u>, row, clash, controversy, contention, feud, quarrel, squabble
● VERB 1 = <u>contest</u>, question, challenge, deny, doubt, oppose, object to, contradict 2 = <u>argue</u>, fight, clash, disagree, fall out (*informal*), quarrel, squabble, bicker

**disqualify** = <u>ban</u>, rule out, prohibit, preclude, debar, declare ineligible

**disregard** VERB = <u>ignore</u>, discount, overlook, neglect, pass over, turn a blind eye to, make light of, pay no heed to ≠ pay attention to
● NOUN = <u>ignoring</u>, neglect, contempt, indifference, negligence, disdain, disrespect

**disrupt** 1 = <u>interrupt</u>, stop, upset, hold up, interfere with, unsettle, obstruct, cut short 2 = <u>disturb</u>, upset, confuse, disorder, spoil, disorganize, disarrange

**disruption** = <u>disturbance</u>, interference, interruption, stoppage

**disruptive** = <u>disturbing</u>, upsetting, disorderly, unsettling, troublesome, unruly ≠ well-behaved

**dissatisfaction** = <u>discontent</u>, frustration, resentment, disappointment, irritation, unhappiness, annoyance, displeasure

**dissatisfied** = <u>discontented</u>, frustrated, unhappy, disappointed, fed up, disgruntled, displeased, unsatisfied ≠ satisfied

**dissent** = <u>disagreement</u>, opposition, protest, resistance, refusal, objection, discord, demur ≠ assent

**dissident** NOUN = <u>protester</u>, rebel, dissenter, demonstrator, agitator
● ADJECTIVE = <u>dissenting</u>, disagreeing, nonconformist, heterodox

**dissolve** 1 = <u>melt</u>, soften, thaw, liquefy, deliquesce 2 = <u>end</u>, suspend, break up, wind up, terminate, discontinue, dismantle, disband

**distance** 1 = <u>space</u>, length, extent, range, stretch, gap, interval, span 2 = <u>aloofness</u>, reserve, detachment, restraint, stiffness, coolness, coldness, standoffishness

**distant** 1 = <u>far-off</u>, far, remote, abroad, out-of-the-way, far-flung, faraway, outlying ≠ close 2 = <u>remote</u> 3 = <u>reserved</u>, withdrawn, cool, remote, detached, aloof, unfriendly, reticent ≠ friendly 4 = <u>faraway</u>, blank, vague, distracted, vacant, preoccupied, oblivious, absent-minded

**distinct** 1 = <u>different</u>, individual, separate, discrete, unconnected ≠ similar 2 = <u>striking</u>, dramatic, outstanding, noticeable, well-defined 3 = <u>definite</u>, marked, clear, decided, obvious, evident, noticeable, conspicuous ≠ vague

**distinction** 1 = <u>difference</u>, contrast, variation, differential, discrepancy, disparity, dissimilarity 2 = <u>excellence</u>, importance, fame, merit, prominence, greatness, eminence, repute 3 = <u>feature</u>, quality, characteristic, mark, individuality, peculiarity, distinctiveness, particularity 4 = <u>merit</u>, honour, integrity, excellence, rectitude

**distinctive** = <u>characteristic</u>, special, individual, unique, typical, peculiar, singular, idiosyncratic ≠ ordinary

**distinctly** 1 = <u>definitely</u>, clearly, obviously, plainly, patently, decidedly, markedly, noticeably 2 = <u>clearly</u>, plainly

**distinguish** 1 = <u>differentiate</u>, determine, separate, discriminate, decide, judge, ascertain, tell the difference 2 = <u>characterize</u>, mark, separate, single out, set apart 3 = <u>make out</u>, recognize, perceive, know, see, tell, pick out, discern

**distinguished** = <u>eminent</u>, noted, famous, celebrated, well-known, prominent, esteemed, acclaimed ≠ unknown

**distort** 1 = <u>misrepresent</u>, twist, bias, disguise, pervert, slant, colour, misinterpret 2 = <u>deform</u>, bend, twist, warp, buckle, mangle, mangulate (Austral. slang), disfigure, contort

**distortion** 1 = <u>misrepresentation</u>, bias, slant, perversion, falsification 2 = <u>deformity</u>, bend, twist, warp, buckle, contortion, malformation, crookedness

**distract** 1 = <u>divert</u>, sidetrack, draw away, turn aside, lead astray, draw or lead away from 2 = <u>amuse</u>, occupy, entertain, beguile, engross

**distracted** = <u>agitated</u>, troubled, puzzled, at sea, perplexed, flustered, in a flap (informal)

**distraction** 1 = <u>disturbance</u>, interference, diversion, interruption 2 = <u>entertainment</u>, recreation, amusement, diversion, pastime

**distraught** = <u>frantic</u>, desperate,

distressed, distracted, worked-up, agitated, overwrought, out of your mind

**distress** NOUN 1 = <u>suffering</u>, pain, worry, grief, misery, torment, sorrow, heartache 2 = <u>need</u>, trouble, difficulties, poverty, hard times, hardship, misfortune, adversity

● VERB = <u>upset</u>, worry, trouble, disturb, grieve, torment, harass, agitate

**distressed** 1 = <u>upset</u>, worried, troubled, distracted, tormented, distraught, agitated, wretched 2 = <u>poverty-stricken</u>, poor, impoverished, needy, destitute, indigent, down at heel, straitened

**distressing** = <u>upsetting</u>, worrying, disturbing, painful, sad, harrowing, heart-breaking

**distribute** 1 = <u>hand out</u>, pass round 2 = <u>circulate</u>, deliver, convey 3 = <u>share</u>, deal, allocate, dispense, allot, dole out, apportion

**distribution** 1 = <u>delivery</u>, mailing, transportation, handling 2 = <u>sharing</u>, division, assignment, rationing, allocation, allotment, apportionment 3 = <u>spread</u>, organization, arrangement, placement

**district** = <u>area</u>, region, sector, quarter, parish, neighbourhood, vicinity, locality

**distrust** VERB = <u>suspect</u>, doubt, be wary of, mistrust, disbelieve, be suspicious of ≠ trust

● NOUN = <u>suspicion</u>, question, doubt, disbelief, scepticism, mistrust, misgiving, wariness ≠ trust

**disturb** 1 = <u>interrupt</u>, trouble, bother, plague, disrupt, interfere with, hassle, inconvenience 2 = <u>upset</u>, concern, worry, trouble, alarm, distress, unsettle, unnerve ≠ calm 3 = <u>muddle</u>, disorder, mix up, mess up, jumble up, disarrange

**disturbance** 1 = <u>disorder</u>, fray, brawl, fracas, commotion, rumpus 2 = <u>upset</u>, bother, distraction, intrusion, interruption, annoyance

**disturbed** 1 (*Psychiatry*) = <u>unbalanced</u>, troubled, disordered, unstable, neurotic, upset, deranged, maladjusted ≠ balanced 2 = <u>worried</u>, concerned, troubled, upset, bothered, nervous, anxious, uneasy ≠ calm

**disturbing** = <u>worrying</u>, upsetting, alarming, frightening, distressing, startling, unsettling, harrowing

**ditch** NOUN = <u>channel</u>, drain, trench, dyke, furrow, gully, moat, watercourse

● VERB 1 (*Slang*) = <u>get rid of</u>, dump (*informal*), scrap, discard, dispose of, dispense with, jettison, throw

out *or* overboard 2 (*Slang*)
= leave, drop, abandon, dump
(*informal*), get rid of, forsake

**dive** VERB 1 = plunge, drop, duck,
dip, descend, plummet 2 = go
underwater 3 = nose-dive,
plunge, crash, swoop, plummet
● NOUN = plunge, spring, jump,
leap, lunge, nose dive

**diverse** 1 = various, mixed,
varied, assorted, miscellaneous,
several, sundry, motley
2 = different, unlike, varying,
separate, distinct, disparate,
discrete, dissimilar

**diversify** = vary, change,
expand, spread out, branch out

**diversion** 1 = distraction,
deviation, digression 2 = pastime,
game, sport, entertainment,
hobby, relaxation, recreation,
distraction (*Chiefly Brit.*)
= detour, roundabout way,
indirect course 4 (*Chiefly Brit.*)
= deviation, departure, straying,
divergence, digression

**diversity** 1 = difference,
multiplicity, heterogeneity,
diverseness 2 = range, variety,
scope, sphere

**divert** 1 = redirect, switch, avert,
deflect, deviate, turn aside
2 = distract, sidetrack, lead astray,
draw *or* lead away from
3 = entertain, delight, amuse,
please, charm, gratify, beguile,
regale

**divide** 1 = separate, split,
segregate, bisect ≠ join
2 *sometimes with* up = share,
distribute, allocate, dispense,
allot, mete, deal out 3 = split,
break up, come between,
estrange, cause to disagree

**dividend** = bonus, share, cut
(*informal*), gain, extra, plus,
portion, divvy (*informal*)

**divine** ADJECTIVE 1 = heavenly,
spiritual, holy, immortal,
supernatural, celestial, angelic,
superhuman 2 = sacred, religious,
holy, spiritual, blessed, revered,
hallowed, consecrated
3 (*Informal*) = wonderful, perfect,
beautiful, excellent, lovely,
glorious, marvellous, splendid
● VERB = guess, suppose, perceive,
discern, infer, deduce, apprehend,
surmise

**division** 1 = separation, dividing,
splitting up, partition, cutting up
2 = sharing, sharing, distribution,
assignment, rationing, allocation,
allotment, apportionment
3 = disagreement, split, rift,
rupture, abyss, chasm, variance,
discord ≠ unity 4 = department,
group, branch 5 = part, bit, piece,
section, class, category, fraction

**divorce** NOUN = separation, split,
break-up, parting, split-up, rift,
dissolution, annulment
● VERB = separate, split up, part
company, dissolve your marriage

**dizzy** 1 = <u>giddy</u>, faint, light-headed, swimming, reeling, shaky, wobbly, off balance 2 = <u>confused</u>, dazzled, at sea, bewildered, muddled, bemused, dazed, disorientated

**do** VERB 1 = <u>perform</u>, achieve, carry out, complete, accomplish, execute, pull off 2 = <u>make</u>, prepare, fix, arrange, look after, see to, get ready 3 = <u>solve</u>, work out, resolve, figure out, decode, decipher, puzzle out 4 = <u>be adequate</u>, be sufficient, satisfy, suffice, pass muster, cut the mustard, meet requirements 5 = <u>produce</u>, make, create, develop, manufacture, construct, invent, fabricate

● NOUN (*Informal, chiefly Brit. & N.Z.*) = party, gathering, function, event, affair, occasion, celebration, reception

● PHRASES **do away with something** = get rid of, remove, eliminate, abolish, discard, put an end to, dispense with, discontinue ◆ **do without something** *or* **someone** = manage without, give up, dispense with, forgo, kick (*informal*), abstain from, get along without

**dock**¹ NOUN = <u>port</u>, haven, harbour, pier, wharf, quay, waterfront, anchorage

● VERB 1 = <u>moor</u>, land, anchor, put in, tie up, berth, drop anchor 2 (*of spacecraft*) = link up, unite, join, couple, rendezvous, hook up

**dock**² 1 = <u>cut</u>, reduce, decrease, diminish, lessen ≠ *increase* 2 = <u>deduct</u>, subtract 3 = <u>cut off</u>, crop, clip, shorten, curtail, cut short

**doctor** NOUN = <u>physician</u>, medic (*informal*), general practitioner, medical practitioner, G.P.

● VERB 1 = <u>change</u>, alter, interfere with, disguise, pervert, tamper with, tinker with, misrepresent 2 = <u>add to</u>, spike, cut, mix something with something, dilute, water down, adulterate

**doctrine** = <u>teaching</u>, principle, belief, opinion, conviction, creed, dogma, tenet, kaupapa (*N.Z.*)

**document** NOUN = <u>paper</u>, form, certificate, report, record, testimonial, authorization

● VERB = <u>support</u>, certify, verify, detail, validate, substantiate, corroborate, authenticate

**dodge** VERB 1 = <u>duck</u>, dart, swerve, sidestep, shoot, turn aside 2 = <u>evade</u>, avoid, escape, get away from, elude 3 = <u>avoid</u>, evade, shirk

● NOUN = <u>trick</u>, scheme, ploy, trap, device, fraud, manoeuvre, deception

**dodgy** 1 (*Brit., Austral., & N.Z.*) = nasty, offensive, unpleasant, revolting, distasteful, repellent, obnoxious, repulsive 2 (*Brit.*, *Austral.*, *& N.Z.*) = **risky**, difficult, tricky, dangerous, delicate, uncertain, dicey (*informal*, *chiefly Brit.*), chancy (*informal*) 3 = **second rate**, poor, inferior, mediocre, shoddy, bush-league (*Austral. & N.Z. informal*), half-pie (*N.Z. informal*), bodger or bodgie (*Austral. slang*)

**dog** NOUN 1 = **hound**, canine, pooch (*slang*), cur, man's best friend, kuri or goorie (*N.Z.*), brak (*S. African*) ● VERB 1 = **plague**, follow, trouble, haunt, hound, torment 2 = **pursue**, follow, track, chase, trail, hound, stalk ● PHRASES **go to the dogs** (*Informal*) = **deteriorate**, degenerate, be in decline, go downhill (*informal*), go down the drain, go to pot, go to ruin

*Related Words*

*adjective:* canine
*female:* bitch
*young:* pup, puppy

**dogged** = **determined**, persistent, stubborn, resolute, tenacious, steadfast, obstinate, indefatigable ≠ irresolute

**dole** NOUN = **share**, grant, gift, allowance, handout, koha (*N.Z.*) ● PHRASES **dole something out** = **give out**, distribute, assign, allocate, hand out, dispense, allot, apportion

**dolphin**

*Related Words*

*collective noun:* school
➤ whales and dolphins

**domestic** ADJECTIVE 1 = **home**, internal, native, indigenous 2 = **household**, home, family, private 3 = **home-loving**, homely, housewifely, stay-at-home, domesticated 4 = **domesticated**, trained, tame, pet, house-trained ● NOUN = **servant**, help, maid, daily, char (*informal*), charwoman

**dominant** 1 = **main**, chief, primary, principal, prominent, predominant, pre-eminent ≠ minor 2 = **controlling**, ruling, commanding, supreme, governing, superior, authoritative

**dominate** 1 = **control**, rule, direct, govern, monopolize, tyrannize, have the whip hand over 2 = **tower above**, overlook, survey, stand over, loom over, stand head and shoulders above

**domination** = **control**, power, rule, authority, influence, command, supremacy, ascendancy

**don** = **put on**, get into, dress in, pull on, change into, get dressed in, clothe yourself in, slip on or into

**donate** = **give**, present, contribute, grant, subscribe, endow, entrust, impart

**donation** = **contribution**, gift, subscription, offering, present, grant, hand-out, koha (*N.Z.*)

**donor** = giver, contributor, benefactor, philanthropist, donator ≠ recipient

**doom NOUN** 1 = <u>destruction</u>, ruin, catastrophe, downfall 2 = <u>fate</u>, fortune

● **VERB** = <u>condemn</u>, sentence, consign, destine

**doomed** = <u>hopeless</u>, condemned, ill-fated, fated, unhappy, unfortunate, cursed, unlucky

**door** = <u>opening</u>, entry, entrance, exit, doorway

**dope NOUN** 1 (*Slang*) = <u>drugs</u>, narcotics, opiates, dadah (*Austral. slang*) 2 (*Informal*) = <u>idiot</u>, fool, twit (*informal, chiefly Brit.*), dunce, simpleton, dimwit (*informal*), nitwit (*informal*), dumb-ass (*slang*), dorba or dorb (*Austral. slang*), bogan (*Austral. slang*)

● **VERB** = <u>drug</u>, knock out, sedate, stupefy, anaesthetize, narcotize

**dorp** (*S. African*) = <u>town</u>, village, settlement, municipality, kainga or kaika (*N.Z.*)

**dose** 1 = <u>measure</u>, amount, allowance, portion, prescription, ration, draught, dosage 2 = <u>quantity</u>, measure, supply, portion

**dot NOUN** = <u>spot</u>, point, mark, fleck, jot, speck, speckle

● **VERB** = <u>spot</u>, stud, fleck, speckle

● **PHRASES on the dot** = <u>on time</u>,

promptly, precisely, exactly (*informal*), to the minute, on the button (*informal*), punctually

**double ADJECTIVE** 1 = <u>matching</u>, coupled, paired, twin, duplicate, in pairs 2 = <u>dual</u>, enigmatic, twofold

● **VERB** 1 = <u>multiply by two</u>, duplicate, increase twofold, enlarge, magnify 2 = <u>fold up or over</u>

● **NOUN** = <u>twin</u>, lookalike, spitting image, clone, replica, dead ringer (*slang*), Doppelgänger, duplicate

● **PHRASES at** *or* **on the double** = <u>at once</u>, now, immediately, directly, quickly, promptly, straight away, right away

◆ **double as something** *or* **someone** = <u>function as</u>, serve as

**doubt NOUN** 1 = <u>uncertainty</u>, confusion, hesitation, suspense, indecision, hesitancy, lack of conviction, irresolution ≠ **certainty** 2 = <u>suspicion</u>, scepticism, distrust, apprehension, mistrust, misgivings, qualms ≠ **belief**

● **VERB** 1 = <u>be uncertain</u>, be sceptical, be dubious 2 = <u>waver</u>, hesitate, vacillate, fluctuate 3 = <u>disbelieve</u>, question, suspect, query, distrust, mistrust, lack confidence in ≠ **believe**

**doubtful** 1 = <u>unlikely</u>, unclear, dubious, questionable, improbable, debatable, equivocal

≠ certain 2 = <u>unsure</u>, uncertain, hesitant, suspicious, hesitating, sceptical, tentative, wavering ≠ certain

**doubtless** = <u>probably</u>, presumably, most likely

**down** ADJECTIVE = <u>depressed</u>, low, sad, unhappy, discouraged, miserable, fed up, dejected
● VERB (*Informal*) = <u>swallow</u>, drink (down), drain, gulp (down), put away (*informal*), toss off

**downfall** = <u>ruin</u>, fall, destruction, collapse, disgrace, overthrow, undoing, comeuppance (*slang*)

**downgrade** = <u>demote</u>, degrade, take down a peg (*informal*), lower *or* reduce in rank ≠ promote

**downright** = <u>complete</u>, absolute, utter, total, plain, outright, unqualified, out-and-out

**down-to-earth** = <u>sensible</u>, practical, realistic, matter-of-fact, sane, no-nonsense, unsentimental, plain-spoken

**downward** = <u>descending</u>, declining, heading down, earthward

**draft** NOUN 1 = <u>outline</u>, plan, sketch, version, rough, abstract 2 = <u>money order</u>, bill (of exchange), cheque, postal order
● VERB = <u>outline</u>, write, plan, produce, create, design, draw, compose

**drag** VERB = <u>pull</u>, draw, haul, trail, tow, tug, jerk, lug

● NOUN (*Slang*) = <u>nuisance</u>, bore, bother, pest, hassle (*informal*), inconvenience, annoyance

**drain** VERB 1 = <u>remove</u>, draw, empty, withdraw, tap, pump, bleed 2 = <u>empty</u> 3 = <u>flow out</u>, leak, trickle, ooze, seep, exude, well out, effuse 4 = <u>drink up</u>, swallow, finish, put away (*informal*), quaff, gulp down 5 = <u>exhaust</u>, wear out, strain, weaken, fatigue, debilitate, tire out, enfeeble 6 = <u>consume</u>, exhaust, empty, use up, sap, dissipate
● NOUN 1 = <u>sewer</u>, channel, pipe, sink, ditch, trench, conduit, duct 2 = <u>reduction</u>, strain, drag, exhaustion, sapping, depletion

**drama** 1 = <u>play</u>, show, stage show, dramatization 2 = <u>theatre</u>, acting, stagecraft, dramaturgy 3 = <u>excitement</u>, crisis, spectacle, turmoil, histrionics

**dramatic** 1 = <u>exciting</u>, thrilling, tense, sensational, breathtaking, electrifying, melodramatic, climactic 2 = <u>theatrical</u>, Thespian, dramaturgical 3 = <u>expressive</u> 4 = <u>powerful</u>, striking, impressive, vivid, jaw-dropping ≠ ordinary

**dramatist** ➤ WORD POWER SUPPLEMENT **dramatists**

**drape** = <u>cover</u>, wrap, fold, swathe

**drastic** = <u>extreme</u>, strong, radical, desperate, severe, harsh

**draught** 1 = <u>breeze</u>, current, movement, flow, puff, gust, current of air 2 = <u>drink</u>

**draw** VERB 1 = <u>sketch</u>, design, outline, trace, portray, paint, depict, mark out 2 = <u>pull</u>, drag, haul, tow, tug 3 = <u>extract</u>, take, remove 4 = <u>deduce</u>, make, take, derive, infer 5 = <u>attract</u> 6 = <u>entice</u>

● NOUN 1 = <u>tie</u>, deadlock, stalemate, impasse, dead heat 2 (*Informal*) = <u>appeal</u>, pull (*informal*), charm, attraction, lure, temptation, fascination, allure

● PHRASES **draw on** or **upon something** = <u>make use of</u>, use, employ, rely on, exploit, extract, take from, fall back on

**drawback** = <u>disadvantage</u>, difficulty, handicap, deficiency, flaw, hitch, snag, downside ≠ advantage

**drawing** = <u>picture</u>, illustration, representation, cartoon, sketch, portrayal, depiction, study

**drawn** = <u>tense</u>, worn, stressed, tired, pinched, haggard

**dread** VERB 1 = <u>fear</u>, shrink from, cringe at the thought of, quail from, shudder to think about, have cold feet about (*informal*), tremble to think about

● NOUN = <u>fear</u>, alarm, horror, terror, dismay, fright, apprehension, trepidation

**dreadful** 1 = <u>terrible</u>, shocking, awful, appalling, horrible, fearful, hideous, atrocious 2 = <u>serious</u>, terrible, awful, horrendous,

monstrous, abysmal 3 = <u>awful</u>, terrible, horrendous, frightful

**dream** NOUN 1 = <u>vision</u>, illusion, delusion, hallucination 2 = <u>ambition</u>, wish, fantasy, desire, pipe dream 3 = <u>daydream</u> 4 = <u>delight</u>, pleasure, joy, beauty, treasure, gem, marvel, pearler (*Austral. slang*)

● VERB 1 = <u>have dreams</u>, hallucinate 2 = <u>daydream</u>, stargaze, build castles in the air or in Spain

● PHRASES **dream of something** or **someone** = <u>daydream about</u>, fantasize about

**dreamer** = <u>idealist</u>, visionary, daydreamer, utopian, escapist, Walter Mitty, fantasist

**dreary** = <u>dull</u>, boring, tedious, drab, tiresome, monotonous, humdrum, uneventful ≠ exciting

**drench** = <u>soak</u>, flood, wet, drown, steep, swamp, saturate, inundate

**dress** NOUN 1 = <u>frock</u>, gown, robe 2 = <u>clothing</u>, clothes, costume, garments, apparel, attire, garb, togs

● VERB 1 = <u>put on clothes</u>, don clothes, slip on or into something ≠ undress 2 = <u>clothe</u> 3 = <u>bandage</u>, treat, plaster, bind up 4 = <u>arrange</u>, prepare, get ready

**dribble** 1 = <u>run</u>, drip, trickle,

drop, leak, ooze, seep, fall in drops
2 = <u>drool</u>, drivel, slaver, slobber

**drift** VERB 1 = <u>float</u>, go (aimlessly),
bob, coast, slip, sail, slide, glide
2 = <u>wander</u>, stroll, stray, roam,
meander, rove, range 3 = <u>stray</u>,
wander, digress, get off the point
4 = <u>pile up</u>, gather, accumulate,
amass, bank up
● NOUN 1 = <u>pile</u>, bank, mass, heap,
mound, accumulation
2 = <u>meaning</u>, point, gist, direction,
import, intention, tendency,
significance

**drill** NOUN 1 = <u>bit</u>, borer, gimlet,
boring tool 2 = <u>training</u>, exercise,
discipline, instruction, preparation,
repetition 3 = <u>practice</u>
● VERB 1 = <u>bore</u>, pierce, penetrate,
sink in, puncture, perforate
2 = <u>train</u>, coach, teach, exercise,
discipline, practise, instruct,
rehearse

**drink** VERB 1 = <u>swallow</u>, sip, suck,
gulp, sup, guzzle, imbibe, quaff
2 = <u>booze</u> (informal), tipple, tope,
hit the bottle (informal)
● NOUN 1 = <u>glass</u>, cup, draught
2 = <u>beverage</u>, refreshment,
potion, liquid 3 = <u>alcohol</u>, booze
(informal), liquor, spirits, the
bottle (informal), hooch or
hootch (informal, chiefly U.S. &
Canad.)

**drip** VERB 1 = <u>drop</u>, splash, sprinkle,
trickle, dribble, exude, plop
● NOUN 1 = <u>drop</u>, bead, trickle,
dribble, droplet, globule, pearl
2 (Informal) = <u>weakling</u>, wet (Brit.
informal), weed (informal), softie
(informal), mummy's boy
(informal), namby-pamby

**drive** VERB 1 = <u>go</u> (by car), ride
(by car), motor, travel by car
2 = <u>operate</u>, manage, direct,
guide, handle, steer 3 = <u>push</u>,
propel 4 = <u>thrust</u>, push, hammer,
ram 5 = <u>herd</u>, urge, impel
6 = <u>force</u>, press, prompt, spur,
prod, constrain, coerce, goad
● NOUN 1 = <u>run</u>, ride, trip, journey,
spin (informal), outing, excursion,
jaunt 2 = <u>initiative</u>, energy,
enterprise, ambition, motivation,
zip (informal), vigour, get-up-and-
go (informal) 3 = <u>campaign</u>, push
(informal), crusade, action, effort,
appeal

**drop** VERB 1 = <u>fall</u>, decline,
diminish 2 often with away
= <u>decline</u>, fall, sink 3 = <u>plunge</u>,
fall, tumble, descend, plummet
4 = <u>drip</u>, trickle, dribble, fall in
drops 5 = <u>sink</u>, fall, descend
6 = <u>quit</u>, give up, axe (informal),
kick (informal), relinquish,
discontinue
● NOUN 1 = <u>decrease</u>, fall, cut,
lowering, decline, reduction,
slump, fall-off 2 = <u>droplet</u>, bead,
globule, bubble, pearl, drip
3 = <u>dash</u>, shot (informal), spot,
trace, sip, tot, trickle, mouthful
4 = <u>fall</u>, plunge, descent

**drought** → **dubious**

- PHRASES **drop off** 1 = <u>fall</u>
<u>asleep</u>, nod (off), doze (off),
snooze (*informal*), have forty
winks (*informal*) 2 = <u>decrease</u>,
lower, decline, shrink, diminish,
dwindle, lessen, subside ◆ **drop**
**out** = <u>leave</u>, stop, give up,
withdraw, quit, pull out, fall by
the wayside ◆ **drop out of**
**something** = <u>discontinue</u>, give
up, quit

**drought** = <u>water shortage</u>,
dryness, dry spell, aridity ≠ flood

**drove** *often plural* = <u>herd</u>,
company, crowds, collection,
mob, flocks, swarm, horde

**drown** 1 = <u>go down</u>, go under
2 = <u>drench</u>, flood, soak, steep,
swamp, saturate, engulf,
submerge 3 = <u>overwhelm</u>,
overcome, wipe out, overpower,
obliterate, swallow up

**drug** NOUN 1 = <u>medication</u>,
medicine, remedy, physic,
medicament 2 = <u>dope</u> (*slang*),
narcotic (*slang*), stimulant, opiate,
dadah (*Austral. slang*)

- VERB 1 = <u>knock out</u>, dope (*slang*),
numb, deaden, stupefy,
anaesthetize

**drum** VERB 1 = <u>pound</u>, beat, tap,
rap, thrash, tattoo, throb, pulsate

- PHRASES **drum something**
**into someone** = <u>drive into</u>,
hammer into, instil into, din into,
harp on about to

**drunk** ADJECTIVE = <u>intoxicated</u>,

plastered (*slang*), drunken, merry
(*Brit. informal*), under the
influence (*informal*), tipsy, legless
(*informal*), inebriated, out to it
(*Austral. & N.Z. slang*), babalas (*S.
African*)

- NOUN = <u>drunkard</u>, alcoholic, lush
(*slang*), boozer (*informal*), wino
(*informal*), inebriate, alko or alco
(*Austral. slang*)

**dry** ADJECTIVE 1 = <u>dehydrated</u>,
dried-up, arid, parched,
desiccated ≠ wet 2 = <u>thirsty</u>,
parched 3 = <u>sarcastic</u>, cynical,
low-key, sly, sardonic, deadpan,
droll, ironical 4 = <u>dull</u>, boring,
tedious, dreary, tiresome,
monotonous, run-of-the-mill,
humdrum ≠ interesting 5 = <u>plain</u>,
simple, bare, basic, stark,
unembellished

- VERB 1 = <u>drain</u>, make dry 2 *often*
*with out* = <u>dehydrate</u>, make dry,
desiccate, sear, parch, dehumidify
≠ wet

- PHRASES **dry up** or **out**
= <u>become dry</u>, harden, wither,
shrivel up, wizen

**dual** = <u>twofold</u>, double, twin,
matched, paired, duplicate,
binary, duplex

**dubious** 1 = <u>suspect</u>, suspicious,
crooked, dodgy (*Brit., Austral., &*
*N.Z. informal*), questionable,
unreliable, fishy (*informal*),
disreputable ≠ trustworthy
2 = <u>unsure</u>, uncertain, suspicious,

hesitating, doubtful, sceptical, tentative, wavering ≠ sure

**duck** 1 = bob, drop, lower, bend, bow, dodge, crouch, stoop 2 (*Informal*) = dodge, avoid, escape, evade, elude, sidestep, shirk 3 = dunk, wet, plunge, dip, submerge, immerse, douse, souse

**due** ADJECTIVE 1 = expected, scheduled 2 = fitting, deserved, appropriate, justified, suitable, merited, proper, rightful 3 = payable, outstanding, owed, owing, unpaid, in arrears
● ADVERB = directly, dead, straight, exactly, undeviatingly
● NOUN = right(s), privilege, deserts, merits, comeuppance (*informal*)
● PLURAL NOUN = membership fee, charges, fee, contribution, levy

**duel** NOUN 1 = single combat, affair of honour 2 = contest, fight, competition, clash, encounter, engagement, rivalry
● VERB = fight, struggle, clash, compete, contest, contend, vie with, lock horns

**duff** (*Brit., Austral., & N.Z. informal*) = bad, poor, useless, inferior, unsatisfactory, defective, imperfect, substandard, bodger or bodgie (*Austral. slang*)

**dull** ADJECTIVE 1 = boring, tedious, dreary, flat, plain, monotonous, run-of-the-mill, humdrum ≠ exciting 2 = lifeless, indifferent, apathetic, listless, unresponsive, passionless ≠ lively 3 = cloudy, dim, gloomy, dismal, overcast, leaden ≠ bright 4 = blunt, blunted, unsharpened ≠ sharp
● VERB = relieve, blunt, lessen, moderate, soften, alleviate, allay, take the edge off

**duly** 1 = properly, fittingly, correctly, appropriately, accordingly, suitably, deservedly, rightfully 2 = on time, promptly, punctually, at the proper time

**dumb** 1 = unable to speak, mute ≠ articulate = silent, mute, speechless, tongue-tied, wordless, voiceless, soundless, mum 3 (*Informal*) = stupid, thick, dull, foolish, dense, unintelligent, asinine, dim-witted (*informal*) ≠ clever

**dummy** NOUN 1 = model, figure, mannequin, form, manikin 2 = imitation, copy, duplicate, sham, counterfeit, replica 3 (*Slang*) = fool, idiot, dunce, oaf, simpleton, nitwit (*informal*), blockhead, dumb-ass (*slang*), dorba or dorb (*Austral. slang*), bogan (*Austral. slang*)
● ADJECTIVE = imitation, false, fake, artificial, mock, bogus, simulated, sham

**dump** VERB 1 = drop, deposit, throw down, let fall, fling down 2 = get rid of, tip, dispose of, unload, jettison, empty out, throw away *or* out 3 = <u>scrap</u>, get rid of, abolish, put an end to, discontinue, jettison, put paid to

● **NOUN** 1 = <u>rubbish tip</u>, tip, junkyard, rubbish heap, refuse heap 2 (*Informal*) = <u>pigsty</u>, hole (*informal*), slum, hovel

**dunny** (*Austral. & N.Z. old-fashioned informal*) = <u>toilet</u>, lavatory, bathroom, loo (*Brit. informal*), W.C., bog (*slang*), Gents *or* Ladies, can (*U.S. & Canad. slang*), bogger (*Austral. slang*), brasco (*Austral. slang*)

**duplicate** **VERB** 1 = <u>repeat</u>, reproduce, copy, clone, replicate 2 = <u>copy</u>

● **ADJECTIVE** = <u>identical</u>, matched, matching, twin, corresponding, twofold

● **NOUN** 1 = <u>copy</u>, facsimile 2 = <u>photocopy</u>, copy, reproduction, replica, carbon copy

**durable** 1 = <u>hard-wearing</u>, strong, tough, reliable, resistant, sturdy, long-lasting ≠ fragile 2 = <u>enduring</u>, continuing, dependable, unwavering, unfaltering

**duration** = <u>length</u>, time, period, term, stretch, extent, spell, span

**dusk** = <u>twilight</u>, evening, evo (*Austral. slang*), nightfall, sunset, dark, sundown, eventide, gloaming (*Scot. poetic*) ≠ dawn

**dust** **NOUN** 1 = <u>grime</u>, grit, powder 2 = <u>particles</u>

● **VERB** = <u>sprinkle</u>, cover, powder, spread, spray, scatter, sift, dredge

**dusty** = <u>dirty</u>, grubby, unclean, unswept

**duty** **NOUN** 1 = <u>responsibility</u>, job, task, work, role, function, obligation, assignment 2 = <u>tax</u>, toll, levy, tariff, excise

● **PHRASES** on duty = <u>at work</u>, busy, engaged, on active service

**dwarf** 1 = <u>tower above</u> *or* over, dominate, overlook, stand over, loom over, stand head and shoulders above 2 = <u>eclipse</u>, tower above *or* over, put in the shade, diminish

● **ADJECTIVE** = <u>miniature</u>, small, baby, tiny, diminutive, bonsai, undersized

● **NOUN** = <u>gnome</u>, midget, Lilliputian, Tom Thumb, pygmy *or* pigmy

**dwell** (*Formal or literary*) = <u>live</u>, reside, lodge, abide

**dwelling** (*Formal or literary*) = <u>home</u>, house, residence, abode, quarters, lodging, habitation, domicile, whare (*N.Z.*)

**dwindle** = <u>lessen</u>, decline, fade, shrink, diminish, decrease, wane, subside ≠ increase

**dye** **VERB** = <u>colour</u>, stain, tint, tinge, pigment

● **NOUN** = <u>colouring</u>, colour, pigment, stain, tint, tinge, colorant

**dying** 1 = <u>near death</u>, moribund, in extremis (*Latin*), at death's

door, not long for this world
2 = **final**, last, parting, departing
3 = **failing**, declining, foundering, diminishing, decreasing, dwindling, subsiding

**dynamic** = **energetic**, powerful, vital, go-ahead, lively, animated, high-powered, forceful ≠ apathetic

**dynasty** = **empire**, house, rule, regime, sovereignty

# E

**each** DETERMINER = **every**, every single

● PRONOUN = **every one**, all, each one, each and every one, one and all

● ADVERB = **apiece**, individually, for each, to each, respectively, per person, per head, per capita

> ### Word Power
>
> **each** – *Each* is a singular pronoun and should be used with a singular verb – for example, *each of the candidates was interviewed separately* (not *were interviewed separately*).

**eager** 1 = **anxious**, keen, hungry, impatient, itching, thirsty ≠ unenthusiastic 2 = **keen**, interested, intense, enthusiastic, passionate, avid (*informal*), fervent ≠ uninterested

**ear** = **sensitivity**, taste, discrimination, appreciation
*(Related Words)*
adjective: aural

**early** ADVERB 1 = **in good time**, beforehand, ahead of schedule, in advance, with time to spare ≠ late 2 = **too soon**, before the usual time, prematurely, ahead of time ≠ late
● ADJECTIVE 1 = **first**, opening, initial, introductory
2 = **premature**, forward, advanced, untimely, unseasonable ≠ belated
3 = **primitive**, first, earliest, young, original, undeveloped, primordial, primeval ≠ developed

**earmark** 1 = **set aside**, reserve, label, flag, allocate, designate, mark out 2 = **mark out**, identify, designate

**earn** 1 = **be paid**, make, get, receive, gain, net, collect, bring in 2 = **deserve**, win, gain, attain, justify, merit, warrant, be entitled to

**earnest** 1 = **serious**, grave, intense, dedicated, sincere, thoughtful, solemn, ardent ≠ frivolous
2 = **determined**, dogged, intent, persistent, persevering, resolute, wholehearted ≠ half-hearted

**earnings** = **income**, pay, wages, revenue, proceeds, salary, receipts, remuneration

**earth** 1 = **world**, planet, globe, sphere, orb, earthly sphere
2 = **ground**, land, dry land, terra

firma3 = <u>soil</u>, ground, land, dust, clay, dirt, turf, silt

**earthly** 1 = <u>worldly</u>, material, secular, mortal, temporal, human ≠ spiritual 2 = <u>sensual</u>, worldly, physical, fleshly, bodily, carnal 3 (*Informal*) = <u>possible</u>, likely, practical, feasible, conceivable, imaginable

**ease** NOUN 1 = <u>straightforwardness</u>, simplicity, readiness 2 = <u>comfort</u>, luxury, leisure, relaxation, prosperity, affluence, rest, repose ≠ hardship 3 = <u>peace of mind</u>, peace, content, quiet, comfort, happiness, serenity, tranquillity ≠ agitation
• VERB 1 = <u>relieve</u>, calm, soothe, lessen, alleviate, lighten, lower, relax ≠ aggravate 2 = <u>reduce</u>, diminish, lessen, slacken 3 = <u>move carefully</u>, edge, slip, inch, slide, creep, manoeuvre

**easily** = <u>without difficulty</u>, smoothly, readily, comfortably, effortlessly, with ease, straightforwardly

**easy** 1 = <u>simple</u>, straightforward, no trouble, not difficult, effortless, painless, uncomplicated, child's play (*informal*) ≠ hard 2 = <u>untroubled</u>, relaxed, peaceful, serene, tranquil, quiet 3 = <u>carefree</u>, comfortable, leisurely, trouble-free, untroubled, cushy (*informal*) ≠ difficult 4 = <u>tolerant</u>, soft, mild, laid-back

(*informal*), indulgent, easy-going, lenient, permissive ≠ strict

**eat** 1 = <u>consume</u>, swallow, chew, scoff (*slang*), devour, munch, tuck into (*informal*), put away 2 = <u>have a meal</u>, lunch, breakfast, dine, snack, feed, graze (*informal*), have lunch

**ebb** VERB 1 = <u>flow back</u>, go out, withdraw, retreat, wane, recede 2 = <u>decline</u>, flag, diminish, decrease, dwindle, lessen, subside, fall away
• NOUN = <u>flowing back</u>, going out, withdrawal, retreat, wane, low water, low tide, outgoing tide

**eccentric** ADJECTIVE = <u>odd</u>, strange, peculiar, irregular, quirky, unconventional, idiosyncratic, outlandish ≠ normal
• NOUN = <u>crank</u> (*informal*), character (*informal*), oddball (*informal*), nonconformist, weirdo or weirdie (*informal*)

**echo** NOUN 1 = <u>reverberation</u>, ringing, repetition, answer, resonance, resounding 2 = <u>copy</u>, reflection, clone, reproduction, imitation, duplicate, double, reiteration
• VERB 1 = <u>reverberate</u>, repeat, resound, ring, resonate 2 = <u>recall</u>, reflect, copy, mirror, resemble, imitate, ape

**eclipse** NOUN = <u>obscuring</u>, covering, blocking, shading, dimming, extinction, darkening, blotting out

● VERB = <u>surpass</u>, exceed, overshadow, excel, transcend, outdo, outclass, outshine

**economic** 1 = <u>financial</u>, industrial, commercial 2 = <u>profitable</u>, successful, commercial, rewarding, productive, lucrative, worthwhile, viable 3 (*Informal*) = <u>economical</u>, cheap, reasonable, modest, low-priced, inexpensive

**economical** 1 = <u>thrifty</u>, sparing, careful, prudent, provident, frugal, parsimonious, scrimping ≠ extravagant 2 = <u>efficient</u>, sparing, cost-effective, money-saving, time-saving ≠ wasteful

**economy** 1 = <u>financial system</u>, financial state 2 = <u>thrift</u>, restraint, prudence, husbandry, frugality, parsimony

**ecstasy** = <u>rapture</u>, delight, joy, bliss, euphoria, fervour, elation ≠ agony

**ecstatic** = <u>rapturous</u>, entranced, joyous, elated, overjoyed, blissful, euphoric, enraptured

**edge** NOUN 1 = <u>border</u>, side, limit, outline, boundary, fringe, verge, brink 2 = <u>verge</u>, point, brink, threshold 3 = <u>advantage</u>, lead, dominance, superiority, upper hand, head start, ascendancy, whip hand 4 = <u>power</u>, force, bite, effectiveness, incisiveness, powerful quality 5 = <u>sharpness</u>, point, bitterness, keenness

● VERB 1 = <u>inch</u>, ease, creep, slink, steal, sidle, move slowly 2 = <u>border</u>, fringe, hem, pipe

● PHRASES on edge = <u>tense</u>, nervous, impatient, irritable, apprehensive, edgy, ill at ease, on tenterhooks

**edit** = <u>revise</u>, improve, correct, polish, adapt, rewrite, condense, redraft

**edition** = <u>version</u>, copy, issue, programme (*TV, Radio*), printing, volume, impression, publication

**educate** = <u>teach</u>, school, train, develop, improve, inform, discipline, tutor

**educated** 1 = <u>cultured</u>, intellectual, learned, sophisticated, refined, cultivated, enlightened, knowledgeable ≠ uncultured 2 = <u>taught</u>, schooled, coached, informed, tutored, instructed, nurtured, well-informed ≠ uneducated

**education** 1 = <u>teaching</u>, schooling, training, development, discipline, instruction, nurture, tuition 2 = <u>learning</u>, schooling, cultivation, refinement

**educational** 1 = <u>academic</u>, school, learning, teaching, scholastic, pedagogical, pedagogic 2 = <u>instructive</u>, useful, cultural, illuminating, enlightening, informative, instructional, edifying

**eerie** = uncanny, strange, frightening, ghostly, weird, mysterious, scary (*informal*), sinister

**effect** NOUN 1 = result, consequence, conclusion, outcome, event, end result, upshot 2 = impression, feeling, impact, influence 3 = purpose, impression, sense, intent, essence, thread, tenor

• PLURAL NOUN = belongings, goods, things, property, stuff, gear, possessions, paraphernalia

• VERB = bring about, produce, complete, achieve, perform, fulfil, accomplish, execute

> ### Word Power
>
> **effect** – It is quite common for the verb *effect* to be mistakenly used where *affect* is intended. *Effect* is relatively uncommon and rather formal, and is a synonym of 'bring about'. Conversely, the noun *effect* is quite often mistakenly written with an initial *a*. The following are correct: *the group is still recovering from the effects of the recession; they really are powerless to effect any change.* The next two examples are incorrect: *the full affects of the shutdown won't be felt for several more days; men whose lack of hair doesn't effect their self-esteem.*

**effective** 1 = efficient, successful, useful, active, capable, valuable, helpful, adequate ≠ ineffective 2 = powerful, strong, convincing, persuasive, telling, impressive, compelling, forceful ≠ weak 3 = virtual, essential, practical, implied, implicit, tacit, unacknowledged 4 = in operation, official, current, legal, active, in effect, valid, operative ≠ inoperative

**efficiency** 1 = effectiveness, power, economy, productivity, organization, cost-effectiveness, orderliness 2 = competence, expertise, capability, proficiency, professionalism, adeptness

**efficient** 1 = effective, successful, structured, productive, systematic, streamlined, cost-effective, methodical ≠ inefficient 2 = competent, professional, capable, organized, productive, proficient, businesslike, well-organized ≠ incompetent

**effort** 1 = attempt, try, endeavour, shot (*informal*), bid, essay, go (*informal*), stab (*informal*) 2 = exertion, work, trouble, energy, struggle, application, graft, toil

**egg** NOUN = ovum, gamete, germ cell

• PHRASES **egg someone on** = incite, push, encourage, urge, prompt, spur, provoke, prod

**eject** 1 = <u>throw out</u>, remove, turn out, expel (*slang*), oust, banish, drive out, evict 2 = <u>bail out</u>, escape, get out

**elaborate ADJECTIVE**
1 = <u>complicated</u>, detailed, studied, complex, precise, thorough, intricate, painstaking 2 = <u>ornate</u>, involved, complex, fancy, complicated, intricate, baroque, ornamented ≠ plain
● **VERB** 1 = <u>develop</u>, flesh out 2 = <u>expand (upon)</u>, extend, enlarge (on), amplify, embellish, flesh out, add detail (to) ≠ simplify

**elastic** 1 = <u>flexible</u>, supple, rubbery, pliable, plastic, springy, pliant, tensile ≠ rigid
2 = <u>adaptable</u>, yielding, variable, flexible, accommodating, tolerant, adjustable, supple ≠ inflexible

**elbow** = <u>joint</u>, angle, curve

**elder ADJECTIVE** = <u>older</u>, first, senior, first-born
● **NOUN** = <u>older person</u>, senior

**elect** 1 = <u>vote for</u>, choose, pick, determine, select, appoint, opt for, settle on 2 = <u>choose</u>, decide, prefer, select, opt

**election** 1 = <u>vote</u>, poll, ballot, referendum, franchise, plebiscite, show of hands 2 = <u>appointment</u>, picking, choice, selection

**electric** 1 = <u>electric-powered</u>, powered, cordless, battery-operated, electrically-charged, mains-operated 2 = <u>charged</u>, exciting, stirring, thrilling, stimulating, dynamic, tense, rousing

**elegance** = <u>style</u>, taste, grace, dignity, sophistication, grandeur, refinement, gracefulness

**elegant** = <u>stylish</u>, fine, sophisticated, delicate, handsome, refined, chic, exquisite ≠ inelegant

**element NOUN** 1 = <u>component</u>, part, unit, section, factor, principle, aspect, foundation 2 = <u>group</u>, faction, clique, set, party, circle 3 = <u>trace</u>, suggestion, hint, dash, suspicion, tinge, smattering, soupçon
● **PLURAL NOUN** = <u>weather conditions</u>, climate, the weather, wind and rain, atmospheric conditions, powers of nature
● **PHRASES be in your element** = be in a situation you enjoy, be in your natural environment, be in familiar surroundings

**elementary** = <u>simple</u>, clear, easy, plain, straightforward, rudimentary, uncomplicated, undemanding ≠ complicated

**elevate** 1 = <u>promote</u>, raise, advance, upgrade, exalt, kick upstairs (*informal*), aggrandize, give advancement to
2 = <u>increase</u>, lift, raise, step up,

intensify, move up, hoist, raise high3 = <u>raise</u>, lift, heighten, uplift, hoist, lift up, raise up, hike up

**elevated** 1 = <u>exalted</u>, important, august, grand, superior, noble, dignified, high-ranking2 = <u>high-minded</u>, fine, grand, noble, inflated, dignified, sublime, lofty ≠ humble3 = <u>raised</u>, high, lifted up, upraised

**elicit** 1 = <u>bring about</u>, cause, derive, bring out, evoke, give rise to, draw out, bring forth 2 = <u>obtain</u>, extract, exact, evoke, wrest, draw out, extort

**eligible** 1 = <u>entitled</u>, fit, qualified, suitable ≠ ineligible2 = <u>available</u>, free, single, unmarried, unattached

**eliminate** = <u>remove</u>, end, stop, withdraw, get rid of, abolish, cut out, dispose of

**elite** = <u>aristocracy</u>, best, pick, cream, upper class, nobility, crème de la crème (*French*), flower ≠ rabble

**eloquent** 1 = <u>silver-tongued</u>, moving, powerful, effective, stirring, articulate, persuasive, forceful ≠ inarticulate 2 = <u>expressive</u>, telling, pointed, significant, vivid, meaningful, indicative, suggestive

**elsewhere** = <u>in *or* to another place</u>, away, abroad, hence (*archaic*), somewhere else, not here, in other places, in *or* to a different place

**elude** 1 = <u>evade</u>, escape, lose, avoid, flee, duck (*informal*), dodge, get away from2 = <u>escape</u>, baffle, frustrate, puzzle, stump, foil, be beyond (someone), thwart

> ### Word Power
>
> **elude** – *Elude* is sometimes wrongly used where *allude* is meant: *he was alluding* (not *eluding*) *to his previous visit to the city.*

**elusive** 1 = <u>difficult to catch</u>, tricky, slippery, difficult to find, evasive, shifty2 = <u>indefinable</u>, fleeting, subtle, indefinite, transient, intangible, indescribable, transitory

> ### Word Power
>
> **elusive** – The spelling of *elusive*, as in *a shy, elusive character*, should be noted. This adjective derives from the verb *elude*, and should not be confused with the rare word *illusive* meaning 'not real' or 'based on illusion'.

**emanate** = <u>flow</u>, emerge, spring, proceed, arise, stem, derive, originate

**embargo** NOUN = <u>ban</u>, bar, restriction, boycott, restraint, prohibition, moratorium, stoppage, rahui (*N.Z.*)

● VERB = <u>block</u>, stop, bar, ban, restrict, boycott, prohibit, blacklist

**embark** VERB = go aboard, climb aboard, board ship, step aboard, go on board, take ship ≠ get off

● PHRASES **embark on something** = <u>begin</u>, start, launch, enter, take up, set out, set about, plunge into

**embarrass** = <u>shame</u>, distress, show up (*informal*), humiliate, disconcert, fluster, mortify, discomfit

**embarrassed** = <u>ashamed</u>, shamed, uncomfortable, awkward, abashed, humiliated, uneasy, unsettled

**embarrassing** = <u>humiliating</u>, upsetting, compromising, delicate, uncomfortable, awkward, sensitive, troublesome, barro (*Austral. slang*)

**embarrassment** 1 = <u>shame</u>, distress, showing up (*informal*), humiliation, discomfort, unease, self-consciousness, awkwardness 2 = <u>problem</u>, difficulty, nuisance, source of trouble, thorn in your flesh 3 = <u>predicament</u>, problem, difficulty (*informal*), mess, jam (*informal*), plight, scrape (*informal*), pickle (*informal*)

**embody** 1 = <u>personify</u>, represent, stand for, manifest, exemplify, symbolize, typify,

actualize 2 = <u>incorporate</u>, include, contain, combine, collect, take in, encompass

**embrace** VERB 1 = <u>hug</u>, hold, cuddle, seize, squeeze, clasp, envelop, canoodle (*slang*) 2 = <u>accept</u>, support, welcome, adopt, take up, seize, espouse, take on board 3 = <u>include</u>, involve, cover, contain, take in, incorporate, comprise, encompass

● NOUN = <u>hug</u>, hold, cuddle, squeeze, clinch (*slang*), clasp

**embroil** = <u>involve</u>, mix up, implicate, entangle, mire, ensnare, enmesh

**embryo** 1 = <u>foetus</u>, unborn child, fertilized egg 2 = <u>germ</u>, beginning, source, root, seed, nucleus, rudiment

**emerge** 1 = <u>come out</u>, appear, surface, rise, arise, turn up, spring up, emanate ≠ withdraw 2 = <u>become apparent</u>, come out, become known, come to light, crop up, transpire, become evident, come out in the wash

**emergence** 1 = <u>coming</u>, development, arrival, surfacing, rise, appearance, arising, turning up 2 = <u>disclosure</u>, publishing, broadcasting, broadcast, publication, declaration, revelation, becoming known

**emergency** NOUN = <u>crisis</u>, danger, difficulty, accident,

disaster, necessity, plight, scrape
(*informal*)
● ADJECTIVE1 = <u>urgent</u>, crisis,
immediate2 = <u>alternative</u>, extra,
additional, substitute,
replacement, temporary,
makeshift, stopgap

**emigrate** = <u>move abroad</u>, move,
relocate, migrate, resettle, leave
your country

**eminent** = <u>prominent</u>, noted,
respected, famous, celebrated,
distinguished, well-known,
esteemed ≠ unknown

**emission** = <u>giving off or out</u>,
release, shedding, leak, radiation,
discharge, transmission,
ejaculation

**emit** 1 = <u>give off</u>, release,
transmit, discharge, send out,
radiate, eject ≠ absorb2 = <u>utter</u>,
produce, voice, give out, let out

**emotion** 1 = <u>feeling</u>, spirit, soul,
passion, excitement, sensation,
sentiment, fervour2 = <u>instinct</u>,
sentiment, sensibility, intuition,
tenderness, gut feeling, soft-
heartedness

**emotional** 1 = <u>psychological</u>,
private, personal, hidden,
spiritual, inner2 = <u>moving</u>,
touching, affecting, stirring,
sentimental, poignant, emotive,
heart-rending3 = <u>passionate</u>,
sentimental, temperamental,
excitable, demonstrative, hot-
blooded4 = <u>emotive</u>, sensitive,

controversial, delicate,
contentious, heated,
inflammatory, touchy

**emphasis** 1 = <u>importance</u>,
attention, weight, significance,
stress, priority, prominence
2 = <u>stress</u>, accent, force, weight

**emphasize** 1 = <u>highlight</u>, stress,
underline, draw attention to,
dwell on, play up, make a point
of, give priority to ≠ minimize
2 = <u>stress</u>, accentuate, lay stress
on

**emphatic** 1 = <u>forceful</u>, positive,
definite, vigorous, unmistakable,
insistent, unequivocal, vehement
≠ hesitant2 = <u>significant</u>,
pronounced, decisive,
resounding, conclusive

**empire** 1 = <u>kingdom</u>, territory,
province, federation,
commonwealth, realm, domain
2 = <u>organization</u>, company,
business, firm, concern,
corporation, consortium, syndicate
*(Related Words)*
*adjective*: imperial

**empirical** or**empiric** = <u>first-
hand</u>, direct, observed, practical,
actual, experimental, pragmatic,
factual ≠ hypothetical

**employ** 1 = <u>hire</u>, commission,
appoint, take on, retain, engage,
recruit, sign up2 = <u>use</u>, apply,
exercise, exert, make use of,
utilize, ply, bring to bear
3 = <u>spend</u>, fill, occupy, involve,

engage, take up, make use of, use up

**employed** 1 = <u>working</u>, in work, having a job, in employment, in a job, earning your living ≠ out of work 2 = <u>busy</u>, active, occupied, engaged, hard at work, in harness, rushed off your feet ≠ idle

**employee** = <u>worker</u>, labourer, workman, staff member, member of staff, hand, wage-earner, white-collar worker

**employer** 1 = <u>boss</u> (informal), manager, head, leader, director, chief, owner, master, baas (S. African) 2 = <u>company</u>, business, firm, organization, establishment, outfit (informal)

**employment** 1 = <u>job</u>, work, position, trade, post, situation, profession, occupation 2 = <u>taking on</u>, commissioning, appointing, hire, hiring, retaining, engaging, appointment 3 = <u>use</u>, application, exertion, exercise, utilization

**empower** 1 = <u>authorize</u>, allow, commission, qualify, permit, sanction, entitle, delegate 2 = <u>enable</u>, equip, emancipate, give means to, enfranchise

**empty ADJECTIVE** 1 = <u>bare</u>, clear, abandoned, deserted, vacant, free, void, desolate ≠ full 2 = <u>meaningless</u>, cheap, hollow, vain, idle, futile, insincere 3 = <u>worthless</u>, meaningless, hollow, pointless, futile, senseless,

## employed → encounter

fruitless, inane ≠ meaningful
● **VERB** 1 = <u>clear</u>, drain, void, unload, pour out, unpack, remove the contents of ≠ fill 2 = <u>exhaust</u>, consume the contents of, void, deplete, use up ≠ replenish 3 = <u>evacuate</u>, clear, vacate

**emulate** = <u>imitate</u>, follow, copy, mirror, echo, mimic, model yourself on

**enable** 1 = <u>allow</u>, permit, empower, give someone the opportunity, give someone the means ≠ prevent 2 = <u>authorize</u>, allow, permit, qualify, sanction, entitle, license, warrant ≠ stop

**enact** 1 = <u>establish</u>, order, command, approve, sanction, proclaim, decree, authorize 2 = <u>perform</u>, play, present, stage, represent, put on, portray, depict

**enchant** = <u>fascinate</u>, delight, charm, entrance, dazzle, captivate, enthral, beguile

**enclose** or **inclose** 1 = <u>surround</u>, circle, bound, fence, confine, close in, wall in, encircle 2 = <u>send with</u>, include, put in, insert

**encompass** 1 = <u>include</u>, hold, cover, admit, deal with, contain, take in, embrace 2 = <u>surround</u>, circle, enclose, close in, envelop, encircle, fence in, ring

**encounter VERB** 1 = <u>experience</u>, meet, face, suffer, have, go through, sustain, endure

2 = <u>meet</u>, confront, come across, bump into (*informal*), run across, come upon, chance upon, meet by chance

● NOUN 1 = <u>meeting</u>, brush, confrontation, rendezvous, chance meeting 2 = <u>battle</u>, conflict, clash, contest, run-in (*informal*), confrontation, head-to-head

**encourage** 1 = <u>inspire</u>, comfort, cheer, reassure, console, hearten, cheer up, embolden ≠ discourage 2 = <u>urge</u>, persuade, prompt, spur, coax, egg on ≠ dissuade 3 = <u>promote</u>, back, support, increase, foster, advocate, stimulate, endorse ≠ prevent

**encouragement**
1 = <u>inspiration</u>, support, comfort, comforting, cheer, cheering, reassurance, morale boosting 2 = <u>urging</u>, prompting, stimulus, persuasion, coaxing, egging on, incitement 3 = <u>promotion</u>, backing, support, endorsement, stimulation, furtherance

**end** NOUN 1 = <u>close</u>, ending, finish, expiry, expiration ≠ beginning 2 = <u>conclusion</u>, ending, climax, completion, finale, culmination, denouement, consummation ≠ start 3 = <u>finish</u>, close, stop, resolution, conclusion, closure, completion, termination 4 = <u>extremity</u>, limit, edge, border, extent, extreme, margin,

boundary 5 = <u>tip</u>, point, head, peak, extremity 6 = <u>purpose</u>, point, reason, goal, target, aim, object, mission 7 = <u>outcome</u>, resolution, conclusion 8 = <u>death</u>, dying, ruin, destruction, passing on, doom, demise, extinction 9 = <u>remnant</u>, butt, stub, scrap, fragment, stump, remainder, leftover

● VERB 1 = <u>stop</u>, finish, halt, cease, wind up, terminate, call off, discontinue ≠ start 2 = <u>finish</u>, close, conclude, wind up, culminate, terminate, come to an end, draw to a close ≠ begin

*Related Words*
adjectives: final, terminal, ultimate

**endanger** = <u>put at risk</u>, risk, threaten, compromise, jeopardize, imperil, put in danger, expose to danger ≠ save

**endearing** = <u>attractive</u>, winning, pleasing, appealing, sweet, engaging, charming, pleasant

**endeavour** (*Formal*) VERB = <u>try</u>, labour, attempt, aim, struggle, venture, strive, aspire
● NOUN = <u>attempt</u>, try, effort, trial, bid, venture, enterprise, undertaking

**ending** = <u>finish</u>, end, close, conclusion, summing up, completion, finale, culmination ≠ start

**endless** = <u>eternal</u>, infinite, continual, unlimited, interminable, incessant,

boundless, everlasting
≠ temporary

**endorse** 1 = <u>approve</u>, back,
support, champion, promote,
recommend, advocate, uphold
2 = <u>sign</u>, initial, countersign, sign
on the back of

**endorsement** = <u>approval</u>,
backing, support, favour,
recommendation, acceptance,
agreement, upholding

**endow** 1 = <u>provide</u>, favour, grace,
bless, supply, furnish, endue
2 = <u>finance</u>, fund, pay for, award,
confer, bestow, bequeath, donate
money to 3 = <u>imbue</u>

**endowment** = <u>provision</u>,
funding, award, grant, gift,
contribution, subsidy, donation,
koha (N.Z.)

**endurance** 1 = <u>staying power</u>,
strength, resolution,
determination, patience, stamina,
fortitude, persistence
2 = <u>permanence</u>, stability,
continuity, duration, longevity,
durability, continuance

**endure** 1 = <u>experience</u>, suffer,
bear, meet, encounter, cope with,
sustain, undergo 2 = <u>last</u>,
continue, remain, stay, stand, go
on, survive, live on

**enemy** = <u>foe</u>, rival, opponent, the
opposition, competitor, the other
side, adversary, antagonist
≠ friend

**energetic** 1 = <u>forceful</u>,

determined, active, aggressive,
dynamic, vigorous, hard-hitting,
strenuous 2 = <u>lively</u>, active,
dynamic, vigorous, animated,
tireless, bouncy, indefatigable
≠ lethargic 3 = <u>strenuous</u>, hard,
taxing, demanding, tough,
exhausting, vigorous, arduous

**energy** 1 = <u>strength</u>, might,
stamina, forcefulness
2 = <u>liveliness</u>, drive,
determination, pep, vitality,
vigour, verve, resilience
3 = <u>power</u>

**enforce** 1 = <u>carry out</u>, apply,
implement, fulfil, execute,
administer, put into effect, put
into action 2 = <u>impose</u>, force,
insist on

**engage** 1 *with in* = <u>participate
in</u>, join in, take part in, undertake,
embark on, enter into, become
involved in, set about
2 = <u>captivate</u>, catch, arrest, fix,
capture 3 = <u>occupy</u>, involve, draw,
grip, absorb, preoccupy, immerse,
engross 4 = <u>employ</u>, appoint,
take on, hire, retain, recruit, enlist,
enrol ≠ dismiss 5 = <u>set going</u>,
apply, trigger, activate, switch on,
energize, bring into operation
6 (*Military*) = <u>begin battle with</u>,
attack, take on, encounter, fall on,
battle with, meet, assail

**engaged** 1 = <u>occupied</u>, working,
employed, busy, tied up
2 = <u>betrothed</u>, promised,

pledged, affianced, promised in marriage ≠ unattached **3** = **in use**, busy, tied up, unavailable ≠ free

**engagement 1** = **appointment**, meeting, interview, date, commitment, arrangement, rendezvous **2** = **betrothal**, marriage contract, troth (*archaic*), agreement to marry **3** = **battle**, fight, conflict, action, struggle, clash, encounter, combat **4** = **participation**, joining, taking part, involvement

**engaging** = **charming**, interesting, pleasing, attractive, lovely, entertaining, winning, fetching (*informal*) ≠ unpleasant

**engine** = **machine**, motor, mechanism, generator, dynamo

**engineer** NOUN **1** = **designer**, producer, architect, developer, deviser, creator, planner, inventor **2** = **worker**, specialist, operator, practitioner, operative, driver, conductor, technician

● VERB **1** = **design**, plan, create, construct, devise **2** = **bring about**, plan, effect, set up (*informal*), scheme, arrange, plot, mastermind

**engraving** = **print**, carving, etching, inscription, plate, woodcut, dry point

**engulf 1** = **immerse**, swamp, submerge, overrun, inundate, envelop, swallow up

**2** = **overwhelm**, overcome, crush, swamp

**enhance** = **improve**, better, increase, lift, boost, add to, strengthen, reinforce ≠ reduce

**enjoy 1** = **take pleasure in** *or* **from**, like, love, appreciate, relish, delight in, be pleased with, be fond of ≠ hate **2** = **have**, use, own, experience, possess, have the benefit of, reap the benefits of, be blessed *or* favoured with

**enjoyable** = **pleasurable**, good, great, fine, nice, satisfying, lovely, entertaining ≠ unpleasant

**enjoyment 1** = **pleasure**, liking, fun, delight, entertainment, joy, happiness, relish **2** = **benefit**, use, advantage, favour, possession, blessing

**enlarge** VERB **1** = **expand**, increase, extend, add to, build up, widen, intensify, broaden ≠ reduce **2** = **grow**, increase, extend, expand, swell, become bigger, puff up, grow larger

● PHRASES **enlarge on something** = **expand on**, develop, add to, fill out, elaborate on, flesh out, expatiate on, give further details about

**enlighten** = **inform**, tell, teach, advise, counsel, educate, instruct, illuminate

**enlightened** = **informed**, aware, reasonable, educated, sophisticated, cultivated, open-

minded, knowledgeable
≠ ignorant

**enlightenment**
= <u>understanding</u>, learning,
education, knowledge,
instruction, awareness, wisdom,
insight

**enlist** 1 = <u>join up</u>, join, enter
(into), register, volunteer, sign up,
enrol 2 = <u>recruit</u>, take on, hire,
sign up, call up, muster, mobilize,
conscript 3 = <u>obtain</u>, get, gain,
secure, engage, procure

**enormous** = <u>huge</u>, massive,
vast, extensive, tremendous,
gross, immense, gigantic ≠ tiny

**enough** DETERMINER = <u>sufficient</u>,
adequate, ample, abundant, as
much as you need, as much as is
necessary

● PRONOUN = <u>sufficiency</u>, plenty,
sufficient, abundance, adequacy,
right amount, ample supply

● ADVERB = <u>sufficiently</u>, amply,
reasonably, adequately,
satisfactorily, abundantly,
tolerably

**enquire** ➤ **inquire**

**enquiry** ➤ **inquiry**

**enrage** = <u>anger</u>, infuriate,
incense, madden, inflame,
exasperate, antagonize, make you
angry ≠ calm

**enrich** 1 = <u>enhance</u>, develop,
improve, boost, supplement,
refine, heighten, augment
2 = <u>make rich</u>, make wealthy,

make affluent, make prosperous,
make well-off

**enrol** 1 = <u>enlist</u>, register, be
accepted, be admitted, join up,
put your name down for, sign up
or on 2 = <u>recruit</u>, take on, enlist

**en route** = <u>on</u> or along the way,
travelling, on the road, in transit,
on the journey

**ensemble** 1 = <u>group</u>, company,
band, troupe, cast, orchestra,
chorus 2 = <u>collection</u>, set, body,
whole, total, sum, combination,
entity 3 = <u>outfit</u>, suit, get-up
(*informal*), costume

**ensue** = <u>follow</u>, result, develop,
proceed, arise, stem, derive, issue
≠ come first

**ensure** 1 = <u>make certain</u>,
guarantee, secure, make sure,
confirm, warrant, certify
2 = <u>protect</u>, defend, secure,
safeguard, guard, make safe

**entail** = <u>involve</u>, require,
produce, demand, call for,
occasion, need, bring about

**enter** 1 = <u>come</u> or go in or into,
arrive, set foot in somewhere,
cross the threshold of
somewhere, make an entrance
≠ exit 2 = <u>penetrate</u>, get in,
pierce, pass into, perforate
3 = <u>join</u>, start work at, begin work
at, enrol in, enlist in ≠ leave
4 = <u>participate in</u>, join (in), be
involved in, get involved in, play a
part in, partake in, associate

yourself with, start to be in 5 = <u>begin</u>, start, take up, move into, commence, set out on, embark upon 6 = <u>compete in</u>, contest, join in, fight, sign up for, go in for 7 = <u>record</u>, note, register, log, list, write down, take down, inscribe

**enterprise** 1 = <u>firm</u>, company, business, concern, operation, organization, establishment, commercial undertaking 2 = <u>venture</u>, operation, project, adventure, undertaking, programme, pursuit, endeavour 3 = <u>initiative</u>, energy, daring, enthusiasm, imagination, drive, ingenuity, originality

**enterprising** = <u>resourceful</u>, original, spirited, daring, bold, enthusiastic, imaginative, energetic

**entertain** 1 = <u>amuse</u>, interest, please, delight, charm, enthral, cheer, regale 2 = <u>show hospitality to</u>, receive, accommodate, treat, put up, lodge, be host to, have company of 3 = <u>consider</u>, imagine, think about, contemplate, conceive of, bear in mind, keep in mind, give thought to

**entertainment** 1 = <u>enjoyable</u>, fun, pleasure, leisure, relaxation, recreation, enjoyment, amusement 2 = <u>pastime</u>, show, sport, performance, treat, presentation, leisure activity

**enthusiasm** = <u>keenness</u>, interest, passion, motivation, relish, zeal, zest, fervour

**enthusiast** = <u>fan</u>, supporter, lover, follower, addict, buff (*informal*), fanatic, devotee

**enthusiastic** = <u>keen</u>, committed, eager, passionate, vigorous, avid, fervent, zealous ≠ apathetic

**entice** = <u>lure</u>, attract, invite, persuade, tempt, induce, seduce, lead on

**entire** = <u>whole</u>, full, complete, total, gross

**entirely** = <u>completely</u>, totally, absolutely, fully, altogether, thoroughly, wholly, utterly ≠ partly

**entitle** 1 = <u>give the right to</u>, allow, enable, permit, sanction, license, authorize, empower 2 = <u>call</u>, name, title, term, label, dub, christen, give the title of

**entity** = <u>thing</u>, being, individual, object, substance, creature, organism

**entrance**[1] 1 = <u>way in</u>, opening, door, approach, access, entry, gate, passage ≠ exit 2 = <u>appearance</u>, coming in, entry, arrival, introduction ≠ exit 3 = <u>admission</u>, access, entry, entrée, admittance, permission to enter, right of entry

**entrance**[2] 1 = <u>enchant</u>, delight,

charm, fascinate, dazzle, captivate, enthral, beguile ≠ **bore** 2 = **mesmerize**, bewitch, hypnotize, put a spell on, cast a spell on, put in a trance

**entrant** 1 = **competitor**, player, candidate, entry, participant, applicant, contender, contestant

**entrenched** or **intrenched** = **fixed**, set, rooted, well-established, ingrained, deep-seated, deep-rooted, unshakeable or unshakable

**entrepreneur** = **businessman** or **businesswoman**, tycoon, executive, industrialist, speculator, magnate, impresario, business executive

**entrust** or **intrust** 1 = **give custody of**, deliver, commit, delegate, hand over, turn over, confide 2 = **assign**

**entry** 1 = **admission**, access, entrance, admittance, entrée, permission to enter, right of entry 2 = **coming in**, entering, appearance, arrival, entrance ≠ **exit** 3 = **introduction**, presentation, initiation, inauguration, induction, debut, investiture 4 = **record**, listing, account, note, statement, item 5 = **way in**, opening, door, approach, access, gate, passage, entrance

**envelope** = **wrapping**, casing, case, covering, cover, jacket, sleeve, wrapper

**environment** 1 = **surroundings**, setting, conditions, situation, medium, circumstances, background, atmosphere 2 = **habitat**, home, surroundings, territory, terrain, locality, natural home

**environmental** = **ecological**, green

**environmentalist** = **conservationist**, ecologist, green

**envisage** 1 = **imagine**, contemplate, conceive (of), visualize, image, fancy, think up, conceptualize 2 = **foresee**, see, expect, predict, anticipate, envision

**envoy** 1 = **ambassador**, diplomat, emissary 2 = **messenger**, agent, representative, delegate, courier, intermediary, emissary

**envy** NOUN = **covetousness**, resentment, jealousy, bitterness, resentfulness, enviousness (informal)

● VERB 1 = **be jealous (of)**, resent, begrudge, be envious (of) 2 = **covet**, desire, crave, aspire to, yearn for, hanker after

**epidemic** 1 = **outbreak**, plague, growth, spread, scourge, contagion 2 = **spate**, plague, outbreak, wave, rash, eruption, upsurge

**episode** 1 = **event**, experience,

happening, matter, affair, incident, adventure, occurrence **2** = instalment, part, act, scene, section, chapter, passage **3** = period, attack, spell, phase, bout

**equal** ADJECTIVE **1** = identical, the same, matching, equivalent, uniform, alike, corresponding ≠ unequal **2** = fair, just, impartial, egalitarian, unbiased, even-handed ≠ unfair **3** = even, balanced, fifty-fifty (*informal*), evenly matched ≠ uneven

● NOUN = match, equivalent, twin, counterpart

● VERB **1** = amount to, make, come to, total, level, parallel, tie with, equate ≠ be unequal to **2** = be equal to, match, reach **3** = be as good as, match, compare with, equate with, measure up to, be as great as

**equality 1** = fairness, equal opportunity, equal treatment, egalitarianism, fair treatment, justness ≠ inequality **2** = sameness, balance, identity, similarity, correspondence, parity, likeness, uniformity ≠ disparity

**equate 1** = identify, associate, connect, compare, relate, mention in the same breath, think of in connection with **2** = make equal, match, even up **3** = be equal to, parallel, compare with, liken, be commensurate

**equation** = equating, comparison, parallel, correspondence

**equilibrium** = stability, balance, symmetry, steadiness, evenness, equipoise

**equip 1** = supply, provide for, stock, arm, array, furnish, fit out, kit out **2** = prepare, qualify, educate, get ready

**equipment** = apparatus, stock, supplies, stuff, tackle, gear, tools, provisions

**equitable** = even-handed, just, fair, reasonable, proper, honest, impartial, unbiased

**equivalent** NOUN = equal, counterpart, twin, parallel, match, opposite number

● ADJECTIVE = equal, same, comparable, parallel, identical, alike, corresponding, tantamount ≠ different

**era** = age, time, period, date, generation, epoch, day *or* days

**eradicate** = wipe out, eliminate, remove, destroy, get rid of, erase, extinguish, obliterate

**erase 1** = delete, cancel out, wipe out, remove, eradicate, obliterate, blot out, expunge **2** = rub out, remove, wipe out, delete

**erect** VERB **1** = build, raise, set up, construct, put up, assemble, put together ≠ demolish **2** = found, establish, form, create, set up, institute, organize, put up

• ADJECTIVE = upright, straight, stiff, vertical, elevated, perpendicular, pricked-up ≠ bent

**erode** 1 = disintegrate, crumble, deteriorate, corrode, break up, grind down, waste away, wear down or away2 = destroy, consume, crumble, eat away, corrode, break up, grind down, abrade3 = weaken, destroy, undermine, diminish, impair, lessen, wear away

**erosion** 1 = disintegration, deterioration, wearing down or away, grinding down
2 = deterioration, undermining, destruction, weakening, attrition, eating away, abrasion, grinding down

**erotic** = sexual, sexy (informal), crude, explicit, sensual, seductive, vulgar, voluptuous

**erratic** = unpredictable, variable, unstable, irregular, inconsistent, uneven, unreliable, wayward ≠ regular

**error** = mistake, slip, blunder, oversight, howler (informal), bloomer (Brit. informal), miscalculation, solecism

**erupt** 1 = explode, blow up, emit lava2 = discharge, expel, emit, eject, spout, throw off, pour forth, spew forth or out3 = gush, burst out, pour forth, belch forth, spew

forth or out4 = start, break out, began, explode, flare up, burst out, boil over5 (Medical) = break out, appear, flare up

**escalate** 1 = grow, increase, extend, intensify, expand, surge, mount, heighten ≠ decrease
2 = increase, develop, extend, intensify, expand, build up, heighten ≠ lessen

**escape** VERB1 = get away, flee, take off, fly, bolt, slip away, abscond, make a break for it
2 = avoid, miss, evade, dodge, shun, elude, duck, steer clear of
3 = leak out, flow out, gush out, emanate, seep out, exude, spill out, pour forth

• NOUN1 = getaway, break, flight, break-out2 = avoidance, evasion, circumvention3 = relaxation, recreation, distraction, diversion, pastime4 = leak, emission, outpouring, seepage, issue, emanation

**escort** NOUN1 = guard, bodyguard, train, convoy, entourage, retinue, cortege
2 = companion, partner, attendant, guide, beau, chaperon

• VERB = accompany, lead, partner, conduct, guide, shepherd, usher, chaperon

**especially** 1 = notably, mostly, strikingly, conspicuously, outstandingly2 = very, specially, extremely, remarkably, unusually, exceptionally, markedly, uncommonly

**espionage** = spying, intelligence, surveillance, counter-intelligence, undercover work

**essay** NOUN = composition, study, paper, article, piece, assignment, discourse, tract

● VERB (Formal) = attempt, try, undertake, endeavour

**essence** 1 = fundamental nature, nature, being, heart, spirit, soul, core, substance 2 = concentrate, spirits, extract, tincture, distillate

**essential** ADJECTIVE 1 = vital, important, needed, necessary, critical, crucial, key, indispensable ≠ unimportant 2 = fundamental, main, basic, principal, cardinal, elementary, innate, intrinsic ≠ secondary

● NOUN = prerequisite, fundamental, necessity, must, basic, sine qua non (Latin), rudiment

**establish** 1 = set up, found, create, institute, constitute, inaugurate 2 = prove, confirm, demonstrate, certify, verify, substantiate, corroborate, authenticate 3 = secure, form, ground, settle

**establishment** NOUN 1 = creation, founding, setting up, foundation, institution, organization, formation, installation 2 = organization, company, business, firm, concern, operation, institution, corporation

● PHRASES the Establishment = the authorities, the system, the powers that be, the ruling class

**estate** 1 = lands, property, area, grounds, domain, manor, holdings 2 = area, centre, park, development, site, zone, plot 3 (Law) = property, capital, assets, fortune, goods, effects, wealth, possessions

**esteem** NOUN = respect, regard, honour, admiration, reverence, estimation, veneration

● VERB = respect, admire, think highly of, love, value, prize, treasure, revere

**estimate** VERB 1 = calculate roughly, value, guess, judge, reckon, assess, evaluate, gauge 2 = think, believe, consider, rate, judge, hold, rank, reckon

● NOUN 1 = approximate calculation, guess, assessment, judgment, valuation, guesstimate (informal), rough calculation, ballpark figure (informal) 2 = assessment, opinion, belief, appraisal, evaluation, judgment, estimation

**estuary** = inlet, mouth, creek, firth, fjord

**etch** 1 = engrave, cut, impress,

stamp, carve, imprint, inscribe
**2** = <u>corrode</u>, eat into, burn into
**etching** = <u>print</u>, impression, carving, engraving, imprint, inscription
**eternal 1** = <u>everlasting</u>, lasting, permanent, enduring, endless, perpetual, timeless, unending ≠ transitory **2** = <u>interminable</u>, endless, infinite, continual, immortal, never-ending, everlasting ≠ occasional
**eternity 1** (*Theology*) = <u>the afterlife</u>, heaven, paradise, the next world, the hereafter
**2** = <u>perpetuity</u>, immortality, infinity, timelessness, endlessness
**3** = <u>ages</u>
**ethical 1** = <u>moral</u>, behavioural
**2** = <u>right</u>, morally acceptable, good, just, fair, responsible, principled ≠ unethical
**ethics** = <u>moral code</u>, standards, principles, morals, conscience, morality, moral values, moral principles, tikanga (*N.Z.*)
**ethnic** *or* **ethnical** = <u>cultural</u>, national, traditional, native, folk, racial, genetic, indigenous
**euphoria** = <u>elation</u>, joy, ecstasy, rapture, exhilaration, jubilation ≠ despondency
**Europe** ► WORD POWER SUPPLEMENT **European Union**
**evacuate 1** = <u>remove</u>, clear, withdraw, expel, move out, send to a safe place **2** = <u>abandon</u>,

leave, clear, desert, quit, withdraw from, pull out of, move out of
**evade 1** = <u>avoid</u>, escape, dodge, get away from, elude, steer clear of, sidestep, duck ≠ face **2** = <u>avoid answering</u>, parry, fend off, fudge, hedge, equivocate
**evaluate** = <u>assess</u>, rate, judge, estimate, reckon, weigh, calculate, gauge
**evaporate 1** = <u>disappear</u>, vaporize, dematerialize, vanish, dissolve, dry up, fade away, melt away **2** = <u>dry up</u>, dry, dehydrate, vaporize, desiccate **3** = <u>fade away</u>, disappear, vanish, dissolve, melt away
**eve 1** = <u>night before</u>, day before, vigil **2** = <u>brink</u>, point, edge, verge, threshold
**even 1** = <u>regular</u>, stable, constant, steady, smooth, uniform, unbroken, uninterrupted ≠ variable
**2** = <u>level</u>, straight, flat, smooth, true, steady, uniform, parallel ≠ uneven **3** = <u>equal</u>, like, matching, similar, identical, comparable ≠ unequal
**4** = <u>equally matched</u>, level, tied, on a par, neck and neck, fifty-fifty (*informal*), all square ≠ ill-matched **5** = <u>square</u>, quits, on the same level, on an equal footing
**6** = <u>calm</u>, composed, cool, well-balanced, placid, unruffled, imperturbable, even-tempered

≠ excitable

**evening** = <u>dusk</u> (*archaic*), night, sunset, twilight, sundown, gloaming (*Scot. poetic*), close of day, evo (*Austral. slang*)

**event** 1 = <u>incident</u>, happening, experience, affair, occasion, proceeding, business, circumstance 2 = <u>competition</u>, game, tournament, contest, bout

**eventual** = <u>final</u>, overall, concluding, ultimate

**eventually** = <u>in the end</u>, finally, one day, after all, some time, ultimately, at the end of the day, when all is said and done

**ever** 1 = <u>at any time</u>, at all, in any case, at any point, by any chance, on any occasion, at any period 2 = <u>always</u>, for ever, at all times, evermore 3 = <u>constantly</u>, continually, perpetually

**every** = <u>each</u>, each and every, every single

**everybody** = <u>everyone</u>, each one, the whole world, each person, every person, all and sundry, one and all
> **everyone**

**everyday** = <u>ordinary</u>, common, usual, routine, stock, customary, mundane, run-of-the-mill
≠ unusual

**everyone** = <u>everybody</u>, each one, the whole world, each person, every person, all and sundry, one and all

---

### Word Power

**everyone** – *Everyone* and *everybody* are interchangeable, and can be used as synonyms of each other in any context. Care should be taken, however, to distinguish between *everyone* as a single word and *every one* as two words, the latter form correctly being used to refer to each individual person or thing in a particular group: *every one of them is wrong*.

---

**everything** = <u>all</u>, the lot, the whole lot, each thing

**everywhere** 1 = <u>all over</u>, all around, the world over, high and low, in every nook and cranny, far and wide *or* near, to *or* in every place 2 = <u>all around</u>, all over, in every nook and cranny, ubiquitously, far and wide *or* near, to *or* in every place

**evidence** NOUN 1 = <u>proof</u>, grounds, demonstration, confirmation, verification, corroboration, authentication, substantiation 2 = <u>sign(s)</u>, suggestion, trace, indication 3 = <u>testimony</u>, statement, submission, avowal
● VERB = <u>show</u>, prove, reveal, display, indicate, witness, demonstrate, exhibit

**evident** = <u>obvious</u>, clear, plain,

apparent, visible, manifest, noticeable, unmistakable ≠ hidden

**evidently** 1 = <u>obviously</u>, clearly, plainly, undoubtedly, manifestly, without question, unmistakably 2 = <u>apparently</u>, seemingly, outwardly, ostensibly, so it seems, to all appearances

**evil** NOUN 1 = <u>wickedness</u>, bad, vice, sin, wrongdoing, depravity, badness, villainy 2 = <u>harm</u>, suffering, hurt, woe 3 = <u>act of cruelty</u>, crime, ill, horror, outrage, misfortune, mischief, affliction
● ADJECTIVE 1 = <u>wicked</u>, bad, malicious, immoral, sinful, malevolent, depraved, villainous 2 = <u>harmful</u>, disastrous, destructive, dire, catastrophic, pernicious, ruinous 3 = <u>demonic</u>, satanic, diabolical, hellish, devilish, infernal, fiendish 4 = <u>offensive</u>, nasty, foul, unpleasant, vile, noxious, disagreeable, pestilential 5 = <u>unfortunate</u>, unfavourable, ruinous, calamitous

**evoke** = <u>arouse</u>, cause, induce, awaken, give rise to, stir up, rekindle, summon up ≠ suppress

**evolution** 1 = <u>rise</u>, development, adaptation, natural selection, Darwinism, survival of the fittest 2 = <u>development</u>, growth, advance, progress, working out, expansion, extension, unfolding

**evolve** 1 = <u>develop</u>, metamorphose, adapt yourself 2 = <u>grow</u>, develop, advance, progress, mature 3 = <u>work out</u>, develop, progress, expand, unfold

**exact** ADJECTIVE = <u>accurate</u>, correct, true, right, specific, precise, definite, faultless ≠ approximate
● VERB 1 = <u>demand</u>, claim, force, command, extract, compel, extort 2 = <u>inflict</u>, apply, administer, mete out, deal out

**exacting** 1 = <u>demanding</u>, hard, taxing, difficult, tough ≠ easy 2 = <u>strict</u>, severe, harsh, rigorous, stringent

**exactly** 1 = <u>accurately</u>, correctly, precisely, faithfully, explicitly, scrupulously, truthfully, unerringly 2 = <u>precisely</u>, specifically, bang on (*informal*), to the letter

**exaggerate** = <u>overstate</u>, enlarge, embroider, amplify, embellish, overestimate, overemphasize, pile it on about (*informal*)

**examination** 1 = <u>checkup</u>, analysis, going-over (*informal*), exploration, health check, check 2 = <u>exam</u>, test, research, paper, investigation, practical, assessment, quiz

**examine** 1 = <u>inspect</u>, study, survey, investigate, explore, analyse, scrutinize, peruse

2 = <u>check</u>, analyse, check over
3 = <u>test</u>, question, assess, quiz,
evaluate, appraise 4 = <u>question</u>,
quiz, interrogate, cross-examine,
grill (*informal*), give the third
degree to (*informal*)

**example** 1 = <u>instance</u>,
specimen, case, sample,
illustration, particular case,
particular instance, typical case
2 = <u>illustration</u>, model, ideal,
standard, prototype, paradigm,
archetype, paragon 3 = <u>warning</u>,
lesson, caution, deterrent

**exceed** 1 = <u>surpass</u>, better, pass,
eclipse, beat, cap (*informal*), top,
be over 2 = <u>go over the limit of</u>,
go beyond, overstep

**excel** VERB = <u>be superior</u>, eclipse,
beat, surpass, transcend, outdo,
outshine
● PHRASES **excel in** *or* **at**
**something** = <u>be good at</u>, shine
at, be proficient in, show talent
in, be skilful at, be talented at

**excellence** = <u>high quality</u>,
merit, distinction, goodness,
superiority, greatness, supremacy,
eminence

**excellent** = <u>outstanding</u>, good,
great, fine, cool (*informal*),
brilliant, very good, superb,
booshit (*Austral. slang*), exo
(*Austral. slang*), sik (*Austral. slang*)
≠ terrible

**except** *or* **except for**
PREPOSITION = <u>apart from</u>, but for,

saving, barring, excepting, other
than, excluding, omitting
● VERB = <u>exclude</u>, leave out, omit,
disregard, pass over

**exception** = <u>special case</u>, freak,
anomaly, inconsistency,
deviation, oddity, peculiarity,
irregularity

**exceptional** 1 = <u>remarkable</u>,
special, excellent, extraordinary,
outstanding, superior, first-class,
marvellous ≠ average
2 = <u>unusual</u>, special, odd, strange,
extraordinary, unprecedented,
peculiar, abnormal ≠ ordinary

**excerpt** = <u>extract</u>, part, piece,
section, selection, passage,
fragment, quotation

**excess** 1 = <u>surfeit</u>, surplus,
overload, glut, superabundance,
superfluity ≠ shortage
2 = <u>overindulgence</u>,
extravagance, profligacy,
debauchery, dissipation,
intemperance, indulgence,
prodigality ≠ moderation

**excessive** 1 = <u>immoderate</u>, too
much, extreme, exaggerated,
unreasonable, disproportionate,
undue, uncontrolled
2 = <u>inordinate</u>, unfair,
unreasonable, disproportionate,
undue, unwarranted, exorbitant,
extortionate

**exchange** VERB = <u>interchange</u>,
change, trade, switch, swap,
barter, give to each other, give to

one another

● **NOUN** 1 = <u>conversation</u>, talk, word, discussion, chat, dialogue, natter, powwow 2 = <u>interchange</u>, trade, switch, swap, trafficking, swapping, substitution, barter

**excite** 1 = <u>thrill</u>, inspire, stir, provoke, animate, rouse, exhilarate, inflame 2 = <u>arouse</u>, provoke, rouse, stir up 3 = <u>titillate</u>, thrill, stimulate, turn on (slang), arouse, get going (informal), electrify

**excitement** = <u>exhilaration</u>, action, activity, passion, thrill, animation, furore, agitation

**exciting** 1 = <u>stimulating</u>, dramatic, gripping, stirring, thrilling, sensational, rousing, exhilarating ≠ boring 2 = <u>titillating</u>, stimulating, arousing, erotic

**exclaim** = <u>cry out</u>, declare, shout, proclaim, yell, utter, call out

**exclude** 1 = <u>keep out</u>, bar, ban, refuse, forbid, boycott, prohibit, disallow ≠ let in 2 = <u>omit</u>, reject, eliminate, rule out, miss out, leave out ≠ include 3 = <u>eliminate</u>, reject, ignore, rule out, leave out, set aside, omit, pass over

**exclusion** 1 = <u>ban</u>, bar, veto, boycott, embargo, prohibition, disqualification 2 = <u>elimination</u>, missing out, rejection, leaving out, omission

**exclusive** 1 = <u>select</u>, fashionable, stylish, restricted, posh (informal, chiefly Brit.), chic, high-class, up-market ≠ unrestricted 2 = <u>sole</u>, full, whole, complete, total, entire, absolute, undivided ≠ shared 3 = <u>entire</u>, full, whole, complete, total, absolute, undivided 4 = <u>limited</u>, unique, restricted, confined, peculiar

**excursion** = <u>trip</u>, tour, journey, outing, expedition, ramble, day trip, jaunt

**excuse** **NOUN** 1 = <u>justification</u>, reason, explanation, defence, grounds, plea, apology, vindication ≠ accusation

● **VERB** 1 = <u>justify</u>, explain, defend, vindicate, mitigate, apologize for, make excuses for ≠ blame 2 = <u>forgive</u>, pardon, overlook, tolerate, acquit, turn a blind eye to, exonerate, make allowances for 3 = <u>free</u>, relieve, exempt, release, spare, discharge, let off, absolve ≠ convict

**execute** 1 = <u>put to death</u>, kill, shoot, hang, behead, decapitate, guillotine, electrocute 2 = <u>carry out</u>, effect, implement, accomplish, discharge, administer, prosecute, enact 3 = <u>perform</u>, carry out, accomplish

**execution** 1 = <u>killing</u>, hanging, the death penalty, the rope, capital punishment, beheading,

the electric chair, the guillotine
2 = **carrying out**, performance, operation, administration, prosecution, enforcement, implementation, accomplishment

**executive** NOUN
1 = **administrator**, official, director, manager, chairman, managing director, controller, chief executive officer
2 = **administration**, government, directors, management, leadership, hierarchy, directorate
● ADJECTIVE = **administrative**, controlling, directing, governing, regulating, decision-making, managerial

**exemplify** = **show**, represent, display, demonstrate, illustrate, exhibit, embody, serve as an example of

**exempt** ADJECTIVE = **immune**, free, excepted, excused, released, spared, not liable to ≠ liable
● VERB = **grant immunity**, free, excuse, release, spare, relieve, discharge, let off

**exemption** = **immunity**, freedom, relief, exception, discharge, release, dispensation, absolution

**exercise** VERB 1 = **put to use**, use, apply, employ, exert, utilize, bring to bear, avail yourself of
2 = **train**, work out, practise, keep fit, do exercises

● NOUN 1 = **use**, practice, application, operation, discharge, implementation, fulfilment, utilization 2 = **exertion**, training, activity, work, labour, effort, movement, toil 3 = **manoeuvre**, campaign, operation, movement, deployment 4 = **task**, problem, lesson, assignment, practice

**exert** VERB = **apply**, use, exercise, employ, wield, make use of, utilize, bring to bear
● PHRASES **exert yourself** = **make an effort**, work, labour, struggle, strain, strive, endeavour, toil

**exhaust** 1 = **tire out**, fatigue, drain, weaken, weary, sap, wear out, debilitate 2 = **use up**, spend, consume, waste, go through, run through, deplete, squander

**exhausted** 1 = **worn out**, tired out, drained, spent, bushed (*informal*), done in (*informal*), all in (*slang*), fatigued ≠ invigorated
2 = **used up**, consumed, spent, finished, depleted, dissipated, expended ≠ replenished

**exhaustion** 1 = **tiredness**, fatigue, weariness, debilitation
2 = **depletion**, emptying, consumption, using up

**exhibit** 1 = **show**, reveal, display, demonstrate, express, indicate, manifest 2 = **display**, show, set out, parade, unveil, put on view

**exhibition** 1 = **show**, display,

representation, presentation, spectacle, showcase, exposition 2 = display, show, performance, demonstration, revelation

exile NOUN 1 = banishment, expulsion, deportation, eviction, expatriation 2 = expatriate, refugee, outcast, émigré, deportee
● VERB = banish, expel, throw out, deport, drive out, eject, expatriate, cast out

exist 1 = live, be present, survive, endure, be in existence, be, have breath 2 = occur, be present 3 = survive, stay alive, make ends meet, subsist, eke out a living, scrape by, scrimp and save, support yourself

existence 1 = reality, being, life, subsistence, actuality 2 = life, situation, way of life, life style

existent 1 = in existence, living, existing, surviving, standing, present, alive, extant

exit NOUN 1 = way out, door, gate, outlet, doorway, gateway, escape route ≠ entry 2 = departure, withdrawal, retreat, farewell, going, goodbye, exodus, decamping
● VERB = depart, leave, go out, withdraw, retire, quit, retreat, go away ≠ enter

exodus = departure, withdrawal, retreat, leaving, flight, exit, migration, evacuation

exotic 1 = unusual, striking, strange, fascinating, mysterious, colourful, glamorous, unfamiliar ≠ ordinary 2 = foreign, alien, tropical, external, naturalized

expand VERB 1 = get bigger, increase, grow, extend, swell, widen, enlarge, become bigger ≠ contract 2 = make bigger, increase, develop, extend, widen, enlarge, broaden, magnify ≠ reduce 3 = spread (out), stretch (out), unfold, unravel, diffuse, unfurl, unroll
● PHRASES expand on something = go into detail about, embellish, elaborate on, develop, flesh out, expound on, enlarge on, expatiate on

expansion 1 = increase, development, growth, spread, magnification, amplification 2 = enlargement, increase, growth, opening out

expatriate NOUN = exile, refugee, emigrant, émigré
● ADJECTIVE = exiled, refugee, banished, emigrant, émigré, expat

expect 1 = think, believe, suppose, assume, trust, imagine, reckon, presume 2 = anticipate, look forward to, predict, envisage, await, hope for, contemplate 3 = require, demand, want, call for, ask for, hope for, insist on

expectation 1 = projection,

supposition, assumption, belief, forecast, likelihood, probability, presumption 2 = **anticipation**, hope, promise, excitement, expectancy, apprehension, suspense

**expedition** = **journey**, mission, voyage, tour, quest, trek

**expel** 1 = **throw out**, exclude, ban, dismiss, kick out (*informal*), ask to leave, turf out (*informal*), debar ≠ let in 2 = **banish**, exile, deport, evict, force to leave ≠ take in 3 = **drive out**, discharge, force out, let out, eject, issue, spew, belch

**expenditure** 1 = **spending**, payment, expense, outgoings, cost, outlay 2 = **consumption**, using, output

**expense** = **cost**, charge, expenditure, payment, spending, outlay

**expensive** = **costly**, high-priced, lavish, extravagant, dear, stiff, steep (*informal*), pricey ≠ cheap

**experience** NOUN
1 = **knowledge**, practice, skill, contact, expertise, involvement, exposure, participation 2 = **event**, affair, incident, happening, encounter, episode, adventure, occurrence
● VERB = **undergo**, feel, face, taste, go through, sample, encounter, endure

**experienced** = **knowledgeable**, skilled, tried, tested, seasoned, expert, veteran, practised ≠ inexperienced

**experiment** NOUN 1 = **test**, trial, investigation, examination, procedure, demonstration, observation, try-out 2 = **research**, investigation, analysis, observation, research and development, experimentation
● VERB = **test**, investigate, trial, research, try, examine, pilot, sample

**experimental** 1 = **test**, trial, pilot, preliminary, provisional, tentative, speculative, exploratory 2 = **innovative**, new, original, radical, creative, ingenious, avant-garde, inventive

**expert** NOUN = **specialist**, authority, professional, master, genius, guru, pundit, maestro, fundi (*S. African*) ≠ amateur
● ADJECTIVE = **skilful**, experienced, professional, masterly, qualified, talented, outstanding, practised ≠ unskilled

**expertise** = **skill**, knowledge, know-how (*informal*), facility, judgment, mastery, proficiency, adroitness

**expire** 1 = **become invalid**, end, finish, conclude, close, stop, run out, cease 2 = **die**, depart, perish, kick the bucket (*informal*), depart this life, meet your maker, cark it (*Austral. & N.Z. slang*), pass away or on

**explain** 1 = <u>make clear</u> or plain, describe, teach, define, resolve, clarify, clear up, simplify 2 = <u>account for</u>, excuse, justify, give a reason for

**explanation** 1 = <u>reason</u>, answer, account, excuse, motive, justification, vindication 2 = <u>description</u>, report, definition, teaching, interpretation, illustration, clarification, simplification

**explicit** 1 = <u>clear</u>, obvious, specific, direct, precise, straightforward, definite, overt ≠ vague 2 = <u>frank</u>, specific, graphic, unambiguous, unrestricted, unrestrained, uncensored ≠ indirect

**explode** 1 = <u>blow up</u>, erupt, burst, go off, shatter 2 = <u>detonate</u>, set off, discharge, let off 3 = <u>lose your temper</u>, rage, erupt, become angry, hit the roof (informal), go crook (Austral. & N.Z. slang) 4 = <u>increase</u>, grow, develop, extend, advance, shoot up, soar, mushroom 5 = <u>disprove</u>, discredit, refute, demolish, repudiate, put paid to, invalidate, debunk

**exploit** VERB 1 = <u>take advantage of</u>, abuse, use, manipulate, milk, misuse, ill-treat, play on or upon 2 = <u>make the best use of</u>, use, make use of, utilize, cash in on (informal), capitalize on, use to good advantage, profit by or from ● NOUN = <u>feat</u>, act, achievement,

enterprise, adventure, stunt, deed, accomplishment

**exploitation** = <u>misuse</u>, abuse, manipulation, using, ill-treatment

**exploration** 1 = <u>expedition</u>, tour, trip, survey, travel, journey, reconnaissance 2 = <u>investigation</u>, research, survey, search, inquiry, analysis, examination, inspection

**explore** 1 = <u>travel around</u>, tour, survey, scout, reconnoitre 2 = <u>investigate</u>, consider, research, survey, search, examine, probe, look into

**explosion** 1 = <u>blast</u>, crack, burst, bang, discharge, report, blowing up, clap 2 = <u>increase</u>, rise, development, growth, boost, expansion, enlargement, escalation 3 = <u>outburst</u>, fit, storm, attack, surge, flare-up, eruption 4 = <u>outbreak</u>, flare-up, eruption, upsurge

**explosive** NOUN = <u>bomb</u>, mine, shell, missile, rocket, grenade, charge, torpedo ● ADJECTIVE 1 = <u>unstable</u>, dangerous, volatile, hazardous, unsafe, perilous, combustible, inflammable 2 = <u>sudden</u>, rapid, marked, unexpected, startling, swift, abrupt 3 = <u>fiery</u>, violent, volatile, stormy, touchy, vehement

**expose** 1 = <u>uncover</u>, show, reveal, display, exhibit, present, unveil, lay bare ≠ hide 2 = <u>make vulnerable</u>, subject, endanger, leave open, jeopardize, put at risk, imperil, lay open

**exposure** 1 = <u>hypothermia</u>, frostbite, extreme cold, intense cold 2 = <u>uncovering</u>, showing, display, exhibition, revelation, presentation, unveiling

**express** VERB 1 = <u>state</u>, communicate, convey, articulate, say, word, voice, declare 2 = <u>show</u>, indicate, exhibit, demonstrate, reveal, intimate, convey, signify
• ADJECTIVE 1 = <u>explicit</u>, clear, plain, distinct, definite, unambiguous, categorical 2 = <u>specific</u>, exclusive, particular, sole, special, singular, clear-cut, especial 3 = <u>fast</u>, direct, rapid, priority, prompt, swift, high-speed, speedy

**expression** 1 = <u>statement</u>, declaration, announcement, communication, utterance, articulation 2 = <u>indication</u>, demonstration, exhibition, display, showing, show, sign, symbol 3 = <u>look</u>, countenance, face, air, appearance, aspect 4 = <u>phrase</u>, saying, word, term, remark, maxim, idiom, adage

**expressive** = <u>vivid</u>, striking, telling, moving, poignant, eloquent ≠ impassive

**expulsion** 1 = <u>ejection</u>, exclusion, dismissal, removal, eviction, banishment 2 = <u>discharge</u>, emission, spewing, secretion, excretion, ejection, seepage, suppuration

**exquisite** 1 = <u>beautiful</u>, elegant, graceful, pleasing, attractive, lovely, charming, comely ≠ unattractive 2 = <u>fine</u>, beautiful, lovely, elegant, precious, delicate, dainty 3 = <u>intense</u>, acute, severe, sharp, keen, extreme

**extend** 1 = <u>spread out</u>, reach, stretch 2 = <u>stretch</u>, stretch out, spread out, straighten out 3 = <u>last</u>, continue, go on, stretch, carry on 4 = <u>protrude</u>, project, stand out, bulge, stick out, hang, overhang, jut out 5 = <u>widen</u>, increase, expand, add to, enhance, supplement, enlarge, broaden ≠ reduce 6 = <u>make longer</u>, prolong, lengthen, draw out, spin out, drag out ≠ shorten 7 = <u>offer</u>, present, confer, stick out, impart, proffer ≠ withdraw

**extension** 1 = <u>annexe</u>, addition, supplement, appendix, appendage 2 = <u>lengthening</u>, extra time, continuation, additional period of time 3 = <u>development</u>, expansion, widening, increase, broadening, enlargement, diversification

**extensive** ADJECTIVE = <u>large</u>, considerable, substantial, spacious, wide, broad, expansive
• ADJECTIVE ≠ confined 2 = <u>comprehensive</u>, complete, wide, pervasive ≠ restricted

3 = **great**, vast, widespread, large-scale, far-reaching, far-flung, voluminous ≠ limited

**extent** 1 = **magnitude**, amount, scale, level, stretch, expanse 2 = **size**, area, length, width, breadth

**exterior** NOUN = **outside**, face, surface, covering, skin, shell, coating, façade
• ADJECTIVE = **outer**, outside, external, surface, outward, outermost ≠ inner

**external** 1 = **outer**, outside, surface, outward, exterior, outermost ≠ internal 2 = **foreign**, international, alien, extrinsic ≠ domestic 3 = **outside**, visiting ≠ inside

**extinct** = **dead**, lost, gone, vanished, defunct ≠ living

**extinction** = **dying out**, destruction, abolition, oblivion, extermination, annihilation, eradication, obliteration

**extra** ADJECTIVE 1 = **additional**, more, added, further, supplementary, auxiliary, ancillary ≠ vital 2 = **surplus**, excess, spare, redundant, unused, leftover, superfluous
• NOUN = **addition**, bonus, supplement, accessory ≠ necessity
• ADVERB 1 = **in addition**, additionally, over and above 2 = **exceptionally**, very, specially, especially, particularly, extremely, remarkably, unusually

**extract** VERB 1 = **take out**, pull, remove, withdraw, pull out, bring out 2 = **pull out**, remove, take out, draw, uproot, pluck out 3 = **elicit**, obtain, force, draw, derive, glean, coerce
• NOUN 1 = **passage**, selection, excerpt, cutting, clipping, quotation, citation 2 = **essence**, solution, concentrate, juice, distillation

> ### Word Power
>
> **extract** – People sometimes use *extract* where *extricate* would be better. Although both words can refer to a physical act of removal from a place, *extract* has a more general sense than *extricate*. Extricate has additional overtones of 'difficulty', and is most commonly used with reference to getting a person – particularly *yourself* – out of a situation. So, for example, you might say *he will find it difficult to extricate himself* (not *extract himself*) *from this situation*.

**extraordinary** 1 = **remarkable**, outstanding, amazing, fantastic, astonishing, exceptional, phenomenal, extremely good ≠ unremarkable 2 = **unusual**, strange, remarkable, uncommon ≠ ordinary

**extravagant** 1 = **wasteful**, lavish, prodigal, profligate,

spendthrift ≠ economical
2 = <u>excessive</u>, outrageous, over
the top (*slang*), unreasonable,
preposterous ≠ moderate

**extreme** ADJECTIVE 1 = <u>great</u>,
highest, supreme, acute, severe,
maximum, intense, ultimate
≠ mild 2 = <u>severe</u>, radical, strict,
harsh, rigid, drastic,
uncompromising 3 = <u>radical</u>,
excessive, fanatical, immoderate
≠ moderate 4 = <u>farthest</u>, furthest,
far, remotest, far-off, outermost,
most distant ≠ nearest
● NOUN = <u>limit</u>, end, edge, opposite,
pole, boundary, antithesis, extremity

**extremely** = <u>very</u>, particularly,
severely, terribly, unusually,
exceptionally, extraordinarily,
tremendously

**extremist** NOUN = <u>radical</u>,
activist, militant, fanatic, die-hard,
bigot, zealot
● ADJECTIVE = <u>extreme</u>, wild,
passionate, frenzied, obsessive,
fanatical, fervent, zealous

**eye** NOUN 1 = <u>eyeball</u>, optic
(*informal*), organ of vision, organ
of sight 2 *often plural* = <u>eyesight</u>,
sight, vision, perception, ability to
see, power of seeing
3 = <u>appreciation</u>, taste,
recognition, judgment,
discrimination, perception,
discernment 4 = <u>observance</u>,
observation, surveillance, vigil,
watch, lookout 5 = <u>centre</u>, heart,

middle, mid, core, nucleus
● VERB = <u>look at</u>, view, study,
watch, survey, observe,
contemplate, check out (*informal*)

(*Related Words*)

*adjectives*: ocular, ophthalmic, optic

# F

**fable** 1 = <u>legend</u>, myth, parable,
allegory, story, tale 2 = <u>fiction</u>,
fantasy, myth, invention, yarn
(*informal*), fabrication, urban
myth, tall story (*informal*) ≠ fact

**fabric** 1 = <u>cloth</u>, material, stuff,
textile, web 2 = <u>framework</u>,
structure, make-up, organization,
frame, foundations, construction,
constitution 3 = <u>structure</u>,
foundations, construction,
framework

**fabulous** 1 (*Informal*)
= <u>wonderful</u>, excellent, brilliant,
superb, spectacular, fantastic
(*informal*), marvellous,
sensational (*informal*) ≠ ordinary
2 = <u>astounding</u>, amazing,
extraordinary, remarkable,
incredible, astonishing,
unbelievable, breathtaking
3 = <u>legendary</u>, imaginary,
mythical, fictitious, made-up,
fantastic, invented, unreal

**façade** 1 = <u>front</u>, face, exterior
2 = <u>show</u>, front, appearance,
mask, exterior, guise, pretence,

semblance

**face** NOUN 1 = <u>countenance</u>, features, profile, mug (*slang*), visage 2 = <u>expression</u>, look, air, appearance, aspect, countenance 3 = <u>side</u>, front, outside, surface, exterior, elevation, vertical surface
● VERB 1 = <u>look onto</u>, overlook, be opposite, look out on, front onto 2 = <u>confront</u>, meet, encounter, deal with, oppose, tackle, experience, brave 3 *often with* up *to* = <u>accept</u>, deal with, tackle, acknowledge, cope with, confront, come to terms with, meet head-on

**facilitate** = <u>further</u>, help, forward, promote, speed up, pave the way for, make easy, expedite ≠ hinder

**facility** 1 *often plural* = <u>amenity</u>, means, aid, opportunity, advantage, resource, equipment, provision 2 = <u>opportunity</u>, possibility, convenience 3 = <u>ability</u>, skill, efficiency, fluency, proficiency, dexterity, adroitness 4 = <u>ease</u>, fluency, effortlessness ≠ difficulty

**fact** 1 = <u>truth</u>, reality, certainty, verity ≠ fiction 2 = <u>event</u>, happening, act, performance, incident, deed, occurrence, fait accompli (*French*)

**faction** 1 = <u>group</u>, set, party, gang, bloc, contingent, clique, coterie 2 = <u>dissension</u>, division, conflict, rebellion, disagreement, variance, discord, infighting

≠ agreement

**factor** = <u>element</u>, part, cause, influence, item, aspect, characteristic, consideration

> ### Word Power
>
> **factor** – In strict usage, *factor* should only be used to refer to something which contributes to a result. It should not be used to refer to a part of something, such as a plan or arrangement; more appropriate alternatives to *factor* in this sense are words such as *component* or *element*.

**factory** = <u>works</u>, plant, mill, workshop, assembly line, shop floor

**factual** = <u>true</u>, authentic, real, correct, genuine, exact, precise, dinkum (*Austral. & N.Z. informal*), true-to-life ≠ fictitious

**faculty** NOUN 1 = <u>ability</u>, power, skill, faculty, capacity, propensity, aptitude ≠ failing 2 = <u>department</u>, school 3 = <u>teaching staff</u>, staff, teachers, professors, lecturers (*chiefly U.S.*)
● PLURAL NOUN = <u>powers</u>, reason, senses, intelligence, wits, capabilities, mental abilities, physical abilities

**fad** = <u>craze</u>, fashion, trend, rage, vogue, whim, mania

**fade** 1 = <u>become pale</u>, bleach, wash out, discolour, lose colour, decolour 2 = <u>make pale</u>, dim, bleach, wash out, blanch,

discolour, decolour 3 = <u>grow dim</u>,
fade away, become less loud
4 = <u>dwindle</u>, disappear, vanish,
melt away, decline, dissolve,
wane, die away

**fail** VERB 1 = <u>be unsuccessful</u>,
founder, fall, break down, flop
(*informal*), fizzle out (*informal*),
come unstuck, miscarry
≠ succeed 2 = <u>disappoint</u>,
abandon, desert, neglect, omit,
let down, forsake, be disloyal to
3 = <u>stop working</u>, stop, die, break
down, stall, cut out, malfunction,
conk out (*informal*) 4 = <u>wither</u>,
perish, sag, waste away, shrivel up
5 = <u>go bankrupt</u>, collapse, fold
(*informal*), close down, go under,
go bust (*informal*), go out of
business, be wound up
6 = <u>decline</u>, deteriorate,
degenerate 7 = <u>give out</u>, dim,
peter out, die away, grow dim
● PHRASES **without fail**
= <u>without exception</u>, regularly,
constantly, invariably, religiously,
unfailingly, conscientiously, like
clockwork

**failing** NOUN = <u>shortcoming</u>,
fault, weakness, defect, deficiency,
flaw, drawback, blemish ≠ strength
● PREPOSITION = <u>in the absence of</u>,
lacking, in default of

**failure** 1 = <u>lack of success</u>,
defeat, collapse, breakdown,
overthrow, miscarriage, fiasco,
downfall ≠ success 2 = <u>loser</u>,

disappointment, flop (*informal*),
write-off, no-hoper (*chiefly
Austral.*), dud (*informal*), black
sheep, washout (*informal*), dead
duck (*slang*) 3 = <u>bankruptcy</u>,
crash, collapse, ruin, closure,
winding up, downfall, going
under ≠ prosperity

**faint** ADJECTIVE 1 = <u>dim</u>, low, soft,
faded, distant, vague, unclear,
muted ≠ clear 2 = <u>slight</u>, weak,
feeble, unenthusiastic, remote,
slim, vague, slender 3 = <u>dizzy</u>,
giddy, light-headed, weak,
exhausted, wobbly, muzzy, woozy
(*informal*) ≠ energetic
● VERB = <u>pass out</u>, black out, lose
consciousness, keel over
(*informal*), go out, collapse, swoon
(*literary*), flake out (*informal*)
● NOUN = <u>blackout</u>, collapse,
coma, swoon (*literary*),
unconsciousness

**faintly** 1 = <u>slightly</u>, rather, a little,
somewhat, dimly 2 = <u>softly</u>,
weakly, feebly, in a whisper,
indistinctly, unclearly

**fair**[1] 1 = <u>unbiased</u>, impartial,
even-handed, unprejudiced, just,
reasonable, proper, legitimate
≠ unfair 2 = <u>respectable</u>, average,
reasonable, decent, acceptable,
moderate, adequate, satisfactory
3 = <u>light</u>, golden, blonde, blond,
yellowish, fair-haired, light-
coloured, flaxen-haired 4 = <u>fine</u>,
clear, dry, bright, pleasant, sunny,

cloudless, unclouded

5 = <u>beautiful</u>, pretty, attractive, lovely, handsome, good-looking, bonny, comely ≠ ugly

**fair²** = <u>carnival</u>, show, fête, festival, exhibition, mart, bazaar, gala

**fairly** 1 = <u>equitably</u>, objectively, legitimately, honestly, justly, lawfully, without prejudice, dispassionately 2 = <u>moderately</u>, rather, quite, somewhat, reasonably, adequately, pretty well, tolerably 3 = <u>positively</u>, really, simply, absolutely 4 = <u>deservedly</u>, objectively, honestly, justifiably, justly, impartially, equitably, without fear or favour

**fairness** = <u>impartiality</u>, justice, equity, legitimacy, decency, disinterestedness, rightfulness, equitableness

**fairy** = <u>sprite</u>, elf, brownie, pixie, puck, imp, leprechaun, peri

**fairy tale** _or_ **fairy story** 1 = <u>folk tale</u>, romance, traditional story 2 = <u>lie</u>, fiction, invention, fabrication, untruth, urban myth, tall story, urban legend

**faith** 1 = <u>confidence</u>, trust, credit, conviction, assurance, dependence, reliance, credence ≠ distrust 2 = <u>religion</u>, church, belief, persuasion, creed, communion, denomination, dogma ≠ agnosticism

**faithful** 1 = <u>loyal</u>, true, committed, constant, devoted, dedicated, reliable, staunch ≠ disloyal 2 = <u>accurate</u>, close, true, strict, exact, precise

**fake ADJECTIVE** = <u>artificial</u>, false, forged, counterfeit, put-on, pretend (_informal_), mock, imitation ≠ genuine

● NOUN 1 = <u>forgery</u>, copy, fraud, reproduction, dummy, imitation, hoax, counterfeit 2 = <u>charlatan</u>, deceiver, sham, quack

● VERB 1 = <u>forge</u>, copy, reproduce, fabricate, counterfeit, falsify 2 = <u>sham</u>, put on, pretend, simulate, feign, go through the motions of

**fall VERB** 1 = <u>drop</u>, plunge, tumble, plummet, collapse, sink, go down, come down ≠ rise 2 = <u>decrease</u>, drop, decline, go down, slump, diminish, dwindle, lessen ≠ increase 3 = <u>be overthrown</u>, surrender, succumb, submit, capitulate, be conquered, pass into enemy hands ≠ triumph 4 = <u>be killed</u>, die, perish, meet your end ≠ survive 5 = <u>occur</u>, happen, come about, chance, take place, befall, come to pass

● NOUN 1 = <u>drop</u>, slip, plunge, dive, tumble, descent, plummet, nose dive 2 = <u>decrease</u>, drop, lowering, decline, reduction, slump, dip, lessening 3 = <u>collapse</u>, defeat, downfall, ruin, destruction, overthrow, submission, capitulation

**false 1** = <u>incorrect</u>, wrong, mistaken, misleading, faulty, inaccurate, invalid, erroneous ≠ correct**2** = <u>untrue</u>, fraudulent, trumped up, fallacious, untruthful ≠ true**3** = <u>artificial</u>, forged, fake, reproduction, replica, imitation, bogus, simulated ≠ real

**falter 1** = <u>hesitate</u>, delay, waver, vacillate ≠ persevere**2** = <u>tumble</u>, totter**3** = <u>stutter</u>, pause, stumble, hesitate, stammer

**fame** = <u>prominence</u>, glory, celebrity, stardom, reputation, honour, prestige, stature ≠ obscurity

**familiar 1** = <u>well-known</u>, recognized, common, ordinary, routine, frequent, accustomed, customary ≠ unfamiliar
**2** = <u>friendly</u>, close, dear, intimate, amicable ≠ formal**3** = <u>relaxed</u>, easy, friendly, comfortable, intimate, casual, amicable
**4** = <u>disrespectful</u>, forward, bold, intrusive, presumptuous, impudent, overfamiliar

**familiarity 1** = <u>acquaintance</u>, experience, understanding, knowledge, awareness, grasp ≠ unfamiliarity**2** = <u>friendliness</u>, intimacy, ease, openness, informality, sociability ≠ formality
**3** = <u>disrespect</u>, forwardness, overfamiliarity, cheek, presumption, boldness ≠ respect

**family 1** = <u>relations</u>, relatives, household, folk (*informal*), kin, nuclear family, next of kin, kith and kin, ainga (*N.Z.*)**2** = <u>children</u>, kids (*informal*), offspring, little ones, littlies (*Austral. informal*)
**3** = <u>ancestors</u>, house, race, tribe, clan, dynasty, line of descent
**4** = <u>species</u>, group, class, system, order, network, genre, subdivision

---

### Word Power

**family** – Some careful writers insist that a singular verb should always be used with collective nouns such as *government*, *team*, *family*, *committee*, and *class*, for example: *the class is doing a project on Vikings*; *the company is mounting a big sales campaign*. In British usage, however, a plural verb is often used with a collective noun, especially where the emphasis is on a collection of individual objects or people rather than a group regarded as a unit: *the family are all on holiday*. The most important thing to remember is never to treat the same collective noun as both singular and plural in the same sentence: *the family is well and sends its best wishes* or *the family are well and send their best wishes*, but not *the family is well and send their best wishes*.

**famine** = <u>hunger</u>, want, starvation, deprivation, scarcity, dearth

**famous** = <u>well-known</u>, celebrated, acclaimed, noted, distinguished, prominent, legendary, renowned ≠ unknown

**fan¹ NOUN** = <u>blower</u>, ventilator, air conditioner

● **VERB** = <u>blow</u>, cool, refresh, air-condition, ventilate

**fan²** = <u>supporter</u>, lover, follower, enthusiast, admirer, buff (*informal*), devotee, aficionado

**fanatic** = <u>extremist</u>, activist, militant, bigot, zealot

**fancy ADJECTIVE** = <u>elaborate</u>, decorative, extravagant, intricate, baroque, ornamental, ornate, embellished ≠ plain

● **NOUN 1** = <u>whim</u>, thought, idea, desire, urge, notion, humour, impulse **2** = <u>delusion</u>, dream, vision, fantasy, daydream, chimera

● **VERB 1** = <u>wish for</u>, want, desire, hope for, long for, crave, yearn for, thirst for **2** = <u>be attracted to</u>, find attractive, lust after, like, take to, be captivated by, have a thing about (*informal*), have eyes for **3** = <u>suppose</u>, think, believe, imagine, reckon, conjecture, think likely

**fantastic 1** (*Informal*) = <u>wonderful</u>, great, excellent, very good, smashing (*informal*),

superb, tremendous (*informal*), magnificent, booshit (*Austral. slang*), exo (*Austral. slang*), sik (*Austral. slang*) ≠ ordinary **2** = <u>strange</u>, bizarre, grotesque, fanciful, outlandish **3** = <u>implausible</u>, unlikely, incredible, absurd, preposterous, cock-and-bull (*informal*)

**fantasy** or (*Archaic*) **phantasy 1** = <u>daydream</u>, dream, wish, reverie, flight of fancy, pipe dream **2** = <u>imagination</u>, fancy, invention, creativity, originality

**far ADVERB 1** = <u>a long way</u>, miles, deep, a good way, afar, a great distance **2** = <u>much</u>, greatly, very much, extremely, significantly, considerably, decidedly, markedly

● **ADJECTIVE** *often with off* = <u>remote</u>, distant, far-flung, faraway, out-of-the-way, far-off, outlying, off the beaten track ≠ near

**farce 1** = <u>comedy</u>, satire, slapstick, burlesque, buffoonery **2** = <u>mockery</u>, joke, nonsense, parody, shambles, sham, travesty

**fare NOUN 1** = <u>charge</u>, price, ticket price, ticket money **2** = <u>food</u>, provisions, board, rations, kai (*N.Z. informal*), nourishment, sustenance, victuals, nutriment

● **VERB** = <u>get on</u>, do, manage, make out, prosper, get along

**farewell INTERJECTION** = <u>goodbye</u>, bye (*informal*), so

long, see you, take care, good
morning, bye-bye (*informal*),
good day, haere ra (*N.Z.*)
● NOUN = goodbye, parting,
departure, leave-taking, adieu,
valediction, sendoff (*informal*)

**farm** NOUN = smallholding, ranch
(*chiefly U.S. & Canad.*), farmstead,
station (*Austral. & N.Z.*), vineyard,
plantation, croft (*Scot.*), grange,
homestead
● VERB = cultivate, work, plant,
grow crops on, keep animals on

**fascinate** = entrance, absorb,
intrigue, rivet, captivate, enthral,
beguile, transfix ≠ bore

**fascinating** = captivating,
engaging, gripping, compelling,
intriguing, very interesting,
irresistible, enticing ≠ boring

**fascination** = attraction, pull,
magic, charm, lure, allure,
magnetism, enchantment

**fashion** NOUN1 = style, look,
trend, rage, custom, mode, vogue,
craze2 = method, way, style,
manner, mode
● VERB = make, shape, cast,
construct, form, create,
manufacture, forge

**fashionable** = popular, in
fashion, trendy (*Brit. informal*), in
(*informal*), modern, with it
(*informal*), stylish, chic
≠ unfashionable

**fast¹** ADJECTIVE1 = quick, flying,
rapid, fleet, swift, speedy, brisk,

hasty ≠ slow2 = fixed, firm,
sound, stuck, secure, tight,
jammed, fastened ≠ unstable
3 = dissipated, wild, exciting,
loose, extravagant, reckless, self-
indulgent, wanton4 = close, firm,
devoted, faithful, steadfast
● ADVERB1 = quickly, rapidly,
swiftly, hastily, hurriedly, speedily,
in haste, at full speed ≠ slowly
2 = securely, firmly, tightly, fixedly
3 = fixedly, firmly, soundly, deeply,
securely, tightly

**fast²** VERB = go hungry, abstain,
go without food, deny yourself
● NOUN = fasting, diet, abstinence

**fasten** 1 = secure, close, do up
2 = tie, bind, tie up3 = fix, join,
link, connect, attach, affix

**fat** ADJECTIVE1 = overweight,
large, heavy, plump, stout, obese,
tubby, portly ≠ thin2 = fatty,
greasy, adipose, oleaginous, oily
≠ lean
● NOUN = fatness, flesh, bulk,
obesity, flab, blubber, paunch,
fatty tissue

**fatal** 1 = disastrous, devastating,
crippling, catastrophic, ruinous,
calamitous, baleful, baneful
≠ minor2 = lethal, deadly, mortal,
causing death, final, killing,
terminal, malignant ≠ harmless

**fate** 1 = destiny, chance, fortune,
luck, the stars, providence, nemesis,
kismet2 = fortune, destiny, lot,
portion, cup, horoscope

**fated** = <u>destined</u>, doomed, predestined, preordained, foreordained

**father** NOUN 1 = <u>daddy</u> (*informal*), dad (*informal*), male parent, pop (*U.S. informal*), old man (*Brit. informal*), pa (*informal*), papa (*old-fashioned informal*), pater 2 = <u>founder</u>, author, maker, architect, creator, inventor, originator, prime mover 3 *usually cap.* = <u>priest</u>, minister, vicar, parson, pastor, cleric, churchman, padre (*informal*) 4 *usually plural* = <u>forefather</u>, predecessor, ancestor, forebear, progenitor, tupuna or tipuna (*N.Z.*)

● VERB = <u>sire</u>, parent, conceive, bring to life, beget, procreate, bring into being, give life to

(Related Words)

adjective: paternal

**fatherly** = <u>paternal</u>, kindly, protective, supportive, benign, affectionate, patriarchal, benevolent

**fatigue** NOUN = <u>tiredness</u>, lethargy, weariness, heaviness, languor, listlessness ≠ freshness

● VERB = <u>tire</u>, exhaust, weaken, weary, drain, wear out, take it out of (*informal*), tire out ≠ refresh

**fatty** = <u>greasy</u>, fat, creamy, oily, adipose, oleaginous, suety, rich

**fault** NOUN 1 = <u>responsibility</u>, liability, guilt, accountability, culpability 2 = <u>mistake</u>, slip, error, blunder, lapse, oversight, indiscretion, howler (*informal*) 3 = <u>failing</u>, weakness, defect, deficiency, flaw, shortcoming, blemish, imperfection ≠ strength

● VERB = <u>criticize</u>, blame, complain, condemn, moan about, censure, hold (someone) responsible, find fault with

● PHRASES **find fault with something** or **someone** = <u>criticize</u>, complain about, whinge about (*informal*), whine about (*informal*), quibble, carp at, take to task, pick holes in ◆ **to a fault** = <u>excessively</u>, unduly, in the extreme, overmuch, immoderately

**faulty** 1 = <u>defective</u>, damaged, malfunctioning, broken, flawed, impaired, imperfect, out of order 2 = <u>incorrect</u>, flawed, unsound

**favour** NOUN 1 = <u>approval</u>, goodwill, commendation, approbation ≠ disapproval 2 = <u>favouritism</u>, preferential treatment 3 = <u>support</u>, backing, aid, assistance, patronage, good opinion 4 = <u>good turn</u>, service, benefit, courtesy, kindness, indulgence, boon, good deed ≠ wrong

● VERB 1 = <u>prefer</u>, opt for, like better, incline towards, choose, pick, desire, go for ≠ object to 2 = <u>indulge</u>, reward, side with, smile upon 3 = <u>support</u>, champion, encourage, approve,

advocate, subscribe to, commend, stand up for ≠ oppose
4 = **help**, benefit

**favourable** 1 = **positive**, encouraging, approving, praising, reassuring, enthusiastic, sympathetic, commending ≠ disapproving2 = **affirmative**, agreeing, confirming, positive, assenting, corroborative
3 = **advantageous**, promising, encouraging, suitable, helpful, beneficial, auspicious, opportune ≠ disadvantageous

**favourite** ADJECTIVE = **preferred**, favoured, best-loved, most-liked, special, choice, dearest, pet
● NOUN = **darling**, pet, blue-eyed boy (*informal*), beloved, idol, fave (*informal*), teacher's pet, the apple of your eye

**fear** NOUN1 = **dread**, horror, panic, terror, fright, alarm, trepidation, fearfulness
2 = **bugbear**, bête noire, horror, nightmare, anxiety, terror, dread, spectre
● VERB1 = **be afraid of**, dread, shudder at, be fearful of, tremble at, be terrified by, take fright at, shake in your shoes about
2 = **regret**, feel, suspect, have a feeling, have a hunch, have a sneaking suspicion, have a funny feeling
● PHRASES **fear for something** or **someone** = **worry about**, be

anxious about, feel concern for

**fearful** 1 = **scared**, afraid, alarmed, frightened, nervous, terrified, petrified ≠ unafraid
2 = **timid**, afraid, frightened, scared, alarmed, nervous, uneasy, jumpy ≠ brave3 = **frightful**, terrible, awful, dreadful, horrific, dire, horrendous, gruesome

**feasible** = **practicable**, possible, reasonable, viable, workable, achievable, attainable, likely ≠ impracticable

**feast** NOUN1 = **banquet**, repast, spread (*informal*), dinner, treat, hakari (*N.Z.*)2 = **festival**, holiday, fête, celebration, holy day, red-letter day, religious festival, saint's day
● VERB = **eat your fill**, wine and dine, overindulge, consume, indulge, gorge, devour, pig out (*slang*)

**feat** = **accomplishment**, act, performance, achievement, enterprise, undertaking, exploit, deed

**feather** NOUN = **plume**
● PLURAL NOUN = **plumage**, plumes, down

**feature** NOUN1 = **aspect**, quality, characteristic, property, factor, trait, hallmark, facet2 = **article**, report, story, piece, item, column
3 = **highlight**, attraction, speciality, main item
● PLURAL NOUN = **face**,

countenance, physiognomy, lineaments

● VERB 1 = <u>spotlight</u>, present, emphasize, play up, foreground, give prominence to 2 = <u>star</u>, appear, participate, play a part

**federation** = <u>union</u>, league, association, alliance, combination, coalition, partnership, consortium

**fed up** = <u>cheesed off</u>, depressed, bored, tired, discontented, dissatisfied, glum, sick and tired (informal), hoha (N.Z.)

**fee** = <u>charge</u>, price, cost, bill, payment, wage, salary, toll

**feeble** 1 = <u>weak</u>, frail, debilitated, sickly, puny, weedy (informal), infirm, effete ≠ strong 2 = <u>inadequate</u>, pathetic, insufficient, lame 3 = <u>unconvincing</u>, poor, thin, tame, pathetic, lame, flimsy, paltry ≠ effective

**feed** VERB 1 = <u>cater for</u>, provide for, nourish, provide with food, supply, sustain, cook for, wine and dine 2 = <u>graze</u>, eat, browse, pasture 3 = <u>eat</u>, drink milk

● NOUN 1 = <u>food</u>, fodder, provender, pasturage 2 (Informal) = <u>meal</u>, spread (informal), dinner, lunch, tea, breakfast, feast, supper

**feel** VERB 1 = <u>experience</u>, bear 2 = <u>touch</u>, handle, manipulate, finger, stroke, paw, caress, fondle 3 = <u>be aware of</u> 4 = <u>perceive</u>,

detect, discern, experience, notice, observe 5 = <u>sense</u>, be aware, be convinced, have a feeling, intuit 6 = <u>believe</u>, consider, judge, deem, think, hold

● NOUN 1 = <u>texture</u>, finish, touch, surface, surface quality 2 = <u>impression</u>, feeling, air, sense, quality, atmosphere, mood, aura

**feeling** 1 = <u>emotion</u>, sentiment 2 = <u>opinion</u>, view, attitude, belief, point of view, instinct, inclination 3 = <u>passion</u>, emotion, intensity, warmth 4 = <u>ardour</u>, love, care, warmth, tenderness, fervour 5 = <u>sympathy</u>, understanding, concern, pity, sensitivity, compassion, sorrow, sensibility 6 = <u>sensation</u>, sense, impression, awareness 7 = <u>sense of touch</u>, perception, sensation 8 = <u>impression</u>, idea, sense, notion, suspicion, hunch, inkling, presentiment 9 = <u>atmosphere</u>, mood, aura, ambience, feel, air, quality

**fell** 1 = <u>cut down</u>, cut, level, demolish, knock down, hew 2 = <u>knock down</u>

**fellow** 1 (Old-fashioned) = <u>man</u>, person, individual, character, guy (informal), bloke (Brit. informal), chap (informal) 2 = <u>associate</u>, colleague, peer, partner, companion, comrade, crony

**fellowship** 1 = <u>society</u>, club, league, association, organization,

guild, fraternity, brotherhood
**2** = <u>camaraderie</u>, brotherhood,
companionship, sociability
**feminine** = <u>womanly</u>, pretty,
soft, gentle, tender, delicate,
ladylike ≠ masculine
**fence** NOUN = <u>barrier</u>, wall,
defence, railings, hedge,
barricade, hedgerow, rampart
● VERB *often within* or *off*
= <u>enclose</u>, surround, bound,
protect, pen, confine, encircle
**ferocious 1** = <u>fierce</u>, violent,
savage, ravening, predatory,
rapacious, wild ≠ gentle **2** = <u>cruel</u>,
bitter, brutal, vicious, ruthless,
bloodthirsty
**ferry** NOUN = <u>ferry boat</u>, boat,
ship, passenger boat, packet
boat, packet
● VERB = <u>transport</u>, bring, carry,
ship, take, run, shuttle, convey
**fertile** = <u>productive</u>, rich, lush,
prolific, abundant, plentiful,
fruitful, teeming ≠ barren
**fertility** = <u>fruitfulness</u>,
abundance, richness, fecundity,
luxuriance, productiveness
**fertilizer** = <u>compost</u>, muck,
manure, dung, bone meal,
dressing
**festival 1** = <u>celebration</u>, fair,
carnival, gala, fête, entertainment,
jubilee, fiesta **2** = <u>holy day</u>,
holiday, feast, commemoration,
feast day, red-letter day, saint's
day, fiesta

**festive** = <u>celebratory</u>, happy,
merry, jubilant, cheery, joyous,
joyful, jovial ≠ mournful
**fetch 1** = <u>bring</u>, pick up, collect,
go and get, get, carry, deliver,
transport **2** = <u>sell for</u>, make, raise,
earn, realize, go for, yield, bring in
**fetching** = <u>attractive</u>, charming,
cute, enticing, captivating,
alluring, winsome
**feud** NOUN = <u>hostility</u>, row,
conflict, argument, disagreement,
rivalry, quarrel, vendetta
● VERB = <u>quarrel</u>, row, clash,
dispute, fall out, contend, war,
squabble
**fever** = <u>excitement</u>, frenzy,
ferment, agitation, fervour,
restlessness, delirium
**few** = <u>not many</u>, one or two,
scarcely any, rare, meagre,
negligible, sporadic, sparse
**fiasco** = <u>flop</u>, failure, disaster,
mess (*informal*), catastrophe,
debacle, cock-up (*Brit. slang*),
washout (*informal*)
**fibre** = <u>thread</u>, strand, filament,
tendril, pile, texture, wisp
**fiction 1** = <u>tale</u>, story, novel,
legend, myth, romance, narration,
creative writing **2** = <u>lie</u>, invention,
fabrication, falsehood, untruth,
urban myth, tall story, urban
legend
**fictional** = <u>imaginary</u>, made-up,
invented, legendary, unreal,
nonexistent

**fiddle** VERB 1 *usually with with* = <u>fidget</u>, play, finger, tamper, mess about *or* around 2 *usually with with* = <u>tinker</u>, adjust, interfere, mess about *or* around 3 (*Informal*) = <u>cheat</u>, cook (*informal*), fix, diddle (*informal*), wangle (*informal*)
● NOUN 1 (*Brit. informal*) = <u>fraud</u>, racket, scam (*slang*), fix, swindle 2 = <u>violin</u>

**fiddling** = <u>trivial</u>, small, petty, trifling, insignificant, unimportant, pettifogging, futile

**fidelity** 1 = <u>loyalty</u>, devotion, allegiance, constancy, faithfulness, dependability, trustworthiness, staunchness ≠ disloyalty 2 = <u>accuracy</u>, precision, correspondence, closeness, faithfulness, exactness, scrupulousness ≠ inaccuracy

**field** NOUN 1 = <u>meadow</u>, land, green, lea (*poetic*), pasture 2 = <u>speciality</u>, line, area, department, territory, discipline, province, sphere 3 = <u>line</u>, reach, sweep 4 = <u>competitors</u>, competition, candidates, runners, applicants, entrants, contestants
● VERB 1 (*Informal*) = <u>deal with</u>, answer, handle, respond to, reply to, deflect, turn aside 2 (*Sport*) = <u>retrieve</u>, return, stop, catch, pick up

**fierce** 1 = <u>ferocious</u>, wild, dangerous, cruel, savage, brutal,

aggressive, menacing, aggers (*Austral. slang*), biffo (*Austral. slang*) ≠ gentle 2 = <u>intense</u>, strong, keen, relentless, cut-throat 3 = <u>stormy</u>, strong, powerful, violent, intense, raging, furious, howling ≠ tranquil

**fiercely** = <u>ferociously</u>, savagely, passionately, furiously, viciously, tooth and nail, tigerishly, with no holds barred

**fiery** 1 = <u>burning</u>, flaming, blazing, on fire, ablaze, aflame, afire 2 = <u>excitable</u>, fierce, passionate, irritable, impetuous, irascible, hot-headed

**fight** VERB 1 = <u>oppose</u>, campaign against, dispute, contest, resist, defy, contend, withstand 2 = <u>battle</u>, combat, do battle 3 = <u>engage in</u>, conduct, wage, pursue, carry on
● NOUN 1 = <u>battle</u>, campaign, movement, struggle 2 = <u>conflict</u>, clash, contest, encounter 3 = <u>brawl</u>, scrap (*informal*), confrontation, rumble (*U.S. & N.Z. slang*), duel, skirmish, tussle, biffo (*Austral. slang*) 4 = <u>row</u>, argument, dispute, quarrel, squabble 5 = <u>resistance</u>, spirit, pluck, militancy, belligerence, pluckiness

**fighter** 1 = <u>boxer</u>, wrestler, pugilist, prize fighter 2 = <u>soldier</u>, warrior, fighting man, man-at-arms

**figure** NOUN 1 = <u>digit</u>, character, symbol, number, numeral
2 = <u>shape</u>, build, body, frame, proportions, physique
3 = <u>personage</u>, person, individual, character, personality, celebrity, big name, dignitary 4 = <u>diagram</u>, drawing, picture, illustration, representation, sketch 5 = <u>design</u>, shape, pattern 6 = <u>price</u>, cost, value, amount, total, sum
• VERB 1 *usually within* = <u>feature</u>, act, appear, contribute to, play a part, be featured 2 = <u>calculate</u>, work out, compute, tot up, total, count, reckon, tally
• PHRASES **figure something** or **someone out** = <u>understand</u>, make out, fathom, see, solve, comprehend, make sense of, decipher

**figurehead** = <u>nominal head</u>, titular head, front man, puppet, mouthpiece

**file**[1] NOUN 1 = <u>folder</u>, case, portfolio, binder 2 = <u>dossier</u>, record, information, data, documents, case history, report, case 3 = <u>line</u>, row, chain, column, queue, procession
• VERB 1 = <u>arrange</u>, order, classify, put in place, categorize, pigeonhole, put in order
2 = <u>register</u>, record, enter, log, put on record 3 = <u>march</u>, troop, parade, walk in line, walk behind one another

**file**[2] = <u>smooth</u>, shape, polish, rub, scrape, rasp, abrade

**fill** 1 = <u>top up</u>, fill up, make full, become full, brim over 2 = <u>swell</u>, expand, become bloated, extend, balloon, fatten 3 = <u>pack</u>, crowd, squeeze, cram, throng 4 = <u>stock</u>, supply, pack, load 5 = <u>plug</u>, close, stop, seal, cork, bung, block up, stop up 6 = <u>saturate</u>, charge, pervade, permeate, imbue, impregnate, suffuse 7 = <u>fulfil</u>, hold, perform, carry out, occupy, execute, discharge 8 *often with up* = <u>satisfy</u>, stuff, glut

**filling** NOUN = <u>stuffing</u>, padding, filler, wadding, inside, insides, contents
• ADJECTIVE = <u>satisfying</u>, heavy, square, substantial, ample

**film** NOUN 1 = <u>movie</u>, picture, flick (*slang*), motion picture
2 = <u>cinema</u>, the movies 3 = <u>layer</u>, covering, cover, skin, coating, dusting, tissue, membrane
• VERB 1 = <u>photograph</u>, record, shoot, video, videotape, take
2 = <u>adapt for the screen</u>, make into a film

**filter** VERB 1 = <u>purify</u>, treat, strain, refine, riddle, sift, sieve, winnow
2 = <u>trickle</u>, seep, percolate, escape, leak, penetrate, ooze, dribble
• NOUN = <u>sieve</u>, mesh, gauze, strainer, membrane, riddle, sifter

**filthy** 1 = <u>dirty</u>, foul, polluted,

squalid, slimy, unclean, putrid, festy (*Austral. slang*) **2** = grimy, muddy, blackened, grubby, begrimed, festy (*Austral. slang*) **3** = <u>obscene</u>, corrupt, indecent, pornographic, lewd, depraved, impure, smutty

**final 1** = <u>last</u>, latest, closing, finishing, concluding, ultimate, terminal ≠ first **2** = <u>irrevocable</u>, absolute, definitive, decided, settled, definite, conclusive, irrefutable

**finale** = <u>climax</u>, ending, close, conclusion, culmination, denouement, last part, epilogue ≠ opening

**finally 1** = <u>eventually</u>, at last, in the end, ultimately, at length, at long last, after a long time **2** = <u>lastly</u>, in the end, ultimately **3** = <u>in conclusion</u>, lastly, in closing, to conclude, to sum up, in summary

**finance** VERB = <u>fund</u>, back, support, pay for, guarantee, invest in, underwrite, endow
● NOUN = <u>economics</u>, business, money, banking, accounts, investment, commerce
● PLURAL NOUN = <u>resources</u>, money, funds, capital, cash, affairs, budgeting, assets

**financial** = <u>economic</u>, business, commercial, monetary, fiscal, pecuniary

**find** VERB **1** = <u>discover</u>, uncover, spot, locate, detect, come across, hit upon, put your finger on ≠ lose **2** = <u>encounter</u>, meet, recognize **3** = <u>observe</u>, learn, note, discover, notice, realize, come up with, perceive
● NOUN = <u>discovery</u>, catch, asset, bargain, acquisition, good buy
● PHRASES **find something out** = <u>learn</u>, discover, realize, observe, perceive, detect, become aware, come to know

**fine**[1] **1** = <u>excellent</u>, good, striking, masterly, very good, impressive, outstanding, magnificent ≠ poor **2** = <u>satisfactory</u>, good, all right, suitable, acceptable, convenient, fair, O.K. or okay (*informal*) **3** = <u>thin</u>, narrow, wispy **4** = <u>delicate</u>, light, thin, sheer, flimsy, wispy, gossamer, diaphanous ≠ coarse **5** = <u>stylish</u>, expensive, elegant, refined, tasteful, quality **6** = <u>exquisite</u>, delicate, fragile, dainty **7** = <u>minute</u>, exact, precise, nice **8** = <u>keen</u>, minute, nice, sharp, acute, subtle, precise, hairsplitting **9** = <u>brilliant</u>, quick, keen, alert, clever, penetrating, astute **10** = <u>sunny</u>, clear, fair, dry, bright, pleasant, clement, balmy ≠ cloudy

**fine**[2] NOUN = <u>penalty</u>, damages, punishment, forfeit, financial penalty
● VERB = <u>penalize</u>, charge, punish

**finger** = touch, feel, handle, play with, manipulate, paw (*informal*), maul, toy with

**finish** VERB 1 = stop, close, complete, conclude, cease, wrap up (*informal*), terminate, round off ≠ start 2 = get done, complete, conclude 3 = end, stop, conclude, wind up, terminate 4 = consume, dispose of, devour, polish off, eat, get through 5 = use up, empty, exhaust 6 = coat, polish, stain, texture, wax, varnish, gild, veneer 7 *usually with* off = destroy, defeat, overcome, bring down, ruin, dispose of, rout, put an end to 8 *usually with* off = kill, murder, destroy, massacre, butcher, slaughter, slay, exterminate ● NOUN 1 = end, close, conclusion, run-in, completion, finale, culmination, cessation ≠ beginning 2 = surface, polish, shine, texture, glaze, veneer, lacquer, lustre

**finished** 1 = over, done, through, ended, closed, complete, executed, finalized ≠ begun 2 = ruined, done for (*informal*), doomed, through, lost, defeated, wiped out, undone

**fire** NOUN 1 = flames, blaze, combustion, inferno, conflagration, holocaust 2 = passion, energy, spirit, enthusiasm, excitement, intensity, sparkle, vitality 3 = bombardment, shooting, firing, shelling, hail, volley, barrage, gunfire ● VERB 1 = let off, shoot, shell, set off, discharge, detonate 2 = shoot, explode, discharge, detonate, pull the trigger 3 (*Informal*) = dismiss, sack (*informal*), get rid of, discharge, lay off, make redundant, cashier, give notice 4 *sometimes with* up = inspire, excite, stir, stimulate, motivate, awaken, animate, rouse

**fireworks** 1 = pyrotechnics, illuminations, feux d'artifice 2 (*Informal*) = trouble, row, storm, rage, uproar, hysterics

**firm** 1 1 = hard, solid, dense, set, stiff, compacted, rigid, inflexible ≠ soft 2 = secure, fixed, rooted, stable, steady, fast, embedded, immovable ≠ unstable 3 = strong, close, tight, steady 4 = strict, unshakeable, resolute, inflexible, unyielding, unbending 5 = determined, resolved, definite, set on, adamant, resolute, inflexible, unyielding ≠ wavering 6 = definite, hard, clear, confirmed, settled, fixed, hard-and-fast, cut-and-dried (*informal*)

**firm** 2 = company, business, concern, association, organization, corporation, venture, enterprise

**firmly** 1 = <u>securely</u>, safely, tightly
2 = <u>immovably</u>, securely, steadily,
like a rock, unflinchingly,
unshakeably 3 = <u>steadily</u>,
securely, tightly, unflinchingly
4 = <u>resolutely</u>, staunchly,
steadfastly, definitely,
unwaveringly, unchangeably

**first** ADJECTIVE 1 = <u>earliest</u>,
original, primordial 2 = <u>initial</u>,
opening, earliest, maiden,
introductory 3 = <u>top</u>, best,
winning, premier 4 = <u>elementary</u>,
key, basic, primary, fundamental,
cardinal, rudimentary, elemental
5 = <u>foremost</u>, highest, greatest,
leading, head, ruling, chief, prime
● ADVERB = <u>to begin with</u>, firstly,
initially, at the beginning, in the
first place, beforehand, to start
with, at the outset
● NOUN = <u>novelty</u>, innovation,
originality, new experience
● PHRASES **from the first** = <u>from</u>
<u>the start</u>, from the beginning,
from the outset, from the very
beginning, from the introduction,
from the starting point, from the
inception, from the
commencement

**fish** = <u>angle</u>, net, cast, trawl
▸ **types of fish** ▸ **sharks**

**fit¹** VERB 1 = <u>adapt</u>, shape, arrange,
alter, adjust, modify, tweak
(*informal*), customize 2 = <u>place</u>,
insert 3 = <u>suit</u>, meet, match,
belong to, conform to,

correspond to, accord with, be
appropriate to 4 = <u>equip</u>, provide,
arm, prepare, fit out, kit out
● ADJECTIVE 1 = <u>appropriate</u>,
suitable, right, becoming, seemly,
fitting, skilled, correct
≠ inappropriate 2 = <u>healthy</u>,
strong, robust, sturdy, well, trim,
strapping, hale ≠ unfit

**fit²** 1 = <u>seizure</u>, attack, bout,
spasm, convulsion, paroxysm
2 = <u>bout</u>, burst, outbreak,
outburst, spell

**fitness** 1 = <u>appropriateness</u>,
competence, readiness, eligibility,
suitability, propriety, aptness
2 = <u>health</u>, strength, good health,
vigour, good condition, wellness,
robustness

**fitting** NOUN = <u>accessory</u>, part,
piece, unit, component,
attachment
● ADJECTIVE = <u>appropriate</u>,
suitable, proper, apt, right,
becoming, seemly, correct
≠ unsuitable

**fix** VERB 1 = <u>place</u>, join, stick,
attach, set, position, plant, link
2 = <u>decide</u>, set, choose, establish,
determine, settle, arrange, arrive
at 3 = <u>arrange</u>, organize, sort out,
see to, fix up, make arrangements
for 4 = <u>repair</u>, mend, service,
correct, restore, see to, overhaul,
patch up 5 = <u>focus</u>, direct at,
fasten on 6 (*Informal*) = <u>rig</u>, set
up (*informal*), influence,

## Types of fish

ahuru (*N.Z.*)
alewife
albacore
alfonsino
amberjack
anabas
anchovy
angelfish
archerfish
argentine
aua (*N.Z.*)
Australian salmon, native salmon,
  salmon trout, bay trout *or*
  kahawai (*N.Z. & Austral.*)
barbel
barracouta *or* (*Austral.*) hake
barracuda
barramundi *or* (*Austral.*) barra *or*
  giant perch
bass
beluga
bib, pout, *or* whiting pout
black cod *or* Māori chief (*N.Z.*)
blackfish *or* (*Austral.*) nigger
bleak
blenny
blowfish *or* (*Austral.*) toado
blue cod, rock cod, *or* (*N.Z.*)
  rawaru, pakirikiri, *or* patutuki
bluefin tuna
bluefish *or* snapper
blue nose (*N.Z.*)
bonito *or* (*Austral.*) horse
  mackerel
bony bream (*Austral.*)
bowfin *or* dogfish
bream *or* (*Austral.*) brim

brill
brook trout *or* speckled trout
brown trout
bullhead
bully *or* (*N.Z.*) pakoko,
  titarakura, *or* toitoi
burbot, eelpout, *or* ling
butterfish, greenbone, *or* (*N.Z.*)
  koaea *or* marari
capelin *or* caplin
carp
catfish
Chinook salmon, quinnat
  salmon, *or* king salmon
chub
cisco *or* lake herring
clingfish
coalfish *or* (*Brit.*) saithe *or* coley
cockabully
cod *or* codfish
coelacanth
coho *or* silver salmon
coley
conger
coral trout
dab
dace
dart (*Austral.*)
darter
dory
dragonet
eel *or* (*N.Z.*) tuna
eelpout
electric eel
fighting fish *or* betta
filefish
flatfish *or* (*N.Z.*) flattie

## Types of fish (continued)

flathead
flounder or (N.Z.) patiki
flying fish
flying gurnard
garpike, garfish, gar, or (Austral.)
  ballahoo
geelbek
gemfish or (Austral.) hake
goby
golden perch, freshwater bream,
  Murray perch, or yellow-belly
  (Austral.)
goldfish
gourami
grayling or (Austral.) yarra
  herring
grenadier or rat-tail
groper or grouper
grunion
grunt
gudgeon
gunnel
guppy
gurnard or gurnet
haddock
hagfish, hag or blind eel
hake
halfbeak
halibut
hapuku (Austral. & N.Z.)
herring
hogfish
hoki (N.Z.)
horse mackerel
jewelfish
jewfish or (Austral. informal)
  jewie

John Dory
kelpfish or (Austral. informal)
  kelpie
killifish
kingfish
kingklip (S. Afr.)
kokanee
kokopu (N.Z.)
lamprey or lamper eel
leatherjacket
lemon sole
ling or (Austral.) beardie
loach
luderick or (N.Z.) parore
lumpfish or lumpsucker
lungfish
mackerel or (colloquial) shiner
mangrove Jack (Austral.)
manta, manta ray, devilfish, or
  devil ray
maomao (N.Z.)
marlin or spearfish
menhaden
miller's thumb
minnow or (Scot.) baggie minnow
mirror carp
moki or blue moki (N.Z.)
molly
monkfish or (U.S.) goosefish
moray
morwong, black perch, or (N.Z.)
  porae
mudfish
mudskipper
opah, moonfish, or kingfish
orange roughy (Austral.)
orfe

## Types of fish (continued)

ouananiche
ox-eye herring (Austral.)
parore, blackfish, black
 rockfish or mangrove fish
 (N.Z.)
parrotfish
pearl perch (Austral.)
perch or (Austral.) redfin
pickerel
pike, luce, or jackfish
pikeperch
pilchard or (Austral. informal)
 pillie
pilot fish
pipefish or needlefish
piranha or piraña
plaice
pollack or pollock
pollan
pompano
porae (N.Z.)
porcupine fish or globefish
porgy or pogy
pout
powan or lake herring
puffer or globefish
rainbow trout
ray
redfin
redfish
red mullet or (U.S.) goatfish
red salmon
red snapper
remora
ribbonfish
roach
rock bass

rockfish or (formerly) rock
 salmon
rockling
rudd
ruffe, ruff, or pope
salmon
sand eel, sand lance, or launce
sardine
sauger
saury or skipper
sawfish
scad
scaldfish
scorpion fish
scup or northern porgy
sea bass
sea bream
sea horse
sea scorpion
sea snail or snailfish
sea trout
Sergeant Baker
shad
shanny
shiner
Siamese fighting fish
sild
silver belly (N.Z.)
silverfish
silverside or silversides
skate
skipjack or skipjack tuna
smelt
smooth hound
snapper, red bream, or (Austral.)
 wollomai or wollamai
snipefish or bellows fish

## Types of fish (continued)

| | |
|---|---|
| snoek | trevalla (*Austral.*) |
| snook | trevally, araara *or* samson fish |
| sockeye *or* red salmon | (*Austral. & N.Z.*) |
| sole | triggerfish |
| Spanish mackerel *or* Queensland | trout |
| kingfish | trunkfish, boxfish, *or* cowfish |
| sprat | tuna *or* tunny |
| steelhead | turbot |
| stickleback | vendace |
| stingray | wahoo |
| stonefish | walleye, walleyed pike, *or* dory |
| sturgeon | warehou (*N.Z.*) |
| sucker | weever |
| sunfish | whitebait |
| surgeonfish | whitefish |
| swordfish | whiting |
| swordtail | witch |
| tailor | wobbegong, wobbygong, *or* |
| tarakihi *or* terakihi (*N.Z.*) | wobegong |
| tarpon | wolffish *or* catfish |
| tarwhine | wrasse |
| tautog *or* blackfish | yellowfin (*N.Z.*) |
| tench | yellow jack |
| toadfish | |
| tommy rough *or* tommy ruff | |
| (*Austral.*) | |

manipulate, fiddle (*informal*)
● NOUN (*Informal*) = mess, corner,
difficulty, dilemma,
embarrassment, plight, pickle
(*informal*), uphill (*S. African*)
● PHRASES **fix someone up**
= provide, supply, bring about,
lay on, arrange for ◆ **fix
something up** = arrange, plan,
settle, fix, organize, sort out, agree

on, make arrangements for
**fixed** 1 = <u>inflexible</u>, set, steady,
resolute, unwavering ≠ wavering
2 = <u>immovable</u>, set, established,
secure, rooted, permanent, rigid
≠ mobile 3 = <u>agreed</u>, set,
planned, decided, established,
settled, arranged, resolved
**fizz** 1 = <u>bubble</u>, froth, fizzle,

effervesce, produce bubbles
2 = <u>sputter</u>, buzz, sparkle, hiss,
crackle

**flag¹** NOUN = <u>banner</u>, standard,
colours, pennant, ensign,
streamer, pennon

● VERB = <u>mark</u>, identify, indicate,
label, pick out, note

● PHRASES **flag something** or
**someone down** = <u>hail</u>, stop,
signal, wave down

**flag²** = <u>weaken</u>, fade, weary, falter,
wilt, wane, sag, languish

**flagging** = <u>weakening</u>,
declining, waning, fading,
deteriorating, wearying, faltering,
wilting

**flair** 1 = <u>ability</u>, feel, talent, gift,
genius, faculty, mastery, knack
2 = <u>style</u>, taste, dash, chic,
elegance, panache, discernment,
stylishness

**flake** NOUN = <u>chip</u>, scale, layer,
peeling, shaving, wafer, sliver

● VERB = <u>chip</u>, peel (off), blister

**flamboyant** 1 = <u>camp</u>
(*informal*), dashing, theatrical,
swashbuckling 2 = <u>showy</u>,
elaborate, extravagant, ornate,
ostentatious 3 = <u>colourful</u>,
striking, brilliant, glamorous,
stylish, dazzling, glitzy (*slang*),
showy

**flame** NOUN 1 = <u>fire</u>, light, spark,
glow, blaze, brightness, inferno
2 (*Informal*) = <u>sweetheart</u>,
partner, lover, girlfriend,

boyfriend, heart-throb (*Brit.*),
beau

● VERB = <u>burn</u>, flash, shine, glow,
blaze, flare, glare

**flank** 1 = <u>side</u>, hip, thigh, loin
2 = <u>wing</u>, side, sector, aspect

**flap** VERB 1 = <u>flutter</u>, wave, flail
2 = <u>beat</u>, wave, thrash, flutter,
wag, vibrate, shake

● NOUN 1 = <u>flutter</u>, beating,
waving, shaking, swinging, swish
2 (*Informal*) = <u>panic</u>, state
(*informal*), agitation, commotion,
sweat (*informal*), dither (*chiefly
Brit.*), fluster, tizzy (*informal*)

**flare** NOUN = <u>flame</u>, burst, flash,
blaze, glare, flicker

● VERB 1 = <u>blaze</u>, flame, glare,
flicker, burn up 2 = <u>widen</u>, spread,
broaden, spread out, dilate, splay

**flash** NOUN = <u>blaze</u>, burst, spark,
beam, streak, flare, dazzle, glare

● VERB 1 = <u>blaze</u>, shine, beam,
sparkle, flare, glare, gleam, light
up 2 = <u>speed</u>, race, shoot, fly, tear,
dash, whistle, streak 3 (*Informal*)
= <u>show quickly</u>, display, expose,
exhibit, flourish, show off, flaunt

● ADJECTIVE (*Informal*)
= <u>ostentatious</u>, smart, trendy,
showy

**flat¹** ADJECTIVE 1 = <u>even</u>, level,
levelled, smooth, horizontal
≠ uneven 2 = <u>punctured</u>,
collapsed, burst, blown out,
deflated, empty 3 = <u>used up</u>,
finished, empty, drained, expired

4 = <u>absolute</u>, firm, positive, explicit, definite, outright, downright, unequivocal5 = <u>dull</u>, dead, empty, boring, depressing, tedious, lacklustre, tiresome ≠ exciting6 = <u>without energy</u>, empty, weak, tired, depressed, drained, weary, worn out
7 = <u>monotonous</u>, boring, dull, tedious, tiresome, unchanging
● ADVERB = <u>completely</u>, directly, absolutely, categorically, precisely, exactly, utterly, outright
● PHRASES flat out (*Informal*) = at full speed, all out, to the full, hell for leather (*informal*), as hard as possible, at full tilt, for all you are worth

**flat²** = <u>apartment</u>, rooms, quarters, digs, suite, penthouse, living quarters

**flatly** = <u>absolutely</u>, completely, positively, categorically, unequivocally, unhesitatingly

**flatten** 1 = <u>level</u>, squash, compress, trample, iron out, even out, smooth off2 = <u>destroy</u>, level, ruin, demolish, knock down, pull down, raze

**flatter** 1 = <u>praise</u>, compliment, pander to, sweet-talk (*informal*), wheedle, soft-soap (*informal*), butter up2 = <u>suit</u>, become, enhance, set off, embellish, do something for, show to advantage

**flattering** 1 = <u>becoming</u>, kind, effective, enhancing, well-chosen ≠ unflattering2 = <u>ingratiating</u>, complimentary, fawning, fulsome, laudatory, adulatory ≠ uncomplimentary

**flavour** NOUN1 = <u>taste</u>, seasoning, flavouring, savour, relish, smack, aroma, zest ≠ blandness2 = <u>quality</u>, feeling, feel, style, character, tone, essence, tinge
● VERB = <u>season</u>, spice, add flavour to, enrich, infuse, imbue, pep up, leaven

**flaw** = <u>weakness</u>, failing, defect, weak spot, fault, blemish, imperfection, chink in your armour

**flawed** 1 = <u>damaged</u>, defective, imperfect, blemished, faulty
2 = <u>erroneous</u>, incorrect, invalid, wrong, mistaken, false, faulty, unsound

**flee** = <u>run away</u>, escape, bolt, fly, take off (*informal*), depart, run off, take flight

**fleet** = <u>navy</u>, task force, flotilla, armada

**fleeting** = <u>momentary</u>, passing, brief, temporary, short-lived, transient, ephemeral, transitory ≠ lasting

**flesh** NOUN1 = <u>fat</u>, muscle, tissue, brawn2 = <u>fatness</u>, fat, adipose tissue, corpulence, weight
3 = <u>meat</u>4 = <u>physical nature</u>, carnality, human nature, flesh and

blood, sinful nature
● PHRASES **your own flesh and blood** = family, blood, relations, relatives, kin, kith and kin, blood relations, kinsfolk, ainga (N.Z.)

**flexibility** 1 = elasticity, pliability, springiness, pliancy, give (informal) 2 = adaptability, openness, versatility, adjustability 3 = complaisance, accommodation, give and take, amenability

**flexible** 1 = pliable, plastic, elastic, supple, lithe, springy, pliant, stretchy ≠ rigid 2 = adaptable, open, variable, adjustable, discretionary ≠ inflexible

**flick** VERB 1 = jerk, pull, tug, lurch, jolt 2 = strike, tap, remove quickly, hit, touch, stroke, flip, whisk
● PHRASES **flick through something** = browse, glance at, skim, leaf through, flip through, thumb through, skip through

**flicker** VERB 1 = twinkle, flash, sparkle, flare, shimmer, gutter, glimmer 2 = flutter, waver, quiver, vibrate
● NOUN 1 = glimmer, flash, spark, flare, gleam 2 = trace, breath, spark, glimmer, iota

**flight**[1] 1 = journey, trip, voyage 2 = aviation, flying, aeronautics 3 = flock, group, unit, cloud, formation, squadron, swarm, flying group

**flight**[2] = escape, fleeing, departure, retreat, exit, running away, exodus, getaway

**fling** VERB = throw, toss, hurl, launch, cast, propel, sling, catapult
● NOUN = binge, good time, bash, party, spree, night on the town, rave-up (Brit. slang)

**flip** VERB 1 = flick, switch, snap, slick 2 = spin, turn, overturn, turn over, roll over 3 = toss, throw, flick, fling, sling
● NOUN = toss, throw, spin, snap, flick

**flirt** VERB 1 = chat up, lead on (informal), make advances at, make eyes at, philander, make sheep's eyes at 2 usually with **with** = toy with, consider, entertain, play with, dabble in, trifle with, give a thought to, expose yourself to
● NOUN = tease, philanderer, coquette, heart-breaker

**float** 1 = glide, sail, drift, move gently, bob, coast, slide, be carried 2 = be buoyant, hang, hover ≠ sink 3 = launch, offer, sell, set up, promote, get going ≠ dissolve

**floating** 1 = uncommitted, wavering, undecided, indecisive, vacillating, sitting on the fence (informal), unaffiliated, independent 2 = free, wandering, variable, fluctuating, unattached, movable

**flock** NOUN 1 = herd, group, flight, drove, colony, gaggle, skein 2 = crowd, company, group, host, collection, mass, gathering, herd
• VERB 1 = stream, crowd, mass, swarm, throng 2 = gather, crowd, mass, collect, assemble, herd, huddle, converge

**flog** = beat, whip, lash, thrash, whack, scourge, hit hard, trounce

**flood** NOUN 1 = deluge, downpour, inundation, tide, overflow, torrent, spate 2 = torrent, flow, rush, stream, tide, abundance, glut, profusion 3 = series, stream, avalanche, barrage, spate, torrent 4 = outpouring, rush, stream, surge, torrent
• VERB 1 = immerse, swamp, submerge, inundate, drown, cover with water 2 = pour over, swamp, run over, overflow, inundate 3 = engulf, sweep into, overwhelm, surge into, swarm into, pour into 4 = saturate, fill, choke, swamp, glut, oversupply, overfill 5 = stream, flow, rush, pour, surge

**floor** NOUN 1 = ground 2 = storey, level, stage, tier
• VERB 1 (Informal) = disconcert, stump, baffle, confound, throw (informal), defeat, puzzle, bewilder 2 = knock down, fell,

knock over, prostrate, deck (slang)

**flop** VERB 1 = slump, fall, drop, collapse, sink 2 = hang down, hang, dangle, sag, droop 3 (Informal) = fail, fold (informal), founder, fall flat, come unstuck, misfire, go belly-up (slang) ≠ succeed
• NOUN (Informal) = failure, disaster, fiasco, debacle, washout (informal), nonstarter ≠ success

**floppy** = droopy, soft, loose, limp, sagging, baggy, flaccid, pendulous

**floral** = flowery, flower-patterned

**flounder** 1 = falter, struggle, stall, slow down, run into trouble, come unstuck (informal), be in difficulties, hit a bad patch 2 = dither, struggle, blunder, be confused, falter, be in the dark, be out of your depth 3 = struggle, struggle, toss, thrash, stumble, fumble, grope

> ### Word Power
> **flounder** – Flounder is sometimes wrongly used where founder is meant: the project foundered (not floundered) because of lack of funds.

**flourish** VERB 1 = thrive, increase, advance, progress, boom, bloom, blossom, prosper ≠ fail

2 = <u>succeed</u>, move ahead, go places (*informal*) 3 = <u>grow</u>, thrive, flower, succeed, bloom, blossom, prosper 4 = <u>wave</u>, brandish, display, shake, wield, flaunt
● NOUN 1 = <u>wave</u>, sweep, brandish, swish, swing, twirl 2 = <u>show</u>, display, parade, fanfare 3 = <u>curlicue</u>, sweep, decoration, swirl, plume, embellishment, ornamentation

**flourishing** = <u>thriving</u>, successful, blooming, prospering, rampant, going places, in the pink

**flow** VERB 1 = <u>run</u>, course, rush, sweep, move, pass, roll, flood 2 = <u>pour</u>, move, sweep, flood, stream 3 = <u>issue</u>, follow, result, emerge, spring, proceed, arise, derive
● NOUN = <u>stream</u>, current, movement, motion, course, flood, drift, tide

**flower** NOUN 1 = <u>bloom</u>, blossom, efflorescence 2 = <u>elite</u>, best, prime, finest, pick, choice, cream, crème de la crème (*French*) 3 = <u>height</u>, prime, peak
● VERB 1 = <u>bloom</u>, open, mature, flourish, unfold, blossom 2 = <u>blossom</u>, grow, develop, progress, mature, thrive, flourish, bloom

*Related Words*
adjective: floral

**fluctuate** 1 = <u>change</u>, swing, vary, alternate, waver, veer, seesaw 2 = <u>shift</u>, oscillate

**fluent** = <u>effortless</u>, natural, articulate, well-versed, voluble

**fluid** NOUN = <u>liquid</u>, solution, juice, liquor, sap
● ADJECTIVE = <u>liquid</u>, flowing, watery, molten, melted, runny, liquefied ≠ solid

**flurry** 1 = <u>commotion</u>, stir, bustle, flutter, excitement, fuss, disturbance, ado 2 = <u>gust</u>, shower, gale, swirl, squall, storm

**flush**[1] VERB 1 = <u>blush</u>, colour, glow, redden, turn red, go red 2 *often with* **out** = <u>cleanse</u>, wash out, rinse out, flood, swill, hose down 3 = <u>expel</u>, drive, dislodge
● NOUN = <u>blush</u>, colour, glow, reddening, redness, rosiness

**flush**[2] 1 = <u>level</u>, even, true, flat, square 2 (*Informal*) = <u>wealthy</u>, rich, well-off, in the money (*informal*), well-heeled (*informal*), replete, moneyed

**flutter** VERB 1 = <u>beat</u>, flap, tremble, ripple, quiver, vibrate, palpitate 2 = <u>flit</u>
● NOUN 1 = <u>tremor</u>, tremble, shiver, shudder, palpitation 2 = <u>vibration</u>, twitching, quiver 3 = <u>agitation</u>, state (*informal*), confusion, excitement, flap (*informal*), dither (*chiefly Brit.*), commotion, fluster

**fly**[1] 1 = <u>take wing</u>, soar, glide,

---

### Types of fly

| | |
|---|---|
| aphid *or* plant louse | gallfly |
| aphis | gnat |
| blackfly *or* bean aphid | green blowfly *or* (*Austral.* |
| blowfly, bluebottle, *or* (*Austral.* | *informal*) blue-arsed fly |
| *informal*) blowie | greenfly |
| botfly | horsefly *or* cleg |
| bushfly | housefly |
| crane fly *or* (*Brit.*) daddy-longlegs | hover fly |
| damselfly | lacewing |
| dragonfly *or* (*colloquial*) devil's | mayfly *or* dayfly |
| darning-needle | sandfly |
| drosophila, fruit fly, *or* vinegar fly | stonefly |
| fly | tsetse fly *or* tzetze fly |
| fruit fly | warble fly |
| gadfly | whitefly |

---

wing, sail, hover, flutter, flit **2** = <u>pilot</u>, control, operate, steer, manoeuvre, navigate **3** = <u>airlift</u>, send by plane, take by plane, take in an aircraft **4** = <u>flutter</u>, wave, float, flap **5** = <u>display</u>, show, flourish, brandish **6** = <u>rush</u>, race, shoot, career, speed, tear, dash, hurry **7** = <u>pass swiftly</u>, pass, glide, slip away, roll on, flit, elapse, run its course **8** = <u>leave</u>, get away, escape, flee, run for it, skedaddle (*informal*), take to your heels

**fly²** ▸ types of fly

**flying** = <u>hurried</u>, brief, rushed, fleeting, short-lived, hasty, transitory

**foam** NOUN = <u>froth</u>, spray, bubbles, lather, suds, spume,

head
● VERB = <u>bubble</u>, boil, fizz, froth, lather, effervesce

**focus** VERB **1** = <u>concentrate</u>, centre, spotlight, direct, aim, pinpoint, zoom in **2** = <u>fix</u>, train, direct, aim
● NOUN **1** = <u>centre</u>, focal point, central point **2** = <u>focal point</u>, heart, target, hub

**foe** = <u>enemy</u>, rival, opponent, adversary, antagonist ≠ friend

**fog** = <u>mist</u>, gloom, haze, smog, murk, miasma, peasouper (*informal*)

**foil¹** = <u>thwart</u>, stop, defeat, disappoint, counter, frustrate, hamper, balk

**foil²** = <u>complement</u>, relief, contrast, antithesis

**fold** VERB 1 = <u>bend</u>, crease, double over 2 (*Informal*) = <u>go bankrupt</u>, fail, crash, collapse, founder, shut down, go under, go bust (*informal*)

● NOUN = <u>crease</u>, gather, bend, overlap, wrinkle, pleat, ruffle, furrow

**folk** 1 = <u>people</u>, persons, individuals, men and women, humanity, inhabitants, mankind, mortals 2 *usually plural* = <u>family</u>, parents, relations, relatives, tribe, clan, kin, kindred, ainga (*N.Z.*)

**follow** 1 = <u>accompany</u>, attend, escort, go behind, tag along behind, come behind 2 = <u>pursue</u>, track, dog, hunt, chase, shadow, trail, hound ≠ avoid 3 = <u>come after</u>, go after, come next ≠ precede 4 = <u>result</u>, issue, develop, spring, flow, proceed, arise, ensue 5 = <u>obey</u>, observe, adhere to, stick to, heed, conform to, keep to, pay attention to ≠ ignore 6 = <u>succeed</u>, replace, come after, take over from, come next, supersede, supplant, take the place of 7 = <u>understand</u>, realize, appreciate, take in, grasp, catch on (*informal*), comprehend, fathom 8 = <u>keep up with</u>, support, be interested in, cultivate, be a fan of, keep abreast of

**follower** = <u>supporter</u>, fan,

disciple, devotee, apostle, pupil, adherent, groupie (*slang*) ≠ leader

**following** ADJECTIVE 1 = <u>next</u>, subsequent, successive, ensuing, later, succeeding, consequent 2 = <u>coming</u>, about to be mentioned

● NOUN = <u>supporters</u>, backing, train, fans, suite, clientele, entourage, coterie

**folly** 1 = <u>foolishness</u>, nonsense, madness, stupidity, indiscretion, lunacy, imprudence, rashness ≠ wisdom

**fond** ADJECTIVE 1 = <u>loving</u>, caring, warm, devoted, tender, adoring, affectionate, indulgent ≠ indifferent 2 = <u>unrealistic</u>, empty, naive, vain, foolish, deluded, overoptimistic, delusive ≠ sensible

● PHRASES **fond of** 1 = <u>attached to</u>, in love with, keen on, attracted to, having a soft spot for, enamoured of 2 = <u>keen on</u>, into (*informal*), hooked on, partial to, having a soft spot for, addicted to

**fondly** 1 = <u>lovingly</u>, tenderly, affectionately, amorously, dearly, possessively, with affection, indulgently 2 = <u>unrealistically</u>, stupidly, vainly, foolishly, naively, credulously

**food** = <u>nourishment</u>, fare, diet, tucker (*Austral. & N.Z. informal*), rations, nutrition, cuisine, refreshment, nibbles, kai (*N.Z. informal*)

**fool** NOUN 1 = <u>simpleton</u>, idiot, mug (*Brit. slang*), dummy (*slang*), git (*Brit. slang*), twit (*informal, chiefly Brit.*), dunce, imbecile (*informal*), dorba or dorb (*Austral. slang*), bogan (*Austral. slang*) ≠ genius 2 = <u>dupe</u>, mug (*Brit. slang*), sucker (*slang*), stooge (*slang*), laughing stock, pushover (*informal*), fall guy (*informal*) 3 = <u>jester</u>, clown, harlequin, buffoon, court jester
● VERB = <u>deceive</u>, mislead, delude, trick, take in, con (*informal*), dupe, beguile

**foolish** = <u>unwise</u>, silly, absurd, rash, senseless, foolhardy, ill-judged, imprudent ≠ sensible

**footing** 1 = <u>basis</u>, foundation, base position, groundwork 2 = <u>relationship</u>, position, basis, standing, rank, status, grade

**footpath** (*Austral. & N.Z.*) = <u>pavement</u>, sidewalk (*U.S. & Canad.*)

**footstep** = <u>step</u>, tread, footfall

**foray** = <u>raid</u>, sally, incursion, inroad, attack, assault, invasion, swoop

**forbid** = <u>prohibit</u>, ban, disallow, exclude, rule out, veto, outlaw, preclude ≠ permit

### Word Power

**forbid** – Traditionally, it has been considered more correct to talk about *forbidding someone to do something*, rather than *forbidding someone from doing something*. Recently, however, the *from* option has become generally more acceptable, so that *he was forbidden to come in* and *he was forbidden from coming in* may both now be considered correct.

**forbidden** = <u>prohibited</u>, banned, vetoed, outlawed, taboo, out of bounds, proscribed

**forbidding** = <u>threatening</u>, severe, frightening, hostile, menacing, sinister, daunting, ominous ≠ inviting

**force** VERB 1 = <u>compel</u>, make, drive, press, oblige, constrain, coerce, impel 2 = <u>push</u>, thrust, propel 3 = <u>break open</u>, blast, wrench, prise, wrest
● NOUN 1 = <u>compulsion</u>, pressure, violence, constraint, oppression, coercion, duress, arm-twisting (*informal*) 2 = <u>power</u>, might, pressure, energy, strength, momentum, impulse, vigour ≠ weakness 3 = <u>intensity</u>, vigour, vehemence, fierceness, emphasis 4 = <u>army</u>, unit, company, host, troop, squad, patrol, regiment
● PHRASES **in force** 1 = <u>valid</u>,

working, current, effective, binding, operative, operational, in operation 2 = **in great numbers**, all together, in full strength

**forced** 1 = **compulsory**, enforced, mandatory, obligatory, involuntary, conscripted ≠ voluntary 2 = **false**, affected, strained, wooden, stiff, artificial, contrived, unnatural ≠ natural

**forceful** 1 = **dynamic**, powerful, assertive ≠ weak 2 = **powerful**, strong, convincing, effective, compelling, persuasive, cogent

**forecast** NOUN = **prediction**, prognosis, guess, prophecy, conjecture, forewarning

● VERB = **predict**, anticipate, foresee, foretell, divine, prophesy, augur, forewarn

**forefront** = **lead**, centre, front, fore, spearhead, prominence, vanguard, foreground

**foreign** = **alien**, exotic, unknown, strange, imported, remote, external, unfamiliar ≠ native

**foreigner** = **alien**, incomer, immigrant, non-native, stranger, settler

**foremost** = **leading**, best, highest, chief, prime, primary, supreme, most important

**foresee** = **predict**, forecast, anticipate, envisage, prophesy, foretell

**forever** 1 = **evermore**, always, ever, for good, for keeps, for all time, in perpetuity, till the cows come home (informal)
2 = **constantly**, always, all the time, continually, endlessly, persistently, eternally, perpetually

---

### Word Power

**forever** – Forever and for ever can both be used to say that something is without end. For all other meanings, forever is the preferred form.

---

**forfeit** VERB = **relinquish**, lose, give up, surrender, renounce, be deprived of, say goodbye to, be stripped of

● NOUN = **penalty**, fine, damages, forfeiture, loss, mulct

**forge** 1 = **form**, build, create, establish, set up, fashion, shape, frame 2 = **fake**, copy, reproduce, imitate, counterfeit, feign, falsify 3 = **create**, make, work, found, form, model, fashion, shape

**forget** 1 = **neglect**, overlook, omit, not remember, be remiss, fail to remember 2 = **leave behind**, lose, lose sight of, mislay

**forgive** = **excuse**, pardon, not hold something against, understand, acquit, condone, let off (informal), turn a blind eye to ≠ blame

**forgiveness** = **pardon**, mercy, absolution, exoneration, amnesty, acquittal, remission

**forgotten** = <u>unremembered</u>, lost, past, left behind, omitted, bygone, past recall

**fork** = <u>branch</u>, part, separate, split, divide, diverge, subdivide, bifurcate

**forked** = <u>branching</u>, split, branched, divided, angled, pronged, zigzag, Y-shaped

**form** NOUN 1 = <u>type</u>, sort, kind, variety, class, style 2 = <u>shape</u>, formation, configuration, structure, pattern, appearance 3 = <u>condition</u>, health, shape, nick (*informal*), fitness, trim, fettle 4 = <u>document</u>, paper, sheet, questionnaire, application 5 = <u>procedure</u>, etiquette, use, custom, convention, usage, protocol, wont, kawa (*N.Z.*), tikanga (*N.Z.*) 6 = <u>class</u>, year, set, rank, grade, stream

• VERB 1 = <u>arrange</u>, combine, line up, organize, assemble, draw up 2 = <u>make</u>, produce, fashion, build, create, shape, construct, forge 3 = <u>constitute</u>, make up, compose, comprise 4 = <u>establish</u>, start, launch 5 = <u>take shape</u>, grow, develop, materialize, rise, appear, come into being, crystallize 6 = <u>draw up</u>, devise, formulate, organize 7 = <u>develop</u>, pick up, acquire, cultivate, contract

**formal** 1 = <u>serious</u>, stiff, detached, official, correct, conventional, remote, precise ≠ informal 2 = <u>official</u>, authorized, endorsed, certified, solemn 3 = <u>ceremonial</u>, traditional, solemn, ritualistic, dressy 4 = <u>conventional</u>, established, traditional

**formality** 1 = <u>correctness</u>, seriousness, decorum, protocol, etiquette 2 = <u>convention</u>, procedure, custom, ritual, rite

**format** = <u>arrangement</u>, form, style, make-up, look, plan, design, type

**formation** 1 = <u>establishment</u>, founding, forming, setting up, starting, production, generation, manufacture 2 = <u>development</u>, shaping, constitution, moulding, genesis 3 = <u>arrangement</u>, grouping, design, structure, pattern, organization, array, configuration

**former** = <u>previous</u>, one-time, erstwhile, earlier, prior, sometime, foregoing ≠ current

**formerly** = <u>previously</u>, earlier, in the past, at one time, before, lately, once

**formidable** 1 = <u>impressive</u>, great, powerful, tremendous, mighty, terrific, awesome, invincible 2 = <u>intimidating</u>, threatening, terrifying, menacing, dismaying, fearful, daunting, frightful ≠ encouraging

**formula** = <u>method</u>, plan, policy,

rule, principle, procedure, recipe, blueprint

**formulate** 1 = <u>devise</u>, plan, develop, prepare, work out, invent, forge, draw up 2 = <u>express</u>, detail, frame, define, specify, articulate, set down, put into words

**fort** NOUN = <u>fortress</u>, keep, camp, tower, castle, garrison, stronghold, citadel, fortified pa (*N.Z.*)
● PHRASES **hold the fort** (*Informal*) = take responsibility, cover, stand in, carry on, take over the reins, deputize, keep things on an even keel

**forte** = <u>speciality</u>, strength, talent, strong point, métier, long suit (*informal*), gift ≠ weak point

**forth** 1 (*Formal or old-fashioned*) = <u>forward</u>, out, away, ahead, onward, outward 2 = <u>out</u>

**forthcoming** 1 = <u>approaching</u>, coming, expected, future, imminent, prospective, impending, upcoming 2 = <u>available</u>, ready, accessible, at hand, in evidence, obtainable, on tap (*informal*) 3 = <u>communicative</u>, open, free, informative, expansive, sociable, chatty, talkative

**fortify** 1 = <u>protect</u>, defend, strengthen, reinforce, support, shore up, augment, buttress 2 = <u>strengthen</u>, add alcohol to

≠ dishearten

**fortitude** = <u>courage</u>, strength, resolution, grit, bravery, backbone, perseverance, valour

**fortress** = <u>castle</u>, fort, stronghold, citadel, redoubt, fastness, fortified pa (*N.Z.*)

**fortunate** 1 = <u>lucky</u>, favoured, jammy (*Brit. slang*), in luck ≠ unfortunate 2 = <u>well-off</u>, rich, successful, wealthy, prosperous, affluent, opulent, well-heeled (*informal*) 3 = <u>providential</u>, fortuitous, felicitous, timely, helpful, convenient, favourable, advantageous

**fortunately** = <u>luckily</u>, happily, as luck would have it, providentially, by good luck, by a happy chance

**fortune** NOUN 1 = <u>wealth</u>, means, property, riches, resources, assets, possessions, treasure ≠ poverty 2 = <u>luck</u>, fluke (*informal*), stroke of luck, serendipity, twist of fate, run of luck 3 = <u>chance</u>, fate, destiny, providence, the stars, Lady Luck, kismet
● PLURAL NOUN = destiny, lot, experiences, history, condition, success, means, adventures

**forward** ADVERB 1 = <u>forth</u>, on, ahead, onwards ≠ backward(s) 2 = <u>on</u>, onward, onwards
● ADJECTIVE 1 = <u>leading</u>, first, head, front, advance, foremost 2 = <u>future</u>, advanced, premature, prospective 3 = <u>presumptuous</u>,

familiar, bold, cheeky, brash,
pushy (*informal*), brazen,
shameless ≠ shy

● VERB 1 = **further**, advance,
promote, assist, hurry, hasten,
expedite 2 = **send on**, send, post,
pass on, dispatch, redirect

**fossick** (*Austral. & N.Z.*) = **search**,
hunt, explore, ferret, check,
forage, rummage

**foster** 1 = **bring up**, mother,
raise, nurse, look after, rear, care
for, take care of 2 = **develop**,
support, further, encourage, feed,
promote, stimulate, uphold
≠ suppress

**foul** ADJECTIVE 1 = **dirty**,
unpleasant, stinking, filthy,
grubby, repellent, squalid,
repulsive, festy (*Austral. slang*),
yucko (*Austral. slang*) ≠ clean
2 = **obscene**, crude, indecent,
blue, abusive, coarse, vulgar, lewd
3 = **unfair**, illegal, crooked, shady
(*informal*), fraudulent, dishonest,
unscrupulous, underhand
4 = **offensive**, bad, wrong, evil,
corrupt, disgraceful, shameful,
immoral ≠ admirable

● VERB = **dirty**, stain, contaminate,
pollute, taint, sully, defile,
besmirch ≠ clean

**found** 1 = **establish**, start, set up,
begin, create, institute, organize,
constitute

**foundation** 1 = **basis** 2 *often
plural* = **substructure**,

underpinning, groundwork,
bedrock, base, footing, bottom
3 = **setting up**, institution,
instituting, organization,
settlement, establishment,
initiating, originating

**founder**[1] = **initiator**, father,
author, architect, creator,
beginner, inventor, originator

**founder**[2] 1 = **fail**, collapse, break
down, fall through, be
unsuccessful, come unstuck,
miscarry, misfire 2 = **sink**, go
down, be lost, submerge, capsize,
go to the bottom

> **Word Power**
>
> **founder** – *Founder* is
> sometimes used wrongly where
> *flounder* is meant: *this
> unexpected turn of events left
> him floundering* (not *foundering*).

**fountain** 1 = **font**, spring,
reservoir, spout, fount, water
feature, well 2 = **jet**, stream, spray,
gush 3 = **source**, fount,
wellspring, cause, origin,
derivation, fountainhead

**fowl** = **poultry**
> ➤ types of fowl

**foyer** = **entrance hall**, lobby,
reception area, vestibule,
anteroom, antechamber

**fraction** = **percentage**, share,
section, slice, portion

**fracture** NOUN 1 = **break**, split,

### Types of fowl

| | |
|---|---|
| barnacle goose | Muscovy duck *or* musk duck |
| brush turkey *or* scrub turkey | mute swan |
| bufflehead | paradise duck |
| Canada goose | pintail |
| canvasback | pochard |
| chicken *or* (*Austral. slang*) chook | redhead |
| cock *or* cockerel | Rhode Island Red chicken |
| duck | scaup *or* scaup duck |
| eider *or* eider duck | screamer |
| gadwall | shelduck |
| goldeneye | shoveler |
| goosander | smew |
| goose | snow goose |
| greylag *or* greylag goose | sultan |
| hen | swan |
| mallard | teal |
| mallee fowl *or* (*Austral.*) gnow | trumpeter swan |
| mandarin duck | turkey |
| megapode | whooper *or* whooper swan |
| merganser *or* sawbill | wigeon *or* widgeon |
| moorhen | |

crack 2 = <u>cleft</u>, opening, split, crack, rift, rupture, crevice, fissure
● VERB 1 = <u>break</u>, crack 2 = <u>split</u>, separate, divide, rend, fragment, splinter, rupture

**fragile** 1 = <u>unstable</u>, weak, vulnerable, delicate, uncertain, insecure, precarious, flimsy
2 = <u>fine</u>, weak, delicate, frail, brittle, flimsy, dainty, easily broken ≠ durable 3 = <u>delicate</u>, fine, charming, elegant, neat, exquisite, graceful, petite
4 = <u>unwell</u>, poorly, weak, delicate,

crook (*Austral. & N.Z. informal*), shaky, frail, feeble, sickly

**fragment** NOUN = <u>piece</u>, bit, scrap, particle, portion, shred, speck, sliver
● VERB 1 = <u>break</u>, shatter, crumble, disintegrate, splinter, come apart, break into pieces, come to pieces ≠ fuse 2 = <u>break up</u>, split up

**fragrance** 1 = <u>scent</u>, smell, perfume, bouquet, aroma, sweet smell, sweet odour, redolence ≠ stink 2 = <u>perfume</u>, scent, cologne, eau de toilette, eau de

Cologne, toilet water, Cologne water

**fragrant** = aromatic, perfumed, balmy, redolent, sweet-smelling, sweet-scented, odorous ≠ stinking

**frail** 1 = feeble, weak, puny, infirm ≠ strong 2 = flimsy, weak, vulnerable, delicate, fragile, insubstantial

**frame** NOUN 1 = casing, framework, structure, shell, construction, skeleton, chassis 2 = physique, build, form, body, figure, anatomy, carcass
● VERB 1 = mount, case, enclose 2 = surround, ring, enclose, encompass, envelop, encircle, hem in 3 = devise, draft, compose, build, sketch, put together, draw up, formulate, map out
● PHRASES frame of mind = mood, state, attitude, humour, temper, outlook, disposition, mind-set

**framework** 1 = system, plan, order, scheme, arrangement, the bare bones 2 = structure, body, frame, foundation, shell, skeleton

**frank** = candid, open, direct, straightforward, blunt, sincere, outspoken, honest ≠ secretive

**frankly** 1 = honestly, sincerely, in truth, candidly, to tell you the truth, to be frank, to be frank with someone, to be honest 2 = openly, freely, directly, plainly,

bluntly, candidly, without reserve

**frantic** 1 = frenzied, wild, furious, distracted, distraught, berserk, at the end of your tether, beside yourself, berko (*Austral. slang*) ≠ calm 2 = hectic, desperate, frenzied, fraught (*informal*), frenetic

**fraternity** 1 = companionship, fellowship, brotherhood, kinship, camaraderie 2 = circle, company, guild 3 = brotherhood, club, union, society, league, association

**fraud** 1 = deception, deceit, treachery, swindling, trickery, duplicity, double-dealing, chicanery ≠ honesty 2 = scam, deception (*slang*) 3 = hoax, trick, con (*informal*), deception, sham, spoof (*informal*), prank, swindle 4 (*Informal*) = impostor, fake, hoaxer, pretender, charlatan, fraudster, swindler, phoney or phony (*informal*)

**fraudulent** = deceitful, crooked (*informal*), untrue, sham, treacherous, dishonest, swindling, double-dealing ≠ genuine

**fray** = wear thin, wear, rub, wear out, chafe

**freak** ADJECTIVE = abnormal, chance, unusual, exceptional, unparalleled
● NOUN 1 (*Informal*) = enthusiast, fan, nut (*slang*), addict, buff (*informal*), fanatic, devotee, fiend (*informal*) 2 = aberration,

eccentric, anomaly, oddity, monstrosity, malformation
**3** = weirdo or weirdie (informal), eccentric, character (informal), oddball (informal), nonconformist

**free** ADJECTIVE
**1** = complimentary, for free (informal), for nothing, unpaid, for love, free of charge, on the house, without charge
**2** = allowed, permitted, unrestricted, unimpeded, clear, able **3** = at liberty, loose, liberated, at large, on the loose ≠ confined **4** = independent, unfettered, footloose
**5** = available, empty, spare, vacant, unused, unoccupied, untaken **6** = generous, liberal, lavish, unstinting, unsparing ≠ mean
● VERB **1** = clear, disengage, cut loose, release, rescue, extricate
**2** = release, liberate, let out, set free, deliver, loose, untie, unchain ≠ confine **3** = disentangle, extricate, disengage, loose, unravel, disconnect, untangle

**freedom 1** = independence, democracy, sovereignty, self-determination, emancipation, autarchy, rangatiratanga (N.Z.)
**2** = liberty, release, discharge, emancipation, deliverance ≠ captivity **3** = licence, latitude, free rein, opportunity, discretion,

carte blanche, blank cheque ≠ restriction

**freely 1** = abundantly, liberally, lavishly, extravagantly, copiously, unstintingly, amply **2** = openly, frankly, plainly, candidly, unreservedly, straightforwardly, without reserve **3** = willingly, readily, voluntarily, spontaneously, without prompting, of your own free will, of your own accord

**freeway** (U.S. & Austral.) = motorway (Brit.), autobahn (German), autoroute (French), autostrada (Italian)

**freeze 1** = ice over or up, harden, stiffen, solidify, become solid **2** = chill **3** = fix, hold, limit, hold up **4** = suspend, stop, shelve, curb, cut short, discontinue

**freezing 1** = icy, biting, bitter, raw, chill, arctic, frosty, glacial **2** = frozen, very cold

**freight 1** = transportation, traffic, delivery, carriage, shipment, haulage, conveyance, transport **2** = cargo, goods, load, delivery, burden, shipment, merchandise, consignment

**French** = Gallic

**frenzied** = uncontrolled, wild, crazy, furious, frantic, frenetic, feverish, rabid

**frenzy** = fury, passion, rage, seizure, hysteria, paroxysm, derangement ≠ calm

**frequent** ADJECTIVE = common, repeated, usual, familiar, everyday, persistent, customary, recurrent ≠ infrequent

● VERB = visit, attend, haunt, be found at, patronize, hang out at (informal), visit often, go to regularly ≠ keep away

**frequently** = often, commonly, repeatedly, many times, habitually, not infrequently, much ≠ infrequently

**fresh** 1 = additional, more, new, other, added, further, extra, supplementary 2 = natural, unprocessed, unpreserved ≠ preserved 3 = new, original, novel, different, recent, modern, up-to-date, unorthodox ≠ old 4 = invigorating, clean, pure, crisp, bracing, refreshing, brisk, unpolluted ≠ stale 5 = cool, cold, refreshing, brisk, chilly, nippy 6 = lively, keen, alert, refreshed, vigorous, energetic, sprightly, spry ≠ weary 7 = cheeky (Informal), impertinent, forward, familiar, audacious, disrespectful, presumptuous, insolent ≠ well-mannered

**fret** = worry, brood, agonize, obsess, lose sleep, upset yourself, distress yourself

**friction** 1 = conflict, hostility, resentment, disagreement, animosity, discord, bad blood, dissension 2 = resistance, rubbing, scraping, grating, rasping, chafing, abrasion 3 = rubbing, scraping, grating, rasping, chafing, abrasion

**friend** 1 = companion, pal, mate (informal), buddy (informal), best friend, close friend, comrade, chum (informal), cobber (Austral. & N.Z.), E hoa (N.Z. old-fashioned informal) ≠ foe 2 = supporter, ally, associate, sponsor, patron, well-wisher

**friendly** = amiable, welcoming, warm, neighbourly, pally (informal), helpful, sympathetic, affectionate ≠ amicable, warm, familiar, pleasant, intimate, informal, cordial, congenial ≠ unfriendly

**friendship** 1 = attachment, relationship, bond, link, association, tie 2 = friendliness, affection, harmony, goodwill, intimacy, familiarity, rapport, companionship ≠ unfriendliness

**fright** 1 = fear, shock, alarm, horror, panic, dread, consternation, trepidation ≠ courage 2 = scare, start, turn, surprise, shock, jolt, the creeps (informal), the willies (slang)

**frighten** 1 = scare, shock, alarm, terrify, startle, intimidate, unnerve, petrify ≠ reassure

**frightened** = afraid, alarmed, scared, terrified, shocked, startled, petrified, flustered

**frightening** = terrifying, shocking, alarming, startling, horrifying, menacing, scary (*informal*), fearful

**fringe** NOUN 1 = border, edging, edge, trimming, hem, frill, flounce 2 = edge, limits, border, margin, outskirts, perimeter, periphery, borderline
• ADJECTIVE = unofficial, alternative, radical, innovative, avant-garde, unconventional, unorthodox

**frog** > amphibians

**front** NOUN 1 = head, start, lead, forefront 2 = exterior, face, façade, frontage 3 = foreground, fore, forefront, nearest part 4 = front line, trenches, vanguard, firing line 5 (*Informal*) = disguise, cover, blind, mask, cover-up, cloak, façade, pretext
• ADJECTIVE 1 = foremost, at the front ≠ back 2 = leading, first, lead, head, foremost, topmost
• VERB = face onto, overlook, look out on, have a view of, look over or onto

**frontier** = border, limit, edge, boundary, verge, perimeter, borderline, dividing line

**frost** = hoarfrost, freeze, rime

**frown** VERB = glare, scowl, glower, make a face, look daggers, knit your brows, lour or lower
• NOUN = scowl, glare, glower, dirty look

**frozen** 1 = icy, hard, solid, frosted, arctic, ice-covered, icebound 2 = chilled, cold, iced, refrigerated, ice-cold 3 = ice-cold, freezing, numb, very cold, frigid, frozen stiff

**fruit** 1 = produce, crop, yield, harvest 2 *often plural* = result, reward, outcome, end result, return, effect, benefit, profit

**frustrate** = thwart, stop, check, block, defeat, disappoint, counter, spoil, crool or cruel (*Austral. slang*) ≠ further

**frustrated** = disappointed, discouraged, infuriated, exasperated, resentful, embittered, disheartened

**frustration** 1 = annoyance, disappointment, resentment, irritation, grievance, dissatisfaction, exasperation, vexation 2 = obstruction, blocking, foiling, spoiling, thwarting, circumvention

**fudge** = misrepresent, hedge, stall, flannel (*Brit. informal*), equivocate

**fuel** = incitement, ammunition, provocation, incentive

**fugitive** = runaway, refugee, deserter, escapee

**fulfil** 1 = carry out, perform, complete, achieve, accomplish ≠ neglect 2 = achieve, realize, satisfy, attain, consummate, bring to fruition 3 = satisfy, please, content, cheer, refresh, gratify, make happy 4 = <u>comply with</u>, meet, fill, satisfy, observe, obey, conform to, answer

**fulfilment** = <u>achievement</u>, implementation, completion, accomplishment, realization, attainment, consummation

**full** 1 = <u>filled</u>, stocked, brimming, replete, complete, loaded, saturated ≠ empty 2 = <u>satiated</u>, having had enough, replete 3 = <u>extensive</u>, complete, generous, adequate, ample, abundant, plentiful ≠ incomplete 4 = <u>comprehensive</u>, complete, exhaustive, all-embracing 5 = <u>rounded</u>, strong, rich, powerful, intense, pungent 6 = <u>plump</u>, rounded, voluptuous, shapely, well-rounded, buxom, curvaceous 7 = <u>voluminous</u>, large, loose, baggy, billowing, puffy, capacious, loose-fitting ≠ tight 8 = <u>rich</u>, strong, deep, loud, distinct, resonant, sonorous, clear ≠ thin

**full-scale** = <u>major</u>, wide-ranging, all-out, sweeping, comprehensive, thorough, in-depth, exhaustive

**fully** 1 = <u>completely</u>, totally, perfectly, entirely, altogether, thoroughly, wholly, utterly 2 = <u>in all respects</u>, completely, totally, entirely, altogether, thoroughly, wholly

**fumble** = <u>grope</u>, flounder, scrabble, feel around

**fume** VERB = <u>rage</u>, seethe, see red (informal), storm, rant, smoulder, get hot under the collar (informal)
● PLURAL NOUN = <u>smoke</u>, gas, exhaust, pollution, vapour, smog

**fun** NOUN 1 = <u>amusement</u>, sport, pleasure, entertainment, recreation, enjoyment, merriment, jollity 2 = <u>enjoyment</u>, pleasure, mirth ≠ gloom
● ADJECTIVE = <u>enjoyable</u>, entertaining, pleasant, amusing, lively, diverting, witty, convivial
● PHRASES **make fun of something** or **someone** = <u>mock</u>, tease, ridicule, poke fun at, laugh at, mimic, parody, send up (Brit. informal)

**function** NOUN 1 = <u>purpose</u>, business, job, use, role, responsibility, task, duty 2 = <u>reception</u>, party, affair, gathering, bash (informal), social occasion, soiree, do (informal)
● VERB 1 = <u>work</u>, run, operate, perform, go 2 = <u>act</u>, operate, perform, behave, do duty, have the role of

**functional** 1 = <u>practical</u>, utilitarian, serviceable, hard-wearing, useful 2 = <u>working</u>, operative, operational, going, prepared, ready, viable, up and running

**fund** NOUN = <u>reserve</u>, stock, supply, store, collection, pool

● PLURAL NOUN = <u>money</u>, capital, cash, finance, means, savings, resources, assets

● VERB = <u>finance</u>, back, support, pay for, subsidize, provide money for, put up the money for

**fundamental** 1 = <u>central</u>, key, basic, essential, primary, principal, cardinal ≠ incidental 2 = <u>basic</u>, essential, underlying, profound, elementary, rudimentary

**fundamentally** 1 = <u>basically</u>, at heart, at bottom 2 = <u>essentially</u>, radically, basically, primarily, profoundly, intrinsically

**fundi** (S. African) = <u>expert</u>

**funeral** = <u>burial</u>, committal, laying to rest, cremation, interment, obsequies, entombment

**funny** 1 = <u>humorous</u>, amusing, comical, entertaining, comic, witty, hilarious, riotous ≠ unfunny 2 = <u>comic</u>, comical 3 = <u>peculiar</u>, odd, strange, unusual, bizarre, curious, weird, mysterious 4 = <u>ill</u>, poorly (informal), sick, odd, crook (Austral. & N.Z. informal), ailing, unhealthy, unwell, off-colour (informal)

**furious** 1 = <u>angry</u>, raging, fuming, infuriated, incensed, enraged, inflamed, very angry, tooshie (Austral. slang) ≠ pleased 2 = <u>violent</u>, intense, fierce, savage, turbulent, vehement, unrestrained

**furnish** 1 = <u>decorate</u>, fit out, stock, equip 2 = <u>supply</u>, give, offer, provide, present, grant, hand out

**furniture** = <u>household goods</u>, furnishings, fittings, house fittings, goods, things (informal), possessions, appliances

**furore** = <u>commotion</u>, to-do, stir, disturbance, outcry, uproar, hullabaloo

**further** or **farther** ADVERB = <u>in addition</u>, moreover, besides, furthermore, also, to boot, additionally, into the bargain

● ADJECTIVE = <u>additional</u>, more, new, other, extra, fresh, supplementary

● VERB = <u>promote</u>, help, develop, forward, encourage, advance, work for, assist ≠ hinder

**furthermore** = <u>moreover</u>, further, in addition, besides, too, as well, to boot, additionally

**furthest** or **farthest** = <u>most distant</u>, extreme, ultimate, remotest, furthermost, outmost

**fury** 1 = <u>anger</u>, passion, rage, madness, frenzy, wrath, impetuosity ≠ calmness 2 = <u>violence</u>, force, intensity, severity, ferocity, savagery, vehemence, fierceness ≠ peace

**fuss** NOUN 1 = <u>commotion</u>, to-do, bother, stir, excitement, ado, hue

and cry, palaver **2=** <u>bother</u>, trouble, struggle, hassle (*informal*), nuisance, inconvenience, hindrance **3=** <u>complaint</u>, row, protest, objection, trouble, argument, squabble, furore
• **VERB** = <u>worry</u>, flap (*informal*), fret, fidget, take pains, be agitated, get worked up

**futile** = <u>useless</u>, vain, unsuccessful, pointless, worthless, fruitless, ineffectual, unprofitable ≠ useful

**future NOUN 1=** <u>time to come</u>, hereafter, what lies ahead **2=** <u>prospect</u>, expectation, outlook
• **ADJECTIVE** = <u>forthcoming</u>, coming, later, approaching, to come, succeeding, fated, subsequent ≠ past

**fuzzy 1=** <u>frizzy</u>, fluffy, woolly, downy **2=** <u>indistinct</u>, blurred, vague, distorted, unclear, bleary, out of focus, ill-defined ≠ distinct

# G

**gadget** = <u>device</u>, thing, appliance, machine, tool, implement, invention, instrument

**gag[1] NOUN** = <u>muzzle</u>, tie, restraint
• **VERB 1=** <u>suppress</u>, silence, muffle, curb, stifle, muzzle, quieten **2=** <u>retch</u>, heave

**gag[2]** (*Informal*) = <u>joke</u>, crack

(*slang*), funny (*informal*), quip, pun, jest, wisecrack (*informal*), witticism

**gain VERB 1=** <u>acquire</u>, get, receive, pick up, secure, collect, gather, obtain ≠ <u>profit</u>, get, land, secure, collect, gather, capture, acquire ≠ lose **3=** <u>put on</u>, increase in, gather, build up **4=** <u>attain</u>, get, reach, get to, secure, obtain, acquire, arrive at
• **NOUN 1=** <u>rise</u>, increase, growth, advance, improvement, upsurge, upturn, upswing **2=** <u>profit</u>, return, benefit, advantage, yield, dividend ≠ loss
• **PLURAL NOUN** = <u>profits</u>, earnings, revenue, proceeds, winnings, takings
• **PHRASES gain on something or someone** = <u>get nearer to</u>, close in on, approach, catch up with, narrow the gap on

**gala** = <u>festival</u>, fête, celebration, carnival, festivity, pageant, jamboree

**gale 1=** <u>storm</u>, hurricane, tornado, cyclone, blast, typhoon, tempest, squall **2**(*Informal*) = <u>outburst</u>, scream, roar, fit, storm, shout, burst, explosion

**gall** = <u>annoy</u>, provoke, irritate, trouble, disturb, madden, exasperate, vex

**gallop 1=** <u>run</u>, race, career, speed, bolt **2=** <u>dash</u>, run, race, career, speed, rush, sprint

**gamble NOUN 1=** <u>risk</u>, chance,

venture, lottery, speculation, uncertainty, leap in the dark ≠ **certainty** 2 = **bet**, flutter (*informal*), punt (*chiefly Brit.*), wager

● VERB 1 = **take a chance**, speculate, stick your neck out (*informal*) 2 = **chance**, hazard, wager 3 = **bet**, play, game, speculate, punt, wager, have a flutter (*informal*)

**game** NOUN 1 = **pastime**, sport, activity, entertainment, recreation, distraction, amusement, diversion ≠ **job** 2 = **match**, meeting, event, competition, tournament, clash, contest, head-to-head 3 = **amusement**, joke, entertainment, diversion 4 = **wild animals** *or* **birds**, prey, quarry 5 = **scheme**, plan, design, trick, plot, tactic, manoeuvre, ploy

● ADJECTIVE 1 = **willing**, prepared, ready, eager, interested, desirous 2 = **brave**, courageous, spirited, daring, persistent, gritty, intrepid, plucky ≠ **cowardly**

**gang** = **group**, crowd, pack, company, band, bunch, mob

**gangster** = **hoodlum** (*chiefly U.S.*), crook (*informal*), bandit, hood (*U.S. slang*), robber, mobster (*U.S. slang*), racketeer, ruffian, tsotsi (*S. African*)

**gap** 1 = **opening**, space, hole, break, crack, slot, aperture, cleft 2 = **interval**, pause, interruption,

respite, lull, interlude, breathing space, hiatus 3 = **difference**, gulf, contrast, disagreement, discrepancy, inconsistency, disparity, divergence

**gape** 1 = **stare**, wonder, goggle, gawp (*Brit. slang*), gawk 2 = **open**, split, crack, yawn

**gaping** = **wide**, great, open, broad, vast, yawning, wide open, cavernous

**garland** NOUN = **wreath**, band, bays, crown, honours, laurels, festoon, chaplet

● VERB = **adorn**, crown, deck, festoon, wreathe

**garment** *often plural* = **clothes**, dress, clothing, gear (*slang*), uniform, outfit, costume, apparel

**garnish** NOUN = **decoration**, embellishment, adornment, ornamentation, trimming

● VERB = **decorate**, adorn, ornament, embellish, trim ≠ **strip**

**garrison** NOUN 1 = **troops**, group, unit, section, command, armed force, detachment 2 = **fort**, fortress, camp, base, post, station, stronghold, fortification, fortified pa (*N.Z.*)

● VERB = **station**, position, post, install, assign, put on duty

**gas** 1 = **fumes**, vapour 2 (*U.S., Canad., & N.Z.*) = **petrol**, gasoline

**gasp** VERB = **pant**, blow, puff, choke, gulp, catch your breath

● NOUN = **pant**, puff, gulp, sharp

intake of breath

**gate** = barrier, opening, door, entrance, exit, gateway, portal

**gather** 1= congregate, assemble, collect, meet, mass, come together, muster, converge ≠ scatter 2= assemble, collect, bring together, muster, call together ≠ disperse 3= collect, assemble, accumulate, mass, muster, garner, amass, stockpile 4= pick, harvest, pluck, reap, garner, glean 5= build up, rise, increase, grow, expand, swell, intensify, heighten 6= understand, believe, hear, learn, assume, conclude, presume, infer 7= fold, tuck, pleat

**gathering** 1= assembly, group, crowd, meeting, conference, company, congress, mass, hui (*N.Z.*), runanga (*N.Z.*) 2= collecting, obtaining, attainment

**gauge** VERB 1= measure, calculate, evaluate, value, determine, count, weigh, compute 2= judge, estimate, guess, assess, evaluate, rate, appraise, reckon
• NOUN = meter, dial, measuring instrument

**gay** ADJECTIVE 1= homosexual, lesbian, queer (*informal or derogatory*), moffie (*S. African slang*) 2= cheerful, lively, sparkling, merry, upbeat (*informal*), buoyant, cheery, carefree ≠ sad 3= colourful, rich, bright, brilliant, vivid, flamboyant, flashy, showy ≠ drab
• NOUN = homosexual, lesbian, auntie *or* aunty (*Austral. slang*), lily (*Austral. slang*) ≠ heterosexual

> ### Word Power
>
> **gay** – By far the most common and up-to-date use of the word *gay* is in reference to being homosexual. Other senses of the word have become uncommon and dated.

**gaze** VERB = stare, look, view, watch, regard, gape
• NOUN = stare, look, fixed look

**gazette** = newspaper, paper, journal, periodical, news-sheet

**gear** NOUN 1= mechanism, works, machinery, cogs, cogwheels, gearwheels 2= equipment, supplies, tackle, tools, instruments, apparatus, paraphernalia, accoutrements 3= clothing, wear, dress, clothes, outfit, costume, garments, togs
• VERB with *to* or *towards* = equip, fit, adjust, adapt

**gem** 1= precious stone, jewel, stone 2= treasure, prize, jewel, pearl, masterpiece, humdinger (*slang*), taonga (*N.Z.*)

**general** 1= widespread, accepted, popular, public, common, broad, extensive, universal ≠ individual 2= overall, complete, total, global, comprehensive, blanket, inclusive, all-embracing ≠ restricted 3 = <u>universal</u>, overall, widespread, collective, across-the-board ≠ exceptional 4 = <u>vague</u>, loose, blanket, sweeping, unclear, approximate, woolly, indefinite ≠ specific

**generally** 1 = <u>usually</u>, commonly, typically, normally, on the whole, by and large, ordinarily, as a rule ≠ occasionally 2 = <u>commonly</u>, widely, publicly, universally, extensively, popularly, conventionally, customarily ≠ individually

**generate** = <u>produce</u>, create, make, cause, give rise to, engender ≠ end

**generation** 1 = <u>age group</u>, peer group 2 = <u>age</u>, period, era, time, lifetime, span, epoch

**generic** = <u>collective</u>, general, common, wide, comprehensive, universal, blanket, inclusive ≠ specific

**generosity** 1 = <u>liberality</u>, charity, bounty, munificence, beneficence, largesse or largess 2 = <u>magnanimity</u>, goodness, kindness, selflessness, charity, unselfishness, high-mindedness, nobleness

**generous** 1 = <u>liberal</u>, lavish, charitable, hospitable, bountiful, open-handed, unstinting, beneficent ≠ mean

2 = <u>magnanimous</u>, kind, noble, good, high-minded, unselfish, big-hearted 3 = <u>plentiful</u>, lavish, ample, abundant, full, rich, liberal, copious ≠ meagre

**genesis** = <u>beginning</u>, origin, start, birth, creation, formation, inception ≠ end

**genius** 1 = <u>brilliance</u>, ability, talent, capacity, gift, bent, excellence, flair 2 = <u>master</u>, expert, mastermind, maestro, virtuoso, whiz (*informal*), hotshot (*informal*), brainbox, fundi (*S. African*) ≠ dunce

**genre** = <u>type</u>, group, order, sort, kind, class, style, species

**gentle** 1 = <u>kind</u>, kindly, tender, mild, humane, compassionate, meek, placid ≠ unkind 2 = <u>slow</u>, easy, slight, moderate, gradual, imperceptible 3 = <u>moderate</u>, light, soft, slight, mild, soothing ≠ violent

**gentlemanly** = <u>chivalrous</u>, refined, polite, civil, courteous, gallant, genteel, well-mannered

**genuine** 1 = <u>authentic</u>, real, actual, true, valid, legitimate, veritable, bona fide, dinkum (*Austral. & N.Z. informal*) ≠ counterfeit 2 = <u>heartfelt</u>, sincere, honest, earnest, real, true, frank, unaffected ≠ affected 3 = <u>sincere</u>, honest, frank, candid, dinkum (*Austral. & N.Z. informal*), guileless ≠ hypocritical

**germ** 1 = <u>microbe</u>, virus, bug (*informal*), bacterium, bacillus, microorganism 2 = <u>beginning</u>, root, seed, origin, spark, embryo, rudiment

**gesture** NOUN = <u>sign</u>, action, signal, motion, indication, gesticulation

● VERB = <u>signal</u>, sign, wave, indicate, motion, beckon, gesticulate

**get** VERB 1 = <u>become</u>, grow, turn, come to be 2 = <u>persuade</u>, convince, induce, influence, entice, incite, impel, prevail upon 3 (*informal*) = <u>annoy</u>, upset, anger, disturb, trouble, bug (*informal*), irritate, gall 4 = <u>obtain</u>, receive, gain, acquire, win, land, net, pick up 5 = <u>fetch</u>, bring, collect 6 = <u>understand</u>, follow, catch, see, realize, take in, perceive, grasp 7 = <u>catch</u>, develop, contract, succumb to, fall victim to, go down with, come down with 8 = <u>arrest</u>, catch, grab, capture, seize, take, nab (*informal*), apprehend

● PHRASES **get at someone** = <u>criticize</u>, attack, blame, put down, knock (*informal*), nag, pick on, disparage ◆ **get at something** 1 = <u>reach</u>, touch, grasp, get (a) hold of, stretch to 2 = <u>find out</u>, learn, reach, reveal, discover, acquire, detect, uncover 3 = <u>imply</u>, mean, suggest, hint, intimate, lead up to, insinuate ◆ **get by** = <u>manage</u>, survive, cope, fare, exist, get along, make do, muddle through ◆ **get something across** = <u>communicate</u>, pass on, transmit, convey, impart, bring home, make known, put over

**ghastly** = <u>horrible</u>, shocking, terrible, awful, dreadful, horrendous, hideous, frightful ≠ lovely

**ghost** 1 = <u>spirit</u>, soul, phantom, spectre, spook (*informal*), apparition, wraith, atua (*N.Z.*), kehua (*N.Z.*), wairua (*N.Z.*) 2 = <u>trace</u>, shadow, suggestion, hint, suspicion, glimmer, semblance

*(Related Words)*

adjective: spectral

**ghostly** = <u>unearthly</u>, phantom, eerie, supernatural, spooky (*informal*), spectral

**giant** ADJECTIVE = <u>huge</u>, vast, enormous, tremendous, immense, titanic, gigantic, monumental ≠ tiny

● NOUN = <u>ogre</u>, monster, titan, colossus

**gidday** or **g'day** (*Austral. & N.Z.*) = <u>hello</u>, hi (*informal*), greetings, how do you do?, good morning, good evening, good afternoon, welcome, kia ora (*N.Z.*)

**gift** 1 = <u>donation</u>, offering, present, contribution, grant,

legacy, hand-out, endowment, bonsela (*S. African*), koha (*N.Z.*)
2 = **talent**, ability, capacity, genius, power, capability, flair, knack

**gifted** = **talented**, able, skilled, expert, masterly, brilliant, capable, clever ≠ talentless

**gigantic** = **huge**, large, giant, massive, enormous, tremendous, immense, titanic ≠ tiny

**giggle** VERB = **laugh**, chuckle, snigger, chortle, titter, twitter
● NOUN = **laugh**, chuckle, snigger, chortle, titter, twitter

**girl** = **female child**, lass, lassie (*informal*), miss, maiden (*archaic*), maid (*archaic*)

**give** VERB 1 = **perform**, do, carry out, execute 2 = **communicate**, announce, transmit, pronounce, utter, issue 3 = **produce**, make, cause, occasion, engender 4 = **present**, contribute, donate, provide, supply, award, grant, deliver ≠ take 5 = **concede**, allow, grant 6 = **surrender**, yield, devote, hand over, relinquish, part with
● PHRASES **give in** = **admit defeat**, yield, concede, collapse, quit, submit, surrender, succumb
◆ **give something away** = **reveal**, expose, leak, disclose, betray, uncover, let out, divulge
◆ **give something off** *or* **out** = **emit**, produce, release, discharge, send out, throw out, exude ◆ **give something up**

= **abandon**, stop, quit, cease, renounce, leave off, desist

**glad** 1 = **happy**, pleased, delighted, contented, gratified, joyful, overjoyed ≠ unhappy
2 (*Archaic*) = **pleasing**, happy, cheering, pleasant, cheerful, gratifying

**gladly** 1 = **happily**, cheerfully, gleefully 2 = **willingly**, freely, happily, readily, cheerfully, with pleasure ≠ reluctantly

**glamorous** 1 = **attractive**, elegant, dazzling ≠ unglamorous
2 = **exciting**, glittering, prestigious, glossy ≠ unglamorous

**glamour** 1 = **charm**, appeal, beauty, attraction, fascination, allure, enchantment
2 = **excitement**, magic, thrill, romance, prestige, glitz (*slang*)

**glance** VERB = **peek**, look, view, glimpse, peep ≠ scrutinize
● NOUN = **peek**, look, glimpse, peep, dekko (*slang*) ≠ good look

> ## Word Power
>
> **glance** – Care should be taken not to confuse *glance* and *glimpse*: *he caught a glimpse* (not *glance*) *of her making her way through the crowd; he gave a quick glance* (not *glimpse*) *at his watch*. A *glance* is a deliberate action, while a *glimpse* seems opportunistic.

**glare** VERB ¹ = <u>scowl</u>, frown, glower, look daggers, lour *or* lower ² = <u>dazzle</u>, blaze, flare, flame

● NOUN ¹ = <u>scowl</u>, frown, glower, dirty look, black look, lour *or* lower ² = <u>dazzle</u>, glow, blaze, flame, brilliance

**glaring** ¹ = <u>obvious</u>, gross, outrageous, manifest, blatant, conspicuous, flagrant, unconcealed ≠ inconspicuous ² = <u>dazzling</u>, strong, bright, glowing, blazing ≠ subdued

**glaze** NOUN = <u>coat</u>, finish, polish, shine, gloss, varnish, enamel, lacquer

● VERB = <u>coat</u>, polish, gloss, varnish, enamel, lacquer

**gleam** VERB = <u>shine</u>, flash, glow, sparkle, glitter, shimmer, glint, glimmer

● NOUN ¹ = <u>glimmer</u>, flash, beam, glow, sparkle ² = <u>trace</u>, suggestion, hint, flicker, glimmer, inkling

**glide** = <u>slip</u>, sail, slide

**glimpse** NOUN = <u>look</u>, sighting, sight, glance, peep, peek

● VERB = <u>catch sight of</u>, spot, sight, view, spy, espy

**glitter** VERB = <u>shine</u>, flash, sparkle, glare, gleam, shimmer, twinkle, glint

● NOUN ¹ = <u>glamour</u>, show, display, splendour, tinsel, pageantry, gaudiness, showiness

² = <u>sparkle</u>, flash, shine, glare, gleam, sheen, shimmer, brightness

**global** ¹ = <u>worldwide</u>, world, international, universal ² = <u>comprehensive</u>, general, total, unlimited, exhaustive, all-inclusive ≠ limited

**globe** = <u>planet</u>, world, earth, sphere, orb

**gloom** ¹ = <u>darkness</u>, dark, shadow, shade, twilight, dusk, obscurity, blackness ≠ light ² = <u>depression</u>, sorrow, woe, melancholy, unhappiness, despondency, dejection, low spirits ≠ happiness

**gloomy** ¹ = <u>dark</u>, dull, dim, dismal, black, grey, murky, dreary ≠ light ² = <u>miserable</u>, sad, pessimistic, melancholy, glum, dejected, dispirited, downcast ≠ happy ³ = <u>depressing</u>, bad, dreary, sombre, dispiriting, disheartening, cheerless

**glorious** ¹ = <u>splendid</u>, beautiful, brilliant, shining, superb, gorgeous, dazzling ≠ dull ² = <u>delightful</u>, fine, wonderful, excellent, marvellous, gorgeous ³ = <u>illustrious</u>, famous, celebrated, distinguished, honoured, magnificent, renowned, eminent ≠ ordinary

**glory** NOUN ¹ = <u>honour</u>, praise, fame, distinction, acclaim, prestige, eminence, renown

≠ shame 2 = <u>splendour</u>, majesty, greatness, grandeur, nobility, pomp, magnificence, pageantry
● **VERB** = <u>triumph</u>, boast, relish, revel, exult, take delight, pride yourself

**gloss[1]** = <u>shine</u>, gleam, sheen, polish, brightness, veneer, lustre, patina

**gloss[2] NOUN** = <u>interpretation</u>, comment, note, explanation, commentary, translation, footnote, elucidation
● **VERB** = <u>interpret</u>, explain, comment, translate, annotate, elucidate

**glossy** = <u>shiny</u>, polished, shining, glazed, bright, silky, glassy, lustrous ≠ dull

**glow NOUN** = <u>light</u>, gleam, splendour, glimmer, brilliance, brightness, radiance, luminosity ≠ dullness
● **VERB** 1 = <u>shine</u>, burn, gleam, brighten, glimmer, smoulder 2 = be pink

**glowing** 1 = <u>complimentary</u>, enthusiastic, rave (informal), ecstatic, rhapsodic, laudatory, adulatory ≠ scathing 2 = <u>aglow</u>, bright, radiant ≠ pale

**glue NOUN** = <u>adhesive</u>, cement, gum, paste
● **VERB** = <u>stick</u>, fix, seal, cement, gum, paste, affix

**go VERB** 1 = <u>move</u>, travel, advance, journey, proceed, pass, set off

≠ stay 2 = <u>leave</u>, withdraw, depart, move out, slope off, make tracks 3 = <u>elapse</u>, pass, flow, fly by, expire, lapse, slip away 4 = <u>be given</u>, be spent, be awarded, be allotted 5 = <u>function</u>, work, run, move, operate, perform ≠ fail 6 = <u>match</u>, blend, correspond, fit, suit, chime, harmonize 7 = <u>serve</u>, help, tend
● **NOUN** 1 = <u>attempt</u>, try, effort, bid, shot (informal), crack (informal) 2 = <u>turn</u>, shot (informal), stint 3 (Informal) = <u>energy</u>, life, drive, spirit, vitality, vigour, verve, force
● **PHRASES go off** 1 = <u>depart</u>, leave, quit, go away, move out, decamp, slope off 2 = <u>explode</u>, fire, blow up, detonate, come about 3 (Informal) = <u>go bad</u>, turn, spoil, rot, go stale ♦ **go out** 1 = <u>see someone</u>, court, date (informal, chiefly U.S.), woo, go steady (informal), be romantically involved with 2 = <u>be extinguished</u>, die out, fade out
♦ **go through something** 1 = <u>suffer</u>, experience, bear, endure, brave, undergo, tolerate, withstand 2 = <u>search</u>, look through, rummage through, rifle through, hunt through, fossick through (Austral. & N.Z.), ferret about in 3 = <u>examine</u>, check, search, explore, look through

**goal** = <u>aim</u>, end, target, purpose, object, intention, objective, ambition

**god** = deity, immortal, divinity, divine being, supreme being, atua (N.Z.)

➤ **gods and goddesses**

**godly** = devout, religious, holy, righteous, pious, good, saintly, god-fearing

**gogga** (S. African) = insect, bug, creepy-crawly (Brit. informal)

**golden** 1 = yellow, blonde, blond, flaxen ≠ dark
2 = successful, glorious, prosperous, rich, flourishing, halcyon ≠ worst  3 = promising, excellent, favourable, opportune ≠ unfavourable

➤ **shades of orange**
➤ **shades of yellow**

**gone** 1 = missing, lost, away, vanished, absent, astray  2 = past, over, ended, finished, elapsed

**good** ADJECTIVE 1 = excellent, great, fine, pleasing, acceptable, first-class, splendid, satisfactory, booshit (Austral. slang), exo (Austral. slang), sik (Austral. slang) ≠ bad  2 = proficient, able, skilled, expert, talented, clever, accomplished, first-class ≠ bad
3 = beneficial, useful, helpful, favourable, wholesome, advantageous ≠ harmful
4 = honourable, moral, worthy, ethical, upright, admirable, honest, righteous ≠ bad  5 = well-behaved, polite, orderly,

obedient, dutiful, well-mannered ≠ naughty  6 = kind, kindly, friendly, obliging, charitable, humane, benevolent, merciful ≠ unkind  7 = true, real, genuine, proper, dinkum (Austral. & N.Z. informal)  8 = full, complete, extensive ≠ scant
9 = considerable, large, substantial, sufficient, adequate, ample  10 = valid, convincing, compelling, legitimate, authentic, persuasive, bona fide ≠ invalid
11 = convenient, timely, fitting, appropriate, suitable ≠ inconvenient

● NOUN 1 = benefit, interest, gain, advantage, use, profit, welfare, usefulness ≠ disadvantage
2 = virtue, goodness, righteousness, worth, merit, excellence, morality, rectitude ≠ evil

● PHRASES **for good** = permanently, finally, for ever, once and for all, irrevocably

**goodbye** NOUN = farewell, parting, leave-taking

● INTERJECTION = farewell, see you, see you later, ciao (Italian), cheerio, adieu, ta-ta, au revoir (French), haere ra (N.Z.)

**goodness** 1 = virtue, honour, merit, integrity, morality, honesty, righteousness, probity ≠ badness
2 = excellence, value, quality, worth, merit, superiority

# Gods and goddesses

## Greek

| | | | |
|---|---|---|---|
| Aeolus | winds | Hephaestus | fire and metalworking |
| Aphrodite | love and beauty | | |
| Apollo | light, youth, and music | Hera | queen of the gods |
| | | Hermes | messenger of the gods |
| Ares | war | | |
| Artemis | hunting and the moon | Horae *or* the Hours | seasons |
| Asclepius | healing | Hymen | marriage |
| Athene *or* Pallas Athene | wisdom | Hyperion | sun |
| | | Hypnos | sleep |
| Bacchus | wine | Iris | rainbow |
| Boreas | north wind | Momus | blame and mockery |
| Cronos | fertility of the earth | | |
| | | Morpheus | sleep and dreams |
| Demeter | agriculture | Nemesis | vengeance |
| Dionysus | wine | Nike | victory |
| Eos | dawn | Pan | woods and shepherds |
| Eros | love | | |
| Fates | destiny | Poseidon | sea and earthquakes |
| Gaea *or* Gaia | the earth | | |
| Graces | charm and beauty | Rhea | fertility |
| | | Selene | moon |
| Hades | underworld | Uranus | sky |
| Hebe | youth and spring | Zephyrus | west wind |
| Hecate | underworld | Zeus | king of the gods |
| Helios | sun | | |

## Roman

| | | | |
|---|---|---|---|
| Aesculapius | medicine | Cupid | love |
| Apollo | light, youth, and music | Cybele | nature |
| | | Diana | hunting and the moon |
| Aurora | dawn | | |
| Bacchus | wine | Faunus | forests |
| Bellona | war | Flora | flowers |
| Bona Dea | fertility | Janus | doors and beginnings |
| Ceres | agriculture | | |

| Roman (continued) | | | |
|---|---|---|---|
| Juno | queen of the gods | Pluto | underworld |
| Jupiter or Jove | king of the gods | Quirinus | war |
| Lares | household | Saturn | agriculture and |
| Luna | moon | | vegetation |
| Mars | war | Sol | sun |
| Mercury | messenger of | Somnus | sleep |
| | the gods | Trivia | crossroads |
| Minerva | wisdom | Venus | love |
| Neptune | sea | Victoria | victory |
| Penates | storeroom | Vulcan | fire and |
| Phoebus | sun | | metalworking |

**3** = <u>nutrition</u>, benefit, advantage, wholesomeness, salubriousness
**4** = <u>kindness</u>, charity, humanity, goodwill, mercy, compassion, generosity, friendliness
**goods 1** = <u>merchandise</u>, stock, products, stuff, commodities, wares **2** = <u>property</u>, things, effects, gear, possessions, belongings, trappings, paraphernalia
**goodwill** = <u>friendliness</u>, friendship, benevolence, amity, kindliness
**gore¹** = <u>blood</u>, slaughter, bloodshed, carnage, butchery
**gore²** = <u>pierce</u>, wound, transfix, impale
**gorge**NOUN = <u>ravine</u>, canyon, pass, chasm, cleft, fissure, defile, gulch
● VERB **1** = <u>overeat</u>, devour, gobble, wolf, gulp, guzzle

**2** usually reflexive = <u>stuff</u>, feed, cram, glut
**gorgeous 1** = <u>magnificent</u>, beautiful, superb, spectacular, splendid, dazzling, sumptuous ≠ shabby **2** = <u>delightful</u>, good, great, wonderful, excellent, lovely, fantastic, pleasant ≠ awful
**3** (Informal) = <u>beautiful</u>, lovely, stunning (informal), elegant, handsome, exquisite, ravishing ≠ ugly
**gospel 1** = <u>doctrine</u>, news, teachings, message, revelation, creed, credo, tidings **2** = <u>truth</u>, fact, certainty, the last word
**gossip**NOUN **1** = <u>idle talk</u>, scandal, hearsay, tittle-tattle, small talk, chitchat, blether, chinwag (Brit. informal)
**2** = <u>busybody</u>, chatterbox (informal), chatterer, scandalmonger, gossipmonger
● VERB = <u>chat</u>, chatter, jaw (slang),

blether

**gourmet** = <u>connoisseur</u>, foodie (*informal*), bon vivant (*French*), epicure, gastronome

**govern** 1 = <u>rule</u>, lead, control, command, manage, direct, guide, handle 2 = <u>restrain</u>, control, check, master, discipline, regulate, curb, tame

**government** 1 = <u>administration</u>, executive, ministry, regime, powers-that-be 2 = <u>rule</u>, authority, administration, sovereignty, governance, statecraft

**governor** = <u>leader</u>, administrator, ruler, head, director, manager, chief, executive, baas (*S. African*)

**gown** = <u>dress</u>, costume, garment, robe, frock, garb, habit

**grab** = <u>snatch</u>, catch, seize, capture, grip, grasp, clutch, snap up

**grace** NOUN 1 = <u>elegance</u>, poise, ease, polish, refinement, fluency, suppleness, gracefulness ≠ ungainliness 2 = <u>manners</u>, decency, etiquette, consideration, propriety, tact, decorum ≠ bad manners 3 = <u>indulgence</u>, mercy, pardon, reprieve 4 = <u>benevolence</u>, favour, goodness, goodwill, generosity, kindness, kindliness ≠ ill will 5 = <u>prayer</u>, thanks, blessing, thanksgiving, benediction

6 = <u>favour</u>, regard, respect, approval, approbation, good opinion ≠ disfavour ● VERB 1 = <u>adorn</u>, enhance, decorate, enrich, set off, ornament, embellish 2 = <u>honour</u>, favour, dignify ≠ insult

**graceful** 1 = <u>elegant</u>, easy, pleasing, beautiful ≠ inelegant 2 = <u>polite</u>, mannerly, charming, gracious, civil, courteous, well-mannered

**gracious** = <u>courteous</u>, polite, civil, accommodating, kind, friendly, cordial, well-mannered ≠ ungracious

**grade** VERB = <u>classify</u>, rate, order, class, group, sort, range, rank ● NOUN 1 = <u>class</u> 2 degree 3 = <u>level</u>, rank, group, class, stage, category, echelon

**gradual** = <u>steady</u>, slow, regular, gentle, progressive, piecemeal, unhurried ≠ sudden

**gradually** = <u>steadily</u>, slowly, progressively, gently, step by step, little by little, by degrees, unhurriedly

**graduate** 1 = <u>mark off</u>, grade, proportion, regulate, gauge, calibrate, measure out 2 = <u>classify</u>, rank, grade, group, order, sort, arrange

**graft** NOUN 1 = <u>shoot</u>, bud, implant, sprout, splice, scion 2 (*Informal*) = <u>labour</u>, work, effort, struggle, sweat, toil, slog, exertion

● **VERB 1** = join, insert, transplant, implant, splice, affix **2** = work, labour, struggle, sweat (*informal*), slave, strive, toil

**grain 1** = seed, kernel, grist **2** = cereal, corn **3** = bit, piece, trace, scrap, particle, fragment, speck, morsel **4** = texture, pattern, surface, fibre, weave, nap

**grand 1** = impressive, great, large, magnificent, imposing, splendid, regal, stately ≠ unimposing **2** = ambitious, great, grandiose **3** = superior, great, dignified, stately **4** = excellent, great (*informal*), fine, wonderful, outstanding, smashing (*informal*), first-class, splendid ≠ bad

**grandeur** = splendour, glory, majesty, nobility, pomp, magnificence, sumptuousness, sublimity

**grant NOUN** = award, allowance, donation, endowment, gift, subsidy, hand-out
● **VERB 1** = give, allow, present, award, permit, assign, allocate, hand out **2** = accept, allow, admit, acknowledge, concede

**graphic 1** = vivid, clear, detailed, striking, explicit, expressive ≠ vague **2** = pictorial, visual, diagrammatic ≠ impressionistic

**grapple 1** = deal, tackle, struggle, take on, confront, get to grips, address yourself to

**2** = struggle, fight, combat, wrestle, battle, clash, tussle, scuffle

**grasp VERB 1** = grip, hold, catch, grab, seize, snatch, clutch, clinch **2** = understand, realize, take in, get, see, catch on, comprehend, catch *or* get the drift of
● **NOUN 1** = grip, hold, possession, embrace, clutches, clasp **2** = understanding, knowledge, grip, awareness, mastery, comprehension **3** = reach, power, control, scope

**grasping** = greedy, acquisitive, rapacious, avaricious, covetous, snoep (*S. African informal*) ≠ generous

**grate 1** = shred, mince, pulverize **2** = scrape, grind, rub, scratch, creak, rasp

**grateful** = thankful, obliged, in (someone's) debt, indebted, appreciative, beholden

**grating**[1] = grille, grid, grate, lattice, trellis, gridiron

**grating**[2] = irritating, harsh, annoying, jarring, unpleasant, raucous, strident, discordant ≠ pleasing

**gratitude** = thankfulness, thanks, recognition, obligation, appreciation, indebtedness, gratefulness ≠ ingratitude

**grave**[1] = tomb, vault, crypt, mausoleum, sepulchre, pit, burying place

**grave**[2] **1** = <u>serious</u>, important, critical, pressing, threatening, dangerous, acute, severe ≠ trifling **2** = <u>solemn</u>, sober, sombre, dour, unsmiling ≠ carefree

**graveyard** = <u>cemetery</u>, churchyard, burial ground, charnel house, necropolis

**gravity** **1** = <u>seriousness</u>, importance, significance, urgency, severity, acuteness, weightiness, momentousness ≠ triviality **2** = <u>solemnity</u>, seriousness, gravitas ≠ frivolity

**graze**[1] = <u>feed</u>, crop, browse, pasture

**graze**[2] VERB **1** = <u>scratch</u>, skin, scrape, chafe, abrade **2** = <u>touch</u>, brush, rub, scrape, shave, skim, glance off

● NOUN = <u>scratch</u>, scrape, abrasion

**greasy** = <u>fatty</u>, slippery, oily, slimy, oleaginous

**great** **1** = <u>large</u>, big, huge, vast, enormous, immense, gigantic, prodigious ≠ small **2** = <u>important</u>, serious, significant, critical, crucial, momentous ≠ unimportant **3** = <u>famous</u>, outstanding, remarkable, prominent, renowned, eminent, illustrious **4** (Informal) = <u>excellent</u>, fine, wonderful, superb, fantastic (informal), tremendous (informal), marvellous (informal), terrific (informal), booshit

(Austral. slang), exo (Austral. slang), sik (Austral. slang) ≠ poor **5** = <u>very</u>, really, extremely, exceedingly

**greatly** = <u>very much</u>, hugely, vastly, considerably, remarkably, enormously, immensely, tremendously

**greatness** **1** = <u>grandeur</u>, glory, majesty, splendour, pomp, magnificence **2** = <u>fame</u>, glory, celebrity, distinction, eminence, note, renown, illustriousness

**greed** or **greediness** **1** = <u>gluttony</u>, voracity **2** = <u>avarice</u>, longing, desire, hunger, craving, selfishness, acquisitiveness, covetousness ≠ generosity

**greedy** **1** = <u>gluttonous</u>, insatiable, voracious, ravenous, piggish **2** = <u>avaricious</u>, grasping, selfish, insatiable, acquisitive, rapacious, materialistic, desirous ≠ generous

**green** ADJECTIVE **1** = <u>verdant</u>, leafy, grassy **2** = <u>ecological</u>, conservationist, environment-friendly, ozone-friendly, non-polluting **3** = <u>inexperienced</u>, new, raw, naive, immature, gullible, untrained, wet behind the ears (informal) **4** = <u>jealous</u>, grudging, resentful, envious, covetous

● NOUN = <u>lawn</u>, common, turf, sward

> **shades of green**

**greet** **1** = <u>salute</u>, hail, say hello to,

### Shades of green

| | | | |
|---|---|---|---|
| apple green | emerald green | Lincoln green | pea green |
| aquamarine | jade | Nile green | pistachio |
| avocado | lime green | olive | sea green |

address, accost 2 = <u>welcome</u>, meet, receive, karanga (*N.Z.*), mihi (*N.Z.*) 3 = <u>receive</u>, take, respond to, react to

**greeting** = <u>welcome</u>, reception, salute, address, salutation, hongi (*N.Z.*), kia ora (*N.Z.*)

**grey** 1 = <u>dull</u>, dark, dim, gloomy, drab 2 = <u>boring</u>, dull, anonymous, faceless, colourless, nondescript, characterless 3 = <u>pale</u>, wan, pallid, ashen 4 = <u>ambiguous</u>, uncertain, neutral, unclear, debatable

➤ **shades from black to white**

**grief** = <u>sadness</u>, suffering, regret, distress, misery, sorrow, woe, anguish ≠ joy

**grievance** = <u>complaint</u>, gripe (*informal*)

**grieve** 1 = <u>mourn</u>, suffer, weep, lament 2 = <u>sadden</u>, hurt, injure, distress, wound, pain, afflict, upset ≠ gladden

**grim** = <u>terrible</u>, severe, harsh, forbidding, formidable, sinister

**grind** VERB 1 = <u>crush</u>, mill, powder, grate, pulverize, pound, abrade, granulate 2 = <u>press</u>, push, crush, jam, mash, force down 3 = <u>grate</u>, scrape, gnash

4 = <u>sharpen</u>, polish, sand, smooth, whet

● NOUN = <u>hard work</u> (*Informal*), labour, sweat (*informal*), chore, toil, drudgery

**grip** VERB 1 = <u>grasp</u>, hold, catch, seize, clutch, clasp, take hold of 2 = <u>engross</u>, fascinate, absorb, entrance, hold, compel, rivet, enthral

● NOUN 1 = <u>clasp</u>, hold, grasp 2 = <u>control</u>, rule, influence, command, power, possession, domination, mastery 3 = <u>hold</u>, purchase, friction, traction 4 = <u>understanding</u>, sense, command, awareness, grasp, appreciation, mastery, comprehension

**gripping** = <u>fascinating</u>, exciting, thrilling, entrancing, compelling, riveting, enthralling, engrossing

**grit** NOUN 1 = <u>gravel</u>, sand, dust, pebbles 2 = <u>courage</u>, spirit, resolution, determination, guts (*informal*), backbone, fortitude, tenacity

● VERB = <u>clench</u>, grind, grate, gnash

**gritty** 1 = <u>rough</u>, sandy, dusty, rasping, gravelly, granular

**²** = courageous, dogged, determined, spirited, brave, resolute, tenacious, plucky

**groan** VERB ¹ = moan, cry, sigh
**²** (*Informal*) = complain, object, moan, grumble, gripe (*informal*), carp, lament, whine

● NOUN ¹ = moan, cry, sigh, whine
**²** (*Informal*) = complaint, protest, objection, grumble, grouse, gripe (*informal*)

**groom** NOUN ¹ = stableman, stableboy, hostler or ostler (*archaic*) **²** = newly-wed, husband, bridegroom, marriage partner

● VERB ¹ = brush, clean, tend, rub down, curry **²** = smarten up, clean, tidy, preen, spruce up, primp **³** = train, prime, prepare, coach, ready, educate, drill, nurture

**groove** = indentation, cut, hollow, channel, trench, flute, trough, furrow

**grope** = feel, search, fumble, flounder, fish, scrabble, cast about, fossick (*Austral. & N.Z.*)

**gross** ADJECTIVE ¹ = flagrant, blatant, rank, sheer, utter, grievous, heinous, unmitigated ≠ qualified **²** = vulgar, offensive, crude, obscene, coarse, indelicate ≠ decent **³** = fat, obese, overweight, hulking, corpulent ≠ slim **⁴** = total, whole, entire, aggregate, before tax, before

deductions ≠ net

● VERB = earn, make, take, bring in, rake in (*informal*)

**grotesque** ¹ = unnatural, bizarre, strange, fantastic, distorted, deformed, outlandish, freakish ≠ natural **²** = absurd, preposterous ≠ natural

**ground** NOUN ¹ = earth, land, dry land, terra firma **²** = arena, pitch, stadium, park (*informal*), field, enclosure

● PLURAL NOUN ¹ = estate, land, fields, gardens, territory **²** = reason, cause, basis, occasion, foundation, excuse, motive, justification **³** = dregs, lees, deposit, sediment

● VERB ¹ = base, found, establish, set, settle, fix **²** = instruct, train, teach, initiate, tutor, acquaint with, familiarize with

**group** NOUN = crowd, party, band, pack, gang, bunch

● VERB = arrange, order, sort, class, classify, marshal, bracket

**grove** = wood, plantation, covert, thicket, copse, coppice, spinney

**grow** ¹ = develop, get bigger ≠ shrink **²** = get bigger, spread, swell, stretch, expand, enlarge, multiply **³** = cultivate, produce, raise, farm, breed, nurture, propagate **⁴** = become, get, turn, come to be **⁵** = originate, spring, arise, stem, issue **⁶** = improve, advance, progress, succeed, thrive, flourish, prosper

**grown-up** NOUN = <u>adult</u>, man, woman

● ADJECTIVE = <u>mature</u>, adult, of age, fully-grown

**growth** 1 = <u>increase</u>, development, expansion, proliferation, enlargement, multiplication ≠ decline 2 = <u>progress</u>, success, improvement, expansion, advance, prosperity ≠ failure 3 (*Medical*) = <u>tumour</u>, cancer, swelling, lump, carcinoma (*Pathology*), sarcoma (*Medical*)

**grudge** NOUN = <u>resentment</u>, bitterness, grievance, dislike, animosity, antipathy, enmity, rancour ≠ goodwill

● VERB = <u>resent</u>, mind, envy, covet, begrudge ≠ welcome

**gruelling** = <u>exhausting</u>, demanding, tiring, taxing, severe, punishing, strenuous, arduous ≠ easy

**gruesome** = <u>horrific</u>, shocking, terrible, horrible, grim, ghastly, grisly, macabre ≠ pleasant

**grumble** VERB 1 = <u>complain</u>, moan, gripe (*informal*), whinge (*informal*), carp, whine, grouse, bleat 2 = <u>rumble</u>, growl, gurgle

● NOUN 1 = <u>complaint</u>, protest, objection, moan, grievance, grouse, gripe (*informal*), grouch (*informal*) 2 = <u>rumble</u>, growl, gurgle

**guarantee** VERB 1 = <u>ensure</u>, secure, assure, warrant, make certain 2 = <u>promise</u>, pledge, undertake

● NOUN 1 = <u>promise</u>, pledge, assurance, certainty, word of honour 2 = <u>warranty</u>, contract, bond

**guard** VERB = <u>protect</u>, defend, secure, mind, preserve, shield, safeguard, watch over

● NOUN 1 = <u>sentry</u>, warder, warden, custodian, watch, lookout, watchman, sentinel 2 = <u>shield</u>, security, defence, screen, protection, safeguard, buffer

**guarded** = <u>cautious</u>, reserved, careful, suspicious, wary, prudent, reticent, circumspect

**guardian** = <u>keeper</u>, champion, defender, guard, warden, curator, protector, custodian

**guerrilla** = <u>freedom fighter</u>, partisan, underground fighter

**guess** VERB 1 = <u>estimate</u>, predict, work out, speculate, conjecture, postulate, hypothesize ≠ know 2 = <u>suppose</u>, think, believe, suspect, judge, imagine, reckon, fancy

● NOUN 1 = <u>estimate</u>, speculation, judgment, hypothesis, conjecture, shot in the dark ≠ certainty 2 = <u>supposition</u>, idea, theory, hypothesis

**guest** = <u>visitor</u>, company, caller,

manu(w)hiri (N.Z.)

**guidance** = <u>advice</u>, direction, leadership, instruction, help, management, teaching, counselling

**guide** NOUN 1 = <u>handbook</u>, manual, guidebook, instructions, catalogue 2 = <u>directory</u>, street map 3 = <u>escort</u>, leader, usher 4 = <u>pointer</u>, sign, landmark, marker, beacon, signpost, guiding light, lodestar 5 = <u>model</u>, example, standard, ideal, inspiration, paradigm
● VERB 1 = <u>lead</u>, direct, escort, conduct, accompany, shepherd, usher, show the way 2 = <u>steer</u>, control, manage, direct, handle, command, manoeuvre 3 = <u>supervise</u>, train, teach, influence, advise, counsel, instruct, oversee

**guild** = <u>society</u>, union, league, association, company, club, order, organization

**guilt** 1 = <u>shame</u>, regret, remorse, contrition, guilty conscience, self-reproach ≠ pride 2 = <u>culpability</u>, blame, responsibility, misconduct, wickedness, sinfulness, guiltiness ≠ innocence

**guilty** 1 = <u>ashamed</u>, sorry, rueful, sheepish, contrite, remorseful, regretful, shamefaced ≠ proud 2 = <u>culpable</u>, responsible, to blame, offending, erring, at fault, reprehensible, blameworthy

≠ innocent

**guise** 1 = <u>form</u>, appearance, shape, aspect, mode, semblance 2 = <u>pretence</u>, disguise, aspect, semblance

**gulf** 1 = <u>bay</u>, bight, sea inlet 2 = <u>chasm</u>, opening, split, gap, separation, void, rift, abyss

**gum** NOUN = <u>glue</u>, adhesive, resin, cement, paste
● VERB = <u>stick</u>, glue, affix, cement, paste

**gun** = <u>firearm</u>, shooter (slang), piece (slang), handgun

**gunman** = <u>armed man</u>, gunslinger (U.S. slang)

**guru** 1 = <u>authority</u>, expert, leader, master, pundit, Svengali, fundi (S. African) 2 = <u>teacher</u>, mentor, sage, master, tutor

**gush** VERB 1 = <u>flow</u>, run, rush, flood, pour, stream, cascade, spurt 2 = <u>enthuse</u>, rave, spout, overstate, effuse
● NOUN = <u>stream</u>, flow, rush, flood, jet, cascade, torrent, spurt

**gut** NOUN = <u>paunch</u> (Informal), belly, spare tyre (Brit. slang), potbelly, puku (N.Z.)
● PLURAL NOUN 1 = <u>intestines</u>, insides (informal), stomach, belly, bowels, innards (informal), entrails 2 (Informal) = <u>courage</u>, spirit, nerve, daring, pluck, backbone, bottle (slang), audacity
● VERB 1 = <u>disembowel</u>, clean 2 = <u>ravage</u>, empty, clean out,

despoil

● ADJECTIVE = <u>instinctive</u>, natural, basic, spontaneous, intuitive, involuntary, heartfelt, unthinking

**gutter** = <u>drain</u>, channel, ditch, trench, trough, conduit, sluice

**guy** (*Informal*) = <u>man</u>, person, fellow, lad, bloke (*Brit. informal*), chap

**Gypsy** or **Gipsy** = <u>traveller</u>, roamer, wanderer, Bohemian, rover, rambler, nomad, Romany

# H

**habit** 1 = <u>mannerism</u>, custom, way, practice, characteristic, tendency, quirk, propensity 2 = <u>addiction</u>, dependence, compulsion

**hack**¹ = <u>cut</u>, chop, slash, mutilate, mangle, mangulate (*Austral. slang*), hew, lacerate

**hack**² = <u>reporter</u>, writer, correspondent, journalist, scribbler, contributor, literary hack

**hail**¹ VERB 1 = <u>acclaim</u>, honour, acknowledge, cheer, applaud ≠ condemn 2 = <u>salute</u>, greet, address, welcome, say hello to, halloo ≠ snub 3 = <u>flag down</u>, summon, signal to, wave down

● PHRASES **hail from somewhere** = <u>come from</u>, be born in, originate in, be a native of, have your roots in

**hail**² NOUN 1 = <u>hailstones</u>, sleet, hailstorm, frozen rain 2 = <u>shower</u>, rain, storm, battery, volley, barrage, bombardment, downpour

● VERB 1 = <u>rain</u>, shower, pelt 2 = <u>batter</u>, rain, bombard, pelt, rain down on, beat down upon

**hair** = <u>locks</u>, mane, tresses, shock, mop, head of hair

**hairdresser** = <u>stylist</u>, barber, coiffeur or coiffeuse

**hairy** 1 = <u>shaggy</u>, woolly, furry, stubbly, bushy, unshaven, hirsute 2 (*Slang*) = <u>dangerous</u>, risky, unpredictable, hazardous, perilous

**hale** (*Old-fashioned*) = <u>healthy</u>, well, strong, sound, fit, flourishing, robust, vigorous

**half** NOUN = <u>fifty per cent</u>, equal part

● ADJECTIVE = <u>partial</u>, limited, moderate, halved

● ADVERB = <u>partially</u>, partly, in part
(*Related Words*)
*prefixes*: bi-, demi-, hemi-, semi-

**halfway** ADVERB = <u>midway</u>, to or in the middle

● ADJECTIVE = <u>midway</u>, middle, mid, central, intermediate, equidistant

**hall** 1 = <u>passage</u>, lobby, corridor, hallway, foyer, entry, passageway, entrance hall 2 = <u>meeting place</u>, chamber, auditorium, concert hall, assembly room

**hallmark** 1 = <u>trademark</u>, sure

sign, telltale sign **2** (*Brit.*) = **mark**, sign, device, stamp, seal, symbol

**halt** VERB **1** = **stop**, break off, stand still, wait, rest ≠ continue **2** = **come to an end**, stop, cease **3** = **hold back**, end, check, block, curb, terminate, cut short, bring to an end ≠ aid
● NOUN = **stop**, end, close, pause, standstill, stoppage ≠ continuation

**halting** = **faltering**, stumbling, awkward, hesitant, laboured, stammering, stuttering

**halve 1** = **cut in half**, reduce by fifty per cent, decrease by fifty per cent, lessen by fifty per cent **2** = **split in two**, cut in half, bisect, divide in two, share equally, divide equally

**hammer 1** = **hit**, drive, knock, beat, strike, tap, bang **2** (*Informal*) = **defeat**, beat, thrash, trounce, run rings around (*informal*), wipe the floor with (*informal*), drub

**hamper** = **hinder**, handicap, prevent, restrict, frustrate, hamstring, interfere with, obstruct ≠ help

**hand** NOUN **1** = **palm**, fist, paw (*informal*), mitt (*slang*) **2** = **worker**, employee, labourer, workman, operative, craftsman, artisan, hired man **3** = **round of applause**, clap, ovation, big hand **4** = **writing**, script, handwriting, calligraphy

● VERB = **give**, pass, hand over, present to, deliver

**handbook** = **guidebook**, guide, manual, instruction book

**handcuff** VERB = **shackle**, secure, restrain, fetter, manacle
● PLURAL NOUN = **shackles**, cuffs (*informal*), fetters, manacles

**handful** = **few**, sprinkling, small amount, smattering, small number ≠ a lot

**handicap** NOUN **1** = **disability**, defect, impairment, physical abnormality **2** = **disadvantage**, barrier, restriction, obstacle, limitation, drawback, stumbling block, impediment ≠ advantage **3** = **advantage**, head start
● VERB = **hinder**, limit, restrict, burden, hamstring, hamper, hold back, impede ≠ help

**handle** NOUN = **grip**, hilt, haft, stock
● VERB **1** = **manage**, deal with, tackle, cope with **2** = **deal with**, manage **3** = **control**, manage, direct, guide, manipulate, manoeuvre **4** = **hold**, feel, touch, pick up, finger, grasp

**handsome 1** = **good-looking**, attractive, gorgeous, elegant, personable, dishy (*informal, chiefly Brit.*), comely ≠ ugly **2** = **generous**, large, princely, liberal, considerable, lavish, ample, abundant ≠ mean

**handy 1** = **useful**, practical,

helpful, neat, convenient, easy to use, manageable, user-friendly ≠ useless 2 = convenient, close, available, nearby, accessible, on hand, at hand, within reach ≠ inconvenient 3 = skilful, skilled, expert, adept, deft, proficient, adroit, dexterous ≠ unskilled

**hang** VERB 1 = dangle, swing, suspend 2 = lower, suspend, dangle 3 = lean 4 = execute, lynch, string up (*informal*)
● PHRASES **get the hang of something** = grasp, understand, learn, master, comprehend, catch on to, acquire the technique of
◆ **hang back** = be reluctant, hesitate, hold back, recoil, demur

**hangover** = aftereffects, morning after (*informal*)

**hang-up** (*informal*) = preoccupation, thing (*informal*), problem, block, difficulty, obsession, mania, inhibition

**hank** = coil, roll, length, bunch, piece, loop, clump, skein

**happen** 1 = occur, take place, come about, result, develop, transpire (*informal*), come to pass 2 = chance, turn out (*informal*)

**happening** = event, incident, experience, affair, proceeding, episode, occurrence

**happily** 1 = luckily, fortunately, providentially, opportunely 2 = joyfully, cheerfully, gleefully,

blithely, merrily, gaily, joyously 3 = willingly, freely, gladly, with pleasure

**happiness** = pleasure, delight, joy, satisfaction, ecstasy, bliss, contentment, elation ≠ unhappiness

**happy** 1 = pleased, delighted, content, thrilled, glad, cheerful, merry, ecstatic 2 = contented, joyful, blissful ≠ sad 3 = fortunate, lucky, timely, favourable, auspicious, propitious, advantageous ≠ unfortunate

**harass** = annoy, trouble, bother, harry, plague, hound, hassle (*informal*), persecute

**harassed** = hassled, worried, troubled, strained, under pressure, tormented, distraught (*informal*), vexed

**harassment** = hassle, trouble, bother, irritation, persecution (*informal*), nuisance, annoyance, pestering

**harbour** NOUN = port, haven, dock, mooring, marina, pier, wharf, anchorage
● VERB 1 = hold, bear, maintain, nurse, retain, foster, entertain, nurture 2 = shelter, protect, hide, shield, provide refuge, give asylum to

**hard** ADJECTIVE 1 = tough, strong, firm, solid, stiff, rigid, resistant, compressed ≠ soft 2 = difficult, involved, complicated, puzzling,

intricate, perplexing,
impenetrable, thorny ≠ easy
**3=** exhausting, tough, exacting,
rigorous, gruelling, strenuous,
arduous, laborious ≠ easy
**4=** harsh, cold, cruel, stern,
callous, unkind, unsympathetic,
pitiless ≠ kind **5=** grim, painful,
distressing, harsh, unpleasant,
intolerable, grievous,
disagreeable
● **ADVERB** **1=** strenuously, steadily,
persistently, doggedly, diligently,
energetically, industriously,
untiringly **2=** intently, closely,
carefully, sharply, keenly
**3=** forcefully, strongly, heavily,
sharply, severely, fiercely,
vigorously, intensely ≠ softly
**harden 1=** solidify, set, freeze,
cake, bake, clot, thicken, stiffen
**2=** accustom, season, toughen,
train, inure, habituate
**hardened 1=** habitual, chronic,
shameless, inveterate, incorrigible
≠ occasional **2=** seasoned,
experienced, accustomed,
toughened, inured, habituated
≠ naive
**hardly 1=** barely, only just,
scarcely, just, with difficulty, with
effort ≠ completely **2=** only just,
just, barely, scarcely
**hardship=** suffering, need,
difficulty, misfortune, adversity,
tribulation, privation ≠ ease
**hardy=** strong, tough, robust,

sound, rugged, sturdy, stout
≠ frail
**hare**

*Related Words*

adjective: leporine
male: buck
female: leveret
habitation: down, husk
**harm** VERB **1=** injure, hurt,
wound, abuse, ill-treat, maltreat
≠ heal **2=** damage, hurt, ruin,
spoil
● **NOUN 1=** injury, suffering,
damage, ill, hurt, distress
**2=** damage, loss, ill, hurt,
misfortune, mischief ≠ good
**harmful=** damaging,
dangerous, negative, destructive,
hazardous, unhealthy,
detrimental, hurtful ≠ harmless
**harmless 1=** safe, benign,
wholesome, innocuous, nontoxic
≠ dangerous **2=** inoffensive,
innocent, innocuous, gentle,
tame, unobjectionable
**harmony 1=** accord, peace,
agreement, friendship, sympathy,
cooperation, rapport,
compatibility ≠ conflict **2=** tune,
melody, unison, tunefulness,
euphony ≠ discord
**harness** VERB **=** exploit, control,
channel, employ, utilize, mobilize
● **NOUN =** equipment, tackle, gear,
tack
**harrowing=** distressing,
disturbing, painful, terrifying,

269

traumatic, tormenting, agonizing, nerve-racking

**harry** = <u>pester</u>, bother, plague, harass, hassle (*informal*), badger, chivvy

**harsh** 1 = <u>severe</u>, hard, tough, stark, austere, inhospitable 2 = <u>bleak</u>, freezing, severe, icy 3 = <u>cruel</u>, savage, ruthless, barbarous, pitiless 4 = <u>hard</u>, severe, cruel, stern, pitiless ≠ kind 5 = <u>drastic</u>, punitive, Draconian 6 = <u>raucous</u>, rough, grating, strident, rasping, discordant, guttural, dissonant ≠ soft

**harshly** = <u>severely</u>, roughly, cruelly, strictly, sternly, brutally

**harvest** NOUN 1 = <u>harvesting</u>, picking, gathering, collecting, reaping, harvest-time 2 = <u>crop</u>, yield, year's growth, produce
● VERB = <u>gather</u>, pick, collect, bring in, pluck, reap

**hassle** (*Informal*) NOUN = <u>trouble</u>, problem, difficulty, bother, grief (*informal*), uphill (*S. African*), inconvenience
● VERB = <u>bother</u>, bug (*informal*), annoy, hound, harass, badger, pester

**hasten** = <u>rush</u>, race, fly, speed, dash, hurry (up), scurry, make haste ≠ dawdle

**hastily** = <u>quickly</u>, rapidly, promptly, speedily 2 = <u>hurriedly</u>, rashly, precipitately, impetuously

**hatch** 1 = <u>incubate</u>, breed, sit on,

brood, bring forth 2 = <u>devise</u>, design, invent, put together, conceive, brew, formulate, contrive

**hate** VERB 1 = <u>detest</u>, loathe, despise, dislike, abhor, recoil from, not be able to bear ≠ love 2 = <u>dislike</u>, detest, shrink from, recoil from, not be able to bear ≠ like 3 = <u>be unwilling</u>, regret, be reluctant, hesitate, be sorry, be loath, feel disinclined
● NOUN = <u>dislike</u>, hostility, hatred, loathing, animosity, aversion, antipathy, enmity ≠ love

**hatred** = <u>hate</u>, dislike, animosity, aversion, revulsion, antipathy, enmity, repugnance ≠ love

**haul** VERB = <u>drag</u>, draw, pull, heave
● NOUN = <u>yield</u>, gain, spoils, catch, harvest, loot, takings, booty

**haunt** VERB = <u>plague</u>, trouble, obsess, torment, possess, stay with, recur, prey on
● NOUN = <u>meeting place</u>, hangout (*informal*), rendezvous, stamping ground

**haunted** 1 = <u>possessed</u>, ghostly, cursed, eerie, spooky (*informal*), jinxed 2 = <u>preoccupied</u>, worried, troubled, plagued, obsessed, tormented

**haunting** = <u>evocative</u>, poignant, unforgettable

**have** VERB 1 = <u>own</u>, keep, possess, hold, retain, boast, be the owner of 2= get, obtain, take, receive, accept, gain, secure, acquire 3= suffer, experience, undergo, sustain, endure, be suffering from 4= give birth to, bear, deliver, bring forth, beget 5= experience, go through, undergo, meet with, come across, run into, be faced with

• PHRASES **have someone on** = tease, kid (informal), wind up (Brit. slang), trick, deceive, take the mickey, pull someone's leg

♦ **have something on** = wear, be wearing, be dressed in, be clothed in, be attired in ♦ **have to** 1= must, should, be forced, ought, be obliged, be bound, have got to, be compelled 2= have got to, must

**haven** = sanctuary, shelter, retreat, asylum, refuge, oasis, sanctum

**havoc** 1= devastation, damage, destruction, ruin 2(Informal) = disorder, confusion, chaos, disruption, mayhem, shambles

**hazard** NOUN = danger, risk, threat, problem, menace, peril, jeopardy, pitfall

• VERB = jeopardize, risk, endanger, threaten, expose, imperil, put in jeopardy

• PHRASES **hazard a guess** = guess, conjecture, presume, take a guess

**hazardous** = dangerous, risky, difficult, insecure, unsafe,

precarious, perilous, dicey (informal, chiefly Brit.) ≠ safe

**haze** = mist, cloud, fog, obscurity, vapour

**head** NOUN 1= skull, crown, pate, nut (slang), loaf (slang) 2= mind, reasoning, understanding, thought, sense, brain, brains (informal), intelligence 3= top, crown, summit, peak, crest, pinnacle 4(Informal) = head teacher, principal 5= leader, president, director, manager, chief, boss (informal), captain, master

• ADJECTIVE = chief, main, leading, first, prime, premier, supreme, principal

• VERB 1= lead, precede, be the leader of, be or go first, be or go at the front of, lead the way 2= top, lead, crown, cap 3= be in charge of, run, manage, lead, control, direct, guide, command

• PHRASES **go to your head** 1= intoxicate 2= make someone conceited, puff someone up, make someone full of themselves

♦ **head over heels** = completely, thoroughly, utterly, intensely, wholeheartedly, uncontrollably

**headache** 1= migraine, head (informal), neuralgia 2= problem (Informal), worry, trouble, bother, nuisance, inconvenience, bane, vexation

**heading** = title, name, caption,

271

headline, rubric

**heady 1** = <u>exciting</u>, thrilling, stimulating, exhilarating, intoxicating **2** = <u>intoxicating</u>, strong, potent, inebriating

**heal 1** *sometimes with* **up** = <u>mend</u>, get better, get well, cure, regenerate, show improvement **2** = <u>cure</u>, restore, mend, make better, remedy, make good, make well ≠ injure

**health 1** = <u>condition</u>, state, shape, constitution, fettle **2** = <u>wellbeing</u>, strength, fitness, vigour, good condition, soundness, robustness, healthiness ≠ illness **3** = <u>state</u>, condition, shape

**healthy 1** = <u>well</u>, fit, strong, active, robust, in good shape (*informal*), in the pink, in fine fettle ≠ ill **2** = <u>wholesome</u>, beneficial, nourishing, nutritious, salutary, hygienic, salubrious ≠ unwholesome **3** = <u>invigorating</u>, beneficial, salutary, salubrious

**heap** NOUN **1** = <u>pile</u>, lot, collection, mass, stack, mound, accumulation, hoard **2** *often plural* (*Informal*) = <u>a lot</u>, lots (*informal*), plenty, masses, load(s) (*informal*), great deal, tons, stack(s)
● VERB *sometimes with* **up** = <u>pile</u>, collect, gather, stack, accumulate, amass, hoard
● PHRASES **heap something on someone** = <u>load with</u>, confer on, assign to, bestow on, shower upon

**hear 1** = <u>overhear</u>, catch, detect **2** = <u>listen to</u> **3** (*Law*) = <u>try</u>, judge, examine, investigate **4** = <u>learn</u>, discover, find out, pick up, gather, ascertain, get wind of (*informal*)

**hearing** = <u>inquiry</u>, trial, investigation, industrial tribunal

**heart** NOUN **1** = <u>emotions</u>, feelings, love, affection **2** = <u>nature</u>, character, soul, constitution, essence, temperament, disposition **3** = <u>root</u>, core, centre, nucleus, hub, gist, nitty-gritty (*informal*), nub **4** = <u>courage</u>, will, spirit, purpose, bottle (*Brit. informal*), resolution, resolve, stomach
● PHRASES **by heart** = <u>from</u> *or* <u>by</u> <u>memory</u>, verbatim, word for word, pat, word-perfect, by rote, off by heart, off pat
(Related Words)
*adjective*: cardiac

**heat** VERB *sometimes with* **up** = <u>warm (up)</u>, cook, boil, roast, reheat, make hot ≠ chill
● NOUN **1** = <u>warmth</u>, hotness, temperature ≠ cold **2** = <u>hot</u> <u>weather</u>, warmth, closeness, high temperature, heatwave, warm weather, hot climate, mugginess **3** = <u>passion</u>, excitement, intensity, fury, fervour, vehemence ≠ calmness
(Related Words)
*adjective*: thermal

**heated 1** = <u>impassioned</u>, intense, spirited, excited, angry,

furious, fierce, lively ≠ **calm**
2 = <u>wound up</u>, worked up, keyed up, het up (*informal*)

**heaven** NOUN 1 = <u>paradise</u>, next world, hereafter, nirvana (*Buddhism, Hinduism*), bliss, Zion (*Christianity*), life everlasting, Elysium or Elysian fields (*Greek myth*) 2 (*Informal*) = <u>happiness</u>, paradise, ecstasy, bliss, utopia, rapture, seventh heaven

● PHRASES **the heavens** (*Old-fashioned*) = <u>sky</u>, ether, firmament

**heavenly** 1 = <u>celestial</u>, holy, divine, blessed, immortal, angelic ≠ **earthly** 2 (*Informal*) = <u>wonderful</u>, lovely, delightful, beautiful, divine (*informal*), exquisite, sublime, blissful ≠ **awful**

**heavily** 1 = <u>excessively</u>, to excess, very much, a great deal, considerably, copiously, without restraint, immoderately
2 = <u>densely</u>, closely, thickly, compactly 3 = <u>hard</u>, clumsily, awkwardly, weightily

**heavy** 1 = <u>weighty</u>, large, massive, hefty, bulky, ponderous ≠ **light** 2 = <u>intensive</u>, severe, serious, concentrated, fierce, excessive, relentless
3 = <u>considerable</u>, large, huge, substantial, abundant, copious, profuse ≠ **slight**

**hectic** = <u>frantic</u>, chaotic, heated, animated, turbulent, frenetic, feverish ≠ **peaceful**

**hedge** VERB = <u>prevaricate</u>, evade, sidestep, duck, dodge, flannel (*Brit. informal*), equivocate, temporize

● PHRASES **hedge against something** = <u>protect against</u>, insure against, guard against, safeguard against, shield against, cover against

**heed** (*Formal*) VERB = <u>pay attention to</u>, listen to, take notice of, follow, consider, note, observe, obey ≠ **ignore**

● NOUN = <u>thought</u>, care, mind, attention, regard, respect, notice ≠ **disregard**

**heel** (*Slang*) = <u>swine</u>, cad (*Brit. informal*), bounder (*Brit. old-fashioned slang*), rotter (*slang, chiefly Brit.*)

**hefty** (*Informal*) = <u>big</u>, strong, massive, strapping, robust, muscular, burly, hulking ≠ **small**

**height** 1 = <u>tallness</u>, stature, highness, loftiness ≠ **shortness**
2 = <u>altitude</u>, measurement, highness, elevation, tallness ≠ **depth** 3 = <u>peak</u>, top, crown, summit, crest, pinnacle, apex ≠ **valley** 4 = <u>culmination</u>, climax, zenith, limit, maximum, ultimate ≠ **low point**

**heighten** = <u>intensify</u>, increase, add to, improve, strengthen, enhance, sharpen, magnify

**heir** = <u>successor</u>, beneficiary, inheritor, heiress (*fem.*), next in

line
**hell** 1 = the underworld, the abyss, Hades (Greek myth), hellfire, the inferno, fire and brimstone, the nether world, the bad fire (informal) 2 (Informal) = torment, suffering, agony, nightmare, misery, ordeal, anguish, wretchedness

**hello** = hi (informal), greetings, how do you do?, good morning, good evening, good afternoon, welcome, kia ora (N.Z.), gidday or g'day (Austral. & N.Z.)

**helm** (Nautical) = tiller, wheel, rudder

**help** VERB 1 sometimes without = aid, support, assist, cooperate with, abet, lend a hand, succour ≠ hinder 2 = improve, ease, relieve, facilitate, alleviate, mitigate, ameliorate ≠ make worse 3 = assist, aid, support 4 = resist, refrain from, avoid, prevent, keep from
● NOUN = assistance, aid, support, advice, guidance, cooperation, helping hand ≠ hindrance

**helper** = assistant, ally, supporter, mate, second, aide, attendant, collaborator

**helpful** 1 = cooperative, accommodating, kind, friendly, neighbourly, sympathetic, supportive, considerate 2 = useful, practical, profitable, constructive 3 = beneficial, advantageous

**helping** = portion, serving, ration, piece, dollop (informal), plateful

**helpless** = powerless, weak, disabled, incapable, paralysed, impotent, infirm ≠ powerful

**hem** NOUN = edge, border, margin, trimming, fringe
● PHRASES **hem something or someone in** 1 = surround, confine, enclose, shut in 2 = restrict, confine, beset, circumscribe

**hence** = therefore, thus, consequently, for this reason, in consequence, ergo, on that account

**herald** VERB = indicate, promise, usher in, presage, portend, foretoken
● NOUN 1 (Often literary) = forerunner, sign, signal, indication, token, omen, precursor, harbinger 2 = messenger, courier, proclaimer, announcer, crier, town crier

**herd** = flock, crowd, collection, mass, drove, mob, swarm, horde

**hereditary** 1 = genetic, inborn, inbred, transmissible, inheritable 2 (Law) = inherited, passed down, traditional, ancestral

**heritage** = inheritance, legacy, birthright, tradition, endowment, bequest

**hero** 1 = protagonist, leading

man 2 = **star**, champion, victor, superstar, conqueror 3 = **idol**, favourite, pin-up (*slang*), fave (*informal*)
**heroic** = **courageous**, brave, daring, fearless, gallant, intrepid, valiant, lion-hearted ≠ **cowardly**
**heroine** 1 = **protagonist**, leading lady, diva, prima donna 2 = **idol**, favourite, pin-up (*slang*), fave (*informal*)

> ### Word Power
> **heroine** – Note that the word *heroine*, meaning 'a female hero', has an *e* at the end. The drug *heroin* is spelled without a final *e*.

**hesitate** 1 = **waver**, delay, pause, wait, doubt, falter, dither (*chiefly Brit.*), vacillate ≠ **be decisive** 2 = **be reluctant**, be unwilling, shrink from, think twice, scruple, demur, hang back, be disinclined ≠ **be determined**
**hesitation** = **reluctance**, reservation(s), misgiving(s), ambivalence, qualm(s), unwillingness, scruple(s), compunction
**hidden** 1 = **secret**, veiled, latent 2 = **concealed**, secret, covert, unseen, clandestine, secreted, under wraps
**hide**¹ 1 = **conceal**, stash (*informal*), secrete, put out of sight ≠ **display** 2 = **go into hiding**, take cover, keep out of sight, hole up, lie low, go underground, go to ground, go to earth 3 = **keep secret**, suppress, withhold, keep quiet about, hush up, draw a veil over, keep dark, keep under your hat ≠ **disclose** 4 = **obscure**, cover, mask, disguise, conceal, veil, cloak, shroud ≠ **reveal**
**hide**² = **skin**, leather, pelt
**hideous** = **ugly**, revolting, ghastly, monstrous, grotesque, gruesome, grisly, unsightly ≠ **beautiful**
**hiding** (*Informal*) = **beating**, whipping, thrashing, licking (*informal*), spanking, walloping (*informal*), drubbing
**hierarchy** = **grading**, ranking, social order, pecking order, class system, social stratum
**high** ADJECTIVE 1 = **tall**, towering, soaring, steep, elevated, lofty ≠ **extreme** 2 = **extreme**, great, acute, severe, extraordinary, excessive ≠ **low** 3 = **strong**, violent, extreme, blustery, squally, sharp 4 = **important**, chief, powerful, superior, eminent, exalted ≠ **lowly** 5 = **high-pitched**, piercing, shrill, penetrating, strident, sharp, acute, piping ≠ **deep** 6 (*Informal*) = **intoxicated**, stoned (*slang*), tripping (*informal*)
● ADVERB = **way up**, aloft, far up, to a great height
**high-flown** = **extravagant**,

elaborate, pretentious, exaggerated, inflated, lofty, grandiose, overblown ≠ straightforward

**highlight** VERB = <u>emphasize</u>, stress, accent, show up, underline, spotlight, accentuate, call attention to ≠ play down

● NOUN = <u>high point</u>, peak, climax, feature, focus, focal point, high spot ≠ low point

**highly** = <u>extremely</u>, very, greatly, vastly, exceptionally, immensely, tremendously

**hijack** = <u>seize</u>, take over, commandeer, expropriate

**hike** NOUN = <u>walk</u>, march, trek, ramble, tramp, traipse

● VERB = <u>walk</u>, march, trek, ramble, tramp, back-pack

**hilarious** 1 = <u>funny</u>, entertaining, amusing, hysterical, humorous, comical, side-splitting 2 = <u>merry</u>, uproarious, rollicking ≠ serious

**hill** = <u>mount</u>, fell, height, mound, hilltop, tor, knoll, hillock, kopje *or* koppie (*S. African*)

**hinder** = <u>obstruct</u>, stop, check, block, delay, frustrate, handicap, interrupt ≠ help

**hint** NOUN 1 = <u>clue</u>, suggestion, implication, indication, pointer, allusion, innuendo, intimation 2 *often plural* = <u>advice</u>, help, tip(s), suggestion(s), pointer(s) 3 = <u>trace</u>, touch, suggestion, dash,

suspicion, tinge, undertone

● VERB *sometimes with* **at** = <u>suggest</u>, indicate, imply, intimate, insinuate

**hire** VERB 1 = <u>employ</u>, commission, take on, engage, appoint, sign up, enlist 2 = <u>rent</u>, charter, lease, let, engage

● NOUN 1 = <u>rental</u>, hiring, rent, lease 2 = <u>charge</u>, rental, price, cost, fee

**hiss** VERB 1 = <u>whistle</u>, wheeze, whiz, whirr, sibilate 2 = <u>jeer</u>, mock, deride

● NOUN = <u>fizz</u>, buzz, hissing, fizzing, sibilation

**historic** = <u>significant</u>, notable, momentous, famous, extraordinary, outstanding, remarkable, ground-breaking ≠ unimportant

> ### Word Power
>
> **historic** – Although *historic* and *historical* are similarly spelt they are very different in meaning and should not be used interchangeably. A distinction is usually made between *historic*, which means 'important' or 'significant', and *historical*, which means 'pertaining to history': *a historic decision*; *a historical perspective*.

**historical** = <u>factual</u>, real, documented, actual, authentic, attested ≠ contemporary

➤ historic

**history** 1 = <u>the past</u>, antiquity,

yesterday, yesteryear, olden days

2 = <u>chronicle</u>, record, story, account, narrative, recital, annals

**hit** VERB1 = <u>strike</u>, beat, knock, bang, slap, smack, thump, clout (*informal*)2 = <u>collide with</u>, run into, bump into, clash with, smash into, crash against, bang into

3 = <u>affect</u>, damage, harm, ruin, devastate, overwhelm, touch, impact on4 = <u>reach</u>, gain, achieve, arrive at, accomplish, attain

● NOUN1 = <u>shot</u>, blow2 = <u>blow</u>, knock, stroke, belt (*informal*), rap, slap, smack, clout (*informal*)

3 = <u>success</u>, winner, triumph, smash (*informal*), sensation

● PHRASEShit it off (*Informal*) = <u>get on (well) with</u>, click (*slang*), be on good terms, get on like a house on fire (*informal*) ◆hit on or upon something = <u>think up</u>, discover, arrive at, invent, stumble on, light upon, strike upon

**hitch** NOUN = <u>problem</u>, catch, difficulty, hold-up, obstacle, drawback, snag, uphill (*S. African*), impediment

● VERB1 (*Informal*) = <u>hitchhike</u>, thumb a lift2 = <u>fasten</u>, join, attach, couple, tie, connect, harness, tether

● PHRASEShitch something up = <u>pull up</u>, tug, jerk, yank

**hitherto** (*Formal*) = <u>previously</u>, so far, until now, thus far, heretofore

**hobby** = <u>pastime</u>, relaxation, leisure pursuit, diversion, avocation, (leisure) activity

**hoist** VERB = <u>raise</u>, lift, erect, elevate, heave

● NOUN = <u>lift</u>, crane, elevator, winch

**hold** VERB1 = <u>embrace</u>, grasp, clutch, hug, squeeze, cradle, clasp, enfold2 = <u>restrain</u> ≠ release

3 = <u>accommodate</u>, take, contain, seat, have a capacity for

4 = <u>consider</u>, think, believe, judge, regard, assume, reckon, deem ≠ deny5 = <u>occupy</u>, have, fill, maintain, retain, possess, hold down (*informal*)6 = <u>conduct</u>, convene, call, run, preside over ≠ cancel7 = <u>detain</u>, confine, imprison, impound ≠ release

● NOUN1 = <u>grip</u>, grasp, clasp

2 = <u>foothold</u>, footing3 = <u>control</u>, influence, mastery, mana (*N.Z.*)

**holder** 1 = <u>owner</u>, bearer, possessor, keeper, proprietor

2 = <u>case</u>, cover, container

**hold-up** 1 = <u>robbery</u>, theft, mugging (*informal*), stick-up (*slang, chiefly U.S.*)2 = <u>delay</u>, wait, hitch, setback, snag, traffic jam, stoppage, bottleneck

**hole** 1 = <u>cavity</u>, pit, hollow, chamber, cave, cavern

2 = <u>opening</u>, crack, tear, gap, breach, vent, puncture, aperture

3 = <u>burrow</u>, den, earth, shelter, lair

**4** (*Informal*) = <u>hovel</u>, dump (*informal*), dive (*slang*), slum **5** (*Informal*) = <u>predicament</u>, spot (*informal*), fix (*informal*), mess, jam (*informal*), dilemma, scrape (*informal*), hot water (*informal*)

**holiday 1** = <u>vacation</u>, leave, break, time off, recess **2** = <u>festival</u>, fête, celebration, feast, gala

**hollow ADJECTIVE 1** = <u>empty</u>, vacant, void, unfilled ≠ solid **2** = <u>worthless</u>, useless, vain, meaningless, pointless, futile, fruitless ≠ meaningful **3** = <u>dull</u>, low, deep, muted, toneless, reverberant ≠ vibrant

● **NOUN 1** = <u>cavity</u>, hole, bowl, depression, pit, basin, crater, trough ≠ mound **2** = <u>valley</u>, dale, glen, dell, dingle ≠ hill

● **VERB** often followed by out = <u>scoop out</u>, dig out, excavate, gouge out

**holocaust 1** = <u>devastation</u>, destruction, genocide, annihilation, conflagration **2** = <u>genocide</u>, massacre, annihilation

**holy 1** = <u>sacred</u>, blessed, hallowed, venerable, consecrated, sacrosanct, sanctified ≠ unsanctified **2** = <u>devout</u>, godly, religious, pure, righteous, pious, virtuous, saintly ≠ sinful

**homage** = <u>respect</u>, honour, worship, devotion, reverence, deference, adulation, adoration ≠ contempt

**home NOUN 1** = <u>dwelling</u>, house, residence, abode, habitation, pad (*slang*), domicile **2** = <u>birthplace</u>, homeland, home town, native land

● **ADJECTIVE 1** = <u>domestic</u>, local, internal, native

● **PHRASES at home 1** = <u>in</u>, present, available **2** = <u>at ease</u>, relaxed, comfortable, content, at peace ◆ **bring something home to someone** = <u>make clear</u>, emphasize, drive home, press home, impress upon

**homeland** = <u>native land</u>, birthplace, motherland, fatherland, country of origin, mother country

**homeless** = <u>destitute</u>, displaced, dispossessed, down-and-out

**homely 1** = <u>comfortable</u>, welcoming, friendly, cosy, homespun **2** = <u>plain</u>, simple, ordinary, modest ≠ elaborate

**homicide** = <u>murder</u>, killing, manslaughter, slaying, bloodshed

**hone 1** = <u>improve</u>, better, enhance, upgrade, refine, sharpen, edge **2** = <u>sharpen</u>, point, grind, edge, file, polish, whet

---

### Word Power

**hone** – *Hone* is sometimes wrongly used where *home* is meant: *this device makes it easier to home in on* (not *hone in on*) *the target.*

**honest** 1 = <u>trustworthy</u>, upright, ethical, honourable, reputable, truthful, virtuous, law-abiding ≠ dishonest 2 = <u>open</u>, direct, frank, plain, sincere, candid, forthright, upfront (*informal*) ≠ secretive

**honestly** 1 = <u>ethically</u>, legally, lawfully, honourably, by fair means 2 = <u>frankly</u>, plainly, candidly, straight (out), truthfully, to your face, in all sincerity

**honesty** 1 = <u>integrity</u>, honour, virtue, morality, probity, rectitude, truthfulness, trustworthiness 2 = <u>frankness</u>, openness, sincerity, candour, bluntness, outspokenness, straightforwardness

**honorary** = <u>nominal</u>, unofficial, titular, in name or title only

**honour** NOUN 1 = <u>integrity</u>, morality, honesty, goodness, fairness, decency, probity, rectitude ≠ dishonour 2 = <u>prestige</u>, credit, reputation, glory, fame, distinction, dignity, renown ≠ disgrace 3 = <u>reputation</u>, standing, prestige, image, status, stature, good name, cachet 4 = <u>acclaim</u>, praise, recognition, compliments, homage, accolades, commendation ≠ contempt 5 = <u>privilege</u>, credit, pleasure, compliment
• VERB 1 = <u>acclaim</u>, praise, decorate, commemorate, commend 2 = <u>respect</u>, value, esteem, prize, appreciate, adore

≠ scorn 3 = <u>fulfil</u>, keep, carry out, observe, discharge, live up to, be true to 4 = <u>pay</u>, take, accept, pass, acknowledge ≠ refuse

**honourable** 1 = <u>principled</u>, moral, ethical, fair, upright, honest, virtuous, trustworthy 2 = <u>proper</u>, respectable, virtuous, creditable

**hook** NOUN = <u>fastener</u>, catch, link, peg, clasp
• VERB 1 = <u>fasten</u>, fix, secure, clasp 2 = <u>catch</u>, land, trap, entrap

**hooked** 1 = <u>bent</u>, curved, aquiline, hook-shaped 2 (*Informal*) = <u>obsessed</u>, addicted, taken, devoted, turned on (*slang*), enamoured 3 (*Informal*) = <u>addicted</u>, dependent, using (*informal*), having a habit

**hooligan** = <u>delinquent</u>, vandal, hoon (*Austral. & N.Z.*), ruffian, lager lout, yob or yobbo (*Brit. slang*), cougan (*Austral. slang*), scozza (*Austral. slang*), bogan (*Austral. slang*)

**hoop** = <u>ring</u>, band, loop, wheel, round, girdle, circlet

**hop** VERB = <u>jump</u>, spring, bound, leap, skip, vault, caper
• NOUN = <u>jump</u>, step, spring, bound, leap, bounce, skip, vault

**hope** VERB = <u>believe</u>, look forward to, cross your fingers
• NOUN = <u>belief</u>, confidence, expectation, longing, dream, desire, ambition, assumption ≠ despair

**hopeful 1** = <u>optimistic</u>, confident, looking forward to, buoyant, sanguine, expectant ≠ despairing **2** = <u>promising</u>, encouraging, bright, reassuring, rosy, heartening, auspicious ≠ unpromising
**hopefully** = <u>optimistically</u>, confidently, expectantly, with anticipation

> ## Word Power
>
> **hopefully**—Some people object to the use of *hopefully* as a synonym for the phrase 'it is hoped that' in a sentence such as *hopefully I'll be able to attend the meeting.* This use of the adverb first appeared in America in the 1960s, but it has rapidly established itself elsewhere. There are really no strong grounds for objecting to it, since we accept other sentence adverbials that fulfil a similar function, for example *unfortunately,* which means 'it is unfortunate that' in a sentence such as *unfortunately I won't be able to attend the meeting.*

**hopeless** = <u>impossible</u>, pointless, futile, useless, vain, no-win, unattainable
**horde** = <u>crowd</u>, mob, swarm, host, band, pack, drove, gang
**horizon** = <u>skyline</u>, view, vista
**horizontal** = <u>level</u>, flat, parallel

**horrible 1** (*Informal*) = <u>dreadful</u>, terrible, awful, nasty, cruel, mean, unpleasant, horrid ≠ wonderful **2** = <u>terrible</u>, appalling, terrifying, shocking, grim, dreadful, revolting, ghastly
**horrific** = <u>horrifying</u>, shocking, appalling, awful, terrifying, dreadful, horrendous, ghastly
**horrify 1** = <u>terrify</u>, alarm, frighten, scare, intimidate, petrify, make your hair stand on end ≠ comfort **2** = <u>shock</u>, appal, dismay, sicken, outrage ≠ delight
**horror 1** = <u>terror</u>, fear, alarm, panic, dread, fright, consternation, trepidation **2** = <u>hatred</u>, disgust, loathing, aversion, revulsion, repugnance, odium, detestation ≠ love
**horse** = <u>nag</u>, mount, mare, colt, filly, stallion, steed (*archaic or literary*), moke (*Austral. slang*), yarraman or yarramin (*Austral.*), gee-gee (*slang*)

**Related Words**

*adjectives:* equestrian, equine
*male:* stallion
*female:* mare
*young:* foal, colt, filly

**hospitality** = <u>welcome</u>, warmth, kindness, friendliness, sociability, conviviality, neighbourliness, cordiality
**host¹** or **hostess** NOUN
**1** = <u>master of ceremonies</u>, proprietor, innkeeper, landlord or

landlady 2 = <u>presenter</u>, compere
(*Brit.*), anchorman or anchorwoman
● VERB = <u>present</u>, introduce,
compere (*Brit.*), front (*informal*)

**host²** 1 = <u>multitude</u>, lot, load
(*informal*), wealth, array, myriad,
great quantity, large number
2 = <u>crowd</u>, army, pack, drove,
mob, herd, legion, swarm

**hostage** = <u>captive</u>, prisoner, pawn

**hostile** 1 = <u>antagonistic</u>,
opposed, contrary, ill-disposed
2 = <u>unfriendly</u>, belligerent,
antagonistic, rancorous, ill-
disposed ≠ friendly
3 = <u>inhospitable</u>, adverse,
uncongenial, unsympathetic,
unwelcoming ≠ hospitable

**hostility** NOUN
1 = <u>unfriendliness</u>, hatred,
animosity, spite, bitterness,
malice, venom, enmity
≠ friendliness 2 = <u>opposition</u>,
resentment, antipathy, aversion,
antagonism, ill feeling, ill-will,
animus ≠ approval
● PLURAL NOUN = <u>warfare</u>, war,
fighting, conflict, combat, armed
conflict ≠ peace

**hot** 1 = <u>heated</u>, boiling, steaming,
roasting, searing, scorching,
scalding 2 = <u>warm</u>, close, stifling,
humid, torrid, sultry, sweltering,
balmy ≠ cold 3 = <u>spicy</u>, pungent,
peppery, piquant, biting, sharp
≠ mild 4 = <u>intense</u>, passionate,
heated, spirited, fierce, lively,

animated, ardent 5 = <u>new</u>, latest,
fresh, recent, up to date, just out,
up to the minute, bang up to
date (*informal*) ≠ old 6 = <u>popular</u>,
hip, fashionable, cool, in demand,
sought-after, must-see, in vogue
≠ unpopular 7 = <u>fierce</u>, intense,
strong, keen, competitive, cut-
throat 8 = <u>fiery</u>, violent, raging,
passionate, stormy ≠ calm

**hound** = <u>harass</u>, harry, bother,
provoke, annoy, torment, hassle
(*informal*), badger

(Related Words)
*collective noun*: pack

**house** NOUN 1 = <u>home</u>, residence,
dwelling, pad (*slang*), homestead,
abode, habitation, domicile,
whare (*N.Z.*) 2 = <u>household</u>,
family, family 3 = <u>firm</u>, company,
business, organization, outfit
(*informal*) 4 = <u>assembly</u>,
parliament, Commons, legislative
body 5 = <u>dynasty</u>, tribe, clan
● VERB 1 = <u>accommodate</u>, quarter,
take in, put up, lodge, harbour,
billet 2 = <u>contain</u>, keep, hold,
cover, store, protect, shelter
3 = <u>take</u>, accommodate, sleep,
provide shelter for, give a bed to
● PHRASES **on the house** = <u>free</u>,
for free (*informal*), for nothing,
free of charge, gratis

**household** = <u>family</u>, home,
house, family circle, ainga (*N.Z.*)

**housing** 1 = <u>accommodation</u>,
homes, houses, dwellings,

domiciles **2**= <u>case</u>, casing, covering, cover, shell, jacket, holder, container

**hover 1**= <u>float</u>, fly, hang, drift, flutter **2**= <u>linger</u>, loiter, hang about *or* around (*informal*) **3**= <u>waver</u>, fluctuate, dither (*chiefly Brit.*), oscillate, vacillate

**however**= <u>but</u>, nevertheless, still, though, yet, nonetheless, notwithstanding, anyhow

**howl**VERB **1**= <u>bay</u>, cry **2**= <u>cry</u>, scream, roar, weep, yell, wail, shriek, bellow
● NOUN **1**= <u>baying</u>, cry, bay, bark, barking, yelping **2**= <u>cry</u>, scream, roar, bay, wail, shriek, clamour, bawl

**hub**= <u>centre</u>, heart, focus, core, middle, focal point, nerve centre

**huddle**VERB **1**= <u>curl up</u>, crouch, hunch up **2**= <u>crowd</u>, press, gather, collect, squeeze, cluster, flock, herd
● NOUN (*Informal*) = <u>discussion</u>, conference, meeting, hui (*N.Z.*), powwow, confab (*informal*), korero (*N.Z.*)

**hue**= <u>colour</u>, tone, shade, dye, tint, tinge

**hug**VERB = <u>embrace</u>, cuddle, squeeze, clasp, enfold, hold close, take in your arms
● NOUN = <u>embrace</u>, squeeze, bear hug, clinch (*slang*), clasp

**huge**= <u>enormous</u>, large, massive, vast, tremendous, immense, gigantic, monumental ≠ tiny

**hui** (*N.Z.*) = <u>meeting</u>, gathering, assembly, conference, congress, rally, convention, get-together (*informal*)

**hull**= <u>framework</u>, casing, body, covering, frame

**hum 1**= <u>drone</u>, buzz, murmur, throb, vibrate, purr, thrum, whir **2**(*Informal*) = <u>be busy</u>, buzz, bustle, stir, pulse, pulsate

**human**ADJECTIVE = <u>mortal</u>, manlike ≠ nonhuman
● NOUN = <u>human being</u>, person, individual, creature, mortal, man *or* woman ≠ nonhuman

**humane**= <u>kind</u>, compassionate, understanding, forgiving, tender, sympathetic, benign, merciful ≠ cruel

**humanitarian**ADJECTIVE **1**= <u>compassionate</u>, charitable, humane, benevolent, altruistic **2**= <u>charitable</u>, philanthropic, public-spirited
● NOUN = <u>philanthropist</u>, benefactor, Good Samaritan, altruist

**humanity 1**= <u>the human race</u>, man, mankind, people, mortals, humankind, Homo sapiens **2**= <u>human nature</u>, mortality **3**= <u>kindness</u>, charity, compassion, sympathy, mercy, philanthropy, fellow feeling, kind-heartedness

**humble**ADJECTIVE **1**= <u>modest</u>, meek, unassuming, unpretentious, self-effacing, unostentatious ≠ proud

**2** = lowly, poor, mean, simple, ordinary, modest, obscure, undistinguished ≠ distinguished

● VERB = humiliate, disgrace, crush, subdue, chasten, put (someone) in their place, take down a peg (*informal*) ≠ exalt

**humidity** = damp, moisture, dampness, wetness, moistness, dankness, clamminess, mugginess

**humiliate** = embarrass, shame, humble, crush, put down, degrade, chasten, mortify ≠ honour

**humiliating** = embarrassing, shaming, humbling, mortifying, crushing, degrading, ignominious, barro (*Austral. slang*)

**humiliation** = embarrassment, shame, disgrace, humbling, put-down, degradation, indignity, ignominy

**humorous** = funny, comic, amusing, entertaining, witty, comical, droll, jocular ≠ serious

**humour** NOUN **1** = comedy, funniness, fun, amusement, funny side, jocularity, facetiousness, ludicrousness ≠ seriousness

**2** = mood, spirits, temper, disposition, frame of mind

**3** = joking, comedy, wit, farce, jesting, wisecracks (*informal*), witticisms

● VERB = indulge, accommodate, go along with, flatter, gratify,

pander to, mollify ≠ oppose

**hunch** NOUN = feeling, idea, impression, suspicion, intuition, premonition, inkling, presentiment

● VERB = crouch, bend, curve, arch, draw in

**hunger** NOUN **1** = appetite, emptiness, hungriness, ravenousness **2** = starvation, famine, malnutrition, undernourishment **3** = desire, appetite, craving, ache, lust, yearning, itch, thirst

● PHRASES **hunger for** or **after something** = want, desire, crave, long for, wish for, yearn for, hanker after, ache for

**hungry 1** = starving, ravenous, famished, starved, empty, voracious, peckish (*informal*, *chiefly Brit.*) **2** = eager, keen, craving, yearning, greedy, avid, desirous, covetous

**hunk** = lump, piece, chunk, block, mass, wedge, slab, nugget

**hunt** VERB = stalk, track, chase, pursue, trail, hound

● NOUN = search, hunting, investigation, chase, pursuit, quest

● PHRASES **hunt for something** or **someone** = search for, look for, seek for, forage for, scour for, fossick for (*Austral. & N.Z.*), ferret about for

**hurdle 1** = obstacle, difficulty, barrier, handicap, hazard, uphill

(S. African), obstruction, stumbling block **2** = fence, barrier, barricade

**hurl** = throw, fling, launch, cast, pitch, toss, propel, sling

**hurricane** = storm, gale, tornado, cyclone, typhoon, tempest, twister (U.S. informal), willy-willy (Austral.)

**hurried 1** = hasty, quick, brief, rushed, short, swift, speedy **2** = rushed, perfunctory, speedy, hasty, cursory

**hurry** VERB **1** = rush, fly, dash, scurry, scoot ≠ dawdle **2** = make haste, rush, get a move on (informal), step on it (informal)

● NOUN = rush, haste, speed, urgency, flurry, quickness ≠ slowness

**hurt** VERB **1** = injure, damage, wound, cut, disable, bruise, scrape, impair ≠ heal **2** = ache, be sore, be painful, burn, smart, sting, throb, be tender **3** = harm, injure, ill-treat, maltreat **4** = upset, distress, pain, wound, annoy, grieve, sadden

● NOUN = distress, suffering, pain, grief, misery, sorrow, heartache, wretchedness ≠ happiness

● ADJECTIVE **1** = injured, wounded, damaged, harmed, cut, bruised, scarred ≠ healed **2** = upset, wounded, crushed, offended, aggrieved, tooshie (Austral. slang) ≠ calmed

**hurtle** = rush, charge, race, shoot, fly, speed, tear, crash

**husband** NOUN = partner, spouse, mate, better half (humorous)

● VERB = conserve, budget, save, store, hoard, economize on, use economically ≠ squander

**hush** VERB = quieten, silence, mute, muzzle, shush

● NOUN = quiet, silence, calm, peace, tranquillity, stillness

**hut 1** = cabin, shack, shanty, hovel, whare (N.Z.) **2** = shed, outhouse, lean-to, lockup

**hybrid 1** = crossbreed, cross, mixture, compound, composite, amalgam, mongrel, half-breed **2** = mixture, compound, composite, amalgam

**hygiene** = cleanliness, sanitation, disinfection, sterility

**hymn 1** = religious song, song of praise, carol, chant, anthem, psalm, paean **2** = song of praise, anthem, paean

**hype** (Slang) = publicity, promotion, plugging (informal), razzmatazz (slang), brouhaha, ballyhoo (informal)

**hypocrisy** = insincerity, pretence, deception, cant, duplicity, deceitfulness ≠ sincerity

**hypothesis** = theory, premise, proposition, assumption, thesis, postulate, supposition

**hysteria** 1 = <u>frenzy</u>, panic, madness, agitation, delirium, hysterics

**hysterical** 1 = <u>frenzied</u>, frantic, raving, distracted, distraught, crazed, overwrought, berko (*Austral. slang*) ≠ calm 2 (*Informal*) = <u>hilarious</u>, uproarious, side-splitting, comical ≠ serious

# I

**icy** 1 = <u>cold</u>, freezing, bitter, biting, raw, chill, chilly, frosty ≠ hot 2 = <u>slippery</u>, glassy, slippy (*informal* or *dialect*), like a sheet of glass 3 = <u>unfriendly</u>, cold, distant, aloof, frosty, frigid, unwelcoming ≠ friendly

**idea** 1 = <u>notion</u>, thought, view, teaching, opinion, belief, conclusion, hypothesis 2 = <u>understanding</u>, thought, view, opinion, concept, impression, perception 3 = <u>intention</u>, aim, purpose, object, plan, objective

---

> ## Word Power
>
> **idea** – It is usually considered correct to say that someone has the *idea of doing something*, rather than *the idea to do something*. For example, you would say *he had the idea of taking a holiday*, not *he had the idea to take a holiday*.

---

**ideal** NOUN 1 = <u>epitome</u>, standard, dream, pattern, perfection, last word, paragon 2 = <u>model</u>, prototype, paradigm ● ADJECTIVE = <u>perfect</u>, best, model, classic, supreme, ultimate, archetypal, exemplary ≠ imperfect

**ideally** = <u>in a perfect world</u>, all things being equal, if you had your way

**identical** = <u>alike</u>, matching, twin, duplicate, indistinguishable, interchangeable ≠ different

**identification** 1 = <u>discovery</u>, recognition, determining, establishment, diagnosis, confirmation, divination 2 = <u>recognition</u>, naming, distinguishing, confirmation, pinpointing 3 = <u>connection</u>, relationship, association 4 = <u>understanding</u>, relationship, involvement, unity, sympathy, empathy, rapport, fellow feeling

**identify** VERB 1 = <u>recognize</u>, place, name, remember, spot, diagnose, make out, pinpoint 2 = <u>establish</u>, spot, confirm, demonstrate, pick out, certify, verify, mark out ● PHRASES **identify something or someone with something or someone** = <u>equate with</u>, associate with ◆ **identify with someone** = <u>relate to</u>, respond to, feel for, empathize with

**identity** = individuality, self, character, personality, existence, originality, separateness

**idiot** = fool, moron, twit (*informal, chiefly Brit.*), chump, imbecile, cretin, simpleton, halfwit, galah (*Austral. & N.Z. informal*), dorba or dorb (*Austral. slang*), bogan (*Austral. slang*)

**idle** ADJECTIVE **1** = unoccupied, unemployed, redundant, inactive ≠ occupied **2** = unused, inactive, out of order, out of service **3** = lazy, slow, slack, sluggish, lax, negligent, inactive, inert ≠ busy **4** = useless, vain, pointless, unsuccessful, ineffective, worthless, futile, fruitless ≠ useful
● VERB *often with away* = fritter, lounge, potter, loaf, dally, loiter, dawdle, laze

**idol 1** = hero, pin-up, favourite, pet, darling, beloved (*slang*), fave (*informal*) **2** = graven image, god, deity

**if 1** = provided, assuming, given that, providing, supposing, presuming, on condition that, as long as **2** = when, whenever, every time, any time

**ignite 1** = catch fire, burn, burst into flames, inflame, flare up, take fire **2** = set fire to, light, set alight, torch, kindle

**ignorance 1** = lack of education, stupidity, foolishness ≠ knowledge **2** *with of*

= unawareness of, inexperience of, unfamiliarity with, innocence of, unconsciousness of

**ignorant 1** = uneducated, illiterate ≠ educated **2** = insensitive, rude, crass **3** *with of* = uninformed of, unaware of, oblivious to, innocent of, unconscious of, inexperienced of, uninitiated about, unenlightened about ≠ informed

**ignore 1** = pay no attention to, neglect, disregard, slight, overlook, scorn, spurn, rebuff ≠ pay attention to **2** = overlook, discount, disregard, reject, neglect, shrug off, pass over, brush aside **3** = snub, slight, rebuff

**ill** ADJECTIVE **1** = unwell, sick, poorly (*informal*), diseased, weak, crook (*Austral. & N.Z. slang*), ailing, frail ≠ healthy **2** = harmful, bad, damaging, evil, foul, unfortunate, destructive, detrimental ≠ favourable
● NOUN = problem, trouble, suffering, worry, injury, hurt, strain, harm ≠ good
● ADVERB **1** = badly, unfortunately, unfavourably, inauspiciously **2** = hardly, barely, scarcely, just, only just, by no means, at a push ≠ well

**illegal** = unlawful, banned, forbidden, prohibited, criminal, outlawed, illicit, unlicensed ≠ legal

**illicit** 1 = illegal, criminal, prohibited, unlawful, illegitimate, unlicensed, unauthorized, felonious ≠ legal 2 = forbidden, improper, immoral, guilty, clandestine, furtive

**illness** = sickness, disease, infection, disorder, bug (*informal*), ailment, affliction, malady

**illuminate** 1 = light up, brighten ≠ darken 2 = explain, interpret, make clear, clarify, clear up, enlighten, shed light on, elucidate ≠ obscure

**illuminating** = informative, revealing, enlightening, helpful, explanatory, instructive ≠ confusing

**illusion** 1 = delusion, misconception, misapprehension, fancy, fallacy, false impression, false belief 2 = false impression, appearance, impression, deception, fallacy ≠ reality 3 = fantasy, vision, hallucination, trick, spectre, mirage, daydream, apparition

**illustrate** 1 = demonstrate, emphasize 2 = explain, sum up, summarize, bring home, point up, elucidate

**illustrated** = pictured, decorated, pictorial

**illustration** 1 = example, case, instance, sample, specimen, exemplar 2 = picture, drawing,

painting, image, print, plate, figure, portrait

**image** 1 = thought, idea, vision, concept, impression, perception, mental picture, conceptualization 2 = figure of speech 3 = reflection, likeness, mirror image 4 = figure, idol, icon, fetish, talisman 5 = replica, copy, reproduction, counterpart, clone, facsimile, spitting image (*informal*), Doppelgänger 6 = picture, photo, photograph, representation, reproduction, snapshot

**imaginary** = fictional, made-up, invented, imagined, unreal, hypothetical, fictitious, illusory ≠ real

**imagination** 1 = creativity, vision, invention, ingenuity, enterprise, originality, inventiveness, resourcefulness 2 = mind's eye, fancy

**imaginative** = creative, original, inspired, enterprising, clever, ingenious, inventive ≠ unimaginative

**imagine** 1 = envisage, see, picture, plan, think of, conjure up, envision, visualize 2 = believe, think, suppose, assume, suspect, guess (*informal, chiefly U.S. & Canad.*), take it, reckon

**imitate** 1 = copy, follow, repeat, echo, emulate, ape, simulate, mirror 2 = do an impression of, mimic, copy

**imitation** NOUN ¹ = <u>replica</u>, fake, reproduction, sham, forgery, counterfeiting, likeness, duplication ² = <u>copying</u>, resemblance, mimicry ³ = <u>impression</u>, impersonation
● ADJECTIVE = <u>artificial</u>, mock, reproduction, dummy, synthetic, man-made, simulated, sham ≠ real

**immaculate** ¹ = <u>clean</u>, spotless, neat, spruce, squeaky-clean, spick-and-span ≠ dirty ² = <u>pure</u>, perfect, impeccable, flawless, faultless, above reproach ≠ corrupt ³ = <u>perfect</u>, flawless, impeccable, faultless, unblemished, untarnished, unexceptionable ≠ tainted

**immediate** ¹ = <u>instant</u>, prompt, instantaneous, quick, on-the-spot, split-second ≠ later ² = <u>nearest</u>, next, direct, close, near ≠ far

**immediately** = <u>at once</u>, now, instantly, straight away, directly, promptly, right away, without delay

**immense** = <u>huge</u>, great, massive, vast, enormous, extensive, tremendous, very big ≠ tiny

**immerse** ¹ = <u>engross</u>, involve, absorb, busy, occupy, engage ² = <u>plunge</u>, dip, submerge, sink, duck, bathe, douse, dunk

**immigrant** = <u>settler</u>, incomer, alien, stranger, outsider, newcomer, migrant, emigrant

**imminent** = <u>near</u>, coming, close, approaching, gathering, forthcoming, looming, impending ≠ remote

**immoral** = <u>wicked</u>, bad, wrong, corrupt, indecent, sinful, unethical, depraved ≠ moral

**immortal** ADJECTIVE ¹ = <u>timeless</u>, eternal, everlasting, lasting, traditional, classic, enduring, perennial ≠ ephemeral ² = <u>undying</u>, eternal, imperishable, deathless ≠ mortal
● NOUN ¹ = <u>hero</u>, genius, great ² = <u>god</u>, goddess, deity, divine being, immortal being, atua (N.Z.)

**immune**
● PHRASES **immune from** = exempt from, free from
♦ **Immune to** ¹ = <u>resistant to</u>, free from, protected from, safe from, not open to, spared from, secure against, invulnerable to ² = <u>unaffected by</u>, invulnerable to

**immunity** ¹ = <u>exemption</u>, amnesty, indemnity, release, freedom, invulnerability ² with to = <u>resistance to</u>, protection from, resilience to, inoculation against, immunization from ≠ susceptibility to

**impact** NOUN ¹ = <u>effect</u>, influence, consequences, impression, repercussions,

# impair → imply

ramifications 2 = <u>collision</u>,
contact, crash, knock, stroke,
smash, bump, thump

● **VERB** = <u>hit</u>, strike, crash, clash,
crush, ram, smack, collide

**impair** = <u>worsen</u>, reduce,
damage, injure, harm, undermine,
weaken, diminish ≠ improve

**impaired** = <u>damaged</u>, flawed,
faulty, defective, imperfect,
unsound

**impasse** = <u>deadlock</u>, stalemate,
standstill, dead end, standoff

**impatient** 1 = <u>cross</u>, annoyed,
irritated, prickly, touchy, bad-
tempered, intolerant, ill-
tempered ≠ easy-going
2 = <u>eager</u>, longing, keen, anxious,
hungry, enthusiastic, restless, avid
≠ calm

**impeccable** = <u>faultless</u>, perfect,
immaculate, flawless, squeaky-
clean, unblemished,
unimpeachable, irreproachable
≠ flawed

**impending** = <u>looming</u>, coming,
approaching, near, forthcoming,
imminent, upcoming, in the
pipeline

**imperative** = <u>urgent</u>, essential,
pressing, vital, crucial
≠ unnecessary

**imperial** = <u>royal</u>, regal, kingly,
queenly, princely, sovereign,
majestic, monarchial

**impetus** 1 = <u>incentive</u>, push,
spur, motivation, impulse,

stimulus, catalyst, goad 2 = <u>force</u>,
power, energy, momentum

**implant** 1 = <u>insert</u>, fix, graft
2 = <u>instil</u>, infuse, inculcate

**implement** **VERB** = <u>carry out</u>,
effect, carry through, complete,
apply, perform, realize, fulfil
≠ hinder

● **NOUN** = <u>tool</u>, machine, device,
instrument, appliance, apparatus,
gadget, utensil

**implicate** **VERB** = <u>incriminate</u>,
involve, embroil, entangle,
inculpate ≠ dissociate

● **PHRASES implicate
something** or **someone in
something** = <u>involve in</u>,
associate with

**implication** **NOUN** = <u>suggestion</u>,
hint, inference, meaning,
significance, presumption,
overtone, innuendo

● **PLURAL NOUN** = <u>consequences</u>,
result, developments, upshot

**implicit** 1 = <u>implied</u>,
understood, suggested, hinted at,
taken for granted, unspoken,
inferred, tacit ≠ explicit
2 = <u>inherent</u>, underlying, intrinsic,
latent, ingrained, inbuilt
3 = <u>absolute</u>, full, complete, firm,
fixed, constant, utter, outright

**implied** = <u>suggested</u>, indirect,
hinted at, implicit, unspoken,
tacit, undeclared, unstated

**imply** 1 = <u>suggest</u>, hint, insinuate,
indicate, intimate, signify

**²** = <u>involve</u>, mean, entail, require, indicate, point to, signify, presuppose

**import** VERB = <u>bring in</u>, buy in, ship in, introduce

● **NOUN** **¹** (*Formal*) = <u>significance</u>, concern, value, weight, consequence, substance, moment, magnitude

**²** = <u>meaning</u>, implication, significance, sense, intention, substance, drift, thrust

**importance** **¹** = <u>significance</u>, interest, concern, moment, value, weight, import, consequence

**²** = <u>prestige</u>, standing, status, rule, authority, influence, distinction, esteem, mana (*N.Z.*)

**important** **¹** = <u>significant</u>, critical, substantial, urgent, serious, far-reaching, momentous, seminal ≠ unimportant

**²** = <u>powerful</u>, prominent, commanding, dominant, influential, eminent, high-ranking, authoritative

**impose**

● **PHRASES** **impose something on** *or* **upon someone** **¹** = <u>levy</u>, introduce, charge, establish, fix, institute, decree, ordain

**²** = <u>inflict</u>, force, enforce, visit, press, apply, thrust, saddle (someone) with

**imposing** = <u>impressive</u>, striking, grand, powerful, commanding, awesome, majestic, dignified ≠ unimposing

**imposition** **¹** = <u>application</u>, introduction, levying

**²** = <u>intrusion</u>, liberty, presumption

**impossible** **¹** = <u>not possible</u>, out of the question, impracticable, unfeasible

**²** = <u>unachievable</u>, out of the question, vain, unthinkable, inconceivable, far-fetched, unworkable, implausible ≠ possible **³** = <u>absurd</u>, crazy (*informal*), ridiculous, outrageous, ludicrous, unreasonable, preposterous, farcical

**impotence** = <u>powerlessness</u>, inability, helplessness, weakness, incompetence, paralysis, frailty, incapacity ≠ powerfulness

**impoverish** **¹** = <u>bankrupt</u>, ruin, beggar, break **²** = <u>deplete</u>, drain, exhaust, diminish, use up, sap, wear out, reduce

**impoverished** = <u>poor</u>, needy, destitute, bankrupt, poverty-stricken, impecunious, penurious ≠ rich

**impress** VERB = <u>excite</u>, move, strike, touch, affect, inspire, amaze, overcome

● **PHRASES** **impress something on** *or* **upon someone** = <u>stress</u>, bring home to, instil in, drum into, knock into, emphasize to, fix in, inculcate in

**impression** **¹** = <u>idea</u>, feeling,

thought, sense, view, assessment, judgment, reaction 2 = <u>effect</u>, influence, impact 3 = <u>imitation</u>, parody, impersonation, send-up (*Brit. informal*), takeoff (*informal*) 4 = <u>mark</u>, imprint, stamp, outline, hollow, dent, indentation

**impressive** = <u>grand</u>, striking, splendid, good, great (*informal*), fine, powerful, exciting ≠ unimpressive

**imprint** NOUN = <u>mark</u>, impression, stamp, indentation
● VERB = <u>engrave</u>, print, stamp, impress, etch, emboss

**imprison** = <u>jail</u>, confine, detain, lock up, put away, intern, incarcerate, send down (*informal*) ≠ free

**imprisoned** = <u>jailed</u>, confined, locked up, inside (*slang*), in jail, captive, behind bars, incarcerated

**imprisonment** = <u>confinement</u>, custody, detention, captivity, incarceration

**improbable** 1 = <u>doubtful</u>, unlikely, dubious, questionable, fanciful, far-fetched, implausible ≠ probable 2 = <u>unconvincing</u>, weak, unbelievable, preposterous ≠ convincing

**improper** 1 = <u>inappropriate</u>, unfit, unsuitable, out of place, unwarranted, uncalled-for ≠ appropriate 2 = <u>indecent</u>, vulgar, suggestive, unseemly, untoward, risqué, smutty, unbecoming ≠ decent

**improve** 1 = <u>enhance</u>, better, add to, upgrade, touch up, ameliorate ≠ worsen 2 = <u>get better</u>, pick up, develop, advance

**improvement**
1 = <u>enhancement</u>, advancement, betterment 2 = <u>advance</u>, development, progress, recovery, upswing

**improvise** 1 = <u>devise</u>, contrive, concoct, throw together 2 = <u>ad-lib</u>, invent, busk, wing it (*informal*), play it by ear (*informal*), extemporize, speak off the cuff (*informal*)

**impulse** = <u>urge</u>, longing, wish, notion, yearning, inclination, itch, whim

**inaccurate** = <u>incorrect</u>, wrong, mistaken, faulty, unreliable, defective, erroneous, unsound ≠ accurate

**inadequacy** 1 = <u>shortage</u>, poverty, dearth, paucity, insufficiency, meagreness, scantiness 2 = <u>incompetence</u>, inability, deficiency, incapacity, ineffectiveness 3 = <u>shortcoming</u>, failing, weakness, defect, imperfection

**inadequate** 1 = <u>insufficient</u>, meagre, poor, lacking, scant, sparse, sketchy ≠ adequate 2 = <u>incapable</u>, incompetent, faulty, deficient, unqualified, not up to scratch (*informal*)

≠ capable

**inadvertently**
= unintentionally, accidentally, by accident, mistakenly, unwittingly, by mistake, involuntarily ≠ deliberately

**inaugural** = first, opening, initial, maiden, introductory

**incarnation** = embodiment, manifestation, epitome, type, personification

**incense** = anger, infuriate, enrage, irritate, madden, inflame, rile (informal), make your blood boil (informal)

**incensed** = angry, furious, fuming, infuriated, enraged, maddened, indignant, irate, tooshie (Austral. slang), off the air (Austral. slang)

**incentive** = inducement, encouragement, spur, lure, bait, motivation, carrot (informal), stimulus ≠ disincentive

**incident** 1 = disturbance, scene, clash, disorder, confrontation, brawl, fracas, commotion 2 = adventure, drama, excitement, crisis, spectacle 3 = happening, event, affair, business, fact, matter, occasion, episode

**incidentally** = by the way, in passing, en passant, parenthetically, by the bye

**inclination** 1 = desire, longing, aspiration, craving, hankering

2 = tendency, liking, disposition, penchant, propensity, predisposition, predilection, proclivity ≠ aversion

**incline** VERB = predispose, influence, persuade, prejudice, sway, dispose
● NOUN = slope, rise, dip, grade, descent, ascent, gradient

**inclined** 1 = disposed, given, prone, likely, liable, apt, predisposed 2 = willing, minded, disposed

**include** 1 = contain, involve, incorporate, cover, consist of, take in, embrace, comprise ≠ exclude 2 = count 3 = add, enter, put in, insert

**inclusion** = addition, incorporation, introduction, insertion ≠ exclusion

**inclusive** = comprehensive, general, global, sweeping, blanket, umbrella, across-the-board, all-embracing ≠ limited

**income** = revenue, earnings, pay, returns, profits, wages, yield, proceeds

**incoming** 1 = arriving, landing, approaching, entering, returning, homeward ≠ departing 2 = new

**incompatible** = inconsistent, conflicting, contradictory, incongruous, unsuited, mismatched ≠ compatible

**incompetence** = ineptitude, inability, inadequacy, incapacity,

ineffectiveness, uselessness, unfitness, incapability
**incompetent** = _inept_, useless, incapable, floundering, bungling, unfit, ineffectual, inexpert ≠ competent
**incomplete** = _unfinished_, partial, wanting, deficient, imperfect, fragmentary, half-pie (_N.Z. informal_) ≠ complete
**inconsistency** 1 = _unreliability_, instability, unpredictability, fickleness, unsteadiness 2 = _incompatibility_, discrepancy, disparity, disagreement, variance, divergence, incongruity
**inconsistent** 1 = _changeable_, variable, unpredictable, unstable, erratic, fickle, capricious, unsteady ≠ consistent 2 = _incompatible_, conflicting, at odds, contradictory, incongruous, discordant, out of step, irreconcilable ≠ compatible
**inconvenience** NOUN = _trouble_, difficulty, bother, fuss, disadvantage, disturbance, disruption, nuisance, uphill (_S. African_)
• VERB = _trouble_, bother, disturb, upset, disrupt, put out, discommode
**incorporate** 1 = _include_, contain, take in, embrace, integrate, encompass, assimilate, comprise of 2 = _integrate_, include, absorb, merge, fuse,

assimilate, subsume 3 = _blend_, combine, compound, mingle
**incorrect** = _false_, wrong, mistaken, flawed, faulty, inaccurate, untrue, erroneous ≠ correct
**increase** VERB = _raise_, extend, boost, expand, develop, advance, strengthen, widen ≠ decrease 2 = _grow_, develop, spread, expand, swell, enlarge, escalate, multiply ≠ shrink
• NOUN = _growth_, rise, development, gain, expansion, extension, proliferation, enlargement
**increasingly** = _progressively_, more and more
**incredible** 1 (_Informal_) = _amazing_, wonderful, stunning, extraordinary, overwhelming, astonishing, staggering, sensational (_informal_) 2 = _unbelievable_, unthinkable, improbable, inconceivable, preposterous, unconvincing, unimaginable, far-fetched
**incumbent** NOUN = _holder_, keeper, bearer
• ADJECTIVE (_Formal_) = _obligatory_, required, necessary, essential, binding, compulsory, mandatory, imperative
**incur** = _sustain_, experience, suffer, gain, earn, collect, meet with, provoke
**indecent** 1 = _obscene_, lewd,

dirty, inappropriate, rude, crude, filthy, improper ≠ decent 2 = underlineunbecoming, unsuitable, vulgar, unseemly, undignified, indecorous ≠ proper

**indeed** 1 = <u>certainly</u>, yes, definitely, surely, truly, undoubtedly, without doubt, indisputably 2 = <u>really</u>, actually, in fact, certainly, genuinely, in truth, in actuality

**indefinitely** = <u>endlessly</u>, continually, for ever, ad infinitum

**independence** = <u>freedom</u>, liberty, autonomy, sovereignty, self-rule, self-sufficiency, self-reliance, rangatiratanga (*N.Z.*) ≠ subjugation

**independent** 1 = <u>separate</u>, unattached, uncontrolled, unconstrained ≠ controlled 2 = <u>self-sufficient</u>, free, liberated, self-contained, self-reliant, self-supporting 3 = <u>self-governing</u>, free, autonomous, liberated, sovereign, self-determining, nonaligned ≠ subject

**independently** = <u>separately</u>, alone, solo, on your own, by yourself, unaided, individually, autonomously

**indicate** 1 = <u>show</u>, suggest, reveal, display, demonstrate, point to, imply, manifest 2 = <u>imply</u>, suggest, hint, intimate, signify, insinuate 3 = <u>point to</u>, point out, specify, gesture

towards, designate 4 = <u>register</u>, show, record, read, express, display, demonstrate

**indication** = <u>sign</u>, mark, evidence, suggestion, symptom, hint, clue, manifestation

**indicator** = <u>sign</u>, mark, measure, guide, signal, symbol, meter, gauge

**indict** = <u>charge</u>, accuse, prosecute, summon, impeach, arraign

**indictment** = <u>charge</u>, allegation, prosecution, accusation, impeachment, summons, arraignment

**indifference** = <u>disregard</u>, apathy, negligence, detachment, coolness, coldness, nonchalance, aloofness ≠ concern

**indifferent** 1 = <u>unconcerned</u>, detached, cold, cool, callous, aloof, unmoved, unsympathetic ≠ concerned 2 = <u>mediocre</u>, ordinary, moderate, so-so (*informal*), passable, undistinguished, no great shakes (*informal*), half-pie (*N.Z. informal*) ≠ excellent

**indignation** = <u>resentment</u>, anger, rage, exasperation, pique, umbrage

**indirect** 1 = <u>related</u>, secondary, subsidiary, incidental, unintended 2 = <u>circuitous</u>, roundabout, curving, wandering, rambling, deviant, meandering, tortuous

≠ direct

**indispensable** = essential, necessary, needed, key, vital, crucial, imperative, requisite
≠ dispensable

**individual** ADJECTIVE
1 = separate, independent, isolated, lone, solitary ≠ collective
2 = unique, special, fresh, novel, exclusive, singular, idiosyncratic, unorthodox ≠ conventional
● NOUN = person, being, human, unit, character, soul, creature

**individually** = separately, independently, singly, one by one, one at a time

**induce** 1 = cause, produce, create, effect, lead to, occasion, generate, bring about ≠ prevent
2 = persuade, encourage, influence, convince, urge, prompt, sway, entice ≠ dissuade

**indulge** VERB 1 = gratify, satisfy, feed, give way to, pander to, gladden 2 = spoil, pamper, cosset, humour, give in to, coddle, mollycoddle, overindulge
● PHRASES **indulge yourself** = treat yourself, splash out, spoil yourself, luxuriate in something, overindulge yourself

**indulgence** 1 = luxury, treat, extravagance, favour, privilege
2 = gratification, satisfaction, fulfilment, appeasement, satiation

**industrialist** = capitalist, tycoon, magnate, manufacturer, captain of industry, big businessman

**industry** 1 = business, production, manufacturing, trade, commerce 2 = trade, world, business, service, line, field, profession, occupation
3 = diligence, effort, labour, hard work, trouble, activity, application, endeavour

**ineffective** 1 = unproductive, useless, futile, vain, unsuccessful, pointless, fruitless, ineffectual
≠ effective 2 = inefficient, useless, poor, powerless, unfit, worthless, inept, impotent

**inefficient** 1 = wasteful, uneconomical, profligate
2 = incompetent, inept, weak, bungling, ineffectual, disorganized ≠ efficient

**inequality** = disparity, prejudice, difference, bias, diversity, irregularity, unevenness, disproportion

**inevitable** = unavoidable, inescapable, inexorable, sure, certain, fixed, assured, fated
≠ avoidable

**inevitably** = unavoidably, naturally, necessarily, surely, certainly, as a result, automatically, consequently

**inexpensive** = cheap, reasonable, budget, bargain, modest, economical ≠ expensive

**inexperienced** = <u>new</u>, green, raw, callow, immature, untried, unpractised, unversed ≠ experienced

**infamous** = <u>notorious</u>, ignominious, disreputable, ill-famed ≠ esteemed

**infancy** = <u>beginnings</u>, start, birth, roots, seeds, origins, dawn, outset ≠ end

**infant** = <u>baby</u>, child, babe, toddler, tot, bairn (*Scot.*), littlie (*Austral. informal*), ankle-biter (*Austral. slang*), tacker (*Austral. slang*)

**infect** 1 = <u>contaminate</u>
2 = <u>pollute</u>, poison, corrupt, contaminate, taint, defile
3 = <u>affect</u>, move, upset, overcome, stir, disturb

**infection** = <u>disease</u>, condition, complaint, illness, virus, disorder, corruption, poison

**infectious** = <u>catching</u>, spreading, contagious, communicable, virulent, transmittable

**inferior** ADJECTIVE = <u>lower</u>, minor, secondary, subsidiary, lesser, humble, subordinate, lowly ≠ superior
● NOUN = <u>underling</u>, junior, subordinate, lesser, menial, minion

**infertility** = <u>sterility</u>, barrenness, unproductiveness, infecundity

**infiltrate** = <u>penetrate</u>, pervade, permeate, percolate, filter through to, make inroads into, sneak into (*informal*), insinuate yourself

**infinite** 1 = <u>vast</u>, enormous, immense, countless, measureless
2 = <u>limitless</u>, endless, unlimited, eternal, never-ending, boundless, everlasting, inexhaustible ≠ finite

**inflame** = <u>enrage</u>, stimulate, provoke, excite, anger, arouse, rouse, infuriate ≠ calm

**inflamed** = <u>swollen</u>, sore, red, hot, infected, fevered

**inflate** 1 = <u>blow up</u>, pump up, swell, dilate, distend, bloat, puff up or out ≠ deflate 2 = <u>increase</u>, expand, enlarge ≠ diminish
3 = <u>exaggerate</u>, embroider, embellish, enlarge, amplify, overstate, overestimate, overemphasize

**inflated** = <u>exaggerated</u>, swollen, overblown

**inflation** = <u>increase</u>, expansion, extension, swelling, escalation, enlargement

**inflict** = <u>impose</u>, administer, visit, apply, deliver, levy, wreak, mete or deal out

**influence** NOUN 1 = <u>control</u>, power, authority, direction, command, domination, supremacy, mastery, mana (*N.Z.*)
2 = <u>power</u>, authority, pull (*informal*), importance, prestige, clout (*informal*), leverage

$^3$ = spell, hold, power, weight, magic, sway, allure, magnetism
● VERB $^1$ = affect, have an effect on, have an impact on, control, concern, direct, guide, bear upon
$^2$ = persuade, prompt, urge, induce, entice, coax, incite, instigate
**influential** 1 = important, powerful, telling, leading, inspiring, potent, authoritative, weighty ≠ unimportant
$^2$ = instrumental, important, significant, crucial
**influx** = arrival, rush, invasion, incursion, inundation, inrush
**inform** VERB = tell, advise, notify, instruct, enlighten, communicate to, tip someone off
● PHRASES **inform on someone** = betray, denounce, shop (slang, chiefly Brit.), give someone away, incriminate, blow the whistle on (informal), grass on (Brit. slang), double-cross (informal), dob someone in (Austral. & N.Z. slang)
**informal** 1 = natural, relaxed, casual, familiar, unofficial, laid-back, easy-going, colloquial
$^2$ = relaxed, easy, comfortable, simple, natural, casual, cosy, laid-back (informal) ≠ formal
$^3$ = casual, comfortable, leisure, everyday, simple $^4$ = unofficial, irregular ≠ official
**information** = facts, news, report, message, notice,

knowledge, data, intelligence, drum (Austral. informal)
**informative** = instructive, revealing, educational, forthcoming, illuminating, enlightening, chatty, communicative
**informed** = knowledgeable, up to date, enlightened, learned, expert, familiar, versed, in the picture
**infuriate** = enrage, anger, provoke, irritate, incense, madden, exasperate, rile ≠ soothe
**infuriating** = annoying, irritating, provoking, galling, maddening, exasperating, vexatious
**ingenious** = creative, original, brilliant, clever, bright, shrewd, inventive, crafty ≠ unimaginative
**ingredient** = component, part, element, feature, piece, unit, item, aspect
**inhabit** = live in, occupy, populate, reside in, dwell in, abide in
**inhabitant** = occupant, resident, citizen, local, native, tenant, inmate, dweller
**inhabited** = populated, peopled, occupied, developed, settled, tenanted, colonized
**inhale** = breathe in, gasp, draw in, suck in, respire ≠ exhale
**inherent** = intrinsic, natural, essential, native, fundamental,

hereditary, instinctive, innate ≠ extraneous

**inherit** = be left, come into, be willed, succeed to, fall heir to

**inheritance** = legacy, heritage, bequest, birthright, patrimony

**inhibit** 1 = hinder, check, frustrate, curb, restrain, constrain, obstruct, impede ≠ further
2 = prevent, stop, frustrate ≠ allow

**inhibited** = shy, reserved, guarded, subdued, repressed, constrained, self-conscious, reticent ≠ uninhibited

**initial** = opening, first, earliest, beginning, primary, maiden, introductory, embryonic ≠ final

**initially** = at first, first, firstly, originally, primarily, in the beginning, at or in the beginning

**initiate** VERB 1 = begin, start, open, launch, kick off (informal), embark on, originate, set about
2 = introduce, admit, enlist, enrol, launch, establish, invest, recruit
● NOUN = novice, member, pupil, convert, amateur, newcomer, beginner, trainee
● PHRASES **initiate someone into something** = instruct in, train in, coach in, acquaint with, drill in, make aware of, teach about, tutor in

**initiative** 1 = advantage, start, lead, upper hand 2 = enterprise, drive, energy, leadership, ambition, daring, enthusiasm, dynamism

**inject** 1 = vaccinate, administer, inoculate 2 = introduce, bring in, insert, instil, infuse, breathe

**injection** 1 = vaccination, shot (informal), jab (informal), dose, booster, immunization, inoculation 2 = introduction, investment, insertion, advancement, dose, infusion

**injunction** = order, ruling, command, instruction, mandate, precept, exhortation

**injure** 1 = hurt, wound, harm, damage, smash, crush, mar, shatter, mangulate (Austral. slang)
2 = damage, harm, ruin, wreck, spoil, impair, crool or cruel (Austral. slang) 3 = undermine, damage

**injured** = hurt, damaged, wounded, broken, cut, crushed, disabled, weakened, crook (Austral. & N.Z. slang)

**injury** 1 = wound, cut, damage, trauma (Pathology), gash, lesion, laceration 2 = harm, suffering, damage, ill, hurt, disability, misfortune, affliction 3 = wrong, offence, insult, detriment, disservice

**injustice** 1 = unfairness, discrimination, prejudice, bias, inequality, oppression, intolerance, bigotry ≠ justice
2 = wrong, injury, crime, error,

offence, sin, misdeed, transgression

**inland** = interior, internal, upcountry

**inner** 1 = inside, internal, interior, inward ≠ outer 2 = central, middle, internal, interior 3 = hidden, deep, secret, underlying, obscure, repressed, unrevealed ≠ obvious

**innocence** 1 = naiveté, simplicity, inexperience, credulity, gullibility, ingenuousness, artlessness, unworldliness ≠ worldliness 2 = blamelessness, clean hands, uprightness, irreproachability, guiltlessness ≠ guilt 3 = chastity, virtue, purity, modesty, celibacy, continence, maidenhood

**innocent** 1 = not guilty, in the clear, blameless, clean, honest, uninvolved, irreproachable, guiltless ≠ guilty 2 = naive, open, trusting, simple, childlike, gullible, unsophisticated, unworldly ≠ worldly 3 = harmless, innocuous, inoffensive, well-meant, unobjectionable, well-intentioned

**innovation** 1 = change, revolution, departure, introduction, variation, transformation, upheaval, alteration 2 = newness, novelty, originality, freshness, modernization, uniqueness

**inquest** = inquiry, investigation, probe, inquisition

**inquire** or **enquire** VERB = ask, question, query, quiz ● PHRASES **inquire into something** = investigate, study, examine, research, explore, look into, probe into, make inquiries into

**inquiry** or **enquiry** 1 = question, query, investigation 2 = investigation, study, review, survey, examination, probe, inspection, exploration 3 = research, investigation, analysis, inspection, exploration, interrogation

**insane** 1 = mad, crazy, mentally ill, crazed, demented, deranged, out of your mind, off the air (Austral. slang), porangi (N.Z.) ≠ sane 2 = stupid, foolish, daft (informal), irresponsible, irrational, senseless, preposterous, impractical ≠ reasonable

**insect** = bug, creepy-crawly (Brit. informal), gogga (S. African informal) ➤ beetles ➤ butterflies and moths ➤ flies ➤ types of insect

**insecure** 1 = unconfident, worried, anxious, afraid, shy, uncertain, unsure, timid ≠ confident 2 = unsafe, exposed, vulnerable, wide-open,

---

### Types of insect

| | |
|---|---|
| body louse, cootie (*U.S. & N.Z.*), or (*N.Z. slang*) kutu | measuring worm, looper, or inchworm |
| bookworm | midge |
| caddis worm *or* caseworm | mosquito |
| cankerworm | nit |
| cochineal *or* cochineal insect | phylloxera |
| cockroach | scale insect |
| crab (*louse*) | silkworm |
| cricket | silverfish |
| earwig, *or* (*Scot. dialect*) clipshears, *or* clipshear | stick insect *or* (*U.S. & Canad.*) walking stick |
| flea | thrips |
| grasshopper | treehopper |
| katydid | weta (*N.Z.*) |
| locust | wireworm |
| louse *or* (*N.Z.*) kutu | woodworm |
| mantis *or* praying mantis | |

---

unprotected, defenceless, unguarded ≠ safe

**insecurity** = <u>anxiety</u>, fear, worry, uncertainty ≠ confidence

**insert** = <u>put</u>, place, position, slip, slide, slot, thrust, stick in

**inside** NOUN = <u>interior</u>, contents, core, nucleus

● PLURAL NOUN (*Informal*) = <u>stomach</u>, guts, belly, bowels, innards (*informal*), entrails, viscera, vitals

● ADJECTIVE 1 = <u>inner</u>, internal, interior, inward ≠ outside

2 = <u>confidential</u>, private, secret, internal, exclusive, restricted, privileged, classified

● ADVERB = <u>indoors</u>, in, within, under cover

**insight** 1 = <u>understanding</u>, perception, sense, knowledge, vision, judgment, awareness, grasp 2 *with* **into** = understanding of, perception of, awareness of, experience of, description of, introduction to, observation of, judgment of

**insignificant** = <u>unimportant</u>, minor, irrelevant, petty, trivial, meaningless, trifling, paltry ≠ important

**insist** 1 lay down the law, put your foot down (*informal*)

2 = <u>demand</u>, order, require, command, dictate, entreat

3 = <u>assert</u>, state, maintain, claim,

declare, repeat, vow, swear

**insistence** 1= <u>demand</u>, command, dictate, entreaty, importunity 2= <u>assertion</u>, claim, statement, declaration, persistence, pronouncement

**inspect** 1= <u>examine</u>, check, look at, view, survey, look over, scrutinize, go over or through 2= <u>check</u>, examine, investigate, look at, survey, vet, look over, go over or through

**inspection** 1= <u>examination</u>, investigation, scrutiny, once-over (*informal*) 2= <u>check</u>, search, investigation, review, survey, examination, scrutiny, once-over (*informal*)

**inspector** = <u>examiner</u>, investigator, supervisor, monitor, superintendent, auditor, censor, surveyor

**inspiration** 1= <u>imagination</u>, creativity, ingenuity, insight, originality, inventiveness, cleverness 2= <u>motivation</u>, example, model, boost, spur, incentive, revelation, stimulus ≠ deterrent 3= <u>influence</u>, spur, stimulus, muse

**inspire** 1= <u>motivate</u>, stimulate, encourage, influence, spur, animate, enliven, galvanize ≠ discourage 2= <u>give rise to</u>, produce, result in, engender

**inspired** 1= <u>brilliant</u>, wonderful, impressive, outstanding, thrilling, memorable, dazzling, superlative 2= <u>stimulated</u>, uplifted, exhilarated, enthused, elated

**inspiring** = <u>uplifting</u>, exciting, moving, stirring, stimulating, rousing, exhilarating, heartening ≠ uninspiring

**instability** 1= <u>uncertainty</u>, insecurity, vulnerability, volatility, unpredictability, fluctuation, impermanence, unsteadiness ≠ stability 2= <u>imbalance</u>, variability, unpredictability, unsteadiness, changeableness

**install** 1= <u>set up</u>, put in, place, position, station, establish, lay, fix 2= <u>institute</u>, establish, introduce, invest, ordain, inaugurate, induct 3= <u>settle</u>, position, plant, establish, lodge, ensconce

**installation** 1= <u>setting up</u>, fitting, instalment, placing, positioning, establishment 2= <u>appointment</u>, ordination, inauguration, induction, investiture

**instalment** 1= <u>payment</u>, repayment, part payment 2= <u>part</u>, section, chapter, episode, portion, division

**instance**NOUN = <u>example</u>, case, occurrence, occasion, sample, illustration

● VERB = <u>name</u>, mention, identify, point out, advance, quote, refer to, point to

**instant**NOUN 1= <u>moment</u>,

second, flash, split second, jiffy (*informal*), trice, twinkling of an eye (*informal*) 2 = <u>time</u>, point, hour, moment, stage, occasion, phase, juncture

● ADJECTIVE 1 = <u>immediate</u>, prompt, instantaneous, direct, quick, on-the-spot, split-second 2 = <u>ready-made</u>, fast, convenience, ready-mixed, ready-cooked, precooked

**instantly** = <u>immediately</u>, at once, straight away, now, directly, right away, instantaneously, this minute

**instead** ADVERB = <u>rather</u>, alternatively, preferably, in preference to, in lieu, on second thoughts

● PHRASES **instead of** = <u>in place of</u>, rather than, in preference to, in lieu of, in contrast with

**instinct** 1 = <u>natural inclination</u>, talent, tendency, faculty, inclination, knack, predisposition, proclivity 2 = <u>talent</u>, skill, gift, capacity, bent, genius, faculty, knack 3 = <u>intuition</u>, impulse

**instinctive** = <u>natural</u>, inborn, automatic, unconscious, inherent, spontaneous, reflex, innate ≠ acquired

**instinctively** = <u>intuitively</u>, naturally, automatically, without thinking, involuntarily, by instinct

**institute** NOUN = <u>establishment</u>, body, centre, school, university,

society, association, college

● VERB = <u>establish</u>, start, found, launch, set up, introduce, fix, organize ≠ end

**institution** 1 = <u>establishment</u>, body, centre, school, university, society, association, college 2 = <u>custom</u>, practice, tradition, law, rule, procedure, convention, ritual

**institutional** = <u>conventional</u>, accepted, established, formal, routine, orthodox, procedural

**instruct** 1 = <u>order</u>, tell, direct, charge, bid, command, mandate, enjoin 2 = <u>teach</u>, school, train, coach, educate, drill, tutor

**instruction** NOUN 1 = <u>order</u>, ruling, command, rule, demand, regulation, dictate, decree 2 = <u>teaching</u>, schooling, training, grounding, education, coaching, lesson(s), guidance

● PLURAL NOUN = <u>information</u>, rules, advice, directions, recommendations, guidance, specifications

**instructor** = <u>teacher</u>, coach, guide, adviser, trainer, demonstrator, tutor, mentor

**instrument** 1 = <u>tool</u>, device, implement, mechanism, appliance, apparatus, gadget, contraption (*informal*) 2 = <u>agent</u>, means, medium, agency, vehicle, mechanism, organ

**instrumental** = <u>active</u>,

involved, influential, useful, helpful, contributory

**insufficient** = inadequate, scant, meagre, short, sparse, deficient, lacking ≠ ample

**insulate** = isolate, protect, screen, defend, shelter, shield, cut off, cushion

**insult** VERB = offend, abuse, wound, slight, put down, snub, malign, affront ≠ praise
• NOUN 1 = jibe, slight, put-down, abuse, snub, barb, affront, abusive remark 2 = offence, slight, snub, slur, affront, slap in the face (*informal*), kick in the teeth (*informal*), insolence

**insulting** = offensive, rude, abusive, degrading, contemptuous, disparaging, scurrilous, insolent ≠ complimentary

**insurance** 1 = assurance, cover, security, protection, safeguard, indemnity 2 = protection, security, guarantee, shelter, safeguard, warranty

**insure** 1 = assure, cover, protect, guarantee, warrant, underwrite, indemnify 2 = protect, cover, safeguard

**intact** = undamaged, whole, complete, sound, perfect, entire, unscathed, unbroken ≠ damaged

**integral** = essential, basic, fundamental, necessary, component, constituent, indispensable, intrinsic ≠ inessential

**integrate** = join, unite, combine, blend, incorporate, merge, fuse, assimilate ≠ separate

**integrity** 1 = honesty, principle, honour, virtue, goodness, morality, purity, probity ≠ dishonesty 2 = unity, unification, cohesion, coherence, wholeness, soundness, completeness

**intellect** = intelligence, mind, reason, understanding, sense, brains (*informal*), judgment

**intellectual** ADJECTIVE = scholarly, learned, academic, lettered, intelligent, cerebral, erudite, scholastic ≠ stupid
• NOUN = academic, expert, genius, thinker, master, mastermind, maestro, highbrow, fundi (*S. African*), acca (*Austral. slang*) ≠ idiot

**intelligence** 1 = intellect, understanding, brains (*informal*), sense, knowledge, judgment, wit, perception ≠ stupidity 2 = information, news, facts, report, findings, knowledge, data, notification ≠ misinformation

**intelligent** = clever, bright, smart, sharp, enlightened, knowledgeable, well-informed, brainy (*informal*) ≠ stupid

**intend** = plan, mean, aim, propose, purpose, have in mind *or* view

**intense** 1 = <u>extreme</u>, great, severe, fierce, deep, powerful, supreme, acute ≠ mild 2 = <u>fierce</u>, tough 3 = <u>passionate</u>, emotional, fierce, heightened, ardent, fanatical, fervent, heartfelt ≠ indifferent

### Word Power

**intense** – *Intense* is sometimes wrongly used where *intensive* is meant: *the land is under intensive* (not *intense*) *cultivation. Intensely* is sometimes wrongly used where *intently* is meant: *he listened intently* (not *intensely*).

**intensify** 1 = <u>increase</u>, raise, add to, strengthen, reinforce, widen, heighten, sharpen ≠ decrease 2 = <u>escalate</u>, increase, widen, deepen

**intensity** 1 = <u>force</u>, strength, fierceness 2 = <u>passion</u>, emotion, fervour, force, strength, fanaticism, ardour, vehemence

**intensive** = <u>concentrated</u>, thorough, exhaustive, full, demanding, detailed, complete, serious

**intent** ADJECTIVE = <u>absorbed</u>, intense, fascinated, preoccupied, enthralled, attentive, watchful, engrossed ≠ indifferent

● NOUN = <u>intention</u>, aim, purpose,

meaning, end, plan, goal, design ≠ chance

**intention** = <u>aim</u>, plan, idea, goal, end, design, target, wish

**inter** = <u>bury</u>, lay to rest, entomb, consign to the grave

**intercept** = <u>catch</u>, stop, block, seize, cut off, interrupt, head off, obstruct

**intercourse** 1 = <u>sexual intercourse</u>, sex (*informal*), copulation, coitus, carnal knowledge 2 = <u>contact</u>, communication, commerce, dealings

**interest** NOUN 1 = <u>hobby</u>, activity, pursuit, entertainment, recreation, amusement, preoccupation, diversion 2 *often plural* = <u>advantage</u>, good, benefit, profit 3 = <u>stake</u>, investment

● VERB = <u>arouse your curiosity</u>, fascinate, attract, grip, entertain, intrigue, divert, captivate ≠ bore

**interested** 1 = <u>curious</u>, attracted, excited, drawn, keen, gripped, fascinated, captivated ≠ uninterested 2 = <u>involved</u>, concerned, affected, implicated

**interesting** = <u>intriguing</u>, absorbing, appealing, attractive, engaging, gripping, entrancing, stimulating ≠ uninteresting

**interface** = <u>connection</u>, link, boundary, border, frontier

**interfere** VERB = <u>meddle</u>,

intervene, intrude, butt in, tamper, pry, encroach, stick your oar in (*informal*)

● PHRASES **interfere with something** *or* **someone** = conflict with, check, clash, handicap, hamper, disrupt, inhibit, thwart

**interference** = intrusion, intervention, meddling, opposition, conflict, obstruction, prying

**interim** = temporary, provisional, makeshift, acting, caretaker, improvised, stopgap

**interior** NOUN = inside, centre, heart, middle, depths, core, nucleus

● ADJECTIVE 1 = inside, internal, inner ≠ exterior 2 = mental, emotional, psychological, private, personal, secret, hidden, spiritual

**intermediary** = mediator, agent, middleman, broker, go-between

**intermediate** = middle, mid, halfway, in-between (*informal*), midway, intervening, transitional, median

**internal** 1 = domestic, home, national, local, civic, in-house, intramural 2 = inner, inside, interior ≠ external

**international** = global, world, worldwide, universal, cosmopolitan, intercontinental

**Internet**
● PHRASES **the Internet** = the information superhighway, the net (*informal*), the web (*informal*), the World Wide Web, cyberspace

**interpret** 1 = take, understand, explain, construe 2 = translate, transliterate 3 = explain, make sense of, decode, decipher, elucidate 4 = understand, read, crack, solve, figure out (*informal*), comprehend, decode, deduce 5 = portray, present, perform, render, depict, enact, act out

**interpretation** 1 = explanation, analysis, exposition, elucidation 2 = performance, portrayal, presentation, reading, rendition 3 = reading, study, review, version, analysis, explanation, examination, evaluation

**interpreter** = translator

**interrogation** = questioning, inquiry, examination, grilling (*informal*), cross-examination, inquisition, third degree (*informal*)

**interrupt** 1 = intrude, disturb, intervene, interfere (with), break in, heckle, butt in, barge in (*informal*) 2 = suspend, stop, end, delay, cease, postpone, shelve, put off

**interruption** 1 = disruption, break, disturbance, hitch, intrusion 2 = stoppage, pause, suspension

**interval** 1 = <u>period</u>, spell, space, stretch, pause, span 2 = <u>break</u>, interlude, intermission, rest, gap, pause, respite, lull 3 = <u>delay</u>, gap, hold-up, stoppage 4 = <u>stretch</u>, space

**intervene** 1 = <u>step in</u> (*informal*), interfere, mediate, intrude, intercede, arbitrate, take a hand (*informal*) 2 = <u>interrupt</u>, involve yourself 3 = <u>happen</u>, occur, take place, follow, arise, ensue, befall, materialize

**intervention** = <u>mediation</u>, interference, intrusion, arbitration, conciliation, agency

**interview** NOUN 1 = <u>meeting</u> 2 = <u>audience</u>, talk, conference, exchange, dialogue, consultation, press conference

● VERB 1 = <u>examine</u>, talk to 2 = <u>question</u>, interrogate, examine, investigate, pump, grill (*informal*), quiz, cross-examine

**interviewer** = <u>questioner</u>, reporter, investigator, examiner, interrogator

**intimacy** = <u>familiarity</u>, closeness, confidentiality ≠ aloofness

**intimate¹** ADJECTIVE 1 = <u>close</u>, dear, loving, near, familiar, thick (*informal*), devoted, confidential ≠ distant 2 = <u>private</u>, personal, confidential, special, individual, secret, exclusive ≠ public 3 = <u>detailed</u>, minute, full, deep, particular, immediate,

comprehensive, profound 4 = <u>cosy</u>, relaxed, friendly, informal, harmonious, snug, comfy (*informal*), warm

● NOUN = <u>friend</u>, close friend, crony, cobber (*Austral. & N.Z. old-fashioned informal*), confidant *or* confidante, (constant) companion, E hoa (*N.Z.*) ≠ stranger

**intimate²** 1 = <u>suggest</u>, indicate, hint, imply, insinuate 2 = <u>announce</u>, state, declare, communicate, make known

**intimately** 1 = <u>closely</u>, personally, warmly, familiarly, tenderly, affectionately, confidentially, confidingly 2 = <u>fully</u>, very well, thoroughly, in detail, inside out

**intimidate** = <u>frighten</u>, pressure, threaten, scare, bully, plague, hound, daunt

**intimidation** = <u>bullying</u>, pressure, threat(s), menaces, coercion, arm-twisting (*informal*), browbeating, terrorization

**intricate** = <u>complicated</u>, involved, complex, fancy, elaborate, tangled, tortuous, convoluted ≠ simple

**intrigue** NOUN 1 = <u>plot</u>, scheme, conspiracy, manoeuvre, collusion, stratagem, chicanery, wile 2 = <u>affair</u>, romance, intimacy, liaison, amour

● VERB 1 = <u>interest</u>, fascinate,

attract, rivet, titillate 2 = plot,
scheme, manoeuvre, conspire,
connive, machinate

**intriguing** = interesting,
fascinating, absorbing, exciting,
engaging, gripping, stimulating,
compelling

**introduce** 1 = bring in,
establish, set up, start, found,
launch, institute, pioneer
2 = present, acquaint, make
known, familiarize 3 = suggest,
air, advance, submit, bring up, put
forward, broach, moot 4 = add,
insert, inject, throw in (informal),
infuse

**introduction** 1 = launch,
institution, pioneering,
inauguration ≠ elimination
2 = opening, prelude, preface,
lead-in, preamble, foreword,
prologue, intro (informal)
≠ conclusion

**introductory** 1 = preliminary,
first, initial, inaugural, preparatory
≠ concluding 2 = starting,
opening, initial

**intruder** = trespasser, invader,
prowler, interloper, infiltrator,
gate-crasher (informal)

**intrusion** 1 = interruption,
interference, infringement,
trespass, encroachment
2 = invasion, breach,
infringement, encroachment,
infraction, usurpation

**intuition** 1 = instinct,

perception, insight, sixth sense
2 = feeling, idea, impression,
suspicion, premonition, inkling,
presentiment

**invade** 1 = attack, storm, assault,
capture, occupy, seize, raid,
overwhelm 2 = infest, swarm,
overrun, ravage, beset, pervade,
permeate

**invader** = attacker, raider,
plunderer, aggressor, trespasser

**invalid**[1] NOUN = patient, sufferer,
convalescent, valetudinarian
● ADJECTIVE = disabled, ill, sick,
ailing, frail, infirm, bedridden

**invalid**[2] 1 = null and void, void,
worthless, inoperative ≠ valid
2 = unfounded, false, illogical,
irrational, unsound, fallacious
≠ sound

**invaluable** = precious, valuable,
priceless, inestimable, worth your
or its weight in gold ≠ worthless

**invariably** = always, regularly,
constantly, repeatedly,
consistently, continually,
eternally, habitually

**invasion** 1 = attack, assault,
capture, takeover, raid, offensive,
occupation, conquering
2 = intrusion, breach, violation,
disturbance, disruption,
infringement, encroachment,
infraction

**invent** 1 = create, make, produce,
design, discover, manufacture,
devise, conceive 2 = make up,

devise, concoct, forge, fake, fabricate, feign, falsify

**invention** 1 = <u>creation</u>, machine, device, design, instrument, discovery, innovation, gadget 2 = <u>development</u>, design, production, setting up, foundation, construction, creation, discovery 3 = <u>fiction</u>, fantasy, lie, yarn, fabrication, falsehood, untruth 4 = <u>creativity</u>, imagination, initiative, enterprise, genius, ingenuity, originality, inventiveness

**inventive** = <u>creative</u>, original, innovative, imaginative, inspired, fertile, ingenious, resourceful ≠ uninspired

**inventor** = <u>creator</u>, maker, author, designer, architect, coiner, originator

**inventory** = <u>list</u>, record, catalogue, listing, account, roll, file, register

**invertebrate** ➤ crustaceans ➤ snails, slugs and other gastropods ➤ spiders and other arachnids ➤ types of invertebrate

**invest** VERB 1 = <u>spend</u>, expend, advance, venture, put in, devote, lay out, sink in 2 = <u>empower</u>, provide, charge, sanction, license, authorize, vest

● PHRASES **invest in something** = <u>buy</u>, get, purchase, pay for, obtain, acquire, procure

**investigate** = <u>examine</u>, study, research, go into, explore, look into, inspect, probe into

**investigation** = <u>examination</u>, study, inquiry, review, search, survey, probe, inspection

**investigator** = <u>examiner</u>, researcher, monitor, detective, analyser, explorer, scrutinizer, inquirer

**investment** 1 = <u>investing</u>, backing, funding, financing, contribution, speculation, transaction, expenditure 2 = <u>stake</u>, interest, share, concern, portion, ante (*informal*) 3 = <u>buy</u>, asset, acquisition, venture, risk, gamble

**invisible** = <u>unseen</u>, imperceptible, indiscernible, unseeable ≠ visible

**invitation** = <u>request</u>, call, invite (*informal*), summons

**invite** 1 = <u>ask</u> 2 = <u>request</u>, look for, bid for, appeal for 3 = <u>encourage</u>, attract, cause, court, ask for (*informal*), generate, foster, tempt

**inviting** = <u>tempting</u>, appealing, attractive, welcoming, enticing, seductive, alluring, mouthwatering ≠ uninviting

**invoke** 1 = <u>apply</u>, implement, initiate, resort to, put into effect 2 = <u>call upon</u>, appeal to, pray to, petition, beseech, entreat, supplicate

# Types of invertebrate

amoeba or (U.S.) ameba
animalcule or animalculum
arthropod
bardy, bardie, or bardi (Austral.)
bivalve
blue-ringed octopus (Austral.)
Bluff oyster (N.Z.)
box jellyfish or (Austral.) sea wasp
brachiopod or lamp shell
brandling
bryozoan or (colloquial) sea mat
centipede
chiton or coat-of-mail shell
clam
cone (shell)
coral
ctenophore or comb jelly
cunjevoi or cunje (Austral.)
cuttlefish or cuttle
daphnia
earthworm
eelworm
gastropodart
horseleech
jellyfish or (Austral. slang)
  blubber
kina (N.Z.)
lancelet or amphioxus
leech
lugworm, lug, or lobworm
millipede, millepede, or
  milleped
mollusc
mussel
octopus or devilfish
oyster

paper nautilus, nautilus, or
  argonaut
pearly nautilus, nautilus, or
  chambered nautilus
piddock
pipi or ugari (Austral.)
Portuguese man-of-war or
  (Austral.) bluebottle
quahog, hard-shell clam, hard-
  shell, or round clam
ragworm or (U.S.) clamworm
razor-shell or (U.S.) razor clam
red coral or precious coral
roundworm
sandworm or (Austral.)
  pumpworm
scallop
sea anemone
sea cucumber
sea lily
sea mouse
sea squirt
sea urchin
seed oyster
sponge
squid
starfish
tapeworm
tardigrade or water bear
teredo or shipworm
trepang or bêche-de-mer
tube worm
tubifex
tusk shell or tooth shell
worm

**involve** 1 = <u>entail</u>, mean, require, occasion, imply, give rise to, necessitate 2 = <u>concern</u>, draw in, bear on

**involved** = <u>complicated</u>, complex, intricate, hard, confused, confusing, elaborate, tangled ≠ straightforward

**involvement** = <u>connection</u>, interest, association, commitment, attachment

**inward** 1 = <u>incoming</u>, entering, inbound, ingoing 2 = <u>internal</u>, inner, private, personal, inside, secret, hidden, interior ≠ outward

**Ireland** = <u>Hibernia</u> (*Latin*)

**iron** ADJECTIVE 1 = <u>ferrous</u>, ferric 2 = <u>inflexible</u>, hard, strong, tough, rigid, adamant, unconditional, steely ≠ weak
● PHRASES **iron something out** = <u>settle</u>, resolve, sort out, get rid of, reconcile, clear up, put right, straighten out

*Related Words*
*adjectives*: ferric, ferrous

**ironic** *or* **ironical** 1 = <u>sarcastic</u>, dry, acid, bitter, mocking, wry, satirical, tongue-in-cheek 2 = <u>paradoxical</u>, contradictory, puzzling, baffling, confounding, enigmatic, incongruous

**irony** 1 = <u>sarcasm</u>, mockery, ridicule, satire, cynicism, derision 2 = <u>paradox</u>, incongruity

**irrational** 1 = <u>illogical</u>, crazy, absurd, unreasonable, preposterous, nonsensical ≠ rational

**irregular** 1 = <u>variable</u>, erratic, occasional, random, casual, shaky, sporadic, haphazard ≠ steady 2 = <u>uneven</u>, rough, ragged, crooked, jagged, bumpy, contorted, lopsided ≠ even 3 = <u>inappropriate</u>, unconventional, unethical, unusual, extraordinary, exceptional, peculiar, unofficial 4 = <u>unofficial</u>, underground, guerrilla, resistance, partisan, rogue, paramilitary, mercenary

**irrelevant** = <u>unconnected</u>, unrelated, unimportant, inappropriate, peripheral, immaterial, extraneous, beside the point ≠ relevant

**irresistible** = <u>overwhelming</u>, compelling, overpowering, urgent, compulsive

**irresponsible** = <u>thoughtless</u>, reckless, careless, unreliable, untrustworthy, shiftless, scatterbrained ≠ responsible

**irritate** 1 = <u>annoy</u>, anger, bother, needle (*informal*), infuriate, exasperate, nettle, irk ≠ placate 2 = <u>inflame</u>, pain, rub, scratch, scrape, chafe

**irritated** = <u>annoyed</u>, cross, angry, bothered, put out, exasperated, nettled, vexed, tooshie (*Austral. slang*), hoha (*N.Z.*)

**irritating** = <u>annoying</u>, trying,

infuriating, disturbing, nagging, troublesome, maddening, irksome ≠ pleasing

**irritation** 1 = <u>annoyance</u>, anger, fury, resentment, gall, indignation, displeasure, exasperation ≠ pleasure
2 = <u>nuisance</u>, irritant, drag (*informal*), pain in the neck (*informal*), thorn in your flesh

**island** = <u>isle</u>, atoll, islet, ait *or* eyot (*dialect*), cay *or* key

(*Related Words*)
adjective: insular

**isolate** 1 = <u>separate</u>, break up, cut off, detach, split up, insulate, segregate, disconnect
2 = <u>quarantine</u>

**isolated** = <u>remote</u>, far, distant, lonely, out-of-the-way, hidden, secluded, inaccessible

**isolation** = <u>separation</u>, segregation, detachment, solitude, seclusion, remoteness

**issue** NOUN 1 = <u>topic</u>, point, matter, problem, question, subject, theme 2 = <u>point</u>, question, bone of contention
3 = <u>edition</u>, printing, copy, publication, number, version
4 = <u>children</u>, offspring, babies, kids (*informal*), heirs, descendants, progeny ≠ parent
● VERB = <u>give out</u>, release, publish, announce, deliver, spread, broadcast, distribute
● PHRASES **take issue with**

something *or* someone = <u>disagree with</u>, question, challenge, oppose, dispute, object to, argue with, take exception to

**itch** VERB 1 = <u>prickle</u>, tickle, tingle
2 = <u>long</u>, ache, crave, pine, hunger, lust, yearn, hanker
● NOUN 1 = <u>irritation</u>, tingling, prickling, itchiness 2 = <u>desire</u>, longing, craving, passion, yen (*informal*), hunger, lust, yearning

**item** 1 = <u>article</u>, thing, object, piece, unit, component
2 = <u>matter</u>, point, issue, case, question, concern, detail, subject
3 = <u>report</u>, story, piece, account, note, feature, notice, article

**itinerary** = <u>schedule</u>, programme, route, timetable

# J

**jab** VERB = <u>poke</u>, dig, punch, thrust, tap, stab, nudge, prod
● NOUN = <u>poke</u>, dig, punch, thrust, tap, stab, nudge, prod

**jacket** = <u>covering</u>, casing, case, cover, skin, shell, coat, wrapping

**jackpot** = <u>prize</u>, winnings, award, reward, bonanza

**jail** NOUN = <u>prison</u>, penitentiary (*U.S.*), confinement, dungeon, nick (*Brit. slang*), slammer (*slang*), reformatory, boob (*Austral. slang*)
● VERB = <u>imprison</u>, confine, detain, lock up, put away, intern,

incarcerate, send down

**jam** NOUN = <u>predicament</u>, tight spot, situation, trouble, hole (*slang*), fix (*informal*), mess, pinch
● VERB 1 = <u>pack</u>, force, press, stuff, squeeze, ram, wedge, cram 2 = <u>crowd</u>, throng, crush, mass, surge, flock, swarm, congregate 3 = <u>congest</u>, block, clog, stick, stall, obstruct

**jar¹** = <u>pot</u>, container, drum, vase, jug, pitcher, urn, crock

**jar²** 1 *usually with on* = <u>irritate</u>, annoy, offend, nettle, irk, grate on, get on your nerves (*informal*) 2 = <u>jolt</u>, rock, shake, bump, rattle, vibrate, convulse

**jargon** = <u>parlance</u>, idiom, usage, argot

**jaw** PLURAL NOUN = <u>opening</u>, entrance, mouth
● VERB (*Informal*) = <u>talk</u>, chat, gossip, chatter, spout, natter

**jealous** 1 = <u>suspicious</u>, protective, wary, doubtful, sceptical, vigilant, watchful, possessive ≠ trusting 2 = <u>envious</u>, grudging, resentful, green, green with envy, desirous, covetous ≠ satisfied

**jealousy** = <u>suspicion</u>, mistrust, possessiveness, doubt, spite, resentment, wariness, dubiety

**jeer** VERB = <u>mock</u>, deride, heckle, barrack, ridicule, taunt, scoff, gibe ≠ cheer
● NOUN = <u>mockery</u>, abuse, ridicule,

taunt, boo, derision, gibe, catcall ≠ applause

**jeopardy** = <u>danger</u>, risk, peril, vulnerability, insecurity

**jerk** VERB = <u>jolt</u>, bang, bump, lurch
● NOUN = <u>lurch</u>, movement, thrust, twitch, jolt

**jet** VERB = <u>stream</u>, current, spring, flow, rush, flood, burst, spray
● VERB = <u>fly</u>, wing, cruise, soar, zoom

**jewel** 1 = <u>gemstone</u>, gem, ornament, sparkler (*informal*), rock (*slang*) 2 = <u>treasure</u>, wonder, darling, pearl, gem, paragon, pride and joy, taonga (*N.Z.*)

**jewellery** = <u>jewels</u>, treasure, gems, trinkets, ornaments, finery, regalia

**job** 1 = <u>position</u>, work, calling, business, field, career, employment, profession 2 = <u>task</u>, duty, work, venture, enterprise, undertaking, assignment, chore

**jobless** = <u>unemployed</u>, redundant, out of work, inactive, unoccupied, idle

**jog** 1 = <u>run</u>, trot, canter, lope 2 = <u>nudge</u>, push, shake, prod 3 = <u>stimulate</u>, stir, prod

**join** 1 = <u>enrol in</u>, enter, sign up for, enlist in 2 = <u>connect</u>, unite, couple, link, combine, attach, fasten, add ≠ detach

**joint** ADJECTIVE = <u>shared</u>, mutual, collective, communal, united, joined, allied, combined
● NOUN = <u>junction</u>, connection,

brace, bracket, hinge, intersection, node, nexus

**jointly** = <u>collectively</u>, together, in conjunction, as one, in common, mutually, in partnership, in league ≠ separately

**joke** NOUN 1 = <u>jest</u>, gag (*informal*), wisecrack (*informal*), witticism, crack (*informal*), quip, pun, one-liner (*informal*) 2 = <u>laugh</u>, jest, jape 3 = <u>prank</u>, trick, practical joke, lark (*informal*), escapade, jape 4 = <u>laughing stock</u>, clown, buffoon

● VERB = <u>jest</u>, kid (*informal*), mock, tease, taunt, quip, banter, play the fool

**joker** = <u>comedian</u>, comic, wit, clown, wag, jester, prankster, buffoon

**jolly** = <u>happy</u>, cheerful, merry, upbeat (*informal*), playful, cheery, genial, chirpy (*informal*) ≠ miserable

**jolt** VERB 1 = <u>jerk</u>, push, shake, knock, jar, shove, jog, jostle 2 = <u>surprise</u>, stun, disturb, stagger, startle, perturb, discompose

● NOUN 1 = <u>jerk</u>, start, jump, shake, bump, jar, jog, lurch 2 = <u>surprise</u>, blow, shock, setback, bombshell, bolt from the blue

**journal** 1 = <u>magazine</u>, publication, gazette, periodical 2 = <u>newspaper</u>, paper, daily, weekly, monthly 3 = <u>diary</u>, record, history, log, notebook, chronicle, annals, yearbook

**journalist** = <u>reporter</u>, writer,

correspondent, newsman *or* newswoman, commentator, broadcaster, hack (*derogatory*), columnist

**journey** NOUN 1 = <u>trip</u>, drive, tour, flight, excursion, trek, expedition, voyage 2 = <u>progress</u>, voyage, pilgrimage, odyssey

● VERB = <u>travel</u>, go, move, tour, progress, proceed, wander, trek, go walkabout (*Austral.*)

**joy** = <u>delight</u>, pleasure, satisfaction, ecstasy, enjoyment, bliss, glee, rapture ≠ sorrow

**jubilee** = <u>celebration</u>, holiday, festival, festivity

**judge** NOUN 1 = <u>magistrate</u>, justice, beak (*Brit. slang*), His, Her or Your Honour 2 = <u>referee</u>, expert, specialist, umpire, mediator, examiner, connoisseur, assessor 3 = <u>critic</u>, assessor, arbiter

● VERB 1 = <u>adjudicate</u>, referee, umpire, mediate, officiate, arbitrate 2 = <u>evaluate</u>, rate, consider, view, value, esteem 3 = <u>estimate</u>, guess, assess, calculate, evaluate, gauge

*Related Words*
adjective: judicial

**judgment** 1 = <u>opinion</u>, view, estimate, belief, assessment, diagnosis, valuation, appraisal 2 = <u>verdict</u>, finding, ruling, decision, sentence, decree, arbitration, adjudication 3 = <u>sense</u>, good sense, understanding, discrimination, perception, wisdom, wit, prudence

**judicial** = <u>legal</u>, official

**jug** = <u>container</u>, pitcher, urn, carafe, creamer (*U.S. & Canad.*), vessel, jar, crock

**juggle** = <u>manipulate</u>, change, alter, modify, manoeuvre

**juice 1** = <u>liquid</u>, extract, fluid, liquor, sap, nectar **2** = <u>secretion</u>

**juicy 1** = <u>moist</u>, lush, succulent **2** (*Informal*) = <u>interesting</u>, colourful, sensational, vivid, provocative, spicy (*informal*), suggestive, racy

**jumble** NOUN = <u>muddle</u>, mixture, mess, disorder, confusion, clutter, disarray, mishmash

● VERB = <u>mix</u>, mistake, confuse, disorder, shuffle, muddle, disorganize

**jumbo** = <u>giant</u>, large, huge, immense, gigantic, oversized ≠ tiny

**jump** VERB **1** = <u>leap</u>, spring, bound, bounce, hop, skip **2** = <u>vault</u>, hurdle, go over, sail over, hop over **3** = <u>spring</u>, bound, bounce **4** = <u>recoil</u>, start, jolt, flinch, shake, jerk, quake, shudder **5** = <u>increase</u>, rise, climb, escalate, advance, soar, surge, spiral **6** = <u>miss</u>, avoid, skip, omit, evade

● NOUN **1** = <u>leap</u>, spring, skip, bound, hop, vault **2** = <u>rise</u>, increase, upswing, advance, upsurge, upturn, increment

**jumped-up** = <u>conceited</u>, arrogant, pompous, overbearing, presumptuous, insolent

**jumper** = <u>sweater</u>, top, jersey, cardigan, woolly, pullover

**junior 1** = <u>minor</u>, lower, secondary, lesser, subordinate, inferior **2** = <u>younger</u> ≠ senior

**junk** = <u>rubbish</u>, refuse, waste, scrap, litter, debris, garbage (*chiefly U.S.*), trash

**jurisdiction 1** = <u>authority</u>, power, control, rule, influence, command, mana (*N.Z.*) **2** = <u>range</u>, area, field, bounds, province, scope, sphere, compass

**just** ADVERB **1** = <u>recently</u>, lately, only now **2** = <u>merely</u>, only, simply, solely **3** = <u>barely</u>, hardly, by a whisker, by the skin of your teeth **4** = <u>exactly</u>, really, quite, completely, totally, perfectly, entirely, truly

● ADJECTIVE **1** = <u>fair</u>, good, legitimate, upright, honest, equitable, conscientious, virtuous ≠ unfair **2** = <u>fitting</u>, due, correct, deserved, appropriate, justified, decent, merited ≠ inappropriate

---

### Word Power

**just** – The expression *just exactly* is considered to be poor style because, since both words mean the same thing, only one or the other is needed. Use *just* – *it's just what they want* – or *exactly* – *it's exactly what they want*, but not both together.

**justice** 1 = <u>fairness</u>, equity, integrity, honesty, decency, rightfulness, right ≠ **injustice** 2 = <u>justness</u>, fairness, legitimacy, right, integrity, honesty, legality, rightfulness 3 = <u>judge</u>, magistrate, beak (*Brit. slang*), His, Her *or* Your Honour

**justification** = <u>reason</u>, grounds, defence, basis, excuse, warrant, rationale, vindication

**justify** = <u>explain</u>, support, warrant, defend, excuse, uphold, vindicate, exonerate

**juvenile** NOUN = <u>child</u>, youth, minor, girl, boy, teenager, infant, adolescent ≠ **adult**
• ADJECTIVE 1 = <u>young</u>, junior, adolescent, youthful, immature ≠ **adult** 2 = <u>immature</u>, childish, infantile, puerile, young, youthful, inexperienced, callow

# K

**kai** (*N.Z. informal*) = <u>food</u>, grub (*slang*), provisions, fare, tucker (*Austral. & N.Z. informal*), refreshment, foodstuffs

**kak** (*S. African taboo*) 1 = <u>faeces</u>, excrement, manure, dung, droppings, waste matter 2 = <u>rubbish</u>, nonsense, garbage (*informal*), rot, drivel, tripe (*informal*), bizzo (*Austral. slang*), bull's wool (*Austral. & N.Z. slang*)

**keen** 1 = <u>eager</u>, intense, enthusiastic, passionate, ardent, avid, fervent, impassioned ≠ **unenthusiastic** 2 = <u>earnest</u>, fierce, intense, vehement, passionate, heightened, ardent, fanatical 3 = <u>sharp</u>, incisive, cutting, edged, razor-like ≠ **dull** 4 = <u>perceptive</u>, quick, sharp, acute, smart, wise, clever, shrewd ≠ **obtuse** 5 = <u>intense</u>, strong, fierce, relentless, cut-throat

**keep**[1] VERB 1 *usually with from* = <u>prevent</u>, restrain, hinder, keep back 2 = <u>hold on to</u>, maintain, retain, save, preserve, nurture, cherish, conserve ≠ **lose** 3 = <u>store</u>, put, place, house, hold, deposit, stack, stow 4 = <u>carry</u>, stock, sell, supply, handle 5 = <u>support</u>, maintain, sustain, provide for, mind, fund, finance, feed 6 = <u>raise</u>, own, maintain, tend, farm, breed, look after, rear 7 = <u>manage</u>, run, administer, be in charge (of), direct, handle, supervise 8 = <u>delay</u>, detain, hinder, impede, obstruct, set back ≠ **release**
• NOUN = <u>board</u>, food, maintenance, living, kai (*N.Z. informal*)
• PHRASES **keep something up** 1 = <u>continue</u>, make, maintain, carry on, persist in, persevere with 2 = <u>maintain</u>, sustain, perpetuate, retain, preserve,

prolong ♦ **keep up** = keep pace

**keep²** = tower, castle

**keeper** = curator, guardian, steward, attendant, caretaker, preserver

**keeping** NOUN = care, charge, protection, possession, custody, guardianship, safekeeping
● PHRASES **in keeping with** = in agreement with, in harmony with, in accord with, in compliance with, in conformity with, in balance with, in correspondence with, in proportion with

**key** NOUN 1 = opener, door key, latchkey 2 = answer
● ADJECTIVE = essential, leading, major, main, important, necessary, vital, crucial ≠ minor

**kia ora** (*N.Z.*) = hello, hi (*informal*), greetings, gidday *or* g'day (*Austral. & N.Z.*), how do you do?, good morning, good evening, good afternoon

**kick** VERB 1 = boot, knock, punt 2 (*Informal*) = give up, break, stop, abandon, quit, cease, eschew, leave off
● NOUN (*Informal*) = thrill, buzz (*slang*), tingle, high (*slang*)
● PHRASES **kick off** (*Informal*) = begin, start, open, commence, initiate, get on the road ♦ **kick someone out** (*Informal*) = dismiss, remove, get rid of, expel, eject, evict, sack (*informal*)

**kid¹** (*Informal*) = child, baby, teenager, youngster, infant, adolescent, juvenile, toddler, littlie (*Austral. informal*), ankle-biter (*Austral. slang*), tacker (*Austral. slang*)

**kid²** = tease, joke, trick, fool, pretend, wind up (*Brit. slang*), hoax, delude

**kidnap** = abduct, capture, seize, snatch (*slang*), hijack, hold to ransom

**kill** 1 = slay, murder, execute, slaughter, destroy, massacre, butcher, cut down 2 (*Informal*) = destroy, crush, scotch, stop, halt, wreck, shatter, suppress

**killer** = murderer, slayer, hit man (*slang*), butcher, gunman, assassin, terminator, executioner

**killing** NOUN = murder, massacre, slaughter, dispatch, manslaughter, elimination, slaying, homicide
● ADJECTIVE (*Informal*) = tiring, taxing, exhausting, punishing, fatiguing, gruelling, sapping, debilitating
● PHRASES **make a killing** (*Informal*) = profit, gain, clean up (*informal*), be lucky, be successful, make a fortune, strike it rich (*informal*), make a bomb (*slang*)

**kind¹** 1 = class, sort, type, variety, brand, category, genre 2 = sort, set, type, family, species, breed

> ## Word Power
>
> **kind** – It is common in
> informal speech to combine
> singular and plural in sentences
> like *children enjoy those kind of
> stories*. However, this is not
> acceptable in careful writing,
> where the plural must be used
> consistently: *children enjoy those
> kinds of stories*.

**kind²** = <u>considerate</u>, kindly,
concerned, friendly, generous,
obliging, charitable, benign
≠ unkind

**kindly** ADJECTIVE = <u>benevolent</u>,
kind, caring, warm, helpful,
pleasant, sympathetic, benign
≠ cruel
● ADVERB = <u>benevolently</u>, politely,
generously, thoughtfully,
tenderly, lovingly, cordially,
affectionately ≠ unkindly

**kindness** = <u>goodwill</u>,
understanding, charity, humanity,
compassion, generosity,
philanthropy, benevolence
≠ malice

**king** = <u>ruler</u>, monarch, sovereign,
leader, lord, Crown, emperor,
head of state

**kingdom** = <u>country</u>, state,
nation, territory, realm

**kiss** VERB 1 = <u>peck</u> (*informal*),
osculate, neck (*informal*)
2 = <u>brush</u>, touch, shave, scrape,
graze, glance off, stroke
● NOUN = <u>peck</u> (*informal*), snog
(*Brit. slang*), smacker (*slang*),
French kiss, osculation

**kit** NOUN 1 = <u>equipment</u>,
materials, tackle, tools, apparatus,
paraphernalia 2 = <u>gear</u>, things,
stuff, equipment, uniform
● PHRASES **kit something** or
**someone out** or **up** = <u>equip</u>, fit,
supply, provide with, arm, stock,
costume, furnish

**knack** = <u>skill</u>, art, ability, facility,
talent, gift, capacity, trick
≠ ineptitude

**kneel** = <u>genuflect</u>, stoop

**knickers** = <u>underwear</u>, smalls,
briefs, drawers, panties, bloomers

**knife** NOUN = <u>blade</u>, carver, cutter
● VERB = <u>cut</u>, wound, stab, slash,
thrust, pierce, spear, jab

**knit** 1 = <u>join</u>, unite, link, tie, bond,
combine, bind, weave 2 = <u>heal</u>,
unite, join, link, bind, fasten,
intertwine 3 = <u>furrow</u>, tighten,
knot, wrinkle, crease, screw up,
pucker, scrunch up

**knob** = <u>ball</u>, stud, knot, lump,
bump, projection, hump,
protrusion

**knock** VERB 1 = <u>bang</u>, strike, tap,
rap, thump, pummel 2 = <u>hit</u>,
strike, punch, belt (*informal*),
smack, thump, cuff 3 (*Informal*)
= <u>criticize</u>, condemn, put down,
run down, abuse, slate (*informal*),
censure, denigrate

● NOUN 1 = <u>knocking</u>, pounding, beating, tap, bang, banging, rap, thump 2 = <u>bang</u>, blow, impact, jar, collision, jolt, smash 3 = <u>blow</u>, hit, punch, crack, clip, slap, bash, smack 4 (*Informal*) = <u>setback</u>, check, defeat, blow, reverse, disappointment, hold-up, hitch
● PHRASES **knock about** or **around** = <u>wander</u>, travel, roam, rove, range, drift, stray, ramble, go walkabout (*Austral.*) ◆ **knock about** or **around with someone** = <u>mix with</u>, associate with, mingle with, consort with, hobnob with, socialize with, accompany ◆ **knock off** (*Informal*) = <u>stop work</u>, get out, call it a day (*Informal*), finish work, clock off, clock out
◆ **knock someone about** or **around** = <u>hit</u>, attack, beat, strike, abuse, injure, assault, batter ◆ **knock someone down** = <u>run over</u>, hit, run down, knock over, mow down ◆ **knock something down** = <u>demolish</u>, destroy, flatten, tear down, level, fell, dismantle, bulldoze ◆ **knock something off** (*Slang*) = <u>steal</u>, take, nick (*slang, chiefly Brit.*), thieve, rob, pinch
**knockout** 1 = <u>killer blow</u>, coup de grâce (*French*), KO or K.O. (*slang*) 2 (*Informal*) = <u>success</u>, hit, winner, triumph, smash, sensation, smash hit ≠ failure

**knot** NOUN = <u>connection</u>, tie, bond, joint, loop, ligature
● VERB = <u>tie</u>, secure, bind, loop, tether
**know** 1 = <u>have knowledge of</u>, see, understand, recognize, perceive, be aware of, be conscious of 2 = <u>be acquainted with</u>, recognize, be familiar with, be friends with, be friendly with, have knowledge of, have dealings with, socialize with ≠ be unfamiliar with 3 *sometimes with* **about** or **of** = <u>be familiar with</u>, understand, comprehend, have knowledge of, be acquainted with, feel certain of, have dealings in, be versed in ≠ be ignorant of
**know-how** (*Informal*) = <u>expertise</u>, ability, skill, knowledge, facility, talent, command, capability
**knowing** = <u>meaningful</u>, significant, expressive, enigmatic, suggestive
**knowledge** 1 = <u>understanding</u>, sense, judgment, perception, awareness, insight, grasp, appreciation 2 = <u>learning</u>, education, intelligence, instruction, wisdom, scholarship, enlightenment, erudition ≠ ignorance 3 = <u>acquaintance</u>, intimacy, familiarity ≠ unfamiliarity
**knowledgeable** 1 = <u>well-</u>

informed, conversant, au fait (*French*), experienced, aware, familiar, in the know (*informal*), cognizant 2 = **intelligent**, learned, educated, scholarly, erudite

**known** = **famous**, well-known, celebrated, noted, acknowledged, recognized, avowed ≠ unknown

**kopje** or**koppie** (*S. African*) = <u>hill</u>, down (*archaic*), fell, mount, hilltop, knoll, hillock, brae (*Scot.*)

# L

**label** NOUN = tag, ticket, tab, marker, sticker
● VERB = <u>tag</u>, mark, stamp, ticket, tab

**labour** NOUN 1 = <u>workers</u>, employees, workforce, labourers, hands 2 = <u>work</u>, effort, employment, toil, industry 3 = <u>childbirth</u>, birth, delivery, parturition
● VERB 1 = <u>work</u>, toil, strive, work hard, sweat (*informal*), slave, endeavour, slog away (*informal*) ≠ rest 2 = <u>struggle</u>, work, strain, work hard, strive, grapple, toil, make an effort
3 = <u>overemphasize</u>, stress, elaborate, exaggerate, strain, dwell on, overdo, go on about
4 *usually with under* = <u>be disadvantaged by</u>, suffer from, be a victim of, be burdened by

**Labour** = left-wing, Democrat (*U.S.*)

**laboured** = <u>difficult</u>, forced, strained, heavy, awkward

**labourer** = <u>worker</u>, manual worker, hand, blue-collar worker, drudge, navvy (*Brit. informal*)

**lace** NOUN 1 = <u>netting</u>, net, filigree, meshwork, openwork
2 = <u>cord</u>, tie, string, lacing, shoelace, bootlace
● VERB 1 = <u>fasten</u>, tie, tie up, do up, secure, bind, thread 2 = <u>mix</u>, drug, doctor, add to, spike, contaminate, fortify, adulterate
3 = <u>intertwine</u>, interweave, entwine, twine, interlink

**lack** NOUN = <u>shortage</u>, want, absence, deficiency, need, inadequacy, scarcity, dearth ≠ abundance
● VERB = <u>miss</u>, want, need, require, not have, be without, be short of, be in need of ≠ have

**lad** = <u>boy</u>, kid (*informal*), guy (*informal*), youth, fellow, youngster, juvenile, nipper (*informal*)

**laden** = <u>loaded</u>, burdened, full, charged, weighed down, encumbered

**lady** 1 = <u>gentlewoman</u>, duchess, noble, dame, baroness, countess, aristocrat, viscountess
2 = <u>woman</u>, female, girl, damsel, charlie (*Austral. slang*), chook (*Austral. slang*), wahine (*N.Z.*)

**lag** = hang back, delay, trail, linger, loiter, straggle, dawdle, tarry

**laid-back** = relaxed, calm, casual, easy-going, unflappable (*informal*), unhurried, free and easy ≠ tense

**lake** = pond, pool, reservoir, loch (*Scot.*), lagoon, mere, lough (*Irish*), tarn

**lame** 1 = disabled, handicapped, crippled, limping, hobbling, game 2 = unconvincing, poor, pathetic, inadequate, thin, weak, feeble, unsatisfactory

**lament** VERB = bemoan, grieve, mourn, weep over, complain about, regret, wail about, deplore
● NOUN 1 = complaint, moan, wailing, lamentation 2 = dirge, requiem, elegy, threnody

**land** NOUN 1 = ground, earth, dry land, terra firma 2 = soil, ground, earth, clay, dirt, sod, loam 3 = countryside, farmland 4 (*Law*) = property, grounds, estate, real estate, realty, acreage 5 = country, nation, region, state, district, territory, province, kingdom
● VERB 1 = arrive, dock, put down, moor, alight, touch down, disembark, come to rest 2 (*Informal*) = gain, get, win, secure, acquire
● PHRASES **land up** = end up, turn up, wind up, finish up, fetch up (*informal*)
(*Related Words*)
*adjective*: terrestrial

**landlord** 1 = owner, landowner, proprietor, freeholder, lessor, landholder 2 = innkeeper, host, hotelier

**landmark** 1 = feature, spectacle, monument 2 = milestone, turning point, watershed, critical point

**landscape** = scenery, country, view, land, scene, prospect, countryside, outlook

**landslide** = landslip, avalanche, rockfall

**lane** = road, street, track, path, way, passage, trail, pathway

**language** 1 = tongue, dialect, vernacular, patois 2 = speech, communication, expression, speaking, talk, talking, discourse, parlance

**languish** 1 = decline, fade away, wither away, flag, weaken, wilt ≠ flourish 2 (*Literary*) = waste away, suffer, rot, be abandoned, be neglected ≠ thrive 3 *often with* for = pine, long, desire, hunger, yearn, hanker

**lap**[1] = circuit, tour, leg, stretch, circle, orbit, loop

**lap**[2] VERB 1 = ripple, wash, splash, swish, gurgle, slosh, purl, plash 2 = drink, sip, lick, swallow, gulp, sup
● PHRASES **lap something up**

= relish, like, enjoy, delight in, savour, revel in, wallow in, accept eagerly

**lapse** NOUN 1 = <u>decline</u>, fall, drop, deterioration 2 = <u>mistake</u>, failing, fault, failure, error, slip, negligence, omission 3 = <u>interval</u>, break, gap, pause, interruption, lull, breathing space, intermission
● VERB 1 = <u>slip</u>, fall, decline, sink, drop, slide, degenerate 2 = <u>end</u>, stop, run out, expire, terminate

**lapsed** = <u>expired</u>, ended, finished, run out, invalid, out of date, discontinued

**large** ADJECTIVE 1 = <u>big</u>, great, huge, heavy, massive, vast, enormous, tall ≠ small
2 = <u>massive</u>, great, big, huge, vast, enormous, considerable, substantial ≠ small
● PHRASES at large 1 = <u>in general</u>, generally, chiefly, mainly, as a whole, in the main 2 = <u>free</u>, on the run, fugitive, at liberty, on the loose, unchained, unconfined
◆ by and large = <u>on the whole</u>, generally, mostly, in general, all things considered, predominantly, in the main, all in all

**largely** = <u>mainly</u>, generally, chiefly, mostly, principally, primarily, predominantly, by and large

**large-scale** = <u>wide-ranging</u>, global, sweeping, broad, wide, vast, extensive, wholesale

**lash**[1] VERB 1 = <u>pound</u>, beat, strike, hammer, drum, smack (*dialect*) 2 = <u>censure</u>, attack, blast, put down, criticize, slate (*informal, chiefly Brit.*), scold, tear into (*informal*) 3 = <u>whip</u>, beat, thrash, birch, flog, scourge
● NOUN = <u>blow</u>, hit, strike, stroke, stripe, swipe (*informal*)

**lash**[2] = <u>fasten</u>, tie, secure, bind, strap, make fast

**last**[1] ADJECTIVE 1 = <u>most recent</u>, latest, previous 2 = <u>hindmost</u>, final, at the end, remotest, furthest behind, most distant, rearmost ≠ foremost 3 = <u>final</u>, closing, concluding, ultimate ≠ first
● ADVERB = <u>in</u> or <u>at the end</u>, after, behind, in the rear, bringing up the rear
● PHRASES the last word 1 = <u>final decision</u>, final say, final statement, conclusive comment 2 = <u>leading</u>, finest, cream, supreme, elite, foremost, pre-eminent, unsurpassed

---

### Word Power

**last** – Since *last* can mean either *after all others* or *most recent*, it is better to avoid using this word where ambiguity might arise, as in *her last novel*. *Final* or *latest* should be used as alternatives in such contexts to avoid any possible confusion.

**last²** = <u>continue</u>, remain, survive, carry on, endure, persist, keep on, abide ≠ end

**lasting** = <u>continuing</u>, long-term, permanent, enduring, remaining, abiding, long-standing, perennial ≠ passing

**latch** NOUN = <u>fastening</u>, catch, bar, lock, hook, bolt, hasp
● VERB = <u>fasten</u>, bar, secure, bolt, make fast

**late** ADJECTIVE 1 = <u>overdue</u>, delayed, last-minute, belated, tardy, behind time, behindhand ≠ early 2 = <u>dead</u>, deceased, departed, passed on, former, defunct ≠ alive 3 = <u>recent</u>, new, advanced, fresh ≠ old
● ADVERB = <u>behind time</u>, belatedly, tardily, behindhand, dilatorily ≠ early

**lately** = <u>recently</u>, of late, just now, in recent times, not long ago, latterly

**later** ADVERB = <u>afterwards</u>, after, eventually, in time, subsequently, later on, thereafter, in a while
● ADJECTIVE = <u>subsequent</u>, next, following, ensuing

**latest** = <u>up-to-date</u>, current, fresh, newest, modern, most recent, up-to-the-minute

**latitude** = <u>scope</u>, liberty, freedom, play, space, licence, leeway, laxity

**latter** PRONOUN = <u>second</u>, last, last-mentioned, second-mentioned
● ADJECTIVE = <u>last</u>, ending, closing, final, concluding ≠ earlier

> ### Word Power
> **latter** – *The latter* should only be used to specify the second of two items, for example in *if I had to choose between the hovercraft and the ferry, I would opt for the latter.* Where there are three or more items, the last can be referred to as *the last-named*, but not *the latter.*

**laugh** VERB = <u>chuckle</u>, giggle, snigger, cackle, chortle, guffaw, titter, be in stitches
● NOUN 1 = <u>chortle</u>, giggle, chuckle, snigger, guffaw, titter 2 (*Informal*) = <u>joke</u>, scream (*informal*), hoot (*informal*), lark, prank 3 (*Informal*) = <u>clown</u>, character (*informal*), scream (*informal*), entertainer, card (*informal*), joker, hoot (*informal*)
● PHRASES **laugh something off** = <u>disregard</u>, ignore, dismiss, overlook, shrug off, minimize, brush aside, make light of

**laughter** = <u>amusement</u>, entertainment, humour, glee, fun, mirth, hilarity, merriment

**launch** VERB 1 = <u>propel</u>, fire, dispatch, discharge, project, send

off, set in motion, send into orbit
2 = **begin**, start, open, initiate,
introduce, found, set up, originate
● **PHRASES launch into
something** = start
enthusiastically, begin, initiate,
embark on, instigate, inaugurate,
embark upon

**laurel**
● **PHRASES rest on your laurels**
= sit back, relax, take it easy, relax
your efforts

**lavatory** = toilet, bathroom, loo
(*Brit. informal*), cloakroom
(*Brit.*), privy, urinal, latrine, washroom,
dunny (*Austral. & N.Z. old-
fashioned informal*), bogger
(*Austral. slang*), brasco (*Austral.
slang*)

**lavish** ADJECTIVE 1 = grand,
magnificent, splendid, abundant,
copious, profuse ≠ stingy
2 = extravagant, wild, excessive,
exaggerated, wasteful, prodigal,
unrestrained, immoderate
≠ thrifty 3 = generous, free,
liberal, bountiful, open-handed,
unstinting, munificent ≠ stingy
● **VERB** = shower, pour, heap,
deluge, dissipate ≠ stint

**law** 1 = constitution, code,
legislation, charter 2 = statute,
act, bill, rule, order, command,
regulation, resolution
3 = principle, code, canon,
precept, axiom, kaupapa (*N.Z.*)
4 = the legal profession, the bar,

barristers

*Related Words*
*adjectives:* legal, judicial

**lawsuit** = case, action, trial, suit,
proceedings, dispute,
prosecution, legal action

**lawyer** = legal adviser, attorney,
solicitor, counsel, advocate,
barrister, counsellor, legal
representative

**lay**[1] VERB 1 = place, put, set,
spread, plant, leave, deposit, put
down 2 = devise, plan, design,
prepare, work out, plot, hatch,
contrive 3 = produce, bear,
deposit 4 = arrange, prepare,
make, organize, position, set out,
devise, put together 5 = attribute,
assign, allocate, allot, ascribe,
impute 6 = put forward, offer,
present, advance, lodge, submit,
bring forward 7 = bet, stake,
venture, gamble, chance, risk,
hazard, wager
● **PHRASES lay someone off**
= dismiss, fire (*informal*), release,
sack (*informal*), pay off, discharge,
let go, make redundant ◆ **lay
someone out** (*Informal*)
= knock out, fell, floor, knock
unconscious, knock for six ◆ **lay
something out** 1 = arrange,
order, design, display, exhibit, put
out, spread out 2 (*Informal*)
= spend, pay, invest, fork out
(*slang*), expend, shell out
(*informal*), disburse

### Word Power

**lay** – In standard English, the verb *to lay* (meaning 'to put something somewhere') always needs an object, for example *the Queen laid a wreath*. By contrast, the verb *to lie* is always used without an object, for example *he was just lying there*.

**lay²** 1 = <u>nonclerical</u>, secular, non-ordained 2 = <u>nonspecialist</u>, amateur, unqualified, untrained, inexpert, nonprofessional

**layer** = <u>tier</u>, level, seam, stratum

**layout** = <u>arrangement</u>, design, outline, format, plan, formation

**lazy** 1 = <u>idle</u>, inactive, indolent, slack, negligent, inert, workshy, slothful ≠ industrious
2 = <u>lethargic</u>, languorous, slow-moving, languid, sleepy, sluggish, drowsy, somnolent ≠ quick

**leach** = <u>extract</u>, strain, drain, filter, seep, percolate

**lead** VERB 1 = <u>go in front (of)</u>, head, be in front, be at the head (of), walk in front (of) 2 = <u>guide</u>, conduct, steer, escort, precede, usher, pilot, show the way
3 = <u>connect to</u>, link, open onto
4 = <u>be ahead (of)</u>, be first, exceed, be winning, excel, surpass, come first, transcend 5 = <u>command</u>, rule, govern, preside over, head, control, manage, direct 6 = <u>live</u>,

have, spend, experience, pass, undergo 7 = <u>result in</u>, cause, produce, contribute, generate, bring about, bring on, give rise to
8 = <u>cause</u>, prompt, persuade, move, draw, influence, motivate, prevail

● NOUN 1 = <u>first place</u>, winning position, primary position, vanguard 2 = <u>advantage</u>, start, edge, margin, winning margin
3 = <u>example</u>, direction, leadership, guidance, model, pattern 4 = <u>clue</u>, suggestion, hint, indication, pointer, tip-off
5 = <u>leading role</u>, principal, protagonist, title role, principal part 6 = <u>leash</u>, line, cord, rein, tether

● ADJECTIVE = <u>main</u>, prime, top, leading, first, head, chief, premier
● PHRASES lead someone on
= <u>entice</u>, tempt, lure, mislead, draw on, seduce, deceive, beguile
♦ lead up to something
= <u>introduce</u>, prepare for, pave the way for

**leader** = <u>principal</u>, president, head, chief, boss (*informal*), director, manager, chairman, baas (*S. African*) ≠ follower

**leadership** 1 = <u>authority</u>, control, influence, command, premiership, captaincy, governance, headship
2 = <u>guidance</u>, government, authority, management,

direction, supervision, domination, superintendency

**leading** = <u>principal</u>, top, major, main, first, highest, greatest, chief ≠ minor

**leaf** NOUN 1 = <u>frond</u>, blade, cotyledon 2 = <u>page</u>, sheet, folio
● PHRASES **leaf through something** (with *book*, *magazine* etc. as object) = <u>skim</u>, glance, scan, browse, look through, dip into, flick through, flip through

**leaflet** = <u>booklet</u>, notice, brochure, circular, flyer, tract, pamphlet, handout

**leafy** = <u>green</u>, shaded, shady, verdant

**league** 1 = <u>association</u>, union, alliance, coalition, group, corporation, partnership, federation 2 (*Informal*) = <u>class</u>, group, level, category

**leak** VERB 1 = <u>escape</u>, pass, spill, release, drip, trickle, ooze, seep 2 = <u>disclose</u>, tell, reveal, pass on, give away, make public, divulge, let slip
● NOUN 1 = <u>leakage</u>, discharge, drip, seepage, percolation 2 = <u>hole</u>, opening, crack, puncture, aperture, chink, crevice, fissure 3 = <u>disclosure</u>, exposé, exposure, admission, revelation, uncovering, betrayal, unearthing

**lean**[1] VERB 1 = <u>bend</u>, tip, slope, incline, tilt, heel, slant 2 = <u>rest</u>,

prop, be supported, recline, repose 3 = <u>tend</u>, prefer, favour, incline, be prone to, be disposed to
● PHRASES **lean on someone** = <u>depend on</u>, trust, rely on, cling to, count on, have faith in

**lean**[2] = <u>thin</u>, slim, slender, skinny, angular, trim, spare, gaunt ≠ fat

**leaning** = <u>tendency</u>, bias, inclination, bent, disposition, penchant, propensity, predilection

**leap** VERB = <u>jump</u>, spring, bound, bounce, hop, skip
● NOUN 1 = <u>jump</u>, spring, bound, vault 2 = <u>rise</u>, change, increase, soaring, surge, escalation, upsurge, upswing
● PHRASES **leap at something** = <u>accept eagerly</u>, seize on, jump at

**learn** 1 = <u>master</u>, grasp, pick up, take in, familiarize yourself with 2 = <u>discover</u>, hear, understand, find out about, become aware, discern, ascertain, come to know 3 = <u>memorize</u>, commit to memory, learn by heart, learn by rote, learn parrot-fashion, get off pat

**learned** = <u>scholarly</u>, academic, intellectual, versed, well-informed, erudite, highbrow, well-read ≠ uneducated

**learner** = <u>student</u>, novice,

beginner, apprentice, neophyte, tyro ≠ **expert**

**learning** = knowledge, study, education, scholarship, enlightenment

**lease** = hire, rent, let, loan, charter, rent out, hire out

**least** = smallest, meanest, fewest, lowest, tiniest, minimum, slightest, minimal

**leave** VERB 1 = depart from, withdraw from, go from, escape from, quit, flee, exit, pull out of ≠ **arrive** 2 = quit, give up, get out of, resign from, drop out of 3 = give up, abandon, dump (*informal*), drop, surrender, ditch (*informal*), chuck (*informal*), discard ≠ **stay with** 4 = entrust, commit, delegate, refer, hand over, assign, consign, allot 5 = bequeath, will, transfer, endow, confer, hand down 6 = forget, leave behind, mislay 7 = cause, produce, result in, generate, deposit

● NOUN 1 = holiday, break, vacation, time off, sabbatical, leave of absence, furlough 2 = permission, freedom, sanction, liberty, concession, consent, allowance, warrant ≠ **refusal** 3 = departure, parting, withdrawal, goodbye, farewell, retirement, leave-taking, adieu ≠ **arrival**

● PHRASES **leave something or**

**someone out** = omit, exclude, miss out, forget, reject, ignore, overlook, neglect

**lecture** NOUN 1 = talk, address, speech, lesson, instruction, presentation, discourse, sermon 2 = telling-off (*informal*), rebuke, reprimand, talking-to (*informal*), scolding, dressing-down (*informal*), reproof

● VERB 1 = talk, speak, teach, address, discourse, spout, expound, hold forth 2 = tell off (*informal*), berate, scold, reprimand, censure, castigate, admonish, reprove

**lees** = sediment, grounds, deposit, dregs

**left** 1 = left-hand, port, larboard (*Nautical*) 2 (*of politics*) = socialist, radical, left-wing, leftist

**left-wing** = socialist, communist, red (*informal*), radical, revolutionary, militant, Bolshevik, Leninist

**leg** NOUN 1 = limb, member, shank, lower limb, pin (*informal*), stump (*informal*) 2 = support, prop, brace, upright 3 = stage, part, section, stretch, lap, segment, portion

● PHRASES **pull someone's leg** (*Informal*) = tease, trick, fool, kid (*informal*), wind up (*Brit. slang*), hoax, make fun of, lead up the garden path

**legacy** = bequest, inheritance,

gift, estate, heirloom

**legal** 1 = <u>judicial</u>, judiciary, forensic, juridical, jurisdictive 2 = <u>lawful</u>, allowed, sanctioned, constitutional, valid, legitimate, authorized, permissible

**legend** 1 = <u>myth</u>, story, tale, fiction, saga, fable, folk tale, folk story 2 = <u>celebrity</u>, star, phenomenon, genius, prodigy, luminary, megastar (informal) 3 = <u>inscription</u>, title, caption, device, motto, rubric

**legendary** 1 = <u>famous</u>, celebrated, well-known, acclaimed, renowned, famed, immortal, illustrious ≠ unknown 2 = <u>mythical</u>, fabled, traditional, romantic, fabulous, fictitious, storybook, apocryphal ≠ factual

**legion** 1 = <u>army</u>, company, force, division, troop, brigade 2 = <u>multitude</u>, host, mass, drove, number, horde, myriad, throng

**legislation** 1 = <u>law</u>, act, ruling, rule, bill, measure, regulation, charter 2 = <u>lawmaking</u>, regulation, prescription, enactment

**legislative** = <u>law-making</u>, judicial, law-giving

**legislator** = <u>lawmaker</u>, lawgiver

**legislature** = <u>parliament</u>, congress, senate, assembly, chamber

**legitimate** ADJECTIVE 1 = <u>lawful</u>, legal, genuine, authentic, authorized, rightful, kosher (informal), dinkum (Austral. & N.Z. informal), licit ≠ unlawful 2 = <u>reasonable</u>, correct, sensible, valid, warranted, logical, justifiable, well-founded ≠ unreasonable

● VERB = <u>legitimize</u>, allow, permit, sanction, authorize, legalize, pronounce lawful

**leisure** = <u>spare</u>, free, rest, ease, relaxation, recreation ≠ work

**lekker** (S. African slang) = <u>delicious</u>, tasty, luscious, palatable, delectable, mouthwatering, scrumptious (informal), appetizing, yummo (Austral. slang)

**lemon**
*Related Words*
adjectives: citric, citrous
➤ shades of yellow

**lend** VERB 1 = <u>loan</u>, advance, sub (Brit. informal) 2 = <u>give</u>, provide, add, supply, grant, confer, bestow, impart

● PHRASES **lend itself to something** = be appropriate for, suit, be suitable for, be appropriate to, be serviceable for

**length** NOUN 1 = <u>distance</u>, reach, measure, extent, span, longitude 2 = <u>duration</u>, term, period, space, stretch, span, expanse 3 = <u>piece</u>, measure, section, segment, portion

● **PHRASES at length 1** = <u>at last</u>, finally, eventually, in time, in the end, at long last 2 = <u>for a long time</u>, completely, fully, thoroughly, for hours, in detail, for ages, in depth

**lengthen 1** = <u>extend</u>, continue, increase, stretch, expand, elongate ≠ shorten 2 = <u>protract</u>, extend, prolong, draw out, spin out, make longer ≠ cut down

**lengthy 1** = <u>protracted</u>, long, prolonged, tedious, drawn-out, interminable, long-winded, long-drawn-out 2 = <u>very long</u>, long, rambling, interminable, long-winded, wordy, discursive, extended ≠ brief

**lesbian** = <u>homosexual</u>, gay, les (slang), sapphic, lesbo (slang)

**less DETERMINER** = <u>smaller</u>, shorter, not so much

● **PREPOSITION** = <u>minus</u>, without, lacking, excepting, subtracting

### Word Power

**less** – Less should not be confused with fewer. Less refers strictly only to quantity and not to number: there is less water than before. Fewer means smaller in number: there are fewer people than before.

**lessen 1** = <u>reduce</u>, lower, diminish, decrease, ease, narrow,

minimize ≠ increase 2 = <u>grow less</u>, diminish, decrease, contract, ease, shrink

**lesser** = <u>lower</u>, secondary, subsidiary, inferior, less important ≠ greater

**lesson 1** = <u>class</u>, schooling, period, teaching, coaching, session, instruction, lecture 2 = <u>example</u>, warning, message, moral, deterrent 3 = <u>Bible reading</u>, reading, text, Bible passage, Scripture passage

**let VERB 1** = <u>allow</u>, permit, authorize, give the go-ahead, give permission 2 = <u>lease</u>, hire, rent, rent out, hire out, sublease

● **PHRASES let on** (Informal) 1 = <u>reveal</u>, disclose, say, tell, admit, give away, divulge, let slip ◆ **let someone down** = <u>disappoint</u>, fail, abandon, desert, disillusion, fall short, leave stranded, leave in the lurch ◆ **let someone off** = <u>excuse</u>, release, discharge, pardon, spare, forgive, exempt, exonerate ◆ **let something or someone in** = <u>admit</u>, include, receive, welcome, greet, take in, incorporate, give access to ◆ **let something down** = <u>deflate</u>, empty, exhaust, flatten, puncture ◆ **let something off 1** = <u>fire</u>, explode, set off, discharge, detonate 2 = <u>emit</u>, release, leak,

exude, give off ◆ **let something
out** 1 = <u>release</u>, discharge
2 = <u>emit</u>, make, produce, give
vent to ◆ **let up** = <u>stop</u>, diminish,
decrease, subside, relax, ease
(up), moderate, lessen

**lethal** = <u>deadly</u>, terminal, fatal,
dangerous, devastating,
destructive, mortal, murderous
≠ harmless

**letter** 1 = <u>message</u>, line, note,
communication, dispatch,
missive, epistle 2 = <u>character</u>,
mark, sign, symbol

**level** NOUN = <u>position</u>, standard,
degree, grade, standing, stage,
rank, status
● ADJECTIVE 1 = <u>equal</u>, balanced, at
the same height 2 = <u>horizontal</u>,
even, flat, smooth, uniform
≠ slanted 3 = <u>even</u>, tied, equal,
drawn, neck and neck, all square,
level pegging
● VERB 1 = <u>equalize</u>, balance, even
up 2 = <u>destroy</u>, devastate,
demolish, flatten, knock down,
pull down, tear down, bulldoze
≠ build 3 = <u>direct</u>, point, turn,
train, aim, focus 4 = <u>flatten</u>, plane,
smooth, even off or out
● PHRASES **on the level**
(*Informal*) = <u>honest</u>, genuine,
straight, fair, square, dinkum
(*Austral. & N.Z. informal*), above
board

**lever** NOUN = <u>handle</u>, bar
● VERB = <u>prise</u>, force

**leverage** 1 = <u>influence</u>,
authority, pull (*informal*), weight,
clout (*informal*) 2 = <u>force</u>, hold,
pull, strength, grip, grasp

**levy** NOUN = <u>tax</u>, fee, toll, tariff,
duty, excise, exaction
● VERB = <u>impose</u>, charge, collect,
demand, exact

**liability** 1 = <u>disadvantage</u>,
burden, drawback,
inconvenience, handicap,
nuisance, hindrance, millstone
2 = <u>responsibility</u>, accountability,
culpability, answerability

**liable** 1 = <u>likely</u>, tending, inclined,
disposed, prone, apt
2 = <u>vulnerable</u>, subject, exposed,
prone, susceptible, open, at risk
of 3 = <u>responsible</u>, accountable,
answerable, obligated

> ### Word Power
> **liable** – In the past, it was
> considered incorrect to use
> *liable* to mean 'probable' or
> 'likely', as in *it's liable to happen
> soon*. However, this usage is
> now generally considered
> acceptable.

**liaison** 1 = <u>contact</u>,
communication, connection,
interchange 2 = <u>intermediary</u>,
contact, hook-up 3 = <u>affair</u>,
romance, intrigue, fling, love
affair, amour, entanglement

**liar** = <u>falsifier</u>, perjurer, fibber,
fabricator

**libel** NOUN = <u>defamation</u>, misrepresentation, denigration, smear, calumny, aspersion

● VERB = <u>defame</u>, smear, slur, blacken, malign, denigrate, revile, vilify

**liberal** 1 = <u>tolerant</u>, open-minded, permissive, indulgent, easy-going, broad-minded ≠ intolerant 2 = <u>progressive</u>, radical, reformist, libertarian, forward-looking, free-thinking ≠ conservative 3 = <u>abundant</u>, generous, handsome, lavish, ample, rich, plentiful, copious ≠ limited 4 = <u>generous</u>, kind, charitable, extravagant, open-hearted, bountiful, magnanimous, open-handed ≠ stingy

**liberate** = <u>free</u>, release, rescue, save, deliver, let out, set free, let loose ≠ imprison

**liberty** NOUN = <u>independence</u>, sovereignty, liberation, autonomy, immunity, self-determination, emancipation, self-government ≠ restraint

● PHRASES **at liberty** 1 = <u>free</u>, escaped, unlimited, at large, not confined, untied, on the loose, unchained 2 = <u>able</u>, free, allowed, permitted, entitled, authorized

◆ **take liberties** or **a liberty** = <u>not show enough respect</u>, show disrespect, act presumptuously, behave too familiarly, behave impertinently

**licence** NOUN 1 = <u>certificate</u>, document, permit, charter, warrant 2 = <u>permission</u>, the right, authority, leave, sanction, liberty, immunity, entitlement ≠ denial 3 = <u>freedom</u>, creativity, latitude, independence, liberty, deviation, leeway, free rein ≠ restraint 4 = <u>laxity</u>, excess, indulgence, irresponsibility, licentiousness, immoderation ≠ moderation

● PHRASES **under licence** = <u>with permission</u>, under a charter, under warrant, under a permit, with authorization, under a patent

**license** = <u>permit</u>, sanction, allow, warrant, authorize, empower, certify, accredit ≠ forbid

**lick** VERB 1 = <u>taste</u>, lap, tongue 2 (*Informal*) = <u>beat</u>, defeat, overcome, rout, outstrip, outdo, trounce, vanquish 3 (*of flames*) = <u>flicker</u>, touch, flick, dart, ripple, play over

● NOUN 1 = <u>dab</u>, bit, touch, stroke 2 (*Informal*) = <u>pace</u>, rate, speed, clip (*informal*)

**lie**[1] NOUN = <u>falsehood</u>, deceit, fabrication, fib, fiction, invention, deception, untruth

● VERB = <u>fib</u>, fabricate, falsify, prevaricate, not tell the truth, equivocate, dissimulate, tell untruths

# lie → light

- **PHRASES give the lie to something** = <u>disprove</u>, expose, discredit, contradict, refute, negate, invalidate, rebut

**lie²** 1 = <u>recline</u>, rest, lounge, sprawl, stretch out, loll, repose 2 = <u>be placed</u>, be, rest, exist, be situated 3 = <u>be situated</u>, sit, be located, be positioned 4 = <u>be buried</u>, remain, rest, be, be entombed

**life** 1 = <u>being</u>, existence, vitality, sentience 2 = <u>existence</u>, being, lifetime, time, days, span 3 = <u>way of life</u>, situation, conduct, behaviour, life style 4 = <u>liveliness</u>, energy, spirit, vitality, animation, vigour, verve, zest 5 = <u>biography</u>, story, history, profile, confessions, autobiography, memoirs, life story

*Related Words*

adjectives: animate, vital

**lifelong** = <u>long-lasting</u>, enduring, lasting, persistent, long-standing, perennial

**lifetime** = <u>existence</u>, time, day(s), span

**lift** VERB 1 = <u>raise</u>, pick up, hoist, draw up, elevate, uplift, heave up, upraise ≠ lower 2 = <u>revoke</u>, end, remove, withdraw, stop, cancel, terminate, rescind ≠ impose 3 = <u>disappear</u>, clear, vanish, disperse, dissipate, rise, be dispelled
- **NOUN** 1 = <u>boost</u>, encouragement, stimulus, pick-me-up, fillip, shot in the arm

(*informal*), gee-up ≠ blow 2 = <u>elevator</u> (*chiefly U.S.*), hoist, paternoster 3 = <u>ride</u>, run, drive, hitch (*informal*)
- **PHRASES lift off** = <u>take off</u>, be launched, blast off, take to the air

**light¹** NOUN 1 = <u>brightness</u>, illumination, luminosity, shining, glow, glare, gleam, brilliance ≠ dark 2 = <u>lamp</u>, torch, candle, flare, beacon, lantern, taper 3 = <u>match</u>, spark, flame, lighter 4 = <u>aspect</u>, context, angle, point of view, interpretation, viewpoint, slant, standpoint
- **ADJECTIVE** 1 = <u>bright</u>, brilliant, shining, illuminated, luminous, well-lit, lustrous, well-illuminated ≠ dark 2 = <u>pale</u>, fair, faded, blonde, blond, bleached, pastel, light-coloured ≠ dark
- **VERB** 1 = <u>illuminate</u>, light up, brighten ≠ darken 2 = <u>ignite</u>, inflame, kindle, touch off, set alight ≠ put out
- **PHRASES light up** 1 = <u>cheer</u>, shine, blaze, sparkle, animate, brighten, lighten, irradiate 2 = <u>shine</u>, flash, beam, blaze, sparkle, flare, glare, gleam

**light²** ADJECTIVE 1 = <u>insubstantial</u>, thin, slight, portable, buoyant, airy, flimsy, underweight ≠ heavy 2 = <u>weak</u>, soft, gentle, moderate, slight, mild, faint, indistinct ≠ strong 3 = <u>digestible</u>, modest, frugal ≠ substantial

4 = insignificant, small, slight, petty, trivial, trifling, inconsequential, inconsiderable ≠ serious 5 = **light-hearted**, funny, entertaining, amusing, witty, humorous, frivolous, unserious ≠ serious 6 = **nimble**, graceful, deft, agile, sprightly, lithe, limber, lissom ≠ clumsy

● PHRASES **light on** or **upon something** 1 = **settle**, land, perch, alight 2 = **come across**, find, discover, encounter, stumble on, hit upon, happen upon

**lighten**[1] = **brighten**, illuminate, light up, irradiate, become light

**lighten**[2] 1 = **ease**, relieve, alleviate, allay, reduce, lessen, mitigate, assuage ≠ intensify 2 = **cheer**, lift, revive, brighten, perk up, buoy up ≠ depress

**lightly** 1 = **moderately**, thinly, slightly, sparsely, sparingly ≠ heavily 2 = **gently**, softly, slightly, faintly, delicately ≠ forcefully 3 = **carelessly**, breezily, thoughtlessly, flippantly, frivolously, heedlessly ≠ seriously 4 = **easily**, simply, readily, effortlessly, unthinkingly, without thought, flippantly, heedlessly ≠ with difficulty

**lightweight** 1 = **thin**, fine, delicate, sheer, flimsy, gossamer, diaphanous, filmy 2 = **unimportant**, shallow, trivial, insignificant, slight, petty,

worthless, trifling ≠ significant

**like**[1] = **similar to**, same as, equivalent to, parallel to, identical to, alike, corresponding to, comparable to ≠ different

> ### Word Power
>
> **like** – The use of *like* to mean 'such as' was in the past considered undesirable in formal writing, but has now become acceptable, for example in *I enjoy team sports like football and rugby*. However, the common use of *look like* and *seem like* to mean 'look or seem as if' is thought by many people to be incorrect or nonstandard. You might say *it looks as if* (or *as though*) *he's coming*, but it is still wise to avoid *it looks like he's coming*, particularly in formal or written contexts.

**like**[2] 1 = **enjoy**, love, delight in, go for, relish, savour, revel in, be fond of ≠ dislike 2 = **admire**, approve of, appreciate, prize, take to, esteem, cherish, hold dear ≠ dislike 3 = **wish**, want, choose, prefer, desire, fancy, care, feel inclined

**likelihood** = **probability**, chance, possibility, prospect

**likely** 1 = **inclined**, disposed, prone, liable, tending, apt 2 = **probable**, expected,

anticipated, odds-on, on the cards, to be expected
3 = plausible, possible, reasonable, credible, feasible, believable

**liken** = similarly, compare, match, relate, parallel, equate, set beside

**likewise** = similarly, the same, in the same way, in similar fashion, in like manner

**liking** = fondness, love, taste, weakness, preference, affection, inclination, penchant ≠ dislike

**limb** 1 = part, member, arm, leg, wing, extremity, appendage
2 = branch, spur, projection, offshoot, bough

**limelight** = publicity, recognition, fame, the spotlight, attention, prominence, stardom, public eye

**limit** NOUN 1 = end, ultimate, deadline, breaking point, extremity 2 = boundary, edge, border, frontier, perimeter
● VERB = restrict, control, check, bound, confine, curb, restrain, ration

**limitation** 1 = restriction, control, check, curb, restraint, constraint 2 = weakness, failing, qualification, reservation, defect, flaw, shortcoming, imperfection

**limited** = restricted, controlled, checked, bounded, confined, curbed, constrained, finite ≠ unlimited

**limp**[1] VERB = hobble, stagger, stumble, shuffle, hop, falter, shamble, totter
● NOUN = lameness, hobble

**limp**[2] = floppy, soft, slack, drooping, flabby, pliable, flaccid ≠ stiff

**line** NOUN 1 = stroke, mark, score, band, scratch, slash, streak, stripe
2 = wrinkle, mark, crease, furrow, crow's foot 3 = row, queue, rank, file, column, convoy, procession
4 = string, cable, wire, rope, thread, cord 5 = trajectory, way, course, track, channel, direction, route, path 6 = boundary, limit, edge, border, frontier, partition, borderline 7 = occupation, work, calling, business, job, area, trade, field
● VERB 1 = border, edge, bound, fringe 2 = mark, crease, furrow, rule, score
● PHRASES in line for = due for, shortlisted for, in the running for

**lined** 1 = wrinkled, worn, furrowed, wizened 2 = ruled, feint

**line-up** = arrangement, team, row, selection, array

**linger** = stay, remain, stop, wait, delay, hang around, idle, dally

**link** NOUN 1 = connection, relationship, association, tie-up, affinity 2 = relationship, association, bond, connection, attachment, affinity
3 = component, part, piece,

element, constituent

● **VERB 1** = <u>associate</u>, relate, identify, connect, bracket **2** = <u>connect</u>, join, unite, couple, tie, bind, attach, fasten ≠ separate

**lip 1** = <u>edge</u>, rim, brim, margin, brink **2** (*Slang*) = <u>impudence</u>, insolence, impertinence, cheek (*informal*), effrontery, backchat (*informal*), brass neck (*informal*)

**liquid NOUN** = <u>fluid</u>, solution, juice, sap

● **ADJECTIVE 1** = <u>fluid</u>, running, flowing, melted, watery, molten, runny, aqueous **2** (*of assets*) = <u>convertible</u>, disposable, negotiable, realizable

**liquor 1** = <u>alcohol</u>, drink, spirits, booze (*informal*), hard stuff (*informal*), strong drink **2** = <u>juice</u>, stock, liquid, extract, broth

**list¹ NOUN** = <u>inventory</u>, record, series, roll, index, register, catalogue, directory

● **VERB** = <u>itemize</u>, record, enter, register, catalogue, enumerate, note down, tabulate

**list² VERB** = <u>lean</u>, tip, incline, tilt, heel over, careen

● **NOUN** = <u>tilt</u>, leaning, slant, cant

**listen 1** = <u>hear</u>, attend, pay attention, lend an ear, prick up your ears **2** = <u>pay attention</u>, observe, obey, mind, heed, take notice, take note of, take heed of

**literacy** = <u>education</u>, learning, knowledge

**literal 1** = <u>exact</u>, close, strict, accurate, faithful, verbatim, word for word **2** = <u>actual</u>, real, true, simple, plain, genuine, bona fide, unvarnished

**literally** = <u>exactly</u>, really, closely, actually, truly, precisely, strictly, faithfully

**literary** = <u>well-read</u>, learned, formal, intellectual, scholarly, erudite, bookish

**literate** = <u>educated</u>, informed, knowledgeable

**literature** = <u>writings</u>, letters, compositions, lore, creative writing

➤ **Shakespeare**

**litigation** = <u>lawsuit</u>, case, action, prosecution

**litter NOUN 1** = <u>rubbish</u>, refuse, waste, junk, debris, garbage (*chiefly U.S.*), trash, muck **2** = <u>brood</u>, young, offspring, progeny

● **VERB 1** = <u>clutter</u>, mess up, clutter up, be scattered about, disorder, disarrange, derange **2** = <u>scatter</u>, spread, shower, strew

**little ADJECTIVE 1** = <u>small</u>, minute, short, tiny, wee, compact, miniature, diminutive ≠ big **2** = <u>young</u>, small, junior, infant, immature, undeveloped, babyish

● **ADVERB 1** = <u>hardly</u>, barely, scarcely ≠ much **2** = <u>rarely</u>, seldom, scarcely, not often, infrequently, hardly ever ≠ always

• **NOUN** = <u>bit</u>, touch, spot, trace, hint, particle, fragment, speck ≠ lot

• **PHRASES a little** = <u>to a small extent</u>, slightly, to some extent, to a certain extent, to a small degree

**live**[1] 1 = <u>dwell</u>, board, settle, lodge, occupy, abide, inhabit, reside 2 = <u>exist</u>, last, prevail, be, have being, breathe, persist, be alive 3 = <u>survive</u>, get along, make a living, make ends meet, subsist, eke out a living, support yourself, maintain yourself 4 = <u>thrive</u>, flourish, prosper, have fun, enjoy yourself, live life to the full

**live**[2] 1 = <u>living</u>, alive, breathing, animate 2 = <u>active</u>, unexploded 3 = <u>topical</u>, important, pressing, current, hot, burning, controversial, prevalent

**livelihood** = <u>occupation</u>, work, employment, living, job, bread and butter (informal)

**lively** 1 = <u>animated</u>, spirited, quick, keen, active, alert, dynamic, vigorous ≠ dull 2 = <u>vivid</u>, strong, striking, bright, exciting, stimulating, bold, colourful ≠ dull 3 = <u>enthusiastic</u>, strong, keen, stimulating, eager, formidable, vigorous, animated

**living** **NOUN** = <u>lifestyle</u>, ways, situation, conduct, behaviour, customs, lifestyle, way of life

• **ADJECTIVE** 1 = <u>alive</u>, existing, moving, active, breathing, animate ≠ dead 2 = <u>current</u>, present, active, contemporary, in use, extant ≠ obsolete

**lizard** > reptiles

**load** **VERB** 1 = <u>fill</u>, stuff, pack, pile, stack, heap, cram, freight 2 = <u>make ready</u>, charge, prime

• **NOUN** 1 = <u>cargo</u>, delivery, haul, shipment, batch, freight, consignment 2 = <u>oppression</u>, charge, worry, trouble, weight, responsibility, burden, onus

• **PHRASES load someone down** = <u>burden</u>, worry, oppress, weigh down, saddle with, encumber, snow under

**loaded** 1 = <u>tricky</u>, charged, sensitive, delicate, manipulative, emotive, insidious, artful 2 = <u>biased</u>, weighted, rigged, distorted 3 (Slang) = <u>rich</u>, wealthy, affluent, well off, flush (informal), well-heeled (informal), well-to-do, moneyed

**loaf**[1] 1 = <u>lump</u>, block, cake, cube, slab 2 (Slang) = <u>head</u>, mind, sense, common sense, nous (Brit. slang), gumption (Brit. informal)

**loaf**[2] = <u>idle</u>, hang around, take it easy, lie around, loiter, laze, lounge around

**loan** **NOUN** = <u>advance</u>, credit, overdraft

• **VERB** = <u>lend</u>, advance, let out

**loathe** = <u>hate</u>, dislike, despise, detest, abhor, abominate

**loathing** = <u>hatred</u>, hate, disgust, aversion, revulsion, antipathy, repulsion, abhorrence

**lobby** VERB = <u>campaign</u>, press, pressure, push, influence, promote, urge, persuade
● NOUN 1 = <u>pressure group</u>, group, camp, faction, lobbyists, interest group, special-interest group, ginger group 2 = <u>corridor</u>, passage, entrance, porch, hallway, foyer, entrance hall, vestibule

**lobola** (*S. African*) = <u>dowry</u>, portion, marriage settlement, dot (*archaic*)

**local** ADJECTIVE 1 = <u>community</u>, regional 2 = <u>confined</u>, limited, restricted
● NOUN = <u>resident</u>, native, inhabitant

**locate** 1 = <u>find</u>, discover, detect, come across, track down, pinpoint, unearth, pin down 2 = <u>place</u>, put, set, position, seat, site, establish, settle

**location** = <u>place</u>, point, setting, position, situation, spot, venue, locale

**lock¹** VERB 1 = <u>fasten</u>, close, secure, shut, bar, seal, bolt 2 = <u>unite</u>, join, link, engage, clench, entangle, interlock, entwine 3 = <u>embrace</u>, press, grasp, clutch, hug, enclose, clasp, encircle
● NOUN = <u>fastening</u>, catch, bolt, clasp, padlock

● PHRASES **lock someone up** = <u>imprison</u>, jail, confine, cage, detain, shut up, incarcerate, send down (*informal*)

**lock²** = <u>strand</u>, curl, tuft, tress, ringlet

**lodge** NOUN 1 = <u>cabin</u>, shelter, cottage, hut, chalet, gatehouse 2 = <u>society</u>, group, club, section, wing, chapter, branch
● VERB 1 = <u>register</u>, enter, file, submit, put on record 2 = <u>stay</u>, room, board, reside 3 = <u>stick</u>, remain, implant, come to rest, imbed

**lodging** *often plural* = <u>accommodation</u>, rooms, apartments, quarters, digs (*Brit. informal*), shelter, residence, abode

**lofty** 1 = <u>noble</u>, grand, distinguished, renowned, elevated, dignified, illustrious, exalted ≠ humble 2 = <u>high</u>, raised, towering, soaring, elevated ≠ low 3 = <u>haughty</u>, proud, arrogant, patronizing, condescending, disdainful, supercilious ≠ modest

**log** NOUN 1 = <u>stump</u>, block, branch, chunk, trunk 2 = <u>record</u>, account, register, journal, diary, logbook
● VERB = <u>record</u>, enter, note, register, chart, put down, set down

**logic** = <u>reason</u>, reasoning, sense,

good sense

**logical 1** = <u>rational</u>, clear, reasoned, sound, consistent, valid, coherent, well-organized ≠ illogical **2** = <u>reasonable</u>, sensible, natural, wise, plausible ≠ unlikely

**lone** = <u>solitary</u>, single, one, only, sole, unaccompanied

**loneliness** = <u>solitude</u>, isolation, desolation, seclusion

**lonely 1** = <u>solitary</u>, alone, isolated, abandoned, lone, withdrawn, single, forsaken ≠ accompanied **2** = <u>desolate</u>, deserted, remote, isolated, out-of-the-way, secluded, uninhabited, godforsaken ≠ crowded

**lonesome** (Chiefly U.S. & Canad.) = <u>lonely</u>, gloomy, dreary, desolate, forlorn, friendless, companionless

**long¹ 1** = <u>elongated</u>, extended, stretched, expanded, extensive, lengthy, far-reaching, spread out ≠ short **2** = <u>prolonged</u>, sustained, lengthy, lingering, protracted, interminable, spun out, long-drawn-out ≠ brief

**long²** = <u>desire</u>, want, wish, burn, pine, lust, crave, yearn

**longing** = <u>desire</u>, hope, wish, burning, urge, ambition, hunger, yen (informal) ≠ indifference

**long-standing** = <u>established</u>, fixed, enduring, abiding, long-lasting, long-established, time-honoured

**look** VERB **1** = <u>see</u>, view, consider, watch, eye, study, survey, examine **2** = <u>search</u>, seek, hunt, forage, fossick (Austral. & N.Z.) **3** = <u>consider</u>, contemplate **4** = <u>face</u>, overlook **5** = <u>hope</u>, expect, await, anticipate, reckon on **6** = <u>seem</u>, appear, look like, strike you as

● NOUN **1** = <u>glimpse</u>, view, glance, observation, sight, examination, gaze, inspection **2** = <u>appearance</u>, bearing, air, style, aspect, manner, expression, impression

● PHRASES **look after something** or **someone** = <u>take care of</u>, mind, protect, tend, guard, nurse, care for, supervise ◆ **look down on** or **upon someone** = <u>disdain</u>, despise, scorn, sneer at, spurn, contemn (formal) ◆ **look forward to something** = <u>anticipate</u>, expect, look for, wait for, await, hope for, long for ◆ **look out for something** = <u>be careful of</u>, beware, watch out for, pay attention to, be wary of, keep an eye out for ◆ **look someone up** = <u>visit</u>, call on, drop in on (informal), look in on ◆ **look something up** = <u>research</u>, find, search for, hunt for, track down, seek out ◆ **look up** = <u>improve</u>, develop, advance, pick up, progress, get better, shape up (informal), perk up ◆ **look up to someone** = <u>respect</u>, honour, admire, esteem, revere, defer to, think highly of

**lookout** 1 = <u>watchman</u>, guard, sentry, sentinel 2 = <u>watch</u>, guard, vigil 3 = <u>watchtower</u>, post, observatory, observation post 4 (*Informal*) = <u>concern</u>, business, worry

**loom** = <u>appear</u>, emerge, hover, take shape, threaten, bulk, menace, come into view

**loop** NOUN = <u>curve</u>, ring, circle, twist, curl, spiral, coil, twirl
● VERB = <u>twist</u>, turn, roll, knot, curl, spiral, coil, wind round

**loophole** = <u>let-out</u>, escape, excuse

**loose** ADJECTIVE 1 = <u>free</u>, detached, insecure, unfettered, unrestricted, untied, unattached, unfastened 2 = <u>slack</u>, easy, relaxed, sloppy, loose-fitting ≠ tight 3 (*Old-fashioned*) = <u>promiscuous</u>, fast, abandoned, immoral, dissipated, profligate, debauched, dissolute ≠ chaste 4 = <u>vague</u>, random, inaccurate, rambling, imprecise, ill-defined, indistinct, inexact ≠ precise
● VERB = <u>free</u>, release, liberate, detach, unleash, disconnect, set free, untie ≠ fasten

**loosen** VERB = <u>untie</u>, undo, release, separate, detach, unloose
● PHRASES **loosen up** = <u>relax</u>, chill (*slang*), soften, unwind, go easy (*informal*), hang loose,

outspan (*S. African*), ease up or off

**loot** VERB = <u>plunder</u>, rob, raid, sack, rifle, ravage, ransack, pillage
● NOUN = <u>plunder</u>, goods, prize, haul, spoils, booty, swag (*slang*)

**lord** NOUN 1 = <u>peer</u>, nobleman, count, duke, gentleman, earl, noble, baron 2 = <u>ruler</u>, leader, chief, master, governor, commander, superior, liege
● PHRASES **lord it over someone** = <u>boss around</u> or <u>about</u> (*informal*), order around, threaten, bully, menace, intimidate, hector, bluster ◆ **the Lord** or **Our Lord** = <u>Jesus Christ</u>, God, Christ, Messiah, Jehovah, the Almighty

**lose** 1 = <u>be defeated</u>, be beaten, lose out, come to grief 2 = <u>mislay</u>, drop, forget, be deprived of, lose track of, misplace 3 = <u>forfeit</u>, miss, yield, be deprived of, pass up (*informal*)

**loser** NOUN 1 = <u>failure</u>, flop (*informal*), also-ran, no-hoper (*Austral. slang*), dud (*informal*), non-achiever

**loss** NOUN 1 = <u>losing</u>, waste, squandering, forfeiture ≠ gain 2 *sometimes plural* = <u>deficit</u>, debt, deficiency, debit, depletion ≠ gain 3 = <u>damage</u>, cost, injury, hurt, harm ≠ advantage
● PHRASES **at a loss** = <u>confused</u>, puzzled, baffled, bewildered, helpless, stumped, perplexed,

mystified

**lost** = <u>missing</u>, disappeared, vanished, wayward, misplaced, mislaid

**lot** NOUN 1 = <u>bunch</u> (*informal*), group, crowd, crew, set, band, quantity, assortment 2 = <u>destiny</u>, situation, circumstances, fortune, chance, accident, fate, doom

● PHRASES **a lot** or **lots** 1 = <u>plenty</u>, scores, masses (*informal*), load(s) (*informal*), wealth, piles (*informal*), a great deal, stack(s) 2 = <u>often</u>, regularly, frequently, a good deal

**lotion** = <u>cream</u>, solution, balm, salve, liniment, embrocation

**lottery** 1 = <u>raffle</u>, draw, lotto (*Brit., N.Z., & S. African*), sweepstake 2 = <u>gamble</u>, chance, risk, hazard, toss-up (*informal*)

**loud** 1 = <u>noisy</u>, booming, roaring, thundering, forte (*Music*), resounding, deafening, thunderous ≠ quiet 2 = <u>garish</u>, bold, glaring, flamboyant, brash, flashy, lurid, gaudy ≠ sombre

**loudly** = <u>noisily</u>, vigorously, vehemently, vociferously, uproariously, lustily, shrilly, fortissimo (*Music*)

**lounge** VERB = <u>relax</u>, loaf, sprawl, lie about, take it easy, loiter, loll, laze, outspan (*S. African*)

● NOUN = <u>sitting room</u>, living room, parlour, drawing room, front room, reception room, television room

**love** VERB 1 = <u>adore</u>, care for, treasure, cherish, prize, worship, be devoted to, dote on ≠ hate 2 = <u>enjoy</u>, like, appreciate, relish, delight in, savour, take pleasure in, have a soft spot for ≠ dislike

● NOUN 1 = <u>passion</u>, affection, warmth, attachment, intimacy, devotion, tenderness, adoration, aroha (*N.Z.*) ≠ hatred 2 = <u>liking</u>, taste, bent for, weakness for, relish for, enjoyment, devotion to, penchant for 3 = <u>beloved</u>, dear, dearest, lover, darling, honey, sweetheart, truelove ≠ enemy 4 = <u>sympathy</u>, understanding, pity, humanity, warmth, mercy, sorrow, kindness, aroha (*N.Z.*)

● PHRASES **make love** = <u>have sexual intercourse</u>, have sex, go to bed, sleep together, do it (*informal*), mate, have sexual relations, have it off (*slang*)

**love affair** = <u>romance</u>, relationship, affair, intrigue, liaison, amour

**lovely** 1 = <u>beautiful</u>, appealing, attractive, charming, pretty, handsome, good-looking, exquisite ≠ ugly 2 = <u>wonderful</u>, pleasing, nice, pleasant, engaging, marvellous, delightful, enjoyable ≠ horrible

**lover** = <u>sweetheart</u>, beloved, loved one, flame (*informal*), mistress, admirer, suitor, woman friend

**loving** 1 = <u>affectionate</u>, dear, devoted, tender, fond, doting, amorous, warm-hearted ≠ cruel 2 = <u>tender</u>, kind, caring, warm, gentle, sympathetic, considerate

**low** 1 = <u>small</u>, little, short, stunted, squat ≠ tall 2 = <u>inferior</u>, bad, poor, inadequate, unsatisfactory, deficient, second-rate, shoddy, half-pie (*N.Z. informal*), bodger or bodgie (*Austral. slang*) 3 = <u>quiet</u>, soft, gentle, whispered, muted, subdued, hushed, muffled ≠ loud 4 = <u>dejected</u>, depressed, miserable, fed up, moody, gloomy, glum, despondent ≠ happy 5 = <u>coarse</u>, common, rough, crude, rude, vulgar, undignified, disreputable 6 = <u>ill</u>, weak, frail, stricken, debilitated ≠ strong

**lower** ADJECTIVE 1 = <u>subordinate</u>, under, smaller, junior, minor, secondary, lesser, inferior 2 = <u>reduced</u>, cut, diminished, decreased, lessened, curtailed ≠ increased

● VERB 1 = <u>drop</u>, sink, depress, let down, submerge, take down, let fall ≠ raise 2 = <u>lessen</u>, cut, reduce, diminish, slash, decrease, prune, minimize ≠ increase

**low-key** = <u>subdued</u>, quiet, restrained, muted, understated, toned down

**loyal** = <u>faithful</u>, true, devoted, dependable, constant, staunch, trustworthy, trusty ≠ disloyal

**loyalty** = <u>faithfulness</u>, commitment, devotion, allegiance, fidelity, homage, obedience, constancy

**luck** NOUN 1 = <u>good fortune</u>, success, advantage, prosperity, blessing, windfall, godsend, serendipity 2 = <u>fortune</u>, lot, stars, chance, accident, fate, destiny, twist of fate

● PHRASES **in luck** = <u>fortunate</u>, successful, favoured, well-off, jammy (*Brit. slang*) ◆ **out of luck** = <u>unfortunate</u>, cursed, unlucky, unsuccessful

**luckily** = <u>fortunately</u>, happily, opportunely

**lucky** = <u>fortunate</u>, successful, favoured, charmed, blessed, jammy (*Brit. slang*), serendipitous ≠ unlucky

**lucrative** = <u>profitable</u>, rewarding, productive, fruitful, well-paid, advantageous, remunerative

**ludicrous** = <u>ridiculous</u>, crazy, absurd, preposterous, silly, laughable, farcical, outlandish ≠ sensible

**luggage** = <u>baggage</u>, things, cases, bags, gear, suitcases, paraphernalia, impedimenta

**lull** NOUN = <u>respite</u>, pause, quiet, silence, calm, hush, let-up

(*informal*)

● VERB = <u>calm</u>, soothe, subdue, quell, allay, pacify, tranquillize

**lumber¹** VERB (*Brit. informal*) = <u>burden</u>, land, load, saddle, encumber

● NOUN (*Brit.*) = <u>junk</u>, refuse, rubbish, trash, clutter, jumble

**lumber²** = <u>plod</u>, shuffle, shamble, trudge, stump, waddle, trundle

**lumbering** = <u>awkward</u>, heavy, hulking, ponderous, ungainly

**lump** NOUN 1 = <u>piece</u>, ball, block, mass, chunk, hunk, nugget 2 = <u>swelling</u>, growth, bump, tumour, bulge, hump, protrusion

● VERB = <u>group</u>, throw, mass, combine, collect, pool, consolidate, conglomerate

**lunatic** NOUN = <u>madman</u>, maniac, psychopath, nutcase (*slang*)

● ADJECTIVE = <u>mad</u>, crazy, insane, irrational, daft, deranged, crackpot (*informal*), crackbrained, off the air (*Austral. slang*)

**lunge** VERB = <u>pounce</u>, charge, dive, leap, plunge, thrust

● NOUN = <u>thrust</u>, charge, pounce, spring, swing, jab

**lurch** 1 = <u>tilt</u>, roll, pitch, list, rock, lean, heel 2 = <u>stagger</u>, reel, stumble, weave, sway, totter

**lure** VERB = <u>tempt</u>, draw, attract, invite, trick, seduce, entice, allure

● NOUN = <u>temptation</u>, attraction, incentive, bait, carrot (*informal*), inducement, enticement, allurement

**lurk** = <u>hide</u>, sneak, prowl, lie in wait, slink, skulk, conceal yourself

**lush** 1 = <u>abundant</u>, green, flourishing, dense, rank, verdant 2 = <u>luxurious</u>, grand, elaborate, lavish, extravagant, sumptuous, plush (*informal*), ornate

**lust** NOUN 1 = <u>lechery</u>, sensuality, lewdness, lasciviousness 2 = <u>desire</u>, longing, passion, appetite, craving, greed, thirst

● PHRASES **lust for** *or* **after someone** = <u>desire</u>, want, crave, yearn for, covet, hunger for *or* after ◆ **lust for** *or* **after something** = <u>desire</u>, crave, yearn for, covet

**luxurious** = <u>sumptuous</u>, expensive, comfortable, magnificent, splendid, lavish, plush (*informal*), opulent

> ### Word Power
>
> **luxurious** – *Luxurious* is sometimes wrongly used where *luxuriant* is meant: *he had a luxuriant* (not *luxurious*) *moustache; the walls were covered with a luxuriant growth of wisteria.*

**luxury** 1 = <u>opulence</u>, splendour, richness, extravagance, affluence, hedonism, a bed of roses, the life of Riley ≠ poverty

2 = <u>extravagance</u>, treat, extra, indulgence, frill ≠ necessity

**lying** NOUN = <u>dishonesty</u>, perjury, deceit, misrepresentation, mendacity, untruthfulness

● ADJECTIVE = <u>deceitful</u>, false, deceiving, treacherous, dishonest, two-faced, mendacious, perfidious ≠ truthful

**lyrical** = <u>enthusiastic</u>, inspired, poetic, impassioned, effusive, rhapsodic

# M

**machine** 1 = <u>appliance</u>, device, apparatus, engine, tool, instrument, mechanism, gadget 2 = <u>system</u>, structure, organization, machinery, setup (informal)

**machinery** = <u>equipment</u>, gear, instruments, apparatus, technology, tackle, tools, gadgetry

**macho** = <u>manly</u>, masculine, chauvinist, virile

**mad** 1 = <u>insane</u>, crazy (informal), nuts (slang), raving, unstable, psychotic, demented, deranged, off the air (Austral. slang) ≠ sane 2 = <u>foolish</u>, absurd, wild, stupid, daft (informal), irrational, senseless, preposterous ≠ sensible 3 (Informal) = <u>angry</u>, furious, incensed, enraged, livid

(informal), berserk, berko (Austral. slang), tooshie (Austral. slang), off the air (Austral. slang) ≠ calm 4 = <u>enthusiastic</u>, wild, crazy (informal), ardent, fanatical, avid, impassioned, infatuated ≠ nonchalant 5 = <u>frenzied</u>, wild, excited, frenetic, uncontrolled, unrestrained

**madden** = <u>infuriate</u>, irritate, incense, enrage, upset, annoy, inflame, drive you crazy ≠ calm

**madly** 1 (Informal) = <u>passionately</u>, wildly, desperately, intensely, to distraction, devotedly 2 = <u>foolishly</u>, wildly, absurdly, ludicrously, irrationally, senselessly 3 = <u>energetically</u>, wildly, furiously, excitedly, recklessly, speedily, like mad (informal) 4 = <u>insanely</u>, frantically, hysterically, crazily, deliriously, distractedly, frenziedly

**madness** 1 = <u>insanity</u>, mental illness, delusion, mania, dementia, distraction, aberration, psychosis 2 = <u>foolishness</u>, nonsense, folly, absurdity, idiocy, wildness, daftness (informal), foolhardiness

**magazine** = <u>journal</u>, publication, supplement, rag (informal), issue, glossy (informal), pamphlet, periodical

**magic** NOUN 1 = <u>sorcery</u>, wizardry, witchcraft,

enchantment, black art, necromancy 2 = **conjuring**, illusion, trickery, sleight of hand, legerdemain, prestidigitation 3 = **charm**, power, glamour, fascination, magnetism, enchantment, allurement

● **ADJECTIVE** = **miraculous**, entrancing, charming, fascinating, marvellous, magical, enchanting, bewitching

**magician 1** = **conjuror**, illusionist, prestidigitator 2 = **sorcerer**, witch, wizard, illusionist, warlock, necromancer, enchanter *or* enchantress

**magistrate** = **judge**, justice, justice of the peace, J.P.

**magnetic** = **attractive**, irresistible, seductive, captivating, charming, fascinating, charismatic, hypnotic ≠ repulsive

**magnificent 1** = **splendid**, impressive, imposing, glorious, gorgeous, majestic, regal, sublime ≠ ordinary 2 = **brilliant**, fine, excellent, outstanding, superb, splendid

**magnify 1** = **enlarge**, increase, boost, expand, intensify, blow up (*informal*), heighten, amplify ≠ reduce 2 = **make worse**, exaggerate, intensify, worsen, exacerbate, increase, inflame 3 = **exaggerate**, overstate, inflate, overplay, overemphasize ≠ understate

**magnitude 1** = **importance**, consequence, significance, moment, note, weight, greatness ≠ unimportance 2 = **immensity**, size, extent, enormity, volume, vastness ≠ smallness 3 = **intensity**, amplitude

**maid 1** = **servant**, chambermaid, housemaid, menial, maidservant, female servant, domestic (*archaic*), parlourmaid 2 (*Literary*) = **girl**, maiden, lass, damsel, lassie (*informal*), wench

**maiden** NOUN (*Literary*) = **girl**, maid, lass, damsel, virgin, lassie (*informal*), wench

● **ADJECTIVE 1** = **first**, initial, inaugural, introductory 2 = **unmarried**, unwed

**mail** NOUN = **letters**, post, correspondence

● **VERB** = **post**, send, forward, e-mail, dispatch

**main** **ADJECTIVE** = **chief**, leading, head, central, essential, principal, foremost ≠ minor

● **PLURAL NOUN 1** = **pipeline**, channel, pipe, conduit, duct 2 = **cable**, line, electricity supply, mains supply

● **PHRASES in the main** = **on the whole**, generally, mainly, mostly, in general, for the most part

**mainly** = **chiefly**, mostly, largely, principally, primarily, on the whole, predominantly, in the main

**mainstream** = <u>conventional</u>, general, established, received, accepted, current, prevailing, orthodox ≠ unconventional

**maintain** 1 = <u>continue</u>, retain, preserve, sustain, carry on, keep up, prolong, perpetuate ≠ end 2 = <u>assert</u>, state, claim, insist, declare, contend, profess, avow ≠ disavow 3 = <u>look after</u>, care for, take care of, conserve, keep in good condition

**maintenance** 1 = <u>upkeep</u>, keeping, care, repairs, conservation, nurture, preservation 2 = <u>allowance</u>, support, keep, alimony 3 = <u>continuation</u>, carrying-on, perpetuation, prolongation

**majestic** = <u>grand</u>, magnificent, impressive, superb, splendid, regal, stately, monumental ≠ modest

**majesty** = <u>grandeur</u>, glory, splendour, magnificence, nobility ≠ triviality

**major** 1 = <u>important</u>, critical, significant, great, serious, crucial, outstanding, notable 2 = <u>main</u>, higher, greater, bigger, leading, chief, senior, supreme ≠ minor

**majority** 1 = <u>most</u>, mass, bulk, best part, better part, lion's share, preponderance, greater number 2 = <u>adulthood</u>, maturity, age of consent, seniority, manhood or womanhood

### Word Power

**majority** – The majority of should always refer to a countable number of things or people. If you are talking about an amount or quantity, rather than a countable number, use *most of*, as in *most of the harvest was saved* (not *the majority of the harvest was saved*).

**make** VERB 1 = <u>produce</u>, cause, create, effect, lead to, generate, bring about, give rise to 2 = <u>perform</u>, do, effect, carry out, execute 3 = <u>force</u>, cause, compel, drive, require, oblige, induce, constrain 4 = <u>create</u>, build, produce, manufacture, form, fashion, construct, assemble 5 = <u>earn</u>, get, gain, net, win, clear, obtain, bring in 6 = <u>amount to</u>, total, constitute, add up to, count as, tot up to (*informal*)
● NOUN = <u>brand</u>, sort, style, model, kind, type, variety, marque
● PHRASES **make for something** = <u>head for</u>, aim for, head towards, be bound for
♦ **make it** (*Informal*) = <u>succeed</u>, prosper, arrive (*informal*), get on, crack it (*informal*) ♦ **make off** = <u>flee</u>, clear out (*informal*), bolt, take to your heels, run away *or* off ♦ **make something up** = <u>invent</u>, create, construct, compose, frame, coin, devise,

originate ♦ **make up** = <u>settle</u>
<u>your differences</u>, bury the
hatchet, call it quits, declare a
truce, be friends again ♦ **make**
**up for something**
= <u>compensate for</u>, make amends
for, atone for, balance out, offset,
make recompense for ♦ **make**
**up something 1** = <u>form</u>,
account for, constitute, compose,
comprise **2** = <u>complete</u>, supply,
fill, round off
**maker** = <u>manufacturer</u>,
producer, builder, constructor
**makeshift** = <u>temporary</u>,
provisional, substitute, expedient,
stopgap
**make-up 1** = <u>cosmetics</u>, paint
(*informal*), powder, face
(*informal*), greasepaint (*Theatre*)
**2** = <u>nature</u>, character,
constitution, temperament,
disposition **3** = <u>structure</u>,
organization, arrangement,
construction, assembly,
constitution, format, composition
**making** NOUN = <u>creation</u>,
production, manufacture,
construction, assembly,
composition, fabrication
● PLURAL NOUN = <u>beginnings</u>,
potential, capacity, ingredients
**male** = <u>masculine</u>, manly, macho,
virile ≠ female
**malicious** = <u>spiteful</u>,
malevolent, resentful, vengeful,
rancorous, ill-disposed, ill-natured

≠ benevolent
**mammal** ► bats ► carnivores
► marsupials ► monkeys,
apes and other primates
► rodents ► sea mammals
► whales and dolphins

| *Extinct mammals* | |
|---|---|
| apeman | mastodon |
| aurochs | megathere |
| australopithecine | quagga |
| eohippus | sabre-toothed |
| glyptodont | tiger *or* cat |
| mammoth | tarpan |

**mammoth** = <u>colossal</u>, huge,
giant, massive, enormous,
immense, gigantic, monumental
≠ tiny
**man** NOUN **1** = <u>male</u>, guy
(*informal*), fellow (*informal*),
gentleman, bloke (*Brit. informal*),
chap (*Brit. informal*), dude (*U.S.*
*informal*), geezer (*informal*)
**2** = <u>human</u>, human being, person,
individual, soul **3** = <u>mankind</u>,
humanity, people, human race,
humankind, Homo sapiens
● VERB = <u>staff</u>, people, crew,
occupy, garrison
**mana** (*N.Z.*) = <u>authority</u>,
influence, power, might, standing,
status, importance, eminence
**manage 1** = <u>be in charge of</u>, run,
handle, direct, conduct,
command, administer, supervise
**2** = <u>organize</u>, use, handle,

regulate 3 = <u>cope</u>, survive, succeed, carry on, make do, get by (*informal*), muddle through 4 = <u>perform</u>, do, achieve, carry out, undertake, cope with, accomplish, contrive 5 = <u>control</u>, handle, manipulate

**management** 1 = <u>administration</u>, control, running, operation, handling, direction, command, supervision 2 = <u>directors</u>, board, executive(s), administration, employers

**manager** = <u>supervisor</u>, head, director, executive, boss (*informal*), governor, administrator, organizer, baas (*S. African*)

**mandate** = <u>command</u>, order, commission, instruction, decree, directive, edict

**mandatory** = <u>compulsory</u>, required, binding, obligatory, requisite ≠ optional

**manhood** = <u>manliness</u>, masculinity, virility

**manifest** ADJECTIVE = <u>obvious</u>, apparent, patent, evident, clear, glaring, noticeable, blatant ≠ concealed
• VERB = <u>display</u>, show, reveal, express, demonstrate, expose, exhibit ≠ conceal

**manifestation** 1 = <u>sign</u>, symptom, indication, mark, example, evidence, proof, testimony 2 = <u>display</u>, show, exhibition, expression, demonstration

**manipulate** 1 = <u>influence</u>, control, direct, negotiate, exploit, manoeuvre 2 = <u>work</u>, use, operate, handle

**mankind** = <u>people</u>, man, humanity, human race, humankind, Homo sapiens

> ### Word Power
>
> **mankind** – Some people object to the use of *mankind* to refer to all human beings on the grounds that it is sexist. A preferable term is *humankind*, which refers to both men and women.

**manly** = <u>virile</u>, masculine, strong, brave, bold, strapping, vigorous, courageous ≠ effeminate

**man-made** = <u>artificial</u>, manufactured, mock, synthetic, ersatz

**manner** NOUN 1 = <u>style</u>, way, fashion, method, custom, mode 2 = <u>behaviour</u>, air, bearing, conduct, aspect, demeanour 3 = <u>type</u>, form, sort, kind, variety, brand, category
• PLURAL NOUN 1 = <u>conduct</u>, behaviour, demeanour 2 = <u>politeness</u>, courtesy, etiquette, refinement, decorum, p's and q's 3 = <u>protocol</u>, customs, social graces

**mannered** = <u>affected</u>, artificial,

pretentious, stilted, arty-farty
(*informal*) ≠ natural

**manoeuvre** VERB 1 = <u>scheme</u>,
wangle (*informal*), machinate
2 = <u>manipulate</u>, arrange,
organize, set up, engineer, fix,
orchestrate, contrive
● NOUN 1 = <u>stratagem</u>, scheme,
trick, tactic, intrigue, dodge, ploy,
ruse 2 *often plural* = <u>movement</u>,
operation, exercise, war game

**mansion** = <u>residence</u>, manor,
hall, villa, seat

**mantle** 1 = <u>covering</u>, screen,
curtain, blanket, veil, shroud,
canopy, pall 2 = <u>cloak</u>, wrap, cape,
hood, shawl

**manual** ADJECTIVE 1 = <u>physical</u>,
human 2 = <u>hand-operated</u>, hand,
non-automatic
● NOUN = <u>handbook</u>, guide,
instructions, bible

**manufacture** VERB 1 = <u>make</u>,
build, produce, construct, create,
turn out, assemble, put together
2 = <u>concoct</u>, make up, invent,
devise, fabricate, think up, cook
up (*informal*), trump up
● NOUN = <u>making</u>, production,
construction, assembly, creation

**manufacturer** = <u>maker</u>,
producer, builder, creator,
industrialist, constructor

**many** DETERMINER = <u>numerous</u>,
various, countless, abundant,
myriad, innumerable, manifold,
umpteen (*informal*)

● PRONOUN = <u>a lot</u>, lots (*informal*),
plenty, scores, heaps (*informal*)

**mar** 1 = <u>harm</u>, damage, hurt,
spoil, stain, taint, tarnish 2 = <u>ruin</u>,
spoil, scar, flaw, impair, detract
from, deform, blemish ≠ improve

**march** VERB 1 = <u>parade</u>, walk, file,
pace, stride, swagger 2 = <u>walk</u>,
strut, storm, sweep, stride, flounce
● NOUN 1 = <u>walk</u>, trek, slog, yomp
(*Brit. informal*), routemarch
2 = <u>progress</u>, development,
advance, evolution, progression

**margin** = <u>edge</u>, side, border,
boundary, verge, brink, rim,
perimeter

**marginal** 1 = <u>insignificant</u>, small,
minor, slight, minimal, negligible
2 = <u>borderline</u>, bordering, on the
edge, peripheral

**marijuana** = <u>cannabis</u>, pot
(*slang*), dope (*slang*), grass (*slang*),
hemp, dagga (*S. African*)

**marine** = <u>nautical</u>, maritime,
naval, seafaring, seagoing

**mariner** = <u>sailor</u>, seaman, sea
dog, seafarer, salt

**marital** = <u>matrimonial</u>, nuptial,
conjugal, connubial

**maritime** 1 = <u>nautical</u>, marine,
naval, oceanic, seafaring
2 = <u>coastal</u>, seaside, littoral

**mark** NOUN 1 = <u>spot</u>, stain, streak,
smudge, line, scratch, scar, blot
2 = <u>characteristic</u>, feature,
standard, quality, measure, stamp,
attribute, criterion 3 = <u>indication</u>,

sign, symbol, token 4 = <u>brand</u>,
impression, label, device, flag,
symbol, token, emblem
5 = <u>target</u>, goal, aim, purpose,
object, objective
● VERB 1 = <u>scar</u>, scratch, stain,
streak, blot, smudge, blemish
2 = <u>label</u>, identify, brand, flag,
stamp, characterize 3 = <u>grade</u>,
correct, assess, evaluate, appraise
4 = <u>distinguish</u>, show, illustrate,
exemplify, denote 5 = <u>observe</u>,
mind, note, notice, attend to, pay
attention to, pay heed to

**marked** = <u>noticeable</u>, clear,
decided, striking, obvious,
prominent, patent, distinct
≠ imperceptible

**markedly** = <u>noticeably</u>, clearly,
obviously, considerably, distinctly,
decidedly, strikingly, conspicuously

**market** NOUN = <u>fair</u>, mart, bazaar,
souk (Arabic)
● VERB = <u>sell</u>, promote, retail,
peddle, vend

**maroon** = <u>abandon</u>, leave,
desert, strand, leave high and dry
(informal)

**marriage** = <u>wedding</u>, match,
nuptials, wedlock, matrimony
(Related Words)
adjectives: conjugal, marital, nuptial

**marry** 1 = <u>tie the knot</u> (informal),
wed, get hitched (slang)
2 = <u>unite</u>, join, link, bond, ally,
merge, knit, unify

**marsh** = <u>swamp</u>, bog, slough,

fen, quagmire, morass

**marshal** 1 = <u>conduct</u>, take, lead,
guide, steer, escort, shepherd,
usher 2 = <u>arrange</u>, group, order,
line up 2 = organize, deploy, array,
draw up

**marsupial** ▸ marsupials

**martial** = <u>military</u>, belligerent,
warlike, bellicose

**marvel** VERB = <u>be amazed</u>,
wonder, gape, be awed
● NOUN 1 = <u>wonder</u>,
phenomenon, miracle, portent
2 = <u>genius</u>, prodigy

**marvellous** = <u>excellent</u>, great
(informal), wonderful, brilliant,
amazing, extraordinary, superb,
spectacular, booshit (Austral.
slang), exo (Austral. slang), sik
(Austral. slang) ≠ terrible

**masculine** = <u>male</u>, manly,
mannish, manlike, virile

**mask** NOUN = <u>façade</u>, disguise,
front, cover, screen, veil, guise,
camouflage
● VERB = <u>disguise</u>, hide, conceal,
obscure, cover (up), screen,
blanket, veil

**mass** NOUN 1 = <u>lot</u>, collection,
load, pile, quantity, bunch, stack,
heap 2 = <u>piece</u>, block, lump, chunk,
hunk 3 = <u>size</u>, matter, weight,
extent, bulk, magnitude, greatness
● ADJECTIVE = <u>large-scale</u>, general,
widespread, extensive, universal,
wholesale, indiscriminate
● VERB = <u>gather</u>, assemble,

348

## Marsupials

bandicoot
Bennett's tree kangaroo *or*
  tcharibeena
bettong
bilby, rabbit(-eared) bandicoot,
  long-eared bandicoot, dalgyte, *or*
  dalgite
bobuck *or* mountain (brushtail)
  possum
boodie (rat), burrowing rat-
  kangaroo, Lesueur's rat-
  kangaroo, tungoo, *or* tungo
boongary *or* Lumholtz's tree
  kangaroo
bridled nail-tail wallaby *or* merrin
brush-tail(ed) possum
burramys *or* (mountain) pygmy
  possum
crest-tailed marsupial mouse,
  Cannings' little dog, *or* mulgara
crescent nail-tail wallaby *or*
  wurrung
cuscus
dasyurid, dasyure, native cat,
  marsupial cat, *or* wild cat
dibbler
diprotodon
dunnart
fluffy glider *or* yellow-bellied
  glider
flying phalanger, flying squirrel,
  glider, *or* pongo
green ringtail possum *or* toolah
hare-wallaby
honey mouse, honey possum,
  noolbenger, *or* tait
jerboa, jerboa pouched mouse,
  jerboa kangaroo, *or* kultarr
kangaroo *or* (*Austral. informal*)
  roo

koala (bear) *or* (*Austral.*) native
  bear
kowari
larapinta *or* Darling Downs
  dunnart
marlu
marsupial mole
marsupial mouse
munning
ningaui
northern native cat *or* satanellus
numbat *or* banded anteater
opossum *or* possum
pademelon *or* paddymelon
phalanger
pitchi-pitchi *or* wuhl-wuhl
platypus, duck-billed platypus, *or*
  duckbill
potoroo
pygmy glider, feather glider, *or*
  flying mouse
quokka
quoll
rat kangaroo
squirrel glider
sugar glider
tammar, damar, *or* dama
Tasmanian devil *or* ursine
  dasyure
thylacine, Tasmanian wolf, *or*
  Tasmanian tiger
tiger cat *or* spotted native cat
tree kangaroo
tuan, phascogale, *or* wambenger
wallaby
wallaroo, uroo, *or* biggada
warabi
wombat *or* (*Austral.*) badger
yapok
yallara

accumulate, collect, rally, swarm, throng, congregate

**massacre** NOUN = <u>slaughter</u>, murder, holocaust, carnage, extermination, annihilation, butchery, blood bath

• VERB = <u>slaughter</u>, kill, murder, butcher, wipe out, exterminate, mow down, cut to pieces

**massage** NOUN = <u>rub-down</u>, manipulation

• VERB 1 = <u>rub down</u>, manipulate, knead 2 = <u>manipulate</u>, alter, distort, doctor, cook (*informal*), fix (*informal*), rig, fiddle (*informal*)

**massive** = <u>huge</u>, big, enormous, immense, hefty, gigantic, monumental, mammoth ≠ tiny

**master** NOUN 1 = <u>lord</u>, ruler, commander, chief, director, manager, boss (*informal*), head, baas (*S. African*) ≠ servant 2 = <u>expert</u>, maestro, ace (*informal*), genius, wizard, virtuoso, doyen, past master, fundi (*S. African*) ≠ amateur 3 = <u>teacher</u>, tutor, instructor ≠ student

• ADJECTIVE = <u>main</u>, principal, chief, prime, foremost, predominant ≠ lesser

• VERB 1 = <u>learn</u>, understand, pick up, grasp, get the hang of (*informal*), know inside out, know backwards 2 = <u>overcome</u>, defeat, conquer, tame, triumph over, vanquish ≠ give in to

**masterly** = <u>skilful</u>, expert, crack (*informal*), supreme, world-class, consummate, first-rate, masterful

**mastermind** VERB = <u>plan</u>, manage, direct, organize, devise, conceive

• NOUN = <u>organizer</u>, director, manager, engineer, brain(s) (*informal*), architect, planner

**masterpiece** = <u>classic</u>, tour de force (*French*), pièce de résistance (*French*), magnum opus, jewel

**mastery** 1 = <u>understanding</u>, skill, know-how, expertise, prowess, finesse, proficiency, virtuosity 2 = <u>control</u>, command, domination, superiority, supremacy, upper hand, ascendancy, mana (*N.Z.*), whip hand

**match** NOUN 1 = <u>game</u>, test, competition, trial, tie, contest, fixture, bout 2 = <u>marriage</u>, pairing, alliance, partnership 3 = <u>equal</u>, rival, peer, counterpart

• VERB 1 = <u>correspond with</u>, go with, fit with, harmonize with 2 = <u>correspond</u>, agree, accord, square, coincide, tally, conform, match up 3 = <u>rival</u>, equal, compete with, compare with, emulate, measure up to

**matching** = <u>identical</u>, like, twin, equivalent, corresponding, coordinating ≠ different

**mate** NOUN 1 (*Informal*) = <u>friend</u>, pal (*informal*), companion, buddy

(*informal*), comrade, chum (*informal*), mucker (*Brit. informal*), crony, cobber (*Austral. & N.Z. old-fashioned informal*), E hoa (*N.Z.*)
2 = <u>partner</u>, lover, companion, spouse, consort, helpmeet, husband *or* wife 3 = <u>assistant</u>, subordinate, apprentice, helper, accomplice, sidekick (*informal*)
4 = <u>colleague</u>, associate, companion
● VERB = <u>pair</u>, couple, breed

**material** NOUN 1 = <u>substance</u>, matter, stuff 2 = <u>cloth</u>, fabric, textile 3 = <u>information</u>, details, facts, notes, evidence, particulars, data, info (*informal*)
● ADJECTIVE 1 = <u>physical</u>, solid, substantial, concrete, bodily, tangible, palpable, corporeal
2 = <u>relevant</u>, important, significant, essential, vital, serious, meaningful, applicable

**materially** = <u>significantly</u>, much, greatly, essentially, seriously, gravely, substantially ≠ insignificantly

**maternal** = <u>motherly</u>, protective, nurturing, maternalistic

**maternity** = <u>motherhood</u>, parenthood, motherliness

**matted** = <u>tangled</u>, knotted, unkempt, knotty, tousled, ratty, uncombed

**matter** NOUN 1 = <u>situation</u>, concern, business, question, event, subject, affair, incident
2 = <u>substance</u>, material, body, stuff
● VERB = <u>be important</u>, make a difference, count, be relevant, make any difference, carry weight, cut any ice (*informal*), be of account

**matter-of-fact**
= <u>unsentimental</u>, plain, sober, down-to-earth, mundane, prosaic, deadpan, unimaginative

**mature** VERB = <u>develop</u>, grow up, bloom, blossom, come of age, age
● ADJECTIVE 1 = <u>matured</u>, seasoned, ripe, mellow
2 = <u>grown-up</u>, adult, of age, fully fledged, full-grown ≠ immature

**maturity** 1 = <u>adulthood</u>, puberty, coming of age, pubescence, manhood *or* womanhood ≠ immaturity
2 = <u>ripeness</u>

**maul** 1 = <u>mangle</u>, claw, lacerate, tear, mangulate (*Austral. slang*)
2 = <u>ill-treat</u>, abuse, batter, molest, manhandle

**maverick** NOUN = <u>rebel</u>, radical, dissenter, individualist, protester, eccentric, heretic, nonconformist ≠ traditionalist
● ADJECTIVE = <u>rebel</u>, radical, dissenting, individualistic, eccentric, heretical, iconoclastic, nonconformist

**maximum** ADJECTIVE = <u>greatest</u>,

highest, supreme, paramount, utmost, most, topmost ≠ minimal
● NOUN = top, peak, ceiling, utmost, upper limit ≠ minimum

**maybe** = perhaps, possibly, perchance (*archaic*)

**mayhem** = chaos, trouble, violence, disorder, destruction, confusion, havoc, fracas

**maze** = web, confusion, tangle, labyrinth, imbroglio, complex network

**meadow** = field, pasture, grassland, lea (*poetic*)

**mean¹** 1 = signify, indicate, represent, express, stand for, convey, spell out, symbolize 2 = imply, suggest, intend, hint at, insinuate 3 = intend, want, plan, expect, design, aim, wish, think

---

### Word Power

**mean** – In standard British English, *mean* should not be followed by *for* when expressing intention. *I didn't mean this to happen* is acceptable, but not *I didn't mean for this to happen.*

---

**mean²** 1 = miserly, stingy, parsimonious, niggardly, mercenary, penny-pinching, ungenerous, tight-fisted, snoep (*S. African informal*) ≠ generous 2 = dishonourable, petty, shameful, shabby, vile, callous, sordid, despicable, scungy (*Austral. & N.Z.*) ≠ honourable

**mean³** NOUN = average, middle, balance, norm, midpoint
● ADJECTIVE = average, middle, standard

**meaning** 1 = significance, message, substance, drift, connotation, gist 2 = definition, sense

**meaningful** = significant, important, material, useful, relevant, valid, worthwhile, purposeful ≠ trivial

**meaningless** = nonsensical, senseless, inconsequential, inane ≠ worthwhile

**means** PLURAL NOUN 1 = method, way, process, medium, agency, instrument, mode 2 = money, funds, capital, income, resources, fortune, wealth, affluence
● PHRASES by all means = certainly, surely, of course, definitely, doubtlessly ◆ by no means = in no way, definitely not, not in the least, on no account

**meantime** or **meanwhile** = at the same time, simultaneously, concurrently

**meanwhile** or **meantime** = for now, in the interim

**measure** VERB = quantify, determine, assess, weigh, calculate, evaluate, compute, gauge
● NOUN 1 = quantity, share, amount, allowance, portion,

quota, ration, allotment
2 = <u>action</u>, act, step, procedure,
means, control, initiative,
manoeuvre 3 = <u>gauge</u>, rule, scale,
metre, ruler, yardstick 4 = <u>law</u>, act,
bill, legislation, resolution, statute
**measured** 1 = <u>steady</u>, even,
slow, regular, dignified, stately,
solemn, leisurely 2 = <u>considered</u>,
reasoned, studied, calculated,
deliberate, sober, well-thought-
out
**measurement** = <u>calculation</u>,
assessment, evaluation, valuation,
computation, calibration,
mensuration
**meat** = <u>food</u>, flesh, kai (*N.Z.
informal*)
**mechanical** 1 = <u>automatic</u>,
automated, mechanized, power-
driven, motor-driven ≠ manual
2 = <u>unthinking</u>, routine,
automatic, instinctive,
involuntary, impersonal, cursory,
perfunctory ≠ conscious
**mechanism** 1 = <u>process</u>, way,
means, system, operation,
agency, method, technique
2 = <u>machine</u>, device, tool,
instrument, appliance, apparatus,
contrivance
**mediate** = <u>intervene</u>, step in
(*informal*), intercede, referee,
umpire, reconcile, arbitrate,
conciliate
**mediation** = <u>arbitration</u>,
intervention, reconciliation,

conciliation, intercession
**mediator** = <u>negotiator</u>,
arbitrator, referee, umpire,
intermediary, middleman, arbiter,
peacemaker
**medicine** = <u>remedy</u>, drug, cure,
prescription, medication,
nostrum, medicament
**mediocre** = <u>second-rate</u>,
average, ordinary, indifferent,
middling, pedestrian, inferior, so-
so (*informal*), half-pie (*N.Z.
informal*) ≠ excellent
**meditation** = <u>reflection</u>,
thought, study, musing,
pondering, contemplation,
rumination, cogitation
**medium** ADJECTIVE = <u>average</u>,
mean, middle, middling, fair,
intermediate, midway, mediocre
≠ extraordinary
● NOUN 1 = <u>spiritualist</u>, seer,
clairvoyant, fortune teller,
channeller 2 = <u>middle</u>, mean,
centre, average, compromise,
midpoint
**meet** 1 = <u>encounter</u>, come
across, run into, happen on, find,
contact, confront, bump into
(*informal*) ≠ avoid 2 = <u>gather</u>,
collect, assemble, get together,
come together, muster, convene,
congregate ≠ disperse 3 = <u>fulfil</u>,
match (up to), answer, satisfy,
discharge, comply with, come up
to, conform to ≠ fall short of
4 = <u>experience</u>, face, suffer, bear,

go through, encounter, endure, undergo 5 = <u>converge</u>, join, cross, touch, connect, come together, link up, intersect ≠ diverge

**meeting** 1 = <u>conference</u>, gathering, assembly, congress, session, convention, get-together (*informal*), reunion, hui (*N.Z.*) 2 = <u>encounter</u>, introduction, confrontation, engagement, rendezvous, tryst, assignation

**melancholy** ADJECTIVE = <u>sad</u>, depressed, miserable, gloomy, glum, mournful, despondent, dispirited ≠ happy
● NOUN = <u>sadness</u>, depression, misery, gloom, sorrow, unhappiness, despondency, dejection ≠ happiness

**mellow** ADJECTIVE 1 = <u>full-flavoured</u>, rich, sweet, delicate 2 = <u>ripe</u>, mature, ripened ≠ unripe
● VERB 1 = <u>relax</u>, improve, settle, calm, mature, soften, sweeten 2 = <u>season</u>, develop, improve, ripen

**melody** 1 = <u>tune</u>, song, theme, air, music, strain 2 = <u>tunefulness</u>, harmony, musicality, euphony, melodiousness

**melt** 1 = <u>dissolve</u>, run, soften, fuse, thaw, defrost, liquefy, unfreeze 2 *often with away* = <u>disappear</u>, fade, vanish, dissolve, disperse, evaporate, evanesce 3 = <u>soften</u>, relax, disarm, mollify

**member** = <u>representative</u>, associate, supporter, fellow, subscriber, comrade, disciple

**membership** 1 = <u>participation</u>, belonging, fellowship, enrolment 2 = <u>members</u>, body, associates, fellows

**memoir** = <u>account</u>, life, record, journal, essay, biography, narrative, monograph

**memoirs** = <u>autobiography</u>, diary, life story, experiences, memories, journals, recollections, reminiscences

**memorable** = <u>noteworthy</u>, celebrated, historic, striking, famous, significant, remarkable, notable ≠ forgettable

**memorandum** = <u>note</u>, minute, message, communication, reminder, memo, jotting

**memorial** NOUN = <u>monument</u>, shrine, plaque, cenotaph
● ADJECTIVE = <u>commemorative</u>, remembrance, monumental

**memory** 1 = <u>recall</u>, mind, retention, ability to remember, powers of recall, powers of retention 2 = <u>recollection</u>, reminder, reminiscence, impression, echo, remembrance 3 = <u>commemoration</u>, respect, honour, recognition, tribute, remembrance, observance

**menace** NOUN 1 (*Informal*) = <u>nuisance</u>, plague, pest, annoyance, troublemaker

2 = <u>threat</u>, warning, intimidation, ill-omen, ominousness
• **VERB** = bully, threaten, intimidate, terrorize, frighten, scare

**menacing** = <u>threatening</u>, frightening, forbidding, looming, intimidating, ominous, louring or lowering ≠ encouraging

**mend** **VERB** 1 = <u>repair</u>, fix, restore, renew, patch up, renovate, refit, retouch 2 = <u>darn</u>, repair, patch, stitch, sew 3 = <u>heal</u>, improve, recover, get better, be all right, be cured, recuperate, pull through 4 = <u>improve</u>, reform, correct, revise, amend, rectify, ameliorate, emend
• **PHRASES** on the mend = <u>convalescent</u>, improving, recovering, getting better, recuperating

**mental** 1 = <u>intellectual</u>, rational, theoretical, cognitive, brain, conceptual, cerebral 2 (*Informal*) = <u>insane</u>, mad, disturbed, unstable, mentally ill, psychotic, unbalanced, deranged

**mentality** = <u>attitude</u>, character, personality, psychology, make-up, outlook, disposition, cast of mind

**mentally** = <u>psychologically</u>, intellectually, inwardly

**mention** **VERB** = <u>refer to</u>, point out, bring up, state, reveal, declare, disclose, intimate
• **NOUN** 1 often with of = <u>reference</u> to, observation, indication, remark on, allusion to 2 = <u>acknowledgment</u>, recognition, tribute, citation, honourable mention

**mentor** = <u>guide</u>, teacher, coach, adviser, tutor, instructor, counsellor, guru

**menu** = <u>bill of fare</u>, tariff (*chiefly Brit.*), set menu, table d'hôte, carte du jour (*French*)

**merchandise** = <u>goods</u>, produce, stock, products, commodities, wares

**merchant** = <u>tradesman</u>, dealer, trader, broker, retailer, supplier, seller, salesman

**mercy** 1 = <u>compassion</u>, pity, forgiveness, grace, kindness, clemency, leniency, forbearance ≠ cruelty 2 = <u>blessing</u>, boon, godsend

**mere** 1 = <u>simple</u>, nothing more than, common, plain, pure 2 = <u>bare</u>, slender, trifling, meagre, just, only, basic, no more than

**merge** 1 = <u>combine</u>, blend, fuse, amalgamate, unite, join, mix, mingle ≠ separate 2 = <u>join</u>, unite, combine, fuse ≠ separate 3 = <u>melt</u>, blend, mingle

**merger** = <u>union</u>, fusion, consolidation, amalgamation, combination, coalition, incorporation

**merit** **NOUN** = <u>advantage</u>, value, quality, worth, strength, asset, virtue, strong point

● **VERB** = <u>deserve</u>, warrant, be entitled to, earn, have a right to, be worthy of

**merry** 1 = <u>cheerful</u>, happy, carefree, jolly, festive, joyous, convivial, blithe ≠ gloomy 2 (*Brit. informal*) = tipsy, happy, mellow, tiddly (*slang, chiefly Brit.*), squiffy (*Brit. informal*)

**mesh NOUN** = <u>net</u>, netting, network, web, tracery

● **VERB** = <u>engage</u>, combine, connect, knit, coordinate, interlock, dovetail, harmonize

**mess NOUN** 1 = <u>untidiness</u>, disorder, confusion, chaos, litter, clutter, disarray, jumble 2 = <u>shambles</u> 3 = <u>difficulty</u>, dilemma, plight, hole (*informal*), fix (*informal*), jam (*informal*), muddle, pickle (*informal*), uphill (*S. African*)

● **PHRASES mess about** *or* **around** = <u>potter about</u>, dabble, amuse yourself, fool about *or* around, muck about *or* around (*informal*), play about *or* around, trifle ◆ **mess something up** 1 = <u>botch</u>, muck something up (*Brit. slang*), muddle something up 2 = <u>dirty</u>, pollute, clutter, disarrange, dishevel ◆ **mess with something** *or* **someone** = <u>interfere</u>, play, fiddle (*informal*), tamper, tinker, meddle

**message** 1 = <u>communication</u>, note, bulletin, word, letter, dispatch, memorandum, communiqué 2 = <u>point</u>, meaning, idea, moral, theme, import, purport

**messenger** = <u>courier</u>, runner, carrier, herald, envoy, go-between, emissary, delivery boy

**messy** 1 = <u>disorganized</u>, sloppy (*informal*), untidy 2 = <u>dirty</u> 3 = <u>untidy</u>, disordered, chaotic, muddled, cluttered, shambolic, disorganized ≠ tidy 4 = <u>dishevelled</u>, ruffled, untidy, rumpled, bedraggled, tousled, uncombed 5 = <u>confusing</u>, difficult, complex, confused, tangled, chaotic, tortuous

**metaphor** = <u>figure of speech</u>, image, symbol, analogy, conceit (*literary*), allegory, trope, figurative expression

**method** 1 = <u>manner</u>, process, approach, technique, way, system, style, procedure 2 = <u>orderliness</u>, planning, order, system, purpose, pattern, organization, regularity

**midday** = <u>noon</u>, twelve o'clock, noonday

**middle NOUN** = <u>centre</u>, heart, midst, halfway point, midpoint, midsection

● **ADJECTIVE** 1 = <u>central</u>, medium, mid, intervening, halfway, intermediate, median 2 = <u>intermediate</u>, intervening

**middle-class** = bourgeois, traditional, conventional

**middling** 1 = mediocre, all right, indifferent, so-so (*informal*), unremarkable, tolerable, run-of-the-mill, passable, half-pie (*N.Z. informal*) 2 = moderate, medium, average, fair, ordinary, modest, adequate

**midnight** = twelve o'clock, middle of the night, dead of night, the witching hour

**midst**
PHRASES **in the midst of** = among, during, in the middle of, surrounded by, amidst, in the thick of

**midway** ADJECTIVE *or* ADVERB = halfway, in the middle of, part-way, equidistant, at the midpoint, betwixt and between

**might** NOUN = power, force, energy, strength, vigour
● PHRASES **with all your might** = forcefully, vigorously, mightily, manfully, lustily

**mighty** = powerful, strong, strapping, robust, vigorous, sturdy, forceful, lusty ≠ weak

**migrant** NOUN = wanderer, immigrant, traveller, rover, nomad, emigrant, itinerant, drifter
● ADJECTIVE = itinerant, wandering, drifting, roving, travelling, shifting, immigrant, transient

**migrate** = move, travel, journey, wander, trek, voyage, roam, emigrate

**migration** = wandering, journey, voyage, travel, movement, trek, emigration, roving

**mild** 1 = gentle, calm, easy-going, meek, placid, docile, peaceable, equable ≠ harsh 2 = temperate, warm, calm, moderate, tranquil, balmy ≠ cold 3 = bland, thin, smooth, tasteless, insipid, flavourless

**militant** = aggressive, active, vigorous, assertive, combative ≠ peaceful

**military** ADJECTIVE = warlike, armed, soldierly, martial
● NOUN = armed forces, forces, services, army

**milk** = exploit, pump, take advantage of
*Related Words*
*adjective*: lactic

**mill** NOUN 1 = grinder, crusher, quern 2 = factory, works, plant, workshop, foundry
● VERB = grind, pound, crush, powder, grate
● PHRASES **mill about** *or* **around** = swarm, crowd, stream, surge, throng

**mimic** VERB = imitate, do (*informal*), take off (*informal*), ape, parody, caricature, impersonate
● NOUN = imitator, impressionist, copycat (*informal*), impersonator, caricaturist

**mince** 1 = <u>cut</u>, grind, crumble, dice, hash, chop up 2 = <u>tone down</u>, spare, moderate, weaken, soften

**mincing** = <u>affected</u>, camp (*informal*), precious, pretentious, dainty, sissy, effeminate, foppish

**mind** NOUN 1 = <u>memory</u>, recollection, remembrance, powers of recollection 2 = <u>intelligence</u>, reason, reasoning, understanding, sense, brain(s) (*informal*), wits, intellect 3 = <u>intention</u>, wish, desire, urge, fancy, leaning, notion, inclination 4 = <u>sanity</u>, reason, senses, judgment, wits, marbles (*informal*), rationality, mental balance
● VERB 1 = <u>take offence at</u>, dislike, care about, object to, resent, disapprove of, be bothered by, be affronted by 2 = <u>be careful</u>, watch, take care, be wary, be cautious, be on your guard 3 = <u>look after</u>, watch, protect, tend, guard, take care of, attend to, keep an eye on 4 = <u>pay attention to</u>, mark, note, listen to, observe, obey, heed, take heed of
(Related Words)
*adjective:* mental

**mine** NOUN 1 = <u>pit</u>, deposit, shaft, colliery, excavation 2 = <u>source</u>, store, fund, stock, supply, reserve, treasury, wealth
● VERB = <u>dig up</u>, extract, quarry, unearth, excavate, hew, dig for

**miner** = <u>coalminer</u>, pitman (*Brit.*), collier (*Brit.*)

**mingle** 1 = <u>mix</u>, combine, blend, merge, unite, join, interweave, intermingle ≠ separate 2 = <u>associate</u>, consort, socialize, rub shoulders (*informal*), hobnob, fraternize, hang about or around ≠ dissociate

**miniature** = <u>small</u>, little, minute, tiny, toy, scaled-down, diminutive, minuscule ≠ giant

**minimal** = <u>minimum</u>, smallest, least, slightest, token, nominal, negligible, least possible

**minimize** 1 = <u>reduce</u>, decrease, shrink, diminish, prune, curtail, miniaturize ≠ increase 2 = <u>play down</u>, discount, belittle, disparage, decry, underrate, deprecate, make light or little of ≠ praise

**minimum** ADJECTIVE = <u>lowest</u>, smallest, least, slightest, minimal, least possible ≠ maximum
● NOUN = <u>lowest</u>, least, lowest level, nadir

**minister** NOUN = <u>clergyman</u>, priest, vicar, parson, preacher, pastor, cleric, rector
● VERB often with to = <u>attend</u>, serve, tend, take care of, cater to, pander to, administer to

**ministry** 1 = <u>department</u>, office, bureau, government department 2 = <u>administration</u>, council 3 = <u>the priesthood</u>, the church, the cloth, holy orders

**minor** = <u>small</u>, lesser, slight, petty, trivial, insignificant, unimportant, inconsequential ≠ major

**mint** = <u>make</u>, produce, strike, cast, stamp, punch, coin

**minute¹** NOUN = <u>moment</u>, second, bit, flash, instant, tick (*Brit. informal*), sec (*informal*), short time
● PLURAL NOUN = <u>record</u>, notes, proceedings, transactions, transcript, memorandum

**minute²** 1 = <u>small</u>, little, tiny, miniature, microscopic, diminutive, minuscule, infinitesimal ≠ huge 2 = <u>precise</u>, close, detailed, critical, exact, meticulous, exhaustive, painstaking ≠ imprecise

**miracle** = <u>wonder</u>, phenomenon, sensation, marvel, amazing achievement, astonishing feat

**miraculous** = <u>wonderful</u>, amazing, extraordinary, incredible, astonishing, unbelievable, phenomenal, astounding ≠ ordinary

**mirror** NOUN = <u>looking-glass</u>, glass (*Brit.*), reflector
● VERB = <u>reflect</u>, follow, copy, echo, emulate

**miscarriage** = <u>failure</u>, error, breakdown, mishap, perversion

**misconduct** = <u>immorality</u>, wrongdoing, mismanagement,
malpractice, impropriety

**miserable** 1 = <u>sad</u>, depressed, gloomy, forlorn, dejected, despondent, sorrowful, wretched ≠ happy 2 = <u>pathetic</u>, sorry, shameful, despicable, deplorable, lamentable ≠ respectable

**misery** 1 = <u>unhappiness</u>, distress, despair, grief, suffering, depression, gloom, torment ≠ happiness 2 (*Brit. informal*) = <u>moaner</u>, pessimist, killjoy, spoilsport, prophet of doom, wet blanket (*informal*), sourpuss (*informal*), wowser (*Austral. & N.Z. slang*)

**misfortune** 1 *often plural* = <u>bad luck</u>, adversity, hard luck, ill luck, infelicity 2 = <u>mishap</u>, trouble, disaster, reverse, tragedy, setback, calamity, affliction ≠ good luck

**misguided** = <u>unwise</u>, mistaken, misplaced, deluded, ill-advised, imprudent, injudicious

**mislead** = <u>deceive</u>, fool, delude, take someone in (*informal*), misdirect, misinform, hoodwink, misguide

**misleading** = <u>confusing</u>, false, ambiguous, deceptive, evasive, disingenuous ≠ straightforward

**miss** VERB 1 = <u>fail to notice</u>, overlook, pass over 2 = <u>long for</u>, yearn for, pine for, long to see, ache for, feel the loss of, regret the absence of 3 = <u>not go to</u>, skip, cut, omit, be absent from, fail to attend, skive off (*informal*), play truant from, bludge (*Austral. & N.Z. informal*) 4 = avoid, beat, escape, skirt, duck, cheat, bypass, dodge

● NOUN = mistake, failure, error, blunder, omission, oversight

**missile** = projectile, weapon, shell, rocket

**missing** = lost, misplaced, not present, astray, unaccounted for, mislaid

**mission** = task, job, commission, duty, undertaking, quest, assignment, vocation

**missionary** = evangelist, preacher, apostle

**mist** = fog, cloud, steam, spray, film, haze, vapour, smog

**mistake** NOUN 1 = error, blunder, oversight, slip, gaffe (*informal*), miscalculation, faux pas
2 = oversight, error, slip, fault, howler (*informal*), erratum

● VERB 1 = confuse with, take for, mix up with 2 = misunderstand, misinterpret, misjudge, misread, misconstrue, misapprehend

**mistaken** 1 = wrong, incorrect, misguided, wide of the mark
≠ correct 2 = inaccurate, false, faulty, erroneous, unsound
≠ accurate

**mistress** = lover, girlfriend, concubine, kept woman, paramour

**misunderstand**
1 = misinterpret, misread,

mistake, misjudge, misconstrue, misapprehend, be at cross-purposes with 2 = miss the point, get the wrong end of the stick

**misunderstanding** = mistake, error, mix-up, misconception, misinterpretation, misjudgment

**misuse** NOUN 1 = waste, squandering 2 = abuse
3 = misapplication, abuse, illegal use, wrong use
4 = perversion, desecration
5 = misapplication

● VERB 1 = abuse, misapply, prostitute 2 = waste, squander, embezzle, misappropriate

**mix** VERB 1 = combine, blend, merge, join, cross, fuse, mingle, jumble 2 = socialize, associate, hang out (*informal*), mingle, circulate, consort, hobnob, fraternize 3 *often with* up = combine, marry, blend, integrate, amalgamate, coalesce, meld

● NOUN = mixture, combination, blend, fusion, compound, assortment, alloy, medley

● PHRASES **mix something up**
1 = confuse, scramble, muddle, confound 2 = blend, beat, mix, stir, fold

**mixed** 1 = varied, diverse, different, differing, cosmopolitan, assorted, jumbled, disparate
≠ homogeneous 2 = combined, blended, united, compound,

composite, mingled, amalgamated ≠ pure

**mixed-up** = confused, disturbed, puzzled, bewildered, at sea, upset, distraught, muddled

**mixture** = blend, mix, variety, fusion, assortment, brew, jumble, medley 2 = composite, compound 3 = cross, combination, blend 4 = concoction, compound, blend, brew, amalgam

**mix-up** = confusion, mistake, misunderstanding, mess, tangle, muddle

**moan** VERB 1 = groan, sigh, sob, whine, lament 2 (Informal) = grumble, complain, groan, whine, carp, grouse, whinge (informal), bleat
● NOUN 1 = groan, sigh, sob, lament, wail, grunt, whine 2 (Informal) = complaint, protest, grumble, whine, grouse, gripe (informal), grouch (informal)

**mob** NOUN 1 = crowd, pack, mass, host, drove, flock, swarm, horde 2 (Slang) = gang, group, set, lot, crew (informal)
● VERB = surround, besiege, jostle, fall on, set upon, crowd around, swarm around

**mobile** = movable, moving, travelling, wandering, portable, itinerant, peripatetic

**mobilize** 1 = rally, organize, stimulate, excite, prompt,

marshal, activate, awaken 2 = deploy, prepare, ready, rally, assemble, call up, marshal, muster

**mock** VERB = laugh at, tease, ridicule, taunt, scorn, sneer, scoff, deride ≠ respect
● ADJECTIVE = imitation, pretended, artificial, fake, false, dummy, sham, feigned ≠ genuine

**mocking** = scornful, scoffing, satirical, contemptuous, sarcastic, sardonic, disrespectful, disdainful

**mode** 1 = method, way, system, form, process, style, technique, manner 2 = fashion, style, trend, rage, vogue, look, craze

**model** NOUN 1 = representation, image, copy, miniature, dummy, replica, imitation, duplicate 2 = pattern, example, standard, original, ideal, prototype, paradigm, archetype 3 = sitter, subject, poser
● VERB 1 = show off (informal), wear, display, sport 2 = shape, form, design, fashion, carve, mould, sculpt

**moderate** ADJECTIVE 1 = mild, reasonable, controlled, limited, steady, modest, restrained, middle-of-the-road ≠ extreme 2 = average, middling, fair, ordinary, indifferent, mediocre, so-so (informal), passable, half-pie (N.Z. informal)
● VERB 1 = soften, control, temper, regulate, curb, restrain, subdue,

lessen 2 = <u>lessen</u>, ease ≠ intensify

**modern** 1 = <u>current</u>, contemporary, recent, present-day, latter-day 2 = <u>up-to-date</u>, fresh, new, novel, newfangled ≠ old-fashioned

**modest** 1 = <u>moderate</u>, small, limited, fair, ordinary, middling, meagre, frugal 2 = <u>unpretentious</u>, reserved, retiring, shy, coy, reticent, self-effacing, demure

**modesty** = <u>reserve</u>, humility, shyness, reticence, timidity, diffidence, coyness, bashfulness ≠ conceit

**modification** = <u>change</u>, variation, qualification, adjustment, revision, alteration, refinement

**modify** 1 = <u>change</u>, reform, convert, alter, adjust, adapt, revise, remodel 2 = <u>tone down</u>, lower, qualify, ease, moderate, temper, soften, restrain

**mogul** = <u>tycoon</u>, baron, magnate, big shot (*informal*), big noise (*informal*), big hitter (*informal*), heavy hitter (*informal*), V.I.P.

**moist** = <u>damp</u>, wet, soggy, humid, clammy, dewy

**moisture** = <u>damp</u>, water, liquid, dew, wetness

**molecule** = <u>particle</u>, jot, speck

**moment** 1 = <u>instant</u>, second, flash, twinkling, split second, jiffy (*informal*), trice 2 = <u>time</u>, point,

stage, juncture

**momentous** = <u>significant</u>, important, vital, critical, crucial, historic, pivotal, fateful ≠ unimportant

**momentum** = <u>impetus</u>, force, power, drive, push, energy, strength, thrust

**monarch** = <u>ruler</u>, king *or* queen, sovereign, tsar, potentate, emperor *or* empress, prince *or* princess

**monarchy** 1 = <u>sovereignty</u>, autocracy, kingship, royalism, monocracy 2 = <u>kingdom</u>, empire, realm, principality

**monastery** = <u>abbey</u>, convent, priory, cloister, nunnery, friary

**monetary** = <u>financial</u>, money, economic, capital, cash, fiscal, budgetary, pecuniary

**money** = <u>cash</u>, capital, currency, hard cash, readies (*informal*), riches, silver, coin

**monitor** VERB = <u>check</u>, follow, watch, survey, observe, keep an eye on, keep track of, keep tabs on

● NOUN 1 = <u>guide</u>, observer, supervisor, invigilator 2 = <u>prefect</u> (*Brit.*), head girl, head boy, senior boy, senior girl

**monk** (*Loosely*) = <u>friar</u>, brother

(Related Words)
*adjective*: monastic

**monkey** 1 = <u>simian</u>, ape, primate 2 = <u>rascal</u>, horror, devil, rogue,

imp, tyke, scallywag, scamp,
nointer (*Austral. slang*)

**Related Words**

*adjective:* simian

> **monkeys, apes and other
primates**

**monster** NOUN 1 = <u>giant</u>,
mammoth, titan, colossus,
monstrosity 2 = <u>brute</u>, devil,
beast, demon, villain, fiend
• ADJECTIVE = <u>huge</u>, massive,
enormous, tremendous, immense,
gigantic, mammoth, colossal

**monstrous** 1 = <u>outrageous</u>,
shocking, foul, intolerable,

disgraceful, scandalous, inhuman,
diabolical ≠ decent 2 = <u>huge</u>,
massive, enormous, tremendous,
immense, mammoth, colossal,
prodigious ≠ tiny 3 = <u>unnatural</u>,
horrible, hideous, grotesque,
gruesome, frightful, freakish,
fiendish ≠ normal

**monument** = <u>memorial</u>, cairn,
marker, shrine, tombstone,
mausoleum, commemoration,
headstone

**monumental** 1 = <u>important</u>,
significant, enormous, historic,
memorable, awesome, majestic,

### Monkeys, apes and other primates

| | |
|---|---|
| baboon | loris |
| Barbary ape | macaque |
| bushbaby *or* galago | mandrill |
| capuchin | mangabey |
| chacma | marmoset |
| chimpanzee *or* chimp | mona |
| colobus | monkey *or* (*archaic*) jackanapes |
| douroucouli | orang-outang, orang-utan, *or* |
| flying lemur *or* colugo | orang |
| gelada | proboscis monkey |
| gibbon | rhesus monkey |
| gorilla | saki |
| green monkey | siamang |
| grivet | sifaka |
| guenon | spider monkey |
| guereza | squirrel monkey |
| howler monkey | tamarin |
| indris *or* indri | tarsier |
| langur | vervet |
| lemur | |

unforgettable ≠ unimportant
**2** (*Informal*) = <u>immense</u>, great,
massive, staggering, colossal
≠ tiny

**mood** = <u>state of mind</u>, spirit,
humour, temper, disposition,
frame of mind

**moody 1** = <u>changeable</u>, volatile,
unpredictable, erratic, fickle,
temperamental, impulsive,
mercurial ≠ stable **2** = <u>sulky</u>,
irritable, temperamental, touchy,
ill-tempered, tooshie (*Austral. slang*)
≠ cheerful **3** = <u>gloomy</u>, sad, sullen,
glum, morose ≠ cheerful **4** = <u>sad</u>,
gloomy, melancholy, sombre

**moon** NOUN = <u>satellite</u>

● VERB = <u>idle</u>, drift, loaf, languish,
waste time, daydream, mope

*Related Words*
adjective: lunar

**moor**[1] = <u>moorland</u>, fell (*Brit.*), heath

**moor**[2] = <u>tie up</u>, secure, anchor,
dock, lash, berth, make fast

**mop** NOUN **1** = <u>squeegee</u>, sponge,
swab **2** = <u>mane</u>, shock, mass,
tangle, mat, thatch

● VERB = <u>clean</u>, wash, wipe,
sponge, swab

**moral** ADJECTIVE = <u>good</u>, just,
right, principled, decent, noble,
ethical, honourable ≠ immoral

● NOUN = <u>lesson</u>, meaning, point,
message, teaching, import,
significance, precept

● PLURAL NOUN = <u>morality</u>,
standards, conduct, principles,
behaviour, manners, habits, ethics

**morale** = <u>confidence</u>, heart,
spirit, self-esteem, team spirit,
esprit de corps

**morality 1** = <u>virtue</u>, justice,
morals, honour, integrity,
goodness, honesty, decency
**2** = <u>ethics</u>, conduct, principles,
morals, manners, philosophy,
mores **3** = <u>rights and wrongs</u>,
ethics

**moratorium** = <u>postponement</u>,
freeze, halt, suspension, standstill

**more** ADJECTIVE = <u>extra</u>,
additional, new, other, added,
further, new-found, supplementary

● ADVERB **1** = <u>to a greater extent</u>,
longer, better, further, some more
**2** = <u>moreover</u>, also, in addition,
besides, furthermore, what's
more, on top of that, to boot

**moreover** = <u>furthermore</u>, also,
further, in addition, too, as well,
besides, additionally

**morning 1** = <u>before noon</u>,
forenoon, morn (*poetic*), a.m.
**2** = <u>dawn</u>, sunrise, first light,
daybreak, break of day

**mortal** ADJECTIVE **1** = <u>human</u>,
worldly, passing, fleshly, temporal,
transient, ephemeral, perishable
**2** = <u>fatal</u>, killing, terminal, deadly,
destructive, lethal, murderous,
death-dealing

● NOUN = <u>human being</u>, being,
man, woman, person, human,
individual, earthling

**mortality** 1 = <u>humanity</u>, transience, impermanence, corporeality, impermanency 2 = <u>death</u>, dying, fatality

**mostly** 1 = <u>mainly</u>, largely, chiefly, principally, primarily, on the whole, predominantly 2 = <u>generally</u>, usually, on the whole, as a rule

**moth**

(Related Words)
*young*: caterpillar
*enthusiast*: lepidopterist
▸ **butterflies and moths**

**mother** NOUN = <u>female parent</u>, mum (*Brit. informal*), ma (*informal*), mater, dam, mummy (*Brit. informal*), foster mother, biological mother
● VERB = <u>nurture</u>, raise, protect, tend, nurse, rear, care for, cherish
● ADJECTIVE = <u>native</u>, natural, innate, inborn

(Related Words)
*adjective*: maternal

**motherly** = <u>maternal</u>, loving, caring, comforting, sheltering, protective, affectionate

**motif** 1 = <u>design</u>, shape, decoration, ornament 2 = <u>theme</u>, idea, subject, concept, leitmotif

**motion** NOUN 1 = <u>movement</u>, mobility, travel, progress, flow, locomotion 2 = <u>proposal</u>, suggestion, recommendation, proposition, submission
● VERB = <u>gesture</u>, direct, wave, signal, nod, beckon, gesticulate

**motivate** 1 = <u>inspire</u>, drive, stimulate, move, cause, prompt, stir, induce 2 = <u>stimulate</u>, drive, inspire, stir, arouse, galvanize, incentivize

**motivation** = <u>incentive</u>, inspiration, motive, stimulus, reason, spur, inducement, incitement

**motive** = <u>reason</u>, ground(s), purpose, object, incentive, inspiration, stimulus, rationale

**motto** = <u>saying</u>, slogan, maxim, rule, adage, proverb, dictum, precept

**mould¹** 1 = <u>cast</u>, shape, pattern 2 = <u>design</u>, style, fashion, build, form, kind, shape, pattern 3 = <u>nature</u>, character, sort, kind, quality, type, stamp, calibre
● VERB 1 = <u>shape</u>, make, work, form, create, model, fashion, construct 2 = <u>influence</u>, make, form, control, direct, affect, shape

**mould²** = <u>fungus</u>, blight, mildew

**mound** 1 = <u>heap</u>, pile, drift, stack, rick 2 = <u>hill</u>, bank, rise, dune, embankment, knoll, hillock, kopje or koppie (*S. African*)

**mount** VERB 1 = <u>increase</u>, build, grow, swell, intensify, escalate, multiply ≠ decrease
2 = <u>accumulate</u>, increase, collect, gather, build up, pile up, amass
3 = <u>ascend</u>, scale, climb (up), go up, clamber up ≠ descend 4 = <u>get (up) on</u>, jump on, straddle, climb

onto, hop on to, bestride, get on the back of ≠ **get off** 5 = display, present, prepare, put on, organize, put on display
● NOUN 1 = **horse**, steed (*literary*)
2 = **backing**, setting, support, stand, base, frame

**mountain** 1 = **peak**, mount, horn, ridge, fell (*Brit.*), berg (*S. African*), alp, pinnacle 2 = **heap**, mass, masses, pile, a great deal, ton, stack, abundance

**mourn** 1 *often with* for = **grieve for**, lament, weep for, wail for
2 = **bemoan**, rue, deplore, bewail

**mourning** 1 = **grieving**, grief, bereavement, weeping, woe, lamentation 2 = **black**, sackcloth and ashes, widow's weeds

**mouth** 1 = **lips**, jaws, gob (*slang*), maw, cakehole (*Brit. slang*) 2 = **entrance**, opening, gateway, door, aperture, orifice
3 = **opening** 4 = **inlet**, outlet, estuary, firth, outfall, debouchment

⟨Related Words⟩
*adjective*: oral

**move** VERB 1 = **transfer**, change, switch, shift, transpose 2 = **go**, advance, progress, shift, proceed, stir, budge, make a move
3 = **relocate**, leave, remove, quit, migrate, emigrate, decamp, up sticks (*Brit. informal*) 4 = **drive**, cause, influence, persuade, shift, inspire, prompt, induce
≠ **discourage** 5 = **touch**, affect,

excite, impress, stir, disquiet
6 = **propose**, suggest, urge, recommend, request, advocate, submit, put forward
● NOUN 1 = **action**, step, manoeuvre 2 = **ploy**, action, measure, step, initiative, stroke, tactic, manoeuvre 3 = **transfer**, posting, shift, removal, relocation
4 = **turn**, go, play, chance, shot (*informal*), opportunity

**movement** 1 = **group**, party, organization, grouping, front, faction 2 = **campaign**, drive, push, crusade 3 = **move**, action, motion, manoeuvre 4 = **activity**, moving, stirring, bustle 5 = **advance**, progress, flow 6 = **transfer**, transportation, displacement
7 = **development**, change, variation, fluctuation
8 = **progression**, progress
9 (*Music*) = **section**, part, division, passage

**movie** 1 = **film**, picture, feature, flick (*slang*)

**moving** 1 = **emotional**, touching, affecting, inspiring, stirring, poignant ≠ **unemotional**
2 = **mobile**, running, active, going, operational, in motion, driving, kinetic ≠ **stationary**

**mow** VERB = **cut**, crop, trim, shear, scythe
● PHRASES **mow something or someone down** = **massacre**, butcher, slaughter, cut down,

# much → murder

shoot down, cut to pieces

**much** ADVERB 1 = <u>greatly</u>, a lot, considerably, decidedly, exceedingly, appreciably ≠ hardly 2 = <u>often</u>, a lot, routinely, a great deal, many times, habitually, on many occasions, customarily
● DETERMINER = <u>great</u>, a lot of, plenty of, considerable, substantial, piles of (*informal*), ample, abundant ≠ little
● PRONOUN = <u>a lot</u>, plenty, a great deal, lots (*informal*), masses (*informal*), loads (*informal*), tons (*informal*), heaps (*informal*) ≠ little

**muck** 1 = <u>dirt</u>, mud, filth, ooze, sludge, mire, slime, gunge (*informal*), kak (*S. African informal*) 2 = <u>manure</u>, dung, ordure

**mud** = <u>dirt</u>, clay, ooze, silt, sludge, mire, slime

**muddle** NOUN = <u>confusion</u>, mess, disorder, chaos, tangle, mix-up, disarray, predicament
● VERB 1 = <u>jumble</u>, disorder, scramble, tangle, mix up 2 = <u>confuse</u>, bewilder, daze, confound, perplex, disorient, stupefy, befuddle

**muddy** 1 = <u>boggy</u>, swampy, marshy, quaggy 2 = <u>dirty</u>, soiled, grimy, mucky, mud-caked, bespattered

**mug**[1] = <u>cup</u>, pot, beaker, tankard

**mug**[2] (*Informal*) 1 = <u>face</u>,

features, countenance, visage 2 = <u>fool</u>, sucker (*slang*), chump (*informal*), simpleton, easy or soft touch (*slang*), dorba or dorb (*Austral. slang*), bogan (*Austral. slang*)

**mug**[3] VERB = <u>attack</u>, assault, beat up, rob, set about or upon
● PHRASES mug up (on) something = <u>study</u>, cram (*informal*), bone up on (*informal*), swot up on (*Brit. informal*)

**multiple** = <u>many</u>, several, various, numerous, sundry, manifold, multitudinous

**multiply** 1 = <u>increase</u>, extend, expand, spread, build up, proliferate ≠ decrease 2 = <u>reproduce</u>, breed, propagate

**multitude** 1 = <u>great number</u>, host, army, mass, horde, myriad 2 = <u>crowd</u>, host, mass, mob, swarm, horde, throng

**mundane** 1 = <u>ordinary</u>, routine, commonplace, banal, everyday, day-to-day, prosaic, humdrum ≠ extraordinary 2 = <u>earthly</u>, worldly, secular, mortal, terrestrial, temporal ≠ spiritual

**municipal** = <u>civic</u>, public, local, council, district, urban, metropolitan

**murder** NOUN = <u>killing</u>, homicide, massacre, assassination, slaying, bloodshed, carnage, butchery
● VERB = <u>kill</u>, massacre, slaughter, assassinate, eliminate (*slang*),

butcher, slay, bump off (*slang*)

**murderer** = <u>killer</u>, assassin, slayer, butcher, slaughterer, cut-throat, hit man (*slang*)

**murderous** = <u>deadly</u>, savage, brutal, cruel, lethal, ferocious, cut-throat, bloodthirsty

**murky** 1 = <u>dark</u>, gloomy, grey, dull, dim, cloudy, misty, overcast ≠ bright 2 = <u>dark</u>, cloudy

**murmur** VERB = <u>mumble</u>, whisper, mutter

● NOUN = <u>whisper</u>, drone, purr

**muscle** NOUN 1 = <u>tendon</u>, sinew 2 = <u>strength</u>, might, power, weight, stamina, brawn

● PHRASES **muscle in** (*Informal*) = <u>impose yourself</u>, encroach, butt in, force your way in

**muscular** = <u>strong</u>, powerful, athletic, strapping, robust, vigorous, sturdy, sinewy

**muse** = <u>ponder</u>, consider, reflect, contemplate, deliberate, brood, meditate, mull over

**music** ➤ **musical expressions and tempo instructions**

**musical** = <u>melodious</u>, lyrical, harmonious, melodic, tuneful, dulcet, sweet-sounding, euphonious ≠ discordant

**must** = <u>necessity</u>, essential, requirement, fundamental, imperative, requisite, prerequisite, sine qua non (*Latin*)

**muster** VERB 1 = <u>summon up</u>, marshal 2 = <u>rally</u>, gather,

assemble, marshal, mobilize, call together 3 = <u>assemble</u>, convene

● NOUN = <u>assembly</u>, meeting, collection, gathering, rally, convention, congregation, roundup, hui (*N.Z.*), runanga (*N.Z.*)

**mutation** 1 = <u>anomaly</u>, variation, deviant, freak of nature 2 = <u>change</u>, variation, evolution, transformation, modification, alteration, metamorphosis, transfiguration

**mute** 1 = <u>close-mouthed</u>, silent 2 = <u>silent</u>, dumb, unspoken, tacit, wordless, voiceless, unvoiced 3 = <u>dumb</u>, speechless, voiceless

**mutter** = <u>grumble</u>, complain, murmur, rumble, whine, mumble, grouse, bleat

**mutual** = <u>shared</u>, common, joint, returned, reciprocal, interchangeable, requited

---

### Word Power

**mutual** – *Mutual* is sometimes used, as in *a mutual friend*, to mean 'common to or shared by two or more people'. This use has sometimes been frowned on in the past because it does not reflect the two-way relationship contained in the origins of the word, which comes from Latin *mutuus* meaning 'reciprocal'. However, this usage is very common and is now generally regarded as acceptable.

## Musical expressions and tempo instructions

| instruction | meaning |
|---|---|
| accelerando | with increasing speed |
| adagio | slowly |
| agitato | in an agitated manner |
| allegretto | fairly quickly or briskly |
| allegro | quickly, in a brisk, lively manner |
| amoroso | lovingly |
| andante | at a moderately slow tempo |
| andantino | slightly faster than andante |
| assai | (in combination) very |
| cantabile | in a singing style |
| con | (in combination) with |
| con amore | lovingly |
| con brio | vigorously |
| con moto | quickly |
| crescendo | gradual increase in loudness |
| diminuendo | gradual decrease in loudness |
| dolce | gently and sweetly |
| doloroso | in a sorrowful manner |
| espressivo | expressively |
| forte | loud or loudly |
| fortissimo | very loud |
| furioso | in a frantically rushing manner |
| giocoso | merry |
| grave | solemn and slow |
| grazioso | graceful |
| largo | slowly and broadly |
| larghetto | slowly and broadly, but less so than largo |
| legato | smoothly and connectedly |
| leggiero | light |
| lento | slowly |
| maestoso | majestically |
| mezzo | (in combination) moderately |
| moderato | at a moderate tempo |
| molto | (in combination) very |

## Musical expressions and
## tempo instructions (continued)

| instruction | meaning |
|---|---|
| non troppo *or* non tanto | (in combination) not too much |
| pianissimo | very quietly |
| piano | softly |
| più | (in combination) more |
| pizzicato | (in music for stringed instruments) to be plucked with the finger |
| poco *or* un poco | (in combination) a little |
| pomposo | in a pompous manner |
| presto | very fast |
| prestissimo | faster than presto |
| quasi | (in combination) almost, as if |
| rallentando | becoming slower |
| rubato | with a flexible tempo |
| scherzando | in jocular style |
| semplice | simple and unforced |
| sforzando | with strong initial attack |
| sostenuto | in a smooth and sustained manner |
| sotto voce | extremely quiet |
| staccato | (of notes) short, clipped, and separate |
| strepitoso | noisy |
| stringendo | with increasing speed |
| tanto | (in combination) too much |
| troppo | (in combination) too much |
| vivace | in a brisk lively manner |

**myriad** NOUN = multitude, host, army, swarm, horde

● ADJECTIVE = innumerable, countless, untold, incalculable, immeasurable, multitudinous

**mysterious** 1 = strange, puzzling, secret, weird, perplexing, uncanny, mystifying, arcane ≠ clear 2 = secretive, enigmatic, evasive, discreet, covert, reticent, furtive, inscrutable

**mystery** = puzzle, problem, question, secret, riddle, enigma, conundrum, teaser

**mystic** *or* **mystical** = supernatural, mysterious, transcendental, occult,

metaphysical, paranormal, inscrutable, otherworldly

**myth** 1 = legend, story, fiction, saga, fable, allegory, fairy story, folk tale 2 = illusion, story, fancy, fantasy, imagination, invention, delusion, superstition

**mythology** = legend, folklore, tradition, lore

# N

**nab** = catch, arrest, apprehend, seize, grab, capture, collar (*informal*), snatch

**nag**[1] VERB = scold, harass, badger, pester, worry, plague, hassle (*informal*), upbraid

● NOUN = scold, complainer, grumbler, virago, shrew, tartar, moaner, harpy

**nag**[2] = horse (*U.S.*), hack

**nagging** 1 = continuous, persistent, continual, niggling, repeated, constant, endless, perpetual 2 = scolding, shrewish

**nail** NOUN 1 = tack, spike, rivet, hobnail, brad (*technical*) 2 = fingernail, toenail, talon, thumbnail, claw

● VERB 1 = fasten, fix, secure, attach, pin, hammer, tack 2 (*informal*) = catch, arrest, capture, apprehend, trap, snare, ensnare, entrap

**naive** *or* **naïve** = gullible,

trusting, credulous, unsuspicious, green, simple, innocent, callow ≠ worldly

**naked** = nude, stripped, exposed, bare, undressed, starkers (*informal*), stark-naked, unclothed ≠ dressed

**name** NOUN = title, nickname, designation, term, handle (*slang*), epithet, sobriquet, moniker *or* monicker (*slang*)

● VERB 1 = call, christen, baptize, dub, term, style, label, entitle 2 = nominate, choose, select, appoint, specify, designate

**namely** = specifically, to wit, viz.

**nap**[1] NOUN = sleep, rest, kip (*Brit. slang*), siesta, catnap, forty winks (*informal*)

● VERB = sleep, rest, drop off (*informal*), doze, kip (*Brit. slang*), snooze (*informal*), nod off (*informal*), catnap

**nap**[2] = pile, down, fibre, weave, grain

**napkin** = serviette, cloth

**narcotic** NOUN = drug, anaesthetic, painkiller, sedative, opiate, tranquillizer, anodyne, analgesic

● ADJECTIVE = sedative, calming, hypnotic, analgesic, soporific, painkilling

**narrative** = story, report, history, account, statement, tale, chronicle

**narrator** = storyteller, writer,

author, reporter, commentator, chronicler

**narrow** ADJECTIVE 1 = <u>thin</u>, fine, slim, slender, tapering, attenuated ≠ broad 2 = <u>limited</u>, restricted, confined, tight, close, meagre, constricted ≠ wide 3 = <u>insular</u>, prejudiced, partial, dogmatic, intolerant, narrow-minded, small-minded, illiberal ≠ broad-minded
● VERB 1 = <u>restrict</u>, limit, reduce, constrict 2 = <u>get narrower</u>, taper, shrink, tighten, constrict

**narrowly** = <u>just</u>, barely, only just, scarcely, by the skin of your teeth

**nasty** 1 = <u>unpleasant</u>, ugly, disagreeable ≠ pleasant 2 = <u>spiteful</u>, mean, offensive, vicious, unpleasant, vile, malicious, despicable ≠ pleasant 3 = <u>disgusting</u>, unpleasant, offensive, vile, distasteful, obnoxious, objectionable, disagreeable, festy (*Austral. slang*), yucko (*Austral. slang*) 4 = <u>serious</u>, bad, dangerous, critical, severe, painful

**nation** 1 = <u>country</u>, state, realm 2 = <u>public</u>, people, society

**national** ADJECTIVE = <u>nationwide</u>, public, widespread, countrywide
● NOUN = <u>citizen</u>, subject, resident, native, inhabitant

**nationalism** = <u>patriotism</u>, loyalty to your country, chauvinism, jingoism, allegiance

**nationality** 1 = <u>citizenship</u>, birth 2 = <u>race</u>, nation

**nationwide** = <u>national</u>, general, widespread, countrywide

**native** ADJECTIVE = <u>mother</u>, indigenous, vernacular
● NOUN = <u>inhabitant</u>, national, resident, citizen, countryman, aborigine (*often offensive*), dweller

**natural** 1 = <u>logical</u>, valid, legitimate 2 = <u>normal</u>, common, regular, usual, ordinary, typical, everyday ≠ abnormal 3 = <u>innate</u>, native, characteristic, inherent, instinctive, intuitive, inborn, essential 4 = <u>unaffected</u>, open, genuine, spontaneous, unpretentious, unsophisticated, dinkum (*Austral. & N.Z. informal*), ingenuous, real ≠ affected 5 = <u>pure</u>, plain, organic, whole, unrefined ≠ processed

**naturally** 1 = <u>of course</u>, certainly 2 = <u>typically</u>, simply, normally, spontaneously

**nature** 1 = <u>creation</u>, world, earth, environment, universe, cosmos, natural world 2 = <u>quality</u>, character, make-up, constitution, essence, complexion 3 = <u>temperament</u>, character, personality, disposition, outlook, mood, humour, temper 4 = <u>kind</u>, sort, style, type, variety, species, category, description

**naughty** 1 = <u>disobedient</u>, bad, mischievous, badly behaved, wayward, wicked, impish, refractory ≠ good 2 = <u>obscene</u>, vulgar, improper, lewd, risqué, smutty, ribald ≠ clean

**nausea** = <u>sickness</u>, vomiting, retching, squeamishness, queasiness, biliousness

**naval** = <u>nautical</u>, marine, maritime

**navigation** = <u>sailing</u>, voyaging, seamanship, helmsmanship

**navy** = <u>fleet</u>, flotilla, armada

**near** 1 = <u>close</u>, neighbouring, nearby, adjacent, adjoining ≠ far 2 = <u>imminent</u>, forthcoming, approaching, looming, impending, upcoming, nigh, in the offing ≠ far-off

**nearby** = <u>neighbouring</u>, adjacent, adjoining

**nearly** 1 = <u>practically</u>, almost, virtually, just about, as good as, well-nigh 2 = <u>almost</u>, approaching, roughly, just about, approximately

**neat** 1 = <u>tidy</u>, trim, orderly, spruce, shipshape, spick-and-span ≠ untidy 2 = <u>methodical</u>, tidy, systematic, fastidious ≠ disorganized 3 = <u>smart</u>, trim, tidy, spruce, dapper, natty (*informal*), well-groomed, well-turned out 4 = <u>graceful</u>, elegant, adept, nimble, adroit, efficient ≠ clumsy 5 = <u>clever</u>, efficient, handy, apt, well-judged ≠ inefficient 6 = <u>cool</u>, great

(*informal*), excellent, brilliant, superb, fantastic (*informal*), tremendous, fabulous (*informal*), booshit (*Austral. slang*), exo (*Austral. slang*), sik (*Austral. slang*) ≠ terrible 7 (*of alcoholic drinks*) = <u>undiluted</u>, straight, pure, unmixed

**neatly** 1 = <u>tidily</u>, smartly, systematically, methodically, fastidiously 2 = <u>smartly</u>, elegantly, tidily, nattily 3 = <u>gracefully</u>, expertly, efficiently, adeptly, skilfully, nimbly, adroitly, dexterously 4 = <u>cleverly</u>, efficiently

**necessarily** 1 = <u>automatically</u>, naturally, definitely, undoubtedly, certainly 2 = <u>inevitably</u>, of necessity, unavoidably, incontrovertibly, nolens volens (*Latin*)

**necessary** 1 = <u>needed</u>, required, essential, vital, compulsory, mandatory, imperative, indispensable ≠ unnecessary 2 = <u>inevitable</u>, certain, unavoidable, inescapable ≠ avoidable

**necessity** NOUN 1 = <u>essential</u>, need, requirement, fundamental, requisite, prerequisite, sine qua non (*Latin*), desideratum 2 = <u>inevitability</u>, certainty ● PLURAL NOUN = <u>essentials</u>, needs, requirements, fundamentals

**need** VERB 1 = <u>want</u>, miss, require,

lack, have to have, demand
2 = <u>require</u>, want, demand, call for, entail, necessitate 3 = <u>have to</u>, be obliged to

● NOUN 1 = <u>requirement</u>, demand, essential, necessity, requisite, desideratum 2 = <u>necessity</u>, call, demand, obligation
3 = <u>emergency</u>, want, necessity, urgency, exigency 4 = <u>poverty</u>, deprivation, destitution, penury

**needed** = <u>necessary</u>, wanted, required, lacked, called for, desired

**needle** = <u>irritate</u>, provoke, annoy, harass, taunt, nag, goad, rile

**needless** = <u>unnecessary</u>, pointless, gratuitous, useless, unwanted, redundant, superfluous, groundless
≠ essential

**needy** = <u>poor</u>, deprived, disadvantaged, impoverished, penniless, destitute, poverty-stricken, underprivileged
≠ wealthy

**negative** ADJECTIVE
1 = <u>pessimistic</u>, cynical, unwilling, gloomy, jaundiced, uncooperative ≠ optimistic
2 = <u>dissenting</u>, contradictory, refusing, denying, rejecting, opposing, resisting, contrary
≠ assenting

● NOUN = <u>denial</u>, no, refusal, rejection, contradiction

**neglect** VERB 1 = <u>disregard</u>,
ignore, fail to look after ≠ look after 2 = <u>shirk</u>, forget, overlook, omit, evade, pass over, skimp, be remiss in *or* about 3 = <u>fail</u>, forget, omit

● NOUN 1 = <u>negligence</u>, inattention ≠ care 2 = <u>shirking</u>, failure, oversight, carelessness, dereliction, slackness, laxity

**neglected** 1 = <u>uncared-for</u>, abandoned, underestimated, disregarded, undervalued, unappreciated 2 = <u>run down</u>, derelict, overgrown, uncared-for

**negligence** = <u>carelessness</u>, neglect, disregard, dereliction, slackness, inattention, laxity, thoughtlessness

**negotiate** 1 = <u>bargain</u>, deal, discuss, debate, mediate, hold talks, cut a deal, conciliate
2 = <u>arrange</u>, work out, bring about, transact 3 = <u>get round</u>, clear, pass, cross, get over, get past, surmount

**negotiation** 1 = <u>bargaining</u>, debate, discussion, transaction, dialogue, mediation, arbitration, wheeling and dealing (*informal*)
2 = <u>arrangement</u>, working out, transaction, bringing about

**negotiator** = <u>mediator</u>, ambassador, diplomat, delegate, intermediary, moderator, honest broker

**neighbourhood** 1 = <u>district</u>, community, quarter, region, locality, locale 2 = vicinity, environs

**neighbouring** = nearby, next, near, bordering, surrounding, connecting, adjacent, adjoining ≠ remote

**neighbourly** = helpful, kind, friendly, obliging, harmonious, considerate, sociable, hospitable

**nerve** NOUN 1 = bravery, courage, bottle (*Brit. slang*), resolution, daring, guts (*informal*), pluck, grit 2 (*Informal*) = impudence, cheek (*informal*), audacity, boldness, temerity, insolence, impertinence, brazenness

● PLURAL NOUN = tension, stress, strain, anxiety, butterflies (in your stomach) (*informal*), nervousness, cold feet (*informal*), worry

● PHRASES **nerve yourself** = brace yourself, prepare yourself, steel yourself, fortify yourself, gear yourself up, gee yourself up

**nervous** = apprehensive, anxious, uneasy, edgy, worried, tense, fearful, uptight (*informal*), toey (*Austral. slang*) ≠ calm

**nest** = refuge, retreat, haunt, den, hideaway

**nestle** = snuggle, cuddle, huddle, curl up, nuzzle

**nestling** = chick, fledgling, baby bird

**net¹** NOUN = mesh, netting, network, web, lattice, openwork

● VERB = catch, bag, capture, trap, entangle, ensnare, enmesh

**net²** or **nett** ADJECTIVE = after taxes, final, clear, take-home

● VERB = earn, make, clear, gain, realize, bring in, accumulate, reap

**network** 1 = web, system, arrangement, grid, lattice 2 = maze, warren, labyrinth

**neurotic** = unstable, nervous, disturbed, abnormal, obsessive, compulsive, manic, unhealthy ≠ rational

**neutral** 1 = unbiased, impartial, disinterested, even-handed, uninvolved, nonpartisan, unprejudiced, nonaligned ≠ biased 2 = expressionless, dull 3 = uncontroversial or noncontroversial, inoffensive 4 = colourless

**never** 1 = at no time, not once, not ever ≠ always 2 = under no circumstances, not at all, on no account, not ever

---

### Word Power

**never** – *Never* is sometimes used in informal speech and writing as an emphatic form of *not*, with simple past tenses of certain verbs: *I never said that* – and in very informal speech as a denial in place of *did not*: *he says I hit him, but I never*. These uses of *never* should be avoided in careful writing.

**nevertheless** = <u>even so</u>, still, however, yet, regardless, nonetheless, notwithstanding, in spite of that

**new** 1 = <u>modern</u>, recent, contemporary, up-to-date, latest, current, original, fresh ≠ old-fashioned2 = <u>brand new</u>
3 = <u>extra</u>, more, added, new-found, supplementary
4 = <u>unfamiliar</u>, strange
5 = <u>renewed</u>, changed, improved, restored, altered, revitalized

**newcomer** 1 = <u>new arrival</u>, stranger2 = <u>beginner</u>, novice, new arrival, parvenu, Johnny-come-lately (*informal*)

**news** = <u>information</u>, latest (*informal*), report, story, exposé, intelligence, rumour, revelation

**next** ADJECTIVE1 = <u>following</u>, later, succeeding, subsequent
2 = <u>adjacent</u>, closest, nearest, neighbouring, adjoining
● ADVERB = <u>afterwards</u>, then, later, following, subsequently, thereafter

**nice** 1 = <u>pleasant</u>, delightful, agreeable, good, attractive, charming, pleasurable, enjoyable ≠ unpleasant2 = <u>kind</u>, helpful, obliging, considerate ≠ unkind
3 = <u>likable or likeable</u>, friendly, engaging, charming, pleasant, agreeable4 = <u>polite</u>, courteous, well-mannered ≠ vulgar
5 = <u>precise</u>, fine, careful, strict,

subtle, delicate, meticulous, fastidious ≠ vague

**nicely** 1 = <u>pleasantly</u>, well, delightfully, attractively, charmingly, agreeably, acceptably, pleasurably ≠ unpleasantly2 = <u>kindly</u>, politely, thoughtfully, amiably, courteously

**niche** 1 = <u>recess</u>, opening, corner, hollow, nook, alcove
2 = <u>position</u>, calling, place, slot (*informal*), vocation, pigeonhole (*informal*)

**nick** VERB1 (*Slang*) = <u>steal</u>, pinch (*informal*), swipe (*slang*), pilfer
2 = <u>cut</u>, mark, score, chip, scratch, scar, notch, dent
● NOUN = <u>cut</u>, mark, scratch, chip, scar, notch, dent

**nickname** = <u>pet name</u>, label, diminutive, epithet, sobriquet, moniker or monicker (*slang*)

**night** = <u>darkness</u>, dark, night-time

*Related Words*
  *adjective:* nocturnal

**nightly** ADJECTIVE = <u>nocturnal</u>, night-time
● ADVERB = <u>every night</u>, nights (*informal*), each night, night after night

**nightmare** 1 = <u>bad dream</u>, hallucination2 = <u>ordeal</u>, trial, hell, horror, torture, torment, tribulation, purgatory

**nil** 1 = <u>nothing</u>, love, zero

2 = <u>zero</u>, nothing, none, naught

**nip**[1] VERB 1 = <u>pop</u>, go, run, rush, dash 2 = <u>bite</u> 3 = <u>pinch</u>, squeeze, tweak

• PHRASES **nip something in the bud** = <u>thwart</u>, check, frustrate

**nip**[2] = <u>dram</u>, shot (*informal*), drop, sip, draught, mouthful, snifter (*informal*)

**nirvana** = <u>paradise</u>, peace, joy, bliss, serenity, tranquillity

**no** INTERJECTION = <u>not at all</u>, certainly not, of course not, absolutely not, never, no way, nay ≠ yes

• NOUN = <u>refusal</u>, rejection, denial, negation ≠ consent

**noble** ADJECTIVE 1 = <u>worthy</u>, generous, upright, honourable, virtuous, magnanimous ≠ despicable 2 = <u>dignified</u>, great, imposing, impressive, distinguished, splendid, stately ≠ lowly 3 = <u>aristocratic</u>, lordly, titled, patrician, blue-blooded, highborn ≠ humble

• NOUN = <u>lord</u>, peer, aristocrat, nobleman ≠ commoner

**nobody** PRONOUN = <u>no-one</u>

• NOUN = <u>nonentity</u>, lightweight (*informal*), zero, cipher ≠ celebrity

**nod** VERB 1 = <u>incline</u>, bow 2 = <u>signal</u>, indicate, motion, gesture 3 = <u>salute</u>, acknowledge

• NOUN 1 = <u>signal</u>, sign, motion, gesture, indication 2 = <u>salute</u>,

greeting, acknowledgment

**noise** = <u>sound</u>, row, racket, clamour, din, uproar, commotion, hubbub ≠ silence, calm

**noisy** 1 = <u>rowdy</u>, strident, boisterous, vociferous, uproarious, clamorous ≠ quiet 2 = <u>loud</u>, piercing, deafening, tumultuous, ear-splitting, cacophonous, clamorous ≠ quiet

**nominal** 1 = <u>titular</u>, formal, purported, in name only, supposed, so-called, theoretical, professed 2 = <u>token</u>, small, symbolic, minimal, trivial, trifling, insignificant, inconsiderable

**nominate** 1 = <u>propose</u>, suggest, recommend, put forward 2 = <u>appoint</u>, name, choose, select, elect, assign, designate

**nomination** 1 = <u>proposal</u>, suggestion, recommendation 2 = <u>appointment</u>, election, selection, designation, choice

**nominee** = <u>candidate</u>, applicant, entrant, contestant, aspirant, runner

**none** 1 = <u>not any</u>, nothing, zero, not one, nil 2 = <u>no-one</u>, nobody, not one

**nonetheless** = <u>nevertheless</u>, however, yet, even so, despite that, in spite of that

**non-existent** *or* **nonexistent** = <u>imaginary</u>, fictional, mythical, unreal, hypothetical, illusory ≠ real

**nonsense** 1 = <u>rubbish</u>, hot air (*informal*), twaddle, drivel, tripe (*informal*), gibberish, claptrap (*informal*), double Dutch (*Brit. informal*), bizzo (*Austral. slang*), bull's wool (*Austral. & N.Z. slang*) ≠ sense2 = <u>idiocy</u>, stupidity

**non-stop** or**nonstop** ADJECTIVE = <u>continuous</u>, constant, relentless, uninterrupted, endless, unbroken, interminable, incessant ≠ occasional

● ADVERB = <u>continuously</u>, constantly, endlessly, relentlessly, perpetually, incessantly, ceaselessly, interminably

**noon** NOUN = <u>midday</u>, high noon, noonday, twelve noon, noontide

● ADJECTIVE = <u>midday</u>, noonday, noontide

**norm** = <u>standard</u>, rule, pattern, average, par, criterion, benchmark, yardstick

**normal** 1 = <u>usual</u>, common, standard, average, natural, regular, ordinary, typical ≠ unusual2 = <u>sane</u>, reasonable, rational, well-adjusted, compos mentis (*Latin*), in your right mind, mentally sound

**normally** 1 = <u>usually</u>, generally, commonly, regularly, typically, ordinarily, as a rule, habitually 2 = <u>as usual</u>, naturally, properly, conventionally, in the usual way

**north** ADJECTIVE = <u>northern</u>, polar, arctic, boreal, northerly

● ADVERB = <u>northward(s)</u>, in a northerly direction

**nose** NOUN = <u>snout</u>, bill, beak, hooter (*slang*), proboscis

● VERB = <u>ease forward</u>, push, edge, shove, nudge

*Related Words*
adjective: nasal

**nostalgia** = <u>reminiscence</u>, longing, pining, yearning, remembrance, homesickness, wistfulness

**nostalgic** = <u>sentimental</u>, longing, emotional, homesick, wistful, maudlin, regretful

**notable** ADJECTIVE
1 = <u>remarkable</u>, striking, unusual, extraordinary, outstanding, memorable, uncommon, conspicuous ≠ imperceptible
2 = <u>prominent</u>, famous ≠ unknown

● NOUN = <u>celebrity</u>, big name, dignitary, luminary, personage, V.I.P.

**notably** = <u>remarkably</u>, unusually, extraordinarily, noticeably, strikingly, singularly, outstandingly, uncommonly

**notch** NOUN1 = <u>level</u> (*Informal*), step, degree, grade2 = <u>cut</u>, nick, incision, indentation, mark, score, cleft

● VERB = <u>cut</u>, mark, score, nick, scratch, indent

**note** NOUN1 = <u>message</u>, letter, communication, memo, memorandum, epistle 2 = <u>record</u>, reminder, memo, memorandum, jotting, minute 3 = <u>annotation</u>, comment, remark 4 = <u>document</u>, form, record, certificate 5 = <u>symbol</u>, mark, sign, indication, token 6 = <u>tone</u>, touch, trace, hint, sound

● **VERB** 1 = <u>notice</u>, see, observe, perceive 2 = <u>bear in mind</u>, be aware, take into account 3 = <u>mention</u>, record, mark, indicate, register, remark 4 = <u>write down</u>, record, scribble, set down, jot down

**notebook** = <u>notepad</u>, exercise book, journal, diary

**noted** = <u>famous</u>, celebrated, distinguished, well-known, prominent, acclaimed, notable, renowned ≠ unknown

**nothing** 1 = <u>nought</u>, zero, nil, not a thing, zilch (slang) 2 = <u>a trifle</u> 3 = <u>nobody</u>, cipher, nonentity 4 = <u>void</u>, emptiness, nothingness, nullity

**notice** **VERB** = <u>observe</u>, see, note, spot, distinguish, perceive, detect, discern ≠ overlook

● **NOUN** 1 = <u>notification</u>, warning, advice, intimation, news, communication, announcement, instruction 2 = <u>attention</u>, interest, note, regard, consideration, observation, scrutiny, heed ≠ oversight 3 = <u>the sack</u> (informal), dismissal, the boot

(slang), the push (slang), marching orders (informal)

**noticeable** = <u>obvious</u>, clear, striking, plain, evident, manifest, conspicuous, perceptible

**notify** = <u>inform</u>, tell, advise, alert to, announce, warn, make known to

**notion** 1 = <u>idea</u>, view, opinion, belief, concept, impression, sentiment, inkling 2 = <u>whim</u>, wish, desire, fancy, impulse, inclination, caprice

**notorious** = <u>infamous</u>, disreputable, opprobrious

**notoriously** = <u>infamously</u>, disreputably

**notwithstanding** = <u>despite</u>, in spite of, regardless of

**nought** or (Archaic or literary) **naught** = <u>zero</u>, nothing, nil

**nourish** 1 = <u>feed</u>, supply, sustain, nurture 2 = <u>encourage</u>, support, maintain, promote, sustain, foster

**nourishing** = <u>nutritious</u>, beneficial, wholesome, nutritive

**novel**[1] = <u>story</u>, tale, fiction, romance, narrative

**novel**[2] = <u>new</u>, different, original, fresh, unusual, innovative, uncommon ≠ ordinary

**novelist** ► **WORD POWER SUPPLEMENT** novelists

**novelty** 1 = <u>newness</u>, originality, freshness, innovation, surprise, uniqueness, strangeness, unfamiliarity 2 = <u>curiosity</u>, rarity, oddity, wonder 3 = <u>trinket</u>, souvenir, memento, bauble, trifle, knick-knack

**novice** = <u>beginner</u>, pupil, amateur, newcomer, trainee, apprentice, learner, probationer ≠ expert

**now** ADVERB 1 = <u>nowadays</u>, at the moment 2 = <u>immediately</u>, promptly, instantly, at once, straightaway

● PHRASES **now and then** or **again** = <u>occasionally</u>, sometimes, from time to time, on and off, intermittently, infrequently, sporadically

**nowadays** = <u>now</u>, today, at the moment, in this day and age

**nucleus** = <u>centre</u>, heart, focus, basis, core, pivot, kernel, nub

**nude** = <u>naked</u>, stripped, bare, undressed, stark-naked, disrobed, unclothed, unclad ≠ dressed

**nudge** VERB 1 = <u>push</u>, touch, dig, jog, prod, elbow, shove, poke 2 = <u>prompt</u>, influence, persuade, spur, prod, coax

● NOUN 1 = <u>push</u>, touch, dig, elbow, bump, shove, poke, jog 2 = <u>prompting</u>, push, encouragement, prod

**nuisance** = <u>trouble</u>, problem, trial, drag (informal), bother, pest, irritation, hassle (informal) ≠ benefit

**numb** ADJECTIVE 1 = <u>unfeeling</u>, dead, frozen, paralysed, insensitive, deadened, immobilized, torpid ≠ sensitive 2 = <u>stupefied</u>, deadened, unfeeling

● VERB 1 = <u>stun</u>, knock out, paralyse, daze 2 = <u>deaden</u>, freeze, dull, paralyse, immobilize, benumb

**number** NOUN 1 = <u>numeral</u>, figure, character, digit, integer 2 = <u>amount</u>, quantity, collection, aggregate ≠ shortage 3 = <u>crowd</u>, horde, multitude, throng 4 = <u>group</u>, set, band, crowd, gang 5 = <u>issue</u>, copy, edition, imprint, printing

● VERB 1 = <u>amount to</u>, come to, total, add up to 2 = <u>calculate</u>, account, reckon, compute, enumerate ≠ guess 3 = <u>include</u>, count

**numerous** = <u>many</u>, several, countless, lots, abundant, plentiful, innumerable, copious ≠ few

**nurse** 1 = <u>look after</u>, treat, tend, care for, take care of, minister to 2 = <u>harbour</u>, have, maintain, preserve, entertain, cherish 3 = <u>breast-feed</u>, feed, nurture, nourish, suckle, wet-nurse

**nursery** = <u>crèche</u>, kindergarten, playgroup

**nurture** VERB = <u>bring up</u>, raise, look after, rear, care for, develop ≠ neglect

● NOUN = <u>upbringing</u>, training, education, instruction, rearing, development

**nut 1** (*Slang*) = <u>madman</u>, psycho (*slang*), crank (*informal*), lunatic, maniac, nutcase (*slang*) **2** (*Slang*) = <u>head</u>, skull

**nutrition** = <u>food</u>, nourishment, sustenance, nutriment

**oath 1** = <u>promise</u>, bond, pledge, vow, word, affirmation, avowal **2** = <u>swear word</u>, curse, obscenity, blasphemy, expletive, four-letter word, profanity

**obedience** = <u>compliance</u>, respect, reverence, observance, subservience, submissiveness, docility ≠ disobedience

**obey 1** = <u>submit to</u>, surrender (to), give way to, bow to, give in to, yield to, do what you are told by ≠ disobey **2** = <u>carry out</u>, follow, implement, act upon, carry through ≠ disregard **3** = <u>abide by</u>, keep, follow, comply with, observe, heed, conform to, keep to

**object¹ 1** = <u>thing</u>, article, body, item, entity **2** = <u>purpose</u>, aim, end, point, plan, idea, goal, design **3** = <u>target</u>, victim, focus, recipient

**object² 1** *with to* = <u>protest</u> against, oppose, argue against, draw the line at, take exception to, cry out against, complain against, expostulate against ≠ accept **2** = <u>disagree</u>, demur,

remonstrate, express disapproval ≠ agree

**objection** = <u>protest</u>, opposition, complaint, doubt, dissent, outcry, protestation, scruple ≠ agreement

**objective** NOUN = <u>purpose</u>, aim, goal, end, plan, hope, idea, target ● ADJECTIVE **1** = <u>factual</u>, real **2** = <u>unbiased</u>, detached, fair, open-minded, impartial, impersonal, disinterested, even-handed ≠ subjective

**objectively** = <u>impartially</u>, neutrally, fairly, justly, without prejudice, dispassionately, with an open mind, equitably

**obligation 1** = <u>duty</u>, compulsion **2** = <u>task</u>, job, duty, work, charge, role, function, mission **3** = <u>responsibility</u>, duty, liability, accountability, answerability

**oblige 1** = <u>compel</u>, make, force, require, bind, constrain, necessitate, impel **2** = <u>help</u>, assist, benefit, please, humour, accommodate, indulge, gratify ≠ bother

**obliged 1** = <u>forced</u>, required, bound, compelled, duty-bound **2** = <u>grateful</u>, in (someone's) debt, thankful, indebted, appreciative, beholden

**obliging** = <u>accommodating</u>, kind, helpful, willing, polite, cooperative, agreeable, considerate ≠ unhelpful

**obscene** 1 = <u>indecent</u>, dirty, offensive, filthy, improper, immoral, pornographic, lewd ≠ decent 2 = <u>offensive</u>, shocking, evil, disgusting, outrageous, revolting, sickening, vile

**obscure** ADJECTIVE 1 = <u>unknown</u>, little-known, humble, unfamiliar, out-of-the-way, lowly, unheard-of, undistinguished ≠ famous 2 = <u>abstruse</u>, complex, confusing, mysterious, vague, unclear, ambiguous, enigmatic ≠ straightforward 3 = <u>unclear</u>, uncertain, confused, mysterious, doubtful, indeterminate ≠ well-known 4 = <u>indistinct</u>, vague, blurred, dark, faint, dim, gloomy, murky ≠ clear
• VERB 1 = <u>obstruct</u>, hinder 2 = <u>hide</u>, screen, mask, disguise, conceal, veil, cloak, camouflage ≠ expose

**observation** 1 = <u>watching</u>, study, survey, review, investigation, monitoring, examination, inspection 2 = <u>comment</u>, thought, note, statement, opinion, remark, explanation, reflection 3 = <u>remark</u>, comment, statement, reflection, utterance 4 = <u>observance of</u>, compliance with, honouring of, fulfilment of, carrying out of

**observe** 1 = <u>watch</u>, study, view, look at, check, survey, monitor, keep an eye on (informal) 2 = <u>notice</u>, see, note, discover, spot, regard, witness, distinguish 3 = <u>remark</u>, say, comment, state, note, reflect, mention, opine 4 = <u>comply with</u>, keep, follow, respect, carry out, honour, discharge, obey ≠ disregard

**observer** 1 = <u>witness</u>, viewer, spectator, looker-on, watcher, onlooker, eyewitness, bystander 2 = <u>commentator</u>, reporter, special correspondent 3 = <u>monitor</u>, watchdog, supervisor, scrutineer

**obsessed** = <u>absorbed</u>, dominated, gripped, haunted, distracted, hung up (slang), preoccupied ≠ indifferent

**obsession** = <u>preoccupation</u>, thing (informal), complex, hang-up (informal), mania, phobia, fetish, fixation

**obsessive** = <u>compulsive</u>, gripping, consuming, haunting, irresistible, neurotic, besetting, uncontrollable

**obsolete** = <u>outdated</u>, old, passé, old-fashioned, discarded, extinct, out of date, archaic ≠ up-to-date

**obstacle** 1 = <u>obstruction</u>, block, barrier, hurdle, snag, impediment, blockage, hindrance 2 = <u>hindrance</u>, bar, difficulty, barrier, handicap, hurdle, hitch, drawback, uphill (S. African)

**≠ help**

**obstruct 1** = <u>block</u>, close, bar, plug, barricade, stop up, bung up (*informal*) **2** = <u>hold up</u>, stop, check, block, restrict, slow down, hamper, hinder **3** ≠ <u>impede</u>, hamper, hold back, thwart, hinder ≠ help **4** = <u>obscure</u>, screen, cover

**obtain 1** = <u>get</u>, gain, acquire, land, net, pick up, secure, procure ≠ lose **2** = <u>achieve</u>, get, gain, accomplish, attain **3** (*Formal*) = <u>prevail</u>, hold, exist, be the case, abound, predominate, be in force, be current

**obvious** = <u>clear</u>, plain, apparent, evident, distinct, manifest, noticeable, conspicuous ≠ unclear

**obviously 1** = <u>clearly</u>, of course, without doubt, assuredly **2** = <u>plainly</u>, patently, undoubtedly, evidently, manifestly, markedly, without doubt, unquestionably

**occasion NOUN 1** = <u>time</u>, moment, point, stage, instance, juncture **2** = <u>function</u>, event, affair, do (*informal*), happening, experience, gathering, celebration **3** = <u>opportunity</u>, chance, time, opening, window **4** = <u>reason</u>, cause, call, ground(s), excuse, incentive, motive, justification

**● VERB** (*Formal*) = <u>cause</u>, produce, lead to, inspire, result in, generate, prompt, provoke

**occasional** = <u>infrequent</u>, odd, rare, irregular, sporadic, intermittent, few and far between, periodic ≠ constant

**occasionally** = <u>sometimes</u>, at times, from time to time, now and then, irregularly, now and again, periodically, once in a while ≠ constantly

**occult NOUN** = <u>magic</u>, witchcraft, sorcery, wizardry, enchantment, black art, necromancy
**● ADJECTIVE** = <u>supernatural</u>, magical, mysterious, psychic, mystical, unearthly, esoteric, uncanny

**occupant** = <u>occupier</u>, resident, tenant, inmate, inhabitant, incumbent, dweller, lessee

**occupation 1** = <u>job</u>, calling, business, line (of work), trade, career, employment, profession **2** = <u>hobby</u>, pastime, diversion, relaxation, leisure pursuit, (leisure) activity **3** = <u>invasion</u>, seizure, conquest, incursion, subjugation **4** = <u>occupancy</u>, residence, holding, control, possession, tenure, tenancy

**occupied 1** = <u>in use</u>, taken, full, engaged, unavailable **2** = <u>inhabited</u>, peopled, lived-in, settled, tenanted ≠ uninhabited **3** = <u>busy</u>, engaged, employed, working, active, hard at work, rushed off your feet

**occupy** 1 = <u>inhabit</u>, own, live in, dwell in, reside in, abide in ≠ vacate<sub>2</sub> = <u>invade</u>, take over, capture, seize, conquer, overrun, annex, colonize ≠ withdraw 3 = <u>hold</u>, control, dominate, possess<sub>4</sub> = <u>take up</u>, consume, tie up, use up, monopolize<sub>5</sub> *often passive* = <u>engage</u>, involve, employ, divert, preoccupy, engross<sub>6</sub> = <u>fill</u>, take up, cover, fill up, pervade, permeate, extend over

**occur** VERB<sub>1</sub> = <u>happen</u>, take place, come about, turn up (*informal*), crop up (*informal*), transpire (*informal*), befall 2 = <u>exist</u>, appear, be found, develop, turn up, be present, manifest itself, present itself
● PHRASES **occur to someone** = <u>come to mind</u>, strike someone, dawn on someone, spring to mind, cross someone's mind, enter someone's head, suggest itself to someone

---

### Word Power

**occur** – It is usually regarded as incorrect to talk of pre-arranged events *occurring* or *happening*. For this meaning a synonym such as *take place* would be more appropriate: *the wedding took place* (not *occurred* or *happened*) *in the afternoon.*

---

**occurrence** 1 = <u>incident</u>, happening, event, fact, matter, affair, circumstance, episode 2 = <u>existence</u>, instance, appearance, manifestation, materialization

**odd** 1 = <u>peculiar</u>, strange, unusual, extraordinary, bizarre, offbeat, freakish<sub>2</sub> = <u>unusual</u>, strange, rare, extraordinary, remarkable, bizarre, peculiar, irregular ≠ normal<sub>3</sub> = <u>occasional</u>, various, random, casual, irregular, periodic, sundry, incidental ≠ regular<sub>4</sub> = <u>spare</u>, remaining, extra, surplus, solitary, leftover, unmatched, unpaired ≠ matched

**odds** PLURAL NOUN<sub>1</sub> = <u>probability</u>, chances, likelihood
● PHRASES **at odds** 1 = <u>in conflict</u>, arguing, quarrelling, at loggerheads, at daggers drawn 2 = <u>at variance</u>, conflicting, contrary to, at odds, out of line, out of step, at sixes and sevens (*informal*) ◆**odds and ends** = <u>scraps</u>, bits, remains, fragments, debris, remnants, bits and pieces, bric-a-brac

**odour** = <u>smell</u>, scent, perfume, fragrance, stink, bouquet, aroma, stench

**odyssey** = <u>journey</u>, tour, trip, quest, trek, expedition, voyage, crusade

**off** ADVERB = <u>away</u>, out, apart,

elsewhere, aside, hence, from here

● **ADJECTIVE 1** = <u>absent</u>, gone, unavailable **2** = <u>cancelled</u>, abandoned, postponed, shelved **3** = <u>bad</u>, rotten, rancid, mouldy, turned, spoiled, sour, decayed

**offence 1** = <u>crime</u>, sin, fault, violation, wrongdoing, trespass, felony, misdemeanour **2** = <u>outrage</u>, shock, anger, trouble, bother, resentment, irritation, hassle (*informal*) **3** = <u>insult</u>, slight, hurt, outrage, injustice, snub, affront, indignity

**offend 1** = <u>distress</u>, upset, outrage, wound, slight, insult, annoy, snub ≠ <u>please</u> **2** = <u>break the law</u>, sin, err, do wrong, fall, go astray

**offended** = <u>upset</u>, hurt, bothered, disturbed, distressed, outraged, stung, put out (*informal*), tooshie (*Austral. slang*)

**offender** = <u>criminal</u>, convict, crook, villain, culprit, sinner, delinquent, felon

**offensive ADJECTIVE**
**1** = <u>insulting</u>, rude, abusive, degrading, contemptuous, disparaging, objectionable, disrespectful ≠ respectful **2** = <u>disgusting</u>, gross, foul, unpleasant, revolting, vile, repellent, obnoxious, festy (*Austral. slang*), yucko (*Austral.*

*slang*) ≠ pleasant **3** = <u>attacking</u>, threatening, aggressive, striking, hostile, invading, combative ≠ defensive

● **NOUN** = <u>attack</u>, charge, campaign, strike, push (*informal*), assault, raid, drive

**offer VERB 1** = <u>provide</u>, present, furnish, afford ≠ withhold **2** = <u>volunteer</u>, come forward, offer your services **3** = <u>propose</u>, suggest, advance, submit **4** = <u>give</u>, show, bring, provide, render, impart **5** = <u>put up for sale</u>, sell **6** = <u>bid</u>, submit, propose, tender, proffer

● **NOUN 1** = <u>proposal</u>, suggestion, proposition, submission **2** = <u>bid</u>, tender, bidding price

**offering 1** = <u>contribution</u>, gift, donation, present, subscription, hand-out **2** = <u>sacrifice</u>, tribute, libation, burnt offering

**office 1** = <u>place of work</u>, workplace, base, workroom, place of business **2** = <u>branch</u>, department, division, section, wing, subdivision, subsection **3** = <u>post</u>, place, role, situation, responsibility, function, occupation

**officer 1** = <u>official</u>, executive, agent, representative, appointee, functionary, office-holder, office bearer **2** = <u>police officer</u>, detective, PC, police constable, police man, police woman

**official** ADJECTIVE[1] = authorized, formal, sanctioned, licensed, proper, legitimate, authentic, certified ≠ unofficial [2] = formal, bureaucratic, ceremonial, solemn, ritualistic

● NOUN = officer, executive, agent, representative, bureaucrat, appointee, functionary, office-holder

**offset** = cancel out, balance, set off, make up for, compensate for, counteract, neutralize, counterbalance

**offspring** 1 = child, baby, kid (informal), youngster, infant, successor, babe, toddler, littlie (Austral. informal), ankle-biter (Austral. slang), tacker (Austral. slang) ≠ parent [2] = children, young, family, issue, stock, heirs, descendants, brood

**often** = frequently, generally, commonly, repeatedly, time and again, habitually, not infrequently ≠ never

**oil** VERB = lubricate, grease
● NOUN[1] = lubricant, grease, lubrication, fuel oil [2] = lotion, cream, balm, salve, liniment, embrocation, solution

**oily** = greasy, slimy, fatty, slippery, oleaginous

**OK** or **okay** ADJECTIVE (Informal) 1 = all right, fine, fitting, in order, permitted, suitable, acceptable,

allowable ≠ unacceptable 2 = fine, good, average, fair, all right, acceptable, adequate, satisfactory ≠ unsatisfactory 3 = well, all right, safe, sound, healthy, unharmed, uninjured

● INTERJECTION = all right, right, yes, agreed, very good, roger, very well, ya (S. African), righto (Brit. informal), yebo (S. African informal)

● VERB = approve, allow, agree to, permit, sanction, endorse, authorize, rubber-stamp (informal)

● NOUN = authorization, agreement, sanction, approval, go-ahead (informal), blessing, permission, consent

**old** 1 = aged, elderly, ancient, mature, venerable, antiquated, senile, decrepit ≠ young 2 = former, earlier, past, previous, prior, one-time, erstwhile 3 = long-standing, established, fixed, enduring, abiding, long-lasting, long-established, time-honoured [4] = stale, worn-out, banal, threadbare, trite, overused, timeworn

**old-fashioned** 1 = out of date, dated, outdated, unfashionable, outmoded, passé, old hat, behind the times ≠ up-to-date 2 = oldfangled, square (informal), outdated, unfashionable, obsolescent

**ominous** = <u>threatening</u>, sinister, grim, fateful, foreboding, unpromising, portentous, inauspicious ≠ promising

**omission** 1 = <u>exclusion</u>, removal, elimination, deletion, excision ≠ inclusion 2 = <u>gap</u>, space, exclusion, lacuna 3 = <u>failure</u>, neglect, negligence, oversight, carelessness, dereliction, slackness, laxity

**omit** 1 = <u>leave out</u>, drop, exclude, eliminate, skip ≠ include 2 = <u>forget</u>, overlook, neglect, pass over, lose sight of

**once** ADVERB 1 = <u>on one occasion</u>, one time, one single time 2 = <u>at one time</u>, previously, formerly, long ago, once upon a time
• CONJUNCTION = <u>as soon as</u>, when, after, the moment, immediately, the instant
• PHRASES **at once** 1 = <u>immediately</u>, now, straight away, directly, promptly, instantly, right away, forthwith 2 = <u>simultaneously</u>, together, at the same time, concurrently

**one-sided** 1 = <u>unequal</u>, unfair, uneven, unjust, unbalanced, lopsided, ill-matched ≠ equal 2 = <u>biased</u>, prejudiced, weighted, unfair, partial, distorted, partisan, slanted ≠ unbiased

**ongoing** = <u>in progress</u>, developing, progressing, evolving, unfolding, unfinished

**onlooker** = <u>spectator</u>, witness, observer, viewer, looker-on, watcher, eyewitness, bystander

**only** ADJECTIVE = <u>sole</u>, one, single, individual, exclusive, unique, lone, solitary
• ADVERB 1 = <u>just</u>, simply, purely, merely 2 = <u>hardly</u>, just, barely, only just, scarcely, at a push

**onset** = <u>beginning</u>, start, birth, outbreak, inception, commencement ≠ end

**onslaught** = <u>attack</u>, charge, campaign, strike, assault, raid, invasion, offensive ≠ retreat

**onward** or **onwards** = <u>forward</u>, on, forwards, ahead, beyond, in front, forth

**ooze**[1] 1 = <u>seep</u>, well, escape, leak, drain, filter, drip, trickle 2 = <u>emit</u>, release, leak, drip, dribble, give off, pour forth 3 = <u>exude</u>, emit

**ooze**[2] = <u>mud</u>, clay, dirt, silt, sludge, mire, slime, alluvium

**open** VERB 1 = <u>unfasten</u>, unlock ≠ close 2 = <u>unwrap</u>, uncover, undo, unravel, untie ≠ wrap 3 = <u>uncork</u> 4 = <u>unfold</u>, spread (out), expand, unfurl, unroll ≠ fold 5 = <u>clear</u>, unblock ≠ block 6 = <u>undo</u>, unbutton, unfasten ≠ fasten 7 = <u>begin business</u> 8 = <u>start</u>, begin, launch, trigger, kick off (*informal*), initiate,

commence, get going ≠ end
9 = <u>begin</u>, start, commence ≠ end
● **ADJECTIVE** 1 = <u>unclosed</u>,
unlocked, ajar, unfastened,
yawning ≠ closed 2 = <u>unsealed</u>,
unstoppered ≠ unopened
3 = <u>extended</u>, unfolded, stretched
out, unfurled, spreading out,
unrolled ≠ shut 4 = <u>frank</u>, direct,
straightforward, sincere,
transparent, honest, candid,
truthful ≠ sly 5 = <u>receptive</u>,
sympathetic, responsive,
amenable 6 = <u>unresolved</u>,
unsettled, undecided, debatable,
moot, arguable 7 = <u>clear</u>,
passable, unhindered,
unimpeded, navigable,
unobstructed ≠ obstructed
8 = <u>available</u>, to hand, accessible,
handy, at your disposal
9 = <u>general</u>, public, free, universal,
blanket, across-the-board,
unrestricted, overarching
≠ restricted 10 = <u>vacant</u>, free,
available, empty, unoccupied,
unfilled
**open-air** = <u>outdoor</u>, outside,
out-of-door(s), alfresco
**opening ADJECTIVE** = <u>first</u>,
earliest, beginning, premier,
primary, initial, maiden, inaugural
● **NOUN** 1 = <u>beginning</u>, start,
launch, dawn, outset, initiation,
inception, commencement
≠ ending 2 = <u>hole</u>, space, tear,
crack, gap, slot, puncture,

aperture ≠ blockage
3 = <u>opportunity</u>, chance, time,
moment, occasion, look-in
(*informal*) 4 = <u>job</u>, position, post,
situation, opportunity, vacancy
**openly** = <u>frankly</u>, plainly,
honestly, overtly, candidly,
unreservedly, unhesitatingly,
forthrightly ≠ privately
**open-minded** = <u>unprejudiced</u>,
liberal, balanced, objective,
reasonable, tolerant, impartial,
receptive ≠ narrow-minded
**operate** 1 = <u>manage</u>, run, direct,
handle, supervise, be in charge of
2 = <u>function</u>, work, act 3 = <u>run</u>,
work, use, control, manoeuvre
4 = <u>work</u>, go, run, perform,
function ≠ break down
**operation** = <u>performance</u>,
action, movement, motion
**operational** = <u>working</u>, going,
running, ready, functioning,
operative, viable, functional
≠ inoperative
**operative ADJECTIVE** = <u>in force</u>,
effective, functioning, active, in
effect, operational, in operation
≠ inoperative
● **NOUN** 1 = <u>worker</u>, employee,
labourer, workman, artisan 2 (*U.S.
& Canad.*) = <u>spy</u>, undercover
agent, mole, nark (*Brit., Austral., &
N.Z. slang*)
**operator** = <u>worker</u>, driver,
mechanic, operative, conductor,

388

technician, handler

**opinion** 1 = <u>belief</u>, feeling, view, idea, theory, conviction, point of view, sentiment, 2 = <u>estimation</u>, view, impression, assessment, judgment, appraisal, considered opinion

**opponent** 1 = <u>adversary</u>, rival, enemy, competitor, challenger, foe, contestant, antagonist ≠ ally 2 = <u>opposer</u>, dissident, objector ≠ supporter

**opportunity** = <u>chance</u>, opening, time, turn, moment, possibility, occasion, slot

**oppose** = <u>be against</u>, fight (against), block, take on, counter, contest, resist, combat ≠ support

**opposed** 1 with to = <u>against</u>, hostile, adverse, in opposition, averse, antagonistic, (dead) set against, 2 = <u>contrary</u>, conflicting, clashing, counter, adverse, contradictory, dissentient

**opposing** 1 = <u>conflicting</u>, different, contrasting, opposite, differing, contrary, contradictory, incompatible, 2 = <u>rival</u>, conflicting, competing, enemy, opposite, hostile

**opposite** PREPOSITION = <u>facing</u>, face to face with, across from, eyeball to eyeball (*informal*)

● ADJECTIVE 1 = <u>facing</u>, other, opposing, 2 = <u>different</u>, conflicting, contrasted, contrasting, unlike, contrary, dissimilar, divergent ≠ alike 3 = <u>rival</u>, conflicting, opposing, competing

● NOUN = <u>reverse</u>, contrary, converse, antithesis, contradiction, inverse, obverse

**opposition** 1 = <u>hostility</u>, resistance, resentment, disapproval, obstruction, animosity, antagonism, antipathy ≠ support, 2 = <u>opponent(s)</u>, competition, rival(s), enemy, competitor(s), other side, challenger(s), foe

**oppress** 1 = <u>subjugate</u>, abuse, suppress, wrong, master, overcome, subdue, persecute ≠ liberate, 2 = <u>depress</u>, burden, discourage, torment, harass, afflict, sadden, vex

**oppression** = <u>persecution</u>, control, abuse, injury, injustice, cruelty, domination, repression ≠ justice

**oppressive** 1 = <u>tyrannical</u>, severe, harsh, cruel, brutal, authoritarian, unjust, repressive ≠ merciful, 2 = <u>stifling</u>, close, sticky, stuffy, humid, sultry, airless, muggy

**opt** VERB = <u>choose</u>, decide, prefer, select, elect ≠ reject

● PHRASES **opt for something** or **someone** = <u>choose</u>, pick, select, adopt, go for, designate, decide on, plump for

**optimistic** 1 = <u>hopeful</u>, positive, confident, encouraged, cheerful, rosy, buoyant, sanguine ≠ pessimistic 2 = <u>encouraging</u>, promising, bright, good, reassuring, rosy, heartening, auspicious ≠ discouraging

**optimum** *or* **optimal** = <u>ideal</u>, best, highest, finest, perfect, supreme, peak, outstanding ≠ worst

**option** = <u>choice</u>, alternative, selection, preference, freedom of choice, power to choose

**optional** = <u>voluntary</u>, open, discretionary, possible, extra, elective ≠ compulsory

**opus** = <u>work</u>, piece, production, creation, composition, work of art, brainchild, oeuvre (*French*)

**oral** = <u>spoken</u>, vocal, verbal, unwritten

**orange**

### Shades of orange

| | |
|---|---|
| amber | peach |
| burnt sienna | tangerine |
| ochre | terracotta |

**orbit** NOUN 1 = <u>path</u>, course, cycle, circle, revolution, rotation, trajectory, sweep 2 = <u>sphere of influence</u>, reach, range, influence, province, scope, domain, compass

● VERB = <u>circle</u>, ring, go round, revolve around, encircle, circumscribe, circumnavigate

**orchestrate** 1 = <u>organize</u>, plan, run, set up, arrange, put together, marshal, coordinate 2 = <u>score</u>, set, arrange, adapt

**ordain** 1 = <u>appoint</u>, name, commission, select, invest, nominate, anoint, consecrate 2 (*Formal*) = <u>order</u>, will, rule, demand, require, direct, command, dictate

**ordeal** = <u>hardship</u>, trial, difficulty, test, suffering, nightmare, torture, agony ≠ pleasure

**order** VERB 1 = <u>command</u>, instruct, direct, charge, demand, require, bid, compel ≠ forbid 2 = <u>decree</u>, rule, demand, prescribe, pronounce, ordain ≠ ban 3 = <u>request</u>, ask (for), book, seek, reserve, apply for, solicit, send away for 4 = <u>arrange</u>, group, sort, position, line up, organize, catalogue, sort out ≠ disarrange

● NOUN 1 = <u>instruction</u>, ruling, demand, direction, command, dictate, decree, mandate 2 = <u>request</u>, booking, demand, commission, application, reservation, requisition 3 = <u>sequence</u>, grouping, series, structure, chain, arrangement, line-up, array 4 = <u>organization</u>, system, method, pattern, symmetry, regularity, neatness, tidiness ≠ chaos 5 = <u>peace</u>,

**orderly → origin**

control, law, quiet, calm, discipline, law and order, tranquillity$_6$ = **society**, company, group, club, community, association, institute, organization$_7$ = **class**, set, rank, grade, caste$_8$ = **kind**, group, class, family, sort, type, variety, category

**orderly 1** = **well-behaved**, controlled, disciplined, quiet, restrained, law-abiding, peaceable ≠ disorderly$_2$ = **well-organized**, regular, in order, organized, precise, neat, tidy, systematic ≠ disorganized

**ordinary 1** = **usual**, standard, normal, common, regular, typical, conventional, routine $_2$ = **commonplace**, plain, modest, humble, mundane, banal, unremarkable, run-of-the-mill ≠ extraordinary

**organ 1** = **body part**, part of the body, element, biological structure$_2$ = **newspaper**, medium, voice, vehicle, gazette, mouthpiece

**organic 1** = **natural**, biological, living, live, animate $_2$ = **systematic**, ordered, structured, organized, integrated, orderly, methodical

**organism** = **creature**, being, thing, body, animal, structure, beast, entity

**organization 1** = **group**, company, party, body, association, band, institution, corporation$_2$ = **management**, running, planning, control, operation, handling, structuring, administration$_3$ = **structure**, form, pattern, make-up, arrangement, construction, format, formation

**organize 1** = **arrange**, run, plan, prepare, set up, devise, put together, take care of, jack up (*N.Z. informal*) ≠ disrupt$_2$ = **put in order**, arrange, group, list, file, index, classify, inventory ≠ muddle

**orient** or**orientate 1** = **adjust**, adapt, alter, accustom, align, familiarize, acclimatize$_2$ = **get your bearings**, establish your location

**orientation 1** = **inclination**, tendency, disposition, predisposition, predilection, proclivity, partiality$_2$ = **induction**, introduction, adjustment, settling in, adaptation, assimilation, familiarization, acclimatization $_3$ = **position**, situation, location, bearings, direction, arrangement, whereabouts

**origin 1** = **beginning**, start, birth, launch, foundation, creation, emergence, onset ≠ end$_2$ = **root**, source, basis, base, seed, foundation, nucleus, derivation

**original** ADJECTIVE 1 = <u>first</u>, earliest, initial 2 = <u>initial</u>, first, starting, opening, primary, introductory ≠ <u>final</u> 3 = <u>new</u>, fresh, novel, unusual, unprecedented, innovative, unfamiliar, seminal ≠ unoriginal 4 = <u>creative</u>, inspired, imaginative, artistic, fertile, ingenious, visionary, inventive
● NOUN = <u>prototype</u>, master, pattern ≠ copy

**originally** = <u>initially</u>, first, firstly, at first, primarily, to begin with, in the beginning

**originate** 1 = <u>begin</u>, start, emerge, come, happen, rise, appear, spring ≠ end 2 = <u>invent</u>, create, design, launch, introduce, institute, generate, pioneer

**ornament** NOUN 1 = <u>decoration</u>, trimming, accessory, festoon, trinket, bauble, knick-knack 2 = <u>embellishment</u>, decoration, embroidery, elaboration, adornment, ornamentation
● VERB = <u>decorate</u>, adorn, array, do up (informal), embellish, festoon, beautify, prettify

**orthodox** 1 = <u>established</u>, official, accepted, received, common, traditional, normal, usual ≠ unorthodox 2 = <u>conformist</u>, conservative, traditional, strict, devout, observant ≠ nonconformist

**orthodoxy** 1 = <u>doctrine</u>, teaching, opinion, principle, belief, convention, creed, dogma 2 = <u>conformity</u>, received wisdom, traditionalism, conventionality ≠ nonconformity

**other** 1 = <u>additional</u>, more, further, new, added, extra, fresh, spare 2 = <u>different</u>, alternative, contrasting, distinct, diverse, dissimilar, separate, alternative

**otherwise** 1 = <u>or else</u>, or, if not, or then 2 = <u>apart from that</u>, in other ways, in (all) other respects 3 = <u>differently</u>, any other way, contrarily

**ounce** = <u>shred</u>, bit, drop, trace, scrap, grain, fragment, atom

**oust** = <u>expel</u>, turn out, dismiss, exclude, exile, throw out, displace, topple

**out** ADJECTIVE 1 = <u>not in</u>, away, elsewhere, outside, gone, abroad, from home, absent 2 = <u>extinguished</u>, ended, finished, dead, exhausted, expired, used up, at an end ≠ alight 3 = <u>in bloom</u>, opening, open, flowering, blooming, in flower, in full bloom 4 = <u>available</u>, on sale, in the shops, to be had, purchasable 5 = <u>revealed</u>, exposed, common knowledge, public knowledge, (out) in the open ≠ kept secret
● VERB = <u>expose</u>

**outbreak** 1 = <u>eruption</u>, burst,

**outburst** explosion, epidemic, rash, outburst, flare-up, upsurge **2** = <u>onset</u>, beginning, outset, opening, dawn, commencement

**outburst** = <u>explosion</u>, fit, surge, outbreak, flare-up, eruption, spasm, outpouring

**outcome** = <u>result</u>, end, consequence, conclusion, payoff (*informal*), upshot

**outcry** = <u>protest</u>, complaint, objection, dissent, outburst, clamour, uproar, commotion

**outdated** = <u>old-fashioned</u>, dated, obsolete, out of date, passé, archaic, unfashionable, antiquated ≠ modern

**outdoor** = <u>open-air</u>, outside, out-of-door(s), alfresco ≠ indoor

**outer** **1** = <u>external</u>, outside, outward, exterior, exposed, outermost ≠ inner **2** = <u>surface</u> **3** = <u>outlying</u>, distant, provincial, out-of-the-way, peripheral, far-flung ≠ central

**outfit** **1** = <u>costume</u>, dress, clothes, clothing, suit, get-up (*informal*), kit, ensemble **2** (*Informal*) = <u>group</u>, company, team, party, unit, crowd, squad, organization

**outgoing** **1** = <u>leaving</u>, former, previous, retiring, withdrawing, prior, departing, erstwhile ≠ incoming **2** = <u>sociable</u>, open, social, warm, friendly,

expansive, affable, extrovert ≠ reserved

**outgoings** = <u>expenses</u>, costs, payments, expenditure, overheads, outlay

**outing** = <u>journey</u>, run, trip, tour, expedition, excursion, spin (*informal*), jaunt

**outlaw** VERB **1** = <u>ban</u>, bar, veto, forbid, exclude, prohibit, disallow, proscribe ≠ legalise **2** = <u>banish</u>, put a price on (someone's) head
  ● NOUN (*History*) = <u>bandit</u>, criminal, thief, robber, fugitive, outcast, felon, highwayman

**outlet** **1** = <u>shop</u>, store, supermarket, market, boutique, emporium, hypermarket **2** = <u>channel</u>, release, medium, avenue, vent, conduit **3** = <u>pipe</u>, opening, channel, exit, duct

**outline** VERB **1** = <u>summarize</u>, draft, plan, trace, sketch (in), sum up, encapsulate, delineate **2** = <u>silhouette</u>, etch
  ● NOUN **1** = <u>summary</u>, review, résumé, rundown, synopsis, précis, thumbnail sketch, recapitulation **2** = <u>shape</u>, lines, form, figure, profile, silhouette, configuration, contour(s)

**outlook** **1** = <u>attitude</u>, opinion, position, approach, mood, perspective, point of view, stance **2** = <u>prospect(s)</u>, future, expectations, forecast, prediction,

# out of date → outspoken

probability, prognosis

**out of date 1** = <u>old-fashioned</u>, dated, outdated, obsolete, démodé (*French*), antiquated, outmoded, passé ≠ modern **2** = <u>invalid</u>, expired, lapsed, void, null and void

**output** = <u>production</u>, manufacture, manufacturing, yield, productivity

**outrage VERB** = <u>offend</u>, shock, upset, wound, insult, infuriate, incense, madden

• **NOUN** = <u>indignation</u>, shock, anger, rage, fury, hurt, resentment, scorn

**outrageous 1** = <u>atrocious</u>, shocking, terrible, offensive, appalling, cruel, savage, horrifying ≠ mild **2** = <u>unreasonable</u>, unfair, steep (*informal*), shocking, extravagant, scandalous, preposterous, unwarranted ≠ reasonable

**outright ADJECTIVE 1** = <u>absolute</u>, complete, total, perfect, sheer, thorough, unconditional, unqualified **2** = <u>definite</u>, clear, certain, flat, absolute, black-and-white, straightforward, unequivocal

• **ADVERB 1** = <u>openly</u>, frankly, plainly, overtly, candidly, unreservedly, unhesitatingly, forthrightly **2** = <u>absolutely</u>, completely, totally, fully,

entirely, thoroughly, wholly, utterly

**outset** = <u>beginning</u>, start, opening, onset, inauguration, inception, commencement, kickoff (*informal*) ≠ finish

**outside NOUN** = <u>exterior</u>, face, front, covering, skin, surface, shell, coating

• **ADJECTIVE 1** = <u>external</u>, outer, exterior, outward, extraneous ≠ inner **2** = <u>remote</u>, small, unlikely, slight, slim, distant, faint, marginal

• **ADVERB** = <u>outdoors</u>, out of the house, out-of-doors

### Word Power

**outside** – The use of *outside of* and *inside of*, although fairly common, is generally thought to be incorrect or nonstandard: *She waits outside* (not *outside of*) *the school.*

**outsider** = <u>stranger</u>, incomer, visitor, newcomer, intruder, interloper, odd one out

**outskirts** = <u>edge</u>, boundary, suburbs, fringe, perimeter, periphery, suburbia, environs

**outspan** (*S. African*) = <u>relax</u>, chill out (*slang, chiefly U.S.*), take it easy, loosen up, put your feet up

**outspoken** = <u>forthright</u>, open, frank, straightforward, blunt, explicit, upfront (*informal*), unequivocal ≠ reserved

**outstanding** 1 = <u>excellent</u>,
good, great, important, special,
fine, brilliant, impressive, booshit
(*Austral. slang*), exo (*Austral.
slang*), sik (*Austral. slang*)
≠ mediocre 2 = <u>unpaid</u>,
remaining, due, pending, payable,
unsettled, uncollected
3 = <u>undone</u>, left, omitted,
unfinished, unfulfilled,
unperformed

**outward** = <u>apparent</u>, seeming,
surface, ostensible ≠ inward

**outwardly** = <u>apparently</u>,
externally, seemingly, it seems
that, on the surface, it appears
that, ostensibly, on the face of it

**outweigh** = <u>override</u>, cancel
(out), eclipse, offset, compensate
for, supersede, neutralize,
counterbalance

**oval** = <u>elliptical</u>, egg-shaped,
ovoid

**ovation** = <u>applause</u>, hand,
cheers, praise, tribute, acclaim,
clapping, accolade ≠ derision

**over** PREPOSITION 1 = <u>above</u>, on
top of 2 = <u>on top of</u>, on, across,
upon 3 = <u>across</u>, (looking) onto
4 = <u>more than</u>, above, exceeding,
in excess of, upwards of
5 = <u>about</u>, regarding, relating to,
concerning, apropos of
● ADVERB 1 = <u>above</u>, overhead, in
the sky, on high, aloft, up above

2 = <u>extra</u>, more, further, beyond,
additional, in addition, surplus, in
excess
● ADJECTIVE = <u>finished</u>, done
(with), through, ended, closed,
past, completed, complete
(*Related Words*)
*prefixes*: hyper-, super-

**overall** ADJECTIVE = <u>total</u>, full,
whole, general, complete, entire,
global, comprehensive
● ADVERB = <u>in general</u>, generally,
mostly, all things considered, on
average, on the whole,
predominantly, in the main

**overcome** VERB 1 = <u>defeat</u>, beat,
conquer, master, overwhelm,
subdue, rout, overpower
2 = <u>conquer</u>, beat, master,
subdue, triumph over, vanquish
● ADJECTIVE = <u>overwhelmed</u>,
moved, affected, emotional,
choked, speechless, bowled over
(*informal*), at a loss for words

**overdue** 1 = <u>delayed</u>, belated,
late, behind schedule, tardy,
unpunctual, behindhand ≠ early
2 = <u>unpaid</u>, owing

**overflow** VERB = <u>spill over</u>, well
over, run over, pour over, bubble
over, brim over
● NOUN 1 = <u>flood</u>, spilling over
2 = <u>surplus</u>, extra, excess,
overspill, overabundance,
additional people *or* things

**overhaul** VERB 1 = <u>check</u>, service,

maintain, examine, restore, tune (up), repair, go over 2 = **overtake**, pass, leave behind, catch up with, get past, outstrip, get ahead of, outdistance

● NOUN = <u>check</u>, service, examination, going-over (*informal*), inspection, once-over (*informal*), checkup, reconditioning

**overhead** ADJECTIVE = <u>raised</u>, suspended, elevated, aerial, overhanging

● ADVERB = <u>above</u>, in the sky, on high, aloft, up above
≠ underneath

**overheads** = <u>running costs</u>, expenses, outgoings, operating costs

**overlook** 1 = <u>look over</u> or <u>out on</u>, have a view of 2 = <u>miss</u>, forget, neglect, omit, disregard, pass over ≠ notice 3 = <u>ignore</u>, excuse, forgive, pardon, disregard, condone, turn a blind eye to, wink at

**overpower** 1 = <u>overcome</u>, master, overwhelm, overthrow, subdue, quell, subjugate, prevail over 2 defeat, crush, triumph over, vanquish 3 = <u>overwhelm</u>, overcome, bowl over (*informal*), stagger

**override** 1 = <u>outweigh</u>, eclipse, supersede, take precedence over, prevail over 2 = <u>overrule</u>, cancel,

overturn, repeal, rescind, annul, nullify, countermand 3 = <u>ignore</u>, reject, discount, overlook, disregard, pass over, take no notice of

**overrun** 1 = <u>overwhelm</u>, attack, assault, occupy, raid, invade, penetrate, rout 2 = <u>spread over</u>, overwhelm, choke, swamp, infest, inundate, permeate, swarm over 3 = <u>exceed</u>, go beyond, surpass, overshoot, run over or on

**overshadow** 1 = <u>spoil</u>, ruin, mar, wreck, blight, crool or cruel (*Austral. slang*), mess up, put a damper on 2 = <u>outshine</u>, eclipse, surpass, dwarf, tower above, leave or put in the shade

**overt** = <u>open</u>, obvious, plain, public, manifest, blatant, observable, undisguised
≠ hidden

**overtake** 1 = <u>pass</u>, leave behind, overhaul, catch up with, get past, outdistance, go by or past 2 = <u>outdo</u>, top, exceed, eclipse, surpass, outstrip, get the better of, outclass 3 = <u>befall</u>, hit, happen to, catch off guard, catch unawares 4 = <u>engulf</u>, overwhelm, hit, strike, swamp, envelop, swallow up

**overthrow** VERB = <u>defeat</u>, overcome, conquer, bring down, oust, topple, rout, overpower
≠ uphold

**overturn** ● NOUN = <u>downfall</u>, fall, defeat, collapse, destruction, ousting, undoing, unseating ≠ preservation

**overturn** 1 = <u>tip over</u>, topple, upturn, capsize, upend, keel over, overbalance 2 = <u>knock over</u> or <u>down</u>, upturn, tip over, upend 3 = <u>reverse</u>, change, cancel, abolish, overthrow, set aside, repeal, quash 4 = <u>overthrow</u>, defeat, destroy, overcome, bring down, oust, topple, depose

**overweight** = <u>fat</u>, heavy, stout, hefty, plump, bulky, chunky, chubby ≠ underweight

**overwhelm** 1 = <u>overcome</u>, devastate, stagger, bowl over (informal), knock (someone) for six (informal), sweep (someone) off his or her feet, take (someone's) breath away 2 = <u>destroy</u>, defeat, overcome, crush, massacre, conquer, wipe out, overthrow

**overwhelming** 1 = <u>overpowering</u>, strong, powerful, towering, stunning, crushing, devastating, shattering ≠ negligible 2 = <u>vast</u>, huge, massive, enormous, tremendous, immense, very large ≠ insignificant

**owe** = <u>be in debt (to)</u>, be in arrears (to), be overdrawn (by), be obligated or indebted (to)

**owing to** = <u>because of</u>, thanks to, as a result of, on account of, by reason of

**own** ADJECTIVE = <u>personal</u>, special, private, individual, particular, exclusive ● VERB = <u>possess</u>, have, keep, hold, enjoy, retain, be in possession of, have to your name

**owner** = <u>possessor</u>, holder, proprietor, titleholder, landlord or landlady

**ownership** = <u>possession</u>, occupation, tenure, dominion

# P

**pace** NOUN 1 = <u>speed</u>, rate, tempo, velocity 2 = <u>step</u>, walk, stride, tread, gait 3 = <u>footstep</u>, step, stride ● VERB = <u>stride</u>, walk, pound, patrol, march up and down

**pack** VERB 1 = <u>package</u>, load, store, bundle, stow 2 = <u>cram</u>, crowd, press, fill, stuff, jam, ram, compress ● NOUN 1 = <u>packet</u>, box, parcel, carton 2 = <u>bundle</u>, parcel, load, burden, rucksack, knapsack, back pack, kitbag 3 = <u>group</u>, crowd, company, band, troop, gang, bunch, mob ● PHRASES **pack someone off** = <u>send away</u>, dismiss, send

packing (*informal*) ♦ **pack**
**something in** 1 (*Brit. informal*)
= <u>resign from</u>, leave, give up, quit
(*informal*), chuck (*informal*), jack
in (*informal*) 2 = <u>stop</u>, give up,
kick (*informal*), cease, chuck
(*informal*)

**package** NOUN 1 = <u>parcel</u>, box,
container, packet, carton
2 = <u>collection</u>, lot, unit,
combination, compilation
● VERB = <u>pack</u>, box, parcel (up)

**packet** 1 = <u>container</u>, box,
package, carton 2 = <u>package</u>,
parcel 3 (*Slang*) = <u>a fortune</u>, a
bomb (*Brit. slang*), a pile
(*informal*), a small fortune, a tidy
sum (*informal*), a king's ransom
(*informal*)

**pact** = <u>agreement</u>, alliance,
treaty, deal, understanding,
bargain, covenant

**pad**[1] NOUN 1 = <u>wad</u>, dressing,
pack, padding, compress,
wadding 2 = <u>cushion</u>, filling,
stuffing, pillow, bolster,
upholstery 3 = <u>notepad</u>, block,
notebook, jotter, writing pad
4 (*Slang*) = <u>home</u>, flat, apartment,
place 5 = <u>paw</u>, foot, sole
● VERB = <u>pack</u>, fill, protect, stuff,
cushion

**pad**[2] = <u>sneak</u>, creep, steal, go
barefoot

**padding** 1 = <u>filling</u>, stuffing,
packing, wadding 2 = <u>waffle</u>

(*informal, chiefly Brit.*), hot air
(*informal*), verbiage, wordiness,
verbosity

**paddle**[1] NOUN = <u>oar</u>, scull
● VERB = <u>row</u>, pull, scull

**paddle**[2] = <u>wade</u>, splash (about),
slop

**pagan** ADJECTIVE = <u>heathen</u>,
infidel, polytheistic, idolatrous
● NOUN = <u>heathen</u>, infidel,
polytheist, idolater

**page**[1] = <u>folio</u>, side, leaf, sheet

**page**[2] VERB = <u>call</u>, summon, send
for
● NOUN 1 = <u>attendant</u>, pageboy
2 = <u>servant</u>, attendant, squire,
pageboy

**pain** NOUN 1 = <u>suffering</u>,
discomfort, hurt, irritation,
tenderness, soreness 2 = <u>ache</u>,
stinging, aching, cramp, throb,
throbbing, pang, twinge
3 = <u>sorrow</u>, suffering, torture,
distress, despair, misery, agony,
sadness
● PLURAL NOUN = <u>trouble</u>, effort,
care, bother, diligence
● VERB 1 = <u>distress</u>, hurt, torture,
grieve, torment, sadden, agonize,
cut to the quick 2 = <u>hurt</u>

**painful** 1 = <u>sore</u>, smarting,
aching, tender ≠ painless
2 = <u>distressing</u>, unpleasant,
grievous, distasteful, agonizing,
disagreeable ≠ pleasant
3 = <u>difficult</u>, arduous, trying, hard,

troublesome, laborious ≠ easy

**painfully** = <u>distressingly</u>, clearly, sadly, unfortunately, dreadfully

**paint** NOUN = <u>colouring</u>, colour, stain, dye, tint, pigment, emulsion

● VERB₁ = <u>colour</u>, cover, coat, stain, whitewash, daub, distemper, apply paint to

2 = <u>depict</u>, draw, portray, picture, represent, sketch

**pair** NOUN₁ = <u>set₂</u> = <u>couple</u>, brace, duo

● VERB = <u>team</u>, match (up), join, couple, twin, bracket

---

### Word Power

**pair** – Like other collective nouns, *pair* takes a singular or a plural verb according to whether it is seen as a unit or as a collection of two things: *the pair are said to dislike each other; a pair of good shoes is essential.*

---

**pal** (*Informal*) = <u>friend</u>, companion, mate (*informal*), buddy (*informal*), comrade, chum (*informal*), crony, cobber (*Austral. & N.Z. old-fashioned informal*), E hoa (*N.Z.*)

**pale** ADJECTIVE₁ = <u>light</u>, soft, faded, subtle, muted, bleached, pastel, light-coloured₂ = <u>dim</u>, weak, faint, feeble, thin, wan, watery₃ = <u>white</u>, pasty, bleached, wan, colourless, pallid, ashen

≠ rosy-cheeked

● VERB = <u>become pale</u>, blanch, whiten, go white, lose colour

**pamper** = <u>spoil</u>, indulge, pet, cosset, coddle, mollycoddle

**pamphlet** = <u>booklet</u>, leaflet, brochure, circular, tract

**pan**¹ NOUN = <u>pot</u>, container, saucepan

● VERB₁ (*Informal*) = <u>criticize</u>, knock, slam (*slang*), censure, tear into (*informal*)₂ = <u>sift out</u>, look for, search for

**pan**² = <u>move along or across</u>, follow, track, sweep

**panic** NOUN = <u>fear</u>, alarm, terror, anxiety, hysteria, fright, trepidation, a flap (*informal*)

● VERB₁ = <u>go to pieces</u>, become hysterical, lose your nerve

2 = <u>alarm</u>, scare, unnerve

**panorama** 1 = <u>view</u>, prospect, vista₂ = <u>survey</u>, perspective, overview, overall picture

**pant** = <u>puff</u>, blow, breathe, gasp, wheeze, heave

**pants** 1 (*Brit.*) = <u>underpants</u>, briefs, drawers, knickers, panties, boxer shorts, broekies (*S. African*), underdaks (*Austral. slang*)₂ (*U.S.*) = <u>trousers</u>, slacks

**paper** NOUN₁ = <u>newspaper</u>, daily, journal, gazette₂ = <u>essay</u>, article, treatise, dissertation

3 = <u>examination</u>, test, exam

4 = <u>report</u>

● PLURAL NOUN 1 = <u>letters</u>, records, documents, file, diaries, archive, paperwork, dossier 2 = <u>documents</u>, records, certificates, identification, deeds, identity papers, I.D. (*informal*)

● VERB = <u>wallpaper</u>, hang

**parade** NOUN 1 = <u>procession</u>, march, pageant, cavalcade 2 = <u>show</u>, display, spectacle

● VERB 1 = <u>march</u>, process, promenade 2 = <u>flaunt</u>, display, exhibit, show off (*informal*) 3 = <u>strut</u>, show off (*informal*), swagger, swank

**paradigm** = <u>model</u>, example, pattern, ideal

**paradise** 1 = <u>heaven</u>, Promised Land, Happy Valley (*Islam*), Elysian fields 2 = <u>bliss</u>, delight, heaven, felicity, utopia

**paradox** = <u>contradiction</u>, puzzle, anomaly, enigma, oddity

**paragraph** = <u>section</u>, part, item, passage, clause, subdivision

**parallel** NOUN 1 = <u>equivalent</u>, counterpart, match, equal, twin, analogue ≠ opposite 2 = <u>similarity</u>, comparison, analogy, resemblance, likeness ≠ difference

● ADJECTIVE 1 = <u>matching</u>, corresponding, like, similar, resembling, analogous ≠ different 2 = <u>equidistant</u>, alongside, side by side

≠ divergent

**paralyse** 1 = <u>disable</u>, cripple, lame, incapacitate 2 = <u>freeze</u>, stun, numb, petrify, halt, immobilize 3 = <u>immobilize</u>, freeze, halt, disable, cripple, incapacitate, bring to a standstill

**paralysis** 1 = <u>immobility</u>, palsy 2 = <u>standstill</u>, breakdown, stoppage, halt

**parameter** (*Informal*) usually plural = <u>limit</u>, restriction, framework, limitation, specification

**paramount** = <u>principal</u>, prime, first, chief, main, primary, supreme, cardinal ≠ secondary

**paranoid** 1 = <u>suspicious</u>, worried, nervous, fearful, antsy (*informal*) 2 = <u>obsessive</u>, disturbed, manic, neurotic, mentally ill, psychotic, deluded, paranoiac

**parasite** = <u>sponger</u> (*informal*), leech, hanger-on, scrounger (*informal*), bloodsucker (*informal*), quandong (*Austral. slang*)

**parcel** NOUN = <u>package</u>, case, box, pack, bundle

● VERB often with **up** = <u>wrap</u>, pack, package, tie up, do up, gift-wrap, box up, fasten together

**pardon** VERB 1 = <u>forgive</u>, excuse ≠ condemn 2 = <u>acquit</u>, let off (*informal*), exonerate, absolve

≠ punish

● NOUN 1 = forgiveness, absolution ≠ condemnation 2 = acquittal, amnesty, exoneration ≠ punishment

**parent** = father or mother, sire, progenitor, procreator, old (*Austral. & N.Z. informal*), patriarch

**parish** 1 = district, community 2 = community, flock, church, congregation

**park** 1 = recreation ground, garden, playground, pleasure garden, playpark, domain (*N.Z.*), forest park (*N.Z.*) 2 = parkland, grounds, estate, lawns, woodland, grassland 3 = field, pitch, playing field

**parliament** 1 = assembly, council, congress, senate, convention, legislature 2 = sitting

**parliamentary** = governmental, legislative, law-making

**parlour** or (*U.S.*)**parlor** 1 (*Old-fashioned*) = sitting room, lounge, living room, drawing room, front room 2 = establishment, shop, store, salon

**parody** NOUN = takeoff (*informal*), satire, caricature, send-up (*Brit. informal*), spoof (*informal*), skit, burlesque

● VERB = take off (*informal*), caricature, send up (*Brit.*

*informal*), burlesque, satirize, do a takeoff of (*informal*)

**parrot** = repeat, echo, imitate, copy, mimic

**parry** 1 = evade, avoid, dodge, sidestep 2 = ward off, block, deflect, repel, rebuff, repulse

**parson** = clergyman, minister, priest, vicar, preacher, pastor, cleric, churchman

**part** NOUN 1 = piece, share, proportion, percentage, bit, section, scrap, portion ≠ entirety 2 often plural = region, area, district, neighbourhood, quarter, vicinity 3 = component, bit, unit, constituent 4 = branch, division, office, section, wing, subdivision, subsection 5 = organ, member, limb 6 (*Theatre*) = role, representation, persona, portrayal, depiction, character part 7 (*Theatre*) = lines, words, script, dialogue 8 = side, behalf

● VERB 1 = divide, separate, break, tear, split, rend, detach, sever ≠ join 2 = part company, separate, split up ≠ meet

● PHRASES **in good part** = good-naturedly, well, cheerfully, without offence

**partial** 1 = incomplete, unfinished, imperfect, uncompleted ≠ complete 2 = biased, prejudiced, discriminatory, partisan, unfair, one-sided, unjust ≠ unbiased

**partially** = partly, somewhat, in part, not wholly, fractionally, incompletely

**participant** = participator, member, player, contributor, stakeholder

**participate** = take part, be involved, perform, join, partake ≠ refrain from

**participation** = taking part, contribution, involvement, sharing in, joining in, partaking

**particle** = bit, piece, scrap, grain, shred, mite, jot, speck

**particular** ADJECTIVE 1 = specific, special, exact, precise, distinct, peculiar ≠ general 2 = special, exceptional, notable, uncommon, marked, unusual, remarkable, singular 3 = fussy, demanding, fastidious, choosy (*informal*), picky (*informal*), finicky, pernickety (*informal*) ≠ indiscriminate

● NOUN *usually plural* = detail, fact, feature, item, circumstance, specification

**particularly** 1 = specifically, expressly, explicitly, especially, in particular, distinctly
2 = especially, notably, unusually, exceptionally, singularly, uncommonly

**parting** 1 = farewell, goodbye
2 = division, breaking, split,

separation, rift, rupture

**partisan** ADJECTIVE = prejudiced, one-sided, biased, partial, sectarian ≠ unbiased

● NOUN 1 = supporter, devotee, adherent, upholder ≠ opponent
2 = underground fighter, guerrilla, freedom fighter, resistance fighter

**partition** NOUN 1 = screen, wall, barrier 2 = division, separation, segregation

● VERB = separate, screen, divide

**partly** = partially, somewhat, slightly ≠ completely

---

### Word Power

**partly** – *Partly* and *partially* are to some extent interchangeable, but *partly* should be used when referring to a part or parts of something: *the building is partly (not partially) made of stone*, while *partially* is preferred for the meaning *to some extent: his mother is partially (not partly) sighted.*

---

**partner** 1 = spouse, consort, significant other (*U.S. informal*), mate, husband *or* wife
2 = companion, ally, colleague, associate, mate, comrade
3 = associate, colleague, collaborator

**partnership** 1 = cooperation, alliance, sharing, union,

connection, participation, copartnership **2** = **company**, firm, house, interest, society, cooperative

**party 1** = **faction**, set, side, league, camp, clique, coterie **2** = **get-together** (*informal*), celebration, do (*informal*), gathering, function, reception, festivity, social gathering **3** = **group**, team, band, company, unit, squad, crew, gang

**pass** VERB **1** = **go by** or **past**, overtake, drive past, lap, leave behind, pull ahead of ≠ **stop 2** = **go**, move, travel, progress, proceed **3** = **run**, move, stroke **4** = **give**, hand, send, transfer, deliver, convey **5** = **be left**, come, be bequeathed, be inherited by **6** = **kick**, hit, loft, head, lob **7** = **elapse**, progress, go by, lapse, wear on, go past, tick by **8** = **end**, go, cease, blow over **9** = **spend**, fill, occupy, while away **10** = **exceed**, beat, overtake, go beyond, surpass, outstrip, outdo **11** = **be successful in**, qualify (in), succeed (in), graduate (in), get through, do, gain a pass in ≠ **fail 12** = **approve**, accept, decree, enact, ratify, ordain, legislate (for) ≠ **ban**

● NOUN **1** = **licence**, ticket, permit, passport, warrant, authorization **2** = **gap**, route, canyon, gorge, ravine

● PHRASES **pass away** or **on** (*Euphemistic*) = **die**, pass on, expire, pass over, snuff it (*informal*), kick the bucket (*slang*), shuffle off this mortal coil, cark it (*Austral. & N.Z. informal*) ◆ **pass out** (*Informal*) = **faint**, black out (*informal*), lose consciousness, become unconscious ◆ **pass something over** = **disregard**, ignore, not dwell on ◆ **pass something up** (*Informal*) = **miss**, let slip, decline, neglect, forgo, abstain from, give (something) a miss (*informal*)

> ### Word Power
>
> **pass** – The past participle of *pass* is sometimes wrongly spelt *past*: *the time for recriminations has passed* (not *past*).

**passage 1** = **corridor**, hall, lobby, vestibule **2** = **alley**, way, close (*Brit.*), course, road, channel, route, path **3** = **extract**, reading, piece, section, text, excerpt, quotation **4** = **journey**, crossing, trip, trek, voyage **5** = **safe-conduct**, right to travel, freedom to travel, permission to travel

**passenger** = **traveller**, rider, fare, commuter, fare payer

**passer-by** = **bystander**, witness, observer, viewer, spectator, looker-on, watcher, onlooker

**passing** 1 = momentary, fleeting, short-lived, transient, ephemeral, brief, temporary, transitory 2 = superficial, short, quick, glancing, casual, summary, cursory, perfunctory

**passion** 1 = love, desire, lust, infatuation, ardour 2 = emotion, feeling, fire, heat, excitement, intensity, warmth, zeal ≠ indifference 3 = mania, enthusiasm, obsession, bug (*informal*), craving, fascination, craze 4 = rage, fit, storm, anger, fury, outburst, frenzy, paroxysm

**passionate** 1 = emotional, eager, strong, intense, fierce, ardent, fervent, heartfelt ≠ unemotional 2 = loving, erotic, hot, ardent, amorous, lustful ≠ cold

**passive** 1 = submissive, compliant, receptive, docile, quiescent ≠ spirited 2 = inactive, uninvolved ≠ active

**past** NOUN 1 = former times, long ago, days gone by, the olden days ≠ future 2 = background, life, history, past life, life story, career to date

● ADJECTIVE 1 = former, early, previous, ancient, bygone, olden ≠ future 2 = previous, former, one-time, ex- 3 = last, previous 4 = over, done, ended, finished, gone

● PREPOSITION 1 = after, beyond, later than 2 = by, across, in front of

● ADVERB 1 = on, by, along

> ## Word Power
>
> **past** – The past participle of *pass* is sometimes wrongly spelt *past*: *the time for recriminations has passed* (not *past*).

**paste** NOUN 1 = adhesive, glue, cement, gum 2 = purée, pâté, spread

● VERB = stick, glue, cement, gum

**pastel** = pale, light, soft, delicate, muted ≠ bright

**pastime** = activity, game, entertainment, hobby, recreation, amusement, diversion

**pastor** = clergyman, minister, priest, vicar, parson, rector, curate, churchman

**pastoral** 1 = ecclesiastical, priestly, ministerial, clerical 2 = rustic, country, rural, bucolic

**pasture** = grassland, grass, meadow, grazing

**pat** VERB = stroke, touch, tap, pet, caress, fondle

● NOUN = tap, stroke, clap

**patch** NOUN 1 = spot, bit, scrap, shred, small piece 2 = plot, area, ground, land, tract 3 = reinforcement, piece of fabric, piece of cloth, piece of material, piece sewn on

**patent** • VERB *often with* **up** = mend, cover, repair, reinforce, stitch (up), sew (up)

**patent** NOUN = copyright, licence, franchise, registered trademark
• ADJECTIVE = obvious, apparent, evident, clear, glaring, manifest

**path** 1 = way, road, walk, track, trail, avenue, footpath, berm (*N.Z.*) 2 = route, way, course, direction 3 = course, way, road, route

**pathetic** = sad, moving, touching, affecting, distressing, tender, poignant, plaintive
≠ funny

**patience** 1 = forbearance, tolerance, serenity, restraint, calmness, sufferance
≠ impatience 2 = endurance, resignation, submission, fortitude, long-suffering, perseverance, stoicism, constancy

**patient** NOUN = sick person, case, sufferer, invalid
• ADJECTIVE 1 = forbearing, understanding, forgiving, mild, tolerant, indulgent, lenient, even-tempered ≠ impatient 2 = long-suffering, resigned, calm, enduring, philosophical, persevering, stoical, submissive

**patriot** = nationalist, loyalist, chauvinist

**patriotic** = nationalistic, loyal, chauvinistic, jingoistic

**patriotism** = nationalism, jingoism

**patrol** VERB = police, guard, keep watch (on), inspect, safeguard, keep guard (on)
• NOUN = guard, watch, watchman, sentinel, patrolman

**patron** 1 = supporter, friend, champion, sponsor, backer, helper, benefactor, philanthropist 2 = customer, client, buyer, frequenter, shopper, habitué

**patronage** = support, promotion, sponsorship, backing, help, aid, assistance

**pattern** 1 = order, plan, system, method, sequence 2 = design, arrangement, motif, figure, device, decoration 3 = plan, design, original, guide, diagram, stencil, template

**pause** VERB = stop briefly, delay, break, wait, rest, halt, cease, interrupt ≠ continue
• NOUN = stop, break, interval, rest, gap, halt, respite, lull
≠ continuance

**pave** = cover, floor, surface, concrete, tile

**paw** (*Informal*) = manhandle, grab, maul, molest, handle roughly

**pay** VERB 1 = reward, compensate, reimburse, recompense, requite, remunerate 2 = spend, give, fork out (*informal*), remit, shell out (*informal*) 3 = settle 4 = bring in, earn, return, net, yield 5 = **be profitable**, make money, make a return 6 = **benefit**, repay, be worthwhile 7 = **give**, extend, present with, grant, hand out, bestow

● NOUN = **wages**, income, payment, earnings, fee, reward, salary, allowance

● PHRASES **pay off** = **succeed**, work, be effective ◆ **pay something off** = **settle**, clear, square, discharge, pay in full

**payable** = **due**, outstanding, owed, owing

**payment** 1 = **remittance**, advance, deposit, premium, instalment 2 = **settlement**, paying, discharge, remittance 3 = **wages**, fee, reward, hire, remuneration

**peace** 1 = **truce**, ceasefire, treaty, armistice ≠ war 2 = **stillness**, rest, quiet, silence, calm, hush, tranquillity, seclusion 3 = **serenity**, calm, composure, contentment, repose, equanimity, peacefulness, harmoniousness 4 = **harmony**, accord, agreement, concord

**peaceful** 1 = **at peace**, friendly, harmonious, amicable, nonviolent ≠ hostile 2 = **peace-loving**, conciliatory, peaceable, unwarlike ≠ belligerent 3 = **calm**, still, quiet, tranquil, restful ≠ agitated 4 = **serene**, placid, undisturbed

**peak** NOUN 1 = **high point**, crown, climax, culmination, zenith, acme 2 = **point**, top, tip, summit, brow, crest, pinnacle, apex

● VERB = **culminate**, climax, come to a head

**peasant** = **rustic**, countryman

**peck** VERB 1 = **pick**, hit, strike, tap, poke, jab, prick 2 = **kiss**, plant a kiss, give someone a smacker, give someone a peck or kiss

● NOUN = **kiss**, smacker, osculation (rare)

**peculiar** 1 = **odd**, strange, unusual, bizarre, funny, extraordinary, curious, weird ≠ ordinary 2 = **special**, particular, unique, characteristic ≠ common

**peddle** = **sell**, trade, push (informal), market, hawk, flog (slang)

**pedestrian** NOUN = **walker**, foot-traveller ≠ driver

● ADJECTIVE = **dull**, ordinary, boring, commonplace, mundane, mediocre, banal, prosaic, half-pie (N.Z. informal) ≠ exciting

**pedigree** ADJECTIVE = **purebred**, thoroughbred, full-blooded

● NOUN = **lineage**, family, line, race, stock, blood, breed, descent

**peel** NOUN = **rind**, skin, peeling

● VERB = **skin**, scale, strip, pare, shuck, flake off, take the skin or rind off

**peep** VERB = peek, look, eyeball (*slang*), sneak a look, steal a look
● NOUN = look, glimpse, peek, look-see (*slang*)

**peer**[1] = squint, look, spy, gaze, scan, inspect, peep, peek

**peer**[2] 1 = noble, lord, aristocrat, nobleman 2 = equal, like, fellow, contemporary, compeer

**peg** NOUN = pin, spike, rivet, skewer, dowel, spigot
● VERB = fasten, join, fix, secure, attach

**pen**[1] = write (down), draft, compose, pencil, draw up, scribble, take down, inscribe

**pen**[2] NOUN = enclosure, pound, fold, cage, coop, hutch, sty
● VERB = enclose, confine, cage, fence in, coop up, hedge in, shut up *or* in

**penalty** = punishment, price, fine, handicap, forfeit

**pending** ADJECTIVE
1 = undecided, unsettled, in the balance, undetermined
2 = forthcoming, imminent, prospective, impending, in the wind
● PREPOSITION = awaiting, until, waiting for, till

**penetrate** 1 = pierce, enter, go through, bore, stab, prick
2 = grasp, work out, figure out (*informal*), comprehend, fathom, decipher, suss (out) (*slang*), get to

the bottom of

**penetrating** 1 = sharp, harsh, piercing, carrying, piping, loud, strident, shrill ≠ sweet
2 = pungent 3 = piercing
4 = intelligent, quick, sharp, keen, acute, shrewd, astute, perceptive ≠ dull 5 = perceptive, sharp, keen ≠ unperceptive

**penetration** 1 = piercing, entry, entrance, puncturing, incision
2 = entry, entrance

**pension** = allowance, benefit, welfare, annuity, superannuation

**pensioner** = senior citizen, retired person, retiree (*U.S.*), old-age pensioner, O.A.P.

**people** PLURAL NOUN 1 = persons, individuals, folk (*informal*), men and women, humanity, mankind, mortals, the human race
2 = nation, public, community, subjects, population, residents, citizens, folk 3 = race, tribe
4 = family, parents, relations, relatives, folk, folks (*informal*), clan, kin
● VERB = inhabit, occupy, settle, populate, colonize

**pepper** NOUN = seasoning, flavour, spice
● VERB 1 = pelt, hit, shower, blitz, rake, bombard, assail, strafe
2 = sprinkle, spot, scatter, dot, fleck, intersperse, speck, spatter

**perceive** 1 = <u>see</u>, notice, note, identify, discover, spot, observe, recognize 2 = <u>understand</u>, gather, see, learn, realize, grasp, comprehend, suss (out) (*slang*) 3 = <u>consider</u>, believe, judge, suppose, rate, deem, adjudge

**perception** 1 = <u>awareness</u>, understanding, sense, impression, feeling, idea, notion, consciousness

2 = <u>understanding</u>, intelligence, observation, discrimination, insight, sharpness, cleverness, keenness

**perch** VERB 1 = <u>sit</u>, rest, balance, settle 2 = <u>place</u>, put, rest, balance 3 = <u>land</u>, alight, roost
• NOUN = <u>resting place</u>, post, branch, pole

**perennial** = <u>continual</u>, lasting, constant, enduring, persistent, abiding, recurrent, incessant

**perfect** ADJECTIVE 1 = <u>faultless</u>, correct, pure, impeccable, exemplary, flawless, foolproof ≠ deficient 2 = <u>excellent</u>, ideal, supreme, superb, splendid, sublime, superlative

3 = <u>immaculate</u>, impeccable, flawless, spotless, unblemished ≠ flawed 4 = <u>complete</u>, absolute, sheer, utter, consummate, unmitigated ≠ partial 5 = <u>exact</u>, true, accurate, precise, correct, faithful, unerring

• VERB = <u>improve</u>, develop, polish, refine ≠ mar

### Word Power

**perfect** – For most of its meanings, the adjective *perfect* describes an absolute state, so that something either is or is not *perfect*, and cannot be referred to in terms of degree – thus, one thing should not be described as *more perfect* or *less perfect* than another thing. However, when *perfect* is used in the sense of 'excellent in all respects', *more* and *most* are acceptable, for example *the next day the weather was even more perfect*.

**perfection** = <u>excellence</u>, integrity, superiority, purity, wholeness, sublimity, exquisiteness, faultlessness

**perfectly** 1 = <u>completely</u>, totally, absolutely, quite, fully, altogether, thoroughly, wholly ≠ partially

2 = <u>flawlessly</u>, ideally, wonderfully, superbly, supremely, impeccably, faultlessly ≠ badly

**perform** 1 = <u>do</u>, achieve, carry out, complete, fulfil, accomplish, execute, pull off 2 = <u>fulfil</u>, carry out, execute, discharge

3 = <u>present</u>, act (out), stage, play, produce, represent, put on, enact

4 = <u>appear on stage</u>, act

5 = <u>function</u>, go, work, run,

operate, handle, respond, behave

**performance** 1 = <u>presentation</u>, playing, acting (out), staging, production, exhibition, rendering, portrayal 2 = <u>show</u>, appearance, concert, gig (*informal*), recital 3 = <u>work</u>, acts, conduct, exploits, feats 4 = <u>carrying out</u>, practice, achievement, execution, completion, accomplishment, fulfilment

**performer** = <u>artiste</u>, player, Thespian, trouper, actor or actress

**perfume** 1 = <u>fragrance</u>, scent 2 = <u>scent</u>, smell, fragrance, bouquet, aroma, odour

**perhaps** = <u>maybe</u>, possibly, it may be, it is possible (that), conceivably, perchance (*archaic*), feasibly, happen (*Northern English dialect*)

**peril** 1 = <u>danger</u>, risk, threat, hazard, menace, jeopardy, perilousness 2 *often plural* = <u>pitfall</u>, problem, risk, hazard ≠ safety

**perimeter** = <u>boundary</u>, edge, border, bounds, limit, margin, confines, periphery ≠ centre

**period** = <u>time</u>, term, season, space, run, stretch, spell, phase

**periodic** = <u>recurrent</u>, regular, repeated, occasional, cyclical, sporadic, intermittent

**peripheral** 1 = <u>secondary</u>, minor, marginal, irrelevant,

unimportant, incidental, inessential 2 = <u>outermost</u>, outside, external, outer, exterior

**perish** 1 = <u>die</u>, be killed, expire, pass away, lose your life, cark it (*Austral. & N.Z. slang*) 2 = <u>be destroyed</u>, fall, decline, collapse, disappear, vanish 3 = <u>rot</u>, waste away, decay, disintegrate, decompose, moulder

**perk** (*Brit. informal*) = <u>bonus</u>, benefit, extra, plus, fringe benefit, perquisite

**permanent** 1 = <u>lasting</u>, constant, enduring, persistent, eternal, abiding, perpetual, everlasting ≠ temporary 2 = <u>long-term</u>, established, secure, stable, steady ≠ temporary

**permission** = <u>authorization</u>, sanction, licence, approval, leave, go-ahead (*informal*), liberty, consent ≠ prohibition

**permit** VERB 1 = <u>allow</u>, grant, sanction, let, entitle, license, authorize, consent to ≠ forbid 2 = <u>enable</u>, let, allow, cause

● NOUN = <u>licence</u>, pass, document, certificate, passport, visa, warrant, authorization ≠ prohibition

**perpetual** 1 = <u>everlasting</u>, permanent, endless, eternal, lasting, perennial, infinite, never-ending ≠ temporary 2 = <u>continual</u>, repeated, constant, endless, continuous, persistent, recurrent, never-ending ≠ brief

**perpetuate** 1 = <u>maintain</u>, preserve, keep going, immortalize ≠ end

**persecute** 1 = <u>victimize</u>, torture, torment, oppress, pick on, ill-treat, maltreat ≠ mollycoddle

2 = <u>harass</u>, bother, annoy, tease, hassle (*informal*), badger, pester ≠ leave alone

**persist** 1 = <u>continue</u>, last, remain, carry on, keep up, linger

2 = <u>persevere</u>, continue, go on, carry on, keep on, keep going, press on, not give up

**persistence** = <u>determination</u>, resolution, grit, endurance, tenacity, perseverance, doggedness, pertinacity

**persistent** 1 = <u>continuous</u>, constant, repeated, endless, perpetual, continual, never-ending, incessant ≠ occasional

2 = <u>determined</u>, dogged, steady, stubborn, persevering, tireless, tenacious, steadfast ≠ irresolute

**person** NOUN = <u>individual</u>, being, body, human, soul, creature, mortal, man *or* woman

● PHRASES **in person**

1 = <u>personally</u>, yourself₂ = <u>in the flesh</u>, actually, physically, bodily

**personal** 1 = <u>own</u>, special, private, individual, particular, peculiar₂ = <u>individual</u>, special,

**perpetuate → persuade**

particular, exclusive₃ = <u>private</u>

4 = <u>offensive</u>, nasty, insulting, disparaging, derogatory

**personality** 1 = <u>nature</u>, character, make-up, identity, temperament, disposition, individuality₂ = <u>character</u>, charm, attraction, charisma, magnetism₃ = <u>celebrity</u>, star, notable, household name, famous name, personage, megastar (*informal*)

**personally** 1 = <u>in your opinion</u>, in your book, for your part, from your own viewpoint, in your own view₂ = <u>by yourself</u>, alone, independently, solely, on your own₃ = <u>individually</u>, specially, subjectively, individualistically

4 = <u>privately</u>, in private, off the record

**personnel** = <u>employees</u>, people, staff, workers, workforce, human resources, helpers

**perspective** 1 = <u>outlook</u>, attitude, context, angle, frame of reference₂ = <u>objectivity</u>, proportion, relation, relativity, relative importance

**persuade** 1 = <u>talk (someone) into</u>, urge, influence, win (someone) over, induce, sway, entice, coax ≠ dissuade₂ = <u>cause</u>, lead, move, influence, motivate, induce, incline, dispose

3 = <u>convince</u>, satisfy, assure, cause

to believe

**persuasion** 1 = <u>urging</u>, inducement, wheedling, enticement, cajolery 2 = <u>belief</u>, views, opinion, party, school, side, camp, faith

**persuasive** = <u>convincing</u>, telling, effective, sound, compelling, influential, valid, credible ≠ unconvincing

**pervasive** = <u>widespread</u>, general, common, extensive, universal, prevalent, ubiquitous, rife

**perverse** 1 = <u>stubborn</u>, contrary, dogged, troublesome, rebellious, wayward, intractable, wilful ≠ cooperative 2 = <u>ill-natured</u>, cross, surly, fractious, churlish, ill-tempered, stroppy (*Brit. slang*), peevish ≠ good-natured 3 = <u>abnormal</u>, unhealthy, improper, deviant

**pervert** VERB 1 = <u>distort</u>, abuse, twist, misuse, warp, misrepresent, falsify 2 = <u>corrupt</u>, degrade, deprave, debase, debauch, lead astray
● NOUN = <u>deviant</u>, degenerate, sicko (*informal*), weirdo or weirdie (*informal*)

**pessimistic** = <u>gloomy</u>, dark, despairing, bleak, depressed, cynical, hopeless, glum ≠ optimistic

**pest** 1 = <u>infection</u>, bug, insect, plague, epidemic, blight, scourge, pestilence, gogga (*S. African informal*) 2 = <u>nuisance</u>, trial, pain (*informal*), drag (*informal*), bother, irritation, annoyance, bane

**pet** ADJECTIVE = <u>favourite</u>, favoured, dearest, cherished, fave (*informal*), dear to your heart
● NOUN = <u>favourite</u>, treasure, darling, jewel, idol
● VERB 1 = <u>fondle</u>, pat, stroke, caress 2 = <u>pamper</u>, spoil, indulge, cosset, baby, dote on, coddle, mollycoddle 3 (*Informal*) = <u>cuddle</u>, kiss, snog (*Brit. slang*), smooch (*informal*), neck (*informal*), canoodle (*slang*)

**petition** NOUN 1 = <u>appeal</u>, round robin, list of signatures 2 = <u>entreaty</u>, appeal, suit, application, request, prayer, plea, solicitation
● VERB = <u>appeal</u>, plead, ask, pray, beg, solicit, beseech, entreat

**petty** 1 = <u>trivial</u>, insignificant, little, small, slight, trifling, negligible, unimportant ≠ important 2 = <u>small-minded</u>, mean, shabby, spiteful, ungenerous, mean-minded ≠ broad-minded

**phantom** = <u>spectre</u>, ghost, spirit, shade (*literary*), spook (*informal*), apparition, wraith, phantasm

**phase** NOUN = <u>stage</u>, time, point,

position, step, development, period, chapter

● PHRASES **phase something in** = introduce, incorporate, ease in, start ● **phase something out** = eliminate, close, remove, withdraw, pull out, wind up, run down, terminate

**phenomenal** = extraordinary, outstanding, remarkable, fantastic, unusual, marvellous, exceptional, miraculous ≠ unremarkable

**phenomenon** 1 = occurrence, happening, fact, event, incident, circumstance, episode
2 = wonder, sensation, exception, miracle, marvel, prodigy, rarity

---

### Word Power

**phenomenon** – Although *phenomena* is often treated as a singular, this is not grammatically correct. *Phenomenon* is the singular form of this word, and *phenomena* the plural; so *several new phenomena were recorded in his notes* is correct, but *that is an interesting phenomena* is not.

---

**philosopher** = thinker, theorist, sage, wise man, logician, metaphysician

**philosophical** or **philosophic** 1 = theoretical, abstract, wise, rational, logical,

## phenomenal → phrase

thoughtful, sagacious ≠ practical
2 = stoical, calm, composed, cool, collected, serene, tranquil, unruffled ≠ emotional

**philosophy** 1 = thought, knowledge, thinking, reasoning, wisdom, logic, metaphysics
2 = outlook, values, principles, convictions, thinking, beliefs, doctrine, ideology

**phone** NOUN 1 = telephone, blower (*informal*) 2 = call, ring (*informal, chiefly Brit.*), tinkle (*Brit. informal*)

● VERB = call, telephone, ring (up) (*informal, chiefly Brit.*), give someone a call, give someone a ring (*informal, chiefly Brit.*), make a call, give someone a tinkle (*Brit. informal*), get on the blower (*informal*)

**photograph** NOUN = picture, photo (*informal*), shot, print, snap (*informal*), snapshot, transparency

● VERB = take a picture of, record, film, shoot, snap (*informal*), take (someone's) picture

**photographic** 1 = pictorial, visual, graphic, cinematic, filmic
2 = accurate, exact, precise, faithful, retentive

**phrase** NOUN = expression, saying, remark, construction, quotation, maxim, idiom, adage

● VERB = express, say, word, put,

voice, communicate, convey, put
into words

**physical** 1 = <u>corporal</u>, fleshly,
bodily, corporeal 2 = <u>earthly</u>,
fleshly, mortal, incarnate
3 = <u>material</u>, real, substantial,
natural, solid, tangible, palpable

**physician** = <u>doctor</u>, doc
(*informal*), medic (*informal*),
general practitioner, medical
practitioner, doctor of medicine,
G.P., M.D.

**pick** VERB 1 = <u>select</u>, choose,
identify, elect, nominate, specify,
opt for, single out ≠ reject
2 = <u>gather</u>, pull, collect, take in,
harvest, pluck, garner
3 = <u>provoke</u>, start, cause, stir up,
incite, instigate 4 = <u>open</u>, force,
crack (*informal*), break into, break
open

● NOUN 1 = <u>choice</u>, decision,
option, selection, preference
2 = <u>best</u>, prime, finest, elect, elite,
cream, jewel in the crown, crème
de la crème (*French*)

● PHRASES **pick on someone**
1 = <u>torment</u>, bully, bait, tease, get
at (*informal*), badger, persecute,
hector 2 = <u>choose</u>, select, prefer,
elect, single out, fix on, settle
upon ◆ **pick something** or
**someone out** = <u>identify</u>,
recognize, distinguish, perceive,
discriminate, make someone or
something out, tell someone or
something apart ◆ **pick**

**something** or **someone up**
1 = <u>lift</u>, raise, gather, take up,
grasp, uplift 2 = <u>collect</u>, get, call
for ◆ **pick something up**
1 = <u>learn</u>, master, acquire, get the
hang of (*informal*), become
proficient in 2 = <u>obtain</u>, get, find,
buy, discover, purchase, acquire,
locate ◆ **pick up** 1 = <u>improve</u>,
recover, rally, get better, bounce
back, make progress, perk up,
turn the corner 2 = <u>recover</u>,
improve, rally, get better, mend,
turn the corner, be on the mend,
take a turn for the better

**picket** VERB = <u>blockade</u>, boycott,
demonstrate outside

● NOUN 1 = <u>demonstration</u>, strike,
blockade 2 = <u>protester</u>,
demonstrator, picketer
3 = <u>lookout</u>, watch, guard, patrol,
sentry, sentinel 4 = <u>stake</u>, post,
pale, paling, upright, stanchion

**pickle** VERB = <u>preserve</u>,
marinade, steep

● NOUN 1 = <u>chutney</u>, relish,
piccalilli 2 (*Informal*)
= <u>predicament</u>, fix (*informal*),
difficulty, bind (*informal*), jam
(*informal*), dilemma, scrape
(*informal*), hot water (*informal*),
uphill (*S. African*)

**pick-up** = <u>improvement</u>,
recovery, rise, rally, strengthening,
revival, upturn, change for the
better

**picnic** = <u>excursion</u>, barbecue,

barbie (*informal*), cookout (*U.S. & Canad.*), alfresco meal, clambake (*U.S. & Canad.*), outdoor meal, outing

**picture** NOUN 1 = <u>representation</u>, drawing, painting, portrait, image, print, illustration, sketch 2 = <u>photograph</u>, photo, still, shot, image, print, frame, slide 3 = <u>film</u>, movie (*U.S. informal*), flick (*slang*), feature film, motion picture 4 = <u>idea</u>, vision, concept, impression, notion, visualization, mental image 5 = <u>description</u>, impression, explanation, report, account, image, sketch, depiction 6 = <u>personification</u>, embodiment, essence, epitome
● VERB 1 = <u>imagine</u>, see, envision, visualize, conceive of, fantasize about, conjure up an image of 2 = <u>represent</u>, show, draw, paint, illustrate, sketch, depict 3 = <u>show</u>, photograph, capture on film

**picturesque** 1 = <u>interesting</u>, pretty, beautiful, attractive, charming, scenic, quaint ≠ unattractive 2 = <u>vivid</u>, striking, graphic, colourful, memorable ≠ dull

**piece** 1 = <u>bit</u>, slice, part, block, quantity, segment, portion, fragment 2 = <u>component</u>, part, section, bit, unit, segment, constituent, module 3 = <u>item</u>, report, story, study, review, article

4 = <u>composition</u>, work, production, opus 5 = <u>work of art</u>, work, creation 6 = <u>share</u>, cut (*informal*), slice, percentage, quantity, portion, quota, fraction

**pier** 1 = <u>jetty</u>, wharf, quay, promenade, landing place 2 = <u>pillar</u>, support, post, column, pile, upright, buttress

**pierce** 1 = <u>penetrate</u>, stab, spike, enter, bore, drill, puncture, prick

**piercing** 1 (*of sound*) = <u>penetrating</u>, sharp, loud, shrill, high-pitched, ear-splitting ≠ low 2 = <u>perceptive</u>, sharp, keen, alert, penetrating, shrewd, perspicacious, quick-witted ≠ unperceptive 3 = <u>sharp</u>, acute, severe, intense, painful, stabbing, excruciating, agonizing 4 (*of weather*) = <u>cold</u>, biting, freezing, bitter, arctic, wintry, nippy

**pig** 1 = <u>hog</u>, sow, boar, swine, porker 2 (*Informal*) = <u>slob</u>, glutton 3 (*Informal*) = <u>brute</u>, monster, scoundrel, rogue, swine, rotter, boor

**pigment** = <u>colour</u>, colouring, paint, stain, dye, tint, tincture

**pile** 1 NOUN 1 = <u>heap</u>, collection, mountain, mass, stack, mound, accumulation, hoard 2 (*Informal*) *often plural* = <u>lot(s)</u>, mountain(s), load(s) (*informal*), oceans, wealth, great deal, stack(s), abundance 3 = <u>mansion</u>, building, residence, manor, country house, seat, big house, stately home

● VERB 1 = load, stuff, pack, stack, charge, heap, cram, lade 2 = crowd, pack, rush, climb, flood, stream, crush, squeeze

● PHRASES pile up = accumulate, collect, gather (up), build up, amass

**pile²** = foundation, support, post, column, beam, upright, pillar

**pile³** = nap, fibre, down, hair, fur, plush

**pile-up** (*Informal*) = collision, crash, smash, accident, smash-up (*informal*), multiple collision

**pilgrim** = traveller, wanderer, devotee, wayfarer

**pilgrimage** = journey, tour, trip, mission, expedition, excursion

**pill** = tablet, capsule, pellet

**pillar** 1 = support, post, column, prop, shaft, upright, pier, stanchion 2 = supporter, leader, mainstay, leading light (*informal*), upholder

**pilot** NOUN 1 = airman, flyer, aviator, aeronaut 2 = helmsman, navigator, steersman

● VERB 1 = fly, operate, be at the controls of 2 = navigate, drive, direct, guide, handle, conduct, steer 3 = direct, conduct, steer

● ADJECTIVE = trial, test, model, sample, experimental

**pin** NOUN 1 = tack, nail, needle,

safety pin 2 = peg, rod, brace, bolt

● VERB 1 = fasten, stick, attach, join, fix, secure, nail, clip 2 = hold fast, hold down, constrain, immobilize, pinion

● PHRASES **pin someone down** = force, pressure, compel, put pressure on, pressurize, nail someone down, make someone commit themselves ◆ **pin something down** = determine, identify, locate, name, specify, pinpoint

**pinch** VERB 1 = nip, press, squeeze, grasp, compress 2 = hurt, crush, squeeze, pain, cramp 3 (*Brit. informal*) = steal, lift (*informal*), nick (*slang, chiefly Brit.*), swipe (*slang*), knock off (*slang*), pilfer, purloin, filch

● NOUN 1 = nip, squeeze 2 = dash, bit, mite, jot, speck, soupçon (*French*) 3 = emergency, crisis, difficulty, plight, scrape (*informal*), strait, uphill (*S. African*), predicament

**pine** VERB = waste, decline, sicken, fade, languish

● PHRASES **pine for something or someone** 1 = long, ache, crave, yearn, eat your heart out over 2 = hanker after, crave, wish for, yearn for, thirst for, hunger for

**pink** NOUN *or* ADJECTIVE = rosy, rose, salmon, flushed, reddish, roseate

➤ **shades of red**

**pinnacle** 1 = <u>summit</u>, top, height, peak, 2 = <u>height</u>, top, crown, crest, zenith, apex, vertex

**pinpoint** 1 = <u>identify</u>, discover, define, distinguish, put your finger on, 2 = <u>locate</u>, find, identify, zero in on

**pioneer** NOUN, 1 = <u>founder</u>, leader, developer, innovator, trailblazer, 2 = <u>settler</u>, explorer, colonist

● VERB = <u>develop</u>, create, establish, start, discover, institute, invent, initiate

**pipe** NOUN, 1 = <u>tube</u>, drain, canal, pipeline, line, main, passage, cylinder

● VERB = <u>convey</u>, channel, conduct

● PHRASES **pipe down** (Informal) = <u>be quiet</u>, shut up (informal), hush, stop talking, quieten down, shush, shut your mouth, hold your tongue

**pipeline** = <u>tube</u>, passage, pipe, conduit, duct

**pirate** NOUN = <u>buccaneer</u>, raider, marauder, corsair, freebooter

● VERB = <u>copy</u>, steal, reproduce, bootleg, appropriate, poach, crib (informal), plagiarize

**pit** NOUN, 1 = <u>coal mine</u>, mine, shaft, colliery, mine shaft, 2 = <u>hole</u>, depression, hollow, crater, trough, cavity, abyss, chasm

● VERB = <u>scar</u>, mark, dent, indent, pockmark

**pitch** NOUN, 1 = <u>sports field</u>, ground, stadium, arena, park, field of play, 2 = <u>tone</u>, sound, key, frequency, timbre, modulation 3 = <u>level</u>, point, degree, summit, extent, height, intensity, high point, (informal)

● VERB, 1 = <u>throw</u>, cast, toss, hurl, fling, chuck (informal), sling, lob (informal), 2 = <u>fall</u>, drop, plunge, dive, tumble, topple, plummet, fall headlong, 3 = <u>set up</u>, raise, settle, put up, erect, 4 = <u>toss</u> (about), roll, plunge, lurch

● PHRASES **pitch in** = <u>help</u>, contribute, participate, join in, cooperate, chip in (informal), get stuck in (Brit. informal), lend a hand

**pitfall** usually plural = <u>danger</u>, difficulty, peril, catch, trap, hazard, drawback, snag, uphill (S. African)

**pity** NOUN, 1 = <u>compassion</u>, charity, sympathy, kindness, fellow feeling ≠ mercilessness 2 = <u>shame</u>, sin (informal), misfortune, bummer (slang), crying shame, 3 = <u>mercy</u>, kindness, clemency, forbearance

● VERB = <u>feel sorry for</u>, feel for, sympathize with, grieve for, weep for, bleed for, have compassion for

**pivotal** = <u>crucial</u>, central, vital, critical, decisive

**place** NOUN 1 = spot, point, position, site, area, location, venue, whereabouts 2 = region, quarter, district, neighbourhood, vicinity, locality, locale, dorp (*S. African*) 3 = position, spot, point, location 4 = space, position, seat, chair 5 = rank, standing, position, footing, station, status, grade, niche 6 = situation, position, circumstances, shoes (*informal*) 7 = job, position, post, situation, office, employment, appointment 8 = home, house, room, property, accommodation, pad (*slang*), residence, dwelling 9 (In this context, the construction is always negative) = duty, right, job, charge, concern, role, affair, responsibility

• VERB 1 = lay (down), put (down), set (down), stand, position, rest, station, stick (*informal*) 2 = put, lay, set, invest, pin 3 = classify, class, group, put, order, sort, rank, arrange 4 = entrust to, give to, assign to, appoint to, allocate to, find a home for 5 = identify, remember, recognize, pin someone down, put your finger on, put a name to

• PHRASES take place = happen, occur, go on, go down (*U.S. & Canad.*), arise, come about, crop up, transpire (*informal*)

**plague** NOUN 1 = disease, infection, epidemic, pestilence 2 = infestation, invasion, epidemic, influx, host, swarm, multitude

• VERB 1 = torment, trouble, torture 2 = pester, trouble, bother, annoy, tease, harry, harass, hassle

**plain** ADJECTIVE 1 = unadorned, simple, basic, severe, bare, stark, austere, spartan ≠ ornate 2 = clear, obvious, patent, evident, visible, distinct, understandable, manifest ≠ hidden 3 = straightforward, open, direct, frank, blunt, outspoken, honest, downright ≠ roundabout 4 = ugly, unattractive, homely (*U.S. & Canad.*), unlovely, unprepossessing, not beautiful, no oil painting (*informal*), ill-favoured ≠ attractive 5 = ordinary, common, simple, everyday, commonplace, unaffected, unpretentious ≠ sophisticated

• NOUN = flatland, plateau, prairie, grassland, steppe, veld

**plan** NOUN 1 = scheme, system, design, programme, proposal, strategy, method, suggestion 2 = diagram, map, drawing, chart, representation, sketch, blueprint, layout

• VERB 1 = devise, arrange, scheme, plot, draft, organize, outline, formulate 2 = intend, aim, mean, propose, purpose 3 = design, outline, draw up a plan of

**plane** NOUN₁ = <u>aeroplane</u>, aircraft, jet, airliner, jumbo jet
₂ = <u>flat surface</u>, the flat, horizontal, level surface₃ = <u>level</u>, position, stage, condition, standard, degree, rung, echelon
● ADJECTIVE = <u>level</u>, even, flat, regular, smooth, horizontal
● VERB = <u>skim</u>, sail, skate, glide

**plant**¹ NOUN = <u>flower</u>, bush, vegetable, herb, weed, shrub
● VERB₁ = <u>sow</u>, scatter, transplant, implant, put in the ground
₂ = <u>seed</u>, sow, implant₃ = <u>place</u>, put, set, fix₄ = <u>hide</u>, put, place, conceal₅ = <u>place</u>, put, establish, found, fix, insert

**plant**² ₁ = <u>factory</u>, works, shop, yard, mill, foundry₂ = <u>machinery</u>, equipment, gear, apparatus

**plaster** NOUN₁ = <u>mortar</u>, stucco, gypsum, plaster of Paris
₂ = <u>bandage</u>, dressing, sticking plaster, Elastoplast®, adhesive plaster
● VERB = <u>cover</u>, spread, coat, smear, overlay, daub

**plastic** = <u>pliant</u>, soft, flexible, supple, pliable, ductile, mouldable ≠ rigid

**plate** NOUN₁ = <u>platter</u>, dish, dinner plate, salver, trencher (*archaic*)₂ = <u>helping</u>, course, serving, dish, portion, platter, plateful₃ = <u>layer</u>, panel, sheet, slab

## plane → play

₄ = <u>illustration</u>, picture, photograph, print, engraving, lithograph
● VERB = <u>coat</u>, gild, laminate, cover, overlay

**plateau** ₁ = <u>upland</u>, table, highland, tableland₂ = <u>levelling off</u>, level, stage, stability

**platform** ₁ = <u>stage</u>, stand, podium, rostrum, dais, soapbox
₂ = <u>policy</u>, programme, principle, objective(s), manifesto, party line

**plausible** ₁ = <u>believable</u>, possible, likely, reasonable, credible, probable, persuasive, conceivable ≠ unbelievable
₂ = <u>glib</u>, smooth, specious, smooth-talking, smooth-tongued

**play** VERB₁ = <u>amuse yourself</u>, have fun, sport, fool, romp, revel, trifle, entertain yourself₂ = <u>take part in</u>, be involved in, engage in, participate in, compete in
₃ = <u>compete against</u>, challenge, take on, oppose, contend against
₄ = <u>perform</u>, carry out₅ = <u>act</u>, portray, represent, perform, act the part of₆ = <u>perform on</u>, strum, make music on
● NOUN₁ = <u>amusement</u>, pleasure, leisure, games, sport, fun, entertainment, relaxation
₂ = <u>drama</u>, show, piece, comedy, tragedy, farce, soapie (*Austral. slang*), pantomime
● PHRASES **play on** *or* **upon something** = <u>take advantage of</u>, abuse, exploit, impose on, trade

on, capitalize on ◆ **play
something down** = <u>minimize</u>,
make light of, gloss over, talk
down, underrate, underplay,
pooh-pooh (*informal*), soft-pedal
(*informal*) ◆ **play something
up** = <u>emphasize</u>, highlight,
underline, stress, accentuate
◆ **play up 1** (*Brit. informal*)
= <u>hurt</u>, be painful, bother you,
trouble you, be sore, pain you
**2** (*Brit. informal*) = <u>malfunction</u>,
not work properly, be on the
blink (*slang*) **3** (*Brit. informal*)
= <u>be awkward</u>, misbehave, give
trouble, be disobedient, be
stroppy (*Brit. slang*)

**playboy** = <u>womanizer</u>,
philanderer, rake, lady-killer
(*informal*), roué, ladies' man

**player 1** = <u>sportsman</u> or
<u>sportswoman</u>, competitor,
participant, contestant
**2** = <u>musician</u>, artist, performer,
virtuoso, instrumentalist
**3** = <u>performer</u>, entertainer,
Thespian, trouper, actor or actress

**plea 1** = <u>appeal</u>, request, suit,
prayer, petition, entreaty,
intercession, supplication
**2** = <u>excuse</u>, defence, explanation,
justification

**plead** = <u>appeal</u>, ask, request, beg,
petition, implore, beseech, entreat

**pleasant 1** = <u>pleasing</u>, nice, fine,
lovely, amusing, delightful,

enjoyable, agreeable, lekker (*S.
African slang*) ≠ horrible
**2** = <u>friendly</u>, nice, agreeable,
likable or likeable, engaging,
charming, amiable, genial
≠ disagreeable

**please** = <u>delight</u>, entertain,
humour, amuse, suit, satisfy,
indulge, gratify ≠ annoy

**pleased** = <u>happy</u>, delighted,
contented, satisfied, thrilled, glad,
gratified, over the moon (*informal*)

**pleasing 1** = <u>enjoyable</u>,
satisfying, charming, delightful,
gratifying, agreeable, pleasurable
≠ unpleasant **2** = <u>likable</u> or
<u>likeable</u>, engaging, charming,
delightful, agreeable ≠ disagreeable

**pleasure 1** = <u>happiness</u>, delight,
satisfaction, enjoyment, bliss,
gratification, gladness,
delectation ≠ displeasure
**2** = <u>amusement</u>, joy ≠ duty

**pledge** NOUN **1** = <u>promise</u>, vow,
assurance, word, undertaking,
warrant, oath, covenant
**2** = <u>guarantee</u>, security, deposit,
bail, collateral, pawn, surety
◆ VERB = <u>promise</u>, vow, swear,
contract, engage, give your word,
give your oath

**plentiful** = <u>abundant</u>, liberal,
generous, lavish, ample,
overflowing, copious, bountiful
≠ scarce

**plenty 1** = <u>abundance</u>, wealth,

prosperity, fertility, profusion, affluence, plenitude, fruitfulness **2** *usually with* **of** = lots of (*informal*), enough, a great deal of, masses of, piles of (*informal*), stacks of, heaps of (*informal*), an abundance of

**plight** = <u>difficulty</u>, condition, state, situation, trouble, predicament

**plot¹** NOUN **1** = <u>plan</u>, scheme, intrigue, conspiracy, cabal, stratagem, machination **2** = <u>story</u>, action, subject, theme, outline, scenario, narrative, story line
● VERB **1** = <u>plan</u>, scheme, conspire, intrigue, manoeuvre, contrive, collude, machinate **2** = <u>devise</u>, design, lay, conceive, hatch, contrive, concoct, cook up (*informal*) **3** = <u>chart</u>, mark, map, locate, calculate, outline

**plot²** = <u>patch</u>, lot, area, ground, parcel, tract, allotment

**plough** VERB = <u>turn over</u>, dig, till, cultivate
● PHRASES **plough through something** = <u>forge</u>, cut, drive, press, push, plunge, wade

**ploy** = <u>tactic</u>, move, trick, device, scheme, manoeuvre, dodge, ruse

**pluck** VERB **1** = <u>pull out</u> *or* off, pick, draw, collect, gather, harvest **2** = <u>tug</u>, catch, snatch, clutch, jerk, yank, tweak, pull at **3** = <u>strum</u>, pick, finger, twang
● NOUN = <u>courage</u>, nerve, bottle

(*Brit. slang*), guts (*informal*), grit, bravery, backbone, boldness

**plug** NOUN **1** = <u>stopper</u>, cork, bung, spigot **2** (*Informal*) = <u>mention</u>, advertisement, advert (*Brit. informal*), push, publicity, hype
● VERB **1** = <u>seal</u>, close, stop, fill, block, stuff, pack, cork **2** (*Informal*) = <u>mention</u>, promote, publicize, advertise, build up, hype
● PHRASES **plug away** (*Informal*) = <u>slog away</u>, labour, toil away, grind away (*informal*), peg away, plod away

**plum** = <u>choice</u>, prize, first-class

**plumb** VERB = <u>delve into</u>, explore, probe, go into, penetrate, gauge, unravel, fathom
● ADVERB = <u>exactly</u>, precisely, bang, slap, spot-on (*Brit. informal*)

**plummet 1** = <u>drop</u>, fall, crash, nose-dive, descend rapidly **2** = <u>plunge</u>, fall, drop, crash, tumble, nose-dive, descend rapidly

**plump** = <u>chubby</u>, fat, stout, round, tubby, dumpy, roly-poly, rotund ≠ scrawny

**plunder** VERB **1** = <u>loot</u>, strip, sack, rob, raid, rifle, ransack, pillage **2** = <u>steal</u>, rob, take, nick (*informal*), pinch (*informal*), embezzle, pilfer, thieve
● NOUN **1** = <u>pillage</u> **2** = <u>loot</u>, spoils, booty, swag (*slang*), ill-gotten gains

**plunge** VERB **1** = <u>descend</u>, fall,

drop, crash, pitch, sink, dive, tumble$_2$ = <u>hurtle</u>, charge, career, jump, tear, rush, dive, dash

**3** = <u>submerge</u>, dip$_4$ = <u>throw</u>, cast, pitch, propel$_5$ = <u>fall steeply</u>, drop, crash (*informal*), slump, plummet, take a nosedive (*informal*)

● NOUN$_1$ = <u>dive</u>, jump, duck, descent$_2$ = <u>fall</u>, crash (*informal*), slump, drop, tumble

**plus** PREPOSITION = <u>and</u>, with, added to, coupled with

● NOUN (*Informal*) = <u>advantage</u>, benefit, asset, gain, extra, bonus, good point

● ADJECTIVE = <u>additional</u>, added, extra, supplementary, add-on

> ### Word Power
>
> **plus** – When you have a sentence with more than one subject linked by *and*, this makes the subject plural and means it should take a plural verb: *the doctor and all the nurses were* (not *was*) *waiting for the patient*. However, where the subjects are linked by *plus*, *together with*, or *along with*, the number of the verb remains just as it would have been if the extra subjects had not been mentioned. Therefore you would say *the doctor, together with all the nurses, was* (not *were*) *waiting for the patient*.

**plush** = <u>luxurious</u>, luxury, lavish,

rich, sumptuous, opulent, de luxe

**ply** = <u>work at</u>, follow, exercise, pursue, carry on, practise

**pocket** NOUN = <u>pouch</u>, bag, sack, compartment, receptacle

● ADJECTIVE = <u>small</u>, compact, miniature, portable, little

● VERB = <u>steal</u>, take, lift (*informal*), appropriate, pilfer, purloin, filch

**pod** = <u>shell</u>, case, hull, husk, shuck

**podium** = <u>platform</u>, stand, stage, rostrum, dais

**poem** = <u>verse</u>, song, lyric, rhyme, sonnet, ode, verse composition

**poet** = <u>bard</u>, rhymer, lyricist, lyric poet, versifier, elegist

> WORD POWER SUPPLEMENT

**poets**

**poetic 1** = <u>figurative</u>, creative, lyric, symbolic, lyrical$_2$ = <u>lyrical</u>, lyric, elegiac, metrical

**poetry** = <u>verse</u>, poems, rhyme, rhyming, verse composition

**poignant** = <u>moving</u>, touching, sad, bitter, intense, painful, distressing, pathetic

**point** NOUN = <u>essence</u>, meaning, subject, question, heart, import, drift, thrust$_2$ = <u>purpose</u>, aim, object, end, reason, goal, intention, objective$_3$ = <u>aspect</u>, detail, feature, quality, particular, respect, item, characteristic

**4** = <u>place</u>, area, position, site, spot, location, locality, locale

**5** = <u>moment</u>, time, stage, period,

phase, instant, juncture, moment in time **6** = **stage**, level, position, condition, degree, pitch, circumstance, extent **7** = **end**, tip, sharp end, top, spur, spike, apex, prong **8** = **score**, tally, mark **9** = **pinpoint**, mark, spot, dot, fleck
● VERB **1** = **aim**, level, train, direct **2** = **indicate**, show, signal, point to, gesture towards **3** = **face**, look, direct
● PHRASES **point at** or **to something** or **someone** = **indicate**, point out, specify, designate, gesture towards

**pointed 1** = **sharp**, edged, acute, barbed **2** = **cutting**, telling, biting, sharp, keen, acute, penetrating, pertinent

**pointer 1** = **hint**, tip, suggestion, recommendation, caution, piece of information, piece of advice **2** = **indicator**, hand, guide, needle, arrow

**pointless** = **senseless**, meaningless, futile, fruitless, stupid, silly, useless, absurd ≠ worthwhile

**poised 1** = **ready**, waiting, prepared, standing by, all set **2** = **composed**, calm, together (informal), collected, dignified, self-confident, self-possessed ≠ agitated

**poison NOUN** = **toxin**, venom, bane (archaic)

● VERB **1** = **murder**, kill, give someone poison, administer poison to **2** = **contaminate**, foul, infect, spoil, pollute, blight, taint, befoul **3** = **corrupt**, colour, undermine, bias, sour, pervert, warp, taint

**poisonous 1** = **toxic**, fatal, deadly, lethal, mortal, virulent, noxious, venomous **2** = **evil**, malicious, corrupting, pernicious, baleful

**poke VERB 1** = **jab**, push, stick, dig, stab, thrust, shove, nudge **2** = **protrude**, stick, thrust, jut
● NOUN = **jab**, dig, thrust, nudge, prod

**pole** = **rod**, post, support, staff, bar, stick, stake, paling

**police NOUN** = **the law** (informal), police force, constabulary, fuzz (slang), boys in blue (informal), the Old Bill (slang), rozzers (slang)
● VERB = **control**, patrol, guard, watch, protect, regulate

**policy 1** = **procedure**, plan, action, practice, scheme, code, custom **2** = **line**, rules, approach

**polish NOUN 1** = **varnish**, wax, glaze, lacquer, japan **2** = **sheen**, finish, glaze, gloss, brightness, lustre **3** = **style**, class (informal), finish, breeding, grace, elegance, refinement, finesse
● VERB **1** = **shine**, wax, smooth, rub, buff, brighten, burnish

**polished** 2 *often with* **up** = <u>perfect</u>, improve, enhance, refine, finish, brush up, touch up

**polished** 1 = <u>elegant</u>, sophisticated, refined, polite, cultivated, suave, well-bred ≠ unsophisticated

2 = <u>accomplished</u>, professional, masterly, fine, expert, skilful, adept, superlative ≠ amateurish

3 = <u>shining</u>, bright, smooth, gleaming, glossy, burnished ≠ dull

**polite** 1 = <u>mannerly</u>, civil, courteous, gracious, respectful, well-behaved, complaisant, well-mannered ≠ rude 2 = <u>refined</u>, cultured, civilized, polished, sophisticated, elegant, genteel, well-bred ≠ uncultured

**politic** = <u>wise</u>, diplomatic, sensible, prudent, advisable, expedient, judicious

**political** = <u>governmental</u>, government, state, parliamentary, constitutional, administrative, legislative, ministerial

**politician** = <u>statesman</u> or <u>stateswoman</u>, representative, senator (*U.S.*), congressman (*U.S.*), Member of Parliament, legislator, public servant, congresswoman (*U.S.*)

**politics** 1 = <u>affairs of state</u>, government, public affairs, civics 2 = <u>political beliefs</u>, party politics, political allegiances, political leanings, political sympathies

3 = <u>political science</u>, statesmanship, civics, statecraft

**poll** NOUN 1 = <u>survey</u>, figures, count, sampling, returns, ballot, tally, census 2 = <u>election</u>, vote, voting, referendum, ballot, plebiscite

● VERB 1 = <u>question</u>, interview, survey, sample, ballot, canvass

2 = <u>gain</u>, return, record, register, tally

**pollute** 1 = <u>contaminate</u>, dirty, poison, soil, foul, infect, spoil, stain ≠ decontaminate 2 = <u>defile</u>, corrupt, sully, deprave, debase, profane, desecrate, dishonour ≠ honour

**pollution** 1 = <u>contamination</u>, dirtying, corruption, taint, foulness, defilement, uncleanness

2 = <u>waste</u>, poisons, dirt, impurities

**pond** = <u>pool</u>, tarn, small lake, fish pond, duck pond, millpond

**ponder** = <u>think about</u>, consider, reflect on, contemplate, deliberate about, muse on, brood on, meditate on

**pool** 1 1 = <u>swimming pool</u>, lido, swimming bath(s) (*Brit.*), bathing pool (*archaic*) 2 = <u>pond</u>, lake, mere, tarn 3 = <u>puddle</u>, drop, patch

**pool²** NOUN 1 = <u>supply</u>, reserve, fall-back 2 = <u>kitty</u>, bank, fund, stock, store, pot, jackpot, stockpile

• VERB = <u>combine</u>, share, merge, put together, amalgamate, lump together, join forces on

**poor** 1 = <u>impoverished</u>, broke (*informal*), hard up (*informal*), short, needy, penniless, destitute, poverty-stricken ≠ rich 2 = <u>unfortunate</u>, unlucky, hapless, pitiful, luckless, wretched, ill-starred, pitiable ≠ fortunate 3 = <u>inferior</u>, unsatisfactory, mediocre, second-rate, rotten (*informal*), low-grade, below par, substandard, half-pie (*N.Z. informal*), bodger or bodgie (*Austral. slang*) ≠ excellent 4 = <u>meagre</u>, inadequate, insufficient, lacking, incomplete, scant, deficient, skimpy ≠ ample

**poorly** ADVERB = <u>badly</u>, incompetently, inadequately, unsuccessfully, insufficiently, unsatisfactorily, inexpertly ≠ well

• ADJECTIVE (*Informal*) = <u>ill</u>, sick, unwell, crook (*Austral. & N.Z. informal*), seedy (*informal*), below par, off colour, under the weather (*informal*), feeling rotten (*informal*) ≠ healthy

**pop** NOUN = <u>bang</u>, report, crack, noise, burst, explosion

• VERB 1 = <u>burst</u>, crack, snap, bang, explode, go off (with a bang) 2 = <u>put</u>, insert, push, stick, slip, thrust, tuck, shove

**pope** = <u>Holy Father</u>, pontiff, His Holiness, Bishop of Rome, Vicar of Christ

**popular** 1 = <u>well-liked</u>, liked, in, accepted, favourite, approved, in favour, fashionable ≠ unpopular 2 = <u>common</u>, general, prevailing, current, conventional, universal, prevalent ≠ rare

**popularity** 1 = <u>favour</u>, esteem, acclaim, regard, approval, vogue 2 = <u>currency</u>, acceptance, circulation, vogue, prevalence

**populate** 1 = <u>inhabit</u>, people, live in, occupy, reside in, dwell in (*formal*) 2 = <u>settle</u>, occupy, pioneer, colonize

**population** = <u>inhabitants</u>, people, community, society, residents, natives, folk, occupants

**pore** = <u>opening</u>, hole, outlet, orifice

**pornography** = <u>obscenity</u>, porn (*informal*), dirt, filth, indecency, smut

**port** = <u>harbour</u>, haven, anchorage, seaport

**portable** = <u>light</u>, compact, convenient, handy, manageable, movable, easily carried

**porter¹** (*Chiefly Brit.*) = <u>doorman</u>,

caretaker, janitor, concierge, gatekeeper

**porter²** = <u>baggage attendant</u>, carrier, bearer, baggage-carrier

**portion** 1 = <u>part</u>, bit, piece, section, scrap, segment, fragment, chunk 2 = <u>helping</u>, serving, piece, plateful 3 = <u>share</u>, allowance, lot, measure, quantity, quota, ration, allocation

**portrait** 1 = <u>picture</u>, painting, image, photograph, representation, likeness 2 = <u>description</u>, profile, portrayal, depiction, characterization, thumbnail sketch

**portray** 1 = <u>play</u>, take the role of, act the part of, represent, personate (*rare*) 2 = <u>describe</u>, present, depict, evoke, delineate, put in words 3 = <u>represent</u>, draw, paint, illustrate, sketch, figure, picture, depict 4 = <u>characterize</u>, represent, depict

**portrayal** 1 = <u>performance</u>, interpretation, characterization 2 = <u>depiction</u>, picture, representation, sketch, rendering 3 = <u>description</u>, account, representation 4 = <u>characterization</u>, representation, depiction

**pose** VERB 1 = <u>position yourself</u>, sit, model, arrange yourself 2 = <u>put on airs</u>, posture, show off (*informal*)

● NOUN 1 = <u>posture</u>, position, bearing, attitude, stance 2 = <u>act</u>, façade, air, front, posturing, pretence, mannerism, affectation

● PHRASES **pose as something** *or* **someone** = <u>impersonate</u>, pretend to be, profess to be, masquerade as, pass yourself off as

**posh** (*Informal, chiefly Brit.*) 1 = <u>smart</u>, grand, stylish, luxurious, classy (*slang*), swish (*informal, chiefly Brit.*), up-market, swanky (*informal*) 2 = <u>upper-class</u>, high-class

**position** NOUN 1 = <u>location</u>, place, point, area, post, situation, station, spot 2 = <u>posture</u>, attitude, arrangement, pose, stance 3 = <u>status</u>, place, standing, footing, station, rank, reputation, importance 4 = <u>job</u>, place, post, opening, office, role, situation, duty 5 = <u>place</u>, standing, rank, status 6 = <u>attitude</u>, view, perspective, point of view, opinion, belief, stance, outlook

● VERB = <u>place</u>, put, set, stand, arrange, locate, lay out

**positive** 1 = <u>beneficial</u>, useful, practical, helpful, progressive, productive, worthwhile, constructive ≠ harmful 2 = <u>certain</u>, sure, convinced, confident, satisfied, assured, free

from doubt ≠ uncertain
3 = <u>definite</u>, real, clear, firm, certain, express, absolute, decisive ≠ inconclusive
4 (*Informal*) = <u>absolute</u>, complete, perfect, right (*Brit. informal*), real, total, sheer, utter

**positively** 1 = <u>definitely</u>, surely, firmly, certainly, absolutely, emphatically, unquestionably, categorically 2 = <u>really</u>, completely, simply, plain (*informal*), absolutely, thoroughly, utterly, downright

**possess** 1 = <u>own</u>, have, hold, be in possession of, be the owner of, have in your possession 2 = <u>be endowed with</u>, have, enjoy, benefit from, be possessed of, be gifted with 3 = <u>seize</u>, hold, control, dominate, occupy, take someone over, have power over, have mastery over

**possession** NOUN = <u>ownership</u>, control, custody, hold, hands, tenure
● PLURAL NOUN = <u>property</u>, things, effects, estate, assets, belongings, chattels

**possibility** 1 = <u>feasibility</u>, likelihood, potentiality, practicability, workableness
2 = <u>likelihood</u>, chance, risk, odds, prospect, liability, probability
3 *often plural* = <u>potential</u>, promise, prospects, talent, capabilities, potentiality

**possible** 1 = <u>feasible</u>, viable, workable, achievable, practicable, attainable, doable, realizable ≠ unfeasible 2 = <u>likely</u>, potential, anticipated, probable, odds-on, on the cards ≠ improbable 3 = <u>conceivable</u>, likely, credible, plausible, hypothetical, imaginable, believable, thinkable ≠ inconceivable 4 = <u>aspiring</u>, would-be, promising, hopeful, prospective, wannabe (*informal*)

> ### Word Power
>
> **possible** – Although it is very common to talk about something's being *very possible* or *more possible*, many people object to such uses, claiming that *possible* describes an absolute state, and therefore something can only be either *possible* or *not possible*. If you want to refer to different degrees of probability, a word such as *likely* or *easy* may be more appropriate than *possible*, for example *it is very likely that he will resign* (not *very possible*).

**possibly** = <u>perhaps</u>, maybe, perchance (*archaic*)

**post¹** NOUN 1 = <u>mail</u>, collection, delivery, postal service, snail mail (*informal*) 2 = <u>correspondence</u>, letters, cards, mail
● VERB = <u>send (off)</u>, forward, mail,

get off, transmit, dispatch, consign

● **PHRASES keep someone posted** = notify, brief, advise, inform, report to, keep someone informed, keep someone up to date, apprise

**post²** NOUN 1 = job, place, office, position, situation, employment, appointment, assignment 2 = position, place, base, beat, station

● VERB = station, assign, put, place, position, situate, put on duty

**post³** NOUN = support, stake, pole, column, shaft, upright, pillar, picket

● VERB = put something up, display, affix, pin something up

**poster** = notice, bill, announcement, advertisement, sticker, placard, public notice

**postpone** = put off, delay, suspend, adjourn, shelve, defer, put back, put on the back burner (informal) ≠ go ahead with

**posture** NOUN = bearing, set, attitude, stance, carriage, disposition

● VERB = show off (informal), pose, affect, put on airs

**pot** = container, bowl, pan, vessel, basin, cauldron, skillet

**potent** 1 = powerful, commanding, dynamic, dominant, influential,

authoritative 2 = strong, powerful, mighty, vigorous, forceful ≠ weak

**potential** ADJECTIVE 1 = possible, future, likely, promising, probable 2 = hidden, possible, inherent, dormant, latent

● NOUN = ability, possibilities, capacity, capability, aptitude, wherewithal, potentiality

**potter** usually with around or about = mess about, tinker, dabble, footle (informal)

**pottery** = ceramics, terracotta, crockery, earthenware, stoneware

**pounce** = attack, strike, jump, leap, swoop

**pound¹** = enclosure, yard, pen, compound, kennels

**pound²** 1 sometimes with on = beat, strike, hammer, batter, thrash, thump, clobber (slang), pummel 2 = crush, powder, pulverize 3 = pulsate, beat, pulse, throb, palpitate 4 = stomp, tramp, march, thunder (informal)

**pour** 1 = let flow, spill, splash, dribble, drizzle, slop (informal), slosh (informal), decant 2 = flow, stream, run, course, rush, emit, cascade, gush 3 = rain, pelt (down), teem, bucket down (informal) 4 = stream, crowd, flood, swarm, gush, throng, teem

## Word Power

**pour** – The spelling of *pour* (as in *she poured cream on her strudel*) should be carefully distinguished from that of *pore over* or *through* (as in *she pored over the manuscript*).

**pout** VERB = <u>sulk</u>, glower, look petulant, pull a long face
● NOUN = <u>sullen look</u>, glower, long face

**poverty** 1 = <u>pennilessness</u>, want, need, hardship, insolvency, privation, penury, destitution ≠ wealth 2 = <u>scarcity</u>, lack, absence, want, deficit, shortage, deficiency, inadequacy ≠ abundance

**powder** NOUN = <u>dust</u>, talc, fine grains, loose particles
● VERB = <u>dust</u>, cover, scatter, sprinkle, strew, dredge

**power** 1 = <u>control</u>, authority, influence, command, dominance, domination, mastery, dominion, mana (*N.Z.*) 2 = <u>ability</u>, capacity, faculty, property, potential, capability, competence, competency ≠ inability 3 = <u>authority</u>, right, licence, privilege, warrant, prerogative, authorization 4 = <u>strength</u>, might, energy, muscle, vigour, potency, brawn ≠ weakness 5 = <u>forcefulness</u>, force, strength, punch (*informal*), intensity,

potency, eloquence, persuasiveness

**powerful** 1 = <u>influential</u>, dominant, controlling, commanding, prevailing, authoritative ≠ powerless 2 = <u>strong</u>, strapping, mighty, vigorous, potent, energetic, sturdy ≠ weak 3 = <u>persuasive</u>, convincing, telling, moving, striking, storming, dramatic, impressive

**powerless** 1 = <u>defenceless</u>, vulnerable, dependent, subject, tied, ineffective, unarmed 2 = <u>weak</u>, disabled, helpless, incapable, frail, feeble, debilitated, impotent ≠ strong

**practical** 1 = <u>functional</u>, realistic, pragmatic ≠ impractical 2 = <u>empirical</u>, real, applied, actual, hands-on, in the field, experimental, factual ≠ theoretical 3 = <u>sensible</u>, ordinary, realistic, down-to-earth, matter-of-fact, businesslike, hard-headed ≠ impractical 4 = <u>feasible</u>, possible, viable, workable, practicable, doable ≠ impractical 5 = <u>useful</u>, ordinary, appropriate, sensible, everyday, functional, utilitarian, serviceable 6 = <u>skilled</u>, experienced, efficient, accomplished, proficient ≠ inexperienced

## Word Power

**practical** – A distinction is usually made between *practical* and *practicable*. *Practical* refers to a person, idea, project, etc., as being more concerned with or relevant to practice than theory: *he is a very practical person; the idea had no practical application. Practicable* refers to a project or idea as being capable of being done or put into effect: *the plan was expensive, yet practicable.*

**practically** 1 = <u>almost</u>, nearly, essentially, virtually, basically, fundamentally, all but, just about 2 = <u>sensibly</u>, reasonably, matter-of-factly, realistically, rationally, pragmatically

**practice** 1 = <u>custom</u>, way, system, rule, method, tradition, habit, routine, tikanga (*N.Z.*) 2 = <u>training</u>, study, exercise, preparation, drill, rehearsal, repetition3 = <u>profession</u>, work, business, career, occupation, pursuit, vocation4 = <u>business</u>, company, office, firm, enterprise, partnership, outfit (*informal*) 5 = <u>use</u>, experience, action, operation, application, enactment

**practise** 1 = <u>rehearse</u>, study, prepare, perfect, repeat, go through, go over, refine2 = <u>do</u>, train, exercise, drill3 = <u>carry out</u>, follow, apply, perform, observe, engage in4 = <u>work at</u>, pursue, carry on

**practised** = <u>skilled</u>, trained, experienced, seasoned, able, expert, accomplished, proficient ≠ inexperienced

**pragmatic** = <u>practical</u>, sensible, realistic, down-to-earth, utilitarian, businesslike, hard-headed ≠ idealistic

**praise** VERB1 = <u>acclaim</u>, approve of, honour, cheer, admire, applaud, compliment, congratulate ≠ criticize2 = <u>give thanks to</u>, bless, worship, adore, glorify, exalt
● NOUN1 = <u>approval</u>, acclaim, tribute, compliment, congratulations, eulogy, commendation, approbation ≠ criticism2 = <u>thanks</u>, glory, worship, homage, adoration

**pray** 1 = <u>say your prayers</u>, offer a prayer, recite the rosary2 = <u>beg</u>, ask, plead, petition, request, solicit, implore, beseech

**prayer** 1 = <u>supplication</u>, devotion2 = <u>orison</u>, litany, invocation, intercession3 = <u>plea</u>, appeal, request, petition, entreaty, supplication

**preach** 1 *often with* to = <u>deliver a sermon</u>, address, evangelize, preach a sermon2 = <u>urge</u>, teach, champion, recommend, advise, counsel, advocate, exhort

**preacher** 1 = <u>clergyman</u>, minister, parson, missionary, evangelist

**precarious** 1 = <u>insecure</u>, dangerous, tricky, risky, dodgy (*Brit., Austral., & N.Z. informal*), unsure, hazardous, shaky ≠ **secure** 2 = <u>dangerous</u>, shaky, insecure, unsafe, unreliable ≠ **stable**

**precaution** 1 = <u>safeguard</u>, insurance, protection, provision, safety measure 2 = <u>forethought</u>, care, caution, prudence, providence, wariness

**precede** 1 = <u>go before</u>, antedate 2 = <u>go ahead of</u>, lead, head, go before 3 = <u>preface</u>, introduce, go before

**precedent** = <u>instance</u>, example, standard, model, pattern, prototype, paradigm, antecedent

**precinct** = <u>area</u>, quarter, section, sector, district, zone

**precious** 1 = <u>valuable</u>, expensive, fine, prized, dear, costly, invaluable, priceless ≠ **worthless** 2 = <u>loved</u>, prized, dear, treasured, darling, beloved, adored, cherished 3 = <u>affected</u>, artificial, twee (*Brit. informal*), overrefined, overnice

**precipitate** VERB 1 = <u>quicken</u>,

trigger, accelerate, advance, hurry, speed up, bring on, hasten 2 = <u>throw</u>, launch, cast, hurl, fling, let fly

● ADJECTIVE 1 = <u>hasty</u>, rash, reckless, impulsive, precipitous, impetuous, heedless 2 = <u>sudden</u>, quick, brief, rushing, rapid, unexpected, swift, abrupt

**precise** 1 = <u>exact</u>, specific, particular, express, correct, absolute, accurate, explicit ≠ **vague** 2 = <u>strict</u>, particular, exact, formal, careful, stiff, rigid, meticulous ≠ **inexact**

**precisely** 1 = <u>exactly</u>, squarely, correctly, absolutely, strictly, accurately, plumb (*informal*), square on 2 = <u>just so</u>, yes, absolutely, exactly, quite so, you bet (*informal*), without a doubt, indubitably 3 = <u>just</u>, entirely, absolutely, altogether, exactly, in all respects 4 = <u>word for word</u>, literally, exactly, to the letter

**precision** = <u>exactness</u>, care, accuracy, particularity, meticulousness, preciseness

**predecessor** 1 = <u>previous job holder</u>, precursor, forerunner, antecedent 2 = <u>ancestor</u>, forebear, antecedent, forefather, tupuna *or* tipuna (*N.Z.*)

**predicament** = <u>fix</u> (*informal*), situation, spot (*informal*), hole (*slang*), mess, jam (*informal*), dilemma, pinch

**predict** = <u>foretell</u>, forecast, divine, prophesy, augur, portend

**predictable** = <u>likely</u>, expected, sure, certain, anticipated, reliable, foreseeable ≠ unpredictable

**prediction** = <u>prophecy</u>, forecast, prognosis, divination, prognostication, augury

**predominantly** = <u>mainly</u>, largely, chiefly, mostly, generally, principally, primarily, for the most part

**prefer** 1 = <u>like better</u>, favour, go for, pick, fancy, opt for, incline towards, be partial to 2 = <u>choose</u>, opt for, pick, desire, would rather, would sooner, incline towards

---

### Word Power

**prefer** – Normally, to (not than) is used after prefer and preferable. Therefore, you would say I prefer skating to skiing, and a small income is preferable to no income at all. However, when expressing a preference between two activities stated as infinitive verbs, for example to skate and to ski, use than, as in I prefer to skate than to ski.

---

**preferable** = <u>better</u>, best, chosen, preferred, recommended, favoured, superior, more suitable ≠ undesirable

**preferably** = <u>ideally</u>, if possible, rather, sooner, by choice, in or for preference

**preference** 1 = <u>liking</u>, wish, taste, desire, leaning, bent, bias, inclination 2 = <u>first choice</u>, choice, favourite, pick, option, selection 3 = <u>priority</u>, first place, precedence, favouritism, favoured treatment

**pregnant** 1 = <u>expectant</u>, expecting (informal), with child, in the club (Brit. slang), big or heavy with child 2 = <u>meaningful</u>, pointed, charged, significant, telling, loaded, expressive, eloquent

**prejudice** NOUN
1 = <u>discrimination</u>, injustice, intolerance, bigotry, unfairness, chauvinism, narrow-mindedness 2 = <u>bias</u>, preconception, partiality, preconceived notion, prejudgment
● VERB 1 = <u>bias</u>, influence, colour, poison, distort, slant, predispose 2 = <u>harm</u>, damage, hurt, injure, mar, undermine, spoil, impair, crool or cruel (Austral. slang)

**prejudiced** = <u>biased</u>, influenced, unfair, one-sided, bigoted, intolerant, opinionated, narrow-minded ≠ unbiased

**preliminary** ADJECTIVE 1 = <u>first</u>, opening, trial, initial, test, pilot, prior, introductory 2 = <u>qualifying</u>,

eliminating
● NOUN = introduction, opening, beginning, start, prelude, preface, overture, preamble

**prelude** 1 = introduction, beginning, start 2 = overture, opening, introduction, introductory movement

**premature** 1 = early, untimely, before time, unseasonable 2 = hasty, rash, too soon, untimely, ill-timed, overhasty

**premier** NOUN = head of government, prime minister, chancellor, chief minister, P.M.
● ADJECTIVE = chief, leading, first, highest, head, main, prime, primary

**premiere** = first night, opening, debut

**premise** = assumption, proposition, argument, hypothesis, assertion, supposition, presupposition, postulation

**premises** = building(s), place, office, property, site, establishment

**premium** NOUN 1 = fee, charge, payment, instalment 2 = surcharge, extra charge, additional fee or charge 3 = bonus, reward, prize, perk (Brit. informal), bounty, perquisite
● PHRASES at a premium = in great demand, rare, scarce, in

short supply, hard to come by

**preoccupation** 1 = obsession, fixation, bee in your bonnet 2 = absorption, abstraction, daydreaming, immersion, reverie, absent-mindedness, engrossment, woolgathering

**preoccupied** 1 = absorbed, lost, wrapped up, immersed, engrossed, rapt 2 = lost in thought, distracted, oblivious, absent-minded

**preparation** 1 = groundwork, preparing, getting ready 2 usually plural = arrangement, plan, measure, provision 3 = mixture, medicine, compound, concoction

**prepare** 1 = make or get ready, arrange, jack up (N.Z. informal) 2 = train, guide, prime, direct, brief, discipline, put someone in the picture 3 = make, cook, put together, get, produce, assemble, muster, concoct 4 = get ready 5 = practise, get ready, train, exercise, warm up, get into shape

**prepared** 1 = willing, inclined, disposed 2 = ready, set 3 = fit, primed, in order, arranged, in readiness

**prescribe** 1 = specify, order, direct, stipulate, write a prescription for 2 = ordain, set, order, rule, recommend, dictate, lay down, decree

**prescription** 1 = instruction,

direction, formula, script
(*informal*), recipe 2 = <u>medicine</u>,
drug, treatment, preparation,
cure, mixture, dose, remedy

**presence** NOUN 1 = <u>being</u>,
existence, residence, attendance,
showing up, occupancy,
inhabitance 2 = <u>personality</u>,
bearing, appearance, aspect, air,
carriage, aura, poise
• PHRASES **presence of mind**
= <u>level-headedness</u>, assurance,
composure, poise, cool (*slang*),
wits, countenance, coolness

**present**[1] ADJECTIVE 1 = <u>current</u>,
existing, immediate,
contemporary, present-day,
existent 2 = <u>here</u>, there, near,
ready, nearby, at hand ≠ absent
3 = <u>in existence</u>, existing, existent,
extant
• PHRASES **the present** = <u>now</u>,
today, the time being, here and
now, the present moment

**present**[2] NOUN 1 = <u>gift</u>, offering,
grant, donation, hand-out,
endowment, boon, gratuity,
bonsela (*S. African*), koha (*N.Z.*)
• VERB 1 = <u>give</u>, award, hand over,
grant, hand out, confer, bestow
2 = <u>put on</u>, stage, perform, give,
show, render 3 = <u>launch</u>, display,
parade, exhibit, unveil
4 = <u>introduce</u>, make known,
acquaint someone with

**presentation** 1 = <u>giving</u>, award,
offering, donation, bestowal,

conferral 2 = <u>appearance</u>, look,
display, packaging, arrangement,
layout 3 = <u>performance</u>,
production, show

**presently** 1 = <u>at present</u>,
currently, now, today, these days,
nowadays, at the present time, in
this day and age 2 = <u>soon</u>,
shortly, directly, before long,
momentarily (*U.S. & Canad.*), by
and by, in a jiffy (*informal*)

**preservation** 1 = <u>upholding</u>,
support, maintenance
2 = <u>protection</u>, safety,
maintenance, conservation,
salvation, safeguarding,
safekeeping

**preserve** VERB 1 = <u>maintain</u>,
keep, continue, sustain, keep up,
prolong, uphold, conserve ≠ end
2 = <u>protect</u>, keep, save, maintain,
defend, shelter, shield, care for
≠ attack
• NOUN = <u>area</u>, department, field,
territory, province, arena, sphere

**preside** = <u>officiate</u>, chair,
moderate, be chairperson

**president** ➤ WORD POWER
SUPPLEMENT presidents

**press** 1 = <u>push (down)</u>, depress,
lean on, press down, force down
2 = <u>push</u>, squeeze, jam, thrust,
ram, wedge, shove 3 = <u>hug</u>,
squeeze, embrace, clasp, crush,
hold close, fold in your arms
4 = <u>urge</u>, beg, petition, exhort,

implore, pressurize, entreat
**5** = **plead**, present, lodge, submit, tender, advance insistently
**6** = **steam**, iron, smooth, flatten
**7** = **compress**, grind, reduce, mill, crush, pound, squeeze, tread
**8** = **crowd**, push, gather, surge, flock, herd, swarm, seethe

**pressing** = **urgent**, serious, vital, crucial, imperative, important, high-priority, importunate ≠ unimportant

**pressure 1** = **force**, crushing, squeezing, compressing, weight, compression **2** = **power**, influence, force, constraint, sway, compulsion, coercion **3** = **stress**, demands, strain, heat, load, burden, urgency, hassle (*informal*), uphill (*S. African*)

**prestige** = **status**, standing, credit, reputation, honour, importance, fame, distinction, mana (*N.Z.*)

**prestigious** = **celebrated**, respected, prominent, great, important, esteemed, notable, renowned ≠ unknown

**presumably** = **it would seem**, probably, apparently, seemingly, on the face of it, in all probability, in all likelihood

**presume 1** = **believe**, think, suppose, assume, guess (*informal, chiefly U.S. & Canad.*), take for granted, infer, conjecture

**2** = **dare**, venture, go so far as, take the liberty, make so bold as

**pretend 1** = **feign**, affect, assume, allege, fake, simulate, profess, sham **2** = **make believe**, suppose, imagine, act, make up

**pretty** ADJECTIVE = **attractive**, beautiful, lovely, charming, fair, good-looking, bonny, comely ≠ plain

● ADVERB (*Informal*) = **fairly**, rather, quite, kind of (*informal*), somewhat, moderately, reasonably

**prevail 1** = **win**, succeed, triumph, overcome, overrule, be victorious **2** = **be widespread**, abound, predominate, be current, be prevalent, exist generally

**prevailing 1** = **widespread**, general, established, popular, common, current, usual, ordinary **2** = **predominating**, ruling, main, existing, principal

**prevalent** = **common**, established, popular, general, current, usual, widespread, universal ≠ rare

**prevent** = **stop**, avoid, frustrate, hamper, foil, inhibit, avert, thwart ≠ help

**prevention** = **elimination**, safeguard, precaution, thwarting, avoidance, deterrence

**preview** = **sample**, sneak preview, trailer, taster, foretaste,

advance showing
**previous** 1 = <u>earlier</u>, former,
past, prior, preceding, erstwhile
≠ later 2 = <u>preceding</u>, past, prior,
foregoing
**previously** = <u>before</u>, earlier,
once, in the past, formerly,
hitherto, beforehand
**prey** 1 = <u>quarry</u>, game, kill
2 = <u>victim</u>, target, mug (*Brit.
slang*), dupe, fall guy (*informal*)
▷ **birds of prey**
**price** NOUN 1 = <u>cost</u>, value, rate,
charge, figure, worth, damage

(*informal*), amount
2 = <u>consequences</u>, penalty, cost,
result, toll, forfeit
● VERB = <u>evaluate</u>, value, estimate,
rate, cost, assess
**priceless** = <u>valuable</u>, expensive,
precious, invaluable, dear, costly
≠ worthless
**prick** VERB = <u>pierce</u>, stab,
puncture, punch, lance, jab,
perforate
● NOUN = <u>puncture</u>, hole, wound,
perforation, pinhole
**prickly** 1 = <u>spiny</u>, barbed, thorny,

### Birds of prey

| | |
|---|---|
| accipiter | kestrel |
| Australian goshawk *or* chicken | kite |
|   hawk | lammergeier, lammergeyer, |
| bald eagle |   bearded vulture, *or* (*archaic*) |
| barn owl |   ossifrage |
| buzzard | lanner |
| caracara | merlin |
| condor | mopoke *or* (*N.Z.*) ruru |
| duck hawk | osprey, fish eagle, *or* (*archaic*) |
| eagle |   ossifrage |
| eagle-hawk *or* wedge-tailed eagle | owl |
| falcon *or* (*N.Z.*) bush-hawk *or* | peregrine falcon |
|   karearea | saker |
| falconet | screech owl |
| golden eagle | sea eagle, erne, *or* ern |
| goshawk | secretary bird |
| gyrfalcon *or* gerfalcon | snowy owl |
| harrier | sparrowhawk |
| hawk | tawny owl |
| hobby | turkey buzzard *or* vulture |
| honey buzzard | vulture |

bristly **2** = <u>itchy</u>, sharp, smarting, stinging, crawling, tingling, scratchy

**pride 1** = <u>satisfaction</u>, achievement, fulfilment, delight, content, pleasure, joy, gratification **2** = <u>self-respect</u>, honour, ego, dignity, self-esteem, self-image, self-worth **3** = <u>conceit</u>, vanity, arrogance, pretension, hubris, self-importance, egotism, self-love ≠ humility

**priest** = <u>clergyman</u>, minister, father, divine, vicar, pastor, cleric, curate

**primarily 1** = <u>chiefly</u>, largely, generally, mainly, essentially, mostly, principally, fundamentally **2** = <u>at first</u>, originally, initially, in the first place, in the beginning, first and foremost, at or from the start

**primary** = <u>chief</u>, main, first, highest, greatest, prime, principal, cardinal ≠ subordinate

**prime** ADJECTIVE **1** = <u>main</u>, leading, chief, central, major, key, primary, supreme **2** = <u>best</u>, top, select, highest, quality, choice, excellent, first-class
● NOUN = <u>peak</u>, flower, bloom, height, heyday, zenith
● VERB **1** = <u>inform</u>, tell, train, coach, brief, fill in (informal), notify, clue in (informal) **2** = <u>prepare</u>, set up, load, equip, get ready, make ready

**prime minister** ➤ WORD POWER SUPPLEMENT prime ministers

**primitive 1** = <u>early</u>, first, earliest, original, primary, elementary, primordial, primeval ≠ modern **2** = <u>crude</u>, simple, rough, rudimentary, unrefined ≠ elaborate

**prince** = <u>ruler</u>, lord, monarch, sovereign, crown prince, liege, prince regent, crowned head

**princely 1** = <u>substantial</u>, considerable, large, huge, massive, enormous, sizable or sizeable **2** = <u>regal</u>, royal, imperial, noble, sovereign, majestic

**princess** = <u>ruler</u>, lady, monarch, sovereign, liege, crowned head, crowned princess, dynast

**principal** ADJECTIVE = <u>main</u>, leading, chief, prime, first, key, essential, primary ≠ minor
● NOUN **1** = <u>headmaster</u> or <u>headmistress</u>, head (informal), dean, head teacher, rector, master or mistress **2** = <u>star</u>, lead, leader, prima ballerina, leading man or lady, coryphée **3** = <u>capital</u>, money, assets, working capital

**principally** = <u>mainly</u>, largely, chiefly, especially, mostly, primarily, above all, predominantly

**principle** NOUN **1** = <u>morals</u>, standards, ideals, honour, virtue, ethics, integrity, conscience, kaupapa (*N.Z.*) 2 = <u>rule</u>, law, truth, precept

● PHRASES **in principle** 1 = <u>in general</u> 2 = <u>in theory</u>, ideally, on paper, theoretically, in an ideal world, en principe (*French*)

> ## Word Power
>
> **principle** – *Principle* and *principal* are often confused: *the principal* (not *principle*) *reason for his departure; the plan was approved in principle* (not *principal*).

**print** VERB 1 = <u>run off</u>, publish, copy, reproduce, issue, engrave 2 = <u>publish</u>, release, circulate, issue, disseminate 3 = <u>mark</u>, impress, stamp, imprint

● NOUN 1 = <u>photograph</u>, photo, snap 2 = <u>picture</u>, plate, etching, engraving, lithograph, woodcut, linocut 3 = <u>copy</u>, photo (*informal*), picture, reproduction, replica

**prior** ADJECTIVE = <u>earlier</u>, previous, former, preceding, foregoing, pre-existing, pre-existent

● PHRASES **prior to** = <u>before</u>, preceding, earlier than, in advance of, previous to

**priority** 1 = <u>prime concern</u> 2 = <u>precedence</u>, preference, primacy, predominance 3 = <u>supremacy</u>, rank, precedence, seniority, right of way, pre-

eminence

**prison** = <u>jail</u>, confinement, nick (*Brit. slang*), cooler (*slang*), jug (*slang*), dungeon, clink (*slang*), gaol, boob (*Austral. slang*)

**prisoner** 1 = <u>convict</u>, con (*slang*), lag (*slang*), jailbird 2 = <u>captive</u>, hostage, detainee, internee

**privacy** = <u>seclusion</u>, isolation, solitude, retirement, retreat

**private** 1 = <u>exclusive</u>, individual, privately owned, own, special, reserved ≠ public 2 = <u>secret</u>, confidential, covert, unofficial, clandestine, off the record, hush-hush (*informal*) ≠ public 3 = <u>personal</u>, individual, secret, intimate, undisclosed, unspoken, innermost, unvoiced 4 = <u>secluded</u>, secret, separate, isolated, sequestered ≠ busy 5 = <u>solitary</u>, reserved, retiring, withdrawn, discreet, secretive, self-contained, reclusive ≠ sociable

**privilege** = <u>right</u>, due, advantage, claim, freedom, liberty, concession, entitlement

**privileged** = <u>special</u>, advantaged, favoured, honoured, entitled, elite

**prize**[1] NOUN 1 = <u>reward</u>, cup, award, honour, medal, trophy, accolade 2 = <u>winnings</u>, haul, jackpot, stakes, purse

- **ADJECTIVE** = <u>champion</u>, best, winning, top, outstanding, award-winning, first-rate

**prize²** = <u>value</u>, treasure, esteem, cherish, hold dear

**prize³** *or* **prise** 1 = <u>force</u>, pull, lever 2 = <u>drag</u>, force, draw, wring, extort

**probability** 1 = <u>likelihood</u>, prospect, chance, odds, expectation, liability, likeliness 2 = <u>chance</u>, odds, possibility, likelihood

**probable** = <u>likely</u>, possible, apparent, reasonable to think, credible, plausible, feasible, presumable ≠ unlikely

**probably** = <u>likely</u>, perhaps, maybe, possibly, presumably, most likely, doubtless, perchance (*archaic*)

**probation** = <u>trial period</u>, trial, apprenticeship

**probe** VERB 1 *often with into* = <u>examine</u>, go into, investigate, explore, search, look into, analyze, dissect 2 = <u>explore</u>, examine, poke, prod, feel around
- **NOUN** = <u>investigation</u>, study, inquiry, analysis, examination, exploration, scrutiny, scrutinization

**problem** 1 = <u>difficulty</u>, trouble, dispute, plight, obstacle, dilemma, headache (*informal*), complication 2 = <u>puzzle</u>, question, riddle, enigma, conundrum, poser

**problematic** = <u>tricky</u>, puzzling, doubtful, dubious, debatable, problematical ≠ clear

**procedure** = <u>method</u>, policy, process, course, system, action, practice, strategy

**proceed** 1 = <u>begin</u>, go ahead 2 = <u>continue</u>, go on, progress, carry on, go ahead, press on ≠ discontinue 3 = <u>go on</u>, continue, progress, carry on, go ahead, move on, move forward, press on ≠ stop 4 = <u>arise</u>, come, issue, result, spring, flow, stem, derive

**proceeding** = <u>action</u>, process, procedure, move, act, step, measure, deed

**proceeds** = <u>income</u>, profit, revenue, returns, products, gain, earnings, yield

**process** NOUN 1 = <u>procedure</u>, means, course, system, action, performance, operation, measure 2 = <u>development</u>, growth, progress, movement, advance, evolution, progression 3 = <u>method</u>, system, practice, technique, procedure
- **VERB** = <u>handle</u>, manage, action, deal with, fulfil

**procession** = <u>parade</u>, train, march, file, cavalcade, cortege

**proclaim** 1 = <u>announce</u>, declare,

advertise, publish, indicate, herald, circulate, profess ≠ keep secret 2 = <u>pronounce</u>, announce, declare

**prod** VERB 1 = <u>poke</u>, push, dig, shove, nudge, jab 2 = <u>prompt</u>, move, urge, motivate, spur, stimulate, rouse, incite
● NOUN 1 = <u>poke</u>, push, dig, shove, nudge, jab 2 = <u>prompt</u>, signal, cue, reminder, stimulus

**prodigy** = <u>genius</u>, talent, wizard, mastermind, whizz (*informal*)

**produce** VERB 1 = <u>cause</u>, effect, generate, bring about, give rise to 2 = <u>make</u>, create, develop, manufacture, construct, invent, fabricate 3 = <u>create</u>, develop, write, turn out, compose, originate, churn out (*informal*) 4 = <u>yield</u>, provide, grow, bear, give, supply, afford, render 5 = <u>bring forth</u>, bear, deliver, breed, give birth to, beget, bring into the world 6 = <u>show</u>, provide, present, advance, demonstrate, offer, come up with, exhibit 7 = <u>display</u>, show, present, proffer 8 = <u>present</u>, stage, direct, put on, do, show, mount, exhibit
● NOUN = <u>fruit and vegetables</u>, goods, food, products, crops, yield, harvest, greengrocery (*Brit.*)

**producer** 1 = <u>director</u>, promoter, impresario 2 = <u>maker</u>, manufacturer, builder, creator, fabricator 3 = <u>grower</u>, farmer

**product** 1 = <u>goods</u>, produce, creation, commodity, invention, merchandise, artefact 2 = <u>result</u>, consequence, effect, outcome, upshot

**production** 1 = <u>producing</u>, making, manufacture, manufacturing, construction, formation, fabrication 2 = <u>creation</u>, development, fashioning, composition, origination 3 = <u>management</u>, administration, direction 4 = <u>presentation</u>, staging, mounting

**productive** 1 = <u>fertile</u>, rich, prolific, plentiful, fruitful, fecund ≠ barren 2 = <u>creative</u>, inventive 3 = <u>useful</u>, rewarding, valuable, profitable, effective, worthwhile, beneficial, constructive ≠ useless

**productivity** = <u>output</u>, production, capacity, yield, efficiency, work rate

**profess** 1 = <u>claim</u>, allege, pretend, fake, make out, purport, feign 2 = <u>state</u>, admit, announce, declare, confess, assert, proclaim, affirm

**professed** 1 = <u>supposed</u>, would-be, alleged, so-called, pretended, purported, self-styled, ostensible 2 = <u>declared</u>, confirmed, confessed, proclaimed, self-confessed, avowed, self-acknowledged

**profession** = occupation, calling, business, career, employment, office, position, sphere

**professional** ADJECTIVE
1 = qualified, trained, skilled, white-collar 2 = expert, experienced, skilled, masterly, efficient, competent, adept, proficient ≠ amateurish
• NOUN = expert, master, pro (informal), specialist, guru, adept, maestro, virtuoso, fundi (S. African)

**professor** = don (Brit.), fellow (Brit.), prof (informal)

**profile** 1 = outline, lines, form, figure, silhouette, contour, side view 2 = biography, sketch, vignette, characterization, thumbnail sketch

**profit** NOUN 1 often plural = earnings, return, revenue, gain, yield, proceeds, receipts, takings ≠ loss 2 = benefit, good, use, value, gain, advantage, advancement ≠ disadvantage
• VERB 1 = make money, gain, earn 2 = benefit, help, serve, gain, promote, be of advantage to

**profitable** 1 = money-making, lucrative, paying, commercial, worthwhile, cost-effective, fruitful, remunerative
2 = beneficial, useful, rewarding, valuable, productive, worthwhile, fruitful, advantageous ≠ useless

**profound** 1 = sincere, acute, intense, great, keen, extreme, heartfelt, deeply felt ≠ insincere
2 = wise, learned, deep, penetrating, philosophical, sage, abstruse, sagacious ≠ uninformed

**programme** 1 = schedule, plan, agenda, timetable, listing, list, line-up, calendar 2 = course, curriculum, syllabus 3 = show, performance, production, broadcast, episode, presentation, transmission, telecast

**progress** NOUN
1 = development, growth, advance, gain, improvement, breakthrough, headway ≠ regression 2 = movement forward, passage, advancement, course, advance, headway ≠ movement backward
• VERB 1 = move on, continue, travel, advance, proceed, go forward, make headway ≠ move back 2 = develop, improve, advance, grow, gain ≠ get behind
• PHRASES in progress = going on, happening, continuing, being done, occurring, taking place, proceeding, under way

**progression** 1 = progress, advance, advancement, gain, headway, furtherance, movement forward 2 = sequence, course, series, chain, cycle, string, succession

**progressive** 1 = enlightened,
liberal, modern, advanced,
radical, revolutionary, avant-
garde, reformist 2 = growing,
continuing, increasing,
developing, advancing, ongoing

**prohibit** 1 = forbid, ban, veto,
outlaw, disallow, proscribe, debar
≠ permit 2 = prevent, restrict,
stop, hamper, hinder, impede
≠ allow

**prohibition** = ban, boycott,
embargo, bar, veto, prevention,
exclusion, injunction

**project** NOUN 1 = scheme, plan,
job, idea, campaign, operation,
activity, venture 2 = assignment,
task, homework, piece of
research
● VERB 1 = forecast, expect,
estimate, predict, reckon,
calculate, gauge, extrapolate
2 = stick out, extend, stand out,
bulge, protrude, overhang, jut

**projection** = forecast, estimate,
reckoning, calculation,
estimation, computation,
extrapolation

**proliferation** = multiplication,
increase, spread, expansion

**prolific** 1 = productive, creative,
fertile, inventive, copious
2 = fruitful, fertile, abundant,
luxuriant, profuse, fecund
≠ unproductive

**prolong** = lengthen, continue,

perpetuate, draw out, extend,
delay, stretch out, spin out
≠ shorten

**prominence** 1 = fame, name,
reputation, importance, celebrity,
distinction, prestige, eminence
2 = conspicuousness,
markedness

**prominent** 1 = famous, leading,
top, important, main,
distinguished, well-known,
notable ≠ unknown
2 = noticeable, obvious,
outstanding, pronounced,
conspicuous, eye-catching,
obtrusive ≠ inconspicuous

**promise** VERB 1 = guarantee,
pledge, vow, swear, contract,
assure, undertake, warrant
2 = seem likely, look like, show
signs of, augur, betoken
● NOUN 1 = guarantee, word,
bond, vow, commitment, pledge,
undertaking, assurance
2 = potential, ability, talent,
capacity, capability, aptitude

**promising** 1 = encouraging,
likely, bright, reassuring, hopeful,
favourable, rosy, auspicious
≠ unpromising 2 = talented, able,
gifted, rising

**promote** 1 = help, back, support,
aid, forward, encourage, advance,
boost ≠ impede 2 = advertise,
sell, hype, publicize, push, plug
(*informal*) 3 = raise, upgrade,

441

**promotion** 1 = <u>rise</u>, upgrading,
move up, advancement,
elevation, exaltation, preferment
2 = <u>publicity</u>, advertising,
plugging (*informal*)
3 = <u>encouragement</u>, support,
boosting, advancement,
furtherance

**prompt** VERB 1 = <u>cause</u>, occasion,
provoke, give rise to, elicit
2 = <u>remind</u>, assist, cue, help out
● ADJECTIVE = <u>immediate</u>, quick,
rapid, instant, timely, early, swift,
speedy ≠ slow
● ADVERB (*Informal*) = <u>exactly</u>,
sharp, promptly, on the dot,
punctually

**promptly** 1 = <u>immediately</u>,
swiftly, directly, quickly, at once,
speedily 2 = <u>punctually</u>, on time,
spot on (*informal*), bang on
(*informal*), on the dot, on the
button (*U.S.*), on the nail

**prone** 1 = <u>liable</u>, given, subject,
inclined, tending, bent, disposed,
susceptible ≠ disinclined 2 = <u>face
down</u>, flat, horizontal, prostrate,
recumbent ≠ face up

**pronounce** 1 = <u>say</u>, speak,
sound, articulate, enunciate
2 = <u>declare</u>, announce, deliver,
proclaim, decree, affirm

**pronounced** = <u>noticeable</u>,
decided, marked, striking,
obvious, evident, distinct, definite

promotion → properly

≠ imperceptible

**proof** NOUN = <u>evidence</u>,
demonstration, testimony,
confirmation, verification,
corroboration, authentication,
substantiation
● ADJECTIVE = <u>impervious</u>, strong,
resistant, impenetrable, repellent

**prop** VERB 1 = <u>lean</u>, place, set,
stand, position, rest, lay, balance
2 *often with* **up** = <u>support</u>,
sustain, hold up, brace, uphold,
bolster, buttress
● NOUN 1 = <u>support</u>, stay, brace,
mainstay, buttress, stanchion
2 = <u>mainstay</u>, support, sustainer,
anchor, backbone, cornerstone,
upholder

**propaganda** = <u>information</u>,
advertising, promotion, publicity,
hype, disinformation

**propel** 1 = <u>drive</u>, launch, force,
send, shoot, push, thrust, shove
≠ stop 2 = <u>impel</u>, drive, push,
prompt, spur, motivate ≠ hold
back

**proper** 1 = <u>real</u>, actual, genuine,
true, bona fide, dinkum (*Austral. &
N.Z. informal*) 2 = <u>correct</u>,
accepted, established,
appropriate, right, formal,
conventional, precise ≠ improper
3 = <u>polite</u>, right, becoming,
seemly, fitting, fit, mannerly,
suitable ≠ unseemly

**properly** 1 = <u>correctly</u>, rightly,

fittingly, appropriately, accurately, suitably, aptly ≠ incorrectly 2 = politely, decently, respectably ≠ badly

**property** 1 = possessions, goods, effects, holdings, capital, riches, estate, assets 2 = land, holding, estate, real estate, freehold 3 = quality, feature, characteristic, attribute, trait, hallmark

**prophecy** 1 = prediction, forecast, prognostication, augury 2 = second sight, divination, augury, telling the future, soothsaying

**prophet** or **prophetess** = soothsayer, forecaster, diviner, oracle, seer, sibyl, prophesier

**proportion** NOUN 1 = part, share, amount, division, percentage, segment, quota, fraction 2 = relative amount, relationship, ratio 3 = balance, harmony, correspondence, symmetry, concord, congruity

● PLURAL NOUN = dimensions, size, volume, capacity, extent, expanse

**proportional** or **proportionate** = correspondent, corresponding, even, balanced, consistent, compatible, equitable, in proportion ≠ disproportionate

**proposal** = suggestion, plan, programme, scheme, offer,

project, bid, recommendation

**propose** 1 = put forward, present, suggest, advance, submit 2 = intend, mean, plan, aim, design, scheme, have in mind 3 = nominate, name, present, recommend 4 = offer marriage, pop the question (*informal*), ask for someone's hand (in marriage)

**proposition** NOUN 1 = task, problem, activity, job, affair, venture, undertaking 2 = theory, idea, argument, concept, thesis, hypothesis, theorem, premiss 3 = proposal, plan, suggestion, scheme, bid, recommendation 4 = advance, pass (*informal*), proposal, overture, improper suggestion, come-on (*informal*)

● VERB = make a pass at, solicit, accost, make an improper suggestion to

**proprietor** or **proprietress** = owner, titleholder, landlord or landlady

**prosecute** (*Law*) = take someone to court, try, sue, indict, arraign, put someone on trial, litigate, bring someone to trial

**prospect** NOUN 1 = likelihood, chance, possibility, hope, promise, odds, expectation, probability 2 = idea, outlook 3 = view, landscape, scene, sight, outlook, spectacle, vista

● PLURAL NOUN = possibilities,

chances, future, potential, expectations, outlook, scope
● VERB = <u>look</u>, search, seek, dowse

**prospective 1** = <u>potential</u>, possible **2** = <u>expected</u>, coming, future, likely, anticipated, forthcoming, imminent

**prospectus** = <u>catalogue</u>, list, programme, outline, syllabus, synopsis

**prosper** = <u>succeed</u>, advance, progress, thrive, get on, do well, flourish

**prosperity** = <u>success</u>, riches, plenty, fortune, wealth, luxury, good fortune, affluence ≠ poverty

**prosperous 1** = <u>wealthy</u>, rich, affluent, well-off, well-heeled (*informal*), well-to-do, moneyed ≠ poor **2** = <u>successful</u>, booming, thriving, flourishing, doing well ≠ unsuccessful

**prostitute** NOUN = <u>whore</u>, hooker (*U.S. slang*), pro (*slang*), tart (*informal*), call girl, harlot, streetwalker, loose woman
● VERB = <u>cheapen</u>, sell out, pervert, degrade, devalue, squander, demean, debase

**protagonist 1** = <u>supporter</u>, champion, advocate, exponent **2** = <u>leading character</u>, principal, central character, hero or heroine

**protect** = <u>keep someone safe</u>,
defend, support, save, guard, preserve, look after, shelter ≠ endanger

**protection 1** = <u>safety</u>, care, defence, protecting, security, custody, safeguard, aegis **2** = <u>safeguard</u>, cover, guard, shelter, screen, barrier, shield, buffer **3** = <u>armour</u>, cover, screen, barrier, shelter, shield

**protective 1** = <u>protecting</u> **2** = <u>caring</u>, defensive, motherly, fatherly, maternal, vigilant, watchful, paternal

**protector 1** = <u>defender</u>, champion, guard, guardian, patron, bodyguard **2** = <u>guard</u>, screen, protection, shield, pad, cushion, buffer

**protest** VERB = <u>object</u>, demonstrate, oppose, complain, disagree, cry out, disapprove, demur **2** = <u>assert</u>, insist, maintain, declare, affirm, profess, attest, avow
● NOUN **1** = <u>demonstration</u>, march, rally, sit-in, demo (*informal*), hikoi (*N.Z.*) **2** = <u>objection</u>, complaint, dissent, outcry, protestation, remonstrance

**protocol** = <u>code of behaviour</u>, manners, conventions, customs, etiquette, propriety, decorum

**prototype** = <u>original</u>, model, first, example, standard

**protracted** = <u>extended</u>,

prolonged, drawn-out, spun out, dragged out, long-drawn-out

**proud** 1 = satisfied, pleased, content, thrilled, glad, gratified, joyful, well-pleased ≠ dissatisfied 2 = conceited, arrogant, lordly, imperious, overbearing, haughty, snobbish, self-satisfied ≠ humble

**prove** 1 = turn out, come out, end up 2 = verify, establish, determine, show, confirm, demonstrate, justify, substantiate ≠ disprove

**proven** = established, proved, confirmed, tested, reliable, definite, verified, attested

**provide** VERB 1 = supply, give, distribute, outfit, equip, donate, furnish, dispense ≠ withhold 2 = give, bring, add, produce, present, serve, afford, yield
● PHRASES **provide for someone** = support, care for, keep, maintain, sustain, take care of, fend for ◆ **provide for something** = take precautions against, plan for, prepare for, anticipate, plan ahead for, forearm for

**provided** often with that = if, given, on condition, as long as

**provider** 1 = supplier, giver, source, donor 2 = breadwinner, supporter, earner, wage earner

**providing** often with that = on condition that, given that, as long as

**province** 1 = region, section, district, zone, patch, colony, domain 2 = area, business, concern, responsibility, line, role, department, field
➤ WORD POWER SUPPLEMENT
**Canadian provinces**
➤ WORD POWER SUPPLEMENT
**South African provinces and provincial capitals**

**provincial** ADJECTIVE 1 = regional, state, local, county, district, territorial, parochial 2 = rural, country, local, rustic, homespun, hick (informal, chiefly U.S. & Canad.), backwoods ≠ urban 3 = parochial, insular, narrow-minded, unsophisticated, limited, narrow, small-town (chiefly U.S.), inward-looking ≠ cosmopolitan

**provision** NOUN 1 = supplying, giving, providing, supply, delivery, distribution, catering, presentation 2 = condition, term, requirement, demand, rider, restriction, qualification, clause
● PLURAL NOUN = food, supplies, stores, fare, rations, foodstuff, kai (N.Z. informal), victuals, edibles

**provisional** 1 = temporary, interim ≠ permanent 2 = conditional, limited, qualified, contingent, tentative ≠ definite

**provocation** 1 = cause, reason, grounds, motivation, stimulus, incitement 2 = <u>offence</u>, challenge, insult, taunt, injury, dare, grievance, annoyance

**provocative** = <u>offensive</u>, provoking, insulting, stimulating, annoying, galling, goading

**provoke** 1 = <u>anger</u>, annoy, irritate, infuriate, hassle (*informal*), aggravate (*informal*), incense, enrage ≠ pacify 2 = <u>rouse</u>, cause, produce, promote, occasion, prompt, stir, induce ≠ curb

**prowess** 1 = <u>skill</u>, ability, talent, expertise, genius, excellence, accomplishment, mastery ≠ inability 2 = <u>bravery</u>, daring, courage, heroism, mettle, valour, fearlessness, valiance ≠ cowardice

**proximity** = <u>nearness</u>, closeness

**proxy** = <u>representative</u>, agent, deputy, substitute, factor, delegate

**prudent** 1 = <u>cautious</u>, careful, wary, discreet, vigilant ≠ careless 2 = <u>wise</u>, politic, sensible, shrewd, discerning, judicious ≠ unwise 3 = <u>thrifty</u>, economical, sparing, careful, canny, provident, frugal, far-sighted ≠ extravagant

**prune** 1 = <u>cut</u>, trim, clip, dock, shape, shorten, snip 2 = <u>reduce</u>, cut, cut back, trim, cut down, pare down, make reductions in

**psyche** = <u>soul</u>, mind, self, spirit, personality, individuality, anima,

wairua (*N.Z.*)

**psychiatrist** = <u>psychotherapist</u>, analyst, therapist, psychologist, shrink (*slang*), psychoanalyst, headshrinker (*slang*)

**psychic** ADJECTIVE 1 = <u>supernatural</u>, mystic, occult 2 = <u>mystical</u>, spiritual, magical, other-worldly, paranormal, preternatural 3 = <u>psychological</u>, emotional, mental, spiritual, inner, psychiatric, cognitive
● NOUN = <u>clairvoyant</u>, fortune teller

**psychological** 1 = <u>mental</u>, emotional, intellectual, inner, cognitive, cerebral 2 = <u>imaginary</u>, psychosomatic, irrational, unreal, all in the mind

**psychology** 1 = <u>behaviourism</u>, study of personality, science of mind 2 (*Informal*) = <u>way of thinking</u>, attitude, behaviour, temperament, mentality, thought processes, mental processes, what makes you tick

**pub** *or* **public house** = <u>tavern</u>, bar, inn, saloon

**public** NOUN = <u>people</u>, society, community, nation, everyone, citizens, electorate, populace
● ADJECTIVE 1 = <u>civic</u>, government, state, national, local, official, community, social 2 = <u>general</u>, popular, national, shared, common, widespread, universal,

collective 3 = <u>open</u>, accessible, communal, unrestricted ≠ private 4 = <u>well-known</u>, leading, important, respected, famous, celebrated, recognized, distinguished 5 = <u>known</u>, open, obvious, acknowledged, plain, patent, overt ≠ secret

**publication** 1 = <u>pamphlet</u>, newspaper, magazine, issue, title, leaflet, brochure, periodical 2 = <u>announcement</u>, publishing, broadcasting, reporting, declaration, disclosure, proclamation, notification

**publicity** 1 = <u>advertising</u>, press, promotion, hype, boost, plug (*informal*) 2 = <u>attention</u>, exposure, fame, celebrity, fuss, public interest, limelight, notoriety

**publish** 1 = <u>put out</u>, issue, produce, print 2 = <u>announce</u>, reveal, spread, advertise, broadcast, disclose, proclaim, circulate

**pudding** = <u>dessert</u>, afters (*Brit. informal*), sweet, pud (*informal*)

**puff** VERB 1 = <u>smoke</u>, draw, drag (*slang*), suck, inhale, pull at or on 2 = <u>breathe heavily</u>, pant, exhale, blow, gasp, gulp, wheeze, fight for breath
● NOUN 1 = <u>drag</u>, pull (*slang*), moke 2 = <u>blast</u>, breath, whiff, draught, gust

**pull** VERB 1 = <u>draw</u>, haul, drag, trail, tow, tug, jerk, yank ≠ push 2 = <u>extract</u>, pick, remove, gather, take out, pluck, uproot, draw out ≠ insert 3 (*Informal*) = <u>attract</u>, draw, bring in, tempt, lure, interest, entice, pull in ≠ repel 4 = <u>strain</u>, tear, stretch, rip, wrench, dislocate, sprain
● NOUN 1 = <u>tug</u>, jerk, yank, twitch, heave ≠ shove 2 = <u>puff</u>, drag (*slang*), inhalation 3 (*Informal*) = <u>influence</u>, power, weight, muscle, clout (*informal*), kai (*N.Z. informal*)
● PHRASES **pull over (of)** 1 = <u>withdraw</u>, quit 2 = <u>leave</u>, abandon, get out, quit, retreat from, depart, evacuate ◆ **pull someone up** = <u>reprimand</u>, rebuke, admonish, read the riot act to, tell someone off (*informal*), reprove, bawl someone out (*informal*), tear someone off a strip (*Brit. informal*) ◆ **pull something off** (*Informal*) = <u>succeed in</u>, manage, carry out, accomplish
◆ **pull something out** = <u>produce</u>, draw, bring out, draw out ◆ **pull up** = <u>stop</u>, halt, brake

**pulp** NOUN 1 = <u>paste</u>, mash, mush 2 = <u>flesh</u>, meat, soft part
● ADJECTIVE = <u>cheap</u>, lurid, trashy, rubbishy
● VERB = <u>crush</u>, squash, mash,

pulverize

**pulse** NOUN = <u>beat</u>, rhythm, vibration, beating, throb, throbbing, pulsation

● VERB = <u>beat</u>, throb, vibrate, pulsate

**pump** 1 = <u>supply</u>, send, pour, inject 2 = <u>interrogate</u>, probe, quiz, cross-examine

**punch¹** VERB = <u>hit</u>, strike, box, smash, belt (*informal*), sock (*slang*), swipe (*informal*), bop (*informal*)

● NOUN 1 = <u>blow</u>, hit, sock (*slang*), jab, swipe (*informal*), bop (*informal*), wallop (*informal*) 2 (*Informal*) = <u>effectiveness</u>, bite, impact, drive, vigour, verve, forcefulness

**punch²** = <u>pierce</u>, cut, bore, drill, stamp, puncture, prick, perforate

**punctuate** = <u>interrupt</u>, break, pepper, sprinkle, intersperse

**puncture** NOUN 1 = <u>flat tyre</u>, flat, flattie (*N.Z.*) 2 = <u>hole</u>, opening, break, cut, nick, leak, slit

● VERB = <u>pierce</u>, cut, nick, penetrate, prick, rupture, perforate, bore a hole

**punish** = <u>discipline</u>, correct, castigate, chastise, sentence, chasten, penalize

**punishing** = <u>hard</u>, taxing, wearing, tiring, exhausting, gruelling, strenuous, arduous

≠ easy

**punishment** 1 = <u>penalizing</u>, discipline, correction, retribution, chastening, chastisement 2 = <u>penalty</u>, penance

**punitive** = <u>retaliatory</u>, in reprisal, retaliative

**punt** VERB = <u>bet</u>, back, stake, gamble, lay, wager

● NOUN = <u>bet</u>, stake, gamble, wager

**punter** 1 = <u>gambler</u>, better, backer 2 (*Informal*) = <u>person</u>, man in the street

**pupil** 1 = <u>student</u>, schoolboy *or* schoolgirl, schoolchild ≠ teacher 2 = <u>learner</u>, novice, beginner, disciple ≠ instructor

**puppet** 1 = <u>marionette</u>, doll, glove puppet, finger puppet 2 = <u>pawn</u>, tool, instrument, mouthpiece, stooge, cat's-paw

**purchase** VERB = <u>buy</u>, pay for, obtain, get, score (*slang*), gain, pick up, acquire ≠ sell

● NOUN 1 = <u>acquisition</u>, buy, investment, property, gain, asset, possession 2 = <u>grip</u>, hold, support, leverage, foothold

**pure** 1 = <u>unmixed</u>, real, simple, natural, straight, genuine, neat, authentic ≠ adulterated 2 = <u>clean</u>, wholesome, sanitary, spotless, sterilized, squeaky-clean, untainted, uncontaminated

≠ contaminated 3 = <u>complete</u>, total, perfect, absolute, sheer, patent, utter, outright ≠ qualified 4 = <u>innocent</u>, modest, good, moral, impeccable, righteous, virtuous, squeaky-clean ≠ corrupt

**purely** = <u>absolutely</u>, just, only, completely, simply, entirely, exclusively, merely

**purge** VERB 1 = <u>rid</u>, clear, cleanse, strip, empty, void 2 = <u>get rid of</u>, remove, expel, wipe out, eradicate, do away with, exterminate

● NOUN = <u>removal</u>, elimination, expulsion, eradication, ejection

**purity** 1 = <u>cleanness</u>, cleanliness, wholesomeness, pureness, faultlessness, immaculateness ≠ impurity 2 = <u>innocence</u>, virtue, integrity, honesty, decency, virginity, chastity, chasteness ≠ immorality

**purple** ▶ shades of purple
**purport** = <u>claim</u>, allege, assert, profess

**purpose** NOUN 1 = <u>reason</u>, point, idea, aim, object, intention 2 = <u>aim</u>, end, plan, hope, goal,

wish, desire, object
3 = <u>determination</u>, resolve, will, resolution, ambition, persistence, tenacity, firmness

● PHRASES on purpose = <u>deliberately</u>, purposely, intentionally, knowingly, designedly

---

### Word Power

**purpose** – The two concepts *purposeful* and *on purpose* should be carefully distinguished. *On purpose* and *purposely* have roughly the same meaning, and imply that a person's action is deliberate, rather than accidental. However, *purposeful* and its related adverb *purposefully* refer to the way that someone acts as being full of purpose or determination.

---

**purposely** = <u>deliberately</u>, expressly, consciously, intentionally, knowingly, with intent, on purpose ≠ accidentally

**purse** NOUN 1 = <u>pouch</u>, wallet, money-bag 2 (U.S.) = <u>handbag</u>, bag, shoulder bag, pocket book,

---

### Shades of purple

| | | | |
|---|---|---|---|
| amethyst | heather | magenta | puce |
| aubergine | indigo | mauve | Tyrian purple |
| burgundy | lavender | mulberry | violet |
| claret | lilac | plum | wine |

clutch bag 3 = <u>funds</u>, means, money, resources, treasury, wealth, exchequer

● **VERB** = <u>pucker</u>, contract, tighten, pout, press together

**pursue** 1 = <u>engage in</u>, perform, conduct, carry on, practise 2 = <u>try for</u>, seek, desire, search for, aim for, work towards, strive for 3 = <u>continue</u>, maintain, carry on, keep on, persist in, proceed in, persevere in 4 = <u>follow</u>, track, hunt, chase, dog, shadow, tail (*informal*), hound ≠ flee

**pursuit** 1 = <u>quest</u>, seeking, search, aim of, aspiration for, striving towards 2 = <u>pursuing</u>, seeking, search, hunt, chase, trailing 3 = <u>occupation</u>, activity, interest, line, pleasure, hobby, pastime

**push** **VERB** 1 = <u>shove</u>, force, press, thrust, drive, knock, sweep, plunge ≠ pull 2 = <u>press</u>, operate, depress, squeeze, activate, hold down 3 = <u>make or force your way</u>, move, shoulder, inch, squeeze, thrust, elbow, shove 4 = <u>urge</u>, encourage, persuade, spur, press, incite, impel ≠ discourage

● **NOUN** 1 = <u>shove</u>, thrust, butt, elbow, nudge ≠ pull 2 (*Informal*) = <u>drive</u>, go (*informal*), energy, initiative, enterprise, ambition, vitality, vigour

● **PHRASES** **the push** (*Informal,*

*chiefly Brit.*) = <u>dismissal</u>, the sack (*informal*), discharge, the boot (*slang*), your cards (*informal*)

**put** **VERB** 1 = <u>place</u>, leave, set, position, rest, park (*informal*), plant, lay 2 = <u>express</u>, state, word, phrase, utter

● **PHRASES** **put someone off** 1 = <u>discourage</u>, intimidate, deter, daunt, dissuade, demoralize, scare off, dishearten 2 = <u>disconcert</u>, confuse, unsettle, throw (*informal*), dismay, perturb, faze, discomfit ◆ **put someone up** 1 = <u>accommodate</u>, house, board, lodge, quarter, take someone in, billet 2 = <u>nominate</u>, put forward, offer, present, propose, recommend, submit ◆ **put something across** *or* **over** = <u>communicate</u>, explain, convey, make clear, get across, make yourself understood ◆ **put something off** = <u>postpone</u>, delay, defer, adjourn, hold over, put on the back burner (*informal*), take a rain check on (*U.S. & Canad. informal*) ◆ **put something up** 1 = <u>build</u>, raise, set up, construct, erect, fabricate 2 = <u>offer</u>, present, mount, put forward

**puzzle** **VERB** = <u>perplex</u>, confuse, baffle, stump, bewilder, confound, mystify, faze

● **NOUN** 1 = <u>problem</u>, riddle,

question, conundrum, poser
2 = <u>mystery</u>, problem, paradox, enigma, conundrum

**puzzling** = <u>perplexing</u>, baffling, bewildering, involved, enigmatic, incomprehensible, mystifying, abstruse ≠ simple

# Q

**quake** = <u>shake</u>, tremble, quiver, move, rock, shiver, shudder, vibrate

**qualification** 1 = <u>eligibility</u>, quality, ability, skill, fitness, attribute, capability, aptitude 2 = <u>condition</u>, proviso, requirement, rider, reservation, limitation, modification, caveat

**qualified** 1 = <u>capable</u>, trained, experienced, seasoned, able, fit, expert, chartered ≠ untrained 2 = <u>restricted</u>, limited, provisional, conditional, reserved, bounded, adjusted, moderated ≠ unconditional

**qualify** 1 = <u>certify</u>, equip, empower, train, prepare, fit, ready, permit ≠ disqualify 2 = <u>restrict</u>, limit, reduce, ease, moderate, regulate, diminish, temper

**quality** 1 = <u>standard</u>, standing, class, condition, rank, grade, merit, classification 2 = <u>excellence</u>, status, merit,

position, value, worth, distinction, virtue 3 = <u>characteristic</u>, feature, attribute, point, side, mark, property, aspect 4 = <u>nature</u>, character, make, sort, kind

**quantity** 1 = <u>amount</u>, lot, total, sum, part, number 2 = <u>size</u>, measure, mass, volume, length, capacity, extent, bulk

> ## Word Power
>
> **quantity** – The use of a plural noun after *quantity of*, as in *a large quantity of bananas*, used to be considered incorrect, the objection being that the word *quantity* should only be used to refer to an uncountable amount, which was grammatically regarded as a singular concept. Nowadays, however, most people consider the use of *quantity* with a plural noun to be acceptable.

**quarrel** NOUN = <u>disagreement</u>, fight, row, argument, dispute, controversy, breach, contention, biffo (*Austral. slang*) ≠ accord
● VERB = <u>disagree</u>, fight, argue, row, clash, dispute, differ, fall out (*informal*) ≠ get on or along (with)

**quarry** = <u>prey</u>, victim, game, goal, aim, prize, objective

**quarter** NOUN 1 = <u>district</u>, region, neighbourhood, place, part, side, area, zone 2 = <u>mercy</u>, pity, compassion, charity, sympathy, tolerance, kindness, forgiveness

● PLURAL NOUN = <u>lodgings</u>, rooms, chambers, residence, dwelling, barracks, abode, habitation

● VERB = <u>accommodate</u>, house, lodge, place, board, post, station, billet

**quash** 1 = <u>annul</u>, overturn, reverse, cancel, overthrow, revoke, overrule, rescind

2 = <u>suppress</u>, crush, put down, beat, overthrow, squash, subdue, repress

**queen** 1 = <u>sovereign</u>, ruler, monarch, leader, Crown, princess, majesty, head of state 2 = <u>leading light</u>, star, favourite, celebrity, darling, mistress, big name

**queer** 1 = <u>strange</u>, odd, funny, unusual, extraordinary, curious, weird, peculiar ≠ <u>normal</u> 2 = <u>faint</u>, dizzy, giddy, queasy, light-headed

### Word Power

**queer** – Although the term *queer* meaning 'gay' is still considered derogatory when used by non-gays, it is now being used by gay people themselves as a positive term in certain contexts, such as *queer politics, queer cinema*. Nevertheless, many gay people would not wish to have the term applied to them, nor would they use it of themselves.

**query** NOUN 1 = <u>question</u>, inquiry, problem 2 = <u>doubt</u>, suspicion, objection

● VERB 1 = <u>question</u>, challenge, doubt, suspect, dispute, object to, distrust, mistrust 2 = <u>ask</u>, inquire or enquire, question

**quest** 1 = <u>search</u>, hunt, mission, enterprise, crusade

2 = <u>expedition</u>, journey, adventure

**question** NOUN 1 = <u>inquiry</u>, enquiry, query, investigation, examination, interrogation ≠ <u>answer</u> 2 = <u>difficulty</u>, problem, doubt, argument, dispute, controversy, query, contention

3 = <u>issue</u>, point, matter, subject, problem, debate, proposal, theme

● VERB 1 = <u>interrogate</u>, cross-examine, interview, examine, probe, quiz, ask questions

2 = <u>dispute</u>, challenge, doubt, suspect, oppose, query, mistrust, disbelieve ≠ accept

● PHRASES **out of the question** = <u>impossible</u>, unthinkable, inconceivable, not on (*informal*), hopeless, unimaginable, unworkable, unattainable

**questionable** = <u>dubious</u>, suspect, doubtful, controversial, suspicious, dodgy (*Brit., Austral., & N.Z. informal*), debatable, moot ≠ indisputable

**queue** = <u>line</u>, row, file, train,

series, chain, string, column

**quick 1** = <u>fast</u>, swift, speedy, express, cracking (*Brit. informal*), smart, rapid, fleet ≠ slow **2** = <u>brief</u>, passing, hurried, flying, fleeting, summary, lightning, short-lived ≠ long **3** = <u>immediate</u>, instant, prompt, sudden, abrupt, instantaneous **4** ≠ <u>excitable</u>, passionate, irritable, touchy, irascible, testy ≠ calm **5** = <u>intelligent</u>, bright (*informal*), alert, sharp, acute, smart, clever, shrewd ≠ stupid

**quicken 1** = <u>speed up</u>, hurry, accelerate, hasten, gee up (*informal*) **2** = <u>stimulate</u>, inspire, arouse, excite, revive, incite, energize, invigorate

**quickly 1** = <u>swiftly</u>, rapidly, hurriedly, fast, hastily, briskly, apace ≠ slowly **2** = <u>soon</u>, speedily, as soon as possible, momentarily (*U.S.*), instantaneously, pronto (*informal*), a.s.a.p. (*informal*) **3** = <u>immediately</u>, at once, directly, promptly, abruptly, without delay

**quiet ADJECTIVE 1** = <u>soft</u>, low, muted, lowered, whispered, faint, suppressed, stifled ≠ loud **2** = <u>peaceful</u>, silent, hushed, soundless, noiseless ≠ noisy **3** = <u>calm</u>, peaceful, tranquil, mild, serene, placid, restful ≠ exciting **4** = <u>still</u>, calm, peaceful, tranquil ≠ troubled **5** = <u>undisturbed</u>, isolated, secluded, private,

sequestered, unfrequented ≠ crowded **6** = <u>silent</u> **7** = <u>reserved</u>, retiring, shy, gentle, mild, sedate, meek ≠ excitable
● **NOUN** = <u>peace</u>, rest, tranquillity, ease, silence, solitude, serenity, stillness ≠ noise

**quietly 1** = <u>noiselessly</u>, silently **2** = <u>softly</u>, inaudibly, in an undertone, under your breath **3** = <u>calmly</u>, serenely, placidly, patiently, mildly **4** = <u>silently</u>, mutely

**quilt** = <u>bedspread</u>, duvet, coverlet, eiderdown, counterpane, doona (*Austral.*), continental quilt

**quip** = <u>joke</u>, sally, jest, riposte, wisecrack (*informal*), retort, pleasantry, gibe

**quirky** = <u>odd</u>, unusual, eccentric, idiosyncratic, peculiar, offbeat

**quit 1** = <u>resign (from)</u>, leave, retire (from), pull out (of), step down (from) (*informal*), abdicate **2** = <u>stop</u>, give up, cease, end, drop, abandon, halt, discontinue ≠ continue **3** = <u>leave</u>, depart from, go out of, go away from, pull out from

**quite 1** = <u>somewhat</u>, rather, fairly, reasonably, relatively, moderately **2** = <u>absolutely</u>, perfectly, completely, totally, fully, entirely, wholly

**quiz NOUN** = <u>examination</u>, questioning, interrogation, interview, investigation, grilling (*informal*), cross-examination, cross-questioning

● VERB = <u>question</u>, ask, interrogate, examine, investigate

**quota** = <u>share</u>, allowance, ration, part, limit, slice, quantity, portion

**quotation** 1 = <u>passage</u>, quote (*informal*), excerpt, reference, extract, citation 2 (*Commerce*) = <u>estimate</u>, price, tender, rate, cost, charge, figure, quote (*informal*)

**quote** 1 = <u>repeat</u>, recite, recall 2 = <u>refer to</u>, cite, give, name, detail, relate, mention, instance

# R

**race¹ NOUN** 1 = <u>competition</u>, contest, chase, dash, pursuit 2 = <u>contest</u>, competition, rivalry

● VERB 1 = <u>compete against</u>, run against 2 = <u>compete</u>, run, contend, take part in a race 3 = <u>run</u>, fly, career, speed, tear, dash, hurry, dart

**race²** NOUN = <u>people</u>, nation, blood, stock, type, folk, tribe

**racial** = <u>ethnic</u>, ethnological, national, folk, genetic, tribal, genealogical

**rack** NOUN = <u>frame</u>, stand, structure, framework

● VERB = <u>torture</u>, torment, afflict, oppress, harrow, crucify, agonize, pain

> ## Word Power
>
> **rack** – The use of the spelling *wrack* rather than *rack* in sentences such as *she was wracked by grief* or *the country was wracked by civil war* is very common, but is thought by many people to be incorrect.

**racket** 1 = <u>noise</u>, row, fuss, disturbance, outcry, clamour, din, pandemonium 2 = <u>fraud</u>, scheme

**radiate** 1 = <u>emit</u>, spread, send out, pour, shed, scatter 2 = <u>shine</u>, be diffused 3 = <u>show</u>, display, demonstrate, exhibit, emanate, give off or out 4 = <u>spread out</u>, diverge, branch out

**radical** ADJECTIVE 1 = <u>extreme</u>, complete, entire, sweeping, severe, thorough, drastic 2 = <u>revolutionary</u>, extremist, fanatical 3 = <u>fundamental</u>, natural, basic, profound, innate, deep-seated ≠ superficial

● NOUN = <u>extremist</u>, revolutionary, militant, fanatic ≠ conservative

**rage** NOUN 1 = <u>fury</u>, temper, frenzy, rampage, tantrum, foulie (*Austral. slang*) ≠ calmness 2 = <u>anger</u>, passion, madness, wrath, ire 3 = <u>craze</u>, fashion, enthusiasm, vogue, fad (*informal*), latest thing

● VERB = <u>be furious</u>, blow up (*informal*), fume, lose it (*informal*), seethe, lose the plot (*informal*), go ballistic (*slang, chiefly U.S.*), lose your temper ≠ stay calm

**ragged** 1 = <u>tatty</u>, worn, torn, run-down, shabby, seedy, scruffy, in tatters ≠ smart 2 = <u>rough</u>, rugged, unfinished, uneven, jagged, serrated

**raid** VERB 1 = <u>steal from</u>, plunder, pillage, sack 2 = <u>attack</u>, invade, assault 3 = <u>make a search of</u>, search, bust (*informal*), make a raid on, make a swoop on
● NOUN 1 = <u>attack</u>, invasion, foray, sortie, incursion, sally, inroad 2 = <u>bust</u> (*informal*), swoop 3 = <u>robbery</u>, sacking

**raider** = <u>attacker</u>, thief, robber, plunderer, invader, marauder

**railing** = <u>fence</u>, rails, barrier, paling, balustrade

**rain** NOUN 1 = <u>rainfall</u>, fall, showers, deluge, drizzle, downpour, raindrops, cloudburst
● VERB 1 = <u>pour</u>, pelt (down), teem, bucket down (*informal*), drizzle, come down in buckets (*informal*) 2 = <u>fall</u>, shower, be dropped, sprinkle, be deposited

**rainy** = <u>wet</u>, damp, drizzly, showery ≠ dry

**raise** 1 = <u>lift</u>, elevate, uplift, heave 2 = <u>set upright</u>, lift, elevate 3 = <u>increase</u>, intensify, heighten, advance, boost, strengthen, enhance, enlarge ≠ reduce

4 = <u>make louder</u>, heighten, amplify, louden 5 = <u>collect</u>, gather, obtain 6 = <u>cause</u>, start, produce, create, occasion, provoke, originate, engender 7 = <u>put forward</u>, suggest, introduce, advance, broach, moot 8 = <u>bring up</u>, develop, rear, nurture 9 = <u>build</u>, construct, put up, erect ≠ demolish

**rake**[1] 1 = <u>gather</u>, collect, remove 2 = <u>search</u>, comb, scour, scrutinize, fossick (*Austral. & N.Z.*)

**rake**[2] = <u>libertine</u>, playboy, swinger (*slang*), lecher, roué, debauchee ≠ puritan

**rally** NOUN 1 = <u>gathering</u>, convention, meeting, congress, assembly, hui (*N.Z.*) 2 = <u>recovery</u>, improvement, revival, recuperation ≠ relapse
● VERB 1 = <u>gather together</u>, unite, regroup, reorganize, reassemble 2 = <u>recover</u>, improve, revive, get better, recuperate ≠ get worse

**ram** 1 = <u>hit</u>, force, drive into, crash, impact, smash, dash, butt 2 = <u>cram</u>, force, stuff, jam, thrust

**ramble** NOUN 1 = <u>walk</u>, tour, stroll, hike, roaming, roving, saunter
● VERB 1 = <u>walk</u>, range, wander, stroll, stray, roam, rove, saunter, go walkabout (*Austral.*) 2 often with **on** = <u>babble</u>, rabbit (on) (*Brit. informal*), waffle (*informal, chiefly Brit.*), witter on (*informal*)

**ramp** = <u>slope</u>, incline, gradient, rise

**rampage** VERB = <u>go berserk</u>, storm, rage, run riot, run amok

● PHRASES **on the rampage** = <u>berserk</u>, wild, violent, raging, out of control, amok, riotous, berko (*Austral. slang*)

**rampant** 1 = <u>widespread</u>, prevalent, rife, uncontrolled, unchecked, unrestrained, profuse, spreading like wildfire 2 (*Heraldry*) = <u>upright</u>, standing, rearing, erect

**random** ADJECTIVE 1 = <u>chance</u>, casual, accidental, incidental, haphazard, fortuitous, hit or miss, adventitious ≠ planned 2 = <u>casual</u>

● PHRASES **at random** = <u>haphazardly</u>, randomly, arbitrarily, by chance, willy-nilly, unsystematically

**randy** (*Informal*) = <u>lustful</u>, hot, turned-on (*slang*), aroused, horny (*slang*), amorous, lascivious

**range** NOUN 1 = <u>series</u>, variety, selection, assortment, lot, collection, gamut 2 = <u>limits</u>, reach 3 = <u>scope</u>, area, bounds, province, orbit, radius

● VERB 1 = <u>vary</u>, run, reach, extend, stretch 2 = <u>roam</u>, wander, rove, ramble, traverse

**rank**¹ NOUN 1 = <u>status</u>, level, position, grade, order, sort, type, division 2 = <u>class</u>, caste 3 = <u>row</u>, line, file, column, group, range, series, tier

● VERB 1 = <u>order</u>, dispose 2 = <u>arrange</u>, sort, line up, array, align

**rank**² 1 = <u>absolute</u>, complete, total, gross, sheer, utter, thorough, blatant 2 = <u>foul</u>, bad, offensive, disgusting, revolting, stinking, noxious, rancid, festy (*Austral. slang*) 3 = <u>abundant</u>, lush, luxuriant, dense, profuse

**ransom** = <u>payment</u>, money, price, payoff

**rant** = <u>shout</u>, roar, yell, rave, cry, declaim

**rap** VERB = <u>hit</u>, strike, knock, crack, tap

● NOUN 1 = <u>blow</u>, knock, crack, tap, clout (*informal*) 2 (*Slang*) = <u>rebuke</u>, blame, responsibility, punishment

**rape** VERB = <u>sexually assault</u>, violate, abuse, ravish, force, outrage

● NOUN = <u>sexual assault</u>, violation, ravishment, outrage

**rapid** 1 = <u>sudden</u>, prompt, speedy, express, swift ≠ gradual 2 = <u>quick</u>, fast, hurried, swift, brisk, hasty ≠ slow

**rapidly** = <u>quickly</u>, fast, swiftly, briskly, promptly, hastily, hurriedly, speedily

**rare** 1 = <u>uncommon</u>, unusual, few, strange, scarce, singular, sparse, infrequent ≠ common

2 = <u>superb</u>, great, fine, excellent, superlative, choice, peerless

**rarely** = <u>seldom</u>, hardly, hardly ever, infrequently ≠ often

> ### Word Power
> **rarely** – Since the meaning of *rarely* is 'hardly ever', the combination *rarely ever* is repetitive and should be avoided in careful writing, even though you may sometimes hear this phrase used in informal speech.

**raring** (in construction *raring to do something*) = <u>eager</u>, impatient, longing, ready, keen, desperate, enthusiastic

**rarity** 1 = <u>curio</u>, find, treasure, gem, collector's item 2 = <u>uncommonness</u>, scarcity, infrequency, unusualness, shortage, strangeness, sparseness

**rash**[1] = <u>reckless</u>, hasty, impulsive, imprudent, careless, ill-advised, foolhardy, impetuous ≠ cautious

**rash**[2] 1 = <u>outbreak of spots</u>, (skin) eruption 2 = <u>spate</u>, series, wave, flood, plague, outbreak

**rate** NOUN 1 = <u>speed</u>, pace, tempo, velocity, frequency 2 = <u>degree</u>, standard, scale, proportion, ratio 3 = <u>charge</u>,

price, cost, fee, figure
● VERB 1 = <u>evaluate</u>, consider, rank, reckon, value, measure, estimate, count 2 = <u>deserve</u>, merit, be entitled to, be worthy of
● PHRASES **at any rate** = <u>in any case</u>, anyway, anyhow, at all events

**rather** 1 = <u>preferably</u>, sooner, more readily, more willingly 2 = <u>to some extent</u>, quite, a little, fairly, relatively, somewhat, moderately, to some degree

> ### Word Power
> **rather** – It is acceptable to use either *would rather* or *had rather* in sentences such as *I would rather* (or *had rather*) *see a film than a play*. *Had rather*, however, is less common than *would rather*, and sounds a little old-fashioned nowadays.

**ratify** = <u>approve</u>, establish, confirm, sanction, endorse, uphold, authorize, affirm ≠ annul

**rating** = <u>position</u>, placing, rate, order, class, degree, rank, status

**ratio** = <u>proportion</u>, rate, relation, percentage, fraction

**ration** NOUN = <u>allowance</u>, quota, allotment, helping, part, share, measure, portion
● VERB = <u>limit</u>, control, restrict,

budget

**rational** = sensible, sound, wise, reasonable, intelligent, realistic, logical, sane ≠ insane

**rationale** = reason, grounds, theory, principle, philosophy, logic, motivation, raison d'être (*French*)

**rattle** 1 = clatter, bang, jangle 2 = shake, jolt, vibrate, bounce, jar 3 (*Informal*) = fluster, shake, upset, disturb, disconcert, perturb, faze

**ravage** VERB = destroy, ruin, devastate, spoil, demolish, ransack, lay waste, despoil
● PLURAL NOUN = damage, destruction, devastation, ruin, havoc, ruination, spoliation

**rave** 1 = rant, rage, roar, go mad (*informal*), babble, be delirious 2 (*Informal*) = enthuse, praise, gush, be mad about (*informal*), be wild about (*informal*)

**raving** = mad, wild, crazy, hysterical, insane, irrational, crazed, delirious, berko (*Austral. slang*), off the air (*Austral. slang*)

**raw** 1 = unrefined, natural, crude, unprocessed, basic, rough, coarse, unfinished ≠ refined 2 = uncooked, natural, fresh ≠ cooked 3 = inexperienced, new, green, immature, callow ≠ experienced 4 = chilly, biting,

cold, freezing, bitter, piercing, parky (*Brit. informal*)

**ray** = beam, bar, flash, shaft, gleam

**re** = concerning, about, regarding, with regard to, with reference to, apropos

---

### Word Power

**re** – In contexts such as *re your letter, your remarks have been noted* or *he spoke to me re your complaint*, *re* is common in business or official correspondence. In spoken and in general written English *with reference to* is preferable in the former case and *about* or *concerning* in the latter. Even in business correspondence, the use of *re* is often restricted to the letter heading.

---

**reach** VERB 1 = arrive at, get to, make, attain 2 = attain, get to 3 = touch, grasp, extend to, stretch to, contact 4 = contact, get in touch with, get through to, communicate with, get hold of
● NOUN 1 = grasp, range, distance, stretch, capacity, extent, extension, scope 2 = jurisdiction, power, influence

**react** = respond, act, proceed, behave

**reaction** 1 = response, answer, reply 2 = counteraction, backlash, recoil 3 = <u>conservatism</u>, the right

## Word Power

**reaction** – Some people say that *reaction* should always refer to an instant response to something (as in *his reaction was one of amazement*), and that this word should not be used to refer to a considered response given in the form of a statement (as in *the Minister gave his reaction to the court's decision*). Use *response* instead.

**reactionary** ADJECTIVE
= <u>conservative</u>, right-wing
● NOUN = <u>conservative</u>, die-hard, right-winger ≠ radical

**read** 1 = <u>scan</u>, study, look at, pore over, peruse 2 = <u>understand</u>, interpret, comprehend, construe, decipher, see, discover
3 = <u>register</u>, show, record, display, indicate

**readily** 1 = <u>willingly</u>, freely, quickly, gladly, eagerly
≠ reluctantly 2 = <u>promptly</u>, quickly, easily, smoothly, effortlessly, speedily, unhesitatingly ≠ with difficulty

**readiness** 1 = <u>willingness</u>, eagerness, keenness
2 = <u>promptness</u>, facility, ease, dexterity, adroitness

**reading** 1 = <u>perusal</u>, study, examination, inspection, scrutiny

2 = <u>learning</u>, education, knowledge, scholarship, erudition
3 = <u>recital</u>, performance, lesson, sermon 4 = <u>interpretation</u>, version, impression, grasp

**ready** 1 = <u>prepared</u>, set, primed, organized ≠ unprepared
2 = <u>completed</u>, arranged
3 = <u>mature</u>, ripe, mellow, ripened, seasoned 4 = <u>willing</u>, happy, glad, disposed, keen, eager, inclined, prone ≠ reluctant 5 = <u>prompt</u>, smart, quick, bright, sharp, keen, alert, clever ≠ slow 6 = <u>available</u>, handy, present, near, accessible, convenient ≠ unavailable

**real** 1 = <u>true</u>, genuine, sincere, factual, dinkum (*Austral. & N.Z. informal*), unfeigned 2 = <u>genuine</u>, authentic, dinkum (*Austral. & N.Z. informal*) ≠ fake 3 = <u>proper</u>, true, valid 4 = <u>true</u>, actual 5 = <u>typical</u>, true, genuine, sincere, dinkum (*Austral. & N.Z. informal*), unfeigned 6 = <u>complete</u>, total, perfect, utter, thorough

**realistic** 1 = <u>practical</u>, real, sensible, common-sense, down-to-earth, matter-of-fact, level-headed ≠ impractical
2 = <u>attainable</u>, sensible
3 = <u>lifelike</u>, true to life, authentic, true, natural, genuine, faithful

**reality** 1 = <u>fact</u>, truth, realism, validity, verity, actuality 2 = <u>truth</u>, fact, actuality

**realization** 1 = <u>awareness</u>, understanding, recognition, perception, grasp, conception, comprehension, cognizance 2 = <u>achievement</u>, accomplishment, fulfilment

**realize** 1 = <u>become aware of</u>, understand, take in, grasp, comprehend, get the message 2 = <u>fulfil</u>, achieve, accomplish, make real 3 = <u>achieve</u>, do, effect, complete, perform, fulfil, accomplish, carry out *or* through

**really** 1 = <u>certainly</u>, genuinely, positively, surely 2 = <u>truly</u>, actually, in fact, indeed, in actuality

**realm** 1 = <u>field</u>, world, area, province, sphere, department, branch, territory 2 = <u>kingdom</u>, country, empire, land, domain, dominion

**reap** 1 = <u>get</u>, gain, obtain, acquire, derive 2 = <u>collect</u>, gather, bring in, harvest, garner, cut

**rear**[1] NOUN 1 = <u>back part</u>, back ≠ front 2 = <u>back</u>, end, tail, rearguard, tail end

● ADJECTIVE = <u>back</u>, hind, last, following ≠ front

**rear**[2] 1 = <u>bring up</u>, raise, educate, train, foster, nurture 2 = <u>breed</u>, keep 3 = <u>rise</u>, tower, soar, loom

**reason** NOUN 1 = <u>cause</u>, grounds, purpose, motive, goal, aim, object, intention 2 = <u>sense</u>, mind,

understanding, judgment, logic, intellect, sanity, rationality ≠ emotion

● VERB = <u>deduce</u>, conclude, work out, make out, infer, think

● PHRASES **reason with someone** = <u>persuade</u>, bring round, urge, win over, prevail upon (*informal*), talk into *or* out of

---

### Word Power

**reason** – Many people object to the expression *the reason is because*, on the grounds that it is repetitive. It is therefore advisable to use either *this is because* or *the reason is that*.

---

**reasonable** 1 = <u>sensible</u>, sound, practical, wise, logical, sober, plausible, sane ≠ irrational 2 = <u>fair</u>, just, right, moderate, equitable, tenable ≠ unfair 3 = <u>within reason</u>, fit, proper ≠ impossible 4 = <u>low</u>, cheap, competitive, moderate, modest, inexpensive 5 = <u>average</u>, fair, moderate, modest, O.K. *or* okay (*informal*)

**reassure** = <u>encourage</u>, comfort, hearten, gee up, restore confidence to, put *or* set your mind at rest

**rebate** = <u>refund</u>, discount, reduction, bonus, allowance, deduction

**rebel** NOUN 1 = <u>revolutionary</u>, insurgent, secessionist, revolutionist 2 = <u>nonconformist</u>, dissenter, heretic, apostate, schismatic
● VERB 1 = <u>revolt</u>, resist, rise up, mutiny 2 = <u>defy</u>, dissent, disobey
● ADJECTIVE = <u>rebellious</u>, revolutionary, insurgent, insurrectionary

**rebellion** 1 = <u>resistance</u>, rising, revolution, revolt, uprising, mutiny 2 = <u>nonconformity</u>, defiance, heresy, schism

**rebellious** 1 = <u>defiant</u>, difficult, resistant, unmanageable, refractory ≠ obedient
2 = <u>revolutionary</u>, rebel, disorderly, unruly, insurgent, disloyal, seditious, mutinous ≠ obedient

**rebound** 1 = <u>bounce</u>, ricochet, recoil 2 = <u>misfire</u>, backfire, recoil, boomerang

**rebuff** VERB = <u>reject</u>, refuse, turn down, cut, slight, snub, spurn, knock back (slang) ≠ encourage
● NOUN = <u>rejection</u>, snub, knock-back, slight, refusal, repulse, cold shoulder, slap in the face (informal) ≠ encouragement

**rebuke** VERB = <u>scold</u>, censure, reprimand, castigate, chide, dress down (informal), admonish, tell off (informal) ≠ praise
● NOUN = <u>scolding</u>, censure,

reprimand, row, dressing down (informal), telling-off (informal), admonition ≠ praise

**recall** VERB 1 = <u>recollect</u>, remember, evoke, call to mind 2 = <u>call back</u> 3 = <u>annul</u>, withdraw, cancel, repeal, revoke, retract, countermand
● NOUN 1 = <u>recollection</u>, memory, remembrance 2 = <u>annulment</u>, withdrawal, repeal, cancellation, retraction, rescindment

**recede** = <u>fall back</u>, withdraw, retreat, return, retire, regress

**receipt** 1 = <u>sales slip</u>, proof of purchase, counterfoil
2 = <u>receiving</u>, delivery, reception, acceptance

**receive** 1 = <u>get</u>, accept, be given, pick up, collect, obtain, acquire, take 2 = <u>experience</u>, suffer, bear, encounter, sustain, undergo 3 = <u>greet</u>, meet, admit, welcome, entertain, accommodate

**recent** = <u>new</u>, modern, up-to-date, late, current, fresh, novel, present-day ≠ old

**recently** = <u>not long ago</u>, newly, lately, currently, freshly, of late, latterly

**reception** 1 = <u>party</u>, gathering, get-together, social gathering, function, celebration, festivity, soirée 2 = <u>response</u>, reaction, acknowledgment, treatment, welcome, greeting

**recess** 1 = <u>break</u>, rest, holiday, interval, vacation, respite, intermission 2 = <u>alcove</u>, corner, bay, hollow, niche, nook

**recession** = <u>depression</u>, drop, decline, slump ≠ boom

**recipe** = <u>directions</u>, instructions, ingredients

**recital** 1 = <u>performance</u>, rendering, rehearsal, reading 2 = <u>account</u>, telling, statement, relation, narrative 3 = <u>recitation</u>

**recite** = <u>perform</u>, deliver, repeat, declaim

**reckless** = <u>careless</u>, wild, rash, precipitate, hasty, mindless, headlong, thoughtless ≠ cautious

**reckon** 1 (*Informal*) = <u>think</u>, believe, suppose, imagine, assume, guess (*informal*, *chiefly U.S. & Canad.*) 2 = <u>consider</u>, rate, account, judge, regard, count, esteem, deem 3 = <u>count</u>, figure, total, calculate, compute, add up, tally, number

**reckoning** = <u>count</u>, estimate, calculation, addition

**reclaim** 1 = <u>retrieve</u>, regain 2 = <u>regain</u>, salvage, recapture

**recognition** 1 = <u>identification</u>, recollection, discovery, remembrance 2 = <u>acceptance</u>, admission, allowance, confession

**recognize** 1 = <u>identify</u>, know, place, remember, spot, notice,

recall, recollect 2 = <u>acknowledge</u>, allow, accept, admit, grant, concede ≠ ignore 3 = <u>appreciate</u>, respect, notice

**recollection** = <u>memory</u>, recall, impression, remembrance, reminiscence

**recommend** 1 = <u>advocate</u>, suggest, propose, approve, endorse, commend ≠ disapprove of 2 = <u>put forward</u>, approve, endorse, commend, praise 3 = <u>advise</u>, suggest, advance, propose, counsel, advocate, prescribe, put forward

**recommendation** 1 = <u>advice</u>, proposal, suggestion, counsel 2 = <u>commendation</u>, reference, praise, sanction, approval, endorsement, advocacy, testimonial

**reconcile** 1 = <u>resolve</u>, settle, square, adjust, compose, rectify, put to rights 2 = <u>reunite</u>, bring back together, conciliate 3 = <u>make peace between</u>, reunite, propitiate

**reconciliation** = <u>reunion</u>, conciliation, pacification, reconcilement ≠ separation

**reconsider** = <u>rethink</u>, review, revise, think again, reassess

**reconstruct** 1 = <u>rebuild</u>, restore, recreate, remake, renovate, remodel, regenerate 2 = <u>build up a picture of</u>, build up, piece together, deduce

**record** NOUN 1 = <u>document</u>, file, register, log, report, account, entry, journal 2 = <u>evidence</u>, trace, documentation, testimony, witness 3 = <u>disc</u>, single, album, LP, vinyl 4 = <u>background</u>, history, performance, career
● VERB 1 = <u>set down</u>, minute, note, enter, register, log, chronicle 2 = <u>make a recording of</u>, video, tape, video-tape, tape-record 3 = <u>register</u>, show, indicate, give evidence of

**recorder** = <u>chronicler</u>, archivist, historian, clerk, scribe, diarist

**recording** = <u>record</u>, video, tape, disc

**recount** = <u>tell</u>, report, describe, relate, repeat, depict, recite, narrate

**recover** 1 = <u>get better</u>, improve, get well, recuperate, heal, revive, mend, convalesce ≠ relapse 2 = <u>rally</u> 3 = <u>save</u>, rescue, retrieve, salvage, reclaim ≠ abandon 4 = <u>recoup</u>, restore, get back, regain, retrieve, reclaim, redeem, recapture ≠ lose

**recovery** 1 = <u>improvement</u>, healing, revival, mending, recuperation, convalescence 2 = <u>retrieval</u>, repossession, reclamation, restoration

**recreation** = <u>leisure</u>, play, sport, fun, entertainment, relaxation, enjoyment, amusement

**recruit** VERB 1 = <u>gather</u>, obtain, engage, procure 2 = <u>assemble</u>, raise, levy, muster, mobilize 3 = <u>enlist</u>, draft, enrol ≠ dismiss
● NOUN = <u>beginner</u>, trainee, apprentice, novice, convert, initiate, helper, learner

**recur** = <u>happen again</u>, return, repeat, persist, revert, reappear, come again

**recycle** = <u>reprocess</u>, reuse, salvage, reclaim, save

**red** NOUN or ADJECTIVE 1 = <u>crimson</u>, scarlet, ruby, vermilion, cherry, coral, carmine 2 = <u>flushed</u>, embarrassed, blushing, florid, shamefaced 3 = <u>chestnut</u>, reddish, flame-coloured, sandy, Titian, carroty
● PHRASES **in the red** (*Informal*) = <u>in debt</u>, insolvent, in arrears, overdrawn ◆ **see red** (*Informal*) = <u>lose your temper</u>, lose it (*informal*), go mad (*informal*), crack up (*informal*), lose the plot (*informal*), go ballistic (*slang, chiefly U.S.*), fly off the handle (*informal*), blow your top
> **shades of red**

**redeem** 1 = <u>reinstate</u>, absolve, restore to favour 2 = <u>make up for</u>, compensate for, atone for, make amends for 3 = <u>buy back</u>, recover, regain, retrieve, reclaim, repurchase 4 = <u>save</u>, free, deliver,

### Shades of red

| | | |
|---|---|---|
| auburn | flesh | raspberry |
| baby pink | foxy | rose |
| burgundy | fuchsia | roseate |
| burnt sienna | ginger | rosy |
| cardinal red | henna | ruby |
| carmine | liver | russet |
| carnation | magenta | rust |
| carroty | maroon | sandy |
| cerise | mulberry | scarlet |
| cherry | old rose | strawberry |
| chestnut | oxblood | tea rose |
| cinnabar | oyster pink | terracotta |
| copper *or* coppery | peach | Titian |
| coral | pink | vermilion |
| crimson | plum | wine |
| damask | poppy | |
| flame | puce | |

liberate, ransom, emancipate

**redemption** 1 = compensation, amends, reparation, atonement 2 = salvation, release, rescue, liberation, emancipation, deliverance

**redress VERB** 1 = make amends for, make up for, compensate for 2 = put right, balance, correct, adjust, regulate, rectify, even up ● NOUN = amends, payment, compensation, reparation, atonement, recompense

**reduce** 1 = lessen, cut, lower, moderate, weaken, diminish, decrease, cut down ≠ increase 2 = degrade, downgrade, break,

humble, bring low ≠ promote

**redundancy** 1 = layoff, sacking, dismissal 2 = unemployment, the sack (*informal*), the axe (*informal*), joblessness

**redundant** 1 = superfluous, extra, surplus, unnecessary, unwanted, inessential, supernumerary ≠ essential

**reel** 1 = stagger, rock, roll, pitch, sway, lurch 2 = whirl, spin, revolve, swirl

**refer VERB** = direct, point, send, guide ● PHRASES **refer to something or someone** 1 = allude to,

mention, cite, speak of, bring up
2 = <u>relate to</u>, concern, apply to, pertain to, be relevant to
3 = <u>consult</u>, go, apply, turn to, look up

> ## Word Power
>
> **refer** – It is usually unnecessary to add *back* to the verb *refer*, since the sense of *back* is already contained in the *re-* part of this word. For example, you might say *This refers to* (not *refers back to*) *what has already been said. Refer back* is only considered acceptable when used to mean 'return a document or question to the person it came from for further consideration', as in *he referred the matter back to me*.

**referee** NOUN = umpire, judge, ref (*informal*), arbiter, arbitrator, adjudicator
● VERB = umpire, judge, mediate, adjudicate, arbitrate

**reference** 1 = <u>allusion</u>, note, mention, quotation 2 = <u>citation</u>
3 = <u>testimonial</u>, recommendation, credentials, endorsement, character reference

**referendum** = <u>public vote</u>, popular vote, plebiscite

**refine** 1 = <u>purify</u>, process, filter, cleanse, clarify, distil 2 = <u>improve</u>, perfect, polish, hone

**refined** 1 = <u>purified</u>, processed, pure, filtered, clean, clarified, distilled ≠ unrefined 2 = <u>cultured</u>, polished, elegant, polite, cultivated, civilized, well-bred ≠ coarse 3 = <u>discerning</u>, fine, sensitive, delicate, precise, discriminating, fastidious

**reflect** 1 = <u>show</u>, reveal, display, indicate, demonstrate, manifest
2 = <u>throw back</u>, return, mirror, echo, reproduce 3 = <u>consider</u>, think, muse, ponder, meditate, ruminate, cogitate, wonder

**reflection** 1 = <u>image</u>, echo, mirror image 2 = <u>consideration</u>, thinking, thought, idea, opinion, observation, musing, meditation

**reflective** = thoughtful, contemplative, meditative, pensive

**reform** NOUN = <u>improvement</u>, amendment, rehabilitation, betterment
● VERB 1 = <u>improve</u>, correct, restore, amend, rectify
2 = <u>mend your ways</u>, go straight (*informal*), shape up (*informal*), turn over a new leaf, clean up your act (*informal*), pull your socks up (*Brit. informal*)

**refrain¹** = <u>stop</u>, avoid, cease, renounce, abstain, leave off, desist, forbear

**refrain²** = <u>chorus</u>, tune, melody

**refresh** 1 = <u>revive</u>, freshen, revitalize, stimulate, brace, enliven, invigorate 2 = <u>stimulate</u>, prompt, renew, jog

**refreshing** 1 = <u>new</u>, original, novel 2 = <u>stimulating</u>, fresh, bracing, invigorating ≠ tiring

**refreshment** = <u>food and drink</u>, drinks, snacks, titbits, kai (*N.Z. informal*)

**refuge** 1 = <u>protection</u>, shelter, asylum 2 = <u>haven</u>, retreat, sanctuary, hide-out

**refugee** = <u>exile</u>, émigré, displaced person, escapee

**refund** NOUN = <u>repayment</u>, reimbursement, return
● VERB = <u>repay</u>, return, restore, pay back, reimburse

**refurbish** = <u>renovate</u>, restore, repair, clean up, overhaul, revamp, mend, do up (*informal*)

**refusal** = <u>rejection</u>, denial, rebuff, knock-back (*slang*)

**refuse**¹ = <u>decline</u>, reject, turn down, say no to 2 = <u>deny</u>, decline, withhold ≠ allow

**refuse**² = <u>rubbish</u>, waste, junk (*informal*), litter, garbage, trash

**regain** 1 = <u>recover</u>, get back, retrieve, recapture, win back, take back, recoup 2 = <u>get back to</u>, return to, reach again

**regal** = <u>royal</u>, majestic, kingly *or* queenly, noble, princely, magnificent

**regard** VERB 1 = <u>consider</u>, see, rate, view, judge, think of, esteem, deem 2 = <u>look at</u>, view, eye, watch, observe, clock (*Brit. slang*), check out (*informal*), gaze at
● NOUN 1 = <u>respect</u>, esteem, thought, concern, care, consideration 2 = <u>look</u>, gaze, scrutiny, stare, glance
● PLURAL NOUN = <u>good wishes</u>, respects, greetings, compliments, best wishes
● PHRASES as regards = <u>concerning</u>, regarding, relating to, pertaining to

### Word Power

**regard** – The word *regard* in the expression *with regard to* is singular, and has no *s* at the end. People often make the mistake of saying *with regards to*, perhaps being influenced by the phrase *as regards*.

**regarding** = <u>concerning</u>, about, on the subject of, re, respecting, as regards, with reference to, in *or* with regard to

**regardless** 1 = <u>in spite of</u> everything, anyway, nevertheless, in any case 2 *with of* = <u>irrespective of</u>, heedless of, unmindful of

**regime** 1 = <u>government</u>, rule, management, leadership, reign 2 = <u>plan</u>, course, system, policy, programme, scheme, regimen

**region** = <u>area</u>, place, part, quarter, section, sector, district, territory

> ➤ **WORD POWER SUPPLEMENT**
administrative regions

**regional** = <u>local</u>, district, provincial, parochial, zonal

**register** NOUN = <u>list</u>, record, roll, file, diary, catalogue, log, archives
● VERB 1 = <u>enrol</u>, enlist, list, note, enter 2 = <u>record</u>, catalogue, chronicle 3 = <u>indicate</u>, show 4 = <u>show</u>, mark, indicate, manifest 5 = <u>express</u>, show, reveal, display, exhibit

**regret** VERB 1 = <u>be or feel sorry about</u>, rue, deplore, bemoan, repent (of), bewail ≠ be satisfied with 2 = <u>mourn</u>, miss, grieve for or over
● NOUN 1 = <u>remorse</u>, compunction, bitterness, repentance, contrition, penitence 2 = <u>sorrow</u> ≠ satisfaction

**regular** 1 = <u>frequent</u> 2 = <u>normal</u>, common, usual, ordinary, typical, routine, customary, habitual ≠ infrequent 3 = <u>steady</u>, consistent 4 = <u>even</u>, level, balanced, straight, flat, fixed, smooth, uniform ≠ uneven

**regulate** 1 = <u>control</u>, run, rule, manage, direct, guide, handle, govern 2 = <u>moderate</u>, control, modulate, fit, tune, adjust

**regulation** 1 = <u>rule</u>, order, law, dictate, decree, statute, edict, precept 2 = <u>control</u>, government, management, direction, supervision

**rehearsal** = <u>practice</u>, rehearsing, run-through, preparation, drill

**rehearse** = <u>practise</u>, prepare, run through, go over, train, repeat, drill, recite

**reign** VERB 1 = <u>be supreme</u>, prevail, predominate, hold sway 2 = <u>rule</u>, govern, be in power, influence, command
● NOUN = <u>rule</u>, power, control, command, monarchy, dominion

---

### Word Power

**reign** – The words rein and reign should not be confused; note the correct spellings in *he gave full rein to his feelings* (not *reign*); and *it will be necessary to rein in public spending* (not *reign in*).

---

**rein** = <u>control</u>, harness, bridle, hold, check, brake, curb, restraint

**reincarnation** = <u>rebirth</u>, transmigration of souls

**reinforce** 1 = <u>support</u>, strengthen, fortify, toughen, stress, prop, supplement, emphasize 2 = <u>increase</u>, extend, add to, strengthen, supplement

**reinforcement** NOUN

1 = <u>strengthening</u>, increase, fortification, augmentation
2 = <u>support</u>, stay, prop, brace, buttress
● PLURAL NOUN = <u>reserves</u>, support, auxiliaries, additional *or* fresh troops
**reinstate** = <u>restore</u>, recall, re-establish, return
**reiterate** (*Formal*) = repeat, restate, say again, do again
**reject** VERB 1 = <u>rebuff</u>, jilt, turn down, spurn, refuse, say no to, repulse ≠ accept 2 = <u>deny</u>, exclude, veto, relinquish, renounce, disallow, forsake, disown ≠ approve 3 = <u>discard</u>, decline, eliminate, scrap, jettison, throw away *or* out ≠ accept
● NOUN 1 = <u>castoff</u>, second, discard ≠ treasure 2 = <u>failure</u>, loser, flop
**rejection** 1 = <u>denial</u>, veto, dismissal, exclusion, disowning, thumbs down, renunciation, repudiation ≠ approval
2 = <u>rebuff</u>, refusal, knock-back (*slang*), kick in the teeth (*slang*), brushoff (*slang*) ≠ acceptance
**rejoice** = <u>be glad</u>, celebrate, be happy, glory, be overjoyed, exult ≠ lament
**rejoin** = <u>reply</u>, answer, respond, retort, riposte
**relate** VERB 1 = <u>tell</u>, recount, report, detail, describe, recite, narrate

● PHRASES **relate to something** *or* **someone** 1 = <u>concern</u>, refer to, apply to, have to do with, pertain to, be relevant to
2 = <u>connect with</u>, associate with, link with, couple with, join with, correlate to
**related** 1 = <u>associated</u>, linked, joint, connected, affiliated, akin, interconnected ≠ unconnected
2 = <u>akin</u>, kindred ≠ unrelated
**relation** NOUN 1 = <u>similarity</u>, link, bearing, bond, comparison, correlation, connection
2 = <u>relative</u>, kin, kinsman *or* kinswoman
● PLURAL NOUN 1 = <u>dealings</u>, relationship, affairs, contact, connections, interaction, intercourse 2 = <u>family</u>, relatives, tribe, clan, kin, kindred, kinsmen, kinsfolk, ainga (*N.Z.*)
**relationship** 1 = <u>association</u>, bond, connection, affinity, rapport, kinship 2 = <u>affair</u>, romance, liaison, amour, intrigue
3 = <u>connection</u>, link, parallel, similarity, tie-up, correlation
**relative** NOUN = <u>relation</u>, kinsman *or* kinswoman, member of your *or* the family
● ADJECTIVE 1 = <u>comparative</u>
2 = <u>corresponding</u> 3 *with* to = <u>in proportion to</u>, proportionate to
**relatively** = <u>comparatively</u>, rather, somewhat

**relax** 1 = be or feel at ease, chill out (slang, chiefly U.S.), take it easy, lighten up (slang), outspan (S. African) ≠ be alarmed 2 = calm down, calm, unwind 3 = make less tense, rest 4 = lessen, reduce, ease, relieve, weaken, loosen, let up, slacken ≠ tighten 5 = moderate, ease, relieve, weaken, slacken ≠ tighten up

**relaxation** = leisure, rest, fun, pleasure, recreation, enjoyment

**relay** = broadcast, carry, spread, communicate, transmit, send out

**release** VERB 1 = set free, free, discharge, liberate, drop, loose, undo, extricate ≠ imprison 2 = acquit, let go, let off, exonerate, absolve 3 = issue, publish, make public, make known, launch, distribute, put out, circulate ≠ withhold
• NOUN 1 = liberation, freedom, liberty, discharge, emancipation, deliverance ≠ imprisonment 2 = acquittal, exemption, absolution, exoneration 3 = issue, publication, proclamation

**relegate** = demote, degrade, downgrade

**relentless** 1 = merciless, fierce, cruel, ruthless, unrelenting, implacable, remorseless, pitiless ≠ merciful 2 = unremitting, persistent, unrelenting, incessant, nonstop, unrelieved

**relevant** = significant, appropriate, related, fitting, to the point, apt, pertinent, apposite ≠ irrelevant

**reliable** 1 = dependable, trustworthy, sure, sound, true, faithful, staunch ≠ unreliable 2 = safe, dependable 3 = definitive, sound, dependable, trustworthy

**reliance** 1 = dependency, dependence 2 = trust, confidence, belief, faith

**relic** = remnant, vestige, memento, trace, fragment, souvenir, keepsake

**relief** 1 = ease, release, comfort, cure, remedy, solace, deliverance, mitigation 2 = rest, respite, relaxation, break, breather (informal) 3 = aid, help, support, assistance, succour

**relieve** 1 = ease, soothe, alleviate, relax, comfort, calm, cure, soften ≠ intensify 2 = help, support, aid, sustain, assist, succour

**religion** = belief, faith, theology, creed
➤ religion

**religious** 1 = spiritual, holy, sacred, devotional 2 = conscientious, faithful, rigid, meticulous, scrupulous, punctilious

**relinquish** (Formal) = give up, leave, drop, abandon, surrender, let go, renounce, forsake

**relish** VERB 1 = enjoy, like, savour,

# Religion

## Religions

animism
Babi *or* Babism
Baha'ism
Buddhism
Christianity
Confucianism
druidism
heliolatry
Hinduism *or* Hindooism
Islam
Jainism
Judaism
Macumba
Manichaeism *or* Manicheism
Mithraism *or* Mithraicism
Orphism

paganism
Rastafarianism
Ryobu Shinto
Santeria
Satanism
Scientology ®
shamanism
Shango
Shembe
Shinto
Sikhism
Taoism
voodoo *or* voodooism
Yezidis
Zoroastrianism *or* Zoroastrism

## Religious festivals

Advent
Al Hijrah
Ascension Day
Ash Wednesday
Baisakhi
Bodhi Day
Candlemas
Chanukah *or* Hanukkah
Ching Ming
Christmas
Corpus Christi
Day of Atonement
Dhammacakka
Diwali
Dragon Boat Festival
Dussehra
Easter
Eid ul-Adha *or* Id-ul-Adha
Eid ul-Fitr *or* Id-ul-Fitr

Epiphany
Feast of Tabernacles
Good Friday
Guru Nanak's Birthday
Hirja
Hola Mohalla
Holi
Janamashtami
Lailat ul-Barah
Lailat ul-Isra Wal Mi'raj
Lailat ul-Qadr
Lent
Mahashivaratri
Maundy Thursday
Michaelmas
Moon Festival
Palm Sunday
Passion Sunday
Passover

| Religious festivals (continued) | |
| --- | --- |
| Pentecost | Sexagesima |
| Pesach | Shavuot |
| Purim | Shrove Tuesday |
| Quadragesima | Sukkoth *or* Succoth |
| Quinquagesima | Trinity |
| Raksha Bandhan | Wesak |
| Ramadan | Whitsun |
| Rama Naumi | Winter Festival |
| Rogation | Yom Kippur |
| Rosh Hashanah | Yuan Tan |
| Septuagesima | |

revel in ≠ dislike 2 = look forward to, fancy, delight in

● NOUN 1 = enjoyment, liking, love, taste, fancy, penchant, fondness, gusto ≠ distaste

2 = condiment, seasoning, sauce

**reluctance** = unwillingness, dislike, loathing, distaste, aversion, disinclination, repugnance

**reluctant** 1 = unwilling, hesitant, loath, disinclined, unenthusiastic ≠ willing

---

### Word Power

**reluctant** – *Reticent* is quite commonly used nowadays as a synonym of *reluctant* and followed by *to* and a verb. In careful writing it is advisable to avoid this use, since many people would regard it as mistaken.

---

**rely on** 1 = depend on, lean on

2 = be confident of, bank on, trust, count on, bet on

**remain** 1 = stay, continue, go on, stand, dwell 2 = stay behind, wait, delay ≠ go 3 = continue, be left, linger

**remainder** = rest, remains, balance, excess, surplus, remnant, residue, leavings

**remains** 1 = remnants, leftovers, rest, debris, residue, dregs, leavings 2 = corpse, body, carcass, cadaver 3 = relics

**remark** VERB 1 = comment, say, state, reflect, mention, declare, observe, pass comment

2 = notice, note, observe, perceive, see, mark, make out, espy

● NOUN = comment, observation, reflection, statement, utterance

**remarkable** = extraordinary, striking, outstanding, wonderful, rare, unusual, surprising, notable ≠ ordinary

**remedy** NOUN = <u>cure</u>, treatment, medicine, nostrum

● VERB = <u>put right</u>, rectify, fix, correct, set to rights

**remember** 1 = <u>recall</u>, think back to, recollect, reminisce about, call to mind ≠ forget 2 = <u>bear in mind</u>, keep in mind 3 = <u>look back (on)</u>, commemorate

**remembrance**
1 = <u>commemoration</u>, memorial
2 = <u>souvenir</u>, token, reminder, monument, memento, keepsake
3 = <u>memory</u>, recollection, thought, recall, reminiscence

**remind** = <u>jog your memory</u>, prompt, make you remember

**reminiscent** = <u>suggestive</u>, evocative, similar

**remnant** = <u>remainder</u>, remains, trace, fragment, end, rest, residue, leftovers

**remorse** = <u>regret</u>, shame, guilt, grief, sorrow, anguish, repentance, contrition

**remote** 1 = <u>distant</u>, far, isolated, out-of-the-way, secluded, inaccessible, in the middle of nowhere ≠ nearby 2 = <u>far</u>, distant 3 = <u>slight</u>, small, outside, unlikely, slim, faint, doubtful, dubious ≠ strong 4 = <u>aloof</u>, cold, reserved, withdrawn, distant, abstracted, detached, uncommunicative

≠ outgoing

**removal** 1 = <u>extraction</u>, withdrawal, uprooting, eradication, dislodgment, taking away or off or out 2 = <u>dismissal</u>, expulsion, elimination, ejection 3 = <u>move</u>, transfer, departure, relocation, flitting (Scot. & Northern English dialect)

**remove** 1 = <u>take out</u>, withdraw, extract ≠ insert 2 = <u>take off</u> ≠ put on 3 = <u>erase</u>, eliminate, take out 4 = <u>dismiss</u>, eliminate, get rid of, discharge, abolish, expel, throw out, oust ≠ appoint 5 = <u>get rid of</u>, erase, eradicate, expunge 6 = <u>take away</u>, detach, displace ≠ put back 7 = <u>delete</u>, get rid of, erase, excise 8 = <u>move</u>, depart, relocate, flit (Scot. & Northern English dialect)

**renaissance** or **renascence** = <u>rebirth</u>, revival, restoration, renewal, resurgence, reappearance, reawakening

**rend** (Literary) = <u>tear</u>, rip, separate, wrench, rupture

**render** 1 = <u>make</u>, cause to become, leave 2 = <u>provide</u>, give, pay, present, supply, submit, tender, hand out 3 = <u>represent</u>, portray, depict, do, give, play, act, perform

**renew** 1 = <u>recommence</u>, continue, extend, repeat, resume, reopen, recreate, reaffirm

2 = reaffirm, resume, recommence 3 = replace, refresh, replenish, restock 4 = restore, repair, overhaul, mend, refurbish, renovate, refit, modernize

**renounce** 1 = disown, quit, forsake, recant, forswear, abjure 2 = disclaim, deny, give up, relinquish, waive, abjure ≠ assert

**renovate** = restore, repair, refurbish, do up (informal), renew, overhaul, refit, modernize

**renowned** = famous, noted, celebrated, well-known, distinguished, esteemed, notable, eminent ≠ unknown

**rent[1]** VERB 1 = hire, lease 2 = let, lease
● NOUN = hire, rental, lease, fee, payment

**rent[2]** 1 = tear, split, rip, slash, slit, gash, hole 2 = opening, hole

**repair** VERB 1 = mend, fix, restore, heal, patch, renovate, patch up ≠ damage 2 = put right, make up for, compensate for, rectify, redress
● NOUN 1 = mend, restoration, overhaul 2 = darn, mend, patch 3 = condition, state, form, shape (informal)

**repay** = pay back, refund, settle up, return, square, compensate, reimburse, recompense

**repeal** VERB = abolish, reverse, revoke, annul, recall, cancel, invalidate, nullify ≠ pass
● NOUN = abolition, cancellation, annulment, invalidation, rescindment ≠ passing

**repeat** VERB 1 = reiterate, restate 2 = retell, echo, replay, reproduce, rerun, reshow
● NOUN 1 = repetition, echo, reiteration 2 = rerun, replay, reshowing

### Word Power

**repeat** – Since the sense of *again* is already contained within the *re-* part of the word *repeat*, it is unnecessary to say that something is *repeated again*.

**repeatedly** = over and over, often, frequently, many times

**repel** 1 = drive off, fight, resist, parry, hold off, rebuff, ward off, repulse ≠ submit to 2 = disgust, offend, revolt, sicken, nauseate, gross out (U.S. slang) ≠ delight

**repertoire** = range, list, stock, supply, store, repertory

**repetition** 1 = recurrence, repeating, echo 2 = repeating, replication, restatement, reiteration, tautology

**replace** 1 = take the place of, follow, succeed, oust, take over from, supersede, supplant 2 = substitute, change, exchange, switch, swap **3** = <u>put back</u>, restore

**replacement 1** = <u>replacing</u>
**2** = <u>successor</u>, double, substitute,
stand-in, proxy, surrogate,
understudy

**replica 1** = <u>reproduction</u>, model,
copy, imitation, facsimile, carbon
copy ≠ original **2** = <u>duplicate</u>,
copy, carbon copy

**replicate** = <u>copy</u>, reproduce,
recreate, mimic, duplicate,
reduplicate

**reply** VERB **1** = <u>answer</u>, respond,
retort, counter, rejoin, retaliate,
reciprocate
● NOUN = <u>answer</u>, response,
reaction, counter, retort,
retaliation, counterattack,
rejoinder

**report** VERB **1** = <u>inform of</u>,
communicate, recount **2** *often
with on* = <u>communicate</u>, tell,
state, detail, describe, relate,
broadcast, pass on **3** = <u>present
yourself</u>, come, appear, arrive,
turn up
● NOUN **1** = <u>article</u>, story, piece,
write-up **2** = <u>account</u>, record,
statement, communication,
description, narrative **3** *often
plural* = <u>news</u>, word **4** = <u>bang</u>,
sound, crack, noise, blast, boom,
explosion, discharge **5** = <u>rumour</u>,
talk, buzz, gossip, hearsay

**reporter** = <u>journalist</u>, writer,
correspondent, hack (*derogatory*),

pressman, journo (*slang*)

**represent 1** = <u>act for</u>, speak for
**2** = <u>stand for</u>, serve as
**3** = <u>express</u>, correspond to,
symbolize, mean **4** = <u>exemplify</u>,
embody, symbolize, typify,
personify, epitomize **5** = <u>depict</u>,
show, describe, picture, illustrate,
outline, portray, denote

**representation 1** = <u>picture</u>,
model, image, portrait,
illustration, likeness **2** = <u>portrayal</u>,
depiction, account, description

**representative** NOUN
**1** = <u>delegate</u>, member, agent,
deputy, proxy, spokesman *or*
spokeswoman **2** = <u>agent</u>,
salesman, rep, commercial
traveller
● ADJECTIVE **1** = <u>typical</u>,
characteristic, archetypal,
exemplary ≠ uncharacteristic
**2** = <u>symbolic</u>

**repress 1** = <u>control</u>, suppress,
hold back, bottle up, check, curb,
restrain, inhibit ≠ release **2** = <u>hold
back</u>, suppress, stifle **3** = <u>subdue</u>,
abuse, wrong, persecute, quell,
subjugate, maltreat ≠ liberate

**repression 1** = <u>subjugation</u>,
control, constraint, domination,
tyranny, despotism
**2** = <u>suppression</u>, crushing,
quashing **3** = <u>inhibition</u>, control,
restraint, bottling up

**reprieve** VERB = <u>grant a stay of</u>

execution to, pardon, let off the hook (*slang*)

● NOUN = <u>stay of execution</u>, amnesty, pardon, remission, deferment, postponement of punishment

**reproduce** 1 = <u>copy</u>, recreate, replicate, duplicate, match, mirror, echo, imitate 2 = <u>print</u>, copy 3 (*Biology*) = <u>breed</u>, procreate, multiply, spawn, propagate

**reproduction** 1 = <u>copy</u>, picture, print, replica, imitation, duplicate, facsimile ≠ original 2 (*Biology*) = <u>breeding</u>, increase, generation, multiplication

**reptile** ► reptiles

**Republican** ADJECTIVE = <u>right-wing</u>, Conservative

● NOUN = <u>right-winger</u>, Conservative

**reputation** = <u>name</u>, standing, character, esteem, stature, renown, repute

**request** VERB 1 = <u>ask for</u>, appeal for, put in for, demand, desire 2 = <u>invite</u>, entreat 3 = <u>seek</u>, ask (for), solicit

● NOUN 1 = <u>appeal</u>, call, demand, plea, desire, entreaty, suit 2 = <u>asking</u>, plea

**require** 1 = <u>need</u>, crave, want, miss, lack, wish, desire 2 = <u>order</u>, demand, command, compel, exact, oblige, call upon, insist upon 3 = <u>ask</u>

> ## Word Power
>
> **require** – The use of *require to* as in *I require to see the manager* or *you require to complete a special form* is thought by many people to be incorrect. Useful alternatives are: *I need to see the manager* and *you are required to complete a special form.*

**requirement** = <u>necessity</u>, demand, stipulation, want, need, must, essential, prerequisite

**rescue** VERB 1 = <u>save</u>, get out, release, deliver, recover, liberate ≠ desert 2 = <u>salvage</u>, deliver, redeem

● NOUN = <u>saving</u>, salvage, deliverance, release, recovery, liberation, salvation, redemption

**research** NOUN = <u>investigation</u>, study, analysis, examination, probe, exploration

● VERB = <u>investigate</u>, study, examine, explore, probe, analyse

**resemblance** = <u>similarity</u>, correspondence, parallel, likeness, kinship, sameness, similitude ≠ dissimilarity

**resemble** = <u>be like</u>, look like, mirror, parallel, be similar to, bear a resemblance to

**resent** = <u>be bitter about</u>, object to, grudge, begrudge, take exception to, take offence at ≠ be

## Reptiles

adder
agama
agamid
alligator
amphisbaena
anaconda or (*Caribbean*) camoodi
asp
bandy-bandy
black snake or red-bellied black snake
blind snake
blue tongue
boa
boa constrictor
box turtle
brown snake or (*Austral.*) mallee snake
bull snake or gopher snake
bushmaster
carpet snake or python
cayman or caiman
chameleon
chuckwalla
cobra
constrictor
copperhead
coral snake
crocodile
death adder or deaf adder
diamondback, diamondback terrapin, or diamondback turtle
diamond snake or diamond python
elapid
fer-de-lance
frill-necked lizard, frilled lizard, bicycle lizard, cycling lizard, or (*Austral. informal*) frillie
gaboon viper
garter snake
gecko
giant tortoise
Gila monster
glass snake
goanna, bungarra (*Austral.*), or go (*Austral. informal*)
grass snake
green turtle
harlequin snake
hawksbill or hawksbill turtle
hognose snake or puff adder
horned toad or lizard
horned viper
iguana
jew lizard, bearded lizard, or bearded dragon
king cobra or hamadryad
king snake
Komodo dragon or Komodo lizard
krait
leatherback or (*Brit.*) leathery turtle
lizard
loggerhead or loggerhead turtle
mamba
massasauga
milk snake
monitor
mud turtle
ngarara (*N.Z.*)

## Reptiles (continued)

| | |
|---|---|
| perentie or perenty | snake |
| pit viper | snapping turtle |
| puff adder | soft-shelled turtle |
| python | taipan |
| rat snake | terrapin |
| rattlesnake or (*U.S. & Canad. informal*) rattler | tiger snake |
| rock snake, rock python, amethystine python, or Schneider python | tokay |
| | tortoise |
| | tree snake |
| saltwater crocodile or (*Austral. informal*) saltie | tuatara or (*technical*) sphenodon (*N.Z.*) |
| sand lizard | turtle |
| sand viper | viper |
| sea snake | wall lizard |
| sidewinder | water moccasin, moccasin, or cottonmouth |
| skink | water snake |
| slowworm or blindworm | whip snake |
| smooth snake | |

content with

**resentment** = <u>bitterness</u>, indignation, ill feeling, ill will, grudge, animosity, pique, rancour

**reservation** 1 *often plural* = <u>doubt</u>, scruples, hesitancy 2 = <u>reserve</u>, territory, preserve, sanctuary

**reserve** VERB 1 = <u>book</u>, prearrange, engage 2 = <u>put by</u>, secure 3 = <u>keep</u>, hold, save, store, retain, set aside, stockpile, hoard
● NOUN 1 = <u>store</u>, fund, savings, stock, supply, reservoir, hoard, cache 2 = <u>park</u>, reservation,

preserve, sanctuary, tract, forest park (*N.Z.*) 3 = <u>shyness</u>, silence, restraint, constraint, reticence, secretiveness, taciturnity 4 = <u>reservation</u>, doubt, delay, uncertainty, indecision, hesitancy, vacillation, irresolution
● ADJECTIVE = <u>substitute</u>, extra, spare, secondary, fall-back, auxiliary

**reserved** 1 = <u>uncommunicative</u>, retiring, silent, shy, restrained, secretive, reticent, taciturn ≠ uninhibited 2 = <u>set aside</u>, taken, kept, held, booked, retained, engaged, restricted

**reservoir** 1 = <u>lake</u>, pond, basin 2 = <u>store</u>, stock, source, supply, reserves, pool

**reside** (*Formal*) = <u>live</u>, lodge, dwell, stay, abide ≠ visit

**residence** = <u>home</u>, house, dwelling, place, flat, lodging, abode, habitation

**resident** 1 = <u>inhabitant</u>, citizen, local ≠ nonresident 2 = <u>tenant</u>, occupant, lodger 3 = <u>guest</u>, lodger

**residue** = <u>remainder</u>, remains, remnant, leftovers, rest, extra, excess, surplus

**resign** VERB 1 = <u>quit</u>, leave, step down (*informal*), vacate, abdicate, give *or* hand in your notice 2 = <u>give up</u>, abandon, yield, surrender, relinquish, renounce, forsake, forgo
● PHRASES **resign yourself to something** = <u>accept</u>, succumb to, submit to, give in to, yield to, acquiesce to

**resignation** 1 = <u>leaving</u>, departure, abandonment, abdication 2 = <u>acceptance</u>, patience, submission, compliance, endurance, passivity, acquiescence, sufferance ≠ resistance

**resigned** = <u>stoical</u>, patient, subdued, long-suffering, compliant, unresisting

**resist** 1 = <u>oppose</u>, battle against, combat, defy, stand up to, hinder ≠ accept 2 = <u>refrain from</u>, avoid, keep from, forgo, abstain from, forbear ≠ indulge in 3 = <u>withstand</u>, be proof against

**resistance** 1 = <u>opposition</u>, hostility, aversion 2 = <u>fighting</u>, fight, battle, struggle, defiance, obstruction, impediment, hindrance

**resistant** 1 = <u>opposed</u>, hostile, unwilling, intractable, antagonistic, intransigent 2 = <u>impervious</u>, hard, strong, tough, unaffected

**resolution** 1 = <u>declaration</u> 2 = <u>decision</u>, resolve, intention, aim, purpose, determination, intent 3 = <u>determination</u>, purpose, resolve, tenacity, perseverance, willpower, firmness, steadfastness

**resolve** VERB 1 = <u>work out</u>, answer, clear up, crack, fathom 2 = <u>decide</u>, determine, agree, purpose, intend, fix, conclude
● NOUN 1 = <u>determination</u>, resolution, willpower, firmness, steadfastness, resoluteness ≠ indecision 2 = <u>decision</u>, resolution, objective, purpose, intention

**resort** 1 = <u>holiday centre</u>, spot, retreat, haunt, tourist centre 2 = <u>recourse to</u>, reference to

**resound** 1 = <u>echo</u>, resonate,

reverberate, re-echo 2 = ring

**resounding** = echoing, full, ringing, powerful, booming, reverberating, resonant, sonorous

**resource** NOUN 1 = facility 2 = means, course, resort, device, expedient

● PLURAL NOUN 1 = funds, holdings, money, capital, riches, assets, wealth 2 = reserves, supplies, stocks

**respect** VERB 1 = think highly of, value, honour, admire, esteem, look up to, defer to, have a good or high opinion of 2 = show consideration for, honour, observe, heed 3 = abide by, follow, observe, comply with, obey, heed, keep to, adhere to ≠ disregard

● NOUN 1 = regard, honour, recognition, esteem, admiration, estimation ≠ contempt 2 = consideration, kindness, deference, tact, thoughtfulness, considerateness 3 = particular, way, point, matter, sense, detail, feature, aspect

**respectable** 1 = honourable, good, decent, worthy, upright, honest, reputable, estimable ≠ disreputable 2 = decent, neat, spruce 3 = reasonable, considerable, substantial, fair, ample, appreciable, sizable or sizeable ≠ small

**respective** = specific, own, individual, particular, relevant

**respite** = pause, break, rest, relief, halt, interval, recess, lull

**respond** 1 = answer, return, reply, counter, retort, rejoin ≠ remain silent 2 often with to = reply to, answer 3 = react, retaliate, reciprocate

**response** = answer, return, reply, reaction, feedback, retort, counterattack, rejoinder

**responsibility** 1 = duty, business, job, role, task, accountability, answerability 2 = fault, blame, liability, guilt, culpability 3 = obligation, duty, liability, charge, care 4 = authority, power, importance, mana (N.Z.) 5 = job, task, function, role 6 = level-headedness, rationality, dependability, trustworthiness, conscientiousness, sensibleness

**responsible** 1 = to blame, guilty, at fault, culpable 2 = in charge, in control, in authority 3 = accountable, liable, answerable ≠ unaccountable 4 = sensible, reliable, rational, dependable, trustworthy, level-headed ≠ unreliable

**responsive** = sensitive, open, alive, susceptible, receptive, reactive, impressionable ≠ unresponsive

**rest¹** VERB 1 = <u>relax</u>, take it easy, sit down, be at ease, put your feet up, outspan (*S. African*) ≠ work 2 = <u>stop</u>, have a break, break off, take a breather (*informal*), halt, cease ≠ keep going 3 = <u>place</u>, repose, sit, lean, prop ≠ <u>be placed</u>, sit, lie, be supported, recline

● NOUN 1 = <u>relaxation</u>, repose, leisure ≠ work 2 = <u>pause</u>, break, stop, halt, interval, respite, lull, interlude 3 = <u>refreshment</u>, release, relief, ease, comfort, cure, remedy, solace 4 = <u>inactivity</u> 5 = <u>support</u>, stand, base, holder, prop 6 = <u>calm</u>, tranquillity, stillness

**rest²** = <u>remainder</u>, remains, excess, remnants, others, balance, surplus, residue

**restaurant** = <u>café</u>, diner (*chiefly U.S. & Canad.*), bistro, cafeteria, tearoom, eatery *or* eaterie

**restless** 1 = <u>unsettled</u>, nervous, edgy, fidgeting, on edge, restive, jumpy, fidgety ≠ relaxed 2 = <u>moving</u>, wandering, unsettled, unstable, roving, transient, nomadic ≠ settled

**restoration** 1 = <u>reinstatement</u>, return, revival, restitution, re-establishment, replacement ≠ abolition 2 = <u>repair</u>, reconstruction, renewal, renovation, revitalization

≠ demolition

**restore** 1 = <u>reinstate</u>, re-establish, reintroduce ≠ abolish 2 = <u>revive</u>, build up, strengthen, refresh, revitalize ≠ make worse 3 = <u>re-establish</u>, replace, reinstate, give back 4 = <u>repair</u>, refurbish, renovate, reconstruct, fix (up), renew, rebuild, mend ≠ demolish 5 = <u>return</u>, replace, recover, bring back, send back, hand back

**restrain** 1 = <u>hold back</u>, control, check, contain, restrict, curb, hamper, hinder ≠ encourage 2 = <u>control</u>, inhibit

**restrained** 1 = <u>controlled</u>, moderate, self-controlled, calm, mild, undemonstrative ≠ hot-headed 2 = <u>unobtrusive</u>, discreet, subdued, tasteful, quiet ≠ garish

**restraint** 1 = <u>limitation</u>, limit, check, ban, embargo, curb, rein, interdict ≠ freedom 2 = <u>self-control</u>, self-discipline, self-restraint, self-possession ≠ self-indulgence 3 = <u>constraint</u>, limitation, inhibition, control, restriction

**restrict** 1 = <u>limit</u>, regulate, curb, ration ≠ widen 2 = <u>hamper</u>, handicap, restrain, inhibit

**restriction** 1 = <u>control</u>, rule, regulation, curb, restraint, confinement 2 = <u>limitation</u>, handicap, inhibition

**result** NOUN 1 = <u>consequence</u>,

effect, outcome, end result, product, sequel, upshot ≠ cause 2 = **outcome**, end

● VERB = **arise**, follow, issue, happen, appear, develop, spring, derive

**resume** = **begin again**, continue, go on with, proceed with, carry on, reopen, restart ≠ discontinue

**résumé** = **summary**, synopsis, précis, rundown, recapitulation

**resumption** = **continuation**, carrying on, reopening, renewal, restart, resurgence, re-establishment

**resurgence** = **revival**, return, renaissance, resurrection, resumption, rebirth, re-emergence

**resurrect** 1 = **revive**, renew, bring back, reintroduce
2 = **restore to life**, raise from the dead

**resurrection** 1 = **revival**, restoration, renewal, resurgence, return, renaissance, rebirth, reappearance ≠ killing off
2 usually caps = **raising or rising from the dead**, return from the dead ≠ demise

**retain** 1 = **maintain**, reserve, preserve, keep up, continue to have 2 = **keep**, save ≠ let go

**retaliate** = **pay someone back**, hit back, strike back, reciprocate, take revenge, get even with

(informal), get your own back (informal) ≠ turn the other cheek

**retaliation** = **revenge**, repayment, vengeance, reprisal, an eye for an eye, reciprocation, requital, counterblow

**retard** = **slow down**, check, arrest, delay, handicap, hinder, impede, set back ≠ speed up

**retire** 1 = **stop working**, give up work 2 = **withdraw**, leave, exit, go away, depart 3 = **go to bed**, turn in (informal), hit the sack (slang), hit the hay (slang)

**retirement** = **withdrawal**, retreat, privacy, solitude, seclusion

**retiring** = **shy**, reserved, quiet, timid, unassuming, self-effacing, bashful, unassertive ≠ outgoing

**retort** VERB = **reply**, return, answer, respond, counter, come back with, riposte

● NOUN = **reply**, answer, response, comeback, riposte, rejoinder

**retreat** VERB = **withdraw**, back off, draw back, leave, go back, depart, fall back, pull back ≠ advance

● NOUN 1 = **flight**, retirement, departure, withdrawal, evacuation ≠ advance 2 = **refuge**, haven, shelter, sanctuary, hideaway, seclusion

**retrieve** 1 = **get back**, regain, recover, restore, recapture

2 = <u>redeem</u>, save, win back, recoup

**retrospect** = <u>hindsight</u>, review, re-examination ≠ foresight

**return** VERB 1 = <u>come back</u>, go back, retreat, turn back, revert, reappear ≠ depart 2 = <u>put back</u>, replace, restore, reinstate ≠ keep 3 = <u>give back</u>, repay, refund, pay back, reimburse, recompense ≠ keep 4 = <u>recur</u>, repeat, persist, revert, happen again, reappear, come again 5 = <u>elect</u>, choose, vote in

● NOUN 1 = <u>reappearance</u> ≠ departure 2 = <u>restoration</u>, reinstatement, re-establishment ≠ removal 3 = <u>recurrence</u>, repetition, reappearance, reversion, persistence 4 = <u>profit</u>, interest, gain, income, revenue, yield, proceeds, takings 5 = <u>statement</u>, report, form, list, account, summary

**revamp** = <u>renovate</u>, restore, overhaul, refurbish, do up (*informal*), recondition

**reveal** 1 = <u>make known</u>, disclose, give away, make public, tell, announce, proclaim, let out ≠ keep secret 2 = <u>show</u>, display, exhibit, unveil, uncover, manifest, unearth, unmask ≠ hide

**revel** VERB = <u>celebrate</u>, carouse, live it up (*informal*), make merry

● NOUN *often plural*

= <u>merrymaking</u>, party, celebration, spree, festivity, carousal

**revelation** 1 = <u>disclosure</u>, news, announcement, publication, leak, confession, divulgence 2 = <u>exhibition</u>, publication, exposure, unveiling, uncovering, unearthing, proclamation

**revenge** NOUN = <u>retaliation</u>, vengeance, reprisal, retribution, an eye for an eye

● VERB = <u>avenge</u>, repay, take revenge for, get your own back for (*informal*)

**revenue** = <u>income</u>, returns, profits, gain, yield, proceeds, receipts, takings ≠ expenditure

**revere** = <u>be in awe of</u>, respect, honour, worship, reverence, exalt, look up to, venerate ≠ despise

**reverse** VERB 1 (*Law*) = <u>change</u>, cancel, overturn, overthrow, undo, repeal, quash, revoke ≠ implement 2 = <u>turn round</u>, turn over, turn upside down, upend 3 = <u>transpose</u>, change, move, exchange, transfer, switch, shift, alter 4 = <u>go backwards</u>, retreat, back up, turn back, move backwards, back ≠ go forward

● NOUN 1 = <u>opposite</u>, contrary, converse, inverse 2 = <u>misfortune</u>, blow, failure, disappointment, setback, hardship, reversal, adversity 3 = <u>back</u>, rear, other

side, wrong side, underside
≠ front
● ADJECTIVE = opposite, contrary,
converse

revert 1 = go back, return, come
back, resume 2 = return

> ### Word Power
>
> revert – Since the concept
> *back* is already contained in the
> re- part of the word *revert*, it is
> unnecessary to say that
> someone *reverts back* to a
> particular type of behaviour.

review NOUN 1 = survey, study,
analysis, examination, scrutiny
2 = critique, commentary,
evaluation, notice, criticism,
judgment 3 = inspection, parade,
march past 4 = magazine,
journal, periodical, zine (informal)
● VERB 1 = reconsider, revise,
rethink, reassess, re-examine, re-
evaluate, think over 2 = assess,
study, judge, evaluate, criticize
3 = inspect, check, survey,
examine, vet 4 = look back on,
remember, recall, reflect on,
recollect

reviewer = critic, judge,
commentator

revise 1 = change, review
2 = edit, correct, alter, update,
amend, rework, redo, emend
3 = study, go over, run through,

cram (informal), swot up on (Brit.
informal)

revision 1 = emendation,
updating, correction 2 = change,
amendment 3 = studying,
cramming (informal), swotting
(Brit. informal), homework

revival 1 = resurgence ≠ decline
2 = reawakening, renaissance,
renewal, resurrection, rebirth,
revitalization

revive 1 = revitalize, restore,
renew, rekindle, invigorate,
reanimate 2 = bring round,
awaken 3 = come round, recover
4 = refresh ≠ exhaust

revolt NOUN 1 = uprising, rising,
revolution, rebellion, mutiny,
insurrection, insurgency
● VERB 1 = rebel, rise up, resist,
mutiny 2 = disgust, sicken, repel,
repulse, nauseate, gross out (U.S.
slang), turn your stomach, make
your flesh creep

revolting = disgusting, foul,
horrible, sickening, horrid,
repellent, repulsive, nauseating,
yucko (Austral. slang) ≠ delightful

revolution 1 = revolt, rising,
coup, rebellion, uprising, mutiny,
insurgency 2 = transformation,
shift, innovation, upheaval,
reformation, sea change
3 = rotation, turn, cycle, circle,
spin, lap, circuit, orbit

revolutionary ADJECTIVE

1 = <u>rebel</u>, radical, extremist, subversive, insurgent
≠ reactionary 2 = <u>innovative</u>, new, different, novel, radical, progressive, drastic, ground-breaking ≠ conventional
● NOUN = <u>rebel</u>, insurgent, revolutionist ≠ reactionary

**revolve** 1 = <u>go round</u>, circle, orbit 2 = <u>rotate</u>, turn, wheel, spin, twist, whirl

**reward** NOUN 1 = <u>punishment</u>, retribution, comeuppance (slang), just deserts 2 = <u>payment</u>, return, prize, wages, compensation, bonus, premium, repayment ≠ penalty
● VERB = <u>compensate</u>, pay, repay, recompense, remunerate ≠ penalize

**rewarding** = <u>satisfying</u>, fulfilling, valuable, profitable, productive, worthwhile, beneficial, enriching ≠ unrewarding

**rhetoric** 1 = <u>hyperbole</u>, bombast, wordiness, verbosity, grandiloquence, magniloquence
2 = <u>oratory</u>, eloquence, public speaking, speech-making, elocution, declamation, grandiloquence, whaikorero (N.Z.)

**rhetorical** = <u>high-flown</u>, bombastic, verbose, oratorical, grandiloquent, declamatory, arty-farty (informal), magniloquent

**rhyme** = <u>poem</u>, song, verse, ode

**rhythm** 1 = <u>beat</u>, swing, accent, pulse, tempo, cadence, lilt
2 = <u>metre</u>, time

**rich** 1 = <u>wealthy</u>, affluent, well-off, loaded (slang), prosperous, well-heeled (informal), well-to-do, moneyed ≠ poor 2 = <u>well-stocked</u>, full, productive, ample, abundant, plentiful, copious, well-supplied ≠ scarce 3 = <u>full-bodied</u>, sweet, fatty, tasty, creamy, luscious, succulent ≠ bland
4 = <u>fruitful</u>, productive, fertile, prolific ≠ barren 5 = <u>abounding</u>, luxurious, lush, abundant

**riches** 1 = <u>wealth</u>, assets, plenty, fortune, substance, treasure, affluence ≠ poverty
2 = <u>resources</u>, treasures

**richly** 1 = <u>elaborately</u>, lavishly, elegantly, splendidly, exquisitely, expensively, luxuriously, gorgeously 2 = <u>fully</u>, well, thoroughly, amply, appropriately, properly, suitably

**rid** VERB = <u>free</u>, clear, deliver, relieve, purge, unburden, make free, disencumber
● PHRASES get rid of something or someone
= <u>dispose of</u>, throw away or out, dump, remove, eliminate, expel, eject

**riddle**[1] 1 = <u>puzzle</u>, problem, conundrum, poser 2 = <u>enigma</u>, question, secret, mystery, puzzle, conundrum, teaser, problem

**riddle²** 1 = <u>pierce</u>, pepper, puncture, perforate, honeycomb 2 = <u>pervade</u>, fill, spread through

**riddled** = <u>filled</u>, spoilt, pervaded, infested, permeated

**ride** VERB 1 = <u>control</u>, handle, manage 2 = <u>travel</u>, be carried, go, move
● NOUN = <u>journey</u>, drive, trip, lift, outing, jaunt

**ridicule** VERB 1 = <u>laugh at</u>, mock, make fun of, sneer at, jeer at, deride, poke fun at, chaff
● NOUN = <u>mockery</u>, scorn, derision, laughter, jeer, chaff, gibe, raillery

**ridiculous** = <u>laughable</u>, stupid, silly, absurd, ludicrous, farcical, comical, risible ≠ sensible

**rife** = <u>widespread</u>, rampant, general, common, universal, frequent, prevalent, ubiquitous

**rifle** = <u>ransack</u>, rob, burgle, loot, strip, sack, plunder, pillage

**rift** 1 = <u>breach</u>, division, split, separation, falling out (*informal*), disagreement, quarrel 2 = <u>split</u>, opening, crack, gap, break, fault, flaw, cleft

**rig** VERB 1 = <u>fix</u>, engineer (*informal*), arrange, manipulate, tamper with, gerrymander 2 (*Nautical*) = <u>equip</u>, fit out, kit out, outfit, supply, furnish

● PHRASES **rig something up** = <u>set up</u>, build, construct, put up, arrange, assemble, put together, erect

**right** ADJECTIVE 1 = <u>correct</u>, true, genuine, accurate, exact, precise, valid, factual, dinkum (*Austral. & N.Z. informal*) ≠ wrong
2 = <u>proper</u>, done, becoming, seemly, fitting, fit, appropriate, suitable ≠ inappropriate 3 = <u>just</u>, good, fair, moral, proper, ethical, honest, equitable ≠ unfair
● ADVERB 1 = <u>correctly</u>, truly, precisely, exactly, genuinely, accurately ≠ wrongly 2 = <u>suitably</u>, fittingly, appropriately, properly, aptly ≠ improperly 3 = <u>exactly</u>, squarely, precisely 4 = <u>directly</u>, straight, precisely, exactly, unswervingly, without deviation, by the shortest route, in a beeline 5 = <u>straight</u>, directly, quickly, promptly, straightaway ≠ indirectly
● NOUN 1 = <u>prerogative</u>, business, power, claim, authority, due, freedom, licence 2 = <u>justice</u>, truth, fairness, legality, righteousness, lawfulness ≠ injustice
● VERB = <u>rectify</u>, settle, fix, correct, sort out, straighten, redress, put right

**right away** = <u>immediately</u>, now, directly, instantly, at once, straightaway, forthwith, pronto (*informal*)

**righteous** = <u>virtuous</u>, good, just, fair, moral, pure, ethical, upright ≠ wicked

**rigid** 1 = <u>strict</u>, set, fixed, exact, rigorous, stringent ≠ flexible
2 = <u>inflexible</u>, uncompromising, unbending 3 = <u>stiff</u>, inflexible, inelastic ≠ pliable

**rigorous** = <u>strict</u>, hard, demanding, tough, severe, exacting, harsh, stern ≠ soft

**rim** 1 = <u>edge</u>, lip, brim 2 = <u>border</u>, edge, trim 3 = <u>margin</u>, border, verge, brink

**ring¹** VERB 1 = <u>phone</u>, call, telephone, buzz (*informal, chiefly Brit.*) 2 = <u>chime</u>, sound, toll, reverberate, clang, peal
3 = <u>reverberate</u>
● NOUN 1 = <u>call</u>, phone call, buzz (*informal, chiefly Brit.*) 2 = <u>chime</u>, knell, peal

---

### Word Power

**ring** – *Rang* is the past tense of the verb *ring*, as in *he rang the bell*. *Rung* is the past participle, as in *he has already rung the bell*, and care should be taken not to use it as if it were a variant form of the past tense.

---

**ring²** NOUN 1 = <u>circle</u>, round, band, circuit, loop, hoop, halo 2 = <u>arena</u>, enclosure, circus, rink 3 = <u>gang</u>, group, association, band, circle, mob, syndicate, cartel

● VERB = <u>encircle</u>, surround, enclose, girdle, gird

**rinse** VERB = <u>wash</u>, clean, dip, splash, cleanse, bathe
● NOUN = <u>wash</u>, dip, splash, bath

**riot** NOUN 1 = <u>disturbance</u>, disorder, confusion, turmoil, upheaval, strife, turbulence, lawlessness 2 = <u>display</u>, show, splash, extravaganza, profusion 3 = <u>laugh</u>, joke, scream (*informal*), hoot (*informal*), lark
● VERB = <u>rampage</u>, run riot, go on the rampage
● PHRASES **run riot** 1 = <u>rampage</u>, go wild, be out of control
2 = <u>grow profusely</u>, spread like wildfire

**rip** VERB 1 = <u>tear</u>, cut, split, burst, rend, slash, claw, slit 2 = <u>be torn</u>, tear, split, burst
● NOUN = <u>tear</u>, cut, hole, split, rent, slash, slit, gash
● PHRASES **rip someone off** (*Slang*) = <u>cheat</u>, rob, con (*informal*), skin (*slang*), fleece, defraud, swindle

**ripe** 1 = <u>ripened</u>, seasoned, ready, mature, mellow ≠ unripe
2 = <u>right</u>, suitable 3 = <u>mature</u>
4 = <u>suitable</u>, timely, ideal, favourable, auspicious, opportune ≠ unsuitable

**rip-off** or **ripoff** (*Slang*) = <u>cheat</u>, con (*informal*), scam (*slang*), con trick (*informal*), fraud, theft, swindle

**rise** VERB 1 = get up, stand up, get to your feet 2 = arise 3 = go up, climb, ascend ≠ descend 4 = loom, tower 5 = get steeper, ascend, go uphill, slope upwards ≠ drop 6 = increase, mount ≠ decrease 7 = grow, go up, intensify 8 = rebel, revolt, mutiny 9 = advance, progress, get on, prosper
● NOUN 1 = upward slope, incline, elevation, ascent, kopje or koppie (*S. African*) 2 = increase, upturn, upswing, upsurge ≠ decrease 3 = pay increase, raise (*U.S.*), increment 4 = advancement, progress, climb, promotion
● PHRASES give rise to something = cause, produce, effect, result in, bring about

**risk** NOUN 1 = danger, chance, possibility, hazard 2 = gamble, chance, speculation, leap in the dark 3 = peril, jeopardy
● VERB 1 = stand a chance of 2 = dare, endanger, jeopardize, imperil, venture, gamble, hazard

**risky** = dangerous, hazardous, unsafe, perilous, uncertain, dodgy (*Brit., Austral., & N.Z. informal*), dicey (*informal*, *chiefly Brit.*), chancy (*informal*) ≠ safe

**rite** = ceremony, custom, ritual, practice, procedure, observance

**ritual** NOUN 1 = ceremony, rite,

observance 2 = custom, tradition, routine, convention, practice, procedure, habit, protocol, tikanga (*N.Z.*)
● ADJECTIVE = ceremonial, conventional, routine, customary, habitual

**rival** NOUN = opponent, competitor, contender, contestant, adversary ≠ supporter
● VERB = compete with, match, equal, compare with, come up to, be a match for
● ADJECTIVE = competing, conflicting, opposing

**rivalry** = competition, opposition, conflict, contest, contention

**river** 1 = stream, brook, creek, waterway, tributary, burn (*Scot.*) 2 = flow, rush, flood, spate, torrent

**riveting** = enthralling, gripping, fascinating, absorbing, captivating, hypnotic, engrossing, spellbinding

**road** 1 = roadway, highway, motorway, track, route, path, lane, pathway 2 = way, path

**roam** = wander, walk, range, travel, stray, ramble, prowl, rove

**roar** VERB 1 = thunder 2 = guffaw, laugh heartily, hoot, split your sides (*informal*) 3 = cry, shout, yell, howl, bellow, bawl, bay
● NOUN 1 = guffaw, hoot 2 = cry,

shout, yell, howl, outcry, bellow

**rob** 1 = steal from, hold up, mug (informal) 2 = raid, hold up, loot, plunder, burgle, pillage 3 = dispossess, con (informal), cheat, defraud 4 = deprive, do out of (informal)

**robber** = thief, raider, burglar, looter, fraud, cheat, bandit, plunderer

**robbery** 1 = burglary, raid, hold-up, rip-off (slang), stick-up (slang, chiefly U.S.) 2 = theft, stealing, mugging (informal), plunder, swindle, pillage, larceny

**robe** = gown, costume, habit

**robot** = machine, automaton, android, mechanical man

**robust** = strong, tough, powerful, fit, healthy, strapping, hardy, vigorous ≠ weak

**rock**[1] = stone, boulder

**rock**[2] 1 = sway, pitch, swing, reel, toss, lurch, roll 2 = shock, surprise, shake, stun, astonish, stagger, astound

**rocky**[1] = rough, rugged, stony, craggy

**rocky**[2] = unstable, shaky, wobbly, rickety, unsteady

**rod** 1 = stick, bar, pole, shaft, cane 2 = staff, baton, wand

**rodent ▸ rodents**

**rogue** 1 = scoundrel, crook (informal), villain, fraud, blackguard, skelm (S. African),

rorter (Austral. slang) 2 = scamp, rascal, scally (Northwest English dialect), nointer (Austral. slang)

**role** 1 = job, part, position, post, task, duty, function, capacity 2 = part, character, representation, portrayal

**roll** VERB 1 = turn, wheel, spin, go round, rotate, whirl, swivel 2 = trundle, go, move 3 = flow, run, course 4 often with up = wind, bind, wrap, swathe, envelop, furl, enfold 5 = level, even, press, smooth, flatten 6 = toss, rock, lurch, reel, tumble, sway

● NOUN 1 = rumble, boom, roar, thunder, reverberation 2 = register, record, list, index, census 3 = turn, spin, rotation, cycle, wheel, revolution, reel, whirl

**romance** 1 = love affair, relationship, affair, attachment, liaison, amour 2 = excitement, colour, charm, mystery, glamour, fascination 3 = story, tale, fantasy, legend, fairy tale, love story, melodrama

**romantic** ADJECTIVE 1 = loving, tender, passionate, fond, sentimental, amorous, icky (informal) ≠ unromantic 2 = idealistic, unrealistic, impractical, dreamy, starry-eyed ≠ realistic 3 = exciting, fascinating, mysterious, colourful,

---

## Rodents

| | |
|---|---|
| agouti | kangaroo rat |
| beaver | kiore (*N.Z.*) |
| capybara | lemming |
| cavy | Māori rat *or* (*N.Z.*) kiore |
| chinchilla | marmot |
| chipmunk | mouse |
| coypu *or* nutria | muskrat *or* musquash |
| desert rat | paca |
| dormouse | pack rat |
| fieldmouse | porcupine |
| flying squirrel | rat |
| gerbil, gerbille, *or* jerbil | red squirrel *or* chickaree |
| gopher *or* pocket gopher | spinifex hopping mouse *or* |
| gopher *or* ground squirrel | (*Austral.*) dargawarra |
| grey squirrel | springhaas |
| groundhog *or* woodchuck | squirrel |
| guinea pig *or* cavy | suslik *or* souslik |
| hamster | viscacha *or* vizcacha |
| harvest mouse | vole |
| hedgehog | water rat |
| house mouse | water vole *or* water rat |
| jerboa | |

---

glamorous ≠ unexciting
● NOUN = <u>idealist</u>, dreamer, sentimentalist

**romp** VERB = <u>frolic</u>, sport, have fun, caper, cavort, frisk, gambol
● NOUN = <u>frolic</u>, lark (*informal*), caper

**room** 1 = <u>chamber</u>, office, apartment 2 = <u>space</u>, area, capacity, extent, expanse
3 = <u>opportunity</u>, scope, leeway, chance, range, occasion, margin

**root**[1] NOUN 1 = <u>stem</u>, tuber, rhizome

2 = <u>source</u>, cause, heart, bottom, base, seat, seed, foundation
● PLURAL NOUN = <u>sense of</u> belonging, origins, heritage, birthplace, home, family, cradle
● PHRASES **root something** *or* **someone out** = <u>get rid of</u>, remove, eliminate, abolish, eradicate, do away with, weed out, exterminate

**root**[2] = <u>dig</u>, burrow, ferret

**rope** NOUN = <u>cord</u>, line, cable, strand, hawser

● PHRASES **know the ropes** = be experienced, be knowledgeable, be an old hand ◆ **rope someone in** or **into something** (*Brit.*) = persuade, involve, engage, enlist, talk into, inveigle

**rosy** ADJECTIVE 1 = glowing, blooming, radiant, ruddy, healthy-looking ≠ pale 2 = promising, encouraging, bright, optimistic, hopeful, cheerful, favourable, auspicious ≠ gloomy

● NOUN = pink, red

➤ **shades of red**

**rot** VERB 1 = decay, spoil, deteriorate, perish, decompose, moulder, go bad, putrefy

2 = crumble 3 = deteriorate, decline, waste away

● NOUN 1 = decay, decomposition, corruption, mould, blight, canker, putrefaction 2 (*Informal*) = nonsense, rubbish, drivel, twaddle, garbage (*chiefly U.S.*), trash, tripe (*informal*), claptrap (*informal*), bizzo (*Austral. slang*), bull's wool (*Austral. & N.Z. slang*)

(Related Words)
*adjective:* putrid

**rotate** 1 = revolve, turn, wheel, spin, reel, go round, swivel, pivot

2 = follow in sequence, switch, alternate, take turns

**rotation** 1 = revolution, turning, turn, wheel, spin, spinning, reel,

orbit 2 = sequence, switching, cycle, succession, alternation

**rotten** 1 = decaying, bad, rank, corrupt, sour, stinking, perished, festering, festy (*Austral. slang*) ≠ fresh 2 = crumbling, perished

3 (*Informal*) = despicable, mean, base, dirty, nasty, contemptible

4 (*Informal*) = inferior, poor, inadequate, duff (*Brit. informal*), unsatisfactory, lousy (*slang*), substandard, crummy (*slang*), bodger or bodgie (*Austral. slang*)

5 = corrupt, immoral, crooked (*informal*), dishonest, dishonourable, perfidious ≠ honourable

**rough** ADJECTIVE 1 = uneven, broken, rocky, irregular, jagged, bumpy, stony, craggy ≠ even

2 = boisterous, hard, tough, arduous 3 = ungracious, blunt, rude, coarse, brusque, uncouth, impolite, uncivil ≠ refined

4 = unpleasant, hard, difficult, tough, uncomfortable ≠ easy

5 = approximate, estimated ≠ exact 6 = vague, general, sketchy, imprecise, inexact

7 = basic, crude, unfinished, incomplete, imperfect, rudimentary, sketchy, unrefined ≠ complete 8 = stormy, wild, turbulent, choppy, squally ≠ calm

9 = harsh, tough, nasty, cruel, unfeeling ≠ gentle

● NOUN = outline, draft, mock-up,

preliminary sketch
● PHRASES **rough and ready**
1 = <u>makeshift</u>, crude, provisional, improvised, sketchy, stopgap
2 = <u>unrefined</u>, shabby, untidy, unkempt, unpolished, ill-groomed ◆ **rough something out** = <u>outline</u>, plan, draft, sketch

**round** NOUN 1 = <u>series</u>, session, cycle, sequence, succession
2 = <u>stage</u>, turn, level, period, division, session, lap 3 = <u>sphere</u>, ball, band, ring, circle, disc, globe, orb 4 = <u>course</u>, tour, circuit, beat, series, schedule, routine
● ADJECTIVE 1 = <u>spherical</u>, rounded, curved, circular, cylindrical, rotund, globular
2 = <u>plump</u>, full, ample, fleshy, rotund, full-fleshed
● VERB = <u>go round</u>, circle, skirt, flank, bypass, encircle, turn
● PHRASES **round something or someone up** = <u>gather</u>, muster, group, drive, collect, rally, herd, marshal

**roundabout** 1 = <u>indirect</u>, devious, tortuous, circuitous, evasive, discursive ≠ direct
2 = <u>oblique</u>, implied, indirect, circuitous

**roundup** = <u>muster</u>, collection, rally, assembly, herding

**rouse** 1 = <u>wake up</u>, call, wake, awaken 2 = <u>excite</u>, move, stir, provoke, anger, animate, agitate, inflame 3 = <u>stimulate</u>, provoke, incite

**rousing** = <u>lively</u>, moving, spirited, exciting, inspiring, stirring, stimulating ≠ dull

**rout** VERB = <u>defeat</u>, beat, overthrow, thrash, destroy, crush, conquer, wipe the floor with (*informal*)
● NOUN = <u>defeat</u>, beating, overthrow, thrashing, pasting (*slang*), debacle, drubbing

**route** 1 = <u>way</u>, course, road, direction, path, journey, itinerary
2 = <u>beat</u>, circuit

---

### Word Power

**route** – When adding *-ing* to the verb *route* to form the present participle, it is more conventional, and clearer, to keep the final *e* from the end of the verb stem: *routeing*. The spelling *routing* in this sense is also possible, but keeping the *e* distinguishes it from *routing*, which is the participle formed from the verb *rout* meaning 'to defeat'.

---

**routine** NOUN = <u>procedure</u>, programme, order, practice, method, pattern, custom
● ADJECTIVE 1 = <u>usual</u>, standard, normal, customary, ordinary, typical, everyday, habitual ≠ unusual 2 = <u>boring</u>, dull, predictable, tedious, tiresome,

humdrum

**row¹** NOUN = <u>line</u>, bank, range, series, file, string, column

● PHRASES **in a row** = <u>consecutively</u>, running, in turn, one after the other, successively, in sequence

**row²** NOUN (*Informal*) 1 = <u>quarrel</u>, dispute, argument, squabble, tiff, trouble, brawl 2 = <u>disturbance</u>, noise, racket, uproar, commotion, rumpus, tumult

● VERB = <u>quarrel</u>, fight, argue, dispute, squabble, wrangle

**royal** 1 = <u>regal</u>, kingly, queenly, princely, imperial, sovereign 2 = <u>splendid</u>, grand, impressive, magnificent, majestic, stately

**rub** VERB 1 = <u>stroke</u>, massage, caress 2 = <u>polish</u>, clean, shine, wipe, scour 3 = <u>chafe</u>, scrape, grate, abrade

● NOUN 1 = <u>massage</u>, caress, kneading 2 = <u>polish</u>, stroke, shine, wipe

● PHRASES **rub something out** = <u>erase</u>, remove, cancel, wipe out, delete, obliterate, efface

**rubbish** 1 = <u>waste</u>, refuse, scrap, junk (*informal*), litter, garbage (chiefly U.S.), trash, lumber 2 = <u>nonsense</u>, garbage (chiefly U.S.), twaddle, rot, trash, hot air (*informal*), tripe (*informal*), claptrap (*informal*), bizzo (*Austral. slang*), bull's wool (*Austral. & N.Z.*)

slang)

**rude** 1 = <u>impolite</u>, insulting, cheeky, abusive, disrespectful, impertinent, insolent, impudent ≠ polite 2 = <u>uncivilized</u>, rough, coarse, brutish, boorish, uncouth, loutish, graceless 3 = <u>vulgar</u> ≠ refined 4 = <u>unpleasant</u>, sharp, sudden, harsh, startling, abrupt 5 = <u>roughly-made</u>, simple, rough, raw, crude, primitive, makeshift, artless ≠ well-made

**rue** (*Literary*) = <u>regret</u>, mourn, lament, repent, be sorry for, kick yourself for

**ruffle** 1 = <u>disarrange</u>, disorder, mess up, rumple, tousle, dishevel 2 = <u>annoy</u>, upset, irritate, agitate, nettle, fluster, peeve (*informal*) ≠ calm

**rugged** 1 = <u>rocky</u>, broken, rough, craggy, difficult, ragged, irregular, uneven ≠ even 2 = <u>strong-featured</u>, rough-hewn, weather-beaten ≠ delicate 3 = <u>well-built</u>, strong, tough, robust, sturdy 4 = <u>tough</u>, strong, robust, muscular, sturdy, burly, husky (*informal*), brawny ≠ delicate

**ruin** VERB 1 = <u>destroy</u>, devastate, wreck, defeat, smash, crush, demolish, lay waste ≠ create 2 = <u>bankrupt</u>, break, impoverish, beggar, pauperize 3 = <u>spoil</u>, damage, mess up, blow (*slang*), screw up (*informal*), botch, make a mess of, crool or cruel (*Austral. slang*) ≠ improve

● NOUN 1 = <u>bankruptcy</u>, insolvency, destitution 2 = <u>disrepair</u>, decay, disintegration, ruination, wreckage 3 = <u>destruction</u>, fall, breakdown, defeat, collapse, wreck, undoing, downfall ≠ preservation

**rule** NOUN 1 = <u>regulation</u>, law, direction, guideline, decree 2 = <u>precept</u>, principle, canon, maxim, tenet, axiom 3 = <u>custom</u>, procedure, practice, routine, tradition, habit, convention 4 = <u>government</u>, power, control, authority, command, regime, reign, jurisdiction, mana (*N.Z.*)

● VERB 1 = <u>govern</u>, control, direct, have power over, command over, have charge of 2 = <u>reign</u>, govern, be in power, be in authority 3 = <u>decree</u>, decide, judge, settle, pronounce 4 = <u>be prevalent</u>, prevail, predominate, be customary, preponderate

● PHRASES **as a rule** = <u>usually</u>, generally, mainly, normally, on the whole, ordinarily ◆ **rule someone out** = <u>exclude</u>, eliminate, disqualify, ban, reject, dismiss, prohibit, leave out ◆ **rule something out** = <u>reject</u>, exclude, eliminate

**ruler** 1 = <u>governor</u>, leader, lord, commander, controller, monarch, sovereign, head of state 2 = <u>measure</u>, rule, yardstick

**ruling** ADJECTIVE 1 = <u>governing</u>, reigning, controlling, commanding 2 = <u>predominant</u>, dominant, prevailing, preponderant, chief, main, principal, pre-eminent ≠ minor

● NOUN = <u>decision</u>, verdict, judgment, decree, adjudication, pronouncement

**rumour** = <u>story</u>, news, report, talk, word, whisper, buzz, gossip

**run** VERB 1 = <u>race</u>, rush, dash, hurry, sprint, bolt, gallop, jog (*Brit. informal*) ≠ dawdle 2 = <u>flee</u>, escape, take off (*informal*), bolt, beat it (*slang*), leg it (*informal*), take flight, do a runner (*slang*) ≠ stay 3 = <u>take part</u>, compete 4 = <u>continue</u>, go, stretch, reach, extend, proceed ≠ stop 5 (*Chiefly U.S. & Canad.*) = <u>compete</u>, stand, contend, be a candidate, put yourself up for, take part 6 = <u>manage</u>, lead, direct, be in charge of, control, operate, handle 7 = <u>go</u>, work, operate, perform, function 8 = <u>perform</u>, carry out 9 = <u>work</u>, go, operate, function 10 = <u>pass</u>, go, move, roll, glide, skim 11 = <u>flow</u>, pour, stream, go, leak, spill, discharge, gush 12 = <u>publish</u>, feature, display, print 13 = <u>melt</u>, dissolve, liquefy, go soft 14 = <u>smuggle</u>, traffic in, bootleg

● NOUN 1 = <u>race</u>, rush, dash, sprint,

gallop, jog, spurt 2 = <u>ride</u>, drive, trip, spin (*informal*), outing, excursion, jaunt 3 = <u>sequence</u>, period, stretch, spell, course, season, series, string

4 = <u>enclosure</u>, pen, coop

● **PHRASES run away** = <u>flee</u>, escape, bolt, abscond, do a runner (*slang*), make a run for it, scram (*informal*), fly the coop (*U.S. & Canad. informal*) ◆ **run into someone** = <u>meet</u>, encounter, bump into, run across, come across *or* upon ◆ **run into something** 1 = <u>be beset by</u>, encounter, come across *or* upon, face, experience 2 = <u>collide with</u>, hit, strike ◆ **run out** 1 = <u>be used up</u>, dry up, give out, fail, finish, be exhausted 2 = <u>expire</u>, end, terminate ◆ **run over something** 1 = <u>exceed</u>, overstep, go over the top of, go over the limit of 2 = <u>review</u>, check, go through, go over, run through, rehearse ◆ **run over something** *or* **someone** = <u>knock down</u>, hit, run down, knock over ◆ **run something** *or* **someone down** 1 = <u>criticize</u>, denigrate, belittle, knock (*informal*), rubbish (*informal*), slag (off) (*slang*), disparage, decry 2 = <u>downsize</u>, cut, reduce, trim, decrease, cut back, curtail 3 = <u>knock down</u>, hit, run into, run over, knock over

**run-down** *or* **rundown**

1 = <u>exhausted</u>, weak, drained, weary, unhealthy, worn-out, debilitated, below par ≠ fit

2 = <u>dilapidated</u>, broken-down, shabby, worn-out, seedy, ramshackle, decrepit

**runner** 1 = <u>athlete</u>, sprinter, jogger 2 = <u>messenger</u>, courier, errand boy, dispatch bearer

**running** NOUN 1 = <u>management</u>, control, administration, direction, leadership, organization, supervision 2 = <u>working</u>, performance, operation, functioning, maintenance

● ADJECTIVE 1 = <u>continuous</u>, constant, perpetual, uninterrupted, incessant 2 = <u>in succession</u>, unbroken 3 = <u>flowing</u>, moving, streaming, coursing

**rupture** NOUN = <u>break</u>, tear, split, crack, rent, burst, breach, fissure

● VERB = <u>break</u>, separate, tear, split, crack, burst, sever

**rural** 1 = <u>agricultural</u>, country 2 = <u>rustic</u>, country, pastoral, sylvan ≠ urban

**rush** VERB 1 = <u>hurry</u>, run, race, shoot, fly, career, speed, tear ≠ dawdle 2 = <u>push</u>, hurry, press, hustle 3 = <u>attack</u>, storm, charge at

● NOUN 1 = <u>dash</u>, charge, race, scramble, stampede 2 = <u>hurry</u>, haste, hustle 3 = <u>surge</u>, flow, gush 4 = <u>attack</u>, charge, assault, onslaught

• **ADJECTIVE** = <u>hasty</u>, fast, quick, hurried, rapid, urgent, swift ≠ leisurely

**rust** NOUN 1 = <u>corrosion</u>, oxidation 2 = <u>mildew</u>, must, mould, rot, blight

• **VERB** = <u>corrode</u>, oxidize

**rusty** 1 = <u>corroded</u>, rusted, oxidized, rust-covered 2 = <u>out of practice</u>, weak, stale, unpractised 3 = <u>reddish-brown</u>, chestnut, reddish, russet, coppery, rust-coloured

> <u>shades of red</u>

**ruthless** = <u>merciless</u>, harsh, cruel, brutal, relentless, callous, heartless, remorseless ≠ merciful

# S

**sabotage** VERB = <u>damage</u>, destroy, wreck, disable, disrupt, subvert, incapacitate, vandalize

• **NOUN** = <u>damage</u>, destruction, wrecking

**sack**[1] NOUN 1 = <u>bag</u>, pocket, sac, pouch, receptacle 2 = <u>dismissal</u>, discharge, the boot (*slang*), the axe (*informal*), the push (*slang*)

• **VERB** (*Informal*) = <u>dismiss</u>, fire (*informal*), axe (*informal*), discharge, kiss off (*slang, chiefly U.S. & Canad.*), give (someone) the push

(*informal*)

**sack**[2] VERB = <u>plunder</u>, loot, pillage, strip, rob, raid, ruin

• **NOUN** = <u>plundering</u>, looting, pillage

**sacred** 1 = <u>holy</u>, hallowed, blessed, divine, revered, sanctified ≠ secular 2 = <u>religious</u>, holy, ecclesiastical, hallowed ≠ unconsecrated 3 = <u>inviolable</u>, protected, sacrosanct, hallowed, inalienable, unalterable

**sacrifice** VERB 1 = <u>offer</u>, offer up, immolate 2 = <u>give up</u>, abandon, relinquish, lose, surrender, let go, do without, renounce

• **NOUN** 1 = <u>offering</u>, oblation 2 = <u>surrender</u>, loss, giving up, rejection, abdication, renunciation, repudiation, forswearing

**sad** 1 = <u>unhappy</u>, down, low, blue, depressed, melancholy, mournful, dejected ≠ happy 2 = <u>tragic</u>, moving, upsetting, depressing, dismal, pathetic, poignant, harrowing 3 = <u>deplorable</u>, bad, sorry, terrible, unfortunate, regrettable, lamentable, wretched ≠ good

**sadden** = <u>upset</u>, depress, distress, grieve, make sad, deject

**saddle** = <u>burden</u>, load, lumber (*Brit. informal*), encumber

**sadness** = <u>unhappiness</u>, sorrow, grief, depression, the blues,

misery, melancholy, poignancy ≠ happiness

**safe** ADJECTIVE 1 = protected, secure, impregnable, out of danger, safe and sound, in safe hands, out of harm's way ≠ endangered 2 = all right, intact, unscathed, unhurt, unharmed, undamaged, O.K. or okay (informal) 3 = risk-free, sound, secure, certain, impregnable
● NOUN = strongbox, vault, coffer, repository, deposit box, safe-deposit box

**safeguard** VERB = protect, guard, defend, save, preserve, look after, keep safe
● NOUN = protection, security, defence, guard

**safely** = in safety, with impunity, without risk, safe and sound

**safety** 1 = security, protection, safeguards, precautions, safety measures, impregnability ≠ risk 2 = shelter, haven, protection, cover, retreat, asylum, refuge, sanctuary

**sag** 1 = sink, bag, droop, fall, slump, dip, give way, hang loosely 2 = drop, sink, slump, flop, droop, loll 3 = decline, tire, flag, weaken, wilt, wane, droop

**saga** 1 = carry-on (informal, chiefly Brit.), performance (informal), pantomime (informal) 2 = epic, story, tale, narrative, yarn

**sage** NOUN = wise man, philosopher, guru, master, elder, tohunga (N.Z.)
● ADJECTIVE = wise, sensible, judicious, sagacious, sapient

**sail** NOUN = sheet, canvas
● VERB 1 = go by water, cruise, voyage, ride the waves, go by sea 2 = set sail, embark, get under way, put to sea, put off, leave port, hoist sail, cast or weigh anchor 3 = pilot, steer 4 = glide, sweep, float, fly, wing, soar, drift, skim

**sailor** NOUN = mariner, marine, seaman, sea dog, seafarer

**sake** NOUN = purpose, interest, reason, end, aim, objective, motive
● PHRASES **for someone's sake** = in someone's interests, to someone's advantage, on someone's account, for the benefit of, for the good of, for the welfare of, out of respect for, out of consideration for

**salary** = pay, income, wage, fee, payment, wages, earnings, allowance

**sale** 1 = selling, marketing, dealing, transaction, disposal 2 = auction, fair, mart, bazaar

**salt** NOUN = seasoning
● ADJECTIVE = salty, saline, brackish, briny

**salute** VERB 1 = greet, welcome, acknowledge, address, hail, mihi (N.Z.) 2 = honour, acknowledge, recognize, pay tribute or homage to

● NOUN = greeting, recognition, salutation, address

**salvage** = save, recover, rescue, get back, retrieve, redeem

**salvation** = saving, rescue, recovery, salvage, redemption, deliverance ≠ ruin

**same** 1 = identical, similar, alike, equal, twin, corresponding, duplicate ≠ different 2 = the very same, one and the same, selfsame 3 = aforementioned, aforesaid 4 = unchanged, consistent, constant, unaltered, invariable, unvarying, changeless ≠ altered

> ### Word Power
>
> **same** – The use of *same* as in *if you send us your order for the materials, we will deliver same tomorrow* is common in business and official English. In general English, however, this use of the word is best avoided, as it may sound rather stilted: *may I borrow your book? I will return it* (not *same*) *tomorrow*.

**sample** NOUN 1 = specimen, example, model, pattern, instance 2 = cross section

● VERB = test, try, experience, taste, inspect

● ADJECTIVE = test, trial, specimen, representative

**sanction** VERB = permit, allow, approve, endorse, authorize ≠ forbid

● NOUN 1 often plural = ban, boycott, embargo, exclusion, penalty, coercive measures ≠ permission 2 = permission, backing, authority, approval, authorization, O.K. or okay (informal), stamp or seal of approval ≠ ban

**sanctuary** 1 = protection, shelter, refuge, haven, retreat, asylum 2 = reserve, park, preserve, reservation, national park, tract, nature reserve, conservation area

**sane** 1 = rational, all there (informal), of sound mind, compos mentis (Latin), in your right mind, mentally sound ≠ insane 2 = sensible, sound, reasonable, balanced, judicious, level-headed ≠ foolish

**sap**[1] 1 = juice, essence, vital fluid, lifeblood 2 (Slang) = fool, jerk (slang, chiefly U.S. & Canad.), idiot, wally (slang), twit (informal), simpleton, ninny, dorba or dorb (Austral. slang), bogan (Austral. slang)

**sap**[2] = weaken, drain, undermine,

exhaust, deplete

**satanic** = <u>evil</u>, demonic, hellish, black, wicked, devilish, infernal, fiendish ≠ godly

**satire** 1 = <u>mockery</u>, irony, ridicule 2 = <u>parody</u>, mockery, caricature, lampoon, burlesque

**satisfaction** 1 = <u>fulfilment</u>, pleasure, achievement, relish, gratification, pride ≠ dissatisfaction

2 = <u>contentment</u>, content, comfort, pleasure, happiness, enjoyment, satiety, repletion ≠ discontent

**satisfactory** = <u>adequate</u>, acceptable, good enough, average, fair, all right, sufficient, passable ≠ unsatisfactory

**satisfy** 1 = <u>content</u>, please, indulge, gratify, pander to, assuage, pacify, quench ≠ dissatisfy 2 = <u>convince</u>, persuade, assure, reassure ≠ dissuade 3 = <u>comply with</u>, meet, fulfil, answer, serve, fill, observe, obey ≠ fail to meet

**saturate** 1 = <u>flood</u>, overwhelm, swamp, overrun 2 = <u>soak</u>, steep, drench, imbue, suffuse, wet through, waterlog, souse

**saturated** = <u>soaked</u>, soaking (wet), drenched, sodden, dripping, waterlogged, sopping (wet), wet through

**sauce** = <u>dressing</u>, dip, relish,

condiment

**savage** ADJECTIVE 1 = <u>cruel</u>, brutal, vicious, fierce, harsh, ruthless, ferocious, sadistic ≠ gentle 2 = <u>wild</u>, fierce, ferocious, unbroken, feral, untamed, undomesticated ≠ tame 3 = <u>primitive</u>, undeveloped, uncultivated, uncivilized 4 = <u>uncultivated</u>, rugged, unspoilt, uninhabited, rough, uncivilized ≠ cultivated

● NOUN = <u>lout</u>, yob (Brit. slang), barbarian, yahoo, hoon (Austral. & N.Z.), boor, cougan (Austral. slang), scozza (Austral. slang), bogan (Austral. slang)

● VERB = <u>maul</u>, tear, claw, attack, mangle, lacerate, mangulate (Austral. slang)

**save** 1 = <u>rescue</u>, free, release, deliver, recover, get out, liberate, salvage ≠ endanger 2 = <u>keep</u>, reserve, set aside, store, collect, gather, hold, hoard ≠ spend 3 = <u>protect</u>, keep, guard, preserve, look after, safeguard, salvage, conserve 4 = <u>put aside</u>, keep, reserve, collect, retain, set aside, put by

**saving** NOUN = <u>economy</u>, discount, reduction, bargain

● PLURAL NOUN = <u>nest egg</u>, fund, store, reserves, resources

**saviour** = <u>rescuer</u>, deliverer, defender, protector, liberator, redeemer, preserver

**Saviour** = <u>Christ</u>, Jesus, the Messiah, the Redeemer

**savour** VERB 1 = <u>relish</u>, delight in, revel in, luxuriate in 2 = <u>enjoy</u>, appreciate, relish, delight in, revel in, luxuriate in

● NOUN = <u>flavour</u>, taste, smell, relish, smack, tang, piquancy

**say** VERB 1 = <u>state</u>, declare, remark, announce, maintain, mention, assert, affirm 2 = <u>speak</u>, utter, voice, express, pronounce 3 = <u>suggest</u>, express, imply, communicate, disclose, give away, convey, divulge 4 = <u>suppose</u>, supposing, imagine, assume, presume 5 = <u>estimate</u>, suppose, guess, conjecture, surmise

● NOUN 1 = <u>influence</u>, power, control, authority, weight, clout (*informal*), mana (*N.Z.*) 2 = <u>chance to speak</u>, vote, voice

**saying** = <u>proverb</u>, maxim, adage, dictum, axiom, aphorism

**scale**[1] = <u>flake</u>, plate, layer, lamina

**scale**[2] NOUN 1 = <u>degree</u>, size, range, extent, dimensions, scope, magnitude, breadth 2 = <u>system of measurement</u>, measuring system 3 = <u>ranking</u>, ladder, hierarchy, series, sequence, progression 4 = <u>ratio</u>, proportion

● VERB = <u>climb up</u>, mount, ascend, surmount, clamber up, escalade

**scan** 1 = <u>glance over</u>, skim, look over, eye, check, examine, check out (*informal*), run over 2 = <u>survey</u>, search, investigate, sweep, scour, scrutinize

**scandal** 1 = <u>disgrace</u>, crime, offence, sin, embarrassment, wrongdoing, dishonourable behaviour, discreditable behaviour 2 = <u>gossip</u>, talk, rumours, dirt, slander, tattle, aspersion 3 = <u>shame</u>, disgrace, stigma, infamy, opprobrium 4 = <u>outrage</u>, shame, insult, disgrace, injustice, crying shame

**scant** = <u>inadequate</u>, meagre, sparse, little, minimal, barely sufficient ≠ adequate

**scapegoat** = <u>fall guy</u>, whipping boy

**scar** NOUN 1 = <u>mark</u>, injury, wound, blemish 2 = <u>trauma</u>, suffering, pain, torture, anguish

● VERB = <u>mark</u>, disfigure, damage, mar, mutilate, blemish, deface

**scarce** 1 = <u>in short supply</u>, insufficient ≠ plentiful 2 = <u>rare</u>, few, uncommon, few and far between, infrequent ≠ common

**scarcely** 1 = <u>hardly</u>, barely 2 (*Often used ironically*) = <u>by no means</u>, hardly, definitely not

## Word Power

**scarcely** – Since *scarcely*, *hardly*, and *barely* already have negative force, it is unnecessary to use another negative word with them. Therefore, say *he had hardly had time to think* (not *he hadn't hardly had time to think*); and *there was scarcely any bread left* (not *there was scarcely no bread left*). When *scarcely*, *hardly*, and *barely* are used at the beginning of a sentence, as in *scarcely had I arrived*, the following clause should start with *when*: *scarcely had I arrived when I was asked to chair a meeting*. The word *before* can be used in place of *when* in this context, but the word *than* used in the same way is considered incorrect by many people, though this use is becoming increasingly common.

**scare** VERB = <u>frighten</u>, alarm, terrify, panic, shock, startle, intimidate, dismay
● NOUN 1 = <u>fright</u>, shock, start 2 = <u>panic</u>, hysteria 3 = <u>alert</u>, warning, alarm

**scared** = <u>afraid</u>, alarmed, frightened, terrified, shaken, startled, fearful, petrified

**scary** (*Informal*) = <u>frightening</u>, alarming, terrifying, chilling, horrifying, spooky (*informal*), creepy (*informal*), spine-chilling

**scatter** 1 = <u>throw about</u>, spread, sprinkle, strew, shower, fling, diffuse, disseminate ≠ gather 2 = <u>disperse</u>, dispel, disband, dissipate ≠ assemble

**scenario** 1 = <u>situation</u> 2 = <u>story line</u>, résumé, outline, summary, synopsis

**scene** 1 = <u>act</u>, part, division, episode 2 = <u>setting</u>, set, background, location, backdrop 3 = <u>site</u>, place, setting, area, position, spot, locality 4 (*Informal*) = <u>world</u>, business, environment, arena 5 = <u>view</u>, prospect, panorama, vista, landscape, outlook 6 = <u>fuss</u>, to-do, row, performance, exhibition, carry-on (*informal*, *chiefly Brit.*), tantrum, commotion

**scenery** 1 = <u>landscape</u>, view, surroundings, terrain, vista 2 (*Theatre*) = <u>set</u>, setting, backdrop, flats, stage set

**scenic** = <u>picturesque</u>, beautiful, spectacular, striking, panoramic

**scent** NOUN 1 = <u>fragrance</u>, smell, perfume, bouquet, aroma, odour 2 = <u>trail</u>, track, spoor
● VERB = <u>smell</u>, sense, detect, sniff, discern, nose out

**scented** = <u>fragrant</u>, perfumed, aromatic, sweet-smelling, odoriferous

**sceptic** 1 = <u>doubter</u>, cynic,

disbeliever 2 = <u>agnostic</u>, doubter, unbeliever, doubting Thomas

**sceptical** = <u>doubtful</u>, cynical, dubious, unconvinced, disbelieving, incredulous, mistrustful ≠ convinced

**scepticism** = <u>doubt</u>, suspicion, disbelief, cynicism, incredulity

**schedule** NOUN = <u>plan</u>, programme, agenda, calendar, timetable

● VERB = <u>plan</u>, set up, book, programme, arrange, organize

**scheme** NOUN 1 = <u>plan</u>, programme, strategy, system, project, proposal, tactics 2 = <u>plot</u>, ploy, ruse, intrigue, conspiracy, manoeuvre, subterfuge, stratagem

● VERB = <u>plot</u>, plan, intrigue, manoeuvre, conspire, contrive, collude, machinate

**scheming** = <u>calculating</u>, cunning, sly, tricky, wily, artful, conniving, underhand ≠ straightforward

**scholar** 1 = <u>intellectual</u>, academic, savant, acca (*Austral. slang*) 2 = <u>student</u>, pupil, learner, schoolboy or schoolgirl

**scholarly** = <u>learned</u>, academic, intellectual, lettered, erudite, scholastic, bookish ≠ uneducated

**scholarship** 1 = <u>grant</u>, award, payment, endowment, fellowship, bursary 2 = <u>learning</u>, education, knowledge, erudition, book-learning

**school** NOUN 1 = <u>academy</u>, college, institution, institute, seminary 2 = <u>group</u>, set, circle, faction, followers, disciples, devotees, denomination

● VERB = <u>train</u>, coach, discipline, educate, drill, tutor, instruct

**science** = <u>discipline</u>, body of knowledge, branch of knowledge

**scientific** = <u>systematic</u>, accurate, exact, precise, controlled, mathematical

**scientist** = <u>researcher</u>, inventor, boffin (*informal*), technophile

**scoff**[1] = <u>scorn</u>, mock, laugh at, ridicule, knock (*informal*), despise, sneer, jeer

**scoff**[2] = <u>gobble (up)</u>, wolf, devour, bolt, guzzle, gulp down, gorge yourself on

**scoop** VERB = <u>win</u>, get, land, gain, achieve, earn, secure, obtain

● NOUN 1 = <u>ladle</u>, spoon, dipper 2 = <u>exclusive</u>, exposé, revelation, sensation

● PHRASES **scoop something** or **someone up** = <u>gather up</u>, lift, pick up, take up, sweep up or away ◆ **scoop something out** 1 = <u>take out</u>, empty, spoon out, bail or bale out 2 = <u>dig</u>, shovel, excavate, gouge, hollow out

**scope** 1 = <u>opportunity</u>, room, freedom, space, liberty, latitude

2 = range, capacity, reach, area, outlook, orbit, span, sphere

**scorch** = burn, sear, roast, wither, shrivel, parch, singe

**scorching** = burning, boiling, baking, flaming, roasting, searing, fiery, red-hot

**score** VERB 1 = gain, win, achieve, make, get, attain, notch up (*informal*), chalk up (*informal*) 2 (*Music*) = arrange, set, orchestrate, adapt 3 = cut, scratch, mark, slash, scrape, graze, gouge, deface

● NOUN 1 = rating, mark, grade, percentage 2 = points, result, total, outcome 3 = composition, soundtrack, arrangement, orchestration 4 = grievance, wrong, injury, injustice, grudge

● PLURAL NOUN = lots, loads, many, millions, hundreds, masses, swarms, multitudes

● PHRASES score something out *or* through = cross out, delete, strike out, cancel, obliterate

**scorn** NOUN = contempt, disdain, mockery, derision, sarcasm, disparagement ≠ respect

● VERB = despise, reject, disdain, slight, be above, spurn, deride, flout ≠ respect

**scour**[1] = scrub, clean, polish, rub, buff, abrade

**scour**[2] = search, hunt, comb, ransack

**scout** NOUN = vanguard, lookout, precursor, outrider, reconnoitrer, advance guard

● VERB = reconnoitre, investigate, watch, survey, observe, spy, probe, recce (*slang*)

**scramble** VERB 1 = struggle, climb, crawl, swarm, scrabble 2 = strive, rush, contend, vie, run, push, jostle 3 = jumble, mix up, muddle, shuffle

● NOUN 1 = clamber, ascent 2 = race, competition, struggle, rush, confusion, commotion, melee *or* mêlée

**scrap**[1] NOUN 1 = piece, fragment, bit, grain, particle, portion, part, crumb 2 = waste, junk, off cuts

● PLURAL NOUN = leftovers, remains, bits, leavings

● VERB = get rid of, drop, abandon, ditch (*slang*), discard, write off, jettison, throw away *or* out ≠ bring back

**scrap**[2] (*Informal*) NOUN = fight, battle, row, argument, dispute, disagreement, quarrel, squabble, biffo (*Austral. slang*)

● VERB = fight, argue, row, squabble, wrangle

**scrape** VERB 1 = rake, sweep, drag, brush 2 = grate, grind, scratch, squeak, rasp 3 = graze, skin, scratch, bark, scuff, rub 4 = clean, remove, scour

● NOUN (*Informal*) = <u>predicament</u>, difficulty, fix (*informal*), mess, dilemma, plight, tight spot, awkward situation

**scratch** VERB 1 = <u>rub</u>, scrape, claw at 2 = <u>mark</u>, cut, score, damage, grate, graze, etch, lacerate

● NOUN = <u>mark</u>, scrape, graze, blemish, gash, laceration, claw mark

● PHRASES **up to scratch** (*Informal*) = <u>adequate</u>, acceptable, satisfactory, sufficient, up to standard

**scream** VERB 1 = <u>cry</u>, yell, shriek, screech, bawl, howl

● NOUN = <u>cry</u>, yell, howl, shriek, screech, yelp

**screen** NOUN = <u>cover</u>, guard, shade, shelter, shield, partition, cloak, canopy

● VERB 1 = <u>broadcast</u>, show, put on, present, air, cable, beam, transmit 2 = <u>cover</u>, hide, conceal, shade, mask, veil, cloak 3 = <u>investigate</u>, test, check, examine, scan 4 = <u>process</u>, sort, examine, filter, scan, evaluate, gauge, sift 5 = <u>protect</u>, guard, shield, defend, shelter

**screw** NOUN = <u>nail</u>, pin, tack, rivet, fastener, spike

● VERB 1 = <u>fasten</u>, fix, attach, bolt, clamp, rivet 2 = <u>turn</u>, twist, tighten 3 (*Informal*) = <u>cheat</u>, do (*slang*), rip (someone) off (*slang*),

skin (*slang*), trick, con, sting (*informal*), fleece 4 (*Informal*) often with *out of* = <u>squeeze</u>, wring, extract, wrest

● PHRASES **screw something up** 1 = <u>contort</u>, wrinkle, distort, pucker 2 (*Informal*) = <u>bungle</u>, botch, mess up, spoil, mishandle, make a mess of (*slang*), make a hash of (*informal*), crool or cruel (*Austral. slang*)

**scribble** = <u>scrawl</u>, write, jot, dash off

**script** NOUN 1 = <u>text</u>, lines, words, book, copy, dialogue, libretto 2 = <u>handwriting</u>, writing, calligraphy, penmanship

● VERB = <u>write</u>, draft

**scripture** = <u>The Bible</u>, The Gospels, The Scriptures, The Good Book, Holy Scripture, Holy Writ, Holy Bible

**scrub** 1 = <u>scour</u>, clean, polish, rub, wash, cleanse, buff 2 (*Informal*) = <u>cancel</u>, drop, give up, abolish, forget about, call off, delete

**scrutiny** = <u>examination</u>, study, investigation, search, analysis, inspection, exploration, perusal

**sculpture** NOUN = <u>statue</u>, figure, model, bust, effigy, figurine, statuette

● VERB = <u>carve</u>, form, model, fashion, shape, mould, sculpt, chisel

**sea** NOUN 1 = <u>ocean</u>, the deep, the waves, main 2 = <u>mass</u>, army, host, crowd, mob, abundance, swarm, horde

● **PHRASES at sea** = <u>bewildered</u>, lost, confused, puzzled, baffled, perplexed, mystified, flummoxed

(Related Words)

*adjectives*: marine, maritime

**sea bird** ► **sea birds**

**seal** VERB = <u>settle</u>, clinch, conclude, consummate, finalize ● NOUN 1 = <u>sealant</u>, sealer, adhesive 2 = <u>authentication</u>, stamp, confirmation, ratification, insignia, imprimatur

**seam** 1 = <u>joint</u>, closure 2 = <u>layer</u>, vein, stratum, lode

**sea mammal**

| Sea mammals | |
|---|---|
| dugong | seal |
| elephant seal | sea lion |
| harp seal | walrus *or* |
| manatee | (*archaic*) sea |
| sea cow | horse |

**sear** = <u>wither</u>, burn, scorch, sizzle

**search** VERB = <u>examine</u>, investigate, explore, inspect, comb, scour, ransack, scrutinize, fossick (*Austral. & N.Z.*) ● NOUN = <u>hunt</u>, look, investigation, examination, pursuit, quest, inspection, exploration ● **PHRASES search for something** *or* **someone** = <u>look</u>

| Sea birds | |
|---|---|
| albatross *or* (*informal*) gooney bird | man-of-war bird *or* frigate bird |
| auk | oystercatcher |
| black-backed gull | petrel |
| coot | razorbill *or* razor-billed auk |
| cormorant | scoter |
| fairy penguin, little penguin, *or* (*N.Z.*) korora | sea eagle, erne, *or* ern |
| fish hawk | seagull |
| fulmar | shearwater |
| gannet | short-tailed shearwater, (Tasmanian) mutton bird, *or* (*N.Z.*) titi |
| guillemot | skua |
| gull *or* (*archaic or dialect*) cob(b) | storm petrel, stormy petrel, *or* Mother Carey's chicken |
| herring gull | wandering albatross |
| kittiwake | |

for, hunt for, pursue

**searching** = <u>keen</u>, sharp, probing, close, intent, piercing, penetrating, quizzical ≠ superficial

**searing** 1 = <u>acute</u>, intense, shooting, severe, painful, stabbing, piercing, gut-wrenching 2 = <u>cutting</u>, biting, bitter, harsh, barbed, hurtful, caustic

**season** NOUN = <u>period</u>, time, term, spell
• VERB = <u>flavour</u>, salt, spice, enliven, pep up

**seasoned** = <u>experienced</u>, veteran, practised, hardened, time-served ≠ inexperienced

**seasoning** = <u>flavouring</u>, spice, salt and pepper, condiment

**seat** NOUN 1 = <u>chair</u>, bench, stall, stool, pew, settle
2 = <u>membership</u>, place, constituency, chair, incumbency
3 = <u>centre</u>, place, site, heart, capital, situation, source, hub
4 = <u>mansion</u>, house, residence, abode, ancestral hall
• VERB 1 = <u>sit</u>, place, settle, set, fix, locate, install 2 = <u>hold</u>, take, accommodate, sit, contain, cater for

**second**[1] ADJECTIVE 1 = <u>next</u>, following, succeeding, subsequent 2 = <u>additional</u>, other, further, extra, alternative

3 = <u>inferior</u>, secondary, subordinate, lower, lesser
• NOUN = <u>supporter</u>, assistant, aide, colleague, backer, helper, right-hand man
• VERB = <u>support</u>, back, endorse, approve, go along with

**second**[2] = <u>moment</u>, minute, instant, flash, sec (*informal*), jiffy (*informal*), trice

**secondary** 1 = <u>subordinate</u>, minor, lesser, lower, inferior, unimportant ≠ main
2 = <u>resultant</u>, contingent, derived, indirect ≠ original

**second-hand** = <u>used</u>, old, hand-me-down (*informal*), nearly new

**secondly** = <u>next</u>, second, moreover, furthermore, also, in the second place

**secrecy** 1 = <u>mystery</u>, stealth, concealment, furtiveness, secretiveness, clandestineness, covertness 2 = <u>confidentiality</u>, privacy 3 = <u>privacy</u>, silence, seclusion

**secret** ADJECTIVE 1 = <u>undisclosed</u>, unknown, confidential, underground, undercover, unrevealed 2 = <u>concealed</u>, hidden, disguised ≠ unconcealed
3 = <u>undercover</u>, furtive ≠ open
4 = <u>secretive</u>, reserved, close ≠ frank 5 = <u>mysterious</u>, cryptic, abstruse, occult, clandestine,

arcane ≠ straightforward

● **NOUN** = private affair

● **PHRASES in secret** = <u>secretly</u>, surreptitiously, slyly

**secretive** = <u>reticent</u>, reserved, close, deep, uncommunicative, tight-lipped ≠ open

**secretly** = <u>in secret</u>, privately, surreptitiously, quietly, covertly, furtively, stealthily, clandestinely

**sect** = <u>group</u>, division, faction, party, camp, denomination, schism

**section** 1 = <u>part</u>, piece, portion, division, slice, passage, segment, fraction 2 = <u>district</u>, area, region, sector, zone

**sector** 1 = <u>part</u>, division 2 = <u>area</u>, part, region, district, zone, quarter

**secular** = <u>worldly</u>, lay, earthly, civil, temporal, nonspiritual ≠ religious

**secure** **VERB** 1 = <u>obtain</u>, get, acquire, score (*slang*), gain, procure ≠ lose 2 = <u>attach</u>, stick, fix, bind, fasten ≠ detach

● **ADJECTIVE** 1 = <u>safe</u>, protected, immune, unassailable ≠ unprotected 2 = <u>fast</u>, firm, fixed, stable, steady, fastened, immovable ≠ insecure 3 = <u>confident</u>, sure, easy, certain, assured, reassured ≠ uneasy

**security** 1 = <u>precautions</u>, defence, safeguards, protection, safety measures 2 = <u>assurance</u>, confidence, conviction, certainty, reliance, sureness, positiveness ≠ insecurity 3 = <u>pledge</u>, insurance, guarantee, hostage, collateral, pawn, gage, surety 4 = <u>protection</u>, safety, custody, refuge, sanctuary, safekeeping ≠ vulnerability

**sediment** = <u>dregs</u>, grounds, residue, lees, deposit

**seduce** 1 = <u>tempt</u>, lure, entice, mislead, deceive, beguile, lead astray, inveigle 2 = <u>corrupt</u>, deprave, dishonour, debauch, deflower

**seductive** = <u>tempting</u>, inviting, attractive, enticing, provocative, alluring, bewitching

**see** **VERB** 1 = <u>perceive</u>, spot, notice, sight, witness, observe, distinguish, glimpse 2 = <u>understand</u>, get, follow, realize, appreciate, grasp, comprehend, fathom 3 = <u>find out</u>, learn, discover, determine, verify, ascertain 4 = <u>consider</u>, decide, reflect, deliberate, think over 5 = <u>make sure</u>, ensure, guarantee, make certain, see to it 6 = <u>accompany</u>, show, escort, lead, walk, usher 7 = <u>speak to</u>, receive, interview, consult, confer with 8 = <u>meet</u>, come across, happen on, bump into, run across, chance on 9 = <u>go out with</u>, court, date (*informal, chiefly U.S.*), go steady with (*informal*)

● **PHRASES seeing as** = <u>since</u>, as, in view of the fact that, inasmuch as

> ### Word Power
>
> **see** – It is common to hear *seeing as how*, as in *seeing as how the bus is always late, I don't need to hurry*. However, the use of *how* here is considered incorrect or nonstandard, and should be avoided.

**seed** NOUN 1 = <u>grain</u>, pip, germ, kernel, egg, embryo, spore, ovum 2 = <u>beginning</u>, start, germ 3 = <u>origin</u>, source, nucleus 4 (*Chiefly Bible*) = <u>offspring</u>, children, descendants, issue, progeny

● **PHRASES go** *or* **run to seed** = <u>decline</u>, deteriorate, degenerate, decay, go downhill (*informal*), let yourself go, go to pot

**seek** 1 = <u>look for</u>, pursue, search for, be after, hunt 2 = <u>try</u>, attempt, aim, strive, endeavour, essay, aspire to

**seem** = <u>appear</u>, give the impression of being, look

**seep** = <u>ooze</u>, well, leak, soak, trickle, exude, permeate

**seethe** 1 = <u>be furious</u>, rage, fume, simmer, see red (*informal*), be livid, go ballistic (*slang, chiefly U.S.*) 2 = <u>boil</u>, bubble, foam, fizz, froth

**segment** = <u>section</u>, part, piece, division, slice, portion, wedge

**segregate** = <u>set apart</u>, divide, separate, isolate, discriminate against, dissociate ≠ unite

**segregation** = <u>separation</u>, discrimination, apartheid, isolation

**seize** 1 = <u>grab</u>, grip, grasp, take, snatch, clutch, snap up, pluck ≠ let go 2 = <u>take by storm</u>, take over, acquire, occupy, conquer 3 = <u>capture</u>, catch, arrest, apprehend, take captive ≠ release

**seizure** 1 = <u>attack</u>, fit, spasm, convulsion, paroxysm 2 = <u>taking</u>, grabbing, annexation, confiscation, commandeering 3 = <u>capture</u>, arrest, apprehension

**seldom** = <u>rarely</u>, not often, infrequently, hardly ever ≠ often

**select** VERB = <u>choose</u>, take, pick, opt for, decide on, single out, adopt, settle upon ≠ reject

● **ADJECTIVE** 1 = <u>choice</u>, special, excellent, superior, first-class, hand-picked, top-notch (*informal*) ≠ ordinary 2 = <u>exclusive</u>, elite, privileged, cliquish ≠ indiscriminate

**selection** 1 = <u>choice</u>, choosing, pick, option, preference 2 = <u>anthology</u>, collection, medley, choice

**selective** = <u>particular</u>,

discriminating, careful, discerning, tasteful, fastidious ≠ indiscriminate

**selfish** = self-centred, self-interested, greedy, ungenerous, egoistic or egoistical, egotistic or egotistical ≠ unselfish

**sell** VERB 1 = trade, exchange, barter ≠ buy 2 = deal in, market, trade in, stock, handle, retail, peddle, traffic in ≠ buy
● PHRASES **sell out of something** = run out of, be out of stock of

**seller** = dealer, merchant, vendor, agent, retailer, supplier, purveyor, salesman or saleswoman

**send** VERB 1 = dispatch, forward, direct, convey, remit 2 = propel, hurl, fling, shoot, fire, cast, let fly
● PHRASES **send something or someone up** (Brit. informal) = mock, mimic, parody, spoof (informal), imitate, take off (informal), make fun of, lampoon

**send-off** = farewell, departure, leave-taking, valediction

**senior** 1 = higher ranking, superior ≠ subordinate 2 = the elder, major (Brit.) ≠ junior

**sensation** 1 = feeling, sense, impression, perception, awareness, consciousness 2 = excitement, thrill, stir, furore, commotion

**sensational** 1 = amazing, dramatic, thrilling, astounding ≠ dull 2 = shocking, exciting, melodramatic, shock-horror (facetious) ≠ unexciting 3 (Informal) = excellent, superb, mean (slang), impressive, smashing (informal), fabulous (informal), marvellous, out of this world (informal), booshit (Austral. slang), exo (Austral. slang), sik (Austral. slang) ≠ ordinary

**sense** NOUN 1 = faculty 2 = feeling, impression, perception, awareness, consciousness, atmosphere, aura 3 = understanding, awareness 4 sometimes plural = intelligence, reason, understanding, brains (informal), judgment, wisdom, wit(s), common sense ≠ foolishness 5 = meaning, significance, import, implication, drift, gist
● VERB = perceive, feel, understand, pick up, realize, be aware of, discern, get the impression ≠ be unaware of

**sensibility** often plural = feelings, emotions, sentiments, susceptibilities, moral sense

**sensible** 1 = wise, practical, prudent, shrewd, judicious ≠ foolish 2 = intelligent, practical, rational, sound, realistic, sage, shrewd, down-to-earth ≠ senseless

**sensitive** 1 = <u>thoughtful</u>, kindly, concerned, patient, attentive, tactful, unselfish 2 = <u>delicate</u>, tender 3 = <u>susceptible to</u>, responsive to, easily affected by 4 = <u>touchy</u>, oversensitive, easily upset, easily offended, easily hurt ≠ insensitive 5 = <u>precise</u>, fine, acute, keen, responsive ≠ imprecise

**sensitivity** 1 = <u>susceptibility</u>, responsiveness, receptiveness, sensitiveness 2 = <u>consideration</u>, patience, thoughtfulness 3 = <u>touchiness</u>, oversensitivity 4 = <u>responsiveness</u>, precision, keenness, acuteness

**sensual** 1 = <u>sexual</u>, erotic, raunchy (*slang*), lewd, lascivious, lustful, lecherous 2 = <u>physical</u>, bodily, voluptuous, animal, luxurious, fleshly, carnal

**sentence NOUN** 1 = <u>punishment</u>, condemnation 2 = <u>verdict</u>, order, ruling, decision, judgment, decree
● **VERB** 1 = <u>condemn</u>, doom 2 = <u>convict</u>, condemn, penalize

**sentiment** 1 = <u>feeling</u>, idea, view, opinion, attitude, belief, judgment 2 = <u>sentimentality</u>, emotion, tenderness, romanticism, sensibility, emotionalism, mawkishness

**sentimental** = <u>romantic</u>, touching, emotional, nostalgic, maudlin, weepy (*informal*), slushy (*informal*), schmaltzy (*slang*) ≠ unsentimental

**separate ADJECTIVE** 1 = <u>unconnected</u>, individual, particular, divided, divorced, isolated, detached, disconnected ≠ connected 2 = <u>individual</u>, independent, apart, distinct ≠ joined
● **VERB** 1 = <u>divide</u>, detach, disconnect, disjoin ≠ combine 2 = <u>come apart</u>, split, come away ≠ connect 3 = <u>sever</u>, break apart, split in two, divide in two ≠ join 4 = <u>split up</u>, part, divorce, break up, part company, get divorced, be estranged 5 = <u>distinguish</u>, mark, single out, set apart ≠ link

**separated** 1 = <u>estranged</u>, parted, separate, apart, disunited 2 = <u>disconnected</u>, parted, divided, separate, disassociated, disunited, sundered

**separately** 1 = <u>alone</u>, apart, not together, severally ≠ together 2 = <u>individually</u>, singly

**separation** 1 = <u>division</u>, break, dissociation, disconnection, disunion 2 = <u>split-up</u>, parting, split, divorce, break-up, rift

**sequel** 1 = <u>follow-up</u>, continuation, development 2 = <u>consequence</u>, result, outcome, conclusion, end, upshot

**sequence** = <u>succession</u>, course, series, order, chain, cycle, arrangement, progression

**series** 1 = <u>sequence</u>, course, chain, succession, run, set, order, train 2 = <u>drama</u>, serial, soap (*informal*), sitcom (*informal*), soap opera, soapie (*Austral. slang*), situation comedy

**serious** 1 = <u>grave</u>, bad, critical, dangerous, acute, severe 2 = <u>important</u>, crucial, urgent, pressing, worrying, significant, grim, momentous ≠ unimportant 3 = <u>thoughtful</u>, detailed, careful, deep, profound, in-depth 4 = <u>deep</u>, sophisticated 5 = <u>solemn</u>, earnest, grave, sober, staid, humourless, unsmiling ≠ light-hearted 6 = <u>sincere</u>, earnest, genuine, honest, in earnest ≠ insincere

**seriously** 1 = <u>truly</u>, in earnest, all joking aside 2 = <u>badly</u>, severely, gravely, critically, acutely, dangerously

**seriousness** 1 = <u>importance</u>, gravity, urgency, significance 2 = <u>solemnity</u>, gravity, earnestness, gravitas

**sermon** = <u>homily</u>, address

**servant** = <u>attendant</u>, domestic, slave, maid, help, retainer, skivvy (*chiefly Brit.*)

**serve** 1 = <u>work for</u>, help, aid, assist, be in the service of 2 = <u>perform</u>, do, complete, fulfil, discharge 3 = <u>be adequate</u>, do,

suffice, suit, satisfy, be acceptable, answer the purpose 4 = <u>present</u>, provide, supply, deliver, set out, dish up

**service** NOUN 1 = <u>facility</u>, system, resource, utility, amenity 2 = <u>ceremony</u>, worship, rite, observance 3 = <u>work</u>, labour, employment, business, office, duty 4 = <u>check</u>, maintenance check
● VERB = <u>overhaul</u>, check, maintain, tune (up), go over, fine tune

**session** = <u>meeting</u>, hearing, sitting, period, conference, congress, discussion, assembly

**set**[1] VERB 1 = <u>put</u>, place, lay, position, rest, plant, station, stick 2 = <u>arrange</u>, decide (upon), settle, establish, determine, fix, schedule, appoint 3 = <u>assign</u>, give, allot, prescribe 4 = <u>harden</u>, stiffen, solidify, cake, thicken, crystallize, congeal 5 = <u>go down</u>, sink, dip, decline, disappear, vanish, subside 6 = <u>prepare</u>, lay, spread, arrange, make ready
● ADJECTIVE 1 = <u>established</u>, planned, decided, agreed, arranged, rigid, definite, inflexible 2 = <u>strict</u>, rigid, stubborn, inflexible ≠ flexible 3 = <u>conventional</u>, traditional, stereotyped, unspontaneous
● NOUN 1 = <u>scenery</u>, setting, scene, stage set 2 = <u>position</u>, bearing,

attitude, carriage, posture

● **PHRASES** **be set on** or **upon something** = <u>be determined to</u>, be intent on, be bent on, be resolute about ◆ **set**

**something up** 1 = <u>arrange</u>, organize, prepare, prearrange 2 = <u>establish</u>, begin, found, institute, initiate 3 = <u>build</u>, raise, construct, put up, assemble, put together, erect 4 = <u>assemble</u>, put up

**set²** 1 = <u>series</u>, collection, assortment, batch, compendium, ensemble 2 = <u>group</u>, company, crowd, circle, band, gang, faction, clique

**setback** = <u>hold-up</u>, check, defeat, blow, reverse, disappointment, hitch, misfortune

**setting** = <u>surroundings</u>, site, location, set, scene, background, context, backdrop

**settle** 1 = <u>resolve</u>, work out, put an end to, straighten out 2 = <u>pay</u>, clear, square (up), discharge 3 = <u>move to</u>, take up residence in, live in, dwell in, inhabit, reside in, set up home in, put down roots in 4 = <u>colonize</u>, populate, people, pioneer 5 = <u>land</u>, alight, descend, light, come to rest 6 = <u>calm</u>, quiet, relax, relieve, reassure, soothe, lull, quell ≠ disturb

**settlement** 1 = <u>agreement</u>,

arrangement, working out, conclusion, establishment, confirmation 2 = <u>payment</u>, clearing, discharge 3 = <u>colony</u>, community, outpost, encampment, kainga or kaika (N.Z.)

**settler** = <u>colonist</u>, immigrant, pioneer, frontiersman

**set-up** (Informal) = <u>arrangement</u>, system, structure, organization, conditions, regime

**sever** 1 = <u>cut</u>, separate, split, part, divide, detach, disconnect, cut in two ≠ join 2 = <u>discontinue</u>, terminate, break off, put an end to, dissociate ≠ continue

**several** **ADJECTIVE** = <u>some</u>, a few, a number of, a handful of

● **PRONOUN** = <u>various</u>, different, diverse, sundry

**severe** 1 = <u>serious</u>, critical, terrible, desperate, extreme, awful, drastic, catastrophic 2 = <u>acute</u>, intense, violent, piercing, harrowing, unbearable, agonizing, insufferable 3 = <u>strict</u>, hard, harsh, cruel, rigid, drastic, oppressive, austere ≠ lenient 4 = <u>grim</u>, serious, grave, forbidding, stern, unsmiling, tight-lipped ≠ genial 5 = <u>plain</u>, simple, austere, classic, restrained, Spartan, unadorned, unfussy ≠ fancy

**severely** 1 = <u>seriously</u>, badly,

extremely, gravely, acutely
2 = <u>strictly</u>, harshly, sternly,
sharply

**severity** = <u>strictness</u>, harshness,
toughness, hardness, sternness,
severeness

**sew** = <u>stitch</u>, tack, seam, hem

**sex** 1 = <u>gender</u> 2 (*Informal*)
= <u>lovemaking</u>, sexual relations,
copulation, fornication, coitus,
coition

**sexual** 1 = <u>carnal</u>, erotic, intimate
2 = <u>sexy</u>, erotic, sensual, arousing,
naughty, provocative, seductive,
sensuous

**sexuality** = <u>desire</u>, lust,
eroticism, sensuality, sexiness
(*informal*), carnality

**sexy** = <u>erotic</u>, sensual, seductive,
arousing, naughty, provocative,
sensuous, suggestive

**shabby** 1 = <u>tatty</u>, worn, ragged,
scruffy, tattered, threadbare
≠ smart 2 = <u>run-down</u>, seedy,
mean, dilapidated 3 = <u>mean</u>, low,
rotten (*informal*), cheap, dirty,
despicable, contemptible, scurvy
≠ fair

**shack** = <u>hut</u>, cabin, shanty,
whare (*N.Z.*)

**shade** NOUN 1 = <u>hue</u>, tone, colour,
tint 2 = <u>shadow</u> 3 = <u>dash</u>, trace,
hint, suggestion 4 = <u>nuance</u>,
difference, degree 5 = <u>screen</u>,
covering, cover, blind, curtain,
shield, veil, canopy 6 (*Literary*)

= <u>ghost</u>, spirit, phantom, spectre,
apparition, kehua (*N.Z.*)
● VERB 1 = <u>darken</u>, shadow, cloud,
dim 2 = <u>cover</u>, protect, screen,
hide, shield, conceal, obscure, veil

**shadow** NOUN 1 = <u>silhouette</u>,
shape, outline, profile 2 = <u>shade</u>,
dimness, darkness, gloom, cover,
dusk
● VERB 1 = <u>shade</u>, screen, shield,
darken, overhang 2 = <u>follow</u>, tail
(*informal*), trail, stalk

**shady** 1 = <u>shaded</u>, cool, dim
≠ sunny 2 (*Informal*) = <u>crooked</u>,
dodgy (*Brit., Austral., & N.Z.
informal*), unethical, suspect,
suspicious, dubious,
questionable, shifty ≠ honest

**shaft** 1 = <u>tunnel</u>, hole, passage,
burrow, passageway, channel
2 = <u>handle</u>, staff, pole, rod, stem,
baton, shank 3 = <u>ray</u>, beam,
gleam

**shake** VERB 1 = <u>jiggle</u>, agitate
2 = <u>tremble</u>, shiver, quake, quiver
3 = <u>rock</u>, totter 4 = <u>wave</u>, wield,
flourish, brandish 5 = <u>upset</u>,
shock, frighten, disturb, distress,
rattle (*informal*), unnerve,
traumatize
● NOUN = <u>vibration</u>, trembling,
quaking, jerk, shiver, shudder, jolt,
tremor

**Shakespeare** ► Shakespeare

**shaky** 1 = <u>unstable</u>, weak,
precarious, rickety ≠ stable

## Shakespeare

| Character | Play |
|---|---|
| Sir Andrew Aguecheek | Twelfth Night |
| Antonio | The Merchant of Venice |
| Antony | Antony and Cleopatra, Julius Caesar |
| Ariel | The Tempest |
| Aufidius | Coriolanus |
| Autolycus | The Winter's Tale |
| Banquo | Macbeth |
| Bassanio | The Merchant of Venice |
| Beatrice | Much Ado About Nothing |
| Sir Toby Belch | Twelfth Night |
| Benedick | Much Ado About Nothing |
| Bolingbroke | Richard II |
| Bottom | A Midsummer Night's Dream |
| Brutus | Julius Caesar |
| Caliban | The Tempest |
| Casca | Julius Caesar |
| Cassio | Othello |
| Cassius | Julius Caesar |
| Claudio | Much Ado About Nothing, Measure for Measure |
| Claudius | Hamlet |
| Cleopatra | Antony and Cleopatra |
| Cordelia | King Lear |
| Coriolanus | Coriolanus |
| Cressida | Troilus and Cressida |
| Demetrius | A Midsummer Night's Dream |
| Desdemona | Othello |
| Dogberry | Much Ado About Nothing |
| Edmund | King Lear |
| Enobarbus | Antony and Cleopatra |
| Falstaff | Henry IV Parts I and II, The Merry Wives of Windsor |
| Ferdinand | The Tempest |
| Feste | Twelfth Night |
| Fluellen | Henry V |
| Fool | King Lear |

## Shakespeare (continued)

| Character | Play |
|---|---|
| Guildenstern | Hamlet |
| Hamlet | Hamlet |
| Helena | All's Well that Ends Well, A Midsummer Night's Dream |
| Hermia | A Midsummer Night's Dream |
| Hero | Much Ado About Nothing |
| Hotspur | Henry IV Part I |
| Iago | Othello |
| Jaques | As You Like It |
| John of Gaunt | Richard II |
| Juliet | Romeo and Juliet |
| Julius Caesar | Julius Caesar |
| Katharina or Kate | The Taming of the Shrew |
| Kent | King Lear |
| Laertes | Hamlet |
| Lear | King Lear |
| Lysander | A Midsummer Night's Dream |
| Macbeth | Macbeth |
| Lady Macbeth | Macbeth |
| Macduff | Macbeth |
| Malcolm | Macbeth |
| Malvolio | Twelfth Night |
| Mercutio | Romeo and Juliet |
| Miranda | The Tempest |
| Oberon | A Midsummer Night's Dream |
| Octavius | Antony and Cleopatra |
| Olivia | Twelfth Night |
| Ophelia | Hamlet |
| Orlando | As You Like It |
| Orsino | Twelfth Night |
| Othello | Othello |
| Pandarus | Troilus and Cressida |
| Perdita | The Winter's Tale |
| Petruchio | The Taming of the Shrew |
| Pistol | Henry IV Part II, Henry V, The Merry Wives of Windsor |

| Character | Play |
|-----------|------|
| *Shakespeare (continued)* | |
| Polonius | Hamlet |
| Puck | A Midsummer Night's Dream |
| Mistress Quickly | The Merry Wives of Windsor |
| Regan | King Lear |
| Romeo | Romeo and Juliet |
| Rosalind | As You Like It |
| Rosencrantz | Hamlet |
| Sebastian | The Tempest, Twelfth Night |
| Shylock | The Merchant of Venice |
| Thersites | Troilus and Cressida |
| Timon | Timon of Athens |
| Titania | A Midsummer Night's Dream |
| Touchstone | As You Like It |
| Troilus | Troilus and Cressida |
| Tybalt | Romeo and Juliet |
| Viola | Twelfth Night |

2 = <u>unsteady</u>, faint, trembling, faltering, quivery 3 = <u>uncertain</u>, suspect, dubious, questionable, iffy (*informal*) ≠ reliable

**shallow** = <u>superficial</u>, surface, empty, slight, foolish, trivial, meaningless, frivolous ≠ deep

**sham** NOUN = <u>fraud</u>, imitation, hoax, pretence, forgery, counterfeit, humbug, impostor ≠ the real thing

● ADJECTIVE = <u>false</u>, artificial, bogus, pretended, mock, imitation, simulated, counterfeit ≠ real

**shambles** 1 = <u>chaos</u>, mess, disorder, confusion, muddle,

havoc, disarray, madhouse

2 = <u>mess</u>, jumble, untidiness

**shame** NOUN 1 = <u>embarrassment</u>, humiliation, ignominy, mortification, abashment ≠ shamelessness 2 = <u>disgrace</u>, scandal, discredit, smear, disrepute, reproach, dishonour, infamy ≠ honour

● VERB 1 = <u>embarrass</u>, disgrace, humiliate, humble, mortify, abash ≠ make proud 2 = <u>dishonour</u>, degrade, stain, smear, blot, debase, defile ≠ honour

**shameful** = <u>disgraceful</u>, outrageous, scandalous, mean, low, base, wicked, dishonourable

≠ admirable

**shape** NOUN 1 = <u>appearance</u>, form, aspect, guise, likeness, semblance 2 = <u>form</u>, profile, outline, lines, build, figure, silhouette, configuration 3 = <u>pattern</u>, model, frame, mould 4 = <u>condition</u>, state, health, trim, fettle

● VERB 1 = <u>form</u>, make, produce, create, model, fashion, mould 2 = <u>mould</u>, form, make, fashion, model, frame

**share** NOUN 1 = <u>part</u>, portion, quota, ration, lot, due, contribution, allowance

● VERB 1 = <u>divide</u>, split, distribute, assign 2 = <u>go halves on</u>, go fifty-fifty on (informal)

**shark** ▸ **sharks**

**sharp** ADJECTIVE 1 = <u>keen</u>, jagged, serrated ≠ blunt 2 = <u>quick-witted</u>, clever, astute, knowing, quick, bright, alert, penetrating ≠ dim 3 = <u>cutting</u>, biting, bitter, harsh, barbed, hurtful, caustic ≠ gentle

4 = <u>sudden</u>, marked, abrupt, extreme, distinct ≠ gradual 5 = <u>clear</u>, distinct, well-defined, crisp ≠ indistinct 6 = <u>sour</u>, tart, pungent, hot, acid, acrid, piquant ≠ bland 7 = <u>acute</u>, severe, intense, painful, shooting, stabbing, piercing, gut-wrenching

● ADVERB 1 = <u>promptly</u>, precisely, exactly, on time, on the dot, punctually ≠ approximately

**sharpen** = <u>make sharp</u>, hone, whet, grind, edge

**shatter** 1 = <u>smash</u>, break, burst, crack, crush, pulverize 2 = <u>destroy</u>, ruin, wreck, demolish, torpedo

**shattered** 1 = <u>devastated</u>, crushed, gutted (slang) 2 (Informal) = <u>exhausted</u>, drained, worn out, done in (informal), all in (slang), knackered (slang), tired out, ready to drop

**shave** 1 = <u>trim</u>, crop 2 = <u>scrape</u>, trim, shear, pare

**shed**¹ = <u>hut</u>, shack, outhouse,

---

### Sharks

| | |
|---|---|
| angel shark, angelfish, or monkfish | nurse shark |
| basking shark or sailfish | porbeagle or mackerel shark |
| blue pointer | requiem shark |
| dogfish or (Austral.) dog shark | shovelnose |
| gummy (shark) | thrasher or thresher shark |
| hammerhead | tiger shark |
| mako | tope |
| | whale shark |

whare (N.Z.)

**shed²** 1 = <u>drop</u>, spill, scatter
2 = <u>cast off</u>, discard, moult, slough
off 3 = <u>give out</u>, cast, emit, give,
radiate

**sheen** = <u>shine</u>, gleam, gloss,
polish, brightness, lustre

**sheer** 1 = <u>total</u>, complete,
absolute, utter, pure, downright,
out-and-out, unmitigated
≠ moderate 2 = <u>steep</u>, abrupt,
precipitous ≠ gradual 3 = <u>fine</u>,
thin, transparent, see-through,
gossamer, diaphanous, gauzy
≠ thick

**sheet** 1 = <u>page</u>, leaf, folio, piece
of paper 2 = <u>plate</u>, piece, panel,
slab 3 = <u>coat</u>, film, layer, surface,
stratum, veneer, overlay, lamina
4 = <u>expanse</u>, area, stretch, sweep,
covering, blanket

**shell** NOUN 1 = <u>husk</u>, case, pod
2 = <u>carapace</u> 3 = <u>frame</u>, structure,
hull, framework, chassis
● VERB = <u>bomb</u>, bombard, attack,
blitz, strafe
● PHRASES **shell something out**
(with money or a specified sum
of money as object) = <u>pay out</u>,
fork out (slang), give, hand over

**shelter** NOUN 1 = <u>cover</u>, screen
2 = <u>protection</u>, safety, refuge,
cover 3 = <u>refuge</u>, haven,
sanctuary, retreat, asylum
● VERB 1 = <u>take shelter</u>, hide, seek
refuge, take cover 2 = <u>protect</u>,

shield, harbour, safeguard, cover,
hide, guard, defend ≠ endanger

**sheltered** 1 = <u>screened</u>,
covered, protected, shielded,
secluded ≠ exposed
2 = <u>protected</u>, screened, shielded,
quiet, isolated, secluded,
cloistered

**shelve** = <u>postpone</u>, defer, freeze,
suspend, put aside, put on ice,
put on the back burner
(informal), take a rain check on
(U.S. & Canad. informal)

**shepherd** NOUN = <u>drover</u>,
stockman, herdsman, grazier
● VERB = <u>guide</u>, conduct, steer,
herd, usher
*(Related Words)*
adjective: pastoral

**shield** NOUN = <u>protection</u>, cover,
defence, screen, guard, shelter,
safeguard
● VERB = <u>protect</u>, cover, screen,
guard, defend, shelter, safeguard

**shift** VERB 1 = <u>move</u>, move
around, budge 2 = <u>remove</u>, move,
displace, relocate, rearrange,
reposition
● NOUN 1 = <u>change</u>, shifting,
displacement 2 = <u>move</u>,
rearrangement

**shimmer** VERB = <u>gleam</u>, twinkle,
glisten, scintillate
● NOUN = <u>gleam</u>, iridescence

**shine** VERB 1 = <u>move</u>,
beam, glow, sparkle, glitter, glare,

radiate 2 = <u>polish</u>, buff, burnish, brush 3 = <u>be outstanding</u>, stand out, excel, be conspicuous
● NOUN 1 = <u>polish</u>, gloss, sheen, lustre 2 = <u>brightness</u>, light, sparkle, radiance

**shining** = <u>bright</u>, brilliant, gleaming, beaming, sparkling, shimmering, radiant, luminous

**shiny** = <u>bright</u>, gleaming, glossy, glistening, polished, lustrous

**ship** = <u>vessel</u>, boat, craft

**shiver** VERB = <u>shudder</u>, shake, tremble, quake, quiver
● NOUN = <u>tremble</u>, shudder, quiver, trembling, flutter, tremor

**shock** NOUN 1 = <u>upset</u>, blow, trauma, bombshell, turn (*informal*), distress, disturbance 2 = <u>impact</u>, blow, clash, collision 3 = <u>start</u>, scare, fright, turn, jolt
● VERB 1 = <u>shake</u>, stun, stagger, jolt, stupefy ≠ <u>horrify</u>, appal, disgust, revolt, sicken, nauseate, scandalize

**shocking** 1 (*Informal*) = <u>terrible</u>, appalling, dreadful, bad, horrendous, ghastly, deplorable, abysmal 2 = <u>appalling</u>, outrageous, disgraceful, disgusting, dreadful, horrifying, revolting, sickening ≠ wonderful

**shoot** VERB 1 = <u>open fire on</u>, blast (*slang*), hit, kill, plug (*slang*), bring down 2 = <u>fire</u>, launch, discharge, project, hurl, fling, propel, emit

3 = <u>speed</u>, race, rush, charge, fly, tear, dash, barrel (along) (*informal, chiefly U.S. & Canad.*)
● NOUN = <u>sprout</u>, branch, bud, sprig, offshoot

**shop** = <u>store</u>, supermarket, boutique, emporium, hypermarket, dairy (*N.Z.*)

**shore** = <u>beach</u>, coast, sands, strand (*poetic*), seashore

**short** ADJECTIVE 1 = <u>brief</u>, fleeting, momentary ≠ long 2 = <u>concise</u>, brief, succinct, summary, compressed, terse, laconic, pithy ≠ lengthy 3 = <u>small</u>, little, squat, diminutive, petite, dumpy ≠ tall 4 = <u>abrupt</u>, sharp, terse, curt, brusque, impolite, discourteous, uncivil ≠ polite 5 = <u>scarce</u>, wanting, low, limited, lacking, scant, deficient ≠ plentiful
● ADVERB = <u>abruptly</u>, suddenly, without warning ≠ gradually

**shortage** = <u>deficiency</u>, want, lack, scarcity, dearth, paucity, insufficiency ≠ abundance

**shortcoming** = <u>failing</u>, fault, weakness, defect, flaw, imperfection

**shorten** 1 = <u>cut</u>, reduce, decrease, diminish, lessen, curtail, abbreviate, abridge ≠ increase 2 = <u>turn up</u>

**shortly** = <u>soon</u>, presently, before long, in a little while

**shot** 1 = <u>discharge</u>, gunfire, crack,

blast, explosion, bang
**2** = <u>ammunition</u>, bullet, slug, pellet, projectile, lead, ball **3** = <u>marksman</u>, shooter, markswoman **4** (*Informal*) = <u>strike</u>, throw, lob **5** = <u>attempt</u>, go (*informal*), try, turn, effort, stab (*informal*), endeavour

**shoulder 1** = <u>bear</u>, carry, take on, accept, assume, be responsible for **2** = <u>push</u>, elbow, shove, jostle, press

**shout VERB** = <u>cry (out)</u>, call (out), yell, scream, roar, bellow, bawl, holler (*informal*)
● **NOUN** = <u>cry</u>, call, yell, scream, roar, bellow
● **PHRASES shout someone down** = <u>drown out</u>, overwhelm, drown, silence

**shove VERB** = <u>push</u>, thrust, elbow, drive, press, propel, jostle, impel
● **NOUN** = <u>push</u>, knock, thrust, elbow, bump, nudge, jostle
● **PHRASES shove off** (*Informal*) = <u>go away</u>, leave, clear off (*informal*), depart, push off (*informal*), scram (*informal*)

**shovel 1** = <u>move</u>, scoop, dredge, load, heap **2** = <u>stuff</u>, ladle

**show VERB 1** = <u>indicate</u>, demonstrate, prove, reveal, display, point out, manifest, testify to ≠ <u>disprove</u> **2** = <u>display</u>, exhibit **3** = <u>guide</u>, lead, conduct, accompany, direct, escort

**4** = <u>demonstrate</u>, describe, explain, teach, illustrate, instruct **5** = <u>be visible</u> ≠ be invisible **6** = express, display, reveal, indicate, register, demonstrate, manifest ≠ hide **7** = <u>turn up</u>, appear, attend **8** = <u>broadcast</u>, transmit, air, beam, relay, televise, put on the air
● **NOUN 1** = <u>display</u>, sight, spectacle, array **2** = <u>exhibition</u>, fair, display, parade, pageant **3** = <u>appearance</u>, display, pose, parade **4** = <u>pretence</u>, appearance, illusion, affectation **5** = <u>programme</u>, broadcast, presentation, production **6** = <u>entertainment</u>, production, presentation
● **PHRASES show off** (*Informal*) = <u>boast</u>, brag, blow your own trumpet, swagger ◆ **show someone up** (*Informal*) = <u>embarrass</u>, let down, mortify, put to shame ◆ **show something off** = <u>exhibit</u>, display, parade, demonstrate, flaunt ◆ **show something up** = <u>reveal</u>, expose, highlight, lay bare

**showdown** (*Informal*) = <u>confrontation</u>, clash, face-off (*slang*)

**shower NOUN** = <u>deluge</u>
● **VERB 1** = <u>cover</u>, dust, spray, sprinkle **2** = <u>inundate</u>, heap, lavish, pour, deluge

**show-off** (*Informal*)
= <u>exhibitionist</u>, boaster, poseur, braggart

**shred** 1 = <u>strip</u>, bit, piece, scrap, fragment, sliver, tatter

2 = <u>particle</u>, trace, scrap, grain, atom, jot, iota

**shrewd** = <u>astute</u>, clever, sharp, keen, smart, calculating, intelligent, cunning ≠ naive

**shriek** VERB = <u>scream</u>, cry, yell, screech, squeal

● NOUN = <u>scream</u>, cry, yell, screech, squeal

**shrink** = <u>decrease</u>, dwindle, lessen, grow or get smaller, contract, narrow, diminish, shorten ≠ grow

**shroud** NOUN 1 = <u>winding sheet</u>, grave clothes 2 = <u>covering</u>, veil, mantle, screen, pall

● VERB = <u>conceal</u>, cover, screen, hide, blanket, veil, cloak, envelop

**shudder** VERB = <u>shiver</u>, shake, tremble, quake, quiver, convulse

● NOUN = <u>shiver</u>, tremor, quiver, spasm

**shuffle** 1 = <u>shamble</u>, stagger, stumble, dodder 2 = <u>scuffle</u>, drag, scrape 3 = <u>rearrange</u>, jumble, mix, disorder, disarrange

**shun** = <u>avoid</u>, steer clear of, keep away from

**shut** VERB = <u>close</u>, secure, fasten, seal, slam ≠ open

● ADJECTIVE = <u>closed</u>, fastened,

sealed, locked ≠ open

● PHRASES shut down = <u>stop</u>
<u>work</u>, halt work, close down

**shuttle** = <u>go back and forth</u>, commute, go to and fro, alternate

**shy** ADJECTIVE 1 = <u>timid</u>, self-conscious, bashful, retiring, shrinking, coy, self-effacing, diffident ≠ confident

2 = <u>cautious</u>, wary, hesitant, suspicious, distrustful, chary ≠ reckless

● VERB sometimes with off or away = <u>recoil</u>, flinch, draw back, start, balk

**sick** 1 = <u>unwell</u>, ill, poorly (*informal*), diseased, crook (*Austral. & N.Z. informal*), ailing, under the weather, indisposed ≠ well 2 = <u>nauseous</u>, ill, queasy, nauseated 3 = <u>tired</u>, bored, fed up, weary, jaded 4 (*Informal*) = <u>morbid</u>, sadistic, black, macabre, ghoulish

**sicken** 1 = <u>disgust</u>, revolt, nauseate, repel, gross out (*U.S. slang*), turn your stomach 2 = <u>fall</u> <u>ill</u>, take sick, ail

**sickening** = <u>disgusting</u>, revolting, offensive, foul, distasteful, repulsive, nauseating, loathsome, yucko (*Austral. slang*) ≠ delightful

**sickness** 1 = <u>illness</u>, disorder, ailment, disease, complaint, bug (*informal*), affliction, malady

2 = <u>nausea</u>, queasiness

3 = <u>vomiting</u>

**side** NOUN 1 = <u>border</u>, margin, boundary, verge, flank, rim, perimeter, edge ≠ middle 2 = <u>face</u>, surface, facet 3 = <u>party</u>, camp, faction, subsidiary, lesser, cause 4 = <u>point of view</u>, viewpoint, position, opinion, angle, slant, standpoint 5 = <u>team</u>, squad, line-up 6 = <u>aspect</u>, feature, angle, facet

● ADJECTIVE = <u>subordinate</u>, minor, secondary, subsidiary, lesser, marginal, incidental, ancillary ≠ main

● PHRASES **side with someone** = <u>support</u>, agree with, stand up for, favour, go along with, take the part of, ally yourself with

**sidewalk** (U.S. & Canad.) = <u>pavement</u>, footpath (Austral. & N.Z.)

**sideways** ADVERB 1 = <u>indirectly</u>, obliquely 2 = <u>to the side</u>, laterally

● ADJECTIVE = <u>sidelong</u>, oblique

**sift** 1 = <u>part</u>, filter, strain, separate, sieve 2 = <u>examine</u>, investigate, go through, research, analyse, work over, scrutinize

**sight** NOUN 1 = <u>vision</u>, eyes, eyesight, seeing, eye 2 = <u>spectacle</u>, show, scene, display, exhibition, vista, pageant 3 = <u>view</u>, range of vision, visibility 4 (Informal) = <u>eyesore</u>, mess, monstrosity

● VERB 1 = <u>spot</u>, see, observe, distinguish, perceive, make out, discern, behold

(**Related Words**)

adjectives: optical, visual

**sign** NOUN 1 = <u>symbol</u>, mark, device, logo, badge, emblem 2 = <u>figure</u> 3 = <u>notice</u>, board, warning, placard 4 = <u>indication</u>, evidence, mark, signal, symptom, hint, proof, gesture 5 = <u>omen</u>, warning, portent, foreboding, augury, auspice

● VERB 1 = <u>gesture</u>, indicate, signal, beckon, gesticulate 2 = <u>autograph</u>, initial, inscribe

**signal** NOUN 1 = <u>flare</u>, beam, beacon 2 = <u>cue</u>, sign, prompting, reminder 3 = <u>sign</u>, gesture, indication, mark, note, expression, token

● VERB = <u>gesture</u>, sign, wave, indicate, motion, beckon, gesticulate

**significance** = <u>importance</u>, consequence, moment, weight

**significant** 1 = <u>important</u>, serious, material, vital, critical, momentous, weighty, noteworthy ≠ insignificant 2 = <u>meaningful</u>, expressive, eloquent, indicative, suggestive ≠ meaningless

**signify** = <u>indicate</u>, mean, suggest, imply, intimate, be a sign of, denote, connote

**silence** NOUN 1 = <u>quiet</u>, peace, calm, hush, lull, stillness ≠ noise 2 = <u>reticence</u>, dumbness, taciturnity, muteness ≠ speech

● VERB = quieten, still, quiet, cut off, stifle, cut short, muffle, deaden ≠ make louder

**silent** 1 = mute, dumb, speechless, wordless, voiceless ≠ noisy 2 = uncommunicative, quiet, taciturn 3 = quiet, still, hushed, soundless, noiseless, muted ≠ loud

**silently** 1 = quietly, in silence, soundlessly, noiselessly, inaudibly, without a sound 2 = mutely, in silence, wordlessly

**silhouette** NOUN = outline, form, shape, profile

● VERB = outline, etch

**silly** 1 = stupid, ridiculous, absurd, daft, inane, senseless, idiotic, fatuous ≠ clever 2 = foolish, stupid, unwise, rash, irresponsible, thoughtless, imprudent ≠ sensible

**similar** 1 = alike, resembling, comparable ≠ different *with to* = like, comparable to, analogous to, close to

> ### Word Power
>
> **similar** – As should not be used after similar – so *Wilson held a similar position to Jones* is correct, but not *Wilson held a similar position as Jones*; and *the system is similar to the one in France* is correct, but not *the system is similar as in France.*

**similarity** = resemblance, likeness, sameness, agreement, correspondence, analogy, affinity, closeness ≠ difference

**simmer** VERB 1 = bubble, boil gently, seethe 2 = fume, seethe, smoulder, rage, be angry

● PHRASES **simmer down** (*Informal*) = calm down, control yourself, cool off *or* down

**simple** 1 = uncomplicated, clear, plain, understandable, lucid, recognizable, comprehensible, intelligible ≠ complicated 2 = easy, straightforward, not difficult, effortless, painless, uncomplicated, undemanding 3 = plain, natural, classic, unfussy, unembellished ≠ elaborate 4 = pure, mere, sheer, unalloyed 5 = artless, innocent, naive, natural, sincere, unaffected, childlike, unsophisticated ≠ sophisticated 6 = unpretentious, modest, humble, homely, unfussy, unembellished ≠ fancy

**simplicity** 1 = straightforwardness, ease, clarity, clearness ≠ complexity 2 = plainness, restraint, purity, lack of adornment ≠ elaborateness

**simplify** = make simpler, streamline, disentangle, dumb

down, reduce to essentials

**simply** 1 = <u>just</u>, only, merely, purely, solely 2 = <u>totally</u>, really, completely, absolutely, wholly, utterly 3 = <u>clearly</u>, straightforwardly, directly, plainly, intelligibly 4 = <u>plainly</u>, naturally, modestly, unpretentiously 5 = <u>without doubt</u>, surely, certainly, definitely, beyond question

**simulate** = <u>pretend</u>, act, feign, affect, put on, sham

**simultaneous** = <u>coinciding</u>, concurrent, contemporaneous, coincident, synchronous, happening at the same time

**simultaneously** = <u>at the same time</u>, together, concurrently

**sin NOUN** 1 = <u>wickedness</u>, evil, crime, error, transgression, iniquity 2 = <u>crime</u>, offence, error, wrongdoing, misdeed, transgression, act of evil, guilt • **VERB** = <u>transgress</u>, offend, lapse, err, go astray, do wrong

**sincere** = <u>honest</u>, genuine, real, true, serious, earnest, frank, candid, dinkum (*Austral. & N.Z. informal*) ≠ false

**sincerely** = <u>honestly</u>, truly, genuinely, seriously, earnestly, wholeheartedly, in earnest

**sincerity** = <u>honesty</u>, truth, candour, frankness, seriousness, genuineness

**sing** 1 = <u>croon</u>, carol, chant, warble, yodel, pipe 2 = <u>trill</u>, chirp, warble

---

### Word Power

**sing** – *Sang* is the past tense of the verb *sing*, as in *she sang sweetly*. *Sung* is the past participle, as in *we have sung our song*, and care should be taken not to use it as if it were a variant form of the past tense.

---

**singer** = <u>vocalist</u>, crooner, minstrel, soloist, chorister, balladeer

**single ADJECTIVE** 1 = <u>one</u>, sole, lone, solitary, only, only one 2 = <u>individual</u>, separate, distinct 3 = <u>unmarried</u>, free, unattached, unwed 4 = <u>separate</u>, individual, exclusive, undivided, unshared 5 = <u>simple</u>, unmixed, unblended • **PHRASES single something** or **someone out** = <u>pick</u>, choose, select, separate, distinguish, fix on, set apart, pick on or out

**singly** = <u>one by one</u>, individually, one at a time, separately

**singular** 1 = <u>single</u>, individual 2 = <u>remarkable</u>, outstanding, exceptional, notable, eminent, noteworthy ≠ ordinary 3 = <u>unusual</u>, odd, strange, extraordinary, curious, peculiar, eccentric, queer ≠ conventional

**sinister** = threatening, evil, menacing, dire, ominous, malign, disquieting ≠ reassuring

**sink 1** = go down, founder, go under, submerge, capsize **2** = slump, drop **3** = fall, drop, slip, plunge, subside, abate **4** = drop, fall **5** = stoop, be reduced to, lower yourself **6** = decline, fade, fail, flag, weaken, diminish, decrease, deteriorate ≠ improve **7** = dig, bore, drill, drive, excavate

**sip** VERB = drink, taste, sample, sup
● NOUN = swallow, drop, taste, thimbleful

**sit 1** = take a seat, perch, settle down **2** = place, set, put, position, rest, lay, settle, deposit **3** = be a member of, serve on, have a seat on, preside on **4** = convene, meet, assemble, officiate

**site** NOUN **1** = area, plot **2** = location, place, setting, point, position, situation, spot
● VERB = locate, put, place, set, position, establish, install, situate

**situation 1** = position, state, case, condition, circumstances, equation, plight, state of affairs **2** = scenario, state of affairs **3** = location, place, setting, position, site, spot

> ### Word Power
>
> **situation** – It is common to hear the word *situation* used in sentences such as *the company is in a crisis situation*. This use of *situation* is considered bad style and the word should be left out, since it adds nothing to the sentence's meaning.

**size** NOUN = dimensions, extent, range, amount, mass, volume, proportions, bulk
● PHRASES **size something** or **someone up** (*Informal*) = assess, evaluate, appraise, take stock of

**sizeable** or **sizable** = large, considerable, substantial, goodly, decent, respectable, largish

**sizzle** = hiss, spit, crackle, fry, frizzle

**skeleton** = bones, bare bones

**sketch** NOUN = drawing, design, draft, delineation
● VERB = draw, outline, represent, draft, depict, delineate, rough out

**skilful** = expert, skilled, masterly, able, professional, clever, practised, competent ≠ clumsy

**skill** = expertise, ability, proficiency, art, technique, facility, talent, craft ≠ clumsiness

**skilled** = expert, professional, able, masterly, skilful, proficient ≠ unskilled

**skim** 1 = <u>remove</u>, separate, cream
2 = <u>glide</u>, fly, coast, sail, float
3 *usually with* over *or* through
= <u>scan</u>, glance, run your eye over

**skin** NOUN 1 = <u>hide</u>, pelt, fell
2 = <u>peel</u>, rind, husk, casing,
outside, crust 3 = <u>film</u>, coating
● VERB 1 = <u>peel</u> 2 = <u>scrape</u>, flay

**skinny** = <u>thin</u>, lean, scrawny,
emaciated, undernourished ≠ fat

**skip** 1 = <u>hop</u>, dance, bob, trip,
bounce, caper, prance, frisk
2 = <u>miss out</u>, omit, leave out,
overlook, pass over, eschew, give
(something) a miss

**skirt** 1 = <u>border</u>, edge, flank
2 *often with* around *or* round
= <u>go round</u>, circumvent 3 *often
with* around *or* round = <u>avoid</u>,
evade, steer clear of, circumvent

**sky** = <u>heavens</u>, firmament, rangi
(*N.Z.*)

*Related Words*
adjective: celestial

**slab** = <u>piece</u>, slice, lump, chunk,
wedge, portion

**slack** ADJECTIVE 1 = <u>limp</u>, relaxed,
loose, lax 2 = <u>loose</u>, baggy ≠ taut
3 = <u>slow</u>, quiet, inactive, dull,
sluggish, slow-moving ≠ busy
4 = <u>negligent</u>, lazy, lax, idle,
inactive, slapdash, neglectful,
slipshod ≠ strict
● VERB = <u>shirk</u>, idle, dodge, skive
(*Brit. slang*), bludge (*Austral. &
N.Z. informal*)

● NOUN 1 = <u>surplus</u>, excess, glut,
surfeit, superabundance,
superfluity 2 = <u>room</u>, excess,
leeway, give (*informal*)

**slam** 1 = <u>bang</u>, crash, smash
2 = <u>throw</u>, dash, hurl, fling

**slant** VERB 1 = <u>slope</u>, incline, tilt,
list, bend, lean, heel, cant 2 = <u>bias</u>,
colour, twist, angle, distort
● NOUN 1 = <u>slope</u>, incline, tilt,
gradient, camber 2 = <u>bias</u>,
emphasis, prejudice, angle, point
of view, one-sidedness

**slanting** = <u>sloping</u>, angled,
inclined, tilted, tilting, bent,
diagonal, oblique

**slap** VERB = <u>smack</u>, beat, clap, cuff,
swipe, spank, clobber (*slang*),
wallop (*informal*)
● NOUN = <u>smack</u>, blow, cuff, swipe,
spank

**slash** VERB 1 = <u>cut</u>, slit, gash,
lacerate, score, rend, rip, hack
2 = <u>reduce</u>, cut, decrease, drop,
lower, moderate, diminish, cut
down
● NOUN = <u>cut</u>, slit, gash, rent, rip,
incision, laceration

**slate** (*Informal, chiefly Brit.*)
= <u>criticize</u>, censure, rebuke, scold,
tear into (*informal*)

**slaughter** VERB 1 = <u>kill</u>, murder,
massacre, destroy, execute,
assassinate 2 = <u>butcher</u>, kill, slay,
massacre
● NOUN = <u>slaying</u>, killing, murder,

massacre, bloodshed, carnage, butchery

**slave** NOUN 1 = <u>servant</u>, serf, vassal 2 = <u>drudge</u>, skivvy (chiefly Brit.)

● VERB = <u>toil</u>, drudge, slog

**slavery** = <u>enslavement</u>, servitude, subjugation, captivity, bondage ≠ freedom

**slay** 1 (Archaic or literary) = <u>kill</u>, slaughter, massacre, butcher 2 = <u>murder</u>, kill, massacre, slaughter, mow down

**sleaze** (Informal) = <u>corruption</u>, fraud, dishonesty, bribery, extortion, venality, unscrupulousness

**sleek** = <u>glossy</u>, shiny, lustrous, smooth ≠ shaggy

**sleep** NOUN = <u>slumber(s)</u>, nap, doze, snooze (informal), hibernation, siesta, forty winks (informal), zizz (Brit. informal)

● VERB = <u>slumber</u>, doze, snooze (informal), hibernate, take a nap, catnap, drowse

**sleepy** = <u>drowsy</u>, sluggish, lethargic, heavy, dull, inactive ≠ wide-awake

**slender** 1 = <u>slim</u>, narrow, slight, lean, willowy ≠ chubby 2 = <u>faint</u>, slight, remote, slim, thin, tenuous ≠ strong 3 = <u>meagre</u>, little, small, scant, scanty ≠ large

**slice** NOUN = <u>piece</u>, segment, portion, wedge, sliver, helping,

share, cut

● VERB = <u>cut</u>, divide, carve, sever, dissect, bisect

**slick** ADJECTIVE 1 = <u>skilful</u>, deft, adroit, dexterous, professional, polished ≠ clumsy 2 = <u>glib</u>, smooth, plausible, polished, specious

● VERB = <u>smooth</u>, sleek, plaster down

**slide** = <u>slip</u>, slither, glide, skim, coast

**slight** ADJECTIVE 1 = <u>small</u>, minor, insignificant, trivial, feeble, trifling, meagre, unimportant ≠ large 2 = <u>slim</u>, small, delicate, spare, fragile, lightly-built ≠ sturdy

● VERB = <u>snub</u>, insult, ignore, affront, scorn, disdain ≠ compliment

● NOUN = <u>insult</u>, snub, affront, rebuff, slap in the face (informal), (the) cold shoulder ≠ compliment

**slightly** = <u>a little</u>, a bit, somewhat

**slim** ADJECTIVE 1 = <u>slender</u>, slight, trim, thin, narrow, lean, svelte, willowy ≠ chubby 2 = <u>slight</u>, remote, faint, slender ≠ strong

● VERB = <u>lose weight</u>, diet ≠ put on weight

**sling** 1 (Informal) = <u>throw</u>, cast, toss, hurl, fling, chuck (informal), lob (informal), heave 2 = <u>hang</u>, suspend

**slip** VERB 1 = <u>fall</u>, skid 2 = <u>slide</u>, slither 3 = <u>sneak</u>, creep, steal

● NOUN = <u>mistake</u>, failure, error, blunder, lapse, omission, oversight

● PHRASES **give someone the slip** = <u>escape from</u>, get away from, evade, elude, lose (someone), flee, dodge ◆ **slip up** = <u>make a mistake</u>, blunder, err, miscalculate

**slippery** 1 = <u>smooth</u>, icy, greasy, glassy, slippy (informal, dialect), unsafe 2 = <u>untrustworthy</u>, tricky, cunning, dishonest, devious, crafty, evasive, shifty

**slit** VERB = <u>cut (open)</u>, rip, slash, knife, pierce, lance, gash

● NOUN 1 = <u>cut</u>, gash, incision, tear, rent 2 = <u>opening</u>, split

**slogan** 1 = <u>catch phrase</u>, motto, tag-line, catchword

**slope** NOUN = <u>inclination</u>, rise, incline, tilt, slant, ramp, gradient

● VERB = <u>slant</u>, incline, drop away, fall, rise, lean, tilt

● PHRASES **slope off** (Informal) = <u>slink away</u>, slip away, creep away

**sloping** = <u>slanting</u>, leaning, inclined, oblique

**sloppy** 1 (Informal) = <u>careless</u>, slovenly, slipshod, messy, untidy 2 (Informal) = <u>sentimental</u>, soppy (Brit. informal), slushy (informal), gushing, mawkish, icky (informal)

**slot** NOUN 1 = <u>opening</u>, hole, groove, vent, slit, aperture 2 (Informal) = <u>place</u>, time, space, opening, position, vacancy

● VERB = <u>fit</u>, insert

**slow** ADJECTIVE 1 = <u>unhurried</u>, sluggish, leisurely, lazy, ponderous, dawdling, laggard, lackadaisical ≠ quick 2 = <u>prolonged</u>, protracted, long-drawn-out, lingering, gradual 3 = <u>late</u>, behind, tardy 4 = <u>stupid</u>, dim, dense, thick, retarded, dozy (Brit. informal), obtuse, braindead (informal) ≠ bright

● VERB 1 often with **down** = <u>decelerate</u>, brake 2 often with **down** = <u>delay</u>, hold up, handicap, retard ≠ speed up

> ### Word Power
>
> **slow** – While not as unkind as *thick* and *stupid*, words like *slow* and *backward*, when used to talk about a person's mental abilities, are both unhelpful and likely to cause offence. It is preferable to say that a person has *special educational needs* or *learning difficulties*.

**slowly** = <u>gradually</u>, unhurriedly ≠ quickly

**slug** ➤ snails, slugs and other gastropods

**sluggish** = <u>inactive</u>, slow, lethargic, heavy, dull, inert,

---

### Snails, slugs and other gastropods

| | |
|---|---|
| abalone *or* ear shell | periwinkle *or* winkle |
| conch | slug |
| cowrie *or* cowry | snail |
| limpet | triton |
| murex | wentletrap |
| nudibranch *or* sea slug | whelk |
| ormer *or* sea-ear | |

---

indolent, torpid ≠ energetic

**slum** = <u>hovel</u>, ghetto, shanty

**slump** VERB 1 = <u>fall</u>, sink, plunge, crash, collapse, slip ≠ increase 2 = <u>sag</u>, hunch, droop, slouch, loll
● NOUN 1 = <u>fall</u>, drop, decline, crash, collapse, reverse, downturn, trough ≠ increase 2 = <u>recession</u>, depression, stagnation, inactivity, hard *or* bad times

**slur** = <u>insult</u>, stain, smear, affront, innuendo, calumny, insinuation, aspersion

**sly** ADJECTIVE 1 = <u>roguish</u>, knowing, arch, mischievous, impish 2 = <u>cunning</u>, scheming, devious, secret, clever, subtle, wily, crafty ≠ open
● PHRASES **on the sly** = <u>secretly</u>, privately, covertly, surreptitiously, on the quiet

**smack** VERB 1 = <u>slap</u>, hit, strike, clap, cuff, swipe, spank 2 = <u>drive</u>, hit, strike
● NOUN = <u>slap</u>, blow, cuff, swipe, spank

● ADVERB (*Informal*) = <u>directly</u>, right, straight, squarely, precisely, exactly, slap (*informal*)

**small** 1 = <u>little</u>, minute, tiny, mini, miniature, minuscule, diminutive, petite ≠ big 2 = <u>young</u>, little, junior, wee, juvenile, youthful, immature 3 = <u>unimportant</u>, minor, trivial, insignificant, little, petty, trifling, negligible ≠ important 4 = <u>modest</u>, humble, unpretentious ≠ grand

**smart** ADJECTIVE 1 = <u>chic</u>, trim, neat, stylish, elegant, spruce, snappy, natty (*informal*) ≠ scruffy 2 = <u>clever</u>, bright, intelligent, quick, sharp, keen, acute, shrewd ≠ stupid 3 = <u>brisk</u>, quick, lively, vigorous
● VERB = <u>sting</u>, burn, hurt

**smash** VERB 1 = <u>break</u>, crush, shatter, crack, demolish, pulverize 2 = <u>shatter</u>, break, disintegrate, crack, splinter 3 = <u>collide</u>, crash, meet head-on, clash, come into collision 4 = <u>destroy</u>, ruin, wreck, trash (*slang*), lay waste

**• NOUN** = <u>collision</u>, crash, accident

**smashing** (*Informal*, *chiefly Brit.*) = <u>excellent</u>, mean (*slang*), wonderful, brilliant (*informal*), cracking (*Brit. informal*), superb, fantastic (*informal*), booshit (*Austral. slang*), exo (*Austral. slang*), sik (*Austral. slang*) = awful

**smear** **VERB** 1 = <u>spread over</u>, daub, rub on, cover, coat, bedaub 2 = <u>slander</u>, malign, blacken, besmirch 3 = <u>smudge</u>, soil, dirty, stain, sully

**• NOUN** 1 = <u>smudge</u>, daub, streak, blot, blotch, splotch 2 = <u>slander</u>, libel, defamation, calumny

**smell** **NOUN** 1 = <u>odour</u>, scent, fragrance, perfume, bouquet, aroma 2 = <u>stink</u>, stench, pong (*Brit. informal*), fetor

**• VERB** 1 = <u>stink</u>, reek, pong (*Brit. informal*) 2 = <u>sniff</u>, scent

**smile** **VERB** = <u>grin</u>, beam, smirk, twinkle, grin from ear to ear

**• NOUN** = <u>grin</u>, beam, smirk

**smooth** **ADJECTIVE** 1 = <u>even</u>, level, flat, plane, flush, horizontal ≠ uneven 2 = <u>sleek</u>, polished, shiny, glossy, silky, velvety ≠ rough 3 = <u>mellow</u>, pleasant, mild, agreeable 4 = <u>flowing</u>, steady, regular, uniform, rhythmic 5 = <u>easy</u>, effortless, well-ordered 6 = <u>suave</u>, slick, persuasive, urbane, glib, facile, unctuous,

smarmy (*Brit. informal*)

**• VERB** 1 = <u>flatten</u>, level, press, plane, iron 2 = <u>ease</u>, facilitate ≠ hinder

**smother** 1 = <u>extinguish</u>, put out, stifle, snuff 2 = <u>suffocate</u>, choke, strangle, stifle 3 = <u>suppress</u>, stifle, repress, hide, conceal, muffle

**smug** = <u>self-satisfied</u>, superior, complacent, conceited

**snack** = <u>light meal</u>, bite, refreshment(s)

**snag** **NOUN** = <u>difficulty</u>, hitch, problem, obstacle, catch, disadvantage, complication, drawback

**• VERB** = <u>catch</u>, tear, rip

**snail** > snails, slugs and other gastropods

**snake** = <u>serpent</u>

*Related Words*

adjective: serpentine

> reptiles

**snap** **VERB** 1 = <u>break</u>, crack, separate 2 = <u>pop</u>, click, crackle 3 = <u>speak sharply</u>, bark, lash out at, jump down (someone's) throat (*informal*) 4 = <u>bite at</u>, bite, nip

**• ADJECTIVE** = <u>instant</u>, immediate, sudden, spur-of-the-moment

**• PHRASES** snap something up = <u>grab</u>, seize, take advantage of, pounce upon

**snare** **NOUN** = <u>trap</u>, net, wire, gin, noose

**• VERB** = <u>trap</u>, catch, net, wire,

seize, entrap

**snatch** VERB 1 = <u>grab</u>, grip, grasp, clutch 2 = <u>steal</u>, take, nick (*slang, chiefly Brit.*), pinch (*informal*), lift (*informal*), pilfer, filch, thieve 3 = <u>win</u> 4 = <u>save</u>, recover, get out, salvage

● NOUN = <u>bit</u>, part, fragment, piece, snippet

**sneak** VERB 1 = <u>slink</u>, slip, steal, pad, skulk 2 = <u>slip</u>, smuggle, spirit

● NOUN = <u>informer</u>, betrayer, telltale, Judas, accuser, stool pigeon, nark (*Brit., Austral., & N.Z. slang*), fizgig (*Austral. slang*)

**sneaking** 1 = <u>nagging</u>, worrying, persistent, uncomfortable 2 = <u>secret</u>, private, hidden, unexpressed, unvoiced, undivulged

**sneer** VERB 1 = <u>scorn</u>, mock, ridicule, laugh, jeer, disdain, deride 2 = <u>say contemptuously</u>, snigger

● NOUN = <u>scorn</u>, ridicule, mockery, derision, jeer, gibe

**sniff** 1 = <u>breathe in</u>, inhale 2 = <u>smell</u>, scent 3 = <u>inhale</u>, breathe in, suck in, draw in

**snub** VERB = <u>insult</u>, slight, put down, humiliate, cut (*informal*), rebuff, cold-shoulder

● NOUN = <u>insult</u>, put-down, affront, slap in the face

**so** = <u>therefore</u>, thus, hence, consequently, then, as a result,

accordingly, thence

**soak** VERB 1 = <u>steep</u> 2 = <u>wet</u>, damp, saturate, drench, moisten, suffuse, wet through, waterlog 3 = <u>penetrate</u>, permeate, seep

● PHRASES **soak something up** = <u>absorb</u>, suck up, assimilate

**soaking** = <u>soaked</u>, dripping, saturated, drenched, sodden, streaming, sopping, wet through

**soar** 1 = <u>rise</u>, increase, grow, mount, climb, go up, rocket, escalate 2 = <u>fly</u>, wing, climb, ascend ≠ plunge 3 = <u>tower</u>, climb, go up

**sob** VERB = <u>cry</u>, weep, howl, shed tears

● NOUN = <u>cry</u>, whimper, howl

**sober** 1 = <u>abstinent</u>, temperate, abstemious, moderate ≠ drunk 2 = <u>serious</u>, cool, grave, reasonable, steady, composed, rational, solemn ≠ frivolous 3 = <u>plain</u>, dark, sombre, quiet, subdued, drab ≠ bright

**so-called** = <u>alleged</u>, supposed, professed, pretended, self-styled

**social** ADJECTIVE 1 = <u>communal</u>, community, collective, group, public, general, common 2 = <u>organized</u>, gregarious

● NOUN = <u>get-together</u> (*informal*), party, gathering, function, reception, social gathering

**society** 1 = <u>the community</u>, people, the public, humanity,

**sofa → solitary**

civilization, mankind 2 = <u>culture</u>, community, population 3 = <u>organization</u>, group, club, union, league, association, institute, circle 4 = <u>upper classes</u>, gentry, elite, high society, beau monde 5 (*Old-fashioned*) = <u>companionship</u>, company, fellowship, friendship

**sofa** = <u>couch</u>, settee, divan, chaise longue

**soft** 1 = <u>velvety</u>, smooth, silky, feathery, downy, fleecy ≠ rough 2 = <u>yielding</u>, elastic ≠ hard 3 = <u>soggy</u>, swampy, marshy, boggy 4 = <u>squashy</u>, sloppy, mushy, spongy, gelatinous, pulpy 5 = <u>pliable</u>, flexible, supple, malleable, plastic, elastic, bendable, mouldable 6 = <u>quiet</u>, gentle, murmured, muted, dulcet, soft-toned ≠ loud 7 = <u>lenient</u>, easy-going, lax, indulgent, permissive, spineless, overindulgent ≠ harsh 8 = <u>kind</u>, tender, sentimental, compassionate, sensitive, gentle, tenderhearted, touchy-feely (*informal*) 9 (*Informal*) = <u>easy</u>, comfortable, undemanding, cushy (*informal*) 10 = <u>pale</u>, light, subdued, pastel, bland, mellow ≠ bright 11 = <u>dim</u>, faint, dimmed ≠ bright 12 = <u>mild</u>, temperate, balmy

**soften** 1 = <u>melt</u>, tenderize 2 = <u>lessen</u>, moderate, temper, ease, cushion, subdue, allay, mitigate

**soil**¹ 1 = <u>earth</u>, ground, clay, dust, dirt 2 = <u>territory</u>, country, land

**soil**² = <u>dirty</u>, foul, stain, pollute, tarnish, sully, defile, besmirch ≠ clean

**soldier** = <u>fighter</u>, serviceman, trooper, warrior, man-at-arms, squaddie *or* squaddy (*Brit. slang*)

**sole** = <u>only</u>, one, single, individual, alone, exclusive, solitary

**solely** = <u>only</u>, completely, entirely, exclusively, alone, merely

**solemn** 1 = <u>serious</u>, earnest, grave, sober, sedate, staid ≠ cheerful 2 = <u>formal</u>, grand, grave, dignified, ceremonial, stately, momentous ≠ informal

**solid** 1 = <u>firm</u>, hard, compact, dense, concrete ≠ unsubstantial 2 = <u>strong</u>, stable, sturdy, substantial, unshakable ≠ unstable 3 = <u>reliable</u>, dependable, upstanding, worthy, upright, trusty ≠ unreliable 4 = <u>sound</u>, real, reliable, good, genuine, dinkum (*Austral. & N.Z. informal*) ≠ unsound

**solidarity** = <u>unity</u>, unification, accord, cohesion, team spirit, unanimity, concordance, like-mindedness, kotahitanga (*N.Z.*)

**solitary** 1 = <u>unsociable</u>, reclusive, unsocial, isolated, lonely, cloistered, lonesome, friendless ≠ sociable 2 = <u>lone</u>, alone 3 = <u>isolated</u>, remote, out-of-the-way, hidden, unfrequented ≠ busy

**solution** 1 = <u>answer</u>, key, result, explanation 2 (*Chemistry*) = <u>mixture</u>, mix, compound, blend, solvent

**solve** = <u>answer</u>, work out, resolve, crack, clear up, unravel, decipher, suss (out) (*slang*)

**sombre** 1 = <u>gloomy</u>, sad, sober, grave, dismal, mournful, lugubrious, joyless ≠ cheerful 2 = <u>dark</u>, dull, gloomy, sober, drab ≠ bright

**somebody** = <u>celebrity</u>, name, star, notable, household name, dignitary, luminary, personage ≠ nobody

**somehow** = <u>one way or another</u>, come what may, come hell or high water (*informal*), by fair means or foul, by hook or (by) crook, by some means or other

**sometimes** = <u>occasionally</u>, at times, now and then ≠ always

**song** = <u>ballad</u>, air, tune, carol, chant, chorus, anthem, number, waiata (*N.Z.*)

**soon** = <u>before long</u>, shortly, in the near future

**soothe** 1 = <u>calm</u>, still, quiet, hush, appease, lull, pacify, mollify ≠ upset 2 = <u>relieve</u>, ease, alleviate,

assuage ≠ irritate

**soothing** 1 = <u>calming</u>, relaxing, peaceful, quiet, calm, restful 2 = <u>emollient</u>, palliative

**sophisticated** 1 = <u>complex</u>, advanced, complicated, subtle, delicate, elaborate, refined, intricate ≠ simple 2 = <u>cultured</u>, refined, cultivated, worldly, cosmopolitan, urbane ≠ unsophisticated

**sophistication** = <u>poise</u>, worldliness, savoir-faire, urbanity, finesse, worldly wisdom

**sore** 1 = <u>painful</u>, smarting, raw, tender, burning, angry, sensitive, irritated 2 = <u>annoyed</u>, cross, angry, pained, hurt, upset, stung, irritated, tooshie (*Austral. slang*), hoha (*N.Z.*) 3 = <u>annoying</u>, troublesome 4 (*Literary*) = <u>urgent</u>, desperate, extreme, dire, pressing, critical, acute

**sorrow** NOUN 1 = <u>grief</u>, sadness, woe, regret, distress, misery, mourning, anguish ≠ joy 2 = <u>hardship</u>, trial, tribulation, affliction, trouble, woe, misfortune ≠ good fortune
● VERB = <u>grieve</u>, mourn, lament, be sad, bemoan, agonize, bewail ≠ rejoice

**sorry** 1 = <u>regretful</u>, apologetic, contrite, repentant, remorseful, penitent, shamefaced, conscience-stricken

≠ unapologetic 2 = sympathetic, moved, full of pity, compassionate, commiserative ≠ unsympathetic 3 = <u>wretched</u>, miserable, pathetic, mean, poor, sad, pitiful, deplorable

**sort** NOUN = <u>kind</u>, type, class, make, order, style, quality, nature
● VERB = <u>arrange</u>, group, order, rank, divide, grade, classify, categorize

> ## Word Power
>
> **sort** – It is common in informal speech to combine singular and plural in sentences like *these sort of distinctions are becoming blurred*. This is not acceptable in careful writing, where the plural must be used consistently: *these sorts of distinctions are becoming blurred*.

**soul** 1 = <u>spirit</u>, essence, life, vital force, wairua (N.Z.)
2 = <u>embodiment</u>, essence, epitome, personification, quintessence, type 3 = <u>person</u>, being, individual, body, creature, man *or* woman

**sound**[1] NOUN 1 = <u>noise</u>, din, report, tone, reverberation
2 = <u>idea</u>, impression, drift 3 = <u>cry</u>, noise, peep, squeak 4 = <u>tone</u>, music, note
● VERB 1 = <u>toll</u>, set off 2 = <u>resound</u>, echo, go off, toll, set off, chime, reverberate, clang 3 = <u>seem</u>, seem to be, appear to be

(Related Words)
*adjectives*: sonic, acoustic

**sound**[2] 1 = <u>fit</u>, healthy, perfect, intact, unhurt, uninjured, unimpaired ≠ frail 2 = <u>sturdy</u>, strong, solid, stable 3 = <u>sensible</u>, wise, reasonable, right, correct, proper, valid, rational
≠ irresponsible 4 = <u>deep</u>, unbroken, undisturbed, untroubled ≠ troubled

**sour** 1 = <u>sharp</u>, acid, tart, bitter, pungent, acetic ≠ sweet
2 = <u>rancid</u>, turned, gone off, curdled, gone bad, off ≠ fresh
3 = <u>bitter</u>, tart, acrimonious, embittered, disagreeable, ill-tempered, waspish, ungenerous ≠ good-natured

**source** 1 = <u>cause</u>, origin, derivation, beginning, author
2 = <u>informant</u>, authority
3 = <u>origin</u>, fount

**souvenir** = <u>keepsake</u>, reminder, memento

**sovereign** ADJECTIVE
1 = <u>supreme</u>, ruling, absolute, royal, principal, imperial, kingly *or* queenly 2 = <u>excellent</u>, efficient, effectual
● NOUN = <u>monarch</u>, ruler, king *or* queen, chief, potentate, emperor *or* empress, prince *or* princess

**sovereignty** = <u>supreme power</u>

domination, supremacy, primacy, kingship, rangatiratanga (N.Z.)

**sow** = scatter, plant, seed, implant

**space** 1 = room, capacity, extent, margin, scope, play, expanse, leeway 2 = period, interval, time, while, span, duration 3 = outer space, the universe, the galaxy, the solar system, the cosmos 4 = blank, gap, interval

**spacious** = roomy, large, huge, broad, extensive, ample, expansive, capacious ≠ limited

**span** NOUN 1 = period, term, duration, spell 2 = extent, reach, spread, length, distance, stretch
• VERB = extend across, cross, bridge, cover, link, traverse

**spar** = argue, row, squabble, scrap (informal), wrangle, bicker

**spare** ADJECTIVE 1 = back-up, reserve, second, extra, additional, auxiliary 2 = extra, surplus, leftover, over, free, odd, unwanted, unused ≠ necessary 3 = free, leisure, unoccupied 4 = thin, lean, meagre, gaunt, wiry ≠ plump
• VERB 1 = afford, give, grant, do without, part with, manage without, let someone have 2 = have mercy on, pardon, leave, let off (informal), go easy on (informal), save (from harm) ≠ show no mercy to

**sparing** ≠ economical, frugal, thrifty, saving, careful, prudent ≠ lavish

**spark** NOUN 1 = flicker, flash, gleam, glint, flare 2 = trace, hint, scrap, atom, jot, vestige
• VERB often with off = start, stimulate, provoke, inspire, trigger (off), set off, precipitate

**sparkle** VERB = glitter, flash, shine, gleam, shimmer, twinkle, dance, glint
• NOUN 1 = glitter, flash, gleam, flicker, brilliance, twinkle, glint 2 = vivacity, life, spirit, dash, vitality, élan, liveliness

**spate** = flood, flow, torrent, rush, deluge, outpouring

**speak** 1 = talk, say something 2 = articulate, say, pronounce, utter, tell, state, talk, express 3 = converse, talk, chat, discourse, confer, commune, exchange views, korero (N.Z.) 4 = lecture, address an audience

**speaker** = orator, public speaker, lecturer, spokesperson, spokesman or spokeswoman

**spearhead** = lead, head, pioneer, launch, set off, initiate, set in motion

**special** 1 = exceptional, important, significant, particular, unique, unusual, extraordinary, memorable ≠ ordinary 2 = specific, particular, distinctive, individual, appropriate, precise ≠ general

**specialist** = <u>expert</u>, authority, professional, master, consultant, guru, buff (*informal*), connoisseur, fundi (*S. African*)

**speciality** = <u>forte</u>, métier, specialty, bag (*slang*), pièce de résistance (*French*)

**species** = <u>kind</u>, sort, type, group, class, variety, breed, category

**specific** 1 = <u>particular</u>, special, characteristic, distinguishing ≠ general 2 = <u>precise</u>, exact, explicit, definite, express, clear-cut, unequivocal ≠ vague 3 = <u>peculiar</u>, appropriate, individual, particular, unique

**specification** = <u>requirement</u>, detail, particular, stipulation, condition, qualification

**specify** = <u>state</u>, designate, stipulate, name, detail, mention, indicate, define

**specimen** 1 = <u>sample</u>, example, model, type, pattern, instance, representative, exemplification 2 = <u>example</u>, model, type

**spectacle** 1 = <u>show</u>, display, exhibition, event, performance, extravaganza, pageant 2 = <u>sight</u>, wonder, scene, phenomenon, curiosity, marvel

**spectacular** ADJECTIVE = <u>impressive</u>, striking, dramatic, stunning (*informal*), grand,

magnificent, splendid, dazzling ≠ unimpressive
● NOUN = <u>show</u>, display, spectacle

**spectator** = <u>onlooker</u>, observer, viewer, looker-on, watcher, bystander ≠ participant

**spectre** = <u>ghost</u>, spirit, phantom, vision, apparition, wraith, kehua (*N.Z.*)

**speculate** 1 = <u>conjecture</u>, consider, wonder, guess, surmise, theorize, hypothesize 2 = <u>gamble</u>, risk, venture, hazard

**speculation** 1 = <u>theory</u>, ● opinion, hypothesis, conjecture, guess, surmise, guesswork, supposition 2 = <u>gamble</u>, risk, hazard

**speculative** = <u>hypothetical</u>, academic, theoretical, notional, conjectural, suppositional

**speech** 1 = <u>communication</u>, talk, conversation, discussion, dialogue 2 = <u>diction</u>, pronunciation, articulation, delivery, fluency, inflection, intonation, elocution 3 = <u>language</u>, tongue, jargon, dialect, idiom, parlance, articulation, diction 4 = <u>talk</u>, address, lecture, discourse, homily, oration, spiel (*informal*), whaikorero (*N.Z.*)

**speed** NOUN 1 = <u>rate</u>, pace 2 = <u>swiftness</u>, rush, hurry, haste, rapidity, quickness ≠ slowness

● VERB 1 = <u>race</u>, rush, hurry, zoom, career, tear, barrel (along) (*informal, chiefly U.S. & Canad.*), gallop ≠ crawl 2 = <u>help</u>, advance, aid, boost, assist, facilitate, expedite ≠ hinder

### Word Power

**speed** – The past tense of *speed up* is *speeded up* (not *sped up*), for example *I speeded up to overtake the lorry*. The past participle is also *speeded up*, for example *I had already speeded up when I spotted the police car*.

**speedy** = <u>quick</u>, fast, rapid, swift, express, immediate, prompt, hurried ≠ slow

**spell**[1] = <u>indicate</u>, mean, signify, point to, imply, augur, portend

**spell**[2] 1 = <u>incantation</u>, charm, makutu (*N.Z.*) 2 = <u>enchantment</u>, magic, fascination, glamour, allure, bewitchment

**spell**[3] = <u>period</u>, time, term, stretch, course, season, interval, bout

**spend** 1 = <u>pay out</u>, fork out (*slang*), expend, disburse ≠ save 2 = <u>pass</u>, fill, occupy, while away 3 = <u>use up</u>, waste, squander, empty, drain, exhaust, consume, run through ≠ save

**sphere** 1 = <u>ball</u>, globe, orb, globule, circle 2 = <u>field</u>, department, function, territory, capacity, province, patch, scope

**spice** 1 = <u>seasoning</u> 2 = <u>excitement</u>, zest, colour, pep, zing (*informal*), piquancy

**spicy** 1 = <u>hot</u>, seasoned, aromatic, savoury, piquant 2 (*Informal*) = <u>risqué</u>, racy, ribald, hot (*informal*), suggestive, titillating, indelicate

**spider** ➤ **spiders and other arachnids**

Related Words

fear of: arachnophobia

**spike** NOUN = <u>point</u>, stake, spine,

### Spiders and other arachnids

| | |
|---|---|
| black widow | red-back (spider) |
| chigger, chigoe, *or* (*U.S. &* *Canad.*) redbug | spider |
| | spider mite |
| chigoe, chigger, jigger, *or* sand flea | tarantula |
| | tick |
| harvestman *or* (*U.S. & Canad.*) daddy-longlegs | trap-door spider |
| | whip scorpion |
| katipo | wolf spider *or* hunting spider |
| mite | |

barb, prong

● VERB = <u>impale</u>, spit, spear, stick

**spill** 1 = <u>tip over</u>, overturn, capsize, knock over 2 = <u>shed</u>, discharge, disgorge 3 = <u>slop</u>, flow, pour, run, overflow

**spin** VERB 1 = <u>revolve</u>, turn, rotate, reel, whirl, twirl, gyrate, pirouette 2 = <u>reel</u>, swim, whirl

● NOUN 1 (*Informal*) = <u>drive</u>, ride, joy ride (*informal*) 2 = <u>revolution</u>, roll, whirl, gyration

● PHRASES **spin something out** = <u>prolong</u>, extend, lengthen, draw out, drag out, delay, amplify

**spine** 1 = <u>backbone</u>, vertebrae, spinal column, vertebral column 2 = <u>barb</u>, spur, needle, spike, ray, quill

**spiral** ADJECTIVE = <u>coiled</u>, winding, whorled, helical

● NOUN = <u>coil</u>, helix, corkscrew, whorl

**spirit** NOUN 1 = <u>soul</u>, life 2 = <u>life force</u>, vital spark, mauri (*N.Z.*) 3 = <u>ghost</u>, phantom, spectre, apparition, atua (*N.Z.*), kehua (*N.Z.*) 4 = <u>courage</u>, guts (*informal*), grit, backbone, spunk (*informal*), gameness 5 = <u>liveliness</u>, energy, vigour, life, force, fire, enthusiasm, animation 6 = <u>attitude</u>, character, temper, outlook, temperament, disposition 7 = <u>heart</u>, sense, nature, soul, core, substance,

essence, quintessence 8 = <u>intention</u>, meaning, purpose, purport, gist 9 = <u>feeling</u>, atmosphere, character, tone, mood, tenor, ambience

● PLURAL NOUN = <u>mood</u>, feelings, morale, temper, disposition, state of mind, frame of mind

**spirited** = <u>lively</u>, energetic, animated, active, feisty (*informal, chiefly U.S. & Canad.*), vivacious, mettlesome ≠ lifeless

**spiritual** 1 = <u>nonmaterial</u>, immaterial, incorporeal ≠ material 2 = <u>sacred</u>, religious, holy, divine, devotional

**spit** VERB 1 = <u>expectorate</u> 2 = <u>eject</u>, throw out

● NOUN = <u>saliva</u>, dribble, spittle, drool, slaver

**spite** NOUN = <u>malice</u>, malevolence, ill will, hatred, animosity, venom, spleen, spitefulness ≠ kindness

● VERB = <u>annoy</u>, hurt, injure, harm, vex ≠ benefit

● PHRASES **in spite of** = <u>despite</u>, regardless of, notwithstanding, (even) though

**splash** VERB 1 = <u>paddle</u>, plunge, bathe, dabble, wade, wallow 2 = <u>scatter</u>, shower, spray, sprinkle, wet, spatter, slop 3 = <u>spatter</u>, mark, stain, speck, speckle

● NOUN 1 = <u>dash</u>, touch, spattering

2 = spot, burst, patch, spurt

3 = <u>blob</u>, spot, smudge, stain, smear, fleck, speck

**splendid** 1 = <u>excellent</u>, wonderful, marvellous, great (*informal*), cracking (*Brit. informal*), fantastic (*informal*), first-class, glorious, booshit (*Austral. slang*), exo (*Austral. slang*), sik (*Austral. slang*) ≠ poor

2 = <u>magnificent</u>, grand, impressive, rich, superb, costly, gorgeous, lavish ≠ squalid

**splendour** = <u>magnificence</u>, grandeur, show, display, spectacle, richness, nobility, pomp ≠ squalor

**splinter** NOUN = <u>sliver</u>, fragment, chip, flake

• VERB = <u>shatter</u>, split, fracture, disintegrate

**split** VERB 1 = <u>break</u>, crack, burst, open, give way, come apart, come undone 2 = <u>cut</u>, break, crack, snap, chop 3 = <u>divide</u>, separate, disunite, disband, cleave

4 = <u>diverge</u>, separate, branch, fork, part 5 = <u>tear</u>, rend, rip

6 = <u>share out</u>, divide, distribute, halve, allocate, partition, allot, apportion

• NOUN 1 = <u>division</u>, breach, rift, rupture, discord, schism, estrangement, dissension

2 = <u>separation</u>, break-up, split-up

3 = <u>crack</u>, tear, rip, gap, rent, breach, slit, fissure

• ADJECTIVE 1 = <u>divided</u>

2 = <u>broken</u>, cracked, fractured, ruptured, cleft

**spoil** VERB 1 = <u>ruin</u>, destroy, wreck, damage, injure, harm, mar, trash (*slang*), crool *or* cruel (*Austral. slang*) ≠ improve

2 = <u>overindulge</u>, indulge, pamper, cosset, coddle, mollycoddle ≠ deprive 3 = <u>indulge</u>, pamper, satisfy, gratify, pander to 4 = <u>go bad</u>, turn, go off (*Brit. informal*), rot, decay, decompose, curdle, addle

• PLURAL NOUN = <u>booty</u>, loot, plunder, prey, swag (*slang*)

**spoken** = <u>verbal</u>, voiced, expressed, uttered, oral, said, told, unwritten

**spokesperson** = <u>speaker</u>, official, spokesman *or* spokeswoman, voice, spin doctor (*informal*), mouthpiece

**sponsor** VERB = <u>back</u>, fund, finance, promote, subsidize, patronize

• NOUN = <u>backer</u>, patron, promoter

**spontaneous** = <u>unplanned</u>, impromptu, unprompted, willing, natural, voluntary, instinctive, impulsive ≠ planned

**sport** NOUN 1 = <u>game</u>, exercise, recreation, play, amusement, diversion, pastime 2 = <u>fun</u>, joking, teasing, banter, jest, badinage

• VERB (*Informal*) = wear, display, flaunt, exhibit, flourish, show off, vaunt

**sporting** = fair, sportsmanlike, game (*informal*) ≠ unfair

**sporty** = athletic, outdoor, energetic

**spot** NOUN 1 = mark, stain, speck, scar, blot, smudge, blemish, speckle 2 = pimple, pustule, zit (*slang*) 3 = place, site, point, position, scene, location 4 (*Informal*) = predicament, trouble, difficulty, mess, plight, hot water (*informal*), quandary, tight spot

• VERB 1 = see, observe, catch sight of, sight, recognize, detect, make out, discern 2 = mark, stain, soil, dirty, fleck, spatter, speckle, splodge

**spotlight** NOUN = attention, limelight, public eye, fame

• VERB = highlight, draw attention to, accentuate

**spotted** = speckled, dotted, flecked, mottled, dappled

**spouse** = partner, mate, husband *or* wife, consort, significant other (*U.S. informal*)

**sprawl** = loll, slump, lounge, flop, slouch

**spray**[1] NOUN 1 = droplets, fine mist, drizzle 2 = aerosol, sprinkler, atomizer

• VERB = scatter, shower, sprinkle, diffuse

**spray**[2] = sprig, floral arrangement, branch, corsage

**spread** VERB 1 = open (out), extend, stretch, unfold, sprawl, unroll 2 = extend, open, stretch 3 = grow, increase, expand, widen, escalate, proliferate, multiply, broaden 4 = circulate, broadcast, propagate, disseminate, make known ≠ suppress 5 = diffuse, cast, shed, radiate

• NOUN 1 = increase, development, advance, expansion, proliferation, dissemination, dispersal 2 = extent, span, stretch, sweep

**spree** = fling, binge (*informal*), orgy

**spring** NOUN = flexibility, bounce, resilience, elasticity, buoyancy

• VERB 1 = jump, bound, leap, bounce, vault 2 *often with* from = originate, come, derive, start, issue, proceed, arise, stem

*Related Words*
adjective: vernal

**sprinkle** = scatter, dust, strew, pepper, shower, spray, powder, dredge

**sprinkling** = scattering, dusting, few, dash, handful, sprinkle

**sprint** = run, race, shoot, tear, dash, dart, hare (*Brit. informal*)

**sprout** 1 = germinate, bud,

shoot, spring 2 = <u>grow</u>, develop, ripen

**spur** VERB = <u>incite</u>, drive, prompt, urge, stimulate, animate, prod, prick

● NOUN = <u>stimulus</u>, incentive, impetus, motive, impulse, inducement, incitement

● PHRASES **on the spur of the moment** = <u>on impulse</u>, impulsively, on the spot, impromptu, without planning

**spurn** = <u>reject</u>, slight, scorn, rebuff, snub, despise, disdain, repulse ≠ accept

**spy** NOUN = <u>undercover agent</u>, mole, nark (*Brit., Austral., & N.Z. slang*)

● VERB = <u>catch sight of</u>, spot, notice, observe, glimpse, espy

**squabble** VERB = <u>quarrel</u>, fight, argue, row, dispute, wrangle, bicker

● NOUN = <u>quarrel</u>, fight, row, argument, dispute, disagreement, tiff

**squad** = <u>team</u>, group, band, company, force, troop, crew, gang

**squander** = <u>waste</u>, spend, fritter away, blow (*slang*), misuse, expend, misspend ≠ save

**square** ADJECTIVE = <u>fair</u>, straight, genuine, ethical, honest, on the level (*informal*), kosher (*informal*), dinkum (*Austral. & N.Z. informal*), above board

● VERB often with with = <u>agree</u>, match, fit, correspond, tally, reconcile

**squash** 1 = <u>crush</u>, press, flatten, mash, smash, distort, pulp, compress 2 = <u>suppress</u>, quell, silence, crush, annihilate 3 = <u>embarrass</u>, put down, shame, degrade, mortify

**squeeze** VERB 1 = <u>press</u>, crush, squash, pinch 2 = <u>clutch</u>, press, grip, crush, pinch, squash, compress, wring 3 = <u>cram</u>, press, crowd, force, stuff, pack, jam, ram 4 = <u>hug</u>, embrace, cuddle, clasp, enfold

● NOUN 1 = <u>press</u>, grip, clasp, crush, pinch, squash, wring 2 = <u>crush</u>, jam, squash, press, crowd, congestion 3 = <u>hug</u>, embrace, clasp

**stab** VERB 1 = <u>pierce</u>, stick, wound, knife, thrust, spear, jab, transfix

● NOUN 1 (*Informal*) = <u>attempt</u>, go, try, endeavour 2 = <u>twinge</u>, prick, pang, ache

**stability** = <u>firmness</u>, strength, soundness, solidity, steadiness ≠ instability

**stable** 1 = <u>secure</u>, lasting, strong, sound, fast, sure, established, permanent ≠ insecure 2 = <u>well-balanced</u>, balanced, sensible, reasonable, rational 3 = <u>solid</u>, firm, fixed, substantial, durable, well-made, well-built, immovable

≠ unstable

**stack** NOUN 1 = <u>pile</u>, heap, mountain, mass, load, mound 2 = <u>lot</u>, mass, load (*informal*), ton (*informal*), heap (*informal*), great amount

● VERB = <u>pile</u>, heap up, load, assemble, accumulate, amass

**staff** NOUN 1 = <u>workers</u>, employees, personnel, workforce, team 2 = <u>stick</u>, pole, rod, crook, cane, stave, wand, sceptre

**stage** = <u>step</u>, leg, phase, point, level, period, division, lap

**stagger** 1 = <u>totter</u>, reel, sway, lurch, wobble 2 = <u>astound</u>, amaze, stun, shock, shake, overwhelm, astonish, confound

**stain** NOUN 1 = <u>mark</u>, spot, blot, blemish, discoloration, smirch 2 = <u>stigma</u>, shame, disgrace, slur, dishonour 3 = <u>dye</u>, colour, tint

● VERB 1 = <u>mark</u>, soil, discolour, dirty, tinge, spot, blot, blemish 2 = <u>dye</u>, colour, tint

**stake**[1] = <u>pole</u>, post, stick, pale, paling, picket, palisade

**stake**[2] NOUN = <u>bet</u>, ante, wager

● VERB 1 = <u>bet</u>, gamble, wager, chance, risk, venture, hazard 2 = <u>interest</u>, share, involvement, concern, investment

**stale** 1 = <u>old</u>, hard, dry, decayed ≠ fresh 2 = <u>musty</u>, fusty 3 = <u>tasteless</u>, flat, sour 4 = <u>unoriginal</u>, banal, trite,

stereotyped, worn-out, threadbare, hackneyed, overused ≠ original

**stalk** = <u>pursue</u>, follow, track, hunt, shadow, haunt

**stall** VERB 1 = <u>play for time</u>, delay, hedge, temporize 2 = <u>stop dead</u>, jam, seize up, catch, stick, stop short

● NOUN = <u>stand</u>, table, counter, booth, kiosk

**stalwart** 1 = <u>loyal</u>, faithful, firm, true, dependable, steadfast 2 = <u>strong</u>, strapping, sturdy, stout ≠ puny

**stamina** = <u>staying power</u>, endurance, resilience, force, power, energy, strength

**stammer** = <u>stutter</u>, falter, pause, hesitate, stumble over your words

**stamp** NOUN = <u>imprint</u>, mark, brand, signature, earmark, hallmark

● VERB 1 = <u>print</u>, mark, impress 2 = <u>trample</u>, step, tread, crush 3 = <u>identify</u>, mark, brand, label, reveal, show to be, categorize

● PHRASES **stamp something out** = <u>eliminate</u>, destroy, eradicate, crush, suppress, put down, scotch, quell

**stance** 1 = <u>attitude</u>, stand, position, viewpoint, standpoint 2 = <u>posture</u>, carriage, bearing, deportment

**stand** VERB 1 = be upright, be erect, be vertical 2 = get to your feet, rise, stand up, straighten up 3 = be located, be, sit, be positioned, be situated *or* located 4 = be valid, continue, exist, prevail, remain valid 5 = put, place, position, set, mount 6 = sit, mellow 7 = resist, endure, tolerate, stand up to 8 = tolerate, bear, abide, stomach, endure, brook 9 = take, bear, handle, endure, put up with (*informal*), countenance

● NOUN 1 = position, attitude, stance, opinion, determination 2 = stall, booth, kiosk, table

● PHRASES **stand by** = be prepared, wait ◆ **stand for something** 1 = represent, mean, signify, denote, indicate, symbolize, betoken 2 (*Informal*) = tolerate, bear, put up with, brook ◆ **stand in for someone** = be a substitute for, represent, cover for, take the place of, deputize for ◆ **stand up for something** *or* **someone** = support, champion, defend, uphold, stick up for (*informal*)

**standard** NOUN 1 = level, grade 2 = criterion, measure, guideline, example, model, average, norm, gauge 3 *often plural* = principles, ideals, morals, ethics 4 = flag, banner, ensign

● ADJECTIVE 1 = usual, normal, customary, average, basic, regular, typical, orthodox ≠ unusual 2 = accepted, official, established, approved, recognized, definitive, authoritative ≠ unofficial

**stand-in** = substitute, deputy, replacement, reserve, surrogate, understudy, locum, stopgap

**standing** NOUN 1 = status, position, footing, rank, reputation, eminence, repute 2 = duration, existence, continuance

● ADJECTIVE 1 = permanent, lasting, fixed, regular 2 = upright, erect, vertical

**staple** = principal, chief, main, key, basic, fundamental, predominant

**star** NOUN 1 = heavenly body, celestial body 2 = celebrity, big name, megastar (*informal*), name, luminary 3 = leading man *or* lady, hero *or* heroine, principal, main attraction

● VERB = play the lead, appear, feature, perform

● ADJECTIVE = leading, major, celebrated, brilliant, well-known, prominent

(*Related Words*)
adjectives: astral, stellar

**stare** = gaze, look, goggle, watch, gape, eyeball (*slang*), gawp (*Brit. slang*), gawk

**stark** ADJECTIVE 1 = <u>plain</u>, harsh, basic, grim, straightforward, blunt 2 = <u>sharp</u>, clear, striking, distinct, clear-cut 3 = <u>austere</u>, severe, plain, bare, harsh 4 = <u>bleak</u>, grim, barren, hard 5 = <u>absolute</u>, pure, sheer, utter, downright, out-and-out, unmitigated

● ADVERB = <u>absolutely</u>, quite, completely, entirely, altogether, wholly, utterly

**start** VERB 1 = <u>set about</u>, begin, proceed, embark upon, take the first step, make a beginning ≠ stop 2 = <u>begin</u>, arise, originate, issue, appear, commence ≠ end 3 = <u>set in motion</u>, initiate, instigate, trigger, originate, get going, kick-start ≠ stop 4 = <u>establish</u>, begin, found, create, launch, set up, institute, pioneer ≠ terminate 5 = <u>start up</u>, activate, get something going ≠ turn off 6 = <u>jump</u>, shy, jerk, flinch, recoil

● NOUN 1 = <u>beginning</u>, outset, opening, birth, foundation, dawn, onset, initiation ≠ end 2 = <u>jump</u>, spasm, convulsion

**startle** = <u>surprise</u>, shock, frighten, scare, make (someone) jump

**starving** = <u>hungry</u>, starved, ravenous, famished

**state** NOUN 1 = <u>country</u>, nation, land, republic, territory, federation, commonwealth, kingdom 2 = <u>government</u>, ministry, administration, executive, regime, powers-that-be 3 = <u>condition</u>, shape 4 = <u>frame of mind</u>, condition, spirits, attitude, mood, humour 5 = <u>ceremony</u>, glory, grandeur, splendour, majesty, pomp 6 = <u>circumstances</u>, situation, position, predicament

● VERB = <u>say</u>, declare, specify, present, voice, express, assert, utter

➤ WORD POWER SUPPLEMENT
**Australian states and territories**
➤ WORD POWER SUPPLEMENT
**US states**

**stately** = <u>grand</u>, majestic, dignified, royal, august, noble, regal, lofty ≠ lowly

**statement** 1 = <u>announcement</u>, declaration, communication, communiqué, proclamation 2 = <u>account</u>, report

**station** NOUN 1 = <u>railway station</u>, stop, stage, halt, terminal, train station, terminus 2 = <u>headquarters</u>, base, depot 3 = <u>position</u>, rank, status, standing, situation 4 = <u>post</u>, place, location, position, situation

● VERB = <u>assign</u>, post, locate, set, establish, install

**stature** 1 = <u>height</u>, build, size 2 = <u>importance</u>, standing, prestige, rank, prominence, eminence

**status** 1 = <u>position</u>, rank, grade
2 = <u>prestige</u>, standing, authority, influence, weight, honour, importance, fame, mana (*N.Z.*) 3 = <u>state of play</u>, development, progress, condition, evolution

**staunch** = <u>loyal</u>, faithful, stalwart, firm, sound, true, trusty, steadfast

**stay VERB** 1 = <u>remain</u>, continue to be, linger, stop, wait, halt, pause, abide ≠ go 2 *often with* **at** = <u>lodge</u>, visit, sojourn, put up at, be accommodated at
3 = <u>continue</u>, remain, go on, survive, endure
● **NOUN** 1 = <u>visit</u>, stop, holiday, stopover, sojourn
2 = <u>postponement</u>, delay, suspension, stopping, halt, deferment

**steady** 1 = <u>continuous</u>, regular, constant, consistent, persistent, unbroken, uninterrupted, incessant ≠ irregular 2 = <u>stable</u>, fixed, secure, firm, safe ≠ unstable
3 = <u>regular</u>, established
4 = <u>dependable</u>, sensible, reliable, secure, calm, supportive, sober, level-headed ≠ undependable

**steal** 1 = <u>take</u>, nick (*slang, chiefly Brit.*), pinch (*informal*), lift (*informal*), embezzle, pilfer, misappropriate, purloin 2 = <u>copy</u>, take, appropriate, pinch

(*informal*) 3 = <u>sneak</u>, slip, creep, tiptoe, slink

**stealth** = <u>secrecy</u>, furtiveness, slyness, sneakiness, unobtrusiveness, stealthiness, surreptitiousness

**steep**[1] 1 = <u>sheer</u>, precipitous, abrupt, vertical ≠ gradual
2 = <u>sharp</u>, sudden, abrupt, marked, extreme, distinct
3 (*Informal*) = <u>high</u>, exorbitant, extreme, unreasonable, overpriced, extortionate ≠ reasonable

**steep**[2] = <u>soak</u>, immerse, marinate (*Cookery*), submerge, drench, moisten, souse

**steeped** = <u>saturated</u>, pervaded, permeated, filled, infused, imbued, suffused

**steer** 1 = <u>drive</u>, control, direct, handle, pilot 2 = <u>direct</u>, lead, guide, conduct, escort

**stem**[1] **NOUN** = <u>stalk</u>, branch, trunk, shoot, axis
● **PHRASES stem from something** = <u>originate from</u>, be caused by, derive from, arise from

**stem**[2] = <u>stop</u>, hold back, staunch, check, dam, curb

**step NOUN** 1 = <u>pace</u>, stride, footstep 2 = <u>footfall</u> 3 = <u>move</u>, measure, action, means, act, deed, expedient 4 = <u>stage</u>, point, phase
5 = <u>level</u>, rank, degree
● **VERB** = <u>walk</u>, pace, tread, move

● PHRASES **step in** (*Informal*)
= <u>intervene</u>, take action, become
involved ◆ **step something up**
= <u>increase</u>, intensify, raise

**stereotype** NOUN = <u>formula</u>,
pattern

● VERB = <u>categorize</u>, typecast,
pigeonhole, standardize

**sterile** 1 = <u>germ-free</u>, sterilized,
disinfected, aseptic ≠ unhygienic
2 = <u>barren</u>, infertile,
unproductive, childless ≠ fertile

**sterling** = <u>excellent</u>, sound, fine,
superlative

**stern** 1 = <u>strict</u>, harsh, hard, grim,
rigid, austere, inflexible ≠ lenient
2 = <u>severe</u>, serious, forbidding
≠ friendly

**stick**¹ 1 = <u>twig</u>, branch 2 = <u>cane</u>,
staff, pole, rod, crook, baton
3 (*Slang*) = <u>abuse</u>, criticism, flak
(*informal*), fault-finding

**stick**² VERB 1 (*Informal*) = <u>put</u>,
place, set, lay, deposit 2 = <u>poke</u>,
dig, stab, thrust, pierce, penetrate,
spear, prod 3 = <u>fasten</u>, fix, bind,
hold, bond, attach, glue, paste
4 = <u>adhere</u>, cling, become joined,
become welded 5 = <u>stay</u>, remain,
linger, persist 6 (*Slang*) = <u>tolerate</u>,
take, stand, stomach, abide

● PHRASES **stick out** = <u>protrude</u>,
stand out, jut out, show, project,
bulge, obtrude ◆ **stick up for
someone** (*Informal*) = <u>defend</u>,
support, champion, stand up for

**sticky** 1 = <u>adhesive</u>, gummed,
adherent 2 = <u>gooey</u>, tacky
(*informal*), viscous, glutinous,
gummy, icky (*informal*), gluey,
clinging 3 (*Informal*) = <u>difficult</u>,
awkward, tricky, embarrassing,
nasty, delicate, unpleasant, barro
(*Austral. slang*) 4 = <u>humid</u>, close,
sultry, oppressive, sweltering,
clammy, muggy

**stiff** 1 = <u>inflexible</u>, rigid,
unyielding, hard, firm, tight, solid,
tense ≠ flexible 2 = <u>formal</u>,
constrained, forced, unnatural,
stilted, unrelaxed ≠ informal
3 = <u>vigorous</u>, great, strong
4 = <u>severe</u>, strict, harsh, hard,
heavy, extreme, drastic
5 = <u>difficult</u>, hard, tough,
exacting, arduous

**stifle** 1 = <u>suppress</u>, repress, stop,
check, silence, restrain, hush,
smother 2 = <u>restrain</u>, suppress,
repress, smother

**stigma** = <u>disgrace</u>, shame,
dishonour, stain, slur, smirch

**still** ADJECTIVE 1 = <u>motionless</u>,
stationary, calm, peaceful, serene,
tranquil, undisturbed, restful
≠ moving 2 = <u>silent</u>, quiet,
hushed ≠ noisy

● VERB = <u>quieten</u>, calm, settle,
quiet, silence, soothe, hush, lull
≠ get louder

● ADVERB = <u>however</u>, but, yet,
nevertheless, notwithstanding

**stimulate** = <u>encourage</u>, inspire, prompt, fire, spur, provoke, arouse, rouse

**stimulating** = <u>exciting</u>, inspiring, stirring, rousing, provocative, exhilarating ≠ boring

**stimulus** = <u>incentive</u>, spur, encouragement, impetus, inducement, goad, incitement, fillip

**sting** 1 = <u>hurt</u>, burn, wound 2 = <u>smart</u>, burn, pain, hurt, tingle

**stink** VERB = <u>reek</u>, pong (*Brit. informal*)
• NOUN = <u>stench</u>, pong (*Brit. informal*), foul smell, fetor

**stint** NOUN = <u>term</u>, time, turn, period, share, shift, stretch, spell
• VERB = <u>be mean</u>, hold back, be sparing, skimp on, be frugal

**stipulate** = <u>specify</u>, agree, require, contract, settle, covenant, insist upon

**stir** VERB 1 = <u>mix</u>, beat, agitate 2 = <u>stimulate</u>, move, excite, spur, provoke, arouse, awaken, rouse ≠ inhibit 3 = <u>spur</u>, drive, prompt, stimulate, prod, urge, animate, prick
• NOUN = <u>commotion</u>, excitement, activity, disorder, fuss, disturbance, bustle, flurry

**stock** NOUN 1 = <u>shares</u>, holdings, securities, investments, bonds, equities 2 = <u>property</u>, capital, assets, funds 3 = <u>goods</u>, merchandise, wares, range, choice, variety, selection, commodities 4 = <u>supply</u>, store, reserve, fund, stockpile, hoard 5 = <u>livestock</u>, cattle, beasts, domestic animals
• VERB 1 = <u>sell</u>, supply, handle, keep, trade in, deal in 2 = <u>fill</u>, supply, provide with, equip, furnish, fit out
• ADJECTIVE 1 = <u>hackneyed</u>, routine, banal, trite, overused 2 = <u>regular</u>, usual, ordinary, conventional, customary

**stomach** NOUN 1 = <u>belly</u>, gut (*informal*), abdomen, tummy (*informal*), puku (*N.Z.*) 2 = <u>tummy</u>, pot 3 = <u>inclination</u>, taste, desire, appetite, relish
• VERB = <u>bear</u>, take, tolerate, endure, swallow, abide
*(Related Words)*
adjective: gastric

**stone** 1 = <u>masonry</u>, rock 2 = <u>rock</u>, pebble 3 = <u>pip</u>, seed, pit, kernel

**stoop** VERB 1 = <u>hunch</u> 2 = <u>bend</u>, lean, bow, duck, crouch
• NOUN = <u>slouch</u>, bad posture, round-shoulderedness

**stop** VERB 1 = <u>quit</u>, cease, refrain, put an end to, discontinue, desist ≠ start 2 = <u>prevent</u>, cut short, arrest, restrain, hold back, hinder, repress, impede ≠ facilitate 3 = <u>end</u>, conclude, finish, terminate ≠ continue 4 = <u>cease</u>, shut down, discontinue, desist ≠ continue 5 = <u>halt</u>, pause ≠ keep going 6 = <u>pause</u>, wait, rest, take a break, have a breather (*informal*), stop briefly 7 = <u>stay</u>, rest, lodge

• NOUN 1 = <u>halt</u>, standstill 2 = <u>station</u>, stage, depot, terminus 3 = <u>stay</u>, break, rest

**store** NOUN 1 = <u>shop</u>, outlet, market, mart 2 = <u>supply</u>, stock, reserve, fund, quantity, accumulation, stockpile, hoard 3 = <u>repository</u>, warehouse, depository, storeroom

• VERB 1 = <u>put by</u>, save, hoard, keep, reserve, deposit, garner, stockpile 2 = <u>put away</u>, put in storage, put in store 3 = <u>keep</u>, hold, preserve, maintain, retain, conserve

**storm** NOUN 1 = <u>tempest</u>, hurricane, gale, blizzard, squall 2 = <u>outburst</u>, row, outcry, furore, outbreak, turmoil, disturbance, strife

• VERB 1 = <u>rush</u>, stamp, flounce, fly 2 = <u>rage</u>, rant, thunder, rave, bluster 3 = <u>attack</u>, charge, rush, assault, assail

**stormy** 1 = <u>wild</u>, rough, raging, turbulent, windy, blustery, inclement, squally 2 = <u>rough</u>, wild, turbulent, raging 3 = <u>angry</u>, heated, fierce, passionate, fiery, impassioned

**story** 1 = <u>tale</u>, romance, narrative, history, legend, yarn 2 = <u>anecdote</u>, account, tale, report 3 = <u>report</u>, news, article, feature, scoop, news item

**stout** 1 = <u>fat</u>, big, heavy, overweight, plump, bulky, burly, fleshy ≠ slim 2 = <u>strong</u>, strapping, muscular, robust, sturdy, stalwart, brawny, able-bodied ≠ puny 3 = <u>brave</u>, bold, courageous, fearless, resolute, gallant, intrepid, valiant ≠ timid

**straight** ADJECTIVE 1 = <u>direct</u> ≠ indirect 2 = <u>level</u>, even, right, square, true, smooth, aligned, horizontal ≠ crooked 3 = <u>frank</u>, plain, straightforward, blunt, outright, honest, candid, forthright ≠ evasive 4 = <u>successive</u>, consecutive, continuous, running, solid, nonstop ≠ discontinuous 5 (*Slang*) = <u>conventional</u>, conservative, bourgeois ≠ fashionable 6 = <u>honest</u>, just, fair, reliable, respectable, upright, honourable, law-abiding ≠ dishonest 7 = <u>undiluted</u>, pure, neat, unadulterated, unmixed 8 = <u>in order</u>, organized, arranged, neat, tidy, orderly, shipshape ≠ untidy

• ADVERB 1 = <u>directly</u>, precisely, exactly, unswervingly, by the shortest route, in a beeline 2 = <u>immediately</u>, directly, promptly, instantly, at once, straight away, without delay, forthwith

**straight away** = immediately, now, at once, directly, instantly, right away

**straighten** = neaten, arrange, tidy (up), order, put in order

**straightforward 1** (*Chiefly Brit.*) = simple, easy, uncomplicated, routine, elementary, easy-peasy (*slang*) ≠ complicated **2** = honest, open, direct, genuine, sincere, candid, truthful, forthright, dinkum (*Austral. & N.Z. informal*) ≠ devious

**strain¹** NOUN **1** = pressure, stress, demands, burden **2** = stress, anxiety **3** = worry, effort, struggle ≠ ease **4** = burden, tension **5** = injury, wrench, sprain, pull
● VERB **1** = stretch, tax, overtax **2** = strive, struggle, endeavour, labour, go for it (*informal*), bend over backwards (*informal*), give it your best shot (*informal*), knock yourself out (*informal*) ≠ relax **3** = sieve, filter, sift, purify

**strain²** **1** = trace, suggestion, tendency, streak **2** = breed, family, race, blood, descent, extraction, ancestry, lineage

**strained 1** = tense, difficult, awkward, embarrassed, stiff, uneasy ≠ relaxed **2** = forced, put on, false, artificial, unnatural ≠ natural

**strait** NOUN *often plural* = channel, sound, narrows
● PLURAL NOUN = difficulty, dilemma, plight, hardship, uphill (*S. African*), predicament, extremity

**strand** = filament, fibre, thread, string

**stranded 1** = beached, grounded, marooned, ashore, shipwrecked, aground **2** = helpless, abandoned, high and dry

**strange 1** = odd, curious, weird, wonderful, extraordinary, bizarre, peculiar, abnormal ≠ ordinary **2** = unfamiliar, new, unknown, foreign, novel, alien, exotic, untried ≠ familiar

**stranger 1** = unknown person **2** = newcomer, incomer, foreigner, guest, visitor, alien, outlander

**strangle 1** = throttle, choke, asphyxiate, strangulate **2** = suppress, inhibit, subdue, stifle, repress, overpower, quash, quell

**strap** NOUN = tie, thong, belt
● VERB = fasten, tie, secure, bind, lash, buckle

**strapping** = well-built, big, powerful, robust, sturdy, husky (*informal*), brawny

**strategic 1** = tactical, calculated, deliberate, planned, politic, diplomatic2 = <u>crucial</u>, important, key, vital, critical, decisive, cardinal

**strategy** 1 = <u>policy</u>, procedure, approach, scheme2 = <u>plan</u>, approach, scheme

**stray** VERB1 = <u>wander</u>, go astray, drift2 = <u>drift</u>, wander, roam, meander, rove3 = <u>digress</u>, diverge, deviate, get off the point
● ADJECTIVE1 = <u>lost</u>, abandoned, homeless, roaming, vagrant
2 = <u>random</u>, chance, accidental

**streak** NOUN1 = <u>band</u>, line, strip, stroke, layer, slash, vein, stripe
2 = <u>trace</u>, touch, element, strain, dash, vein
● VERB = <u>speed</u>, fly, tear, flash, sprint, dart, zoom, whizz (*informal*)

**stream** NOUN1 = <u>river</u>, brook, burn (*Scot.*), beck, tributary, bayou, rivulet2 = <u>flow</u>, current, rush, run, course, drift, surge, tide
● VERB1 = <u>flow</u>, run, pour, issue, flood, spill, cascade, gush
2 = <u>rush</u>, fly, speed, tear, flood, pour

**streamlined** = <u>efficient</u>, organized, rationalized, slick, smooth-running

**street** = <u>road</u>, lane, avenue, terrace, row, roadway

**strength** 1 = <u>might</u>, muscle, brawn ≠ weakness2 = <u>will</u>, resolution, courage, character,

nerve, determination, pluck, stamina3 = <u>health</u>, fitness, vigour
4 = <u>mainstay</u>5 = <u>toughness</u>, soundness, robustness, sturdiness
6 = <u>force</u>, power, intensity ≠ weakness7 = <u>potency</u>, effectiveness, efficacy8 = <u>strong point</u>, skill, asset, advantage, talent, forte, speciality ≠ failing

**strengthen** 1 = <u>fortify</u>, harden, toughen, consolidate, stiffen, gee up, brace up ≠ weaken
2 = <u>reinforce</u>, support, intensify, bolster, buttress3 = <u>bolster</u>, harden, reinforce4 = <u>heighten</u>, intensify5 = <u>make stronger</u>, build up, invigorate, restore, give strength to6 = <u>support</u>, brace, reinforce, consolidate, harden, bolster, augment, buttress
7 = <u>become stronger</u>, intensify, gain strength

**stress** VERB1 = <u>emphasize</u>, underline, dwell on2 = <u>place the emphasis on</u>, emphasize, give emphasis to, lay emphasis upon
● NOUN1 = <u>emphasis</u>, significance, force, weight2 = <u>strain</u>, pressure, worry, tension, burden, anxiety, trauma3 = <u>accent</u>, beat, emphasis, accentuation

**stretch** VERB1 = <u>extend</u>, cover, spread, reach, put forth, unroll
2 = <u>last</u>, continue, go on, carry on, reach3 = <u>expand</u>4 = <u>pull</u>, distend, strain, tighten, draw out, elongate

● NOUN 1 = <u>expanse</u>, area, tract, spread, distance, extent

2 = <u>period</u>, time, spell, stint, term, space

**strict** 1 = <u>severe</u>, harsh, stern, firm, stringent ≠ easy-going

2 = <u>stern</u>, firm, severe, harsh, authoritarian 3 = <u>exact</u>, accurate, precise, close, true, faithful, meticulous, scrupulous

4 = <u>absolute</u>, total, utter

**strife** = <u>conflict</u>, battle, clash, quarrel, friction, discord, dissension

**strike** NOUN = <u>walkout</u>, industrial action, mutiny, revolt

● VERB 1 = <u>walk out</u>, down tools, revolt, mutiny 2 = <u>hit</u>, smack, thump, beat, knock, punch, hammer, slap 3 = <u>drive</u>, hit, smack, wallop (informal)

4 = <u>collide with</u>, hit, run into, bump into 5 = <u>knock</u>, smack, thump, beat 6 = <u>affect</u>, touch, devastate, overwhelm, leave a mark on 7 = <u>attack</u>, assault someone, set upon someone, lay into someone (informal)

8 = <u>occur to</u>, hit, come to, register (informal), dawn on or upon

9 = <u>seem to</u>, appear to, look to, give the impression to

10 = <u>move</u>, touch, hit, affect, overcome, stir, disturb, perturb

**striking** = <u>impressive</u>, dramatic, outstanding, noticeable, conspicuous, jaw-dropping ≠ unimpressive

**string** 1 = <u>cord</u>, twine, fibre

2 = <u>series</u>, line, row, file, sequence, succession, procession

3 = <u>sequence</u>, run, series, chain, succession

**stringent** = <u>strict</u>, tough, rigorous, tight, severe, rigid, inflexible ≠ lax

**strip**[1] 1 = <u>undress</u>, disrobe, unclothe 2 = <u>plunder</u>, rob, loot, empty, sack, ransack, pillage, divest

**strip**[2] 1 = <u>piece</u>, shred, band, belt

2 = <u>stretch</u>, area, tract, expanse, extent

**strive** = <u>try</u>, labour, struggle, attempt, toil, go all out (informal), bend over backwards (informal), do your best

**stroke** VERB = <u>caress</u>, rub, fondle, pet

● NOUN 1 = <u>apoplexy</u>, fit, seizure, attack, collapse 2 = <u>blow</u>, hit, knock, pat, rap, thump, swipe

**stroll** VERB = <u>walk</u>, ramble, amble, promenade, saunter

● NOUN = <u>walk</u>, promenade, constitutional, ramble, breath of air

**strong** 1 = <u>powerful</u>, muscular, tough, athletic, strapping, hardy, sturdy, burly ≠ weak 2 = <u>fit</u>, robust, lusty 3 = <u>durable</u>, substantial, sturdy, heavy-duty, well-built, hard-wearing ≠ flimsy

4 = <u>extreme</u>, radical, drastic, strict, harsh, rigid, forceful, uncompromising 5 = <u>decisive</u>, firm, forceful, decided, determined, resolute, incisive 6 = <u>persuasive</u>, convincing, compelling, telling, sound, effective, potent, weighty 7 = <u>keen</u>, deep, acute, fervent, zealous, vehement 8 = <u>intense</u>, deep, passionate, ardent, fierce, fervent, vehement, fervid 9 = <u>staunch</u>, firm, fierce, ardent, enthusiastic, passionate, fervent 10 = <u>distinct</u>, marked, clear, unmistakable ≠ slight 11 = <u>bright</u>, brilliant, dazzling, bold ≠ dull

**stronghold** 1 = <u>bastion</u>, fortress, bulwark 2 = <u>refuge</u>, haven, retreat, sanctuary, hide-out

**structure** NOUN
1 = <u>arrangement</u>, form, make-up, design, organization, construction, formation, configuration 2 = <u>building</u>, construction, erection, edifice
● VERB = <u>arrange</u>, organize, design, shape, build up, assemble

**struggle** VERB 1 = <u>strive</u>, labour, toil, work, strain, go all out (*informal*), give it your best shot (*informal*), exert yourself
2 = <u>fight</u>, battle, wrestle, grapple, compete, contend
● NOUN 1 = <u>effort</u>, labour, toil, work, pains, scramble, exertion

2 = <u>fight</u>, battle, conflict, clash, contest, brush, combat, tussle, biffo (*Austral. slang*)

**strut** = <u>swagger</u>, parade, peacock, prance

**stubborn** = <u>obstinate</u>, dogged, inflexible, persistent, intractable, tenacious, recalcitrant, unyielding ≠ compliant

**stuck** 1 = <u>fastened</u>, fast, fixed, joined, glued, cemented
2 (*Informal*) = <u>baffled</u>, stumped, beaten

**student** 1 = <u>undergraduate</u>, scholar 2 = <u>pupil</u>, scholar, schoolchild, schoolboy *or* schoolgirl 3 = <u>learner</u>, trainee, apprentice, disciple

**studied** = <u>planned</u>, deliberate, conscious, intentional, premeditated ≠ unplanned

**studio** = <u>workshop</u>, workroom, atelier

**study** VERB 1 = <u>learn</u>, cram (*informal*), swot (up) (*Brit. informal*), read up, mug up (*Brit. slang*) 2 = <u>examine</u>, survey, look at, scrutinize 3 = <u>contemplate</u>, read, examine, consider, go into, pore over
● NOUN 1 = <u>examination</u>, investigation, analysis, consideration, inspection, scrutiny, contemplation 2 = <u>piece of research</u>, survey, report, review, inquiry, investigation

3 = <u>learning</u>, lessons, school work, reading, research, swotting (*Brit. informal*)

**stuff** NOUN 1 = <u>things</u>, gear, possessions, effects, equipment, objects, tackle, kit 2 = <u>substance</u>, material, essence, matter

● VERB 1 = <u>shove</u>, force, push, squeeze, jam, ram 2 = <u>cram</u>, fill, pack, crowd

**stuffing** = <u>wadding</u>, filling, packing

**stumble** VERB 1 = <u>trip</u>, fall, slip, reel, stagger, falter, lurch 2 = <u>totter</u>, reel, lurch, wobble

● PHRASES **stumble across** *or* **on** *or* **upon something** *or* **someone** = <u>discover</u>, find, come across, chance upon

**stump** NOUN 1 = <u>tail end</u>, end, remnant, remainder

● VERB = <u>baffle</u>, confuse, puzzle, bewilder, perplex, mystify, flummox, nonplus

**stun** 1 = <u>overcome</u>, shock, confuse, astonish, stagger, bewilder, astound, overpower 2 = <u>daze</u>, knock out, stupefy, numb, benumb

**stunning** (*Informal*) = <u>wonderful</u>, beautiful, impressive, striking, lovely, spectacular, marvellous, splendid ≠ unimpressive

**stunt** = <u>feat</u>, act, trick, exploit, deed

**stunted** = <u>undersized</u>, little, small, tiny, diminutive

**stupid** 1 = <u>unintelligent</u>, thick, simple, slow, dim, dense, simple-minded, moronic ≠ intelligent 2 = <u>silly</u>, foolish, daft (*informal*), rash, pointless, senseless, idiotic, fatuous ≠ sensible 3 = <u>senseless</u>, dazed, groggy, insensate, semiconscious

**sturdy** 1 = <u>robust</u>, hardy, powerful, athletic, muscular, lusty, brawny ≠ puny 2 = <u>substantial</u>, solid, durable, well-made, well-built ≠ flimsy

**style** NOUN 1 = <u>manner</u>, way, method, approach, technique, mode 2 = <u>elegance</u>, taste, chic, flair, polish, sophistication, panache, élan 3 = <u>design</u>, form, cut 4 = <u>type</u>, sort, kind, variety, category, genre 5 = <u>fashion</u>, trend, mode, vogue, rage 6 = <u>luxury</u>, ease, comfort, elegance, grandeur, affluence

● VERB 1 = <u>design</u>, cut, tailor, fashion, shape, arrange, adapt 2 = <u>call</u>, name, term, label, entitle, dub, designate

**stylish** = <u>smart</u>, chic, fashionable, trendy (*Brit. informal*), modish, dressy (*informal*), voguish ≠ scruffy

**subdue** 1 = <u>overcome</u>, defeat, master, break, control, crush, conquer, tame 2 = <u>moderate</u>, suppress, soften, mellow, tone down, quieten down ≠ arouse

**subdued** 1 = quiet, serious, sad, chastened, dejected, downcast, crestfallen, down in the mouth ≠ lively 2 = hushed, soft, quiet, muted ≠ loud

**subject** NOUN 1 = topic, question, issue, matter, point, business, affair, object 2 = citizen, resident, native, inhabitant, national 3 = dependant, subordinate

• ADJECTIVE = subordinate, dependent, satellite, inferior, obedient

• VERB = put through, expose, submit, lay open

• PHRASES subject to 1 = liable to, open to, exposed to, vulnerable to, prone to, susceptible to 2 = bound by 3 = dependent on, contingent on, controlled by, conditional on

**subjective** = personal, prejudiced, biased, nonobjective ≠ objective

**sublime** = noble, glorious, high, great, grand, elevated, lofty, exalted ≠ lowly

**submerge** 1 = flood, swamp, engulf, overflow, inundate, deluge 2 = immerse, plunge, duck 3 = sink, plunge, go under water 4 = overwhelm, swamp, engulf, deluge

**submission** 1 = surrender, yielding, giving in, cave-in (informal), capitulation 2 = presentation, handing in, entry, tendering 3 = compliance, obedience, meekness, resignation, deference, passivity, docility

**submit** 1 = surrender, yield, give in, agree, endure, tolerate, comply, succumb 2 = present, hand in, tender, put forward, table, proffer

**subordinate** NOUN = inferior, junior, assistant, aide, second, attendant ≠ superior

• ADJECTIVE = inferior, lesser, lower, junior, subject, minor, secondary, dependent ≠ superior

**subscribe** 1 = support, advocate, endorse 2 = contribute, give, donate

**subscription** (Chiefly Brit.) = membership fee, dues, annual payment

**subsequent** = following, later, succeeding, after, successive, ensuing ≠ previous

**subsequently** = later, afterwards

**subside** 1 = decrease, diminish, lessen, ease, wane, ebb, abate, slacken ≠ increase 2 = collapse, sink, cave in, drop, lower, settle

**subsidiary** NOUN = branch, division, section, office, department, wing, subdivision, subsection

• ADJECTIVE = secondary, lesser,

subordinate, minor, supplementary, auxiliary, ancillary ≠ main

**subsidy** = <u>aid</u>, help, support, grant, assistance, allowance

**substance** 1 = <u>material</u>, body, stuff, fabric 2 = <u>importance</u>, significance, concreteness 3 = <u>meaning</u>, main point, gist, import, significance, essence 4 = <u>wealth</u>, means, property, assets, resources, estate

**substantial** = <u>big</u>, significant, considerable, large, important, ample, sizable or sizeable ≠ small

**substitute** VERB = <u>replace</u>, exchange, swap, change, switch, interchange
● NOUN = <u>replacement</u>, reserve, surrogate, deputy, sub, proxy, locum
● ADJECTIVE = <u>replacement</u>, reserve, surrogate, second, alternative, fall-back, proxy

> ### Word Power
>
> **substitute** – Although *substitute* and *replace* have the same meaning, the structures they are used in are different. You replace A *with* B, while you substitute B *for* A. Accordingly, *he replaced the worn tyre with a new one*, and *he substituted a new tyre for the worn one* are both correct ways of saying the same thing.

**subtle** 1 = <u>faint</u>, slight, implied, delicate, understated ≠ obvious 2 = <u>crafty</u>, cunning, sly, shrewd, ingenious, devious, wily, artful ≠ straightforward 3 = <u>muted</u>, soft, subdued, low-key, toned down 4 = <u>fine</u>, minute, narrow, tenuous, hair-splitting

**subtlety** 1 = <u>fine point</u>, refinement, sophistication, delicacy 2 = <u>skill</u>, ingenuity, cleverness, deviousness, craftiness, artfulness, slyness, wiliness

**subversive** ADJECTIVE = <u>seditious</u>, riotous, treasonous
● NOUN = <u>dissident</u>, terrorist, saboteur, fifth columnist

**succeed** 1 = <u>triumph</u>, win, prevail 2 = <u>work out</u>, work, be successful 3 = <u>make it</u> (*informal*), do well, be successful, triumph, thrive, flourish, make good, prosper ≠ fail 4 = <u>take over from</u>, assume the office of 5 *with* **to** = <u>take over</u>, assume, attain, come into, inherit, accede to, come into possession of 6 = <u>follow</u>, come after, follow after ≠ precede

**success** 1 = <u>victory</u>, triumph ≠ failure 2 = <u>prosperity</u>, fortune, luck, fame 3 = <u>hit</u> (*informal*), winner, smash, sensation ≠ flop (*informal*) 4 = <u>big name</u>, star, hit (*informal*), celebrity, sensation, megastar (*informal*) ≠ nobody

**successful** 1 = triumphant, victorious, lucky, fortunate 2 = thriving, profitable, rewarding, booming, flourishing, fruitful ≠ unprofitable 3 = top, prosperous, wealthy

**successfully** = well, favourably, with flying colours, victoriously

**succession** 1 = series, run, sequence, course, order, train, chain, cycle 2 = taking over, assumption, inheritance, accession

**successive** = consecutive, following, in succession

**succumb** 1 *often with to* = surrender, yield, submit, give in, cave in (*informal*), capitulate ≠ beat 2 *with to* (with an illness as object) = catch, fall ill with

**suck** 1 = drink, sip, draw 2 = take, draw, pull, extract

**sudden** = quick, rapid, unexpected, swift, hurried, abrupt, hasty ≠ gradual

**suddenly** = abruptly, all of a sudden, unexpectedly

**sue** (*Law*) = take (someone) to court, prosecute, charge, summon, indict

**suffer** 1 = be in pain, hurt, ache 2 = be affected, have trouble with, be afflicted, be troubled with 3 = undergo, experience, sustain, bear, go through, endure

4 = tolerate, stand, put up with (*informal*), bear, endure

**suffering** = pain, distress, agony, misery, ordeal, discomfort, torment, hardship

**suffice** = be enough, do, be sufficient, be adequate, serve, meet requirements

**sufficient** = adequate, enough, ample, satisfactory ≠ insufficient

**suggest** 1 = recommend, propose, advise, advocate, prescribe 2 = indicate 3 = hint at, imply, intimate 4 = bring to mind, evoke

**suggestion**
1 = recommendation, proposal, proposition, plan, motion
2 = hint, insinuation, intimation
3 = trace, touch, hint, breath, indication, whisper, intimation

**suit** NOUN 1 = outfit, costume, ensemble, dress, clothing, habit 2 = lawsuit, case, trial, proceeding, cause, action, prosecution
● VERB 1 = be acceptable to, please, satisfy, do, gratify 2 = agree with, become, match, go with, harmonize with

**suitable** 1 = appropriate, right, fitting, fit, becoming, satisfactory, apt, befitting ≠ inappropriate 2 = seemly, fitting, becoming, proper, correct ≠ unseemly 3 = suited, appropriate, in keeping with ≠ out of keeping

4 = <u>pertinent</u>, relevant, applicable, fitting, appropriate, to the point, apt ≠ irrelevant
5 = <u>convenient</u>, timely, appropriate, well-timed, opportune ≠ inopportune

**suite** = <u>rooms</u>, apartment

**sum** 1 = <u>amount</u>, quantity, volume 2 = <u>calculation</u>, figures, arithmetic, mathematics, maths (*Brit. informal*), tally, math (*U.S. informal*), arithmetical problem 3 = <u>total</u>, aggregate 4 = <u>totality</u>, whole

**summarize** = <u>sum up</u>, condense, encapsulate, epitomize, abridge, précis

**summary** = <u>synopsis</u>, résumé, précis, review, outline, rundown, abridgment

**summit** 1 = <u>peak</u>, top, tip, pinnacle, apex, head ≠ base 2 = <u>height</u>, pinnacle, peak, zenith, acme ≠ depths

**summon** 1 = <u>send for</u>, call, bid, invite 2 *often with* **up** = <u>gather</u>, muster, draw on

**sumptuous** = <u>luxurious</u>, grand, superb, splendid, gorgeous, lavish, opulent ≠ plain

**sunny** 1 = <u>bright</u>, clear, fine, radiant, sunlit, summery, unclouded ≠ dull 2 = <u>cheerful</u>, happy, cheery, buoyant, joyful, light-hearted ≠ gloomy

**sunset** = <u>nightfall</u>, dusk, eventide, close of (the) day

**superb** 1 = <u>splendid</u>, excellent, magnificent, fine, grand, superior, marvellous, world-class, booshit (*Austral. slang*), exo (*Austral. slang*), sik (*Austral. slang*) ≠ inferior 2 = <u>magnificent</u>, superior, marvellous, exquisite, superlative ≠ terrible

**superficial** 1 = <u>shallow</u>, frivolous, empty-headed, silly, trivial ≠ serious 2 = <u>hasty</u>, cursory, perfunctory, hurried, casual, sketchy, desultory, slapdash ≠ thorough 3 = <u>slight</u>, surface, external, on the surface, exterior ≠ profound

**superintendent** = <u>supervisor</u>, director, manager, chief, governor, inspector, controller, overseer

**superior** ADJECTIVE 1 = <u>better</u>, higher, greater, grander, surpassing, unrivalled ≠ inferior 2 = <u>first-class</u>, excellent, first-rate, choice, exclusive, exceptional, de luxe, booshit (*Austral. slang*), sik (*Austral. slang*), exo (*Austral. slang*) ≠ average 3 = <u>supercilious</u>, patronizing, condescending, haughty, disdainful, lordly, lofty, pretentious
● NOUN = <u>boss</u>, senior, director, manager, chief (*informal*), principal, supervisor, baas (*S. African*) ≠ subordinate

> ### Word Power
> **superior** – Superior should
> not be used with than: he is a
> better (not a superior) poet than
> his brother; his poetry is superior
> to (not than) his brother's.

**superiority** = <u>supremacy</u>, lead,
advantage, excellence,
ascendancy, predominance

**supernatural** – <u>paranormal</u>,
unearthly, uncanny, ghostly,
psychic, mystic, miraculous,
occult

**supervise** 1 = <u>observe</u>, guide,
monitor, oversee, keep an eye on
2 = <u>oversee</u>, run, manage, control,
direct, handle, look after,
superintend

**supervision**
= <u>superintendence</u>, direction,
control, charge, care,
management, guidance

**supervisor** = <u>boss</u> (informal),
manager, chief, inspector,
administrator, foreman, overseer,
baas (S. African)

**supplement** VERB = <u>add to</u>,
reinforce, augment, extend
● NOUN 1 = <u>pull-out</u>, insert
2 = <u>appendix</u>, add-on, postscript
3 = <u>addition</u>, extra

**supply** VERB 1 = <u>provide</u>, give,
furnish, produce, stock, grant,
contribute, yield 2 = <u>furnish</u>,

provide, equip, endow
● NOUN = <u>store</u>, fund, stock,
source, reserve, quantity, hoard,
cache
● PLURAL NOUN = <u>provisions</u>,
necessities, stores, food, materials,
equipment, rations

**support** VERB 1 = <u>help</u>, back,
champion, second, aid, defend,
assist, side with ≠ oppose
2 = <u>provide for</u>, maintain, look
after, keep, fund, finance, sustain
≠ live off 3 = <u>bear out</u>, confirm,
verify, substantiate, corroborate
≠ refute 4 = <u>bear</u>, carry, sustain,
prop (up), reinforce, hold, brace,
buttress
● NOUN 1 = <u>furtherance</u>, backing,
promotion, assistance,
encouragement 2 = <u>help</u>, loyalty
≠ opposition 3 = <u>aid</u>, help,
benefits, relief, assistance
4 = <u>prop</u>, post, foundation, brace,
pillar 5 = <u>supporter</u>, prop,
mainstay, tower of strength,
second, backer ≠ antagonist
6 = <u>upkeep</u>, maintenance, keep,
subsistence, sustenance

**supporter** = <u>follower</u>, fan,
advocate, friend, champion,
sponsor, patron, helper
≠ opponent

**supportive** = <u>helpful</u>,
encouraging, understanding,
sympathetic

**suppose** 1 = <u>imagine</u>, consider,
conjecture, postulate,

hypothesize 2 = <u>think</u>, imagine, expect, assume, guess (*informal*, *chiefly U.S. & Canad.*), presume, conjecture

supposed 1 *usually with to* = <u>meant</u>, expected, required, obliged 2 = <u>presumed</u>, alleged, professed, accepted, assumed

supposedly 1 = <u>presumably</u>, allegedly, ostensibly, theoretically, hypothetically ≠ actually

suppress 1 = <u>stamp out</u>, stop, check, crush, conquer, subdue, put an end to, overpower ≠ encourage 2 = <u>check</u>, inhibit, subdue, stop, quell 3 = <u>restrain</u>, stifle, contain, silence, conceal, curb, repress, smother

suppression 1 = <u>elimination</u>, crushing, check, quashing 2 = <u>inhibition</u>, blocking, restraint, smothering

supremacy = <u>domination</u>, sovereignty, sway, mastery, primacy, predominance, supreme power

supreme 1 = <u>paramount</u> ≠ least 2 = <u>chief</u>, leading, principal, highest, head, top, prime, foremost ≠ lowest 3 = <u>ultimate</u>, highest, greatest

supremo (*Brit. informal*) = <u>head</u>, leader, boss (*informal*), director, master, governor, commander, principal, baas (*S. African*)

sure 1 = <u>certain</u>, positive, decided, convinced, confident, assured, definite ≠ uncertain 2 = <u>inevitable</u>, guaranteed, bound, assured, inescapable ≠ unsure 3 = <u>reliable</u>, accurate, dependable, undoubted, undeniable, foolproof, infallible, unerring ≠ unreliable

surely 1 = <u>it must be the case that</u> 2 = <u>undoubtedly</u>, certainly, definitely, without doubt, unquestionably, indubitably, doubtlessly

surface NOUN 1 = <u>covering</u>, face, exterior, side, top, veneer 2 = <u>façade</u>
● VERB 1 = <u>emerge</u>, come up, come to the surface 2 = <u>appear</u>, emerge, arise, come to light, crop up (*informal*), transpire, materialize

surge NOUN 1 = <u>rush</u>, flood 2 = <u>flow</u>, wave, rush, roller, gush, outpouring 3 = <u>tide</u>, swell, billowing 4 = <u>rush</u>, wave, storm, torrent, eruption
● VERB 1 = <u>rush</u>, pour, rise, gush 2 = <u>roll</u>, rush, heave 3 = <u>sweep</u>, rush, storm

surpass = <u>outdo</u>, beat, exceed, eclipse, excel, transcend, outstrip, outshine

surpassing = <u>supreme</u>, extraordinary, outstanding, exceptional, unrivalled, incomparable, matchless

**surplus** NOUN = <u>excess</u>, surfeit
≠ shortage

● ADJECTIVE = <u>extra</u>, spare, excess, remaining, odd, superfluous
≠ insufficient

**surprise** NOUN 1 = <u>shock</u>, revelation, jolt, bombshell, eye-opener (*informal*) 2 = <u>amazement</u>, astonishment, wonder, incredulity

● VERB 1 = <u>amaze</u>, astonish, stun, startle, stagger, take aback 2 = <u>catch unawares</u> or <u>off-guard</u>, spring upon

**surprised** = <u>amazed</u>, astonished, speechless, thunderstruck

**surprising** = <u>amazing</u>, remarkable, incredible, astonishing, unusual, extraordinary, unexpected, staggering

**surrender** VERB 1 = <u>give in</u>, yield, submit, give way, succumb, cave in (*informal*), capitulate ≠ resist 2 = <u>give up</u>, abandon, relinquish, yield, concede, part with, renounce, waive

● NOUN = <u>submission</u>, cave-in (*informal*), capitulation, resignation, renunciation, relinquishment

**surround** = <u>enclose</u>, ring, encircle, encompass, envelop, hem in

**surrounding** ADJECTIVE

= nearby, neighbouring

● PLURAL NOUN = <u>environment</u>, setting, background, location, milieu

**surveillance** = <u>observation</u>, watch, scrutiny, supervision, inspection

**survey** NOUN 1 = <u>poll</u>, study, research, review, inquiry, investigation 2 = <u>examination</u>, inspection, scrutiny 3 = <u>valuation</u>, estimate, assessment, appraisal

● VERB 1 = <u>interview</u>, question, poll, research, investigate 2 = <u>look over</u>, view, examine, observe, contemplate, inspect, eyeball (*slang*), scrutinize 3 = <u>measure</u>, estimate, assess, appraise

**survive** 1 = <u>remain alive</u>, last, live on, endure 2 = <u>continue</u>, last, live on 3 = <u>live longer than</u>, outlive, outlast

**susceptible** 1 = <u>responsive</u>, sensitive, receptive, impressionable, suggestible ≠ unresponsive 2 *usually with to* = <u>liable</u>, inclined, prone, given, subject, vulnerable, disposed ≠ resistant

**suspect** VERB 1 = <u>believe</u>, feel, guess, consider, suppose, speculate ≠ know 2 = <u>distrust</u>, doubt, mistrust ≠ trust

● ADJECTIVE = <u>dubious</u>, doubtful, questionable, iffy (*informal*) ≠ innocent

**suspend** 1 = <u>postpone</u>, put off, cease, interrupt, shelve, defer, cut short, discontinue ≠ continue 2 = <u>hang</u>, attach, dangle

**suspension** = <u>postponement</u>, break, breaking off, interruption, abeyance, deferment, discontinuation

**suspicion** 1 = <u>distrust</u>, scepticism, mistrust, doubt, misgiving, qualm, wariness, dubiety 2 = <u>idea</u>, notion, hunch, guess, impression 3 = <u>trace</u>, touch, hint, suggestion, shade, streak, tinge, soupçon (French)

**suspicious** 1 = <u>distrustful</u>, sceptical, doubtful, unbelieving, wary ≠ trusting 2 = <u>suspect</u>, dubious, questionable, doubtful, dodgy (Brit., Austral., & N.Z. informal), fishy (informal) ≠ beyond suspicion

**sustain** 1 = <u>maintain</u>, continue, keep up, prolong, protract 2 = <u>suffer</u>, experience, undergo, feel, bear, endure, withstand 3 = <u>help</u>, aid, assist 4 = <u>keep alive</u>, nourish, provide for 5 = <u>support</u>, bear, uphold

**sustained** = <u>continuous</u>, constant, steady, prolonged, perpetual, unremitting, nonstop ≠ periodic

**swallow** 1 = <u>eat</u>, consume, devour, swig (informal) 2 = <u>gulp</u>, drink

**swamp** NOUN = <u>bog</u>, marsh, quagmire, slough, fen, mire, morass, pakihi (N.Z.)
● VERB 1 = <u>flood</u>, engulf, submerge, inundate 2 = <u>overload</u>, overwhelm, inundate

**swap** or **swop** = <u>exchange</u>, trade, switch, interchange, barter

**swarm** NOUN = <u>multitude</u>, crowd, mass, army, host, flock, herd, horde
● VERB 1 = <u>crowd</u>, flock, throng, mass, stream 2 = <u>teem</u>, crawl, abound, bristle

**swathe** NOUN = <u>area</u>, section, tract
● VERB = <u>wrap</u>, drape, envelop, cloak, shroud, bundle up

**sway** VERB 1 = <u>move from side to side</u>, rock, roll, swing, bend, lean 2 = <u>influence</u>, affect, guide, persuade, induce
● NOUN = <u>power</u>, control, influence, authority, clout (informal)

**swear** 1 = <u>curse</u>, blaspheme, be foul-mouthed 2 = <u>vow</u>, promise, testify, attest 3 = <u>declare</u>, assert, affirm

**swearing** = <u>bad language</u>, cursing, profanity, blasphemy, foul language

**sweat** NOUN 1 = <u>perspiration</u> 2 (Informal) = <u>panic</u>, anxiety, worry, distress, agitation
● VERB 1 = <u>perspire</u>, glow

2 (*Informal*) = <u>worry</u>, fret, agonize, torture yourself

**sweep** VERB 1 = <u>brush</u>, clean 2 = <u>clear</u>, remove, brush, clean 3 = <u>sail</u>, pass, fly, tear, zoom, glide, skim

● NOUN 1 = <u>movement</u>, move, swing, stroke 2 = <u>extent</u>, range, stretch, scope

**sweeping** 1 = <u>indiscriminate</u>, blanket, wholesale, exaggerated, overstated, unqualified 2 = <u>wide-ranging</u>, global, comprehensive, wide, broad, extensive, all-inclusive, all-embracing ≠ limited

**sweet** ADJECTIVE 1 = <u>sugary</u>, cloying, saccharine, icky (*informal*) ≠ sour 2 = <u>fragrant</u>, aromatic ≠ stinking 3 = <u>fresh</u>, clean, pure 4 = <u>melodious</u>, musical, mellow, dulcet ≠ harsh 5 = <u>charming</u>, kind, agreeable ≠ nasty 6 = <u>delightful</u>, appealing, cute, winning, engaging, lovable, likable or likeable ≠ unpleasant

● NOUN 1 *usually plural* = <u>confectionery</u>, candy (*U.S.*), lolly (*Austral. & N.Z.*), bonbon 2 (*Brit.*) = <u>dessert</u>, pudding

**sweetheart** 1 = <u>dearest</u>, beloved, sweet, angel, treasure, honey, dear, sweetie (*informal*) 2 = <u>love</u>, boyfriend or girlfriend, beloved, lover, darling

**swell** VERB 1 = <u>increase</u>, rise, grow, mount, expand, accelerate, escalate, multiply ≠ decrease 2 = <u>expand</u>, increase, grow, rise, balloon, enlarge, bulge, dilate ≠ shrink

● NOUN = <u>wave</u>, surge, billow

**swelling** = <u>enlargement</u>, lump, bump, bulge, inflammation, protuberance, distension

**swift** 1 = <u>quick</u>, prompt, rapid 2 = <u>fast</u>, quick, rapid, hurried, speedy ≠ slow

**swiftly** = <u>quickly</u>, rapidly, speedily 2 = <u>fast</u>, promptly, hurriedly

**swing** VERB 1 = <u>brandish</u>, wave, shake, flourish, wield, dangle 2 = <u>sway</u>, rock, wave, veer, oscillate 3 *usually with round* = <u>turn</u>, swivel, curve, rotate, pivot 4 = <u>hit out</u>, strike, swipe, lash out at, slap 5 = <u>hang</u>, dangle, suspend

● NOUN 1 = <u>swaying</u>, wave 2 = <u>fluctuation</u>, change, shift, switch, variation

**swirl** = <u>whirl</u>, churn, spin, twist, eddy

**switch** NOUN 1 = <u>control</u>, button, lever, on/off device 2 = <u>change</u>, shift, reversal

● VERB 1 = <u>change</u>, shift, divert, deviate 2 = <u>exchange</u>, swap, substitute

**swollen** = <u>enlarged</u>, bloated, inflamed, puffed up, distended

**swoop** 1 = <u>pounce</u>, attack,

charge, rush, descend 2 = **drop**, plunge, dive, sweep, descend, pounce, stoop

**symbol** 1 = <u>metaphor</u>, image, sign, representation, token 2 = <u>representation</u>, sign, figure, mark, image, token, logo, badge

**symbolic** 1 = <u>representative</u>, emblematic, allegorical 2 = <u>representative</u>, figurative

**sympathetic** 1 = <u>caring</u>, kind, understanding, concerned, interested, warm, pitying, supportive ≠ uncaring 2 = <u>like-minded</u>, compatible, agreeable, friendly, congenial, companionable ≠ uncongenial

**sympathy** 1 = <u>compassion</u>, understanding, pity, commiseration, aroha (*N.Z.*) ≠ indifference 2 = <u>affinity</u>, agreement, rapport, fellow feeling ≠ opposition

**symptom** 1 = <u>sign</u>, mark, indication, warning 2 = <u>manifestation</u>, sign, indication, mark, evidence, expression, proof, token

**synthetic** = <u>artificial</u>, fake, man-made ≠ real

**system** 1 = <u>arrangement</u>, structure, organization, scheme, classification 2 = <u>method</u>, practice, technique, procedure, routine

**systematic** = <u>methodical</u>, organized, efficient, orderly ≠ unmethodical

# T

**table** NOUN 1 = <u>counter</u>, bench, stand, board, surface, work surface 2 = <u>list</u>, chart, tabulation, record, roll, register, diagram, itemization
● VERB (*Brit.*) = <u>submit</u>, propose, put forward, move, suggest, enter, file, lodge

**taboo** NOUN = <u>prohibition</u>, ban, restriction, anathema, interdict, proscription, tapu (*N.Z.*)
● ADJECTIVE = <u>forbidden</u>, banned, prohibited, unacceptable, outlawed, anathema, proscribed, unmentionable ≠ permitted

**tack** NOUN = <u>nail</u>, pin, drawing pin
● VERB 1 = <u>fasten</u>, fix, attach, pin, nail, affix 2 (*Brit.*) = <u>stitch</u>, sew, hem, bind, baste
● PHRASES **tack something on to something** = <u>append</u>, add, attach, tag

**tackle** VERB 1 = <u>deal with</u>, set about, get stuck into (*informal*), come or get to grips with 2 = <u>undertake</u>, attempt, embark upon, get stuck into (*informal*), have a go or stab at (*informal*) 3 = <u>intercept</u>, stop, challenge
● NOUN 1 = <u>block</u>, challenge,

2 = <u>rig</u>, apparatus

**tactic** NOUN = <u>policy</u>, approach, move, scheme, plans, method, manoeuvre, ploy

● PLURAL NOUN = <u>strategy</u>, campaigning, manoeuvres, generalship

**tactical** = <u>strategic</u>, shrewd, smart, diplomatic, cunning ≠ impolitic

**tag** NOUN = <u>label</u>, tab, note, ticket, slip, identification, marker, flap

● VERB = <u>label</u>, mark

**tail** NOUN 1 = <u>extremity</u>, appendage, brush, rear end, hindquarters, hind part 2 = <u>train</u>, end, trail, tailpiece

● VERB (Informal) = <u>follow</u>, track, shadow, trail, stalk

● PHRASES **turn tail** = <u>run away</u>, flee, run off, retreat, cut and run, take to your heels

**tailor** NOUN = <u>outfitter</u>, couturier, dressmaker, seamstress, clothier, costumier

● VERB = <u>adapt</u>, adjust, modify, style, fashion, shape, alter, mould

**taint** = <u>spoil</u>, ruin, contaminate, damage, stain, corrupt, pollute, tarnish ≠ purify

**take** VERB 1 = <u>grip</u>, grab, seize, catch, grasp, clasp, take hold of 2 = <u>carry</u>, bring, bear, transport, ferry, haul, convey, fetch ≠ send 3 = <u>accompany</u>, lead, bring, guide, conduct, escort, convoy

usher 4 = <u>remove</u>, draw, pull, fish, withdraw, extract 5 = <u>steal</u>, appropriate, pocket, pinch (informal), misappropriate, purloin ≠ return 6 = <u>capture</u>, seize, take into custody, lay hold of ≠ release 7 = <u>tolerate</u>, stand, bear, stomach, endure, abide, put up with (informal), withstand ≠ avoid 8 = <u>require</u>, need, involve, demand, call for, entail, necessitate 9 = <u>understand</u>, follow, comprehend, get, see, grasp, apprehend 10 = <u>regard as</u>, believe to be, consider to be, perceive to be, presume to be 11 = <u>have room for</u>, hold, contain, accommodate, accept

● PHRASES **take off** 1 = <u>lift off</u>, take to the air 2 (Informal) = <u>depart</u>, go, leave, disappear, abscond, decamp, slope off ◆ **take someone in** = <u>deceive</u>, fool, con (informal), trick, cheat, mislead, dupe, swindle ◆ **take someone off** (Informal) = <u>parody</u>, imitate, mimic, mock, caricature, send up (Brit. informal), lampoon, satirize

◆ **take something in** = <u>understand</u>, absorb, grasp, digest, comprehend, assimilate, get the hang of (informal)

◆ **take something up** 1 = <u>start</u>, begin, engage in, adopt, become involved in 2 = <u>occupy</u>, absorb, consume, use up, cover, fill, waste, squander

**takeover** = merger, coup, incorporation

**tale** = <u>story</u>, narrative, anecdote, account, legend, saga, yarn (*informal*) fable

**talent** = <u>ability</u>, gift, aptitude, capacity, genius, flair, knack

**talented** = <u>gifted</u>, able, expert, master, masterly, brilliant, ace (*informal*), consummate

**talk** VERB 1 = <u>speak</u>, chat, chatter, converse, communicate, natter 2 = <u>discuss</u>, confer, negotiate, parley, confabulate, korero (*N.Z.*) 3 = <u>inform</u>, grass (*Brit. slang*), tell all, give the game away, blab, let the cat out of the bag
● NOUN = <u>speech</u>, lecture, presentation, report, address, discourse, sermon, symposium, whaikorero (*N.Z.*)

**talking-to** (*Informal*) = <u>reprimand</u>, lecture, rebuke, scolding, criticism, reproach, ticking-off (*informal*), dressing-down (*informal*) ≠ praise

**tall** 1 = <u>lofty</u>, big, giant, long-legged, lanky, leggy 2 = <u>high</u>, towering, soaring, steep, elevated, lofty ≠ short 3 (*Informal*) = <u>implausible</u>, incredible, far-fetched, exaggerated, absurd, unbelievable, preposterous, cock-and-bull (*informal*) ≠ plausible 4 = <u>difficult</u>, hard, demanding,

unreasonable, well-nigh impossible

**tally** NOUN = <u>record</u>, score, total, count, reckoning, running total
● VERB = <u>agree</u>, match, accord, fit, square, coincide, correspond, conform ≠ disagree

**tame** ADJECTIVE 1 = <u>domesticated</u>, docile, broken, gentle, obedient, amenable, tractable ≠ wild 2 = <u>submissive</u>, meek, compliant, subdued, manageable, obedient, docile, unresisting ≠ stubborn 3 = <u>unexciting</u>, boring, dull, bland, uninspiring, humdrum, uninteresting, insipid ≠ exciting
● VERB 1 = <u>domesticate</u>, train, break in, house-train ≠ make fiercer 2 = <u>subdue</u>, suppress, master, discipline, humble, conquer, subjugate ≠ arouse

**tangible** = <u>definite</u>, real, positive, material, actual, concrete, palpable, perceptible ≠ intangible

**tangle** NOUN 1 = <u>knot</u>, twist, web, jungle, coil, entanglement 2 = <u>mess</u>, jam, fix (*informal*), confusion, complication, mix-up, shambles, entanglement
● VERB = <u>twist</u>, knot, mat, coil, mesh, entangle, interweave, ravel ≠ disentangle
● PHRASES **tangle with someone** = <u>come into conflict with</u>, come up against, cross swords with, dispute with,

contend with, contest with, lock horns with

**tantrum** = <u>outburst</u>, temper, hysterics, fit, flare-up, foulie (*Austral. slang*)

**tap**[1] VERB = <u>knock</u>, strike, pat, rap, beat, touch, drum

● NOUN = <u>knock</u>, pat, rap, touch, drumming

**tap**[2] NOUN = <u>valve</u>, stopcock

● VERB = <u>listen in on</u>, monitor, bug (*informal*), spy on, eavesdrop on, wiretap

● PHRASES **on tap** 1 (*Informal*) = <u>available</u>, ready, standing by, to hand, on hand, at hand, in reserve 2 = <u>on draught</u>, cask-conditioned, from barrels, not bottled *or* canned

**tape** NOUN = <u>binding</u>, strip, band, string, ribbon

● VERB[1] = <u>record</u>, video, tape-record, make a recording of 2 *sometimes with* **up** = <u>bind</u>, secure, stick, seal, wrap

**target** 1 = <u>mark</u>, goal[2] = <u>goal</u>, aim, objective, end, mark, object, intention, ambition[3] = <u>victim</u>, butt, prey, scapegoat

**tariff** 1 = <u>tax</u>, duty, toll, levy, excise[2] = <u>price list</u>, schedule

**tarnish** VERB[1] = <u>damage</u>, taint, blacken, sully, smirch ≠ enhance 2 = <u>stain</u>, discolour, darken, blot, blemish ≠ brighten

● NOUN = <u>stain</u>, taint, discoloration, spot, blot, blemish

**tart**[1] = <u>pie</u>, pastry, pasty, tartlet, patty

**tart**[2] = <u>sharp</u>, acid, sour, bitter, pungent, tangy, piquant, vinegary ≠ sweet

**tart**[3] (*Informal*) = <u>slut</u>, prostitute, whore, call girl, trollop, floozy (*slang*)

**task** NOUN = <u>job</u>, duty, assignment, exercise, mission, enterprise, undertaking, chore

● PHRASES **take someone to task** = <u>criticize</u>, blame, censure, rebuke, reprimand, reproach, scold, tell off (*informal*)

**taste** NOUN[1] = <u>flavour</u>, savour, relish, smack, tang ≠ blandness 2 = <u>bit</u>, bite, mouthful, sample, dash, spoonful, morsel, titbit 3 = <u>liking</u>, preference, penchant, fondness, partiality, fancy, appetite, inclination ≠ dislike 4 = <u>refinement</u>, style, judgment, discrimination, appreciation, elegance, sophistication, discernment ≠ lack of judgment

● VERB[1] = <u>have a flavour of</u>, smack of, savour of[2] = <u>sample</u>, try, test, sip, savour 3 = <u>distinguish</u>, perceive, discern, differentiate[4] = <u>experience</u>, know, undergo, partake of, encounter, meet with ≠ miss

**tasty** = <u>delicious</u>, luscious, palatable, delectable, savoury, full-flavoured, scrumptious (*informal*), appetizing, lekker (*S. African slang*), yummo (*Austral. slang*) ≠ bland

**taunt** VERB = jeer, mock, tease, ridicule, provoke, insult, torment, deride

● NOUN = jeer, dig, insult, ridicule, teasing, provocation, derision, sarcasm

**tavern** = inn, bar, pub (*informal, chiefly Brit.*), public house, hostelry, alehouse (*archaic*)

**tax** NOUN = charge, duty, toll, levy, tariff, excise, tithe

● VERB 1 = charge, rate, assess 2 = strain, stretch, try, test, load, burden, exhaust, weaken

**teach** VERB = instruct, train, coach, inform, educate, drill, tutor, enlighten

● VERB = show, train

**teacher** = instructor, coach, tutor, guide, trainer, lecturer, mentor, educator

**team** NOUN 1 = side, squad 2 = group, company, set, body, band, gang, line-up, bunch

● PHRASES **team up** = join, unite, work together, cooperate, couple, link up, get together, band together

**tear** VERB 1 = rip, split, rend, shred, rupture 2 = run 3 = scratch, cut (open), gash, lacerate, injure, mangle, cut to pieces, cut to

ribbons, mangulate (*Austral. slang*) 4 = pull apart, claw, lacerate, mutilate, mangle, mangulate (*Austral. slang*) 5 = rush, run, charge, race, fly, speed, dash, hurry

● NOUN = hole, split, rip, rent, snag, rupture

**tears** PLURAL NOUN = crying, weeping, sobbing, wailing, blubbering

● PHRASES **in tears** = weeping, crying, sobbing, blubbering

**tease** 1 = mock, provoke, torment, taunt, goad, pull someone's leg (*informal*), make fun of 2 = tantalize, lead on, flirt with, titillate

**technical** = scientific, technological, skilled, specialist, specialized, hi-tech *or* high-tech

**technique** 1 = method, way, system, approach, means, style, manner, procedure 2 = skill, performance, craft, touch, execution, artistry, craftsmanship, proficiency

**tedious** = boring, dull, dreary, monotonous, drab, tiresome, laborious, humdrum ≠ exciting

**teenager** = youth, minor, adolescent, juvenile, girl, boy

**telephone** NOUN = phone, mobile (phone), handset, dog and bone (*slang*)

● VERB = call, phone, ring (*chiefly*

*Brit.*), dial

**telescope** NOUN = glass, scope (*informal*), spyglass
● VERB = <u>shorten</u>, contract, compress, shrink, condense, abbreviate, abridge ≠ lengthen

**television** = <u>TV</u>, telly (*Brit. informal*), small screen (*informal*), the box (*Brit. informal*), the tube (*slang*)

**tell** VERB[1] = <u>inform</u>, notify, state to, reveal to, express to, disclose to, proclaim to, divulge
2 = <u>describe</u>, relate, recount, report, portray, depict, chronicle, narrate 3 = <u>instruct</u>, order, command, direct, bid
4 = <u>distinguish</u>, discriminate, discern, differentiate, identify
5 = <u>have</u> or <u>take effect</u>, register, weigh, count, take its toll, carry weight, make its presence felt
● PHRASES **tell someone off** = <u>reprimand</u>, rebuke, scold, lecture, censure, reproach, berate, chide

**telling** = <u>effective</u>, significant, considerable, marked, striking, powerful, impressive, influential ≠ unimportant

**temper** NOUN[1] = <u>irritability</u>, irascibility, passion, resentment, petulance, surliness, hot-headedness ≠ good humour
2 = <u>frame of mind</u>, nature, mind, mood, constitution, humour,

temperament, disposition
3 = <u>rage</u>, fury, bad mood, passion, tantrum, foulie (*Austral. slang*)
4 = <u>self-control</u>, composure, cool (*slang*), calmness, equanimity ≠ anger
● VERB[1] = <u>moderate</u>, restrain, tone down, soften, soothe, lessen, mitigate, assuage ≠ intensify
2 = <u>strengthen</u>, harden, toughen, anneal ≠ soften

**temperament** 1 = <u>nature</u>, character, personality, make-up, constitution, bent, humour, temper 2 = <u>moods</u>, anger, volatility, petulance, excitability, moodiness, hot-headedness ≠ anger

**temple** = <u>shrine</u>, church, sanctuary, house of God

**temporarily** = <u>briefly</u>, for the time being, momentarily, fleetingly, pro tem

**temporary** 1 = <u>impermanent</u>, transitory, brief, fleeting, interim, short-lived, momentary, ephemeral ≠ permanent
2 = <u>short-term</u>, acting, interim, supply, stand-in, fill-in, caretaker, provisional

**tempt** 1 = <u>attract</u>, allure
2 = <u>entice</u>, lure, lead on, invite, seduce, coax ≠ discourage

**temptation** 1 = <u>enticement</u>, lure, inducement, pull, seduction, allurement, tantalization
2 = <u>appeal</u>, attraction

**tempting** = inviting, enticing, seductive, alluring, attractive, mouthwatering, appetizing ≠ uninviting

**tenant** = leaseholder, resident, renter, occupant, inhabitant, occupier, lodger, boarder

**tend**[1] = be inclined, be liable, have a tendency, be apt, be prone, lean, incline, gravitate

**tend**[2] 1 = take care of, look after, keep, attend, nurture, watch over ≠ neglect 2 = maintain, take care of, nurture, cultivate, manage ≠ neglect

**tendency** = inclination, leaning, liability, disposition, propensity, susceptibility, proclivity, proneness

**tender**[1] 1 = gentle, loving, kind, caring, sympathetic, affectionate, compassionate, considerate ≠ harsh 2 = vulnerable, young, sensitive, raw, youthful, inexperienced, immature, impressionable ≠ experienced 3 = sensitive, painful, sore, raw, bruised, inflamed

**tender**[2] NOUN = offer, bid, estimate, proposal, submission
● VERB = offer, present, submit, give, propose, volunteer, hand in, put forward

**tense** ADJECTIVE 1 = strained, uneasy, stressful, fraught, charged, difficult, worrying,

exciting 2 = nervous, edgy, strained, anxious, apprehensive, uptight (*informal*), on edge, jumpy ≠ calm 3 = rigid, strained, taut, stretched, tight ≠ relaxed
● VERB = tighten, strain, brace, stretch, flex, stiffen ≠ relax

**tension** 1 = strain, stress, nervousness, pressure, anxiety, unease, apprehension, suspense ≠ calmness 2 = friction, hostility, unease, antagonism, antipathy, enmity 3 = rigidity, tightness, stiffness, pressure, stress, stretching, tautness

**tentative** 1 = unconfirmed, provisional, indefinite, test, trial, pilot, preliminary, experimental ≠ confirmed 2 = hesitant, cautious, uncertain, doubtful, faltering, unsure, timid, undecided ≠ confident

**term** NOUN 1 = word, name, expression, title, label, phrase 2 = period, time, spell, while, season, interval, span, duration
● PLURAL NOUN 1 = conditions, particulars, provisions, provisos, stipulations, qualifications, specifications 2 = relationship, standing, footing, relations, status
● VERB = call, name, label, style, entitle, tag, dub, designate

**terminal** ADJECTIVE 1 = fatal, deadly, lethal, killing, mortal, incurable, inoperable, untreatable 2 = final, last, closing, finishing, concluding, ultimate, terminating ≠ initial

● NOUN = <u>terminus</u>, station, depot, end of the line

**terminate** 1 = <u>end</u>, stop, conclude, finish, complete, discontinue ≠ begin2 = <u>cease</u>, end, close, finish3 ≠ <u>abort</u>, end

**terrain** = <u>ground</u>, country, land, landscape, topography, going

**terrestrial** = <u>earthly</u>, worldly, global

**terrible** 1 = <u>awful</u>, shocking, terrifying, horrible, dreadful, horrifying, fearful, horrendous 2 (*Informal*) = <u>bad</u>, awful, dreadful, dire, abysmal, poor, rotten (*informal*) ≠ wonderful 3 = <u>serious</u>, desperate, severe, extreme, dangerous, insufferable ≠ mild

**terribly** 1 = <u>very much</u>, very, dreadfully, seriously, extremely, desperately, thoroughly, decidedly2 = <u>extremely</u>, very, dreadfully, seriously, desperately, thoroughly, decidedly, awfully (*informal*)

**terrific** 1 (*Informal*) = <u>excellent</u>, wonderful, brilliant, amazing, outstanding, superb, fantastic (*informal*), magnificent, booshit (*Austral. slang*), exo (*Austral. slang*), sik (*Austral. slang*), ka pai (*N.Z.*) ≠ awful2 = <u>intense</u>, great, huge, enormous, tremendous,

fearful, gigantic

**terrified** = <u>frightened</u>, scared, petrified, alarmed, panic-stricken, horror-struck

**terrify** = <u>frighten</u>, scare, alarm, terrorize

**territory** = <u>district</u>, area, land, region, country, zone, province, patch

➤ **WORD POWER SUPPLEMENT**
**New Zealand territories**

**terror** 1 = <u>fear</u>, alarm, dread, fright, panic, anxiety 2 = <u>nightmare</u>, monster, bogeyman, devil, fiend, bugbear

**test** VERB1 = <u>check</u>, investigate, assess, research, analyse, experiment with, try out, put something to the test 2 = <u>examine</u>, put someone to the test

● NOUN1 = <u>trial</u>, research, check, investigation, analysis, assessment, examination, evaluation2 = <u>examination</u>, paper, assessment, evaluation

**testament** 1 = <u>proof</u>, evidence, testimony, witness, demonstration, tribute2 = <u>will</u>, last wishes

**testify** = <u>bear witness</u>, state, swear, certify, assert, affirm, attest, corroborate ≠ disprove

**testimony** 1 = <u>evidence</u>, statement, submission, affidavit, deposition2 = <u>proof</u>, evidence, demonstration, indication, support, manifestation, verification, corroboration

**testing** = <u>difficult</u>, demanding, taxing, challenging, searching, tough, exacting, rigorous ≠ undemanding

**text** 1 = <u>contents</u>, words, content, wording, body, subject matter 2 = <u>words</u>, wording 3 = <u>transcript</u>, script

**texture** = <u>feel</u>, consistency, structure, surface, tissue, grain

**thank** = <u>say thank you to</u>, show your appreciation to

**thanks** PLURAL NOUN = <u>gratitude</u>, appreciation, credit, recognition, acknowledgment, gratefulness
● PHRASES **thanks to** = <u>because of</u>, through, due to, as a result of, owing to

**thaw** = <u>melt</u>, dissolve, soften, defrost, warm, liquefy, unfreeze ≠ freeze

**theatrical** 1 = <u>dramatic</u>, stage, Thespian 2 = <u>exaggerated</u>, dramatic, melodramatic, histrionic, affected, mannered, showy, ostentatious ≠ natural

**theft** = <u>stealing</u>, robbery, thieving, fraud, embezzlement, pilfering, larceny, purloining

**theme** 1 = <u>motif</u>, leitmotif 2 = <u>subject</u>, idea, topic, essence, subject matter, keynote, gist

**theological** = <u>religious</u>,

ecclesiastical, doctrinal

**theoretical** 1 = <u>abstract</u>, speculative ≠ practical 2 = <u>hypothetical</u>, academic, notional, unproven, conjectural, postulatory

**theory** = <u>belief</u>, feeling, speculation, assumption, hunch, presumption, conjecture, surmise

**therapeutic** = <u>beneficial</u>, healing, restorative, good, corrective, remedial, salutary, curative ≠ harmful

**therapist** = <u>psychologist</u>, analyst, psychiatrist, shrink (*informal*), counsellor, healer, psychotherapist, psychoanalyst

**therapy** = <u>remedy</u>, treatment, cure, healing, method of healing

**therefore** = <u>consequently</u>, so, thus, as a result, hence, accordingly, thence, ergo

**thesis** 1 = <u>proposition</u>, theory, hypothesis, idea, view, opinion, proposal, contention 2 = <u>dissertation</u>, paper, treatise, essay, monograph

**thick** 1 = <u>bulky</u>, broad, big, large, fat, solid, substantial, hefty ≠ thin 2 = <u>wide</u>, across, deep, broad, in extent *or* diameter 3 = <u>dense</u>, close, heavy, compact, impenetrable, lush ≠ thin 4 = <u>heavy</u>, heavyweight, dense, chunky, bulky, woolly 5 = <u>opaque</u>, heavy, dense, impenetrable 6 = <u>viscous</u>, concentrated, stiff, condensed, gelatinous, semi-solid, viscid ≠ runny7 = <u>crowded</u>, full, covered, bursting, bristling, brimming ≠ empty8 (*Informal*) = <u>stupid</u>, slow, dense, dopey (*informal*), moronic, obtuse, brainless, dumb-ass (*informal*) ≠ clever9 (*Informal*) = <u>friendly</u>, close, intimate, familiar, pally (*informal*), devoted, inseparable ≠ unfriendly

**thicken** = <u>set</u>, condense, congeal, clot, jell, coagulate ≠ thin

**thief** = <u>robber</u>, burglar, stealer, plunderer, shoplifter, embezzler, pickpocket, pilferer

**thin** 1 = <u>narrow</u>, fine, attenuated ≠ thick2 = <u>slim</u>, spare, lean, slight, slender, skinny, skeletal, bony ≠ fat3 = <u>meagre</u>, sparse, scanty, poor, scattered, inadequate, insufficient, deficient ≠ plentiful 4 = <u>fine</u>, delicate, flimsy, sheer, skimpy, gossamer, diaphanous, filmy ≠ thick5 = <u>unconvincing</u>, inadequate, feeble, poor, weak, superficial, lame, flimsy ≠ convincing6 = <u>wispy</u>, thinning, sparse, scarce, scanty

**thing** NOUN1 = <u>substance</u>, stuff, being, body, material, fabric, entity2 (*Informal*) = <u>phobia</u>, fear, complex, horror, terror, hang-up (*informal*), aversion, neurosis 3 (*Informal*) = <u>obsession</u>, liking, preoccupation, mania, fetish, fixation, soft spot, predilection
● PLURAL NOUN1 = <u>possessions</u>, stuff, gear, belongings, effects, luggage, clobber (*Brit. slang*), chattels2 = <u>equipment</u>, gear, tools, stuff, tackle, implements, kit, apparatus3 = <u>circumstances</u>, the situation, the state of affairs, matters, life, affairs

**think** VERB1 = <u>believe</u>, be of the opinion, be of the view2 = <u>judge</u>, consider, estimate, reckon, deem, regard as3 = <u>ponder</u>, reflect, contemplate, deliberate, meditate, ruminate, cogitate, be lost in thought
● PHRASES**think something up** = <u>devise</u>, create, come up with, invent, contrive, visualize, concoct, dream something up

**thinker** = <u>philosopher</u>, intellect (*informal*), wise man, sage, brain (*informal*), theorist, mastermind

**thinking** NOUN = <u>reasoning</u>, idea, view, position, theory, opinion, judgment, conjecture
● ADJECTIVE = <u>thoughtful</u>, intelligent, reasoning, rational, philosophical, reflective, contemplative, meditative

**thirst** 1 = <u>dryness</u>, thirstiness, drought2 = <u>craving</u>, appetite, longing, desire, passion, yearning, hankering, keenness ≠ aversion

**thorn** = <u>prickle</u>, spike, spine, barb

**thorough** 1 = <u>comprehensive</u>, full, complete, sweeping, intensive, in-depth, exhaustive ≠ cursory 2 = <u>careful</u>, conscientious, painstaking, efficient, meticulous, exhaustive, assiduous ≠ careless 3 = <u>complete</u>, total, absolute, utter, perfect, outright, unqualified, out-and-out ≠ partial

**thoroughly** 1 = <u>carefully</u>, fully, efficiently, meticulously, painstakingly, scrupulously, assiduously, intensively ≠ carelessly 2 = <u>fully</u> 3 = <u>completely</u>, quite, totally, perfectly, absolutely, utterly, downright, to the hilt ≠ partly

**though** CONJUNCTION = <u>although</u>, while, even if, even though, notwithstanding
● ADVERB = <u>nevertheless</u>, still, however, yet, nonetheless, for all that, notwithstanding

**thought** 1 = <u>thinking</u>, consideration, reflection, deliberation, musing, meditation, rumination, cogitation 2 = <u>opinion</u>, view, idea, concept, notion, judgment 3 = <u>consideration</u>, study, attention, care, regard, scrutiny, heed 4 = <u>intention</u>, plan, idea, design, aim, purpose, object, notion 5 = <u>hope</u>, expectation, prospect, aspiration, anticipation

**thoughtful** 1 = <u>reflective</u>, pensive, contemplative, meditative, serious, studious, deliberative, ruminative ≠ shallow 2 = <u>considerate</u>, kind, caring, kindly, helpful, attentive, unselfish, solicitous ≠ inconsiderate

**thrash** VERB 1 = <u>defeat</u>, beat, crush, slaughter (*informal*), rout, trounce, run rings around (*informal*), wipe the floor with (*informal*) 2 = <u>beat</u>, wallop, whip, belt (*informal*), cane, flog, scourge, spank 3 = <u>thresh</u>, flail, jerk, writhe, toss and turn
● PHRASES **thrash something out** = <u>settle</u>, resolve, discuss, debate, solve, argue out, have something out, talk something over

**thrashing** 1 = <u>defeat</u>, beating, hammering (*informal*), hiding (*informal*), rout, trouncing, drubbing 2 = <u>beating</u>, hiding (*informal*), belting (*informal*), whipping, flogging

**thread** NOUN 1 = <u>strand</u>, fibre, yarn, filament, line, string, twine 2 = <u>theme</u>, train of thought, direction, plot, drift, story line
● VERB = <u>move</u>, pass, ease, thrust, squeeze through, pick your way

**threat** 1 = <u>danger</u>, risk, hazard, menace, peril 2 = <u>threatening remark</u>, menace 3 = <u>warning</u>,

foreshadowing, foreboding
**threaten** 1 = <u>intimidate</u>, bully, menace, terrorize, lean on (*slang*), pressurize, browbeat ≠ defend
2 = <u>endanger</u>, jeopardize, put at risk, imperil, put in jeopardy, put on the line ≠ protect 3 = <u>be imminent</u>, impend

**threshold** 1 = <u>entrance</u>, doorway, door, doorstep 2 = <u>start</u>, beginning, opening, dawn, verge, brink, outset, inception ≠ end
3 = <u>limit</u>, margin, starting point, minimum

**thrift** = <u>economy</u>, prudence, frugality, saving, parsimony, carefulness, thriftiness ≠ extravagance

**thrill** NOUN = <u>pleasure</u>, kick (*informal*), buzz (*slang*), high, stimulation, tingle, titillation ≠ tedium
● VERB = <u>excite</u>, stimulate, arouse, move, stir, electrify, titillate, give someone a kick

**thrilling** = <u>exciting</u>, gripping, stimulating, stirring, sensational, rousing, riveting, electrifying ≠ boring

**thrive** = <u>prosper</u>, do well, flourish, increase, grow, develop, succeed, get on ≠ decline

**thriving** = <u>successful</u>, flourishing, healthy, booming, blooming, prosperous, burgeoning ≠ unsuccessful

**throb** VERB 1 = <u>pulsate</u>, pound, beat, pulse, thump, palpitate
2 = <u>vibrate</u>, pulsate, reverberate, shake, judder (*informal*)
● NOUN 1 = <u>pulse</u>, pounding, beat, thump, thumping, pulsating, palpitation 2 = <u>vibration</u>, throbbing, reverberation, judder (*informal*), pulsation

**throng** NOUN = <u>crowd</u>, mob, horde, host, pack, mass, crush, swarm
● VERB 1 = <u>crowd</u>, flock, congregate, converge, mill around, swarm around ≠ disperse
2 = <u>pack</u>, crowd

**throttle** = <u>strangle</u>, choke, garrotte, strangulate

**through** PREPOSITION 1 = <u>via</u>, by way of, by, between, past, from one side to the other of
2 = <u>because of</u>, by way of, by means of 3 = <u>using</u>, via, by way of, by means of, by virtue of, with the assistance of 4 = <u>during</u>, throughout, for the duration of, in
● ADJECTIVE = <u>completed</u>, done, finished, ended
● PHRASES **through and through** = <u>completely</u>, totally, fully, thoroughly, entirely, altogether, wholly, utterly

**throughout** PREPOSITION
1 = <u>right through</u>, everywhere in, during the whole of, through the whole of 2 = <u>all over</u>, everywhere

in, through the whole of
● ADVERB 1 = from start to finish, right through 2 = all through, right through

**throw** VERB 1 = hurl, toss, fling, send, launch, cast, pitch, chuck (*informal*) 2 = toss, fling, chuck (*informal*), cast, hurl, sling 3 (*Informal*) = confuse, baffle, faze, astonish, confound, disconcert, dumbfound
● NOUN = toss, pitch, fling, sling, lob (*informal*), heave

**thrust** VERB = push, force, shove, drive, plunge, jam, ram, propel
● NOUN 1 = stab, pierce, lunge 2 = push, shove, poke, prod 3 = momentum, impetus, drive

**thug** = ruffian, hooligan, tough, heavy (*slang*), gangster, bully boy, bruiser (*informal*), tsotsi (*S. African*)

**thump** VERB = strike, hit, punch, pound, beat, knock, smack, clout (*informal*)
● NOUN 1 = blow, knock, punch, rap, smack, clout (*informal*), whack, swipe = thud, crash, bang, clunk, thwack

**thunder** NOUN = rumble, crash, boom, explosion
● VERB 1 = rumble, crash, boom, roar, resound, reverberate, peal 2 = shout, roar, yell, bark, bellow

**thus** 1 = therefore, so, hence, consequently, accordingly, for

this reason, ergo, on that account 2 = in this way, so, like this, as follows

**thwart** = frustrate, foil, prevent, snooker, hinder, obstruct, outwit, stymie ≠ assist

**tick** NOUN 1 = check mark, mark, line, stroke, dash 2 = click, tapping, clicking, ticktock 3 (*Brit. informal*) = moment, second, minute, flash, instant, twinkling, split second, trice
● VERB 1 = mark, indicate, check off 2 = click, tap, ticktock

**ticket** 1 = voucher, pass, coupon, card, slip, certificate, token, chit 2 = label, tag, marker, sticker, card, slip, tab, docket

**tide** 1 = current, flow, stream, ebb, undertow, tideway 2 = course, direction, trend, movement, tendency, drift

**tidy** ADJECTIVE 1 = neat, orderly, clean, spruce, well-kept, well-ordered, shipshape ≠ untidy 2 = organized, neat, methodical 3 (*Informal*) = considerable, large, substantial, goodly, healthy, generous, handsome, ample ≠ small
● VERB = neaten, straighten, order, clean, groom, spruce up ≠ disorder

**tie** VERB 1 = fasten, bind, join, link, connect, attach, knot ≠ unfasten 2 = tether, secure 3 = restrict, limit, confine, bind, restrain, hamper, hinder ≠ **free**[4] = <u>draw</u>, be level, match, equal

- **NOUN**[1] = <u>fastening</u>, binding, link, bond, knot, cord, fetter, ligature[2] = <u>bond</u>, relationship, connection, commitment, liaison, allegiance, affiliation[3] = <u>draw</u>, dead heat, deadlock, stalemate

**tier** = <u>row</u>, bank, layer, line, level, rank, storey, stratum

**tight** 1 = <u>close-fitting</u>, narrow, cramped, snug, constricted, close ≠ **loose**[2] = <u>secure</u>, firm, fast, fixed 3 = <u>taut</u>, stretched, rigid ≠ **slack** 4 = <u>close</u>, even, well-matched, hard-fought, evenly-balanced ≠ **uneven**[5] (*Informal*) = <u>miserly</u>, mean, stingy, grasping, parsimonious, niggardly, tightfisted ≠ **generous** 6 (*Informal*) = <u>drunk</u>, intoxicated, plastered (*slang*), under the influence (*informal*), tipsy, paralytic (*informal*), inebriated, out to it (*Austral. & N.Z. slang*) ≠ **sober**

**tighten** = <u>close</u>, narrow, strengthen, squeeze, harden, constrict ≠ **slacken**

**till**[1] = <u>cultivate</u>, dig, plough, work

**till**[2] = <u>cash register</u>, cash box

**tilt** **VERB** = <u>slant</u>, tip, slope, list, lean, heel, incline

- **NOUN**[1] = <u>slope</u>, angle, inclination, list, pitch, incline,

slant, camber[2] (*Medieval history*) = <u>joust</u>, fight, tournament, lists, combat, duel

**timber** 1 = <u>beams</u>, boards, planks[2] = <u>wood</u>, logs

**time** **NOUN**[1] = <u>period</u>, term, space, stretch, spell, span 2 = <u>occasion</u>, point, moment, stage, instance, point in time, juncture[3] = <u>age</u>, duration 4 = <u>tempo</u>, beat, rhythm, measure

- **VERB** = <u>schedule</u>, set, plan, book, programme, set up, fix, arrange

**timeless** = <u>eternal</u>, lasting, permanent, enduring, immortal, everlasting, ageless, changeless ≠ **temporary**

**timely** = <u>opportune</u>, appropriate, well-timed, suitable, convenient, judicious, propitious, seasonable ≠ **untimely**

**timetable** 1 = <u>schedule</u>, programme, agenda, list, diary, calendar[2] = <u>syllabus</u>, course, curriculum, programme, teaching programme

**tinge** **NOUN**[1] = <u>tint</u>, colour, shade 2 = <u>trace</u>, bit, drop, touch, suggestion, dash, sprinkling, smattering

- **VERB** = <u>tint</u>, colour

**tinker** = <u>meddle</u>, play, potter, fiddle (*informal*), dabble, mess about

**tint** **NOUN**[1] = <u>shade</u>, colour, tone, hue[2] = <u>dye</u>, wash, rinse, tinge, tincture

● VERB = <u>dye</u>, colour

**tiny** = <u>small</u>, little, minute, slight, miniature, negligible, microscopic, diminutive ≠ huge

**tip¹** NOUN 1 = <u>end</u>, point, head, extremity, sharp end, nib, prong 2 = <u>peak</u>, top, summit, pinnacle, zenith, spire, acme, vertex

● VERB = <u>cap</u>, top, crown, surmount, finish

**tip²** VERB 1 = <u>reward</u>, remunerate, give a tip to, sweeten (*informal*) 2 = <u>predict</u>, back, recommend, think of

● NOUN 1 = <u>gratuity</u>, gift, reward, present, sweetener (*informal*) 2 = <u>hint</u>, suggestion, piece of advice, pointer

**tip³** VERB 1 = <u>pour</u>, drop, empty, dump, drain, discharge, unload, jettison 2 (*Brit.*) = <u>dump</u>, empty, unload, pour out

● NOUN (*Brit.*) = <u>dump</u>, midden, rubbish heap, refuse heap

**tire** 1 = <u>exhaust</u>, drain, fatigue, weary, wear out ≠ refresh 2 = <u>flag</u>, become tired, fail 3 = <u>bore</u>, weary, exasperate, irritate, irk

**tired** 1 = <u>exhausted</u>, fatigued, weary, flagging, drained, sleepy, worn out, drowsy, tuckered out (*Austral. & N.Z. informal*) ≠ energetic 2 = <u>bored</u>, fed up, weary, sick, hoha (*N.Z.*)

≠ enthusiastic about 3 = <u>hackneyed</u>, stale, well-worn, old, corny (*slang*), threadbare, trite, clichéd ≠ original

**tiring** = <u>exhausting</u>, demanding, wearing, tough, exacting, strenuous, arduous, laborious

**title** 1 = <u>name</u>, designation, term, handle (*slang*), moniker or monicker (*slang*) 2 (*Sport*) = <u>championship</u>, trophy, bays, crown, honour 3 (*Law*) = <u>ownership</u>, right, claim, privilege, entitlement, tenure, prerogative, freehold

**toast¹** 1 = <u>brown</u>, grill, crisp, roast 2 = <u>warm (up)</u>, heat (up), thaw, bring back to life

**toast²** NOUN 1 = <u>tribute</u>, compliment, salute, health, pledge, salutation 2 = <u>favourite</u>, celebrity, darling, talk, pet, focus of attention, hero or heroine, blue-eyed boy or girl (*Brit. informal*)

● VERB = <u>drink to</u>, honour, salute, drink (to) the health of

**together** ADVERB 1 = <u>collectively</u>, jointly, as one, with each other, in conjunction, side by side, mutually, in partnership ≠ separately 2 = <u>at the same time</u>, simultaneously, concurrently, contemporaneously, at one fell swoop

● **ADJECTIVE** (*Informal*) = self-possessed, composed, well-balanced, well-adjusted

**toil** VERB1 = labour, work, struggle, strive, sweat (*informal*), slave, graft (*informal*), slog
2 = struggle, trek, slog, trudge, fight your way, footslog
● **NOUN** = hard work, effort, application, sweat, graft (*informal*), slog, exertion, drudgery ≠ idleness

**toilet** 1 = lavatory, bathroom, loo (*Brit. informal*), privy, cloakroom (*Brit.*), urinal, latrine, washroom, dunny (*Austral. & N.Z. old-fashioned informal*), bogger (*Austral. slang*), brasco (*Austral. slang*)2 = bathroom, gents or ladies (*Brit. informal*), privy, latrine, water closet, ladies' room, W.C.

**token** NOUN = symbol, mark, sign, note, expression, indication, representation, badge
● **ADJECTIVE** = nominal, symbolic, minimal, hollow, superficial, perfunctory

**tolerance** 1 = broad-mindedness, indulgence, forbearance, permissiveness, open-mindedness ≠ intolerance
2 = endurance, resistance, stamina, fortitude, resilience, toughness, staying power, hardiness3 = resistance, immunity, resilience, non-susceptibility

**tolerant** = broad-minded, understanding, open-minded, catholic, long-suffering, permissive, forbearing, unprejudiced ≠ intolerant

**tolerate** 1 = endure, stand, take, stomach, put up with (*informal*)
2 = allow, accept, permit, take, brook, put up with (*informal*), condone ≠ forbid

**toll¹** VERB = ring, sound, strike, chime, knell, clang, peal
● **NOUN** = ringing, chime, knell, clang, peal

**toll²** 1 = charge, tax, fee, duty, payment, levy, tariff2 = damage, cost, loss, roll, penalty, sum, number, roster3 = adverse effects, price, cost, suffering, damage, penalty, harm

**tomb** = grave, vault, crypt, mausoleum, sarcophagus, catacomb, sepulchre

**tone** NOUN1 = pitch, inflection, intonation, timbre, modulation
2 = volume, timbre3 = character, style, feel, air, spirit, attitude, manner, mood4 = colour, shade, tint, tinge, hue
● **VERB** = harmonize, match, blend, suit, go well with
● **PHRASE** tone something down = moderate, temper, soften, restrain, subdue, play down = reduce, moderate

**tongue** = language, speech, dialect, parlance

**tonic** = stimulant, boost, pick-me-up (*informal*), fillip, shot in the arm (*informal*), restorative

**too** 1 = also, as well, further, in addition, moreover, besides, likewise, to boot 2 = excessively, very, extremely, overly, unduly, unreasonably, inordinately, immoderately

**tool** 1 = implement, device, appliance, machine, instrument, gadget, utensil, contraption 2 = puppet, creature, pawn, stooge (*slang*), minion, lackey, flunkey, hireling

**top** NOUN 1 = peak, summit, head, crown, height, ridge, brow, crest ≠ bottom 2 = lid, cover, cap, plug, stopper, bung 3 = first place, head, peak, lead, high point
● ADJECTIVE 1 = highest, loftiest, furthest up, uppermost 2 = leading, best, first, highest, head, finest, elite, foremost ≠ lowest 3 = chief, most important, principal, most powerful, highest, head, leading, main 4 = prime, best, select, first-class, quality, choice, excellent, premier
● VERB 1 = lead, head, be at the top of, be first in 2 = cover, garnish, finish, crown, cap 3 = surpass, better, beat, improve on, cap, exceed, eclipse, excel ≠ not be as good as

**topic** = subject, point, question, issue, matter, theme, subject matter

**topical** = current, popular, contemporary, up-to-date, up-to-the-minute, newsworthy

**topple** 1 = fall over, fall, collapse, tumble, overturn, totter, keel over, overbalance 2 = knock over 3 = overthrow, overturn, bring down, oust, unseat, bring low

**torment** NOUN = suffering, distress, misery, pain, hell, torture, agony, anguish ≠ bliss
● VERB 1 = torture, distress, rack, crucify ≠ comfort 2 = tease, annoy, bother, irritate, harass, hassle (*informal*), pester, vex

**torn** 1 = cut, split, rent, ripped, ragged, slit, lacerated 2 = undecided, uncertain, unsure, wavering, vacillating, in two minds (*informal*), irresolute

**tornado** = whirlwind, storm, hurricane, gale, cyclone, typhoon, tempest, squall

**torture** VERB 1 = torment, abuse, persecute, afflict, scourge, molest, crucify, mistreat ≠ comfort 2 = distress, torment, worry, trouble, rack, afflict, harrow, inflict anguish on
● NOUN 1 = ill-treatment, abuse, torment, persecution,

maltreatment, harsh treatment
2 = **agony**, suffering, anguish, distress, torment, heartbreak ≠ bliss

**toss** VERB1 = **throw**, pitch, hurl, fling, launch, cast, flip, sling
2 = **shake3** = **thrash (about)**, twitch, wriggle, squirm, writhe
● NOUN = **throw**, pitch, lob (*informal*)

**tot** NOUN1 = **infant**, child, baby, toddler, mite, littlie (*Austral. informal*), ankle-biter (*Austral. slang*), tacker (*Austral. slang*)
2 = **measure**, shot (*informal*), finger, nip, slug, dram, snifter (*informal*)
● PHRASEStot something up = **add up**, calculate, total, reckon, compute, tally, enumerate, count up

**total** NOUN = **sum**, entirety, grand total, whole, aggregate, totality, full amount, sum total ≠ part
● ADJECTIVE = **complete**, absolute, utter, whole, entire, undivided, overarching, thoroughgoing ≠ partial
● VERB1 = **amount to**, make, come to, reach, equal, run to, number, add up to2 = **add up**, work out, compute, reckon, tot up ≠ subtract

**totally** = **completely**, entirely, absolutely, fully, comprehensively, thoroughly, wholly, utterly ≠ partly

**touch** VERB1 = **feel**, handle, finger, stroke, brush, make contact with, caress, fondle
2 = **come into contact**, meet, contact, border, graze, adjoin, be in contact, abut3 = **tap4** = **affect**, influence, inspire, impress
5 = **consume**, take, drink, eat, partake of6 = **move**, stir, disturb
7 = **match**, rival, equal, compare with, parallel, hold a candle to (*informal*)
● NOUN1 = **contact**, push, stroke, brush, press, tap, poke, nudge
2 = **feeling**, handling, physical contact3 = **bit**, spot, trace, drop, dash, small amount, jot, smattering4 = **style**, method, technique, way, manner, trademark
● PHRASEStouch and go = **risky**, close, near, critical, precarious, nerve-racking ◆touch on or upon something = **refer to**, cover, raise, deal with, mention, bring in, speak of, hint at

**touching** = **moving**, affecting, sad, stirring, pathetic, poignant, emotive, pitiable

**tough** ADJECTIVE1 = **strong** ≠ weak2 = **hardy**, strong, seasoned, strapping, vigorous, sturdy, stout3 = **violent**, rough, ruthless, pugnacious, hard-bitten
4 = **strict**, severe, stern, hard, firm, resolute, merciless, unbending ≠ lenient5 = **hard**, difficult,

troublesome, uphill, strenuous, arduous, laborious ≠ **resilient**, hard, resistant, durable, strong, solid, rugged, sturdy ≠ fragile

● NOUN = **ruffian**, bully, thug, hooligan, bruiser (*informal*), roughneck (*slang*), tsotsi (*S. African*)

**tour** NOUN = **journey**, expedition, excursion, trip, outing, jaunt, junket

● VERB 1 = **travel round**, travel through, journey round, trek round, go on a trip through 2 = **visit**, explore, go round, inspect, walk round, drive round, sightsee

**tourist** = **traveller**, voyager, tripper, globetrotter, holiday-maker, sightseer, excursionist

**tournament** = **competition**, meeting, event, series, contest

**tow** = **drag**, draw, pull, haul, tug, yank, lug

**towards** 1 = **in the direction of**, to, for, on the way to, en route for 2 = **regarding**, about, concerning, respecting, in relation to, with regard to, with respect to, apropos

**tower** = **column**, pillar, turret, belfry, steeple, obelisk

**toxic** = **poisonous**, deadly, lethal, harmful, pernicious, noxious, septic, pestilential ≠ harmless

**toy** NOUN = **plaything**, game, doll

● PHRASES **toy with something** = **play with**, consider, trifle with, dally with, entertain the possibility of, amuse yourself with, think idly of

**trace** VERB 1 = **search for**, track, unearth, hunt down 2 = **find**, track (down), discover, detect, unearth, hunt down, ferret out, locate 3 = **outline**, sketch, draw 4 = **copy**, map, draft, outline, sketch, reproduce, draw over

● NOUN 1 = **bit**, drop, touch, shadow, suggestion, hint, suspicion, tinge 2 = **remnant**, sign, record, mark, evidence, indication, vestige 3 = **track**, trail, footstep, path, footprint, spoor, footmark

**track** NOUN 1 = **path**, way, road, route, trail, pathway, footpath 2 = **course**, line, path, orbit, trajectory 3 = **line**, tramline

● VERB = **follow**, pursue, chase, trace, tail (*informal*), shadow, trail, stalk

● PHRASES **track something** or **someone down** = **find**, discover, trace, unearth, dig up, hunt down, sniff out, run to earth or ground

**tract**[1] = **area**, region, district, stretch, territory, extent, plot, expanse

**tract**[2] = **treatise**, essay, booklet, pamphlet, dissertation, monograph, homily

**trade** NOUN 1 = commerce, business, transactions, dealing, exchange, traffic, truck, barter 2 = job, employment, business, craft, profession, occupation, line of work, métier

● VERB 1 = deal, do business, traffic, truck, bargain, peddle, transact, cut a deal 2 = exchange, switch, swap, barter 3 = operate, run, deal, do business

**trader** = dealer, supplier, merchant, seller, purveyor

**tradition** 1 = customs, institution, ritual, folklore, lore, tikanga (N.Z.) 2 = established practice, custom, convention, habit, ritual

**traditional** 1 = old-fashioned, old, established, conventional, usual, accustomed, customary, time-honoured ≠ revolutionary 2 = folk, old

**traffic** NOUN 1 = transport, vehicles, transportation, freight 2 = trade, commerce, business, exchange, truck, dealings, peddling

● VERB = trade, deal, exchange, bargain, do business, peddle, cut a deal, have dealings

**tragedy** = disaster, catastrophe, misfortune, adversity, calamity ≠ fortune

**tragic** 1 = distressing, sad, appalling, deadly, unfortunate, disastrous, dreadful, dire ≠ fortunate 2 = sad, miserable, pathetic, mournful ≠ happy

**trail** NOUN 1 = path, track, route, way, course, road, pathway, footpath 2 = tracks, path, marks, wake, trace, scent, footprints, spoor 3 = wake, stream, tail

● VERB 1 = follow, track, chase, pursue, dog, hunt, shadow, trace 2 = drag, draw, pull, sweep, haul, tow, dangle, droop 3 = lag, follow, drift, wander, linger, trudge, plod, meander

**train** VERB 1 = instruct, school, prepare, coach, teach, guide, educate, drill 2 = exercise, prepare, work out, practise, do exercise, get into shape 3 = aim, point, level, position, direct, focus, sight, zero in

● NOUN = sequence, series, chain, string, set, cycle, trail, succession

**trainer** = coach, manager, guide, adviser, tutor, instructor, counsellor, guru

**trait** = characteristic, feature, quality, attribute, quirk, peculiarity, mannerism, idiosyncrasy

**traitor** = betrayer, deserter, turncoat, renegade, defector, Judas, quisling, apostate, fizgig (Austral. slang) ≠ loyalist

**tramp** VERB 1 = trudge, stump, toil, plod, traipse (informal)

2 = hike, walk, trek, roam, march, ramble, slog, rove
● NOUN1 = vagrant, derelict, drifter, down-and-out, derro (Austral. slang)2 = tread, stamp, footstep, footfall3 = hike, march, trek, ramble, slog

**trample** often with on = stamp, crush, squash, tread, flatten, run over, walk over

**trance** = daze, dream, abstraction, rapture, reverie, stupor, unconsciousness

**transaction** = deal, negotiation, business, enterprise, bargain, undertaking

**transcend** = surpass, exceed, go beyond, rise above, eclipse, excel, outstrip, outdo

**transcript** = copy, record, manuscript, reproduction, duplicate, transcription

**transfer** VERB = move, transport, shift, relocate, transpose, change
● NOUN = transference, move, handover, change, shift, transmission, translation, relocation

**transform** 1 = change, convert, alter, transmute2 = make over, remodel, revolutionize

**transformation** 1 = change, conversion, alteration, metamorphosis, transmutation
2 = revolution, sea change

**transit** = movement, transfer,

transport, passage, crossing, transportation, carriage, conveyance

**transition** = change, passing, development, shift, conversion, alteration, progression, metamorphosis

**transitional** 1 = changing, passing, fluid, intermediate, unsettled, developmental
2 = temporary, working, acting, short-term, interim, fill-in, caretaker, provisional

**translate** = render, put, change, convert, interpret, decode, construe, paraphrase

**translation** = interpretation, version, rendering, rendition, decoding, paraphrase

**transmission** 1 = transfer, spread, spreading, passing on, circulation, dispatch, relaying, mediation2 = broadcasting, showing, putting out, relaying, sending3 = programme, broadcast, show, production, telecast

**transmit** 1 = broadcast, televise, relay, air, radio, send out, disseminate, beam out2 = pass on, carry, spread, send, bear, transfer, hand on, convey

**transparent** 1 = clear, sheer, see-through, lucid, translucent, crystalline, limpid, diaphanous
≠ opaque2 = obvious, plain,

patent, evident, explicit, manifest, recognizable, unambiguous ≠ uncertain

**transplant** 1 = <u>implant</u>, transfer, graft 2 = <u>transfer</u>, take, bring, carry, remove, transport, shift, convey

**transport** NOUN 1 = <u>vehicle</u>, transportation, conveyance 2 = <u>transference</u>, carrying, delivery, distribution, transportation, shipment, freight, haulage 3 *often plural* = <u>ecstasy</u>, delight, heaven, bliss, euphoria, rapture, enchantment, ravishment ≠ despondency
● VERB 1 = <u>convey</u>, take, move, bring, send, carry, bear, transfer 2 = <u>enrapture</u>, move, delight, entrance, enchant, captivate, ravish 3 (*History*) = <u>exile</u>, banish, deport

**trap** NOUN 1 = <u>snare</u>, net, gin, pitfall, noose 2 = <u>ambush</u>, set-up (*informal*) 3 = <u>trick</u>, set-up (*informal*), deception, ploy, ruse, trickery, subterfuge, stratagem
● VERB 1 = <u>catch</u>, snare, ensnare, entrap, take, corner, bag, lay hold of 2 = <u>trick</u>, fool, cheat, lure, seduce, deceive, dupe, beguile 3 = <u>capture</u>, catch, arrest, seize, take, secure, collar (*informal*), apprehend

**trash** 1 = <u>nonsense</u>, rubbish, rot, drivel, twaddle, tripe (*informal*), moonshine, hogwash, kak (S.

African taboo slang), bizzo (*Austral. slang*), bull's wool (*Austral. & N.Z. slang*) ≠ sense 2 (*Chiefly U.S. & Canad.*) = <u>litter</u>, refuse, waste, rubbish, junk (*informal*), garbage, dross

**trauma** 1 = <u>shock</u>, suffering, pain, torture, ordeal, anguish 2 = <u>injury</u>, damage, hurt, wound, agony

**traumatic** = <u>shocking</u>, upsetting, alarming, awful, disturbing, devastating, painful, distressing ≠ calming

**travel** VERB = <u>go</u>, journey, move, tour, progress, wander, trek, voyage
● NOUN *usually plural* = <u>journey</u>, wandering, expedition, globetrotting, tour, trip, voyage, excursion

**traveller** or (*U.S.*) **traveler** = <u>voyager</u>, tourist, explorer, globetrotter, holiday-maker, wayfarer

**tread** VERB = <u>step</u>, walk, march, pace, stamp, stride, hike
● NOUN = <u>step</u>, walk, pace, stride, footstep, gait, footfall

**treason** = <u>disloyalty</u>, mutiny, treachery, duplicity, sedition, perfidy, lese-majesty, traitorousness ≠ loyalty

**treasure** NOUN 1 = <u>riches</u>, money, gold, fortune, wealth, valuables, jewels, cash

2 (*Informal*) = <u>angel</u>, darling, jewel, gem, paragon, nonpareil
● **VERB** = <u>prize</u>, value, esteem, adore, cherish, revere, hold dear, love

**treasury** = <u>storehouse</u>, bank, store, vault, hoard, cache, repository

**treat** **VERB1** = <u>behave towards</u>, deal with, handle, act towards, use, consider, serve, manage
2 = <u>take care of</u>, minister to, attend to, give medical treatment to, doctor (*informal*), nurse, care for, prescribe medicine for
3 = <u>provide</u>, stand (*informal*), entertain, lay on, regale
● **NOUN1** = <u>entertainment</u>, party, surprise, gift, celebration, feast, outing, excursion2 = <u>pleasure</u>, delight, joy, thrill, satisfaction, enjoyment, source of pleasure, fun

**treatment** 1 = <u>care</u>, medical care, nursing, medicine, surgery, therapy, healing, medication
2 = <u>cure</u>, remedy, medication, medicine3 *often with*of = <u>handling</u>, dealings with, behaviour towards, conduct towards, management, manipulation, action towards

**treaty** = <u>agreement</u>, pact, contract, alliance, convention, compact, covenant, entente

**trek** **VERB1** = <u>journey</u>, march,

hike, tramp, rove, go walkabout (*Austral.*)2 = <u>trudge</u>, traipse (*informal*), footslog, slog
● **NOUN1** = <u>slog</u>, tramp
2 = <u>journey</u>, hike, expedition, safari, march, odyssey

**tremble** **VERB1** = <u>shake</u>, shiver, quake, shudder, quiver, totter
2 = <u>vibrate</u>, shake, quake, wobble
● **NOUN** = <u>shake</u>, shiver, quake, shudder, wobble, tremor, quiver, vibration

**tremendous** 1 = <u>huge</u>, great, enormous, terrific, formidable, immense, gigantic, colossal ≠ tiny
2 = <u>excellent</u>, great, wonderful, brilliant, amazing, extraordinary, fantastic (*informal*), marvellous, booshit (*Austral. slang*), exo (*Austral. slang*), sik (*Austral. slang*) ≠ terrible

**trench** = <u>ditch</u>, channel, drain, gutter, trough, furrow, excavation

**trend** 1 = <u>tendency</u>, swing, drift, inclination, current, direction, flow, leaning2 = <u>fashion</u>, craze, fad (*informal*), mode, thing, style, rage, vogue

**trendy** (*Brit. informal*) = <u>fashionable</u>, with it (*informal*), stylish, in fashion, in vogue, modish, voguish

**trial** 1 (*Law*) = <u>hearing</u>, case, court case, inquiry, tribunal, lawsuit, appeal, litigation2 = <u>test</u>, experiment, evaluation, audition, dry run (*informal*), assessment, probation, appraisal **3** = **hardship**, suffering, trouble, distress, ordeal, adversity, affliction, tribulation

**tribe** = **race**, people, family, clan, hapu (*N.Z.*), iwi (*N.Z.*)

**tribunal** = **hearing**, court, trial

**tribute** = **accolade**, testimonial, eulogy, recognition, compliment, commendation, panegyric ≠ criticism

**trick** NOUN **1** = **joke**, stunt, spoof (*informal*), prank, practical joke, antic, jape, leg-pull (*Brit. informal*) **2** = **deception**, trap, fraud, manoeuvre, ploy, hoax, swindle, ruse **3** = **sleight of hand**, stunt, legerdemain **4** = **secret**, skill, knack, hang (*informal*), technique, know-how (*informal*) **5** = **mannerism**, habit, characteristic, trait, quirk, peculiarity, foible, idiosyncrasy
● VERB = **deceive**, trap, take someone in (*informal*), fool, cheat, con (*informal*), kid (*informal*), mislead

**trickle** VERB = **dribble**, run, drop, stream, drip, ooze, seep, exude
● NOUN = **dribble**, drip, seepage, thin stream

**tricky 1** = **difficult**, sensitive, complicated, delicate, risky, hairy (*informal*), problematic, thorny ≠ simple **2** = **crafty**, scheming, cunning, slippery, sly, devious, wily, artful ≠ open

**trifle** = **knick-knack**, toy, plaything, bauble, bagatelle

**trifling** = **insignificant**, trivial, worthless, negligible, unimportant, paltry, measly ≠ significant

**trigger** = **bring about**, start, cause, produce, generate, prompt, provoke, set off ≠ prevent

**trim** ADJECTIVE **1** = **neat**, smart, tidy, spruce, dapper, natty (*informal*), well-groomed, shipshape ≠ untidy **2** = **slender**, fit, slim, sleek, streamlined, shapely, svelte, willowy
● VERB **1** = **cut**, crop, clip, shave, tidy, prune, pare, even up **2** = **decorate**, dress, array, adorn, ornament, embellish, deck out, beautify
● NOUN **1** = **decoration**, edging, border, piping, trimming, frill, embellishment, adornment **2** = **condition**, health, shape (*informal*), fitness, wellness, fettle **3** = **cut**, crop, clipping, shave, pruning, shearing, tidying up

**trimming** NOUN = **decoration**, edging, border, piping, frill, embellishment, adornment, ornamentation
● PLURAL NOUN = **extras**, accessories, ornaments, accompaniments, frills, trappings,

paraphernalia

**trinity** = threesome, trio, triad, triumvirate

**trio** = threesome, trinity, trilogy, triad, triumvirate

**trip** NOUN¹ = journey, outing, excursion, day out, run, drive, tour, spin (*informal*) ² = stumble, fall, slip, misstep

● VERB¹ = stumble, fall, fall over, slip, tumble, topple, stagger, misstep² = skip, dance, hop, gambol

● PHRASE **trip someone up** = catch out, trap, wrongfoot

**triple** ADJECTIVE¹ = treble, three times² = three-way, threefold, tripartite

● VERB = treble, increase threefold

**triumph** NOUN¹ = success, victory, accomplishment, achievement, coup, feat, conquest, attainment ≠ failure 2 = joy, pride, happiness, rejoicing, elation, jubilation, exultation

● VERB¹ *often with* over = succeed, win, overcome, prevail, prosper, vanquish ≠ fail 2 = rejoice, celebrate, glory, revel, gloat, exult, crow

**triumphant** 1 = victorious, winning, successful, conquering ≠ defeated² = celebratory, jubilant, proud, elated, exultant, cock-a-hoop

**trivial** = unimportant, small, minor, petty, meaningless, worthless, trifling, insignificant ≠ important

**troop** NOUN = group, company, team, body, unit, band, crowd, squad

● PLURAL NOUN = soldiers, men, armed forces, servicemen, army, soldiery

● VERB = flock, march, stream, swarm, throng, traipse (*informal*)

**trophy** 1 = prize, cup, award, laurels² = souvenir, spoils, relic, memento, booty, keepsake

**tropical** = hot, stifling, steamy, torrid, sultry, sweltering ≠ cold

**trot** VERB = run, jog, scamper, lope, canter

● NOUN = run, jog, lope, canter

**trouble** NOUN¹ = bother, problems, concern, worry, stress, difficulty (*informal*), anxiety, distress² *usually plural* = distress, problem, worry, pain, anxiety, grief, torment, sorrow ≠ pleasure 3 = ailment, disease, failure, complaint, illness, disorder, defect, malfunction⁴ = disorder, fighting, conflict, bother, unrest, disturbance, to-do (*informal*), furore, biffo (*Austral. slang*) ≠ peace⁵ = effort, work, thought, care, labour, pains, hassle (*informal*), inconvenience ≠ convenience

**● VERB 1** = <u>bother</u>, worry, upset, disturb, distress, plague, pain, sadden ≠ please **2** = <u>afflict</u>, hurt, bother, cause discomfort to, pain, grieve **3** = <u>inconvenience</u>, disturb, burden, put out, impose upon, incommode ≠ relieve **4** = <u>take pains</u>, take the time, make an effort, exert yourself ≠ avoid

**troublesome 1** = <u>bothersome</u>, trying, taxing, demanding, difficult, worrying, annoying, tricky ≠ simple **2** = <u>disorderly</u>, violent, turbulent, rebellious, unruly, rowdy, undisciplined, uncooperative ≠ well-behaved

**trough** = <u>manger</u>, water trough

**truce** = <u>ceasefire</u>, peace, moratorium, respite, lull, cessation, let-up (*informal*), armistice

**true 1** = <u>correct</u>, right, accurate, precise, factual, truthful, veracious ≠ false **2** = <u>actual</u>, real, genuine, proper, authentic, dinkum (*Austral. & N.Z. informal*) **3** = <u>faithful</u>, loyal, devoted, dedicated, steady, reliable, staunch, trustworthy ≠ unfaithful **4** = <u>exact</u>, perfect, accurate, precise, spot-on (*Brit. informal*), on target, unerring ≠ inaccurate

**truly 1** = <u>genuinely</u>, correctly, truthfully, rightly, precisely, exactly, legitimately, authentically ≠ falsely **2** = <u>really</u>, very, greatly,

indeed, extremely **3** = <u>faithfully</u>, steadily, sincerely, staunchly, dutifully, loyally, devotedly

**trumpet** NOUN = <u>horn</u>, clarion, bugle

**● VERB** = <u>proclaim</u>, advertise, tout (*informal*), announce, broadcast, shout from the rooftops ≠ keep secret

**trunk 1** = <u>stem</u>, stalk, bole **2** = <u>chest</u>, case, box, crate, coffer, casket **3** = <u>body</u>, torso **4** = <u>snout</u>, nose, proboscis

**trust** VERB **1** = <u>believe in</u>, have faith in, depend on, count on, bank on, rely upon ≠ distrust **2** = <u>entrust</u>, commit, assign, confide, consign, put into the hands of, allow to look after, hand over **3** = <u>expect</u>, hope, suppose, assume, presume, surmise

**● NOUN** = <u>confidence</u>, credit, belief, faith, expectation, conviction, assurance, certainty ≠ distrust

**trusting** *or* **trustful** = <u>unsuspecting</u>, naive, gullible, unwary, credulous, unsuspicious ≠ suspicious

**truth 1** = <u>reality</u>, fact(s), real life **2** = <u>truthfulness</u>, fact, accuracy, precision, validity, legitimacy, veracity, genuineness ≠ inaccuracy

**try** VERB **1** = <u>attempt</u>, seek, aim, strive, struggle, endeavour, have a go, make an effort

2 = <u>experiment with</u>, try out, put to the test, test, taste, examine, investigate, sample

● NOUN = <u>attempt</u>, go (*informal*), shot (*informal*), effort, crack (*informal*), stab (*informal*), bash (*informal*), whack (*informal*)

**trying** = <u>annoying</u>, hard, taxing, difficult, tough, stressful, exasperating, tiresome
≠ straightforward

**tuck** VERB = <u>push</u>, stick, stuff, slip, ease, insert, pop (*informal*)

● NOUN1 (*Brit. informal*) = <u>food</u>, grub (*slang*), kai (*N.Z. informal*), nosh (*slang*)2 = <u>fold</u>, gather, pleat, pinch

**tug** VERB1 = <u>pull</u>, pluck, jerk, yank, wrench2 = <u>drag</u>, pull, haul, tow, lug, heave, draw

● NOUN = <u>pull</u>, jerk, yank

**tuition** = <u>training</u>, schooling, education, teaching, lessons, instruction, tutoring, tutelage

**tumble** VERB = <u>fall</u>, drop, topple, plummet, stumble, flop

● NOUN = <u>fall</u>, drop, trip, plunge, spill, stumble

**tumour** = <u>growth</u>, cancer, swelling, lump, carcinoma (*Pathology*), sarcoma (*Medical*)

**tune** NOUN1 = <u>melody</u>, air, song, theme, strain(s), jingle, ditty

2 = <u>harmony</u>, pitch, euphony

● VERB1 = <u>tune up</u>, adjust

2 = <u>regulate</u>, adapt, modulate, harmonize, attune, pitch

**tunnel** NOUN = <u>passage</u>, underpass, passageway, subway, channel, hole, shaft

● VERB = <u>dig</u>, burrow, mine, bore, drill, excavate

**turbulent** = <u>stormy</u>, rough, raging, tempestuous, furious, foaming, agitated, tumultuous
≠ calm

**turf** NOUN1 = <u>grass</u>, sward2 = <u>sod</u>

● PHRASES the turf = <u>horse-racing</u>, the flat, racing

**turmoil** = <u>confusion</u>, disorder, chaos, upheaval, disarray, uproar, agitation, commotion ≠ peace

**turn** VERB1 = <u>change course</u>, swing round, wheel round, veer, move, switch, shift, swerve

2 = <u>rotate</u>, spin, go round (and round), revolve, roll, circle, twist, spiral3 = <u>change</u>, transform, shape, convert, alter, mould, remodel, mutate4 = <u>shape</u>, form, fashion, cast, frame, mould, make

5 = <u>go bad</u>, go off (*Brit. informal*), curdle6 = <u>make rancid</u>, spoil, sour, taint

● NOUN1 = <u>rotation</u>, cycle, circle, revolution, spin, twist, whirl, swivel2 = <u>change of direction</u>, shift, departure, deviation

3 = <u>direction</u>, course, tack, tendency, drift4 = <u>opportunity</u>, go, time, try, chance, crack

(*informal*), stint 5 = <u>deed</u>, service, act, action, favour, gesture

● **PHRASES turn on someone** = <u>attack</u>, assault, fall on, round on, lash out at, assail, lay into (*informal*), let fly at ◆ **turn someone on** (*Informal*) = <u>arouse</u>, attract, excite, thrill, stimulate, please, titillate ◆ **turn something down** 1 = <u>refuse</u>, decline, reject, spurn, rebuff, repudiate 2 = <u>lower</u>, soften, mute, lessen, muffle, quieten ◆ **turn something in** = <u>hand in</u>, return, deliver, give up, hand over, submit, surrender, tender ◆ **turn something off** = <u>switch off</u>, turn out, put out, stop, cut out, shut down, unplug, flick off ◆ **turn something on** = <u>switch on</u>, activate, start, start up, ignite, kick-start ◆ **turn something up** 1 = <u>find</u>, reveal, discover, expose, disclose, unearth, dig up 2 = <u>increase</u>, raise, boost, enhance, intensify, amplify ◆ **turn up** 1 = <u>arrive</u>, come, appear, show up (*informal*), attend, put in an appearance, show your face 2 = <u>come to light</u>, show up, pop up, materialize

**turning** NOUN = <u>turn-off</u>, turn, bend, curve, junction, crossroads, side road, exit

**turning point** = <u>crossroads</u>, change, crisis, crux, moment of truth

**turnout** = <u>attendance</u>, crowd, audience, gate, assembly, congregation, number, throng

**turnover** 1 = <u>output</u>, business, productivity 2 = <u>movement</u>, coming and going, change

**turtle** ➤ reptiles

**tutor** NOUN = <u>teacher</u>, coach, instructor, educator, guide, guardian, lecturer, guru

● VERB = <u>teach</u>, educate, school, train, coach, guide, drill, instruct

**twig** = <u>branch</u>, stick, sprig, shoot, spray

**twilight** 1 = <u>dusk</u>, evening, sunset, early evening, nightfall, sundown, gloaming (*Scot. poetic*), close of day, evo (*Austral. slang*) ≠ dawn 2 = <u>half-light</u>, gloom, dimness, semi-darkness

**twin** NOUN = <u>double</u>, counterpart, mate, match, fellow, clone, duplicate, lookalike

● VERB = <u>pair</u>, match, join, couple, link, yoke

**twinkle** VERB = <u>sparkle</u>, flash, shine, glitter, gleam, blink, flicker, shimmer

● NOUN = <u>sparkle</u>, flash, spark, gleam, flicker, shimmer, glimmer

**twist** VERB 1 = <u>coil</u>, curl, wind, wrap, screw, twirl 2 = <u>intertwine</u> 3 = <u>distort</u>, screw up, contort, mangle, mangulate (*Austral. slang*) ≠ straighten

● NOUN 1 = <u>surprise</u>, change, turn,

development, revelation

**2** = <u>development</u>, emphasis, variation, slant**3** = <u>wind</u>, turn, spin, swivel, twirl**4** = <u>curve</u>, turn, bend, loop, arc, kink, zigzag, dog-leg

**twitch** VERB**1** = jerk, flutter, jump, squirm**2** = <u>pull (at)</u>, tug (at), pluck (at), yank (at)

• NOUN = jerk, tic, spasm, jump, flutter

**tycoon** = <u>magnate</u>, capitalist, baron, industrialist, financier, fat cat (*slang, chiefly U.S.*), mogul, plutocrat

**type** = <u>kind</u>, sort, class, variety, group, order, style, species

**typical 1** = <u>archetypal</u>, standard, model, normal, stock, representative, usual, regular ≠ unusual**2** = <u>characteristic</u>

**3** = <u>average</u>, normal, usual, routine, regular, orthodox, predictable, run-of-the-mill

**tyranny** = <u>oppression</u>, cruelty, dictatorship, authoritarianism, despotism, autocracy, absolutism, high-handedness ≠ liberality

# U

**ubiquitous** = <u>ever-present</u>, pervasive, omnipresent, everywhere, universal

**ugly 1** = <u>unattractive</u>, homely (*chiefly U.S.*), plain, unsightly, unlovely, unprepossessing, ill-favoured ≠ beautiful

**2** = <u>unpleasant</u>, shocking, terrible, nasty, distasteful, horrid, objectionable, disagreeable ≠ pleasant**3** = <u>bad-tempered</u>, dangerous, menacing, sinister, baleful

**ulcer** = <u>sore</u>, abscess, peptic ulcer, gumboil

**ultimate 1** = <u>final</u>, last, end

**2** = <u>supreme</u>, highest, greatest, paramount, superlative**3** = <u>worst</u>, greatest, utmost, extreme

**4** = <u>best</u>, greatest, supreme, optimum, quintessential

**ultimately 1** = <u>finally</u>, eventually, in the end, after all, at last, sooner or later, in due time

**2** = <u>fundamentally</u>, essentially, basically, primarily, at heart, deep down

**umpire** NOUN = <u>referee</u>, judge, arbiter, arbitrator

• VERB = <u>referee</u>, judge, adjudicate, arbitrate

**unable** = <u>incapable</u>, powerless, unfit, impotent, unqualified, ineffectual ≠ able

**unanimous 1** = <u>agreed</u>, united, in agreement, harmonious, like-minded, of the same mind ≠ divided**2** = <u>united</u>, common, concerted, solid, consistent, harmonious, undivided, congruent ≠ split

**unarmed** = defenceless, helpless, unprotected ≠ armed

**unaware** = ignorant, unconscious, oblivious, uninformed, unknowing, not in the loop (*informal*) ≠ aware

**unbearable** = intolerable, insufferable, too much (*informal*), unacceptable ≠ tolerable

**unborn** = expected, awaited, embryonic

**uncertain** = unsure, undecided, vague, unclear, dubious, hazy, irresolute ≠ sure

**uncertainty**
1 = unpredictability, precariousness, ambiguity, unreliability, fickleness, chanciness, changeableness ≠ predictability 2 = doubt, confusion ≠ confidence
3 = hesitancy, indecision

**uncomfortable** 1 = uneasy, troubled, disturbed, embarrassed, awkward, discomfited ≠ comfortable 2 = painful, awkward, rough

**uncommon** 1 = rare, unusual, odd, novel, strange, peculiar, scarce, queer ≠ common
2 = extraordinary, remarkable, special, outstanding, distinctive, exceptional, notable ≠ ordinary

**uncompromising** = inflexible, strict, rigid, firm, tough, inexorable, intransigent, unbending

**unconditional** = absolute, full, complete, total, positive, entire, outright, unlimited ≠ qualified

**unconscious** 1 = senseless, knocked out, out cold (*informal*), out, stunned, dazed, in a coma, stupefied ≠ awake 2 = unaware, ignorant, oblivious, unknowing ≠ aware 3 = unintentional, unwitting, inadvertent, accidental ≠ intentional

**uncover** 1 = reveal, expose, disclose, divulge, make known ≠ conceal 2 = open, unveil, unwrap, show, strip, expose, bare, lay bare

**under** PREPOSITION 1 = below, beneath, underneath ≠ over
2 = subordinate to, subject to, governed by, secondary to
● ADVERB = below, down, beneath ≠ up

**undercover** = secret, covert, private, hidden, concealed ≠ open

**underdog** = weaker party, little fellow (*informal*), outsider

**underestimate**
1 = undervalue, understate, diminish, play down, minimize, downgrade, miscalculate, trivialize ≠ overestimate
2 = underrate, undervalue, belittle ≠ overrate

> **Word Power**
>
> **underestimate**
>
> *Underestimate is sometimes wrongly used where overestimate is meant: the importance of his work cannot be overestimated (not cannot be underestimated).*

**undergo** = experience, go through, stand, suffer, bear, sustain, endure

**underground** ADJECTIVE
1 = subterranean, basement, lower-level, sunken, covered, buried, subterrestrial 2 = secret, covert, hidden, guerrilla, revolutionary, confidential, dissident, closet
● PHRASES **the underground**
1 = the tube (Brit.), the subway, the metro 2 = the Resistance, partisans, freedom fighters

**underline** 1 = emphasize, stress, highlight, accentuate ≠ minimize
2 = underscore, mark

**underlying** = fundamental, basic, prime, primary, elementary, intrinsic

**undermine** = weaken, sabotage, subvert, compromise, disable ≠ reinforce

**understand** 1 = comprehend, get, take in, perceive, grasp, see, follow, realize 2 = believe, gather, think, see, suppose, notice,

assume, fancy

**understandable** = reasonable, natural, justified, expected, inevitable, legitimate, predictable, accountable

**understanding** NOUN
1 = perception, knowledge, grasp, sense, know-how (informal), judgment, awareness, appreciation ≠ ignorance
2 = agreement, deal, promise, arrangement, accord, contract, bond, pledge ≠ disagreement
3 = belief, view, opinion, impression, interpretation, feeling, idea, notion
● ADJECTIVE = sympathetic, kind, compassionate, considerate, patient, sensitive, tolerant ≠ unsympathetic

**undertake** = agree, promise, contract, guarantee, engage, pledge

**undertaking** 1 = task, business, operation, project, attempt, effort, affair, venture 2 = promise, commitment, pledge, word, vow, assurance

**underwear** = underclothes, lingerie, undies (informal), undergarments, underthings, brookies (S. African informal), underdaks (Austral. slang)

**underworld** 1 = criminals, gangsters, organized crime, gangland (informal) 2 = nether world, Hades, nether regions

**underwrite** = <u>finance</u>, back, fund, guarantee, sponsor, insure, ratify, subsidize

**undesirable** = <u>unwanted</u>, unwelcome, disagreeable, objectionable, unacceptable, unsuitable, unattractive, distasteful ≠ desirable

**undo** 1 = <u>open</u>, unfasten, loose, untie, unbutton, disentangle 2 = <u>reverse</u>, cancel, offset, neutralize, invalidate, annul 3 = <u>ruin</u>, defeat, destroy, wreck, shatter, upset, undermine, overturn

**undone** = <u>unfinished</u>, left, neglected, omitted, unfulfilled, unperformed ≠ finished

**undoubtedly** = <u>certainly</u>, definitely, surely, doubtless, without doubt, assuredly

**unearth** 1 = <u>discover</u>, find, reveal, expose, uncover 2 = <u>dig up</u>, excavate, exhume, dredge up

**unearthly** = <u>eerie</u>, strange, supernatural, ghostly, weird, phantom, uncanny, spooky (*informal*)

**uneasy** 1 = <u>anxious</u>, worried, troubled, nervous, disturbed, uncomfortable, edgy, perturbed ≠ relaxed 2 = <u>precarious</u>, strained, uncomfortable, tense, awkward, shaky, insecure

**unemployed** = <u>out of work</u>,

redundant, laid off, jobless, idle ≠ working

**unfair** 1 = <u>biased</u>, prejudiced, unjust, one-sided, partial, partisan, bigoted 2 = <u>unscrupulous</u>, dishonest, unethical, wrongful, unsporting ≠ ethical

**unfit** 1 = <u>out of shape</u>, feeble, unhealthy, flabby, in poor condition ≠ healthy 2 = <u>incapable</u>, inadequate, incompetent, no good, useless, unqualified ≠ capable 3 = <u>unsuitable</u>, inadequate, useless, unsuited ≠ suitable

**unfold** 1 = <u>reveal</u>, tell, present, show, disclose, uncover, divulge, make known 2 = <u>open</u>, spread out, undo, expand, unfurl, unwrap, unroll

**unfortunate** 1 = <u>disastrous</u>, calamitous, adverse, ill-fated ≠ opportune 2 = <u>regrettable</u>, deplorable, lamentable, unsuitable, unbecoming ≠ becoming 3 = <u>unlucky</u>, unhappy, doomed, cursed, unsuccessful, hapless, wretched ≠ fortunate

**unhappy** 1 = <u>sad</u>, depressed, miserable, blue, melancholy, mournful, dejected, despondent ≠ happy 2 = <u>unlucky</u>, unfortunate, hapless, cursed, wretched, ill-fated ≠ fortunate

**unhealthy** 1 = <u>harmful</u>, detrimental, unwholesome, insanitary, insalubrious ≠ <u>beneficial</u> 2 = <u>sick</u>, sickly, unwell, delicate, crook (*Austral. & N.Z. informal*), ailing, frail, feeble, invalid ≠ <u>well</u> 3 = <u>weak</u>, ailing ≠ strong

**unification** = <u>union</u>, uniting, alliance, coalition, federation, confederation, amalgamation, coalescence

**uniform** NOUN 1 = <u>regalia</u>, suit, livery, colours, habit 2 = <u>outfit</u>, dress, costume, attire, gear (*informal*), get-up (*informal*), ensemble, garb

● ADJECTIVE 1 = <u>consistent</u>, unvarying, similar, even, same, matching, regular, constant ≠ <u>varying</u> 2 = <u>alike</u>, similar, like, same, equal

**unify** = <u>unite</u>, join, combine, merge, consolidate, confederate, amalgamate ≠ divide

**union** 1 = <u>joining</u>, uniting, unification, combination, coalition, merger, mixture, blend 2 = <u>alliance</u>, league, association, coalition, federation, confederacy

**unique** 1 = <u>distinct</u>, special, exclusive, peculiar, only, single, lone, solitary 2 = <u>unparalleled</u>, unmatched, unequalled, matchless, without equal

> ### Word Power
> **unique** – *Unique* with the meaning 'being the only one' or 'having no equal' describes an absolute state: *a case unique in British law.* In this use it cannot therefore be qualified; something is either *unique* or *not unique.* However, *unique* is also very commonly used in the sense of 'remarkable' or 'exceptional', particularly in the language of advertising, and in this meaning it can be used with qualifying words such as *rather, quite,* etc. Since many people object to this use, it is best avoided in formal and serious writing.

**unit** 1 = <u>entity</u>, whole, item, feature 2 = <u>section</u>, company, group, force, detail, division, cell, squad 3 = <u>measure</u>, quantity, measurement 4 = <u>part</u>, section, segment, class, element, component, constituent, tutorial

**unite** 1 = <u>join</u>, link, combine, couple, blend, merge, unify, fuse ≠ <u>separate</u> 2 = <u>cooperate</u>, ally, join forces, band, pool, collaborate ≠ split

**unity** 1 = <u>union</u>, unification, coalition, federation, integration, confederation, amalgamation 2 = <u>wholeness</u>, integrity, oneness, union, entity, singleness

≠ disunity 3 = **agreement**, accord, consensus, harmony, solidarity, unison, assent, concord ≠ disagreement

**universal** 1 = **widespread**, general, common, whole, total, unlimited, overarching 2 = **global**, worldwide, international, pandemic

**universally** = **without exception**, everywhere, always, invariably

**universe** = **cosmos**, space, creation, nature, heavens, macrocosm, all existence

**unknown** 1 = **strange**, new, undiscovered, uncharted, unexplored, virgin, remote, alien 2 = **unidentified**, mysterious, anonymous, unnamed, nameless, incognito 3 = **obscure**, humble, unfamiliar ≠ famous

**unlike** 1 = **different from**, dissimilar to, distinct from, unequal to ≠ similar to 2 = **contrasted with**, not like, in contradiction to, in contrast with or to, as opposed to, differently from, opposite to

**unlikely** 1 = **improbable**, doubtful, remote, slight, faint ≠ probable 2 = **unbelievable**, incredible, implausible, questionable ≠ believable

**unload** 1 = **empty**, clear, unpack, dump, discharge 2 = **unburden**

**unnatural** 1 = **abnormal**, odd, strange, unusual, extraordinary, perverted, queer, irregular ≠ normal 2 = **false**, forced, artificial, affected, stiff, feigned, stilted, insincere ≠ genuine

**unpleasant** 1 = **nasty**, bad, horrid, distasteful, displeasing, objectionable, disagreeable ≠ nice 2 = **obnoxious**, rude ≠ likable or likeable

**unravel** 1 = **solve**, explain, work out, resolve, figure out (*informal*) 2 = **undo**, separate, disentangle, free, unwind, untangle

**unrest** = **discontent**, rebellion, protest, strife, agitation, discord, sedition, dissension ≠ peace

**unsettled** 1 = **unstable**, shaky, insecure, disorderly, unsteady 2 = **restless**, tense, shaken, confused, disturbed, anxious, agitated, flustered 3 = **inconstant**, changing, variable, uncertain

**unstable** 1 = **changeable**, volatile, unpredictable, variable, fluctuating, fitful, inconstant ≠ constant 2 = **insecure**, shaky, precarious, unsettled, wobbly, tottering, unsteady 3 = **unpredictable**, irrational, erratic, inconsistent, temperamental, capricious, changeable ≠ level-headed

**unthinkable** 1 = **impossible**, out of the question,

inconceivable, absurd, unreasonable 2 = **inconceivable**, incredible, unimaginable

**untold** 1 = **indescribable**, unthinkable, unimaginable, undreamed of, unutterable, inexpressible 2 = **countless**, incalculable, innumerable, myriad, numberless, uncountable

**untrue** 1 = **false**, lying, wrong, mistaken, incorrect, inaccurate, dishonest, deceptive ≠ **true** 2 = **unfaithful**, disloyal, deceitful, treacherous, faithless, false, untrustworthy, inconstant ≠ **faithful**

**unusual** 1 = **rare**, odd, strange, extraordinary, different, curious, queer, uncommon ≠ **common** 2 = **extraordinary**, unique, remarkable, exceptional, uncommon, singular, unconventional ≠ **average**

**upbeat** (*Informal*) = **cheerful**, positive, optimistic, encouraging, hopeful, cheery

**upbringing** = **education**, training, breeding, rearing, raising

**update** = **bring up to date**, improve, correct, renew, revise, upgrade, amend, overhaul

**upgrade** = **improve**, better, update, reform, add to, enhance, refurbish, renovate 2 = **promote**, raise, advance, boost, move up, elevate, kick upstairs (*informal*),

give promotion to ≠ demote

**upheaval** = **disturbance**, revolution, disorder, turmoil, disruption

**uphill** 1 = **ascending**, rising, upward, mounting, climbing ≠ descending 2 = **arduous**, hard, taxing, difficult, tough, exhausting, gruelling, strenuous

**uphold** 1 = **support**, back, defend, aid, champion, maintain, promote, sustain 2 = **confirm**, endorse

**uplift** VERB = **improve**, better, raise, advance, inspire, refine, edify

● NOUN = **improvement**, enlightenment, advancement, refinement, enhancement, enrichment, edification

**upper** 1 = **topmost**, top ≠ bottom 2 = **higher**, high ≠ lower 3 = **superior**, senior, higher-level, greater, top, important, chief, most important ≠ inferior

**upper class** = **aristocratic**, upper-class, noble, high-class, patrician, blue-blooded, highborn

**upright** 1 = **vertical**, straight, standing up, erect, perpendicular, bolt upright ≠ horizontal 2 = **honest**, good, principled, just, ethical, honourable, righteous, conscientious ≠ dishonourable

**uprising** = **rebellion**, rising,

revolution, revolt, disturbance, mutiny, insurrection, insurgence

**uproar** 1 = <u>commotion</u>, noise, racket, riot, turmoil, mayhem, din, pandemonium² = <u>protest</u>, outrage, complaint, objection, fuss, stink (*informal*), outcry, furore

**upset** ADJECTIVE¹ = <u>distressed</u>, shaken, disturbed, worried, troubled, hurt, bothered, unhappy² = <u>sick</u>, queasy, bad, ill 3 = <u>overturned</u>, upside down, capsized, spilled
● VERB¹ = <u>distress</u>, trouble, disturb, worry, alarm, bother, grieve, agitate² = <u>tip over</u>, overturn, capsize, knock over, spill 3 = <u>mess up</u>, spoil, disturb, change, confuse, disorder, unsettle, disorganize
● NOUN¹ = <u>distress</u>, worry, trouble, shock, bother, disturbance, agitation 2 = <u>reversal</u>, shake-up (*informal*), defeat² = <u>illness</u>, complaint, disorder, bug (*informal*), sickness, malady

**upside down** *or* **upside-down** ADVERB = <u>wrong side up</u>
● ADJECTIVE¹ = <u>inverted</u>, overturned, upturned 2 (*Informal*) = <u>confused</u>, disordered, chaotic, muddled, topsy-turvy, higgledy-piggledy (*informal*)

**up-to-date** = <u>modern</u>, fashionable, trendy (*Brit. informal*), current, stylish, in vogue, up-to-the-minute ≠ <u>out of date</u>

**urban** = <u>civic</u>, city, town, metropolitan, municipal, dorp (*S. African*)

**urge** VERB¹ = <u>beg</u>, exhort, plead, implore, beseech, entreat 2 = <u>advocate</u>, recommend, advise, support, counsel ≠ <u>discourage</u>
● NOUN = <u>impulse</u>, longing, wish, desire, drive, yearning, itch (*informal*), thirst ≠ <u>reluctance</u>

**urgency** = <u>importance</u>, need, necessity, gravity, pressure, hurry, seriousness, extremity

**urgent** = <u>crucial</u>, desperate, pressing, great, important, crying, critical, immediate ≠ <u>unimportant</u>

**usage** 1 = <u>use</u>, operation, employment, running, control, management, handling 2 = <u>practice</u>, method, procedure, habit, regime, custom, routine, convention

**use** VERB¹ = <u>employ</u>, utilize, work, apply, operate, exercise, practise, resort to² *sometimes with* **up** = <u>consume</u>, exhaust, spend, run through, expend³ = <u>take advantage of</u>, exploit, manipulate
● NOUN¹ = <u>usage</u>, employment, operation, application 2 = <u>purpose</u>, end, reason, object

3 = <u>good</u>, point, help, service, value, benefit, profit, advantage

**used** = <u>second-hand</u>, cast-off, nearly new, shopsoiled ≠ new

**used to** = <u>accustomed to</u>, familiar with

**useful** = <u>helpful</u>, effective, valuable, practical, profitable, worthwhile, beneficial, fruitful ≠ useless

**useless** 1 = <u>worthless</u>, valueless, impractical, fruitless, unproductive, ineffectual, unsuitable ≠ useful 2 = <u>pointless</u>, futile, vain ≠ worthwhile 3 (*Informal*) = <u>inept</u>, no good, hopeless, incompetent, ineffectual

**usher** VERB = <u>escort</u>, lead, direct, guide, conduct
● NOUN = <u>attendant</u>, guide, doorman, escort, doorkeeper

**usual** = <u>normal</u>, customary, regular, general, common, standard, ordinary, typical ≠ unusual

**usually** = <u>normally</u>, generally, mainly, commonly, mostly, on the whole, as a rule, habitually

**utility** = <u>usefulness</u>, benefit, convenience, practicality, efficacy, serviceableness

**utilize** = <u>use</u>, employ, deploy, take advantage of, make use of, put to use, bring into play, avail yourself of

**utmost** ADJECTIVE 1 = <u>greatest</u>, highest, maximum, supreme, paramount, pre-eminent 2 = <u>farthest</u>, extreme, last, final
● NOUN = <u>best</u>, greatest, maximum, highest, hardest

**utter**[1] = <u>say</u>, state, speak, voice, express, deliver, declare, mouth

**utter**[2] = <u>absolute</u>, complete, total, sheer, outright, thorough, downright, unmitigated

**utterly** = <u>totally</u>, completely, absolutely, perfectly, fully, entirely, extremely, thoroughly

# V

**vacancy** 1 = <u>opening</u>, job, post, place, position, role, situation, opportunity 2 = <u>room</u>, space, available accommodation, unoccupied room

**vacant** 1 = <u>empty</u>, free, available, abandoned, deserted, for sale, on the market, void ≠ occupied 2 = <u>unfilled</u>, unoccupied ≠ taken 3 = <u>blank</u>, vague, dreamy, empty, abstracted, idle, vacuous, inane ≠ thoughtful

**vacuum** 1 = <u>gap</u>, lack, absence, space, deficiency, void 2 = <u>emptiness</u>, space, void, gap, nothingness, vacuity

**vague** 1 = <u>unclear</u>, indefinite, hazy, confused, loose, uncertain, unsure, superficial ≠ clear

**2** = <u>imprecise</u>, unspecified, generalized, rough, loose, ambiguous, hazy, equivocal

**3** = <u>absent-minded</u>, distracted, vacant, preoccupied, oblivious, inattentive **4** = <u>indistinct</u>, unclear, faint, hazy, indeterminate, nebulous, ill-defined ≠ distinct

**vain** ADJECTIVE **1** = <u>futile</u>, useless, pointless, unsuccessful, idle, worthless, senseless, fruitless ≠ successful **2** = <u>conceited</u>, narcissistic, proud, arrogant, swaggering, egotistical, self-important ≠ modest

● PHRASES **in vain 1** = <u>useless</u>, to no avail, unsuccessful, fruitless, vain **2** = <u>uselessly</u>, to no avail, unsuccessfully, fruitlessly, vainly, ineffectually

**valid 1** = <u>sound</u>, good, reasonable, telling, convincing, rational, logical, viable ≠ unfounded **2** = <u>legal</u>, official, legitimate, genuine, authentic, lawful, bona fide ≠ invalid

**validity 1** = <u>soundness</u>, force, power, weight, strength, cogency **2** = <u>legality</u>, authority, legitimacy, right, lawfulness

**valley** = <u>hollow</u>, dale, glen, vale, depression, dell

**valuable** ADJECTIVE **1** = <u>useful</u>, important, profitable, worthwhile, beneficial, helpful ≠ useless

**2** = <u>treasured</u>, prized, precious

**3** = <u>precious</u>, expensive, costly, dear, high-priced, priceless, irreplaceable ≠ worthless

● PLURAL NOUN = <u>treasures</u>, prized possessions, precious items, heirlooms, personal effects, costly article

**value** NOUN **1** = <u>importance</u>, benefit, worth, merit, point, service, sense, profit ≠ worthlessness **2** = <u>cost</u>, price, worth, rate, market price, face value, asking price, selling price

● PLURAL NOUN = <u>principles</u>, morals, ethics, mores, standards of behaviour, (moral) standards

● VERB **1** = <u>appreciate</u>, rate, prize, regard highly, respect, admire, treasure, esteem ≠ undervalue

**2** = <u>evaluate</u>, price, estimate, rate, cost, assess, set at, appraise

**vanish 1** = <u>disappear</u>, dissolve, evaporate, fade away, melt away, evanesce ≠ appear **2** = <u>die out</u>, disappear, pass away, end, fade, dwindle, cease to exist, become extinct

**vanity** = <u>pride</u>, arrogance, conceit, narcissism, egotism, conceitedness ≠ modesty

**variable** = <u>changeable</u>, unstable, fluctuating, shifting, flexible, uneven, temperamental, unsteady ≠ constant

**variant** NOUN = <u>variation</u>, form,

599

# variation → veiled

version, development, alternative, adaptation, revision, modification • **ADJECTIVE** = **different**, alternative, modified, divergent

**variation** 1 = **alternative**, variety, modification, departure, innovation, variant 2 = **variety**, change, deviation, difference, diversity, diversion, novelty ≠ uniformity

**varied** = **different**, mixed, various, diverse, assorted, miscellaneous, sundry, motley ≠ unvarying

**variety** 1 = **diversity**, change, variation, difference, diversification, heterogeneity, multifariousness ≠ uniformity 2 = **range**, selection, assortment, mix, collection, line-up, mixture, array 3 = **type**, sort, kind, class, brand, species, breed, strain

**various** 1 = **different**, assorted, miscellaneous, varied, distinct, diverse, disparate, sundry ≠ similar 2 = **many**, numerous, countless, several, abundant, innumerable, sundry, profuse

### Word Power

**various** – The use of *different* after *various*, which seems to be most common in speech, is unnecessary and should be avoided in serious writing: *the disease exists in various forms* (not *in various different forms*).

**varnish** NOUN = **lacquer**, polish, glaze, gloss • **VERB** = **lacquer**, polish, glaze, gloss

**vary** 1 = **differ**, be different, be dissimilar, disagree, diverge 2 = **change**, shift, swing, alter, fluctuate, oscillate, see-saw 3 = **alternate**

**vast** = **huge**, massive, enormous, great, wide, immense, gigantic, monumental ≠ tiny

**vault**[1] = **strongroom**, repository, depository 2 = **crypt**, tomb, catacomb, cellar, mausoleum, charnel house, undercroft

**vault**[2] = **jump**, spring, leap, clear, bound, hurdle

**veer** = **change direction**, turn, swerve, shift, sheer, change course

**vehicle** 1 = **conveyance**, machine, motor vehicle 2 = **medium**, means, channel, mechanism, organ, apparatus

**veil** NOUN 1 = **mask**, cover, shroud, film, curtain, cloak 2 = **screen**, mask, disguise, blind 3 = **film**, cover, curtain, cloak, shroud • **VERB** = **cover**, screen, hide, mask, shield, disguise, conceal, obscure ≠ reveal

**veiled** = **disguised**, implied, hinted at, covert, masked, concealed, suppressed

**vein** 1 = <u>blood vessel</u> 2 = <u>mood</u>, style, note, tone, mode, temper, tenor 3 = <u>seam</u>, layer, stratum, course, current, bed, deposit, streak

**velocity** = <u>speed</u>, pace, rapidity, quickness, swiftness

**vengeance** = <u>revenge</u>, retaliation, reprisal, retribution, requital ≠ forgiveness

**vent** NOUN = <u>outlet</u>, opening, aperture, duct, orifice
● VERB = <u>express</u>, release, voice, air, discharge, utter, emit, pour out ≠ hold back

**venture** NOUN = <u>undertaking</u>, project, enterprise, campaign, risk, operation, activity, scheme
● VERB 1 = <u>go</u>, travel, journey, set out, wander, stray, plunge into, rove 2 = <u>dare</u>, presume, have the courage to, be brave enough, hazard, go out on a limb (*informal*), take the liberty, go so far as 3 = <u>put forward</u>, volunteer

**verbal** = <u>spoken</u>, oral, word-of-mouth, unwritten

**verdict** = <u>decision</u>, finding, judgment, opinion, sentence, conclusion, conviction, adjudication

**verge** NOUN 1 = <u>brink</u>, point, edge, threshold 2 = <u>border</u>, edge, margin, limit, boundary, threshold, brim
● PHRASE **verge on something** = <u>come near to</u>, approach, border on, resemble, incline to, be similar to, touch on, be more or less

**verify** 1 = <u>check</u>, make sure, examine, monitor, inspect 2 = <u>confirm</u>, prove, substantiate, support, validate, bear out, corroborate, authenticate ≠ disprove

**versatile** 1 = <u>adaptable</u>, flexible, all-round, resourceful, multifaceted ≠ unadaptable 2 = <u>all-purpose</u>, variable, adjustable ≠ limited

**versed** = <u>knowledgeable</u>, experienced, seasoned, familiar, practised, acquainted, well-informed, proficient ≠ ignorant

**version** 1 = <u>form</u>, variety, variant, sort, class, design, style, model 2 = <u>adaptation</u>, edition, interpretation, form, copy, rendering, reproduction, portrayal 3 = <u>account</u>, report, description, record, reading, story, view, understanding

**vertical** = <u>upright</u> sheer, perpendicular, straight (up and down), erect, plumb, on end, precipitous, vertiginous ≠ horizontal

**very** ADVERB = <u>extremely</u>, highly, greatly, really, deeply, unusually, profoundly, decidedly
● ADJECTIVE 1 = <u>exact</u>, precise, selfsame 2 = <u>ideal</u>

stager ≠ novice

● ADJECTIVE = long-serving, seasoned, experienced, old, established, qualified, mature, practised

veto VERB = ban, block, reject, rule out, turn down, forbid, boycott, prohibit ≠ pass

● NOUN = ban, dismissal, rejection, vetoing, boycott, embargo, prohibiting, prohibition ≠ ratification

viable = workable, practical, feasible, suitable, realistic, operational, applicable, usable ≠ unworkable

vibrant 1 = energetic, dynamic, sparkling, vivid, spirited, storming, alive, vigorous 2 = vivid, brilliant, intense, clear, rich, glowing

vice 1 = fault, failing, weakness, limitation, defect, deficiency, flaw, shortcoming ≠ good point 2 = wickedness, evil, corruption, sin, depravity, immorality, iniquity, turpitude ≠ virtue

vice versa = the other way round, conversely, in reverse, contrariwise

vicious 1 = savage, brutal, violent, cruel, ferocious, barbarous ≠ gentle 2 = malicious, vindictive, spiteful, mean, cruel, venomous

victim 1 = casualty, sufferer,

---

### Word Power

**very** – In strict usage, adverbs of degree such as *very*, *too*, *quite*, *really*, and *extremely* are used only to qualify adjectives: *he is very happy; she is too sad*. By this rule, these words should not be used to qualify past participles that follow the verb *to be*, since they would then be technically qualifying verbs. With the exception of certain participles, such as *tired* or *disappointed*, that have come to be regarded as adjectives, all other past participles are qualified by adverbs such as *much, greatly, seriously*, or *excessively*: *he has been much* (not *very*) *inconvenienced*; *she has been excessively* (not *too*) *criticized*.

---

vessel 1 = ship, boat, craft 2 = container, receptacle, can, bowl, tank, pot, drum, barrel

vest VERB
● PHRASES vest in something or someone *usually passive* = place, invest, entrust, settle, confer, endow, bestow, consign
◆ vest with something *usually passive* = endow with, entrust with

vet = check, examine, investigate, review, appraise, scrutinize

veteran NOUN = old hand, past master, warhorse (*informal*), old fatality ≠ survivor2 = scapegoat, sacrifice, martyr

**victor** = winner, champion, conqueror, vanquisher, prizewinner ≠ loser

**victorious** = winning, successful, triumphant, first, champion, conquering, vanquishing, prizewinning ≠ losing

**victory** = win, success, triumph, conquest, walkover (*informal*) ≠ defeat

**vie** = compete, struggle, contend, strive

**view** NOUN1 *sometimes plural* = opinion, belief, feeling, attitude, impression, conviction, point of view, sentiment2 = scene, picture, sight, prospect, perspective, landscape, outlook, spectacle3 = vision, sight, visibility, perspective, eyeshot
● VERB = regard, see, consider, perceive, treat, estimate, reckon, deem

**viewer** = watcher, observer, spectator, onlooker

**vigorous** 1 = strenuous, energetic, arduous, hard, taxing, active, rigorous2 = spirited, lively, energetic, active, dynamic, animated, forceful, feisty (*informal*) ≠ lethargic3 = strong, powerful, lively, lusty ≠ weak

**vigorously** 1 = energetically, hard, forcefully, strongly, strenuously, lustily2 = forcefully, strongly, vehemently, strenuously

**vigour** *or (U.S.)***vigor** = energy, vitality, power, spirit, strength, animation, verve, gusto ≠ weakness

**vile** 1 = wicked, evil, corrupt, perverted, degenerate, depraved, nefarious ≠ honourable
2 = disgusting, foul, revolting, offensive, nasty, sickening, horrid, repulsive, yucko (*Austral. slang*) ≠ pleasant

**villain** 1 = evildoer, criminal, rogue, scoundrel, wretch, reprobate, miscreant, blackguard
2 = baddy (*informal*), antihero ≠ hero

**vindicate** 1 = clear, acquit, exonerate, absolve, let off the hook, exculpate ≠ condemn
2 = support, defend, excuse, justify

**vintage** NOUN (always used of wines) = harvest
● ADJECTIVE1 (always used of wines) = high-quality, best, prime, quality, choice, select, superior2 = classic, old, veteran, historic, heritage, enduring, antique, timeless

**violate** 1 = break, infringe, disobey, transgress, ignore, defy, disregard, flout ≠ obey
2 = invade, infringe on, disturb,

upset, shatter, disrupt, impinge
on, encroach on 3 = <u>desecrate</u>,
profane, defile, abuse, pollute,
deface, dishonour, vandalize
≠ honour 4 = <u>rape</u>, molest,
sexually assault, ravish, abuse,
assault, interfere with, sexually
abuse

**violation** 1 = <u>breach</u>, abuse,
infringement, contravention,
abuse, trespass, transgression,
infraction 2 = <u>invasion</u>, intrusion,
trespass, breach, disturbance,
disruption, interruption,
encroachment 3 = <u>desecration</u>,
sacrilege, defilement,
profanation, spoliation 4 = <u>rape</u>,
sexual assault, molesting,
ravishing (old-fashioned), abuse,,
sexual abuse, indecent assault,
molestation

**violence** 1 = <u>brutality</u>,
bloodshed, savagery, fighting,
terrorism 2 = <u>force</u>, power,
strength, might, ferocity,
forcefulness, powerfulness
3 = <u>intensity</u>, force, cruelty,
severity, fervour, vehemence

**violent** 1 = <u>brutal</u>, aggressive,
savage, wild, fierce, bullying, cruel,
vicious ≠ gentle 2 = <u>sharp</u>
3 = <u>passionate</u>, uncontrollable,
unrestrained 4 = <u>fiery</u>, fierce,
passionate

**VIP** = <u>celebrity</u>, big name, star,
somebody, luminary, big hitter
(informal), heavy hitter (informal)

**virgin** NOUN = <u>maiden</u>, girl (archaic)
● ADJECTIVE = <u>pure</u>, chaste,
immaculate, virginal, vestal,
uncorrupted, undefiled
≠ corrupted

**virtual** = <u>practical</u>, essential, in all
but name

**virtually** = <u>practically</u>, almost,
nearly, in effect, in essence, as
good as in, in all but name

**virtue** 1 = <u>goodness</u>, integrity,
worth, morality, righteousness,
probity, rectitude, incorruptibility
≠ vice 2 = <u>merit</u>, strength, asset,
plus (informal), attribute, good
point, strong point ≠ failing
3 = <u>advantage</u>, benefit, merit,
credit, usefulness, efficacy

**visible** = <u>perceptible</u>,
observable, clear, apparent,
evident, manifest, in view,
discernible ≠ invisible

**vision** 1 = <u>image</u>, idea, dream,
plans, hopes, prospect, ideal,
concept 2 = <u>hallucination</u>,
illusion, apparition, revelation,
delusion, mirage, chimera
3 = <u>sight</u>, seeing, eyesight, view,
perception 4 = <u>foresight</u>,
imagination, perception, insight,
awareness, inspiration,
innovation, creativity

**visionary** NOUN 1 = <u>idealist</u>,
romantic, dreamer, daydreamer
≠ realist 2 = <u>prophet</u>, diviner,
mystic, seer, soothsayer, sibyl,

scryer, spaewife (*Scot.*)

● ADJECTIVE[1] = idealistic, romantic, unrealistic, utopian, speculative, impractical, unworkable, quixotic ≠ realistic

2 = prophetic, mystical, predictive, oracular, sibylline

**visit** VERB[1] = call on, drop in on (*informal*), stay at, stay with, stop by, spend time with, look someone up, go see (*U.S.*)

2 = stay in, stop by

● NOUN[1] = call, social call[2] = trip, stop, stay, break, tour, holiday, vacation (*informal*), stopover

**visitor** = guest, caller, company, manu(w)hiri (*N.Z.*)

**vista** = view, scene, prospect, landscape, panorama, perspective

**visual** 1 = optical, optic, ocular

2 = observable, visible, perceptible, discernible ≠ imperceptible

**vital** 1 = essential, important, necessary, key, basic, significant, critical, crucial ≠ unnecessary

2 = lively, vigorous, energetic, spirited, dynamic, animated, vibrant, vivacious ≠ lethargic

**vitality** = energy, vivacity, life, strength, animation, vigour, exuberance, liveliness ≠ lethargy

**vivid** 1 = clear, detailed, realistic, telling, moving, affecting, arresting, powerful ≠ vague

2 = bright, brilliant, intense, clear,

rich, glowing, colourful ≠ dull

**vocabulary** 1 = language, words, lexicon[2] = wordbook, dictionary, glossary, lexicon

**vocal** 1 = outspoken, frank, forthright, strident, vociferous, articulate, expressive, eloquent ≠ quiet[2] = spoken, voiced, uttered, oral, said

**vocation** = profession, calling, job, trade, career, mission, pursuit

**vogue** = fashion, trend, craze, style, mode, passing fancy, dernier cri (*French*)

**voice** NOUN[1] = tone, sound, articulation[2] = utterance

3 = opinion, will, feeling, wish, desire[4] = say, view, vote, comment, input

● VERB = express, declare, air, raise reveal, mention, mouth, pronounce

*Related Words*

adjective: vocal

**void** NOUN[1] = gap, space, lack, hole, emptiness[2] = emptiness, space, vacuum, oblivion, blankness, nullity, vacuity

● ADJECTIVE = invalid, null and void, inoperative, useless, ineffective, worthless

● VERB = invalidate, nullify, cancel, withdraw, reverse, undo, repeal, quash

**volatile** 1 = changeable, shifting, variable, unsettled, unstable, explosive, unreliable, unsteady ≠ **stable** 2 = **temperamental**, erratic, mercurial, up and down (*informal*), fickle, over-emotional ≠ **calm**

**volley** = <u>barrage</u>, blast, burst, shower, hail, bombardment, salvo, fusillade

**volume** 1 = <u>amount</u>, quantity, level, body, total, measure, degree, mass 2 = <u>capacity</u>, size, mass, extent, proportions, dimensions, bulk, measurements 3 = <u>book</u>, work, title, opus, publication, manual, tome, treatise 4 = <u>loudness</u>, sound, amplification

**voluntarily** = <u>willingly</u>, freely, by choice, off your own bat, of your own accord, of your own volition

**voluntary** 1 = <u>intentional</u>, deliberate, planned, calculated, wilful ≠ **unintentional** 2 = **optional**, discretionary, up to the individual, open, unforced, at your discretion, open to choice ≠ **obligatory** 3 = **unpaid**, free, willing, pro bono (*Law*)

**volunteer** = <u>offer</u>, step forward ≠ **refuse**

**vomit** 1 = <u>be sick</u>, throw up (*informal*), spew, chuck (*Austral. & N.Z. informal*), heave (*slang*), retch 2 *often with up* = <u>bring up</u>, throw up, regurgitate, emit (*informal*), disgorge, spew out *or* up

**vote** NOUN = <u>poll</u>, election, ballot, referendum, popular vote, plebiscite, straw poll, show of hands
● VERB = <u>cast your vote</u>

**voucher** = <u>ticket</u>, token, coupon, pass, slip, chit, chitty (*Brit. informal*), docket

**vow** VERB = <u>promise</u>, pledge, swear, commit, engage, affirm, avow, bind yourself
● NOUN = <u>promise</u>, commitment, pledge, oath, profession, avowal

**voyage** NOUN = <u>journey</u>, trip, passage, expedition, crossing, sail, cruise, excursion
● VERB = <u>travel</u>, journey, tour, cruise, steam, take a trip, go on an expedition

**vulgar** 1 = <u>tasteless</u>, common ≠ **tasteful** 2 = <u>crude</u>, rude, coarse, indecent, tasteless, risqué, ribald 3 = <u>uncouth</u>, unrefined, impolite, ill-bred ≠ **refined**

**vulnerable** 1 = <u>susceptible</u>, helpless, unprotected, defenceless, exposed, weak, sensitive, tender ≠ **immune** 2 = **exposed**, open, unprotected, defenceless, accessible, wide open, assailable ≠ **well-protected**

# W

**waddle** = <u>shuffle</u>, totter, toddle, sway, wobble

# wade → wake

**wade** 1 = <u>paddle</u>, splash, splash about, slop2 = <u>walk through</u>, cross, ford, travel across

**wag** VERB1 = <u>wave</u>, shake, waggle, stir, quiver, vibrate, wiggle2 = <u>waggle</u>, wave, shake, flourish, brandish, wobble, wiggle 3 = <u>shake</u>, bob, nod
● NOUN1 = <u>wave</u>, shake, quiver, vibration, wiggle, waggle 2 = <u>nod</u>, bob, shake

**wage** NOUN often plural = <u>payment</u>, pay, remuneration, fee, reward, income, allowance, recompense
● VERB = <u>engage in</u>, conduct, pursue, carry on, undertake, practise, prosecute, proceed with

**wail** VERB = <u>cry</u>, weep, grieve, lament, howl, bawl, yowl
● NOUN = <u>cry</u>, moan, howl, lament, yowl

**wait** VERB1 = <u>stay</u>, remain, stop, pause, rest, linger, loiter, tarry ≠ go2 = <u>stand by</u>, hold back, hang fire3 = <u>be postponed</u>, be suspended, be delayed, be put off, be put back, be deferred, be put on hold (*informal*), be shelved
● NOUN = <u>delay</u>, gap, pause, interval, stay, rest, halt, hold-up

**waiter** or**waitress** = <u>attendant</u>, server, flunkey, steward *or* stewardess, servant

**waive** 1 = <u>give up</u>, relinquish, renounce, forsake, drop, abandon, set aside, dispense with ≠ claim 2 = <u>disregard</u>, ignore, discount, overlook, set aside, pass over, dispense with, brush aside

**wake**[1] VERB1 = <u>awake</u>, stir, awaken, come to, arise, get up, rouse, get out of bed ≠ fall asleep 2 = <u>awaken</u>, arouse, rouse, waken 3 = <u>evoke</u>, recall, renew, stimulate, revive, induce, arouse, call up
● NOUN = <u>vigil</u>, watch, funeral, deathwatch, tangi (*N.Z.*)

---

### Word Power

**wake** – Both *wake* and its synonym *waken* can be used either with or without an object: *I woke/wakened my sister*, and also *I woke/wakened (up) at noon*. *Wake*, *wake up*, and occasionally *waken*, can also be used in a figurative sense, for example *seeing him again woke painful memories*; and *it's time he woke up to his responsibilities*. The verbs *awake* and *awaken* are more commonly used in the figurative than in the literal sense, for example *he awoke to the danger he was in*.

---

**wake**[2] NOUN = <u>slipstream</u>, wash, trail, backwash, train, track, waves, path
● PHRASESin the wake of = <u>in the aftermath of</u>, following, because of, as a result of, on

account of, as a consequence of

**walk** VERB 1 = <u>stride</u>, stroll, go, move, step, march, pace, hike 2 = <u>travel on foot</u> 3 = <u>escort</u>, take, see, show, partner, guide, conduct, accompany

● NOUN 1 = <u>stroll</u>, hike, ramble, march, trek, trudge, promenade, saunter 2 = <u>gait</u>, step, bearing, carriage, tread 3 = <u>path</u>, footpath, track, way, road, lane, trail, avenue, berm (N.Z.)

● PHRASES **walk of life** = <u>area</u>, calling, business, line, trade, class, field, career

**walker** = <u>hiker</u>, rambler, wayfarer, pedestrian

**wall** 1 = <u>partition</u>, screen, barrier, enclosure 2 = <u>barrier</u>, obstacle, barricade, obstruction, check, bar, fence, impediment

**wallet** = <u>purse</u>, pocketbook, pouch, case, holder, money-bag

**wander** VERB = <u>roam</u>, walk, drift, stroll, range, stray, ramble, prowl

● NOUN = <u>excursion</u>, walk, stroll, cruise, ramble, meander, promenade, mosey (*informal*)

**wanderer** = <u>traveller</u>, rover, nomad, drifter, gypsy, explorer, rambler, voyager

**wane** 1 = <u>decline</u>, weaken, diminish, fail, fade, decrease, dwindle, lessen ≠ grow 2 = <u>diminish</u>, decrease, dwindle ≠ wax

**want** VERB 1 = <u>wish for</u>, desire, long for, crave, covet, hope for, yearn for, thirst for ≠ have 2 = <u>need</u>, demand, require, call for 3 = <u>should</u>, need, must, ought 4 = <u>desire</u>, long for, yearn for, thirst for, hanker after, burn for 5 = <u>lack</u>, need, require, miss

● NOUN 1 = <u>lack</u>, need, absence, shortage, deficiency, famine, scarcity, dearth ≠ abundance 2 = <u>poverty</u>, hardship, privation, penury, destitution, neediness, pennilessness ≠ wealth 3 = <u>wish</u>, will, need, desire, requirement, longing, appetite, craving

**wanting** 1 = <u>deficient</u>, poor, inadequate, insufficient, faulty, defective, imperfect, unsound, bodger *or* bodgie (*Austral. slang*) ≠ adequate 2 = <u>lacking</u>, missing, absent, incomplete, short, shy ≠ complete

**war** NOUN 1 = <u>conflict</u>, drive, attack, fighting, fight, operation, battle, movement ≠ peace 2 = <u>campaign</u>, drive, attack, operation, movement, push, mission, offensive

● VERB = <u>fight</u>, battle, clash, wage war, campaign, combat, do battle, take up arms ≠ make peace

**ward** NOUN 1 = <u>room</u>, department, unit, quarter, division, section, apartment, cubicle 2 = <u>district</u>, constituency, area, division, zone, parish, precinct3 = <u>dependant</u>, charge, pupil, minor, protégé

● PHRASES**ward someone off** = <u>drive off</u>, resist, fight off, hold off, repel, fend off ●**ward something off** 1 = <u>avert</u>, fend off, stave off, avoid, frustrate, deflect, repel2 = <u>parry</u>, avert, deflect, avoid, repel, turn aside

**warden** 1 = <u>steward</u>, guardian, administrator, superintendent, caretaker, curator, custodian 2 = <u>jailer</u>, prison officer, guard, screw (*slang*)3 = <u>governor</u>, head, leader, director, manager, chief, executive, commander, baas (*S. African*)4 = <u>ranger</u>, keeper, guardian, protector, custodian, official

**wardrobe** 1 = <u>clothes cupboard</u>, cupboard, closet (*U.S.*), cabinet 2 = <u>clothes</u>, apparel, attire

**warehouse** = <u>store</u>, depot, storehouse, repository, depository, stockroom

**wares** = <u>goods</u>, produce, stock, products, stuff, commodities, merchandise

**warfare** = <u>war</u>, fighting, battle, conflict, combat, hostilities, enmity ≠ peace

**warm** ADJECTIVE1 = <u>balmy</u>, mild, temperate, pleasant, fine, bright, sunny, agreeable ≠ cool2 = <u>cosy</u>, snug, toasty (*informal*), comfortable, homely, comfy (*informal*)3 = <u>moderately hot</u>, heated ≠ cool4 = <u>thermal</u>, winter, thick, chunky, woolly ≠ cool 5 = <u>mellow</u>, relaxing, pleasant, agreeable, restful6 = <u>affable</u>, kindly, friendly, affectionate, loving, tender, amicable, cordial ≠ unfriendly7 = <u>near</u>, close, hot, near to the truth

● VERB = <u>warm up</u>, heat, thaw (out), heat up ≠ cool down

● PHRASES**warm something** or **someone up** = <u>heat</u>, thaw, heat up

**warmth** 1 = <u>heat</u>, snugness, warmness, warmer, homeliness, hotness ≠ coolness2 = <u>affection</u>, feeling, love, goodwill, kindness, tenderness, cordiality, kindliness ≠ hostility

**warn** 1 = <u>notify</u>, tell, remind, inform, alert, tip off, give notice, make someone aware2 = <u>advise</u>, urge, recommend, counsel, caution, commend, exhort, admonish

**warning** 1 = <u>caution</u>, information, advice, injunction, notification2 = <u>notice</u>, notification, sign, alarm, announcement, alert, tip-off (*informal*)3 = <u>omen</u>, sign, forecast, indication, prediction, prophecy, foreboding, portent, rahui (*N.Z.*)4 = <u>reprimand</u>, admonition

**warp** VERB 1 = <u>distort</u>, bend, twist, buckle, deform, disfigure, contort, malform 2 = <u>become distorted</u>, bend, twist, contort, become deformed, become misshapen 3 = <u>pervert</u>, twist, corrupt, degrade, deprave, debase, debauch, lead astray

● NOUN = <u>twist</u>, bend, defect, flaw, distortion, imperfection, kink, contortion

**warrant** VERB 1 = <u>call for</u>, demand, require, rate, earn, deserve, permit 2 = <u>guarantee</u>, declare, pledge, promise, ensure, affirm, certify, attest

● NOUN 1 = <u>authorization</u>, permit, licence, permission, authority, sanction 2 = <u>justification</u>, reason, grounds, basis, licence, rationale, vindication, authority

**warranty** = <u>guarantee</u>, promise, contract, bond, pledge, certificate, assurance, covenant

**warrior** = <u>soldier</u>, combatant, fighter, gladiator, trooper, man-at-arms

**wary** 1 = <u>suspicious</u>, sceptical, guarded, distrustful, chary 2 = <u>watchful</u>, careful, alert, cautious, vigilant, circumspect, heedful ≠ careless

**wash** VERB 1 = <u>clean</u>, scrub, sponge, rinse, scour, cleanse 2 = <u>launder</u>, clean, rinse, dry-clean 3 = <u>rinse</u>, clean, scrub, lather 4 = <u>bathe</u>, bath, clean yourself, soak, douse, scrub yourself down 5 = <u>move</u>, overcome, touch, upset, stir, disturb, perturb, surge through 6 (*Informal*) (always used in negative constructions) = <u>be plausible</u>, stand up, hold up, pass muster, hold water, stick, carry weight, be convincing

● NOUN 1 = <u>laundering</u>, cleaning, clean, cleansing 2 = <u>bathe</u>, dip, soak, scrub, rinse 3 = <u>backwash</u>, slipstream, path, trail, train, track, waves, aftermath 4 = <u>splash</u>, surge, swell, rise and fall, undulation 5 = <u>coat</u>, film, covering, layer, coating, overlay

● PHRASES **wash something** *or* **someone away** = <u>sweep away</u>, carry off, bear away ◆ **wash something away** = <u>erode</u>, wear something away

**wasp** ➤ ants, bees, and wasps

**waste** VERB 1 = <u>squander</u>, throw away, blow (*slang*), lavish, misuse, dissipate, fritter away ≠ save 2 = <u>wear out</u>, wither

● NOUN 1 = <u>squandering</u>, misuse, extravagance, frittering away, dissipation, wastefulness, prodigality ≠ saving 2 = <u>rubbish</u>, refuse, debris, scrap, litter, garbage, trash, leftovers

● PLURAL NOUN = <u>desert</u>, wilderness, wasteland

● ADJECTIVE 1 = <u>unwanted</u>, useless,

worthless, unused, leftover,
superfluous, unusable,
supernumerary ≠ necessary

2 = uncultivated, wild, bare,
barren, empty, desolate,
unproductive, uninhabited
≠ cultivated

● PHRASES waste away
= decline, dwindle, wither, fade,
crumble, decay, wane, wear out

### Word Power

**waste** – *Waste* and *wastage*
are to some extent interchangeable,
but many people think that
*wastage* should not be used to
refer to loss resulting from
human carelessness,
inefficiency, etc.: *a waste* (not *a
wastage*) *of time, money, effort,*
etc.

**watch** VERB 1 = look at, observe,
regard, eye, see, view,
contemplate, eyeball (*slang*)

2 = spy on, follow, track, monitor,
keep an eye on, stake out, keep
tabs on (*informal*), keep watch on

3 = guard, keep, mind, protect,
tend, look after, shelter, take care
of

● NOUN 1 = wristwatch, timepiece,
chronometer 2 = guard,
surveillance, observation, vigil,
lookout

**watchdog** 1 = guardian,
monitor, protector, custodian,
scrutineer 2 = guard dog

**water** NOUN = liquid, $H_2O$, wai
(*N.Z.*)

● PLURAL NOUN = sea, main, waves,
ocean, depths, briny

● VERB 1 = sprinkle, spray, soak,
irrigate, hose, dampen, drench,
douse 2 = get wet, cry, weep,
become wet, exude water

● PHRASES water something
down = dilute, weaken, water,
doctor, thin

(Related Words)
*adjective*: aquatic

**waterfall** = cascade, fall,
cataract

**wave** VERB 1 = signal, sign,
gesture, gesticulate 2 = guide,
point, direct, indicate, signal,
motion, gesture, nod

3 = brandish, swing, flourish, wag,
shake 4 = flutter, flap, stir, shake,
swing, wag, oscillate

● NOUN 1 = gesture, sign, signal,
indication, gesticulation

2 = ripple, breaker, swell, ridge,
roller, billow 3 = outbreak, rash,
upsurge, flood, surge, ground
swell 4 = stream, flood, surge,
spate, current, flow, rush, tide

**waver** 1 = hesitate, dither (*chiefly
Brit.*), vacillate, falter, fluctuate,
seesaw, hum and haw ≠ be
decisive 2 = flicker, shake,
tremble, wobble, quiver, totter

**wax** 1 = increase, grow, develop,
expand, swell, enlarge, magnify

≠ wane2 = <u>become fuller</u>, enlarge

**way** 1 = <u>method</u>, means, system, process, technique, manner, procedure, mode2 = <u>manner</u>, style, fashion, mode3 *often plural* = <u>custom</u>, manner, habit, style, practice, nature, personality, wont, tikanga (*N.Z.*) ≠ <u>route</u>, direction, course, road, path
5 = <u>access</u>, road, track, channel, route, path, trail, pathway
6 = <u>journey</u>, approach, passage
7 = <u>distance</u>, length, stretch

**wayward** = <u>erratic</u>, unruly, unmanageable, unpredictable, capricious, ungovernable, inconstant ≠ obedient

**weak** 1 = <u>feeble</u>, frail, debilitated, fragile, sickly, puny, unsteady, infirm ≠ strong2 = <u>slight</u>, faint, feeble, pathetic, hollow
3 = <u>fragile</u>, brittle, flimsy, fine, delicate, frail, dainty, breakable
4 = <u>unsafe</u>, exposed, vulnerable, helpless, unprotected, defenceless, unguarded ≠ secure
5 = <u>unconvincing</u>, unsatisfactory, lame, flimsy, pathetic
≠ convincing6 = <u>tasteless</u>, thin, diluted, watery, runny, insipid
≠ strong

**weaken** 1 = <u>reduce</u>, undermine, moderate, diminish, lessen, sap
≠ boost2 = <u>wane</u>, diminish, dwindle, lower, flag, fade, lessen
≠ grow3 = <u>sap the strength of</u>

≠ strengthen

**weakness** 1 = <u>frailty</u>, fatigue, exhaustion, fragility, infirmity, feebleness, decrepitude
≠ strength2 = <u>liking</u>, appetite, penchant, soft spot, passion, inclination, fondness, partiality
≠ aversion3 = <u>powerlessness</u>, vulnerability, meekness, spinelessness, timorousness, cravenness, cowardliness
4 = <u>inadequacy</u>, deficiency, transparency, lameness, hollowness, implausibility, flimsiness, unsoundness
5 = <u>failing</u>, fault, defect, deficiency, flaw, shortcoming, blemish, imperfection ≠ strong point

**wealth** 1 = <u>riches</u>, fortune, prosperity, affluence, money, opulence ≠ poverty2 = <u>property</u>, capital, fortune3 = <u>abundance</u>, plenty, richness, profusion, fullness, cornucopia, copiousness
≠ lack

**wealthy** = <u>rich</u>, prosperous, affluent, well-off, flush (*informal*), opulent, well-heeled (*informal*), well-to-do ≠ poor

**wear** VERB1 = <u>be dressed in</u>, have on, sport (*informal*), put on
2 = <u>show</u>, present, bear, display, assume, put on, exhibit
3 = <u>deteriorate</u>, fray, wear thin
● NOUN1 = <u>clothes</u>, things, dress, gear (*informal*), attire, costume,

garments, apparel 2 = <u>damage</u>, wear and tear, erosion, deterioration, attrition, corrosion, abrasion ≠ repair

● **PHRASES wear off** = <u>subside</u>, disappear, fade, diminish, decrease, dwindle, wane, peter out

**wearing** = <u>tiresome</u>, trying, fatiguing, oppressive, exasperating, irksome, wearisome ≠ refreshing

**weary** ADJECTIVE 1 = <u>tired</u>, exhausted, drained, worn out, done in (*informal*), flagging, fatigued, sleepy, clapped out (*Austral. & N.Z. informal*) ≠ energetic 2 = <u>tiring</u>, arduous, tiresome, laborious, wearisome ≠ refreshing

● VERB = <u>grow tired</u>, tire, become bored ≠ invigorate

**weather** NOUN = <u>climate</u>, conditions, temperature, forecast, outlook, meteorological conditions, elements

● VERB = <u>withstand</u>, stand, survive, overcome, resist, brave, endure, come through ≠ surrender to

**weave** 1 = <u>knit</u>, intertwine, plait, braid, entwine, interlace 2 = <u>zigzag</u>, wind, crisscross 3 = <u>create</u>, tell, recount, narrate, build, relate, make up, spin

**web** 1 = <u>cobweb</u>, spider's web 2 = <u>mesh</u>, lattice 3 = <u>tangle</u>, network

**wed** 1 = <u>get married to</u>, be united to ≠ divorce 2 = <u>get married</u>, marry, be united, tie the knot (*informal*), take the plunge (*informal*) ≠ divorce 3 = <u>unite</u>, combine, join, link, ally, blend, merge, interweave ≠ divide

**wedding** = <u>marriage</u>, nuptials, wedding ceremony, marriage service, wedding service

**wedge** VERB = <u>squeeze</u>, force, lodge, jam, crowd, stuff, pack, thrust

● NOUN = <u>block</u>, lump, chunk

**weep** = <u>cry</u>, shed tears, sob, whimper, mourn, lament, blubber, snivel ≠ rejoice

**weigh** 1 = <u>have a weight of</u>, tip the scales at (*informal*) 2 *often with* up = <u>consider</u>, examine, contemplate, evaluate, ponder, think over, reflect upon, meditate upon 3 = <u>compare</u>, balance, contrast, juxtapose, place side by side 4 = <u>matter</u>, carry weight, count

**weight** NOUN 1 = <u>heaviness</u>, mass, poundage, load, tonnage 2 = <u>importance</u>, force, power, value, authority, influence, impact, import, mana (*N.Z.*)

● VERB 1 *often with* down = <u>load</u> 2 = <u>bias</u>, load, slant, unbalance

**weird** 1 = <u>strange</u>, odd, unusual, bizarre, mysterious, queer, eerie, unnatural ≠ normal2 = <u>bizarre</u>, odd, strange, unusual, queer, unnatural, creepy (*informal*), freakish ≠ ordinary

**welcome** VERB1 = <u>greet</u>, meet, receive, embrace, hail, karanga (*N.Z.*), mihi (*N.Z.*) ≠ reject

2 = <u>accept gladly</u>, appreciate, embrace, approve of, be pleased by, give the thumbs up to (*informal*), be glad about, express pleasure *or* satisfaction at

• NOUN = <u>greeting</u>, welcoming, reception, acceptance, hospitality, salutation ≠ rejection

• ADJECTIVE1 = <u>pleasing</u>, appreciated, acceptable, pleasant, desirable, refreshing, delightful, gratifying ≠ unpleasant

2 = <u>wanted</u> ≠ unwanted3 = <u>free</u>

**weld** 1 = <u>join</u>, link, bond, bind, connect, fuse, solder2 = <u>unite</u>, combine, blend, unify, fuse

**welfare** 1 = <u>wellbeing</u>, good, interest, health, security, benefit, safety, protection2 = <u>state benefit</u>, support, benefits, pensions, dole (*slang*), social security, unemployment benefit, state benefits

**well**[1] ADVERB1 = <u>skilfully</u>, expertly, adeptly, professionally, correctly, properly, efficiently, adequately ≠ badly2 = <u>satisfactorily</u>, nicely, smoothly, successfully, pleasantly, splendidly, agreeably ≠ badly

3 = <u>thoroughly</u>, completely, fully, carefully, effectively, efficiently, rigorously4 = <u>intimately</u>, deeply, fully, profoundly ≠ slightly

5 = <u>favourably</u>, highly, kindly, warmly, enthusiastically, approvingly, admiringly, with admiration ≠ unfavourably

6 = <u>considerably</u>, easily, very much, significantly, substantially, markedly7 = <u>fully</u>, highly, greatly, amply, very much, thoroughly, considerably, substantially

8 = <u>possibly</u>, probably, certainly, reasonably, conceivably, justifiably9 = <u>decently</u>, right, kindly, fittingly, fairly, properly, politely, suitably ≠ unfairly

10 = <u>prosperously</u>, comfortably, splendidly, in comfort, in (the lap of) luxury, without hardship

• ADJECTIVE1 = <u>healthy</u>, sound, fit, blooming, in fine fettle, in good condition ≠ ill2 = <u>satisfactory</u>, right, fine, pleasing, proper, thriving ≠ unsatisfactory

3 = <u>advisable</u>, proper, agreeable ≠ inadvisable

**well**[2] NOUN = <u>hole</u>, bore, pit, shaft

• VERB1 = <u>flow</u>, spring, pour, jet, surge, gush, spurt, spout2 = <u>rise</u>, increase, grow, mount, surge, intensify

**wet** ADJECTIVE1 = <u>damp</u>, soaking, saturated, moist, watery, soggy, sodden, waterlogged ≠ dry

2 = <u>rainy</u>, damp, drizzly, showery, raining, pouring, drizzling,

teeming ≠ sunny 3 (*Informal*)
= <u>feeble</u>, soft, weak, ineffectual,
weedy (*informal*), spineless,
effete, timorous

● VERB = <u>moisten</u>, spray, dampen,
water, soak, saturate, douse,
irrigate ≠ dry

● NOUN 1 = <u>rain</u>, drizzle ≠ fine
weather 2 = <u>moisture</u>, water,
liquid, damp, humidity,
condensation, dampness,
wetness ≠ dryness

**whack** (*Informal*) VERB = <u>strike</u>,
hit, belt (*informal*), bang, smack,
thrash, thump, swipe

● NOUN 1 = <u>blow</u>, hit, stroke, belt
(*informal*), bang, smack, thump,
swipe 2 (*Informal*) = <u>share</u>, part,
cut (*informal*), bit, portion, quota
3 (*Informal*) = <u>attempt</u>, go
(*informal*), try, turn, shot
(*informal*), crack (*informal*), stab
(*informal*), bash (*informal*)

**whale ▸ whales and
dolphins**

**wharf** = <u>dock</u>, pier, berth, quay,
jetty, landing stage

**wheel** NOUN = <u>disc</u>, ring, hoop

● VERB 1 = <u>push</u>, trundle, roll
2 = <u>turn</u>, swing, spin, revolve,
rotate, whirl, swivel 3 = <u>circle</u>, go
round, twirl, gyrate

**whereabouts** = <u>position</u>,
situation, site, location

**whiff** = <u>smell</u>, hint, scent, sniff,
aroma, odour

**whim** = <u>impulse</u>, caprice, fancy,
urge, notion

**whine** VERB 1 = <u>cry</u>, sob, wail,
whimper, sniffle, snivel, moan
2 = <u>complain</u>, grumble, gripe
(*informal*), whinge (*informal*),
moan, grouse, grizzle (*informal*,
*chiefly Brit.*), grouch (*informal*)

● NOUN 1 = <u>cry</u>, moan, sob, wail,
whimper 2 = <u>drone</u>, note, hum
3 = <u>complaint</u>, moan, grumble,
grouse, gripe (*informal*), whinge
(*informal*), grouch (*informal*)

**whip** NOUN = <u>lash</u>, cane, birch,
crop, scourge, cat-o'-nine-tails

● VERB 1 = <u>lash</u>, cane, flog, beat,
strap, thrash, birch, scourge
2 = <u>dash</u>, shoot, fly,
tear, rush, dive, dart, whisk
3 = <u>whisk</u>, beat, mix vigorously,
stir vigorously 4 = <u>incite</u>, drive,
stir, spur, work up, get going,
agitate, inflame

**whirl** VERB 1 = <u>spin</u>, turn, twist,
rotate, twirl 2 = <u>rotate</u>, roll, twist,
revolve, swirl, twirl, pirouette
3 = <u>feel dizzy</u>, swim, spin, reel, go
round

● NOUN 1 = <u>revolution</u>, turn, roll,
spin, twist, swirl, rotation, twirl
2 = <u>bustle</u>, round, series,
succession, flurry, merry-go-
round 3 = <u>confusion</u>, daze, dither
(*chiefly Brit.*), giddiness
4 = <u>tumult</u>, spin

**whisk** VERB 1 = <u>flick</u>, whip, sweep,

## Whales and dolphins

beluga
baleen whale
blue whale *or* sulphur-bottom
bottlenose dolphin
bowhead
humpback whale
killer whale, grampus, *or* orca
narwhal

porpoise
right whale *or* (*Austral.*) bay
 whale
rorqual
sperm whale *or* cachalot
toothed whale
whalebone whale
white whale

brush[2] = <u>beat</u>, mix vigorously,
stir vigorously, whip, fluff up
● NOUN[1] = <u>flick</u>, sweep, brush,
whip[2] = <u>beater</u>, mixer, blender

**whisper** VERB[1] = <u>murmur</u>,
breathe ≠ shout[2] = <u>rustle</u>, sigh,
hiss, swish
● NOUN[1] = <u>murmur</u>, mutter,
mumble, undertone[2] (*Informal*)
= <u>rumour</u>, report, gossip,
innuendo, insinuation[3] = <u>rustle</u>,
sigh, hiss, swish

**white** = <u>pale</u>, wan, pasty, pallid,
ashen
➤**shades from black to
white**

**white-collar** = <u>clerical</u>,
professional, salaried, nonmanual

**whittle** VERB = <u>carve</u>, cut, hew,
shape, trim, shave, pare
● PHRASES**whittle something
or someone down** = <u>reduce</u>,
cut down, cut, decrease, prune,
scale down ◆**whittle
something away** = <u>undermine</u>,
reduce, consume, erode, eat
away, wear away

**whole** NOUN = <u>unit</u>, ensemble,
entirety, totality ≠ part
● ADJECTIVE[1] = <u>complete</u>, full,
total, entire, uncut, undivided,
unabridged ≠ partial
[2] = <u>undamaged</u>, intact,
unscathed, unbroken, untouched,
unharmed, in one piece
≠ damaged
● PHRASES**on the whole** [1] = <u>all
in all</u>, altogether, all things
considered, by and large
[2] = <u>generally</u>, in general, as a rule,
chiefly, mainly, mostly, principally,
on average

**wholesale** ADJECTIVE
= <u>extensive</u>, total, mass,
sweeping, broad, comprehensive,
wide-ranging, blanket ≠ limited
● ADVERB = <u>extensively</u>,
comprehensively, across the
board, indiscriminately

**wholly** = <u>completely</u>, totally,
perfectly, fully, entirely,
altogether, thoroughly, utterly

≠ partly

**whore** = prostitute, tart (*informal*), streetwalker, call girl

**wide** ADJECTIVE 1 = <u>spacious</u>, broad, extensive, roomy, commodious ≠ confined 2 = <u>baggy</u>, full, loose, ample, billowing, roomy, voluminous, capacious 3 = <u>expanded</u>, dilated, distended ≠ shut 4 = <u>broad</u>, extensive, wide-ranging, large, sweeping, vast, immense, expansive ≠ restricted 5 = <u>extensive</u>, general, far-reaching, overarching 6 = <u>large</u>, broad, vast, immense 7 = <u>distant</u>, remote, off course, off target

● ADVERB 1 = <u>fully</u>, completely ≠ partly 2 = <u>off target</u>, astray, off course, off the mark

**widen** 1 = <u>broaden</u>, expand, enlarge, dilate, spread, extend, stretch ≠ narrow 2 = <u>get wider</u>, spread, extend, expand, broaden ≠ narrow

**widespread** = <u>common</u>, general, popular, broad, extensive, universal, far-reaching, pervasive ≠ limited

**width** = <u>breadth</u>, extent, span, scope, diameter, compass, thickness, girth

**wield** 1 = <u>brandish</u>, flourish, manipulate, swing, use, manage, handle, employ 2 = <u>exert</u>, maintain, exercise, have, possess

**wife** = <u>spouse</u>, partner, mate, bride, better half (*humorous*), vrou (*S. African*), wahine (*N.Z.*)

**wild** ADJECTIVE 1 = <u>untamed</u>, fierce, savage, ferocious, unbroken, feral, undomesticated, free, warrigal (*Austral. literary*) ≠ tame 2 = <u>uncultivated</u>, natural ≠ cultivated 3 = <u>stormy</u>, violent, rough, raging, choppy, tempestuous, blustery 4 = <u>excited</u>, crazy (*informal*), enthusiastic, raving, hysterical ≠ unenthusiastic 5 = <u>uncontrolled</u>, disorderly, turbulent, wayward, unruly, rowdy, unfettered, riotous ≠ calm 6 = <u>mad</u> (*informal*), furious, fuming, infuriated, incensed, enraged, very angry, irate, tooshie (*Austral. slang*), off the air (*Austral. slang*) 7 = <u>uncivilized</u>, fierce, savage, primitive, ferocious, barbaric, brutish, barbarous ≠ civilized

● PLURAL NOUN = <u>wilderness</u>, desert, wasteland, middle of nowhere (*informal*), backwoods, back of beyond (*informal*)

**wilderness** = <u>wilds</u>, desert, wasteland, uncultivated region

**will** NOUN 1 = <u>determination</u>, drive, purpose, commitment, resolution, resolve, spine, backbone 2 = <u>wish</u>, mind, desire, intention, fancy, preference, inclination 3 = <u>choice</u>, prerogative, volition[4] = **decree**, wish, desire, command, dictate, ordinance[5] = **testament**, bequest(s), last wishes, last will and testament

● VERB[1] = **wish**, want, prefer, desire, see fit[2] = **bequeath**, give, leave, transfer, gift, hand on, pass on, confer

**willing** 1 = **inclined**, prepared, consenting, agreeable, compliant, amenable ≠ **unwilling**[2] = **ready**, game (*informal*) ≠ reluctant

**willingly** = **readily**, freely, gladly, happily, eagerly, voluntarily, cheerfully, by choice ≠ unwillingly

**willingness** = **inclination**, will, agreement, wish, consent, volition ≠ reluctance

**wilt** 1 = **droop**, wither, sag, shrivel 2 = **weaken**, languish, droop 3 = **wane**, flag, fade

**win** VERB[1] = **be victorious in**, succeed in, prevail in, come first in, be the victor in ≠ lose[2] = **be victorious**, succeed, triumph, overcome, prevail, conquer, come first, sweep the board ≠ lose 3 = **gain**, get, land, achieve, earn, secure, obtain, acquire ≠ forfeit

● NOUN = **victory**, success, triumph, conquest ≠ defeat

● PHRASES **win someone over** or **round** = **convince**, influence, persuade, convert, sway, prevail

upon, bring or talk round

**wince** VERB = **flinch**, start, shrink, cringe, quail, recoil, cower, draw back

● NOUN = **flinch**, start, cringe

**wind**[1] NOUN[1] = **air**, blast, hurricane, breeze, draught, gust, zephyr[2] = **flatulence**, gas 3 = **breath**, puff, respiration 4 = **nonsense**, talk, boasting, hot air, babble, bluster, humbug, twaddle (*informal*), bizzo (*Austral. slang*), bull's wool (*Austral. & N.Z. slang*)

● PHRASES **get wind of something** = **hear about**, learn of, find out about, become aware of, be told about, be informed of, be made aware of, hear tell of

**wind**[2] VERB[1] = **meander**, turn, bend, twist, curve, snake, ramble, twist and turn[2] = **wrap**, twist, reel, curl, loop, coil[3] = **coil**, curl, spiral, encircle

● PHRASES **wind someone up** (*Informal*)[1] = **irritate**, excite, anger, annoy, exasperate, nettle, work someone up, pique 2 = **tease**, kid (*informal*), have someone on (*informal*), annoy, rag (*informal*), rib (*informal*), josh (*informal*), vex ◆ **wind something up** 1 = **end**, finish, settle, conclude, tie up, wrap up, finalize[2] = **close down**, close, dissolve, terminate, put something into liquidation

◆ **wind up** = end up, be left, finish up, fetch up (*informal*), land up

**windfall** = godsend, find, jackpot, bonanza, manna from heaven ≠ misfortune

**windy** = breezy, wild, stormy, windswept, blustery, gusty, squally, blowy ≠ calm

**wing** NOUN = faction, group, arm, section, branch
● VERB 1 = fly, soar, glide, take wing 2 = wound, hit, clip

**wink** VERB 1 = blink, bat, flutter 2 = twinkle, flash, shine, sparkle, gleam, shimmer, glimmer
● NOUN = blink, flutter

**winner** = victor, champion, master, champ (*informal*), conqueror, prizewinner ≠ loser

**winning** ADJECTIVE 1 = victorious, first, top, successful, unbeaten, conquering, triumphant, undefeated 2 = charming, pleasing, attractive, engaging, cute, disarming, enchanting, endearing ≠ unpleasant
● PLURAL NOUN = spoils, profits, gains, prize, proceeds, takings

**wipe** VERB 1 = clean, polish, brush, rub, sponge, mop, swab 2 = erase, remove
● NOUN = rub, brush
● PHRASES wipe something or someone out = destroy, massacre, erase, eradicate, obliterate, annihilate, exterminate, expunge

**wisdom** = understanding, learning, knowledge, intelligence, judgment, insight, enlightenment, erudition ≠ foolishness

**wise** 1 = sage, clever, intelligent, sensible, enlightened, discerning, perceptive, erudite ≠ foolish 2 = sensible, clever, intelligent, prudent, judicious ≠ unwise

**wish** NOUN = desire, want, hope, urge, intention, fancy (*informal*), ambition, yen (*informal*) ≠ aversion
● VERB = want, feel, choose, please, desire, think fit
● PHRASES wish for something = desire, want, hope for, long for, crave, aspire to, yearn for, hanker for

**wit** 1 = humour, quips, banter, puns, repartee, wordplay, witticisms, badinage ≠ seriousness 2 = humorist, card (*informal*), comedian, wag, joker, dag (*N.Z. informal*) 3 *often plural* = cleverness, sense, brains, wisdom, common sense, intellect, ingenuity, acumen ≠ stupidity

**witch** = enchantress, magician, hag, crone, sorceress, Wiccan

**witchcraft** = magic, voodoo, wizardry, black magic, enchantment, occultism, sorcery,

Wicca, makutu (*N.Z.*)

**withdraw** 1 = <u>remove</u>, take off, pull out, extract, take away, pull back, draw out, draw back

2 = <u>take out</u>, extract, draw out

**withdrawal** = <u>removal</u>, ending, stopping, taking away, abolition, elimination, cancellation, termination

**withdrawn** = <u>uncommunicative</u>, reserved, retiring, distant, shy, taciturn, introverted, unforthcoming ≠ outgoing

**wither** 1 = <u>wilt</u>, decline, decay, disintegrate, perish, shrivel ≠ flourish2 = <u>waste</u>, decline, shrivel3 = <u>fade</u>, decline, perish ≠ increase

**withering** = <u>scornful</u>, devastating, humiliating, snubbing, hurtful, mortifying

**withhold** 1 = <u>keep secret</u>, refuse, hide, reserve, retain, conceal, suppress, hold back ≠ reveal

2 = <u>hold back</u>, suppress, keep back ≠ release

**withstand** = <u>resist</u>, suffer, bear, oppose, cope with, endure, tolerate, stand up to ≠ give in to

**witness** NOUN1 = <u>observer</u>, viewer, spectator, looker-on, watcher, onlooker, eyewitness, bystander2 = <u>testifier</u>

● VERB1 = <u>see</u>, view, watch, note, notice, observe, perceive

2 = <u>countersign</u>, sign, endorse, validate

**witty** = <u>humorous</u>, funny, clever, amusing, sparkling, whimsical, droll, piquant ≠ dull

**wizard** = <u>magician</u>, witch, shaman, sorcerer, occultist, magus, conjuror, warlock, tohunga (*N.Z.*)

**wobble** VERB1 = <u>shake</u>, rock, sway, tremble, teeter, totter

2 = <u>tremble</u>, shake

● NOUN1 = <u>unsteadiness</u>, shake, tremble2 = <u>unsteadiness</u>, shake, tremor

**woe** 1 = <u>misery</u>, distress, grief, agony, gloom, sadness, sorrow, anguish ≠ happiness

2 = <u>problem</u>, grief, misery, sorrow

**woman** = <u>lady</u>, girl, female, sheila (*Austral. & N.Z. informal*), vrou (*S. African*), adult female, charlie (*Austral. slang*), chook (*Austral. slang*), wahine (*N.Z.*) ≠ man

**womanly** 1 = <u>feminine</u>, motherly, female, warm, tender, matronly, ladylike2 = <u>curvaceous</u>, ample, voluptuous, shapely, curvy (*informal*), busty (*informal*), buxom, full-figured

**wonder** VERB1 = <u>think</u>, question, puzzle, speculate, query, ponder, meditate, conjecture2 = <u>be amazed</u>, stare, marvel, be astonished, gape

● NOUN1 = <u>amazement</u>, surprise,

admiration, awe, fascination, astonishment, bewilderment, wonderment 2 = <u>phenomenon</u>, sight, miracle, spectacle, curiosity, marvel, prodigy, rarity

**wonderful** 1 = <u>excellent</u>, great (*informal*), brilliant, outstanding, superb, fantastic (*informal*), tremendous, magnificent, booshit (*Austral. slang*), exo (*Austral. slang*), sik (*Austral. slang*) ≠ terrible 2 = <u>remarkable</u>, amazing, extraordinary, incredible, astonishing, staggering, startling, phenomenal ≠ ordinary

**woo** 1 = <u>seek</u>, cultivate 2 = <u>court</u>, pursue

**wood** 1 = <u>timber</u>, planks, planking, lumber (*U.S.*) 2 or **woods** = <u>woodland</u>, forest, grove, thicket, copse, coppice 3 = <u>firewood</u>, fuel, logs, kindling

**wooded** = <u>tree-covered</u>, forested, timbered, sylvan (*poetic*), tree-clad

**wooden** 1 = <u>made of wood</u>, timber, woody, ligneous 2 = <u>expressionless</u>, lifeless, deadpan, unresponsive

**wool** 1 = <u>fleece</u>, hair, coat 2 = <u>yarn</u>

**word** NOUN 1 = <u>term</u>, name, expression 2 = <u>chat</u>, tête-à-tête, talk, discussion, consultation, confab (*informal*), heart-to-heart,

powwow (*informal*) 3 = <u>comment</u>, remark, utterance 4 = <u>message</u>, news, report, information, notice, intelligence, dispatch, communiqué 5 = <u>promise</u>, guarantee, pledge, vow, assurance, oath 6 = <u>command</u>, order, decree, bidding, mandate ● VERB = <u>express</u>, say, state, put, phrase, utter, couch, formulate

*Related Words*
adjectives: lexical, verbal

**wording** = <u>phraseology</u>, words, language, phrasing, terminology

**work** VERB 1 = <u>be employed</u>, be in work 2 = <u>labour</u>, sweat, slave, toil, slog (away), drudge, peg away, exert yourself ≠ relax 3 = <u>function</u>, go, run, operate, be in working order ≠ be out of order 4 = <u>succeed</u>, work out, pay off (*informal*), be successful, be effective, do the trick (*informal*), do the business (*informal*), get results 5 = <u>cultivate</u>, farm, dig, till, plough 6 = <u>operate</u>, use, move, control, drive, manage, handle, manipulate 7 = <u>manipulate</u>, form, fashion, shape, mould, knead ● NOUN 1 = <u>employment</u>, business, job, trade, duty, profession, occupation, livelihood ≠ play 2 = <u>effort</u>, industry, labour, sweat, toil, exertion, drudgery, elbow grease (*facetious*) ≠ leisure 3 = <u>task</u>, jobs, projects, commissions, duties, assignments, chores, yakka (*Austral. & N.Z. informal*) **4** = <u>handiwork</u>, doing, act, feat, deed⁵ = <u>creation</u>, piece, production, opus, achievement, composition, handiwork

● **PLURAL NOUN**¹ = <u>factory</u>, plant, mill, workshop² = <u>writings</u>, output, canon, oeuvre (*French*) **3** = <u>mechanism</u>, workings, parts, action, movement, machinery

● **PHRASES work something out** = <u>solve</u>, find out, calculate, figure out

**worker** = <u>employee</u>, hand, labourer, workman, craftsman, artisan, tradesman

**workman** = <u>labourer</u>, hand, worker, employee, mechanic, operative, craftsman, artisan

**workshop 1** = <u>factory</u>, plant, mill² = <u>workroom</u>, studio

**world 1** = <u>earth</u>, planet, globe **2** = <u>mankind</u>, man, everyone, the public, everybody, humanity, humankind³ = <u>sphere</u>, area, field, environment, realm, domain **4** (usually used in phrase *a world of difference*) = <u>huge amount</u>, mountain, wealth, great deal, good deal, abundance, enormous amount, vast amount

**worldly 1** = <u>earthly</u>, physical, secular, terrestrial, temporal, profane ≠ spiritual

**2** = <u>materialistic</u>, grasping, selfish, greedy ≠ nonmaterialistic

**3** = <u>worldly-wise</u>, knowing, experienced, sophisticated, cosmopolitan, urbane, blasé ≠ naive

**worn** = <u>ragged</u>, frayed, shabby, tattered, tatty, threadbare, the worse for wear

**worried** = <u>anxious</u>, concerned, troubled, afraid, frightened, nervous, tense, uneasy ≠ unworried

**worry VERB 1** = <u>be anxious</u>, be concerned, be worried, obsess, brood, fret, agonize, get in a lather (*informal*) ≠ be unconcerned² = <u>trouble</u>, upset, bother, disturb, annoy, unsettle, pester, vex ≠ soothe

● **NOUN**¹ = <u>anxiety</u>, concern, fear, trouble, unease, apprehension, misgiving, trepidation ≠ peace of mind² = <u>problem</u>, care, trouble, bother, hassle (*informal*)

**worsen 1** = <u>deteriorate</u>, decline, sink, decay, get worse, degenerate, go downhill (*informal*) ≠ improve

**2** = <u>aggravate</u>, damage, exacerbate, make worse ≠ improve

**worship VERB**¹ = <u>revere</u>, praise, honour, adore, glorify, exalt, pray to, venerate ≠ dishonour² = <u>love</u>, adore, idolize, put on a pedestal

≠ despise

• NOUN = <u>reverence</u>, praise, regard, respect, honour, glory, devotion, adulation

**worth** 1 = <u>value</u>, price, rate, cost, estimate, valuation ≠ worthlessness 2 = <u>merit</u>, value, quality, importance, excellence, goodness, worthiness ≠ unworthiness 3 = <u>usefulness</u>, value, quality, importance, excellence, goodness ≠ uselessness

**worthless** 1 = <u>valueless</u>, rubbishy, negligible ≠ valuable 2 = <u>useless</u>, unimportant, ineffectual, negligible ≠ useful 3 = <u>good-for-nothing</u>, despicable, contemptible ≠ honourable

**worthwhile** = <u>useful</u>, valuable, helpful, profitable, productive, beneficial, meaningful, constructive ≠ useless

**worthy** = <u>praiseworthy</u>, deserving, valuable, worthwhile, admirable, virtuous, creditable, laudable ≠ disreputable

**would-be** = <u>budding</u>, self-styled, wannabe (informal), unfulfilled, self-appointed

**wound** NOUN 1 = <u>injury</u>, cut, hurt, trauma (Pathology), gash, lesion, laceration 2 often plural = <u>trauma</u>, offence, slight, insult

• VERB 1 = <u>injure</u>, cut, wing, hurt, pierce, gash, lacerate 2 = <u>offend</u>, hurt, annoy, sting, mortify, cut to the quick

**wrangle** VERB = <u>argue</u>, fight, row, dispute, disagree, contend, quarrel, squabble

• NOUN = <u>argument</u>, row, dispute, quarrel, squabble, bickering, tiff, altercation

**wrap** VERB 1 = <u>cover</u>, enclose, shroud, swathe, encase, enfold, bundle up 2 = <u>pack</u>, package, parcel (up), tie up, gift-wrap ≠ unpack 3 = <u>bind</u>, swathe ≠ unwind

• NOUN = <u>cloak</u>, cape, stole, mantle, shawl

• PHRASES **wrap something up** 1 = <u>giftwrap</u>, pack, package, bundle up 2 (Informal) = <u>end</u>, conclude, wind up, terminate, finish off, round off, polish off

**wrath** = <u>anger</u>, rage, temper, fury, resentment, indignation, ire, displeasure ≠ satisfaction

**wreck** VERB 1 = <u>destroy</u>, break, smash, ruin, devastate, shatter, spoil, demolish ≠ build 2 = <u>spoil</u>, ruin, devastate, shatter, crool or cruel (Austral. slang) ≠ save

• NOUN = <u>shipwreck</u>, hulk

**wreckage** = <u>remains</u>, pieces, ruin, fragments, debris, rubble

**wrench** VERB 1 = <u>twist</u>, force, pull, tear, rip, tug, jerk, yank 2 = <u>sprain</u>, strain, rick

● NOUN[1] = <u>twist</u>, pull, rip, tug, jerk, yank[2] = <u>sprain</u>, strain, twist

3 = <u>blow</u>, shock, upheaval, pang

4 = <u>spanner</u>, adjustable spanner

**wrestle** = <u>fight</u>, battle, struggle, combat, grapple, tussle, scuffle

**wrinkle** NOUN[1] = <u>line</u>, fold, crease, furrow, crow's-foot, corrugation[2] = <u>crease</u>, fold, crumple, furrow, crinkle, corrugation

● VERB = <u>crease</u>, gather, fold, crumple, furrow, rumple, pucker, corrugate ≠ smooth

**writ** = <u>summons</u>, document, decree, indictment, court order, subpoena, arraignment

**write** 1 = <u>record</u>, scribble, inscribe, set down, jot down

2 = <u>compose</u>, draft, pen, draw up

3 = <u>correspond</u>, get in touch, keep in touch, write a letter, drop a line, drop a note

**writer** = <u>author</u>, novelist, hack, scribbler, scribe, wordsmith, penpusher

**writing** = <u>script</u>, hand, printing, fist (*informal*), scribble, handwriting, scrawl, calligraphy

**wrong** ADJECTIVE 1 = <u>amiss</u>, faulty, unsatisfactory, not right, defective, awry[2] = <u>incorrect</u>, mistaken, false, inaccurate, untrue, erroneous, wide of the mark, fallacious

3 = <u>inappropriate</u>, incorrect, unsuitable, unacceptable, undesirable, incongruous, unseemly, unbecoming ≠ correct

4 = <u>bad</u>, criminal, illegal, evil, unlawful, immoral, unjust, dishonest ≠ moral[5] = <u>defective</u>, faulty, awry, askew

● ADVERB[1] = <u>incorrectly</u>, badly, wrongly, mistakenly, erroneously, inaccurately ≠ correctly

2 = <u>amiss</u>, astray, awry, askew

● NOUN = <u>offence</u>, injury, crime, error, sin, injustice, misdeed, transgression ≠ good deed

● VERB = <u>mistreat</u>, abuse, hurt, harm, cheat, take advantage of, oppress, malign ≠ treat well

# X

**X-ray** = <u>radiograph</u>, x-ray image

# Y

**yank** VERB = <u>pull</u>, tug, jerk, seize, snatch, pluck, hitch, wrench

● NOUN = <u>pull</u>, tug, jerk, snatch, hitch, wrench, tweak

**yarn** 1 = <u>thread</u>, fibre, cotton, wool[2] (*Informal*) = <u>story</u>, tale, anecdote, account, narrative, fable, reminiscence, urban myth

**yawning** = <u>gaping</u>, wide, huge, vast, cavernous

### Shades of yellow

| | | | |
|---|---|---|---|
| amber | daffodil | oatmeal | straw |
| buff | gold *or* golden | ochre | tea rose |
| canary yellow | lemon | old gold | topaz |
| champagne | maize | primrose | tortoiseshell |
| cinnamon | mustard | saffron | |

**yearly** ADJECTIVE = <u>annual</u>, each year, every year, once a year

● ADVERB = <u>annually</u>, every year, by the year, once a year, per annum

**yearn** *often with* for = <u>long</u>, desire, hunger, ache, crave, covet, itch, hanker after

**yell** VERB = <u>scream</u>, shout, cry out, howl, call out, wail, shriek, screech ≠ whisper

● NOUN = <u>scream</u>, cry, shout, roar, howl, shriek, whoop, screech ≠ whisper

**yellow** ➤ shades of yellow

**yen** = <u>longing</u>, desire, craving, yearning, passion, hunger, ache, itch

**yet** ADVERB 1 = <u>so far</u>, until now, up to now, still, as yet, even now, thus far, up till now 2 = <u>now</u>, right now, just now, so soon 3 = <u>still</u>, in addition, besides, to boot, into the bargain

● CONJUNCTION = <u>nevertheless</u>, still, however, for all that, notwithstanding, just the same, be that as it may

**yield** VERB 1 = <u>bow</u>, submit, give in, surrender, succumb, cave in (*informal*), capitulate 2 = <u>relinquish</u>, resign, hand over, surrender, turn over, make over, give over, bequeath ≠ retain ≠ resist 3 = <u>produce</u>, give, provide, return, supply, bear, net, earn ≠ use up

● NOUN 1 = <u>produce</u>, crop, harvest, output 2 = <u>profit</u>, return, income, revenue, earnings, takings ≠ loss

**yielding** 1 = <u>soft</u>, pliable, springy, elastic, supple, spongy, unresisting 2 = <u>submissive</u>, obedient, compliant, docile, flexible, accommodating, pliant, acquiescent ≠ obstinate

**yob** *or* **yobbo** = <u>thug</u>, hooligan, lout, hoon (*Austral. & N.Z. slang*), ruffian, roughneck (*slang*), tsotsi (*S. African*), cougan (*Austral. slang*), scozza (*Austral. slang*), bogan (*Austral. slang*)

**young** ADJECTIVE 1 = <u>immature</u>, juvenile, youthful, little, green, junior, infant, adolescent ≠ old 2 = <u>early</u>, new, undeveloped, fledgling ≠ advanced

● PLURAL NOUN = <u>offspring</u>, babies,

litter, family, issue, brood, progeny ≠ parents

**youngster** = youth, girl, boy, kid (*informal*), lad, teenager, juvenile, lass

**youth 1** = immaturity, adolescence, boyhood *or* girlhood, salad days ≠ old age

**2** = boy, lad, youngster, kid (*informal*), teenager, young man, adolescent, teen (*informal*) ≠ adult

**youthful** = young, juvenile, childish, immature, boyish, girlish ≠ elderly

# Z

**zeal** = enthusiasm, passion, zest, spirit, verve, fervour, eagerness, gusto ≠ apathy

**zero 1** = nought, nothing, nil

**2** = rock bottom, the bottom, an all-time low, a nadir, as low as you can get

**zip** VERB = speed, shoot, fly, flash, zoom, whizz (*informal*)

● NOUN (*Informal*) = energy, drive, vigour, verve, zest, gusto, liveliness ≠ lethargy

**zone** = area, region, section, sector, district, territory, belt, sphere

**zoom** = speed, shoot, fly, rush, flash, dash, whizz (*informal*), hurtle

# WORD POWER

Supplement

# CONTENTS

WORD POWER

# CONTENTS

**WORD POWER**

*WORD POWER*

### Male

| | |
|---|---|
| Woody Allen (*U.S.*) | Chris Cooper (*U.S.*) |
| Fred Astaire (*U.S.*) | Gary Cooper (*U.S.*) |
| Richard Attenborough (*English*) | Kevin Costner (*U.S.*) |
| Jean-Louis Barrault (*French*) | Noel Coward (*English*) |
| John Barrymore (*U.S.*) | Michael Crawford (*English*) |
| Alan Bates (*English*) | Tom Cruise (*U.S.*) |
| Warren Beatty (*U.S.*) | James Dean (*U.S.*) |
| Jean-Paul Belmondo (*French*) | Robert De Niro (*U.S.*) |
| Alan Bennett (*English*) | Gerard Depardieu (*French*) |
| Dirk Bogarde (*English*) | Vittorio de Sica (*Italian*) |
| Humphrey Bogart (*U.S.*) | John Dexter (*English*) |
| Charles Boyer (*French*) | Leonardo DiCaprio (*U.S.*) |
| Kenneth Branagh (*English*) | Kirk Douglas (*U.S.*) |
| Marlon Brando (*U.S.*) | Michael Douglas (*U.S.*) |
| Adrien Brody (*U.S.*) | Clint Eastwood (*U.S.*) |
| Mel Brooks (*U.S.*) | Douglas Fairbanks Jr. (*U.S.*) |
| Richard Burbage (*English*) | Douglas Fairbanks Snr. (*U.S.*) |
| Richard Burton (*Welsh*) | WC Fields (*U.S.*) |
| Glen Byam Shaw (*English*) | Albert Finney (*English*) |
| James Cagney (*U.S.*) | Errol Flynn (*Australian*) |
| Michael Caine (*English*) | Henry Fonda (*U.S.*) |
| Simon Callow (*English*) | Harrison Ford (*U.S.*) |
| Robert Carlyle (*Scottish*) | Jean Gabin (*France*) |
| Jim Carrey (*Canadian*) | Clark Gable (*U.S.*) |
| Charlie Chaplin (*English*) | David Garrick (*English*) |
| Maurice Chevalier (*French*) | Mel Gibson (*Australian*) |
| John Cleese (*English*) | John Gielgud (*English*) |
| George Clooney (*U.S.*) | Cary Grant (*English-U.S.*) |
| Sean Connery (*Scottish*) | Alec Guinness (*English*) |
| Peter Cook (*English*) | Gene Hackman (*U.S.*) |
| | Tom Hanks (*U.S.*) |

*Male (continued)*

Oliver Hardy (*U.S.*)
Rex Harrison (*English*)
Dustin Hoffman (*U.S.*)
Bob Hope (*U.S.*)
Anthony Hopkins (*Welsh*)
Michael Hordern (*English*)
Leslie Howard (*English*)
Trevor Howard (*English*)
Rock Hudson (*U.S.*)
Barry Humphries (*Australian*)
John Hurt (*English*)
Jeremy Irons (*English*)
Henry Irving (*English*)
Derek Jacobi (*English*)
Al Jolson (*U.S.*)
Boris Karloff (*English*)
Edmund Kean (*English*)
Buster Keaton (*U.S.*)
Harvey Keitel (*U.S.*)
Gene Kelly (*U.S.*)
John Kemble (*English*)
Ben Kingsley (*English*)
Burt Lancaster (*U.S.*)
Charles Laughton (*English-U.S.*)
Stan Laurel (*English-U.S.*)
Bruce Lee (*U.S.*)
Christopher Lee (*English*)
Harold Lloyd (*U.S.*)
Bela Lugosi (*Hungarian*)
Ewan McGregor (*Scottish*)

Ian McKellen (*English*)
Steve McQueen (*U.S.*)
William Macready (*English*)
James Mason (*English*)
Raymond Massey (*Canadian*)
Marcello Mastroianni (*Italian*)
Bernard Miles (*English*)
John Mills (*English*)
Robert Mitchum (*U.S.*)
Dudley Moore (*English*)
Robert Morley (*English*)
Sam Neill (*N.Z.*)
Paul Newman (*U.S.*)
Jack Nicholson (*U.S.*)
Liam Neeson (*Irish*)
David Niven (*English*)
Gary Oldman (*English*)
Laurence Olivier (*English*)
Peter O'Toole (*Irish-British*)
Al Pacino (*U.S.*)
Gregory Peck (*U.S.*)
Donald Pleasence (*English*)
Anthony Quayle (*English*)
Anthony Quinn (*U.S.*)
Daniel Radcliffe (*English*)
Ronald Reagan (*U.S.*)
Robert Redford (*U.S.*)
Michael Redgrave (*English*)
Fernando Rey (*Spanish*)
Ralph Richardson (*English*)
Paul Robeson (*U.S.*)

**WORD POWER**

**WORD POWER**

### Male (continued)

Edward G Robinson (*U.S.*)
Tim Roth (*English*)
Arnold Schwarzenegger (*Austrian-U.S.*)
Paul Scofield (*English*)
Peter Sellers (*English*)
Sam Shepard (*U.S.*)
Sylvester Stallone (*U.S.*)
Konstantin Stanislavsky (*Russian*)
James Stewart (*U.S.*)
Donald Sutherland (*Canadian*)

Jacques Tati (*French*)
Spencer Tracy (*U.S.*)
John Travolta (*U.S.*)
Peter Ustinov (*English*)
Rudolph Valentino (*Italian-U.S.*)
Max Von Sydow (*Swedish*)
John Wayne (*U.S.*)
Johnny Weissmuller (*U.S.*)
Orson Welles (*U.S.*)
Elijah Wood (*U.S.*)

### Female

Yvonne Arnaud (*French*)
Peggy Ashcroft (*English*)
Tallulah Bankhead (*U.S.*)
Brigitte Bardot (*French*)
Ingrid Bergman (*Swedish-U.S.*)
Sarah Bernhardt (*French*)
Clara Bow (*U.S.*)
Fanny Brice (*U.S.*)
Glenn Close (*U.S.*)
Claudette Colbert (*French-U.S.*)
Joan Crawford (*U.S.*)
Bette Davis (*U.S.*)
Geena Davis (*U.S.*)
Judy Davis (*Australian*)

Judi Dench (*English*)
Catherine Deneuve (*French*)
Marlene Dietrich (*German*)
Faye Dunaway (*U.S.*)
Edith Evans (*English*)
Jane Fonda (*U.S.*)
Jodie Foster (*U.S.*)
Greta Garbo (*Swedish*)
Ava Gardner (*U.S.*)
Judy Garland (*U.S.*)
Lillian Gish (*U.S.*)
Joyce Grenfell (*English*)
Jean Harlow (*U.S.*)
Audrey Hepburn (*Belgian-U.S.*)
Katharine Hepburn (*U.S.*)

*Female (continued)*

Wendy Hiller (*English*)
Holly Hunter (*U.S.*)
Isabelle Huppert (*French*)
Glenda Jackson (*English*)
Diane Keaton (*U.S.*)
Grace Kelly (*U.S.*)
Fanny Kemble (*English-U.S.*)
Nicole Kidman (*Australian*)
Jessica Lange (*U.S.*)
Gertrude Lawrence (*English*)
Vivien Leigh (*English*)
Lotte Lenya (*Austrian*)
Margaret Lockwood (*English*)
Jennifer Lopez (*Puerto Rican*)
Sophia Loren (*Italian*)
Siobhan McKenna (*Irish*)
Shirley MacLaine (*U.S.*)
Melina Mercouri (*Greek*)
Liza Minnelli (*U.S.*)
Helen Mirren (*English*)
Marilyn Monroe (*U.S.*)
Jeanne Moreau (*French*)
Michelle Pfeiffer (*U.S.*)
Mary Pickford (*U.S.*)
Joan Plowright (*English*)
Jian Qing (*Chinese*)

Vanessa Redgrave (*English*)
Julia Roberts (*U.S.*)
Flora Robson (*English*)
Ginger Rogers (*U.S.*)
Margaret Rutherford (*English*)
Susan Sarandon (*U.S.*)
Delphine Seyrig (*French*)
Sarah Siddons (*English*)
Simone Signoret (*French*)
Maggie Smith (*English*)
Meryl Streep (*U.S.*)
Barbra Streisand (*U.S.*)
Janet Suzman (*South African*)
Elizabeth Taylor (*English-U.S.*)
Shirley Temple (*U.S.*)
Ellen Terry (*English*)
Emma Thompson (*English*)
Sybil Thorndike (*English*)
Sigourney Weaver (*U.S.*)
Raquel Welch (*U.S.*)
Mae West (*U.S.*)
Billie Whitelaw (*English*)
Kate Winslet (*English*)
Peg Woffington (*Irish*)
Catherine Zeta-Jones (*Welsh*)

WORD POWER

WORD POWER

### French regions

| | |
|---|---|
| Alsace | Île-de-France |
| Aquitaine | Languedoc-Roussillon |
| Auvergne | Limousin |
| Basse-Normandie | Lorraine |
| Brittany | Midi-Pyrénées |
| Burgundy | Nord-Pas-de-Calais |
| Centre | Pays de Loire |
| Champagne-Ardenne | Picardie |
| Corsica | Poitou-Charentes |
| Franche-Comté | Provence-Alpes-Côte d'Azur |
| Haute-Normandie | Rhône-Alpes |

### French départements

| | | |
|---|---|---|
| Ain | Corse | Haute Marne |
| Aisne | Cote d'Or | Haute Savoie |
| Allier | Côtes du Nord | Haute Vienne |
| Alpes de Haute Provence | Creuse | Hautes Alpes |
| Alpes Maritimes | Deux Sèvres | Hautes Pyrénées |
| Ardèche | Dordogne | Hauts de Seine |
| Ardennes | Doubs | Hérault |
| Ariège | Drôme | Ille et Vilaine |
| Aube | Essone | Indre |
| Aude | Eure | Indre et Loire |
| Aveyron | Eure et Loir | Isère |
| Bas Rhin | Finistère | Jura |
| Bouches du Rhône | Gard | Landes |
| Calvados | Gers | Loir et Cher |
| Cantal | Gironde | Loire |
| Charente | Guadeloupe | Loire Atlantique |
| Charente Maritime | Guyane | Loiret |
| Cher | Haut Rhin | Lot |
| Corrèze | Haute Garonne | Lot et Garonne |
| | Haute Loire | Lozère |

# ADMINISTRATIVE REGIONS

## French départements (continued)

Maine et Loire
Manche
Marne
Martinique
Mayenne
Meurthe et Moselle
Meuse
Morbihan
Moselle
Niveres
Nord
Oise
Orne
Paris

Pas de Calais
Puy de Dôme
Pyrénées Atlantiques
Pyrénées Orientales
Réunion
Rhône
Saône
Saône et Loire
Sarthe
Savoie
Seine et Marne
Seine Maritime
Seine Saint Denis
Somme

Tarn
Tarn et Garonne
Territoire de
 Belfort
Val d'Oise
Val de Marne
Var
Vaucluse
Vendée
Vienne
Vosges
Yonne
Yvelines

## German states

Baden-Württemberg
Bavaria
Berlin
Brandenburg
Bremen
Hamburg
Hessen
Lower Saxony

Mecklenburg-West Pomerania
North Rhine-Westphalia
Rhineland-Palatinate
Saarland
Saxony
Saxony-Anhalt
Schleswig-Holstein
Thuringia

## Italian regions

Abruzzo
Basilicata
Calabria
Campania
Emilia-Romagna
Friuli-Venezia
 Giulia

Lazio
Liguria
Lombardy
Marche
Molise
Piedmont
Puglia

Sardinia
Sicily
Trentino-Alto Adige
Tuscany
Umbria
Valle d'Aosta
Veneto

**WORD POWER**

*Italian provinces*

WORD POWER

| | | |
|---|---|---|
| Agrigento | Forlì | Pescara |
| Alessandria | Frosinone | Piacenza |
| Ancona | Genova | Pisa |
| Aosta | Gorizia | Pistoia |
| Arezzo | Grosseto | Pordenone |
| Ascoli Piceno | Imperia | Potenza |
| Asti | Isernia | Prato |
| Avellino | L'Aquila | Ragusa |
| Bari | La Spezia | Ravenna |
| Belluno | Latina | Reggio di Calabria |
| Benevento | Lecce | Reggio Emilia |
| Bergamo | Lecco | Rieti |
| Bologna | Livorno | Rimini |
| Bolzano | Lodi | Roma |
| Brescia | Lucca | Rovigo |
| Brindisi | Macerata | Salerno |
| Cagliari | Mantova | Sassari |
| Caltanissetta | Massa Carrara | Savona |
| Campobasso | Matera | Siena |
| Caserta | Messina | Siracusa |
| Catania | Milano | Sondrio |
| Catanzaro | Modena | Taranto |
| Chieti | Napoli | Teramo |
| Como | Novara | Terni |
| Cosenza | Nuoro | Torino |
| Cremona | Oristano | Trapani |
| Crotone | Padova | Trento |
| Cuneo | Palermo | Treviso |
| Enna | Parma | Trieste |
| Ferrara | Pavia | Udine |
| Firenze | Perugia | Varese |
| Foggia | Pesaro | Venezia |

# ADMINISTRATIVE REGIONS

*Italian provinces (continued)*

| | | |
|---|---|---|
| Verbania | Vibo Valentia | Repubblica di San |
| Vercelli | Vicenza | Marino |
| Verona | Viterbo | |

*Spanish regions*

| | | |
|---|---|---|
| Andalucía | Castilla-La Mancha | Murcia |
| Aragón | Castilla-León | Navarra |
| Asturias | Catalonia | Valencian |
| Balearic Islands | Extremadura | Community |
| Basque Country | Galicia | Ceuta |
| Canary Islands | La Rioja | Melilla |
| Cantabria | Madrid | |

*Spanish provinces*

| | | |
|---|---|---|
| Álava | Ciudad Real | Orense |
| Albacete | Girona | Palencia |
| Alhucemas | Granada | Pontevedra |
| Alicante | Gualalajara | Salamanca |
| Almeria | Guipúzcoa | Santa Cruz de |
| Asturias | Huelva | Tenerife |
| Ávila | Huesca | Segovia |
| Badajoz | Jaén | Sevilla |
| Balearics | La Coruna | Soria |
| Barcelona | La Rioja | Tarragona |
| Burgos | Las Palmas | Teruel |
| Cácares | León | Toledo |
| Cádiz | Lleida | Valencia |
| Cantabria | Lugo | Valladolid |
| Castellón | Madrid | Vélez de la Gomera |
| Chafarinas | Málaga | Vizcaya |
| Cordoba | Melilla | Zamora |
| Cuenca | Murcia | Zaragoza |
| Ceuta | Navarra | |

**WORD POWER**

11

Agostino di Duccio (*Italian*)

Josef Albers (*German-U.S.*)

Leon Battista Alberti (*Italian*)

Washington Allston (*U.S.*)

Lawrence Alma-Tadema
(*Dutch-English*)

Albrecht Altdorfer (*German*)

Fra Angelico (*Italian*)

Pietro Annigoni (*Italian*)

Antonello da Messina (*Italian*)

Apelles (*Greek*)

Karel Appel (*Dutch*)

Aleksandr Porfiryevich
Archipenko (*Russian*)

Giuseppe Arcimboldo
(*Italian*)

Jean *or* Hans Arp (*French*)

John James Audubon (*U.S.*)

Frank Auerbach (*English-
German*)

Francis Bacon (*Irish*)

Leon Nikolayevich Bakst
(*Russian*)

Balthus (*Polish-French*)

Frédéric August Bartholdi
(*French*)

Fra Bartolommeo (*Italian*)

Max Beckmann (*German*)

Vanessa Bell (*English*)

Giovanni Bellini (*Italian*)

Thomas Hart Benton
(*U.S.*)

Gian Lorenzo Bernini (*Italian*)

Joseph Beuys (*German*)

Peter Blake (*English*)

William Blake (*English*)

Umberto Boccioni (*Italian*)

David Bomberg (*English*)

Rosa Bonheur (*French*)

Pierre Bonnard (*French*)

Richard Parkes Bonnington
(*English*)

Gutzon Borglum (*U.S.*)

Hieronymus Bosch (*Dutch*)

Sandro Botticelli (*Italian*)

Francois Boucher (*French*)

Eugène Boudin (*French*)

Arthur Boyd (*Australian*)

Donato Bramante (*Italian*)

Constantin Brancusi
(*Romanian*)

Georges Braque (*French*)

Brassaï (*French*)

Agnolo Bronzino (*Italian*)

Ford Madox Brown (*English*)

Jan Brueghel (*Flemish*)

Pieter Brueghel the Elder
(*Flemish*)

Pieter Brueghel the Younger
(*Flemish*)

Bernard Buffet (*French*)

Edward Burne-Jones (*English*)

Edward Burra (*English*)

Reg Butler (*English*)

WORD POWER

# ARTISTS

Alexander Calder (*U.S.*)

Callimachus (*Greek*)

Robert Campin (*Flemish*)

Antonio Canova (*Italian*)

Michelangelo Merisi da Caravaggio (*Italian*)

Anthony Caro (*English*)

Vittore Carpaccio (*Italian*)

Agostino Carracci (*Italian*)

Annibale Carracci (*Italian*)

Ludovico Carracci (*Italian*)

Mary Cassatt (*U.S.*)

Pietro Cavallini (*Italian*)

Benvenuto Cellini (*Italian*)

Lynn Chadwick (*English*)

Marc Chagall (*Russian-French*)

Philippe de Champaigne (*French*)

Jean-Baptiste Siméon Chardin (*French*)

Giorgio de Chirico (*Italian*)

Giovanni Cimabue (*Italian*)

Claude Lorrain (*French*)

François Clouet (*French*)

Jean Clouet (*French*)

John Constable (*English*)

John Copley (*U.S.*)

Jean Baptiste Camille Corot (*French*)

Antonio Allegri da Corregio (*Italian*)

Gustave Courbet (*French*)

David Cox (*English*)

Antoine Coypel (*French*)

Lucas Cranach (*German*)

Walter Crane (*English*)

John Crome (*English*)

Aelbert Cuyp or Kuyp (*Dutch*)

Paul Cézanne (*French*)

Richard Dadd (*English*)

Salvador Dalí (*Spanish*)

Francis Danby (*Irish*)

Charles François Daubigny (*French*)

Honoré Daumier (*French*)

Jacques Louis David (*French*)

Peter de Wint (*English*)

Hilaire Germain Edgar Degas (*French*)

Eugène Delacroix (*French*)

Paul Delaroche (*French*)

Robert Delaunay (*French*)

Paul Delvaux (*Belgian*)

Maurice Denis (*French*)

André Derain (*French*)

William Dobell (*Australian*)

Domenichino (*Italian*)

Domenico del Barbiere (*Italian*)

Donatello (*Italian*)

Gerrit Dou (*Dutch*)

George Russell Drysdale (*Australian*)

13

# ARTISTS

Jean Dubuffet (*French*)

Duccio di Buoninsegna (*Italian*)

Marcel Duchamp (*French-U.S.*)

Raoul Dufy (*French*)

Albrecht Dürer (*German*)

Thomas Eakins (*U.S.*)

El Greco (*Greek-Spanish*)

James Ensor (*Belgian*)

Jacob Epstein (*British*)

Max Ernst (*German*)

Henri Fantin-Latour (*French*)

Lyonel Feininger (*U.S.*)

John Flaxman (*English*)

Jean Fouquet (*French*)

Jean Honoré Fragonard (*French*)

Lucian Freud (*English*)

Caspar David Friedrich (*German*)

Roger Fry (*English*)

Henry Fuseli (*Swiss*)

Naum Gabo (*Russian-U.S.*)

Thomas Gainsborough (*English*)

Henri Gaudier-Brzeska (*French*)

Paul Gauguin (*French*)

Gentile da Fabriano (*Italian*)

Lorenzo Ghiberti (*Italian*)

Domenico Ghirlandaio (*Italian*)

Alberto Giacometti (*Swiss*)

Giambologna (*Italian*)

Grinling Gibbons (*Dutch*)

Gilbert (Proesch) and George (Passmore) (*English*)

Eric Gill (*English*)

Giorgione da Castelfranco (*Italian*)

Giotto di Bondone (*Italian*)

Giulio Romano (*Italian*)

Hugo van der Goes (*Flemish*)

Julio González (*Spanish*)

Arshile Gorky (*U.S.*)

Francisco de Goya (*Spanish*)

Jan van Goyen (*Dutch*)

Duncan Grant (*Scottish*)

Jean Baptiste Greuze (*French*)

Juan Gris (*Spanish*)

Antoine Jean Gros (*French*)

George Grosz (*German-U.S.*)

Grünewald (*German*)

Francesco Guardi (*Italian*)

François Gérard (*French*)

Théodore Géricault (*French*)

Frans Hals (*Dutch*)

Richard Hamilton (*English*)

Ando Hiroshige (*Japanese*)

Damien Hirst (*English*)

Meindert Hobbema (*Dutch*)

# ARTISTS

David Hockney (*English*)
Hans Hofmann (*German-U.S.*)
William Hogarth (*English*)
Katsushika Hokusai (*Japanese*)
Hans Holbein (*German*)
Winslow Homer (*U.S.*)
Pieter de Hooch or Hoogh (*Dutch*)
Edward Hopper (*U.S.*)
Jean Antoine Houdon (*French*)
William Holman Hunt (*English*)
Jean Auguste Dominique Ingres (*French*)
Augustus John (*Welsh*)
Gwen John (*Welsh*)
Jasper Johns (*U.S.*)
Johan Barthold Jongkind (*Dutch*)
Jacob Jordaens (*Flemish*)
Wassily Kandinsky (*Russian*)
Angelica Kauffmann (*Swiss*)
Ernst Ludwig Kirchner (*German*)
Ron B. Kitaj (*U.S.*)
Paul Klee (*Swiss*)
Gustav Klimt (*Austrian*)
Franz Kline (*U.S.*)
Godfrey Kneller (*German-English*)

Laura Knight (*English*)
Oscar Kokoschka (*Austrian*)
Willem de Kooning (*Dutch-U.S.*)
Leon Kossoff (*English*)
Georges de La Tour (*French*)
Edwin Landseer (*English*)
Thomas Lawrence (*English*)
Charles Lebrun (*French*)
Fernand Léger (*French*)
Wilhelm Lehmbruck (*German*)
Frederic Leighton (*English*)
Peter Lely (*Dutch-English*)
Leonardo da Vinci (*Italian*)
Wyndham Lewis (*British*)
Roy Lichtenstein (*U.S.*)
Norman Alfred William Lindsay (*Australian*)
Jacques Lipchitz (*Lithuanian-U.S.*)
Filippino Lippi (*Italian*)
L(awrence) S(tephen) Lowry (*English*)
Lysippus (*Greek*)
Jan Mabuse (*Flemish*)
Charles Rennie Mackintosh (*Scottish*)
René Magritte (*Belgian*)
Aristide Maillol (*French*)
Kasimir Severinovich Malevich (*Russian*)

**WORD POWER**

15

**WORD POWER**

Edouard Manet (*French*)
Andrea Mantegna (*Italian*)
Franz Marc (*German*)
John Martin (*English*)
Simone Martini (*Italian*)
Masaccio (*Italian*)
Quentin Massys (*Flemish*)
Henri Matisse (*French*)
Hans Memling *or* Memlinc (*Flemish*)
Franz Xavier Messerschmidt (*Austrian*)
Ivan Mestrovic (*Yugoslav-U.S.*)
Michelangelo Buonarroti (*Italian*)
Michelozzi Michelozzo (*Italian*)
John Everett Millais (*English*)
Jean François Millet (*French*)
Joan Miró (*Spanish*)
Amedeo Modigliani (*Italian*)
László Moholy-Nagy (*Hungarian*)
Piet Mondrian (*Dutch*)
Claude Oscar Monet (*French*)
Henry Moore (*British*)
Gustave Moreau (*French*)
Berthe Morisot (*French*)
William Morris (*English*)
Samuel Finley Breese Morse (*U.S.*)
Grandma Moses (*U.S.*)

Edvard Munch (*Norwegian*)
Alfred Munnings (*English*)
Bartolomé Esteban Murillo (*Spanish*)
Myron (*Greek*)
Paul Nash (*English*)
Ernst Wilhelm Nay (*German*)
Barnett Newman (*U.S.*)
Ben Nicholson (*English*)
Sidney Nolan (*Australian*)
Emil Nolde (*German*)
Joseph Nollekens (*Dutch-English*)
Georgia O'Keefe (*U.S.*)
Claes Oldenburg (*Swedish-U.S.*)
Orcagna (*Italian*)
José Clemente Orozco (*Mexican*)
Jean Baptiste Oudry (*French*)
Palma Vecchio (*Italian*)
Samuel Palmer (*English*)
Eduardo Paolozzi (*Scottish*)
Parmigianino (*Italian*)
Victor Pasmore (*English*)
Joachim Patinir *or* Patenier (*Flemish*)
Perugino (*Italian*)
Baldassare Peruzzi (*Italian*)
Antoine Pevsner (*Russian-French*)
Phidias (*Greek*)

Francis Picabia (*French*)

Pablo Picasso (*Spanish*)

Piero della Francesca (*Italian*)

Piero di Cosimo (*Italian*)

Pietro da Cortona (*Italian*)

Jean Baptiste Pigalle (*French*)

Germain Pilon (*French*)

Pinturicchio (*Italian*)

John Piper (*English*)

Pisanello (*Italian*)

Andrea Pisano (*Italian*)

Giovanni Pisano (*Italian*)

Nicola Pisano (*Italian*)

Camille Pissarro (*French*)

Antonio del Pollaiuolo (*Italian*)

Piero del Pollaiuolo (*Italian*)

Jackson Pollock (*U.S.*)

Polyclitus (*Greek*)

Polygnotus (*Greek*)

Pontormo (*Italian*)

Paulus Potter (*Dutch*)

Nicolas Poussin (*French*)

Praxiteles (*Greek*)

Pierre Paul Prud'hon (*French*)

Pierre Puget (*French*)

Pierre Puvis de Chavannes (*French*)

Jacopa della Quercia (*Italian*)

Arthur Rackham (*English*)

Henry Raeburn (*Scottish*)

Allan Ramsay (*Scottish*)

Raphael (*Italian*)

Robert Rauschenberg (*U.S.*)

Man Ray (*U.S.*)

Odilon Redon (*French*)

Rembrandt Harmensz van Rijn (*Dutch*)

Guido Reni (*Italian*)

Pierre Auguste Renoir (*French*)

Joshua Reynolds (*English*)

José de Ribera (*Spanish*)

Bridget Riley (*English*)

Diego Rivera (*Mexican*)

Andrea della Robbia (*Italian*)

Luca della Robbia (*Italian*)

Alexander Mikhailovich Rodchenko (*Russian*)

Auguste Rodin (*French*)

George Romney (*English*)

Salvator Rosa (*Italian*)

Dante Gabriel Rossetti (*English*)

Mark Rothko (*U.S.*)

Geroges Rouault (*French*)

Louis-François Roubiliac or Roubillac (*French*)

Henri Julien Rousseau (*French*)

Théodore Rousseau (*French*)

Peter Paul Rubens (*Flemish*)

Rublyov or Rublev Andrei (*Russian*)

**WORD POWER**

**WORD POWER**

Jacob van Ruisdael (*Dutch*)

Philipp Otto Runge (*German*)

Salomen van Ruysdael (*Dutch*)

John Singer Sargent (*U.S.*)

Egon Schiele (*Austrian*)

Martin Schongauer (*German*)

Kurt Schwitters (*German*)

Scopas (*Greek*)

Maurice Sendak (*U.S.*)

Sesshu (*Japanese*)

Georges Seurat (*French*)

Ben Shahn (*U.S.*)

Walter Richard Sickert (*British*)

Paul Signac (*French*)

Luca Signorelli (*Italian*)

David Alfaro Siqueiros (*Mexican*)

Alfred Sisley (*French*)

John Sloan (*U.S.*)

Claus Sluter (*Dutch*)

David Smith (*U.S.*)

Chaim Soutine (*Lithuanian-French*)

Stanley Spencer (*English*)

Jan Steen (*Dutch*)

Veit Stoss (*German*)

George Stubbs (*English*)

Graham Sutherland (*English*)

Yves Tanguy (*French*)

Vladimir Tatlin (*Russian*)

David Teniers the Elder (*Flemish*)

David Teniers the Younger (*Flemish*)

Gerard Ter Borch or Terborch (*Dutch*)

Hendrik Terbrugghen (*Dutch*)

James Thornhill (*English*)

Bertel Thorvaldsen (*Danish*)

Giambattista Tiepolo (*Italian*)

Jacopo Tintoretto (*Italian*)

James Jacques Joseph Tissot (*French*)

Titian (*Italian*)

Henri Marie Raymond de Toulouse-Lautrec (*French*)

J(oseph) M(allord) W(illiam) Turner (*English*)

Paolo Uccello (*Italian*)

Utagawa Kuniyoshi (*Japanese*)

Maurice Utrillo (*French*)

Adriaen van de Velde (*Dutch*)

Willem van de Velde the Elder (*Dutch*)

Willem van de Velde the Younger (*Dutch*)

Rogier van der Weyden (*Flemish*)

Anthony Van Dyck (*Flemish*)

Jan van Eyck (*Flemish*)

Vincent van Gogh (*Dutch*)

## ARTISTS

Victor Vasarely (*Hungarian-French*)

Giorgio Vasari (*Italian*)

Diego Rodríguez de Silva y Velázquez (*Spanish*)

Jan Vermeer (*Dutch*)

Paolo Veronese (*Italian*)

Andrea del Verrocchio (*Italian*)

Élisabeth Vigée-Lebrun (*French*)

Jacques Villon (*French*)

Maurice de Vlaminck (*French*)

Andy Warhol (*U.S.*)

Jean Antoine Watteau (*French*)

George Frederick Watts (*English*)

Benjamin West (*U.S.*)

James Abbott McNeill Whistler (*U.S.*)

Richard Wilson (*Welsh*)

Joseph Wright (*English*)

Xia Gui *or* Hsia Kuei (*Chinese*)

Zeuxis (*Greek*)

Johann Zoffany (*German*)

Anders Zorn (*Swedish*)

Gaetano Giulio Zumbo (*Italian*)

Francisco Zurbarán (*Spanish*)

WORD POWER

# — AUSTRALIAN STATES AND TERRITORIES —

Australian Capital Territory

New South Wales

Northern Territory

Queensland

South Australia

Tasmania

Victoria

Western Australia

## —— CANADIAN PROVINCES ——

| Province | Abbreviation | Province | Abbreviation |
|---|---|---|---|
| Alberta | AB | Nova Scotia | NS |
| British Columbia | BC | Nunavut | NU |
| Manitoba | MB | Ontario | ON |
| New Brunswick | NB | Prince Edward Island | PE |
| Newfoundland and | NFL | Quebec | QC |
| Labrador | | Saskatchewan | SK |
| Northwest Territories | NT | Yukon | YT |

**WORD POWER**

| *City* | *Country* |
|---|---|
| Abu Dhabi | United Arab Emirates |
| Abuja | Nigeria |
| Accra | Ghana |
| Addis Ababa | Ethiopia |
| Astana | Kazakhstan |
| Algiers | Algeria |
| Amman | Jordan |
| Amsterdam | Netherlands |
| Andorra la Vella | Andorra |
| Ankara | Turkey |
| Antananarivo | Madagascar |
| Apia | Samoa |
| Ashkhabad | Turkmenistan |
| Asmara | Eritrea |
| Asunción | Paraguay |
| Athens | Greece |
| Baghdad | Iraq |
| Baku | Azerbaijan |
| Bamako | Mali |
| Bandar Seri Begawan | Brunei |
| Bangkok | Thailand |
| Bangui | Central African Republic |
| Banjul | Gambia |
| Basseterre | St. Kitts and Nevis |
| Beijing | People's Republic of China |
| Beirut *or* Beyrouth | Lebanon |
| Belfast | Northern Ireland |
| Belgrade | Yugoslavia (Serbia and Montenegro) |
| Belmopan | Belize |
| Berlin | Germany |

WORD POWER

# —— CAPITAL CITIES ——

WORD POWER

| City | Country |
|------|---------|
| *Berne* | Switzerland |
| Bishkek | Kyrgyzstan |
| Bissau | Guinea-Bissau |
| Bloemfontein | judicial capital of South Africa |
| Bogotá | Colombia |
| Brasília | Brazil |
| Bratislava | Slovakia |
| Brazzaville | Congo (Republic of) |
| Bridgetown | Barbados |
| Brussels | Belgium |
| Bucharest | Romania |
| Budapest | Hungary |
| Buenos Aires | Argentina |
| Bujumbura | Burundi |
| Cairo | Egypt |
| Canberra | Australia |
| Cape Town | legislative capital of South Africa |
| Caracas | Venezuela |
| Cardiff | Wales |
| Castries | St. Lucia |
| Cayenne | French Guiana |
| Colombo | Sri Lanka |
| Conakry *or* Konakry | Guinea |
| Copenhagen | Denmark |
| Dakar | Senegal |
| Damascus | Syria |
| Delhi | India |
| Dhaka *or* Dacca | Bangladesh |
| Dili | East Timor |
| Djibouti *or* Jibouti | Djibouti *or* Jibouti |
| Dodoma | Tanzania |

22

# —— CAPITAL CITIES ——

| City | Country |
|------|---------|
| Doha | Qatar |
| Douglas | Isle of Man |
| Dublin | Republic of Ireland |
| Dushanbe | Tajikistan |
| Edinburgh | Scotland |
| Fort-de-France | Martinique |
| Freetown | Sierra Leone |
| Funafuti | Tuvalu |
| Gaborone | Botswana |
| Georgetown | Guyana |
| Guatemala | Guatemala City |
| Hanoi | Vietnam |
| Harare | Zimbabwe |
| Havana | Cuba |
| Helsinki | Finland |
| Honiara | Solomon Islands |
| Islamabad | Pakistan |
| Jakarta *or* Djakarta | Indonesia |
| Jerusalem | Israel |
| Kabul | Afghanistan |
| Kampala | Uganda |
| Katmandu *or* Kathmandu | Nepal |
| Khartoum *or* Khartum | Sudan |
| Kiev | Ukraine |
| Kigali | Rwanda |
| Kingston | Jamaica |
| Kingstown | St. Vincent and the Grenadines |
| Kinshasa | Congo (Democratic Republic of) |
| Kishinev | Moldova |
| Palikir | Micronesia |
| Koror | Palau |

23

**WORD POWER**

| *City* | *Country* |
|--------|-----------|
| Kuala Lumpur | Malaysia |
| Kuwait | Kuwait |
| La Paz | administrative capital of Bolivia |
| Libreville | Gabon |
| Lilongwe | Malawi |
| Lima | Peru |
| Lisbon | Portugal |
| Ljubljana | Slovenia |
| Lomé | Togo |
| London | United Kingdom |
| Luanda | Angola |
| Lusaka | Zambia |
| Luxembourg | Luxembourg |
| Madrid | Spain |
| Majuro | Marshall Islands |
| Malabo | Equatorial Guinea |
| Malé | Maldives |
| Managua | Nicaragua |
| Manama | Bahrain |
| Manila | Philippines |
| Maputo | Mozambique |
| Maseru | Lesotho |
| Mbabane | Swaziland |
| Mexico City | Mexico |
| Minsk | Belarus |
| Mogadishu | Somalia |
| Monaco-Ville | Monaco |
| Monrovia | Liberia |
| Montevideo | Uruguay |
| Moroni | Comoros |
| Moscow | Russia |

# —— CAPITAL CITIES ——

| *City* | *Country* |
|--------|-----------|
| Muscat | Oman |
| Nairobi | Kenya |
| Nassau | Bahamas |
| Ndjamena | Chad |
| Niamey | Niger |
| Nicosia | Cyprus |
| Nouakchott | Mauritania |
| Nuku'alofa | Tonga |
| Nuuk | Greenland |
| Oslo | Norway |
| Ottawa | Canada |
| Ouagadougou | Burkina-Faso |
| Panama City | Panama |
| Paramaribo | Suriname |
| Paris | France |
| Phnom Penh | Cambodia |
| Pishpek | Kirghizia |
| Port-au-Prince | Haiti |
| Port Louis | Mauritius |
| Port Moresby | Papua New Guinea |
| Port of Spain | Trinidad and Tobago |
| Porto Novo | Benin |
| Prague | Czech Republic |
| Praia | Cape Verde |
| Pretoria | administrative capital of South Africa |
| Pristina | Kosovo (Federal Republic of Yugoslavia) |
| Pyongyang | North Korea |
| Quito | Ecuador |
| Rabat | Morocco |

WORD POWER

# CAPITAL CITIES

| City | Country |
|---|---|
| Reykjavik | Iceland |
| Riga | Latvia |
| Riyadh | Saudi Arabia |
| Rome | Italy |
| Roseau | Dominica |
| Sana'a | Yemen |
| San José | Costa Rica |
| San Juan | Puerto Rico |
| San Marino | San Marino |
| San Salvador | El Salvador |
| Santiago | Chile |
| Santo Domingo | Dominican Republic |
| São Tomé | São Tomé and Principe |
| Sarajevo | Bosnia and Herzegovina |
| Seoul | South Korea |
| Singapore | Singapore |
| Skopje | Macedonia |
| Sofia | Bulgaria |
| St. George's | Grenada |
| St. John's | Antigua and Barbuda |
| Stockholm | Sweden |
| Sucre | legislative and judicial capital of Bolivia |
| Suva | Fiji |
| Taipei | Taiwan |
| Tallinn | Estonia |
| Tarawa | Kiribati |
| Tashkent | Uzbekistan |
| Tbilisi | Georgia |
| Tegucigalpa | Honduras |
| Tehran | Iran |

| City | Country |
|------|---------|
| Tel Aviv | Israel |
| Thimphu | Bhutan |
| Tirana | Albania |
| Tokyo | Japan |
| Tripoli | Libya |
| Tunis | Tunisia |
| Ulan Bator | Mongolia |
| Vaduz | Liechtenstein |
| Valletta | Malta |
| Vatican City | Vatican City |
| Victoria | Seychelles |
| Vienna | Austria |
| Vientiane | Laos |
| Port Vila | Vanuatu |
| Vilnius | Lithuania |
| Warsaw | Poland |
| Washington DC | United States of America |
| Wellington | New Zealand |
| Windhoek | Namibia |
| Yamoussoukro | Côte d'Ivoire |
| Yangon (Rangoon) | Myanmar (Burma) |
| Yaoundé or Yaunde | Cameroon |
| Yaren | Nauru |
| Yerevan | Armenia |
| Zagreb | Croatia |

**WORD POWER**

27

# COUNTIES

*English counties*

Bedfordshire
Berkshire
Bristol
Buckinghamshire
Cambridgeshire
Cheshire
Cornwall
Cumbria
Derbyshire
Devon
Dorset
Durham
East Riding of Yorkshire
East Sussex
Essex
Gloucestershire
Greater London
Greater Manchester
Hampshire
Herefordshire
Hertfordshire
Isle of Wight
Kent
Lancashire

Leicestershire
Lincolnshire
Merseyside
Norfolk
Northamptonshire
Northumberland
North Yorkshire
Nottinghamshire
Oxfordshire
Rutland
Shropshire
Somerset
South Yorkshire
Staffordshire
Suffolk
Surrey
Tyne and Wear
Warwickshire
West Midlands
West Sussex
West Yorkshire
Wiltshire
Worcestershire

*Scottish counties*

Aberdeen City
Aberdeenshire
Angus
Argyll and Bute
City of Edinburgh
Clackmannanshire

Dumfries and Galloway
Dundee City
East Ayrshire
East Dunbartonshire
East Lothian
East Renfrewshire

# ——— COUNTIES ———

*Scottish counties (continued)*

| | |
|---|---|
| Falkirk | Perth and Kinross |
| Fife | Renfrewshire |
| Glasgow City | Scottish Borders |
| Highland | Shetland |
| Inverclyde | South Ayrshire |
| Midlothian | South Lanarkshire |
| Moray | Stirling |
| North Ayrshire | West Dunbartonshire |
| North Lanarkshire | Western Isles (Eilean Siar) |
| Orkney | West Lothian |

*Welsh counties*

| | | |
|---|---|---|
| Clwyd | Gwynedd | South Glamorgan |
| Dyfed | Mid Glamorgan | West Glamorgan |
| Gwent | Powys | |

*Northern Irish counties*

| | | |
|---|---|---|
| Antrim | Down | Londonderry City |
| Armagh | Fermanagh | Tyrone |
| Belfast City | Londonderry | |

*Republic of Ireland counties*

| | | |
|---|---|---|
| Carlow | Kilkenny | Offaly |
| Cavan | Laois | Roscommon |
| Clare | Leitrim | Sligo |
| Cork | Limerick | Tipperary |
| Donegal | Longford | Waterford |
| Dublin | Louth | Westmeath |
| Galway | Mayo | Wexford |
| Kerry | Meath | Wicklow |
| Kildare | Monaghan | |

WORD POWER

WORD POWER

| | |
|---|---|
| Afghanistan | Chad |
| Albania | Chile |
| Algeria | Colombia |
| American Samoa | Comoros |
| Andorra | Congo (Republic of) |
| Angola | Congo (Democratic Republic of) |
| Antigua and Barbuda | |
| Argentina | Costa Rica |
| Armenia | Côte d'Ivoire |
| Australia | Croatia |
| Austria | Cuba |
| Azerbaijan | Cyprus |
| Bahamas | Czech Republic |
| Bahrain | Denmark |
| Bangladesh | Djibouti |
| Barbados | Dominica |
| Belarus | Dominican Republic |
| Belau | East Timor |
| Belgium | Ecuador |
| Belize | Egypt |
| Benin | El Salvador |
| Bhutan | England |
| Bolivia | Equatorial Guinea |
| Bosnia and Herzegovina | Eritrea |
| Botswana | Estonia |
| Brazil | Ethiopia |
| Brunei | Fiji |
| Bulgaria | Finland |
| Burkina-Faso | France |
| Burundi | Gabon |
| Cambodia | Gambia |
| Cameroon | Georgia |
| Canada | Germany |
| Cape Verde | Ghana |
| Central African Republic | Greece |

# —— COUNTRIES ——

| | |
|---|---|
| Greenland | Malawi |
| Grenada | Malaysia |
| Guatemala | Mali |
| Guinea | Malta |
| Guinea-Bissau | Marshall Islands |
| Guyana | Mauritania |
| Haiti | Mauritius |
| Honduras | Mexico |
| Hungary | Micronesia |
| Iceland | Moldova |
| India | Monaco |
| Indonesia | Mongolia |
| Iran | Morocco |
| Iraq | Mozambique |
| Israel | Myanmar |
| Italy | Namibia |
| Jamaica | Nauru |
| Japan | Nepal |
| Jordan | Netherlands |
| Kazakhstan | New Zealand |
| Kenya | Nicaragua |
| Kirghizia | Niger |
| Kiribati | Nigeria |
| Kuwait | Northern Ireland |
| Laos | North Korea |
| Latvia | Norway |
| Lebanon | Oman |
| Lesotho | Pakistan |
| Liberia | Panama |
| Libya | Papua New Guinea |
| Liechtenstein | Paraguay |
| Lithuania | People's Republic of China |
| Luxembourg | Peru |
| Macedonia | Philippines |
| Madagascar | Poland |

31

Portugal
Puerto Rico
Qatar
Republic of Ireland
Republic of Maldives
Romania
Russia
Rwanda
St Kitts and Nevis
St Lucia
St Vincent and the Grenadines
Samoa
San Marino
São Tomé and Principe
Saudi Arabia
Scotland
Senegal
Seychelles
Sierra Leone
Singapore
Slovakia
Slovenia
Solomon Islands
Somalia
South Africa
South Korea
Spain
Sri Lanka
Sudan
Surinam
Swaziland

Sweden
Switzerland
Syria
Taiwan
Tajikistan
Tanzania
Thailand
Togo
Tonga
Trinidad and Tobago
Tunisia
Turkey
Turkmenistan
Tuvalu
Uganda
Ukraine
United Arab Emirates
United Kingdom
United States of America
Uruguay
Uzbekistan
Vanuatu
Vatican City
Venezuela
Vietnam
Wales
Yemen
Yugoslavia (Serbia and
    Montenegro)
Zambia
Zimbabwe

WORD POWER

| Country | Currency |
| --- | --- |
| Afghanistan | afghani |
| Albania | lek |
| Algeria | Algerian dinar |
| Andorra | euro |
| Angola | kwanza |
| Antigua and Barbuda | East Caribbean dollar |
| Argentina | peso |
| Armenia | dram |
| Australia | Australian dollar |
| Austria | euro |
| Azerbaijan | manat |
| Bahamas | Bahamian dollar |
| Bahrain | dinar |
| Bangladesh | taka |
| Barbados | Barbados dollar |
| Belarus | rouble |
| Belgium | euro |
| Belize | Belize dollar |
| Benin | CFA franc |
| Bhutan | ngultrum |
| Bolivia | boliviano |
| Bosnia-Herzegovina | convertible marka |
| Botswana | pula |
| Brazil | real |
| Brunei | Brunei dollar |
| Bulgaria | lev |
| Burkina-Faso | CFA franc |
| Burundi | Burundi franc |
| Cambodia | riel |
| Cameroon | CFA franc |
| Canada | Canadian dollar |
| Cape Verde | escudo |
| Central African Republic | CFA franc |

33

| Country | Currency |
| --- | --- |
| *Country* | *Currency* |
| Chad | CFA franc |
| Chile | peso |
| China | yuan |
| Colombia | peso |
| Comoros | Comorian franc |
| Congo (Republic of) | CFA franc |
| Congo (Democratic Republic of) | Congolese franc |
| Costa Rica | cólon |
| Côte d'Ivoire | CFA franc |
| Croatia | kuna |
| Cuba | peso |
| Cyprus | pound |
| Czech Republic | koruna |
| Denmark | krone |
| Djibouti | Djibouti franc |
| Dominica | East Caribbean dollar |
| Dominican Republic | peso |
| East Timor | US dollar |
| Ecuador | US dollar |
| Egypt | pound |
| El Salvador | cólon |
| Equatorial Guinea | CFA franc |
| Eritrea | nakfa |
| Estonia | kroon |
| Ethiopia | birr |
| Fiji | Fiji dollar |
| Finland | euro |
| France | euro |
| French Guiana | French franc |
| Gabon | CFA franc |
| Gambia | dalasi |
| Germany | euro |
| Ghana | cedi |

| Country | Currency |
|---|---|
| Greece | euro |
| Greenland | Danish krone |
| Grenada | East Caribbean dollar |
| Guatemala | quetzal |
| Guinea | Guinea franc |
| Guinea-Bissau | CFA franc |
| Guyana | Guyana dollar |
| Haiti | gourde |
| Honduras | lempira |
| Hungary | forint |
| Iceland | krona |
| India | rupee |
| Indonesia | rupiah |
| Iran | rial |
| Iraq | dinar |
| Ireland (Republic of) | euro |
| Israel | shekel |
| Italy | euro |
| Jamaica | Jamaican dollar |
| Japan | yen |
| Jordan | dinar |
| Kazakhstan | tenge |
| Kenya | shilling |
| Kirghizia | som |
| Kiribati | Australian dollar |
| Kosovo | dinar; euro |
| Kuwait | dinar |
| Kyrgyzstan | som |
| Laos | kip |
| Latvia | lat |
| Lebanon | pound |
| Lesotho | loti |
| Liberia | Liberian dollar |

**WORD POWER**

## CURRENCIES

| Country | Currency |
|---------|----------|
| Libya | dinar |
| Liechtenstein | Swiss franc |
| Lithuania | litas |
| Luxembourg | euro |
| Macedonia | denar |
| Madagascar | Malagasy franc |
| Malawi | kwacha |
| Malaysia | ringgit |
| Maldives (Republic of) | rufiyaa |
| Mali | CFA franc |
| Malta | lira |
| Marshall Islands | U.S. dollar |
| Mauritania | ouguiya |
| Mauritius | rupee |
| Mexico | peso |
| Micronesia | U.S. dollar |
| Moldova | leu |
| Monaco | French franc |
| Mongolia | tugrik |
| Montenegro | euro |
| Montserrat | East Caribbean dollar |
| Morocco | dirham |
| Mozambique | metical |
| Myanmar | kyat |
| Namibia | Namibian dollar |
| Nauru | Australian dollar |
| Nepal | rupee |
| Netherlands | euro |
| New Zealand | New Zealand dollar |
| Nicaragua | córdoba |
| Niger | CFA franc |
| Nigeria | naira |
| North Korea | won |

WORD POWER

| Country | Currency |
|---------|----------|
| Norway | krone |
| Oman | rial |
| Pakistan | rupee |
| Palau | U.S. dollar |
| Panama | balboa |
| Papua New Guinea | kina |
| Paraguay | guarani |
| Peru | new sol |
| Philippines | Philippine peso |
| Poland | zloty |
| Portugal | euro |
| Qatar | riyal |
| Romania | leu |
| Russia | rouble |
| Rwanda | Rwanda franc |
| St. Kitts and Nevis | East Caribbean dollar |
| St. Lucia | East Caribbean dollar |
| St. Vincent and the Grenadines | East Caribbean dollar |
| Samoa | tala |
| San Marino | euro |
| São Tomé and Principe | dobra |
| Saudi Arabia | riyal |
| Senegal | CFA franc |
| Seychelles | rupee |
| Sierra Leone | leone |
| Singapore | Singapore dollar |
| Slovakia | koruna |
| Slovenia | tolar |
| Solomon Islands | Solomon Islands dollar |
| Somalia | shilling |
| South Africa | rand |
| South Korea | won |
| Spain | euro |

WORD POWER

37

| Country | Currency |
| --- | --- |
| Sri Lanka | rupee |
| Sudan | dinar |
| Surinam | guilder |
| Swaziland | lilangeni |
| Sweden | krona |
| Switzerland | Swiss franc |
| Syria | pound |
| Taiwan | Taiwan dollar |
| Tajikistan | somoni |
| Tanzania | shilling |
| Thailand | baht |
| Togo | CFA franc |
| Tonga | pa'anga |
| Trinidad and Tobago | Trinidad and Tobago dollar |
| Tunisia | dinar |
| Turkey | Turkish lira |
| Turkmenistan | manat |
| Tuvalu | Australian dollar |
| Uganda | shilling |
| Ukraine | hryvna |
| United Arab Emirates | dirham |
| United Kingdom | pound sterling |
| United States of America | U.S. dollar |
| Uruguay | peso |
| Uzbekistan | sum |
| Vanuatu | vatu |
| Vatican City | euro |
| Venezuela | bolívar |
| Vietnam | dong |
| Yemen | riyal |
| Yugoslavia (Serbia) | dinar |
| Zambia | kwacha |
| Zimbabwe | Zimbabwe dollar |

Aeschylus (*Greek*)

Edward Albee (*U.S.*)

Robert Amos (*Australian*)

Jean Anouilh (*French*)

Aristophanes (*Greek*)

Alan Ayckbourn (*English*)

Pierre Augustin Caron de Beaumarchais (*French*)

Francis Beaumont (*English*)

Samuel Beckett (*Irish*)

Brendan Behan (*Irish*)

Richard Beynon (*Australian*)

Alan Bleasdale (*English*)

Edward Bond (*English*)

Bertolt Brecht (*German*)

Eugene Brieux (*French*)

Pedro Calderón de la Barca (*Spanish*)

George Chapman (*English*)

Anton Pavlovich Chekhov (*Russian*)

William Congreve (*English*)

Pierre Corneille (*French*)

Noël (Pierce) Coward (*English*)

Thomas Dekker (*English*)

John Dryden (*English*)

T(homas) S(tearns) Eliot (*U.S.-British*)

Louis Esson (*Australian*)

Euripides (*Greek*)

John Fletcher (*English*)

Dario Fo (*Italian*)

John Ford (*English*)

Brian Friel (*English*)

John Galsworthy (*English*)

Jean Genet (*French*)

W(illiam) S(chwenk) Gilbert (*English*)

(Hippolyte) Jean Giraudoux (*French*)

Johann Wolfgang von Goethe (*German*)

Nikolai Gogol (*Russian*)

Oliver Goldsmith (*Irish*)

Oriel Gray (*Australian*)

Robert Greene (*English*)

David Hare (*English*)

Gerhart Johann Robert Hauptmann (*German*)

Václav Havel (*Czech*)

Alfred Hayes (*U.S.*)

(Christian) Friedrich Hebbel (*German*)

Dorthy Hewett (*Australian*)

Thomas Heywood (*English*)

Jack Hibberd (*Australian*)

Sidney Howard (*U.S.*)

Henrik Ibsen (*Norwegian*)

William Motter Inge (*U.S.*)

Eugène Ionesco (*Romanian-French*)

Ben Jonson (*English*)

George Kaiser (*German*)

39

# DRAMATISTS

Tony Kushner (*U.S.*)
Thomas Kyd (*English*)
Ray Lawler (*Australian*)
Liz Lochhead (*Scottish*)
Lope de Vega (*Spanish*)
Federico Garcia Lorca (*Spanish*)
Maurice Maeterlinck (*Belgian*)
David Mamet (*U.S.*)
Christopher Marlowe (*English*)
John Marston (*English*)
Menander (*Greek*)
Arthur Miller (*U.S.*)
Molière (*French*)
Barry Oakley (*Australian*)
Sean O'Casey (*Irish*)
Eugene (Gladstone) O'Neill (*U.S.*)
Joe Orton (*English*)
John Osborne (*English*)
Thomas Otway (*English*)
John Patrick (*U.S.*)
Arthur Wing Pinero (*English*)
Harold Pinter (*English*)
Luigi Pirandello (*Italian*)
Titus Maccius Plautus (*Roman*)
Hal Porter (*Australian*)
Aleksander Sergeyevich Pushkin (*Russian*)
Jean Baptiste Racine (*French*)

Terence Mervyn Rattigan (*English*)
John Romeril (*Australian*)
Willy Russell (*English*)
Thomas Sackville (*English*)
Jean-Paul Sartre (*French*)
Johann Christoph Friedrich von Schiller (*German*)
Lucius Annaeus Seneca (*Roman*)
Alan Seymour (*Australian*)
Peter Shaffer (*English*)
William Shakespeare (*English*)
George Bernard Shaw (*Irish*)
Sam Shepard (*U.S.*)
Richard Brinsley Sheridan (*Irish*)
Robert Sherwood (*U.S.*)
Sophocles (*Greek*)
Wole Soyinka (*Nigerian*)
Tom Stoppard (*Czech-English*)
August Strindberg (*Swedish*)
John Millington Synge (*Irish*)
John Webster (*English*)
Oscar Wilde (*Irish*)
Thornton Wilder (*U.S.*)
Tennessee Williams (*U.S.*)
David Keith Williamson (*Australian*)
William Wycherly (*English*)

# EUROPEAN UNION

*EU member states*

| | |
|---|---|
| 1958 Belgium | 1973 United Kingdom |
| 1958 France | 1981 Greece |
| 1958 Germany | 1986 Portugal |
| 1958 Italy | 1986 Spain |
| 1958 Luxembourg | 1995 Finland |
| 1958 The Netherlands | 1995 Sweden |
| 1973 Denmark | 1995 Austria |
| 1973 Republic of Ireland | |

*EU applications under consideration*

| | |
|---|---|
| Cyprus | Poland |
| Estonia | Switzerland |
| Hungary | Czech Republic |

# NEW ZEALAND TERRITORIES

| | |
|---|---|
| Cook Islands | the Ross Dependency |
| Niue | Tokelau *or* Union Islands |

WORD POWER

Peter Abrahams (*South African*)
Chinua Achebe (*Nigerian*)
Peter Ackroyd (*English*)
Douglas Adams (*English*)
Richard Adams (*English*)
Alain-Fournier (*French*)
Brian Aldiss (*English*)
James Aldridge (*Australian*)
Al Alvarez (*English*)
Eric Ambler (*English*)
Kingsley Amis (*English*)
Martin Amis (*English*)
Mulk Raj Anand (*Indian*)
Maya Angelou (*U.S.*)
Lucius Apuleius (*Roman*)
Jeffrey Archer (*English*)
Isaac Asimov (*U.S.*)
Margaret Atwood (*Canadian*)
Louis Auchincloss (*U.S.*)
Jane Austen (*English*)
Beryl Bainbridge (*English*)
R M Ballantyne (*Scottish*)
J G Ballard (*English*)
Honoré de Balzac (*French*)
Iain Banks (*Scottish*)
Lynne Reid Banks (*English*)
Elspeth Barker (*Scottish*)
Pat Barker (*English*)
Julian Barnes (*English*)
Stanley Barstow (*English*)
John Barth (*U.S.*)
H E Bates (*English*)

Nina Bawden (*English*)
Simone de Beauvoir (*French*)
Sybille Bedford (*British*)
Max Beerbohm (*English*)
Aphra Behn (*English*)
Saul Bellow (*Canadian*)
Andrei Bely (*Russian*)
David Benedictus (*English*)
(Enoch) Arnold Bennett (*English*)
John Berger (*English*)
Thomas Berger (*U.S.*)
Maeve Binchy (*Irish*)
R(ichard) D(oddridge) Blackmore (*English*)
Alan Bleasdale (*English*)
Heinrich Böll (*German*)
Elizabeth Bowen (*Irish*)
Paul Bowles (*U.S.*)
William Boyd (*Scottish*)
Malcolm Bradbury (*English*)
Barbara Taylor Bradford (*English*)
Melvin Bragg (*English*)
John Braine (*English*)
André Brink (*South African*)
Vera Brittain (*English*)
Louis Bromfield (*U.S.*)
Anne Brontë (*English*)
Charlotte Brontë (*English*)
Emily (Jane) Brontë (*English*)
Christina Brooke-Rose (*English*)

Anita Brookner (*English*)

Brigid Brophy (*English*)

George Douglas Brown (*Scottish*)

George Mackay Brown (*Scottish*)

John Buchan (*Scottish*)

Pearl Buck (*U.S.*)

Mikhail Afanaseyev Bulgakov (*Russian*)

John Bunyan (*English*)

Anthony Burgess (*British*)

Fanny Burney (*English*)

Edgar Rice Burroughs (*U.S.*)

William Burroughs (*U.S.*)

Samuel Butler (*English*)

A S Byatt (*English*)

Italo Calvino (*Italian*)

Albert Camus (*French*)

Elias Canetti (*Bulgarian*)

Truman Capote (*U.S.*)

Peter Carey (*Australian*)

Angela Carter (*English*)

Barbara Cartland (*English*)

Willa Cather (*U.S.*)

Camilo José Cela (*Spanish*)

Miguel de Cervantes (*Spanish*)

Raymond Chandler (*U.S.*)

G K Chesterton (*English*)

Agatha (Mary Clarissa) Christie (*English*)

Arthur C Clarke (*English*)

James Clavell (*U.S.*)

Jon Cleary (*Australian*)

J M Coetzee (*South African*)

Colette (*French*)

(William) Wilkie Collins (*English*)

Ivy Compton-Burnett (*English*)

Richard Condon (*U.S.*)

Evan Connell (*U.S.*)

Joseph Conrad (*Polish-British*)

Catherine Cookson (*English*)

James Fenimore Cooper (*U.S.*)

Jilly Cooper (*English*)

William Cooper (*English*)

Maria Correlli (*English*)

Stephen Crane (*U.S.*)

Lionel Davidson (*English*)

(William) Robertson Davies (*Canadian*)

Daniel Defoe (*English*)

Len Deighton (*English*)

E M Delafield (*English*)

Don DeLillo (*U.S.*)

Thomas de Quincy (*English*)

Anita Desai (*Indian*)

Peter De Vries (*U.S.*)

Charles (John Huffam) Dickens (*English*)

Monica Dickens (*English*)

Joan Didion (*U.S.*)

Isak Dinesen (*Danish*)

Benjamin Disraeli (*English*)

J P Donleavy (*Irish*)

WORD POWER

43

# —— NOVELISTS ——

John Roderigo Dos Passos (*U.S.*)

Fyodor Mikhailovich Dostoevsky (*Russian*)

Arthur Conan Doyle (*Scottish*)

Roddy Doyle (*Irish*)

Margaret Drabble (*English*)

Maureen Duffy (*English*)

Alexandre Dumas (*French*)

Daphne Du Maurier (*English*)

Nell Dunn (*English*)

Gerald Durrell (*English*)

Laurence Durrell (*English*)

Umberto Eco (*Italian*)

Maria Edgeworth (*English*)

George Eliot (*English*)

Stanley Elkin (*U.S.*)

Alice Thomas Ellis (*English*)

Ben Elton (*English*)

Zöe Fairbairns (*English*)

Philip José Farmer (*U.S.*)

Howard Fast (*U.S.*)

William Faulkner (*U.S.*)

Elaine Feinstein (*English*)

Helen Fielding (*English*)

Henry Fielding (*English*)

Eva Figes (*British*)

F(rancis) Scott (Key) Fitzgerald (*U.S.*)

Penelope Fitzgerald (*English*)

Gustave Flaubert (*French*)

Ian Fleming (*English*)

Ford Madox Ford (*English*)

Richard Ford (*U.S.*)

C S Forester (*English*)

E M Forster (*English*)

Frederick Forsyth (*English*)

John Fowles (*English*)

Janet Paterson Frame (*New Zealand*)

Dick Francis (*English*)

Antonia Fraser (*English*)

Michael Frayn (*English*)

Nicholas Freeling (*English*)

Marilyn French (*U.S.*)

Roy Fuller (*English*)

William Gaddis (*U.S.*)

Janice Galloway (*Scottish*)

John Galsworthy (*English*)

Gabriel García Márquez (*Colombian*)

Helen Garner (*Australian*)

Elizabeth Gaskell (*English*)

William Alexander Gerhardie (*English*)

Lewis Grassic Gibbon (*Scottish*)

Stella Gibbons (*English*)

André Gide (*French*)

Penelope Gilliat (*English*)

George Gissing (*English*)

Ellen Glasgow (*U.S.*)

(Margaret) Rumer Godden (*English*)

William Godwin (*English*)

# NOVELISTS

Johann Wolfgang von Goethe (German)

Nikolai Vasilievich Gogol (Russian)

Herbert Gold (U.S.)

William (Gerald) Golding (English)

William Goldman (U.S.)

Oliver Goldsmith (Anglo-Irish)

Ivan Aleksandrovich Goncharov (Russian)

Nadine Gordimer (South African)

Maxim Gorky (Russian)

Edmund Gosse (English)

Winston Graham (English)

Günter (Wilhelm) Grass (German)

Robert Graves (English)

Alasdair Gray (Scottish)

Graham Greene (English)

John Grisham (U.S.)

George Grossmith (English)

Weedon Grossmith (English)

David Guterson (U.S.)

Rider Haggard (English)

Arthur Hailey (Anglo-Canadian)

Thomas Hardy (English)

L(eslie) P(oles) Hartley (English)

Nathaniel Hawthorne (U.S.)

Shirley Hazzard (U.S.)

Robert A Heinlein (U.S.)

Joseph Heller (U.S.)

Ernest Hemingway (U.S.)

Hermann Hesse (German)

Georgette Heyer (English)

Patricia Highsmith (U.S.)

Susan Hill (English)

James Hilton (English)

Barry Hines (English)

Russell Hoban (U.S.)

James Hogg (Scottish)

Winifred Holtby (English)

Anthony Hope (English)

Paul Horgan (U.S.)

Elizabeth Jane Howard (English)

Thomas Hughes (English)

Victor (Marie) Hugo (French)

Keri Hulme (New Zealand)

Evan Hunter (U.S.)

Zora Neale Hurston (U.S.)

Aldous Huxley (English)

Hammond Innes (English)

John Irving (U.S.)

Christopher Isherwood (English-U.S.)

Kazuo Ishiguro (British)

Henry James (U.S.-British)

P D James (English)

Ruth Prawer Jhabvala (Anglo-Polish)

Erica Jong (U.S.)

James Joyce (*Irish*)
Franz Kafka (*Czech*)
Johanna Kaplan (*U.S.*)
Nikos Kazantzakis (*Greek*)
Molly Keane (*Anglo-Irish*)
James Kelman (*Scottish*)
Thomas Keneally (*Australian*)
Margaret Kennedy (*English*)
Jack Kerouac (*U.S.*)
Ken Kesey (*U.S.*)
Francis King (*English*)
Stephen King (*U.S.*)
Charles Kingsley (*English*)
Rudyard Kipling (*English*)
Milan Kundera (*French-Czech*)
Pierre Choderlos de Laclos (*French*)
George Lamming (*Barbadian*)
Guiseppe Tomasi di Lampedusa (*Italian*)
D H Lawrence (*English*)
John Le Carré (*English*)
Harper Lee (*U.S.*)
Laurie Lee (*English*)
Sheridan Le Fanu (*Irish*)
Ursula Le Guin (*U.S.*)
Rosamond Lehmann (*English*)
Mikhail Yurievich Lermontov (*Russian*)
Doris Lessing (*Rhodesian*)
Primo Levi (*Italian*)
(Harry) Sinclair Lewis (*U.S.*)
Penelope Lively (*English*)

David Lodge (*English*)
Jack London (*U.S.*)
(Clarence) Malcolm Lowry (*English*)
Alison Lurie (*U.S.*)
Rose Macauley (*English*)
Carson McCullers (*U.S.*)
George MacDonald (*Scottish*)
Ian McEwan (*English*)
William McIlvanney (*Scottish*)
Colin MacInnes (*English*)
Compton MacKenzie (*English*)
Henry MacKenzie (*Scottish*)
Bernard McLaverty (*Irish*)
Alistair MacLean (*Scottish*)
Naguib Mahfouz (*Egyptian*)
Norman Mailer (*U.S.*)
Bernard Malamud (*U.S.*)
David Malouf (*Australian*)
(Cyril) Wolf Mankowitz (*English*)
Thomas Mann (*German*)
Olivia Manning (*English*)
Kamala Markandaya (*Indian*)
Frederick Marryat (*English*)
Ngaio Marsh (*New Zealand*)
Allan Massie (*Scottish*)
Somerset Maugham (*English*)
Guy de Maupassant (*French*)
Francois Mauriac (*French*)
Herman Melville (*U.S.*)
George Meredith (*English*)
James A Michener (*U.S.*)

Henry Miller (*U.S.*)
Yukio Mishima (*Japanese*)
Julian Mitchell (*English*)
Margaret Mitchell (*U.S.*)
Naomi Mitchison (*Scottish*)
Nancy Mitford (*English*)
Timothy Mo (*British*)
Nicholas Monsarrat (*English*)
Michael Moorcock (*English*)
Brian Moore (*Irish-Canadian*)
Toni Morrison (*U.S.*)
John Mortimer (*English*)
Penelope Mortimer (*Welsh*)
Nicholas Mosley (*English*)
Iris Murdoch (*Irish*)
Vladimir Vladimirovich
  Nabokov (*Russian-U.S.*)
V S Naipaul (*Trinidadian*)
P H Newby (*English*)
Ngugi wa Thiong'o (*Kenyan*)
Robert Nye (*English*)
Joyce Carol Oates (*U.S.*)
Edna O'Brien (*Irish*)
Kenzaburo Oë (*Japanese*)
Liam O'Flaherty (*Irish*)
John O'Hara (*U.S.*)
Ben Okri (*Nigerian*)
Margaret Oliphant (*Scottish*)
Michael Ondaatje (*Canadian*)
Baroness Emmuska Orczy
  (*Hungarian-British*)
George Orwell (*English*)
Ouida (*English*)

Cynthia Ozick (*U.S.*)
Boris Leonidovich Pasternak
  (*Russian*)
Allan Paton (*South African*)
Thomas Love Peacock
  (*English*)
Mervyn Peake (*English*)
Harold Porter (*Australian*)
Katherine Anne Porter (*U.S.*)
Anthony Powell (*English*)
John Cowper Powys (*English*)
Terry Pratchett (*English*)
J B Priestley (*English*)
V S Pritchett (*English*)
E Annie Proulx (*U.S.*)
Marcel Proust (*French*)
Mario Puzo (*U.S.*)
Thomas Pynchon (*U.S.*)
Ellery Queen (*U.S.*)
Ann Radcliffe (*English*)
Raja Rao (*Indian*)
Frederic Raphael (*U.S.*)
Piers Paul Read (*English*)
Erich Maria Remarque
  (*German*)
Mary Renault (*English*)
Ruth Rendell (*English*)
Jean Rhys (*British*)
Dorothy Richardson (*English*)
Samuel Richardson (*English*)
Mordecai Richler
  (*Canadian*)
Harold Robbins (*U.S.*)

WORD POWER

# NOVELISTS

Frederick William Rolfe (*English*)

Henry Roth (*U.S.*)

(Ahmed) Salman Rushdie (*Indian-British*)

Vita Sackville-West (*English*)

Marquis de Sade (*French*)

Antoine de Saint-Exupéry (*French*)

Saki (*British*)

J D Salinger (*U.S.*)

George Sand (*French*)

William Saroyan (*U.S.*)

Jean-Paul Sartre (*French*)

Dorothy L Sayers (*English*)

Olive Schreiner (*South African*)

Walter Scott (*Scottish*)

Hubert Selby Jr (*U.S.*)

Tom Sharpe (*English*)

Mary Shelley (*English*)

Carol Shields (*Canadian-American*)

Mikhail Alexandrovich Sholokhov (*Russian*)

Nevil Shute (*Anglo-Austrian*)

Alan Sillitoe (*English*)

Georges Simenon (*Belgian*)

Claude Simon (*French*)

Isaac Bashevis Singer (*U.S.*)

Iain Crichton Smith (*Scottish*)

Zadie Smith (*British*)

Tobias George Smollett (*Scottish*)

C P Snow (*English*)

Alexander Isayevich Solzhenitsyn (*Russian*)

Muriel Spark (*Scottish*)

Howard Spring (*Welsh*)

C K Stead (*New Zealand*)

Gertrude Stein (*U.S.*)

John Steinbeck (*U.S.*)

Stendhal (*French*)

Laurence Sterne (*Irish-British*)

Robert Louis Stevenson (*Scottish*)

J I M Stewart (*Scottish*)

Mary Stewart (*English*)

Bram Stoker (*Irish*)

Robert Stone (*U.S.*)

David Storey (*English*)

Harriet Elizabeth Beecher Stowe (*U.S.*)

William Styron (*U.S.*)

Patrick Süskind (*German*)

Graham Swift (*English*)

Jonathan Swift (*Irish*)

Julian Symons (*English*)

Emma Tennant (*English*)

William Makepeace Thackeray (*English*)

Paul Theroux (*U.S.*)

J(ohn) R(onald) R(euel) Tolkien (*English*)

Leo Tolstoy (*Russian*)

John Kennedy Toole (*U.S.*)
Nigel Tranter (*Scottish*)
Rose Tremain (*English*)
William Trevor (*Irish*)
Anthony Trollope (*English*)
Joanna Trollope (*English*)
Frank Tuohy (*English*)
Ivan Sergeyevich Turgenev (*Russian*)
Amos Tutuola (*Nigerian*)
Mark Twain (*U.S.*)
Anne Tyler (*U.S.*)
John Updike (*U.S.*)
Edward (Falaise) Upward (*English*)
Leon Uris (*U.S.*)
Laurens Van der Post (*South African*)
Peter Vansittart (*English*)
Mario Vargas Llosa (*Peruvian*)
Jules Verne (*French*)
Gore Vidal (*U.S.*)
Voltaire (*French*)
Kurt Vonnegut (*U.S.*)
John Wain (*English*)
Alice Walker (*U.S.*)
Horace Walpole (*English*)
Marina Warner (*English*)
Robert Penn Warren (*U.S.*)
Keith Waterhouse (*English*)
Evelyn Waugh (*English*)
Fay Weldon (*English*)

H G Wells (*English*)
Irvine Welsh (*Scottish*)
Eudora Welty (*U.S.*)
Mary Wesley (*English*)
Morris West (*Australian*)
Rebecca West (*Irish*)
Edith Wharton (*U.S.*)
Antonia White (*English*)
Patrick White (*Australian*)
T H White (*English*)
Oscar Wilde (*Irish*)
Thornton Wilder (*U.S.*)
Michael Wilding (*Australian*)
A(ndrew) N(orman) Wilson (*English*)
Jeanette Winterson (*English*)
P(elham) G(renville) Wodehouse (*English-U.S.*)
Thomas Clayton Wolfe (*U.S.*)
Tom Wolfe (*U.S.*)
Tobias Wolff (*U.S.*)
Virginia Woolf (*English*)
Herman Wouk (*U.S.*)
Richard Nathaniel Wright (*U.S.*)
Frank Yerby (*U.S.*)
Marguerite Yourcenar (*French*)
Evgeny Ivanovich Zamyatin (*Russian*)
Emile Zola (*French*)

WORD POWER

Dannie Abse (*Welsh*)

(Karen) Fleur Adcock (*New Zealander*)

Conrad (Potter) Aiken (*U.S.*)

Anna Akhamatova (*Russian*)

Maya Angelou (*U.S.*)

Guillaume Apollinaire (*French*)

Ludovico Ariosto (*Italian*)

Matthew Arnold (*English*)

W(ystan) H(ugh) Auden (*English-U.S.*)

Charles Pierre Baudelaire (*French*)

Patricia Beer (*English*)

Hilaire Belloc (*British*)

John Berryman (*U.S.*)

John Betjeman (*English*)

Elizabeth Bishop (*U.S.*)

William Blake (*English*)

Edmund Blunden (*English*)

Joseph Brodsky (*Russian-American*)

Rupert (Chawner) Brooke (*English*)

Gwendolyn Brooks (*U.S.*)

Elizabeth Barrett Browning (*English*)

Robert Browning (*English*)

Robert Burns (*Scottish*)

(George Gordon) Byron (*British*)

Callimachus (*Greek*)

Luis Vaz de Camoëns (*Portuguese*)

Thomas Campion (*English*)

Raymond Carver (*U.S.*)

Gaius Valerius Catullus (*Roman*)

Charles Causley (*English*)

Geoffrey Chaucer (*English*)

Amy Clampitt (*U.S.*)

John Clare (*English*)

Samuel Taylor Coleridge (*English*)

William Cowper (*English*)

George Crabbe (*English*)

e(dward) e(stlin) cummings (*U.S.*)

Dante (Alighieri) (*Italian*)

Cecil Day Lewis (*Irish*)

Walter de la Mare (*English*)

Emily Dickinson (*U.S.*)

John Donne (*English*)

H D (Hilda Doolittle) (*U.S.*)

John Dryden (*English*)

Carol Ann Duffy (*Scottish*)

William Dunbar (*Scottish*)

Douglas Dunn (*Scottish*)

Geoffrey Dutton (*Australian*)

T(homas) S(tearns) Eliot (*U.S.-British*)

Ebenezer Elliot (the Corn Law Rhymer) (*English*)

WORD POWER

Paul Éluard (*French*)

Ralph Waldo Emerson (*U.S.*)

William Empson (*English*)

Edward Fitzgerald (*English*)

Robert Fitzgerald (*Australian*)

Robert (Lee) Frost (*U.S.*)

Allen Ginsberg (*U.S.*)

Johann Wolfgang von Goethe (*German*)

Robert Graves (*English*)

Thomas Gray (*English*)

Thom Gunn (*English*)

Seamus Heaney (*Irish*)

Adrian Henri (*English*)

Robert Henryson (*Scottish*)

George Herbert (*English*)

Robert Herrick (*English*)

Hesiod (*Greek*)

Geoffrey Hill (*English*)

Ralph Hodgson (*English*)

Homer (*Greek*)

Thomas Hood (*English*)

Gerard Manley Hopkins (*English*)

Horace (*Roman*)

A(lfred) E(dward) Housman (*English*)

Ted Hughes (*English*)

Elizabeth Jennings (*English*)

Samuel Johnson (*English*)

Ben Jonson (*English*)

Juvenal (*Roman*)

Patrick Kavanagh (*Irish*)

John Keats (*English*)

Sidney Keyes (*English*)

(Joseph) Rudyard Kipling (*English*)

Jean de La Fontaine (*French*)

Alphonse Marie Louis de Prat de Lamartine (*French*)

Walter Savage Landor (*English*)

William Langland (*English*)

Philip Larkin (*English*)

Tom Leonard (*Scottish*)

Henry Wadsworth Longfellow (*U.S.*)

Amy Lowell (*U.S.*)

Robert Lowell (*U.S.*)

Richard Lovelace (*English*)

Lucretius (*Roman*)

Thomas Macauley (*English*)

Norman MacCaig (*Scottish*)

Hugh MacDiarmid (*Scottish*)

Roger McGough (*English*)

Sorley MacLean (*Scottish*)

Louis MacNeice (*Irish*)

Stéphane Mallarmé (*French*)

Martial (*Roman*)

Andrew Marvell (*English*)

John Masefield (*English*)

Edna St Vincent Millay (*U.S.*)

John Milton (*English*)

Marianne Moore (*U.S.*)

**WORD POWER**

# POETS

Edwin Morgan (*Scottish*)

Andrew Motion (*English*)

Edwin Muir (*Scottish*)

Ogden Nash (*U.S.*)

Pablo Neruda (*Chilean*)

Frank O'Hara (*U.S.*)

Omar Khayyam (*Persian*)

Ovid (*Roman*)

Wilfred Owen (*British*)

Brian Patten (*English*)

Octavio Paz (*Mexican*)

Petrarch (*Italian*)

Pindar (*Greek*)

Sylvia Plath (*U.S.*)

Alexander Pope (*English*)

Peter Porter (*Australian*)

Ezra (Loomis) Pound (*U.S.*)

Sextus Propertius (*Roman*)

Aleksander Sergeyevich Pushkin (*Russian*)

Kathleen Raine (*English*)

Adrienne Rich (*U.S.*)

Laura Riding (*U.S.*)

Rainer Maria Rilke (*Austro-German*)

Arthur Rimbaud (*French*)

(John Wilmot) Rochester (*English*)

Theodore Huebner Roethke (*U.S.*)

Isaac Rosenberg (*English*)

Christina Georgina Rossetti (*English*)

Dante Gabriel Rossetti (*English*)

Saint-John Perse (*French*)

Sappho (*Greek*)

Siegfried Sassoon (*English*)

Johann Christoph Friedrich von Schiller (*German*)

Delmore Schwarz (*U.S.*)

Sir Walter Scott (*Scottish*)

Jaroslav Seifert (*Czech*)

William Shakespeare (*English*)

Percy Bysshe Shelley (*English*)

Sir Philip Sidney (*English*)

Edith Sitwell (*English*)

John Skelton (*English*)

Christopher Smart (*English*)

Stevie Smith (*English*)

Robert Southey (*English*)

Stephen Spender (*English*)

Edmund Spenser (*English*)

Wallace Stevens (*U.S.*)

Algernon Charles Swinburne (*English*)

Wislawa Szymborska (*Polish*)

Torquato Tasso (*Italian*)

Alfred, Lord Tennyson (*English*)

Dylan (Marlais) Thomas (*Welsh*)

Edward Thomas (*English*)

# POETS

R(onald) S(tuart) Thomas (*Welsh*)
James Thomson (*Scottish*)
Paul Verlaine (*French*)
Alfred Victor de Vigny (*French*)
François Villon (*French*)
Virgil (*Roman*)
Derek Walcott (*West Indian*)

Francis Charles Webb (*Australian*)
Walt Whitman (*U.S.*)
William Wordsworth (*English*)
Judith Wright (*Australian*)
Thomas Wyatt (*English*)
W(illiam) B(utler) Yeats (*Irish*)

WORD POWER

## *British Prime Ministers*

| Prime Minister | Party | Term of office |
|---|---|---|
| Robert Walpole | Whig | 1721–42 |
| Earl of Wilmington | Whig | 1742–43 |
| Henry Pelham | Whig | 1743–54 |
| Duke of Newcastle | Whig | 1754–56 |
| Duke of Devonshire | Whig | 1756–57 |
| Duke of Newcastle | Whig | 1757–62 |
| Earl of Bute | Tory | 1762–63 |
| George Grenville | Whig | 1763–65 |
| Marquess of Rockingham | Whig | 1765–66 |
| Duke of Grafton | Whig | 1766–70 |
| Lord North | Tory | 1770–82 |
| Marquess of Rockingham | Whig | 1782 |
| Earl of Shelburne | Whig | 1782–83 |
| Duke of Portland | Coalition | 1783 |
| William Pitt | Tory | 1783–1801 |
| Henry Addington | Tory | 1801–04 |
| William Pitt | Tory | 1804–06 |
| Lord Grenville | Whig | 1806–07 |
| Duke of Portland | Tory | 1807–09 |
| Spencer Perceval | Tory | 1809–12 |
| Earl of Liverpool | Tory | 1812–27 |
| George Canning | Tory | 1827 |
| Viscount Goderich | Tory | 1827–28 |
| Duke of Wellington | Tory | 1828–30 |
| Earl Grey | Whig | 1830–34 |
| Viscount Melbourne | Whig | 1834 |
| Robert Peel | Conservative | 1834–35 |
| Viscount Melbourne | Whig | 1835–41 |
| Robert Peel | Conservative | 1841–46 |

**WORD POWER**

## *British Prime Ministers (continued)*

| Prime Minister | Party | Term of office |
|---|---|---|
| Lord John Russell | Liberal | 1846–52 |
| Earl of Derby | Conservative | 1852 |
| Lord Aberdeen | Peelite | 1852–55 |
| Viscount Palmerston | Liberal | 1855–58 |
| Earl of Derby | Conservative | 1858–59 |
| Viscount Palmerston | Liberal | 1859–65 |
| Lord John Russell | Liberal | 1865–66 |
| Earl of Derby | Conservative | 1866–68 |
| Benjamin Disraeli | Conservative | 1868 |
| William Gladstone | Liberal | 1868–74 |
| Benjamin Disraeli | Conservative | 1874–80 |
| William Gladstone | Liberal | 1880–85 |
| Marquess of Salisbury | Conservative | 1885–86 |
| William Gladstone | Liberal | 1886 |
| Marquess of Salisbury | Conservative | 1886–92 |
| William Gladstone | Liberal | 1892–94 |
| Earl of Rosebery | Liberal | 1894–95 |
| Marquess of Salisbury | Conservative | 1895–1902 |
| Arthur James Balfour | Conservative | 1902–05 |
| Henry Campbell-Bannerman | Liberal | 1905–08 |
| Herbert Henry Asquith | Liberal | 1908–15 |
| Herbert Henry Asquith | Coalition | 1915–16 |
| David Lloyd George | Coalition | 1916–22 |
| Andrew Bonar Law | Conservative | 1922–23 |
| Stanley Baldwin | Conservative | 1923–24 |
| James Ramsay MacDonald | Labour | 1924 |
| Stanley Baldwin | Conservative | 1924–29 |
| James Ramsay MacDonald | Labour | 1929–31 |
| James Ramsay MacDonald | Nationalist | 1931–35 |

**WORD POWER**

## *British Prime Ministers (continued)*

| Prime Minister | Party | Term of office |
|---|---|---|
| Stanley Baldwin | Nationalist | 1935–37 |
| Arthur Neville Chamberlain | Nationalist | 1937–40 |
| Winston Churchill | Coalition | 1940–45 |
| Clement Attlee | Labour | 1945–51 |
| Winston Churchill | Conservative | 1951–55 |
| Anthony Eden | Conservative | 1955–57 |
| Harold Macmillan | Conservative | 1957–63 |
| Alec Douglas-Home | Conservative | 1963–64 |
| Harold Wilson | Labour | 1964–70 |
| Edward Heath | Conservative | 1970–74 |
| Harold Wilson | Labour | 1974–76 |
| James Callaghan | Labour | 1976–79 |
| Margaret Thatcher | Conservative | 1979–90 |
| John Major | Conservative | 1990–97 |
| Tony Blair | Labour | 1997– |

WORD POWER